CONTENTS

Cover design: Kim Ludlow

Maps: prepared by
the Cartographic Department of
The Automobile Association
© The Automobile Association 1992

Head of Advertisement Sales:
Christopher Heard Tel: (0256) 20123
Advertisement Production:
Karen Weeks Tel: (0256) 20123

Distributed by: AA Publishing

Typeset by: Avonset, Midsomer
Norton, Bath
Colour reproduction by: Scantran
PTE, Singapore
Printed and bound by: Redwood
Press Limited

© The Automobile Association
April 1992

A CIP catalogue record for this book is
available from the British Library .

ISBN 0 7495 0425 0

Published by
The Automobile Association,
Fanum House, Basingstoke,
Hampshire RG21 2EA

**In association with
Kodak Limited**

PHOTOGRAPHS

Scotland's greatest Adam
mansion, Hopetoun House,
accommodates some remarkable
paintings and fine furniture.

The romantic medieval fantasies of
Victorian architect William Burges
were brought to life in the rooms of
Cardiff Castle.

There are details of well over 2,000 places to visit in this guide, in England, Scotland, Wales, Ireland, the Channel Islands and the Isle of Man, so wherever you are you should find just the place for your day out. Each place has been colour coded (see key) so that you can easily choose the kind of day out which will most interest you, and each entry in the book will tell you exactly what you need to know. Entries are arranged in county order to make it easy to see what's on offer in your area – whether you are at home or on holiday. As well as all this, we have included a handy location atlas at the end of the book to help you find your way around.

We hope that, with the help of this guide, you will enjoy the best possible days out.

Museum and

Historic building or ancient site

Theme park

Garden or area of countryside

Zoo or wildlife park

Industrial site or
preserved railway

Town or city
of outstanding interest

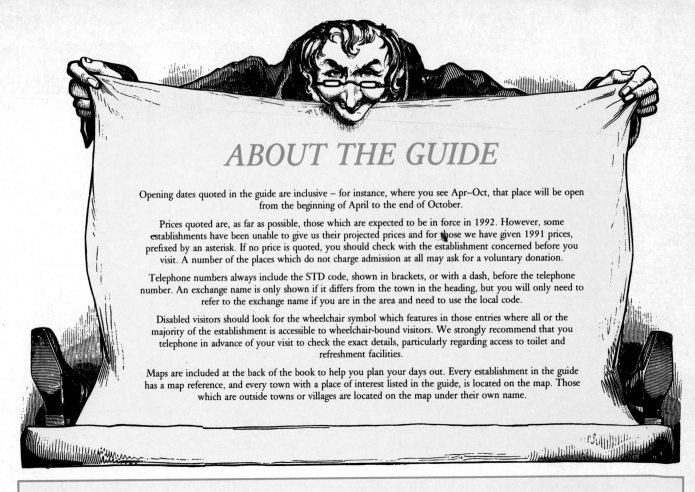

ABOUT THE GUIDE

Opening dates quoted in the guide are inclusive – for instance, where you see Apr–Oct, that place will be open from the beginning of April to the end of October.

Prices quoted are, as far as possible, those which are expected to be in force in 1992. However, some establishments have been unable to give us their projected prices and for those we have given 1991 prices, prefixed by an asterisk. If no price is quoted, you should check with the establishment concerned before you visit. A number of the places which do not charge admission at all may ask for a voluntary donation.

Telephone numbers always include the STD code, shown in brackets, or with a dash, before the telephone number. An exchange name is only shown if it differs from the town in the heading, but you will only need to refer to the exchange name if you are in the area and need to use the local code.

Disabled visitors should look for the wheelchair symbol which features in those entries where all or the majority of the establishment is accessible to wheelchair-bound visitors. We strongly recommend that you telephone in advance of your visit to check the exact details, particularly regarding access to toilet and refreshment facilities.

Maps are included at the back of the book to help you plan your days out. Every establishment in the guide has a map reference, and every town with a place of interest listed in the guide, is located on the map. Those which are outside towns or villages are located on the map under their own name.

SYMBOLS

In order to give you as much information as possible in the space available, we have used the following symbols in the guide:

	ENGLISH	FRANÇAIS	DEUTSCH	ITALIANO	ESPAÑOL
☎	Telephone number	Numéro de telephone	Telefonnummer	Numero telefonico	Número telefonico
♿	Suitable for visitors in wheelchairs	Les invalidens fauteuils reulants pourront y accéder	Für Rollstuhltahrer zugänglich	Addato per visitatori in sedia a rotelle	Adacuado para visitas en silla de reudas
＊	Indicates 1991 price	Prix 1991	1991 Preise	Indica i prezzi del 1991	Indica los precios de 1991
Ⓟ	Parking at Establishment	Stattionment à l'établissement	Parken an Ort und Stelle	Parcheggio sul posto	Aparcamiento en el estabiecimiento
	Refreshments	Rafraîchissements	Erfischungen	Snacks	Refrescos
✕	Restaurant	Restaurant	Restaurant	Ristorante	Restaurante
🐕	No Dogs	Chiens non permis	Hundeverbot	Prohibito ai cani	Se prohiben los perros
🚌	No coaches	Les groupes en cars pas admis	Keine Reisebus-gesellschaften	Non si accettano commitive en gita turistica	Non se acception los grupos de viajeros en coches de linea

ABBREVIATIONS

In the same way, we have abbreviated certain pieces of information:

	ENGLISH	FRANÇAIS	DEUTSCH	ITALIANO	ESPAÑOL
AM	Ancient Monument	Monument ancien	Historiches Gebaude	Monumento storico	Monumento histórico
AM(Cadw)	Ancient Monument (Wales)	Monument ancien (Pays de Galles)	Historiches Gebaude (Walisland)	Monumento storico (Il Paese di Galles)	Monumento historico (Gales)
EH	English Heritage	English Heritage	English Heritage	English Heritage	English Heritage
NT	National Trust	National Trust	National Trust	The National Trust	The National Trust
NTS	National Trust for Scotland	National Trust en Ecosse	National Trust in Schottland	The National Trust for Scozia	The National Trust for Escocia
BH	Bank Holidays	Jours fériés	Bankfeiertage	Festività nazionale	Dia festivo para los bancos y el comercio en general
PH	Public Holidays	Jours fériés	Feiertage	Festività nazionale	Dias festivos
Etr	Easter	Pâques	Ostern	Pasqua	Pascua de Resurrección
ex	except	sauf	ausser	Eccetto	Excepto
IR£	Irish punts	Punts irlandais	Punts irrisch	Punts irlandese	Punts irlandés
Free	Admission free	Entrée libre	Freier eintritt	Entrata libera	Entrada libre
£1	Admission £1	Entrée £1	Eintritt £1	Entrata £1	Entrada £1
ch 50p	Children 50p	Enfants 50p	Kinder 50p	Bambini 50p	Niños 50p
ch 15 50p	Children under 15 50p	Enfants de moins de 15 ans 50p	Kinder unter 15 Jahren 50p	Bambini sotto i 15 anni 50p	Los niños de mendos de 15 años 50p
Pen	Senior Citizens	Retraites	Rentner	Pensionati	Jubilados
Party	Special or reduced rates for parties booked in advance	Tarifs spéciaux ou réduits pour groupes réservés d'advance	Sondertarife oder Ermässi-gungen für im voraus bestellte Gesellschaften	Tariffe speciali o ridotte per comitive prenotano in anticipo	Tarifas especiales o reducidas para los grupos de vaijeros que reserven de anternano
Party 30+	Special or reduced rates for parties of 30 or more booked in advance	Tarifs spéciaux ou réduits pour groupes de 30 et plus réservés d'advance	Sondertarife oder Ermässi-gungem für im voraus bestellte Gessellsschaften von wenigstens 30 30 Personen	Tariffe speciali o ridotte per comitive di 30 o piú persone che prenotano in anticipo	Tarifas especiales o reducidas para grupos de 30 viajeros, o más, que reserven de anternano

Whatever life may be, it's never dull on 'Kodak' GOLD II Film.

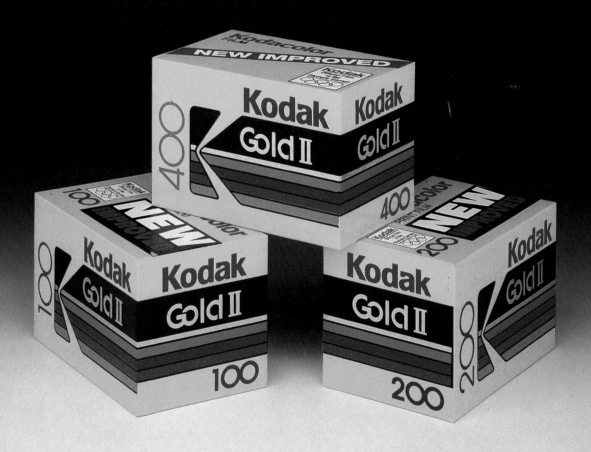

PUT YOURSELF TO THE TEST AND WIN A 'KODAK' COMPACT CAMERA AND NEW 'KODAK' GOLD II FILM OR A 'KODAK' FUN SINGLE-USE CAMERA

Capture those memories of your days out with your friends and family in one of the best ways there is – on 'Kodak' film. Whatever the occasion – a day at the beach, a trip to one of Britain's majestic stately homes or castles, or a leisurely walk in the forest, dale or hill – record the unique memory of that day to look back on and cherish.

Here are some simple hints and tips from Kodak to help you get the most from your camera.

PICK THE RIGHT SPEED OF FILM

The first thing you must do is make sure you have the right speed of film. The speed of a film is indicated by a number. The higher the number, the faster the film.

A "fast" film is one that is highly sensitive to light and should be used if the lighting conditions are dim or for action shots where there is lots of movement.

A "slow" film is less sensitive to light and will give you a very high degree of sharpness and colour accuracy in bright light conditions or still life photography.

REMEMBER to adjust the speed indicator on your camera each time you use a different speed of film or check the instructions for your camera to see if it does it automatically.

New 'Kodak' GOLD II film is available in three speeds – 100, 200 and 400.

'Kodak' GOLD II 100 with its excellent colour saturation is the ideal film for use in bright sunlight, perfect for holidays in the sun.

'Kodak' GOLD II 200 is the ideal film for everyday activities outside or indoors. It has the best balance of colour accuracy, richness and speed, with green, magentas, yellows and oranges more vivid.

'Kodak' GOLD II 400 is the ideal film for use with flash indoors and for "movement" and "action" shoots.

PHOTOGRAPHIC HINTS AND TIPS

Here are ten easy to re-member hints and tips from Kodak to help you take great photographs.

1 Move in Closer

Move in closer to your subject to ensure you capture the most important elements of your photograph such as a child's face, a family group or an animal feeding.

2 Frame Your Pictures

By framing your picture you can create a sensation of depth and

Move in closer to your subject.

direct attention into the picture – use natural frames for pictures such as archways or branches of trees.

3 Use Leading Lines

To direct attention of the picture to your subject use "leading lines" such as a stream, a fence or a pathway, or even a beam of light or shadow.

4 One Focus Point

Make sure there is one focus point in your pictures so as not to distract or confuse the viewer. The focus point could be a person or group, a doorway or an entire house.

5 Action

Make your pictures natural, include action and movement.

6 Flash Pictures

For good flash pictures, make sure your subject is within the flash range for your camera – usually about 4 metres (13 feet). If you are taking a picture of a group, make sure everyone is the same distance from the camera so that each receives the same amount of light.

Also, when using flash, check that your batteries are working and make sure you have some spare in case they

Use leading lines to direct attention to your subject.

run down. Don't use flash directly in front of mirrors or any shiny surfaces – the flash will be reflected back and cause a bright glare in the picture.

Ask your subject to look slightly away from the camera to avoid "red eye".

7 Light Direction

Watch the direction of light in daylight pictures. People tend to squint in bright, direct light. Light from the side creates highlights and shadows that reveal texture and help to show the shape of the subject.

Experiment with lighting a subject from behind. This can be very effective particularly with flowers or leaves.

8 Fresh Film

Make sure your film is "fresh" and not one which has been sitting in your camera for ages. Always ensure the film is within the "develop before" date. Get film developed promptly too.

9 Buy Quality Film

Buy top quality film, like 'Kodak' GOLD II, to ensure top quality results. Why risk those memories to anything else?

10 Capture Those Memories

Remember to carry your camera with you everywhere to catch that unexpected, hilarious, candid or touching photograph.

Action and movement give your pictures a natural feel.

On your next day out remember, there is a suitable 'Kodak' Single-use Camera for taking great pictures in the jungle, dungeon or lagoon.

'Kodak' Single-use Cameras are available from many of the attractions featured in this publication.

LONDON

Modern London offers its 24 million annual visitors some extraordinary contrasts. Its ceremonial and historic ties continue in the annual enactments of events such as the Lord Mayor of Westminster's New Year's Day Parade, the Trooping of the Colour and the State Opening of Parliament, while present day London expands its imaginative riverside developments and tourist attractions in London Docklands and in the London Bridge City on the south bank of the Thames.

Throughout the capital there are fascinating things to see and do, in addition to the places of interest listed in this guide, and below we give details of some of them. You might like your visit to London to coincide with one of the events, do some statue-spotting as you journey around or visit one of the lovely old churches, perhaps for a lunchtime concert. We hope that the pages which follow will help you to make the most of London.

TOURIST INFORMATION

The London Tourist Board is the capital's official information centre and whatever information you need can be obtained from one of the following locations:

Victoria Station Forecourt, SW1
Open Easter–Oct, daily 8am–8pm, Nov–Easter, Mon–Sat 8am–5pm, Sun 8am–4pm, Apr–Oct 8am–6pm; bookshop and Britain Desk Mon–Sat 8am–7.30pm, Sun 8am–5.30pm.

Selfridges Store, Oxford Street, W1
In the basement services arcade. Open store hours.

Liverpool Street Underground Station
Open Mon–Sat 9am–4.30pm, Sun 8.30am–3.30pm.

In addition to these, there are several local Tourist Information Centres around London.

GETTING AROUND
Generally speaking, bringing your car into London is a bad idea. Traffic congestion is a problem and parking can be difficult, not to mention the one-way systems which can easily confuse visitors who are not accustomed to their complexities.

The Underground is the quickest and most efficient way to travel and covers a wide area, with 273 stations. Each entry in this guide quotes the

Built in 1869, the record-breaking tea clipper, the Cutty Sark, is now open to visitors – just one of the many attractive and popular sights of Greenwich.

nearest underground station, or a choice if they are equidistant, and you will find the plan of the underground system on page 9. There is almost always an underground station close at hand and trains run frequently between 5.30am and just after midnight. However, some stations are closed at weekends.

The Docklands Light Railway is London's newest and highly automated transport system which links the City to the revitalised docklands area – 8.5 square miles of what was once a forgotten and largely derelict backwater, but now full of innovative projects including leisure facilities, office and shopping developments. The railway line has been extended to Bank Underground station and runs to Tower Gateway and Island Gardens (opposite Greenwich), with another section from Stratford to Island Gardens. An extension east to Beckton in the Royal Docks is due to open December 1992. Trains run on weekdays only, until 9.30pm.

London Buses can offer a wonderful, cheap alternative to the sightseeing tours (mentioned below), especially from the vantage point of the upper deck, but traffic can be slow at times. That may not matter if you are simply looking around, but could take up valuable visiting time if you are heading for somewhere particular. You can pick up a free, detailed bus map from any Travel Enquiry Office or Underground station.

Concessionary Fares include a reduced flat fare until 10pm for under 14s, and for 14–15 year olds with a Child Rate Photocard, available from Post Offices in the London area. Up to two under-fives per person travel free. If you intend to use public transport extensively, a One Day Travelcard will give you unlimited travel on the Underground, British Rail Network South East, Docklands Light Railway and most London buses. They not only save money, but cut out queuing time for tickets and can be used any time after 9.30am on weekdays and all day at weekends. They can be bought from any London Transport or London Tourist Board Information Centre, any Underground Station and nearly 2000 newsagents. Travelcards are also available for periods longer than one day, but for these you will need a Photocard, so take along a passport-type photograph. Give at least 12 hours notice if you want your Travelcard to be valid for periods other than one day, one week or one month.

London Taxis are a friendly sight and a salvation for those who get lost! After midnight they are a godsend and the only way to get around. Taxi drivers are also a useful source of information as they know London inside out – they have to to get their licence. Charges vary depending on distance and time taken, but are recorded on a meter with additional charges made for extra people and luggage and for night journeys.

The Rush Hour
From Monday to Friday the buses and trains of London carry a daily average of over 6 million passengers. Between 8am–9.30am and from 4pm–6pm travelling on public transport will be uncomfortable so try to arrange your day to avoid these times.

SIGHTSEEING
Bus Tours
These provide an excellent introduction to London, taking in most of the famous sights. London Transport's Official Sightseeing Tours, on red double-deckers, start from Piccadilly Circus (Haymarket), Marble Arch (Speakers' Corner), Baker Street Station and Victoria Station for an 18-mile route lasting about 1½ hours. They leave every half hour between 10am and 5pm and may be open-topped in summer. You can just pay as you board the bus, but it is cheaper if you buy tickets in advance from any London Transport or London Tourist Board Information Centre. There is also a special tour which includes direct entrance (no boring queuing) to Madame Tussaud's. Details of all tours are available from London Transport, 55 Broadway, SW1. tel 071-227 3456.

Apply for a ticket in advance for a guided tour of the Houses of Parliament; the visitors' galleries are open every weekday if you just want to watch the battle of the politicians.

Other sightseeing tour operators include:

Evan Evans Tours Ltd
071-930 2377

Frames Rickards
071-837 3111

Golden Tours
081-743 3300

London Cityrama
071-720 6663

Travellers Check-In
071-580 8284

Harrods Sightseeing
071-581 3603

London Crusader
071-437 0124

Thomas Cook Ltd
071-499 4000

The Big Bus Company
071-498 9345

River and Canal Boat Trips
River Bus and passenger boat services offer an exciting trip and a unique view of the capital. They operate from Westminster Pier, Charing Cross Pier and Tower Pier downstream to Greenwich; from Westminster and Charing Cross downstream to the Tower; and from Westminster Pier upstream to Kew, Richmond and Hampton Court. London Transport's River Bus leaves about every 20–30 minutes, or telephone River Boat Information Service on 071-730 4812 for other departure times. London also has two canals – the Grand Union and the Regent's Canal, with boat trips mainly on the latter. The London Waterbus Company goes from Camden Lock to Little Venice, via Regents Park and London Zoo –

telephone 071-482 2550 for details.

Guided Walks
If you want to discover London on foot, one of the best ways to get to know any city, several companies organise guided walking tours:

City Walks
071-937 4281

Citysights (archaeological)
081-806 4325

Cockney Walks
081-504 9159

Footloose in London
071-435 0259

Footsteps
0622 682072

London Walks
071-624 3978

S J Harris
071-624 9981

Historical Tours
081-668 4019

Tour Guides Ltd
071-839 2498

Should you prefer to explore London on your own, the **Silver Jubilee Walkway** covers ten miles of historic London. It was created in 1977 to commemorate the 25th Anniversary of the Queen's accession to the throne. The entire route is signposted by silver plaques in the shape of a crown set into the pavement, and Parliament Square is a good place to start.

Blue Plaques
Scattered throughout London are the homes of the famous and houses where history was made. Such buildings are marked with a blue plaque recording the event and there are now more than 600 plaques commemorating important events and lives.

DAILY EVENTS
The Changing of the Guard at Buckingham Palace
The ceremony takes place inside the Palace railings and starts at approximately 11.25am, daily from May to mid August, then on alternate days. You will need to arrive early if you want a good view.

Mounting Guard at Whitehall
This colourful spectacle takes place at 11am every weekday and 10am on Sundays.

Ceremony of the Keys
At the Tower of London, the Ceremony of the Keys has taken place every night for the last 700 years. You will need a special pass, obtainable by writing to the Resident Governor, to attend the ceremony, which takes place a few minutes before 10pm nightly and lasts for about 20 minutes.

CALENDAR OF ANNUAL EVENTS
January
Lord Mayor of Westminster's New Year's Day Parade
Starts at 1pm from Piccadilly and proceeds along Regent Street and Oxford Street to finish in Hyde Park, where entertainment continues throughout the day, culminating in a fireworks display.

February
Chinese New Year
(sometimes late January)
On the Sunday nearest to the

Chinese New Year, Soho is alive with Lion Dances, colourful costumes and street decorations. Celebrations start at around 11.40am.

Clown Service
At 4pm on the first Sunday in February, at Holy Trinity Church, Beechwood Road, Dalston E8. Many clowns in full costume and make up attend the service, a wreath is laid to Grimaldi (who originated the clown character) and a free clown show follows.

Gun Salute on Ascension Day
(6 February)

March
Head of the River Race
Takes place on the Thames, from Mortlake to Putney, starting times varying from year to year according to the tides. It is a professional race for eights and up to 420 crews set off at 10 second intervals.

April
Oxford and Cambridge Boat Race
From Putney to Mortlake, the two University teams battle it out along the Thames.

Easter Parade (sometimes in March)
The parade takes place in Battersea Park SW11 and starts at 3pm, but from 12.30pm colourful floats and marching bands circle the park.

London Marathon
The 1992 marathon is scheduled to take place on Sunday 12 April, starting at Greenwich at 8.45am and covering a 26.2-mile course through docklands, along the Thames Embankments and through the City to finish at Westminster Bridge.

Gun Salute, Queen's Birthday
Takes place on 21 April.

Harness Horse Parade
This takes place in Regent's Park NW1 and involves working horses competing for prizes. The event ends with a Grand Parade of winners which lasts from 12 noon to about 1pm.

May
Chelsea Flower Show
Held at Chelsea Royal Hospital in the 3rd week in May, with public days on Wednesday, Thursday and Friday.

June
2 Gun Salute: Coronation Day
To celebrate the 40th anniversary of The Queen's accession to the throne, this will be held in Hyde Park at 12.00 noon and in the Tower of London at 1pm.

Beating Retreat
A military display of marching and drilling bands of the Household Division takes place at Horse Guards

Parade SW1, with floodlit performances in the evening.

Trooping the Colour
On the second Saturday in June, the Queen's Official Birthday is celebrated by Trooping the Colour at Horse Guards Parade. Before and after the event, the Queen, members of her family and her troops go in procession from and to Buckingham Palace along The Mall.

July
Swan Upping
The swans on the Thames belong either to the Queen or to the Companies of Dyers and Vintners, and on the third week of July the birds are rounded up and marked. The Companies' swanherds and the Queen's Keeper of Swans, dressed in colourful garments, travel up the river in decorated skiffs.

Doggett's Coat and Badge Race
Towards the end of July, this Thames race for single sculls starts at London Bridge and ends at Cadogan Pier in Chelsea. It is the oldest annually contested event in the British sporting calendar and celebrates the accession of George I to the throne. The prize of a badge of silver and money to pay for a livery coat for the winner was instigated in 1715 by Thomas Doggett, comedian and manager of London's oldest theatre, The Drury Lane.

August
London Riding Horse Parade
Starting at 1pm at Rotton Row, Hyde Park W2, this competition selects the best turned out horse and rider.

Notting Hill Carnival
Now 25 years old, this is the largest street festival in Europe and is held over the August Bank Holiday weekend, with dancing in the streets to steel and brass bands and participants in spectacular costumes. On Sunday the main attraction is the Children's Carnival.

September
Thamesday
This carnival of festivities is held on the South Bank and includes boat races, fireworks and events for children.

October
State Opening of Parliament
The Queen rides in the Irish State Coach from Buckingham Palace to the Palace of Westminster via the Mall and Whitehall. The royal party enters the Houses of Parliament and the Queen makes her speech in a ceremony not open to the public.

Trafalgar Day Parade
Sea cadets from all over Britain are on Parade in Trafalgar Square at 11am to commemorate Nelson's great victory.

Central London

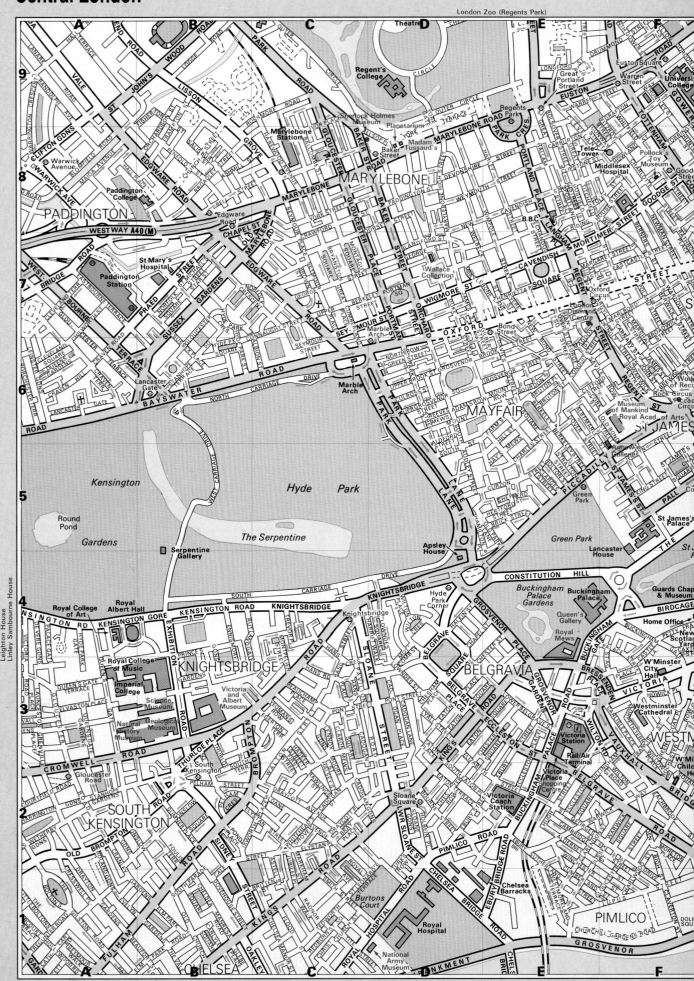

London Zoo (Regents Park)

Chelsea Physic Garden

G
H
I
J
K
L
BLOOMSBURY
HOLBORN
CITY
SOUTHWARK
NEWINGTON
VAUXHALL
RIVER THAMES
Mount Pleasant Post Office
Russell Square
Hospitals
Dicken's House
Museum of the Order of St. John
Royal Britain
Wesley's House
Police Station
Jeanetta Cochrane Theatre
Gray's Inn
Farringdon
Barbican
Smithfield Market
The Barbican
St Giles
Moorgate
Broadgate
Liverpool Street
British Museum
Chancery Lane
Museum of London
St Barts Hospital
National Postal Mus.
Sir John Soane's Mus.
Lincoln's Inn
Patent Office
Public Records Office
Old Curiosity Shop
Holborn
St Paul's (Thames-link)
Central Criminal Court
St Paul's Cathedral
Guildhall
Bank of England
Royal Exchange
Lloyds
Leadenhall Market
Contemporary Applied Arts
Dr Johnson's House
Law Courts
Mansion House
Bush House
Middle Temple Hall
Telecom Technology Showcase
Aldwych
Temple
Covent Garden
London Trans. Mus
Covent Gdn Mkt Hall
Theatre Museum
Somerset House
Courtauld Inst. Gall.
HQS Wellington
HMS President
Blackfriars Station
City of London School
Vintner's Hall
Cannon Street Station
Monument
The Monument
Fishmongers Hall
Custom House
Leicester Square
Portrait & National Gallery
St Martin in-the-Fields
Trafalgar Square
Charing Cross Station
Embankment
National Film Theatre
South Bank TV Centre (LWT)
Royal National Theatre
Bankside Gallery
Schooner Kathleen and May
London Dungeon
HMS Belfast
Southwark Cathedral
London Bridge City
Hay's Galleria
Museum of the Moving Image
London Nautical School
Schiller Int Univ
Admiralty Arch
Mall Galleries
Admiralty
Banqueting House
Royal Festival Hall
Jubilee Gardens
Waterloo (East) Station
Borough Mkt
London Bridge
London Bridge Sta.
Guy's Hospital
Government Offices
Waterloo Sta.
Old Vic
County Hall
Westminster
Borough
Post Office
New Caledonian Mkt
Westminster Hall
Florence Nightingale Museum
St Thomas' Hospital
Lambeth North
Police Station
Westminster Abbey
Houses of Parliament
South Bank Technopark
Tabard Gdns
Arch-bishops Park
Imperial War Museum
Gardens
Lambeth Palace
Elephant and Castle
Westminster Hospital
Museum of Garden History
Rec Centre
Cuming Museum
Tate Gallery
Kennington
Vauxhall
Post Office
The Oval
Kenn-ington Park
Burgess
AA
Pirate Ships at Tabacco Dock
Tower of London
Tower Bridge Walk
Design Museum
Butlers Wharf
FLEET STREET
STRAND
EMBANKMENT
KINGSWAY
HIGH HOLBORN
NEW OXFORD ST
CLERKENWELL ROAD
HOLBORN VIADUCT
NEWGATE ST
CHEAPSIDE
CANNON STREET
QUEEN VICTORIA STREET
UPPER THAMES STREET
LOWER THAMES STREET
LONDON WALL
OLD STREET
CITY ROAD
CHISWELL ST
BEECH STREET
ALDERSGATE
THREADNEEDLE ST
CORNHILL
LEADENHALL ST
FENCHURCH ST
EASTCHEAP
KING WILLIAM ST
GRACECHURCH ST
BISHOPSGATE
LONDON BRIDGE
SOUTHWARK BRIDGE
BLACKFRIARS BRIDGE
WATERLOO BRIDGE
WESTMINSTER BRIDGE
LAMBETH BR.
VAUXHALL BR.
SOUTHWARK STREET
STAMFORD STREET
TOOLEY STREET
BOROUGH HIGH STREET
BLACKFRIARS ROAD
WATERLOO ROAD
YORK ROAD
BOROUGH ROAD
NEWINGTON C'SEWAY
LONG LANE
GREAT DOVER STREET
NEW KENT ROAD
OLD KENT ROAD
KENNINGTON ROAD
KENNINGTON LANE
KENNINGTON PARK ROAD
NEWINGTON BUTTS
WALWORTH ROAD
ST GEORGE'S ROAD
LAMBETH ROAD
LAMBETH PALACE ROAD
ALBERT EMBANKMENT
MILLBANK
WHITEHALL
ABINGDON ST
FARRINGDON ROAD
GOSWELL ROAD
ST JOHN STREET
GRAY'S INN ROAD
THEOBALD'S ROAD
SOUTHAMPTON ROW
WOBURN PLACE
BERMONDSEY STREET
TOWER BRIDGE ROAD
ALBANY ROAD
HARLEYFORD RD
NINE ELMS LANE
KENNINGTON OVAL

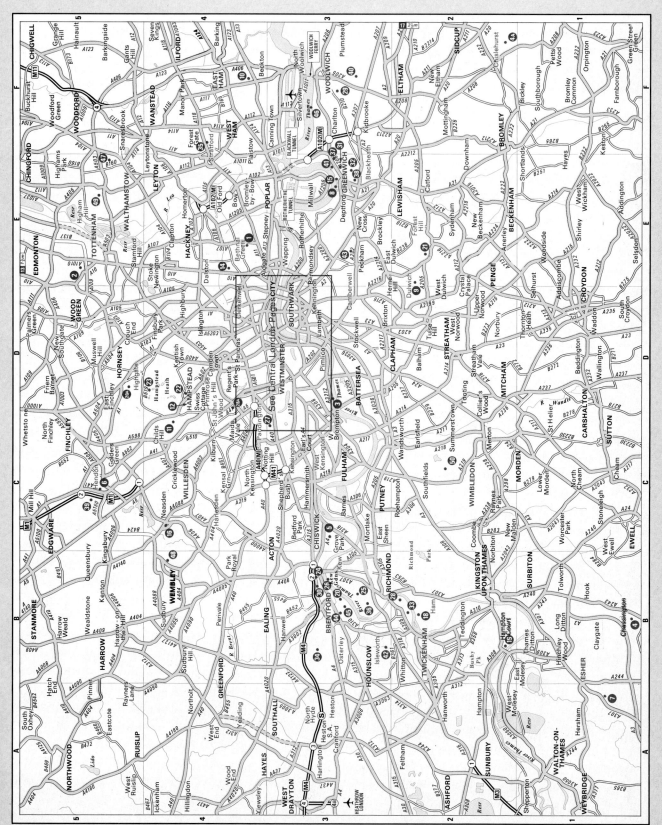

Outer London

KEY TO OUTER LONDON PLAN

		Listed under	Grid ref.			Listed under	Grid ref.
1	Bethnal Green Museum of Childhood	E2	E4	**26**	Kew Palace	Kew	B3
2	Bruce Castle Museum	N17	E5	**27**	London Toy & Model Museum	W2	C3
	Bushy Park	Teddington	B2	**28**	Marble Hill House	Twickenham	B2
3	Carlyle's House	SW3	D3	**28A**	The MCC Museum	NW8	D4
4	Chessington World of Adventures	Chessington	B1	**29**	Museum of Artillery in the Rotunda	SE18	F3
4A	Chislehurst Caves	Chislehurst	F2	**30**	Musical Museum	Brentford	B3
5	Chiswick House	W4	C3	**31**	National Maritime Museum	SE10	E3
6	Church Farm House Museum	NW4	C5	**32**	Old Royal Observatory	SE10	E3
7	Claremont Landscape Garden	Esher	A1	**33**	Orleans House Gallery	Twickenham	B2
8	Cutty Sark Clipper Ship	SE10	E3	**34**	Osterley Park House	Osterley	B3
9	Dulwich Picture Gallery	SE21	E2	**35**	Passmore Edwards Museum	E15	F4
10	East Ham Nature Reserve	E6	F4		Primrose Hill	NW8	D4
11	Fenton House	NW3	C4	**36**	Queen Charlotte's Cottage	Kew	B3
12	Freud Museum	NW3	D4	**37**	The Queens House	SE10	E3
13	Forty Hall Museum	Enfield	E5	**38**	Rangers House	SE3	E3
14	Geffrye Museum	E2	E4		Richmond Park	Richmond	B/C2
15	Gipsy Moth IV	SE10	E3	**39**	Royal Air Force Museum	NW9	C5
16	Grange Museum of Community History	NW10	C4	**40**	Royal Artillery Regimental Museum	SE18	F3
	Greenwich Park	SE10	E3	**41**	Royal Naval College	SE10	E3
17	Hall Place	Bexley	F2	**42**	Rugby Football Union	Twickenham	B3
18	Ham House	Ham	B2	**43**	South London Art Gallery	SE5	E3
19	Hampton Court Palace	Hampton Court	B2	**44**	Syon House	Isleworth	B3
20	Heritage Motor Museum (Syon Park)	Isleworth	B3	**45**	Syon Park	Isleworth	B3
20A	Highgate Cemetery	N6	D5	**46**	Thames Barrier Visitors Centre	SE18	F3
21	Horniman Museum	SE23	E2	**47**	Vestry House Museum	E17	E5
22	Keats House	NW3	D4	**48**	Wembley Stadium	Wembley	B4
23	Kenwood, Iveagh Bequest	NW3	D4	**49**	William Morris Gallery	E17	E5
24	Kew Bridge Steam Museum	Brentford	B3	**50**	Wimbledon Lawn Tennis Museum	SW19	C2
25	Kew Gardens (Royal Botanic Gardens)	Kew	B3				

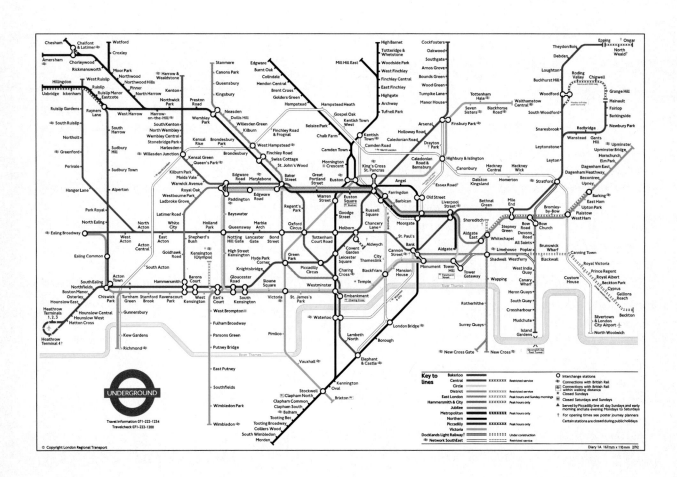

See how we make electricity with a hollow mountain and a fish ladder.

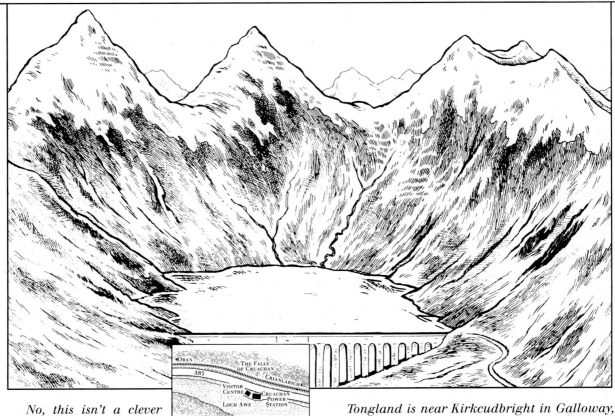

No, this isn't a clever little trick from Blue Peter, but an invitation to visit Cruachan and Tongland, two of our power stations which offer guided tours in the summer months.

Cruachan, set in the rugged grandeur of the Highlands next to Loch Awe, is 15 miles from Oban on the A85. Here you are taken by electric coach deep inside Ben Cruachan, the Hollow Mountain, to the power station turbine hall, where water is drawn down 364 metres from the reservoir above to drive the turbines. Back on the surface there's a Visitor's Centre with a video, display material, shop and a pleasant picnic area.

Tongland is near Kirkcudbright in Galloway, Scotland's bonnie south west, and although much smaller than Cruachan, is the largest power station in the Galloway Hydro Scheme. Your tour starts with a video featuring popular radio and TV personality, Jimmie MacGregor, and features a look at Tongland's turbine hall, still producing power 50 years after being commissioned. The impressive dam and fish ladder, set among the tranquil beauty on the Galloway countryside, offer a most enjoyable holiday trip.

For full details call 086 62 673 for Cruachan and 0557 30114 for Tongland during summer months.

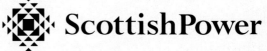

IF YOU'RE NUTS ABOUT CHOCOLATE, YOU'LL BE MAD NOT TO COME.

HAVE YOU EVER WONDERED WHERE CHOCOLATE CAME FROM?

Cadbury World takes you on a magical journey through the history of the world's favourite treat. From the jungles of Central America, where the natives once worshipped gods of chocolate, through 16th century Spain and the London of Samuel Pepys, to Georgian England, where drinking chocolate was all the rage with the fashion-conscious 'dandies.'

All in the setting of the world-famous Cadbury 'Factory in a Garden' in Bournville. Truly something for all the family!

HAVE YOU EVER WONDERED WHAT MADE CADBURY SO FAMOUS?

The fascinating story of the Cadbury family is brought to breathtaking life with stunning displays and tableaux. See how George and Richard Cadbury made their pioneering decision to move from the grime of the city to the green fields of Bournville.

'A DAY IN THE LIFE…'

You can step back into "the good old days" between the Wars, and experience life at Bournville as it was in an age gone by.

All this as well as seeing chocolate actually being made in our special demonstration area; and the chance to visit, on a guided tour, the newest Cadbury packaging plant! Where you can see how these famous bars are wrapped, packed and sent on their way.

EVER WONDERED WHY THE LADY LOVES MILK TRAY?

Take another look at some of Britain's most famous T.V. commercials over the years, including Milk Tray, Cadbury's Dairy Milk, Roses, Flake and Creme Eggs.

EVER WONDERED WHERE TO TAKE THE FAMILY FOR AN EXCITING AFTERNOON OUT?

Without doubt, Cadbury World is the newest, most colourful, and definitely tastiest outing for all the family. There's so much to do and see, and plenty of free parking too.

By road, we're four miles South West of Birmingham City Centre, off the A38 Bristol Road.

By rail, Bournville station is just 10 minutes walk around the corner.

OPENING TIMES AND ADMISSION PRICES

For further information on opening times and admission prices telephone 021-433 4334.

Please note this is not a factory tour.

Cadbury WORLD
THE CHOCOLATE EXPERIENCE

Cadbury World
Linden Road
Bournville
BIRMINGHAM

*Cadbury World regret disabled access to packaging plant is not possible.

FREE PARKING

CHOCOLATE AND GIFT SHOP

SELF-SERVICE RESTAURANT

DISABLED FACILITIES*

IF YOU'RE NUTS ABOUT CHOCOLATE, YOU'LL BE MAD ABOUT CADBURY WORLD

Buckingham Palace

The Queen's Gallery displays changing exhibitions based on the Royal Collection, one of the finest private art collections in the world. The Royal Mews, where The Queen's horses and carriages are housed, provides a rare insight into this unique aspect of the monarchy.

Visitor Information: 071-799 2331

Windsor Castle

The State Apartments, Queen Mary's Dolls' House and the Exhibition of The Queen's Presents and Royal Carriages combine with the regular Changing of the Guard to reveal Windsor Castle's fundamental and continuing role as an Official Residence of the Sovereign.

Visitor Information: 0753 831118

Palace of Holyroodhouse

Throughout the history of Scotland, the Palace of Holyroodhouse has been the scene of the most turbulent and extraordinary events and today provides an unrivalled view of Scotland's past.

Visitor Information: 031 556 1096

BEAULIEU

BLENHEIM PALACE

BROADLANDS

CASTLE HOWARD

TREASURE HOUSES

Eight of the country's most celebrated and historic houses, all with outstanding architectural features, priceless collections and a variety of unique attractions. Most are still owned and cared for by the noble families who have lived in them for generations, and all are set in acres of beautiful parklands.

They offer you and your family a day out of unrivalled excitement, interest and value for money.

For more information on all eight Treasure Houses simply contact Lesley Ann Harnett, Dept. **AA** John Montagu Building, Beaulieu, Brockenhurst, Hampshire, SO42 7ZN or phone any of the individual numbers listed below.

BEAULIEU
(Hampshire)
(0590) 612345.

BLENHEIM PALACE
(Oxfordshire)
(0993) 811325.

BROADLANDS
(Hampshire)
(0794) 516878.

CASTLE HOWARD
(North Yorkshire)
(065 384) 333.

CHATSWORTH
(Derbyshire)
(0246) 582204.

HAREWOOD HOUSE
(West Yorkshire)
(0532) 886225.

WARWICK CASTLE
(Warwickshire)
(0926) 495421.

WOBURN ABBEY
(Bedfordshire)
(0525) 290666.

CHATSWORTH

HAREWOOD HOUSE

WARWICK CASTLE

WOBURN ABBEY

ENGLAND

LONDON CENTRAL

Agnew's Galleries   W1

London Central Plan F5
43 Old Bond St (Underground – Green Park)
☎ 071-629 6176
If you happen to be shopping for Old Masters, then Thomas Agnew & Son's Ltd is the place to visit. They have a worldwide reputation for exhibiting some of the finest Old Master paintings and drawings, and many works pass through their hands on their way to famous art galleries and museums. Some contemporary English works are also displayed.
Open Mon-Fri, 9.30-5.30, 6.30 on Thu during major exhibitions. (Closed BH).
&. ⌨
Details not confirmed for 1992

Banqueting House   SW1

London Central Plan G5
Whitehall (Underground – Westminster)
☎ 071-930 4179 & 071-839 8918
A building which has seen many historic events including the execution of Charles I, the restoration of Charles II and the offer of the throne to William of Orange and Princess Mary. It was the centre of 17th-century London court life and has a sumptuous interior, enriched by Rubens' painted ceiling. The only surviving part of the original Palace of Whitehall, it was designed by Inigo Jones and built in 1619.
Open all year, Mon-Sat 10-5. (Closed Good Fri, 23 Dec-2 Jan & BH's). Liable to close at short notice for Government functions.
shop ✱
Details not confirmed for 1992

British Museum   WC1

London Central Plan G8
Great Russell St (Underground – Russell Sq,Tottenham Court Rd)
☎ 071-580 1788 (recorded information) & 071-323 8599

The stern facade of the British Museum belies the rich and varied treasures within which make it one of the great museums of the world, showing the works of man from many civilisations, from prehistoric to comparatively recent times. Founded in 1753, the nucleus of the museum was the collections of Sir Hans Sloane and Sir Robert Cotton. The galleries are the responsibility of the following departments: Egyptian, Greek and Roman, Western Asiatic, Japanese, Prehistoric and Romano-British, Medieval and later, Coins and Medals, Oriental Prints and Drawings and Ethnography (based at the Museum of Mankind). The museum also displays famous books and manuscripts from the British Library collections. The original building, Montagu House was demolished, and Sir Robert Smirke commissioned to build a more suitable replacement on the site, which was completed in 1852; the famous domed Reading Room was added in 1857. Among the treasures not to be missed are the Egyptian mummies, the notorious and superb Elgin marbles, two of the four existing copies of the Magna Carta, Shakespeare's signature, Nelson's plan of the Battle of Trafalgar and the Sutton Hoo treasure. There is a regular programme of gallery talks, lectures and films, and young visitors can enjoy special children's trails.
Open all year, Mon-Sat 10-5, Sun 2.30-6. (Closed Good Fri, May Day, Xmas & 1 Jan).
Free.
☕ ✕ *licensed* &. *(parking by arrangement; touch tour for visually impaired) toilets for disabled shop* ✱

Cabinet War Rooms   SW1

London Central Plan G4
Clive Steps, King Charles St (Underground – Westminster)
☎ 071-930 6961
The underground emergency accommodation provided to protect the Prime Minister, Winston Churchill, his War Cabinet and the Chiefs of Staff during the Second World War provide a fascinating insight into those tense days and nights. Among the 21 rooms are the Cabinet Room, the Map Room (where information about operations on all fronts was collected) and the Prime Minister's room, which have been carefully preserved since the end of the war. Other rooms have been restored to their original appearance.
Open all year, daily 10-6. Last admission 5.15 (Closed 24-26 Dec & 1 Jan).
£3.60 (ch £1.80, students & pen £2.70). Party 10+.
&. *toilets for disabled shop* ✱

Chelsea Physic Garden   SW3

London Central Plan C1
66 Royal Hospital Rd (Underground – Sloane Square)
☎ 071-352 5646
The second oldest botanic garden in England was begun in 1673 for the study of plants used in medicine by the Society of Apothecaries. By the late 18th century it was famous throughout Europe for its rare and unusual plants, and it is still used for botanical and medicinal research. For the visitor it offers displays of many fascinating plants, and is an oasis of peace and quiet amidst the hubbub of Chelsea. Exhibition of painters of the garden – for sale during Chelsea week.
Open 22 Mar-18 Oct, Wed & Sun 2-5. Additional opening during Chelsea Flower Show week, 19-22 May. Groups at other times by appointment.
£2.50 (ch 5-16 & students £1.30).
&. *garden centre* ✱

Commonwealth Institute   W8

London Central Plan A4
Kensington High St (Underground – High Street Kensington)
☎ 071-603 4535
Discover the history, landscapes, wildlife, crafts and economies of the 50 countries of the Commonwealth on three floors of spectacular galleries, where you can visit the Caribbean, see Canada from a skidoo, climb up Mount Kenya or take a rickshaw across Bangladesh. There are also cultural events and exhibitions as well as educational programmes and special activity sheets for children, and holiday workshops. The Commonwealth Shop sells gifts and crafts from around the world. Special for 1992 is the New Worlds series of programmes in which exhibitions, visual, verbal and performing arts events, conferences etc focus on periods of history to explore the relationships between the Commonwealth and Europe.
Open all year, Mon-Sat 10-5, Sun 2-5. (Closed Good Fri, May Day, 24-26 Dec & 1 Jan).
✱ *Free. Occasional charge for special exhibitions.*
🅿 ✕ *licensed* &. *(lift from car park) toilets for disabled shop* ✱

Contemporary Applied Arts   WC2

London Central Plan G7
43 Earlham St, Covent Garden (Underground – Covent Garden, Leicester Sq)
☎ 071-836 6993
Current arts and crafts are to be found in this centre which runs a programme of special exhibitions and retail displays including wallhangings, furniture, ceramics, pottery and jewellery. There are also books and magazines on craft and design for sale.
Open all year, Mon-Sat 10-5.30pm (Closed Sun, BH Mon, Xmas & New Year).
Free.
&. *shop* ✱

Courtauld Institute Galleries   WC2

London Central Plan H6
Somerset House, Strand (Underground – Temple, Embankment)
☎ 071-873 2526
The Galleries moved from the Woburn Square premises in March 1990 and opened at Somerset House on 15th June 1990. They contain the superb collection of paintings begun by Samuel Courtauld in the 1930s and presented to the University of London in memory of his wife. This is the most important collection of Impressionist and post-Impressionist works in Britain and includes paintings by Monet, Renoir, Degas, Cezanne, Van Gogh and Gauguin. There are also works by Michelangelo, Rubens, Goya, and other notable masters, as well as early Italian paintings. British and French 20th-century works given to the University by Roger Fry are also displayed here. Exhibitions are changed. Special events for 1992 include: 6 Nov-20 Dec, Exhibition of Mexican 19th Century Prints.
Open all year, Mon-Sat 10-6, Sun 2-6. (Closed Good Fri, Xmas & New Year).
✱ *£3 (ch, pen & students £1.50).*
☕ &. *(parking arranged, lift) toilets for disabled shop* ✱

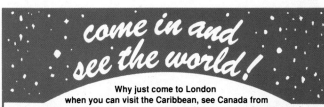

Cuming Museum   SE17

London Central Plan K2
155-157 Walworth Rd (Underground
– Elephant & Castle)
☎ 071-701 1342
The museum of Southwark's history.
The worldwide collections of the
Cuming family joined with the local
history of Southwark, from Roman
times through the days of Chaucer,

Shakespeare and Dickens to the present
day. Special exhibitions on local themes.
Special events for 1992 include: 6 Jun-
Apr 1993, major temporary exhibition
on medieval Southwark.
*Open all year, Tue-Sat 10-5. School &
adult parties daily by appointment. (Closed
BH's & Sat of BH wknd).
Free. shop ✗*

The Design Museum at Butler's Wharf   SE1

London Central Plan L5
Butler's Wharf, Shad Thames
(Underground – London Bridge)
☎ 071-403 6933
A museum of everyday objects. It is the
first of its kind to show design in mass
production and in the context of our
museum of everyday objects. It is the
first of its kind to show design in mass

production and in the context of our
lives. As well as the cafe and restaurant
there is also a library and a lecture
theatre.
*Open all year, Tue-Sun 11.30-6.30.
(Closed Mon ex BH's).*
P (charged) 🍽 ✗ licensed ♿ toilets for
disabled shop ✗
Details not confirmed for 1992

Dickens House   WC1

London Central Plan H9
48 Doughty St (Underground – Russell
Square)
☎ 071-405 2127
Charles Dickens lived in Doughty Street
in his twenties and it was here he wrote
his first full-length novel, *The Pickwick
Papers* and later *Oliver Twist* and *Nicholas
Nickelby*, celebrated for their acute
observation of society on all levels, and
their sympathy for the often unfortunate
characters. Pages of the original
manuscripts of Dickens's books are on
view together with valuable first editions

in the original paper parts, his special
marriage licence and many other
personal mementos. A reconstruction of
the Dingly Dell kitchen, as described in
The Pickwick Papers, is displayed in the
basement and on the first floor, Dickens'
drawing room has been reconstructed.
*Open all year, Mon-Sat 10-5, last
admission 4.30pm. (Closed Sun, BH, Good
Fri & Xmas wk).*
*£2 (ch under 16 £1, pen & students
£1.30). Family ticket £4.*
♿ shop ✗

Dr Johnson's House   EC4

London Central Plan I7
17 Gough Square (Underground –
Temple, Blackfriars)
☎ 071-353 3745
The celebrated literary figure, Dr Samuel
Johnson, lived at 17 Gough Square
between 1749 and 1759. It was here
that he wrote his English Dictionary,
and a first edition is on display at the
house. The dictionary took eight and a
half years to complete and contained
40,000 words. (He then undertook the
formidable task of editing the complete
works of Shakespeare).

The house in Gough Square, tucked
away behind Fleet Street, is a handsome
example of early 18th-century
architecture. It was opened as a museum
in 1914 and exhibits include a fine
collection of prints, letters and other
memorabilia from the life of a man who
was to become the most quoted
Englishman after Shakespeare.
*Open all year, May-Sep, daily 11-5.30;
Oct-Apr 11-5. (Closed Sun, BH's, Good Fri
& 24 Dec).*
✱ *£2 (ch, students & pen £1.50).*
shop ✗

Florence Nightingale Museum   SE1

London Central Plan H4
2 Lambeth Palace Rd (Underground –
Westminster, Waterloo)
☎ 071-620 0374
Florence Nightingale needs no introduction, but this museum shows clearly
that she was more than 'The Lady with
the Lamp'. Beautifully designed, the
museum creates a personal setting in
which are displayed Florence's prized
possessions, a lamp from the Crimean
War and nursing artefacts. The centrepiece

is a recreated ward scene from the
Crimea and audio-visual technology
takes the museum beyond its four walls.
Set on the site of the first School of
Nursing, this museum is an interesting
experience, showing the continued
relevance of this remarkable woman.
*Open all year, Tue-Sun 10-4 (last
admission). (Closed Xmas, 1 Jan, Good Fri
& Etr Sun).*
£2.50 (ch, students & pen £1.50).
🍽 ♿ toilets for disabled shop ✗

Green Park   SW1

London Central Plan E5
(Underground – Green Park)
The smallest of the central London
parks, Green Park is aptly named, for
the Tyburn stream runs just below the
surface, maintaining its lush verdancy. It
is situated in the triangle formed by
Piccadilly, The Mall and Constitution

Hill (where Charles II used to take his
constitutional stroll) and was formerly
meadowland. This informal character is
still maintained today, for there are no
flower borders here – just the springtime
crocuses and daffodils which grow
among the grass.

The Guildhall   EC2

London Central Plan K7
Gresham St (Underground – Bank, St
Paul's)
☎ 071-606 3030
The Court of Common Council
(presided over by the Lord Mayor)
administers the City of London and
meets in the Guildhall. Dating from
1411, when the Livery Companies
raised money for its construction, the
building was badly damaged in the Great
Fire and again in the Blitz. The great
hall, traditionally used for the Lord
Mayor's Banquet and other important
civic functions, is impressively decorated
with the banners and shields of the

livery companies, of which there are
more than 90. Beneath it lies a 15th-
century crypt, the largest of its kind in
London. The Clock Museum, which has
a collection of 700 exhibits, charts the
history of 500 years of time-keeping.
The Guildhall Library has an unrivalled
collection of manuscripts, books and
illustrations on all aspects of the capital
city.
*Open all year, May-Sep, daily 10-5; Oct-
Apr, Mon-Sat 10-5. (Closed Xmas, New
Year, Good Fri, Etr Mon & infrequently
for Civic occasions).*
♿ shop ✗
Details not confirmed for 1992

Guinness World of Records Exhibitions   W1

London Central Plan F6
The Trocadero, Coventry St,
Piccadilly Circus (Underground –
Piccadilly Circus)
☎ 071-439 7331
Through the use of life sized models,
videos and the latest audio-technology,
thousands of world records come alive at
the touch of a button. Six themed areas
depict: The Human World, The Animal
World, Our Planet Earth, Structures and
Machines, The Sports World and The
World of Entertainment.
   Visitors can watch original newsreel

footage whilst measuring up to the
world's tallest man; select their choice of
sporting records from the Sports Recall
Data Bank; watch an exciting chronicle
of man's exploration of space; listen to
the songs that sold millions on a 50s
style juke box, and much more.
*Open all year, Mon-Sat 10am-10pm (last
admission), Sun 10-9.30pm (last
admission). (Closed 25 Dec).*
*£5 (ch 4-16 £3.20, under 3 free, pen &
students £3.95). Group 10+.*
♿ *toilets for disabled shop* ✗

HMS Belfast   SE1

London Central Plan L5
Morgans Ln, Tooley St (Underground
– London Bridge)
☎ 071-407 6434
The largest cruiser ever built for the
Royal Navy dates from 1939. She
served in the Second World War, and
was saved from the breaker's yard to
become a floating naval museum. She is
owned by the Imperial War Museum
and is now permanently moored in the
Pool of London, with seven decks to
explore. New sound and light displays,
exhibitions, art gallery and cinema bring
the ship to life. Recorded audio guides

available. Special events take place
throughout the year. Exhibitions in
1992 include Damage Control Display
opening in April and Falklands
Exhibition: 10th Anniversary, opening
July.
*Open all year, daily. 20 Mar-Oct 10-6,
last admission 5.20; Nov-19 Mar 10-4.30,
last admission 4. (Closed 24-26 Dec & 1
Jan).*
✱ *£3.60 (ch, students & pen £1.80).
Party.*
🍽 ♿ *(wheelchair lift for access on board)
shop* ✗

Houses of Parliament   SW1

London Central Plan G4
Westminster (Underground –
Westminster)
☎ 071-219 4272

From the time of Edward the Confessor
to Henry VIII, the site of the present-
day Houses of Parliament was the main
residence of the monarch. Hence the
often-used term the 'Palace of
Westminster'. It was not until Henry
VIII moved to Whitehall Palace in 1529
that the building was turned over to
state institutions. A disastrous fire in
1834 destroyed most of the medieval
palace and a competition was held for

the design of a new Parliament building.;
Charles Barry was awarded the
commission with his Gothic-style design
(although Pugin was responsible for
much of the creative detail). Today the
building stands at 940ft long, covers
eight acres and includes 1100
apartments. There are over two miles of
passages. To the south stands the lofty
Victorial Tower where the Union Jack
flies when Parliament is in session. At
the north end of the building is the
clock tower which contains Big Ben, the
13¼-ton hour bell.
*To gain admission to the Strangers'
Galleries join the queue at St Stephens
entrance from approx. 5.30pm Mon-Thu,
approx 9.30am Fri (House of Commons).
From approx 2.30pm Tue, Wed & some
Mons, 3pm Thu & 11am Fri (House of
Lords) or by arrangement with MP (House
of Commons) or Peer (House of Lords).
Free but guides require payment if used.*
♿ *(by arrangement) toilets for disabled shop
(bookstall)* ✗ 🚻

Hyde Park   W2

London Central Plan C5
(Underground – Hyde Park Corner,
Marble Arch)
Situated to the west of Park Lane,
between Knightsbridge and Bayswater,
and formerly a Royal hunting park,
Hyde Park now consists of 340 acres of
grass and trees, intersected by paths. The
Serpentine, at its centre, provides a

habitat for wild creatures which cannot
find sanctuary elsewhere in the city
centre. It was the venue for the Great
Exhibition in 1851, but is probably best
known for Speakers' Corner, near
Marble Arch, where, every Sunday,
anyone can stand up and say just what
they please.

Imperial War Museum   SE1

London Central Plan I3
Lambeth Rd (Underground – Lambeth
North)
☎ 071-416 5000

Founded in 1917 and established in
1920 by an Act of Parliament, this
museum illustrates and records all
aspects of the two World Wars and
other military operations involving
Britain and the Commonwealth since
1914. It has recently undergone major

renovations and although the vast
collections are still housed within the
imposing walls of the original building in
Lambeth Road, it is now a thoroughly
modern museum employing all the latest
technology to make its exhibitions more
vital and atmospheric for the visitor.
Improvements include a new, large
exhibition hall, art galleries and a shop
and licensed restaurant. There are always
special exhibitions and the programme of
events includes film shows and lectures.
The Imperial War Museum has a wealth
of military reference material, although
some reference departments are open to
the public by appointment only.
*Open all year, daily 10-6. (Closed 24-26
Dec & 1 Jan).*
✱ *£3 (ch 5-16, students, UB40 & pen
£1.50). Party 10+.*
✗ *licensed* ♿ *toilets for disabled shop* ✗

The Jewish Museum   WC1

London Central Plan G9
Woburn House, Tavistock Square
(Underground – Russell Square, Euston
Square)
☎ 071-388 4525
A fascinating exhibition displaying a
collection of ceremonial art, portraits
and antiques illustrating Jewish life,
history and religion. Two audio-visual
programmes explain Jewish festival and
ceremonies. Special event for 1992: Apr-
Oct, exhibition on London's 18th-
century Portuguese Jewish Comunity.
*Open Tue-Thu 10-4 & Sun am (Fri Apr-
Sep 10-4, Oct-Mar 10-12.45). (Closed Sat,
Mon, Public & Jewish Hols).*
Donations
& shop ✻

Kensington Gardens   W8

London Central Plan A5
(Underground – Queensway, Lancaster
Gate)
This was part of Hyde Park until
William III enclosed his palace gardens
and today, again, the two areas are not
physically divided. A change of character
is apparent, though, once you cross the
invisible boundary which runs from
north to south across the Serpentine
Bridge. Kensington Gardens are noted
for their tranquility and formality and
include the Round Pond, Queen Anne's
Orangery, the Sunken Garden and
Flower Walk.

Kensington Palace State Apartments & Court Dress Collection   W8

London Central Plan A4
Kensington Gardens (Underground –
High Street Kensington)
☎ 071-937 9561
The birthplace of Queen Victoria and
today the London residence of the
Prince and Princess of Wales, Princess
Margaret and Prince and Princess
Michael of Kent, Kensington Palace
looks out over lovely gardens and an
expanse of green parkland. When the
house was bought by William III in
1689, it was a more modest town
house. He commissioned Sir
Christopher Wren to remodel the
building and it was enlarged again and
decorated by William Kent for George I.
It was the principal private royal
residence until George II died. The State
Apartments display pictures and
furniture from the Royal Collection and
there is a section on the Great
Exhibition. The colourful Court Dress
Collection exhibits some of the
magnificent costumes worn at court
from 1750 onwards.
*Open all year, Mon-Sat 9-5, Sun 1-5. Last
admission 4.15. (Closed Good Fri, 24-26
Dec & 1 Jan).*
& *toilets for disabled shop* ✻
Details not confirmed for 1992

Leighton House   W14

London Central Plan A4
12 Holland Park Rd (Underground –
Holland Park)
☎ 071-602 3316
A uniquely opulent and exotic example
of High Victorian taste, Leighton House
was built for the President of the Royal
Academy, Frederic Lord Leighton, by
George Aitchison. The main body of the
house was built in 1866 but the
fabulous Arab Hall, an arresting
'Arabian Nights' creation, was not
completed until 13 years later. The hall
is decorated with gilt, ancient tiles from
the Middle East and a fountain.
Leighton was one of the great Victorian
artists, and much of his work is
displayed here, along with that of his
contemporaries. His sculptures are
exhibited in the quiet garden and there
are two galleries containing both modern
and historic art.
*Open all year, daily 11-5 (6pm during
temporary exhibitions). Garden open Apr-
Sep 11-5. (Closed Sun & BH).*
Free.
✻

Linley Sambourne House   W8

London Central Plan A4
18 Stafford Ter (Underground – High
Street Kensington)
☎ 081-994 1019
The home of Linley Sambourne
(1844-1910), chief political cartoonist at
Punch, has had its magnificent artistic
interior preserved, almost unchanged,
since the late 19th century. Also
displayed are many of Sambourne's own
drawings and photographs.
Open Mar-Oct, Wed 10-4, Sun 2-5.
£2.
shop ✻

Lloyd's of London   EC3

London Central Plan L7
1 Lime St (Underground – Bank)
☎ 071-623 7100
Controversy surrounded the innovative
design of the new Lloyds building when
it was completed in 1986 and the
world's leading insurance market moved
into its new headquarters. A purpose-
built exhibition which explains how
Lloyds works today adds interest to a
visit to one of London's most fascinating
examples of modern architecture. The
famous Lutine Bell is housed in the
Underwriting Room.
*Open all year, Mon-Fri, 10-3.45 (pre-
booked groups) 10-2.30 (general public).
Visiting times subject to change, telephone
for details. At the time of going to press –
only pre-booked groups are allowed entry for
security reasons.*
& *shop* ✻
Details not confirmed for 1992

The London Diamond Centre   W1

London Central Plan E7
10 Hanover St (Underground – Oxford
Circus)
☎ 071-629 5511
Everything you ever needed to know
about diamonds and their related craft is
displayed at the London Diamond
Centre. Visitors can watch diamond
cutters and polishers at work; a
goldsmith creating settings; walk in to a
reconstructed diamond mine and see a
collection of replicas of some of the
world's most famous and historic stones.
A video explains other interesting aspects
of the industry.
*Open all year, Mon-Fri 9.30-5.30, Sat
9.30-1.30.*
& ✻
Details not confirmed for 1992

The London Dungeon   SE1

London Central Plan L5
28-34 Tooley St (Underground –
London Bridge)
☎ 071-403 0606
The London Dungeon has won the
British Tourist Authority's Award for
Outstanding Tourist Enterprise. Its
modest entrance off a street near
London Bridge station will lead the
visitor through to a series of slimy vaults
where the seamy side of life in past
centuries is convincingly re-created.
Methods of torture and death, the tools
of witchcraft and black magic and some
of the more grisly medicinal practices are
well represented. Viewing takes about an
hour; this museum is not recommended
for the faint-hearted.
Entry includes the 'Great Fire of
London' and 'Theatre of the Guillotine'
shows, both using the latest in
interactive technology.
*Open all year, daily, Apr-Sep 10-5.30; Oct-
Mar 10-4.30.*
£5 (ch 14 & pen £3, students £4).
▨ & *toilets for disabled shop* ✻

The London Planetarium   NW1

London Central Plan D8
Marylebone Rd (Underground – Baker
Street)
☎ 071-486 1121

'Solar Swoop' is the new star show at

the London Planetarium, which
incorporates laser effects for the first
time. Two eagles come to life under the
Planetarium dome and describe their
adventures through the Solar System to
audiences. 'Space Trail' is the new
interactive 'lift-off' zone at the
Planetarium, where visitors can receive
up-to-date information about space
through the use of touch-sensitive
screens.
*Open all year, daily (ex 25 Dec), star shows
from 12.40, every 40 mins (earlier during
wknds & holidays).*
Admission fee payable.
shop ✻

London Transport Museum   WC2

London Central Plan H6
The Piazza, Covent Garden
(Underground – Covent Garden,
Leicester Sq)
☎ 071-379 6344

The former flower market in Covent
Garden (now moved to a site in Nine
Elms, SW8) has been converted to
house the London Transport Museum.
It is devoted to the story of London's
public transport from the earliest
beginnings up to the present day, and
vehicles on show include steam
locomotives, trams, buses, trolleybuses,
railway coaches and horse buses. There
are also extensive displays using working
models and audio-visual material, and
visitors can 'drive' a modern bus, a tram
and a tube train. There are special events
for children and families in the school
holidays and a reference library is
available by appointment. There are a
number of exhibitions planned for 1992;
telephone for details.
*Open all year, daily 10-6, last admission
5.15pm. (Closed 24-26 Dec).*
*£3 (ch 5-16, students, UB40s & pen
£1.50). Disabled & ch 5 free. Family ticket
£7. Party 20+.*
& *(wheelchair available) toilets for disabled
shop* ✻

✳ An asterisk indicates that up-to-date information
was not available at the time of our
research – 1991 information has been
published as an indication of
what you may expect.

London Zoo NW1

London Central Plan D9
Regents Park (Underground – Camden Town, Gt Portland St)
☎ 071-722 3333

London Zoo is home to over 5000 animals, insects, reptiles and fish. Founded by Sir Stamford Raffles, the Zoo was opened to the public in 1847, and can claim the world's first aquarium, insect and reptile house. Visitors today can view rare and exotic animals, many of which are participating in captive breeding programmes. Daily events such as Animals in Action, feeding times and Animal Encounters, give visitors an insight into animal behaviour. There are reductions for groups, and free guided tours can be arranged. For youngsters there is a Children's Zoo and Discovery Centre, and a whole range of educational programmes for schools. New exhibits include the African Aviary, offering unrivalled viewing of the birds within, and the Moonlight World where day and night are reversed. Favourites at the Zoo include black rhinos Rosie and Jos, two pairs of Asiatic Lions, the first of their kind in Europe, and of course, Ming the Giant Panda.
Open all year, daily from 10am.
✳ *£5.20 (ch £3.20, students & pen £4.30). Party.*
🅿 *(charged)* ☛ ✕ *licensed* ও *(wheelchairs available) toilets for disabled shop* ⋈

Madame Tussaud's NW1

London Central Plan D8
Marylebone Rd (Underground – Baker Street)
☎ 071-935 6861
 Madame Tussaud's world-famous waxwork collection was founded in Paris in 1770. It moved to England in 1802 and found a permanent home in London's Marylebone Road in 1884. It is Britain's top visitor attraction with over two and a half million visitors a year. The wax models are extremely life-like and the collection is being changed constantly: historical figures, film stars, kings, queens, sportsmen and other popular figures are represented. There are new themed areas within the exhibition, and these include the Garden Party, 200 Years of Madame Tussauds, and Hollywood Legends. The latest figures include John Major, Nelson Mandela, Just William, Neil Kinnock, and Nick Faldo.
Open all year 10-5.30 (9.30am wknds, 9am summer). (Closed 25 Dec).
Admission fee payable.
☛ ✕ *licensed* ও *(Lift access to all exhibition areas with guide escort) toilets for disabled shop* ⋈

Mall Galleries SW1

London Central Plan G5
The Mall (Underground – Charing Cross)
☎ 071-930 6844
These galleries are the exhibition venue for the Federation of British Artists. Eight art societies administered by the federation hold their exhibitions here.
Open all year, daily 10-5.
ও *(chairlft to galleries)* ⋈
Details not confirmed for 1992

Middle Temple Hall EC4

London Central Plan I7
The Temple (Underground – Temple, Blackfriars)
☎ 071-353 4355
Between Fleet Street and the Thames are the Middle and Inner Temples of the Temple Inn of Court, so named because of the Knights Templar who occupied the site from about 1160. Middle Temple Hall is a fine example of Tudor architecture and was built during the reign of Elizabeth I (completed in about 1570). The hall has a double hammerbeam room and beautiful stained glass showing the shields of past readers. The 29ft-long high table was made from a single oak tree from Windsor Forest; and portraits of George I, Elizabeth I, Anne, Charles I and Charles II, James, Duke of York and William II line the walls behind it. Sir Francis Drake was a member of the Middle Temple, and a table made from timbers from the *Golden Hind* – the ship in which he sailed around the world – is shown.
Open all year, Mon-Fri 10-12 & 3-4 (Closed BH).
Free.
⋈ 🚐

The Monument EC3

London Central Plan L6
Monument St (Underground – Monument)
☎ 071-626 2717
Designed by Wren and Hooke and erected in 1671-7, the Monument commemorates the Great Fire of 1666 which is reputed to have started in nearby Pudding Lane. The fire destroyed nearly 90 churches and about 13,000 houses. This fluted Doric column stands 202ft high (Pudding Lane is exactly 202ft from its base) and visitors can climb the 311 steps to a platform at its summit. The views over the City and beyond are splendid. Because of the steps, access is almost impossible for persons with severe disabilities: there is no lift or escalator.
Open all year (ex 25-26 Dec, 1 Jan, Good Fri & May Day) 31 Mar-Sep, Mon-Fri 9-6, Sat & Sun 2-6; Oct-30 Mar, Mon-Sat 9-4. Last admission 20 mins before closing.
✳ *£1 (ch 16 25p).*
⋈

Museum of Garden History SE1

London Central Plan H3
St Mary-at-Lambeth, Lambeth Palace Rd (Underground – Lambeth North)
☎ 071-261 1891 (between 11am-3pm)
Adjoining the south gateway of Lambeth Palace is the former church of St Mary, now the Museum of Garden History, and founded in memory of Charles I's gardener, John Tradescant. The newly made period knot garden is delightful and contains many plants popular in the 17th century. Captain William Bligh of the *Bounty* is buried here.
Open 4 Mar-9 Dec, Mon-Fri 11-3, Sun 10.30-5.
☛ ও *shop*
Details not confirmed for 1992

Museum of London EC2

London Central Plan J8
London Wall (Underground – St Paul's, Barbican)
☎ 071-600 3699 ext 240 or 280

Early December 1976 saw the official opening of the Museum of London. The collections of the former London and Guildhall museums were brought together in one specially designed building, located near the Barbican development. The site adjoins a stretch of the original Roman wall which surrounded the city.
 Devoted to and detailing all aspects of London life from pre-history to contemporary times, the museum offers a fascinating display presented in chronological order. The exhibits and tableaux are arranged to give the visitor a realistic view of life in the capital through the ages; archaeological levels are illustrated by a relief model of the Thames Valley which provides an apt starting point for the story. Features of special interest include the superb models of William the Conqueror's White Tower and old St Pauls; the audio-visual reconstruction of the Great Fire of London in 1666 (superbly atmospheric) and the exhibition of ceremonial London with the Lord Mayor's State Coach as its centrepiece. It is also worth looking out for the medieval hen's egg, a lift from Selfridges department store, and a 1930s Ford motor car. There is also a programme of temporary exhibitions, lunchtime lectures and evening films throughout the year.
 Special events for 1992 include: 19 May-21 Jun, London Documentary Photographers; 15 Sep-Jun 1993, The Purple, White and Green (the suffragettes in London).
Open all year, Tue-Sat 10-6, Sun 2-6 (Closed 24-26 Dec, 1 Jan & every Mon ex BH's). Parties by arrangement.
£3 (concessions £1.50, ch under 5 free). Family ticket £7.50.
✕ *licensed* ও *(wheelchairs available, lifts & induction loops) toilets for disabled shop* ⋈

Museum of Mankind W1

London Central Plan F6
6 Burlington Gardens (Underground – Piccadilly Circus)
☎ 071-636 1555 ext 8043

The ethnographical department of the British Museum was re-housed in 1970 at Burlington Gardens to form the Museum of Mankind. Its vast collections embrace the art and material culture of tribal, village and pre-industrial societies from most areas of the world other than Western Europe. It also houses archaeological collections from the Americas and Africa. The museum's policy is to mount a number of fascinating temporary exhibitions (usually lasting for at least a year) rather than have permanent displays on show, although there are a number of outstanding exhibits on permanent display. The reserve collection is stored in Shoreditch and can be made available for serious study. Film shows and educational services are provided.
Open all year, Mon-Sat 10-5, Sun 2.30-6. (Closed Good Fri, May Day, Xmas & 1 Jan).
Free.
☛ ও *shop* ⋈

Museum of the Moving Image SE1

London Central Plan H5
South Bank, Waterloo (Underground – Waterloo)
☎ 071-401 2636
A journey through cinematic history from the earliest experiments to all the technical wizardry of modern animation is what this museum offers the visitor. There are artefacts to handle, buttons to press and films to watch as well as a detailed explanation of the operations of a television studio. A fascinating insight into the world of films and television with each chapter as exciting as the last.
Open all year, daily 10-6. (Closed 24-26 Dec).
£5.50 (ch, UB40's, disabled & pen £4, students £4.70). Party 10+.
☛ ✕ *licensed* ও *toilets for disabled shop* ⋈
See advertisement on page 22.

Museum of The Order of St John EC1

London Central Plan J9
St John's Gate, St John's Ln (Underground – Farringdon)
☎ 071-253 6644 ext 135
One of London's more obscure museums shows a collection of paintings, silver and furniture belonging to the Order of St John. The interesting medieval gatehouse also houses items relating to the history of the St John Ambulance. Guided tours are available of the 16th-century Gatehouse and the 12th-century Crypt. A major exhibition on the Order's properties in London is planned for Aug/Sep 1992.
Open all year, Mon-Fri 10-5, Sat 10-4 (Closed Etr, Xmas wk & BH's). Guided tours 11 & 2.30 Tue, Fri & Sat.
Donations requested
ও *toilets for disabled shop* ⋈

National Army Museum SW3

London Central Plan D1
Royal Hospital Rd, Chelsea (Underground – Sloane Square)
☎ 071-730 0717
 The history of the British, Indian and Colonial forces from 1485 onwards unfolds in this museum. Displayed, in chronological order, are uniforms, weapons, prints, photographs, relics and mementos together with a special display of the orders and decorations of the Duke of Windsor and those five great Field Marshals – Lord Roberts, Gough, Kitchener, Wolseley and Sir George White VC. The Picture Gallery includes portraits by Gainsborough and Reynolds as well as battle scenes and pictures of the Indian regiments. A new display looks at the British Army in the Napoleonic Wars and includes a 400-square-foot model of the Battle of Waterloo. 1992 special exhibitions will cover the Civil War, the Falklands, and the Burma Campaign.
Open all year, daily 10-5.30. (Closed Good Fri, May Day, 24-26 Dec & 1 Jan).
Free.
🅿 ☛ ও *toilets for disabled shop* ⋈

How do they make you believe a man can fly?

National Gallery   WC2

London Central Plan G6
Trafalgar Square (Underground –
Charing Cross)
☎ 071-839 3321 & recorded
information 071-839 3526

In 1824 the government bought the
collection of pictures accumulated by
John Julius Angerstein, a London
underwriter, and exhibited them at his
former residence in Pall Mall. These
formed the major part of the collections
of the National Gallery. Further
bequests and purchases were made and
by 1831 space had become limited, so
plans were made for a special building to
house the works of art. The present neo-
classical building in Trafalgar Square was
opened in 1838. All the great periods of
European painting are represented here
although only a limited selection of
British works is displayed, as most of the
national collection is housed at the Tate.

The gallery's particular treasures include
Van Eyck's *Arnolfini Marriage*,
Velazquez's *Toilet of Venus*, Leonardo da
Vinci's cartoon (the Virgin and Child
with Saints Anne and John the Baptist),
Rembrandt's *Belshazzar's Feast* and
Titian's *Bacchus and Ariadne*. The British
paintings include Gainsborough's *Mr
and Mrs Andrews* and Constable's
Haywain. There are many more
captivating masterpieces to be seen at the
National Gallery which houses one of
the finest and most extensive collections
in the world. The Sainsbury Wing
opened in 1991 and contains the early
Renaissance works from 1260-1510.
Lectures, guided tours, children's
worksheets and quizzes are available.
Exhibitions for 1992 include: 26 Mar-24
May, Rembrandt: The Master and his
Workshop; 1 Jul-27 Sep, Manet and the
Execution of Maximilian; 12 Nov-7 Feb
1993, Edvard Munch: The Frieze of
Life.
*Open all year, Mon-Sat 10-6, Sun 2-6.
(Closed Good Fri, May Day, 24-26 Dec &
1 Jan).
Free. Admission charged for major
exhibitions.*
♨ ✕ *licensed* ♿ *(wheelchairs available,
induction loop in theatre, lifts) toilets for
disabled shop* ✻

National Portrait Gallery   WC2

London Central Plan G6
2 St Martin's Place (Underground –
Charing Cross)
☎ 071-306 0055

With the aim of illustrating British
history by means of a collection of
portraits of famous, and infamous, men
and women, the gallery's first home was
established in George Street,
Westminster. After several moves the
collection was finally housed in its
present accommodation in 1896.

Located behind the National Gallery,
the building was designed in the style of
an Italian palazzo. A further wing was
added in 1933. The portraits are
arranged in chronological order from the
top floor, starting with the medieval
period and finishing with the present
day. As well as paintings, there are
sculptures, miniatures, engravings,
photographs and cartoons among the
displays. Special exhibitions include
Michael Faraday 1791-1867 (Sep'91-19
Jan), The Portrait in British art
(Nov'91-9 Feb), Eve Arnold in Britain
(Nov'91-23 Feb), George Bernard Shaw
(10 Apr-5 Jul), BP Portrait Award (5
Jun-6 Sep), and Allan Ramsay (16
Oct-17 Jan'92).
*Open all year 10-5, Sat 10-6 & Sun 2-6.
(Closed Good Fri, May Day, 24-26 Dec &
1 Jan).
Free (ex special exhibitions)
shop* ✻

National Postal Museum   EC1

London Central Plan J7
**King Edward Building, King Edward
St** (Underground – St Paul's)
☎ 071-239 5420
This museum is a philatelist's paradise; it
contains the most comprehensive
collection of postage stamps in the
world. Established in 1965, the National
Postal Museum has obtained a vast
collection of material charting the
history of the postal system since its
inception. Exhibits include a display of
numerous stamps issued worldwide since
1878; the R M Phillips collection of
19th-century British stamps, including
the celebrated 'Penny Black', the Frank
Staff collections of 'postal history'

material, and Great Britains reference
display of stamps from King Edward VII
to the present day. The museum also
holds the Thomas de la Rue
correspondence archives, and a large
amount of unique philatelic material,
most of which is available for research
by prior arrangement. Temporary
displays are held throughout the year,
including People in the Post (from 6
May).
*Open all year, Mon-Thu (ex BH)
9.30-4.30, Fri 9.30-4.
Free.*
♿ *(main gallery accessible by prior
arrangement) shop* ✻

The Natural History Museum   SW7

London Central Plan A3
Cromwell Rd (Underground – South
Kensington)
☎ 071-938 9123

The museum's collections were built up
around the specimens collected by Sir
Hans Sloane and which formed a part of
the nucleus of the British Museum. By
1860 the continued expansion of the
collections meant that a separate natural
history museum was required; it was not
until 1881, though, that the new
museum – since 1962 officially the
British Museum (Natural History) – was
opened. The vast and elaborate
Romanesque-style building, with its
terracotta facing showing relief
mouldings of animals, birds and fishes,
continued . . .

covers an area of four acres. The exhibits
cover most aspects of biology and
geology. In the Whale Hall a life size
model of the enormous Blue Whale can
be seen, and in the Hall of Human
Biology visitors can learn about the way
their bodies work (including how it feels
to be in the womb). Creepy Crawlies
shows you how insects, spiders, crabs,
and their relatives are important to
humans, as both friends and foes.
Ecology stresses our relationship with,
and responsibility for, the natural world.
The opening of a major new permanent
exhibition on dinosaurs takes place in
Easter. This includes new skeletons,
recreated robotic models, and displays
on how dinosaurs lived, why they
became extinct, and how they were dug
up and studied by scientists. The Earth
Galleries were formerly the Geological
Museum, which contains the largest
exhibition on basic earth science in the
world, as well as a notable collection of
gemstones and a piece of the Moon.
The entrance to the Earth Galleries is on
Exhibition Road, separate from the
Cromwell Road entrance to the main
museum, but is covered by the same
entrance fee. Public lectures and films
are given on Tue, Thu and Sat. Leaflet
available on request.
*Open all year, Mon-Sat 10-6, Sun 11-6.
(Closed Good Fri, May Day, 24-26 Dec &
1 Jan).*
✳ *£3.50 (ch 5-18, student, UB40s & pen
£1.75). Family ticket £8. Party.*
♨ ♿ *toilets for disabled shop* ✻

Pirate Ships at Tobacco Dock   E1

London Central Plan L6
The Highway (Underground –
Shadwell & Wapping)
☎ 071-702 9681
These two replica sailing ships, moored
alongside Tobacco Dock, paint a
gruesome picture of piracy on the high
seas, their decks strewn with corpses as a
result of a sudden and bloody raid.

Below decks, 'The Three Sisters' houses
an animated history.of piracy, and 'The
Sea Lark' vividly brings to life the story
of Robert Louis Stevenson's *Treasure
Island*.
*Open all year, daily 10-6.
Three Sisters £2.50 (ch £1.50). Sea Lark
£1.*
Ⓟ *shop*

Pollock's Toy Museum   W1

London Central Plan F8
1 Scala St (Underground – Goodge
Street)
☎ 071-636 3452
Teddy bears, board games, toy theatres,
tin toys, mechanical and optical toys,
folk toys and nursery furniture, are
among the attractions to be seen in this
appealing museum. Items from all over

the world and from all periods are
displayed in two small, interconnecting
houses with winding staircases and
charming little rooms.
*Open all year, Mon-Sat 10-5. (Closed Sun
& Xmas).
£1.50 (ch 3-16, students & pen 50p).*
♿ *shop*

Public Record Office Museum   WC2

London Central Plan I7
Chancery Ln (Underground – Temple,
Blackfriars)
☎ 081-876 3444
The Public Record Office houses one of
the finest, most complete archives in
Europe, comprising the records of the
central government and law courts from
the Norman Conquest to the present
century. It is a mine of information and
some of the most interesting material is

exhibited in its museum. Domesday
Book is on permanent display, and a
rotating exhibition of temporary displays
on the theme 'Records and the People',
concerning the impact of social change
on the lives of ordinary people, will
continue in 1992.
*Open all year, Mon-Fri 10-5. Parties at
other times by arrangement.
Free.*
shop ✻ 🖾

The Queen's Gallery   SW1

London Central Plan E4
**Buckingham Palace, Buckingham
Palace Rd** (Underground – Victoria)
☎ 071-799 2331
The Queen's Gallery at Buckingham
Palace was first opened to the public in
1962 to display paintings, drawings,
furniture and other works of art in the
Royal Collection, one of the finest in
the world. The Gallery is sited in a
building originally designed as a
conservatory by John Nash in 1831 and
later converted into a chapel by Blore.
The building suffered severe bomb

damage in the Second World War and
was not reconstructed until 1962; part
of it still remains the private chapel of
Buckingham Palace. 1992 will see a
special exhibition on 'A King's Purchase;
George III and the Consul Smith
Collection' (6 Mar-24 Dec).
*Open Tue-Sat & BH Mon 10-5, Sun 2-5
(ex for short periods between exhibitions).
Telephone 071-799 2331 for detailed
information.
£2.50 (ch 17 £1.50, pen £2)*
♿ *shop* ✻

Regent's Park   NW1

London Central Plan D9
(Underground – Baker Street)
The elegant charm of this park, north of
Marylebone Road, can be attributed to
John Nash, who laid it out, along with
the imposing surrounding terraces, as
part of a plan for a new palace which
was never built. It now contains London

Zoo (see separate entry), a boating lake,
open-air theatre, the Regent's Canal and
the lovely Queen Mary's Rose Garden.
There are a number of Victorian garden
ornaments around the park and a group
of fossil tree trunks are the only
reminders that the Royal Botanic
Gardens were once situated here.

Rock Circus   W1

London Central Plan F6
London Pavilion, Piccadilly Circus
(Underground – Piccadilly Circus)
☎ 071-734 7203
This is the story of rock and pop music
from the 1950s to the present day, told
through animated wax figures and stereo
sound through headsets. Rock Circus re-
enacts the great performances of stars
such as The Beatles, Elvis Presley, Stevie
Wonder and Madonna by use of special

effects, memorabilia and, often, original
clothing and instruments. Waxwork
figures to be unveiled during 1992
include: Bryan Ferry, James Brown, Cliff
Richard.
*Open all year, daily 11-9, Tue 12-9, Fri &
Sat 11-10pm, holiday periods in summer
10am-10pm, Tue 12-10.
£5.95 (ch £3.95, students & pen £4.95).
Family ticket £15.85.*
♿ *toilets for disabled shop* ✻

Royal Academy Of Arts W1

London Central Plan F6
Burlington House, Piccadilly
(Underground – Piccadilly Circus)
☎ 071-439 7438
George III founded the Royal Academy in 1768 and it was moved to Burlington House from the National Gallery in 1869. Its Summer Exhibition runs from May to August to show the work of living artists, and major exhibitions of international importance are held during the rest of the year. The Academy owns a splendid collection of masterpieces including work by Michelangelo and Constable, but these are not always on public view.
Open all year, daily 10-6. (Closed 24-26 Dec).
licensed toilets for disabled shop
Details not confirmed for 1992

Royal Britain EC2

London Central Plan K8
Aldersgate St (Underground – Barbican, Moorgate)
☎ 071-588 0588
All the technical wizardry of the 20th century is employed in this unique exhibition on the history of Britain's monarchy. The visitor walks through time, beginning in the mists of prehistory and ending with a revealing look at royalty today.
Open all year, daily 9-5.30. (Closed 25 Dec).
licensed toilets for disabled shop
Details not confirmed for 1992

The Royal Mews SW1

London Central Plan E4
Buckingham Palace, Buckingham Palace Rd (Underground – Victoria)
☎ 071-799 2331
Designed by John Nash and completed in 1825, the Royal Mews houses the State Coaches. These include the gold, fairy-tale state coach made in 1762, with panels painted by the Florentine artist Cipriani. It has been used for every coronation since that date. The collection also includes the Irish State Coach, private driving carriages and royal sleighs. The Windsor greys and Cleveland Bay carriage horses are stabled here. When the Royal Mews re-opens in April, all seven State Carriages will be displayed together for the first time.
Open all year, Apr-mid Jul, Wed & Thu; mid Jul-Sep, Wed-Fri; Oct-Mar, Wed only noon-4. (Closed if carriage procession or state visit).
£2 (ch 17 £1, pen £1.50).
toilets for disabled shop

St James's Park SW1

London Central Plan F5
(Underground – St James's Park)
Situated between Buckingham Palace and Whitehall, this is the oldest of the Royal Parks in London, drained and converted into a deer park by Henry VIII in 1532. Charles II had the park redesigned in the style of Versailles, but the park as it exists today, with its lake, plantations and walks, was created by Nash for George IV. It remains one of the most delightful and popular places to relax, both for visitors and for workers, who frequently share their sandwiches with the large variety of waterfowl on the lake. There are also band concerts and refreshment facilities.

Schooner Kathleen & May SE1

London Central Plan K6
St Mary Overy Dock, Cathedral St
(Underground – London Bridge)
☎ 071-403 3965
The last British wooden, three-masted topsail schooner, is on show to the public in a berth at St Mary Overy Dock, on the South Bank of the River Thames. Exhibitions on board, and film and audio-visual displays provide added interest.
Open all year, daily 10-5 (4 at wknds); Nov-Mar 11-4. (Closed Xmas, New Year & wknds Nov-Feb).
£1 (ch, students & pen 50p). Family ticket £2.50.
shop

Places to visit in this guide are pinpointed on the atlas at the back of the book.

Science Museum SW7

London Central Plan B3
Exhibition Rd, South Kensington
(Underground – South Kensington)
☎ 071-938 8000

Of all the Exhibition Road museums, the Science Museum is the most attractive to children (and often adults too). Among the displays are many working models with knobs to press, handles to turn and buttons to push to various different effects: exhibits are set in motion, light up, rotate and make noises. The collections cover the application of science to technology and illustrate the development of engineering and industry through the ages; there are galleries dealing with printing, chemistry, nuclear physics, electricity, photography, communications and medicine. A popular feature of the museum is the 'Launch Pad', an interactive children's gallery where children of all ages can carry out their own fun experiments. 'Food for Thought' is a permanent gallery which explains the impact of science and technology on today's food. The centrepiece of the Exploration of Space exhibition is the Apollo 10 space capsule, whilst the world's oldest steam locomotive and Stephenson's *Rocket* can be seen in the huge gallery devoted to rail and road transport. The Wellcome Museum of the History of Medicine features numerous reconstructions of important events in medical history.
Open all year, Mon-Sat 10-6, Sun 11-6. (Closed 24-26 Dec & 1 Jan).
* *£3.50 (ch & concessions £1.75, pen £2).*
toilets for disabled shop

The National Museum of Science & Industry

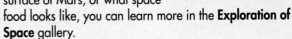

Science Museum

The Science Museum, Exhibition Road, London SW7 2DD
Telephone: 071-938 8000
Opening Times: Monday-Saturday 10.00-18.00
Sunday 11.00-18.00
Closed Christmas Eve, Christmas Day, Boxing Day and New Years Day
Exhibits of actual equipment, instruments and machinery tell the story of the history of science and industry, from the first steam locomotive to man's first flight in space.
There are more than six hundred working exhibits and plenty of fun activities for you to try.
Includes **Launch Pad,** an interactive children's gallery where children of all ages can carry out their own challenging and fun experiments.
In **Food for Thought** you can find out more about the food you eat.
If you've ever wondered what the surface of Mars, or what space food looks like, you can learn more in the **Exploration of Space** gallery.

Sherlock Holmes Museum NW1

London Central Plan C8
221b Baker St (Underground – Baker Street)
☎ 071-935 8866
221b Baker Street, that famous address of super-sleuth Sherlock Holmes, was opened as a museum in March 1990 to the great delight of admirers of the great detective. The first-floor rooms contain all the features familiar to the Holmes enthusiast, and an authentic Victorian atmosphere has been maintained throughout the house. The museum is of unique interest and visitors are encouraged to take photographs.
Open all year, daily 10-6. (Closed 25 Dec).
* *£5 (ch 8-16 £3 & pens £3). Party*
shop

Sir John Soane's Museum WC2

London Central Plan H8
13 Lincoln's Inn Fields (Underground – Holborn)
☎ 071-405 2107 & 071-430 0175 (Info)
Sir John Soane was responsible for some of the most splendid architecture in London, and his house, built in 1812, contains his collections of antiquities, sculpture, paintings, drawings and books. Included amongst his treasures are the *Rake's Progess* and *Election* series of paintings by William Hogarth, and the Sarcophagus of Seti 1 dating from 129BC. The architectural drawing collection can be viewed, but by appointment only.
Open all year, Tue-Sat 10-5. Also first Tue of month 6-9pm. (Closed BH). Lecture tour Sat 2.30.
Free.
shop

* An asterisk indicates that up-to-date information was not available at the time of our research – 1991 information has been published as an indication of what you may expect.

The Story of Telecommunications EC4

London Central Plan J6
145 Queen Victoria St (Underground – Blackfriars)
☎ 071-248 7444
A fascinating exhibition featuring the past, present and future of Britain's telecommunications. The many working exhibits chart 200 years of progress from the earliest telegraphs to satellites and optical fibres. Examples of the different styles of domestic telephones through the decades are displayed among the collection of interesting exhibits.
Open all year, Mon-Fri 10-5. (Closed BH). Also open Lord Mayors Show day.
Free.
(inductive loops) shop

Tate Gallery   SW1

London Central Plan G2
Millbank (Underground – Pimlico)
☎ 071-821 1313 & 071-821 7128

In 1892 Sir Henry Tate, the sugar magnate and prominent collector of contemporary British painting and sculpture, offered to finance the building of a new and permanent home for his growing collection of British Art. Sidney J R Smith was commissioned to design the new gallery on the site of the former Millbank Prison and the building was officially opened to the public in 1897. A number of extensions to the building have followed, the most recent being the Clore Gallery in 1987 which houses the Turner Bequest. In the early part of this century the gallery was able to expand its collection to include foreign 20th-century art.

Amongst the displays for 1992 will be rooms devoted to Hogarth and his circle, Constable and Early 19th-century Landscape, Romanticism and Pre-Raphaelitism, Whistler and his Circle, Art in Germany 1900-1945, Dadd and Surrealism, British Art in the 1930s, British Surrealism and Post-War painting in Britain and France. The Duveen Sculpture Galleries, restored in 1989, will show British Sculpture from Epstein, Moore and Hepworth to contemporaries such as Barry Flanagan, Stephen Cox and Anish Kapoor.

Open Mon-Sat 10-5.50, Sun 2-5.50. (Closed Good Fri, May Day BH, 24-26 Dec & 1 Jan). Opening days may be subject to alteration.
Free. Charge for major loan exhibitions.
♥ ✗ *licensed ⟨ (wheelchairs available on request, parking by arrangement). toilets for disabled shop* ✖

Theatre Museum   WC2

London Central Plan H6
Russell St, Covent Garden
(Underground – Covent Garden, Leicester Sq)
☎ 071-836 7891

Major developments, events and personalities from the performing arts are illustrated in this appealing exhibition. Stage models, costumes, prints, drawings, posters, puppets, props and a variety of other theatre memorabilia are displayed. Special exhibitions include 'Slap – the Art of Stage Make-up', and 'From Page to Stage with the *Wind in the Willows*, based on the National Theatre production. There are children's Saturday clubs, evening 'live' theatre productions, and a monthly 'Masterclass' with members of the acting profession talking about their roles in the theatre.

Open all year, Tue-Sun 11-7.
✳ *£3 (ch under 5 free, ch, students, disabled, UB40's & pen £1.50). Party. Family ticket.*
♥ ⟨ *toilets for disabled shop* ✖

✖ The 'No Dogs' symbol does not normally apply to guide dogs – these are permitted in most establishments.

Tower Bridge   SE1

London Central Plan L6
Walkway (Underground – Tower Hill)
☎ 071-407 0922 & 071-407 5247

Nearly a century old, the fairy-tale outline of Tower Bridge remains one of the capital's most popular landmarks. Its glass-covered walkway stands 142ft above the Thames, affording a panoramic view of the river. Much of the original machinery for working the bridge is still in place and can be seen in the museum.

Open all year, Apr-Oct, 10-6.30; Nov-Mar 10-4.45 (last ticket sold 45 mins before closing). (Closed Good Fri, 24-26 Dec & 1 Jan).
£2.50 (ch 15 & pen £1, ch 5 free). Party.
⟨ *toilets for disabled shop* ✖

Tower of London   EC3

London Central Plan L6
Tower Hill (Underground – Tower Hill)
☎ 071-709 0765

Perhaps the most famous castle in the world, the Tower of London has played a central part in British history throughout the ages. The nucleus of the complex is the original White Tower, built by William the Conqueror as a show of strength to the population of London; it remains one of the most outstanding examples of Norman military architecture in Europe. Today it houses the Royal Armouries, the national collection of arms and armour based on the great arsenal of Henry VIII. For a great part of its history, the Tower of London was used, among other things, as the State Prison. It was here that King Henry VIII had two of his wives executed, here that Lady Jane Grey died and here that Sir Walter Raleigh was imprisoned for 13 years. From the reign of Charles II its main use was as an arsenal, administrative centre and the headquarters of the Royal Mint (until 1812) but during both World Wars it reverted to a state prison and was used to incarcerate German spies. The unique Yeoman Warders, or 'Beefeater' guards are not present merely as a tourist attraction: they guard the Crown Jewels which are exhibited here. Another feature of the Tower are the ravens whose continued residence is said to ensure that the Kingdom does not fail. The first new raven for 300 years was hatched in May 1989, bringing their numbers up to nine.

Open all year, Mar-Oct, Mon-Sat 9.30-5.45, Sun 2-5.30 (last admission 5); Nov-Feb, Mon-Sat 9.30-4.30 (last admission 4). (Closed Good Fri, 24-26 Dec & 1 Jan. Jewel House closed 7 Jan-3 Feb).
⟨ *toilets for disabled shop* ✖
Details not confirmed for 1992

Victoria & Albert Museum   SW7

London Central Plan B3
Cromwell Rd (Underground – South Kensington)
☎ 071-938 8500

Covering art and design, from all countries and from all periods and styles, this museum has over seven miles of galleries. It is impossible to take it all in on one visit, and so it is advisable to buy a guide book and plan a route before setting off to see the displays. The collection was founded at Marlborough House after the Great Exhibition, and was known as the Museum of Manufactures. In 1857 it moved to its present site and was called the South Kensington Museum. Enlarged and re-designed by Sir Aston Webb at the end of the 19th century it was re-opened in 1909 by Edward VII as the Victoria and Albert Museum. There are two types of galleries: the primary ones which give a comprehensive picture of a period or civilisation; and subject galleries which contain the specialised collections. Features include a series of rooms decorated and equipped with the paintings, furniture and household accessories of particular periods in British history including the enormous 16th-century Great Bed of Ware. The Toshiba Gallery of Japanese Art and Design, the Constable Paintings, Raphael Cartoons and the costume exhibition displayed in the Octagon Court all contribute toward one of the world's outstanding collections of fine and applied arts. Exhibitions for 1992 include 'Sovereign – A celebration of 40 years of Her Majesty The Queen's accession to the throne' (Apr-Sep) and 'The Art of Death' (8 Jan-22 Mar).

Open all year, Mon-Sat 10-5.50, Sun 2.30-5.50. (Closed Good Fri, May Day, 27 Aug, 24-26 Dec & 1 Jan).
✳ *Donations-suggested £3 (students, UB40 & pen 50p).*
✗ *licensed ⟨ toilets for disabled shop* ✖

This is just one of many guidebooks published by the AA. The full range is available at any AA shop or good bookshop.

Wallace Collection   W1

London Central Plan D7
Hertford House, Manchester Square
(Underground – Bond Street)
☎ 071-935 0687

An elegant 18th-century town house makes an appropriate gallery for this outstanding collection of art. Founded by the 1st Marquis of Hertford and brought to England from Paris in the late 19th century by Richard Wallace (son of the 4th Marquis), it was bequeathed to the nation in 1897 and came on public display three years later. As well as an unrivalled representation of 18th-century French art with paintings by Boucher, Watteau and Fragonard, Hertford House displays a wealth of furniture, porcelain and beautiful works of art. It is the home of Frans Hals' Laughing Cavalier and of paintings by Gainsborough, Rubens, Delacroix and Titian. It also houses the largest collection of arms and armours outside the Tower of London. A special exhibition of Rembrandt will be held on 5 Mar-5 Jul.

Open all year, Mon-Sat 10-5, Sun 2-5. (Closed Good Fri, May Day, 24-26 Dec & 1 Jan).
Free.
⟨ *(ramps over steps, prior telephone call appreciated) shop* ✖

Wesley's House, Museum & Chapel   EC1

London Central Plan L9
49 City Rd (Underground – Old Street)
☎ 071-253 2262

Wesley's Chapel has been the Mother Church of World Methodism since its construction in 1778. The crypt houses a museum which traces the development of Methodism from the 18th century to the present day. John Wesley's personal possessions, including clothes, books and furniture, are on display in the adjacent house, in which the founder of Methodism lived and died. Some areas of the site are undergoing refurbishment, but these will be re-opened to the public in July, offering greater access for the disabled, picnic areas and a cafeteria.

Open all year, Mon-Sat 10-4 (Closed 25 & 26 Dec). Main service 11am Sun followed by an opportunity to tour the museum and house.
✳ *House & museum £1.60 (ch, students, UB40's & pen 80p); House or museum £1 (ch, students, UB40's & pen 50p).*
⟨ *shop* ✖

Westminster Hall SW1

London Central Plan G4
Westminster (Underground –
Westminster Hall)
☎ 071-219 4272
The great Westminster Hall, where
Charles I was tried in 1649, has survived
virtually intact since it was remodelled at
the end of the 14th century. It even
escaped the fire in 1834 which destroyed
much of the medieval Palace of
Westminster. The magnificent
hammerbeam roof is the earliest
surviving example of its kind.
*Open for tours by arrangement with MP
only. Mon-Thu am (Closed Sat & BH's).
Free although guides require payment if
employed.*
& *toilets for disabled* ✖

For an explanation of the symbols and abbreviations,
see page 2.

LONDON OUTER

London Toy & Model Museum BAYSWATER (W2)

London Outer Plan C3
21-23 Craven Hill (Underground –
Bayswater)
☎ 071-262 9450 & 071-262 7905
A fine collection of commercially-made
models and toys with emphasis on trains,
cars and boats. To add to the interest
there is an extensive garden railway.
*Open all year, Mon-Sat 10-5.30, Sun
11-5.30. (Closed 25-26 Dec & 1 Jan).*
✱ £2.70 (ch 5-15 £1.20, pen, students &
UB40 £1.70). Family ticket £6. Party
15+.
🍴 *shop* ✖

Bethnal Green Museum of Childhood BETHNAL GREEN (E2)

London Outer Plan E4
Cambridge Heath Rd (Underground –
Bethnal Green)
☎ 081-980 2415 & 081-980 3204
This prefabricated Victorian hall houses
a multitude of childhood delights. Toys,
dolls and dolls' houses, model soldiers,
puppets, games, model theatres and
children's costume are all included in its
well planned displays.
*Open all year, Mon-Thu & Sat 10-6, Sun
2.30-6 (Closed Fri, May Day, Spring BH
Mon, 24-26 Dec & 1 Jan).
Free.*
🅿 & *toilets for disabled shop* ✖

Geffrye Museum BETHNAL GREEN (E2)

London Outer Plan E4
Kingsland Rd (Underground – Old
Street)
☎ 071-739 9893 & 071-739 8368
The former almshouses of the
Ironmongers' Company, built in the
18th century, have now been converted
to house this interesting and well
presented museum. A series of period
room sets have been arranged in
chronological order which contain an
impressive collection of furniture and
woodwork dating from Elizabethan
times to the end of the 1930s. Special
exhibitions and events run all year
round, on anything from antiques and
period style to Asian cookery and jazz.
*Open all year, Tue-Sat 10-5, Sun 2-5 &
BH Mons 10-5 (Closed Mon, Good Fri,
24-26 Dec & 1 Jan).*
🍴 & *(wheelchair available) toilets for
disabled shop* ✖
Details not confirmed for 1992

Hall Place BEXLEY

London Outer Plan F2
Bourne Rd (near jct of A2 & A233)
☎ Crayford (0322) 526574
Hall Place is an attractive mansion of
chequered flint and brick, but it is most
interesting for its garden. This has
topiary in the form of the 'Queen's
Beasts'; rose, rock, peat and water
gardens; and a herb garden with a
fascinating range of plants (labelled in
braille) for medicine and cooking. There
is also a conservatory, a local studies
centre and museum and a programme of
exhibitions. On Spring Bank Holiday
1992 (25 May) there will be an Arts
Fayre. Exhibitions will include children's
art (8 Feb-7 Mar),'Boswell's Bexley:
Photographs and mementoes from
Arthur Boswell' (21 Mar-7 Jun), and
100 years of fashion (20 Jun-6 Sep).
*Open all year, House: Mon-Sat 10-5, Sun
& BHs 2-6 (summer); Mon-Sat 10-dusk
(winter). Gardens: Mon-Fri 7.30-dusk, Sat
& Sun 9-dusk.*
✱ *Admission under review*
🅿 🍴 & *shop* ✖

Rangers House BLACKHEATH (SE3)

London Outer Plan E3
Chesterfield Walk
☎ 081-853 0035
This beautiful villa, the former home of
Philip Stanhope, the 4th Earl of
Chesterfield, houses the important
Suffolk collection of Jacobean and Stuart
portraits. Also featured is the Dolmetsch
collection of musical instruments and
some fine furniture. There is a busy
programme of chamber concerts, poetry
readings, holiday projects and
workshops.
*Open all year, Apr-Sep, daily 10-6; Oct-
Mar, daily 10-4. (Closed 24-25 Dec).
Free.*
& *toilets for disabled shop* ✖
(EH)

Kew Bridge Steam Museum　　　　　　　　BRENTFORD

London Outer Plan B3
**The Pumping Station, Green Dragon
Ln** (Underground – Gunnersbury)
☎ 081-568 4757
The Victorian pumping station has
model engines, steam engines and six
beam engines, of which five are working
and one is the largest in the world. A

forge, diesel house and old workshops
can also be seen. Various events are held
including a Magic of Meccano show
(24/5 Apr), historic engine rally ((25
May), and great model steam trials (Sep).
*Open all year, daily 11-5. In steam wknds
& BHs. (Closed Xmas wk).*
🅿 🖦 ♿ *shop*

Musical Museum　　　　　　　　　　BRENTFORD

London Outer Plan B3
368 High St (Underground –
Gunnersbury)
☎ 081-560 8108
This is an extensive collection of
automatic musical instruments, from
musical boxes to music rolls which play
huge orchestrations. There are

demonstrations during opening hours,
and a series of Saturday evening concerts
planned (prior booking essential).
*Open Apr-Oct, Sat & Sun 2-5. Also Jul-
Aug, Wed-Fri 2-4. (Tour 1hr 30mins).
£2 (ch & pen £1.50). Party.*
♿ *shop* 🐕

South London Art Gallery　　　　CAMBERWELL (SE5)

London Outer Plan E3
65 Peckham Rd
☎ 071-703 6120
This art gallery presents ten exhibitions a
year and draws mainly from local
sources. Collections include drawings,

paintings and prints by English artists,
from 1700 onwards.
*Open only when exhibitions are in progress,
Tue-Sat 10-6, Sun 3-6 (Closed Mon).*
🐕
Details not confirmed for 1992

Carlyle's House　　　　　　　　　CHELSEA (SW3)

London Outer Plan D3
24 Cheyne Row (Underground –
Sloane Square)
☎ 071-352 7087
'The Sage of Chelsea' – distinguished
essayist and writer of historical works,
Thomas Carlyle – lived in this 18th-
century town house from 1834 until his
death in 1881. His soundproofed study
and the kitchen, where such literary

notables as Tennyson, Thackeray and
Browning were entertained have been
preserved exactly as the Carlyles knew
them.
*Open Apr-Oct, Wed-Sun & BH Mons
11-5. Last admission 4.30. (Closed Good
Fri)
£2.50. No parties over 20 persons.*
🐕 ▱
(NT)

Chessington World of Adventures　　CHESSINGTON

London Outer Plan B1
(on A243, M25 off junc 9)
☎ Epsom (0372) 727227
Dare you ride the Vampire, the UK's
only hanging roller coaster and the
Dragon River Water Ride with the most
exciting single drop in the UK? Plus
Chessington's latest attraction, Professor
Burp's Bubble Works, a unique crazy
colourful musical indoor water ride for
all the family. Over 100 rides and
attractions including the Canyon, 5th
Dimension, Smugglers' Galleon, Magic
Carpet, Safari Skyway Monorail, Old

Crocks Rally, the Juggler, an
international circus & world famous zoo.
Special Saturdays are allocated to
Scouts, Cubs, Guides, Brownies and
youth clubs, etc. Please telephone for
details.
*Open – Theme Park 28 Mar-1 Nov.
Zoological Gardens open all year. Last
admissions 3pm.*
✳ *£10.50 (£9.50). High season £10.75
(£9.75). Party 20 + .*
🅿 🖦 ✕ *licensed* ♿ *(some rides not
accessible) toilets for disabled shop* 🐕

Chislehurst Caves　　　　　　　　CHISLEHURST

London Outer Plan F2
Old Hill (off A222)
☎ 081-467 3264
This labyrinth of caves has been called
the enigma of Kent. Miles of mysterious
caverns and passages hewn out of the
chalk over some 8,000 years can be

explored with experienced guides to tell
the history and legends of the caves.
*Open all year, daily 11-4.30. (Closed 25
Dec).
£2.50 (ch £1.20); longer tours: Sun &
BH's only £4 (ch £2).*
🅿 🖦 ♿ *toilets for disabled shop*

Chiswick House　　　　　　　　　CHISWICK (W4)

London Outer Plan C3
Burlington Ln, Chiswick (Underground
– Gunnersbury)
☎ 081-995 0508
Considered to be one of the finest
Palladian buildings in Britain, this
domed mansion was built between 1725
and 1730 with magnificent interior

detailing by William Kent. It has been
restored to all its former glory.
*Open all year, Apr-Sep, daily 10-6; Oct-
Mar, daily 10-4. (Closed 24 & 25 Dec).
£2 (ch £1, pen, students & UB40 £1.50).*
♿ *shop* 🐕
(EH)

Royal Air Force Museum　　　　COLINDALE (NW9)

London Outer Plan C5
Grahame Park Way, Hendon
(Underground – Colindale)
☎ 081-205 2266

Over 65 full-size original aeroplanes and
other exhibits, all under cover, tell the
fascinating story of flight through the

ages. Extensive galleries show the
political and historical impact of this
means of transport and communication
– including the incredible 'Battle of
Britain Experience', the story of history's
most famous air battle. Visitor facilities
include personal stereo-audio tours, a
daily free cinema programme, a Tornado
flight simulator, guided tours and a
regular programme of special events and
exhibitions (telephone for details).
*Open daily 10-6. (Closed 24-26 Dec & 1
Jan).*
✳ *£4.10 (ch & concessions £2.05). Family
ticket £10. Party 10 + .*
🅿 ✕ *licensed* ♿ *(wheelchair available)
toilets for disabled shop* 🐕

🐕 The 'No Dogs' symbol does not normally apply
to guide dogs – these are permitted in
most establishments.

Craft Centre of Silk　　　　　　　　CRAYFORD

Map 04 TQ57
Bourne Rd
☎ (0322) 559401
A guided tour will take visitors along a
kind of 'silk road' through the working
mill and craft centre which shows the
history of silk, associated craft tools and
sericulture. As well as the audio-visual
presentation, craftsmen can be seen at
work hand printing silk. The Mill Shop

offers a wide range of silk gifts at mill
prices – and it has a sale in January,
April and October.
*Open all year, Mon-Sat 9.30-5 (4.30 Sat).
(Closed BH's).*
✳ *Craft Centre £1.25 (pen 75p). Guided
Tour of Craft Centre & Mill by
appointment £1.50 (pen £1).*
🅿 🖦 ♿ *(craft centre,shop & coffee shop
only) toilets for disabled shop* 🐕

Darwin Museum, Down House　　　　　DOWNE

Map 04 TQ46
Luxted Rd (Off A233, signposted)
☎ Farnborough (Kent) (0689) 859119
Down House was the home of Charles
Darwin from 1842 until his death in
1882. The drawing room and Old Study
are restored and furnished as they were
when Darwin was working on his
famous, and still controversial book *On
the Origin of Species by means of Natural
Selection*, first published in 1859. The
Museum also includes collections and
memorabilia from Darwin's voyage on
HMS Beagle. There is one room
dedicated to his illustrious grandfather

Dr Erasmus Darwin. The garden is
maintained as laid out by the Darwins,
retaining the original landscaping, flint
and brick walls and glass house, beyond
which lies the famous Sand Walk or
thinking path, along which Darwin took
his daily walk. There will be a bulb
display in March, and other displays to
be arranged; please telephone for
recorded message.
*Open all year, Wed-Sun 1-6 (last admission
5.30). Also BH Mon. (Closed 14 Dec-1
Jan & Feb).*
✳ *£1.50 (ch 5-15 50p, pen & student £1).*
🅿 ♿ *shop* 🐕

Dulwich Picture Gallery   DULWICH (SE21)

London Outer Plan E2
College Rd (N of South Circular A205)
☎ 081-693 5254
The oldest public picture gallery in England is also one of the most beautiful. Housed in a building designed by Sir John Soane in the early part of the 19th century, it displays a fine cross-section of European art, including many

Old Masters. Temporary exhibitions are held throughout the year, including 'Stanislas, Patron and Collector – treasures from Poland' (May-Aug).
Open all year, Tue-Fri 10-1 & 2-5, Sat 11-5, Sun 2-5. (Closed Mon & BHs).
Guided tours Sat & Sun 3pm.
£2 (pen, students & UB40 50p, ch 16 free).
🅿 ♿ *shop* ✶

East Ham Nature Reserve   EAST HAM (E6)

London Outer Plan F4
Visitor Centre, Norman Rd
☎ 081-470 4525
This 10-acre nature reserve with grassland and woodland, has two nature trails with printed guides (braille version in preparation). One trail is suitable for all disabled visitors. There is a visitor centre with displays relating to natural

history and the history of the churchyard nature reserve.
Open Visitor Centre: wknds 2-5. Nature Reserve: summer, Mon-Fri 9-5, wknds 2-5; winter, Mon-Fri 9-4, wknds 2-4.
Free.
♿ *(trails for wheelchairs & blind) toilets for disabled shop* ✶

Forty Hall Museum   ENFIELD

London Outer Plan E5
Forty Hill
☎ 081-363 8196
The mansion of Forty Hall was built in 1629 for Sir Nicholas Raynton, Lord Mayor of London, and then altered in the 18th century. It has fine plaster

ceilings and collections of 17th- and 18th-century furniture, paintings, ceramics and glass. There are also local history displays and temporary exhibitions.
Open all year, Tue-Sun 10-5.
Free.
🅿 ♨ ♿ *toilets for disabled shop* ✶

Claremont Landscape Garden   ESHER

London Outer Plan A1
(E of A307)
☎ (0372) 469421
Laid out by Vanbrugh and Bridgeman before 1720, extended and naturalised by Kent, this is the earliest surviving example of an English landscaped garden. Its 50 acres include a lake with an island pavilion, a grotto and a turf amphitheatre. There are also avenues and viewpoints. A Fête Champetre will

be held on 15-19 July, telephone for details after 26 May.
Open all year, Apr-Oct Mon-Fri 10-6, Sat-Sun & BH Mon 10-7 (15-19 Jul, closes 4pm); Nov-Mar Tue-Sun 10-5 or sunset if earlier.
✶ *Sun & BH Mon £2.50; Mon-Sat £1.50*
🅿 ♨ ♿ *toilets for disabled shop* ✶ *(except guide dogs Apr-Oct)*
(NT)

Horniman Museum   FOREST HILL (SE23)

London Outer Plan E2
London Rd
☎ 081-699 2339
A rather eccentric museum with displays from different cultures, natural history collections (including living creatures) and an extensive exhibition of musical instruments from all over the world. There is also a large library for

reference. Lectures, concerts, special exhibitions and educational workshops are often given.
Open all year, Mon-Sat 10.30-6, Sun 2-6. (Closed 24-26 Dec).
♨ ♿ *(stair lift being installed during 1991) toilets for disabled shop* ✶
Details not confirmed for 1992

Cutty Sark Clipper Ship   GREENWICH (SE10)

London Outer Plan E3
Greenwich Pier
☎ 081-858 3445 & 081-853 3589
The fastest tea clipper to be built (in 1869) once sailed 363 miles in a single day. She has been preserved in dry dock since 1957 and her graceful lines dominate the riverside at Greenwich. Exhibitions and a video presentation on board tell the story of the ship and there

is a magnificent collection of ships' figureheads. Major restoration work can be seen while the ship is open to visitors, ie shipwrights, riggers etc.
Open all year, daily 10-5, Sun 12-5; 6pm in summer. (Closed 24-26 Dec). Last ticket 30 mins before closing.
✶ *£3 (concessions £2). Party 15 +.*
♿ *(between deck & lower hold deck only) shop* ✶

Gipsy Moth IV   GREENWICH (SE10)

London Outer Plan E3
Greenwich Pier, King William Walk
☎ 081-858 3445 or 081-853 3589
Standing near the famous tea clipper is the yacht in which Sir Francis Chichester made the first single-handed

sailing trip around the world, in 1966-7.
Open Apr-Oct, daily 10-6. (Sun 12-6). Last ticket 30 mins before closing.
✶ *50p (ch 30p).*
✶

Greenwich Park   GREENWICH (SE10)

London Outer Plan E3
On the northern perimeter of this delightful park is the largest children's playground in any Royal Park. It is famous, though, as the home of the Old Royal Observatory (see separate entry) and the Meridien which marks Nought Degrees Longitude, where you can stand

in the eastern and western hemispheres at the same time. Mostly laid out by Le Notre, whose love of symmetry is very noticeable, the park has wonderful views down over the Royal Naval College to the Thames. The Wilderness is 13 acres of woodland and wild flowers, inhabited by a herd of fallow deer.

National Maritime Museum   GREENWICH (SE10)

London Outer Plan E3
Romney Rd
☎ 081-858 4422
The National Maritime Museum tells the story of Britain and the Sea, from ancient boats and Roman trade, through centuries of boatbuilding, battles and exploration to 20th-century trade and pleasurecraft. Features include items from Henry VIII's naval fleet, skilled 17th-century Navy Board models of

wooden warships, great masterpieces of battles at Trafalgar and in the Americas. See Nelson's uniform and elegant gilded Royal barges and shalltops.
Open all year, Mon-Sat 10-5 (6pm in summer), Sun 2-5 (6pm in summer). (Closed Good Fri, May Day, 24-27 Dec & 1 Jan).
♨ ♿ *(wheelchair available, touch tours on request) toilets for disabled shop* ✶
Details not confirmed for 1992

Old Royal Observatory   GREENWICH (SE10)

London Outer Plan E3
Greenwich Park
☎ 081-858 4422
Charles II founded the Royal Observatory in 1675 'for perfecting navigation and astronomy'. It stands at zero meridian longitude and is the original home of Grenwich Mean Time. Set in the beautiful grounds of Greenwich Park, which were laid out to plans by the French gardener, Le Nôtre,

who planned the grounds at Versailles, the Royal Observatory is part of the National Maritime Museum. It houses an extensive collection of historic timekeeping, astronomical and navigational instruments.
Open all year, daily 10-5 (6pm in summer). (Closed Good Fri, May Day, 24-27 Dec & 1 Jan).
🅿 ♿ *shop* ✶
Details not confirmed for 1992

♿ This symbol indicates that much or all of the attraction is accessible to wheelchairs. However, there may be some restrictions, so it would be wise to check in advance.

The Queens House   GREENWICH (SE10)

London Outer Plan E3
Romney Rd
☎ 081-858 4422
The first Palladian-style villa in England, designed by Inigo Jones for Anne of Denmark and completed for Queen Henrietta Maria, wife of Charles I. The recent restoration has been carried out to show the house as it appeared when new, with bright silks and furnishings. The Great Hall, the State Rooms and a Loggia overlooking Greenwich Park are

notable features. There is a fine collection of Dutch marine paintings, including some of the finest seascapes ever painted.
Open all year, Mon-Sat 10-5 (6pm in summer), Sun 2-5 (6pm in summer). (Closed Good Fri, May Day, 24-27 & 29-31 Dec & 1 Jan).
♿ *(induction loop commentary) toilets for disabled shop* ✶
Details not confirmed for 1992

Royal Naval College   GREENWICH (SE10)

London Outer Plan E3
☎ 081-858 2154
With the Queen's House as its focal point, this group of buildings was designed by Webb in the late 17th century and Wren in the early 18th century. Additions were subsequently made by such notables as Vanbrugh, Hawksmoor and Ripley. The College

was formerly used as a naval hospital (until 1873) and particularly splendid features include the chapel and the painted hall.
Open all year (Painted Hall and Chapel only), daily (ex Thu) 2.30-5 (last admission 4.30).
shop ✶ �︎

Ham House   HAM

London Outer Plan B2
(W of A307)
☎ 081-940 1950
This lovely house was built in 1610 and redecorated by the Duke and Duchess of Lauderdale in the 1670s. The duke was a member of Charles II's government, and followed the most fashionable style. There is a restored 17th-century garden.

House closed for restoration during 1992.
Open gardens: all year, Tue-Sun (open BH Mon) 10.30-6 pm dusk if earlier. House closed in 1992 for major restoration.
✶ *House closed. Garden free.*
♨ ♿ *toilets for disabled* ✶
(NT)

Fenton House
HAMPSTEAD (NW3)

London Outer Plan C4
Windmill Hill (Underground – Hampstead)
☎ 071-435 3471
A William and Mary mansion built about 1693 and set in a walled garden, Fenton House is now owned by the National Trust. It contains a display of furniture and some notable pieces of Oriental and European porcelain as well as the Benton Fletcher collection of early

keyboard instruments, including a harpsichord once played by Handel. Summer concerts are arranged.
Open Mar, Sat & Sun only; Apr-Oct, Sat-Sun & BH Mon 11-6, Mon, Tue & Wed 1-7. Last admission 30mins before closing.
£3
& ✗
(NT)

Freud Museum
HAMPSTEAD (NW3)

London Outer Plan D4
20 Maresfield Gardens (Underground – Hampstead)
☎ 071-435 2002 & 071-435 5167
In 1938, Sigmund Freud left his home in Vienna as a refugee from the Nazi occupation and chose exile in England, transferring his entire domestic and working environment to the house at 20 Maresfield Gardens. He resumed work until his death here a year later. Freud's extraordinary collection of Egyptian, Greek, Roman and Oriental antiquities,

his working library and papers, and his fine furniture including the famous desk and couch are all here. The house was bequeathed by his daughter Anna Freud (1895-1982), whose pioneering development of her father's work is also represented. The museum has exhibitions on display and historic videos for viewing.
Open all year, Wed-Sun 12-5 (Closed BH's).
& *(personal tours can be arranged if booked in advance) shop* ✗
Details not confirmed for 1992

Keats House
HAMPSTEAD (NW3)

London Outer Plan D4
Keats Grove (Underground – Hampstead)
☎ 071-435 2062
The two Regency houses were occupied by John Keats and his lover and nurse Fanny Brawne. They have now been converted into one building and form a museum devoted to the life of this famous poet. Manuscripts, letters and

personal mementos are displayed. Shelley Bicentenary exhibition (May-Sep).
Open all year, Apr-Oct Mon-Fri 10-1 & 2-6, Sat 10-1 & 2-5, Sun & BH 2-5; Nov-Mar Mon-Fri 1-5, Sat 10-1 & 2-5, Sun 2-5. (Closed Good Fri, Etr eve, May Day, 25-26 Dec & 1 Jan).
Free.
& *shop* ✗

Kenwood, Iveagh Bequest
HAMPSTEAD (NW3)

London Outer Plan D4
Hampstead Ln (Underground – Hampstead)
☎ 081-348 1286
Forming the most beautiful part of Hampstead Heath, the wooded grounds of Kenwood were laid out in the 18th century by the first Earl of Mansfield. He engaged Robert Adam to enlarge the house and transform it into a mansion, and the orangery and library are Adam's design. The first Earl of Iveagh bought the estate in 1925 and bequeathed the grounds, house and its contents to the nation two years later. It contains a fine

collection of paintings including old masters and 18th and 19th-century portraits by the likes of Gainsborough and Reynolds. An exhibition of 18th-century shoebuckles and jewellery makes interesting viewing. Kenwood is a popular venue for outdoor summer events and musical evenings.
Open all year, daily. Good Fri-Sep 10-6; Oct-Maundy Thursday 10-4. (Closed 24-25 Dec).
Free.
P ♨ ✗ *licensed* & *toilets for disabled shop* ✗ *(ex grounds)*

Hampton Court Palace
HAMPTON COURT

London Outer Plan B2
☎ 081-977 8441

The palace was started in the early 16th century by Cardinal Wolsey, Lord Chancellor to Henry VIII. When he fell out of favour he presented it to the king as a placatory gesture. Henry VIII expanded the palace by adding the hammer-beamed great hall, the immense kitchens and the Royal Tennis courts. Later monarchs (and Cromwell) left their

own mark: Elizabeth I added plants from the New World to the garden, and William and Mary commissioned Wren to remodel part of the building. The result was the handsome Fountain Court, part of which was devastated by fire in recent years.
Today pictures, furniture and tapestries can be seen, and there are handsome gardens and parkland close to the River Thames. Special attractions are the kitchens, the great gatehouse, the orangery with its Mantegna paintings, the Hampton Court vine, and the maze, laid out in the time of William III. *Open all year, Palace & maze, daily 9.30-6 (4.30pm mid Oct-mid Mar). (Closed 23-26 Dec & 1 Jan).*
P *(charged)* ♨ ✗ *licensed* & *toilets for disabled shop* ✗ *(ex in gardens)*
Details not confirmed for 1992

Church Farm House Museum
HENDON (NW4)

London Outer Plan C5
Greyhound Hill (Underground – Hendon Central)
☎ 081-203 0130
Dating from the 1660s, this gabled house is a museum of local interest. It features a period furnished kitchen and dining room. Different exhibitions are held throughout the year. Temporary

exhibitions are planned for 1992, including American Comics (summer) and Early Plastics (winter).
Open all year, Mon-Sat 10-1 & 2-5.30 (Tue 10-1 only), Sun 2-5.30. (Closed Good Fri, 25-26 Dec & 1 Jan).
Free.
P & *shop* ✗

Highgate Cemetery
HIGHGATE (N6)

London Outer Plan D5
Swains Ln (Underground – Archway)
☎ 081-340 1834
Highgate Cemetery is the most impressive of a series of large, formally arranged and landscaped cemeteries which were established around the perimeter of London during the first decades of Queen Victoria's reign. Visitors will discover a wealth of fine sculpture and architecture amongst the tombstones, monuments and mausoleums as well as the graves of such

notables as the Rossetti family, George Eliot, Michael Faraday and Karl Marx. *Open all year. Eastern Cemetery: daily 10-5 (4 in winter). Western Cemetery by guided tour only: Sat & Sun 11-4 (3 in winter); midweek tours 12,2 & 4 (12, 2 & 3 in winter). Other times by arrangement. (Closed 25 Dec & during funerals). East cemetery £1. Tour of West cemetery £3 (ch 12-17 £1, under 12 free, pen, students & UB40's £2).*
P *shop* ✗

Syon House
ISLEWORTH

London Outer Plan B3
(Approach via Park Rd off Twickenham Rd)
☎ 081-560 0881/3
The house stands on the site of a monastery, founded by Henry V. After the Dissolution it passed into the hands of the Duke of Somerset but he was accused of treason by John Dudley. Dudley was created Earl of Northumberland and Syon House became his property. The Earldom was made a Dukedom, and in 1750 the 1st Duke of Northumberland engaged Robert Adam to renovate the mansion.

Adam not only adapted the architecture but also was responsible for the furnishings and decoration – the result is spectacular, particularly in the superbly coloured ante-room and gallery library. The Tudor brick was refaced with Bath stone in the late 19th century; this gives the exterior a rather harsh appearance but in no way detracts from the splendours inside.
Open Apr-Sep, Sun-Thu 12-5 (last ticket 4.15). Oct, Sun only.
P ✗ *licensed* & *toilets for disabled shop garden centre* ✗
Details not confirmed for 1992

Syon Park
ISLEWORTH

London Outer Plan B3
(A315 off A310 to Busch Cnr, entry Park Rd)
☎ 081-560 0881/3
Contained within the 55 acres that make up Syon Park is one of the inspirations for the Crystal Palace at the Great Exhibition of 1851: a vast crescent of metal and glass, the first construction of its kind in the world and known as the Great Conservatory. It was designed by Fowler in 1829. The park also boasts a six-acre rose garden which, at the right time of year, assaults the visitor's eye with its brilliant colour; a butterfly house and the largest garden centre in

England. Although the horticultural reputation of Syon Park goes back to the 16th century – when the use of trees purely as ornaments was looked upon as unique – its beauty today is thanks to the master of landscape design, 'Capability' Brown. It is hardly believable that the peaceful haven he has created beside the River Thames is just nine miles from the centre of London.
Open all year, Apr-Oct, daily 10-6; Nov-Mar, 10-dusk. (Closed Xmas). Conservatory closed during winter months.
P ✗ *licensed* & *toilets for disabled shop garden centre* ✗
Details not confirmed for 1992
See advertisement on page 26.

Heritage Motor Museum (Syon Park)
ISLEWORTH

London Outer Plan B3
☎ 081-560 1378
Yet another attraction of this glorious park is an exhibition of more than 100 vehicles covering much of the story of the British motor industry. Special displays are mounted during August and September. Car club meets are held most summer weekends. The museum will be relocated to Warwickshire in

October 1992.
Open all year, daily 10-5.30 (4pm Nov-Mar). (Closed 25-26 Dec). Closing at the end of October. Museum relocating to Gaydon, Warwickshire.
£2.50 (ch & pen £1.75). Family ticket £5.50.
P ♨ ✗ *licensed* & *(wheelchair available) toilets for disabled shop garden centre* ✗

Kew Gardens (Royal Botanic Gardens)
KEW

London Outer Plan B3
(Underground – Kew Bridge)
☎ 081-940 1171

The world-famous gardens at Kew started as a mere nine-acre site, laid out by George III's mother, Princess Augusta in 1759 (she lived in the White House at Kew which has long since been demolished). In 1841 the gardens were given to the State and by 1904, after Queen Victoria had presented more of the surrounding land to the country, the gardens covered 300 acres – their present size. The 19th-century botanist, Sir Joseph Banks, and head gardener, William Aiton (later curator), were

largely responsible for laying the foundations of the great collection of plants, shrubs and trees which exist here today; a collection which not only gives great public enjoyment but also forms part of the world's foremost botanical research centre. The west of the gardens is largely woodland and arboretum, while the formal gardens, with their lawns and neatly manicured beds are in the eastern half. The site has inspired some notable architectural features, both old and very modern. The Palm House is perhaps the most elegant: an early example of glass and wrought iron, it was completed in 1848. But the most famous landmark at Kew is the Chinese Pagoda; it stands 163ft high in ten storeys. Plants that would not otherwise be seen in Britain are grown in houses which reproduce special climatic conditions and among many other features are art galleries, one showing works for sale the other exhibiting the work of Victorian artist Marianne North. Wheelchairs are available
continued . . .

(booking advisable) free of charge and there are purpose-built toilets for wheelchair users. Art exhibitions are changed every 6-8 weeks, and there are jazz concerts with a firework finale in the last week in July. Telephone for details.
Open all year, Gardens daily 9.30-between 4 & 6.30pm on weekdays, between 4-8pm Suns & PH, depending on the time of sunset.
Admission fee payable.
P ▼ ✕ *licensed* ♿ *toilets for disabled shop* ✖

Kew Palace   KEW

London Outer Plan B3
Royal Botanic Gardens (Underground – Kew Bridge)
☎ 081-940 3321
A favourite country residence during the reign of the first three Hanoverian Kings, Kew was the site of several royal houses although only three of the buildings now remain. A fairly modest red-brick building, built in the Dutch style with gables, Kew Palace was built in 1631 and used for nearly a century until 1818 when Queen Charlotte died. It was opened to the public in 1899 and remains much as it was in George III's time, reflecting the quiet country life his family enjoyed here. Family paintings and personal relics, furniture and tapestries are on display, and a charming 17th-century garden has been recreated.
Open Apr-Sep, daily 11-5.30.
shop ✖
Details not confirmed for 1992

Queen Charlotte's Cottage   KEW

London Outer Plan B3
Royal Botanic Gardens (Underground – Kew Bridge)
☎ 081-977 9518
The cottage is typical of the rustic-style edifices built by the gentry in the 18th century and was used by the royal family as a summer house and a place to take tea. The interior is designed to give the impression of a tent.
Open Apr-Sep, Sat, Sun & BH 11-5.30.
shop ✖
Details not confirmed for 1992

Osterley Park House   OSTERLEY

London Outer Plan B3
(Underground – Osterley)
☎ 081-560 3918
This Elizabethan mansion has been transformed into an 18th-century villa, its elegant interior decoration designed in neo-classical style by Robert Adam. The State Apartments include a Gobelin tapestry ante-room and a dressing-room decorated in the Etruscan style.
Open all year: Park, daily 9-7 or sunset if earlier. House: 30 Mar-Oct, Wed-Fri 1-5, Sat-Sun & BH Mon 11-5. (Closed Good Fri & 25-26 Dec).
£2.50
P *(charged)* ▼ ♿ *toilets for disabled* ✖
(NT)

Richmond Park   RICHMOND

London Outer Plan B2
(Underground – Richmond)
With its herds of deer, abundant wild life and centuries-old oaks, Richmond is a favourite haunt for visitors and naturalists. There is a formal garden at Pembroke Lodge, and the various plantations show a wealth of exotic shrubs and wild flowers. Model sail boats are allowed on Adam's Pond, where the deer drink, and the 18-acre Pen Ponds have been specially made for angling (permit required).

The M.C.C. Museum   ST JOHNS WOOD (NW8)

London Outer Plan D4
Lord's Ground (Underground – St John's Wood)
☎ 071-289 1611
Located in the best known cricket ground in the country, this gallery was founded in 1865. It contains a collection of cricket memorabilia, including the ashes urn, and 18th-century paintings of the sport. There is also a fine library of cricketing literature, a 'living image' of W.G.Grace and a video area showing moments from famous matches.
Open, Match days Mon-Sat 10.30-5 to visitors who have paid ground admission. Guided tours throughout year (details 071-266 3025).
Museum £1 (concessions 50p). Guided tour £4 (concessions £2.50). Party 20+.
♿ *toilets for disabled shop* ✖

♿ This symbol indicates that much or all of the attraction is accessible to wheelchairs. However, there may be some restrictions, so it would be wise to check in advance.

Primrose Hill   ST JOHNS WOOD (NW8)

London Outer Plan D4
Once part of the same hunting forest as Regent's Park, Primrose Hill retains in its name the rural character and charm that it undoubtedly had in the past. The view from the summit is panoramic and encompasses virtually the whole of central London. In 1842 its 62 acres gained gaslights, a gymnasium and respectability as a Royal Park.

Passmore Edwards Museum   STRATFORD (E15)

London Outer Plan F4
Romford Rd (Underground – Stratford)
☎ 081-519 4296
The story of Essex and Greater London is pieced together in this Victorian building. The museum draws from archaeology, geology and biology to make up a picture of the varied and fascinating history of the area. Very often there are special exhibitions.
Open all year, Wed-Fri 11-5, Sat 1-5, Sun & BH's 2-5.
♿ *shop* ✖
Details not confirmed for 1992

Bushy Park   TEDDINGTON

London Outer Plan B2
Situated close to Hampton Court, this is one of London's ten Royal parks, formerly hunting preserves, which were opened to the public by Charles I and Charles II. Bushy Park has a famous Chestnut Avenue which runs from Hampton Court to the Teddington Gate. This superb double row of enormous trees, laid out by Wren, is best seen in springtime.

Bruce Castle Museum   TOTTENHAM (N17)

London Outer Plan E5
Lordship Ln (Underground – Turnpike Lane)
☎ 081-808 8772
Standing in a small park this E-shaped part-Elizabethan, part-Jacobean and Georgian building contains a museum with sections on local history, postal history and the Middlesex Regiment. A circular 16th-century tower standing adjacent to the castle adds to the eclectic mix of architectural styles.
Opening times, please telephone for details.
Free.
P ♿ *shop* ✖

Marble Hill House — TWICKENHAM

London Outer Plan B2
Richmond Rd
☎ 081-892 5115
An example of the English Palladian school of architecture, Marble Hill House was built between 1724 and 1729 for Henrietta Howard, mistress of George II and later Countess of Suffolk. The house is furnished with Georgian furniture and paintings. The Great Room has fine Italian paintings by Panini. In the grounds, the Richmond Shakespeare Society perform plays during the summer, and 'Picnic Promenade' concerts are often held during July and August.
Open all year, daily, Good Fri-Sep, 10-6; Oct-Maundy Thu, 10-4. (Closed 24-25 Dec).
Free.
P ☕ ✕ *licensed* ♿ *toilets for disabled shop* 🐕 *(ex in grounds)*

Orleans House Gallery — TWICKENHAM

London Outer Plan B2
Riverside
☎ 081-892 0221
The art gallery holds temporary exhibitions throughout the year and is adjacent to James Gibbs's baroque Octagon Room. Built about 1720, it is all that remains of Orleans House, where Louis Philippe, Duc d'Orleans, King of France 1830-48, lived during his exile. The house was demolished in 1927.
Open all year, Tue-Sat 1-5.30 (4.30pm Oct-Mar), Sun & BH 2-5.30 (Oct-Mar 2-4.30). (Closed Good Fri & 24-26 Dec). Woodland Gardens daily, 9-dusk.
Free.
P ♿ *(handling objects & large print tags for some exhibitions) toilets for disabled* 🐕

Places to visit in this guide are pinpointed on the atlas at the back of the book.

Rugby Football Union — TWICKENHAM

London Outer Plan B3
Rugby Rd
☎ 081-892 8161
A visit to the Twickenham Rugby Football ground captures the marvellous atmosphere of this popular sport on match days. Visitors are given a tour of the changing rooms, the famous double baths and the medical room, and are shown a video which lasts about 15 minutes.

There are also displays of kits and trophies presented to the RFU by other unions around the world, with a museum of the game's past history and a souvenir shop.
Open Mon-Fri, tours 10.30 & 2.15. (Closed wk before Internationals. By prior arrangement, telephone for reservations).
P ✕ *licensed* ♿ *toilets for disabled shop*
Details not confirmed for 1992

Vestry House Museum — WALTHAMSTOW (E17)

London Outer Plan E5
Vestry Road, nr Hoe St (Underground – Walthamstow Central)
☎ 081-527 5544 ext 439 & 081-509 1917
Exhibits of local interest are shown in this small museum housed in a former 18th-century workhouse. It boasts an interesting collection of domestic objects but perhaps its most fascinating piece is the Bremer car: Britain's first vehicle driven by an internal combustion engine. The building is located in Walthamstow Village, a conservation area which is worth a visit in itself. Temporary exhibitions are held throughout the year.
Open all year, Mon-Fri 10-1 & 2-5.30, Sat 10-1 & 2-5 (Closed BH).
♿ *shop* 🐕
Details not confirmed for 1992

William Morris Gallery — WALTHAMSTOW (E17)

London Outer Plan E5
Water House, Lloyd Park, Forest Rd (Underground – Walthamstow Central)
☎ 081-527 5544 ext 4390 & 081-527 3782
William Morris was a great Victorian artist, craftsman, poet and free thinker. This house, his home from 1848 to 1856 and then known as the Water House, has been devoted to the life and work of Morris, his followers, contemporaries and the Morris Company. Exhibits include fabrics, wallpaper and furniture, much of which is still fashionable today. To complete the picture of this innovative period in the history of art and philosophy there are also Pre-Raphaelite paintings, sculpture by Rodin, ceramics and a collection of pictures by Frank Brangwyn, who worked briefly for Morris. A varied programme of events is run by the museum throughout the year.
A major new display will take place during 1992-3, so there is likely to be a short period when the main display is not available. However, a smaller display will be on show in the temporary exhibition room.
Open all year, Tue-Sat 10-1 & 2-5, and 1st Sun in each month 10-12 & 2-5. (Closed Mon & BH's).
Free.
♿ *shop* 🐕

Wembley Stadium — WEMBLEY

London Outer Plan B4
Empire Way
☎ 081-902 8833
Wembley is Britain's largest and most important stadium. It was built in 1923 for the British Empire Exhibition and has a capacity of 100,000. The 1948 Olympic Games were held here, it is the home of the England football team, and it is also the venue for the annual Cup Final and other cup competitions. Other large audience events held here have included the Live Aid rock concert, and in 1977 a large conference centre attached to the stadium was opened.

The tour around the complex includes a visit to the dressing rooms. A walk up the player's tunnel, accompanied by sound effects of a roaring crowd, is one of the highlights of the visit.
Open all year, daily 9.45-last tour departs 4. (Closed on days of events & 25 Dec).
£3.50 (cb & pen £2.50). Party
P *(charged)* ☕ ♿ *toilets for disabled shop* 🐕

Grange Museum of Community History — WILLESDEN (NW10)

London Outer Plan C4
Neasden Ln (Underground – Neasden)
☎ 081-452 8311
This museum includes a display on the British Empire Exhibition for which Wembley Stadium was built, two period room-sets (19th century and 1930s) and a re-constructed drapers' shop. Set in a building dating from around 1700, it also tells the story of the area that now forms the London Borough of Brent. There is a local history library and a comprehensive temporary exhibitions programme.
Open all year, Tue-Thu 12-5, Sat 10-12 & 1-5.
* *Donations*
P ♿ *shop* 🐕

Wimbledon Lawn Tennis Museum — WIMBLEDON (SW19)

London Outer Plan C2
All England Club, Church Rd
(Underground – Wimbledon Park)
☎ 081-946 6131
Wimbledon is synonymous with lawn tennis and the museum in the grounds of the All England Lawn Tennis Club is the only one of its kind in the world. Trophies, pictures, displays and memorabilia trace the development of the game over the last century. A new modern section was opened in April 1991. See also the famous Centre Court.
Open all year, Tue-Sat 11-5, Sun 2-5. (Closed Mon, BHs & Fri-Sun before Championships & middle Sun of Championships). Phone for Xmas/New Year opening times.
£1.50 (cb & pen 75p, student card £1). Party 20+.
P ♿ *(lift) toilets for disabled shop* 🐕

Museum of Artillery in the Rotunda　　　　WOOLWICH (SE18)

London Outer Plan F3
Repository Rd
☎ 081-316 5402
The guns, muskets, rifles and edged
weapons that form the collections in this
museum are contained in a rotunda
designed by John Nash that once stood
in St James's Park. The collection tells
the story of the gun from its beginning

in the 13th-century to the present day,
in an unrivalled display of ordnance,
including ammunition.
Open all year, Mon-Fri 12-5 (4pm Oct-
Mar); Sat & Sun 1-5 (4pm Oct-Mar).
(Closed Good Fri, 24-26 Dec & 1 Jan).
Free.
P & *shop* ✈

Places to visit in this guide are pinpointed on the atlas at the back of the book.

Royal Artillery Regimental Museum　　　　WOOLWICH (SE18)

London Outer Plan F3
Old Royal Military Academy
☎ 081-781 5628
The story of the Royal Regiment of
Artillery from its formation in 1716 is
told in this exhibition housed in the
elegant buildings of the Old Royal

Military Academy at Woolwich.
Open all year, Mon-Fri 12.30-4.30, Sat &
Sun 2-4. (Closed Good Fri, 24-26 Dec & 1
Jan). Subject to closure at short notice, please
telephone for further details.
Free.
✈

Thames Barrier Visitors Centre　　　　WOOLWICH (SE18)

London Outer Plan F3
Unity Way
☎ 081-854 1373

Built to prevent the possibility of
disastrous flooding, the Thames Barrier
spans a third of a mile and is the world's
largest movable flood barrier. It is

sometimes described as the eighth
wonder of the world. The nearby
visitors' centre and exhibition on the
South Bank explains the flood threat and
the construction of this £480 million
project. Each month a test closure,
lasting over 2 hours, is carried out and
the annual full day closure of all ten
gates takes place in the autumn.
Open all year, daily 10.30-5 (5.30 Sat &
Sun). (Closed Xmas – telephone for details).
Evening openings in summer and for
groups – telephone for details.
✳ £2.25 (ch & pen £1.40). Car park 50p
Coach park Free. Family ticket £6.10.
Party.
P *(charged)* ☕ ✕ *licensed* & *(lift) toilets*
for disabled shop ✈

American Museum　　　　BATH

Map 03 ST76
Claverton Manor (2.5m E off A36)
☎ (0225) 460503
Claverton Manor is two miles east of
Bath, in a beautiful setting above the
River Avon. The house was built in
1820 by Sir Jeffrey Wyatville, and is
now a museum of American decorative
arts. A series of rooms show American
life from the 17th to 19th centuries,
with special sections on American

Indians and the Shakers, and a
distinctive collection of quilts. The
gardens are also well worth seeing, and
include an American arboretum.
Winston Churchill made his first
political speech in the grounds in 1897.
Open 29 Mar-3 Nov, Tue-Sun 2-5.
Gardens 1-6. BH Sun & Mon 11-5.
P ☕ & *toilets for disabled shop* ✈
Details not confirmed for 1992

✳ An asterisk indicates that up-to-date information was
not available at the time of our research – 1991
information has been published as an
indication of what you may expect.

Bath Industrial Heritage Centre — BATH

Map 03 ST76
Camden Works, Julian Rd
☎ (0225) 318348

The centre houses the Bowler collection, the entire stock-in-trade of a Victorian brass founder, general engineer and aerated water manufacturer, displayed so as to capture the atmosphere of the original premises. Also here is 'the Story of Bath Stone', with a replica of a mine face before mechanisation, and a Bath cabinet-maker's workshop, complete with tools and original drawings. A series of temporary exhibitions will include displays from the collection of travelling exhibitions, and there will be a series of lectures throughout the year.
Open all year, winter 10-4 (last entry 3pm), summer 10-5. (Closed 24-26 Dec).
✱ *£2.50 (ch, pen & students £1.50).*
Family ticket £7.
♿ *shop* 🐕

Bath Postal Museum — BATH

Map 03 ST76
8 Broad St
☎ (0225) 460333
Ralph Allen, 18th-century postmaster of Bath, helped to reform England's post, and the first letters with stamps were probably posted in Bath. Together with Mr John Palmer, another Bath citizen, Mr Allen introduced the first nationwide mail coach service. The museum has displays on written communications throughout history, exhibitions and films, and of course stamps. A special exhibition will be held from April to December – Pictures in the Post.
Open all year, Mon-Sat 11-5; Sun 2-5 (Apr-Oct). Parties by appointment. (Closed Good Fri, 25-26 Dec & 1 Jan).
£1.70 (ch 50p, pen, UB40 & students £1). Party 10+.
♿ ♿ *shop* 🐕

🐕 **The 'No Dogs' symbol does not normally apply to guide dogs – these are permitted in most establishments.**

Holburne Museum & Crafts Study Centre — BATH

Map 03 ST76
Great Pulteney St
☎ (0225) 466669
This elegant and historic building in a lovely garden setting, has 17th and 18th-century collections of fine and decorative art, notably silver, porcelain, glass, maiolica, furniture and Old Masters, including Gainsborough. These are displayed together with work by 20th-century artists and crafts people, which embraces ceramics, woven and printed textiles, calligraphy and furniture. Annual programme of exhibitions, lectures, and events. Study facilities by appointment.
Open mid Feb-mid Dec, Mon-Sat 11-5, Sun 2.30-6. (Closed Mon Nov-Etr).
✱ *£2 (ch & unemployed £1, students & pen £1.50)*
🅿 ♿ *toilets for disabled shop* 🐕

Museum of Bookbinding & Book Collecting — BATH

Map 03 ST76
Manvers St
☎ (0225) 466000
The Museum includes an exhibition of first and early editions of authors who lived in Bath, such as Jane Austen and Charles Dickens.
Open all year, Mon-Fri 9-1 & 2.15-5.30. (Closed 25 Dec & BH).
£1 (ch 50p). Family ticket £2.50.
shop 🐕 📷

Museum of English Naive Art — BATH

Map 03 ST76
Countess of Huntingdon Chapel, The Vineyard/Paragon
☎ (0225) 446020
This gallery displays the work of English itinerant and artisan artists between about 1750 and 1900, depicting ordinary people, pursuits and incidents. The Chapel was founded by Selina, Countess of Huntingdon (1741-1791) to provide a fashionable non-conformist centre. The same sect built the school next door, in 1842, which now houses the collection.
Open 2 Mar-22 Dec, daily 10.30-5 & Sun 2-6.
£2 (ch, pen, students & UB40's £1).
shop 🐕

No 1 Royal Crescent — BATH

Map 03 ST76
☎ (0225) 428126

Bath is very much a Georgian city, but most of its houses have naturally altered over the years to suit changing tastes and lifestyles. Built in 1768 by John Wood the Elder, No 1 Royal Crescent has been restored to look as it would have done some 200 years ago. Two floors are furnished as they might have been in the 18th century, with pictures, china and furniture of the period, and there is also an interesting kitchen. Note also the first-floor windows, which are the original length: all the others in the Royal Crescent were lengthened downwards in the 19th century. The house was once the home of the Duke of York, famed for marching his 10,000 men up the hill and down again.
Open Apr-Sep, daily 11-5; Mar & Oct-13 Dec, Tue-Sun 11-4. (Closed Good Fri). Last admission 30 mins before closing.
£3 (ch, students & pen £2)
shop 🐕

Roman Baths & Pump Room — BATH

Map 03 ST76
Abbey Church Yard
☎ (0225) 461111 ext 2785

The descent to the Roman baths is a step back in time. The remains give a vivid impression of life nearly 2000 years ago. The Baths, built next to Britain's only hot spring, served the sick and the pilgrims visiting the adjacent Temple of Sulis Minerva. The Spring was a sacred site lying within the courtyard of the Temple. Votive offerings and temple treasures discovered during the excavations of the Spring can be seen in the museum display.

Today, the Temple Courtyard is beneath the Pump Room. This building became a popular meeting place in the 18th century when Bath became the leading resort for fashionable society. Inside the present Pump Room there is now a restaurant where morning coffee, lunches and teas can be taken to the accompaniment of music from the Pump Room Trio. The hot spa water can also be sampled.
Open all year, Mar-Jul & Sep-Oct daily 9-6, Aug daily 9-6 & 8pm-10pm, Nov-Feb Mon-Sat 9-5, Sun 10-5. Disabled visitors free admission to ground floor areas. Last admission 30 minutes before closing. Admission fee payable.
✗ *licensed* ♿ *toilets for disabled shop* 🐕

The Royal Photographic Society — BATH

Map 03 ST76
The Octagon, Milsom St
☎ (0225) 462841
The Octagon was built in 1796 as a chapel, but is now the headquarters of the world's oldest photographic society. A huge collection of cameras, the first photograph, and other classics are displayed. Temporary exhibitions often include top contemporary work. A variety of workshops, seminars and talks will be held throughout the year.
Open all year, daily 9.30-5.30, last admission 5. (Closed 25-26 Dec).
£2.50 (ch, pen, students & UB40 £1.25, ch 7 & disabled free). Parties 12+.
♿ ✗ *licensed* ♿ *(chair lift to all floors) toilets for disabled shop* 🐕

Sally Lunn's Refreshment House & Museum — BATH

Map 03 ST76
4 North Pde Passage
☎ (0225) 461634
The history of this Tudor building can be traced to Roman times. It is the oldest home in Bath, and became a popular meeting place in the 18th century. In the cellars, a fascinating museum reveals the findings of recent excavations. Here too is the original kitchen, with its faggot oven, Georgian cooking range and a collection of baking utensils. The traditional 'Sally Lunn' is still served in the restaurant: it is a bread like the French 'brioche', made with eggs and butter, popularly believed to have been named after its first maker, who came to Bath in 1680.
Open all year, museum – Mon-Sat 10-5 & Sun 12-6; refreshment rooms – Mon 10-6, Tue-Sat 10am-10.30pm & Sun 12-10.30pm. (Closed 25-26 Dec & 1 Jan).
30p (ch & pen free).
♿ ✗ *licensed shop* 🐕 📷

This is just one of many guidebooks published by the AA. The full range is available at any AA shop or good bookshop.

Blaise Castle House Museum — BRISTOL

Map 03 ST57
Henbury Rd, Henbury (4m NW of city, off B4057)
☎ (0272) 506789
The 'castle' is an 18th-century mansion built for a Quaker banker, and is now Bristol's Museum of Social History. It stands in extensive grounds which were planned by Humphry Repton. Nearby Blaise Hamlet is an interesting little estate village designed by John Nash.
Open all year, Sat-Wed 10-1 & 2-5. Please check for BH closures.
Free.
♿ *shop* 🐕

Bristol Industrial Museum — BRISTOL

Map 03 ST57
Prince's Wharf, Prince St
☎ (0272) 251470
The museum is housed in a converted dockside transit shed. Motor and horse-drawn vehicles from the Bristol area are shown, with locally built aircraft and aero-engines. Railway exhibits include the industrial locomotive 'Henbury', steamed about once a month. There are also machines used in local industry, and displays on the history of the port.
Open all year, Sat-Wed 10-1 & 2-5. Please check for BH closures.
Free.
🅿 *(charged)* ♿ *toilets for disabled shop* 🐕

Cabot Tower & Brandon Hill Nature Reserve — BRISTOL

Map 03 ST57
Brandon Hill, Great George St
☎ (0272) 223856
The tower stands over 100ft high and was built in 1897-8 to commemorate Cabot's arrival in North America on 24 June 1497. It stands on Brandon Hill, a municipal park since 1924, and is surrounded by a rock garden and ornamental ponds. There is also a nature reserve.
Open all year, daily 7.30am-dusk.
Free.
♿

City Museum & Art Gallery — BRISTOL

Map 03 ST57
Queen's Rd
☎ (0272) 223571
The museum has regional and international collections representing ancient history, natural sciences, and fine and applied arts. Various exhibitions are held.
Open all year, daily 10-5. Please check for BH closures.
Free.
♿ ♿ *(lift) toilets for disabled shop* 🐕

The Exploratory Hands-on-Science Centre   BRISTOL

Map 03 ST57
Bristol Old Station, Temple Meads
☎ (0272) 252008
As its name suggests, this is a museum which invites the visitor to try things out. Bubbles and bridges, light and lasers, mechanics and mirrors – they are all here to discover and enjoy. Come to the Exploratory and find out for

yourself! There will be a special exhibition held during the summer, telephone for details.
Open all year, daily 10-5 (Closed Xmas wk).
£3.50 (ch, pen & student £2.30, ch 5 free)
Family ticket £22 (allows 10 visits/visitors, valid for 1 year). Party 10+.
🅿 & toilets for disabled shop ✖

The Georgian House   BRISTOL

Map 03 ST57
7 Great George St
☎ (0272) 211362
A carefully preserved example of a late-18th-century town house, with

suitable fixtures and fittings.
Open all year, Mon-Sat, 10-1 & 2-5.
Please check for BH closure.
Free.
✖ 🚐

John Wesley's Chapel (The New Room)   BRISTOL

Map 03 ST57
36 The Horsefair, Broadmead
☎ (0272) 264740
This is the oldest Methodist chapel in the world. It was built in 1739 and rebuilt in 1748, both times by John Wesley. Both chapel and living rooms above are preserved in their original form. Special event for 1992: 21 May,

Charles Wesley Day and 253rd anniversary of New Room.
Open all year, daily 10-4. (Closed Sun, Weds in winter & BH). Upstairs rooms closed 1-2pm.
50p Donation; £1 donation for group tours.
🅿 & shop ✖

Maritime Heritage Centre   BRISTOL

Map 03 ST57
Gas Ferry Rd
☎ (0272) 260680
The centre explores 200 years of Bristol shipbuilding, with special reference to Charles Hill & Son, and their

predecessor, James Hillhouse.
Open all year, daily 10-6, 5pm in winter; (Closed 24 & 25 Dec).
Free.
🅿 (charged) & toilets for disabled ✖

Red Lodge   BRISTOL

Map 03 ST57
Park Row
☎ (0272) 211360
The house was built in the 16th century and then altered in the 18th. It has fine oak carvings and furnishings of both

periods.
Open all year, Mon-Sat 10-1 & 2-5. Please check for BH closures.
Free.
✖ 🚐

SS Great Britain   BRISTOL

Map 03 ST57
Great Western Dock, Gas Ferry Rd
(off Cumberland Rd)
☎ (0272) 260680

Designed by Isambard Kingdom Brunel, the ship was the first iron, screw-propelled ocean-going vessel, and was launched in 1843. She was restored in the dry dock where she was built, and is now the centrepiece of the revitalised Bristol docks.
Open all year daily 10-6, 5pm in winter. (Closed 24 & 25 Dec).
🅿 (charged) 🖢 & shop ✖
Details not confirmed for 1992

Zoological Gardens   BRISTOL

Map 03 ST57
Clifton Down
☎ (0272) 738951
Set in extensive gardens, the zoo has a varied collection of mammals, birds and reptiles, and the 'World of Water' There are outdoor activities in the school holidays, and a full programme of

special events.
Open all year, daily (ex 25 Dec) from 9am. Closing times vary with season.
£4.50 (ch 3-13 £2.20, pen £2.20 on Mon ex BHs).
🅿 (charged) 🖢 ✕ licensed & toilets for disabled shop ✖

For an explanation of the symbols and abbreviations, see page 2.

Clevedon Court   CLEVEDON

Map 03 ST47
(off B3130)
☎ (0272) 872257
Clevedon Court, is a remarkably complete manor house of around 1320. Additions have been made in each century, so it is now a pleasing variety of styles, with an 18th-century terraced garden. One owner, Sir Edmund Elton,

was a celebrated potter, and there is a display of his work.
Open Apr-Sep, Wed, Thu, Sun & BH Mon 2.30-5.30. Last admission 5pm.
£2.80 (ch £1.40, ch under 17 must be accompanied).
🅿 🖢 ✖
(NT)

Dyrham Park   DYRHAM

Map 03 ST77
☎ Abson (027582) 2501
Dyrham Park is a splendid William and Mary house, with interiors which have hardly altered since the late 17th century. It has contemporary Dutch-style furnishings, Dutch pictures and blue-and-white Delft ware. Around the

house is an ancient park with fallow deer.
Open – House & garden Apr-1 Nov, Sat-Wed 12-5.30. (Last admission 5pm or dusk). Park open all year, daily 12-5.30 or dusk if earlier. (Closed 25 Dec).
£4.40. Park only £1.40.
🅿 🖢 & ✖ (ex in dog walk area).
(NT)

Priston Mill   PRISTON

Map 03 ST66
Priston Mill Farm (6m SW, off A39)
☎ (0225) 423894
Once run by the monks of Bath Abbey, this is one of the mills that have supplied flour to the citizens for hundreds of years. Set in rolling countryside, the history and workings of the watermill

are described by staff, and other attractions include a trailer ride, a nature trail, and children's play areas.
Open Etr-Sep, daily 2.15-5.30, Sat, Sun & BH 11-5.30.
£2.10 (ch & pen £1.40). Party. Free admission for disabled in wheelchairs.
🅿 ✕ licensed & shop ✖

Radstock, Midsomer Norton & District Museum   RADSTOCK

Map 03 ST65
Barton Meade House, Haydon (1m S on Haydon/Kilmersden rd)
☎ (0761) 437722
A local history museum, run by volunteers, housed in the 18th-century barn of a former dairy and cheese-making farm located in the old North Somerset coalfield. Features include a reconstructed coalface, miner's cottage,

model railway, agricultural implements, a 1930's Co-op shop, a blacksmith's shop, mining photographs, chapel china and leisure bygones. There is also a Victorian school room and a display on the history of Duchy of Cornwall Lands in North Somerset.
Open all year, Sat 10-4, Sun & BH's 2-5.
✱ £1 (ch, pen & students 50p)
🅿 🖢 & shop

International Helicopter Museum   WESTON-SUPER-MARE

Map 03 ST36
Weston Airport, Locking Moor Rd
☎ (0934) 635227
A unique collection of more than 40 helicopters and autogyros is on display. This is given a further dimension by exhibits of models, photographs and components to illustrate how the aircraft work. There is a ride simulator, and the third Sun in summer months is 'Open Cockpit Day' when visitors can try out the pilots seat of a real helicopter, and

enjoy a pleasure flight (weather/serviceablility permitting). Helicopters from this museum are also featured in the Weston-Super Helidays (25/26 July), which take place on the seafront.
Open all year, Mar-Oct, daily 10-6 & Nov-Feb, Thu-Sun 10.30-4.
£2.50 (ch under 5 free, 5-15 & pen £1.50). Family ticket £6.50. Party 15+.
🅿 🖢 & toilets for disabled shop

Woodspring Museum   WESTON-SUPER-MARE

Map 03 ST36
Burlington St
☎ (0934) 621028
This museum, housed in the workshops of the Edwardian Gaslight Company, is set around a central courtyard with displays of the Victorian seaside holiday, an old chemist's shop, a dairy, and a lion fountain with Victorian pavement mosaics. Adjoining the museum is Clara's Cottage, a Westonian home of the 1900s with period kitchen, parlour, bedroom and back yard. One of the rooms has an additional display of Peggy

Nisbet dolls. Other displays in the museum include a gallery of wildlife in the district, Mendip minerals, mining and local archaeology. There are also costume rooms, an exhibition of transport, cameras, and a display on the dentist in 1900. Changing exhibitions are held in the Temporary Exhibitions Gallery.
Open all year, Mon-Sat 10-5. (Closed Xmas, New Year & Good Fri).
Free.
🖢 & toilets for disabled shop ✖

BEDFORDSHIRE

Houghton House   AMPTHILL

Map 04 TL03
(N off A418)
Now a ruin, the mansion was built for Mary Countess of Pembroke, the sister of Sir Philip Sidney. Inigo Jones is thought to have been involved in work on the house, which is said to be the

'House Beautiful' in Bunyan's 'Pilgrim's Progress'.
Open all reasonable times.
Free.
🅿 &
(EH)

Bedford Museum   BEDFORD

Map 04 TL04
Castle Ln
☎ (0234) 353323
The museum is devoted to local history and natural history, with 19th-century room sets and displays of birds and mammals, agriculture, archaeology, fossils and minerals. Special events and exhibitions for 1992 include: 18 Jan-16 Feb, Games and Sports Worldwide; 16 May-2 Aug, 40th anniversary

exhibition: The American Air Force in Britain; 24 Oct-22 Nov, Fur Feathers and Fashion. Other events details available on application.
Open all year, Tue-Sat 11-5, Sun 2-5. (Closed Mon ex BH Mon afternoon, Good Fri & Xmas).
Free.
& (lift available on request) toilets for disabled shop ✖

Cecil Higgins Art Gallery & Museum — BEDFORD

Map 04 TL04
Castle Close
☎ (0234) 211222
The rooms in this award-winning recreated Victorian mansion are arranged in the manner of a house still lived in, to authenticate the atmosphere. The adjoining gallery has an outstanding collection of ceramics, glass and watercolours, and is set in gardens leading down to the river embankment. A regular programme of thematic exhibitions is taken from the gallery's own collection of watercolours, prints and drawings.
Open all year, Tue-Fri 12.30-5, Sat 11-5, Sun 2-5, BH Mon 12.30-5. (Closed Mon, Good Fri & 25-26 Dec).
Free.
& *toilets for disabled shop* ✱

Moot Hall — ELSTOW

Map 04 TL04
☎ Bedford (0234) 228330 (office hrs)
The restored medieval timber-framed market hall has a collection of 17th-century furniture and items relating to the life and times of John Bunyan, who was born near by. These include a fine collection of his works, notably Pilgrim's Progress. Local Heritage Day (19 Jul) is an annual festival of arts, crafts, and industries, held on the Green where John Bunyan played as a child. Telephone for details.
Open Etr-30 Oct, Tue-Sat & BH's 2-5; Sun 2-5.30. (Closed Mon ex BH's).
✱ *50p (ch 5-16 & pen 25p). School Party. Disabled visitors Free.*
P & *shop* ✱

Leighton Buzzard Railway — LEIGHTON BUZZARD

Map 04 SP92
Pages Park Station, Billington Rd
(.75m SE on A4146)
☎ (0525) 373888
The original light railway was built to carry sand in 1919, and after its redundancy in 1967 the railway society took over its three and a half mile length. It is now a 2ft gauge passenger-carrying line through varied scenery with over 30 locomotives, including nine resident steam engines from West Africa, India, Spain and Britain. 1992 is the 25th anniversary of the preservation, and a major Steam Festival will be held on 2 Aug-13 Sep. Other events include a Teddy Bears' Outing (10 May), a 25th Birthday Steam Gala (21 Jun), and special Christmas trains in Dec.
Open, operating dates Suns, 5 Apr-4 Oct, Etr wknd & BH Mons. Also Wed & Thu 5 Aug-3 Sep. Trains run to Stonehenge Works. Return journey lasts 1hr. Trains run between 11am-3.10pm (4.30 Sun & BH Mons).
Return ticket £3.50 (ch 5-15 £1.75, pen £2.80, ch under 5 free).
P ☛ & *shop*

Luton Hoo (The Wernher Collection) — LUTON

Map 04 TL02
(entrance at Park Street gates)
☎ (0582) 22955
Set in parkland landscaped by Capability Brown is a magnificent country mansion originally designed by Robert Adam, and remodelled in 1903 for Sir Julius Wernher, a diamond magnate. Thoroughly equal to the splendid exterior is the fabulous Wernher Collection of art treasures, the finest private collection in Great Britain, which includes continental items rarely seen in English country houses. The famous Russian collection with works by Carl Fabergé, the Russian court jeweller, paintings, costume and other personal possessions of the Imperial Family, has been redesigned and redisplayed in and around the beautiful chapel, recently restored to its original decorative splendour, consecrated in 1991 into the Russian Orthodox Church and dedicated to the memory of Tsar Nicholas II and the Imperial family.
Other treasures in the house include Old Master paintings, magnificent tapestries, English and French porcelain, Byzantine and medieval ivories, sculpture, bronzes and Renaissance jewellery. A large 3-day craft show will be held in Sept.
Open 14 Apr-18 Oct, daily 1.30-5.45 (Closed Mon ex BH's). Last admission 5pm.
Houses & Gardens £4.30 (ch £1.75, pen £3.70). Gardens only £1.85 (ch 60p, pen £1.60).
P ✕ *licensed* & *toilets for disabled shop* ✱

Luton Museum & Art Gallery — LUTON

Map 04 TL02
Wardown Park, Old Bedford Rd
☎ (0582) 36941
A Victorian mansion standing in Wardown Park contains displays illustrating the natural and cultural history, archaeology and industries of the area, with particular emphasis on the straw hat and pillow lace trade. One gallery includes a reconstructed street. The museum also houses the Bedfordshire & Hertfordshire Regiment collection. A two-day Lace Extravaganza Weekend will be held on 8/9 Feb, featuring talks, demonstrations and lace suppliers of all descriptions. A look behind the scenes at the museum's internationally renowned lace collections is available by arrangement. Telephone for details.
Open all year, Mon-Sat 10-5, Sun 1-5 (Closed Xmas & 1 Jan).
Free.
P & *shop* ✱

The Shuttleworth Collection — OLD WARDEN

Map 04 TL14
(2m W from rdbt on A1, Biggleswade by-pass)
☎ Northill (076727) 288
Housed in seven hangars in a classic grass aerodrome, 30 working historic aeroplanes span the progress of aviation with exhibits ranging from a 1909 Bleriot to a 1941 Spitfire. A garage of roadworthy motor vehicles explores the era of the 1898 Panhard Levassor and there is a coach room of carriages from earlier years.
Open all year, daily 10-4 (3pm Nov-Mar). Closed 1 wk at Xmas.
P ☛ ✕ *licensed* & *toilets for disabled shop* ✱
Details not confirmed for 1992

Wrest Park House & Gardens   SILSOE

Map 04 TL03
☎ (0525) 60718
Notable 18th-century garden layout
with formal canals and alterations by
'Capability' Brown. The early 18th-
century Baroque banqueting house is by
Thomas Archer and Bowling Green

House by Betty Langley.
*Open Apr-Sep, wknds & BH's 10-6.
£1.50 (ch 75p, pen, students & UB40
£1.10).*
🅿 ⬛ ✖
(EH)

Stagsden Bird Gardens   STAGSDEN

Map 04 SP94
(5m W of Bedford, on the A422)
☎ Oakley (02302) 2745
A breeding centre for many species of
birds, including owls, cranes, pheasants,
waterfowl and old breeds of poultry.

There is also a fine collection of shrub
roses.
*Open all year, daily 11-6 or dusk. (Closed
25 Dec)
£2.50 (ch £1 & pen £2).*
🅿 & shop ✖

Whipsnade Wild Animal Park   WHIPSNADE

Map 04 TL01
☎ (0582) 872171
The Park is set in 600 acres of beautiful
parkland and is the home to almost
3000 animals. Wallabies, peacocks, mara
and Chinese water deer roam freely
among the woods, and many of the
animals here are rare and endangered
species in the wild. Whipsnade's
conservation and breeding programmes
for endangered species are known and
respected worldwide. Things to see and
do include Bird of Prey demonstrations,
World of Sealions, Elephants at Work,
Animal Encounters, Discovery Centre,
Woodland Bird Walk, Wolf Wood,
Chimpanzee Centre, Passage through

Asia, Children's Farm, Duck Island, a
steam railway and a new tiger enclosure
called Tiger Falls, which allows visitors
to look down into the enclosure at
different points. Events at Whipsnade
include an Easter Egg Hunt (17-20
May), Steam Weekend (2-4 May),
Conservation Matters (25/26 July), and
Bank Holiday Teddy '92 (29-31 August)
– subject to change, telephone for
details.
*Open all year, Mon-Sat 10-6, Sun & BH
10-7 or sunset. (Closed 25 Dec). Closes
earlier in winter.*
✳ *£5.95 (ch 4 free, 4-15 £3.95, pen &
disabled £4.95) Cars £6.*
🅿 ⬛ ✖ *licensed* & *toilets for disabled shop* ✖

Woburn Abbey & Deer Park   WOBURN

Map 04 SP93
☎ (0525) 290666
This palatial 18th-century mansion is the
home of the Duke of Bedford. The
house dates from 1744 but was
remodelled in 1802 by Henry Holland.
Originally a Cistercian abbey, the Dukes
of Bedford have lived at Woburn since
1547. There is a valuable art collection
in the house with paintings by
Canaletto, Rembrandt, Van Dyck,
Gainsborough and many others. There is
also an extensive collection of 18th-
century furniture, both French and
English. There are 14 state apartments
on view and the private apartments are
shown when not in use by the family.
The house stands in 3,000 acres of

parkland, famous for its collection of
varieties of deer. Special events are held
during the year; please telephone for
details.
*Open, Abbey Sat & Sun only Jan-28 Mar,
11-4.45; 29 Mar-1 Nov daily 11-5.45
(6.15pm Sun). Last admission 45 mins
before closing time. Deer Park Sat & Sun
only Jan-28 Mar, 10.30-3.45; 29 Mar-1
Nov daily 10-4.45 (5.45 Sun).*
✳ *Abbey & Deer Park £5.50 (ch 7-16 £2,
pen £4. Family ticket (2 adults & 2-4 ch)
£12.50-£15.50. Deer Park only car &
passengers £2.50. Motorcycles & passengers
£1.25.*
🅿 ⬛ ✖ *licensed* & *(wheelchairs
accommodated by prior arrangement) toilets
for disabled shop garden centre* ✖

Woburn Wild Animal Kingdom & Leisure Park   WOBURN

Map 04 SP93
☎ (0525) 290407

Within the 3,000 acres of parkland
belonging to Woburn Abbey, is an area
of over 300 acres set aside as a wild

animal kingdom. A collection of many
species of animal has made Woburn
justifiably famous among Safari Parks.
Woburn's own safari road passes
through an African plains area stocked
with eland, zebra, hippos and rhinos.
Then through the well-keepered tiger
and lion enclosures and on past bears
and monkeys. The Pets Corner, Sea
Lion and Parrot Shows, and Elephant
Displays, are all popular attractions. The
large leisure complex also offers a
boating lake and adventure playground.
*Open 7 Mar-1 Nov, daily 10-5.
£7 (ch & pen £4.50).*
🅿 ✖ *licensed* & *toilets for disabled shop* ✖

BERKSHIRE

Basildon Park   BASILDON

Map 04 SU67
☎ Pangbourne (0734) 843040
This lovely 18th-century house, built of
golden Bath stone, fell into decay in the
20th century, but was rescued and
beautifully restored by Lord and Lady
Iliffe. The first feature to impress the
visitor is the classical front with its
splendid central portico and pavilions.

Inside there are delicate plasterwork
decorations on the walls and ceilings and
an elegant staircase. The most impressive
room is the Octagon drawing room,
with its fine pictures and furniture, and
three big windows overlooking the River
Thames. The Shell Room and Bamboo
Room are also notable for their
continued . . .

decorations. There is a small formal
garden, and a pretty terrace garden
overlooks the grounds.
*Open Apr-Oct, Wed-Sat 2-6; Sun & BH
Mon noon-6. Last admission 5.30. (Closed*

*Good Fri & Wed following BH).
House & grounds £3; Grounds only £2.*
🅿 ⬛ & *toilets for disabled shop* ✖ *(ex in
grounds)
(NT)*

Beale Bird Park   BASILDON

Map 04 SU67
Church Farm, Lower Basildon
☎ Upper Basildon (0491) 671325 or
(0734) 845172
Ornamental pheasants, peacocks, parrots,
owls, cranes and wildfowl can be seen
here in a pleasant riverside setting (a
designated area of Outstanding Natural
Beauty), together with Highland cattle
and rare breeds of sheep, a pets corner
and a tropical house. There is a craft
centre, and a children's playground with
paddling pools and sandpits. There is
also excellent fishing in season. The park
has an information/education facility,
and numerous events and exhibitions are
held during the year. River trips are
another attraction, and a narrow gauge
railway runs around the park every day.

Amidst all this is the unusual focal point
of the mausoleum, built by Mr Child
Beale in memory of his parents,
surrounded by a large and varied
collection of statues, fountains and
walks. Wheelchairs are available at the
park and there are purpose-built toilets
for wheelchair users. Events for 1992
include a craft show (14-16 Aug),
Multiple Sclerosis Family Fun day (12
or 19 Jul), and various horse shows and
car club days throughout the year.
*Open daily, Mar-Sep 10-6. Last admission
5pm. Oct-23 Dec 10-5. Last admission
4pm.
£4 (ch under 3 free, 3-16 & disabled £2,
pen £3) Party 15 +.*
🅿 ⬛ & *toilets for disabled shop* ✖ 🖼

Elcot Park Resort Hotel   ELCOT

Map 04 SU36
☎ Kintbury (0488) 58100
The hotel's 16-acre garden overlooks the
Kennet valley, and has beautiful lawns
and woodland. There is a magnificent
display of daffodils and blossom in
spring, with rhododendrons and other

shrubs coming into flower a little later.
It was first laid out by Sir William
Paxton.
Open all year, daily.
🅿 ✖ *licensed* &
Details not confirmed for 1992

> & This symbol indicates that much or all of the
> attraction is accessible to wheelchairs.
> However, there may be some restrictions,
> so it would be wise to check
> in advance.

Dorney Court   ETON

Map 04 SU97
Dorney
☎ Burnham (0628) 604638
This enchanting brick and timber house
stands in a tranquil setting. It has tall
Tudor chimneys and a splendid great
hall and has been the home of the

present family since 1510.
*Open Etr wknd, then Sun & BH Mon in
May; Jun-Sep, Sun-Tue 2-5.30 (last
admission 5pm).
£3 (ch 9 £1.50).*
🅿 ⬛ *shop* ✖

Courage Shire Horse Centre   MAIDENHEAD

Map 04 SU88
**Cherry Garden Ln, Maidenhead
Thicket** (off A4 .5m W of
A4/A423/A423M jct)
☎ Littlewick Green (062882) 4848
Visitors are free to wander around and
meet the horses, or take a free tour with
an experienced guide who will introduce
you to the horses and explain the care
and history of the 'gentle giants' of the
equestrian world. See the harness maker

at work, and certain days will find the
farrier or cooper in attendance. Dray
rides are also available. Events include
Vintage Day (17 May), Rural Craft
Fayre (6/7 Jun), Exemption Dog Show
(19 Jul), Owl Hawk and Falconry Day
(13 Sep), and Heavy horse Show (17/18
Oct).
*Open Mar-Oct, daily 10.30-5.
£2.80 (ch & pen £2).*
🅿 ⬛ & *toilets for disabled shop*

Blake's Lock Museum   READING

Map 04 SU77
Gasworks Rd
☎ (0734) 390918
Housed in an attractive Victorian
building, the museum illustrates the
history of industrial and commercial
development in the town, with

reconstructed bakery, barbers shop and
printers workshop. A traditional gipsy
caravan is also on display.
*Open all year, Tue-Fri 10-5, Sat, Sun &
BH Mon 2-5. Parties by arrangement.
Free.*
& *toilets for disabled shop* ✖

Museum of English Rural Life   READING

Map 04 SU77
**University of Reading, Whiteknights
Park** (2m SE on A327)
☎ (0734) 318660
This museum houses a fascinating
national collection of agricultural,
domestic and crafts exhibits, including
wagons, tools and a wide range of other
equipment used in the English
countryside over the last 150 years.
Family groups will find the exhibitions

especially attractive, and special facilities
such as videos and teaching packs are
available for school parties, on request.
The museum also contains very
extensive documentary and photographic
archives, which can be studied by
appointment.
*Open all year, Tue-Sat, 10-1 & 2-4.30.
(Closed BH's & Xmas-New Year).
£1 (ch free).*
🅿 & *shop* ✖

Wellington Country Park & National Dairy Museum — RISELEY

Map 04 SU76
(off B3349)
☎ Reading (0734) 326444
The park consists of 600 acres of woodland and meadows, set around a lake in the countryside between Reading and Basingstoke. The National Dairy Museum in the grounds outlines the history of the dairy industry in Britain. There is also a Thames Valley Time Trail, which traces the development of earth and mineral resources in the area. Other attractions are the collections of small domestic animals, a deer park and a miniature steam railway. Five nature trails are marked out, in addition to a fitness course and adventure playground. It is also possible to do some fishing, sailing, windsurfing or rowing. Events for 1992 include Easter fun and crafts (19/20 Apr), a horticultural show (2 Aug), and a Shetland Pony show (5 Sep).
Open all year, Mar-Oct, daily 10-5.30 & winter wknds 10-dusk.
£2.70 (ch 5-15 £1.20). Party 20+.
🅿 ☕ ♿ *(fishing platform for disabled) toilets for disabled shop*

Every effort is made to provide accurate information, but details might change during the currency of this guide.

Exhibition of The Queen's Presents & Royal Carriages — WINDSOR

Map 04 SU97
Windsor Castle
☎ (0753) 831118
A regularly changing display of gifts given by foreign governments to The Queen.
Open all year, times vary with season.
£1.50 (ch 70p & pen £1.30).
♿ *toilets for disabled* ⊘

Frogmore House — WINDSOR

Map 04 SU97
Home Park (entrance from B3021)
☎ (0753) 831118 (recorded info)
The long and distinguished history of Frogmore House dates back even further than the present building of 1618, being previously owned by Henry VIII. Subsequent residents have included Charles II's architect, Hugh May, who built the present house, a Duke of Northumberland, Queen Charlotte, Queen Victoria and Queen Mary. It has 19 rooms, and an original mural, discovered only five years ago during redecoration, can be seen on the stairway.
Open Aug-Sep.
£3 (ch £1.50, pen £2.50)
🅿 *shop* ⊘

Household Cavalry Museum — WINDSOR

Map 04 SU97
Combermere Barracks, St Leonards Rd
☎ (0735) 868222 ext 5203
This is one of the finest military museums in Britain. There are comprehensive displays of the uniforms, weapons, horse furniture (tack, regalia, etc.) and armour used by the Household Cavalry from 1600 to the present day.
Open all year Mon-Fri (ex BH) 9-12.30 & 2-4.30.
♿ *shop* ⊘
Details not confirmed for 1992

Queen Mary's Dolls' House — WINDSOR

Map 04 SU97
Windsor Castle
☎ (0753) 831118
The exquisite dolls' house, designed for Queen Mary in the 1920s by Lutyens, is displayed at Windsor Castle. Every piece of furniture, decoration, tableware and equipment in the miniature house has been carried out in perfect detail on a scale of 1:12.
Open all year, times vary with season.
£1.50 (ch 70p, pen £1.30).
shop ⊘

Royalty & Empire Exhibition — WINDSOR

Map 04 SU97
Windsor & Eton Central Station, Thames St
☎ (0753) 857837
Situated opposite Windsor Castle, Royalty and Empire recreates the events which celebrated Queen Victoria's Diamond Jubilee in 1897, using full-size wax figures created by the famous Tussaud's waxworks and displayed in the original surroundings of the historical events to evoke the atmosphere of the times.

One particularly outstanding feature of the exhibition is a theatre show, unique in Europe, which has moving and speaking life-size models of famous Victorians.
Open all year, daily 9.30-5.30 (4.30 in winter). (Closed 25 Dec & part Jan).
☕ ♿ *toilets for disabled shop* ⊘
Details not confirmed for 1992

St George's Chapel — WINDSOR

Map 04 SU97
☎ (0753) 865538
The chapel is an impressive feature of Windsor Castle. Begun in 1475 by Edward IV, and completed in the reign of Henry VIII, it is a fine example of Perpendicular architecture which, with its large windows, gives a light and spacious effect. The magnificent fan vaulting on the ceiling, the chantries, the ironwork and intricate carving on the choir stalls, all add to this superb building. The choir stalls are dedicated to the Order of Knights of the Garter founded by Edward III. Each stall displays the arms of every knight who has sat there and above it are the banner and crested helm of the present holder. To celebrate the Queen's 40th accession to the trone, a Flower and Music Festival will be held on 6-11 May (to be confirmed).
Open weekdays 10-4, Sun 2-4. (Closed 6 Jan-3 Feb, 26 Apr, 12-16 Jun, 24-25 Dec & occasionally at short notice).
* *£2.50 (ch & pen £1.50) Family ticket £6.*
♿ *shop* ⊘

Savill Garden (Windsor Great Park) — WINDSOR

Map 04 SU97
(via Wick Ln, Engelfield Green, near Egham)
☎ (0753) 860222
The Savill Garden covers some 35 acres of woodland and includes hundreds of different varieties of plants. It is at its peak in spring but, with its range of shrubs like magnolias and rhododendrons, rock plants, herbaceous borders and formal rose gardens, there is a wealth of colour and interest throughout the year.
Open all year, daily 10-6 or sunset when earlier. (Closed 25-28 Dec).
£2.50 (ch 16 free, pen £2.30). Party 20+.
🅿 ✕ *licensed* ♿ *toilets for disabled shop garden centre* ⊘

State Apartments — WINDSOR

Map 04 SU97
Windsor Castle
☎ (0753) 831118
There are 16 State Rooms in the Castle, each one not only historically interesting in itself but also a treasure house of superb furniture, porcelain, armour and, especially, paintings. The rooms are decorated with carvings by Grinling Gibbons and ceilings by Verrio. On the walls is a selection from The Queen's unique collection of pictures by painters such as Van Dyck and Rembrandt. These apartments are generally open to the public but may have to be closed at short notice for some Royal functions.
Open all year, except when Her Majesty The Queen is in official residence. Telephone (0753) 831118 for information.
£4 (ch £1.50, pen £2.50)
♿ *toilets for disabled shop* ⊘

Valley Gardens (Windsor Great Park) — WINDSOR

Map 04 SU97
(off A30)
☎ (0753) 860222
These gardens are near Virginia Water, a lake created in the 18th century. The gardens cover some 400 acres of woodland and are noted especially for their outstanding range of rhododendrons, camellias, magnolias and other trees and shrubs. It is worth visiting at any time of the year as there are plants for each season.
Open all year, daily sunrise-sunset.
Free to pedestrians.
🅿 *(charged)* ♿ *toilets for disabled*

Windsor Castle — WINDSOR

Map 04 SU97
☎ (0753) 831118

The castle, which covers 13 acres is the official residence of H.M. The Queen and the largest inhabited castle in the world. It was begun as a wooden fort by William the Conqueror, but has been added to by almost every other monarch. Henry II erected the first stone building, including the famous Round Tower. Among the many alterations since then were those made in the 14th century by Edward III; the 17th century when the Castle began to be altered from a fortress to a palace; and the 19th century. Edward III enlarged the royal apartments and also founded the Order of Knights of the Garter, based at Windsor. Substantial rebuilding was done during the reign of Charles II and Sir Jeffrey Wyattville (1766-1840) was the architect for alterations made by George IV. The castle is in three parts – the Upper Ward which includes the State Apartments, the Middle Ward, with its Round Tower, and the Lower Ward where St George's Chapel is situated. From the Round Tower there are views of 12 counties.
Open all year - Castle precincts, but subject to closure at short notice.
Precincts - free.
♿ *toilets for disabled shop* ⊘

Windsor Safari Park — WINDSOR

Map 04 SU97
Winkfield Rd (SW of town on B3022)
☎ (0753) 830886
Windsor Safari Park offers visitors an 'African Adventure' in the heart of Berkshire! Explore the new Egyptian Entrance and Moroccan Village. Catch one of the new Safari Roadtrains to come close to some of nature's most spectacular and dangerous animals, and don't miss the new Funicular Railway which passes the Elephant Gardens. See the many exciting shows including the Birds of Prey display and the famous Seaworld Show. Enjoy the Port Livingstone area which contains a host of exciting attractions including Limpopo Crocodiles, Swamp Devils and African Queen Riverboat Ride. The entrance price includes admission to all the shows and attractions.
Open all year, daily from 10am. (Closed 25 Dec).
* *Telephone for admission prices.*
🅿 ☕ ✕ *licensed* ♿ *toilets for disabled shop* ⊘

Places to visit in this guide are pinpointed on the atlas at the back of the book.

BUCKINGHAMSHIRE

Buckinghamshire County Museum — AYLESBURY

Map 04 SP81
St Mary's Square, Church St
☎ (0296) 88849
Old parish rooms next to the churchyard now house displays on local history and temporary exhibitions.
Open all year, Mon-Sat 10-1.30 & 2-5. (Closed Good Fri, 25-26 Dec & 1 Jan).
Free.
♿ *shop* ⊘

Bekonscot Model Village   BEACONSFIELD

Map 04 SU99
Warwick Rd, New Town (2m junc 2
M40, 4m junc 16 M25).
☎ (0494) 672919

Bekonscot is the oldest model village in
the world, first opened in 1929. The
layout of little cottages, farms and
countryside (including a gauge 'one'
railway) is based on a scale of 1 inch to
1 foot. There is a purpose-built toilet for
wheelchair users and four narrow-gauge
wheelchairs are available on loan.
Open 29 Feb-1 Nov daily 10-5.
£2.50 (ch £1.25, pen & students £2).
Party 13+.
🅿 ♿ ⚇ *toilets for disabled shop* ✱

Chiltern Open Air Museum   CHALFONT ST GILES

Map 04 SU99
Newland Park, Gorelands Ln (off
B4442)
☎ (02407) 71117
The museum aims to preserve
traditional Chilterns buildings by
rebuilding them here. Among the
buildings dismantled and brought to the
site are a toll house, cart sheds, stables,
granaries, a forge, barns and an Iron Age
house. There is a nature trail through
the 45 acres of parkland and there is also

an adventure playground. Numerous
events are held throughout the year
including Children's Day (4 May), a
Transport Festival (16-17 May), a
Harvest Celebration (10-11 October),
and a Victorian Christmas Weekend (5-6
Dec).
Open Apr-1 Nov, Wed-Sun & BH 2-6.
£2.50 (ch 16 & over 60's £2, ch 5 free).
Family ticket £8.
🅿 ♿ ⚇ *toilets for disabled shop*

Milton's Cottage   CHALFONT ST GILES

Map 04 SU99
Dean Way
☎ (02407) 2313
This timber-framed, 16th-century
cottage with its charming garden, is the
only surviving home in which John
Milton lived and worked. He completed
Paradise Lost and started *Paradise*

Regained here. First editions of these
works are among the many rare books
on display.
*Open Mar-Oct, Tue-Sat 10-1 & 2-6, Sun
2-6. Also open Spring & Summer BH.*
£1.50 (ch 15 60p). Party 20+.
🅿 ⚇ *shop* ✱

Chicheley Hall   CHICHELEY

Map 04 SP94
(A422 between Newport Pagnell and
Bedford)
☎ North Crawley (023065) 252
Built for Sir John Chester between 1719
and 1723, this is one of the finest and
least-altered 18th-century houses in
England, with wonderful Georgian
craftsmanship in its brickwork, carving,

joinery and plasterwork. It has a naval
museum, English sea pictures and
furniture, and an 18th-century dovecote.
*Open 19 Apr-May & Aug, Sun & BH
Mon 2.30-6. Last entry 5pm. Booked
parties at most times.*
£3 (ch £1.50). Parties 20+.
🅿 ♿ ⚇ *shop* ✱

Cliveden   CLIVEDEN

Map 04 SU98
☎ Burnham (0628) 605069

The 375 acres of garden and woodland

overlook the River Thames, and include
a magnificent parterre, topiary, lawns
with box hedges, and rose and water
gardens. The palatial house, home of the
Astors, is now a hotel, but is open on
certain afternoons.
*Open Grounds Mar-Oct daily 11-6, Nov-
Dec daily 11-4. House Apr-Oct, Thu &
Sun 3-6 by timed ticket. (Last admission
5.30)*
Grounds: £3. House: £1 extra
🅿 ✗ ⚇ *toilets for disabled shop* ✱ *(ex in
woodland)*
(NT)

Wycombe Local History & Chair Museum   HIGH WYCOMBE

Map 04 SU89
Castle Hill House, Priory Av
☎ (0494) 421895
Set in Victorian grounds on a medieval
site, the museum is housed in a 17th-
century building with later additions.
The museum explores the history, crafts
and industry of the Wycombe district
and has an impressive collection of rural
furniture. A variety of activities for both

children and adults is planned for 1992,
including a Shakespeare festival in July,
craft demonstrations, and the annual
exhibition in the Guildhall (mid-July –
mid-October).
*Open all year, Mon-Fri 10-5; Sat 10-1 &
2-5; Sun (seasonal-please telephone for
details).*
🅿 ⚇ *shop* ✱

Hughenden Manor   HUGHENDEN

Map 04 SU89
☎ High Wycombe (0494) 532580

Benjamin Disraeli, later Earl of
Beaconsfield and twice Prime Minister,

bought the house in 1847 and lived
there until his death in 1881. It still has
many of his books and other
possessions. There are purpose-built
toilets for wheelchair users, and a braille
leaflet and taped guide is available.
*Open Mar, Sat & Sun only 2-6. Apr-Oct,
House & Gardens, Wed-Sat 2-6 & Sun &
BH Mon 12-6. Last admission 5.30.
(Closed Good Fri.)*
£3 (ch £1.50)
🅿 ⚇ *toilets for disabled shop* ✱ *(ex in park
& car park only)*
(NT)

This is just one of many guidebooks published by the AA.
The full range is available at any AA shop or good bookshop.

Courthouse   LONG CRENDON

Map 04 SP60
Probably built as a wool store in the
early 1400s, but also used as a manorial
courthouse until the late 19th century,
the timber-framed building stands out,
even in a picturesque village of 16th-
and 17th-century cottages. Although the
windows and doors have been altered

and the chimney stack is Tudor, the
magnificent timber roof is original.
*Open, Upper storey Apr-Sep, Wed 2-6, Sat,
Sun & BH Mons 11-6.*
£1
✱
(NT)

Claydon House   MIDDLE CLAYDON

Map 04 SP72
(off A413, entrance by North drive
only)
☎ Steeple Claydon (0296) 730349
The rather sober exterior of this 18th-
century house gives no clue to the
extravagances that lie inside, in the form
of fantastic rococo carvings. Ceilings,
cornices, walls and overmantels are
adorned with delicately carved fruits,
birds, beasts and flowers by Luke
Lightfoot, and his Chinese room is
particularly splendid. The second Earl of
Verney commissioned Lightfoot to
decorate the rooms and built many other

additions to the house besides; but his
ambition eventually bankrupted him and
by 1783 he had to sell up. His successor
proceeded to demolish two-thirds of the
house. Florence Nightingale was a
frequent visitor and relics of her
Crimean experiences are displayed here.
*Open Apr-Oct, Sat-Wed 1-5, BH Mon 1-5
or dusk if earlier. Last admission half hour
before closing.*
£3
🅿 ♿ ⚇ *(Braille guide) toilets for disabled*
✱ *(ex car park)*
(NT)

Pitstone Windmill   PITSTONE

Map 04 SP91
(off B488)
Now restored and fully operative, this is
one of England's oldest postmills, and
still contains part of the original
structure built in 1627.

*Open May-Sep, Sun & BH Mon 2.30-6.
(Last admission 5.30).*
60p
✱
(NT)

Buckinghamshire Railway Centre   QUAINTON

Map 04 SP72
Quainton Rd Station (off A41)
☎ (029675) 720 & 450 (info)
This is one of the largest collections
pertaining to industrial and main-line
standard-gauge railways, with many
items from the last century. Visitors can
take a ride in a vintage steam train and
see a display of locomotives and rolling
stock. A small museum houses other
memorabilia. Fans of Thomas the Tank

Engine will enjoy the chance to meet the
Fat Controller and his friendly engines,
and will even be able to climb aboard
the coaches and take a ride – May 3 &
4, September 26 & 28; toddlers 18
months-5 years – £3, everyone over 5 –
£5.
*Open Apr-Oct, Sun & BH Mon; Jun-Aug,
Wed; 5-20 Dec, Sat & Sun.*
£3.50 (ch & pen £2). Family ticket £9.50.
🅿 ♿ ⚇ *toilets for disabled shop*

Stowe House   STOWE

Map 04 SP63
☎ Buckingham (0280) 813650
The fine 18th-century mansion is now a
public school. The grounds are splendid,
with statuary and garden temples.

*Open 1-13 Apr & 6 Jul-6 Sep, 11-5. May
occasionally be closed if booked for private
functions. Please ring for confirmation.*
£2 (ch £1).
🅿 ⚇ *shop*

Stowe Landscape Gardens   STOWE

Map 04 SP63
☎ Buckingham (0280) 822850
One of the supreme creations of the Georgian era, where the first formal layout was adorned with many buildings by Vanbrugh, Kent and Gibbs. In the 1930s Kent designed the Elysian Fields in a more naturalistic style, depicting one of the earliest examples of the reaction against formality, leading to the evolution of the landscape garden.
Open 28 Mar-20 Apr, 28 Jun-6 Sep, 24

Oct-1 Nov, 19-24 & 27-31 Dec, 1-10 Jan 1993, 27 Mar-18 Apr 1993 – daily 10-6 (or dusk if earlier); Also 22 Apr-26 Jun, 7 Sep-23 Oct, Mon, Wed & Fri 10-5 (or dusk if earlier). Last admission 1hr before closing. Other times, telephone for details. (Closed Good Fri & 25-26 Dec)
£3
🅿 🍴 ♿ *(self-drive battery cars available) toilets for disabled*
(NT)

Waddesdon Manor   WADDESDON

Map 04 SP71
(gates off A41)
☎ Aylesbury (0296) 651211
In 1874 Baron Ferdinand de Rothschild acquired this Buckinghamshire hilltop which became the site for the Destailleur designed château, around which is set one of the finest late Victorian formal gardens and parks designed by Laine. Restoration plans for the gardens include shrubberies and additional bedding to

the fountain terrace. The elegant caste iron rococo-style aviary, built in 1889, contains mainly softbill birds and some parrots.
Open, Grounds & Aviary only 18 Mar-23 Dec, Wed-Fri 12-5, Sat, Sun, Good Fri & BH Mon 12-6.
Grounds & Aviary £3 (ch 5 free, ch 5-17 £1.50).
🅿 🍴 ♿ *toilets for disabled shop* ✗
(NT)

West Wycombe Caves   WEST WYCOMBE

Map 04 SU89
(on A40)
☎ High Wycombe (0494) 524411

halfway up the hill that dominates the village. On the summit stands the parish church and the mausoleum of the Dashwood family. The caves are not natural but were dug on the orders of Sir Francis Dashwood between 1748 and 1752. Sir Francis, the Chancellor of the Exchequer, was also the founder of the Hell Fire Club, whose members were reputed to have practised black magic. The caves, which extend to approximately one-third of a mile underground, are supposed to have been one of their venues. The entrance

The entrance to West Wycombe caves is   *continued . . .*

consists of a large forecourt with flint walls, from which a brick tunnel leads into the caves, where tableaux and curiosities are exhibited in various chambers, including the Great Hall

of Statues.
Open all year, Mar-Oct, daily 11-6; Nov-Feb, Sat & Sun 1-5.
£2.50 (ch & pen £1.25). Party 20+.
🅿 🍴 ♿ *shop garden centre* ✗

West Wycombe Park   WEST WYCOMBE

Map 04 SU89
☎ High Wycombe (0494) 524411
Set in 300 acres of beautiful parkland, the house was rebuilt in the Palladian style, between 1745 and 1771, for Sir Francis Dashwood. Inside there is a good collection of tapestries, furniture and paintings. Of particular note are the painted ceilings by Borgnis.
    The park was laid out in the 18th century and given an artificial lake and classical temples, some of which were designed by Nicholas Revett. The

Temple of Venus has recently been reconstructed. The park was later rearranged by a follower of 'Capability' Brown.
Open, House & grounds Jun-Aug, Sun-Thu 2-6. Grounds only Apr & May, Sun & Wed 2-6 & Etr, May Day & Spring BH Sun & Mon 2-6. Last admission 5.15. Entry by timed tickets on wkdays.
✷ *£4. Grounds only £2.50.*
🅿 ♿ ✗
(NT)

Ascott   WING

Map 04 SP82
☎ Aylesbury (0296) 688242
The house, once the property of the de Rothschilds, was given to the National Trust in 1950. The bequest included a collection of French and Chippendale furniture, pictures by such notable painters as Hogarth, Gainsborough and Rubens. There is also a collection of paintings by Hobbema, Cuyp and other Dutch painters. The collection of Oriental porcelain has some outstanding pieces of K'ang Hsi and of the Ming and Sung dynasties.
    Outside there are 260 acres of land of

which 12 are garden. There are many unusual trees, with thousands of naturalised bulbs, and also a formal garden.
Open, House & garden: 14 Apr-17 May & Sep, Tue-Sun 2-6. Also BH Mon 20 Apr & 4 May (but closed Tue 21 Apr & 5 May). Garden only: 20 May-Aug, every Wed & last Sun of month & BH Mon 25 May & 31 Aug 2-6. Last admission to house 5pm.
House & garden £4 (ch £2). Garden only £2.50.
🅿 ♿ ✗
(NT)

CAMBRIDGESHIRE

CAMBRIDGE

Map 04 TL45
The heart of the ancient university city is the row of colleges which lines the River Cam and overlooks the Backs on the other side of the river. This area of lawns and trees was reclaimed from rough marshland by Richard Bently, Master of Trinity College from 1669 to 1734, and it makes a lovely place to walk. In medieval times, this would have been a very different scene: the Cam was a busy commercial river, and the town was a centre for trade. The university is considered to have begun in 1209, when a group of students arrived after fleeing from riots in Oxford. The colleges are open to the public on most days during daylight, though there are certain restrictions during term time. A good place to start is King's College Chapel, with its glorious fan vaulting. There is a permanent exhibition, 'Kings: The Building of a Chapel', which brings together the chapel's history, architecture, art, heraldry and music. From here, the colleges of Trinity, St John's, Clare and others can easily be reached on foot – or hire a bicycle to see the city in the authentic way.

Cambridge & County Folk Museum   CAMBRIDGE

Map 04 TL45
2/3 Castle St
☎ (0223) 355159
The timber-framed White Horse Inn is an appealing setting for the folk museum. It houses items covering the everyday life of the people of Cambridgeshire from 1650 to the present day. There are also temporary exhibitions. Special exhibitions and craft days take place throughout the year, including 'To Market, To Market' – an

exhibition on shops and shopping through the ages (Mar-May); Roman and Victorian Cambridge (Jun-Oct); and a Christmas exhibition in Dec.
Open all year, Mar-Sep, Mon-Sat 10.30-5, Sun 2-5. Oct-Feb, Tue-Sat 10.30-5, Sun 2-5. (Closed Mon ex school hols & pre-booked school parties). Last admissions 30 mins before closing.
£1 (ch 5-16, students, UB40s & pen 50p).
♿ *(braille & tape guides) shop* ✗

Fitzwilliam Museum   CAMBRIDGE

Map 04 TL45
Trumpington St
☎ (0223) 332900
The Fitzwilliam is one of the oldest museums in Britain, and is housed in an imposing building designed for the purpose in 1834. In the early days, it was only open to 'properly dressed' members of the public, and then only three days a week. The museum has particularly good English and Continental ceramics and English glass, with some outstanding Oriental work, and paintings by Titian, Veronese, Canaletto and many other famous

names, including leading French Impressionists. There are Egyptian, Greek and Roman antiquities, and other treasures include medieval illuminated manuscripts, ivories, miniatures, carvings and armour. There are special exhibitions throughout the year.
Open all year Tue-Sat 10-5, Sun 2.15-5 plus Etr Mon, Spring & Summer BH. (Closed Good Fri, May Day & 24 Dec-1 Jan).
Free.
🍴 ♿ *(preferably pre-arranged) toilets for disabled shop* ✗

Scott Polar Research Institute   CAMBRIDGE

Map 04 TL45
Lensfield Rd
☎ (0223) 336540
The institute is an international centre for polar studies, and has a museum with displays of Arctic and Antarctic expeditions, with special emphasis on those of Captain Scott. Other exhibits include Eskimo work and other arts of

the polar regions. Also shown are displays on current scientific exploration. A special exhibition is shown every summer.
Open all year, Mon-Sat 2.30-4. (Closed some public & university bols).
Free.
shop ✖

University Botanic Garden   CAMBRIDGE

Map 04 TL45
Cory Lodge, Bateman St
☎ (0223) 336265
The garden was founded in 1762, mainly for the study of medicinal plants. It now covers a 40-acre site and has interesting collections of plants in botanical groups, a chronological bed (with plants in order of introduction), a

scented garden, and a conservation garden containing rare species.
Open all year Mon-Sat 8-6, Sun 10-6 (dusk in winter).Glassbouse 11-12.30 & 2-4. Entry on Sun by Bateman St only.
✳ *Sun only £1 (ch 3-17 50p). Free for ticket bolders-particulars from Director*
♿ *toilets for disabled* ✖

University Museum of Archaeology & Anthropology   CAMBRIDGE

Map 04 TL45
Downing St
☎ (0223) 337733
The museum covers man's development from the earliest times throughout the world, with extensive sections on British archaeology and local archaeology in particular. New anthropology displays

and a special exhibition facility are now open. Summer 1992 will see the opening of 'The Americas 1492' exhibition.
Open all year Mon-Fri 2-4, Sat 10-12.30. (Closed 1 wk Etr & 24 Dec-2 Jan)
Free.
♿ *shop* ✖

Duxford Airfield   DUXFORD

Map 04 TL44
(off junc 10 of M11 on A505)
☎ Cambridge (0223) 835000

This former Battle of Britain fighter station has hangars dating from the First World War. It is now home to most of the Imperial War Museum's collection of military aircraft, armoured fighting vehicles, midget submarines and other large exhibits. There are over 120 historic aircraft on the airfield, and also

on display is the Duxford Aviation Society's collection of civil aircraft, including the prototype Concorde 01. Special themed exhibits include a US 8th Air Force Exhibition. Major flying displays are held in summer, and pleasure flights can be taken during summer weekends. Those with aircraft may apply to land them at the airfield; those without can try the popular flight simulator. Cinema shows are held on summer Sundays, and there is an adventure playground. 1992 events include Classic Fighter Display (4/5 July), and Duxford '92 (13 Sep).
Open all year, mid Mar-Oct daily 10-6; Nov-mid Mar daily 10-4. (Closed 24-26 Dec & 1 Jan)
✳ *Telephone for admission prices.*
🅿 🍴 ♿ *(wheelchair available) toilets for disabled shop* ✖

The Stained Glass Museum   ELY

Map 04 TL58
The Cathedral
☎ Cambridge (0223) 327367
The museum is situated in the cathedral and was established in 1972 to rescue and preserve fine stained glass, which might otherwise be lost and is the only one of its kind in the country. Models show how stained-glass windows are

designed and made. There is an exhibition of approximately 80 panels dating from the 13th century to the present day.
Open Mar-Oct, Mon-Fri 10.30-4, Sat & BH 10.30-4.30 & Sun 12-3. Also wknds throughout year.
✳ *£1 (ch & students 50p). Party 12 +.*
🍴 *shop* ✖

Hamerton Wildlife Centre   HAMERTON

Map 04 TL17
☎ (08323) 362
A wildlife breeding centre, dedicated to the practical conservation of endangered species including otters, gibbons, monkeys, marmosets, lemurs, wildcats, meerkats and many more. There is also a large and varied bird collection, with several species unique to Hamerton. Over 120 species in all, many new for 1992. Other attractions include a

children's play area, and undercover viewing of many mammals. Special events for 1992 include falconry demonstrations, teddy bear's picnic and an annual birthday party.
Open Summer daily 10.30-6; winter daily 10.30-4. (Closed Xmas)
£3 (pen £2.50 & ch 5-14 £1.50). Party 15 +
🅿 🍴 ✖ ♿ *shop* ✖

Cromwell Museum   HUNTINGDON

Map 04 TL27
Grammar School Walk
☎ (0480) 425830
The museum is in a restored Norman building, which was first a hospital and then became a school in the 16th century. Oliver Cromwell (born in the town in 1599) was a pupil, so was

Samuel Pepys (born 1640). It now houses some of Cromwell's possessions.
Open all year, Apr-Oct, Tue-Fri 11-1 & 2-5, Sat & Sun 11-1 & 2-4; Nov-Mar, Tue-Fri 1-4, Sat 11-1 & 2-4, Sun 2-4. (Closed BH's ex Good Fri)
Free.
shop ✖

Linton Zoological Gardens   LINTON

Map 04 TL54
Hadstock Rd
☎ Cambridge (0223) 891308
Conservation and education are the
main concerns of this zoo which was
established in 1972. The many species of
animals and birds are housed in
landscaped enclosures as like their
natural habitats as possible. Especially
interesting are the Sumatran tigers, giant
Aloabra tortoises – the largest herd
outside the tropics, a fine collection of
owls, binturongs and the famous Toco
toucans – the only young to be bred in
Britain were born here. All around the
enclosures are fine shrubberies and
exotic trees. Special events are planned
and details can be obtained from the
zoo.
*Open daily 10-6 or dusk (ex 25 Dec). Last
admission 45 minutes before closing time.*
P ▪ & *toilets for disabled shop* ✠
Details not confirmed for 1992

Anglesey Abbey   LODE

Map 04 TL56
☎ Cambridge (0223) 811200
A medieval undercroft has survived from
the priory founded here in 1135, but the
house dates mainly from 1600. Thomas
Hobson of 'Hobson's choice' was one of
the owners. A later owner was Lord
Fairhaven, who amassed the huge
collection of pictures, including
hundreds of views of Windsor Castle. He
also laid out the beautiful Georgian-
style gardens, which are set with urns
and statues.
*Open House: 28 Mar-18 Oct, Wed-Sun &
BH Mon 1.30-5.30. Garden: 28 Mar-12
Jul, Wed-Sun & BH Mon; 13 Jul-8 Sep,
daily; 9 Sep-18, Oct Wed-Sun 11-5.30.
Lode Mill: 28 Mar-18 Oct Sat, Sun &
BH Mons 1.30-5.30.
£4.60 (ch £2.30). Sun & BH Mon £5.50.
Garden only £2.25 (ch £1). Sun & BH
Mon £2.50. Party 15+.*
P ✕ *licensed* & *(braille guide) toilets for
disabled shop* ✠
(NT)

✱ An asterisk indicated that up-to-date information was
not available at the time of our research – 1991
information has been published as an
indication of what you may expect.

Wildfowl & Wetlands Trust   PEAKIRK

Map 04 TF10
☎ Peterborough (0733) 252271
Over 600 ducks, geese and swans
represent more than 100 different
species in an attractive water garden.
There is a magnificent flock of Chilean
flamingoes and trumpeter, black necked
and coscoroba swans. Andean geese and
many other rare and unusual waterfowl
can be seen. A visitor centre provides
information on the birds and the Trust.
*Open all year, daily. Summer 9.30-6.30
(Last admission 5.30). Winter 9.30-dusk.
(Closed 24-25 Dec).*
P ▪ & *toilets for disabled shop* ✠
Details not confirmed for 1992

City of Peterborough Museum & Art Gallery   PETERBOROUGH

Map 04 TL19
Priestgate
☎ (0733) 343329
Articles made by Napoleonic prisoners-
of-war at Norman Cross prison camp are
on display here as well as exhibits of
local geology, archaeology, social and
natural history. Paintings are displayed
along with a small collection of ceramics
and glass, and there are regular
temporary exhibitions.
*Open all year, Tue-Sat 10-5; Also open
BH Mon. (Closed Good Fri & 25-26 Dec).
Please telephone before weekend visits.
Free.
shop* ✠

Longthorpe Tower   PETERBOROUGH

Map 04 TL19
☎ (0733) 268482
Rare wall paintings of religious and
educational subjects are on show in this
13th- to 14th-century fortified house,
which formerly belonged to the de
Thorpe family.
*Open all year, Apr-Sep, daily 10-6; Oct-
Mar, wknds 10-4. (Closed 24-26 Dec & 1
Jan).
£1.10 (ch 55p, students, pen & UB40
85p).*
✠
(EH)

Nene Valley Railway
**Wansford Station, next to A1,
Stibbington, Peterborough PE8 6LR
Telephone: (0780) 782854**

A preserved steam railway with 7½ miles of track,
locomotives and carriages from Europe and the UK.
The ideal outing for those who love steam and for the younger
members of the family. See THOMAS the children's favourite
Engine. Visit the Buffet, Bar, Souvenir shop, Museum and
Model Railway on operating days.

Services operate in 1992 — Sats & Suns from March to
October and some midweek days in June, July & August. In
addition Santa Specials operate in December.

Abbey Gatehouse   RAMSEY

Map 04 TL28
The ruins of this 15th-century
gatehouse, together with the 13th-
century Lady Chapel, are all that remain
of the abbey. Half of the gatehouse was
taken away after the Dissolution. Built
in ornate late-Gothic style, it has
panelled buttresses, and friezes around
both the doorway and the oriel window
above it.
*Open Apr-Oct, daily 10-5 (or dusk).
Free.*
✠
(NT)

Norris Museum   ST IVES

Map 04 TL37
The Broadway
☎ (0480) 65101
The Norris Museum has a
comprehensive collection of
Huntingdonshire local history. Exhibits
include fossils, archaeology and bygones.
Also displayed is some fine work in
bone and straw carried out by French
prisoners at Norman Cross, and
Huntingdonshire lace.
*Open all year, May-Sep, Mon-Fri 10-1 &
2-5, Sat 10-12 & 2-5, Sun 2-5; Oct-Apr,
Tue-Fri 10-1 & 2-4, Sat 10-12. (Closed
BH's).
Free.*
& *shop*

For an explanation of the symbols and abbreviations, see page 2.

Nene Valley Railway   WANSFORD

Map 04 TL09
Wansford Station (A1 west of
Peterborough)
☎ Stamford (0780) 782854
This standard-gauge steam railway runs
between Peterborough and Wansford
and onto Yarwell Junction. It is based at
Wansford Station, which also has an
international collection of steam
locomotives and rolling stock. There is a
small museum of railway memorabilia
from the days of steam. Special events
are arranged throughout the year for
steam enthusiasts and their families.
*Open mid Jul-Aug, Tue-Fri; Mar-Dec,
Sun; Apr-Oct & Dec, Sat & BH Mon.
Also other selected dates – telephone for
details.*
P ▪ & *(disabled access to trains) toilets for
disabled shop
Details not confirmed for 1992*

Wimpole Hall   WIMPOLE

Map 04 TL35
(junc of A14 and A603)
☎ Cambridge (0223) 207257

Although Wimpole Hall is one of the
grandest mansions in East Anglia, it is
perhaps the 360 acres of parkland that
make it unusual. The parkland was
devised and planted by no less than four
of the country's celebrated landscape
designers, Charles Bridgeman,
'Capability' Brown, Sanderson Miller
and Humphrey Repton. Under the
pasture lie the remains of a medieval
village with evidence of tracks and ridge-
and-furrow farming. The house, which
was given to the National Trust in
1976, dates back to 1640, but was
altered into a large 18th-century
mansion with a Georgian façade. The
inside is the work of a number of
important architects. Lord Harley's
library and the gallery are the work of
James Gibbs, and the Yellow Drawing
Room was designed by Sir John Soane
in about 1793. The chapel has a
wonderful painted *trompe l'oeil* ceiling by
Sir James Thornhill.
*Open 28 Mar-1 Nov, Tue-Thu, Sat, Sun
1-5, BH Sun & Mon 11-5. (Closed Good
Fri).
£4.40 (ch £2). Party 15+.*
P ✕ *licensed* & *(braille guide) toilets for
disabled shop* ✠ *(ex park only)*
(NT)

Wimpole Home Farm   WIMPOLE

Map 04 TL35
☎ Cambridge (0223) 207257
When built in 1794, the Home Farm
was one of the most advanced
agricultural enterprises in the country.
The group of thatched and timbered
buildings was designed by Sir John
Soane for the 3rd Earl of Hardwicke.
The Great Barn, now restored, holds a
display of farm machinery and
implements of the kind used at Wimpole
over the past two centuries. On the farm
there is a wide selection of rare breeds of
domestic animals, including the black-
and-white Bagot goat which was rescued
from extinction. In the stables, there are
once more the rare breed of Suffolk
Punch horses. A special children's corner
and a woodland play area are additional
attractions.
*Open 28 Mar-1 Nov, daily (ex Mon &
Fri) 10.30-5. Open BH Mons. (Closed
Good Fri).*
✱ *£3.40 (ch £1.50). Party 15+.*
P ▪ & *(braille guide) toilets for disabled
shop* ✠
(NT)

Peckover House   WISBECH

Map 04 TF40
☎ (0945) 583463
In a town with many elegant Georgian
merchant's houses, Peckover House is
one of the finest. It is named after a
banker who purchased the house in
1777. His bank was part of the group
which formed Barclays Bank in 1896.
The house dates from 1722 and the
interior has Rococo decoration in plaster
and wood. The two- acre garden is a
delightful and colourful example of
Victorian planting, still having its 19th-
century design. In the kitchen garden
there are greenhouses with orange trees
still bearing fruit after 250 years.
*Open, House & garden: 28 Mar-1 Nov,
Sun, Wed & BH Mon. Garden only: 28
Mar-1 Nov, Sat-Wed 2-5.30.
House & garden £2.20 (ch £1). Party 20+.
Garden only £1.*
▪ & ✠
(NT)

Wisbech & Fenland Museum   WISBECH

Map 04 TF40
☎ (0945) 583817
The museum contains a fine collection of ceramics and *objets d'art*. There are exhibits on the archaeology and natural history of Wisbech and the surrounding Fenland. Many items relate to Fenland life. Also of interest are the pictures; oils, water colours and photographs; the European and Oriental art; and Thomas Clarkson's African collection. Parish Registers, and a collection of over 20,000 books including early

manuscripts, originally forming the library of the literary society, are in the town library. Early 1992 will see the opening of a new gallery of geology, and later events include an exhibition of the work and collection of photographer Samuel Smith (27 Jun-29 Aug) and a rose fair (1-4 July).
Open all year, Tue-Sat 10-5 (4pm Oct-Mar). (Closed BH).
Free (Museum libraries & archives available by appointment only).
shop ✻

CHESHIRE

Adlington Hall   ADLINGTON

Map 07 SJ98
(3m N of Macclesfield, 0.5m off A523)
☎ Prestbury (0625) 829206
This fine house is a lovely blend of Tudor timber-framing and 18th-century brick. Handel is said to have played the Bernard Smith organ in the Great Hall.

The grounds have a yew walk and a lime avenue, and craft and antique fairs are held between April and September.
Open Good Fri-Sep, Sun & BH 2-5.30. Parties on weekdays by arrangement.
✳ *£2.50 (ch £1). Gardens £1. Party 25 +*
🅿 ♨ ⅁ *shop* ✻

Beeston Castle   BEESTON

Map 07 SJ55
(off A49)
☎ Bunbury (0829) 260464
This ruined stronghold dates back to around 1220 and was built by the Earl of Chester in an almost inaccessible position. Set on a steep hill, the ruins include the remains of the inner and outer wards, and give spectacular views of the surrounding countryside. An

exhibition explains the history of the castle.
Open all year, Apr-Sep, daily 10-6; Oct-Mar, Tue-Sun 10-4. (Closed 24-26 Dec & 1 Jan).
£1.80 (ch 90p, pen, students & UB40 £1.40).
🅿 ✻
(EH)

Bridgemere Garden World   BRIDGEMERE

Map 07 SJ74
☎ (09365) 381

See advertisement opposite for details.

Capesthorne Hall   CAPESTHORNE

Map 07 SJ87
(On A34 between Congleton and Wimslow)
☎ Chelford (0625) 861221 & 861779
Home of the Bromley-Davenport family, the house was built in 1722 and contains interesting furniture, pictures, silver and Americana. There is a Georgian chapel, and a family theatre. The grounds include a children's play area, and angling is available in season. There are gardens, lakes, a nature trail and woodland walks, and numerous

events are held throughout the year, including craft fairs in costume (11/12 Apr and 26/27 Sep), kit car show (17 May), firework and laser concert (13 Jun) and horse trials (19 Aug).
Open Apr Suns; May & Aug-Sep Wed & Sun; Jun-Jul Tue-Thu & Sun. Park & Garden 12-6, Hall 2-4.
Park, Garden & Chapel £1.75 (ch 50p). Park, Gardens, Chapel & Hall £3.50 (ch £1 & pen £3). Family ticket £7.50. Party 20 +
🅿 ♨ ✕ *licensed* ⅁ *toilets for disabled shop*

CHESTER

Map 07 SJ46
Chester is one of Britain's most appealing cities. It is famed for its picturesque black and white buildings, but is its also a lively town that does not simply live on its past. The best way to start a visit is to walk around the medieval walls; there are small museums in some of the towers. The star attraction within the walls is the group of double-decker streets called the Rows, where stairs lead up to first-floor shops. The town is filled with timber-framed buildings, many of which are more Victorian than medieval, but are nonetheless attractive. There is also a Norman cathedral, extensively restored by Sir George Gilbert Scott. Roman Chester should not be forgotten. The city began as an important Roman military base, and the remains of a Roman amphitheatre lie outside the walls. To get a feel of Roman times, visit the Grosvenor Museum, which has evocative items such as memorial stones to Roman soldiers and their families.

The Cheshire Military Museum   CHESTER

Map 07 SJ46
The Castle
☎ (0244) 347203 & 327617
Exhibits from the history of the Cheshire Regiment, Cheshire Yeomanry, 5th Royal Inniskillin Dragoon Guards,

and 3rd Carabiniers.
Open all year, daily 9-5. (Closed 30 mins lunchtime & 1-2 Jan, Good Fri & 19-31 Dec).
50p (ch 20p).
shop

Chester Heritage Centre   CHESTER

Map 07 SJ46
St Michael's Church, Bridge St Row
☎ (0244) 317948
The centre has displays on Chester's history and architecture, with an audio-visual show. There are exhibitions on various historical and other themes.
Open from Mar, telephone (0244) 321616 for further details.
✳ *Admission fee payable.*
shop ✸

Chester Visitor Centre   CHESTER

Map 07 SJ46
Vicars Ln (opposite Roman Amphitheatre)
☎ (0244) 318916 & 351609
Over 2000 years of Chester's history are illustrated by a video and a life-size reconstruction of a scene in the Chester Rows during Victorian times. There is a tourist information desk and guided tours depart regularly from the Centre. Craft fairs take place on Bank Holiday weekends.
Open all year daily, Apr-Oct 9am-9pm, Nov-Mar 9am-7pm.
♿ ♨ shop
Details not confirmed for 1992

Chester Zoo   CHESTER

Map 07 SJ46
Upton-By-Chester (2m N of city centre off A41)
☎ (0244) 380280
This is one of Europe's finest zoological gardens, with 5500 animals in 110 acres of enclosures and landscaped gardens. There is a tropical house and an aquarium, and waterbus rides can be taken. A new mono-rail system is the latest attraction.
Open all year, daily 10-dusk. Last admission 3.30 Winter, 5.30 Summer. (Closed 25 Dec).
✳ £5 (ch 3-15 & pen £2.50).
🅿 ♨ ✕ *licensed* ♿ *(wheelchairs for hire) toilets for disabled shop* ✸

Grosvenor Museum   CHESTER

Map 07 SJ46
27 Grosvenor St
☎ (0244) 321616
The museum has an outstanding collection of Roman items, including a Roman Army gallery. The museum houses an art gallery, and there are Victorian and Georgian rooms. Temporary exhibitions are held and new galleries are planned for 1992 for natural history, Roman tombstones, and silver.
Open all year, Mon-Sat 10.30-5, Sun 2-5. (Closed Good Fri & Xmas).
Free.
♿ shop ✸

Cholmondeley Castle Gardens   CHOLMONDELEY

Map 07 SJ55
(off A49/A41)
☎ (0829) 720383
Ornamental gardens, with an ancient private chapel, a lakeside picnic area, and some rare breeds of farm animals. There are lovely lakeside and woodland walks. Special events are held throughout the year, please telephone for details.
*Open Etr-Sep, Sun & BH 12-5.30.
£2.50 (ch 75p, pen £1.50). Party.*
🅿 ♨ ♿ *toilets for disabled shop garden centre*

Lyme Park   DISLEY

Map 07 SJ98
☎ (0663) 762023
Surrounded by wild moorland, Lyme Park is an Elizabethan house at the core, but it was transformed in the 17th and 18th centuries. Notable features include the handsome Palladian front and courtyard, the elaborate Baroque ceiling of the grand staircase, and the intricate woodcarvings in the saloon, probably by Grinling Gibbons. Earlier Elizabethan decorative carving can be seen in the drawing room and the Long Gallery. The house's fine pictures and furnishings include Mortlake tapestries. The Hall is interpreted in 1910 with guides in costume of the Edwardian servants of Lord Newton. The house is set amidst 15 acres of formal and informal Victorian gardens, and is surrounded by a 1377 acre country park. Other attractions include a Visitors' Centre, 1910 Tearooms, an Adventure Playground, Orienteering, a Countryside Centre, Pitch and Putt, and Fishing. Details of events are available on request.
Open – Hall, Good Fri-4 Oct, 2-5. (Closed Mon & Fri ex BH's). Freeflow – 23
continued . . .

May-13 Jun & 18 Jul-3 Sep, & all Sun, otherwise Guided Tours. Telephone for Xmas opening times. Park all year, Gardens all year (ex 25 & 26 Dec).
✳ *Admission for Car & Occupants (Park & Garden incl) £3. Hall £1.95 (ch & pen £1, under 5 free). NT members free. Party ticket (5 persons) £4.95.*
🅿 ♨ ♿ *(by arrangement) toilets for disabled shop (NT)*

Boat Museum   ELLESMERE PORT

Map 07 SJ47
Dockyard Rd
☎ 051-355 5017
The museum occupies a historic dock complex at the junction of the Shropshire Union and Manchester Ship Canals. These docks were one of the most important points for transferring goods between sea-going vessels and the smaller craft of the inland waterways. There are over 60 craft to see, ranging from a small weedcutter to a 300-ton coaster. Visitors may go aboard some of them, and there is a boat trip. Other attractions include restored warehouses, workshops, blacksmith's forge and dock workers' cottages. Four of the original steam engines which once drove the hydraulic power system survive, and two are in steam on the first Sunday of each month and Bank Holidays. Craft fairs and other special events take place throughout the year, including Easter craft fair and boaters gathering (Good Friday – Easter Monday), International dance festival (May Bank Holiday), model boats convention (August Bank Holiday), and Christmas Craft Fair with Santa (Nov 28/29). The museum also has displays on canals, canal horses and the town.
Open Summer daily 10-5. Winter daily (ex Fri) 11-4. (Closed 25 & 26 Dec).
✳ £4 (ch £2.70, pen & students £3). Family ticket £12.50.
🅿 ♨ ♿ *(resources pack for blind & deaf) toilets for disabled shop*

Gawsworth Hall   GAWSWORTH

Map 07 SJ86
(2m S of Macclesfield off A536)
☎ North Rode (0260) 223456
This fine Tudor black-and-white manor house was the birthplace of Mary Fitton, thought by some to be the 'Dark Lady' of Shakespeare's sonnets. Pictures and armour can be seen in the house, which also has a tilting ground – now thought to be a rare example of an Elizabethan pleasure garden. Special events for 1992 include: Mid Jun-mid Aug, Open Air Theatre (Shakespeare, Gilbert and Sullivan, brass band and concerts); May and Aug Bank Holiday weekends, craft fairs.
*Open 11 Apr-4 Oct, 2-5.30.
£3 (ch £1.50). Party 20+.*
🅿 ♨ ♿ shop ✸

Jodrell Bank Science Centre & Arboretum — JODRELL BANK SCIENCE CENTRE & ARBORETUM

Map 07 SJ77
☎ Lower Withington (0477) 71339
The Science Centre stands at the feet of one of the largest, fully steerable radio telescopes in the world, the Lovell telescope, a landmark both in Cheshire and in the world of astronomy. Interactive exhibits enable visitors to 'get to grips' with science. There are shows every half-hour in the Planetarium and outside, visitors may walk through 35 acres of tree-lined walkways in the Arboretum, beautiful in every season, and visit the Environmental Discovery Centre. 1992 is International Space

Year, so there will be a number of events held in connection with BISY'92 – British Industry In Space Year. These include the official opening of the Environmental Discovery Centre and the new exhibition 'The Tree Planet'.
Open Sat before Etr-Oct, daily 10.30-5.30; Nov-Sat before Etr, wknds only 12-5 (daily Xmas hols). (Closed 25, 26 Dec & 1 Jan). £3.20 (ch 5-16 £1.80, pen £2.40) includes Exhibition, Planetarium, Arboretum & Environmental Discovery Centre. Family ticket £10. Infants not admitted to the Planetarium.
🅿 ♨ & *toilets for disabled shop* ✖

Tatton Park — KNUTSFORD

Map 07 SJ77
(3.5m from M6, junc 19, or M56 junc 7)
☎ (0565) 654822

Tatton Park is one of the great playgrounds of the north-west, with gardens and a 1000-acre country park offering fishing, swimming, sailing and walking, as well as various events throughout the year. The centrepiece is the great Georgian mansion, whose gardens were first laid out by Humphry Repton, followed in the 19th century by Sir Joseph Paxton, who designed the Italian-style terraces in front of the house. Later, in the 20th century,

Japanese gardeners created a Japanese garden with a Shinto temple beside one of the lakes, and also to be seen are an orangery and a fern house, as well as colourful expanses of flowers.

The park is big enough to absorb its visitors and still provide room for wildlife, and the mere is especially interesting for its wildfowl in winter. A variety of signposted walks includes an historic landscape trail.

The house itself has sumptuous furnishings and pictures including two Canalettos. Also of interest are the kitchens and cellars. The home Farm is stocked with animals and working as it was fifty years ago. Old Hall is the original medieval manor house and a guided tour transports you through five hundred years of Tatton history. An adventure playground is the newest feature. There is a regular programme of special events.
Open Good Fri or Apr-Sep, Park 11-7, Mansion, Gardens, Old Hall & Farm

continued . . .

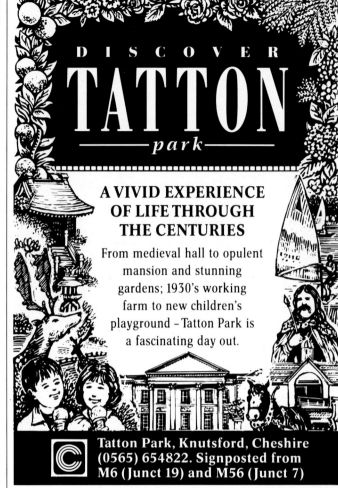
12-5. (Closed Mon ex BH Mon); Oct-Good Fri or Mar, Park 11-5, Gardens 12-4. (Closed Mon & 24-25 Dec), Farm Sun only 12-4, Shop 11.30-4.30. (Last admissions 1hr before closure).
🅿 *(charged)* ♨ ✖ *licensed* & *(Old Hall & Farm not accessible) toilets for disabled shop garden centre* ✖ *(ex in Park & Gardens) (NT)*
Details not confirmed for 1992

& This symbol indicates that much or all of the attraction is accessible to wheelchairs. However, there may be some restrictions, so it would be wise to check in advance.

Hare Hill — MACCLESFIELD

Map 07 SJ97
(4m N off B5087)
☎ (0625) 828981
The beautiful parkland at Hare Hill also features a pretty walled garden and pergola. A brilliant display of rhododendrons and azaleas can be seen in late spring.
Open Apr-25 Oct Wed, Thu, Sat, Sun &

BH Mons 10-5.30. Parties by written appointment with the Head Gardener. Special openings (to see rhododenrons & azaleas) 18 May-5 Jun daily 10-5.30; Nov-Mar 1993, Sat & Sun 10-5.30. £1 (ch 50p). £1 per car (refundable on entry to garden).
🅿 & ✖
(NT)

Every effort is made to provide accurate information, but details might change during the currency of this guide.

Macclesfield Silk Museum — MACCLESFIELD

Map 07 SJ97
Heritage Centre, Roe St
☎ (0625) 613210
The silk museum presents the story of silk in Macclesfield through a colourful audio-visual programme, exhibitions, textiles, garments, models and room settings. It is situated in the Heritage Centre, formerly a Sunday school for child labourers. Special musical events

include: 7 Mar, Vienna After Mozart, with Amanda Roocroft; 16 May, Good Things in Small Packages, with John Lill.
Open all year, Tue-Sat 11-5, Sun & BH Mon 1-5. (Closed Good Fri, 24-26 Dec & 1 Jan)
Admission charged.
🅿 *(charged)* ♨ & *toilets for disabled shop* ✖

Paradise Mill   MACCLESFIELD

Map 07 SJ97
Park Ln
☎ (0625) 618228
An award-winning museum where
knowledgable guides, many of them
former silk mill workers, illustrate the
silk production process with the help of
demonstrations from weavers. The
museum was a working silk mill until
1981 when the last handloom weaver

retired, and 26 handlooms have been
fully restored in their original setting.
Exhibitions and room settings give an
impression of working conditions at the
mill during the 1930s
*Open all year, BH Mon & Tue-Sun 1-5.
(Closed Good Fri, 24-26 Dec & 1 Jan).
Admission charged.*
& *shop* ✻

✳ An asterisk indicates that up-to-date information was
not available at the time of our research – 1991
information has been published as an
indication of what you may expect.

West Park Museum   MACCLESFIELD

Map 07 SJ97
West Park, Prestbury Rd
☎ (0625) 619831
A small but significant collection of
Egyptian antiquities can be seen at this
museum, together with a wide range of
fine and decorative arts. The paintings
on display are from the 19th and early
20th centuries and include the work of
the bird artist, Charles Tunnicliffe. Items
relating to local history are also shown.
The museum was established in 1898 by

the Brocklehurst family, and is on the
edge of one of the earliest parks founded
by voluntary subscriptions. Special
events for 1992 include: 7 Mar-5 Apr,
The Bookmarks of Thomas Stevens and
his Contemporaries; 7 Apr-30 Apr, a
photographic exhibition of popular art;
16 May-28 Jun, Lace in Fashion.
*Open all year, Tue-Sun 2-5. (Closed Mon
ex BH, Good Fri, 25-26 Dec & 1 Jan).
Free.*
& *shop* ✻

Stapeley Water Gardens   NANTWICH

Map 07 SJ65
London Rd, Stapeley (off junc 16 M6,
1m S of Nantwich on A51)
☎ (0270) 623868 & 628628
Claiming to be the World's largest water
garden centre, Stapeley Water Gardens
has 50 acres of display lakes, gardens,
pools and fountains plus 'The Palms'
with sharks, piranhas, koi carp, giant
Amazon water lilies and exotic blooming
plants. The Stapeley Yesteryear
Collection displays fully restored
military, vintage cars, and a Churchill
tank. Special event for 1992: 14 Jun-

19 Jul, The Wildlife Photographer of
the Year.
*Open daily 9-6, wknds & BHs 10-7.
(Winter 9-5, wknds & BHs 10-6). The
Palms Tropical Oasis open from 10am,
closing times as Garden Centre.
The Palms Tropical Oasis £2.50 (ch
£1.25, pen £1.85). The Yesteryear
collection £2.50 (ch £1.25, pen £1.85).
Joint ticket £4.50 (ch £2.20, pen £3.30).*
🅿 ✗ *licensed* & *(wheelchair loan
service) toilets for disabled shop garden centre*
✻

Liverpool University Botanic Gardens (Ness Gardens)   NESTON

Map 07 SJ27
Ness Gardens (off A540 near Ness-on-
Wirral)
☎ 051-336 2135 & 051-336 7769
A place of learning and also a place of
beauty containing fine trees and shrubs,
rock terraces, water gardens, herbaceous
borders and rose collections. The visitor
centre has a slide show and exhibitions.
Plants may be purchased in the gift
shop. For children there is an exciting

adventure playground. There is also a
regular programme of lectures, courses
and special events throughout the year
for which tickets must be obtained in
advance.
*Open all year, Nov-Feb, daily 9.30-4;
Mar-Sep, daily 9.30-dusk.*
✳ *£2.80 (ch 10-18 & pen £1.80). Family
ticket £7.*
🅿 ☕ ✗ *licensed* & *toilets for disabled shop
garden centre* ✻

Nether Alderley Mill   NETHER ALDERLEY

Map 07 SJ87
Congleton Rd (1.5m S of Alderley Edge
on E side of A34)
☎ Wilmslow (0625) 523012
This fascinating water mill was originally
built in the 15th century, and is a lot
larger inside than its outward appearance
would suggest. Inside there are two
overshot water wheels, original
Elizabethan timber work, and Victorian
machinery which has been restored to
full working order after being derelict

for 30 years. The original atmosphere of
a working mill has been preserved as far
as possible, and wheat is ground
occasionally for demonstration purposes,
water permitting.
*Open Apr-Jun & Oct, Wed, Sun & BH
Mon 2-5.30; Jul-Sep, Tue-Sun & BH
Mon 2-5.30. Parties by arrangement.
£1.50. (ch 70p) Parties by prior
arrangement.*
🅿 ✻
(NT)

Arley Hall & Gardens   NORTHWICH

Map 07 SJ67
Nr Great Budworth (5m N)
☎ (0565) 777353
Built in early Victorian times, Arley
House has a private chapel built by
Salvin, and contains interesting examples
of plasterwork, wood carvings, pictures
and furniture. The gardens, winners of
the Christie's/HHA Garden of the Year
award, contain double herbaceous
borders and an unusual avenue of

clipped holly trees. There is a walled
garden, herb garden and a scented
garden – of particular interest to those
visitors who have impaired sight. The
woodland walk provides a contrast to
the well-tended gardens.
*Open 29 Mar-6 Oct, Tue-Sun & BH 2-6.
(Jun-Aug Gardens open 12 noon).*
🅿 ☕ ✗ *licensed* & *toilets for disabled shop*
Details not confirmed for 1992

Norton Priory Museum & Gardens   RUNCORN

Map 07 SJ58
Tudor Rd
☎ (0928) 569895
The site of this medieval priory was the
subject of the largest excavation of any
monastic site in Britain carried out by
modern methods. The landscaped priory
remains include a fine 12th-century
undercroft with a beautifully carved
passage, a St Christopher statue, and a
Norman doorway, all set in 16 acres of
beautiful woodland gardens. Norton has
the most comprehensive exhibition
about medieval monastic life anywhere
in Britain. There are displays of
excavated floor tiles, carved stonework,
ceramics and other artefacts. Facilities
include an auditorium and a museum
shop; and temporary exhibitions and

events are held throughout the year.
Three weeks of sculpture workshops,
run by an artist in residence, take place
in August. Toilet suitable for wheelchair
users; ramps at doors wherever feasible;
bird hide for wheelchair users.
Five minutes' walk away is the 18th-
century walled garden filled with historic
varieties of fruit and flowers. Also a
small exhibition on the history of the
garden.
*Open all year, Apr-Oct, Mon-Fri 12-5;
Sat, Sun & BHs 12-6; Nov-Mar daily
12-4. (Closed 24-26 Dec & 1 Jan). Walled
Garden closed Nov-Feb.
£2.20 (ch 5-16, students, UB40's & pen
£1.10).*
🅿 ☕ & *toilets for disabled shop* ✻ *(ex
museum)*

Little Moreton Hall   SCHOLAR GREEN

Map 07 SJ85
☎ Congleton (0260) 272018

Perhaps one of the best examples of half-
timbered architecture in England, Little
Moreton Hall stands with moat and
gatehouse in all its original and ornate
glory. Although building began about

100 years earlier, by 1580 the house
was much as it is today. Inside the long
gallery, the chapel and the great hall are
its most splendid features and notable
too are some of the pieces of oak
furniture. For details of concerts and
open-air theatre apply to administrators.
*Open Apr-Sep, Wed-Sun 12-5; BH
Mon 11-5.30; Oct, Wed, Sat & Sun
12-5.30. (Closed Good Fri).
£3 wknds & BH, £2.50 wkdays (ch half
price). Family ticket £7.50. Parties.
Parking £2, refundable on entry to Hall.*
🅿 *(charged)* ✗ *licensed* & *(wheelchair &
electric vehicle available) toilets for disabled
shop* ✻
(NT)

✻ The 'No Dogs' symbol does not normally apply
to guide dogs – these are permitted in
most establishments.

Quarry Bank Mill & Styal Country Park   STYAL

Map 07 SJ88
Quarry Bank Mill
☎ Wilmslow (0625) 527468

This 18th-century cotton mill and the
village built by the owners for the
millworkers form one of the most
fascinating Industrial Revolution sites in
Britain. The mill is set in a lovely valley
and there are pleasant walks through
woodland or by the deep ravine of the
River Bollin. It has been restored to
working order and the great iron
waterwheel is turning once again to help

produce cloth (on sale). There are three
floors of textile machinery and also
demonstrations of hand-spinning and
weaving, with galleries illustrating the
millworker's world, textile-finishing
processes and the founders (the Greggs)
as pioneers of the factory system.
In the village are well-preserved millhands cottages, chapels and shops, plus
the house where the young pauper
apprentices lived.
*Mill open all year, Apr & May, Tue-Sun
& BH Mon 11-5; Jun-Sep, daily 11-5;
Oct-Mar, Tue-Sun 11-4. Apprentice House
& Gardens, Tue-Fri, as Mill opening times
during School Hols, Wed-Fri 2pm-Mill
closing time during school term. Sat & Sun
as for Mill. (Closed Mon all year ex BH
Mon).*
🅿 *(charged)* ☕ ✗ *licensed* & *toilets for
disabled shop* ✻ *(ex in Park)*
(NT)
Details not confirmed for 1992

Every effort is made to provide accurate information,
but details might change during the currency
of this guide.

Catalyst – The Museum of the Chemical Industry   WIDNES

Map 07 SJ58
Mersey Rd
☎ 051-420 1121
A unique museum exploring the
chemical industry and its impact on our
lives, past and present, with working
exhibits, computer games and films. A
rooftop observation gallery offers superb
views, and the adjacent Spike Island

Waterside Park offers walks by the River
Mersey, St Helens Canal and an
industrial archaeology trail.
*Open all year, Tue-Sun daily 10-5. (Closed
Mon ex BH's, Good Fri, 24-26 Dec & 1
Jan).*
& *toilets for disabled shop* ✻
Details not confirmed for 1992

CLEVELAND

Gisborough Priory — GUISBOROUGH

Map 08 NZ61
☎ (0287) 638301
The remains of the east end of the 14th-century church make a dramatic sight here. The priory was founded in the 12th century for Augustinian canons.

Open all year, Apr-Sep, daily 10-6; Oct-Mar, Tue-Sun 10-4. (Closed 24-26 Dec & 1 Jan).
75p (ch 40p, students, pen & UB40 55p)
& ✠
(EH)

Gray Art Gallery & Museum — HARTLEPOOL

Map 08 NZ53
Clarence Rd
☎ (0429) 266522 ext 2609
Displays include local history, archaeology and engineering, a picture collection, Oriental items and porcelain. There is a working blacksmith's shop in the grounds. Temporary exhibitions this year include Hartlepool Renaissance

Open Art Exhibition, paintings by John Bratby, and contemporary photography by David Wise, Kodak Young Photographer of the Year 1991.
Open all year, Mon-Sat 10-5.30, Sun 2-5. (Closed Good Fri, 25 Dec & 1 Jan).
Free.
🅿 & toilets for disabled shop ✠

Maritime Museum — HARTLEPOOL

Map 08 NZ53
Northgate
☎ (0429) 272814
The collections illustrate the town's shipbuilding industry and maritime history (in 1900 it was Britain's fifth-largest shipping port). Special features

include a reconstructed fisherman's cottage, a ship's bridge and an early lighthouse lantern.
Open all year, Mon-Sat 10-5 (Closed Good Fri, Xmas & 1 Jan).
Free.
🅿 shop ✠

& This symbol indicates that much or all of the attraction is accessible to wheelchairs. However, there may be some restrictions, so it would be wise to check in advance.

Captain Cook Birthplace Museum — MIDDLESBROUGH

Map 08 NZ42
Stewart Park, Marton (3m S on A172 at Stewart Park, Marton)
☎ (0642) 311211
Opened to mark the 250th anniversary of the birth of the voyager in 1728, this museum illustrates the early life of James Cook and his discoveries with temporary exhibitions. Located in spacious and rolling parkland, the site also offers outside attractions for the visitor, including a conservatory of tropical

plants, and assorted animals and fowl housed in small and accessible paddocks. There are Captain Cook Birthday Celebrations on 25th October.
Open all year, summer Tue-Sun 10-6, winter 9-4. Last ticket 30 mins before closing. (Closed 25-26 Dec & 1 Jan).
✳ 85p (ch & pen 40p). Family ticket £1.80.
🅿 ♨ & (lift to all floors) toilets for disabled shop ✠

Dorman Museum — MIDDLESBROUGH

Map 08 NZ42
Linthorpe Rd
☎ (0642) 813781
Middlesbrough has a rich industrial heritage and is now the administrative centre of Teeside. This museum illustrates its social and industrial growth, its natural history and geological features, by permanent exhibitions and a

varied programme of temporary displays, including one of life before the Romans during a period of Celtic splendour – 'Barbarians' (8 May-22 August).
Open all year Tue-Sat 10-6. (Closed 25-26 Dec & 1 Jan).
Free.
🅿 & toilets for disabled shop ✠

Ormesby Hall — ORMESBY

Map 08 NZ51
☎ Middlesbrough (0642) 324188
An 18th-century mansion, Ormesby Hall has stables attributed to John Carr of York. Plasterwork, furniture and 18th-century pictures can be seen. Special events for 1992 include Spring Flower Weekend (11-12 Apr), sugar craft exhibition and demonstration (18-20 Apr), working model railway

exhibition (2- 31 May), and a country crafts exhibition (6-7 Jun).
Open Apr wknds & 18-20 inc; May-Sep, Wed, Thu, Sat, Sun & BH Mon; Oct, Wed, Sat & Sun 2-5.30. Last admission 5pm.
House & Gardens £1.80 (ch 90p). Garden only 70p (30p).
🅿 ♨ & toilets for disabled shop ✠
(NT)

RNLI Zetland Museum — REDCAR

Map 08 NZ62
5 King St
☎ (0642) 484402
The museum portrays the lifeboat, maritime, fishing and local history of the area, including its main exhibit 'The Zetland' – the oldest lifeboat in the world dating from 1800. There is also a

replica of a fisherman's cottage circa 1900 and almost 2000 other exhibits. The museum is housed in an early lifeboat station, now a listed building.
Open May-Sep, daily 11-4. Other times by appointment.
Free.
🅿 & shop

Tom Leonard Mining Museum — SKINNINGROVE

Map 08 NZ71
Deepdale
☎ (0287) 642877
The museum offers visitors an exciting and authentic underground experience on the site of the old Loftus mine, and a chance to see how the stone was drilled, charged with explosives and fired. Exhibits include a collection of original

tools, lamps, safety equipment, old photographs and domestic objects, providing a glimpse of mining life both above and below ground.
Open Etr-Oct, daily 1-5 (last admission 4pm). Parties by arrangement.
£1 (ch 50p)
🅿 & shop ✠

Preston Hall Museum — STOCKTON-ON-TEES

Map 08 NZ41
Yarm Rd (2m S A19)
☎ (0642) 781184
The museum illustrates Victorian social history, with reconstructions of period rooms and a street with working craftsmen including blacksmiths and farriers. The collections include costume,

toys, arms and armour.
Open all year, Mon-Sat 9.30-5.30, Sun 2-5.30. Last admission 5 (Closed Good Fri, 25-26 Dec & New Year).
Free.
🅿 (charged) ♨ & toilets for disabled shop ✠

CORNWALL & ISLES OF SCILLY

The Duke of Cornwall's Light Infantry Museum — BODMIN

Map 02 SX06
The Keep, Victoria Barracks
☎ (0208) 72810
The museum was started at the Depot in 1925 and contains Armoury and Medals displays, a Uniforms room, and the Main Gallery which displays pictures

and relics devoted to the major campaigns of the Regiment from 1702 to 1945.
Open all year Mon-Fri, 8-4.45 (ex BH).
✳ 50p
🅿 shop

Pencarrow — BODMIN

Map 02 SX06
Washaway (4m N on unclass road off A389)
☎ St Mabyn (020884) 369
This Georgian house is still a family home, and has a superb collection of pictures, furniture and china. The 50 acres of formal and woodland gardens include a Victorian rockery, Italian and American gardens, a lake, an ice house and an ancient British encampment. There are over 600 different

rhododendrons and an internationally acclaimed conifer collection. There are also a craft centre and a children's play area.
Open Etr-15 Oct, Mon-Thu & Sun, 1.30-5; BH Mon & Jun-10 Sep 11-5. (Last tour of the House 5pm).
✳ House & Garden £3 (ch £1.20). Gardens only £1 (ch 50p). Party.
🅿 ♨ & toilets for disabled shop & plant shop ✠ (ex gardens)

Cotehele — CALSTOCK

Map 03 SX46
St Dominick (2m E of St Dominick)
☎ Liskeard (0579) 50434 & 51222

The granite house dates from 1485 and was built for the Edgcumbe family. They moved south to Mount Edgcumbe in the 16th century, and have left Cotehele virtually untouched, apart from

some building work in 1627. Inside there are tapestries, embroideries, furniture and armour; and outside there is a beautiful garden on different levels. It has a medieval dovecote. There is a restored manorial water mill in the valley below, and an outstation of the National Maritime Museum. The restored sailing barge 'Shamrock' can be seen from the quay.
Open Apr-Oct, daily 11-5.30; (11-5 in Oct). Last admission 30 mins before closing. House only closed Fri. Nov-Mar garden only open daylight hours.
House, Garden & Mill £4.80. Garden, Grounds & Mill £2.40. Party.
🅿 ✗ licensed & (Braille guide) toilets for disabled shop ✠
(NT)

North Cornwall Museum & Gallery — CAMELFORD

Map 02 SX18
The Clease
☎ (0840) 212954
The museum is set in a building that was used for making coaches and wagons. There are sections on agriculture, slate and granite quarrying, and wheelwright's tools, and other displays include

cobbling, dairy work and the domestic scene from lace bonnets to early vacuum cleaners. The gallery holds various exhibitions.
Open Apr-Sep, Mon-Sat 10.30-5.
✳ £1 (ch 50p, pen & students 75p).
& shop ✠

Chysauster Ancient Village — CHYSAUSTER ANCIENT VILLAGE

Map 02 SW43
☎ (0736) 61889
Eight drystone masonry houses leading off a courtyard and incorporating a characteristic Cornish underground chamber or 'fogou'. Adjoining the dwellings are byres. Inhabited between 1st and 3rd centuries AD.

Open all year, Apr-Sep, daily 10-6; Oct-Mar, Tue-Sun 10-4. (Closed 24-26 Dec & 1 Jan).
£1.20 (ch 60p, pen, students & UB40 90p).
✠
(EH)

Dobwalls Family Adventure Park   DOBWALLS

Map 03 SX26
(0.5 N of A38)
☎ Liskeard (0579) 20325 & 21129
Dobwalls invites visitors to ride on its two-mile stretch of miniature American railroads. There are steam and diesel locos, and visitors can take the Rio Grande ride through the forests or the Union Pacific route over the prairies. Ten scaled-down locomotives include the Union Pacific Big Boy, and there are tunnels, embankments, lakes and canyons. Also at Dobwalls is

Adventureland – eight action-packed areas filled with adventure play equipment including aerial cableways and three totally enclosed slides. There are also remote-controlled model boats and American-style trucks and trailers, a shooting gallery, Aquablasters and an Edwardian 'penny' amusement arcade.
Open Etr-Oct, daily 10-6 (last admission 4.30pm). Nov-Etr telephone for details. Admission fee payable.
🅿 ♿ & *(motorised & manual wheelchairs available) toilets for disabled shop*

Thorburn Museum & Gallery   DOBWALLS

Map 03 SX26
(N of A38)
☎ Liskeard (0579) 20325 & 21129
'Mr Thorburn's Edwardian Countryside' is a unique combination of art and audio-visual display opened by HRH Prince Charles in 1986. A collection of major paintings by the wildlife artist Archibald Thorburn

(1860-1935) are set in a reconstruction of the countryside, complete with sights, sounds and smells.
Open Etr-Oct daily, 10-6 (last admission 4.30pm). Nov-Etr, telephone for details.
✱ *Admission fee payable.*
🅿 ♿ & *(audio tour, braille, induction loop. Wheelchairs available) toilets for disabled shop*

Pendennis Castle   FALMOUTH

Map 02 SW83
☎ (0326) 316594
Pendennis was built to guard the waterways of the Carrick Roads, and was one of Henry VIII's many coastal forts. It is surrounded by later 16th-century fortifications, and now houses an exhibition of coastal defences of the

Tudor period.
Open all year, Apr-Sep, daily 10-6; Oct-Mar, Tue-Sun 10-4. (Closed 24-26 Dec & 1 Jan).
£1.80 (ch 90p, pen, students & UB40 £1.40).
🅿 ♿ ✈
(EH)

St Catherine's Castle   FOWEY

Map 03 SX15
The ruined stronghold was one of the many castles built by Henry VIII to defend the coast. It was restored in 1855.

Open all year daily, any reasonable time. Free.
(EH)

Godolphin House   GODOLPHIN CROSS

Map 02 SW63
(situated between Townshend and Godolphin)
☎ Penzance (0736) 762409
The former home of the Earls of Godolphin dates from the 15th century, but is most notable for the colonnades added in 1635. Inside is Wootton's painting of the 'Godolphin Arabian', one of the three Arab stallion ancestors of all British bloodstock. The original stables house a small display of maps and interesting documents, and also old farm

wagons. During August, there will be a small reinactment by members of 'The Sealed Knot', of the significant part played by the Godolphins during the Civil War – telephone for details.
Open May & Jun, Thu 2-5; Jul-Sep, Tue & Thu 2-5; Aug, Tue 2-5, Thu 10-1 & 2-5. Open BH Mons. Parties by arrangement at anytime throughout the year including Sun.
£2 (ch £1). Party 8 + .
🅿 ♿ ✈

World in Miniature   GOONHAVERN

Map 02 SW75
Bodmin Rd
☎ Truro (0872) 572828
There are four major attractions for the price of one at this enchanting theme park. Visitors can stroll amongst the world's most famous landmarks such as the Taj Mahal and the Statue of Liberty, all in miniature scale, set in spectacular gardens. Then there is Tombstone, a wild-west town complete with saloon, bank, shops, livery stable and jail. The Adventure Dome is the original super

cinema 180 direct from the USA where you experience the thrills and spills of two great films without leaving your seat. Finally, there are the Gardens, twelve acres of beautifully landscaped garden with over 70,000 plants and shrubs.
Open Apr-Jun & Sep-Oct, daily 10-4 (5pm Jul-Aug).
✱ £3.95 (ch 4-14 £2.75, pen £3.50).
🅿 ♿ & *toilets for disabled shop garden centre*

Seal Sanctuary & Marine Animal Rescue Centre   GWEEK

Map 02 SW72
☎ Mawgan (032622) 361

A hospital and 10 pools are provided here for sick and injured seals washed in on Cornwall's beaches. There is an

exhibition centre with audio-visual displays on seals and their relations. Other attractions include a nature trail and an aquarium. Visitors will also find indentification of the Helford River Wildlife and bird species by means of viewing and interpretation areas. Conservation is a very important aspect of the work here, reflected in the imaginative pollution exhibition on display.
Open all year, daily 9.30-6. (4pm in winter).
✱ £3.80 (ch £1.85).
🅿 ♿ & *(wheelchairs available) toilets for disabled shop*

Flambards Village Theme Park   HELSTON

Map 02 SW62
Culdrose Manor (.5m S on A3083)
☎ (0326) 573404 & 574549
Three award-winning, all-weather attractions can be visited on one site here. Flambards Victorian Village is an evocative recreation of streets, shops and house interiors from the turn of the century, including a 'time capsule' chemist's shop. Britain in the Blitz is a lifesize wartime street featuring shops, a pub and a living room with Morrison shelter; and Cornwall Aero Park covers the history of aviation from 'those magnificent men in their flying machines' to Concorde. Cornwall's Exploratorium, is a 'hands on' science playground for the whole family. There is an adventure playground and many rides from the gentle to the daring, including Flambards Family Log Flume, The fabulous Cyclopter Monorail, Balloon Race, Space Mission, Superbob and Dragon Coaster. There will be new rides for 1992, plus The Amazing

Flambards Maze, Hall of Miscellany, exciting games of skill, and a huge children's playground and picnic area. Facilities for the disabled include purpose-built toilets for wheelchair users, free loan of wheelchairs and a free map guide. On Easter Monday 1992 the annual Easter Bonnet Parade and competition takes place. 1992 will also see the introduction of 'Images of the Blitz', an exhibition of some of the most remarkable photographs of our time by some of the world's best photographers. A telethon charity fund raising event will take place on 4th May.
Open 15 Apr-1 Nov, daily 10-last admission 4pm. Extended opening 27 Jul-3 Sep, last admission 5.30pm. Park closes 8pm.
£7.50 (ch 4-13 £6.50, pen £3.95).
🅿 ⬛ ⚬ *(wheelchairs available) toilets for disabled shop garden centre* ✈
See advertisement on page 47.

Helston Folk Museum   HELSTON

Map 02 SW62
Old Butter Market
☎ (03265) 564027 & 561672
The Old Butter Market has been converted into a lively folk museum dealing with the town and the Lizard Peninsula.

Various exhibitions are held in summer.
Open all year, Mon, Tue & Thu-Sat 10.30-1 & 2-4.30, Wed 10.30-noon.
⚬ *shop* ✈
Details not confirmed for 1992

Land's End   LAND'S END

Map 02 SW32
☎ Penzance (0736) 871501
The most westerly point of mainland England draws countless visitors to its dramatic cliff scenery. On a clear day the Isles of Scilly, 28 miles away, can be seen together with the Wolf Rock Lighthouse and the Seven Stones Reef, where the Torrey Canyon met its end in 1967. The 200-acre site is the setting for wild coastal walks and amazing natural rock formations; and innovative exhibitions have been set up to trace the

geology, wildlife and maritime history of the area. On the southernmost tip of the peninsula are two small smugglers' coves linked by a tunnel which local miners carved through the headland. On view are the last labyrinth, an audio-visual show and the art gallery.
Open all year, site & exhibitions 10-dusk. Times adjustable during winter. £4.95 (ch £2.50 & pen £4.50). Disabled visitors free.
🅿 *(charged)* ⬛ ✕ *licensed* ⚬ *toilets for disabled shop* ✈ *(ex grounds)*

Lanhydrock   LANHYDROCK

Map 02 SX06
☎ Bodmin (0208) 73320

Lanhydrock is approached along an avenue of beeches through a wooded park. It looks Tudor, but only the charming gatehouse, entrance porch and north wing date from the 16th century. The rest was rebuilt after a fire in 1881, and the house now gives a vivid picture

of life in Victorian times. The 'below stairs' sections are particularly interesting and include a mighty kitchen, larders, dairy, bakehouse, cellars, and servants' quarters. Notable among the grander rooms is the long gallery, which has a moulded ceiling showing Old Testament scenes. The windows overlook the formal gardens with their clipped yews and bronze urns.
Open Apr-Oct: House daily (ex Mon), but open BH Mon 11-5.30 (11-5 in Oct). Gardens daily. Last admission half hour before closing. Winter Gardens Nov-Mar during daylight hours.
£4.80 Gardens only £2.40. Party.
🅿 ✕ *licensed* ⚬ *(Braille guide) toilets for disabled shop* ✈ *(ex in Park)*
(NT)

Lanreath Farm & Folk Museum   LANREATH

Map 03 SX15
Churchtown
☎ (0503) 20321
Implements and equipment from the farmhouse, dairy and farmyard are displayed, together with mill workings rescued from a derelict mill house.

Demonstrations of local crafts are given on weekday afternoons from 2 – 4pm.
Open Etr-May & Oct, daily 11-1 & 2-5; Jun-Sep, daily 10-1 & 2-6.
✳ *£1.75 (ch £1). Party.*
🅿 ⚬ *shop*

Launceston Castle   LAUNCESTON

Map 03 SX38
☎ (0566) 772365
Dominating this old market town is the ruin of the 12th- and 13th-century castle. It was stormed and changed hands four times during the Civil Wars, despite its impregnable appearance. The town that grew up outside the walls was the

capital of Cornwall until 1838, when the assizes were moved to Bodmin.
Open all year, Apr-Sep, daily 10-6; Oct-Mar, Tue-Sun 10-4. (Closed 24-26 Dec & 1 Jan).
£1.10 (ch 55p, students, pen & UB40 85p).
⚬ *(outer bailey only)* ✈
(EH)

Launceston Steam Railway   LAUNCESTON

Map 03 SX38
Newport
☎ (0566) 775665
A four-mile round trip behind a century-old steam locomotive is an appealing prospect; there are also displays of stationary steam engines and a model railway. A motor and motorcycle museum and a specialist bookshop on

transport are other features of a visit here.
Open Good Fri-21 Apr & Oct, Tue & Sun, then Jun-Sep, daily 10.30-4.30. (Closed Sat). Also Santa Specials Dec, Sat & Sun 1-4, also 24 & 26 Dec.
✳ *£3.30 (ch £2.20, pen £2.80). Family ticket £10.50. Dogs 50p.*
🅿 ⬛ ⚬ *shop*

Lawrence House   LAUNCESTON

Map 03 SX38
9 Castle St
☎ (0566) 773277 & 773047
The local history museum of this proudly Cornish town is housed in one of several well-preserved red brick Georgian houses, and was once a rendezvous for French officer prisoners

during the Napoleonic wars. The displays and artefacts all relate to the history and social history of Launceston.
Open Apr-early Oct, Mon-Fri 10.30-4.30. Other times by appointment. Closed BH's. Free but donations requested.
(NT)

Monkey Sanctuary   LOOE

Map 03 SX25
St Martins (4m E off B3253)
☎ (05036) 2532
A protected breeding colony of rare Amazon woolly monkeys enjoys life here in the wooded grounds of Murrayton monkey sanctuary. Visitors can get close to the monkeys but are

advised to bring children under four on dry days only. Talks are given morning and afternoon.
Open 2 wks Etr then May-Sep, Sun-Thu 10.30-5.
✳ *£3.50 (ch £1.70 & pen £2.50).*
🅿 ⬛ ⚬ *toilets for disabled shop* ✈

For an explanation of the symbols and abbreviations, see page 2.

Trengwainton Garden   MADRON

Map 02 SW43
Penzance
☎ Penzance (0736) 63021
Rhododendrons and magnolias grow in profusion at Trengwainton, along with many plants that won't usually grow outdoors in Britain. The mild climate means that seed collected on expeditions

to the Far East and southern hemisphere have flourished to produce a magnificent display in this 20th-century garden.
Open Mar-Oct, Wed-Sat also BH Mon & Good Fri 10.30-5.30. (Mar & Oct 11-5). £2.20.
🅿 ⚬ *(Braille guide) toilets for disabled* ✈
(NT)

St Michael's Mount   MARAZION

Map 02 SW53
(.5m S of A394)
☎ (0736) 710507
Rising like a fairytale castle from the sea, St Michael's Mount can be reached on foot by a causeway at low tide, or by ferry in the summer. It has been a church, priory, fortress and a private home in its time, and is still the home of Lord St Levan, whose ancestor St John Aubyn acquired it in 1660. The house is a medieval castle to which a magnificent

east wing was added in the 1870s. There are splendid plaster reliefs of hunting scenes, Chippendale furniture in the elegant Blue Drawing Room, and collections of armour and pictures.
Open Apr-end Oct, Mon-Fri 10.30-5.45. Mar-May special educational visits by prior arrangement, Tue only.
£2.90. Family ticket £8.
⬛ ✕ *licensed shop (Apr-Oct)* ✈
(NT)

Glendurgan   MAWNAN SMITH

Map 02 SW72
☎ Bodmin (0208) 74281
This delightful garden, set in a valley above the River Helford, was started by Alfred Fox in 1820. The informal landscape contains beautiful trees and shrubs from all over the world, including the Japanese loquat, Mexican cypress and tree ferns from New Zealand. There

is also a walled garden, a maze and a Giant's Stride which are popular with children. House not open.
Open Mar-Oct, Tue-Sat & BH Mon 10.30-5.30 (last admission 4.30). (Closed Good Fri).
£2.50.
🅿 ⚬ *(Braille guide) toilets for disabled* ✈
(NT)

Folk Museum   MEVAGISSEY

Map 02 SX04
East Quay
☎ (0726) 843568
The museum is housed in an 18th-century boat builder's shed. It stands at the far end of the north quay in this old fishing village, famous in its day for

pilchards and smuggling. Displays include fishing gear, china clay industry implements, and a cider press.
Open Etr wk 11-6; Etr-May 2-4; Jun-Sep 11-6.
30p (ch & pen 10p).
⚬ ✈

World of Model Railways   MEVAGISSEY

Map 02 SX04
Meadow St
☎ (0726) 842457
Over 2000 British, Continental and American models are on display in this museum, which also features an impressively realistic layout for the models to run through, with urban and

rural areas, a 'working' fairground, an Alpine ski resort with cable cars, and a Cornish china clay pit, all reproduced in miniature.
Open 2 wks Etr, then Spring BH-Oct 11-5. (Closed half term in Oct). £1.95 (ch & pen £1.45).
⚬ *shop*

Dairy Land — NEWQUAY

Map 02 SW86
Tresillian Barton, Summercourt (on A3058)
☎ Mitchell (0872) 510246
Dairy Land was the first farm diversification of its kind in the UK. Here, visitors can watch while the cows are milked to music on a spectacular merry-go-round milking machine. The life of a Victorian farmer and his neighbours is explored in the Countrylife Museum, and a Farm Nature Trail demonstrates farming and nature in harmony with informative displays along pleasant peaceful walks. Children will have fun getting to know the farm animals in the safety of the Farm Park and Playground.
Open Etr & May-Sep, daily 10.30-5.30; Apr & Oct, daily 12-5.
✱ *£3.95 (ch 3-15 £2.80, pen & disabled £3.65). Party.*
🅿 ✗ *licensed ⅋ (wheelchairs for loan; disabled viewing gallery – milking) toilets for disabled shop* ✗

Newquay Zoo — NEWQUAY

Map 02 SW86
Trenance Park
☎ (0637) 873342
Education and conservation are the key issues at this exciting Zoological Theme Park. Apart from the usual attractions such as the Monkey enclosures, penguin pool, tropical house and lion house all of which have been designed for maximum 'creature comfort' the park also boasts a Maze, an Oriental Garden an activity Play Park and a Tarzan Trail Assault Course. The latest attraction is a Tortoise enclosure to house the tortoises that the Zoo is given each year.
Open Apr-Nov, daily 10-5.
✱ *£3.60 (ch £2.20).*
🅿 *(charged)* ✿ ⅋ *shop* ✗

For an explanation of the symbols and abbreviations, see page 2.

Padstow Tropical Bird Gardens — PADSTOW

Map 02 SW97
Fentonluna Ln
☎ (0841) 532262
These well established gardens continue to breed many birds from all corners of the world. Many of the sub-tropical plants growing here are labelled – a thoughtful gesture to gardeners – and a heated walk-in tropical house enables visitors to see free-flying exotic birds at close quarters in a near-natural habitat. Similarly, the planted butterfly house gives the opportunity to view all stages in the life-cycle of butterflies. 'Butterfly World' is a comprehensive exhibition of the world's butterflies, many displayed in their natural habitat.
Open all year 10.30-7 (4pm in winter) last admission 1hr before closing. (Closed 25 Dec.)
✿ ⅋ *shop*
Details not confirmed for 1992.

Geevor Tin Mines — PENDEEN

Map 02 SW33
☎ Penzance (0736) 788662
A working tin mine and museum provide an insight into the methods and equipment used in the mining of tin. Guided tours enable visitors to see the tin treatment plant and a video film illustrates the techniques employed. An underground tour in what is pobably Europe's deepest visitor mine completes an enjoyable day out.
Open Etr-Oct 10-5.30. Last surface tour 4pm. Last admission 5pm. Other times by appointment.
🅿 ✿ ⅋ *toilets for disabled shop*
Details not confirmed for 1992

The Maritime Museum — PENZANCE

Map 02 SW43
19 Chapel St (opposite the Admiral Benbow)
☎ (0736) 68890
Treasures recovered from wrecks by the diving teams of Roland Morris are on display here, including gold and silver from the first treasure found in British waters. A man-o'-war display shows an full-scale section of a 1730 warship, including the gun-decks.
Open Apr-Oct, daily 10-5
shop ✗
Details not confirmed for 1992

Penzance and District Museum & Art Gallery — PENZANCE

Map 02 SW43
Penlee Park
☎ (0736) 63625
The history and development of the district from the times of earliest man to the present day is covered in this museum. There is also an exhibition of the Newlyn school of painting and an open-air theatre.
Open all year, museum & gallery, Mon-Fri 10.30-4.30, Sat 10.30-12.30.
⅋ *shop* ✗
Details not confirmed for 1992

Land of Legend & Model Village — POLPERRO

Map 03 SX25
The Old Forge
☎ (0503) 72378
A glimpse of old Cornwall may be caught here through animated models in a replica of old Polperro, set amid a garden of exotic plants. There are commentary listening posts to guide visitors around and a photographic exhibition of Polperro's history.
Open Etr-Oct, Sun-Fri 10-9.
✿ *shop*
Details not confirmed for 1992

Cornish Engines — POOL

Map 02 SW64
East Pool
☎ Redruth (0209) 216657
Impressive relics of the tin mining industry, these great beam engines were used for pumping water from 2000ft below. They also lifted men and ore from the workings below ground.
Open Apr-Oct, daily 11-5.30 (Oct 11-5). Last admission 30 mins before closing.
£1.60.
🅿 *shop* ✗
(NT)

County Demonstration Garden — PROBUS

Map 02 SW84
☎ Truro (0872) 74282 ext 3400
Permanent displays show many aspects of garden layout, plant selection and the effects of climate. Propagation of plants and trees is shown and there are exhibitions of fruit, herbs, vegetables and cultural trials. The emphasis here is on choosing the right foliage and flowers to suit individual requirements and environment. There is a historical plant collection, geological displays and an outdoor exhibition of sculpture. Special events are advertised in the local press.
Open all year, May-Sep, daily 10-5; Oct-Apr, Mon-Fri 10-4.30. Adviser on duty Thu 2-5.
£2 (ch free).
🅿 ✿ ⅋ *shop* ✗

Trewithen — PROBUS

Map 02 SW84
Grampound Rd (on A390)
☎ St Austell (0726) 882763 & 882418
The Hawkins family has lived in this charming, intimate country house since it was built in 1720. The internationally renowned landscaped garden covers some 20 acres and grows camellias, magnolias and rhododendrons as well as many rare trees and shrubs seldom seen elsewhere. The nurseries are open all year. Open days for 1992 are: 30 May, NSPCC; 13 Jun, Cancer Research Units for Cornwall; 24 Sep, Cornwall County CCA.
Open, House Apr-Jul & Aug BH, Mon & Tue 2-4.30. Gardens open Mar-Sep, Mon-Sat 10-4.30.
House £2.80; Gardens Mar-Jun £2 (ch £1), Jul-Sep £1.75 (ch £1).
🅿 ⅋ *toilets for disabled garden centre*

Restormel Castle — RESTORMEL

Map 02 SX16
☎ (020887) 2687
With a commanding view over the Fowey Valley, Restormel is the best-preserved castle of its period in this area. Much of what survives dates from the 13th century, including a notable round keep; the castle was abandoned in the 16th century.
Open all year, Apr-Sep, daily 10-6; Oct-Mar, Tue-Sun 10-4. (Closed 24-26 Dec & 1 Jan).
£1.10 (ch 55p, student, pen & UB40 85p).
🅿 ⅋ ✗
(EH)

St Agnes Leisure Park — ST AGNES

Map 02 SW75
(S on B3277)
☎ (087255) 2793
The leisure park is set in several acres of mature landscaped gardens. Attractions include Cornwall in miniature, the Lost World of the Dinosaurs, a Super X Simulator, an animated circus, the haunted house and fairyland. The park is illuminated after dark.
Open 29 Mar-5 Jul & 11 Sep-1 Nov, daily 10-6; 6 Jul-10 Sep, daily 10am-10pm.
Admission fee payable.
🅿 ✿ ⅋ *shop*

Charlestown Shipwreck & Heritage Museum — ST AUSTELL

Map 02 SX05
Quay Rd, Charlestown (1.25m SE A3061)
☎ (0726) 69897
Charlestown is a small and unspoilt village with a unique sea-lock china-clay port. It was purpose built in the 18th century by Charles Rashleigh. The Shipwreck and Heritage Centre has a large collection of shipwreck items, and a series of tableaux and photgraphs depicting village life. An important 'History of Diving' display is a recent addition to the Centre. The Charlestown Regatta offers a week of varied activities over Jul/Aug.
Open Etr-Oct, daily 10-5 (later in high season). Last admission 1 hour before closing.
✱ *£2 (ch £1.25, pen £1.50). Family £5. Party.*
🅿 *(charged)* ✿ ⅋ *toilets for disabled shop* ✗

Wheal Martyn Museum — ST AUSTELL

Map 02 SX05
(2m N on A391)
☎ (0726) 850362
The Wheal Martyn Museum tells the story of Cornwall's most important present-day industry: china clay production. The open-air site includes a complete 19th-century clayworks, restored for this purpose. There are huge granite-walled settling tanks, working water-wheels and a wooden slurry pump. Other exhibits include a 220ft pan kiln, horse-drawn wagons and two steam locomotives used in the industry, and a restored 1914 Peerless lorry.
The story of china clay in Cornwall over two centuries is shown using indoor displays. There is also a short slide and sound programme, and a working pottery.
Outside again there are nature trails, a children's adventure trail and the spectacular viewing area of a modern china-clay pit.
Open Apr-Oct, 10-6 (last admission 5pm).
🅿 ✿ ⅋ *toilets for disabled shop*
Details not confirmed for 1992

⅋ This symbol indicates that much or all of the attraction is accessible to wheelchairs. However, there may be some restrictions, so it would be wise to check in advance.

ST IVES

Map 02 SW54
(Park your car at Lelant Station and take advantage of the park and ride service. The fee includes parking and journeys on the train between Lelant and St Ives during the day).

Barbara Hepworth Museum & Sculpture Garden — ST IVES

Map 02 SW54
Barnoon Hill
☎ Penzance (0736) 796226
Turner visited St Ives in 1811. Then, after the railway was established in 1880, the town became a popular haunt for artists; what was once a busy fishing port took on a distinctly Bohemian atmosphere as the net-lofts and fish-cellars were converted into studios. The house and garden that Dame Barbara Hepworth called home from 1949 until her death in 1975 is now a museum

administered by the Tate Gallery and devoted to her life and work. The visitor can see letters, documents and many personal photographs as well as a good selection of her sculptures displayed in both the garden and the house.
Open all year, Apr-Jun & Sep, Mon-Sat 10-5.30; Jul-Aug Mon-Sat 10-6.30, Sun 2-6; Oct-Mar, Mon-Sat 10-4.30. (Closed Good Fri, 25 & 26 Dec).
50p (ch, students, pen 25p).
shop

St Mawes Castle — ST MAWES

Map 02 SW83
☎ (0326) 270526
The castle at St Mawes was built by Henry VIII in the 1540s, roughly the same time as Pendennis Castle in Falmouth. Together they were to guard the mouth of the Fal estuary; their present state of excellent preservation is largely due to their comparatively trouble-free history. Smaller but built in the same 'clover leaf' design as Pendennis, St Mawes particularly is

renowned as a fine example of military architecture. The dungeons, barrack rooms and canon lined walls provide great interest for both adults and children.
Open all year, Apr-Sep, daily 10-6; Oct-Mar, Tue-Sun 10-4. (Closed 24-26 Dec & 1 Jan).
£1.20 (ch 60p, students, pen & UB40 90p).
🅿 🚻
(EH)

Carn Euny Ancient Village — SANCREED

Map 02 SW42
(1m SW)
Four courtyard houses and a number of round houses dating from the 1st century BC can be seen at Carn Euny. There is also a 66ft long 'fogou': a subterranean passage leading to a circular

chamber and used as a hiding place by the ancient inhabitants of this site.
Open any reasonable time.
Free.
🅿
(EH)

Old Post Office — TINTAGEL

Map 02 SX08
☎ (0804) 770024
A small, 14th-century manor house, with an ancient roof of thick uneven slates, it served as a receiving office for letters from 1844 to 1892, hence its

name.
Open Apr-Oct, daily 11-5.30, (Oct 11-5). Last admission 30 mins before closing.
£1.80.
🚹 *(Braille guide) shop*
(NT)

Tintagel Castle — TINTAGEL

Map 02 SX08
☎ Camelford (0840) 770328

The romantic castle ruins have been divided by the erosion of the sea and make a dramatic sight. The castle was built by Reginald, Earl of Cornwall, in about 1145, and most of the remaining

ruins date from the 13th century. They became famous in the 19th century as the site of King Arthur's birthplace and castle; and in fact there is some evidence of a stronghold here in the 5th-8th centuries which covers Arthur's time. There are also the remains of a Celtic monastery, founded on the peninsula about AD500 and abandoned by 1086. A small site exhibition covers the history of the site.
Open all year, Apr-Sep, daily 10-6; Oct-Mar, Tue-Sun 10-4. (Closed 24-26 Dec & 1 Jan).
£1.80 (ch 90p, pen, students & UB40 £1.40).
shop 🚻
(EH)

Antony House — TORPOINT

Map 03 SX45
(2m NW, off A374)
☎ Plymouth (0752) 812191
A fine, largely unaltered mansion, built in brick and Pentewan stone for Sir William Carew between 1711 and 1721. The stable block and outhouses remain from an earlier 17th-century building. Most of the rooms in the house are panelled and contain contemporary furniture and family portraits.
The grounds, which overlook the

River Lynher, were redesigned by Humphry Repton. They include an 18th-century dovecote and, near the river estuary, the Bath Pond House, with plunge bath and a panelled changing room (may be seen only after previous written application to the adminstrator).
Open Apr-Oct, Tue-Thu & BH Mons (also Sun Jun-Aug), 1.30-5.30.
£3.20. Party.
🅿 🚹 *(Braille guide) shop* 🚻
(NT)

Cornish Shire Horse Centre — TREDINNICK

Map 02 SW97
Trelow Farm (off A39)
☎ Rumford (0841) 540276
This 120-acre farm specialises in Shire Horses, and visitors can see mares with foals. There are two horse shows a day which take place under cover and are fully seated, and cart rides are also

available. The work of the blacksmith is also on display and there is a museum of carriages, a video room and the largest display of show harnesses in the country.
Open Good Fri-Oct daily 10-5.
£3.95 (ch £2.50 & pen £3.50)
🅿 🎫 🚻 *licensed* 🚹 *shop*

Trelissick Garden — TRELISSICK GARDEN

Map 02 SW83
☎ Truro (0872) 862090 & 865808
A beautiful woodland park of some 370 acres overlooking the Falmouth estuary. The park was mainly laid out between 1844 and 1913 but the gardens were designed later, between 1937 and 1955. The grounds have been immaculately kept and offer spectacular views from walks through beech trees and oaks.
The location of the garden, near the sea and sheltered by woodland, has allowed many unusual and exotic plants to be grown. There are sub-tropical plants and some from such distant places as Chile and Tasmania. The gardens are particularly noted for their camellias,

magnolias and hydrangeas, of which there are over 100 kinds. There is also a large walled garden with fig trees and climbers, and a shrub garden. Plants are available in the garden shop. There is also an Art and Craft Gallery by the House Farm Courtyard.
Open Mar-Oct, Mon-Sat 10.30-5.30, Sun 1-5.30 (closes at 5 in Mar & Oct).
Woodland walks open Nov-Feb. Last admission 30 mins before closing.
£2.80.
🅿 *(charged)* 🚹 *licensed* 🚹 *(Braille guide) toilets for disabled shop* 🚻 *(ex in woodland walk & park)*
(NT)

Trerice — TRERICE

Map 02 SW85
☎ Newquay (0637) 875404
Built in 1571 for Sir John Arundell, the picturesque Elizabethan house has unusual curved and scrolled gables, which may have been influenced by Sir John's stay in the Netherlands. The hall has an imposing window of 576 panes of glass, and throughout the house are fine plasterwork ceilings. A museum of

lawnmowers is housed in the barn. The garden includes an orchard of Cornish fruit trees.
Open Apr-Oct, Wed-Mon 11-5.30, (Oct 11-5). Last admission 30 mins before closing.
House £3.40. Party.
🅿 🚹 *licensed* 🚹 *(Braille guide) toilets for disabled shop* 🚻
(NT)

Royal Cornwall Museum — TRURO

Map 02 SW84
River St
☎ (0872) 72205
The museum has interesting and well-laid out displays on the history of the county, and it also has a world-famous collection of minerals. There are paintings and drawings, including a number of Old Masters, and some excellent exhibits of pottery, pewter, Japanese ivories, lacquerwork and toys. A new extension was opened recently, housing two temporary exhibition

galleries and a cafe. Two new galleries are due to be opened in 1992 – a decorative arts gallery in April and a minstrals' gallery in September. There is a varied programme of exhibitions throughout the year, including a Civil War commemorative exhibition during Nov/Dec.
Open all year, Mon-Sat 9-5. Library closes 1-2. (Closed BHs).
75p (unaccompanied ch & pen 35p).
🚻 🚹 🚹 *(lift) toilets for disabled shop* 🚻

Poldark Mine and Heritage Complex — WENDRON

Map 02 SW63
(on B3297)
☎ Helston (0326) 573173
This Cornish tin mine has three levels open to the public; an 18th-century village, museums and a cinema showing a film on the history of Cornish mining. On the surface there are restaurants, shops, gardens and children's amusements. The area around the mine

has been laid to lawn and shows the West Country's largest collection of working antiquities, including a 40ft beam engine.
Open Etr-Jun & Sep-Oct, daily 10.30-5.30 (last admission 4); Jul-Aug daily 10-6. (last admission 4.30).
Admission fee payable.
🅿 🎫 🚹 *licensed* 🚹 *shop garden centre* 🚻 *(ex grounds)*

Wayside Museum — ZENNOR

Map 02 SW43
☎ Penzance (0736) 796945
This unique private museum was founded in 1935. It covers every aspect of life in the village of Zennor and the surrounding area. There is information, geological and archeological findings and

other artefacts covering 5000 years of history from 3000BC to the 1930s. Beside the museum is a fully-restored water mill.
Open 18 Mar-Oct, daily 10-6.
✳ *£1.50 (ch & pen £1)*
🅿 🎫 🚹 *shop* 🚻

Every effort is made to provide accurate information, but details might change during the currency of this guide.

CUMBRIA

South Tynedale Railway — ALSTON

Map 11 NY74
The Railway Station, Hexham Rd
☎ (0434) 381696
Running along the beautiful South Tyne valley, this narrow-gauge railway follows the route of the former Alston to Haltwhistle branch. At present the line runs between Alston and Gilderdale. Special events for 1992 include: 27 May, Children's Day; 25-26 Jul, Steam

Enthusiasts' Weekend; 11 Oct, Open Day.
Open 17-26 Apr daily; May, wknds, BHs & daily 23-31; Jun-Sep, Tue-Thu & wknds (daily Jul-Aug & 1-6 Sep); Oct Sun only. Trains leave at 11.15, 12, 2, 3 & 4pm. Santa specials in Dec.
£1.60 (ch 80p) return fare. Party 10+.
🅿 🎫 🚹 *toilets for disabled shop*

Appleby Castle Conservation Centre — APPLEBY-IN-WESTMORLAND

Map 11 NY62
☎ (07683) 51402
The grounds of this beautifully preserved Castle provide a natural setting for a Rare Breeds Survival Trust Approved Centre, featuring rare breeds of British Farm animals and also a large collection of waterfowl and unusual birds. The fine Norman Keep and Great Hall of the house are open to the public. Clifford family paintings and some items of the Nanking cargo are on display in the Hall. The information centre has an exhibition of watercolours by local artists, open daily.
Open 16 Apr-Sep, daily 10-5.
✳ *Admission prices not confirmed.*
🅿 ☕ ♿ *toilets for disabled shop*

Furness Abbey — BARROW-IN-FURNESS

Map 07 SD26
(1.5m NE on unclass road)
☎ (0229) 823420
Built in 1147, Furness Abbey is impressive even as a ruin. The extensive remains of the church and other buildings are a reminder that this was a very wealthy Cistercian establishment, and the setting is the beautiful 'Glen of Deadly Nightshade' near Barrow.
Open all year, Apr-Sep, daily 10-6; Oct-Mar, Tue-Sun 10-4. (Closed 24-26 Dec & 1 Jan).
£1.80 (ch 90p, students, pen & UB40 £1.40). Admission price includes a free Personal Stereo Guided Tour.
🅿 ♿ ✖
(EH)

Lanercost Priory — BRAMPTON

Map 11 NY56
(2.5m NE)
☎ (06977) 3030
The priory was founded in around 1166 by William de Vaux, for Augustinian canons. The nave of the church has survived and is still used, and makes a strange contrast with the ruined priory buildings around.
Open Apr-Sep, daily 10-6.
75p (ch 40p, pen, students & UB40 55p).
🅿 ♿ ✖
(EH)

Brough Castle — BROUGH

Map 11 NY71
(on A66)
☎ (0228) 31777
Standing on the site of the Roman Verterae, the castle was built in the 12th and 13th centuries to replace a stronghold destroyed by the Scots. The later castle also fell into ruin, but was restored in the 17th century by Lady Ann Clifford. The keep and curtain walls can be seen.
Open all year, Apr-Sep, daily 10-6; Oct-Mar, Tue-Sun 10-4. (Closed 24-26 Dec & 1 Jan).
75p (ch 40p, pen, students & UB40 55p).
✖
(EH)

Brougham Castle — BROUGHAM

Map 11 NY52
(off A66)
☎ (0768) 62488
12th- to 14th-century castle, repaired in late 17th-century.
Open all year, Apr-Sep, daily 10-6; Oct-Mar, Tue-Sun 10-4. (Closed 24-26 Dec & 1 Jan).
£1.10 (ch 55p, pen, student & UB40 85p) (EH)

CARK
See Holker

The Border Regiment & King's Own Royal Border Regiment Museum — CARLISLE

Map 11 NY45
Queen Mary's Tower, The Castle
☎ (0228) 32774
Three hundred years of the regiment's history are illustrated with trophies, weaponry, models, silver and pictures. The story of Cumbria's part-time soldiers is also told.
Open all year, daily 15 Mar-1 Oct, 9.30-6.30; 2 Oct-14 Mar, 9.30-4.
✳ *£1.60 (ch 80p, pen & students £1.20). Price includes entry to Carlisle Castle.*
♿ *(parking for disabled at Castle) shop* ✖

The Guildhall Museum — CARLISLE

Map 11 NY45
Green Market
☎ (0228) 819925
The Guildhall was once the meeting place of Carlisle's eight trade guilds, and it still has an atmosphere of medieval times. It is an early 15th-century building with exposed timber work and wattle and daub walls. The displays include items relating to the guilds, and other reminders of life in medieval Carlisle.
Open from 31 Mar, Tue-Sun 11-4. Winter by arrangment.
shop ✖

Tullie House Museum & Art Gallery — CARLISLE

Map 11 NY45
Castle St
☎ (0228) 34781
Travel back into the mists of time and let the real stories of historic Carlisle and Border history unfold before you. Curiosity entices you to begin a journey of discovery as you stroll through LUGUVALIUM (Roman Carlisle), climb part of Hadrian's turf Wall and experience a land inhabited by eagles and peregrines. Peep into Isaac Tullie's study as it might have been when he sat down to record in his diary how the Roundheads laid siege to his Royalist city in 1644, or sit in the 1st-class compartment of a railway carriage and recall the days of steam locomotion. There is a programme of exhibitions planned for 1992.
Open all year, Mon-Fri & Sat 10-5, Thu 10am-10pm, Sun noon-5.
✳ *Ground floor (including Art Gallery) – Free. Upper floors – £2.80 (concessions £1.40).*
☕ ✕ *licensed* ♿ *(chair lift) toilets for disabled shop* ✖

Wordsworth House — COCKERMOUTH

Map 11 NY13
Main St
☎ (0900) 824805
William Wordsworth was born here on 7th April 1770, and happy memories of the house had a great effect on his work. He played on the garden terrace with his sister Dorothy, and the inside staircase, panelling and other features are original.

Portraits and other items connected with the poet are displayed.
Open Apr-1 Nov daily (ex Thu) 11-5, Sun 2-5. (Last admission 4.30). (Winter closed Thu, Sun & wk after Xmas).
£2.30 (ch £1.20)
💺 *shop* ✖
(NT)

Brantwood — CONISTON

Map 07 SD39
(2.5m SE off B5285, unclass rd)
☎ (05394) 41396
Former home of John Ruskin. One of the most beautifully situated houses in the Lake District with fine views across Coniston Water. Large collection of Ruskin paintings and other memorabilia. Delightful nature walks through Brantwood Estate. There are special

events planned every Thursday night from the end of May to the end of October including a dinner and theatre evening 'Meet John Ruskin' with supper, theatre and music.
Open mid Mar-mid Nov, daily 11-5.30. Rest of year, Wed-Sun 11-4.
£2.75 (ch £1.40). Family ticket £7. Party.
🅿 💺 ✗ *licensed* 🚻 *toilets for disabled shop*
✖

Ruskin Museum — CONISTON

Map 07 SD39
The Institute
☎ (05394) 41387
The Victorian writer John Ruskin lived nearby, and the museum displays photocopies of letters and sketchbooks and other relics, with portraits of the writer and his circle. There are also

minerals and examples of Ruskin Lace, based on a design which he brought back from Italy and which became popular with local lace makers.
Open Etr-Oct, daily 10-5.30.
50p
✖

Steam Yacht Gondola — CONISTON

Map 07 SD39
Pier Cottage
☎ (05394) 41288
Launched in 1859, the graceful 'Gondola' worked on Coniston Water until 1937, came back into service in 1980. Now visitors can once again enjoy her silent progress and old-fashioned comfort.

Open Apr-1 Nov to scheduled daily timetable. Trips commence 11 at Coniston; on Sat 12.05. Piers at Coniston, Park-a-Moor at SE end of lake & Brantwood. Ticket prices on application & published locally.
🅿 ✖
(NT)

Dalemain — DACRE

Map 11 NY42
☎ Pooley Bridge (07684) 86450
The stately home of Dalemain was originally a medieval pele tower, which was added to in Tudor times and later, with the imposing Georgian façade completed in 1745. It has splendid oak panelling, Chinese wallpaper, Tudor plasterwork and fine Queen Anne and Georgian furniture. The rooms include a Victorian nursery and a housekeeper's room. The tower contains the Westmorland and Cumberland Yeomanry Museum, and there is a

countryside museum in the 16th-century cobbled courtyard. The grounds include a deerpark and gardens, and there is an adventure playground. The 7th annual Rainbow Craft Fair will be held on 25-26 July.
Open 19 Apr-4 Oct, Sun-Thu 11.15-5. Last entry 5pm.
£3.50 (ch 5 free, ch 16 £2.50). Family Ticket £9. Gardens only £2.50 (ch free). Wheelchair users free.
🅿 💺 ✗ *licensed* 🚻 *toilets for disabled shop garden centre* ✖

✱ An asterisk indicates that up-to-date information was not available at the time of our research – 1991 information has been published as an indication of what you may expect.

Dove Cottage & The Wordsworth Museum — GRASMERE

Map 11 NY30
(S, off A591)
☎ (05394) 35544 & 35547
Wordsworth called Grasmere 'the loveliest spot that man hath ever found.' He lived at Dove Cottage from 1799 to 1808, and during that time wrote much of his best-known poetry. The house is kept in its original condition, as described in the journals of his sister Dorothy, and the award-winning

museum displays manuscripts, paintings and various items associated with the poet. Near the cottage is the former schoolroom where he taught; and Wordsworth, his wife and sister, and other members of the family, are buried in the churchyard.
Open daily 9.30-5.30, last admission 5pm. (Closed 24-26 Dec & 14 Jan-11 Feb).
🅿 ✗ *licensed* 🚻 *toilets for disabled shop* ✖
Details not confirmed for 1992

Theatre in the Forest — GRIZEDALE

Map 07 SD39
☎ Satterthwaite (0229) 860291
Dance and drama, classical and jazz music, variety and folk concerts have all been featured at this unique theatre. It was founded in 1970, with an emphasis on quality, and is open during the day

for exhibitions. Also of interest is a long-distance Sculpture Trail with around sixty sculptures, and The Gallery in the Forest which houses art, sculpture and craft exhibitions.
Open all year, Tue-Sat 11-4.
🅿 *(charged)* 💺 🚻 *toilets for disabled* ✖

Visitor Centre — GRIZEDALE

Map 07 SD39
Forestry Commission
☎ Satterthwaite (0229) 860373
Grizedale Forest was the first Forestry Commission estate where special efforts were made to provide information and other facilities for visitors. The centre illustrates the story of Grizedale from wildwood to its present role as an area managed for timber, wildlife and recreation. There is a conservation tree nursery, and a number of waymarked walks can be followed, ranging from the

one-mile Millwood Habitat Trail to the nine-mile Silurian Way. Routes for cyclists are also provided, and there are woodland sculptures, observation hides, orienteering, children's play area and many picnic sites. The area gives wonderful views, with the possibility of seeing some of the woodland red and roe deer.
Open 29 Mar-4 Nov, daily 10-5. Craft/Sculpture Gallery 50p
🅿 *(charged)* 🚻 *(woodland trails suitable for wheelchairs) toilets for disabled shop*

For an explanation of the symbols and abbreviations, see page 2.

Hardknott Castle Roman Fort — HARDKNOTT CASTLE ROMAN FORT

Map 11 NY20
The fort is at the western end of the hair-pinned (and hair-raising) Hardknott Pass, which has gradients of 1 in 3. On this astonishing site above Eskdale, the Romans built a walled and ramparted

fort covering nearly three acres, with a bath house and parade ground outside. The remains of the building can be seen.
Open any reasonable time.
Free.
(EH)

The Beatrix Potter Gallery — HAWKSHEAD

Map 07 SD39
Main St
☎ (09666) 355
An award-winning exhibition of selected original Beatrix Potter drawings and illustrations from her children's storybooks. Housed in the former office of her husband, solicitor William Heelis.

Also a display of her life as an author, artist, farmer and determined preserver of her beloved Lake District.
Open Apr-30 Oct, Mon-Fri & BH Sun 10.30-4.30 (last admission 4).
£2.30 (ch £1.20)
shop ✖ 🚌
(NT)

Holker Hall & Gardens — HOLKER

Map 07 SD37
Grange-over-Sands
☎ Flookburgh (05395) 58328
The hall dates from the 16th century, although it was rebuilt in grand Victorian style after a fire, and has been owned by the Cavendish family for over 200 years. It has notable woodcarving and stonework, and fine paintings and furniture. The 25 acres of formal and woodland gardens include water features such as the limestone cascade. Given world-class status for the last two years by the Good Gardens Guide, they are a source of beauty and tranquillity. Other

attractions include patchwork and printing displays, a Victorian/Edwardian kitchens exhibition, a craft and countryside exhibition, an adventure playground, a toddlers area, and the magnificent Lakeland motor museum. Holker is also home to the Great Garden and Countryside Festival in June each year. There are also horse trials in July, and a hot air balloon rally in September.
Open Apr-Oct, Sun-Fri 10.30-6. Last admission 4.30 (Motor Museum 5pm). Admission charged.
🅿 💺 🚻 *toilets for disabled shop*

Abbot Hall Art Gallery — KENDAL

Map 07 SD59
Kirkland
☎ (0539) 722464
The ground floor rooms of this splendid house, reputedly designed in 1759 by John Carr of York, have been restored to their period decor, including the original carvings and fine panelling. The rooms make a perfect setting for the Gillow furniture and objets d'art displayed here, while the walls are hung with paintings by Romney, Gardner,

Turner and Ruskin. A further collection of period and contemporary, fine and decorative arts are contained in the modern galleries. Changing temporary exhibitions include sculpture and crafts as well as paintings. The adjoining shop sells crafts by local artist craftsmen.
Open all year, Mon-Fri 10.30-5, Sat & Sun 2-5, (Sat 10.30-5, Spring BH-Oct). (Closed 25-26 Dec & 1 Jan).
🅿 *shop* ✖
Details not confirmed for 1992

Abbot Hall Museum of Lakeland Life & Industry — KENDAL

Map 07 SD59
Kirkland
☎ (0539) 722464
The life and history of the Lake District has a uniqueness which is captured by the displays in this museum, housed in Abbot Hall's stable block. The working and social life of the area, its people and places are well illustrated by a variety of exhibits including period rooms, a

Victorian Cumbrian street scene and a farming display. One of the rooms is devoted to the memory of Arthur Ransome.
Open all year, Mon-Fri 10.30-5, Sat & Sun 2-5. (Sat 10.30-5 Spring BH-Oct. (Closed 25-26 Dec & 1 Jan).
🅿 *shop* ✠
Details not confirmed for 1992

Kendal Museum — KENDAL

Map 07 SD59
Station Rd
☎ (0539) 721374
The archaeology and natural history of the area is dealt with by this small museum which features a New World Wildlife Gallery and many changing exhibitions. Permanent exhibitions include the Alfred Wainwright 'Cabinet of Curiosities', a display of his original

drawings and memorabilia.
Open all year, Mon-Fri 10.30-5, Sat 2-5 (Spring BH-Oct 10.30-5) & Sun 2-5. (Closed 25-26 Dec & 1 Jan).
✻ *£1.50 (ch 5-16, students & pen 75p). Family tickets £4. Treble ticket including Abbot Hall Museum & Abbot Hall Gallery £3 (ch, students & pen £1.50). Family ticket £7.50.*
🅿 &. *(chair lift) toilets for disabled shop* ✠

For an explanation of the symbols and abbreviations, see page 2.

Cars of the Stars Motor Museum — KESWICK

Map 11 NY22
Standish St
☎ (07687) 73757
This unusual museum features celebrity TV and film vehicles, displayed in authentic 'sets'. Some notable exhibits to look out for are *Chitty Chitty Bang Bang*, James Bond's Lotus cars, Laurel and Hardy's Model T, the *MASH* Jeep and

Noddy's car. 1992 will see the introduction to the collection of the original Batmobile. A Road Safety Week will be held in June and in August there will be a James Bond Weekend – details on application.
Open 2 Mar-2 Jan, daily 10-5.
£1.80 (ch & pen £1.20). Family ticket £5.
🅿 ☕ &. *toilets for disabled shop*

Keswick Museum & Art Gallery — KESWICK

Map 11 NY22
Fitz Park, Station Rd
☎ (07687) 73263
A mecca for writers, poets and artists, Keswick's attractions are well illustrated in this museum and gallery. Names such as Coleridge, Shelley, Wordsworth, Southey, Lamb and Walpole can be found among the exhibits which include letters, manuscripts and other relics from the time these literary luminaries spent in the Lake District. One of Ruskin's paintings is among the collections in the art gallery and there is a fine scale model of the Lakes dating from 1834. The

comprehensive geology collection is of regional importance and contains magnificent mineral examples from the Caldbeck Fells. The natural history displays cover animal and bird life of the region, including a golden eagle, and butterfly and moth cabinets. Fitz Park contains formal gardens and a childrens adventure playground.
Open Etr-Oct, Sun-Fri (incl BH) 10-12 & 1-4.
80p (ch, pen, students, UB40's & disabled 40p). Party 10+.
&. *shop* ✠

Lingholm Gardens — KESWICK

Map 11 NY22
(S of A66, signposted from Portincale village)
☎ (07687) 72003
Both formal and woodland gardens are seen at Lingholm, which is at its most spectacular when the rhododendrons and azaleas are in bloom. The gardens

include meconopsis primulas, magnificent trees and shrubs. In Spring, they are alive with daffodils, and the colours of Autumn are breathtaking.
Open Apr-Oct, daily 10-5.
£2.20 (ch accompanied free)
🅿 ☕ &. *(wheelchair route) toilets for disabled* ✠

Mirehouse — KESWICK

Map 11 NY22
(3m N on A591)
☎ (07687) 72287
Undoubtedly a great place for children – there are four adventure playgrounds – but Mirehouse has its fair share of cultural interest, and a walk along the beautiful lake shore will take you past the place where Tennyson wrote much of 'Morte d'Arthur'. Inside the 17th-century house there is much original furniture adorning the graceful rooms.

Portraits and manuscripts of Francis Bacon, Carlyle and, of course, Tennyson are on display. Outside, the flowers in the walled garden attract the bees and butterflies, and make this sheltered spot perfect for picnics.
Open Apr-Oct. House: Wed, Sun & BH Mon 2-5. Grounds: daily 10.30-5.30. Parties by arrangement.
✻ *House & grounds £2.20 (ch £1.10). Grounds only 70p (ch 50p)*
🅿 ☕ &. ✠ *(ex in grounds on lead)*

Levens Hall — LEVENS

Map 07 SD48
(5m S of Kendal, on A6)
☎ Sedgwick (05395) 60321
The most remarkable feature is the topiary garden, laid out in 1692 and little changed. The Elizabethan mansion was built onto a 13th-century pele tower and has fine plasterwork and panelling. A steam engine collection adds further

interest.
Open – House & gardens Etr Sun-Sep, Sun-Thu 11-5. Steam collection 2-5. House & garden £3.50 (ch £1.90 & pen £3), garden only £2.20 (ch £1.10 & pen £2). Party 20+.
🅿 ☕ &. *toilets for disabled shop (plants on sale)* ✠

Flying Buzzard & VIC 96 — MARYPORT

Map 11 NY03
Elizabeth Dock, South Quay, Maryport Harbour
☎ (0900) 815954
Full guided tours of the Flying Buzzard, a 1951 Clyde tug, bringing to life the story of the ship and her crew. Also explore the VIC 96, and visit the hold – a new hands on display for all the

family. A chance to try your hand at tying knots, raising and lowering sails and climbing into a hammock. Special events for 1992 include Steam Weekends.
Open all year – Etr-Oct daily 10.30-4.30; Nov-Etr, telephone to confirm details.
£1.50 (ch £1). Family ticket £4.25
shop

Maritime Museum — MARYPORT

Map 11 NY03
1 Senhouse St
☎ (0900) 813738
Material of local and general maritime interest is displayed, along with photographs illustrating the town's

history.
Open all year, Etr-Oct Mon-Thu 10-5, Fri-Sat 10-1 & 2-5, Sun 2-5; Nov-Etr Mon-Sat 10-1 & 2-4.30.
Free.
&. *shop*

Millom Folk Museum — MILLOM

Map 07 SD18
St Georges Rd
☎ (0229) 772555
All the exhibits in this museum illustrate local life, and they are presented in an informative and captivating way with reconstructed room sets of a miner's cottage, a blacksmith's forge, complete with tools, a corner shop and a full scale

model of a drift of the Hodbarrow Iron Ore Mine. There is also a tribute to the late Dr Norman C Nicholson, poet and author of 'A Man of Millom'.
Open Etr wk; May Day wknd & Spring BH-Sep, Mon-Sat 10-5.
60p (ch 30p). Party.
&. *shop*

Places to visit in this guide are pinpointed on the atlas at the back of the book.

Muncaster Castle & Owl Centre — MUNCASTER

Map 07 SD19
☎ Ravenglass (0229) 717203 & 717393 (owl centre)

Diverse attractions are offered at this castle, the seat of the Pennington family since the 13th century. Inside is a fine collection of 16th- and 17th- century furnishings, embroideries and portraits, whilst the grounds have a nature trail, a

commando course and a profusion of rhododendrons, camellias, magnolias and azaleas. There is also an extensive exhibition of owls, as this is the headquarters of the British Owl Breeding and Release Scheme. Closed circuit television on some nests allows a closer look, and there are continuous owl videos throughout the day in the Old Dairy Theatre. Flying displays take place daily at 2.30pm, weather permitting.
Open Apr-Nov, Castle Tue-Sun & BH 1.30-4.30; Garden & Owl Centre, all year, daily 12-5. Parties by arrangement in the morning.
Castle & Gardens £4.50 (ch 14 £2.50). Gardens & Owl Centre only £2.80 (ch 14 £1.50). Family ticket available. Party.
🅿 ☕ ✕ &. *toilets for disabled shop garden centre*

Muncaster Mill — MUNCASTER

Map 07 SD19
(1m NW on A595 by railway bridge)
☎ Ravenglass (0229) 717232
There has been a mill on this site since the 15th century, and flour and oatmeal are still ground on the premises. The water is brought three-quarters of a mile from the River Mite to the 13ft overshot water wheel, and all the milling

equipment is water driven. This old manorial mill is served by the Ravenglass and Eskdale Railway.
Open Apr, May, Sep & Oct, Mon-Fri, Sun 11-5; Jun-Aug 10-6. Party. Other times by appointment.
✻ *£1 (ch 50p). Family ticket £2.50. Party 12+.*
🅿 &.

&. *This symbol indicates that much or all of the attraction is accessible to wheelchairs. However, there may be some restrictions, so it would be wise to check in advance.*

Hill Top — NEAR SAWREY

Map 07 SD39
☎ Hawkshead (09666) 269
Beatrix Potter wrote many Peter Rabbit books in this little 17th-century house which contains her furniture and china; her 'New Room', where she did much of her work, was restored in 1986.

Open Apr-1 Nov, Mon-Wed, Sat & Sun 11-5. Last admission 4.30. (Closed Thu & Fri (ex Good Fri)).
£3.20 (ch £1.60).
🅿 *shop* ✠
(NT)

PENRITH
See Dacre

Ravenglass & Eskdale Railway   RAVENGLASS

Map 07 SD09
(close to the A595)
☎ (0229) 717171

This narrow gauge (15inch) miniature steam railway was laid in the 19th century to carry iron ore from the mines at Boot. It began to carry passengers and then other freight, including quarried stone, once the mines were closed. The railway was given the nickname 'Owd

Ratty' after its contractor, a man called Ratcliffe. It is now a passenger line, where both steam and diesel locomotives are used during the summer months to pull the open and saloon coaches. The railway runs through beautiful countryside for the seven mile journey from Ravenglass, on the coast, up to the terminus at Dalegarth. Purpose-built toilets for wheelchair users at Ravenglass and Eskdale; special coaches on trains for wheelchair passengers (prior notice advisable).
Open: trains operate daily 4 Apr-1 Nov & 26 Dec-1 Jan; wknds only 15 Feb-29 Mar & 7-15 Nov.
Return fare £5.20 (ch 5-15 £2.60). Family ticket £13.
🅿 *(charged)* ♨ ✗ *licensed* ♿ *(special coach) toilets for disabled shop*

Rydal Mount   RYDAL

Map 11 NY30
☎ Ambleside (05394) 33002

The family home of William Wordsworth from 1813 until his death in 1850, Rydal Mount incorporates a pre-1574 farmer's cottage. Now owned by a descendant of Wordsworth, the

house contains an important group of family portraits, furniture, and many of the poet's personal possessions, together with first editions of his work. Placed in a lovely setting overlooking Windermere and Rydal Water, the house is surrounded by what have been described as the most interesting small gardens in England. They were designed by Wordsworth himself. Evening visits for groups can be organised on request, including a tour of the house and gardens, with poetry readings, wine and gingerbread at a small charge.
Open Mar-Oct daily 9.30-5; Nov-Feb daily (ex Tue) 10-4 (Closed 10 Jan-1 Feb).
£2 (ch 16 80p). Party 10+
🅿 ♿ *shop* ✖

🐕 The 'No Dogs' symbol does not normally apply to guide dogs – these are permitted in most establishments.

National Park Centre   SEDBERGH

Map 07 SD69
72 Main St
☎ (05396) 20125
With the Yorkshire Dales to the south and east and the Lake District just over the border, Sedbergh is set below the hills of the Howgill Fells. The rich natural history of the area and the

beautiful scenery has given rise to this Visitor Centre; maps, walks, guides, local information and interpretative displays are all found here.
Open Apr-Nov, daily mid morning-late afternoon.
Free.
♿ *shop* ✖

Shap Abbey   SHAP

Map 11 NY51
Shap Abbey was founded by the Premonastratensian order in 1199, and dedicated to St Mary Magdalene. The abbey was dissolved in 1540 and most of the ruins date from the 13th century, some of which are standing to first floor

height. The most impressive feature is the 16th-century west tower of the church.
Open any reasonable time.
Free.
🅿 ♿
(EH)

Sizergh Castle   SIZERGH

Map 07 SD48
(3.5m S of Kendal)
☎ Sedgwick (05395) 60070
The castle has a 60-foot high pele tower, built in the 14th century, but most of the castle dates from the 15th to the 18th centuries. There is a Great Hall and some panelled rooms with fine

carved overmantles and adze-hewn floors. The gardens were laid out in the 18th century.
Open Apr-29 Oct, Sun-Thu 1.30-5.30; Garden open 12.30. Last admission 5pm.
£3.10 (ch £1.60). Garden £1.60.
🅿 ♨ ♿ *shop* ✖
(NT)

Hutton-in-the-Forest   SKELTON

Map 11 NY43
☎ (08534) 449
One of the major stately homes in the Lake District, the house has been occupied by the Vane family since the 17th century. The original 14th-century pele tower was added to mainly in the 17th and 19th centuries. The house contains pictures, tapestries and furniture of many periods. The gardens, park and woodland include a walled garden,

topiary, fine specimen trees, a lake and a nature trail. 'Meet the Gardener' afternoons can be arranged.
Open 28 May-27 Sep, Thu, Fri & Sun; BH Sun & Mon (fr Etr) 1-4. Grounds daily May-Oct 11-5. Groups any day booked in advance from 1 Apr.
£2.80 (accompanied ch 7 free, ch £1). Grounds £1 (ch 50p).
🅿 ♨

Acorn Bank Garden   TEMPLE SOWERBY

Map 11 NY62
☎ (07683) 61893
The small but delightful garden of some two and a half acres has a particularly interesting walled kitchen garden. It has been turned into a herb garden with an extensive collection of over 180 varieties of medicinal and culinary herbs. Scented

plants are grown in the small greenhouse.
Open Apr-1 Nov, daily 10-6 (last admission 5.30).
£1.40 (ch 70p).
🅿 ♿ *toilets for disabled shop* ✖
(NT)

Townend   TROUTBECK

Map 11 NY40
☎ (05394) 32628
The house is one of the finest examples of a 'statesmen' (wealthy yeoman) farmer's house in Cumbria. It was built in 1626 for George Browne, and the Browne family lived there until 1944. Inside is the original homemade carved

furniture, with domestic utensils, letters and papers of the farm.
Open Apr-1 Nov, Tue-Fri, Sun & BH Mon 1-5 or dusk if earlier. Last admission 4.30.
£2.30 (ch £1.20).
🅿 ✖
(NT)

This is just one of many guidebooks published by the AA. The full range is available at any AA shop or good bookshop.

Conishead Priory   ULVERSTON

Map 07 SD27
Priory Rd
☎ (0229) 54029
Since the Dissolution there has been a succession of buildings at this site on the shores of Morecambe Bay. The most recent is a huge, 19th-century Gothic mansion set in a 70-acre estate of woods and gardens. In the 1970s the neglected

house was taken over by a Buddhist group, who are now restoring it. There are woodland trails to the bay. Donations towards the restoration work are welcomed.
Open Etr-end Sep, wknds & BH 2-5.
✱ *£1.50 (ch 75p & pen £1).*
🅿 ♨ ♿ *shop*

Laurel & Hardy Museum   ULVERSTON

Map 07 SD27
4c Upper Brook St
☎ (0229) 52292 & 861614
Ulverston was the birthplace of Stan Laurel, so perhaps it is not then so surprising that the town should boast the world's only Laurel and Hardy museum, now extended to more than double the original floor area. Special events include

a display of Oliver Hardy memorabilia obtained from Harlem, Georgia (Ollie's birthplace). To celebrate Oliver Hardy's 100th birthday, January 18th will see the beginning of a month of solo films.
Open all year, daily 10-5.
£1 (ch & pen 50p). Family ticket £2.
♨ ♿ *shop*

Lake District National Park Visitor Centre   WINDERMERE

Map 07 SD49
Brockhole (on A591)
☎ (05394) 46601
Brockhole, built in 1899 for a wealthy businessman, is a large house, set in 32 acres of landscaped gardens, standing on the eastern shore of Lake Windermere. It became England's first National Park Visitor Centre in 1969. It offers a 'Living Lakeland' exhibition on the evolution and development of the National Park, audio-visual displays and

films on the Lake District. In the grounds there is a Nature Trail, a children's Squirrel Nutkin Trail and the Beatrix Potter Grotto. Special events during the school holidays are a big attraction. There are also a Compass Course and daily boat trips on the lake.
Open 12 Apr-1 Nov, daily from 10am. (Closing time varies with season).
✱ *£2 (ch 5-16 £1). Party 15+.*
🅿 ♨ ✗ *licensed* ♿ *(scented garden) toilets for disabled shop* ✖ *(ex in grounds)*

Windermere Steamboat Museum   WINDERMERE

Map 07 SD49
Rayrigg Rd (.25m N Bowness Bay)
☎ (05394) 45565

A unique display of Victorian and Edwardian steamboats which reflects the enormous part boating has played over many years in the history of Lake

Windermere – a popular lake for both motorboat and sailboat enthusiasts. Many of the exhibits in this extensive collection are still afloat and in working order. The museum also contains various displays concerning life on and around the lake. A Model Boat Regatta is held on 16/17th May and other special events and exhibitions are added attractions during the summer, including in 1992 a Classic Motor Boat Rally on 1st and 2nd August.
Open Etr-Oct daily, 10-5. Steamboat trips subject to availability & weather.
✱ *£2.20 (ch £1.40). Family ticket £5.80. Party 12+*
🅿 ♨ ♿ *toilets for disabled shop*

Helena Thompson Museum   WORKINGTON

Map 11 NY02
Park End Rd
☎ (0900) 62598
Costumes, glass, ceramics and other decorative arts and objects of local historical interest form the core of exhibits in this small museum. The items are displayed in a pleasant 18th-century

house and temporary exhibitions are shown in the former stable block.
Open all year, Apr-Oct Mon-Sat 10.30-4; Nov-Mar 11-3. Parties by prior arrangement.
🅿 ♿ *toilets for disabled shop* ✖
Details not confirmed for 1992

DERBYSHIRE

Magpie Mine
BAKEWELL

Map 07 SK26
Sheldon (3m W off B5055)
☎ Matlock (0629) 583834
The surface remains of the mine arc the best example in Britain of a 19th-century lead mine. It was last worked (unsuccessfully) in 1958, and then stabilised in the 1970s. For further information contact the Peak District Mining Museum, Matlock Bath, Derbyshire.
Open at all times.
Free.

Bolsover Castle
BOLSOVER

Map 08 SK47
(on A632)
☎ Chesterfield (0246) 823349
The castle dates back to Norman times, but was rebuilt as a mock castle by Bess of Hardwick's son, in around 1613. His son and grandson continued work on the building, which is unusual because mock castles did not come into vogue until 200 years later. There are fine fireplaces, pseudo-Gothic vaulted ceilings, and ornate panelling. The 'star chamber' is so called because of the stars painted on the ceiling, while the Elysium room has a group of gods on the ceiling, and the Heaven room shows the Ascension of Christ, all elaborately done. There is also an attractive 170ft long riding school, now used by Riding for the Disabled.
Open all year, Apr-Sep, daily 10-6; Oct-Mar, Tue-Sun 10-4. (Closed 24-26 Dec & 1 Jan).
£1.80 (ch 90p, pen, students & UB40 £1.40).
& *(keep not accessible)* ✠
(EH)

For an explanation of the symbols and abbreviations, see page 2.

Buxton Micrarium
BUXTON

Map 07 SK07
The Crescent
☎ (0298) 78662
The Micrarium is a fascinating museum, and the first of its kind. Visitors view the displays through push-button, remote-controlled microscopes, seeing the wonders of nature magnified.
Open 4 Apr-Sep, daily 10-5 (Feb-Mar wknds only).
£2.25 (ch £1.25 & pen £1.75)
& *shop* ✠

Poole's Cavern (Buxton Country Park)
BUXTON

Map 07 SK07
Green Ln
☎ (0298) 26978
The natural limestone cavern lies in 100 acres of woodland. There is a visitor centre with a video show and Roman exhibition. Also on show is an exhibition on the cave and woodland, including archaeological finds from a cave dig.
Open Good Fri-end Oct, daily 10-5. (Closed Wed in Apr, May & Oct).
🅿 & *(wheelchairs available) toilets for disabled shop* ✠ *(ex in park)*
Details not confirmed for 1992

Calke Abbey
CALKE

Map 08 SK32
☎ Melbourne (0332) 863822
This fine baroque mansion dating from the early 18th century was built for Sir John Harpur and remained the family home until its recent acquisition by the National Trust who describe it as the 'house that time forgot'. Among its treasures are an extensive natural history collection, a magnificent Chinese silk state bed (its hangings in mint condition), and a spectacular red and white drawing room. The house stands in extensive wooded parkland and also has walled flower gardens.
Open Apr-Oct Sat-Wed (incl BH Mon); House 1-5.30 Gardens & Church from 11am. Last admission 5pm.
£4 (ch £2)
🅿 *(charged)* ✕ & *toilets for disabled shop* ✠
(NT)

Blue-John Cavern & Mine
CASTLETON

Map 07 SK18
Buxton Rd
☎ Hope Valley (0433) 620638 & 620642
The cavern is a remarkable example of a water-worn cave, and measures over a third of a mile long, with chambers 200ft high. It contains 8 of the 14 veins of Blue John stone, and has been the major source of this unique form of fluorspar for nearly 300 years.
Open all year daily 9.30-6 (or dusk) (telephone for winter opening times); (Closed 25-26 Dec & 1 Jan).
✱ *£3.50 (ch £1.50, pen £2.50). Party. shop*

Peak Cavern
CASTLETON

Map 07 SK18
(on A625)
☎ Hope Valley (0433) 620285
This is one of the most spectacular natural limestone caves in the Peak District, and has an electrically lit underground walk of about half a mile. Ropes have been made for over 500 years in the 'Grand Entrance Hall', and traces of a row of cottages can be seen.
Open Etr-end Oct, daily 10-5.
£2.40 (ch £1.20)
🅿 *shop*

Peveril Castle
CASTLETON

Map 07 SK18
Market Place
☎ Hope Valley (0433) 620613
Henry II built the keep in the 12th century. It stands in an impregnable-looking position high above the town, and gives magnificent views.
Open all year, Apr-Sep, daily 10-6; Oct-Mar, Tue-Sun 10-4. (Closed 24-26 Dec & 1 Jan).
£1.10 (ch 55p, pen, students & UB40 85p)
✠
(EH)

Speedwell Cavern
CASTLETON

Map 07 SK18
Winnats Pass (off A625, 5m W of Castleton Village).
☎ Hope Valley (0433) 620512
Visitors descend 105 steps to a boat which takes them on a one-mile underground exploration of the floodlit cavern with its 'bottomless pit'.
Open all year, daily 9.30-5.30. (Closed 25-26 Dec & 1 Jan).
✱ *£4 (ch 14 £2.50). Party.*
🅿 *shop*

Chatsworth
CHATSWORTH

Map 07 SK27
☎ Baslow (0246) 582204

Chatsworth is the palatial home of the Duke and Duchess of Devonshire, and has one of the richest collections of fine and decorative arts in private hands. Inside there is a splendid painted hall, and a great staircase leads to the even finer chapel, which is decorated with marble, paintings, statues and paintings on walls and ceiling. There are magnificent pictures, furniture and porcelain, and a memorable *trompe l'oeil* painting of a violin on the music room door. The park is one of the finest in Britain. It was laid out by 'Capability' Brown, but is most famous as the work of Joseph Paxton (later Sir Joseph), who became head gardener in the 19th century. Notable features include the Cascade and the Emperor Fountain, which sends up a jet of water to 290ft. Other attractions are the farming and forestry exhibition and the adventure playground. Guided tours are available at extra cost. Numerous events are held throughout the year, including an Angling Fair on 9th and 10th May and a Country Fair on 5th and 6th September.
Open – House & Garden open 29 Mar-Nov, daily 11-4.30. Farmyard & Adventure Playground, 29 Mar-Sep 10.30-4.30.
House & Garden £4.75 (ch £2.20 & pen £3.75). Family ticket £11. Garden only £2.25 (ch £1.10). Farmyard & Adventure Playground prices under review.
🅿 *(charged)* ♨ ✕ *licensed* & *toilets for disabled shop garden centre* ✠ *(ex gardens)*

Peacock Information & Heritage Centre — CHESTERFIELD

Map 08 SK37
Low Pavement
☎ (0246) 207777
The centre is housed in a medieval timber-framed building which is thought to have been a guildhall before becoming the Peacock Inn. The first floor is now used as an exhibition room, and an

audio-visual commentary on the history of Chesterfield is available on request.
Open all year, Mon-Sat. Information Centre Apr-Oct 9-6, Jan-Mar & Nov-Dec 9.30-5. Heritage Centre Mon-Sat 11-4. (Closed 25-27 Dec & 1 Jan).
Free.
& *shop*

Creswell Crags Visitor Centre — CRESWELL

Map 08 SK57
off Crags Rd (1m E off B6042)
☎ Worksop (0909) 720378
The deep narrow gorge of Creswell Crags is pitted with 24 caves and rock shelters which were used for seasonal camps by Stone Age hunter-gatherers. Unusual finds from within the caves include pieces of decorated animal bone and the remains of animals which have long since become extinct, such as the woolly mammoth and hyena. A visitor centre at one end of the gorge explains the importance of the site, with an

exhibition and an audio-visual showing what life was like in prehistoric times. From there, a trail leads through the gorge, where visitors can look into the caves through grills, although the caves cannot be entered. There is a picnic site at the centre, and various events are held. There are purpose-built toilets for wheelchair users, and wheelchairs are available on loan.
Open all year, Feb-Oct, daily, 10.30-4.30; Nov-Jan, Sun only 10.30-4.30.
Free.
P & *toilets for disabled shop*

National Tramway Museum — CRICH

Map 08 SK35
Matlock Rd (off B5035)
☎ Ambergate (0773) 852565
Vintage electric, horse-drawn and steam tramcars from Britain and other parts of the world can be seen at this unique museum. Many of the trams are in working order, and visitors can take unlimited rides on the trams which may once have clanged through the streets of Oporto, Prague or Paisley, but now run along a one-mile tramway with wonderful views over the Derwent Valley. The tramway period street includes the reconstructed façade of the Georgian assembly rooms from Derby.

There are also depots, a video theatre, and numerous exhibitions and displays throughout the year, including an Electric Trams Easter Parade (19 & 20 April), Father's Day Special – dad's chance to drive a train (21 June), and a Teddy Bear's Outing (12 & 13 September).
Open 4 Apr-1 Nov Sat, Sun & BH's. 13 Apr-24 Sep, Mon-Thu. Also Fri 17 & 24 Apr, 29 May, 4 Jul-28 Aug. Additional opening during 19-30 Oct 10-5.30 (6.30 Sat, Sun & BH).
£3.70 (ch £2.10 & pen £3.10). Family £10.50. Party 10+.
P ⬤ & *(ex trams) toilets for disabled shop*

Cromford Mill — CROMFORD

Map 07 SK35
Mill Ln
☎ Matlock (0629) 824297
Sir Richard Arkwright established the world's first successful water-powered cotton mill at Cromford in 1771. The Arkwright Society are involved in a

major restoration to create a lasting monument to an extraordinary genius.
Open all year, daily 10-5. (Closed 25 Dec).
Guided tour & exhibitions £1.50 (ch & pen £1.50). Mill Free.
P ✗ & *toilets for disabled shop*

Denby Pottery Visitors Centre — DERBY

Map 08 SK33
(6m N)
☎ Ripley (0773) 743644
Guided factory tours, with a knowledgeable escort, show the intricate skills of the potters craft including throwing, turning, jolleying, casting, handling and glazing. There is also a museum which illustrates the history of Denby pottery and, not surprisingly, a large factory shop. There is also a

children's play area. The Great Denby Tableware Exchange takes place in Nov, and there is a craft fair in Jun (12-14).
Open all year. Full factory tours, Mon-Thu 9.30-3.30, Fri 9-11. Craftroom only Sat-Sun 10-4. Craftsman's Pantry, daily 9.30-4.30. Factory shop, daily 9-5. Factory tours £2 (ch & pen £1). Craftroom only £1.25 (ch & pen £1). Party.
P ⬤ & *toilets for disabled shop garden centre* ✈

Derby Museum & Art Gallery — DERBY

Map 08 SK33
The Strand
☎ (0332) 255586 & 255587
The museum has a huge range of displays, notably of Derby porcelain and of paintings by the local artist Joseph Wright (1734-97). Also antiquities, natural history and militaria, as well as

many temporary exhibitions, including the paintings and studies of JMW Turner (Apr/May).
Open all year, Mon 11-5, Tue-Sat 10-5, Sun & BHs 2-5. (Closed 25-26 Dec).
Free.
& *(lift to all floors) toilets for disabled shop*
✈

Industrial Museum — DERBY

Map 08 SK33
The Silk Mill, off Full St
☎ (0332) 293111 ext 740
The museum is set in an early 18th-century silk mill and adjacent flour mill. Displays cover local mining, quarrying and industries, and include a major collection of Rolls Royce aero-engines

from 1915 to the present. There is also a new railway section. Temporary exhibitions are held.
Open all year, Mon 11-5, Tue-Sat 10-5, Sun & BHs 2-5.
30p (ch, students, disabled & UB40's 10p).
& *(lift to all floors) toilets for disabled shop*
✈

Pickford's House Social History Museum — DERBY

Map 08 SK33
41 Friar Gate
☎ (0332) 255363
The house was built in 1770 by the architect Joseph Pickford as a combined workplace and family home, and stands in Derby's most handsome street. Pickford's house now shows domestic life at different periods, with Georgian and Edwardian reception rooms and service areas and a 1930s bathroom. Other galleries are devoted to temporary

exhibitions, especially on social history, textiles and costume themes. There is also a display on the growth of Georgian Derby, and on Pickford's contribution to Midlands architecture. The garden has been reconstructed in the Georgian style.
Open all year, Mon 11-5, Tue-Sat 10-5, Sun & BHs 2-5. Times may vary, telephone for details.
30p (ch & concessions 10p). Free on Sun.
P & *shop* ✈

✳ An asterisk indicates that up-to-date information was not available at the time of our research – 1991 information has been published as an indication of what you may expect.

Elvaston Castle Country Park — ELVASTON

Map 08 SK43
Borrowash Rd
☎ Derby (0332) 571342
The 200-acre park was landscaped in the early 19th century, and became one of Britain's first country parks in 1968. Restored after 30 years of neglect, it includes elaborate topiary gardens from the 19th-century scheme, and a walled kitchen garden now planted out as an Old English Garden with herbaceous borders, roses and scented herbs. The

old estate workshops have been restored as an Estate Museum, with exhibitions of blacksmithing, saddlery and other traditional crafts associated with country houses at the turn of the century. There are also nature trails and numerous walks, exhibitions and displays, and a caravan and campsite.
Open all year, daily 9-dusk. Museum Etr-Oct, Wed-Sat 1-5, Sun & BH's 10-6.
P *(charged)* ⬤ & *toilets for disabled shop*
Details not confirmed for 1992

Eyam Hall — EYAM

Map 08 SK27
(W of church)
☎ (0433) 31976
A beautiful 17th-century manor house built and still occupied by the Wright family. It has accumulated furniture, portraits, tapestries and objects of

interest over the centuries, and these are all on display.
Open 29 Mar-25 Oct, Wed, Thu, Sun & BH Mon 11-4.30(last tour).
£2.75 (ch £1.50, pen & concessions £2). Family ticket £7
&

For an explanation of the symbols and abbreviations, see page 2.

Haddon Hall — HADDON HALL

Map 07 SK26
(1.5 S of Bakewell off A6)
☎ Bakewell (0629) 812855 & 814629

Romantic, battlemented Haddon Hall is like a house trapped in time: it has hardly changed for 400 years. It was started in the 12th century; then in the 17th century it was left to lie fallow by its owners, who were Earls and then Dukes of Rutland. They lived at Belvoir

Castle instead, leaving Haddon Hall as perhaps the most perfect example of a medieval manor house in England. The oldest part is the painted chapel; the kitchen and the banqueting hall with its minstrels' gallery are of the 14th century; and there is a later long gallery leading to beautiful terraced rose gardens. Dorothy Vernon, a daughter of the house, is said to have eloped from here with John Manners in 1567. The steps and bridge linked with the elopement were not built until the 17th century – but the marriage of Dorothy and John certainly took place, so perhaps the story is true.
Open Apr-Sep, Tue-Sun (Tue-Sat in Jul-Aug) 11-6. Last entry 5.15.
£3.20 (ch £1.90 & pen £2.60). Party.
P *(charged)* ⬤ *shop* ✈
See advertisement on page 57.

HADDON HALL

BAKEWELL
Derbyshire Seat of the Duke of Rutland

See life as it was lived over 400 years ago - The Great Banqueting Hall, the Medieval Kitchens and Storerooms, the beautiful Long Gallery leading to the famous terraced rose gardens, where in 1567 Dorothy Vernon eloped with her lover John Manners. Haddon Hall is open daily exept Mondays (and Sundays in July and August) from 1st April - 30th September, open all Bank Holiday Mondays.
Haddon Hall is on the A6 one and a half miles south of Bakewell.

For more information contact
The Comptroller, The Estate Office, Haddon Hall, Bakewell, Derbyshire. DE4 1LA
Telephone: Bakewell (0629) 812855

Hardwick Hall — HARDWICK HALL

Map 08 SK46
(2m S M1 Junc 29)
☎ Chesterfield (0246) 850430

The splendid Elizabethan mansion is celebrated as the creation of Bess of Hardwick, a redoubtable character, who was married and widowed four times and became immensely rich in the process. She began the magnificent building at 70 after the death of her fourth husband, the Earl of Shrewsbury. They quarrelled and separated, but he left her even richer than before.

The house is remarkable for its vast area of windows, which become taller from the ground floor up. The six towers are topped by Bess's monogram, ES. Inside, the house and contents, such as Bess's great jewel chest, have escaped change because her descendants lived mainly at Chatsworth instead. The High Great Chamber and the long gallery were probably designed to display the tapestries which line them. The latter room is also hung with Cavendish portraits. There are numerous other tapestries, with some fine needlework by Bess and her ladies, and by Mary, Queen of Scots, who was the Earl of Shrewsbury's prisoner for 15 years. In the kitchen are hundreds of 18th- and 19th-century pots, pans and plates, all marked with a ducal coronet. The gardens are laid out in walled courtyards, and there is a large park.

Open Apr-Oct Wed, Thu, Sat, Sun & BH Mon 12.30-5 or sunset. (Closed Good Fri). Last admission 5. Park all year. Garden Apr-end Oct daily 12-5.30.
House & garden £5 (ch £2.50). Garden only £2 (ch £1)
P ✕ *licensed* ♿ *shop* 🐕 *(ex in park)*
(NT)

For an explanation of the symbols and abbreviations, see page 2.

The American Adventure Theme Park — ILKESTON

Map 08 SK44
Pit Ln
☎ Langley Mill (0773) 769931 & 531521

This is one of Britain's few fully themed parks, based on the legend of a whole continent. The experiences of a day out here are widely varied, from the heartpounding action of the Missile Rollercoaster in Spaceport USA, the wet and wild excitement of the Great Niagara Rapids ride or the Cherokee Falls log flume to the gentle excursion across Lake Reflection aboard a Mississippi paddle steamer, watching a shoot-out in Silver City, seeing the glamour of Lazy Lil's Saloon Show or experiencing the carnival atmosphere of Mexicoland.

Open fr Etr. Telephone for details.
* *£8.70 (ch £7.70, pen & disabled £4.10).*
P ☕ ✕ *licensed* ♿ *(free wheelchair hire) toilets for disabled shop* 🐕

Kedleston Hall — KEDLESTON HALL

Map 07 SK33
☎ Derby (0332) 842191

Thought by many to be the finest Robert Adam house in the country, Kedleston has been the Derbyshire home of the Curzon family for over eight centuries. The original house was demolished at the end of the 17th century when the rather muddled start to the building of the present mansion began. The architect Matthew Brettingham gave Kedleston its present day plan of a main block and two wings linked by corridors; James Paine is responsible for the imposing north front. It wasn't until 1760 that Adam appeared on the scene. He built the south front and designed most of the interior including the awe-inspiring marble hall, regarded as one of the most splendid rooms in Europe. There are some notable pictures, furniture and china displayed in the house together with an Indian Museum containing the collection accumulated by Lord Curzon, Viceroy of India from 1898 to 1905. The charming boathouse and bridge in the gardens were also designed by Adam. A flock of Canada Geese complement the scene.

Open Apr-Oct, Sat-Wed & BH Mons. Park from 11am. Gardens & tearoom 12-5. House & shop 1-5.30.
£3.75 (ch £1.80)
P ✕ *shop* 🐕 *(ex in park)*
(NT)

Lea Gardens — LEA

Map 07 SK35
(3m SE Matlock off A6)
☎ Dethick (0629) 534380

Three and a half acres of attractive woodland gardens with rhododendrons, azaleas and rock plants are open for public enjoyment.

Open 20 Mar-Jul, daily 10-7.
£2 (ch 50p, disabled free). Season ticket £3.
P ☕ ♿ *shop garden centre*

Every effort is made to provide accurate information, but details might change during the currency of this guide.

Riber Castle Wildlife Park — MATLOCK

Map 07 SK36
(off A615)
☎ (0629) 582073

Dominated by the ruins of the fairy-tale fortress built by the larger-than-life figure of John Smedley, who made Matlock a fashionable Victorian health resort, the Riber Castle Wildlife Park covers 25 acres of land at the top of the 853ft high Riber Hill. Specialising in rare breeds and endangered species of birds and animals, the park is home to lynx, otters, reindeer, Arctic foxes, and owls, many on breeding and release programmes; there is also a children's playground. The house is now a roofless shell but still looks imposing and is a good vantage point from which to view the local gorge. The 'Riber Round Up' MG rally is held in September.

Open all year, daily from 10am. (Summer last admission 5pm, winter 3-4.30pm).
* *£3.50 (ch 5-15 £2, pen £3).*
P ☕ ♿ *toilets for disabled shop* 🐕 *(in animal section)*

The Heights of Abraham — MATLOCK BATH

Map 07 SK25
(on A6)
☎ Matlock (0629) 582365

High on a hill above the village of Matlock Bath are the Grounds of the Heights of Abraham. Until recently the climb to the summit was only for the very energetic, but now alpine-style cable cars provide a leisurely and spectacular way of reaching the top from their starting point near Matlock Bath Railway Station. Once inside the Grounds there is plenty to do for the whole family. Two famous show caverns provide fascinating tours, one is introduced by a multivision programme and the other tells the story of a 17th-century lead miner. A coffee shop, licensed restaurant and picnic sites take advantage of the superb views. There is also a nature trail, the Victoria Prospect Tower and play area. In a sparkling waterscaped setting is the High Falls Gallery and a gift shop.

Open daily Etr-Oct 10-5 (later in high season) for Autumn & Winter opening telephone for details.
* *£4.50 (ch £2.50, pen £3.75). Party 20+.*
☕ ✕ *licensed* ♿ *toilets for disabled shop*
See advertisement on page 58.

Peak District Mining Museum — MATLOCK BATH

Map 07 SK25
The Pavilion (off A6)
☎ Matlock (0629) 583834

This rewarding display, ideal for families, explains the history of Derbyshire lead industry from Roman times to the present day. The geology of the area, mining and smelting processes, the quarrying and the people who worked in the industry, are all illustrated by a series of static and moving exhibits and an audio-visual display. The museum also features an early 19th-century water pressure pumping engine – the only one of its kind in Britain.

Open all year, daily 11-4 (later in summer season). (Closed 25 Dec).
£1 (ch, students, disabled & pen 50p). Family £2.50. Party.
P *(charged)* ♿ *shop* 🐕

Temple Mine — MATLOCK BATH

Map 07 SK25
Temple Rd (off A6)
☎ Matlock (0629) 583834

In the process of being restored to how it was in the 1920s and 1930s, this old lead and fluorspar workings makes interesting viewing. A self-guided tour illustrates the geology, mineralisation and mining techniques.

Open Etr-Oct, daily 11-4, (longer hours in summer); Oct-Nov & Jan-Etr, wknds only 1-4.
80p (ch, students, disabled & pen 40p)
shop 🐕

Melbourne Hall — MELBOURNE

Map 08 SK32
(9m S of Derby on A514)
☎ Derby (0332) 862502
In 1133 Henry I gave his royal manor of Melbourne to the first Bishop of Carlisle; hence the surprisingly large parish church of St Michael and St Mary. The lease was then sold to Sir John Coke (Charles I's Secretary of State) in 1628 and the house is still owned by his descendants. Through the centuries the hall has been converted from manor house to a much grander residence which has been the home of two of Britain's most famous Prime Ministers: Lord Melbourne and Lord Palmerston. It features fine collections of pictures and antique furniture, but its chief appeal is its intimate and 'lived in' atmosphere. The glorious formal gardens are among the finest in Britain, and were laid out in about 1700 by royal gardeners London and Wise, who followed the style of the great French garden designer, Le Nôtre. Special events are held each Sunday in August, featuring the Charnwood Archers, the Breedon Handbell Ringers and Mathern Junior Band.
Open, house daily throughout Aug only (ex 3, 10 & 17) 2-5. Prebooked parties by appointment in Aug. Gardens Apr-Sep, Wed, Sat, Sun & BH Mon 2-6.
House Tue-Sat (guided tour) £2 (ch 75p, pen £1.50), Sun & BH Mon (no guided tour) £1.50 (ch 75p, pen £1). House & Garden (Aug only) £3 (ch £1.75), pen £2.50). Garden only £2 (pen £1). Family £5.
☕ ♿ *toilets for disabled shop* ✗

* An asterisk indicates that up-to-date information was not available at the time of our research – 1991 information has been published as an indication of what you may expect.

Middleton Top Engine House — MIDDLETON BY WIRKSWORTH

Map 07 SK25
(.5m S from B5036 Cromford/Wirksworth road)
☎ Wirksworth (0629) 823204
Set above the village of Middleton, site of one of Britain's very few limestone mines, a beam engine built in 1829 for the Cromford & High Peak Railway can be seen in its octagonal engine house. The engine's job was to haul wagons up the Middleton Incline, and its last trip was in 1963 after 134 years' work. The visitor centre tells the story of this historic railway, and there is also a picnic area alongside the High Peak Trail, popular with cyclists, walkers and riders.
Open: High Peak Trail all year; Information Centre, wknds all year, wkdays in summer; Bicycle hire, summer season daily (Etr-Dec wknds only). Engine House Etr-Oct every Sun (engine static) and first wknd in month (engine in motion).
Static Engine 35p (ch 15p). Working Engine 60p (ch 30p).
🅿 *(charged)* ♿ *(ex Engine house) toilets for disabled shop*

Revolution House — OLD WHITTINGTON

Map 08 SK37
High St (on B6052 off A61, signposted)
☎ Chesterfield (0246) 453554 & 231224
Originally the Cock and Pynot alehouse, this 17th century cottage was the scene of a meeting between local noblemen to plan their part in the Revolution of 1688. The house is now furnished in 17th-century style. A video relates the story of the Revolution and there is a small exhibition room.
Open all year, Sat & Sun; 17 Apr-1 Nov, daily 10-4.
Free.
shop ✗

Midland Railway Centre — RIPLEY

Map 08 SK35
Butterley Station (1m N on B6179)
☎ (0773) 747674 & 749788
This centre not only operates a regular steam-train passenger service, but also provides the focal point for a fascinating industrial museum project. Its aim is to depict every aspect of the golden days of the Midland Railway, and its successors. The working section of the railway line extends for some three and a half miles between Butterley Station and Riddings. Exhibits range from the steam locomotives of 1866 to the diesels of 1967. There is also a large section of rolling stock spanning the last 100 years. 'Specials' run from the centre include Wine and Dine trains and Santa Specials. Also of interest is the narrow-gauge railway and an award-winning country park. There are purpose-built toilets for wheelchair users at Butterley Station and special accommodation is available on the trains. Every Sunday from 29th March to 27th September will be a Gala Day.
Open: trains operate all year Sun; Apr-Oct & Dec Sat; 17-26 Apr, 23-31 May, Aug-6 Sep & 26-31 Oct daily; 30 Jun-16 Jul Tue-Thu & Sat-Sun; 21-31 Jul Tue-Sun. Train times 1130-1615.
* *£3.95 (ch £2 & pen £3.50). Family ticket £9.90. Party 15+. Sun & BH Mon (Apr-Oct) £4.50 (ch £2.25 & pen £4). Family ticket £11.25.*
🅿 *(charged)* ☕ ✕ *licensed* ♿ *toilets for disabled shop*

Sudbury Hall — SUDBURY

Map 07 SK13
☎ Barton-on-Trent (0283) 585305
This fine country house was started in 1664 by Lord George Vernon. It has unusual diapered brickwork, a carved two-storey stone frontispiece, a cupola and a large number of tall chimneys. The interior is particularly interesting, with work by some of the best craftsmen of the day: there are plasterwork ceilings by Bradbury and Pettifer, ceiling paintings by Laguerre, a fine carved staircase by Edward Pierce and an overmantel by Grinling Gibbons. Also here is an excellent Museum of Childhood.
Open Apr-Oct, Wed-Sun & BH Mons, 1-5.30 or sunset, last admission 5pm. (Closed Good Fri & Tue after BH Mons)
£3 (ch £1.50). Party. Museum of Childhood £2.
🅿 ☕ ♿ *toilets for disabled shop* ✗ *(ex in grounds)*
(NT)

Wirksworth Heritage Centre — WIRKSWORTH

Map 07 SK25
Crown Yard
☎ (0629) 825225
The Centre has been created in an old silk and velvet mill. The three floors of the mill have interpretative displays of the town's past history as the hub of a prosperous lead-mining industry, the present town and plans for the future. Each floor offers many features of interest including a computer game called 'Rescue the injured lead-miner' and a mock-up of a natural cavern. The lifestyle of a quarryman in the early 1900's is recreated in the Quarryman's House Place. Some unusual local customs such as tap dressing and 'clypping the church' are explained. There are also workshops showing the skills of cabinetmakers, silversmiths and blacksmiths. If you visit Wirksworth during Spring Bank Holiday, you can also see the famous Well Dressings.
Open 8 Feb-12 Apr & 19 Sep-18 Dec, Wed-Sat 11-3, Sun 12.30-3; 14 Apr-26 Jul, Tue-Sat 10.30-4.30, Sun 12.30-4; 27 Jul-18 Sep, daily 10.30-4.30. Also open BH wknds (ex Xmas & New Year). Last admission 30 mins before closing.
75p (ch & pen 40p) Family ticket £1.90. Party 20+.
☕ ✕ *licensed shop* ✗

DEVON

North Devon Maritime Museum — APPLEDORE

Map 03 SS43
Odun House, Odun Rd
☎ Bideford (0237) 474852
Appledore's traditional activities of boat-building and fishing make the village a suitable home for the museum. Each room shows a different aspect of north Devon's maritime history, including steam and motor coasters. There is also a full-size reconstruction of an Appledore kitchen of around 1900.
Open Etr-Oct, daily 2-5.30, also May-Sep, Mon-Fri 11-1pm.
£1 (ch 30p & pen 70p).
shop ✗

Arlington Court — ARLINGTON

Map 03 SS64
☎ Shirwell (0271) 850296
Built in 1822, Arlington Court is filled with a fascinating collection of *objets d'art:* pewter, shells and model ships as well as furniture and costumes from the 19th century. The biggest attraction, however, is the collection of carriages and horsedrawn vehicles, and rides are available. Around the house is a landscaped park grazed by Shetland ponies and sheep. There is a Victorian garden and a conservatory, and nature trails may be followed through the woods and by the lake.
Open Apr-1 Nov, Sun-Fri 11-5.30; also Sat of BH wknds. Footpaths through Park open all year during daylight hours.
House & grounds £4.40. Grounds only £2.20.
🅿 ✕ *licensed* ♿ *(wheelchairs available) toilets for disabled shop* ✗ *(ex in park)*
(NT)

Marwood Hill Gardens — BARNSTAPLE

Map 03 SS53
☎ (0271) 42528
The gardens with their three small lakes cover 18 acres and have many rare trees and shrubs. There is a large bog garden and a walled garden, collections of clematis, camellias and eucalyptus. Alpine plants are also a feature, and there are plants for sale.
Open daily dawn to dusk.
£1
🅿 *shop (plants sold)*

Pecorama Pleasure Gardens — BEER

Map 03 SY28
Underleys
☎ Seaton (0297) 21542
The gardens are high on a hillside, overlooking the delightful fishing village of Beer. A miniature steam and diesel passenger line offers visitors a stunning view of Lyme Bay as it runs through the Pleasure Gardens. These feature 'Melody Close' and the 'Top Spot' where entertainment is staged during high season. Other attractions include an aviary, putting green, crazy golf and children's activity area. The main building houses an exhibition of railway modelling in various small gauges, displayed in settings around the house and gardens. There are souvenir and railway model shops, plus full catering facilities.
Opening times & days vary according to season.
Admission fee payable.
🅿 ⬤ ✕ *& toilets for disabled shop ✼ (ex in certain areas)*

Gorse Blossom Miniature Railway and Woodland Park — BICKINGTON

Map 03 SX77
☎ (0626) 821361
Unlimited rides are allowed on the three-quarter mile, seven and a quarter inch gauge steam railway line, set amid 35 acres of woodland, about half of which is open to the public. Other attractions include woodland walks, a nature trail, woodland assault course, toytown village and children's play area.
Open 28 Mar-6 Oct, daily 10-last admission 4.30.
🅿 ⬤ *& toilets for disabled shop ✼*
Details not confirmed for 1992

Bickleigh Castle — BICKLEIGH

Map 03 SS90
(off A396 take A3072 from Bickleigh Bridge)
☎ (0884) 855363
The 'castle' is really a moated and fortified manor house, and was formerly the romantic home of the heirs of the Earls of Devon and later of the Carew family. The small detached thatched chapel is said to be the oldest complete building in Devon. It dates from the Norman period and, like the medieval Gatehouse, survived the destruction which followed the Civil War. The Carew family acquired the house in the 16th century, and it was Admiral Sir George Carew who commanded the 'Mary Rose' on her first and last voyage. He drowned with his men when the ship capsized and sank. There is an exhibition on the ship and on Tudor maritime history, with a feature on peacetime maritime disasters, mainly that of the 'Titanic'. Also in the house is a museum of domestic objects and toys from the 18th century onwards, and a display of gadgets used by World War II spies and POWs – the most complete collection known. More traditional features of interest include the Great Hall, armoury (including fine Civil War armour), guardroom, Elizabethan bedroom and the 17th-century farmhouse. The garden is moated and the tower can be climbed for views of the Exe Valley and of the castle complex.
Open Etr wk (Good Fri-Fri), then Wed, Sun & BH to late May BH, then daily (ex Sat) to early Oct.
£2.80 (ch 5-15 £1.40). Family ticket £7.50. Party 20+
🅿 ⬤ *& shop ✼*

Bickleigh Mill-Devonshire's Centre — BICKLEIGH

Map 03 SS90
☎ (08845) 419

The picturesque old working watermill on the River Exe has been converted into a most comprehensive Craft, Gift and Garment Centre with attractive restaurant. Cows and goats are milked by hand at the adjacent Heritage Farm. The land is worked by shire horses who support the many rare breeds of animals and poultry. The Agricultural Museum and popular Motor Centre are situated alongside.
Additionally the complex has its own fishing, bird and otter centres with riverside picnic and children's areas serviced by its own shop. A British Tourist Authority award winner.
Open all year, Jan-Mar Sat & Sun only 10-5, Apr-Dec, daily 10-6 (5pm Nov & Dec)
🅿 ⬤ ✕ *licensed & toilets for disabled shop*
Details not confirmed for 1992

Bicton Park Gardens — BICTON

Map 03 SY08
East Budleigh (2m N of Budleigh Salterton on A376)
☎ Colaton Raleigh (0395) 68465
Bicton Park offers many attractions, but the central one is over 50 acres of colourful gardens, shrubs, woodlands, lakes, ponds and fountains, with an Italian garden and a wonderful restored palm house. This has tropical and sub-tropical areas, where bananas and other exotica flourish. There are also fuchsia, geranium and orchid houses.
A modern building houses the James Countryside Museum, which has farm tools, wagons and a cider press among its fascinating displays. Not to be forgotten either are the fun world and adventure playground, Bicton Woodland Railway, crazy golf, bird garden and tropical house. There is also an open-air arena for equestrian and other events. 9 August 1992 is Clowns International Charity Day and around 70 clowns from around the world will gather at Bicton to entertain the visitors and help raise money for local children's charities.
Open Apr-Sep daily, 10-6; Mar & Oct, daily 10-4.
£4.70 (ch 3-15 £3.70, pen £3.95). Return ticket £1.50 (ch £1). Party 20+.
🅿 ✕ *licensed & (adapted carriage on woodland railway) toilets for disabled shop garden centre*

Exmoor Bird Gardens — BLACKMOOR GATE

Map 03 SS64
South Stowford (off B3226)
☎ Parracombe (05983) 352
These landscaped gardens have a waterfall, streams and a lake with penguins, swans and other water birds. There are aviaries with tropical and other birds, and some animals can also be seen, such as wallabies, guanaco, pigs, coati, chipmunks, ponies, monkeys and goats. There is a 'Tarzanland' for children.
Open daily, Apr-Oct 10-6; Nov-Mar 10-4.
£3.50 (ch 3-16 £2.25, under 3 free).
🅿 ⬤ ✕ *licensed & toilets for disabled shop ✼*

Parke Rare Breeds Farm — BOVEY TRACEY

Map 03 SX87
Parke Estate
☎ (0626) 833909

Over 200 acres of parkland in the wooded valley of the River Bovey make a beautiful setting for the farm, which was established to preserve pure old breeds of domestic animal. Some of the breeds at Parke were common in the Middle Ages, and can be traced back to prehistoric times. They may not be very commercial, but they are an essential reservoir of genes which have been lost in the development of modern farm breeds. In the walled garden there is a fascinating collection of poultry, peafowl, ducks and geese, while in the fields there are pigs, goats, sheep and cattle, including the rare Belted Welsh Black cattle. There is also a pets corner and a play area. Another great attraction of Parke is the walks which can be taken through woodland beside the river and along the route of the old railway track. The headquarters of the Dartmoor National Park is also here, and has an information centre.
Open Good Fri-Oct, daily 10-6 (last admission 5pm).
🅿 ⬤ *& toilets for disabled shop (NT)*
Details not confirmed for 1992

Brixham Museum — BRIXHAM

Map 03 SX95
Bolton Cross
☎ (0803) 856267
A museum of general local interest, including the history of fishing in Brixham. It includes HM Coastguard Collection.
Open Etr-Oct, Mon-Sat 10-5.30.
£1.20 (ch & pen 60p). Family ticket £3.
& shop

Buckfast Abbey — BUCKFASTLEIGH

Map 03 SX76
☎ (0364) 42519

The story of Buckfast Abbey is a remarkable one. The monastery was originally founded in 1018, but the monks left during the Dissolution in the 16th century. Monks returned to the site in 1882 and considered restoring it; in 1907 four (mostly inexperienced) monks began rebuilding the church; and now Buckfast Abbey is once again a religious community. The church was built on the old foundations, using local blue limestone and Ham Hill stone. One of the most beautiful features is the great modern east window, which was the work of Father Charles, a craftsman in stained glass. Other monks have other skills: in beekeeping, farming, and the making of Buckfast tonic wine. Monthly concerts are held at the abbey, and there is a flower festival in July (20-25), and there are children's activity days on Wednesdays throughout August.
Open all year daily 5.30am-9.30pm. (Shops, tea room 9-5.30). Etr-Oct (exhibition) 10.30-4.30.
Free. (Exhibition 60p, ch 30p).
🅿 *(charged) ⬤ ✕ licensed & (braille plan, wheelchair available) toilets for disabled shop ✼*

Buckfast Butterfly Farm & Dartmoor Otter Sanctuary — BUCKFASTLEIGH

Map 03 SX76
(off A38)
☎ (0364) 42916
Visitors can wander around a specially designed, undercover tropical garden, where free-flying butterflies and moths from many parts of the world can be seen. The otter sanctuary has four large enclosures with underwater viewing and there are special observation holts.
Open Good Fri-Oct, daily 10-5.30 or dusk (whichever is earlier).
✱ *£3.25 (ch £2 & pen £2.75)*
🅿 ⬤ *& shop ✼*

South Devon Railway — BUCKFASTLEIGH

Map 03 SX76
Buckfastleigh Station
☎ (0364) 42338

The Buckfastleigh & Totnes line was a rural branch which served the middle of the Dart Valley for 98 years before it was closed by British Rail. It is run now as an educational charity, and makes an interesting way to see the Dart Valley and learn about its past. The store of Great Western rolling stock includes a number of locomotives, and there are extensive grounds at Buckfastleigh. The steam-hauled trains run from Buckfastleigh on a one-hour round trip. Special events include: Vintage Car Gathering, Thomas the Tank Engine Day, Autumn Transport Gathering and Santa Trains.
Open daily Etr-Sep, 10-5.30. Also selected days early & late season. Santa trains in Dec.
£5 (ch £3.60, pen £4.50) includes train fare, station & grounds. Party.
🅿 ⬤ *& toilets for disabled shop*

Buckland Abbey — BUCKLAND ABBEY

Map 03 SX46
☎ Yelverton (0822) 853607
Originally a prosperous Cistercian Abbey, and then home of the Grenville family, Buckland Abbey was sold to Sir Francis Drake in 1581. By then the abbey church had been converted into a handsome house with oak panelling and fine plasterwork, and it was his home until he died at sea in 1596. It belonged to the Drake family until 1946. Several restored buildings house a fascinating exhibition about the abbey's history. Among the exhibits is Drake's drum, which is wreathed in legend and is said to give warning of danger to England. There are also craft workshops and some lovely walks.
Open all year Apr-Oct, daily (ex Thu) 10.30-5.30; Nov-Mar Wed (booked parties only), Sat & Sun 2-5.
Abbey & grounds £3.80. Grounds only £1.80. Car park charge refundable against purchase of admission ticket.
🅿 (charged) ➽ ✕ *licensed* & (*wheelchairs & motorised buggy available) toilets for disabled shop* ✖ (*ex in car park)*
(NT)

& This symbol indicates that much or all of the attraction is accessible to wheelchairs. However, there may be some restrictions, so it would be wise to check in advance.

Cobbaton Combat Collection — CHITTLEHAMPTON

Map 03 SS62
Cobbaton
☎ Chittlehamholt (0769) 540740
Second World War British and Canadian military vehicles, war documents and military equipment can be seen in this private collection. There are over fifty vehicles including tanks and a recent Warsaw pact section. There is also a section on 'Mum's War' and the home front. The children's play area includes a Sherman tank.
Open Apr-Oct, daily 10-6. Winter Mon-Fri 10-4.
£2.75 (ch £1.50, pen £2.25)
🅿 & *shop*

CHUDLEIGH
See Lower Ashton

The Milky Way — CLOVELLY

Map 03 SS32
(on the main A39, 2m from Clovelly)
☎ Bideford (0237) 431255
This award-winning attraction gives visitors the opportunity to try hand milking one of their 160 dairy cows or help with the feeding of baby animals (12.30-4pm). The high-tech milking parlour is also on show and there is an adventure playground and a Countryside Collection of machinery, implements and farmhouse scenes of yesteryear. There is also a working pottery on site, and, new for 1992, the North Devon Bird of Prey Centre, with twice daily falconry displays.
Open Apr-Oct, daily 10.30-6.
£3.50 (ch £2, under 3 free, pen £3).
🅿 ➽ & *toilets for disabled shop*

Bodstone Barton Farmworld — COMBE MARTIN

Map 03 SS54
Berrydown (2m S, off A3123)
☎ (0271) 883654
Set in an area of outstanding natural beauty, Bodstone Barton is a 17th-century farm covering 160 acres. The farm is run by both traditional and modern methods, and visitors can see goats and cows being milked by hand or machine. Attractions include an adventure playground, and rides by tractor, trailer and horse-drawn cart. There is a nature trail to follow, with an abundance of wildlife to be seen. A large collection of agricultural and domestic items are on show, with 20,000 square feet under cover. Many crafts are demonstrated here, including spinning, spar-making and pottery; there is a blacksmith and visitors can watch heavy horses being groomed, harnessed and worked. There are lots of rides and regular live entertainment, including a weekly barn dance and barbeque in the season. Please phone for details.
Open all year, daily May-Sep 10-6, Oct-Apr 12-5.
£3.75 (ch £2.50, disabled £1.50 & pen £3).
🅿 ➽ ✕ *licensed* & *toilets for disabled shop* ✖

The Combe Martin Motorcycle Collection — COMBE MARTIN

Map 03 SS54
Cross St
☎ (0271) 882346
The collection was formed in 1979 and contains old and new British motorcycles, displayed against a background of old petrol pumps, signs and garage equipment, exhibiting motoring nostalgia in an old world atmosphere.
Open Etr then end May-end Sep, daily 10-6.
£1.50 (ch & pen 75p, ch 7 free). Party 10+.
& *shop*

Combe Martin Wildlife Park — COMBE MARTIN

Map 03 SS54
(off A399)
☎ (0271) 882486
Twenty acres of woodland complete with streams, cascading waterfalls, ornamental gardens, tropical plants and rare trees make this the most natural wildlife park in Britain. Otters living in the streams have produced 29 young in the last five years and for something completely different, visitors can see Meerkats 'on guard', living in the largest enclosure in the world – a man-made desert. There is also a large selection of primates, mammals and birds. Special events for 1992 include 'Prehistoric World'.
Open Mar-Nov, daily 10-4.30.
£4 (ch & pen £3). Party 10+.
🅿 ➽ ✕ *licensed* & (*car service) shop* ✖

Compton Castle — COMPTON

Map 03 SX86
(off A381 near Marldon)
☎ Kingskerwell (0803) 872112
A fortified house of the 14th to 16th centuries, Compton has been the home of the Gilbert family (related to Sir Walter Raleigh) for 600 years. Much of the appeal of Compton is due to its completeness. The Great Kitchen still has its bread ovens and knife-sharpening marks, and the withdrawing room has squints through which occupants could watch services in the chapel. The original 14th-century hall was restored in the 20th century, complete with the solar, or living room, above. The towers, portcullis entrances and curtain walls were added in the 16th century, when there were French raids in the area. A look-out squint in the wall allows a watch to be kept from the hall door. There is a rose garden outside.
Open Apr-1 Nov Mon, Wed & Thu 10-12.15 & 2-5.
Castle & garden £2.40
✖
(NT)

Bayard's Cove Fort — DARTMOUTH

Map 03 SX85
The low, circular ruined stronghold was built by the townspeople to protect the harbour. It stands at the southern end of the cove, where the cobbled quay was used as a location for *The Onedin Line*.
Open at all reasonable times.
Free.
🅿
(EH)

Butterwalk Museum — DARTMOUTH

Map 03 SX85
6 Butterwalk
☎ (0803) 832923
The timber-framed 17th-century house is part of a restored colonnaded arcade, and is encrusted with carvings. It houses a small maritime museum with over 150 ship models and many pictures and artcrafts relating to the history of this ancient little town.
Open all year, Nov-Etr, Mon-Sat 1.15-4; Etr-Oct, Mon-Sat 11-5.
70p (ch 5 free, ch 5-15 20p & pen 50p). shop

Dartmouth Castle — DARTMOUTH

Map 03 SX85
☎ (0803) 833588
The castle dates from 1481 and was one of the first to be designed for artillery. It faces Kingswear Castle on the other side of the Dart estuary, and a chain could be drawn between the two in times of war. The timber-framed opening for the chain can still be seen.
Open all year, Apr-Sep, daily 10-6; Oct-Mar, Tue-Sun 10-4. (Closed 24-26 Dec & 1 Jan).
£1.50 (ch 75p, students, pen & UB40 £1.10).
🅿 ✖
(EH)

Newcomen Memorial Engine — DARTMOUTH

Map 03 SX85
Royal Av Gardens
☎ (0803) 832281
Thomas Newcomen helped to keep open Devon's mines by inventing a steam-driven pump to clear them of water. This building was erected to commemorate the 300th anniversary of his birth (1663) and houses one of his atmospheric pumping engines of 1725. It may be seen working.
Open Etr-Oct, Mon-Fri 12-3.
20p (ch 5p). Family 50p.

Woodland Leisure Park — DARTMOUTH

Map 03 SX85
Blackawton (W, off B3207)
☎ Blackawton (080421) 598
A beautiful 60-acre park with ten play zones featuring Tarzan swings, death slides, mega assault course, tube slide, a three-stage free-fall slide and a special toddlers' play village. There is an international bird and fish collection, an undercover bee observatory, and a new 15-acre animal farm complex with hundreds of animals under cover. Beautiful Sika deer, tiny Russian hamsters, and many more friendly pets to meet and feed. There are also 30 acres of woodland with super nature walks and ornamental ponds. Live entertainers appear daily during school holidays, and special events during the summer season include a teddy bears' picnic, an army display team, and a country fun day.
Open all year, 31 Mar-Oct, daily 9.30-6.30; Nov-30 Mar, daily 10-dusk.
£3.50 (ch £2.50 & pen £2)
🅿 ➽ & *toilets for disabled shop*

✱ An asterisk indicates that up-to-date information was not available at the time of our research – 1991 information has been published as an indication of what you may expect.

Castle Drogo — DREWSTEIGNTON

Map 03 SX79
☎ Chagford (0647) 433306
The granite castle is one of the most remarkable designs of Sir Edwin Lutyens, and was built between 1910 and 1930 for Julius Drews, a poor man's son who retired at 33 after founding the Home and Colonial Stores. It is a fascinating combination of medieval might and 20th-century luxury, with its own telephone and hydro-electric systems, and craftsmanship of a high order. The castle stands at 900ft, on a rocky crag overlooking the gorge of the River Teign. There are wonderful views from the gardens.
Open Apr-1 Nov, daily (ex Fri) 11-5.30. Garden open daily, 10.30-5.30.
✱ *Castle & grounds £4.40. Grounds only £2.*
🅿 ➽ ✕ *licensed* & (*wheelchairs available) toilets for disabled shop garden centre* ✖
(NT)

EXETER

Map 03 SX99
Exeter's history goes back to before the Romans, when the line of the present High Street was already established as an ancient ridgeway. The city prospered under the Romans, who built the wall and a bath house, and in the Middle Ages when the cathedral was built. This is where most visits begin, and it is well worth seeing for its magnificent nave, where clusters of pillars soar up into the web of fan vaulting in the roof. Other notable features are the intricately decorated bishop's throne, and the misericord carvings under the choir seats, including a crocodile and an elephant. Outside the cathedral is the Close, surrounded by charming buildings, and near by there are a number of interesting small churches. Highlights of the city include Rougemont House and its gardens, the Guildhall and the Maritime Museum. A more unusual attraction is the network of underground passages which brought water to the medieval city and can now be explored: the entrance is in the Princesshay shopping precinct.

Guildhall   EXETER

Map 03 SX99
High St
☎ (0392) 77888
This is one of the oldest municipal buildings still in use. It was built in 1330 and then altered in 1446, and the arches and façade were added in 1592-5. The roof timbers rest on bosses of bears holding staves, and there are portraits of Exeter dignitaries, guild crests, civic silver and regalia.
Open all year, Mon-Sat 10-5.15. (ex when used for civic functions).
Free.
& ✗

Maritime Museum   EXETER

Map 03 SX99
The Haven
☎ (0392) 58075

Afloat, ashore and under cover, there are over 130 boats at the museum, which is at the heart of the lively quay area. The boats come from all over the world and are very varied, ranging from the oldest working steam dredger, *Bertha*, believed to have been built by Brunel, to dhows and coracles, a junk and a sampan, and a Venetian gondola. There are African dug-out canoes and frail-looking craft from the Pacific, and there is a large Danish harbour tug. One section is occupied by the fascinating Ellerman collection of Portugese craft, and elsewhere is the Ocean Rowers' collection, featuring boats which have been rowed across the Atlantic. The museum started with 23 vessels in the 1960s. It aims to rescue types of boats which are going out of use, and now has one of the world's largest collections. Visitors can look at, touch and also climb aboard some of the exhibits. The museum buildings appeared in the television series *The Onedin Line*. Pleasant river and canal walks can be taken nearby. 1991 saw the opening of a new adventure play ship.
Open all year, daily 10-6 summer, 10-5 winter (Closed Xmas).
🅿 ▼ & *toilets for disabled shop*
Details not confirmed for 1992

Rougemont House Museum   EXETER

Map 03 SX99
Castle St
☎ (0392) 265858
The elegant Regency building was opened as a museum in 1986, and has rapidly become very popular. It houses an important collection of lace and a series of major temporary exhibitions. The gardens of the house are in the moat of Rougemont, Exeter's former Norman castle. A fine Norman gateway can still be seen.
Open all year, Mon-Sat 10-5.30.
✳ *£1.50 (ch, pen & students 75p). Family ticket £3.50.*
▼ ✗ *licensed shop* ✗

Royal Albert Memorial Museum   EXETER

Map 03 SX99
Queen St
☎ (0392) 265858
Founded in 1865, the museum is especially interesting for Exeter silver, regional archaeology and Devon paintings. Other displays include a traditional natural history display, a Victorian collection of shells, and beautiful African wood carvings.
Open all year, Tue-Sat 10-5.30.
Free.
shop ✗

St Nicholas' Priory   EXETER

Map 03 SX99
Mint Ln, off Fore St
☎ (0392) 265858
The Benedictine priory was founded in 1070, and its remains include unusual survivals such as the Norman undercroft, a Tudor room and a 15th-century kitchen. Some fine plaster decoration can be seen, and there are displays of pewter, furniture and wood carving.
Open all year, Tue-Sat 10-1 & 2-5.30. May be closed in winter.
Free.
✗

Underground Passages   EXETER

Map 03 SX99
Boots Arcade, High St
☎ (0392) 265858 & 265887
A unique medieval water system with an introductory exhibition. Not recommended unless fit and healthy – definitely not suitable for those inclined to claustrophobia. Flat shoes are essential. All tours are guided, and there is an introductory 10-minute videoplus exhibition.
Open Etr-Oct, daily, tours variable. Nov-Etr afternoons only.
✳ *£1.25 (ch, students & pen 75p).*
shop ✗

Farway Countryside Park   FARWAY

Map 03 SY19
(1.5m S on unclass rd AA signed on B3174)
☎ (040487) 224 & 367
A collection of traditional and modern breeds of farm animals can be seen in the park, which covers 108 acres of beautiful countryside with magnificent views over the Coly Valley. Attractions include pony and donkey cart rides and trekking, nature trails and a grass ski slope.
Open Good Fri-Oct, daily 10-6 (last admission 5pm).
✳ *£2 (ch £1, pen £1.50).*
🅿 *(charged)* ▼ & *toilets for disabled shop*

Hartland Quay Museum   HARTLAND

Map 03 SS22
Hartland Quay
☎ Morwenstow (028883) 353
The displays cover four centuries of shipwrecks on the coasts of Hartland, Welcombe, Clovelly and Morwenstow. Other exhibits include geology, natural history, trade and smuggling.
Open Etr wk then Whitsun-Sep, daily 11-5.
50p (ch 20p).
🅿 ✗

Allhallows Museum   HONITON

Map 03 ST10
High St (next to parish church of St Paul)
☎ (040487) 397
The museum has a wonderful display of Honiton lace, and there are lace demonstrations from June to August. The town's pottery and clock industries are also illustrated, and the museum is interesting for its setting in a chapel built in about 1200.
Open Etr Sat & Mon, then mid May-Sep, Mon-Sat 10-5; Oct 10-4.
60p (ch 20p)
& *shop* ✗

✳ An asterisk indicates that up-to-date information was not available at the time of our research – 1991 information has been published as an indication of what you may expect.

Chambercombe Manor   ILFRACOMBE

Map 03 SS54
(1m E off A399)
☎ (0271) 862624
This is one of England's oldest houses, circa 1066, although there are 16th- and 17th-century additions. It boasts a priest's room, private chapel (dating from about 1086) and inevitably, a ghost. The garden includes an ancient wishing well and waterfowl ponds among its many charms.
Open Good Fri-Sep, Mon-Fri 10.30-5, Sun 2-5 (Closed Sat)
£2.50 (ch £1.50, pen £2)
🅿 ▼ & ✗

Hele Mill   ILFRACOMBE

Map 03 SS54
Hele Bay (1m E)
☎ (0271) 863162
Dating back to 1525, this mill still produces wheatflakes and different grades of wholemeal flour. Inside, many interesting items of mill machinery are on view.
Open Etr Sun-Oct, Mon-Fri 10-5, Sun 2-5.
✳ *£1.60 (ch 5-14 80p)*
🅿 *shop* ✗

Ilfracombe Museum   ILFRACOMBE

Map 03 SS54
Runnymede Gardens, Wilder Rd
☎ (0271) 863541
Ilfracombe was an important trading port from the 14th to the 16th centuries and during the Napoleonic Wars became a popular resort. The history, archaeology, geology, natural history and maritime of the area are illustrated here, along with Victoriana, costumes, photographs and china. There is also a brass-rubbing centre. 1992 is the Diamond Jubilee of Ilfracombe Museum; various activities and events are planned – telephone for details.
Open all year, Etr-Oct 10-5.30 (Jul-Aug 7.30-10), Nov-Etr Mon-Sat 10-1.
✳ *50p (ch 10p, under 5 free, pen 30p). Disabled free.*
& *shop* ✗

Watermouth Castle — ILFRACOMBE

Map 03 SS54
(3m NE off A399)
☎ (0271) 863879
Overlooking a beautiful bay, this 19th-century castle is one of North Devon's finest. It caters enthusiastically for the public, offering such unique experiences as a mechanical musical demonstration and the Watermouth Waltzing Waters. Other attractions include a tube slide,

carousel and Gnomeland.
Open Good Fri & 31 Mar-4 Apr, Sun-Thu 11-4; 7 Apr-16 May & 23 Sep-24 Oct, Sun-Thu 2-4; 19 May-28 Jun & 2-22 Sep, Mon-Fri 11-4, Sun 1-4; 30 Jun-1 Sep Sun-Fri 10-4; 27 Oct-3 Nov Sun-Thu 1-4.
✳ *£4.50 (ch £3.50 & pen £4)*
🅿 ➽ ⅋ *(special wheelchair route) toilets for disabled shop* ✖

Killerton House & Garden — KILLERTON HOUSE & GARDEN

Map 03 SS90
☎ Exeter (0392) 881345

Although the 18th-century house is rather plain, it is not unattractive, especially with the sweeping lawns, shrub borders and planted beds that surround it. A majestic avenue of beech trees runs from the formal 18th and 19th-century gardens, up the hillside past

an arboretum of rhododendrons and conifers. The dining-room, drawing room and upstairs rooms of the house are used to display the Paulise de Bush collection of period costumes: these are shown in a series of room settings, furnished in different periods and ranging from the 18th century to the present day. The family chapel, built in 1840, lies at the eastern edge of the park.
Open: House, Apr-1 Nov, daily 11-5.30. Gardens all year, daily from 10.30. House & grounds £4.20. Grounds only £2.40.
🅿 ➽ ✖ *licensed* ⅋ *(wheelchairs & motorised buggy available) toilets for disabled shop garden centre* ✖ *(ex in park)*
(NT)

Cookworthy Museum of Rural Life — KINGSBRIDGE

Map 03 SX74
The Old Grammar School, 108 Fore St
☎ (0548) 853235
The 17th-century schoolrooms of this former grammar school are now the setting for another kind of education. Reconstructed room-sets of a Victorian kitchen, scullery and pharmacy, a costume room and extensive collection of local historical items are gathered to illustrate South Devon life. A walled

garden and farm gallery are also features of this museum, founded to commemorate William Cookworthy, 'father' of the English china clay industry.
Open all year, Apr-Sep Mon-Sat 10-5; Oct Mon-Fri 10.30-4. Nov-Mar by arrangement.
£1.20 (ch 60p, pen 80p).Family ticket £3.20. Party
⅋ *(Braille labels on selected exhibits) shop*

Coleton Fishacre Garden — KINGSWEAR

Map 03 SX85
Coleton (1.75m E on unclass roads)
☎ (080425) 466
The exotic figure of Lady Dorothy D'Oyley Carte created this equally exotic garden in a stream-fed valley between 1925 and 1940. A wide variety

of uncommon trees and rare shrubs were planted.
Open Mar, Sun only 2-5; Apr-1 Nov, Wed-Fri & Sun 10.30-5.30.
£2.40.
🅿 ✖
(NT)

Knightshayes Court — KNIGHTSHAYES COURT

Map 03 SS91
☎ Tiverton (0884) 254665
This ornate 19th-century house was designed by William Burges, the creator of the fantastic Gothic towers of Cardiff Castle. He was also partly responsible for the rich Gothic-style interior decoration, although an artist/designer called Crace installed the painted ceilings and stencilled wall decorations which were so popular at the time. The court is most noted for its gardens: both formal and woodland, and containing unique shrubs, azaleas, rhododendrons and carpets of spring bulbs. A 50-year-

old topiary of a fox and hounds can be seen, a survivor from one of the older gardens which have all but disappeared. Wheelchairs are available on loan and there are purpose-built toilets for wheelchair users.
Open Apr-1 Nov, House Sat-Thu & Good Fri 1.30-5.30. Garden daily 10.30-5.30. House & garden £4.60. Garden only £2.60.
🅿 ✖ *licensed* ⅋ *(wheelchairs available) toilets for disabled shop garden centre* ✖ *(ex in park)*
(NT)

Canonteign Falls & Country Park — LOWER ASHTON

Map 03 SX88
☎ Christow (0647) 52666
Lakes, wildfowl, a children's play area and miniature horses can be found in this beautiful country park. Covering 80 acres of ancient woodland, this unspoilt

valley is also the setting of the highest waterfall in England.
Open all year, Apr-Oct, daily 10-6; Nov-Mar Sun only 10-5.
🅿 ➽ ✖ *licensed shop*
Details not confirmed for 1992

Lydford Castle — LYDFORD

Map 03 SX58
The great square stone keep dates from 1195. It is not built on a mound, as it seems to be, but had earth piled against the walls. The upper floor was a Stannary Court, which administered local tin mines, and the lower floor was

used to imprison those who broke the forest and stannary laws.
Open all reasonable times.
Free.
🅿
(EH)

Lydford Gorge — LYDFORD

Map 03 SX58
(off A386)
☎ (082282) 441 & 320
The spectacular gorge has been formed by the River Lyd, which has cut into the rock and caused swirling boulders to scoop out potholes in the stream bed. This has created some dramatic features, notably the Devil's Cauldron close to

Lydford Bridge. At the end of the gorge is the 90ft-high White Lady Waterfall.
Open Apr-1 Nov, daily 10-5.30. (Nov-Mar, waterfall entrance only, daily 10.30-3).
£2.60
🅿 ➽ *shop*
(NT)

Lyn & Exmoor Museum — LYNTON

Map 03 SS74
Market St
One of the oldest buildings in Lynton, this delightful, 18th-century whitewashed cottage was saved from demolition to be run as a museum. The displays reflect the life and occupations of the local population and include

traditional arts, crafts and implements, a reconstruction of an Exmoor kitchen and a scale model of the old Lynton – Barnstaple narrow-gauge railway.
Open Apr-Oct, Mon-Fri 10-12.30 & 2-5. Sun 2-5.
✳ *70p (ch 30p)*
✖

Morwellham Quay — MORWELLHAM

Map 03 SX46
☎ Tavistock (0822) 832766 & 833808

When copper was discovered in the hills near Tavistock the town reached new heights of prosperity. Morwellham was the nearest point to which sea-going ships could navigate and became the greatest copper port in Queen Victoria's Empire. Once the mines were exhausted the port area disintegrated into unsightly

wasteland, until 1970 when a charitable trust was set up for its restoration. It is now a thriving and delightful open-air museum. Cottages have been faithfully renovated, complete with pig in the back yard, and visitors can meet a blacksmith, cooper, assayer, quay workers and coachmen, all dressed in period costume to help recreate history in this picturesque old port. There are also underground rides into a copper mine, heavy horse-drawn wagons, slide shows and other displays. Unspoilt countryside, riverside and woodland trails surround the museum.
Open all year (ex Xmas wk) 10-5.30 (4.30 in winter). Last admission 3.30 (2.30 in winter).
✳ *£5.60 (ch £3.95, pen & students £4.95). Party.*
🅿 ➽ ✖ *licensed shop*

Bradley Manor   NEWTON ABBOT

Map 03 SX87
(on A381)
☎ (0626) 54513
A National Trust property of 70 acres,
the 15th-century house and chapel are
surrounded by woodland. The river

Lemon and a millstream flow through
the estate.
*Open Apr-Sep, Wed only 2-5; also Thu, 2
& 9 Apr, 24 Sep & 1 Oct.*
�
(NT)

Museum of Dartmoor Life   OKEHAMPTON

Map 03 SX59
The Dartmoor Centre, West St
☎ (0837) 52295
An attractive three-storey watermill
houses this museum, and the Dartmoor
Tourist Information Centre and working
craft studios are to be found in an
adjoining courtyard. There is a cradle-to-
grave display of Victorian life, and
descriptive reconstructions of local tin
and copper mines are complemented by
a geological display of the moor. Local
history, prehistory, domestic life and
industry are explored, and a 1922
Bullnose Morris farm pickup with a

wooden back shares pride of place with
an ancient David Brown tractor in the
agricultural section. A shop sells crafts
and books and an exhibition gallery
changes its displays regularly. New
exhibition galleries feature a
reconstructed blacksmith's forge and
wheelwright's shop, a cider press and
railway relics.
*Open Mar-mid Nov, Mon-Sat, also Jun-
Sep, Sun 10-5. Other times by
arrangement.*
✱ *£1 (ch 5-16 & students 60p & pen
80p). Party 10+.*
P ☕ & *shop*

Okehampton Castle   OKEHAMPTON

Map 03 SX59
(0.5m S in Castle Lane)
☎ (0837) 52844
The chapel, keep and hall date from the
11th to 14th centuries and stand on the
northern fringe of Dartmoor National
Park.

*Open all year, Apr-Sep, daily 10-6; Oct-
Mar, Tue-Sun 10-4. (Closed 24-26 Dec &
1 Jan).*
*£1.50 (ch 75p, students, pen & UB40
£1.10).*
P
(EH)

Otterton Mill Centre   OTTERTON

Map 03 SY08
(off A376)
☎ Colaton Raleigh (0395) 68521
Mentioned in the Domesday Book, this
water-powered mill grinds wholemeal
flour used in the baking of bread, cakes
and pies sold on the premises. A gallery
houses a series of exhibitions through
the summer and autumn, and there are

studio workshops for stained glass,
blown glass and stone carving as well as
pottery, woodturning and printing.
There is a 'Millhands' co-operative craft
shop.
*Open all year, daily Summer 10.30-5.30;
Winter 11.30-dusk.*
✱ *£1.25 (ch 60p). Party.*
P ☕ & *toilets for disabled garden centre*

Cadhay   OTTERY ST MARY

Map 03 SY19
(near jct of A30 & B3167)
☎ (0404) 812432
A mile north-west of Ottery, over
Cadhay Bridge, this beautiful Tudor and
Georgian house is well worth a visit. It
was begun in 1550 and stands around a

courtyard.
*Open 24 & 25 May then each Tue, Wed
& Thu during Jul-Aug, also 30 & 31 Aug
2-6 (last admission 5.30).*
✱ *£2.50 (ch £1). Party 20+ by
appointment.*
P & ✖ *(ex in garden)*

✱ An asterisk indicates that up-to-date information was
not available at the time of our research – 1991
information has been published as an
indication of what you may expect.

Paignton & Dartmouth Steam Railway   PAIGNTON

Map 03 SX86
Queens Park Station, Torbay Rd
☎ (0803) 555872
Steam trains run for seven miles from
Paignton to Kingswear on the former
Great Western line, stopping at
Goodrington Sands, a popular beach,
and at Churston, connecting with the

ferry crossing to Dartmouth. The line
runs Santa Specials during December,
and dining specials are also available.
*Open Jun-Sep daily 9-5.30 & selected days
Oct-Nov & Mar-May.*
✱ *Dartmouth return £5.50 (ch £3.80).
Family ticket £17. Party 20+*
☕ & *shop (at Paignton & Kingswear)*

Paignton Zoo   PAIGNTON

Map 03 SX86
Totnes Rd (1m, on A385)
☎ (0803) 527936
This is one of England's largest zoos set
in 75 acres of botanical gardens. Animals
in the collection, which first opened
nearly 70 years ago, include lions, tigers,
elephants, giraffe, rhinoceros, zebra,
flamingos, crocodiles and ostrich. The
Zoo is very committed to conservation
and participates in captive breeding
programmes for endangered species. A
special feature is the lake with Gibbon
islands where five Gibbon families roam
freely. Children are well catered for with
an adventure playground, 'meet the

animals' area and the Ark family activity
centre – an indoor area with lots to do
and learn about wildlife on our planet.
Other features include a nature trail
which follows a route past disused lime
kilns, and a jungle express miniature
railway and keeper talks during the
summer.
*Open all year, daily 10-6.30 (5pm in
winter). Last admission 5pm (4pm in
winter). (Closed 25 Dec).*
✱ *£4.90 (ch 3-14 £3, pen £4.20). Party
15+. Reduction for disabled.*
P ☕ ✗ *licensed & (free wheelchair loan-
booking advisable) toilets for disabled shop
garden centre ✖ (kennels available)*

City Museum & Art Gallery   PLYMOUTH

Map 03 SX45
Drake Circus
☎ (0752) 264878
A fine building with varied local and
worldwide collections of natural history,
archaeology, fine and decorative art.
Special collections include the Cottonian
library of prints and Old Master
drawings, paintings from the Newlyn
School, prehistoric finds from Mount
Batten and minerals from Cornwall.
There is a lively programme of

contemporary art exhibitions, and from
March to May, there is an exhibition by
the RSPCA, while from July to
December, the two exhibitions are
'Joshua Reynolds Anniversary', and
'Plymouth in the Age of Discovery'.
*Open all year, Tue-Sat 10-5.30, Sun 2-5,
BH Mon 10-5. (Closed Good Fri & 25-26
Dec).*
Free.
& *toilets for disabled shop* ✖

Merchant's House Museum   PLYMOUTH

Map 03 SX45
33 St Andrews St
☎ (0752) 264878
A fine 16th-century house, modernised
in 1601 by William Parker, an
Elizabethan sea dog and Mayor of
Plymouth. Plymouth's history is told
here in lively displays through the rhyme

'Tinker, Tailor, Soldier, Sailor,
Apothecary, Thief'.
*Open all year Tue-Sat 10-5.30 (Closed
1-2), Sun 2-5, BH Mon 10-5 (Closed
25-26 Dec & Sun in winter).*
✱ *75p (ch 20p)*
& *shop* ✖

✖ The 'No Dogs' symbol does not normally apply
to guide dogs – these are permitted in
most establishments.

Plymouth Dome   PLYMOUTH

Map 03 SX45
The Hoe
☎ (0752) 603300 & 600608 (recorded
message)
This high-tech visitor centre takes you
on a journey through time, exploring the
sounds and smells of an Elizabethan
street, walking the gun-deck of a galleon,
sailing with the epic voyages from
Plymouth Sound, dodging the press
gang, strolling with film stars on an
ocean liner and witnessing the
devastation of the blitz. Use high-
resolution cameras to zoom in on ships
and shoreline, or access computers to
identify naval vessels. Examine satellite

weather pictures as they arrive from
space, keep up to date with shipping
movements and monitor the busy
harbour on radar. An excellent
introduction to Plymouth and a
colourful interpretation of the past.
*Open all year, daily, Etr-May 9-6; Jun-15
Sep 9-7.30pm; 15 Sep-Nov 9-6; Dec-Mar
9-5.30. (Closed 25 Dec).*
✱ *Jul-Sep £2.50 (ch £1.65 & pen £2); rest
of year £2.10 (ch £1.45 & pen £1.85).
Family ticket £7.10. Party.*
☕ & *(induction loop for hard of hearing,
wheelchairs available) toilets for disabled
shop* ✖

Prysten House   PLYMOUTH

Map 03 SX45
Finewell St
☎ (0752) 661414 (Mon-Fri 8.30-1.30)
Thought to have been erected as a town
house by Plymouth and London
merchant Thomas Yogge, who bought
the site in two lots in 1487 and 1498. It
is also believed to have been used as a
'priest's house' by the Augustinian
Order of preaching canons from
Plympton Priory. After the dissolution
of the monasteries in 1539 it fell into
secular use for such purposes as a wine

store, provisions merchants and a bacon
factory. Since 1923, it has been owned
by St Andrew's Church and the people
who give it life are in the main, ordinary
Plymouthians, interested in preserving
part of our national heritage.
Embroiderers are working on a 253ft-
long New World Tapestry – 28ft of it is
now on show.
*Open Apr-Oct, Mon-Sat 10-4. (Other times
by appointment).*
50p (ch & pen 25p). Party 15+.
✖

Royal Citadel   PLYMOUTH

Map 03 SX45
Probably designed by Sir Thomas Fitz,
this magnificent gateway was built in
1670 for the stronghold commenced by
Charles II in 1666. The remaining
buildings of the fort include the

Guardhouse, Governor's House and
Chapel.
Open any reasonable time.
Free.
(EH)

Smeaton Tower   PLYMOUTH

Map 03 SX45
The Promenade, Plymouth Hoe
☎ (0752) 66800 ext 4386
This former Eddystone Lighthouse was
re-erected here in 1882.

*Open end Apr-early Oct, 10.30-1hr before
sunset. Parties by appointment.*
✱ *60p (ch 30p).*
✖

Dartmoor Wildlife Park & Westcountry Falconry Centre   PLYMPTON

Map 03 SX55
(3m NE at Sparkwell, N of A38)
☎ Cornwood (075537) 209 & 343
The collection of over 100 species of
animals and birds is set in 30 acres of
Devonshire countryside. Special
attractions include a large group of big
cats, bears, wolves, seals, deer, waterfowl
and reptiles. You may touch, talk to and
learn about living animals in 'Close

Encounters of the Animal Kind' – an
indoor attraction giving first hand
experience of wild creatures. Falconry
displays are given (weather permitting)
and there are pony rides at weekends
and bank holidays.
Open daily, 10-dusk.
P ✗ *licensed & toilets for disabled shop*
Details not confirmed for 1992

Saltram House   PLYMPTON

Map 03 SX55
(2m W between A38 & A379)
☎ Plymouth (0752) 336546
Built on the site of a Tudor Mansion, this magnificent George II house still has its original contents. The collection of paintings was begun at the suggestion of Reynolds and includes many of his portraits. The saloon and dining room were designed by Robert Adam and have superb decorative plasterwork and period furniture. Set in beautiful surroundings with a shrub garden and 18th-century summer house, Saltram House has a lovely view of the Plym estuary. Wheelchairs are available on loan and there are purpose-built toilets for wheelchair users.
Open Apr-1 Nov, Sun-Thu; House 12.30-5.30. Garden 10.30-5.30. £4.80. Gardens only £2.
🅿 ⬤ ✗ *licensed* ♿ *(wheelchairs available) toilets for disabled shop* ✖ *(ex park) (NT)*

Powderham Castle   POWDERHAM

Map 03 SX98
(signposted off A379 Exeter/Dawlish road)
☎ Starcross (0626) 890243
Built between 1390 and 1420, this ancestral home of the Earls of Devon was damaged in the Civil War. Restored and altered in later times throughout fine furnishings and portraits are displayed. The house is set in beautiful rose gardens with views over the deer park to the Exe Estuary.
Open mid May-mid Sep, 2-5.30 (last admission 5pm). (Closed Fri & Sat).
✱ *£3.20 (ch 5-16 £1)*
🅿 ⬤ ♿ *shop* ✖

Overbecks Museum & Garden   SALCOMBE

Map 03 SX73
Sharpitor (1.5m SW)
☎ (054884) 2893
The garden at Overbecks is particularly stunning when the magnolias are in bloom; but its situation, on the most southerly tip of Devon, allows many tender and exotic plants to flourish; one of the most varied collections of trees, shrubs and flowering plants in the country is grown here. The Edwardian house displays toys, dolls, a natural history collection and a section on shipbuilding.
Open Apr-1 Nov, daily (ex Sat) 11-5.30. Garden all year, daily 10-8 or sunset if earlier.
Museum & gardens £3. Gardens only £2.
🅿 *(charged)* ⬤ *shop* ✖ *(ex in gardens)* ▨ *(NT)*

Sidmouth Museum   SIDMOUTH

Map 03 SY18
Church St
☎ (0395) 516139
An elegant Regency house next to the parish church, the museum contains an interesting collection of local prints, many mementoes of Sidmouth's heyday as a Victorian resort, a costume gallery and a good display of old lace.
Open Etr-Oct, Mon-Sat 10-12.30 & 2-4.30, Sun 2-4.30. Other times by appointment.
✱ *40p (ch 5-16 20p).*
shop

Vintage Toy & Train Museum   SIDMOUTH

Map 03 SY18
1st Floor, Fields Department Store, Market Place
☎ (0395) 515124 ext 34
A splendid display of toys, games and children's books, covering the 50 years from 1925 to 1975. The exhibits include the first and last Dinky Toy, Hornby '0' gauge trains and Minic clockwork vehicles, together with a selection of Britain's military and farm figures and Cadbury's free gift with cocoa – Cococubs. 1992 will see a special display of French Hornby Gauge '0' trains made in the Paris Meccano factory during the 1930s.
Open 14 Apr-Oct, Mon-Sat 10-5. (Closed BH).
£1 (ch 3-14 & pen 50p).
🅿 ⬤ *shop* ▨

Quince Honey Farm   SOUTH MOLTON

Map 03 SS72
(3.5m W on A361)
☎ (0769) 572401
This is the largest wild-bee farm in the world. Visitors can view the honey-bees, without disturbing them, in a specially designed building with glass booths and tunnels. Observation hives enable visitors to see into the centre of the colony and view larvae and newly-hatched bees in the cells of the comb. Even the queen may be seen at the very heart of the hive. The farm shop sells a wide range of honey, including the local heather honey, as well as pure beeswax candles and polish.
Open daily, mid Apr-Sep 9-6; Oct 9-5; Shop only Nov-Etr 9-5. (Closed 25-26 Dec & 1 Jan).
£2.90 (ch 5-16 £1.30, pen £2.20)
🅿 ⬤ *shop* ✖

South Molton Museum   SOUTH MOLTON

Map 03 SS72
Town Hall, The Square
☎ (0769) 572951
The museum is in part of the Guildhall, a Portland stone-fronted building erected in about 1743. The entrance is through an open arcaded frontage. In the museum are objects relating to local history such as old charters, weights and measures, old fire engines and a giant cider press. There are monthly art and craft displays.
Open Mar-Nov, Tue, Thu & Fri 10.30-1 & 2-4; Wed & Sat 10.30-12.30.
✱ *Free. Donations accepted.*
♿ *shop* ✖

Museum of Waterpower & Finch Foundry   STICKLEPATH

Map 03 SX69
☎ Okehampton (0837) 840046
Finch Foundry was, in the 19th century, a water-powered factory for making sickles, scythes, shovels and other hand tools. Although no longer in production, three waterwheels can still be seen driving huge hammers, shears, grindstone and other machinery. There is also a display of hand tools and a gallery devoted to water power. A series of craft days will be held in 1992, telephone for details.
Open Mar-mid Nov, Mon-Sat; Jun-Sep, Sun 10-5.
✱ *£1.50 (ch 50p, pen £1.20).*
🅿 ⬤ ♿ *shop*

Tiverton Castle   TIVERTON

Map 03 SS91
☎ (0884) 253200 & 071-727 4854
Dating from 1106, the castle dominates the River Exe. It was originally moated on three sides with the Exe as the fourth defence. One remaining circular Norman tower remains from the original four, and there is also a medieval gatehouse with walls 5ft thick. The castle was a Royalist stronghold during the Civil War but was taken by the Roundheads in 1645. It houses a fascinating clock collection in the tower, and one of the finest collections of Civil War armour and arms in the country. Visitors are encouraged to add their stitches in history to the New World tapestry. The 350th anniversary of the start of the English Civil War will be commemorated at the Castle this year..
Open 17 Apr-Sep, Sun-Thu 2.30-5.30. £2.50 (ch 7-16 £1.50, disabled half price).
🅿 ⬤ ♿ *shop*

Tiverton Museum   TIVERTON

Map 03 SS91
Saint Andrew St
☎ (0884) 256295
This large and comprehensive museum is housed in a restored 19th-century school. The numerous local exhibits include a Heathcote Lace Gallery featuring relics of the local lacemaking industry (started by John Heathcote). There is also an agricultural section with a collection of farm wagons and a complete smithy. Other large exhibits include two waterwheels and a railway gallery that houses a GWR 0-4-2T Locomotive No.1442, other railway relics and a display on the Grand Western Canal.
Open Mon-Sat 10.30-4.30. (Closed 21 Dec-29 Jan).
✱ *Admission charged.*
♿ *shop* ✖

Babbacombe Model Village   TORQUAY

Map 03 SX96
Hampton Av, Babbacombe
☎ (0803) 328669
Set in four acres of beautifully maintained, miniature landscaped garden, the village contains over 400 models and 1200ft of model railway. Authentic sound effects have been added, to create a whole new dimension. In summer, when the village is open until late, it is illuminated. Special 'Close Encounters' can be seen early and late season, featuring UFOs and a laser show.
Open all year, Etr-Sep, daily 9am-10pm; Oct 9-9pm; Nov-Etr 9am-dusk. (Closed 25 Dec).
£3.20 (ch £2)
🅿 *(charged)* ♿ *('touch & see' board for blind) toilets for disabled shop garden centre*

'Bygones'   TORQUAY

Map 03 SX96
Fore St, St Marychurch
☎ (0803) 326108
Step back in time in this life-size Victorian exhibition street including a forge, pub and period display rooms, housed in a former cinema. Exhibits include a large Hornby railway layout, illuminated fantasyland, railwayana and military exhibits. At Christmas the street is turned into a winter wonderland
Open all year, Jun-Sep 10am-10pm; Oct, Apr & May 10-5; Nov-Mar 10-1. (Last admission 1 hour before closing). (Closed 25 Dec).
£2.25 (ch 5-13 £1.25) (pen £1.95 out of season)
⬤ ♿ *shop* ✖

Kents Cavern Showcaves   TORQUAY

Map 03 SX96
The Caves, Wellswood (1.25m NE off B3199)
☎ (0803) 294059 & 215136
Recognised as one of the most important archaeological sites in Britain, these showcaves provide a set of unique experiences. This is not only a world of spectacular natural beauty, but also a priceless record of past times, where a multitude of secrets of mankind, animals and nature have become trapped and preserved over the last 500,000 years. One hundred and seventy years after the first excavations and with over 70,000 remains already unearthed, modern research is still discovering new clues to our past.
The showcaves are visited along well-lit paths and tours are accompanied by 'storytellers' who bring to life past scenes using props and the natural setting of the caves.
Open daily (ex 25 Dec). Apr-Jun & Sep-Oct 10-6; Jul & Aug 10-9 (6pm Sat); Nov-Mar 10-5. Last tour 45mins before closing time.
£2.90 (ch 5-15 £1.90 ch under 5 free). Party 20+.
🅿 ⬤ ♿ *shop* ✖

Torquay Museum   TORQUAY

Map 03 SX96
529 Babbacombe Rd
☎ (0803) 293975
The museum was purpose built in 1875 by the Torquay Natural History Society. The impressive natural history collection includes the remains of extinct animals from South Devon caves. There are pictorial archives, Victoriana and a new Archaeological Gallery.
Open all year, Mon-Fri (also Sat, Etr-Sep) 10-4.45; also Sun, Jul-Sep 1.45-4.45. (Closed Good Fri, Etr Sun, Xmas & New Year).
🅿 *shop* ✖ ▨
Details not confirmed for 1992

Torre Abbey   TORQUAY

Map 03 SX96
The Kings Dr
☎ (0803) 293593
Founded in 1196, the remains of the abbey include the entrance to the chapter house, a 14th-century gatehouse, the guest hall and the great barn. The present house, converted from part of the original abbey in the 17th and 18th centuries, has newly restored furnished period rooms, and serves as Torquay's art gallery. There is a Festival of Flowers on 11-14 Sep.
Open daily Apr, May & Oct, 10-5. (Last admission 4). Jun-Sep 10-6.(Last admission 5).
✱ *£2 (ch 15 & pen £1, under 8 free). Family ticket £4.50.*
⬤ ✖
See advertisement on page 65.

TORRE ABBEY, TORQUAY

The Kings Drive, Torquay TQ2 5JX. Tel: 0803 293593

Torbay's oldest and most historic building. Founded in 1196 as a monastery, it was converted for use as a private home following the dissolution of the monasteries by King Henry VIII in 1539. The home of the Cary family from 1662 until 1930. Art galleries, furnished period rooms, Cary family chapel, Agatha Christie Memorial Room, extensive gardens, ruins of original Abbey Church, and much, much more. Exhibitions including local artists are held in the upper gallery throughout the season and families who want a little more from their visit can take part in the Torre Abbey "Quest". Ask for details at the Reception Desk.

Open daily from April to October, from 10.00 am until 6.00 pm (last admission 5.00 pm)
Adults £2.00 – Children (8-15) and OAPs £1.00 – Under 8s free
Family Ticket (2 adults and up to 3 children) £4.50

Dartington Crystal — TORRINGTON, GREAT

Map 03 SS41
Linden Close
☎ Torrington (0805) 24233
Tours of the factory are conducted from the safety of viewing galleries that overlook the craftsmen. They can be seen carrying out the age-old techniques of glass manufacture and processing, and there are also studio glass-making demonstrations. The factory has a permanent exhibition tracing the history of glass and crystal over the past 300 years, including items from 1650 and a replica 18th-century glass cone. A video theatre adds a further dimension. A shop sells decanters, goblets and other items of glassware, at attractive prices.
Open all year. Tours & Glass Centre: Mon-Fri 9.30-4. Shop & Restaurant: Mon-Sat 9-5. All facilities (ex factory tours) open wknds in high season.
Full tour (inc Glass Centre) £1.95 (ch 6-16 80p, pen £1.60). Glass Centre only: 85p (ch 6-16 30p). Party 10+.
🅿 ☕ ✕ *licensed* ♿ *toilets for disabled shop* ⛌

RHS Garden Rosemoor — TORRINGTON, GREAT

Map 03 SS41
(1m SE of town on B3220)
☎ Torrington (0805) 24067
Started in 1959, the garden contains many rare plants. It is sheltered in a wooded valley and covers about eight acres. There are species and hybrid rhododendrons, shrub roses and a wide variety of ornamental trees and shrubs. A new 32-acre garden is being developed over the next ten years. It already contains two thousand roses of two hundred varieties, two large colour theme gardens, a herb garden and potager, an extensive herbaceous border, and stream and bog gardens.
Open: Gardens all year; Visitor centre Mar & Oct 10-5, Apr-Sep 10-6.
£2.25 (ch 50p). Party 20+.
🅿 ✕ *licensed* ♿ *(Herb garden for disabled) toilets for disabled shop garden centre* ⛌

Bowden House & The British Photographic Museum — TOTNES

Map 03 SX86
☎ (0803) 863664
At Bowden House visitors are welcomed by guides in 1740 Georgian dress. Parts of the house date back as far as the 12th century, but most of it was built in 1510 by John Giles, supposedly the wealthiest man in Devon. In 1704 the Queen Anne façade was added. The Grand Hall is decorated in neo-Classical Baroque style, and the Great Hall is adorned with 18th-and 19th-century weaponry. The rooms have been beautifully restored.
The museum has a large collection of vintage cameras, a replica Victorian studio, Edwardian darkroom and some shops. Other attractions are the Les Allen movie pioneer display and a changing monthly exhibition of old photographs. The house is set in twelve acres of attractive grounds.
Open – 19 Apr-1 Oct, from noon. Bowden House Tue-Thu & BH Sun & Mon. Museum open Tue-Thu.
Museum £2.25. House Tour £2.75. Combined Ticket £4. (Reductions for children).
🅿 ✕ *licensed* ♿ *(museum only suitable) toilets for disabled shop* ⛌

The Guildhall — TOTNES

Map 03 SX86
off High St
☎ (0803) 862147
Originally the refectory, kitchens, brewery and bakery for the Benedictine Priory of Totnes (1088-1536), the building was established as the Guildhall in 1553 during the reign of Henry VIII. A magistrates court and a prison opened in 1624, the same year of the refurbishment of the council chamber which is still used today. There are also relics of the Civil War, and lists of the manors since 1359.
Open Etr-Sep, Mon-Fri 10-1 & 2-5; Oct-Etr by appointment.
✱ *50p (ch 25p).*

Totnes Castle — TOTNES

Map 03 SX86
☎ (0803) 864406
A classic example of the Norman motte-and-bailey castle, Totnes dates from the 11th century. The circular shell-keep is protected by a curtain wall erected in the 13th century and reconstructed in the 14th. There are marvellous views from the walls of the keep across the town to the Dart valley.
Open all year, Apr-Sep, daily 10-6; Oct-Mar, Tue-Sun 10-4. (Closed 24-26 Dec & 1 Jan).
£1.20 (ch 60p, pen, students & UB40 90p)
⛌
(EH)

Totnes Motor Museum — TOTNES

Map 03 SX86
Steamer Quay
☎ (0803) 862777
This is a private collection of vintage, sports and racing cars and motorcycles, most of which are currently raced. There are also engines and other paraphernalia, and the whole collection covers a 70-year span.
Open Etr-Oct, daily 10-5.30.
£2.25 (ch £1.50 & pen £1.75). Family ticket £6.50. 🅿 ♿ *shop*

Totnes Museum — TOTNES

Map 03 SX86
70 Fore St
☎ (0803) 863821
This four-storey, partly timbered house, complete with connecting gallery to an additional kitchen/buttery block, dates from about 1575. It has a cobbled courtyard, elaborate plaster ceilings and 16th-century fireplaces. It is now a museum of furniture, domestic objects, toys, dolls, costumes and archaeology. One room is dedicated to Charles Babbage who invented the ancestor of modern computers.
Open Etr-30 Oct, Mon-Fri & BHs 10.30-1 & 2-5.
75p (ch 5-16 25p).
shop ⛌ *(ex small dogs)*

Coldharbour Mill Working Wool Museum — UFFCULME

Map 03 ST01
Coldharbour Mill (off B3181)
☎ Craddock (0884) 840960
Originally an important centre for the wool trade, the Culme Valley now has only one working mill. This was built as a grist mill in 1753, but was converted to a wool mill in 1797 by a Somerset woollen manufacturer, Thomas Fox. He added a large red-brick and stone factory in which serge, flannel and worsted yarn was produced for nearly 200 years. The mill closed in 1981 but was reopened as a Working Wool Museum. Visitors can watch every stage in the process of producing woollen cloth and yarn on the two working levels of the mill. There are also displays of interesting machinery and artefacts connected with the wool trade, plus a weaver's cottage, and dye and carpenters' workshops. Visitors can see the 18ft diameter water wheel awaiting restoration, and the 300HP Pollit and Wigzell steam engine which powered the Mill until its closure. Knitting, yarn and made-up garments can be bought in the mill shop. There are 'Steam-ups' planned for 1992, when the Pollit and Wigzell steam engine will be in steam; please ring for details.
Open Etr-Oct, daily 11-5. Winter Mon-Fri (telephone for times). Last tour 4pm.
£2.85 (ch 5-16 £1.60). Family ticket £7.50. Party 20+.
🅿 ☕ ✕ *licensed* ♿ *shop* ⛌

The National Shire Horse Centre — YEALMPTON

Map 03 SX55
(On A379, Plymouth to Kingsbridge)
☎ Plymouth (0752) 880268 & 880806 (recorded info)

Some fine old farm buildings are at the hub of this 60-acre farm with over 40 Shire horses. With the revival of interest in the gentle giants, the farm has become the National Shire Horse Centre. Visitors are able to see not only the heavy horses and their foals, but a variety of other creatures as well. A butterfly house permits a range of exotic butterflies to be seen in their real habitat. A craft centre, showing the skills of the saddler and the falconer, among others, is in the barns. Daily displays of falconry (at 1pm and 3.30pm) and parades of the Shire horses (at 11.30, 2.30 and 4.15) are given throughout the year. Children are well catered for with a pets area, cart rides and an adventure playground with free-fall slide. Special events include Bank Holiday Specials, a Western Weekend (3rd wknd Jul), a Steam and Vintage Rally (2nd wknd Aug), and a Classic Car Show (1st Sunday in Sep).
Open all year, daily 10-5. (Closed 24-26 Dec).
✱ *£4.40 (ch £2.99, pen £3.95)*
🅿 ☕ ✕ *licensed* ♿ *toilets for disabled shop garden centre*

Paperweight Centre — YELVERTON

Map 03 SX56
4 Buckland Ter, Leg O'Mutton
☎ (0822) 854250
This unusual centre is the home of the Broughton Collection – a glittering display of paperweights of all sizes and designs. The centre also has an extensive range of modern glass paperweights for sale. Prices range from a few pounds to over £500. There is also a series of oil and watercolour paintings by talented local artists, a collection of which are scenes of Dartmoor.
Open all year, 30 Mar-Oct, Mon-Sat 10-5. Also Sun end May-mid Sep; Nov-Etr, Wed 1-5 & Sat 10-5; 1-24 Dec, Mon-Sat 10-5. Other times by appointment.
Free.
♿ *(ramp on request) shop*

Yelverton Paperweight Centre
YELVERTON PAPERWEIGHT CENTRE
West Devon
An impressive display of over 800 glass paperweights.
Open: 2 weeks before Easter to end October, Mon-Sat 10am-5pm, Sundays end May-Mid Sept 10am-5pm. All winter Wed 1pm-5pm, Sat 10am-5pm. Dec 1-24 Mon-Sat 10am-5pm. ADMISSION FREE.
Leg O'Mutton, Yelverton, Devon PL20 6AD
Telephone: Yelverton 0822 854250
Signposted on A386 at Yelverton

DORSET

Abbotsbury Sub Tropical Gardens　　　　　　ABBOTSBURY

Map 03 SY58
Beach Rd (on B3157)
☎ (0305) 871387
Sheltered by a curtain of trees, the twenty acre Sub Tropical Gardens have a Mediterranean-type climate that allows rare and tender plants to flourish. The gardens were started in 1760, and have a

walled garden in the centre which is a mass of azaleas, camellias and rhododendrons.
Open mid Mar-mid Oct, daily 10-6. Open in winter months at reduced rate.
P ♿ & (wheelchair for hire) toilets for disabled shop garden centre
Details not confirmed for 1992

Abbotsbury Swannery　　　　　　　　　　　　ABBOTSBURY

Map 03 SY58
New Barn Rd
☎ Weymouth (0305) 871242 & 871684
Monks founded the swannery in the 14th century, and it is still a breeding ground for the only managed colonial herd of mute swans. The swans can be seen safely at close quarters, and the site is also home or stopping point for many wild birds. Reeds are harvested for thatching, and there is a 17th-century duck decoy. Mid-July this year sees the

biennial swan round-up. A spectacular event where around eight hundred swans are herded toward the head of Fleet Lagoon. This enables staff to give each bird a general health check and repair or renew any damaged rings.
Open Apr-Oct, daily 9.30-4.30. Winter visiting for waterfowl is available, phone for details.
P & (wheelchair loan, herb garden for blind) toilets for disabled ✖
Details not confirmed for 1992

Athelhampton House　　　　　　　　　　　ATHELHAMPTON

Map 03 SY79
(on A35 1m E of Puddletown)
☎ Puddletown (0305) 848363
The house is built on the legendary site of King Athelstan's palace, and dates from the 15th century. A family home for 500 years, it is one of the finest medieval houses in southern England. The baronial great hall is worth seeing just for its roof structure. Around the

house are 10 acres of formal and landscaped gardens, with river gardens and a 15th-century dovecote. Craft fairs will be held here over the Easter and August Bank Holidays.
Open Etr-Oct, Wed, Thu, Sun, BH & also Tue May-Sep & Mon Aug, 2-6.
✱ *House & Garden £3.20. Garden only £1.60.*
P ♿ ✗ *licensed* & *shop* ✖

✖ **The 'No Dogs' symbol does not normally apply to guide dogs – these are permitted in most establishments.**

Mapperton Gardens　　　　　　　　　　　　BEAMINSTER

Map 03 ST40
(2m SE off A356 & B3163)
☎ (0308) 862645
Set around a manor house dating back to the 16th century are several acres of terraced hillside gardens, with specimen trees and shrubs, and formal borders. There are also fountains, grottoes, stone fishponds and an orangery, and the

garden offers good views and walks. The annual Courtyard Fair will be held on 12th September, with craft demonstrations, house tours and local displays.
Open Mar-Oct, daily 2-6.
Gardens £2.50 (ch 5-18 £1.50, under 5 free).
P & ✖

Parnham　　　　　　　　　　　　　　　　　BEAMINSTER

Map 03 ST40
(1m S on A3066)
☎ Bridport (0308) 862204
The house is a fine Tudor mansion, but it is most famous as the home of John Makepeace and his furniture-making workshop. The workshop is open to visitors, and complete pieces are shown in the house. There are also continuous

exhibitions by living designers and craftsmen. Surrounding the house are 14 acres of restored gardens, formal terraces and woodlands.
Open Etr-Oct Sun, Wed & BHs 10-5.
£3 (ch £1.50, under 10 free)
P ♿ ✗ *licensed* & *toilets for disabled shop* ✖ *(ex in grounds)*

Royal Signals Museum　　　　　　　　　BLANDFORD FORUM

Map 03 ST80
Blandford Camp
☎ Blandford (0258) 482248
The history of army radio and line communications is illustrated with paintings, uniforms, medals and badges,

vehicles and signalling equipment.
Open all year, Mon-Fri 10-5; Jun-Sep, Sat, Sun & BH 10-4. (Closed 10 days over Xmas).
Free.
P & *shop* ✖

Russell-Cotes Art Gallery & Museum　　　　BOURNEMOUTH

Map 03 SZ09
East Cliff
☎ (0202) 551009
The museum was built in 1894 as East Cliff Hall. Together with a new extension called The Display Space, it houses collections of 17th to 20th century paintings, watercolours, sculpture, miniatures, ceramics and furniture. There is a large ethnographic

collection and one section of the museum is devoted to the actor Sir Henry Irving. Temporary exhibitions are regularly displayed on a wide variety of subjects.
Open all year, Mon-Sat 10-5. (Closed Good Fri & 25-26 Dec).
£1 (ch, students, UB40's & pen 50p). Free on Sat.
& *shop* ✖

The Shelley Rooms　　　　　　　　　　　　BOURNEMOUTH

Map 03 SZ09
Beechwood Av, Boscombe
☎ (0202) 303571
The Shelley Rooms contain a small museum display commemorating the life and work of Percy Byshe Shelley. Also

on show is a collection of romantic literature and reference books.
Open all year Mon-Sat 2-5. (Closed BH's, Good Fri & 25 Dec).
P & ✖

Terracotta Warriors　　　　　　　　　　　BOURNEMOUTH

Map 03 SZ09
Old Christchurch Ln
☎ (0202) 293544
The Terracotta Warriors experience transports you back to the third century BC to see the First Emperor, Quin Shi Huang in life and death. Descend to a dramatic life-size reconstruction of part

of the Terracotta Army excavation, and finally see the especially-recreated Terracotta Warriors displayed in all their glory.
Open all year, daily 9.30-5.30 (9pm Jul-Aug). (Closed 24-26 Dec).
✱ *£2.85 (ch £1.70 & pen £2.35).*
shop ✖

Clouds Hill　　　　　　　　　　　　　　BOVINGTON CAMP

Map 03 SY88
(4m SW of Bere Regis)
T E Lawrence ('Lawrence of Arabia') bought this cottage in 1925 when he was a private in the Tank Corps at Bovington. He would escape here to play records and entertain friends to feasts of baked beans and China tea. Lawrence's sleeping bag, marked

'Meum', can be seen, together with his furniture and other memorabilia. Three rooms only are on show.
Open Apr-1 Nov, Wed-Fri, Sun & BH Mon 2-5; 8 Nov-Mar Sun 1-4 or dusk if earlier.
£2.20. No photography.
✖ 🚗
(NT)

The Tank Museum　　　　　　　　　　　BOVINGTON CAMP
(Royal Armoured Corps & Royal Tank Regiment)

Map 03 SY88
(off A352)
☎ Bindon Abbey (0929) 403463 & 403329
You can climb inside some of the exhibits at Bovington Camp as well as look at them. There are over 250 examples of wheeled and tracked armoured fighting vehicles from 17 different countries, dating from 1915

onwards and including a cut-away Centurion tank. There are also separate displays of armaments, uniforms, medals, guns and other equipment. Videos and working models can be seen, and four new exhibition halls cover the development of the tank. Special events include: Military Model and Wargamers Fair (23-25 May), Tank Militaria and
continued . . .

Auto Jumble (13 & 14 Jun), and Military Day/Battle Day (26 July).
Open all year, daily 10-5. Last admission 4.30. (Closed 10 days over Xmas).
* *£4 (ch & pen £2). Family ticket £8. Party 10+. Servicemen free.*
P X *licensed* ♿ *(wheelchair available) toilets for disabled shop* ✗

Bridport Museum — BRIDPORT

Map 03 SY49
South St
☎ (0308) 22116
Housed in a Tudor building, this local history museum tells the story of Bridport and its surroundings. There is a variety of displays, including natural history, agriculture, costume and the history of the town, also an extensive local history reference centre. Special event for 1992: Apr, the opening of the Harbour Museum in West Bay (1.5 miles south of Bridport) covering the history of the harbour and the rope and net-making industry..
Open all year, Etr-Oct, Mon-Sat 10-4.30, Sun 2-4.30; Nov-Etr, Wed & Sat 10-4.30, Sun 2-4.30.
70p (ch 35p).
♿ *shop* ✗

Brownsea Island — BROWNSEA ISLAND

Map 03 SZ08
(located in Poole Harbour)
☎ Canford Cliffs (0202) 707744
Although it is popular and easy to reach from Poole, Brownsea still offers peace, seclusion and a sense of timelessness. Visitors can wander along woodland paths, lounge on beautiful beaches, admire the fine views of Corfe Castle and the Dorset coast, or join a guided tour of the 250-acre nature reserve managed by the Dorset Naturalists' Trust. The island is perhaps most famous, however, as the site of the first scout camp, held by Lord Baden- Powell in 1907. Scouts and Guides are still the only people allowed to stay here overnight.
The lack of development on the island is due to its last private owner, Mrs Bonham Christie. She kept it as a kind of huge garden for animals, birds and flowers, and let peacocks roam free. Their descendants still thrive here, as do native red squirrels, and sika deer, introduced in 1896. A less welcome newcomer is the destructive mink. The island is also famous for its dragonflies, moths and butterflies, but most of all for its birds. The brackish lagoon supports a colony of Sandwich and common terns, with numerous waders in autumn and spring, and ducks in winter. There is also a heronry, one of Britain's largest.
Open Apr-11 Oct, daily 10-8 or dusk if earlier; check for time of last boat.
£1.90 (ch £1). Family ticket £5. (Apr, May, Jun & Sep). Party 15+.
☕ ♿ *toilets for disabled shop* ✗
(NT)

This is just one of many guidebooks published by the AA.
The full range is available at any AA shop or good bookshop.

Compton Acres Gardens — CANFORD CLIFFS

Map 03 SZ08
Canford Cliffs Rd (on B3065)
☎ (0202) 700778

The nine and a half acres of Compton Acres incorporate Japanese, Roman and Italian gardens, rock and water gardens, and heather gardens. There are fine views over Poole Harbour and the Purbeck Hills.
Open Mar-Oct, daily 10.30-6.30.
£3.30 (ch £1, student & pen £2.40). Party.
P ☕ ♿ *toilets for disabled shop garden centre* ✗

Chettle House — CHETTLE

Map 03 ST91
(6m NE of Blandford Forum off A354)
☎ Tarrant Hinton (025889) 209
This small country house was designed by Thomas Archer, and is praised as a fine example of the English Baroque. Around the house there are beautifully laid-out gardens. There is a vineyard, and a gallery where landscapes and wildlife paintings by leading artists are displayed. There is a craft fair held in May (23-25), and an exhibition of the work of David Shepherd in July (25-26).
Open 17 Apr-11 Oct, daily 11-5. (Closed Tue).
£1.50
P ♿ ✗

Christchurch Castle & Norman House — CHRISTCHURCH

Map 03 SZ19
All that remains of the castle buildings is a ruined keep and a Norman house, which was probably where the castle constable lived. The house is unusually well preserved, and still has its original windows and tall chimney. The keep is more dilapidated, but parts of the thick walls can be seen.
Open any reasonable time.
Free.
(EH)

Red House Museum & Gardens — CHRISTCHURCH

Map 03 SZ19
Quay Rd
☎ (0202) 482860
Local history, archaeology, natural history, Victoriana, dolls and costumes are displayed in this Georgian house. New displays tell the story of early human settlement from the Old Stone Age to the Normans, and there is also an exhibition of fashionable dress from 1865-1914. Temporary exhibitions are shown, and there are gardens with a woodland walk and herb garden.
Open all year, Tue-Sat 10-5, Sun 2-5. (Closed Mon ex BH).
* *75p (ch & pen 50p).*
♿ *shop* ✗

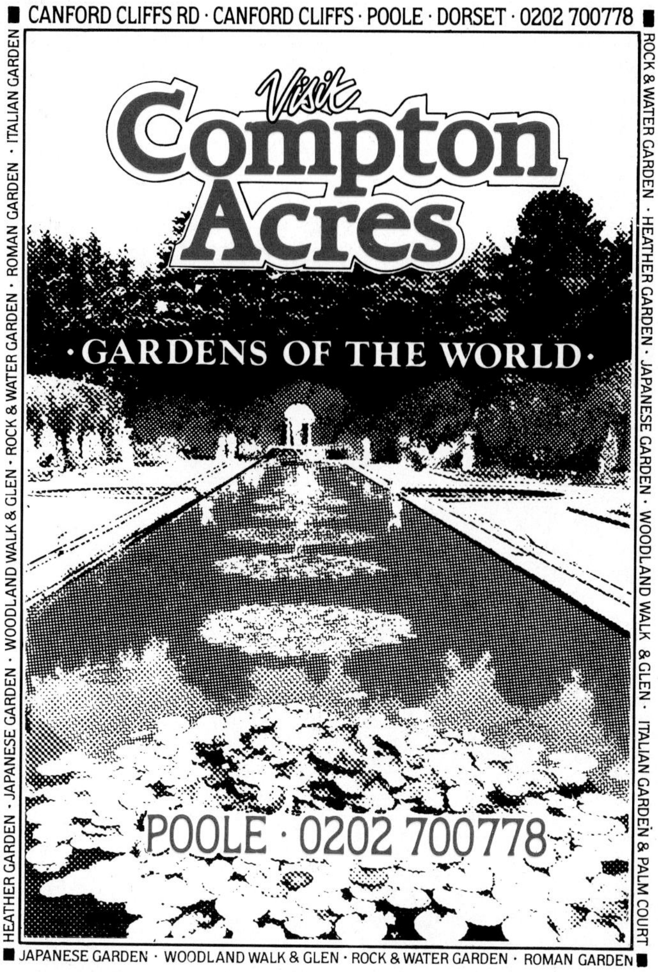

Corfe Castle — CORFE CASTLE

Map 03 SY98
☎ (0929) 480921
The castle was first built in Norman times, and was added to by King John. It was defended during the Civil War by Lady Bankes, who surrendered after a stout resistance. Parliament ordered the demolition of the castle, and today it is one of the most impressive ruins in England.
Open 9 Feb-Oct, daily 10-5.30 or dusk if earlier; Nov-Feb wknds only 12-3.30.
£2.50 (ch £1.30). Party 15+ by arrangement.
☕ X *licensed shop*
(NT)

Corfe Castle Museum — CORFE CASTLE

Map 03 SY98
West St
☎ Corfe (0929) 480415
The tiny, rectangular building was partly rebuilt in brick after a fire in 1680. It has old village relics and dinosaur footprints 130 million years old. A council chamber on the first floor is reached by a staircase at one end. The Ancient Order of Marblers meets here each Shrove Tuesday.
Open all year, May-Sep, daily 9-7; Oct-Apr 10-4 (limited opening phone for details).
Free.
♿ ✗

Cranborne Manor Private Gardens & Garden Centre — CRANBORNE

Map 03 SU01
☎ (07254) 248
The 17th-century gardens are privately owned and include a Jacobean Mount garden and herb garden. The river garden is particularly beautiful in the spring, with flowering cherries, daffodils and tulips. There are fine avenues of beech and lime and a magnificent yew hedge.
Garden Centre all year, Tue-Sat 9-5, (Sun 2-5. Mar-Dec). Manor Gardens Apr-Sep, Wed only 9-5.
P ☕ ♿ *shop garden centre* ✗
Details not confirmed for 1992

For an explanation of the symbols and abbreviations, see page 2.

Dinosaur Museum — DORCHESTER

Map 03 SY69
Icen Way
☎ (0305) 269880
Britain's only museum devoted to dinosaurs has an appealing mixture of fossils, skeletons, life-size reconstructions and interactive displays such as the 'feelies'. There are audio-visual presentations, and the idea is to provide an all-round family attraction with new displays each year.
Open all year, daily 9.30-5.30. (Closed 24-26 Dec).
* *£2.35 (ch £1.70, pen £2.05).*
♿ *shop*

Dorset County Museum   DORCHESTER

Map 03 SY69
High West St
☎ (0305) 262735
A visit to the museum is a must for anyone interested in the Dorset area and its fascinating archaeology. Displays cover prehistoric and Roman times, including sites such as Maiden Castle. There are also sections on the Dorset poet William Barnes, and on the poet and novelist Thomas Hardy, with a reconstruction of his study. Geology, natural history and rural crafts are also

explored in the museum which has twice won the Museum of the Year Award. Various exhibitions are planned for 1992, including The Contemporary Work of Art Teachers in the County (1 March – 3 April), Stained Glass by Henry Haig (23 May – 4 July), and The Building Stones of Dorset (mid-July – mid-Sep).
Open daily 10-5. (Closed Sun, Good Fri, 24-26 Dec & 1 Jan).
£2 (ch & pen £1, ch 5 free).
  shop

Dorset Military Museum   DORCHESTER

Map 03 SY69
The Keep, Bridport Rd
☎ (0305) 264066
Nearly 300 years of military history are covered, with displays on the Dorset Regiment, Dorset Militia and Volunteers, the Queen's Own Dorset

Yeomanry, and Devonshire and Dorset Regiment (from 1958).
Open all year, Mon-Sat 9-1 & 2-5, (Oct-Jun Sat 10-1).
£1 (ch & pen 50p).
P shop ✶

Hardy's Cottage   DORCHESTER

Map 03 SY69
Higher Bockhampton (3m E off A35)
☎ (0305) 262366
Thomas Hardy was born in this thatched house in 1840. It was built by his great-grandfather and has not changed much in appearance since. The

inside can only be seen by appointment with the tenant.
Open Apr-1 Nov, daily (ex Thu) 11-6 or dusk if earlier.
£2.30. Interior by appointment.
P & ✶
(NT)

Maiden Castle   DORCHESTER

Map 03 SY69
(1m SW)

The Iron Age fort of Maiden Castle ranks among the finest in Britain. It covers 47 acres, and has daunting earthworks which must once have been even bigger, with a complicated defensive system around the entrances. One of the main purposes of such castles

may have been to protect grain from marauding bands, and the need for such protection seems to have grown during the Iron Age. The first fort was built in around 700BC on the site of an earlier Neolithic camp, and had just a single rampart. By the time it was completed, probably around 100BC, it embraced the whole plateau and had outer earthworks as well. It was excavated in the 1930s by Sir Mortimer Wheeler, who found a cemetery of defenders killed when the castle was attacked and then taken by Roman troops in AD43. There are good views.
Open any reasonable time.
Free.
P
(EH)

Tutankhamun Exhibition   DORCHESTER

Map 03 SY69
High West St
☎ (0305) 269571
The exhibition recreates the excitement of one of the world's greatest discoveries of ancient treasure using sight, sound and smell. A reconstruction of the tomb

and facsimiles of its contents are displayed.
Open all year, daily 9.30-5.30. (Closed 24-26 Dec).
✶ *£2.85 (ch £1.70, pen £2.35).*
& shop ✶

✶ An asterisk indicates that up-to-date information was not available at the time of our research – 1991 information has been published as an indication of what you may expect.

Minterne Gardens   MINTERNE MAGNA

Map 03 ST60
(2m N of Cerne Abbas on A352)
☎ Cerne Abbas (0300) 341370
Lakes, cascades, streams and many fine and rare trees will be found in these lovely landscaped gardens. The 18th-

century design is a superb setting for the spring shows of rhododendrons, azaleas and spring bulbs.
Open Apr-Oct, daily 10-7.
£2 (accompanied ch free).
P

Great Poole Model Railway   POOLE

Map 03 SZ09
Henning's Wharf, The Quay
☎ (0202) 687240
A '00' gauge scenic layout covers more than 1000 sq ft of this model museum. 'Life in Space' and 'Smugglers and Pirates' are two of the displays on show.

Open all year daily Apr-May 9.30-5.30, Jun-Sep from 9.30, Oct-Nov 10-5, Dec-Mar 10.30-5, later at wknd. (Closed 25 Dec).
£2.25 (ch £1.25, pen £1.95). Family ticket £6.
  & shop

Guildhall Museum   POOLE

Map 03 SZ09
Market St
☎ (0202) 683138
Set in an impressive Georgian building, once the meeting place of the local council and also a court room, the musum displays facets of Poole's

fascinating history.
Open all year, Mon-Sat 10-5, Sun 2-5. (Closed Good Fri, 25-26 Dec & 1 Jan).
60p (ch 30p). Combined ticket to all 3 museums £3.55 (ch £1.80).
shop ✶

Poole Pottery   POOLE

Map 03 SZ09
The Quay
☎ (0202) 668681
Founded in 1873, this well-known establishment has been producing its distinctive Poole Pottery since 1921. There is also a display of past and

present pottery manufacture. An extensive Craft Centre is open Mar-Dec.
Open all year, Mon-Sat, 10-5. (Closed Xmas).
Free.
  shop ✶

Scaplen's Court   POOLE

Map 03 SZ09
High St
☎ (0202) 683138
This delightful medieval Merchant House is the setting for the continuing 'Poole Story'. Here the subject of the exhibition is the domestic life of the people of the town. On certain days the kitchen comes alive as the fire is lit in the cooking range and food is prepared

as in days gone by. There are also fine examples of Georgian furnishings, an Explorer's Room, displays of children's toys and examples of fine needlework.
Open all year, Mon-Sat 10-1 & 2-5, Sun 2-5. (Closed Good Fri, 25-26 Dec & 1 Jan).
60p (ch 30p). Combined ticket to all 3 museums £3.55 (ch £1.80).
shop ✶

Waterfront Museum   POOLE

Map 03 SZ09
4 High St, The Quay
☎ (0202) 683138
Waterfront marks the beginning of 'The Poole Story'. Housed in the medieval Town Cellars and the 18th century Oakley's Mill, it offers visitors a fascinating insight into the history of the town and port of Poole. Exhibits include The Romans Invade, Smugglers and Pirates, and the Golden Age of Sail. Visitors can step back in time with a walk along Oakley's Row, a Victorian

street scene complete with Pharmacy and Old Curiosity Shop. The Scout Movement began on Brownsea Island in Poole Harbour and its history is celebrated here in a special gallery.
Open all year, Mon-Sat, 10-5 & Sun 2-5. (Closed Good Fri, 25-26 Dec & 1 Jan).
£2.95 (ch £1.50, pen £2.25). Family ticket £7.25. Combined ticket to all 3 museums £3.55 (ch £1.80, pen £2.85).
& *(ex Town Cellars) toilets for disabled shop*
✶

For an explanation of the symbols and abbreviations, see page 2.

Portland Castle   PORTLAND

Map 03 SY67
Castle Town
☎ (0305) 820539
Erected by Henry VIII and added to in the 17th and 18th centuries, Portland Castle defended the southernmost coast

of Wessex.
Open Apr-Sep, daily 10-6.
£1.10 (ch 55p, students, pen & UB40 85p).
P & ✶
(EH)

Portland Museum   PORTLAND

Map 03 SY67
217 Wakeham
☎ (0305) 821804
Avice's cottage in Thomas Hardy's book 'The Well-Beloved', this building is now a museum of local and historical interest, with varied displays such as domestic bygones and maritime relics. Regular temporary exhibitions are held, including a shipwreck and smuggling exhibition. A

new gallery displays Portland history from the Stone Age to the 19th century.
Open all year, Etr-Sep, daily 10.30-1 & 1.30-5.45 (9 on Fri). Oct-Etr, Tue-Sun 10.30-1 & 1.30-4.30.
✶ *£1 (ch, students & UB40's free, pen 50p).*
& *(talking tapes for blind & partially sighted) shop*

Purse Caundle Manor   PURSE CAUNDLE

Map 03 ST61
(off A30)
☎ Milborne Port (0963) 250400
This excellent example of a medieval manor has a great hall, minstrels' gallery, chamber, bedchambers and gardens. It is

still a family home, a fact which adds to its charm.
Open Etr Mon-Sep, Thu, Sun & BH Mon 2-5. Other times by appointment.
£1.75 (ch 50p).
P & ✶

Abbey Ruins & Museum   SHAFTESBURY

Map 03 ST82
Park Walk
☎ (0747) 52910
The abbey at Shaftesbury was part of a nunnery founded by King Alfred in 888. It became one of the wealthiest in the country but was destroyed during the Dissolution in 1539. The excavated ruins show the foundations of the abbey. A museum on the site displays carved

stones, decorated floor tiles and other artefacts found during the excavations. A guided trail around the ruins can be followed using a numbered leaflet. An attractive recent addition is the Anglo/Saxon herb garden.
Open Apr-Oct daily, 10-5.30.
✶ *75p (ch 25p, pen & student 50p).*
Parties
& shop

Local History Museum   SHAFTESBURY

Map 03 ST82
Gold Hill
☎ (0747) 52157
The museum is situated at the top of a
steep, quaint hill with a cobbled
roadway and 18th-century cottages.
Inside are exhibits of needlework, toys,
agricultural and domestic items, fans,
pottery and finds from local excavations.
There is also an interesting fire engine of
1744.
*Open Etr-Sep, daily 11-5, Sun 2.30-5
(other times by appointment).*
50p (ch 10p)
& garden centre ✖

Sherborne Castle   SHERBORNE

Map 03 ST61
☎ (0935) 813182
This 16th-century house, built by Sir
Walter Raleigh, is the 'new' castle and
has been the home of the Digby family
since 1617. The house was built beside
the ruins of the old castle (see entry
below), and in 1625 four wings were
added to the original 1594 building. The
house contains some fine furniture,
paintings, porcelain and many items of
historical interest. The grounds, with an
artificial lake, were designed by
Capability Brown in the 18th century.
Tea and refreshments are served in a
Gothic dairy which is by the lake. There
are two events planned for August; a
craft fair (1-2) and an Elizabethan
weekend (15-16)
*Open Etr Sat-Sep, Thu, Sat, Sun & BH
Mons 2-5.30 (grounds 12-5.30).*
£3.60 (ch £1.80, pen £3). Grounds only
£1.50 (ch 80p). Party 25 +.
🅿 ☕ shop ✖ (ex in grounds)

Sherborne Museum   SHERBORNE

Map 03 ST61
Abbey Gate House, Church Ln
☎ (0935) 812252
On show in this museum is a model of
Sherborne's original Norman castle, as
well as a fine Victoria doll's house and
other domestic and agricultural bygones.
There are also items of local geological,
natural history and archeological
interest, including Roman material.
Photographs of the Sherborne Missal of
1400 are on display. The latest addition
is a 15th-century wall painting originally
from a house near the museum. 1992
will see a temporary exhibition in the
spring celebrating the 40th anniversary
of the accession of Queen Elizabeth II,
and an exhibition in the summer entitled
'It's a small world'.
*Open Apr-Oct, Tue-Sat 10.30-12.30 &
2.30-4.30, Sun 2.30-4.30; Nov-Dec, Tue,
Thu & Sat 10.30-12.30 & 2.30-4.30.
(Closed end Dec-Mar).*
50p (ch 15p).
& shop ✖

Sherborne Old Castle   SHERBORNE

Map 03 ST61
☎ (0935) 812730
The castle was built between 1107 and
1135 by Roger, Bishop of Salisbury but
was captured and destroyed by
Cromwell's forces in the Civil War. The
ruins of the main buildings, the curtain
wall and the towers and gates date from
Norman times. The castle came into Sir
Walter Raleigh's possession in 1592.
*Open all year, Apr-Sep, daily 10-6; Oct-
Mar, Tue-Sun 10-4. (Closed 24-26 Dec &
1 Jan).*
£1.10 (ch 55p, students, pen & UB40
85p).
🅿 & ✖
(EH)

Worldwide Butterflies & Lullingstone Silk Farm   SHERBORNE

Map 03 ST61
Compton House, Over Compton
(entrance on A30, 2.5m W)
☎ Yeovil (0935) 74608

Set in the grounds of lovely Compton
House is the superb collection of
butterflies from all over the world, flying
free in reconstructions of their natural
habitats, including natural jungle and a
tropical palmhouse. The collection has
been built up over 30 years and there
are active breeding and hatching areas on
view as well as an extensive specialist
library for research. Compton is also the
home of the Lullingstone Silk Farm
which produced unique English-reared
silk for the last two coronations and the
Queen's and the Princess of Wales's
wedding dresses. At the farm the
complete process of silk production is
shown by exhibits and film.
Open Apr-Oct, daily 10-5.
Admission fee payable.
🅿 ☕ & shop ✖

---

*Every effort is made to provide accurate information,
but details might change during the currency
of this guide.*

Swanage Railway   SWANAGE

Map 03 SZ07
Station House
☎ (0929) 425800 & 424276 (timetable)
When the branch railway line from
Wareham was closed in 1972, Swanage
railway station was fortunately saved
from destruction, and a band of
enthusiasts started work on rebuilding
the line. As part of the reconstruction of
the railway serving the Isle of Purbeck,
steam train rides of about six miles are
available. There is an exhibition with a
model railway in a museum coach at the
station, and special events are held
throughout the year for the railway
enthusiast. 1992 special events include a
Victorian weekend on 20-21 June.
*Open all year, wknds & BH; Jun-Sep,
daily 10.30-5.30; Santa Specials every
wknd in Dec.*
£3.90 (ch 5-15 £1.95, under 4 free)
return. Family ticket £9.
🅿 (charged) (wine & dine specials on Sat
eves) & (special disabled persons coach) toilets
for disabled shop

SWANAGE RAILWAY

Station House, Swanage, Dorset
Enjoy a nostalgic steam train ride on the
Purbeck Line. Steam trains run every
weekend throughout the year, with daily running June to September,
Christmas week and Easter week.
Many special events are held during the year, see our brochure for
details. Every Sunday from Easter to the end of September, and some
weekdays during the peak season, our vintage open top bus connects
at Harman's Cross for Corfe Castle.
Open top bus connections to other
tourist attractions are planned for
1992. The Swanage Railway is an
authorised British Rail Ticket Agent.
The booking office is open daily,
except Christmas Day.
For further information telephone the
booking office on (0929) 425800.

PURBECK

Tolpuddle Museum   TOLPUDDLE

Map 03 SY79
(on A35)
☎ Puddletown (0305) 848237
Tolpuddle is celebrated for the
agricultural workers from the village
who united to improve their wages and
conditions of employment. They were
arrested and transported in 1834 and
became known as the Tolpuddle
Martyrs. In the 1930s the TUC built a
museum of six cottages named after
them. Also in the village is the 'Martyrs'
Tree', an old sycamore under which it is
thought the Martyrs met. The museum
within the cottages depicts the story of
the martyrs. The Tolpuddle Martyrs
Rally is held on 19th July, 12.30-4pm.
*Open all year, Apr-Oct, Tue-Sat 10-5.30,
Sun 11-5.30; Nov-Mar, Tue-Sat 10-4,
Sun 11-4. (Closed 24 Dec-1 Jan).*
Free.
shop ✖

Dorset Heavy Horse Centre   VERWOOD

Map 03 SU00
Edmondsham Rd (1.25m NW,
signposted from Verwood).
☎ (0202) 824040
The Horse Centre has become home to
some of the finest champion heavy
horses in the country. Breeds kept here
include the Shire, Percheron, Ardennes,
Clydesdale, Canadian-Belgian and
Suffolk Punch. There are commentaries
at 11.30, 2.30 and 4.15. There are also
Shetland ponies, and a display of harness
farm wagons and farm implements.
*Open Good Fri-Oct, daily 10-5.30.
Commentaries at 11.30, 2.30 & 4.15.*
£2.95 (ch £1.95, pen £2.50). Party 12 +.
🅿 ☕ & toilets for disabled shop

✖ The 'No Dogs' symbol does not normally apply
to guide dogs – these are permitted in
most establishments.

Lulworth Cove Heritage Centre   WEST LULWORTH

Map 03 SY88
☎ (092941) 587
Permanent exhibitions at the centre
include Smuggling (1700-1850), Paddle
Steamers, Oil in Dorset (BP
Exploration), and Country Wines. There
are also displays on Dorset buttons and
Featherstitchery, local flora and fauna,
the Lulworth Skipper butterfly, the.
history of the village, and a small Poets'
Corner. A large room is available for
field study groups, meetings, film shows,
etc. Details on request.
*Open – high season, daily 10-6; low season,
Tue-Thu & Sat-Sun 10-6.*
£1.50 (ch 5-14 & pen 80p). Family ticket
£4
& toilets for disabled shop ✖

The Deep Sea Adventure & Titanic Story   WEYMOUTH

Map 03 SY67
9 Custom House Quay, Old Harbour
☎ (0305) 760690
This exciting exhibition is an adventure
story detailing the struggle to recover
wealth from the sea. The exhibition
brings the subject to life by the use of
animation, lighting and sound effects.
The latest addition to the exhibition is
'The Titanic Story: Signals of Disaster',
a major collection of actual Titanic
signals. Events for 1992 include: Titanic
Week (12-18 Apr), Oyster Festival
(23/24 May), Trawler Race (25 May),
and the National Historic Diving Rally
(6 Sep). There are also diving displays,
given at set times mainly, during July
and August.
*Open all year, daily 10-5.30; winter
10-4.30. Jul & Aug also open
10am-10pm. (Closed 24-26 Dec).*
£2.95 (ch 14 £1.95, ch 15-16 , pen &
students £2.50). Party 10 +.
& (lift) toilets for disabled shop ✖

Sea Life Park   WEYMOUTH

Map 03 SY67
Lodmoor Country Park
☎ (0305) 788255
The Sea Life Park is part of the beautiful
Lodmoor Country Park. Here you can
marvel at the mysteries of the deep and
discover exotic tropical creatures through
the spectacular marine life displays, the
ocean film theatre, the shark
observatory, tropical jungle and blue
whale splash pool. There is also Captain
Kid's Adventureland and a lakeside
picnic area. Special events throughout
the year; please telephone for details.
*Open all year, daily from 10am. (Closed 25
Dec).*
✱ Admission fee payable.
🅿 (charged) ☕ & toilets for disabled shop
✖

Kingston Lacy House, Garden & Park — WIMBORNE

Map 03 SZ09
(1.5m W on B3082)
☎ (0202) 883402
One of the finest houses of its period in Dorset, Kingston Lacy House and 1,500 of its 9,000 acres were bequeathed to the National Trust in 1981 and opened to the public only in 1986. Until then, the house had been the home of the Bankes family for over 300 years. The original house was built between 1663 and 1665, but in the 1830s it was altered and given a stone façade by Sir Charles Barry for WJ Bankes.

WJ Bankes was a traveller and a collector and, not only did he add the grand Italian marble staircase and a superb Venetian ceiling, but treasures from Spain and an Egyptian obelisk. There is also a quite outstanding picture collection with works by Titian, Rubens, Velasquez, Reynolds and family portraits by Van Dyck and Lely.
Open Apr-1 Nov, Sat-Wed 12-5.30. Last admission 4.30; Park 11.30-6. Last admission 5.
£4.80 (ch £2.40). Park & Gardens only: £1.70. Party 20+.
P ✕ *licensed* & *(parking by arrangement) toilets for disabled shop* ✖ *(ex in north park) (NT)*

Knoll Gardens — WIMBORNE

Map 03 SZ09
Stapehill Rd (3m E)
☎ (0202) 873931
A rare, unusual and exotic collection of plants from all over the world, begun some 20 years ago, now boasts well over 3000 different species of named plants. The gardens are a compact six-acre site of beautiful water gardens, ponds, waterfalls, streams, rockeries, herbaceous borders, woodland glens, colourful formal areas and other exciting features.
Open from Mar, daily 10-6.
£2.95 (ch £1.43, pen £2.40). Party 20+.
P ☛ ✕ *licensed* & *toilets for disabled shop garden centre* ✖

Priest's House Museum — WIMBORNE

Map 03 SZ09
23-27 High St
☎ (0202) 882533
Explore Wimborne's past through this award-winning local history museum set in an historic house with a working kitchen, regular special exhibitions and a beautiful walled garden. Parties are welcome by arrangement.
Open Apr-Oct & 27 Dec-10 Jan, Mon-Sat 10.30-4.30, Sun 2-4.30. Nov-Xmas wknds only. (Closed 29 Jul).
✳ *£1 (ch 25p).*
☛ & *shop* ✖

CO DURHAM

Bowes Museum — BARNARD CASTLE

Map 11 NZ01
☎ Teesdale (0833) 690606
This splendid French château-style mansion was built in 1869 by John Bowes, who made his fortune in Durham coal and married a French actress. They amassed an outstanding collection of works of art, and built the flamboyant château to house them. The museum is now run by the county council, and its collections include paintings by El Greco, Goya and Canaletto among others, porcelain and silver, furniture, ceramics and tapestries. There is a children's room and a local history section, and a formal garden. Temporary exhibitions are held. In 1992 special celebrations and exhibitions are being organised for a centenary year.
Open May-Sep, Mon-Sat 10-5.30, Sun 2-5; Nov-Feb closes 4pm; Mar, Apr & Oct closes 5pm. (Closed 20-25 Dec & 1 Jan).
✳ *£1.75 (ch, pen & UB40 85p).*
P ☛ & *toilets for disabled shop* ✖

The Castle — BARNARD CASTLE

Map 11 NZ01
☎ (0833) 38212
The town's name comes from Bernard Baliol, who built the castle in 1125. The castle clings to the steep banks of the Tees and is now a ruin, but it still has a 12th-century keep, and the remains of a 14th-century hall.
Open all year, Apr-Sep, daily 10-6; Oct-Mar, Tue-Sun 10-4. (Closed 24-26 Dec & 1 Jan)
£1.10 (ch 55p, students, pen & UB40 85p)
& *shop*
(EH)

Egglestone Abbey — BARNARD CASTLE

Map 11 NZ01
(1m SE)
The remains of this Premonstratensian abbey make a picturesque sight on the right bank of the River Tees. A large part of the church can be seen, as can remnants of monastic buildings.
Open any reasonable time.
Free.
P &
(EH)

The North of England Open Air Museum — BEAMISH

Map 11 NZ25
(off A693 & A6076)
☎ Stanley (0207) 231811

This open air museum, set in 200 acres of beautiful Co. Durham countryside, vividly recreates life in the North of England around the turn of the century. Visitors are able to take a tram ride into the living past and stroll down the cobbled street of The Town to see the fully stocked Co-operative shops, the Dentist's home and surgery, the Solicitor's office, the Music Teacher's home and then quench their thirst in the Sun Inn. Nearby is the Railway Station, with signal box, goods yard and
continued...

weighbridge house, where locomotives are often in steam. Just a tram ride away at the Colliery Village, guided tours are given underground at a real drift mine, a steam winding engine demonstrates how coal was drawn to the surface and visitors can see the cosy pit cottages, where home-made bread is often baked in a coal-fired oven. The farmyard at Home Farm is a lively place, with lots of ducks, geese and hens, and the farmer's wife can be seen going about her daily chores in the farmhouse kitchen. In the dairy the delicious Beamish cheese is made. Events for 1992 include the Northern Vintage Transport Association Display (23-25 May), an MG car club meet (25 July), and a Prize Leek Show (19/20 Sep).
Open all year, Apr-Oct daily 10-6; Nov-Mar daily (ex Mon) 10-5. Last admission 4pm. Phone for details of Xmas opening.
✳ *Summer:£5-£6 (ch & pen £4). Winter £3 (ch & pen £2.50). Party.*
P ☛ & *toilets for disabled shop* ✖ *(ex in grounds)*

Bowes Castle — BOWES

Map 11 NY91
(on A66)
Built inside the earthworks of the Roman fort of 'Lavatrae', the castle is a ruin now, but the great Norman keep still stands three storeys high. It was built between 1171 and 1187.
Open any reasonable time.
Free.
🚐
(EH)

Killhope Wheel Lead Mining Centre — COWSHILL

Map 11 NY84
(3m W off A689)
☎ Weardale (0388) 537505
The lead mine and 19th-century crushing mill have been restored to look as they would have done in the 1870s. Visitors are invited to get involved in activities such as panning for lead and working machinery. A path leads to displays of lead mining through the ages. The 84ft water wheel is now restored and turning.
Open Etr-Oct, daily 10.30-5. Last entry 4.30. (Jul & Aug 5.30. Last entry 5.); Nov, Sun 10.30-5.
£1.50 (ch & pen 75p). Party 10+.
P ☛ & *toilets for disabled shop*

Art Gallery — DARLINGTON

Map 11 NZ21
Crown St
☎ (0325) 462034
The gallery has a permanent collection of pictures but also shows temporary exhibitions throughout the year. A 'Silver Longboat' art competition will be open to artists in the northern region during 1992.
Open all year, Mon-Fri 10-8, Sat 10-5.30 (Closed Sun & all weekend BH)
Free.
✖

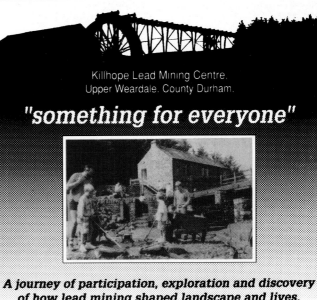

Darlington Museum · DARLINGTON

Map 11 NZ21
Tubwell Row
☎ (0325) 463795
Displays on local history, wildlife and archaeology are shown, with various bygones. There is also an observation beehive, which can be seen from about

May to September.
Open all year, Mon-Wed & Fri 10-1 & 2-6; Thu 10-1; Sat 10-1 & 2-5.30 (Closed Good Fri, May Day, Xmas & 1 Jan)
Free.
& *shop* ✖

Darlington Railway Centre & Museum · DARLINGTON

Map 11 NZ21
North Rd Station (0.75m N off A167)
☎ (0325) 460532
The museum is housed in North Road Station, built 17 years after the world's first passenger train ran along the Stockton and Darlington line. The building has been carefully restored and part is still in use for train services. The prize exhibit is 'Locomotion', which pulled the first passenger train and was built by Robert Stephenson & Co in 1825. Several other steam locomotives

are also shown, together with an early railway coach of about 1845 and a chaldron (coal) wagon. There are also models and other exhibits relating to the Stockton and Darlington and the North Eastern Railway companies. Locomotive restoration work takes place in the former goods shed nearby. There is a Railway Carnival in September (tel for details).
Open daily 9.30-5 (Closed Xmas & New Year); Last admission 4.30pm.
✱ *£1.40 (ch 5-15 70p & pen £1). Party.*
P & *toilets for disabled shop* ✖

Durham Light Infantry Museum & Durham Art Gallery · DURHAM

Map 11 NZ24
Aykley Heads
☎ 091-384 2214
The history of the Regiment is told in displays of artefacts, medals, uniforms and vehicles. The Art Gallery has a continuous programme of temporary exhibitions, and it holds regular lectures and concerts. A military vehicle rally is held on the August Bank Holiday

Sunday and Monday and brass band concerts are held on Sunday afternoons in summer. This year there will be an exhibition to celebrate Durham's new First Class County Cricket status – 'Cricket' (4 Apr-7 Jun).
Open all year, Tue-Sat 10-5 & Sun 2-5. (Closed Mon, ex BHs).
✱ *70p (ch & pen 30p)*
P ⚲ & *toilets for disabled shop* ✖

Finchale Priory · DURHAM

Map 11 NZ24
(3m NE)
The lovely setting of the priory was chosen by St Godric in 1110 as a place for years of solitary meditation. The priory was begun in 1180, and was used by monks from Durham Cathedral. There are considerable remains of the

13th-century church.
Open all year, Apr-Sep, daily 10-6; Oct-Mar, Tue-Sun 10-4. (Closed 24-26 Dec & 1 Jan).
Free.
P & ✖
(EH)

Oriental Museum · DURHAM

Map 11 NZ24
University of Durham, Elvet Hill
☎ 091-374 2911
The museum has a remarkable collection of Oriental artefacts, ranging from Ancient Egypt to Japan. Special exhibitions are held throughout the year,

including photographs of Kashgar by Jimmy Holmes (Feb-Apr), and Chinese Gods loaned by Keith Stevens (Jun-Oct).
Open Mon-Fri 9.30-1 & 2-5, Sat & Sun 2-5. (Closed Xmas-New Year).
✱ *50p (ch, pen & students 30p)*
P & *shop* ✖

St Aidan's College Grounds · DURHAM

Map 11 NZ24
Windmill Hill (1m S off A1050)
☎ 091-374 3269
The college was designed by Sir Basil Spence and built in the early 1960s. The grounds were landscaped by Professor Brian Hackett, and are at their best in July, when the shrub beds are in flower.

There is a laburnum walk and a reflecting pool, well stocked with plants and fish. Good views of Durham Cathedral.
Open, daily 9-dusk.
Free, but donations to National Gardens Scheme.
P & *toilets for disabled* ✖

Raby Castle · STAINDROP

Map 11 NZ12
(1m N, off A688)
☎ (0833) 60202

The stronghold of the powerful Nevill family until 1569, and the home of the Vane family since 1626. The fortress is built around a courtyard and surrounded by a moat (now dry). The castle was erected during Saxon times but is

substantially 14th century, with parts added in nearly every century. It has an impressive gateway; and nine towers of which the tallest is 80ft; a vast medieval hall; and a Victorian octagonal drawing-room. The 14th-century kitchen, with its collection of Victorian copper cooking utensils, was in use daily until 1954. The castle contains fine pictures from English, Dutch and Italian schools, interesting furniture and ceramics, and a good carriage collection. There are about five acres of gardens and an additional 200-acre park with both red and fallow deer. Home Farm Open Days are on 3/4 June, 10-4pm.
Open 18 Mar-22 Apr; May-Jun, Wed & Sun; Jul-Sep, Sun-Fri; BHs May, Spring & Aug, Sat-Wed 1-5. Park & gardens
continued . . .

11-5.30, (last admission 4.30).
*Castle, Gardens & Carriage Collection
£2.75 (ch £1.30, pen £2.25). Park,
Gardens & Carriage Collection £1 (ch &*

pen 75p). Party.
P ⚑ ⅌ *toilets for disabled shop* ✠ *(ex in
Park)*

Tanfield Railway — TANFIELD

Map 11 NZ15
(on A6076)
☎ 091-274 2002
The Causey Arch, the first large railway
bridge and the largest single span arch in
Britain of its era, is the centrepiece of a
woodland full of picturesque walks
around a deep valley. The story of the
early railway and collieries is told on a
series of display boards, giving an
interesting break in a return journey
from Tanfield. You can ride in carriages
that first saw use in Victorian times, and

visit Marley Hill shed, built in 1854,
inside which you can see the stationary
steam engine at work driving some of
the vintage machine tools. The
blacksmith is also often at work forging
new parts for the restoration work.
*Open all year, summer daily 10-5; winter
daily 10-4. Trains – Etr-Sep, Sun & BH
Mon (also Thu & Sat Jun-Aug); Oct-Nov
& Jan-Etr, Sun pm service; Dec, North
Pole Express. Telephone for details.
Admission charged.*
See advertisement on page 71.

EAST SUSSEX

Clergy House — ALFRISTON

Map 04 TQ50
☎ (0323) 870001

The thatched and timber-framed parish
priests' house was built in about 1350

and had not changed very much by
1896, when it was acquired by the
National Trust. (It was the first building
to be taken over by the Trust.) Now
carefully and sensitively restored, it gives
a vivid idea of medieval living
conditions. Outside the house is a pretty
cottage garden.
*Open Apr-Oct daily 11-6 (or dusk if
earlier). Last admission 30 mins before
closing.
Apr, May, Sep & Oct £1.20 (ch 60p);
Jun-Aug £1.70 (ch 90p)
shop
(NT)*

Drusillas Park — ALFRISTON

Map 04 TQ50
☎ Eastbourne (0323) 870234
This famous small zoo features many
special areas including 'Out of Africa'
with its meerkat mound, otter valley,
world of owls, flamingo lagoon and
beaver country. There are also beautiful
gardens, an adventure playground, a
railway, and a farm area introduced in
1991. Special events for 1992 include

many charity days, half-term activities,
and a Rose and Gardeners Day (Jul).
*Open all year, daily 10-5 or dusk if earlier,
(ex Xmas).
£4.50 (ch 3-12 £3.95, concessions £2.95).
Incl zoo & railway ride & children 3-12
playland. Grounds free.*
P ⚑ ⅌ ✗ *licensed* & *toilets for disabled shop
garden centre* ✠

For an explanation of the symbols and abbreviations, see page 2.

Battle & District Historical Society Museum — BATTLE

Map 04 TQ71
Langton House
☎ (04246) 2714
The focal point is a diorama of the
Battle of Hastings and a reproduction of
the Bayeux Tapestry. There are also
local history exhibits. A Summer Arts

Festival is held, and the Battle Festival
takes place in June/July. Special displays
(eg, old photographs, toys etc) are
arranged throughout the season.
Open Etr-Sep, daily.
✱ *70p (ch 20p, ch accompanied free).
shop* ✠

Battle Abbey — BATTLE

Map 04 TQ71
☎ (04246) 3792
Built by William to commemorate his
victory over Harold at the Battle of
Hastings, today one can visit the
excavated foundations of the abbey, and
the monks' dormitory and common
room which survived the Dissolution. A
new exhibition in the Great Gatehouse

opens in the spring; it tells the day-to-
day story of a monk's life at the abbey.
*Open all year, Apr-Sep, daily 10-6. Oct-
Mar, daily 10-4. (Closed 24-26 Dec & 1
Jan).
£2.50 (ch £1.30, pen, students & UB40
£1.90)*
P &
(EH)

Buckleys Yesterday's World — BATTLE

Map 04 TQ71
90 High St
☎ (04246) 4269
The shopping and social habits of the
past are explored in this unique
exhibition of over 30,000 nostalgic
exhibits. See Queen Victoria's
nightdress, Victorian toys and dolls,
Pennyfarthing bicycles and many
everyday objects now made quaint with

age (dating from 1850 to 1950). The
grand re-opening will take place in the
1st week of June, and special events and
exhibitions will take place throughout
the summer.
*Open all year, daily 10-5.30 (last
admission) (open longer Jul-Aug).
£2.95 (ch £1.95, pen £2.75). Party 10+.*
⅌ & *shop*

Bexhill Museum of Costume & Social History — BEXHILL-ON-SEA

Map 04 TQ70
Old Manor Gardens, Old Town
☎ Bexhill (0424) 215361
Costumes from 1740 to 1960 can be
seen here, with interesting accessories,
toys, dolls, sewing machines, radios and
other evocative homely items. The

museum has a pleasant setting in the
grounds of the Old Manor House.
*Open Apr-Sep, Tue-Fri & BH Mons
10.30-1 & 2.30-5.30, Sat & Sun
2.30-5.30.*
P & *toilets for disabled shop
Details not confirmed for 1992*

Bodiam Castle — BODIAM

Map 04 TQ72
(off A229)
☎ Staplecross (058083) 436

Small and picturesque, Bodiam is like
the castles that children draw. Its tall
curtain walls form a rectangular court
with round drum towers at each corner,
all reflected in the water of the moat. It
was built in 1386-8 by Sir Edward
Dalrymple, not for show but as a

working fortification. The walls measure
some 6ft 6in thick, and the great
gatehouse was defended by gun loops
and three portcullises, of which one has
survived. The castle walls have remained
remarkably intact, and although the
castle was gutted in the Civil War it still
has over 30 fireplaces and 28 garderobes
(latrines), each with a drain shaft to the
moat. The remains of the chapel, halls,
chambers and kitchens (with fireplaces)
can be seen and the circular stairs to the
battlements give access to some lovely
views.
*Open all year, Apr-Oct 10-6; Nov-Mar,
Mon-Sat 10-sunset. Last admission half
hour before closing. (Closed 25-29 Dec).
£2 (ch £1). Parties (Mon-Fri) by prior
arrangement.*
P ⅌ ✗ *licensed* & *toilets for disabled shop
(NT)*

Booth Museum of Natural History — BRIGHTON

Map 04 TQ30
194 Dyke Rd
☎ (0273) 552586
The museum was built in 1874 to house
the bird collection of Edward Thomas
Booth (1840-1890). His collection is still
on display, but the museum has
expanded considerably since Booth's day
and now includes thousands of butterfly
and insect specimens, geology galleries
with fossils, rocks and local dinosaur
bones and a magnificent collection of
animal skeletons, largely collected by

F W Lucas (1842-1932), a Brighton
solicitor. Conservation is also covered,
with displays on the major habitats of
Sussex showing how, over the ages,
humans have managed and altered them.
There is also a programme of exciting
temporary exhibitions.
*Open all year, Mon-Sat (ex Thu) 10-5,
Sun 2-5. (Closed Good Fri, Xmas & 1
Jan).*
& *shop* ✠
Details not confirmed for 1992

Museum & Art Gallery — BRIGHTON

Map 04 TQ30
Church St
☎ (0273) 603005
The museum was built as the Prince
Regent's stables and riding school. It
now houses paintings and displays of
musical instruments, Sussex archaeology,
folklife and history, with the Willett
collection of ceramics. A section on

20th-century fine and applied art has Art
Nouveau, Art Deco and costume. The
Art Gallery has an exciting programme
of temporary exhibitions.
*Open all year, Tue-Sat 10-5.45, Sun 2-5.
(Closed Mon (ex BH), Good Fri, Xmas &
1 Jan). Opening times subject to variation.
Free.*
⅌ & *shop* ✠

Preston Manor — BRIGHTON

Map 04 TQ30
194 Preston Rd (off A23)
☎ (0273) 603005 ext 3239
This attractive Georgian house was
bequeathed to the town in 1932 by Sir
Charles Thomas-Sandford. It has been
left much as it was in his day, with
furniture, silver, and ceramics, and the
servants' quarters can be visited. The
house is set in beautiful grounds with

scented and walled gardens.
*Open all year, Tue-Sat 10-5, Sun 2-5.
(Closed Mon (ex BH Mon), Good Fri &
25-26 Dec).*
✱ *£2.30 (ch £1.20, pen, students & UB40
£1.80). Family ticket £3.40-£5.30. Party
20+.*
P ✠

See advertisement on page 73.

Royal Pavilion — BRIGHTON

Map 04 TQ30
Old Steine
☎ (0273) 603005

The pavilion was the marine palace of
the Prince Regent (George IV). It began
as a farmhouse which the prince rented
after his secret marriage to Mrs
Fitzherbert. The farmhouse was

transformed into a neo-classical villa by
Henry Holland, and the villa was in
turn transformed by John Nash into the
present building. The prince was
interested in Indian exteriors and in the
fantastic Chinoiserie decorations inside.
Today the furniture includes pieces lent
by HM the Queen. Queen Victoria's
Apartments and the extensive structural
restoration of the pavilion are now
complete.
*Open all year, Jun-Sep, daily 10-6; Oct-
May, daily 10-5. (Closed 25-26 Dec).*
✱ *£3.10 (ch £1.60, pen, students &
UB40's £2.30). Party 20+.*
⅌ & *(facilities for the blind by
arrangement) toilets for disabled shop* ✠

See advertisement on page 73.

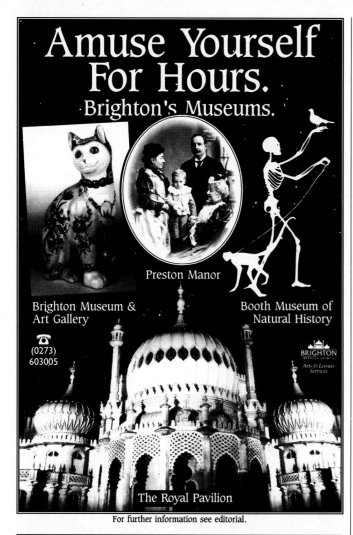

Sea Life Centre — BRIGHTON

Map 04 TQ30
Marine Pde
☎ (0273) 604233 & 604234
This is one of eight sea life centres in Britain specialising in British marine creatures from all around the coast of Britain. On show is everything from worms to octopus, from sharks to stingrays as well as special pools where you can actually touch the sea creatures.
A special section of the Sea Life

Centre is devoted to the recreation of the Victorian aquarium as it was 130 years ago. This includes many weird and wonderful fish – look out for George, the Centre's 3ft grouper!
Open all year, daily (ex Xmas day), from 10am. Last admission 5.15 (4.15 in winter).
✱ *£3.75 (ch 14 £2.75, pen £3, under 3 free). Family ticket £11. Party 10+.*
🍴 ♿ *toilets for disabled shop* ✖

Bateman's — BURWASH

Map 04 TQ62
(1m SW)
☎ (0435) 882302
Rudyard Kipling lived at this lovely 17th-century ironmaster's house from 1902 to 1936. Kipling's study is kept much as it was then and among his many possessions to be seen around the property is his 1928 Rolls Royce. There are attractive gardens, with a restored watermill which grinds flour for sale. On

8 August Bateman's Concert will be held – this is an orchestral concert with fireworks: bring picnics.
Open Apr-Oct, Sat-Wed 11-5.30 (last admission 4.30).
Sat & Mon-Wed £3.20 (ch £1.60); Sun & BH's £3.70 (ch £1.90).
🅿 🍴 ✖ *licensed* ♿ *toilets for disabled shop* ✖
(NT)

Every effort is made to provide accurate information, but details might change during the currency of this guide.

Coastal Defence Museum — EASTBOURNE

Map 04 TV69
King Edward's Pde
☎ (0323) 410440
The museum is housed in one of the Martello towers built in the 1800s to fend off invasion by Napoleon. After the Napoleonic Wars they were used by a predecessor of the coastguard service. This one now has displays on defence

methods and equipment of the Napoleonic period to the Second World War and an exhibition of over 1,000 model soldiers provided by the British Model Soldier Society..
Open Etr-Oct, daily 9.30-5.30.
60p (ch & pen 30p). Party 10+.
shop ✖

Eastbourne Redoubt Fortress — EASTBOURNE

Map 04 TV69
Royal Pde
☎ (0323) 410300
This huge fortification was built in 1804 in case of invasion by Napoleon, and has places for 11 guns. It is now the home of the Sussex Combined Services Museum (The Royal Sussex Regiment and the Queen's Royal Irish Hussars).

The fort also has an aquarium grotto with marine and freshwater fish. During the summer months many concerts are held, including the spectacular '1812 Nights'.
Open Etr-Oct, 9.30-5.30.
£1.35 (ch & pen 85p). Party.
🍴 *shop*

"How We Lived Then" Museum of Shops & Social History — EASTBOURNE

Map 04 TV69
20 Cornfield Ter
☎ (0323) 37143
Over the last 30 years, Jan and Graham Upton have collected over 50,000 items which are now displayed on three floors of authentic old shop settings, transporting visitors back to the age of their grandparents. Grocers, chemists, iron-mongers, tailors, cobblers, photographers, jewellers, music and toy shops are all represented in fascinating detail, as well as a Post Office, complete

with dour post mistress. Other displays, such as seaside souvenirs, wartime rationing and Royal mementoes, help to capture 100 years of social history. The gift shop includes old fashioned sweets, reproduction tins, advertisements and tin-plate and Victorian-style greetings cards.
Open daily Feb-Dec, 10-5.30 (last entry 5pm).
£1.50 (ch 5-15 85p, pen £1.25). Party
♿ *shop*

Lifeboat Museum — EASTBOURNE

Map 04 TV69
Grand Pde
☎ (0323) 30717
The work of lifeboats which have been stationed at Eastbourne is illustrated here, as is the work of the Royal National Lifeboat Institution in general. Lifeboat models are shown, with the

sails and oars from the last sailing lifeboat at the station, and gear worn by lifeboat men. There are also descriptions and photographs of notable rescues.
Open Jan-Mar, wknds only; Apr-Dec, daily 9.30-6.
♿ *shop* ✖
Details not confirmed for 1992

Towner Art Gallery & Local History Museum — EASTBOURNE

Map 04 TV69
Manor Gardens, High St, Old Town
☎ (0323) 411688 & 25112
This 18th-century manor house is in delightful public gardens. The gallery contains collections of mainly 19th- and 20th-century British art. There is a lively programme of temporary exhibitions of historical, modern and contemporary art; local history and craft; workshops, talks; concerts and other events. In the Local History Museum, you can see Eastbourne and area from prehistoric

times to the Edwardian era. Exhibitions planned for 1992 include 18 Jan-26 Apr, A view of Sussex; 16 May-14 Jun, People in Place – sculptures by Philip Cox; 2 Aug-20 Sep, Eric Ravilious – Eastbourne artist; and 26 Sep-1 Nov, Peter Kennard – photographs on theme of Britannia.
Open all year, Tue-Sat 10-5, Sun & BH Mon 2-5. (Closed Mon, Good Fri, 24-26 Dec & 1 Jan).
Free.
♿ *shop* ✖

The Living World — EXCEAT

Map 04 TV59
Seven Sisters Country Park
☎ Alfriston (0323) 870100
This is a living exhibition of small creatures: butterflies, bees, spiders, snails, moths, scorpions, marine life and others, in settings that are as near to nature as possible. The displays of this unique

mini zoo are based in two old Sussex barns, situated in a 700-acre Country Park within the Heritage Coastline.
Open all year, mid Mar-1 Nov, daily; Nov-mid Mar, wknds & school holidays 10-5.
✱ *£2 (ch & pen £1.20, ch 5 free). Family ticket £5.70. Wheelchair users free.*
🅿 🍴 ✖ ♿ *toilets for disabled shop*

Firle Place — FIRLE

Map 04 TQ40
☎ Glynde (0273) 858335
Home of the Gage family for over 500 years, the house has a Tudor core but was remodelled in the 18th century. Its treasures include important European and English Old Master paintings, fine English and French furniture, and especially porcelain, including notable examples from Sèvres and English

factories. There are family monuments and brasses in the church at West Firle.
Open May-Sep, Sun, Wed & Thu; also Etr, Spring, May & Aug BH Sun & Mon 2-5.
£3.25 (ch £1). Groups 25+. Connoisseurs Day £3.75. Private viewing 25+ by appointment only.
🅿 ✖ *licensed* ♿ *shop* ✖ *(ex in garden)*
See advertisement on page 74.

Bedgebury National Pinetum — FLIMWELL

Map 04 TQ73
(1.5m N off A21 onto B2079)
☎ Goudhurst (0580) 211044
The 160-acre pinetum is a kind of dictionary of conifers – it is the national collection of the trees – and was planted by the Forestry Commission and the Royal Botanic Gardens. Experts and non-experts alike can enjoy wandering along the marked paths and rides to the imaginatively arranged groups of individual species, which spread over two valleys and round a lake. The

colours of the conifers themselves are much more varied than one might expect, and among them there are interesting deciduous trees which make a fine display in autumn. A new trail is planned for 1992 called 'Around the world in 80 minutes.'
Open all year, daily 10-8 or dusk. Visitor centre Etr-Sep, daily 11-5, & Oct Mon-Fri 12-4.
£1.50 (ch 75p, pen £1)
🅿 ♿ *toilets for disabled shop*

Firle Place

Nr. Lewes on A27 Eastbourne Road
Glynde (0273) 858335

In parkland setting under South Downs, beautiful home of the Viscount Gage. Connoisseurs collection of European and English Old Masters, notable Sèvres and English porcelain and fine French and English furniture. Historic American connections.

OPEN: SUNDAYS, WEDNESDAYS & THURSDAYS
(2.00pm till last ticket 5.00pm). May 3rd – end Sept also B.H. Suns/Mons during season.

ADMISSION:

Adults	£3.25
Child	£1.00
Pre-Booked Groups of 25+	£2.85
Connoisseurs (NO Group reduction)	£3.75
Private Weekday Exclusive Viewing	£4.75 (£118.75 min.)
Private Saturday (these for Groups of 30+)	£6.50 (£195 min.)

(Children = 5-15 inclusive, under 5 no charge)

Glynde Place — GLYNDE

Map 04 TQ40
Lewes (off A27)
☎ (0273) 858337
A lovely Elizabethan manor with 18th-century additions, in a beautiful downland setting. A connoisseur's day is held on the last Wednesday of every month.
*Open Jun-Sep, Wed & Thu 2.15-5. Also 1st and last Sun of month.
£3 (ch £1.50). Garden only 75p. Party 20+*
P ⬤ ✕

Michelham Priory — HAILSHAM

Map 04 TQ50
Upper Dicker (2.5m W off A22)
☎ (0323) 844224
This Augustinian priory was founded in 1229, and the site includes a 14th-century gatehouse and a 16th-century house with interesting furniture, stained glass, tapestries and examples of Sussex iron work. The six-acre garden includes a physic garden, and also here are a blacksmith's and wheelwright's shop, a working watermill and a museum on the traditional local industry of ropemaking. Art is shown in the Tudor barn, and facilities include a Sussex crafts shop and
continued . . .

GLYNDE PLACE
Nr LEWES

A very beautiful example of 16th century architecture. The house, which is built round a courtyard, is of flint and brick and stands in the picturesque village of Glynde. Interesting collection of pictures, bronzes and historical documents.

Open: June to September, Weds & Thurs and first and last Sun of each month. 2.15 – 5.30pm (last adm 5pm).
Open: Easter Sun & Mon and Bank Hols.
House open for guided tours by prior arrangement (25 or more £2.50).
Admission: £3.00, children £1.50. Garden only 75p (rebate on entry into house). Free parking.
Refreshments: Home baked teas in Coach House (parties to book in advance).

---

a children's playground. A full programme of events is planned throughout 1992 which will include art and crafts exhibitions, Morris dancing, plays and a vintage car rally.
*Open 25 Mar-Oct, daily 11-5.30. Nov, Feb-24 Mar, Sun 11-4.
£3 (ch 5-16 £1.70). Family ticket £8. Party.
⬤ ✕ licensed ♿ (braille guide available) toilets for disabled shop ✕ (ex in gardens)*

Bentley Wildfowl & Motor Museum — HALLAND

Map 04 TQ51
☎ (0825) 840573
Hundreds of swans, geese and ducks from all over the world can be seen on lakes and ponds and also flamingoes, cranes and peacocks. There is a fine array of veteran, Edwardian and vintage vehicles, and the house has splendid antiques and wildfowl paintings. On 3-4
May there will be a Craft Fair here.
*Open 21 Mar-Oct, daily 10.30-4.30 (5pm Jul & Aug). Nov-Feb & part of Mar, wknds (Closed Jan).
£3.10 (ch 4-15 £1.50, pen £2.40). Family ticket £8.
P ⬤ ♿ (wheelchairs available) toilets for disabled shop ✕*

Fishermen's Museum — HASTINGS

Map 04 TQ80
Rock a Nore Rd
☎ (0424) 424787
This was once the fishermen's church, and now houses such exhibits as paintings, photographs, model craft, and
the last of Hastings' luggers built for sail.
*Open May-Sep, Mon-Fri 10.30-12 & 2.30-5, Sun 2.30-5.
♿
Details not confirmed for 1992*

Hastings Castle & 1066 Story — HASTINGS

Map 04 TQ80
Castle Hill
☎ (0424) 718888
The ruins of the Norman castle stand on the cliffs, close to the site of William the Conqueror's first motte-and-bailey castle in England. It was excavated in 1825 and 1968, and old dungeons were discovered in 1894. 'The Story of
1066', which opened recently in the Castle grounds, is an exciting audio-visual experience about the Castle and that famous battle.
*Open 11 Apr-27 Sep, daily 10 (last admission 5.30);28 Sep-1 Nov, daily 11 (last admission 4).
✳ £2 (ch £1.50, pen £1.75).
shop ✕*

Hastings Embroidery — HASTINGS

Map 04 TQ80
Town Hall, Queen's Rd
☎ (0424) 718888
The 80yd embroidery illustrates great events in British history from 1066 to modern times. It was sewn by the Royal School of Needlework, using threads, cords, metals, lace, jewels and
appropriate cloths. Dolls in period costume and a scale model of the Battle of Hastings are also shown.
*Open Jun-Sep, Tue-Fri 10-5; Oct-Apr, Tue-Fri 11.30. May 10-5 (Closed Mon & Sat) Last admission 30 mins before close.
✳ £1 (ch & pen 50p).
♿ toilets for disabled shop ✕*

Hastings Museum & Art Gallery — HASTINGS

Map 04 TQ80
Cambridge Rd
☎ (0424) 721202
The exhibits cover local history, archaeology and wildlife, with examples of Sussex ironwork and pottery. The
fine and applied art includes an extensive collection of pictures, and there is a special exhibition gallery.
*Open Mon-Fri 10-5, Sat 10-1,Sun 2-5.
P ✕
Details not confirmed for 1992*

Museum of Local History — HASTINGS

Map 04 TQ80
Old Town Hall, High St
☎ (0424) 721209
The archaeology and history of Hastings are featured, with an emphasis on the fishing industry and the role of Hastings
as one of the Cinque Ports.
*Open Etr-27 Sep, Mon-Sat 10-1 & 2-5; 28 Sep-Etr Sun only 3-5.
♿ shop ✕
Details not confirmed for 1992*

Smugglers Adventure — HASTINGS

Map 04 TQ80
St Clements Cave, West Hill
☎ (0424) 422964
A Smuggler's Adventure is a themed experience housed in a labyrinth of caverns and passages deep below the West Hill. Visitors first tour a comprehensive exhibition and museum, followed by a video theatre, before embarking on the Adventure Walk – a
trip through several acres of caves with life-size tableaux, push-button automated models and dramatic scenic effects depicting life in the days of 18th-century smuggling.
*Open all year daily, Etr-Sep 10-5.30; Oct-Etr 11-4.30. (Closed 25 Dec).
£3 (ch £2, pen & students £2.50). Family ticket £9.35.
shop ✕*

For an explanation of the symbols and abbreviations, see page 2.

British Engineerium — HOVE

Map 04 TQ20
off Nevill Rd
☎ Brighton (0273) 559583
This restored Victorian water pumping station has an original working beam engine of 1876, and a French Corliss horizontal engine which won first prize at the Paris International Exhibition of
1889. There are also traction engines, fire engines, and many hundreds of other full-size and model engines of all sorts. Exhibitions throughout the year.
*Open all year, daily 10-5 (Closed wk prior to Xmas). In Steam Sun & BH.
✳ £3 (ch, students & pen £2).
P ♿ shop ✕*

Anne of Cleves House Museum   LEWES

Map 04 TQ41
52 Southover High St
☎ (0273) 474610
This 16th-century town house was given
to Anne of Cleves by her ex-husband,
Henry VIII as part of her divorce
settlement. It is now devoted to Sussex
arts and crafts, agricultural, industrial

and domestic life, with a notable
collection of Sussex ironwork including
early gun-founding material. There is a
medieval herb garden outside.
*Open Etr or Apr-Oct, Mon-Sat 10-5.30.
Sun 2-5.30.*
£1.60 (ch 80p). Party.
& *shop* ✝

Castle & Museum of Sussex Archaeology   LEWES

Map 04 TQ41
169 High St
☎ (0273) 474379
Not much is left of the Norman and
13th-century castle, but the site offers a
good view of the town. The 16th- to
18th-century Barbican House has a
museum with displays on prehistoric,
Roman, Saxon and medieval Sussex.
Lewes Living History Model is a 25

minute tape/slide presentation exploring
the town's 1,000 year history, using an
accurate model of Lewes in the 1880s as
a background.
*Open all year, Castle & Museum Mon-Sat
10-5.30; Sun 11-5.30.*
*Apr-Oct £2.80 (ch £1.40). Nov-Mar
£1.60 (ch 80p).(Includes Lewes Living
History Model). Party.*
⬤ & *shop* ✝ *(ex in Castle grounds)*

Great Dixter   NORTHIAM

Map 04 TQ82
(off A28)
☎ (0797) 253160
Dating back to the 15th century, this
half-timbered house has a notable great
hall and fine gardens.
*Open Apr-11 Oct & also 17, 18, 24, 25
Oct, Tue-Sun & BH Mon 2-5; Gardens*

*open as house and also from 11am on
23-25 May, Sun in Jul & Aug & 31
Aug.*
*House & Gardens £3.20 (ch 50p). Gardens
only £2 (ch 25p). Concessions NT members
& pen on Fri £2.50.*
🅿 ⬤ *shop garden centre* ✝

Pevensey Castle   PEVENSEY

Map 04 TQ60
☎ (0323) 762604
Built on the site of a 3rd-century Roman
fort, Pevensey Castle has Norman and
13th century additions. It has never been
taken by force. Ancient fireplaces,
dungeons and an oubliette can be seen.

*Open all year, Apr-Sep, daily 10-6; Oct-
Mar, Tue-Sun 10-4. (Closed 24-26 Dec &
1 Jan).*
*£1.50 (ch 75p, students, pen & UB40
£1.10).*
🅿 & ✈ ✝
(EH)

Lamb House   RYE

Map 04 TQ92
West St
This 18th-century house was the home
of novelist Henry James from 1898 until
his death in 1916, and was later
occupied by E F Benson writer of the
Lucia books, who was at one time

Mayor of Rye. The house is surrounded
by an attractive garden.
*Open three rooms only Apr-Oct, Wed &
Sat 2-6 (last admission 5.30).*
£1.60.
✝ 🚃
(NT)

Rye Museum   RYE

Map 04 TQ92
Ypres Tower, Gun Garden
☎ (0797) 223254
The museum is housed in a 13th
century tower which was used as a
prison for nearly three centuries. It now
contains Cinque Ports material, militaria,

shipping, medieval and other pottery
from Rye kilns, as well as toys, dolls etc.
*Open Etr-Oct, Mon-Sat 10.30-1 &
2.15-5.30, Sun 11.30-1 & 2.15-5.30 (last
admission 30 mins before close).*
Prices under review.
✝

& This symbol indicates that much or all of the
attraction is accessible to wheelchairs.
However, there may be some restrictions,
so it would be wise to check
in advance.

Sheffield Park Garden   SHEFFIELD PARK

Map 04 TQ42
(5m E of Haywards Heath off A275)
☎ Danehill (0825) 790655

Originally landscaped by Capability
Brown, in about 1775, to create a
beautiful park with five lakes and a
cascade, further extensive planting was

done at the beginning of the 20th
century. This has given Sheffield Park a
superb collection of trees, with particular
emphasis on trees that give good autumn
colour. In May and June masses of
azaleas and rhododendrons give colour
and later there are magnificent waterlilies
on the lakes. The gardens and woodland
cover nearly 200 acres.
*Open Apr-8 Nov, Tue-Sat 11-6 or sunset if
earlier, Sun & BH Mon 2-6 or sunset;
Sun in Oct, 1pm-sunset. Last admission
1hr before closing. (Closed Good Fri & Tue
following BH Mon).*
*£3.20 (ch £1.60) Apr & Jun-Sep; £3.70
(ch £1.90) May, Oct & Nov.*
🅿 ⬤ & *toilets for disabled shop* ✝
(NT)

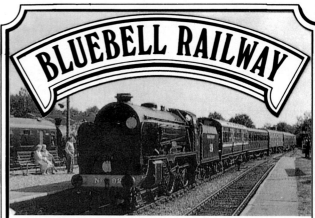

Sheffield Park Station,   SHEFFIELD PARK STATION
Bluebell Railway & Museum

Map 04 TQ42
(4.5m E of Haywards Heath, off A275)
☎ Newick (082572) 3777 & 2370
(Train Information)
As its name suggests this five-mile long,
revived steam-railway line runs through
woodland that is a mass of bluebells
in the springtime. There is a regular service
throughout the year and on certain
Saturdays between April and October
there are Evening Pullman Dinner trains.
It is also possible to charter trains with
catering for private functions. Part of the
station is a museum and there is the
largest collection of locomotives and
carriages in the region. There are many

special events organised for 1992, among
them the English Food and Wine Fair
on 20-21 Jun, and the Autumn Steam
Gala on 12-13 Sep.
*Open all year, trains run Jan & Feb Sun;
Mar, Apr & Nov wknds; May Wed, Sat
& Sun; Jun-Sep daily; Oct wknds & Half
Term week; Dec Santa Specials. For
timetable and information regarding trains
contact above.*
✳ *3rd class return fare £4.50 (ch 3-13
£2.25). Family ticket £11. Museum &
locomotive sheds only, £1 (ch 50p).
Supplementary available for 1st class travel
& new extension section.*
🅿 ⬤ ✗ *licensed* & *toilets for disabled shop*

✝ The 'No Dogs' symbol does not normally apply
to guide dogs – these are permitted in
most establishments.

Wilmington Priory   WILMINGTON

Map 04 TQ50
(off A27)
☎ Eastbourne (0323) 870537
The ruins of this Benedictine priory date
from Norman times. There were
additions in the early Tudor period and
there is still a Tudor crypt. The ruins

now house a small agricultural museum
with some items over 150 years old.
*Open 25 Mar-Oct, Mon & Wed-Sat
11-5.30, Sun 2-5.30.*
£1.50 (ch 5-16 50p).
& *shop* ✝

Winchelsea Museum   WINCHELSEA

Map 04 TQ91
Court Hall
☎ Rye (0797) 226365
The Court Hall, one of the oldest
buildings in Winchelsea, now houses the
museum with the old prison cells
underneath. Dating back to the 13th
century, it was restored in the 16th and

later centuries. There is a model of the
town as it was in 1292, collections of
clay pipes, bottles and other exhibits of
local interest.
*Open mid Apr-Sep, Mon-Sat 10.30-12.30
& 2-5; Sun 2.30-5.30.*
50p (ch under 14 20p).
shop ✝

ESSEX

Audley End House — AUDLEY END

Map 04 TL53
☎ Saffron Walden (0799) 522399

A 17th-century house built by Thomas Howard, Earl of Suffolk, with some work by Robert Adam. Pictures and furnishings in state room. Miniature railway in grounds.
Open Apr-Sep, Tue-Sun & BHs 1-6; Park & Gardens open noon.
£4.50 (ch £2.30, pen, students & UB40 £3.40).
P *(charged)* ☕ ♿ 🐕
(EH)

Colne Valley Railway & Museum — CASTLE HEDINGHAM

Map 04 TL73
Castle Hedingham Station (4m NW of Halstead on A604)
☎ Hedingham (0787) 61174
The old Colne Valley and Halstead railway buildings have been rebuilt here. Stock includes seven steam locomotives plus forty other engines, carriages and wagons, in steam from Easter to December. There is also a five-acre riverside nature and picnic area. Visitors may also dine in style in restored Pullman carriages while travelling along the line. There are several 'Specials' running during 1992.
Open all year, daily 10-dusk. Steam days, rides from 12-4.30. (Closed 23 Dec-1 Feb). Steam days £3 (ch £1.50, pen £2); Family ticket £9. Non-steam days (to view static exhibits only) £1.50 (ch 75p, pen £1); Family ticket £4.50.
P ☕ ✕ *licensed* ♿ *shop* 🐕

This is just one of many guidebooks published by the AA.
The full range is available at any AA shop or good bookshop.

Hedingham Castle — CASTLE HEDINGHAM

Map 04 TL73
(1m off A604)
☎ Hedingham (0787) 60261
This majestic Norman castle was built in 1140. It was besieged by King John, and visited by King Henry VII, King Henry VIII and Queen Elizabeth and was the home of the de Veres, Earls of Oxford, for over 500 years. The Keep is one of the finest in Western Europe and stands almost 100ft high. The banqueting hall and minstrels' gallery and other features are also in good condition. Visitors can enjoy peaceful woodland walks and perhaps a picnic by the lake.
Open Etr wknd-Oct, daily 10-5
£2.50 (ch £1.25). Family ticket £6.
P ☕ *shop* 🐕

Chelmsford & Essex Museum, Essex Regiment Museum — CHELMSFORD

Map 04 TL70
Oaklands Park, Moulsham St
☎ (0245) 353066 & 260614
The long-term exhibitions cover local history, archaeology and other subjects, with displays of costume, glass, paintings, coins and local products. The regimental museum traces the regiment's history.
Open all year, Mon-Sat 10-5, Sun 2-5. (Closed Good Fri, 25-26 Dec, plus other days as advertised).
Free.
P ♿ *toilets for disabled shop* 🐕

Every effort is made to provide accurate information, but details might change during the currency of this guide.

Paycocke's — COGGESHALL

Map 04 TL82
West St
☎ (0376) 561305
This timber-framed house is a fine example of a medieval merchant's home. It was completed in about 1505 and has interesting carvings on the outside timbers, including the Paycocke trade sign. Inside there are further elaborate carvings and linenfold panelling. Behind the house is a pretty garden.
Open 29 Mar-4 Oct Tue, Thu, Sun & BH Mon 2-5.30. (Closed Good Fri).
£1.40 (ch 75p).
♿ 🐕
(NT)

The Beth Chatto Gardens Ltd — COLCHESTER

Map 04 TL92
Elmstead Market (7m E on A133)
☎ Wivenhoe (0206) 822007
The gardens were begun only 28 years ago, when Beth Chatto and her husband began working on four acres of wasteland. Today the wasteland has become a garden of three areas, each with their own distinctive character and plants. First is the south-west facing dry garden, which is on gravel and has plants which can cope with drought, such as yucca and pineapple broom. It faces a group of oaks which shade the second area, with woodland and other shade-loving plants, including some chosen for their fine foliage. Lastly, there is the wetland garden, with five large pools filled with fish and surrounded by swathes of exotic and native bog plants. The nursery has over 1000 different plants.
Open all year, Mar-Oct, Mon-Sat 9-5; Nov-Feb, Mon-Fri 9-4. (Closed BHs).
* *£1.*
P 🐕

Colchester Castle Museum — COLCHESTER

Map 04 TL92
Castle Park, High St
☎ (0206) 712931

This is the largest Norman Castle Keep in Europe. It was built over the remains of the magnificent Roman Temple of Claudius which was destroyed by Boudicca in AD60.
Colchester was the first capital of Roman Britain, and the archeaological collections on display are among the finest in the country.
Open all year, Mon-Sat 10-5, Sun (Apr-Oct) 2-5. Last admission 4.30. (Closed 24-26 Dec).
* *£1 (ch 5-16, pen, students & UB40 50p).*
♿ *shop* 🐕

Colchester Zoo — COLCHESTER

Map 04 TL92
Stanway Hall, Maldon Rd (3m W of town B1022)
☎ (0839) 222000
The zoo has one hundred and fifty types of animal, the most exciting collection in East Anglia. Visitors can meet the elephants, handle a snake, and see parrots, seals, penguins and birds of prey all appearing in fun, informative daily displays. There is also a lakeside miniature railway, amusement complex, several eating places and gift shops, all set in forty acres of beautiful gardens. Special events include a Teddy Bears' Picnic, special days for Brownies, Scouts and Mother and Toddler groups; please phone for details.
Open all year, daily from 9.30. Last admission 5.30pm (1hr before dusk out of season). (Closed 25 Dec).
* *£4.50 (ch 3-13 £2.50, pen £4, disabled £1.90).*
P ✕ *licensed* ♿ *toilets for disabled shop* 🐕

Hollytrees Museum — COLCHESTER

Map 04 TL92
High St
☎ (0206) 712931
Two centuries of fascinating toys, costume, decorative arts and curios are displayed in this attractive Georgian town house.
Open all year, Mon-Sat 10-1 & 2-5. (Closed Good Fri & 23-27 Dec).
Free.
♿ *shop* 🐕

Natural History Museum — COLCHESTER

Map 04 TL92
All Saints Church, High St
☎ (0206) 712931
Displays of the distintive natural history of North-east Essex, including impressive dioramas, are housed in the former All Saints Church.
Open all year, Mon-Sat 10-1 & 2-5. (Closed Sun, Good Fri & pm 23-27 Dec).
Free.
♿ *shop* 🐕

Trinity Museum — COLCHESTER

Map 04 TL92
Holy Trinity Church, Trinity Sq
☎ (0206) 712931
Town and country life in the Colchester area over the last two hundred years are displayed in this medieval former Church of Holy Trinity complete with Saxon tower.
Open all year, Mon-Sat 10-1 & 2-5. (Closed Sun, Good Fri & 23-27 Dec).
Free.
♿ *shop* 🐕

Tymperleys Clock Museum — COLCHESTER

Map 04 TL92
Trinity St
☎ (0206) 712931 & 712932
A fine collection of Colchester-made clocks on display in this restored, late 15th-century house.
Open Apr-Oct, Mon-Sat 10-1 & 2-5.
Free.
♿ *shop* 🐕

Thurrock Museum — GRAYS

Map 04 TQ67
Orsett Rd
☎ Grays Thurrock (0375) 390000 ext 2414
Local history, agriculture, trades and industries are illustrated, with a display on archaeology from the Stone Age to the Saxons.
Open all year, Mon-Sat 9-8. (Closed BH).
Free.
♿ *toilets for disabled shop* 🐕

Hadleigh Castle — HADLEIGH

Map 04 TQ88
A familiar sight from Constable's paintings, the castle was first built by Hubert de Burgh and has fine views of the Thames estuary. It is defended by ditches on three sides, and the north-east and south-east towers are still impressive. The latter has a fireplace and three garderobe (latrine) shafts.
Open any reasonable time.
Free.
(EH)

Harlow Museum — HARLOW

Map 04 TL41
Passmores House, Third Av
☎ (0279) 446422
Harlow is best known as a new town, but the museum tells its story from Prehistoric and Roman to modern times, with a section on the Harlow Potters and the New Town. It is housed in an early Georgian building set in gardens. Part of the medieval moat from an earlier house can be seen.
Open all year, Tue & Thu 10-9, Wed & Fri-Mon 10-5. (Closed 12.30-1.30 Sat-Sun & Xmas).
Free.
P ♿ *shop* 🐕

Mark Hall Cycle Museum & Gardens — HARLOW

Map 04 TL41
Muskham Rd off First Av
☎ (0279) 39680
The history of the bicycle is illustrated with over 60 examples, from an 1819 hobby horse to a plastic machine of 1982, and a wide range of accessories

and memorabilia. There are also three walled gardens, a Tudor herb garden and a cottage garden.
Open all year, daily 10-5, gardens dusk in winter. (Closed 1-2 Mon-Fri & Xmas). Free.
🅿 🚻 *toilets for disabled shop* 🐕

The Redoubt — HARWICH

Map 05 TM23
☎ (0255) 503429
The 180ft-diameter circular fort was built in 1808 in case of invasion by Napoleon. It has a dry moat and 8ft-thick walls, with 18 rooms for stores, ammunition and quarters for 300 men. The Redoubt is being restored by the Harwich Society, and contains three

small museums. Ten guns can be seen on the battlements. On 25 May the annual fete will be held.
*Open all year, Sun 10-12 & 2-5. Also 25 May, Sat in Jul & daily in Aug, 2-5. (Closed 27 Dec-24 May).
£1 (accompanied ch free).
shop*

HEDINGHAM
See Castle Hedingham

🐕 The 'No Dogs' symbol does not normally apply to guide dogs – these are permitted in most establishments.

Layer Marney Tower — LAYER MARNEY

Map 04 TL91
(off B1022)
☎ Colchester (0206) 330784
The only parts of the grand mansion planned by Sir Henry Marney to be completed were the remarkable gatehouse and west wing. However, the red-brick and terracotta-patterned gatehouse is grander than those of some royal palaces, and remains one of the great buildings of the 16th century. The west wing has similar architecture. Also

of interest is a rare breeds farm, the formal gardens, a medieval barn, a church, a farm shop and the deer park. Many special events organised for 1992 include the Grail Fair on 24-25 May with medieval healing and magical arts and jousting tournament.
*Open Jul-Aug, daily (ex Sat) 2-6; Apr-Jun & Sep, Thu & Sun 2-6; BHs 11-6.
£3 (ch £1.50). Party 20+.*
🅿 ♨ 🚻 *shop* 🐕

Mistley Towers — MISTLEY

Map 04 TM13
All that remains of the grand hall and church, commissioned by Richard Rigby and designed by Robert Adam, are the lodges built in 1782 for the hall, and two square, classic towers topped with

drums and domes which Adam had added to an earlier church.
*Open all reasonable times.
Free.*
🚻 *(exterior only)*
(EH)

Mole Hall Wildlife Park — NEWPORT

Map 04 TL53
Widdington
☎ Saffron Walden (0799) 40400
Set within the grounds of a part-Elizabethan hall, which is not open to the public, this wildlife park has a large collection of birds and animals in pools and enclosures. It offers a rare opportunity to see otters feeding and at play, and other creatures are housed in attractive pens within a garden setting where many waterfowl roam free. A signposted walk takes visitors through a deer paddock. The butterfly house and insect pavillion allow visitors to wander

through a tropical environment with exotic plants and beautiful free-flying butterflies. A small tea shop provides a welcome break, and a gift shop sells interesting items pertaining to natural history, displays of butterflies and mementos. From March 1992 onwards there will be a large pool for Koi and other fish (open to adults only).
*Open all year, daily 10.30-6 (or dusk). (Closed 25 Dec). Butterfly House open mid Mar-mid Nov.
£3.50 (ch £2.25, pen £3). Party.*
🅿 ♨ *shop* 🐕

Saffron Walden Museum — SAFFRON WALDEN

Map 04 TL53
Museum St
☎ (0799) 22494
Built in 1834, the museum lies near the castle ruins on the east side of the town. Its collections include local archaeology, natural history, ceramics, glass, costume, furniture, and toys, and special

exhibitions are held.
Open all year, Apr-Sep, Mon-Sat 11-5, Sun & BHs 2.30-5; Oct-Mar,Mon-Sat, 11-4, Sun & BHs 2.30-5. (Closed Good Fri, 24 & 25 Dec).
🅿 🚻 *toilets for disabled shop* 🐕
Details not confirmed for 1992

Central Museum & Planetarium — SOUTHEND-ON-SEA

Map 04 TQ88
Victoria Av
☎ (0702) 330214
A fine Edwardian building housing displays of archaeology, natural history and local history, telling the story of man in the south east Essex area. Also the only planetarium in the South East outside London. Special events for 1992 include: 16 May onwards, Prehistoric

Technology – an exhibition illustrating the life and achievements of prehistoric people in Northern Europe; Jul-Oct, A Century and More of Southend.
*Open – Central Museum Mon 1-5, Tue-Sat 10-5 (Closed Sun & BH); Planetarium Wed-Sat, shows at 10, 11, noon, 2, 3 & 4.
✱ Central Museum free. Planetarium admission charged.*
🚻 *(planetarium not accessible) shop* 🐕

Tilbury Fort — TILBURY

Map 04 TQ67
☎ (0375) 858489
The fort dates from the reign of Henry VIII, but is most famous for Queen Elizabeth I's review of the fleet and army gathered to fight the Spanish Armada. In about 1670 the fort was extensively altered for defence against the Dutch and the French – ironically, it

was designed by a Dutchman in the French style.
*Open all year, Apr-Sep, daily 10-6; Oct-Mar, Tue-Sun 10-4. (Closed 24-26 Dec & 1 Jan).
£1.50 (ch 75p, pen, students & UB40 £1.10).*
🅿 🚻 🐕
(EH)

Hayes Hill Farm — WALTHAM ABBEY

Map 04 TL30
Stubbings Hall Ln, Crooked Mile
☎ Nazeing (099289) 2291
A traditional-style farmyard which has been opened to the public. Visitors can see a range of farm animals, kept in the traditional way, plus tools and machinery from earlier times. The centrepiece of the farm is a restored 16th-century barn. On Sundays and Bank Holidays there are demonstrations

of traditional crafts. Your visit also includes a look around Holyfield Hall Farm, a working commercial dairy and arable farm of some 435 acres. There are 150 Fresian cows, and milking takes place at 2.45pm every day. Booked guided tours are available.
*Open all year, Mon-Fri 10-4.30, wknds & BH 10-6.
✱ £1.60 (ch & pen £1). Party.*
🅿 🚻 *toilets for disabled shop*

Waltham Abbey Gatehouse, Bridge & Entrance to Cloisters — WALTHAM ABBEY

Map 04 TL30
Beside the great Norman church at Waltham are the ruins of the abbey buildings. Little remains but a 14th-century bridge and gatehouse, with both pedestrian and vehicle entrances, and part of the 12th-century north cloister.

The bridge is named after King Harold, founder of the abbey. The church has an undercroft museum.
*Open any reasonable time.
Free.*
🅿
(EH)

GLOUCESTERSHIRE

Barnsley House Garden — BARNSLEY

Map 03 SP00
(4m NE of Cirencester on B4425)
☎ Bibury (0285740) 281
This lovely garden is the creation of Rosemary Verey, who since 1962 has transformed the older garden that was here. There are herbs and a knot garden, and best of all a vegetable garden planted as a French 'potager orne', with small paths forming a chequerboard around fruit trees trained as pyramids, ornamental brassicas and other decorative kitchen plants. They are planted for effect in groups rather than

allotment-style rows, but not simply for show, being constantly cut, picked and used by the family. The garden is also interesting for its use of ground cover in the borders. Other features include a laburnum walk (good in early June) and a lime walk. Two 18th-century summerhouses, one Gothic, the other classical, complete the picture.
*Open all year Mon, Wed, Thu & Sat 10-6; Parties & guided tours by appointment. House not open.
£2 (ch free, pen £1). Party.*
🅿 🚻 *garden centre* 🐕

Berkeley Castle — BERKELEY

Map 03 ST69
(on B4509 1.5m W of A38)
☎ Dursley (0453) 810332
Home of the Berkeleys for over 800 years, the castle is all one might expect – a great rambling place surrounded by 14ft thick walls, with a Norman keep, a great hall, medieval kitchens and some splendid apartments. It is most famous for the dungeon where Edward II was gruesomely murdered in 1327, at the instigation of his wife and the Earl of

Mortimer. Outside there are Elizabethan terraced gardens and an extensive park. There is also a particularly good butterfly farm, with hundreds of exotic butterflies in free flight.
*Open Apr, daily 2-5; May-Sep weekdays 11-5, Sun 2-5. Oct Sun only 2-4.30; BH Mon 11-5. (Closed Mon ex BH).
£3.40 (ch £1.60, pen £2.80).*
🅿 ♨ *shop* 🐕

See advertisement on page 78.

Jenner Museum — BERKELEY

Map 03 ST69
Church Ln, High St
☎ Dursley (0453) 810631
This beautiful Georgian house was the home of Edward Jenner, the discoverer of vaccination against smallpox. The house and the garden, with its Temple of Vaccinia, are much as they were in Jenner's day. He is buried in the nearby

church, which also has some fine monuments to the Berkeley family.
*Open 17 Apr-Sep, Tue-Sat 12.30-5.30, Sun 1-5.30. Oct, Sun 1-5.30. (Closed Mon, ex BH Mon 12.30-5.30).
£1.20 (ch 7 30p, students 50p, pen 80p). Family ticket.*
🅿 🚻 *toilets for disabled shop* 🐕

Birdland — BOURTON-ON-THE-WATER

Map 03 SP12
(on A429)
☎ Cotswold (0451) 20689 & 20480
The eight-acre garden of birds was created by Len Hill, nicknamed the 'Penguin Millionaire' because of his conservation interests. It contains a fine collection of penguins, new aviaries, a

tropical house and birds at liberty, including macaws, parrots, cockatoos and lorikeets.
*Open all year, Apr-Oct, daily 10-6; Nov-Mar, daily 10-4. (Closed 25 Dec).
✱ £3.50 (ch £2.80 & pen £3). Party 10+.*
🚻 *shop*

BERKELEY CASTLE
Gloucestershire

England's oldest inhabited castle was completed in 1153 at the command of Henry II. Ever since it has been the home of the Berkeleys who have given their name to numerous locations all over the world, from Berkeley Square in London to Berkeley University in California.

24 generations have preserved this ancient castle and transformed a savage Norman fortress into a truly stately home full of treasures. Paintings by primarily English and Dutch masters, tapestries, furniture of an interesting diversity, silver and porcelain.

Just off the A38 midway between Bristol and Gloucester. Leave M5 at exit 14 or 13.

Opening times — please see editorial reference.

Cotswolds Motor Museum   BOURTON-ON-THE-WATER

Map 03 SP12
☎ Cotswold (0451) 21255
Housed in a water mill on the River Windrush, the museum has cars and motorcycles from the vintage years up to the 1950s, with a collection of 800 advertising signs and some 8000 pieces of automobilia. Also here is the Childhood Toy Collection and Father Christmas Workshop.
Open Feb-Nov, daily 10-6.
& *shop*
Details not confirmed for 1992

Folly Farm Waterfowl   BOURTON-ON-THE-WATER

Map 03 SP12
(2.5 W on A436)
☎ (0451) 20285
Two miles from Bourton, this conservation centre in the Cotswolds has a series of pools and lakes with over 160 types of waterfowl, ducks, geese and poultry, including many rare and endangered species.
Open all year, Apr-Sep daily 10-6; Oct-Mar 10-4.
£2.70 (ch £1.60, pen £2).
🅿 🍽 & *toilets for disabled shop garden centre*

✳ An asterisk indicates that up-to-date information was not available at the time of our research – 1991 information has been published as an indication of what you may expect.

Model Village   BOURTON-ON-THE-WATER

Map 03 SP12
Old New Inn
☎ Cotswold (0451) 20467
The model is built of Cotswold stone to a scale of one-ninth, and is a perfect replica of the village. It includes a miniature River Windrush, a working model waterwheel, churches and shops, with tiny trees, shrubs and alpine plants.
Open all year 9-6.30 (summer), 10-dusk (winter). (Closed 25 Dec).
£1.20 (ch 90p, pen £1). Party 20+.
🅿 🍽 ✗ *licensed shop*

Village Life Exhibition   BOURTON-ON-THE-WATER

Map 03 SP12
The Old Mill
☎ Cotswold (0451) 21255
A complete Edwardian village shop is displayed with bathroom, kitchen and bedroom above. There is also a blacksmith's forge, a model of the old mill, photographs and toys, with a large display of street jewellery.
Open Feb-Nov, daily 10-6.
shop
Details not confirmed for 1992

Chedworth Roman Villa   CHEDWORTH

Map 03 SP01
Yanworth (off A429)
☎ Withington (024289) 256
The remains of a Romano-British villa, excavated 1864-66. Mosaics and two bath houses are well preserved. The museum houses the smaller finds and there is a 10-minute video programme.
Open Mar-Oct, Tue-Sun & BH Mon 10-5.30. (Closed Good Fri). Last admission 5; Nov-6 Dec, Wed-Sun 11-4 (or sunset) also 12-13 Dec.
£2.40. Family £6.60.
🅿 & *(wheelchair available) toilets for disabled shop* ✖
(NT)

Art Gallery & Museum   CHELTENHAM

Map 03 SO92
Clarence St
☎ (0242) 237431
The museum has an outstanding collection of furniture and metalwork by followers of William Morris such as C R Ashbee and Sidney Barnsley. There are also fine paintings from the 1600s onwards, including a group of 17th-century Dutch works, and exhibits relating to the social history and archaeology of the Cotswolds and the town. Temporary exhibitions are held at regular intervals throughout the year.
Open all year, Mon-Sat 10-5.20; May-Sep, Sun 2-5.20. (Closed BHs).
Free.
🍽 & *toilets for disabled shop* ✖

Holst Birthplace Museum   CHELTENHAM

Map 03 SO92
4 Clarence Rd, Pittville
☎ (0242) 524846 & 237431
The composer of *The Planets* was born at this Regency house in 1874. The rooms are furnished in the style of the period, and include a drawing room, housemaid's parlour, bedroom nursery and working Victorian kitchen and laundry.
Open all year, Tue-Fri 12-5.20, Sat 11-5.20. (Closed Mon, BHs & 10-14 Feb).
Free.
shop ✖

Pittville Pump Room & Museum   CHELTENHAM

Map 03 SO92
Pittville Park
☎ (0242) 512740 & 237431
The pump room is generally considered Cheltenham's finest building. It was built in Greek Revival style in the 19th century, and has a colonnaded façade and a pillared and balconied hall. The first pump room was more humble, just a thatched shelter over a spring where pigeons had been noticed pecking at salt crystals.
  The Pittville Pump Room was bought by the borough in 1890 and has since been restored and the spa fountain was repositioned in 1960. Various functions are held and there is a museum showing the story of the town from the 18th century. Imaginative use of original costumes brings to life the history of Cheltenham from its Regency heyday to the Swinging Sixties. Temporary exhibitions are held throughout the year on the theme of costume, textiles and jewellery.
Open all year, Tue-Sat 10.30-5; Apr-Oct, Sun 10.30-5; also Etr Mon, Spring & Summer BH's. Last admission 4.40.
Apr-Oct £1 (concessions 50p). Nov-Mar 60p (30p). Pump room free. Family ticket available. Party.
🅿 & *toilets for disabled shop* ✖

For an explanation of the symbols and abbreviations, see page 2.

Corinium Museum   CIRENCESTER

Map 03 SP00
Park St
☎ (0285) 655611
Cirencester was an important Roman city, and the museum has impressive displays of Roman mosaic floors, sculpture, everyday items, an unusual five-letter square palindrome, and a new Cotswold Prehistory gallery. Special exhibitions are held throughout the year. 'Building for the Disabled' award winner.
Open all year, Apr-Oct, Mon-Sat 10-5.30, Sun 2-5.30; Nov-Mar, Tue-Sat 10-5, Sun 2-5. Also open BHs. (Closed Xmas).
✳ £1 (ch 50p, students & pen 75p). Party.
& *toilets for disabled shop*
See advertisement on page 79.

Clearwell Caves Ancient Iron Mines   CLEARWELL

Map 03 SO50
☎ Dean (0594) 32535
The mines were worked in Iron Age times, and the industry grew under the Romans. Over half a million tons of ore were extracted in the 19th century, and the last commercial mining was in 1945. Today nine large caverns can be seen, with deeper trips for the more adventurous. There are engine rooms and exhibits of local mining and geology from the Forest of Dean, including several vintage stationary engines. Educational visits are a speciality. Special events for 1992 include: 20 Jun, Midsummer Party (100ft underground); 31 Oct, Hallowe'en Party; 1-24 Dec, A Christmas Fantasy.
Open Mar-Oct daily 10-5. Other times by arrangement. Santa's secret workshop 1-24 Dec – Mon-Fri 2-6, Sat-Sun 10-5.
£2.50 (ch £1.50, pen £2)
🅿 🍽 ✗ & *shop* ✖

Prinknash Abbey   CRANHAM

Map 03 SO81
(on A46)
☎ Painswick (0452) 812239
The abbey has become famous for its pottery in the 20th century, but its origins lie in the Middle Ages. Set in a large park, the old abbey building is a 12th- to 16th-century house which was used by Benedictine monks and guests of Gloucester Abbey until 1539. It became a priory and later an abbey for Benedictine monks from Caldey in 1928. Rich beds of clay were discovered when foundations were being dug for a new building, and so the pottery was established. It has a distinctive style, and is sold in many parts of the world. The monks are skilled in other crafts as well, and make many articles for the abbey church.
Open all year. Abbey Church: daily 5am-8pm. Pottery: Mon-Sat 10.30-4.30 (Sun pm). Pottery shop 9-5.30. (Closed Good Fri, 25 & 26 Dec).
75p (ch 40p).
🅿 🍽 & *toilets for disabled shop*

COTSWOLD MUSEUMS

the museum service of Cotswold District Council

CORINIUM MUSEUM at CIRENCESTER

Award-winning presentation of one of the finest collections of antiquities from Roman Britain. Full-scale reconstructions plus displays of Cotswold archaeology and local history and special exhibitions throughout the year.

Open daily throughout the year except winter Mondays in Park Street, close to town centre. Tel: (0285) 655611.

COTSWOLD COUNTRYSIDE COLLECTION at NORTHLEACH

Cotswold rural life museum housed in the 18th century Northleach House of Correction. Preserved cells and restored courtroom capture the atmosphere! Home of the Lloyd-Baker Collection of agricultural history plus special exhibitions on country themes.

Open: April to October (incl) daily 10 to 5.30 and Sundays 2 to 5.30 plus all Bank Holidays. Free car parking and picnic area; tourist information; museum shop; refreshments.
Telephone (0451) 60715 or (0285) 655611.

GLOUCESTER CITY MUSEUMS AND ART GALLERY

FOLK MUSEUM
- Timber-framed buildings
- Severn fishing and farming tools
- Wheelwright's shop

CITY MUSEUM & ART GALLERY
- Roman mosaics and sculptures
- Freshwater aquarium
- Antique furniture and barometers

CITY EAST GATE
- Roman and medieval towers

Prinknash Bird Park	CRANHAM

Map 03 SO81
Prinknash Abbey
☎ Gloucester (0452) 812727
Nine acres of parkland and lakes make a beautiful home for black swans, geese and other water birds. There are also exotic birds such as white and Indian blue peacocks and crown cranes, and the park supports fallow deer and pygmy goats. The Golden Wood is stocked with ornamental pheasants, and leads to the restored (and reputedly haunted) monks' fishpond, which contains trout. There is a very different kind of Pets Corner, with the emphasis on beauty.
Open all year, daily 10-5 (4 in winter). Park closes at 6pm (5 in winter).
✱ *£2.20 (ch & pen £1.10). Party.*
🅿 ♨ *shop* ✖

Odda's Chapel	DEERHURST

Map 03 SO82
(off B4213 near River Severn)
The rare Saxon chapel was built by Earl Odda and dedicated in 1056. It was discovered as part of a farmhouse and has been restored.
Open any reasonable time.
Free.
(EH)

Places to visit in this guide are pinpointed on the atlas at the back of the book.

City East Gate	GLOUCESTER

Map 03 SO81
Eastgate St
☎ (0452) 524131
Gloucester was Roman 'Glevum', and the Normans built their walls on Roman foundations. At City East Gate, there are Roman and medieval gate towers and a moat in an underground exhibition chamber. From 27 July to 29 August the adjacent city wall, and bastion in King's Walk are also open.
Open May-Sep, Wed & Fri 2.15-5, Sat 10-12 & 2.15-5.
✱ *30p (UB40s 10p).*
shop ✖

City Museum & Art Gallery	GLOUCESTER

Map 03 SO81
Brunswick Rd
☎ (0452) 524131
The museum houses the Marling bequest of 18th-century walnut furniture, barometers and domestic silver. The archaeology displays include Roman mosaics and sculptures, and the natural history section has a freshwater aquarium. There are paintings by Richard Wilson, Gainsborough, Turner and others, and art exhibitions are held throughout the year.
Open all year, Mon-Sat 10-5.
Free.
♿ *(lift) shop* ✖

Folk Museum	GLOUCESTER

Map 03 SO81
99-103 Westgate St
☎ (0452) 526467
A group of Tudor and Jacobean timber-framed houses now illustrates local history, domestic life and rural crafts. Exhibits range from Civil War armour to Victorian toys, wooden ploughs and Severn fishing tackle. There are also reconstructions of a Double Gloucester dairy and a wheelwright's shop, and a pin factory with an 18th-century forge.
Open all year, Mon-Sat 10-5.
Free.
♿ *shop* ✖

National Waterways Museum	GLOUCESTER

Map 03 SO81
Llanthony Warehouse, The Docks
☎ (0452) 307009
In October 1990, this museum was judged to be one of the top seven museums in Europe in the European Museum of the Year Awards. The judge's report said 'It has used a strong poetic sense to unlock the images always latent in technology, and has revealed canal and river travel not only as a means of transport, but as a way of life with a character of its own'.
For centuries goods were transferred at Gloucester Docks between inland craft bound for Wales and the Midlands, and larger vessels which could negotiate the Severn Estuary. The heyday of the docks came after the opening of the Gloucester and Berkeley Canal in 1827, and many of the warehouses built in the 19th century still stand. The museum is housed in the Llanthony warehouse, a seven-storey brick building with cast-iron columns, which now shows the role of inland waterways in Britain's fortunes. A traditional canal maintenance yard has been re-created alongside, there are boats to visit, and demonstrations are given of the crafts and skills needed to run the canals. Special events for 1992 include a Crafts Weekend on 3-4 May and a Tugs Weekend on 20-21 June.
Open all year, daily 10-6; (winter 10-5). (Closed 25 Dec).
✱ *Admission fee payable.*
🅿 *(charged)* ♨ ♿ *toilets for disabled shop* ✖

The Robert Opie Collection Museum of Packaging & Advertising	GLOUCESTER

Map 03 SO81
Albert Warehouse, Gloucester Docks
☎ (0452) 302309
This museum is both a feast of nostalgia and an interesting exploration of changing tastes in design, with tins, cartons, hoardings, boxes, bottles and other ephemera from Victorian times onwards on display. Quiz sheets for children.
Open all year, daily, 10-6; winter Tue-Fri 10-5, Sat & Sun 10-6. (Closed 25-26 Dec). £2.25 (ch 85p, pen & students £1.75). Family tickets £5.95. Party 10+.
🅿 *(charged)* ♨ ✖ *licensed* ♿ *shop* ✖

Cotswold Farm Park
GUITING POWER

Map 03 SP02
Bemborough (3.5m NE on unclass road)
☎ Cotswold (0451) 850307
Cotswold sheep, Old Gloucester cows and many other rare breeds of farm animals can be seen here in a typical Cotswold farm setting. The aim is to ensure the survival of the old breeds, and

education is an important part of the farm's work. There are seasonal events such as lambing in April, shearing in June (list of events available on application), and local crafts are on sale.
Open Apr-Sep, daily 10.30-6.
£2.50 (ch £1.25, pen £1.75).
P & toilets for disabled shop ✝

Hailes Abbey
HAILES

Map 03 SP02
☎ (0242) 602398
In the Middle Ages the Cistercian abbey attracted numerous pilgrims because it owned a phial said to contain the blood of Christ. Today the abbey is a beautiful ruin, and the museum has roof bosses, ornate tiles and other evidence of past

magnificence.
Open all year, Apr-Sep, daily 10-6; Oct-Mar, daily 10-4. (Closed 24-26 Dec & 1 Jan).
£1.60 (ch 80p, students, pen & UB40 £1.20).
P &
(EH & NT)

Littledean Hall
LITTLEDEAN

Map 03 SO61
☎ Dean (0594) 824213
The largest known Roman temple in rural Britain was unearthed here in 1984 and the manor itself was built in Norman times; its north front is on the site of a Saxon hall of the 11th century. The house has always been lived in, and remains relatively untouched since the 19th century. Inside there are

interpretive displays and a reconstruction of a Saxon lord's hall. The grounds offer beautiful walks, some of the oldest trees in Dean, fish pools in the walled garden and, of course, the Roman excavations. A new museum is currently under development.
Open Apr-Oct, daily 2-5.30. (Closed Sat).
✱ *£2.50 (ch £2, pen £2.25).*
P & ✝ *(ex in grounds)*

Dean Forest Railway
LYDNEY

Map 03 SO60
Norchard Steam Centre, New Mills
(1m N at New Mills on B4234)
☎ Dean (0594) 843423
Just north of Lydney lies the headquarters of the Dean Forest Railway where a number of locomotives, coaches, wagons and railway equipment are on show and guided tours are available by arrangement. There are also a gift shop, museum, riverside walk and forest trail. Events for 1992 will include

a Vintage Rally (18 Oct), Thomas the Tank Engine (20/21 Jun and 19/20 Sep), and 'Santa Specials' in Nov and Dec.
Open all year, daily for static displays. Steam days: Sun, Apr-Sep; Wed in Jun & Jul; Tue-Thu Aug & all BH's (ex Xmas & New Year).
✱ *£2.50 (ch £1.50 & pen £2). Party 20+. Prices include train ride (steam days only).*
P ☕ & toilets for disabled shop

For an explanation of the symbols and abbreviations, see page 2.

Hidcote Manor Garden
MICKLETON

Map 03 SP14
(1m E of B4632)
☎ (0386) 438333
One of the most delightful gardens in England, created this century by the great horticulturist Major Laurence Johnston and comprising a series of small gardens within the whole, separated by walls and hedges of different species. The gardens are famous

for rare shrubs, trees, herbaceous borders, 'old' roses and interesting plant species.
Open, Gardens only Apr-Oct, daily (ex Tue & Fri) 11-7, no entry after 6pm or 1hr before sunset.
£4.20. Family ticket £11.60. Parties by prior written arrangement.
P ✗ *licensed & toilets for disabled shop ✝*
(NT)

Kiftsgate Court Garden
MICKLETON

Map 03 SP14
Mickleton (0.5 m S off A46, adjacent Hidcote NT garden)
Standing adjacent to Hidcote is a magnificently situated house with a garden that is also open to the public. Its chief attraction lies in its collection of old-fashioned roses, including the largest

rose in England, the R Filipes Kiftsgate. A wide variety of unusual plants and shrubs and fine trees can be seen.
Open Apr-Sep, Wed, Thu, Sun & BH 2-6. Also Sat, Jun-Jul.
£2.20 (ch 80p).
P ☕ ✝

Batsford Arboretum
MORETON-IN-MARSH

Map 04 SP23
(1.5m W, off A44)
☎ (0608) 50722 & (0386) 700409(wknds)
This arboretum, although privately owned, boasts one of the largest

collections of trees in Great Britain. The 50 acres of land contain many rare and very beautiful species.
Open Mar-early Nov 10-5.
✱ *£2 (ch 16 & pen £1). Party.*
P ☕ shop garden centre

Cotswold Falconry Centre
MORETON-IN-MARSH

Map 04 SP23
Batsford Park (1m E on A44)
☎ Blockley (0386) 701043
Conveniently located by the Batsford Park Arboretum, the Cotswold Falconry gives daily demonstrations in the art of falconry. The emphasis here is on

breeding and conservation, and eagles, hawks, owls and falcons may be seen flying.
Open Mar-Nov, 10.30-5.30. (Last admission 5pm).
P & shop garden centre ✝
Details not confirmed for 1992

Sezincote
MORETON-IN-MARSH

Map 04 SP23
(1.5m off A44 Evesham rd)
The Indian-style house at Sezincote was the inspiration for Brighton Pavilion; its charming water garden adds to its exotic aura and features trees of unusual size.
Open: House, May-Jul & Sep, Thu & Fri

2.30-5.30. Garden only, all year (ex Dec) Thu, Fri & BH Mon 2-6 or dusk if earlier.
✱ *House & garden £3.50. Garden only £2.50 (ch £1 under 5 free). Groups by appointment only.*
P ✝

The National Birds of Prey Centre
NEWENT

Map 03 SO72
(1m SW on unclass Clifford's Mesne Road)
☎ (0531) 820286

Jemima Parry-Jones is becoming increasingly famous for her displays of falconry at shows and fairs all over the country. This is the 'home-base' for her exceptional collection of birds of prey. Trained birds can be seen at close quarters in the 'Hawk Walk' and there are also breeding aviaries, a gift shop, bookshop, coffee shop and children's play area. Weather permitting, birds are flown four times daily, giving an exciting and educational display.
Open Feb-Nov, daily 10.30-5.30.
✱ *£3.75 (ch £1.95).*
P ☕ & toilets for disabled shop ✝

Newent Butterfly & Natural World Centre
NEWENT

Map 03 SO72
Springbank, Birches Ln
☎ (0531) 821800
In a beautiful setting with magnificent views, The Butterfly Centre has a collection of tropical butterflies flying free in an exotic environment. There is also a live insect gallery, a reptile area

and a children's zoo. Aviaries of birds include fancy fowl, waterfowl, peacocks, and many others.
Open Etr-Oct, daily 10-5.
✱ *£2.95 (ch £1.95, ch under 4 free, pen £2.75).*
P & shop ✝

The Shambles
NEWENT

Map 03 SO72
Church St
☎ (0531) 822144
Victorian life is recreated here, around cobbled streets and a square flanked by shops and a four-storey house,

illustrating the way of life in a bygone age. A small Victorian town.
Open Etr-Xmas, Tue-Sun & BH's 10-6 (or dusk).
£2.35 (ch £1.35, pen £1.95).
☕ ✗ *licensed & toilets for disabled shop*

Cotswold Countryside Collection — NORTHLEACH

Map 03 SP11
Fosseway
☎ Cotswold (0451) 60715
The story of everyday rural life in the Cotswolds is told in this museum, housed in the remaining buildings of the Northleach House of Correction. It was one of a group of Gloucestershire's 'country prisons' built around 1789 by Sir Onesiphorus Paul. The Lloyd-Baker agricultural collection, one of the best in the country, exhibits a unique collection of Gloucestershire harvest-wagons. There is a 'below stairs' gallery showing a dairy, kitchen and laundry. There are also special exhibitions.
Open Apr-Oct, Mon-Sat 10-5.30, Sun 2-5.30 & BHs.
✱ *£1 (ch 50p, students & pen 75p). Party.*
🅿 🍴 ♿ *toilets for disabled shop*

Keith Harding's World of Mechanical Music — NORTHLEACH

Map 03 SP11
Oak House, High St
☎ Cotswold (0451) 60181
A fascinating collection of antique clocks, musical boxes, automata and mechanical musical instruments, restored and maintained in the world-famous workshops, displayed in a period setting, and played during regular tours. Winner of 'Come to Britain' award 1988.
Open all year, daily 10-6.
£3.50 (ch 16 £1.50, under 3 free, pen £2.75). Family ticket £8.50. Disabled-helpers Free.
🅿 ♿ *(brochure in braille) toilets for disabled shop* ✱

Painswick Rococo Garden — PAINSWICK

Map 03 SO80
The Stables, Painswick House
☎ (0452) 813204
This beautiful Rococo garden (a compromise between formality and informality) – the only one of its period to survive completely – is currently in the process of being restored. There are fascinating contemporary garden buildings with vistas, ponds and woodland walks, famous for snowdrops in the early spring.
Open Feb-mid Dec, 11-5.
£2.40 (ch £1.20, pen £2).
🅿 🍴 ✕ *licensed* ♿ *toilets for disabled shop*

Wildfowl & Wetlands Trust — SLIMBRIDGE

Map 03 SO70
(off A38 and M5 junc 13 or 14)
☎ Cambridge (Glos) (0453) 890333

Slimbridge was started as a wildfowl reserve in 1946 by Sir Peter Scott. Since then it has become one of the most famous in the world, having the largest and most varied collection of swans, geese and ducks to be seen. Slimbridge has six flocks of flamingos, which is the largest gathering of these birds in any country. There are both captive and wild birds and a substantial number of rare and endangered birds at Slimbridge. In a severe winter, up to 8000 birds may fly into the refuge, which now covers some 800 acres of flat fields, marsh and mudflats on the River Severn. First-class viewing facilities are available and, in winter, towers and hides provide remarkable views of the migrating birds. There is a permanent educational exhibition and also a Tropical House. Facilities for the disabled include purpose-built toilets for wheelchair users, and a braille trail with taped commentaries.
Open all year, daily from 9.30 (Closed 24-25 Dec)
🅿 🍴 ✕ *licensed* ♿ *toilets for disabled shop* ✱
Details not confirmed for 1992

Snowshill Manor — SNOWSHILL

Map 03 SP03
(3m SW of Broadway)
☎ Broadway (0386) 852410
Snowshill Manor is a Tudor house with a 17th-century façade. It has 21 rooms containing Charles Paget Wade's collection of craftmanship, including musical instruments, clocks, toys, bicycles, weavers' and spinners' tools, and Japanese armour.
Open Etr Sat-Mon 11-1 & 2-6; Apr & Oct, Sat & Sun 11-1 & 2-5; May-Sep Wed-Sun 11-1 & 2-6. Last admission to house 30 mins before closing.
£3.80 (ch £1.90). Family ticket £10.40.
🅿 *shop* ✱
(NT)

Dean Heritage Centre — SOUDLEY

Map 03 SO61
Camp Mill (on B4227)
☎ Dean (0594) 822170
Set around an old watermill and its tranquil mill pond in a beautiful wooded valley, the unique heritage of the Forest of Dean is portrayed through museum displays entitled 'Dean – the Story of a Forest', with a reconstructed cottage, coal mine, 12ft overshot waterwheel, beam engine and audio-visual sequences. There are also nature trails, including one suitable for wheelchairs, picnic areas and barbecue hearths as well as a smallholding. Added attractions are an adventure playground, craft shop and craft workshops. Many special events take place throughout the year.
Open all year, daily, Apr-Oct 10-6, Nov-Mar 10-5. (Closed 25-26 Dec).
✱ *£2.30 (ch £1.25, students, pen & UB40 £1.75). Party 20+. Season tickets available.*
🅿 🍴 ♿ *toilets for disabled shop* ✱ *(ex in grounds)*

Stanway House — STANWAY

Map 03 SP03
(0.5m E of B4632 or B4077)
☎ Stanton (038673) 469
A thoroughly lived-in Jacobean manor house with unusual furniture, set in formal landscaped parkland. There is also a tithe barn.
Open Jun-Aug, Tue & Thu 2-5.
£2 (ch £1, pen £1.75). Party.
🅿 ♿

Chavenage — TETBURY

Map 03 ST89
(2m NW signposted off B4014)
☎ (0666) 502329
Built in about 1576, this unspoilt Elizabethan house contains some stained glass from the 17th-century and earlier, and some good furniture and tapestries. The owner during the Civil War was a Parliamentarian, and the house also contains Cromwellian relics. In more recent years, the house has been the location for the television series 'Are You Being Served?' and 'Poirot'. There is a Shakespeare Week in July.
Open May-Sep, Thu, Sun & BHs 2-5. Also Etr Sun & Mon. Other days by appointment only.
£2.50 (ch £1.25).
🅿 ♿ ✱ *(ex in grounds)*

Nature in Art — TWIGWORTH

Map 03 SO82
Wallsworth Hall, Tewkesbury Rd (on A38)
☎ Gloucester (0452) 731422
An ever changing and ever growing collection portraying wildlife in any art medium, from any period and from all over the world, makes this the first museum of its kind. Dedicated to wildlife art of the highest international standards, there are myriads of outstanding exhibits including sculpture (both indoor and outdoor), tapestries
continued . . .

and ceramics. There is a comprehensive 'artist in residence' programme for nine months of the year. Awarded a Special Commendation in the National Heritage Museum of the Year Awards. Events include BBC Wildlife Photographer of the Year exhibition (11 Feb-15 Mar), Art in Nature exhibition (14 Jul-16 Aug), Animals and Nature Jewellery

(Nov/Dec), and a monthly programme of talks, films and demonstrations (programme published January 1992). *Open all year, Tue-Sun & BH's 10-5. (Closed 24-26 Dec).* £2.50 (ch, pen & students £1.75, ch under 8 free). 🅿 ➤ ♿ *(lift) toilets for disabled shop* ✖ *(ex grounds)*

Uley Tumulus   ULEY

Map 03 ST79
(1m N)
This 180ft long barrow is known as Hetty Pegler's Tump. The Neolithic burial mound is about 85ft wide and is surrounded by a dry-built wall. It

contains a central passage, built of stone, and three burial chambers.
Open any reasonable time.
Free.
(EH)

Westbury Court Garden   WESTBURY-ON-SEVERN

Map 03 SO71
☎ (045276) 461
This formal water garden with canals and yew hedges was laid out between 1696 and 1705. It is the earliest of its kind remaining in England and was restored in 1971 and planted with species dated from pre 1700, including

apple, pear and plum trees.
Open Apr-Oct, Wed-Sun & BH Mon 11-6. (Closed Good Fri). Other months by appointment only.
£1.80. *Party.*
🅿 ♿ *toilets for disabled* ✖
(NT)

Westonbirt Arboretum   WESTONBIRT

Map 03 ST88
(3m S Tetbury on A433)
☎ (066688) 220
This large arboretum was started in 1829 and now has one of the largest collections of temperate trees and shrubs in Europe. The trees are laid out in 600 acres of ground, in a series of wide sweeping rides and paths covering 17 miles. Waymarked trails and the great variety of trees provides interest and

colour throughout the year, even in winter, when the distinctive barks of the birches and maple are visible. There is a Visitor Centre with an exhibition, shop, and interesting video programme. The arboretum is managed by the Forestry Commission.
Open all year, daily 10-8 or sunset. Visitor centre & shop Etr-Xmas.
✳ £2 *(ch & pen £1).*
🅿 ➤ ♿ *toilets for disabled shop*

Sudeley Castle & Gardens   WINCHCOMBE

Map 03 SP02
☎ (0242) 602308
Little remains of the original medieval castle, once the home of Catherine Parr, the last wife of Henry VIII. There was considerable destruction during the Civil War, including Catherine Parr's tomb, and the castle was reconstructed in 1858 by Sir Gilbert Scott who incorporated the 15th-century remains into his design. Good furniture, porcelain and tapestries can be seen, and the art collection includes notable paintings by Turner, Rubens and Van Dyck. The award-winning gardens have been extended recently; centrepiece is the Queen's

Garden, a traditional Tudor rose garden. The eight-acre garden is complemented by Sudeley Castle Roses, a specialist plant centre. A special events programme runs throughout the year including jousting, craft fairs and concerts. There is also a waterfowl collection and a children's log fortress.
Open Apr-Oct daily; grounds 11-5.30, castle apartments noon-5.
£4.75 *(ch £2.50). Grounds only* £3.10 *(ch* £1.40). *Family ticket* £12. *Season ticket* £17.25 *(ch* £8.50). *Family ticket* £34.50. *Ground season ticket* £11. *Party 20+.*
🅿 ✖ *licensed* ♿ *shop garden centre* ✖

Witcombe Roman Villa   WITCOMBE, GREAT

Map 03 SO91
The remains of a large Roman Villa, built around three sides of a courtyard. Several mosaic pavements have been preserved and there is also evidence of

underfloor heating from a hypocaust.
Open any reasonable time.
Free.
🅿 ♿
(EH)

GREATER MANCHESTER

Dunham Massey Hall   ALTRINCHAM

Map 07 SJ78
(3m SW off A56, junc 19 off M6 or 7 off M56)
☎ 061-941 1025

A fine 18th-century house and park, home of the Earls of Stamford until 1976. Originally a 16th-century moated courtyard house, it was remodelled in the early 1730s by the 2nd Earl of Warrington and altered again in the early 1900s. It contains some fine 18th-century furniture and magnificent

silverware made by Huguenot smiths. Portraits of the Booth and Grey families (Earls of Warrington and Stamford) include one of Lady Jane Grey. A fully-equipped kitchen, butlers' pantry and laundry are not to be missed. Fallow deer roam the park, which also has a working Elizabethan saw mill. The 20-acre garden is on an ancient site with moat, mount and orangery. There are mature trees and fine lawns with an extensive range of shrubs and water-loving plants.
Open Apr-1 Nov. House daily (ex Fri) 1-5, Sun & BH Mon 12-5. (Last admission 4.30). Gardens open daily 12-5.30, Sun & BH Mon 11-5.30. Park always open. House & Garden £4. *Garden only* £2. *Family ticket* £10. *Park only* £1.50 *per car (NT members free), coaches free.*
🅿 *(charged)* ✖ *licensed* ♿ *toilets for disabled shop* ✖ *(ex in Park)*
(NT)

Museum of the Manchesters   ASHTON-UNDER-LYNE

Map 07 SJ99
Market Place
☎ 061-344 3078
This is an interesting museum illustrating the history of the Manchester Regiment and its relationship with the local

community, from the early 19th century to National Service.
Open all year, Mon-Sat, 10-4. (Closed Sun & BH's)
Free.
♿ *toilets for disabled shop* ✖

Portland Basin Industrial Heritage Centre   ASHTON-UNDER-LYNE

Map 07 SJ99
1 Portland Place, Portland St South (off A635)
☎ 061-308 3374
The story of the area over the last 200 years is unfolded here. The harsh times of the Industrial Revolution are highlighted, and there are special sections on political and religious movements.

Temporary exhibitions and summer children's activities are planned for 1992.
Open all year, Apr-Sep, Tue-Sat 10-6, Sun 12-6; Oct-Mar, Tue-Sat 10-4, Sun 12-4. Closed Mon (ex BH's).
Free.
🅿 ♿ *toilets for disabled shop* ✖

✖ The 'No Dogs' symbol does not normally apply to guide dogs – these are permitted in most establishments.

Tonge Moor Textile Museum   BOLTON

Map 07 SD70
Tonge Moor Library, Tonge Moor Rd
☎ (0204) 21394
Samuel Crompton lived in Bolton at Hall i' th' Wood, and his 1779 spinning mule is shown, together with other historic machines such as Arkwright's

water frame (1768) and Hargreave's spinning jenny (1764).
Open all year, Mon & Thu 2-7.30, Tue & Fri 9.30-5.30, Sat 9.30-12.30. (Closed Sun & Wed).
Free.
♿ ✖ ▱

Bramall Hall, Bramhall Park   BRAMHALL

Map 07 SJ88
☎ 061-485 3708
The large timber-framed hall dates from
the 14th century, and is one of the finest
black-and-white houses in Cheshire. It
has rare 16th-century wall paintings and
period furniture, and was the home of
the Davenport family for 500 years

before coming into the care of the
Metropolitan Borough of Stockport.
*Open all year, Apr-Sep daily 1-5, Oct-Mar
Tue-Sun 1-4. (Closed 25, 26 Dec & 2-31
Jan).*
P ✿ & *toilets for disabled shop* ✕
Details not confirmed for 1992

East Lancashire Railway & The Bury Transport Museum   BURY

Map 07 SD81
Bolton St Station
☎ 061-764 7790 (wknds) & 061-705
5111(day)
Opened in 1987, the track is 8.5 miles
long, stretching along the scenic Irwell
Valley and reviving memories of the
golden age of steam. The journey
includes two tunnels, viaducts and views
of the West Pennine Moors between
Bury, Ramsbottom and Rawtenstall.

Special events for 1992 include: Big
Engine weekends on 27 January and
22nd February; a Mother's Day special
on 29 March and Diesel weekends in
June and October.
*Weekend service & BHs, Santa specials Dec;
(Closed Xmas & New Year).
Bury-Rawtenstall £5 (ch £2.50). Bury-
Ramsbottom £3 (ch £1.50).*
P ✿ & *(station area c... table) toilets
for disabled shop*

City Art Galleries   MANCHESTER

Map 07 SJ89
Mosley St/Princess St
☎ 061-236 5244
The Mosley Street Galleries have
permanent displays of European art,
ceramics and silver which are displayed
with furniture in an elaborate decorative
scheme. The strength of this Gallery lies
in the superb collection of Victorian art,
especially the group of major Pre-
Raphaelite paintings. Decorative and
applied arts, including porcelain from

early times to the 19th century,
furniture and sculpture are also included
in this magnificent collection. The
Princess Street Galleries house major
temporary exhibitions.
*Open Mon-Sat 10-5.45, Sun 2-5.45
(Closed May Day BH, 25-26 Dec & 1
Jan).
Free.*
✿ ✕ *licensed* & *(notify gallery prior to a
visit) toilets for disabled shop* ✕

Gallery of English Costume   MANCHESTER

Map 07 SJ89
Platt Hall, Rusholme
☎ 061-224 5217
With one of the most comprehensive
costume collections in Great Britain, this
gallery makes captivating viewing.
Housed in a fine Georgian mansion, the
displays focus on the changing styles of
everyday fashion and accessories, looking
back over 400 years. Contemporary
fashion is also illustrated and because of
the vast amount of material in the

collection, exhibitions are constantly
changing and no one period is
permanently illustrated. The costume
library is available for research purposes,
by appointment only. New for 1992:
The New Woman – the change in
women's fashions and women's roles,
1939-1980.
*Open all year, daily (ex Tue) 10-5.45, Sun
2-5.45, Nov-Feb closes at 4pm.
Free.*
P & *shop* ✕

Granada Studios Tour   MANCHESTER

Map 07 SJ89
Water St
☎ 061-832 9090 & 061-833 0880
Enter the world of television at Granada
Studios Tour in the heart of the City
Centre. Only here can you walk down
Coronation Street, Downing Street and
Baker Street in just one day.
Visit the Giant Room, from the popular
children's programme Return of the
Antelope, where chairs loom overhead.
See the spectacular Magic Show, then
take part in a comedy debate in the
House of Commons. Explore the history
of cinema at Projections, experience
Motion Master where the seats move
with the action, and see a spectacular
3-D and laser show, the latest addition

to this award-winning tour. You should
allow a possible five hours for your visit.
Special events for 1992 include :16
Apr, Charlie Chaplin's birthday
promotion; 4 Jul, American
Independence Day.
*Open all year, 26 Mar-29 Sep, Tue, Thu-
Sun & BH Mon 9.45-7pm, Wed
9.45-11.30pm. (Closed Mon); 2 Oct-12
Apr, Wed-Fri 9.45-5.30, Sat, Sun & BH
Mon 9.45-6.30. (Closed Mon & Tue).
Telephone for details during school half
term. (Closed 24 & 25 Dec.)*
✲ *£8.75 (ch 12 £5.95). Family ticket
£26.50. Party.*
P *(charged)* ✿ ✕ *licensed* & *(ex Theatre)
toilets for disabled shop* ✕

The John Rylands University Library of Manchester   MANCHESTER

Map 07 SJ89
150 Deansgate
☎ 061-834 5343
Founded as a memorial to Manchester
cotton-magnate and millionaire John
Rylands (1801-88) this former private
library now comprises the Special
Collections Division of the John Rylands
University Library of Manchester. It is a
library of international renown, both for
its manuscript and printed-book
resources as well as its medieval-jewelled
bindings. In total its holdings extend to
five million books, manuscripts and
archival items representing some fifty
cultures and ranging in date from the
third millenium BC to the present day.
It is perhaps best known for its 2nd-
century St John Fragment, the earliest

known piece of New Testament writing
in existence; its St Christopher Woodcut
(1423), the earliest piece of western
printing with an undisputed date; and its
Gutenberg Bible (1455/6), the first book
printed using moveable type. The
Library's treasures are more than
matched by the magnificent neo-Gothic
surroundings designed by architect Basil
Champneys at the instigation of
Enriqueta Augustina Rylands, third wife
and widow of John Rylands. Notable
items from stock are always displayed as
part of the Library's varied exhibitions
programme which in 1992 includes: 4
Jun-3 Sep, Happy Every After (folktales
and fairytales) and on 9 Sep, Middle
Eastern Manuscripts.
continued . . .

THE MANCHESTER MUSEUM

The University, Manchester M13 9PL. Tel: 061 275 2634

Museum of the Year 1987. Superb collections of Botany (living plant
display), Geology (Stratigraphical Hall with fossil Ichthyosaur),
Entomology and Zoology (Cannon Aquarium, observation bee-hive).
New Mammal Gallery displays include human evolution and marine
biology. New displays of Daily Life in Ancient Egypt and mummies.
Large ethnographic collections, Simon Archery collection and
Numismatics.

Open daily 10.00-5.00 (closed Sundays). Admission free.
How to get there: Buses from Central Manchester to the University,
Oxford Road. The museum is part of Manchester University.

---

*Open all year, Mon-Fri 10-5.30, Sat 10-1
(Closed BH & Xmas-New Year). Pre-booked
groups only at other times.*

*Free.
shop* ✕

Manchester Jewish Museum   MANCHESTER

Map 07 SJ89
190 Cheetham Hill Rd *(1m from city
centre on A665)*
☎ 061-834 9879 & 061-832 7353
The history of Manchester Jewry is
illustrated by a permanent exhibition
housed in the former
Spanish/Portuguese Synagogue built in
1874. There are also temporary
exhibitions which change about three

times a year (for details send SAE to
Administrator).
*Open all year, Mon-Thu, 10.30-4, Sun
10.30-5. (Closed Jewish Hols).
£1 (ch, pen, student & UB40 50p) Family
ticket £3. Heritage Trails £4.50, £1.50 &
75p.*
& *(wheelchair access at rear door by
arrangement) shop* ✕

Manchester Museum   MANCHESTER

Map 07 SJ89
The University, Oxford Rd
☎ 061-275 2634
Famous for its Lloyd Japanese collection,
the museum also houses an aquarium,
numerous items from Ancient Egypt,
rocks, minerals, fossils, coins and native

craftsmanship among the millions of
exhibits. Frequent temporary exhibitions
are shown; lectures are provided.
*Open all year, Mon-Sat 10-5. (Closed Good
Fri, May Day & Xmas-New Year).*
P *(charged)* & *shop* ✕
Details not confirmed for 1992

Manchester Museum of Transport   MANCHESTER

Map 07 SJ89
Boyle St, Cheetham
☎ 061-205 2122 & 061-205 1082
The City's travel through the ages is
illustrated here; among the many
interesting exhibits include over 70 buses
and other vehicles from the area together
with old photographs, tickets and other
memorabilia. Special events for 1992

will be the Spring and Autumn Festival
of Transport; Historic Vehicle Rally and
a special weekend for disabled and
handicapped people.
*Open all year, Wed, Sat, Sun & BH 10-5.
Parties at other times by arrangement.
£1.25 (ch accompanied 50p). Family ticket
£3.*
P ✿ & *toilets for disabled shop*

Manchester United Museum & Tour Centre   MANCHESTER

Map 07 SJ89
Old Trafford *(2m from city centre, off
A56)*
☎ 061-877 4002
This Museum was opened in 1986 and
is the first purpose-built British football
museum. It covers the history of
Manchester United in word, pictures,
sound and vision, from its inception in
1878 to the present day. A new Trophy
Room was added in September 1991.
More than 400 exhibits are regularly on
display.

Subject to availability, a tour includes
a visit to the Museum, then into the
stadium, players' lounge, dressing rooms
and down the players' tunnel to view
the pitch and stadium.
*Open all year Tue-Sun & most BH Mons
9.30-4. (Closed 25 Dec).
Ground Tour, Museum & Trophy Room
£4.95 (ch & pen £2.95). Museum &
Trophy Room only £2.95 (ch & pen
£1.95).*
P ✿ & *toilets for disabled shop* ✕
See advertisement on page 84.

Museum of Science and Industry   MANCHESTER

Map 07 SJ89
Liverpool Rd, Castlefield
☎ 061-832 2244

National Heritage Museum of the Year
in 1990, the Museum of Science and
Industry offers endless fascination for
adults and children. Located on the site
of the oldest passenger railway in the
world, its permanent exhibitions include
the Power Hall, the Air and Space
Gallery, the 'Making of Manchester' and
'Underground Manchester' – an
exhibition of water sanitation and
sewerage. Other exhibitions include the
Electricity Gallery, the 'Out of This
World' Space Gallery, cameras and
continued . . .

MANCHESTER UNITED MUSEUM AND VISITOR CENTRE

Old Trafford, Manchester. Tel: 061-877-4002

The first purpose built Museum in British Football covers the history of Manchester United in words, pictures, sound and vision. More than 400 exhibits on display including Shirts, Trophies, Tickets, Programmes and International Caps.
Ground Tours available which usually include Dressing Rooms, walk down the players tunnel to view the pitch and stadium.
The Museum includes murals painted by the world famous Walter Kershaw.

Museum open: 9.30 am-4.00 pm every day except Mondays.

Admission Prices: £4.95 for adults £2.95 for Juniors/Senior Citizens. **Ground Tours and Museum.**

£2.95 for adults and £1.95 Juniors/Senior citizens. **Museum only.**

Under fives free.

Coffee Shop, Souvenir Shop and free parking.

Salford Mining Museum — SALFORD

Map 07 SJ89
Buile Hill Park, Eccles Old Rd
☎ 061-736 1832
Two reproduction coal mines, a gallery to illustrate the history and development of coal mining and an exhibition of mining art are housed in this listed Georgian building. The reference library and archives are only available for research purposes.
Open all year, Mon-Fri 10-12.30 & 1.30-5, Sun 2-5. (Closed Good Fri, 24-26 Dec & 1 Jan).
Free.
Ⓟ *shop* ✷

Salford Museum & Art Gallery — SALFORD

Map 07 SJ89
Peel Park, Crescent
☎ 061-736 2649
The pride of this provincial gallery has to be its collection of L S Lowry's works which are displayed in the art gallery together with Victorian paintings and decorative arts. The small museum is equally revealing with its street scene reconstructed in the typical style of a northern industrial town at the turn of the century.
Open all year, Mon-Fri 10-4.45, Sun 2-5. (Closed Good Fri, 25 & 26 Dec, 1 Jan).
Free.
Ⓟ ☕ ♿ *toilets for disabled shop* ✷

STOCKPORT
See Bramhall

Wigan Pier — WIGAN

Map 07 SD50
Wallgate
☎ (0942) 323666

Wigan Pier was once a music hall joke but today the pier, and its warehouses have been converted into a lively museum. The 'pier' was a wharf for loading coal on the Leeds-Liverpool Canal, and the theme of the museum is life as it was in the town at the turn of the century. There is a mock-up of a coal mine, and an escalator for sorting coal, as well as the interior of a pub, a miner's house and a school. Actors bring these to life by involving visitors as guests to the house or pupils in the school. There is also an exhibition called The Way We Were. Across the canal is a textile mill with the world's largest working mill engine and other textile, colliery and rope-making machines. The two parts are connected by a waterbus or by bridges and a canal walk. Since 1984 several festivals have been held at Wigan Pier each year: a Jazz Festival in July, an Arts Festival in September and another in December.
Open all year, daily 10-5. (Closed 25-26 Dec).
Ⓟ ☕ ♿ *(ex for steam engine) toilets for disabled shop* ✷
Details not confirmed for 1992

HAMPSHIRE

Airborne Forces Museum — ALDERSHOT

Map 04 SU85
Browning Barracks, Queens Av
☎ (0252) 349619
Aldershot is the home of the 5th Airborne Brigade, and paratroopers can often be seen practising their drops above the town, so it is an appropriate home for the Airborne Forces Museum. It is easily identified by the World War II Dakota outside, and tells the story of the creation and operation of the parachute forces from 1940 onwards. There are aircraft models and briefing models for World War II operations, and a post-war display includes captured enemy arms, vehicles, dioramas of actions, parachutes, equipment and many scale models. There are Victoria and George Crosses among the medals on show. The Airborne Forces Day Parade and Display is held on the first Saturday in July.
Open all year, daily 10-4.30. (Closed Mon & 22-29 Dec).
✷ *£1.25 (ch, students, pen and ex-servicemen 60p)*
Ⓟ ♿ *shop* ✷

Aldershot Military Museum — ALDERSHOT

Map 04 SU85
Evelyn Woods Rd, Queens Av
☎ (0252) 314598
A look behind the scenes at the daily life of both soldiers and civilians as Aldershot and Farnborough grew up around the military camps to become the home of the British Army. Displays include a Victorian barrack room and military tailor's shop, the birth of British aviation, the Canadian Army in Aldershot during World War II, and the Rushmoor Local History Gallery.
Special events for 1992 include: 19 Jul, Special Events Day, including displays by military societies and historical re-enactment groups etc.
Open Mar-Oct, daily 10-5; Nov-Feb, daily 10-4.30. (Closed 14-26 Dec & 1 Jan)
✷ *£1.50 (ch 40p & pen £1)*
Ⓟ ♿ *shop*

Royal Corps of Transport Museum — ALDERSHOT

Map 04 SU85
Buller Barracks
☎ (0252) 348834
General militaria, uniforms and badges of the corps and its predecessors are displayed here. There are also models and photographs of vehicles used from 1794 to the present day.
Open all year, Mon-Fri 9-12.30 & 2-4.30. (Closed Public bols)
Free.
Ⓟ ♿ *(assistance given) shop* ✷

---

microscopes, the printing and textile galleries, Machine Tools Gallery and 'Xperiment' – the interactive science centre. Recent additions include 'Energy for the Future' and the new Gas Gallery, telling the story of 200 years of Britain's gas history in a lively and entertaining way.
Open all year, daily 10-5. Last admission 4.30. (Closed 23-25 Dec).
£3.50 (ch, students, pen, UB40 & disabled £1.50 ch under 5 free). Party 10+.
Ⓟ *(charged)* ☕ ✕ *licensed* ♿ *toilets for disabled shop* ✷

Whitworth Art Gallery — MANCHESTER

Map 07 SJ89
University of Manchester, Oxford Rd
☎ 061-273 4865 & 061-273 5958
The Whitworth Art Gallery runs an exciting programme of temporary exhibitions and displays, many of which highlight our rich and varied permanent collections. Whether you like modern art or gentle English landscapes, there is something for everyone. Surprisingly, we also have important collections of textiles and wallpapers which are frequently on show. Artists represented include Albrecht Durer, William Blake, JMW Turner, William Morris, Barbara Hepworth and Gilbert and George. Items not on public display can be viewed by appointment.
Open Mon-Sat 10-5, Thu until 9pm. (Closed Good Fri & Xmas-New Year).
Free.
Ⓟ ✕ *licensed* ♿ *toilets for disabled shop* ✷ 🚌

Heaton Hall — PRESTWICH

Map 07 SD80
Heaton Park (on A665)
☎ 061-773 1231 or 061- 236 5244 ext 123
The finest neo-classical house in the north-west is surrounded by extensive parkland. Designed by James Wyatt for Sir Thomas Egerton in 1772, the house has magnificent period interiors decorated with fine plasterwork, paintings and furniture. Other attractions include a unique circular room with Pompeiian-style paintings, and an original Samuel Green organ. Changing exhibitions are put on throughout the summer.
Telephone for details
Ⓟ *(charged)* ☕ ✕ *licensed* ♿ *toilets for disabled shop* ✷
Details not confirmed for 1992

Ordsall Hall Museum — SALFORD

Map 07 SJ89
Taylorson St
☎ 061-872 0251
A Victorian farmhouse kitchen, local and social history displays and some interesting Tudor, and earlier and later, architecture are features of this half-timbered manor house; the erstwhile home of the Radclyffe family.
Open all year, Mon-Fri 10-12.30 & 1.30-5, Sun 2-5. (Closed Good Fri, 25-26 Dec & 1 Jan).
♿ *toilets for disabled shop* ✷
Details not confirmed for 1992

Mid Hants Railway   ALRESFORD

Map 04 SU53
Watercress Line
☎ (0962) 733810 & 734200
Best known as the Watercress Line, this steam railway runs along ten miles of the old Winchester to Alton line, between Alresford and Alton. The train travels through beautiful Hampshire countryside with views of hills and watercress beds. At Ropley several steam locomotives are being restored. There

are special activities throughout the year; telephone for details.
Open main operating periods: Sun, Jan-Mar. wknds & BH's end Mar-Oct. Mid wk running begins Jun-mid Jul. Daily mid Jul-1st wk Sep (check timetable). "Santa Special" wknds Dec, booking essential.
P ☕ ✗ *licensed ♿ (ramps for trains) toilets for disabled shop*
Details not confirmed for 1992

ALTON
See East Tisted

Sir Harold Hillier Gardens & Arboretum   AMPFIELD

Map 04 SU42
Jermyn's Ln
☎ Braishfield (0794) 68787
This is the largest collection of trees and shrubs of its kind in the British Isles. The plants come from different parts of the world, and include many rarities. The setting is 160 acres of attractive landscape, with something of interest at all times of the year. Superb colour is provided in particular during the spring and autumn seasons. Special events for

1992 include: May, guided walks every Wed and Sun at 2.30pm to look at collection of azaleas or rhododendrons; Oct, guided walks every Wed and Sun at 2.30pm to look at autumn colour and interest in the gardens.
Open all year, Mon-Fri 10.30-5; Mar-Nov, wknds & BH's 10.30-6.
✳ *£1.80 (ch 5-15 free wk days, wknds & BHs 50p, pen £1.40). Party 30 +.*
P ☕ ♿ *toilets for disabled garden centre* ✘

Andover Museum & Museum of The Iron Age   ANDOVER

Map 04 SU34
Church Close
☎ (0264) 366283
The museum is housed in a fine Georgian building. Among its displays are locally manufactured agricultural machinery and an aquarium to display local fish found in the Test Valley: new local history displays are opening in 1992. There is a natural history gallery,

and temporary exhibitions are held. The Museum of the Iron Age, which interprets Danebury Hill Fort, is housed in an adjacent building.
Open Apr-Oct, Tue-Sat 10-5. Also Museum of Iron Age Apr-Sep, Sun 2-5.
✳ *Admission fee payable for "Museum of the Iron Age" £1.10 (ch & pen 55p). Party.*
P ♿ *shop* ✘

10 miles of nostalgia.

Steam trains. Running through the rolling Hampshire countryside between Alton and Alresford. A living, breathing part of our heritage. Experience them for yourself on Hampshire's preserved steam railway. There's a direct link through Network South East to Alton, giving you reduced fares and, for cardholders, even greater reductions. Or take advantage of the easy road access. Once you've arrived, we'll transport you back to another age.

Open: *Sundays: January–Easter. Saturdays and Bank Holidays: Easter–end of October*
Mid-week running: *Mid-June–mid-July*
Daily running: *Mid-July–1st Week September (check timetable)*
Further details contact: *Marketing Officer, Mid-Hants Railway PLC, Alresford Station, Hampshire, SO24 9JG.* **Tel:** *(0962) 733810.*

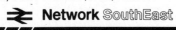

Finkley Down Farm Park   ANDOVER

Map 04 SU34
(signposted from A303 & A343)
☎ (0264) 352195
A wide range of farm animals and poultry can be seen here, including some rare breeds. The pets corner has tame, hand-reared baby animals that can be stroked and petted. There is also a

Countryside Museum, housed in a barn, Romany caravans and rural bygones to see, an adventure playground and a large picnic area.
Open Apr-1 Oct, daily 10.30-6. Last admission 5pm.
Admission charged.
P ☕ ♿ *toilets for disabled shop*

Every effort is made to provide accurate information,
but details might change during the currency
of this guide.

New Forest Butterfly Farm   ASHURST

Map 04 SU31
Longdown (off A35)
☎ Southampton (0703) 292166
The butterfly reserve is set in a glasshouse planted as a tropical garden, with lemon and banana trees, passion flowers and a mass of other plants and shrubs needed by the different types of butterfly. The species come from all over the world, with a separate area

devoted to butterflies of Britain. There are also dragonfly ponds, and other creatures to be seen include tarantulas, scorpions, praying mantises, ants and locusts.
Open 11 Apr-1 Nov, daily 10-5.
£3.30 (ch 3-14 £2.30 & pen £3). Party 15 +.
P ☕ ♿ *(ex woodland walk) toilets for disabled shop garden centre* ✘

✘ The 'No Dogs' symbol does not normally apply
to guide dogs – these are permitted in
most establishments.

Willis Museum   BASINGSTOKE

Map 04 SU65
Old Town Hall, Market Place
☎ (0256) 465902
The museum is housed in the handsome Old Town Hall. Displays include a New Town history gallery, exhibits of horology, embroidery, local interest and

a natural history gallery. There is also a gallery for temporary exhibitions and a local Tourist Information Centre.
Open all year, Tue-Fri 10-5, Sat 10-4. Free.
shop ✘

Beaulieu: National Motor Museum | BEAULIEU

Map 04 SU30
(on B3054)
☎ (0590) 612345

The venerable 16th-century house of Beaulieu is worth seeing just for its lovely setting by the Beaulieu River, but it has become most famous as the home of the National Motor Museum. This is one of the world's largest collections of vehicles and motoring memorabilia, with the extra attraction of 'Wheels', a feature which takes visitors on an automated trip through a spectacular display of 100 years of motoring. Other attractions are a high-level monorail through the grounds, veteran bus rides and a model railway. Special events are held throughout the year, including, in 1992, Boat Jumble on 12 Apr; Day for the Disabled 6 Jun; Countryside Show 28 Jun; Autojumble & Automart 12-13 Sep, and a Fireworks Fair on 31 Oct.

The main house itself has a collection of fine paintings and furnishings, with costumed figures showing generations of the Montagu family, which has lived here since 1538. The house is only the gatehouse of the great abbey which once stood here, and ruins of other monastic buildings can be seen in the grounds. There is also an exhibition of monastic life.

Open all year – Palace House & Gardens, National Motor Museum, Beaulieu Abbey & Exhibition of Monastic Life, Etr-Sep 10-6; Oct-Etr 10-5. (Closed 25 Dec).
✱ *£6.50 (ch £4.50, pen & students £5).*
Party 15 +.
🅿 ☕ Ᏽ *toilets for disabled shop*

Places to visit in this guide are pinpointed on the atlas at the back of the book.

Bishop's Waltham Palace | BISHOP'S WALTHAM

Map 04 SU51
(on A333)
☎ (0489) 892460
The town may have been laid out by the bishops of Winchester, and the remains of their palace are still impressive. It dates from the 12th century, and consists of state apartments round a cloister court, with a great hall and a four-storey tower. It was surrendered to Parliamentary forces in the Civil War.

Open all year, Apr-Sep, daily 10-6; Oct-Mar, Tue-Sun 10-4. (Closed 24-26 Dec & 1 Jan).
£1.50 (ch 75p, pen, students & UB40 £1.10).
🅿 Ᏽ ✖
(EH)

Beaulieu
Memories are made of this

Rolls Royce Silver Ghost 1909.

The Upper Drawing Room, reputedly haunted.

Wheels, a fascinating journey through motoring, past, present & future.

After the Ghost in the Museum...find out about the ghost in the House...... Once you've been back

Former Great Gatehouse of Beaulieu Abbey.

Donald Campbell's 1961 Bluebird.

Riverside walk in the grounds.

to the future...go on to the past... ...after seeing the Bluebird, relax and feed the ducks...

Miniature Veteran Car Ride.

The tranquil 13th century Beaulieu Abbey.

The magnificent collection of Grand Prix cars.

after viewing the veteran cars, why not ride in one?...retreat to a Monastery..then see life in the fast lane.

The National Motor Museum • Palace House and Grounds • Abbey and Exhibition • Wheels, A Sensational Journey Through 100 Years of Motoring • Rides and Drives • Costume Drama • Shops • Restaurants
Open Every Day Except Christmas Day 10am–6pm(Oct–Easter 10am–5pm) Tel: Beaulieu (0590) 612123(24 Hrs) Availability of some Features changes. Phone for details.

Spinners | BOLDRE

Map 04 SZ39
School Ln (off A337)
☎ Lymington (0590) 673347
The garden has been entirely created by the owners since 1960. It has azaleas, rhododendrons, camellias and magnolias, interspersed with primulas, blue poppies and other woodland and ground cover plants. The nusery (open all year) is famed for its rare and less common trees, shrubs and plants and attracts visitors from all over the world.
Open 20 Apr-1 Sep daily 10-6. Other times on application. Nursery open all year.
✱ *£1 (accompanied ch under 7 free).*
🅿 *garden centre* ✖

Breamore House, Countryside & Carriage Museums | BREAMORE

Map 03 SU11
(on A338)
☎ Downton (0725) 22468
The handsome manor house was built in around 1583 and has a fine collection of paintings, china and tapestries. The museum has good examples of coaches and steam engines, and uses reconstructed workshops and other displays to show how people lived, worked and travelled a century or so ago. On the weekend of 9th and 10th May the Breamore Museum Special (11am – 6pm) is a mini rally almost all under cover; on Sunday 14th June the Breamore Horse Show is in aid of the Wessex Medical School Trust. Other special events include: 23-25 May, Breamore Craft Show, open 10.30am; 19-20 Sep, Craft Show, open 10.30am.
Open Apr Tue, Wed & Sun & Etr, May-Jul & Sep, Tue-Thu & Sat, Sun & all BH, Aug, daily 2-5.30.
Combined tickets £3.50 (ch £2); Party & pen rate available.
🅿 ☕ Ᏽ *toilets for disabled shop* ✖

Bucklers Hard Village & Maritime Museum | BUCKLER'S HARD

Map 04 SU40
(off B3054)
☎ Bucklers Hard (0590) 616203
This is a historic shipbuilding village, where wooden warships, including some of Nelson's fleet, were built from New Forest oak. In its busy days the wide main street would have been used for rolling great logs to the 'hard' where the ships were built, and the village would have been stacked high with timber. The 18th-century homes of a shipwright and labourer, and a master shipbuilder's office can be seen. A typical inn scene has been reconstructed, complete with costumed figures, smells and conversation. The Maritime Museum tells the story of the local shipbuilding industry, and also has items from the voyages of Sir Francis Chichester, who moored his boats here. On the last Sunday in July 1992 The Bucklers Hard Village Festival recaptures all the atmosphere of the village fjte.
Open all year, Etr-Spring BH 10-6; Spring BH-Sep 10-9; Oct-Etr 10-4.30. (Closed 25 Dec).
£2.30 (ch £1.50, pen & student £1.85).
Party 15 +
🅿 ☕ ✖ *licensed* Ᏽ *shop*

Sandham Memorial Chapel | BURGHCLERE

Map 04 SU46
(4m S Newbury off A34)
☎ (063527) 292
The chapel was built in 1926-7 in memory of H W Sandham, who was killed in the First World War, and its walls are filled with 19 frescoes by Stanley Spencer. He based the work on his own wartime experiences, which included a period in Salonica and a spell as a hospital orderly. This had helped to make Spencer acutely aware of the humdrum life of the ordinary men. His pictures include soldiers coping with laundry and rubbish, moving baggage and dressing wounds, and laying out kit for inspection. These unsung aspects of war create a haunting and poignant series. Its climax is a resurrection scene that fills one wall. In the foreground is a tangled mass of crosses, each one handed in by a soldier.
Open Apr-Oct, Wed-Sun 11.30-6. Nov-Mar, Sat & Sun 11.30-4. Also open BH Mons.
£1.20 (ch 60p).
Ᏽ ✖
(NT)

Jane Austen's House | CHAWTON

Map 04 SU73
☎ Alton (0420) 83262
The house stands in the village street, and is where Jane Austen lived and wrote from 1809 to 1817. It has been restored to look as it would have done in the early 1800s, and items such as the author's donkey cart and writing table can be seen. Visitors are welcome to picnic in the garden in daylight hours. Refreshments are available in the village.
continued . . .

Special event for 1992: 18 Jul (175th anniversary of Jane Austen's death), an evening of music and readings.
Open daily Apr-Oct, 11-4.30 also Nov, Dec

& Mar, Wed-Sun. Jan & Feb, Sat & Sun. (Closed 25 & 26 Dec). £1.50 (ch 8-18 50p). Party 15 +.
& toilets for disabled shop ✖

Rotherfield Park   EAST TISTED

Map 04 SU73
☎ Tisted (042058) 204
The house is a fine example of Victorian Gothic architecture, and has been the home of the same family for over 170 years. There are large and varied gardens with good views.

Open, House & Gardens 1-7 Jun, 1-7 Jul, 1-7 Aug & Sun & Mon of BH's 2-5. Gardens, Apr-Sep, Sun & Thu 2-5. House & garden £2.50. Garden only £1 (ch free).
P *& garden centre ✖ (ex in grounds)*
See advertisement on page 85

Exbury Gardens   EXBURY

Map 04 SU40
Exbury Estate
☎ Fawley (0703) 891203

Exbury Gardens is a 200-acre landscape woodland garden on the East bank of the Beaulieu River and contains one of the finest collections of rhododendrons,

azaleas, camellias and magnolias in the world – as well as many rare and beautiful shrubs and trees. A labyrinth of tracks and paths enable the visitor to explore and enjoy the countless intricate plantings, the cascades and ponds, a sensational Rock Garden, Heather Garden and Iris Garden, Daffodil Meadow and River Walk. The Autumn colours are spectacular.
Open 2 Mar-7 Jul & 7 Sep-20 Oct, daily 10-5.30 (or dusk if earlier). Plant Centre & Gift Shop, all year, daily (ex 25 & 26 Dec).
P 🛒 *& toilets for disabled shop garden centre*
Details not confirmed for 1992

Royal Navy Submarine Museum & HMS Alliance   GOSPORT

Map 04 SZ69
Haslar Jetty Rd
☎ (Portsmouth) (0705) 529217
The great attraction of this museum is the chance to see inside a submarine. There are guided tours of *HMS Alliance*, a World War II vessel. *Holland I*, which was the Royal Navy's first submarine and dates from 1901. It was salvaged in December 1982 after 69 years under the sea. The more conventional part of the museum covers the development of submarines from their earliest days.

There is an emphasis on British boats, but an international view is also given, and there are models of practically every kind. Outside, the dominant presence of the modern Royal Navy gives an exciting, topical flavour to a visit.
Open all year, Apr-Oct 10-4.30, Nov-Mar 10-3.30. (Closed 24-25 Dec & 1 Jan). £3 (ch & pen £2). Party 12 + .Joint tickets available for HMS Warrior or Royal Marines Museum.
P 🛒 *& shop ✖*

For an explanation of the symbols and abbreviations, see page 2.

Havant Museum   HAVANT

Map 04 SU70
East St
☎ (0705) 451155
The museum shares this late 19th-century building with a flourishing arts centre. There are brand new displays of local history exhibits and a firearms collection, made by the engineer Cecil G

Vokes (he also developed the automatic windscreen wiper). There is also a regular programme of temporary exhibitions.
Open all year, Tue-Sat 10-5. Free.
P *& shop ✖*

Highclere Castle   HIGHCLERE

Map 04 SU46
☎ (0635) 253210
This splendid early Victorian mansion stands in beautiful parkland. It has sumptuous interiors and numerous Old Master pictures. Also shown are early finds by the 5th Earl of Carnarvon, one of the discoverers of Tutankhamun's tomb. Special events for 1992 include:

23-25 May, Craft Fair; 27 Jun, Classical Concert with Fireworks; 3-5 Jul, Flower Festival.
Open Jul-Sep, Wed-Sun 2-6; Aug BH Mon 11-6. Last admission to Castle 5pm. £3.90 (ch £2.50, pen £3.40)
P 🛒 *& (wheelchair available) toilets for disabled shop garden centre ✖*

Hinton Ampner   HINTON AMPNER

Map 04 SU62
(off A272)
☎ (0962) 771305 & 771023
It is the site and surroundings which provide the principal charm of Hinton Ampner. The house which now stands with wide views over the placid Hampshire landscape has suffered a chequered history. It was remodelled in the Georgian style in 1936 by Ralph Dutton, the 8th and last Lord Sherborne, and is a tribute to the energy and devotion of this man. Having lovingly restored and refurnished his home, he relinquished it to a school during the war and then saw it

decimated by fire in 1960. Undaunted, he rebuilt and refurnished the house with fine Regency furniture, pictures and porcelain.
The gardens juxtapose formality of design and informality of planting, and there are delightful walks with many prospects and unexpected vistas.
Open 29 Apr-Sep. Garden: Sat, Sun, Tue, Wed, Good Fri & BH Mon 1.30-5.30. House: Tue & Wed only plus Sat & Sun in Aug 1.30-5.30. Last admission 5pm. ✳ Garden £2 (ch £1). House £1.30 extra (ch 65p extra).
P *& toilets for disabled ✖*
(NT)

Hurst Castle   HURST CASTLE

Map 04 SZ38
☎ (0590) 642344
The castle is one of the many coastal forts built by Henry VIII in case of invasion, and was occupied in the Civil War and then fortified again in the 19th century. It can be reached on foot or by boat from Keyhaven (weather

permitting).
Open all year, Apr-Sep, daily 10-6; Oct-Mar, Tue-Sun 10-4. (Closed 24-26 Dec & 1 Jan). £1.50 (ch 75p, students, pen & UB40 £1.10).
🛒
(EH)

Bohunt Manor   LIPHOOK

Map 04 SU83
(on A3)
☎ (0428) 722208
Bohunt includes woodland gardens with a lakeside walk, a water garden, roses and herbaceous borders, and a collection of ornamental ducks, geese and cranes.

Several unusual trees and shrubs include a handkerchief tree and a Judas tree. The property has been given to the Worldwide Fund for Nature.
Open all year, daily.
✳ £1.50 (ch free, pen £1).
P *& toilets for disabled ✖*

Hollycombe Steam Collection   LIPHOOK

Map 04 SU83
(1.5m SE on unclass rd)
☎ (0428) 724900
This all-encompassing collection of steam-driven equipment includes a Bioscope show, a fairground organ, a steam roundabout, a big wheel, a steam farm, an engine room of a paddle steamer, demonstrations of threshing and steam rolling, traction engine rides and a steam locomotive which runs through a

woodland setting up to spectacular views of the South Downs. As if all this wasn't enough there are also woodland gardens for walks and a miniature railway.
Special events take place on 23-25 May, a Festival of Steam; 6-7 Jun; 29-31 Aug and 19-20 Sep.
Open 18 Apr-11 Oct, BH & Sun, also 17-31 Aug, rides 2-6. £4 (ch £3 & pen £3.50). Party 15 +
P 🛒 *& shop ✖*

New Forest Museum & Visitor Centre   LYNDHURST

Map 04 SU30
Main Car Park, High St
☎ (0703) 283914
The story of the New Forest, including its history, traditions, character and wildlife, told through an audio-visual show and exhibition displays. The show

features lifesize models of Forest characters, and the famous New Forest embroidery.
Open all year, daily from 10am (Closed 25 Dec)
Admission charged
P *& toilets for disabled shop ✖*

Marwell Zoological Park　　　　　　　　MARWELL

Map 04 SU52
Colden Common
☎ Owslebury (0962) 777406 & 777407

Devoted to the conservation and breeding of rare wild animals, Marwell has a worldwide reputation. The animals are housed in spacious enclosures or can be seen grazing in paddocks, and there is an enclosure where animals can be approached and stroked by children. Covering 100 acres of parkland, the collection includes over 1000 animals, and some of the species here no longer exist in the wild. New animals are being added constantly. There is also a gift shop and many attractions for younger children, including a children's farmyard, Wallaby Wood and road trains. Numerous events are held throughout the year, including a Christmas 'Winter Wonderland'.
Open all year, daily (ex 25 Dec), 10-6 (or dusk). Last admission 4.30pm or 1 hour before dusk (whichever is earliest).
£5.20 (ch 3-14 £4) Party 20+. Free to orange badge holders.
🅿 ▄ ✕ *licensed* ♿ *toilets for disabled shop* ✿

Museum of Army Flying　　　MIDDLE WALLOP

Map 04 SU23
(on A343)
☎ Andover (0264) 384421
This award-winning museum tells the story of army flying from the 19th-century to the present day. Exhibits include kites, balloons, photographs, dioramas, vintage aircraft and 'hands on' exhibits. Pilot training flights can be seen during the week and museum aircraft often fly at weekends (weather permitting). There is a restaurant with panoramic views over the airfield. Special events for 1992 include, amongst others: 9-10 May, Middle Wallop International Air Show; 21 Jun, Tiger Moth Rally; 1 Aug, Kite Flying Championships; 8 Aug, Model Aircraft International Rally.
Open all year, daily 10-4.30. (Closed Xmas-New Year). Evening visits by special arrangement.
✳ *£3 (ch, pen £2). Family ticket £8. Party.*
🅿 ✕ *licensed* ♿ *(lifts to upper levels) toilets for disabled shop* ✿ *(ex in grounds)*

Furzey Gardens　　　　　　　　　　MINSTEAD

Map 04 SU21
☎ Southampton (0703) 812464
The ancient cottage which stands in Furzey Gardens dates from 1560 and provides a charming venue for displays of local arts and crafts. The eight acres of peaceful glades which surround the cottage include winter and summer heathers, rare flowering trees and shrubs and a mass of spring bulbs which produce a wonderful display after the winter months.
Open daily 10-5 (dusk in winter). (Closed Xmas).
Gardens, cottage & gallery £1.95 (ch 5-14 95p). Nov-Feb reduced admission charge. Party 20+.
🅿 ♿ *shop* ✿

Mottisfont Abbey　　　　　　　　MOTTISFONT

Map 04 SU32
(4m S Newbury off A34)
☎ Lockerly (0794) 41220 & 40757
Set picturesquely by the River Test, Mottisfont Abbey is an 18th-century house adapted from a 13th-century priory. The north front shows its medieval church origins quite clearly, and the monks' 'cellarium' is virtually complete. Above it is the extraordinary Whistler Room, with its walls and ceiling decorated with *trompe l'oeil* paintings by Rex Whistler. The garden has splendid old trees and a walled garden planted with historic roses. Details for open air events in summer can be obtained by ringing the National Rose Garden Event Tel 0794 40757, and Abbey Plays (not NT) Tel 0794 40846.
Open Apr-Sep, Grounds daily (ex Fri & Sat) 2-6. Rose garden also open 7pm-9pm Tue, Wed, Thu & Sun during Rose Season. House (Whistler Room & Cellarium) special openings Wed only 2-5. (Last admission to house 5pm; Rose Gardens 8.30pm).
✳ *Grounds £2.30. House 50p extra.*
🅿 ♿ *toilets for disabled shop* ✿ *(NT)*

For an explanation of the symbols and abbreviations, see page 2.

Netley Abbey　　　　　　　　　　　　NETLEY

Map 04 SU40
☎ (0703) 453076
A romantic ruin, set among green lawns and trees, this was a 13th-century Cistercian abbey founded by Peter des Roches, tutor to Henry III. During the Dissolution part of the early English-style abbey was converted into a house; all that remains is an impressive shell. Nearby is the 19th-century Gothic- style Netley Castle.
Open all year, Apr-Sep, daily 10-6; Oct-Mar, wknds only 10-4. (Closed 24-26 Dec & 1 Jan).
£1.10 (ch 55p, students, pen & UB40 85p).
🅿 ♿ ✿ *(EH)*

Sammy Miller Museum　　　　　NEW MILTON

Map 04 SZ29
Gore Rd
☎ (0425) 619696
This museum has machines dating back to 1900 and is accepted as the world's most interesting Motor Cycle Museum with many machines that are the only surviving ones in the world. The Racing collection is of exceptional interest with the opportunity to see these wonderful World Record Breaking Bikes and their history, including the first bike to lap a Grand Prix Course at over 100 miles per hour, the 4 cylinder supercharged 500c.c. AJS. There are also DKW, NSU, Motoguzzi MV, Norton, Rudge, Velocette, Sunbeam etc., and of course three-wheel Morgan.
Open all year, daily 10-4.30.
🅿 ▄ ♿ *shop* ✿
Details not confirmed for 1992

Basing House　　　　　　　　　　OLD BASING

Map 04 SU65
Redbridge Ln
☎ Basingstoke (0256) 467294
A two-year siege in 1645 ended in the destruction of the largest house of Tudor England. Built on the site of a Norman castle in 1530, the ruins of Basing House (torches required) are a fascinating study. There is a re-creation of a garden of 1600 and exhibitions showing the history of the house. A fine 16th-century tithe barn stands nearby. Special events for 1992 include: 31 Aug-12 Sep, Community Arts Festival.
Open Apr-Sep, Wed-Sun & BH 2-6.
✳ *£1.10 (ch & pen 60p).*
🅿 *(tea shop on Sun only)* ♿ *toilets for disabled shop*

Paultons Park　　　　　　　　　　　　OWER

Map 04 SU31
(exit junc 2 M27, signed off A36)
☎ Southampton (0703) 814455
Paultons Park has 140 acres of beautiful parkland, extensive gardens and stands on the edge of the New Forest. Around 1000 exotic species of animals, birds and wildfowl have their home here. There are hours of pleasure for children in Kids Kingdom, the Magic Forest, Pet's Corner and Land of the Dinosaurs. There is a 10-acre lake with a working waterwheel and a miniature Rio Grande Railway. Other attractions include the Bumper Boats, Go-Karts and a six-lane Astroglide. Visitors can also enjoy a glimpse of the past in the Romany and Village Life Museums, and during the summer holidays there is live entertainment.
Open 14 Mar-1 Nov, daily 10-6.30. Last admission 4.30pm. Rides close 5.30pm. Earlier closing spring & autumn. Admission fee payable.
🅿 ▄ ✕ ♿ *(free wheelchair available) toilets for disabled shop* ✿

✳ An asterisk indicated that up-to-date information was not available at the time of our research – 1991 information has been published as an indication of what you may expect.

The Bear Museum　　　　　　　　PETERSFIELD

Map 04 SU72
38 Dragon St
☎ (0730) 65108
Teddy Bears are the theme of this museum, which children will love because they are allowed to cuddle and play with the exhibits. A variety of dolls and bears are displayed in the Victorian-style nursery while downstairs is the 'Teddy Bear's Picnic' where children are encouraged to sing along to the famous song and join in the fun of the large picnic scene. Dolls and bears can be brought here for repair and there is also a shop.
Open Mon-Sat 10-5 & Sun 11-5. (Closed 2 weeks in summer, phone for details). Free.
🅿 ♿ *shop* ✿

Portchester Castle　　　　　　　PORTCHESTER

Map 04 SU60
(off A27)
☎ (0705) 378291
Evidence of the 3rd-century Roman fort can still be seen on this nine-acre site. A church built in 1133 still stands, showing its fine west front and carved font. Robert Assheton built the great tower in 1367, and buildings within the inner courtyard were converted to a palace by Richard II, and the remains of the kitchen, hall and great chamber are still apparent. This was the palace from which Henry V embarked for Agincourt, and Henry VIII stayed here with Anne Boleyn. In later times, although falling into disrepair, the castle was home to prisoners from the Napoleonic Wars.
Open all year, Apr-Sep, daily 10-6; Oct-Mar, Tue-Sun 10-4. (Closed 24-26 Dec & 1 Jan).
£1.50 (ch 75p, students, pen & UB40 £1.10).
🅿 ♿ ✿ *(EH)*

Charles Dickens' Birthplace Museum　PORTSMOUTH & SOUTHSEA

Map 04 SZ69
393 Old Commercial Rd
☎ (0705) 827261
Built in 1805, this is the birthplace and early home of the famous novelist. Now restored and furnished to illustrate the middle-class taste of the early 19th century, the museum displays items pertaining to Dickens' work and the couch on which he died. There will be a special 'birthday' opening on 7 February from 10.30am-5.30pm.
Open Mar-Oct, daily 10.30-5.30 (last admission 5pm).
High season: £1 (ch & student 60p, pen 75p). Family ticket £2.60. Low season: 75p (ch & student 45p, pen 55p). Family ticket £1.95.
shop ✿

City Museum　　　　　　PORTSMOUTH & SOUTHSEA

Map 04 SZ69
Museum Rd, Old Portsmouth
☎ (0705) 827261
The museum features the new 'Story of Portsmouth' exhibition. This includes an introduction to the history of Portsmouth, local archaeology, the early history of the town, room settings showing life in the home from the 17th century to the 1950s, and a gallery of local pictures. Extensive use is made of audio-visuals and new sections will be added in 1993. Other displays include furniture and decorative arts from the 17th-20th centuries, a specialist contemporary crafts gallery and a regular programme of temporary exhibitions. Special events for 1992: 19-20 Apr, family activity weekend; 21 May-3 Jul, Football Exhibition.
Open all year, daily 10.30-5.30. Last admission 5pm. (Closed 24-26 Dec).
High season: 80p (ch 13 & students 50p, ch under 13 free, pen 60p); Low season: 60p (ch 13 & students 35p, ch under 13 free, pen 45p).
🅿 ♿ *(induction loops) toilets for disabled shop* ✿

Cumberland House Natural Science Museum & Butterfly House
PORTSMOUTH & SOUTHSEA

Map 04 SZ69
Eastern Pde
☎ (0705) 827261
The geology and natural history of the area are explained, with a full-size reconstruction of a dinosaur, and aquarium and free-flying butterflies. There are seasonal displays of woodland, downland and marshland ecology.
Open all year, daily 10.30-5.30. Last admission 5pm. (Closed 24-26 Dec).
✱ *£1 (ch 60p, pen 75p). Family ticket £2.60. Oct-Mar: 75p (ch 45p, pen 55p). Family ticket £1.95.*
🅿 *shop* ✖

This is just one of many guidebooks published by the AA. The full range is available at any AA shop or good bookshop.

D-Day Museum & Overlord Embroidery
PORTSMOUTH & SOUTHSEA

Map 04 SZ69
Clarence Esplanade (adjacent to Southsea Castle)
☎ (0705) 827261
The story of D-Day is told from the viewpoint of those involved in both sides of history's biggest seaborne invasion, through audio-visual shows, displays, military vehicles and the 272ft long
Overlord Embroidery.
Open all year, daily 10-5.30. Last admission 4.30. (Closed 24-26 Dec).
£3 (ch £1.80, pen £2.25). Family ticket £7.80. Oct-Mar: £2.25 (ch £1.35, pen £1.70). Family ticket £5.85.
&. *(Induction loops available for the hard of hearing). toilets for disabled shop* ✖

For an explanation of the symbols and abbreviations, see page 2.

Eastney Industrial Museum
PORTSMOUTH & SOUTHSEA

Map 04 SZ69
Henderson Rd, Eastney
☎ (0705) 827261
The engine house contains a pair of James and Watt beam engines and reciprocal pumps built in 1887 and now restored to their original condition. Normally 'in steam' at weekends, the engines are electrically operated at other times. An adjacent building of 1904
houses Crossley Gas Engines. A display, 'Steam and Water in Portsmouth', opened recently. Young persons must be accompanied by an adult.
Open & In Steam Apr-Sep, wknds & BHs 1.30-5.30; Oct-Mar, 1st Sun of month in steam).
£1 (ch 60p, pen 75p). Family ticket £2.60. shop ✖

HMS Victory
PORTSMOUTH & SOUTHSEA

Map 04 SZ69
HM Naval Base
☎ (0705) 839766

Still in commission and manned by regular serving officers and men, Lord Nelson's famous flagship at the Battle of

Trafalgar is, because of her age and historic significance, the world's most outstanding example of maritime restoration. A tour around her decks gives some idea of the sailors' way of life in Nelson's day, and visitors can see the spot where the Admiral received his fatal wound, and the surgery below decks where he eventually died.
Open Mar-Oct, daily 10-4.50; Nov-Feb, daily 10.30-4.30. (Closed 25 Dec).
£3.90 (ch £ 2.50, pen £3). Family £10.50. Prices include Royal Naval Museum.
🅿 *(charged)* &. *(lower gun deck) toilets for disabled shop* ✖

Every effort is made to provide accurate information, but details might change during the currency of this guide.

HMS Warrior 1860
PORTSMOUTH & SOUTHSEA

Map 04 SZ69
Victory Gate, HM Naval Base
☎ (0705) 291379

Originally launched in 1860, HMS Warrior was the world's first iron-hulled armoured warship. Restored, with

painstaking accuracy over a period of eight years in Hartlepool, she is now a permanent feature beside The Hard in Portsmouth. She gives an insight into life aboard a 19th-century warship, enhanced by the staff on board dressed in the correct uniform of the period. Special events are planned in August for 'Victorian Navy Days'.
Open all year, Mar-Jun & Sep-Oct 10-5.30; Jul-Aug 10-7; Nov-Feb 10.30-5. (Last admission 1 hr before closing).
£3.70 (ch & student £2.20, pen £3). Family ticket £10-£13. Party.
♨ ✖ &. *(upper deck only) toilets for disabled shop* ✖

The Mary Rose Ship Hall & Exhibition — PORTSMOUTH & SOUTHSEA

Map 04 SZ69
HM Naval base
☎ (0705) 839766 & 750521
The spectacular raising of the Mary Rose in 1982 is remembered by millions. Remarkably preserved in the Solent silts for 437 years, Henry VIII's warship was a Tudor time capsule, complete with everyday possessions, clothing, food, tools and weapons of her 700 men. Now the Mary Rose is one of Britain's major tourist attractions, offering a fascinating family day out. In her special dry dock workshop in Portsmouth's historic dockyard, the great oak hull is constantly sprayed with chilled water to conserve her timbers. Visitors can witness the reinstatement of much of the decking removed before the recovery, and will also enjoy special hi-tech 'Acoustiguide' radio commentary which is provided. In the Mary Rose Exhibition a twelve minute audio-visual presentation on the discovery, raising and conservation of the ship highlights the enormous endeavour which has gone into the world's most ambitious

underwater archaeological project. The visitor will then enjoy all the more the fascinating exhibition of the Mary Rose's treasures: a themed display of many of the 20,000 artefacts recovered, including longbows, cannon, gaming boards, clothing, combs, pewterware, lanterns, a shaving bowl – even the contents of the barber surgeon's chest, with syringes and jars of ointment! Special events for 1992 include: 10-11 Oct, a weekend of celebrations – the 10th Anniversary of the Raising. On 4-5 Jul there will be a summer celebration of the same. EASTER HOLIDAY SPECIAL OFFER: £1.50 OFF A FAMILY TICKET. Show this guide to reception on your way in for this seasonal discount. Valid 11-26 April.
Open all year, daily, Mar-Oct 10-5.30 (last visitors 4.30pm), Jul & Aug 10-6.45 (last visitor 5.45); Nov-Feb, daily 10.30-5 (last visitors 4pm). (Closed 25 Dec).
£3.90 (ch & students £2.50, pen £3). Family ticket £10.50-£13.
& *(to all but one gallery of Ship Hall) toilets for disabled shop* ✈

Round Tower — PORTSMOUTH & SOUTHSEA

Map 04 SZ69
Broad St, Old Portsmouth
☎ (0705) 827261
Dating from the early 15th century, this is the first permanent defensive work to be built in Portsmouth. Now an

excellent vantage point, it commands the entrance to the Harbour.
Open all year, daily.
Free.
P

The Royal Marines Museum — PORTSMOUTH & SOUTHSEA

Map 04 SZ69
☎ (0705) 819385
The Royal Marines Museum offers a series of exhibitions depicting the history of the corps through the ages. An audio-

visual show demonstrates the Marine involvement in the Falklands War, there's a chance to walk through a chilled display of conditions in the far

continued ...

north, and a 16th-century gallery showing life at sea, with graphic descriptions of punishments and food. Outside there is a junior commando assault course, and the chance to climb aboard a Falklands landing craft.

Open all year, Etr-Aug daily 10-5.30; Sep-Etr daily 10-4.30. (Closed 3 days Xmas)
£2.50 (ch & students £1.25, pen £1.50)
Family ticket £6
P *shop* ✈

Royal Naval Museum — PORTSMOUTH & SOUTHSEA

Map 04 SZ69
HM Naval Base
☎ (0705) 733060
This is the only museum exclusively devoted to the overall history of the Navy. A panorama of Trafalgar, with sound-effects, is complemented by relics of Lord Nelson, his officers and men. Uniforms, medals, figureheads and model ships are on show, and there are displays on such subjects as 'The Rise of

the Royal Navy', 'Sailing Navy', 'The Victorian Navy', 'The Navy in the 20th Century', and to bring the picture right up to date, 'The Modern Navy'.
Open all year, daily 10.30-5. (Closed 25 Dec).
£1.80 (ch & pen £1.30). Family ticket £4.90.
♥ & *(exhibit for sight impaired groups by prior arrangement) toilets for disabled shop* ✈

Southsea Castle & Museum — PORTSMOUTH & SOUTHSEA

Map 04 SZ69
Clarence Esp
☎ (0705) 827261
Part of Henry VIII's national coastal defences, this fort was built in 1545 and contains displays illustrating Portsmouth's development as a military fortress, aspects of naval history and the archaeology of the area. Special events for 1992 include: 27 Jun-5 Jul Free

Week, commemorating Henry VIII's birthday
Open all year, daily 10.30-5.30. Last admission 5pm. (Closed 24-26 Dec).
£1 (ch & students 60p, ch under 3 free, pen 75p). Family ticket £2.60. Oct-Mar: 75p (ch & students 45p, ch under 3 free, pen 55p). Family ticket £1.95.
P *(charged)* & *(wheelchair available) shop* ✈

Spitbank Fort — PORTSMOUTH & SOUTHSEA

Map 04 SZ69
☎ Fareham (0329) 664286 & (0831) 608383
This massive granite and iron fortress was built in the 1860s as part of the coastal defences against Napoleon. The interior is a maze of passages connecting over 50 rooms on two levels. A Victorian cooking range is still in working order, as are the forge and

402ft well from which fresh water is obtained. Because of its location one mile out to sea, it provides a panoramic viewpoint of the Solent.
Open Etr-Oct. (Weather permitting).
✱ *£4 (ch £2.50) includes ferry charge. Boat ride takes approx 20 mins, visitors should allow 2hr to view. Ferries depart Gosport & Clarence Pier.*
♥

BROADLANDS

*F*amous for royal honeymoons and as the home of Lord Mountbatten, Broadlands has countless mementoes of the Mountbatten and Palmerston eras and of its many royal visitors.

One of the finest Palladian houses in England, Broadlands is also home to a magnificent collection of paintings and furniture.

Enjoying an idyllic setting on the banks of the Test with superb views from the riverside lawns.

The Mountbatten Exhibition traces the eventful lives of Lord and Lady Mountbatten, while history is brought vividly to life

in 'The Life and Times of Lord Mountbatten' multi-screen audio-visual presentation.

SPECTACULAR MOUNTBATTEN AUDIO-VISUAL

Facilities include self-service restaurant, picnic area and two gift shops.

1992 opening 16th April-27th September. Admission 10am - 4pm. Closed Fridays, except Good Friday and in August. All-inclusive admission charge. Children under 12 free when accompanied by parent. Free parking.

For further information, call Romsey (0794) 516878.

OFF A31, ROMSEY. SIGNPOSTED FROM JUNCTIONS 2 AND 3, M27

Roman Villa   ROCKBOURNE

Map 03 SU11
☎ (07253) 541
Discovered in 1942, about a mile outside the village, these remains of a 40 room Roman Villa are the largest in the area and represent a fine display of mosaics and hypocaust. The site museum reveals discoveries excavated over many years and displayed in

context. These range from a coin hoard, jewellery and leather shoes to pottery vessels, architectural fragments and human skeletons.
Open Good Fri-Oct, Mon-Fri 2-6, Sat, Sun & BH 10.30-6; Jul & Aug daily 10.30-6.
✻ *£1.10 (concessions 55p).*
🅿 ё *shop* ✖

Broadlands   ROMSEY

Map 04 SU32
(main entrance on A31 Romsey by-pass)
☎ (0794) 516878

Famous as the venue chosen by the Prince and Princess of Wales for their honeymoon, Broadlands was the home of the late Lord Mountbatten and is now lived in by his grandson, Lord Romsey. An elegant Palladian mansion in a beautiful landscaped setting on the

banks of the River Test, Broadlands was also the country residence of Lord Palmerston, the great Victorian prime minister. Visitors may view the House with its fine furniture and pictures and mementoes of the famous, enjoy the superb views from the Riverside Lawns or relive Lord Mountbatten's life and times in the Mountbatten Exhibition and spectacular new Mountbatten A-V Presentation. Special events for 1992 include: 13-14 Jun, Broadlands Country Fair; 7-9 Aug, Hampshire Craft Show; 12 Sep, Romsey Show.
Open 16 Apr-27 Sep, 10-4. (Closed Fri ex Good Fri & Aug).
£4.75 (ch 12-16 £3.15, (ch under 12 free), pen, students & disabled £3.80). Party 15+
🅿 ✖ ё *toilets for disabled shop* ✖
See advertisement on page 90.

This is just one of many guidebooks published by the AA. The full range is available at any AA shop or good bookshop.

Oates Memorial Library & Museum and the   SELBORNE
Gilbert White Museum

Map 04 SU73
The Wakes
☎ (042050) 275
The pioneer naturalist and author, the Rev. Gilbert White, had his home here and enjoyed, as visitors can enjoy today, the extensive gardens. Captain Oates of Antarctic fame and his relation and explorer of Southern Africa, Frank Oates, are commemorated here in

separate galleries. The 18th-century rooms in the house are open to the public.
Open Mar-Oct, Wed-Sun & BH 11-5.30 (last admission 5pm). Also open Jul-Sep, Tue. (Closed Mon & Tue ex BH).
£1.60 (ch 80p, pen & students £1) Party 10+.
ё *shop* ✖

The Vyne   SHERBORNE ST JOHN

Map 04 SU65
(0.5m NE)
☎ Basingstoke (0256) 881337
The Vyne was built at the beginning of the 16th century by William Sandys and later came into the Chute family, who owned the property until 1956 when it was bequeathed to the National Trust. Much of the exterior of the house is still 16th century but there have been several major alterations, including the earliest classical portico on an English country house. Inside, the chapel with its original 16th-century stained glass, and the Oak

Gallery, are both of note. The Gallery has superb linenfold panelling. There is also an 18th-century tomb chamber and an elegant staircase. The house is set in a pleasant garden with a small lake.
Open Apr-24 Oct, Tue-Thu, Sat & Sun. House: 1.30-5.30, BH Mon 11-5.30. Garden: 12.30-5.30. Tea Room: 12.30-2.30 & 3-5.30. Last admission 5pm. (Closed Tue following BH).
✻ *House & Garden £3.80. Garden only £1.90.*
🅿 ⬤ ё *shop* ✖
(NT)

Calleva Museum   SILCHESTER

Map 04 SU66
"Sawyers Lands"
☎ (0734) 700362
The museum deals with the Roman town of Calleva Atrebatum, the remains of which have been excavated nearby. Little is visible of the actual remains except some of the mile long city wall

and a 9000-seat amphitheatre. Objects from the site, photos, maps and other material give a brief account of the town. (See also Reading Museum).
Open daily 9am-sunset.
✖
Details not confirmed for 1992

Places to visit in this guide are pinpointed on the atlas at the back of the book.

God's House Tower   SOUTHAMPTON

Map 04 SU41
Winkle St
☎ (0703) 220007 & 632493
An early fortified building, dating from the 1400s and taking its name from the nearby medieval hospital, it now houses the city's Museum of Archeology with

exhibits on the Roman, Saxon and medieval towns of Southampton.
Open Tue-Fri 10-12 & 1-5; Sat 10-12 & 1-4; Sun 2-5.
shop ✖
Details not confirmed for 1992

Southampton City Art Gallery   SOUTHAMPTON

Map 04 SU41
Civic Centre, Commercial Rd
☎ (0703) 231375
The largest gallery in the south of England, with the finest collection of paintings and sculpture. The collection spans six centuries of British and European art. It is particularly strong on

20th-century British art. The gallery has many exhibitions, films and schools workshops, quizzes, and projects.
Open all year, Tue-Fri 10-5, Sun 2-5. Late opening Thu (8pm seasonal). (Closed 25-27 & 31 Dec).
ё *toilets for disabled shop* ✖
Details not confirmed for 1992

Southampton Hall of Aviation   SOUTHAMPTON

Map 04 SU41
Albert Rd South
☎ (0703) 635830
The Hall of Aviation was inspired by the development of the famous Spitfire aeroplane at the nearby Supermarine Aviation Works at Woolston. The Spitfire evolved from aircraft built for the Schneider Trophy air races, which the company won in 1931 with the Supermarine 6B. There is a Supermarine S6A on display as well as one of the last Spitfires produced, the Mark 24, and other aircraft of local interest.
The museum is built around a huge

Sandringham flying-boat which visitors can board. It was operated out of Southampton Airport by Imperial Airways (BOAC) to all parts of the British Empire. There are also exhibits on aviation production and engineering in the south of England.
Open all year, Tue-Sat 10-5, Sun 12-5. Also BH Mon & School Holidays. (Closed Xmas).
£2.50 (ch £1.50, pen & students £2). Family ticket available. Party.
ё *(lift to all levels) toilets for disabled shop* ✖

Southampton Maritime Museum   SOUTHAMPTON

Map 04 SU41
The Wool House, Town Quay
☎ (0703) 223941 & 224216
The Wool House was built in the 14th century. It was a warehouse for wool and has buttressed stone walls and chestnut roof timbering. It currently houses an interesting maritime museum

with models and displays telling the history of the Victorian and modern port of Southampton.
Open all year, Tue-Fri 10-1 & 2-5, Sat 10-1 & 2-4, Sun 2-5. (Closed Mon & BHs).
ё *shop* ✖
Details not confirmed for 1992

Tudor House Museum   SOUTHAMPTON

Map 04 SU41
St Michael's Square
☎ (0703) 332513 & 224216
This fine half-timbered house, built at the end of the 15th century and therefore much older than its name suggests, is now a museum. The collection is mainly of Victorian domestic items, including dolls, costume

and some interesting mourning jewellery. There is a Tudor garden at the rear.
Open all year, Tue-Fri 10-5, Sat 10-4, Sun 2-5. (Closed Mon & BHs). Lunchtime closing 12-1.
ё *toilets for disabled shop* ✖
Details not confirmed for 1992

Stratfield Saye House   STRATFIELD SAYE

Map 04 SU66
(off A33)
☎ Basingstoke (0256) 882882

The house was built in 1630 and given by the nation to the first Duke of Wellington in 1817, after his victory

over Napoleon at the Battle of Waterloo. Stratfield Saye has remained the home of the Dukes of Wellington and contains a unique collection of paintings, prints, and furniture as well as many momentoes of the lst Duke, including his magnificent funeral carriage. It weighs 18 tons and is 17ft high. The Wellington Exhibition shows the life and times of the great statesman soldier, and in the grounds is the grave of Copenhagen, his mighty horse.
Open May-last Sun in Sep, daily ex Fri.
🅿 ✖ *licensed* ё *toilets for disabled shop* ✖
(ex in grounds)
Details not confirmed for 1992

Wellington Country Park & National Dairy Museum — STRATFIELD SAYE

Map 04 SU66
☎ Reading (0734) 326444

(For full entry see Riseley, Berkshire)

Titchfield Abbey — TITCHFIELD

Map 04 SU50
Also known as 'Palace House', this used to be the seat of the Earl of Southampton. The abbey was founded in 1232 and closed during the Dissolution, allowing the Earl to build a fine Tudor mansion on the site in 1538.

He incorporated the nave of the 13th-century church and the gatehouse into his new home.
Open Apr-Sep, daily 10-6.
Free.
P & ✗
(EH)

Eling Tide Mill — TOTTON

Map 04 SU31
Eling Toll Bridge
☎ Southampton (0703) 869575
Eling is one of the very few remaining mills still using tidal energy to grind wheat into flour. There has been a mill on this site for at least 900 years – a predecessor appeared in the Domesday Book. The present mill was extensively restored and reopened in 1980.

It has two sets of millstones, each separately driven, but only one set has been restored to working condition. The waterwheels were cast in iron and installed by Armfields of Ringwood at the beginning of the century. Flour ground at the mill is on sale.
Open all year, Wed-Sun, 10-4.
£1 (ch 60p, pen 75p).
P & shop ✗

✻ An asterisk indicates that up-to-date information was not available at the time of our research – 1991 information has been published as an indication of what you may expect.

The Hawk Conservancy — WEYHILL

Map 04 SU34
(off A303)
☎ Andover (0264) 772252
In the heart of attractive Hampshire countryside, this conservancy has a specialist collection of birds of prey from all over the world. The enclosures in which the birds are kept are very simple and the range of hawks, falcons, eagles, owls, vultures and kites are easily seen.

There are impressive demonstrations of falconry every day (at noon, 2pm, 3pm and 4pm), weather permitting, and also the exciting opportunity for visitors to hold or fly some of the birds themselves.
Open Mar-last Sun in Oct, daily from 10.30 (last admission spring & winter 4pm, summer 5pm).
P ✗ & *toilets for disabled shop* ✗
Details not confirmed for 1992

The Great Hall of Winchester Castle — WINCHESTER

Map 04 SU42
The Castle
☎ (0962) 846476
The only remaining portion of William the Conqueror's first castle, it was completed in 1235 and is a fine example of 13th-century architecture. Purbeck marble columns support the roof and on the west wall hangs the Round Table

purported to belong to King Arthur. A small medieval garden known as Queen Eleanor's Garden, leads off the Hall.
Open all year, Mar-Oct daily 10-5; Nov-Feb, daily 10-4. (Closed Good Fri & 25-26 Dec).
Donations.
& shop ✗

Guildhall Gallery — WINCHESTER

Map 04 SU42
The Broadway
☎ (0962) 848296 & 52874
Situated in the refurbished 19th-century Guildhall, the Gallery has a display of topographical views and frequently

changing temporary exhibitions.
Open during exhibitions, Tue-Sat 10-5, Sun & Mon 2-5. (Closed Mon, Sep-Mar).
Subject to alteration.
Free.
✗ *licensed* & *toilets for disabled shop* ✗

Gurkha Museum — WINCHESTER

Map 04 SU42
Peninsula Barracks, Romsey Rd
☎ (0962) 842832
This museum tells the fascinating story of the Gurkha's involvement with the British Army. Travel from Nepal to the North-West Frontier and beyond, with the help of life-sized dioramas, interactive exhibits and sound displays. Experience life in the Malayan jungle and the Falklands campaign. Special

events include: 25-29 Feb, Half Term Treasure Trail; 14-20 Apr, Great Easter Egg Hunt; 10-14 Nov, Curry Event; 1-23 Dec, Christmas Shopping.
Open all year, BH Mon, Tue-Sat 10-5. Last entry 4.30. (Closed Tue following BH Mon).
✻ *£1.50 (ch & pen 75p). Armed forces free. Party 15 +.*
P & *(lift & stair lift) toilets for disabled shop* ✗

Hospital of St Cross — WINCHESTER

Map 04 SU42
(1.5m S of city, on A333)
☎ (0962) 851375
The hospital was founded in 1136 for the benefit of 13 poor men and it is still functioning. Throughout the Middle Ages the hospital handed out the Dole – bread and beer – to travellers, and this is still done. The Chapel of St Cross (12th

century); Tim Brethrens Hall and medieval kitchen, and the walled Master's Garden are all worthy of close inspection.
Open all year, Apr-Sep, Mon-Fri 9.30-12.30 & 2-5; Oct-Mar 10.30-12.30 & 2-3.30. (Closed Sun, Good Fri & 25 Dec).
& *toilets for disabled shop* ✗

Royal Hampshire Regiment Museum & Memorial Gardens — WINCHESTER

Map 04 SU42
Serle's House, Southgate St
☎ (0962) 863658
This fine, 18th-century Baroque-style house now incorporates an excellent collection of militaria from the history of the Royal Hampshire Regiment. The

gardens are a memorial to the Regimental dead.
Open all year, Mon-Fri 10-12.30 & 2-4; Etr-Oct wknds & BH noon-4.
Free.
& ✗

Royal Hussars (PWO) Regimental Museum — WINCHESTER

Map 04 SU42
Peninsula Barracks, Romsey Rd
☎ (0962) 863751
The Royal Hussars (Prince of Wales Own) were formed by the amalgamation of the 10th Royal Hussars (Prince of Wales Own) and the 11th Hussars (Prince Alberts Own) in 1969, both regiments having been raised at the time of the Jacobite Rebellion in 1715. Visitors to this museum will learn the story of the Royal Hussars (Prince of Wales Own) from its founding to the present day. The displays are laid out in

chronological order and the various themes are lavishly illustrated with paintings, prints, photographs and many artefacts, including, weapons, medals, uniforms and a collection of gold and silver. Another interesting exhibit is the cupboard in which one Private Fowler of the 11th Hussars spent three years and nine months whilst hiding from the Germans in World War II.
Open 6 Jan-18 Dec, Tue-Fri 10-4, Sat, Sun & BH's 12-4.
£1.50 (ch & pen 50p). Party.
P & *toilets for disabled shop* ✗

✗ The 'No Dogs' symbol does not normally apply to guide dogs – these are permitted in most establishments.

Westgate Museum — WINCHESTER

Map 04 SU42
High St
☎ (0962) 848269
This small museum of arms, armour and historical objects from Winchester's past, is housed in the rooms over the medieval Westgate of the city. From the

roof there is an excellent panorama of the city and surrounding country.
Open all year, Mon-Fri 10-5, Sat 10-1 & 2-5, Sun 2-5 (4pm Oct-Mar). (Closed Mon Oct-Mar, Good Fri, 25 Dec & 1 Jan).
✻ *30p (ch & pen 20p).*
shop ✗

Winchester City Museum — WINCHESTER

Map 04 SU42
The Square
☎ (0962) 848269
Located on the edge of the cathedral precinct, the museum has a well-laid-out display relating to the archaeology and history of the city and central Hampshire. An interesting exhibit is the

interior of a 19th-century chemist's shop, which used to be in the High Street.
Open all year, Mon-Sat 10-5, Sun 2-5 (4pm Oct-Mar). (Closed Mon Oct-Mar, Good Fri, Xmas & 1 Jan).
Free.
& *shop* ✗

Every effort is made to provide accurate information, but details might change during the currency of this guide.

Winchester College — WINCHESTER

Map 04 SU42
College St
☎ (0962) 868778
Founded and built by Bishop William of Wykeham in 1382, Winchester College is one of the oldest public schools in England. The college has greatly expanded over the years but the original buildings remain intact. The chapel, and during school term, the cloisters and

Fromond's Chantry are open to the public. Also open is the War Cloister, which is reached by Commoners' Gate. Dedicated in 1924, it contains memorials to Wykhamists who died in World War I and all battles since then.
Guided tours Apr-Sep daily (ex Sun am) 11, 1 & 3.15.
✻ *£2 (ch £1.50).*
& *toilets for disabled shop* ✗

HEREFORD & WORCESTER

Berrington Hall — ASHTON

Map 03 SO56
Berrington (3m N off A49)
☎ Leominster (0568) 615721
An elegant neo-classical house of the late 18th century, designed by Henry Holland and set in a park landscape by 'Capability' Brown; the formal exterior belies the delicate interior with beautifully decorated ceilings and fine furniture, including the Digby collection and a recently restored bedroom suite, nursery, Victorian laundry and pretty tiled Georgian dairy; attractive garden

with interesting plants and a recently planted apple orchard in the walled garden.
Open Apr, Sat & Sun 1.30-5.30; May-Sep daily (ex Mon or Tue but open BH Mon) 1.30-5.30; Oct, Sat & Sun 1.30-4.30. Last admission 30 mins before closing.
£3 (ch £1.50). Family ticket £8.25. Grounds only £1.20.
P ♿ & *toilets for disabled shop* ✗
(NT)

Bewdley Museum · BEWDLEY

Map 07 SO77
The Shambles, Load St
☎ (0299) 403573

The Shambles is an 18th-century row of butcher's shops, and makes an interesting setting for the attractive museum devoted to the crafts and industries of the Bewdley area, with displays of charcoal burning, basket making and coopering. There are also craft workshops within the museum, where demonstrations are often held. For those interested in the industrial side, there is a restored brass foundry and the sawyard area gives occasional demonstrations of a 19th-century horizontal reciprocal saw. A working water wheel and hydraulic ram pump can also be seen and there are daily demonstrations of rope-making and clay-pipe making. A range of events, demonstrations and exhibitions take place throughout the year. These will include workshops on coracle making, stickdressing, working in willow, and skepmaking.
Open Mar-Nov, Mon-Sat 10-5.30 (inc BH), Sun 11-5.30.
✱ *55p (ch & pen 20p, accom ch free). School party Free.*
& *shop*

Severn Valley Railway · BEWDLEY

Map 07 SO77
☎ (0299) 403816 & (0746) 764361

(For full entry see Bridgnorth, Shropshire)

West Midland Safari & Leisure Park · BEWDLEY

Map 07 SO77
Spring Grove (on A456)
☎ (0299) 402114
A wildlife park with over 40 species of wild and exotic animals. Ride tickets can also be bought for the variety of rides in the leisure area. Attractions include a pets corner, a sealion show, a reptile house, a parrot show, and a deer park.
Open Apr-Oct, daily 10-5.
✱ *£3.50 (ch 4 free). Book of ride tickets 5-£1.50, 10-£3 or 20-£5. Unlimited ride wristband £3.50.*
🅿 🍴 & *toilets for disabled shop garden centre*

✕ The 'No Dogs' symbol does not normally apply to guide dogs – these are permitted in most establishments.

Broadway Tower Country Park · BROADWAY

Map 03 SP03
☎ (0386) 852390

This 65ft tower was designed by James Wyatt for the 6th Earl of Coventry, and was built in 1799. There are exhibitions on three floors, and an observation room with telescope, giving wonderful views over 12 counties. Around the tower is a country park with farm animals, an adventure playground, nature walks, a barbeque, ball game areas and giant chess and draughts boards.
Open Apr-Oct, daily 10-6.
£2.25 (ch & pen £1.50). Family ticket £7. Party.
🅿 🍴 ✕ *licensed & toilets for disabled shop*

Lower Brockhampton · BROCKHAMPTON

Map 03 SO65
(2m E of Bromyard)
This timber-framed and moated 14th-century manor house is unusual for its 15th-century gatehouse – a rare example of this type of structure. The house also has a ruined 12th-century chapel and is reached down a long, secluded lane. It lies north of the A44 and is part of a larger National Trust property covering over 1600 acres of Herefordshire countryside.
Open; Medieval Hall & Parlour open Apr-Sep, Wed-Sun & BH Mon 10-1 & 2-6. (Closed Good Fri). Oct: Wed-Sun 10-1 & 2-4.
£1.30 (ch 65p). Family ticket £3.50. Party.
🅿 & ✕
(NT)

Avoncroft Museum of Buildings · BROMSGROVE

Map 07 SO97
Redditch Rd, Stoke Heath (2m S, off A38)
☎ (0527) 31886
The aim of the museum is to save interesting buildings by re-erecting and restoring them here. A working post mill and a blacksmith's shop, a cockpit and a merchant's house are neighbours on the 15-acre site with an 18th-century dovecote, an earth closet and a 1946 prefab. One of the more unusual exhibits is a Georgian icehouse from Tong Castle in Shropshire. It consists of a deep, brick-built pit, where ice could be stored in winter for use in summer. The latest acquistion is the great 14th-century roof from the Gueston Hall, once a monastic establishment adjoining Worcester Cathedral. An interesting feature of the museum is that the people who work on the buildings have had to relearn traditional skills such as building in wattle and daub. Visitors can sometimes see the skills being used as buildings are added to the museum. There are wheelchair ramps to the shop and tearoom, and a wheelchair is available on loan.
Open Jun-Aug daily 11-5.30; Apr, May, Sep & Oct 11-5.30 (Closed Mon). Mar & Nov 11-4.30 (Closed Mon & Fri). Open BHs.
£2.80 (ch £1.40, pen £1.95). Family ticket £7.40.
🅿 🍴 & *toilets for disabled shop*

The Bromsgrove Museum · BROMSGROVE

Map 07 SO97
26 Birmingham Rd
☎ (0527) 77934
The museum displays past industries and crafts of Bromsgrove with a street scene showing fifteen Victorian/Edwardian shops. There is a picture gallery and a craft, toy and model shop next to the museum. Various exhibitions are held.
Open all year Mon-Sat 10-5 (Closed 12.30-1.30), Sun 2-5.
shop ✕
Details not confirmed for 1992

Croft Castle · CROFT

Map 03 SO46
(off B4362)
☎ Yarpole (056885) 246
Home of the Croft family since Domesday (with a break of 170 years from 1750); walls and towers date from the 14th and 15th centuries; the interior is mainly 18th century, when the fine Georgian-Gothic staircase and plasterwork ceilings were added. There is a splendid avenue of 350-year-old Spanish chestnuts, and an Iron Age Fort (Croft Ambrey) may be reached by footpath.
Open Apr & Oct, Sat & Sun 2-5; Etr, Sat-Mon 2-6; May-Sep, Wed-Sun & BH Mon 2-6. Last admission half hour before closing. Parkland open all year. £2.70. Family ticket £7.40.
🅿 & *(parking available)* ✕ *(ex in parkland)*
(NT)

Dinmore Manor · DINMORE

Map 03 SO45
(off A49)
☎ Canon Pyon (043271) 322
From its spectacular hillside location, the manor enjoys outstanding views of the surrounding countryside. The cloisters, South Room, Roof Walk, Chapel, Music Room (Great Hall), and Grotto are all open to the public. The chapel, dating back to the 12th century, is in a unique setting next to the rock garden, pools, the collection of old acers, and the 1200-year-old yew tree. Among the many attractions here are the remarkable collection of 1930s stained glass, an 18th-century chamber organ, a Victorian aeolian pipe organ, and two medieval sundials.
Open all year, daily 10-6.
✱ *£2 (ch & pen £1, accompanied ch 14 free).*
🅿 & ✕

The Almonry Museum & Heritage Centre · EVESHAM

Map 03 SP04
Abbey Gate
☎ (0386) 446944
The 14th-century stone and timber building was the home of the Almoner of the Benedictine Abbey in Evesham. It now houses the Almonry Heritage Centre which has exhibitions relating to the history of Evesham Abbey, the battle
continued . . .

of Evesham, and the culture and trade of
Evesham. Evesham Tourist Information
Centre is also located here.
Open all year, Mon-Sat & BHs (ex Xmas)
&. *shop* ✻

Goodrich Castle   GOODRICH

Map 03 SO51
☎ Symonds Yat (0600) 890538

The castle stands above the River Wye,
and gives wonderful views in all
directions. It was built in around 1150
and then expanded in the 13th and 14th
century, using the red sandstone rock on

which it stands, so that rock and castle
seem to merge together. The castle was
not severely tested until the Civil War,
when it was held by Royalists and was
battered by 'Roaring Meg' – a cannon.
said to have fired 200-pound balls. The
siege ended after four and a half months,
by which time the castle had lost its
water supply. Parliament ordered the
slighting of the castle, but the remains
are still extensive and impressive.
*Open all year, Apr-Sep, daily 10-6; Oct-
Mar, Tue-Sun 10-4. (Closed 24-26 Dec &
1 Jan).*
*£1.50 (ch 75p, pen, students & UB40
£1.10)*
🅿
(EH)

**Every effort is made to provide accurate information,
but details might change during the currency
of this guide.**

Hanbury Hall   HANBURY

Map 03 SO96
☎ (052784) 214
This William and Mary style red-brick
house, completed in 1701, is a typical
example of an English country house
built by a prosperous local family. The
house contains outstanding painted
ceilings and staircase by Thornhill and
the Watney collection of porcelain,

while outside there are both a
contemporary orangery and an ice
house.
*Open Apr-Oct, Sat-Mon 2-6. Last
admission 30 mins before closing.*
£2.80. Family ticket £7.70. Party.
🅿 ☕ &. *(Braille guide) toilets for disabled
shop* ✻ *(ex in park)*
(NT)

Harvington Hall   HARVINGTON

Map 07 SO87
☎ Chaddesley Corbett (0562) 777267
An extraordinary number of hiding
places makes this moated manor house
especially interesting, including false
chimneys and a false step in a staircase.
The house also has Elizabethan murals,

and there is a Georgian chapel in the
garden.
*Open Mar-Oct, daily 11.30-5.30. (Closed
Good Fri).*
✻ *£2 (ch £1, pen £1.50).*
🅿 ✗ *licensed* &. *toilets for disabled shop* ✻

Churchill Gardens Museum & Brian Hatton Art Gallery   HEREFORD

Map 03 SO54
3 Venn's Ln
☎ (0432) 268121 or 267409
The museum is laid out in a Regency
house with fine grounds, and has 18th-
and early 19th-century rooms, displays
of costume, and a gallery devoted to

works by the local artist Brian Hatton.
*Open all year, 2-5, Apr-Sep, Tue-Sun; Oct-
Mar, Tue-Sat.*
✻ *70p (ch & pen 35p) Joint ticket with Old
House £1.20 (ch & pen 60p)*
🅿 &. *shop* ✻

Cider Museum & King Offa Distillery   HEREFORD

Map 03 SO54
Pomona Place, Whitecross Rd (A438
to Brecon)
☎ (0432) 354207
Cider-making through the ages – the
exhibits include a huge 17th-century
French beam press, an old farm cider
house and travelling cidermakers 'tack',

original champagne cider cellars, a 1920s
bottling line and a working cider brandy
distillery.
*Open all year, Apr-Oct, daily 10-5.30;
Nov-Mar, Mon-Sat 1-5.*
*£1.80 (ch, pen & students £1.25). Party
20 +.*
🅿 &. *shop*

Hereford Museum & Art Gallery   HEREFORD

Map 03 SO54
Broad St
☎ (0432) 268121 ext 207
Displays range from Roman mosaic
pavements to folklife and beekeeping,
including an observation hive. English
watercolours, local geology and

archaeology are also featured. The art
gallery has monthly exhibitions.
*Open all year, Tue, Wed & Fri 10-6, Thu
10-5, Sat 10-5 (Apr-Sep); Sat 10-4 (Oct-
Mar). (Closed Mon ex BH'S).*
&. *(wheelchairs available) toilets for disabled
shop* ✻

Old House   HEREFORD

Map 03 SO54
High Town
☎ (0432) 268121 ext 225 or 207
This good example of a Jacobean house
was built in around 1621, and was once
in a row of similar houses. It has
bedrooms with four-poster beds, and a
number of wall paintings.

*Open all year, Tue-Fri 10-1 & 2-5.30.
(Sat, Apr-Sep 10-1 & 2-5.30; Oct-Mar
10-1). Mon 10-1. Also open BH Mons
10-1 & 2-5.15.*
✻ *70p (ch & pen 35p). Joint ticket with
Churchill Gardens Museum £1.20 (ch &
pen 60p).*
&. *shop* ✻

Hartlebury Castle State Rooms   KIDDERMINSTER

Map 07 SO87
Hartlebury (5m S)
☎ Hartlebury (0299) 250410
The elegant interior of this castle, the
seat of the Bishops of Worcester since
850, reveals little of its long and
sometimes troubled history. Its present

Gothic appearance dates from the 18th
century.
*Open Etr-6 Sep, 1st Sun in month plus
BH Mon & Tue 2-5. Also Wed (Etr-Aug)
2-4.*
75p (ch 25p, pen 50p).
🅿 &. *shop* ✻

Hereford & Worcester County Museum   KIDDERMINSTER

Map 07 SO87
Hartlebury Castle, Hartlebury (5m S,
off A449)
☎ Hartlebury (0299) 250416
Housed in the north wing of Hartlebury
Castle, the Country Museum contains a
delightful display of crafts and industries.
There are unique collections of toys,
costume, domestic life, room settings
and horse-drawn vehicles as well as a

reconstructed forge, schoolroom,
wheelwright's and tailor's shop. Special
events for 1992 include Childhood and
Toy exhibitions from June to August
inclusive. Telephone the museum for
details.
*Open Mar-Nov, Mon-Thu & B's 10-5,
Fri & Sun 2-5. (Closed Sat & Good Fri).*
£1 (ch & pen 50p). Family ticket.
🅿 ☕ &. *shop* ✻ *(ex in grounds)*

Severn Valley Railway   KIDDERMINSTER

Map 07 SO87
☎ Bewdley (0299) 403816 & (0746)
764361

(For full entry see Bridgnorth,
Shropshire)

Hergest Croft Gardens   KINGTON

Map 03 SO25
(0.25m W off A44)
☎ (0544) 230160
An old-fashioned kitchen garden is a
rarity which can be seen at Hergest
Croft. The trees, shrubs and herbaceous

borders of the rest of these large gardens
are set against a woodland valley filled
with vast rhododendron bushes.
Open 30 Apr-29 Oct daily, 1.30-6.30.
🅿 ☕ &. *shop garden centre*
Details not confirmed for 1992

✻ **An asterisk indicated that up-to-date information was
not available at the time of our research – 1991
information has been published as an
indication of what you may expect.**

Malvern Museum   MALVERN

Map 03 SO74
Abbey Gateway, Abbey Rd
☎ (0684) 567811
The local history exhibits range from the
story of the Malvern Hills to the Water
Cure and the lives of Sir Edward Elgar
and Bernard Shaw, and from the first
British motor car to radar and the

silicone chip. The museum is housed in
one of the two buildings that survive
from the Benedictine monastery.
*Open Etr-Oct, daily 10.30-5 (ex closed Wed
in term time).*
✻ *40p (ch 7 10p).*
shop ⚕

Forge Mill Needle Museum &
Bordesley Abbey Visitor Centre   REDDITCH

Map 03 SP06
Forge Mill, Needle Mill Ln, Riverside
(off A441)
☎ (0527) 62509
The museum is housed in the only
remaining water-driven, needle-scouring
mill, with machinery from the 18th
century which is demonstrated regularly.
Displays of finds from the nearby 12th-
century Cistercian Abbey are shown in

the new Visitor Centre (opening Feb
1992). Both the museum and the visitor
centre are set in attractive surroundings
within the Arrow Valley Park.
*Open Feb-Oct, Sat 2-5, Sun-Thu 11-4.30;
Nov, Mon-Thu. Parties by arrangement.*
✻ *£1.25 (ch 50p, pen 75p). Family ticket
£3. Party.*
🅿 &. *toilets for disabled shop*

The Lost Street Museum — ROSS-ON-WYE

Map 03 SO52
Palma Court, 27 Brookend St
☎ (0989) 62752
Discover this unique Edwardian Street, lost in time, with its fully stocked, life-size shops. This is probably the largest privately-owned collection of music boxes, toys, dolls, wireless, gramaphones, motor cycles, costumes

and advertising in the country. There are demonstrations of musical boxes and automata, quizes with cash prizes and the pub boasts a fine collection of old amusement machines.
Open Feb-Nov, Mon-Sat 10-5; Sun 11-5. Dec-Jan, telephone for opening times.
💺 &
Details not confirmed for 1992

Spetchley Park Gardens — SPETCHLEY

Map 03 SO85
☎ (090565) 213 or 224
The 140-acre deer park and the gardens surround an early 19th-century mansion (not open), with sweeping lawns and herbaceous borders, a rose lawn and enclosed gardens with low box and yew hedges. The interesting trees include a

17th-century cedar of Lebanon.
Open 29 Mar-Sep, Mon-Fri 11-5, Sun 2-5; BH Mons 11-5. Other days by appointment. Garden centre within gardens open same hours.
✱ £1.70 (ch 90p). Party 25 +.
🅿 💺 & *garden centre* ✖

Stone House Cottage Gardens — STONE

Map 07 SO87
(2m SE on A448)
☎ Kidderminster (0562) 69902
An unusual walled garden with towers provides a sheltered area of about one acre for rare shrubs, climbers and interesting herbaceous plants. Adjacent

to the garden is a nursery with a large selection of unusual plants.
Open Gardens & nursery Mar-Oct, Wed-Sat 10-6; May & Jun, Sun, in aid of the National Garden Scheme.
£1.50 (in collection box for charity).
🅿 & *garden centre* ✖

The Weir Gardens — SWAINSHILL

Map 03 SO44
The gardens are at their best in spring when there are lovely displays of naturalised bulbs set in woodland and grassland walks. Cliff garden walks can be taken here, with fine views of the

River Wye and the Welsh hills.
Open 17 Feb-Oct, Wed-Sun 11-6.
✖ ▭
(NT)
Details not confirmed for 1992

The Jubilee Park — SYMONDS YAT (WEST)

Map 03 SO51
☎ (0600) 890360
The world-famous Jubilee Maze, built to celebrate the Queen's Jubilee in 1977, and the Museum of Mazes showing paths of mazes and labyrinths through the ages. Also The World of Butterflies, where hundreds of colourful butterflies from all over the world fly free in their large tropical indoor garden. Special events for 1992 include: Spring Festival and Easter Maze Festival; Sep-Oct,

Autumn Crafts Exhibition; Nov 1-Christmas, Winter Wonderland.
Open Feb-24 Dec, attractions – daily 11-5.30, restaurant and information – daily 10.30-5.30. Open evenings Aug until 10pm, Nov-Dec Thu-Sat until 8pm.
✱ £2.50 (ch £1.50 & pen £2). Prices include admission to Jubilee Maze, Museum of Mazes and Amazing Puzzle Shop.
🅿 💺 ✖ & *toilets for disabled shop garden centre* ✖ *(ex in grounds)*

Dovecote — WICHENFORD

Map 03 SO76
This large 17th-century dovecote has nearly 600 nesting boxes and is unusual in its timber-framed, wattle and daub construction, which was rarely used for dovecotes. The gabled roof appears to have a chimney, but it is actually an entrance for the birds.

Open Apr-Oct, daily 9-6 or sunset. (Closed Good Fri). Other times by prior appointment with Severn Regional Office, tel (0684) 850051.
60p.
✖
(NT)

City Museum & Art Gallery — WORCESTER

Map 03 SO85
Foregate St
☎ (0905) 25371
The gallery has temporary art exhibitions from both local and national sources, while the museum exhibits geology, local and natural history displays. Of particular interest is a complete 19th-century chemists shop. There are also collections relating to the

Worcestershire Regiment and the Worcestershire Yeoman Cavalry. New River Severn displays and activities will open in the summer.
Open all year, Mon, Tue Wed & Fri 9.30-6, Sat 9.30-5.
Free.
💺 & *(Lift to all floors from Taylor's Lane entrance). toilets for disabled shop* ✖

The Commandery — WORCESTER

Map 03 SO85
Sidbury
☎ (0905) 355071
This fine 15th-century, timber-framed building was the headquarters of Charles II's army during the Battle of Worcester in 1651. It has an impressive Great Hall with some good 15th-century stained glass, and the building is now England's only Civil War centre. There are spectacular audio-visual displays, including the trial of King Charles I – join the jury and decide the King's fate,

and see the Scots' camp on the eve of the Battle of Worcester. The Commandery is the base of the Worcester Militia who stage regular 17th-century live action weekends.
1992 is the 350th anniversary of the outbreak of the Civil War, and there will be a series of spectacular events throughout the year to mark this momentous occasion.
Open all year, Mon-Sat 10-5, Sun 1.30-5.30. (Closed 25 Dec & 1 Jan).
continued . . .

✱ £2.85 (concessions £1.50). Family ticket £6.95. Season ticket £8 (concessions £4.65).
💺 & *shop* ✖

Family season ticket £19.95. Party.
💺 & *shop* ✖

Dyson Perrins Museum — WORCESTER

Map 03 SO85
Severn St (off A44)
☎ (0905) 23221
This museum holds the world's largest and finest collection of Worcester's famous porcelain. Some of the pieces date from 1751 when the porcelain factory was opened in the city. There are also examples on show from services made for the Royal family and European

aristocracy, including the dinner service made for the Prince and Princess of Wales.
Open all year, Mon-Fri 9.30-5 & Sat 10-5. Royal Worcester factory tours Mon-Fri by prior arrangement.
Free.
🅿 *(charged)* ✖ *licensed* & *(ex factory) shop* ✖

Elgar's Birthplace Museum — WORCESTER

Map 03 SO85
Crown East Ln, Lower Broadheath
(3m W, off A44 to Leominster).
☎ Cotheridge (0905) 333224
The cottage where Sir Edward Elgar, the composer, was born in 1857 is now a museum. There is a comprehensive

display of musical scores, photographs, letters and personal effects.
Open daily ex Wed, May-Sep 10.30-6. Oct-15 Jan & 16 Feb-Apr 1.30-4.30. £2 (ch 50p, students £1 & pen £1.50). Party.
& *shop* ✖ *(ex in gardens)*

Hawford Dovecote — WORCESTER

Map 03 SO85
(3m N on A449)
An unusual square, half-timbered 16th-century dovecote. Access on foot only via the entrance drive to the adjoining house.

Open Apr-Oct 9-6 or sunset. (Closed Good Fri). Other times by prior appointment only with regional office.
60p.
✖
(NT)

Tudor House Museum — WORCESTER

Map 03 SO85
Friar St
☎ (0905) 25371
This interesting 500-year-old timber-framed house has a squint and an ornate plaster ceiling. It is now a museum of local life featuring a children's room, an Edwardian bathroom and displays of the

Home Front of World War II. In the yard at the back there are large agricultural exhibits.
Open all year, Mon-Wed & Fri-Sat 10.30-5.
& *shop* ✖
Details not confirmed for 1992

HERTFORDSHIRE

Shaw's Corner — AYOT ST LAWRENCE

Map 04 TL11
(at SW end of village)
☎ Stevenage (0438) 820307
George Bernard Shaw lived here from 1906 until his death in 1950. He gave the house to the National Trust in 1946, and the contents are much as they were in his time. Among other items to be seen are his hats, including a soft

homburg he wore for 60 years, his exercise machine, fountain pen, spectacles and several pictures.
Open Apr-Oct Wed-Sat 2-6, Sun & BH Mon noon-6. Last admission 5.30. (Closed Good Fri)
£2.50.
🅿 & ✖
(NT)

Berkhamsted Castle — BERKHAMSTED

Map 04 SP90
Roads and a railway have cut into the castle site, but its huge banks and ditches remain impressive. The original motte and bailey was probably built by William the Conqueror's half brother, and there is a later stone keep. The

castle was owned by the Black Prince, and King John of France was imprisoned here.
Open any reasonable time.
Free.
🅿 &
(EH)

Hatfield House — HATFIELD

Map 04 TL20
(2m from junc 4 A1(M) on A1000)
☎ (0707) 262823

Robert Cecil built the great Jacobean mansion in 1607-11. It replaced an older palace where Elizabeth I had spent much of her childhood, and is full of Elizabethan associations, important portraits of the queen, and historic

possessions such as her silk stockings, perhaps the first pair worn in England. There are also other celebrated pictures, tapestries and armour, including some from the Spanish Armada. Newer attractions include a William IV kitchen (1833) and the National Collection of Model Soldiers.
Around the house are the great park and gardens, including a parterre planted with yews and roses, a scented garden and knot garden with typical plants of the 15th to 17th centuries. Hatfield is still the home of the Cecils, who at one point had a private waiting room at the nearby railway station.
Special events for 1992 are: Living crafts: 7-10 May; National Patchwork Championships 4-7 Jun; Festival of
continued . . .

Gardening 20-21 Jun; Bentley Drivers Club Concours 27 Jun.
Open 25 Mar-11 Oct. House: weekdays 12-4.15, Sun 1.30-5. (Closed Mon ex BH 11-5 & Good Fri). Gardens: daily 11-6. House Park & Gardens £4.30 (ch £2.90, pen £3.50). Park, Gardens & Exhibitions £2.40 (ch £1.80, pen £2.20). Party 20+.
P ☕ ✕ *licensed* ♿ *toilets for disabled shop garden centre* 🐕 *(ex in park)*

Hitchin Museum & Art Gallery — HITCHIN

Map 04 TL12
Paynes Park
☎ (0462) 434476
The gallery houses displays on local domestic and working life. The costume gallery covers two centuries of fashion, and the regimental collection of the Hertfordshire yeomanry is housed here. There is a fascinating reconstructed Victorian chemist's shop, complemented by a physic garden outside. Temporary art exhibitions change monthly.
Open all year, Mon-Sat 10-5, Sun 2-4.30. (Closed BHs).
Free.
P ♿ *shop* 🐕

Knebworth House, Gardens & Country Park — KNEBWORTH

Map 04 TL22
(direct access from junc 7 A1(M) at Stevenage
☎ Stevenage (0438) 812661

Home of the Lytton family since 1490, the original Tudor manor was transformed in 1843 by the spectacular high Gothic decoration of Victorian novelist Sir Edward Bulwer Lytton. The interior includes a superb Jacobean Great Hall with a splendid plaster ceiling and magnificent panelling (the reredos, which stretches across the width of the room, is 17th century). He was a well known statesman and author and counted among his friends many famous people, including Dickens and Disraeli, who were all guests at Knebworth. There is a fascinating exhibition on the British Raj and some fine furniture and portraits. Outside, the formal-style gardens were simplified by Lutyens (who built several buildings in the town) and the 250-acre park now includes many attractions for visitors. There is a miniature railway, an extensive adventure playground, and a deer park. Knebworth is a popular venue for special events and activities, including in 1992 jousting tournaments (3/4 May), car rallies, and a fireworks and laser symphony concert (5 Jul). Telephone for details.
Open 4 Apr-17 May, Sat, Sun, BH & school holidays; 23 May-6 Sep, daily (ex Mon). Also wknds 12 Sep-4 Oct. House & Garden 12-5; Park 11-5.30. (Closed Mon ex BHs, 27 Jun & 31 Jul-3 Aug).
£4 (ch & pen £3.50); Park & Playground only: £2.50. Party.
P ☕ ✕ *licensed* ♿ *shop* 🐕 *(ex in park)*

First Garden City Heritage Museum — LETCHWORTH

Map 04 TL23
296 Norton Way South
☎ (0462) 683149
Designed by Barry Parker and Raymond Unwin, Letchworth was the first of the garden cities. The museum, housed in the original, thatched offices of the architects, explains the development of this innovative architectural and social concept.
Open all year, Mon-Fri 2-4.30, Sat 10-1 & 2-4. Other times by appointment. (Closed 25-26 Dec).
♿ *shop* 🐕
Details not confirmed for 1992

Museum & Art Gallery — LETCHWORTH

Map 04 TL23
Broadway
☎ (0462) 685647
Art exhibitions are changed at monthly intervals in the gallery, while the more permanent collections in the museum include displays of archaeological items found in north Hertfordshire. Important Iron Age and Roman finds from Baldock are exhibited and there is also a natural history gallery.
Open all year Mon-Sat 10-5. (Closed BHs).
Free.
♿ *shop* 🐕

Mosquito Aircraft Museum — LONDON COLNEY

Map 04 TL20
Salisbury Hall
☎ Bowmansgreen (0727) 22051
Photographs, memorabilia and aero-engine displays are extra attractions of this museum which exhibits 18 De Havilland aircraft, including three Mosquitoes, a Vampire, Venom and Horsa. Visitors may walk through the workshops. A wheelchair is available for disabled visitors.
Open Etr-Oct, Sun & BH Mons 10.30-5.30 also Jul-Sep, Thu 2-5.30.
P ♿ *shop*
Details not confirmed for 1992

For an explanation of the symbols and abbreviations, see page 2.

Royston Museum — ROYSTON

Map 04 TL34
Lower King St
☎ (0763) 242587
Housed in the former chapel schoolroom, the museum contains exhibits which trace the history and development of the town.
The museum also holds regular temporary exhibitions including one this year on the American Air Force, to be held in April.
Open all year, Wed, Thu & Sat 10-5. Other times by appointment with the Curator.
Free.
♿ *shop* 🐕

Clock Tower ST ALBANS

Map 04 TL10
Market Pl
☎ (0727) 53301
This early 15th-century curfew tower, which faces the High Street, provides fine views over the city (especially of the abbey) and the surrounding countryside. This is one of the only two medieval

clock towers in the country. It has a bell which strikes on the hour and is older than the tower itself.
Open Good Fri–mid Sep, Sat, Sun & BH 10.30-5.
✱ 20p (ch 5 10p).
shop ✖

The Gardens of The Rose (Royal National Rose Society) ST ALBANS

Map 04 TL10
Chiswell Green (2m S off Watford Rd in Chiswell Green Ln)
☎ (0727) 50461
These are the showgrounds of the Royal National Rose Society, and include the International Trial Ground for new roses. The gardens contain over 30,000 plants in 1,650 different varieties. These include old-fashioned roses, modern

roses and the roses of the future. The National Miniature Rose Show takes place on 1-2 Aug – entry free to visitors to the gardens.
Open 13 Jun-18 Oct, Mon-Sat 9-5, Sun & BH 10-6.
£3 (accompanied ch free, registered disabled £2). Party 20+.
🅿 ⚊ ♿ *toilets for disabled shop*

Gorhambury ST ALBANS

Map 04 TL10
(entry via lodge gates on A414)
☎ (0727) 54051
Pleasant house built by Sir Robert Taylor (1774-1784) to house an extensive picture collection of 17th-century portraits of the Grimston and

Bacon families and their contempories. Also of note is the 16th-century enamelled glass collection and an early English pile carpet.
Open May-Sep, Thu 2-5.
£2.50 (ch & pen £1.50). Party.
🅿 *shop* ✖

This is just one of many guidebooks published by the AA. The full range is available at any AA shop or good bookshop.

Kingsbury Watermill Museum ST ALBANS

Map 04 TL10
Saint Michael's St
☎ (0727) 53502
This 16th-century corn mill still has a working waterwheel and is now a museum. Exhibits include a collection of old farm implements, and there is also

an art gallery. The mill is on the River Ver half a mile from the city.
Open all year, Mar-Oct, Tue-Sat 11-6, Sun 12-6; Nov-Feb, Wed-Sat 11-5, Sun 12-5. (Closed Mon & 25 Dec-2 Jan).
✱ 75p (ch 40p, pen & students 50p).
🅿 ⚊ *shop* ✖ ▨

Museum of St Albans ST ALBANS

Map 04 TL10
Hatfield Rd
☎ (0727) 56679 & 66100 ext 2927
The museum displays collections relating to the natural history and geology of the south-east Hertfordshire. Exhibits include the Salaman collection of craft tools, and reconstructed workshops.

The history of St Albans is traced from the departures of the Romans up to the present day. There are also two new galleries.
Open all year, daily 10-5, Sun 2-5.
🅿 ♿ *shop* ✖
Details not confirmed for 1992

Roman Theatre of Verulamium ST ALBANS

Map 04 TL10
St Michaels (off A4147)
☎ (0727) 835035
The theatre was first discovered on the Gorhambury Estate in 1847 and was fully excavated by Dr Kathleen Kenyon in 1935. It is unique in England. First constructed around AD160, it is semi-

circular in shape, 180ft across and could hold 1,600 spectators. Following modification over two centuries, the theatre was used for religious processions, ceremonies and plays.
Open all year, daily 10-5 (4 in winter).
£1 (ch 40p, students 80p).
🅿 ♿ *shop* ✖

COME TO THE GARDENS OF THE ROSE

OPEN from June to October, Mondays to Saturdays 9am to 5pm. Sundays and Bank Holidays 10am to 6pm
Enjoy the spectacle of this world-renowned rose collection – species, historical, modern and roses of the future.
Over 30,000 plants in 1,650 varieties.
Admission: Adults £3. Children under 16 Free. Members free. Car and Coach Park Free. Party rates on application. Gift Shop and Licensed Cafeteria. Facilities for the disabled.
THE ROYAL NATIONAL ROSE SOCIETY
Chiswell Green Lane, St. Albans, Herts. Telephone 0727 50461.

St Albans Organ Museum ST ALBANS

Map 04 TL10
320 Camp Rd
☎ (0727) 869693 & 51557
This unusual museum contains a unique collection of automatically operated organs and other musical instruments. It also has Wurlitzer and Rutt theatre organs. There are recitals every Sunday, 2.15 to 4.30, but they can also be arranged at other times for party

bookings. Saturday evening theatre organ concerts are planned for Feb 22, Mar 21, Apr 11, May 23, Jun 27 and Jul 25, and there will be a Summer Soirée and a Christmas Concert.
Open all year, Recitals 2.15-4.30 (ex 25 Dec). Parties at other times by appointment.
£1.50 (ch 60p, concessions £1). Party.
🅿 ♿ *shop* ✖

Verulamium Museum ST ALBANS

Map 04 TL10
St Michaels
☎ (0727) 819339
Verulamium was one of the largest and most important Roman towns in Britain. By the 1st century it was declared a 'municipium', which gave its inhabitants the rights of Roman citizenship. No other British city was granted this honour. The town was attacked by Boadicea in AD61, but rebuilt after her defeat.
The site is set within a 100-acre park. A mosaic and under floor heating system can be seen in situ, and the museum shows finds, including mosaics, wall

paintings, jewellery, pottery and other domestic items.
Following refurbishment in 1991, the museum has new displays including recreated Roman rooms, excavation videos, hands-on discovery areas and computer data bases accessible to visitors. Regular talks and demonstrations at weekends.
Open Apr-Oct, weekdays 10-5.30, Sun 2-5.30; Nov-Feb, weekdays 10-4, Sun 2-4.
£1.80 (ch, pen & students 90p). Family ticket £3.95.
🅿 (charged) ♿ *shop* ✖
See advertisement on page 98.

Benington Lordship Gardens STEVENAGE

Map 04 TL22
Benington (off A602)
☎ Benington (043885) 668
On the site of the ruins of a Norman castle with a keep and moat, this seven-acre terraced garden was made at the beginning of the century, and overlooks lakes and parkland. It has fine herbaceous borders, roses and a rock garden and is renowned for a stunning

display of snowdrops. Ring for details of events throughout the year including an autumn spectacular on the third Sunday in October.
Open Feb, Wed & Sun 12-5; Etr, Spring & Summer BH Mon 12-5; Apr-Sep, Wed 12-5; Apr-Aug, Sun 2-5. Open all year for pre-booked parties.
£2.20 (ch free).
🅿 *shop* ✖

Stevenage Museum STEVENAGE

Map 04 TL22
St George's Way
☎ (0438) 354292
The museum, in the undercroft of the parish church of St George, tells the story of Stevenage from earliest times to the present day. There are also temporary exhibitions. Special events in

1992: Pet Parade 15 Feb-18 Jul; Paper People 27 Jul-24 Aug; Badgers 31 Aug-2 Nov; Sport in Stevenage 30 Nov-30 April 1993.
Open all year, Mon-Sat & BH's 10-5. (Closed Sun).
Free.
♿ *toilets for disabled shop* ✖

✖ The 'No Dogs' symbol does not normally apply to guide dogs – these are permitted in most establishments.

Zoological Museum TRING

Map 04 SP91
Akeman St
☎ (044282) 4181
This most unusual museum was founded in the 1890s by Lionel Walter, 2nd Baron Rothschild, scientist, eccentric and natural history enthusiast. It is famous for its magnificent collection of thousands of mammals and birds, and there are also displays of reptiles, fishes,

insects and domestic dogs. There is even a well known exhibition of dressed fleas. Extinct, rare, exotic and bizarre specimens in a unique Victorian setting. Exhibitions are organised throughout the year (details on request).
Open all year, Mon-Sat 10-5, Sun 2-5. (Closed Good Fri, 24-26 Dec & 1 Jan).
✱ £1 (ch 15, UB40 & pen 50p).
🅿 ♿ *toilets for disabled shop* ✖

Scott's Grotto WARE

Map 04 TL31
Scott's Rd (off A119)
☎ (0920) 464131
Scott's Grotto, built in the 1760s by the Quaker poet John Scott, has been described by English Heritage as "one of the finest in England". Recently restored by the Ware Society, it consists of

underground passages and chambers decorated with flints, shells, minerals and stones, and extends 67ft into the side of the hill. Please wear flat shoes and bring a torch.
Open Apr-Sep, Sat & BH's 2-4.30. Other times by appointment only.
Donations

Watford Museum WATFORD

Map 04 TQ19
194 High St
☎ (0923) 32297
A good art gallery and a museum specialising in the history of Watford from the earliest times to the present day. There are special features on the local industries of printing and brewing, together with a display on wartime

Watford, based on the *Dad's Army* TV series, written by Jimmy Perry from his experiences in Watford. Temporary exhibitions take place throughout the year.
Open all year, Mon-Sat 10-5. (Closed 25 & 26 Dec).
Free.
♿ (lift) *toilets for disabled shop* ✖

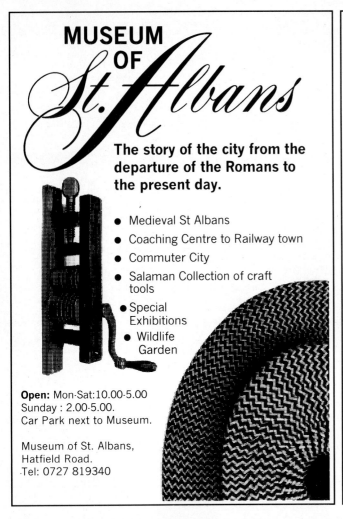

HUMBERSIDE

Art Gallery & Museum   BEVERLEY

Map 08 TA03
Champney Rd
☎ Hull (0482) 882255
Local antiquities, Victorian bygones and china are displayed, along with pictures of Beverley and other works of art. Notable among these is the bust of Sir

Winston Churchill by Bryant Baker of New York. Solo art exhibitions are held.
Open all year, Mon-Wed & Fri 9.30-12.30 & 2-5, Thu 9.30-12, Sat 9.30-4.
Free.
✈

The Guildhall   BEVERLEY

Map 08 TA03
Register Sq
☎ Hull (0482) 867430
The Guildhall was established in 1500 and then rebuilt in handsome classical style in 1762. It is now used as a county court and Mayor's Parlour, but can be visited for its notable ceiling painting in the courtroom, its display of civic

regalia, ancient charters and other treasures. A guide service is available.
Open Etr-Sep, daily 10-4.30; Oct-Etr, Mon-Fri 10-4.30, Sat 10-1. For opening times of Mayor's Parlour please telephone for details.
Free. Admission charged for some exhibits.
& ✈

For an explanation of the symbols and abbreviations, see page 2.

The Hall, Lairgate   BEVERLEY

Map 08 TA03
☎ Hull (0482) 882255

Now used as council offices, the Hall is an 18th-century building with an interesting late 18th-century stucco ceiling, and a Chinese room with rare hand-painted wallpaper.
Open all year, Mon-Thu 8.45-5.30 & Fri 9-4 (subject to availability). Groups at other times by arrangement.
Free.
& ✈

Museum of Army Transport   BEVERLEY

Map 08 TA03
Flemingate
☎ Hull (0482) 860445
The museum tells the story of army transport from horse drawn waggons to the recent Gulf conflict: everything from prototype vehicles to Montgomery's Rolls Royce and the last Blackburn Beverley aircraft. There are also other exhibits to be explored including 'Women at the wheel' (their role in the war) and an area for children. Special events in 1992 include a Toy and Train Fair on 1 Mar and 10 May, and the 'El Alamein' exhibition on 23 Oct.
Open all year, daily 10-5. (Closed 24-26 Dec).
✱ *£2.50 (ch 5-16 & pen £1.50). Children under 16 must be accompanied. Party 10+.*
P ☕ & *toilets for disabled shop* ✈

✱ An asterisk indicated that up-to-date information was not available at the time of our research – 1991 information has been published as an indication of what you may expect.

Sewerby Hall, Park & Zoo — BRIDLINGTON

Map 08 TA16
☎ (0262) 673769 (Park) & 677874 (Hall)
The house was built around 1714-20, and is now an art gallery and museum of history and archaeology. It contains the Amy Johnson Trophy Room, and the gardens are full of interest, especially the walled gardens. There is also a miniature

zoo and aviary.
Open all year, Park & grounds 9-dusk. From Spring BH-mid Sep game facilities are available to public. Art gallery & museum, Good Fri-last Sun in Sep.
P *(charged)* ⚑ ⑁ *(garden for the blind) toilets for disabled shop*
Details not confirmed for 1992

Burton Agnes Hall — BURTON AGNES

Map 08 TA16
Estate Office (on A166)
☎ (026289) 324 due to change to (0262) 490324
Built in 1598, this is a magnificent Elizabethan house, with furniture, pictures, china and tapestries amassed by the family owners over four centuries. There is an old gatehouse, and the woodland gardens and herbaceous borders can also be seen. The ghost of a

young girl is said to haunt the property.
Special events for 1992 include a Gala day on 3 May; Flower Festival 25-26 Jul and 'An Elizabethan Experience' 2-3 Sep. Admission charges vary on these days.
Open Apr-Oct, daily 11-5.
£2.50 (ch & pen £2). Grounds only £1 (ch 50p). Party.
P ⚑ ⑁ *toilets for disabled shop* ✹

Norman Manor House — BURTON AGNES

Map 08 TA16
This is the house that Burton Agnes Hall replaced. It is a rare survivor from Norman times, and though later encased in brick it still has its Norman piers and the groined roof of a lower chamber. An

upper room and an old donkey wheel can also be seen.
Open all year.
Free.
(EH)

Elsham Hall Country Park — ELSHAM

Map 08 TA01
(on M180/A15 Humber Bridge junc)
☎ Barnetby (0652) 688698

Attractions include an animal farmyard, clocktower shop and art gallery, carp-feeding jetty, an arboretum and an

adventure playground. There are nature trails and quizzes, a Craft Centre with working craftsfolk, a tea room and an award-winning restaurant. The latest addition is a Falconry Centre with an excellent selection of birds of prey. There are special events planned throughout the year, especially during the school holidays.
Open all year, mid Sep-Maundy Thu, Sun & BH 11-4; Etr Sat-mid Sep, daily 11-5. (Closed Good Fri & 25-26 Dec).
✹ £3 (ch & pen £2, ch under 3 free). Party 20+.
P ⚑ ✗ *licensed* ⑁ *(fishing facilities for disabled) toilets for disabled shop garden centre* ✹

Old Rectory — EPWORTH

Map 08 SE70
☎ (0427) 872268
John and Charles Wesley were brought up in the handsome rectory, which was built in 1709 and restored in 1957. Epworth itself is interesting as the centre

of the Isle of Axholme, which has been inhabited for some 10,000 years.
Open Mar-Oct, Mon-Sat 10-12 & 2-4, Sun 2-4.
£1.50 (ch 75p).
P ⑁ *shop* ✹

✳ An asterisk indicated that up-to-date information was not available at the time of our research – 1991 information has been published as an indication of what you may expect.

National Fishing Heritage Centre — GRIMSBY

Map 08 TA20
Alexandra Dock
☎ (0472) 242000
The National Fishing Heritage Centre tells the story of the British Fishing Industry, arguably the nation's most gruelling and demanding occupation, as seen through the eyes of one of the world's greatest fishing ports – Grimsby. Visitors are given a rare opportunity to experience life at sea on a Grimsby

trawler in the mid 1950's; they can see, hear, smell and touch a series of recreated environments which take them from the back streets of Grimsby to the distant fishing grounds of the Arctic Circle – and back again.
Open from 8 May, daily 10-6. (Closed Xmas).
✳ £2.85 (ch £2.10, pen £2.35). Family ticket £8.35.
P ⚑ ⑁ *toilets for disabled shop* ✹

Welholme Galleries — GRIMSBY

Map 08 TA20
Welholme Rd
☎ (0472) 242000 ext 1385
A collection of Napoleonic and later 19th-century ship models, marine paintings and fine china is a notable feature of the museum. It also has folk items and interesting photographs of

Lincolnshire life from the collections of W E R Hallgarth. Various exhibitions are held during the year.
Open all year, Tue-Sat 10-5. (Closed Xmas & BHs).
P ⑁ *shop* ✹
Details not confirmed for 1992

Hornsea Museum — HORNSEA

Map 08 TA24
11 Newbegin
☎ (0964) 533443 & 533430
A former farmhouse and its outbuildings now illustrate local life and history, with 19th-century farmhouse rooms and a dairy, craft tools and farming implements. Photographs, industries and local personalities are also featured. Craft

demonstrations take place in the summer and Victorian activity sessions can be arranged for groups of any age.
Open Etr-Oct, Mon-Sat 10-5, Sun 2-5. Nov-Etr by appointment.
£1.25 (ch & pen 85p). Family ticket £3.25.
shop ✹ *(ex garden)*

Hornsea Pottery Leisure Park — HORNSEA

Map 08 TA24
Rolston Rd
☎ (0964) 534211
This retail and leisure park on Yorkshire's east coast combines bargain factory shopping – everything from clothes, toys, shoes, pottery, furniture, and bedding plus designer clothes shops. Family leisure attractions include Butterfly World, Birds of Prey Conservation Centre, Yorkshire Car Collection, Minidale Farmyard and

Model Village plus adventure playground. Special events for 1992 include unusual car rallies and a Santa's party and Children in Need 'aerobathon' in November.
Open all year, daily from 10-5 (Closing at 6pm school summer holidays, 4pm Nov-Feb). Xmas week phone for details. Amenities charged individually.
P ⚑ ✗ *licensed* ⑁ *toilets for disabled shop* ✹ *(ex in park)*
See advertisement on page 100.

✳ An asterisk indicates that up-to-date information was not available at the time of our research – 1991 information has been published as an indication of what you may expect.

Hull & East Riding Museum — HULL

Map 08 TA02
36 High St
☎ (0482) 593902
The transport section looks at road transport through the ages; and the displays on the archaeology of Humberside include the 'Horkstow Pavement' and other Roman mosaics. The iron age Hasholme Boat is

undergoing preservation in its specially built boat lab. Celtic World displays have recently opened.
Open all year, Mon-Sat 10-5 & Sun 1.30-4.30. (Closed 25-26 Dec, 1 Jan & Good Fri).
Free.
⑁ *(access with prior arrangement) shop* ✹

Maister House   HULL

Map 08 TA02
160 High St
☎ (0482) 24114
The house is a mid-18th-century rebuilding, notable for its splendid stone and wrought-iron staircase, ornate stucco work and finely carved doors. Only the staircase and entrance hall are open.
Open all year, Mon-Fri 10-4 (Closed BH). 80p (incl guide book).
✖
(NT)

Town Docks Museum   HULL

Map 08 TA02
Queen Victoria Square
☎ (0482) 593902
Hull's maritime history is illustrated here, with displays on whales and whaling, ships and shipping, and other aspects of this Humber port. There is also a Victorian court room. The restored dock area, with its fine Victorian and Georgian buildings, is well worth exploring too. Special events for 1992 include: 11 Apr-31 May, Arms and Armoury Exhibition; 26 Sep-29 Nov, Folk Art from Yorkshire; 12 Dec-6 Feb 93, How We Used to Live.
Open all year, Mon-Sat 10-5 & Sun 1.30-4.30. (Closed 25-26 Dec, 1 Jan & Good Fri).
Free.
♿ *shop* ✖

Wilberforce House   HULL

Map 08 TA02
23-25 High St
☎ (0482) 593902
The early 17th-century mansion was the birthplace of William Wilberforce, who went on to become a leading campaigner against slavery. There are Jacobean and Georgian rooms and displays on slavery. The house also has secluded gardens.
Open all year, Mon-Sat 10-5 & Sun 1.30-4.30. (Closed 25-26 Dec, 1 Jan & Good Fri).
Free.
🅿 ♿ *shop* ✖

For an explanation of the symbols and abbreviations, see page 2.

Burnby Hall Garden & Stewart Collection   POCKLINGTON

Map 08 SE84
The Balk
☎ (0759) 302068
The two lakes in this garden have an outstanding collection of 50 varieties of hardy water lilies recently designated a National Collection, and are complemented by a fine rose garden. The museum contains sporting trophies and ethnic material gathered on world-wide travels.
Open 4 Apr-mid Oct, 10-6.
£1.50 (ch 50p, pen £1) Jun-Sep; £1 (ch 50p, pen 80p) Etr-May & Oct.
🅿 ♿ *wheelchairs available toilets for disabled shop* ✖

Penny Arcadia   POCKLINGTON

Map 08 SE84
Ritz Cinema, Market Place
☎ (0759) 303420
This museum houses the world's most comprehensive collection of antique and veteran coin-operated amusement machines. An audio-visual screen show, stage presentation, guided tours and demonstrations introduce you to the world of the slot-machine.
Open May-Sep, daily 10-5 (Jun-Aug), 12.30-5 (May & Sep). Other times by arrangement.
£3 (ch 15 & pen £2). Party.
🅿 ♿

✳ An asterisk indicates that up-to-date information was not available at the time of our research – 1991 information has been published as an indication of what you may expect.

Sandtoft Transport Centre   SANDTOFT

Map 08 SE70
Belton Rd
☎ Weybridge (0932) 851650
Set up primarily for the preservation and operation of trolley buses this developing museum now boasts over 60 vehicles from many parts of Britain and the Continent. There are some working models among the exhibits which include motorbuses and other transport memorabilia.
(Leave M180 at junction 2, S of motorway on A161 for about quarter of a mile, then take unclassed road.)
Open Etr-Sep, Sun & BH's 12-6.
🅿 ♿ *shop*
Details not confirmed for 1992

Borough Museum & Art Gallery   SCUNTHORPE

Map 08 SE81
Oswald Rd
☎ (0724) 843533
The local history gallery in this regional museum includes a reconstruction of a 19th-century ironworker's cottage, a Victorian parlour and a visual display on the iron and steel industries. Other exhibits embrace the natural history, natural science and archeology of the area together with temporary exhibitions of contemporary arts, crafts and photography. Special events for 1992 include: 1 Feb-28 Mar, How we used to live, the Victorians; 4 Apr-31 May, Sky Delights – Kites; 4 Jul-16 Aug, Salt & Silk from Germany; 22 Aug-20 Sep, Comedy Festival Exhibition.
Open all year, Mon-Sat & BH 10-5, Sun 2-5. (Closed Xmas).
✳ *Admission free, but a charge is made for group visits in the evenings.*
🅿 ♿ *toilets for disabled shop* ✖

Normanby Hall Country Park — SCUNTHORPE

Map 08 SE81
Normanby (5m N on B1430)
☎ (0724) 720588
A whole host of activities and attractions are offered in the 350 acres of grounds that surround Normanby Hall including golf, riding, nature trails, gift shop and a farming museum. Deer herds can be spotted grazing in the parkland and many species of wildfowl have their home here. Inside the Regency mansion there are fine rooms decorated and furnished in period style. Special events include car rallies, craft fairs, demonstrations and guided walks
Open, Park all year, daily. Hall: Etr-Oct, Mon-Fri 11-5, Sat & Sun 1-5; Nov-Etr by appointment only. Farming Museum: Etr-Oct, daily 1-5; Nov-Etr by appointment only.
Free.
🅿 (charged) 🍴 ✕ licensed ♿ toilets for disabled shop

Burton Constable Hall — SPROATLEY

Map 08 TA13
Burton Constable (1.5m N)
☎ Hornsea (0964) 562400
This superb Elizabethan house was built in 1570, but much of the interior was remodelled in the 18th century. There are magnificent reception rooms and a Tudor long gallery with a pendant roof: the contents range from pictures and furniture (much of it by Thomas Chippendale) to a unique collection of 18th-century scientific instruments.
Outside are 200 acres of parkland landscaped by Capability Brown, with oaks and chestnuts, and a lake with an island. Camping and caravanning sites are available in the park and there is also seasonal fishing.
Open, Hall & grounds Etr, May Day & Spring BH Sun & Mon; Jun & Jul, Sun; 19 Jul-6 Sep, Sun-Thu. (Grounds 12 noon, House 1pm. Last admission 4.30).
House £3 (ch £1.20, pen £2.25).
🅿 🍴 ♿ shop

Thornton Abbey — THORNTON

Map 08 TA11
☎ (0469) 40357
A magnificent 14th-century gatehouse and the ruins of the church and other buildings survive from the Augustinian abbey, founded in 1139. The gate is approached across a dry moat, spanned by a long bridge with arcaded walls and circular towers.
Open all year, Apr-Sep, daily 10-6; Oct-Mar wknds only 10-4. (Closed 24-26 Dec & 1 Jan).
£1.10 (ch 55p, pen, students & UB40 85p)
♿ ✈
(EH)

KENT

Aylesford Priory — AYLESFORD

Map 04 TQ75
The Friars
☎ Maidstone (0622) 717272
Built in the 13th and 14th centuries and then closed down in the reformation, the priory has been restored and is now a house of prayer, guest house, conference centre and a place of pilgrimage and retreat. It has fine cloisters, and displays sculpture and ceramics by modern artists and potters.
Open all year, daily 9-dusk. Gift & book shop 10-4.45. Guided tours of the priory by arrangement.
Donations
🅿 🍴 ♿ toilets for disabled shop ✈

Howletts Zoo Park — BEKESBOURNE

Map 04 TR15
(off A257)
☎ Canterbury (0227) 721286
Howletts is one of John Aspinall's animal collections in Kent. It has the world's largest breeding gorilla colony, and also to be seen are tigers, small cats, free running deer and antelope, snow leopards, bison, ratel and the UK's only herd of breeding elephants.
Open all year, daily 10-5 or dusk. (Closed 25 Dec).
🅿 🍴 ♿ toilets for disabled shop ✈
Details not confirmed for 1992

Whitbread Hop Farm — BELTRING

Map 04 TQ64
☎ Maidstone (0622) 872068
Set amidst picturesque countryside and hop gardens, this is the largest group of Victorian oast houses and galleried barns in the world. They house two award-winning museums, one on rural crafts, the other devoted to hop farming through the ages. There are also displays of farming machinery, carts and other bygones, but perhaps the greatest attractions are the Whitbread Shire Horses. The many facilites include a gift shop and restaurant, coarse fishing, a craft centre and a play area for children, and there are nature trails to follow. Numerous events are held throughout the year, including jazz festivals, country fairs, motor shows, flower and garden shows, a hot air balloon show, and even Highland games.
Open 4 Mar-23 Dec, daily 10-6. (Last admission 5pm).
£4.25 (ch, pen & disabled £3). Extra charges on special event days.
🅿 🍴 ✕ licensed ♿ (audio tours for partially sighted) toilets for disabled shop

Biddenden Vineyards and Cider — BIDDENDEN

Map 04 TQ83
Little Whatmans (0.5m S off A262)
☎ (0580) 291726
The present vineyard was established in 1969 and now covers 22 acres. Visitors are welcome to stroll around the vineyard and to taste wines, ciders and apple juice available at the shop. Special events are held during the year, including the Apple Yowling in Jan; telephone for details.
Open all year, Shop: Mon-Fri 9-5, Sat 11-5 (3pm Nov-Feb), Sun 12-5 (3pm Nov-Dec), BH 11-5 (Mar-Oct). (Closed midday 24 Dec-2 Jan).
🅿 🍴 ♿ shop
Details not confirmed for 1992

Great Comp Garden — BOROUGH GREEN

Map 04 TQ65
(2m E off B2016)
☎ (0732) 882669
The garden has been planned and created over the last 34 years. There is an interesting collection of trees, shrubs, herbaceous plants and heathers, with fine lawns and paths. The 17th-century house is not open.
Open Apr-Oct, daily 11-6.
🅿 🍴 ♿ garden centre ✈
Details not confirmed for 1992

Emmett's Garden — BRASTED

Map 04 TQ45
Ide Hill
☎ Ide Hill (073275) 367
Emmett's is a charming hillside shrub garden, with bluebells in spring and fine autumn colours. It has magnificent views over Bough Beech Reservoir and the Weald. Emmett's Country Fair (22-23 Aug) has over 100 craft stands, with displays and demonstrations all day.
Open Apr-Oct, Wed-Sun & BH Mon 2-6 (last admission 5pm).
£2.20 (ch £1.10).
🅿 🍴 ♿ toilets for disabled
(NT)

Places to visit in this guide are pinpointed on the atlas at the back of the book.

Bleak House Dickens Maritime & Smuggling Museum — BROADSTAIRS

Map 05 TR36
Fort Rd
☎ Thanet (0843) 62224
The house was a favourite seaside residence of Charles Dickens. He wrote the greater parts of 'David Copperfield' and other work here, and worked out the idea for 'Bleak House'. There are special exhibitions of relics salvaged from the Goodwin sands, and of 'The Golden Age of Smuggling'.
Open Etr-Jun & Oct-Nov 10-6, Jul-Sep 10-9.
£1.50 (ch 12 85p, pen £1.30). Party 10+
♿ shop

Dickens House Museum — BROADSTAIRS

Map 05 TR36
Victoria Pde
☎ Thanet (0843) 62853
The house was immortalised by Dickens as the home of Betsy Trotwood in 'David Copperfield'. Dickens letters and possessions are shown, with local and Dickensian prints, costumes and general Victoriana. The parlour is furnished as described in the book.
Open Apr-Oct, daily 2.30-5.30.
75p (ch 25p).
shop ✈

CANTERBURY

Map 04 TR15
A visit to Canterbury must naturally start at the cathedral. This is where Chaucer's pilgrims and countless others came to visit the shrine of Thomas à'Becket, who was murdered near the steps to the north transept in the 12th century. The treasures of the shrine were carried off during the Dissolution, but its site is still marked, with the tomb of the Black Prince close by. The cathedral has an awe-inspiring high, narrow nave, and the cathedral's medieval stained glass is well worth studying for the stories it tells. Next to the cathedral are the ruins of the former monastery, and the medieval and later buildings of the King's School. An interesting walk can be taken from Christ Church Gate around streets with picturesque old buildings like Queen Elizabeth's Guest Chamber and the weavers' cottages beside the Stour. A short walk leads up the hill to St Martin's church, which was old in the time of the Venerable Bede and is probably the oldest church in England still in use. Older still is the prehistoric tumulus topped by a 19th-century obelisk in Dane John garden.

Blean Bird Park — CANTERBURY

Map 04 TR15
Honey Hill, Blean (3m NW on A290)
☎ (0227) 471666
Exotic tropical birds can be seen flying in a natural setting among the trees. The garden has the largest breeding collection of macaws, cockatoos and parakeets in England. There are also owls, peacocks, pheasants and other birds, with a pets' corner, a small collection of mammals, and a woodland walk.
Open Mar-Nov 10-6.
✻ *£2.50 (ch £1.50, pen £2).*
P ☕ ♿ *toilets for disabled shop* 🐕

Canterbury Heritage — CANTERBURY

Map 04 TR15
Poor Priests' Hospital, Stour St
☎ (0227) 452747
An award-winning new museum in a breath-taking medieval building on the riverbank close to the Cathedral, shops and other attractions. The tour starts in Roman times and continues up to the present day. Some of the most exciting of the city's treasures are shown: Roman cavalry swords and a silver spoon hoard, Anglo-Saxon gold, and Viking finds. The displays include (among many others) a reconstruction of Becket's tomb; a medieval street with a pilgrim badge shop; Christopher Marlowe (he was born in Canterbury); the city in the Civil War; and Stephenson's locomotive 'Invicta'. The latest feature to be added is the Rupert Bear Collection.
Open all year, Mon-Sat 10.30-5 & Sun (Jun-Oct) 1.30-5 (last admission 4pm). (Closed Good Fri & Xmas).
♿ *shop* 🐕
Details not confirmed for 1992

For an explanation of the symbols and abbreviations, see page 2.

The Canterbury Tales — CANTERBURY

Map 04 TR15
Saint Margaret's St
☎ (0227) 454888
At Canterbury Tales you can step back in time to the 17th-century and experience the sights, sounds and even the smells of the period. Meet the people, see their animals and visit their homes, inns and workshops and become one of Chaucer's happy band of pilgrims walking from Southwark to Canterbury and the miracle-working tomb of St Thomas Becket. The whole thing is brought vividly to life using the latest electronic presentation techniques. Commentary is available in English, French, Dutch, German, Italian and Spanish. A special children's tape is available, with 24 hours' notice. Events for 1992 include a medieval street theatre.
Open all year, Apr-Sep daily 9.30-5.30; Jan-Mar & Oct-Dec, Mon-Fri 10-4.30 & Sat-Sun 9.30-5.30.
✻ *£3.75 (ch 6-16 £2.50, under 6 free, students & pen £3). Family ticket £11.*
☕ ♿ *toilets for disabled shop* 🐕

Royal Museum, Art Gallery & Buffs Regimental Museum — CANTERBURY

Map 04 TR15
High St
☎ (0227) 452747
Displays include fine porcelain, glass, clocks and watches, and east Kent archaeology, including Roman and Anglo-Saxon jewellery. The work of the famous animal painter, Thomas Sidney Cooper, RA, is featured, as is the local regiment, the Buffs. There is a gallery for temporary exhibitions.
Open all year, Mon-Sat 10-5.
shop 🐕
Details not confirmed for 1992

St Augustine's Abbey — CANTERBURY

Map 04 TR15
☎ (0227) 767345
The abbey was founded by St Augustine on land given by King Ethelbert in AD598, and the foundations of a 7th-century church can be seen. The remains of a round church of the 11th-century underlie the extensive ruins of the medieval Benedictine abbey.
Open all year, Apr-Sep, daily 10-6; Oct-Mar, Tue-Sun 10-4. (Closed 24-26 Dec & 1 Jan).
£1.10 (ch 55p, pen, students & UB40 85p).
(EH)

West Gate Museum — CANTERBURY

Map 04 TR15
Saint Peter's St
☎ (0227) 452747
The last of the city's fortified gatehouses sits astride the London road with the river as a moat. Rebuilt in around 1380 by Archbishop Sudbury, it was used as a prison for many years. The battlements give a panoramic view of the city. Arms and armour can be seen in the guardroom, and there are cells in the towers.
Open all year, Mon-Sat; Apr-Sep 10-1 & 2-5; Oct-Mar 2-4 only. Dates under review.
shop 🐕
Details not confirmed for 1992

Chartwell — CHARTWELL

Map 04 TQ45
☎ Edenbridge (0732) 866368
The former home of Sir Winston Churchill is filled with reminders of the great statesman, from his hats and uniforms to gifts presented by Stalin and Roosevelt. There are paintings of Churchill and other works by notable artists, and also many paintings by Churchill himself. His studio is arranged with easel and paintbox at the ready. The garden has walls and ponds laid out by Churchill, and gives fine views. Events for 1992 include sheep dog trials (31 Jul) and a 1940s dance in a marquee to the Syd Lawrence Orchestra (19/20 Jun).
Open: House only Mar & Nov, Wed, Sat & Sun 11-4.30; House, Garden & Studio, Apr-Oct, Tue-Thu 12-5.30, Sat, Sun & BH Mon 11-5.30 (Closed 21 Mar & Good Fri).
House & Garden £3.80 (ch £1.90). Studio 50p. Gardens only £1.60 (ch 80p). Entrance by numbered ticket at times in summer to avoid congestion, waiting time can be spent in garden.
P ✕ *licensed* ♿ *toilets for disabled shop* 🐕 *(ex garden)*
(NT)

For an explanation of the symbols and abbreviations, see page 2.

Fort Amherst — CHATHAM

Map 04 TQ76
Dock Rd
☎ Medway (0634) 847747
The fort is the finest surviving Napoleonic fortress in the country. It has massive ditches, gun positions, impressive bastions and a warren of tunnels. The restored barracks have a working and firing gun battery, and other areas are also part of a major restoration scheme.
Open daily 15 Jan-21 Dec.
£2.50 (ch, pen & students £1.25).
P ☕ *shop* ✠

Historic Dockyard — CHATHAM

Map 04 TQ76
☎ Medway (0634) 812551

A Royal dockyard until 1984, now an 80-acre working museum with 47 Scheduled Ancient Monuments which form the most complete Georgian/early Victorian dockyard in the world. Eight museum galleries cover 400 years of shipbuilding history, and include the award-winning 'Wooden Walls' which shows through sights, sounds and smells, how 18th-century warships such as HMS Victory were built here. Visitors can see a working ropery, sail and flag-making, crafts workshops in action, and witness the restoration of the Victorian sloop, Gannet, in dry dock. Impressive buildings include huge covered slips, a Georgian Officers' Terrace, and the Commissioner's House (1703), Britain's oldest intact naval building whose pleasant garden is open to visitors. Guided tours and horse-drawn wagon rides are available. Special events for 1992 include a Mad Hatter's Tea Party (20 Apr), a model railway exhibition (13-14 Jun), and a heavy horse day (26 Jul).
Open all year, Apr-Oct, Wed-Sun 10-6 (last admission 5); Nov-Mar, Wed, Sat & Sun 10-4.30 (last admission 3.30).
£5.20 (ch 5-16 £2.60, student & pen £4.50). Party.
P ✗ *licensed* ♿ *(wheelchair available) toilets for disabled shop*

Places to visit in this guide are pinpointed on the atlas at the back of the book.

Chiddingstone Castle — CHIDDINGSTONE

Map 04 TQ54
(off B2027, at Bough Beech)
☎ Penshurst (0892) 870347
The 'castle' is a 17th-century house, almost completely rebuilt in the castle style c1800 by William Atkinson. It contains Stewart and Jacobite paintings and other relics. Egyptian and Oriental antiquities, and a fine collection of Japanese lacquer and swords. Fishing in the lake at £8 a day.
Open Apr-Oct. Apr-May & Oct, Sat & Sun & Etr; Jun-Sep, Tue-Sun; all BH's. Weekdays 2-5.30, Sun & BH 11.30-5.30. Other times for parties by arrangement.
£3 (ch 5-15 £1.50). Party 20+.
P ☕ ✗ *licensed* ♿ *shop* ✠

Chilham Castle Gardens — CHILHAM

Map 04 TR05
☎ Canterbury (0227) 730319
The 'castle' is an imposing hexagonal Jacobean house with an older keep, overlooking the the River Stour. It is not open, but the spacious gardens can be visited. Immediately below the house are terraces planted with roses and wisteria, then come trees and yew hedges, a rose garden, a vegetable garden and a herb garden. There is some handsome topiary, and there are wide lawns adorned with stone urns. Woodland and lakeside walks can be taken, and various events are held in the grounds during the year. Also there is the Raptor Centre, where birds of prey can be seen. Events for 1992 include horse trials (16/17 May), a festival of transport (24/25 May), a country fair (1/2 August), Midsummer Mania (23/24 Aug), and a Firework Fantasia (1 Nov).
Open, Garden only 12 Apr-18 Oct, daily 11-6. (Last admission 5pm).
Garden: Tue-Thu, Sat & Sun £3 (ch £1.50); Mon & Fri £2.50 (ch £1.25). Parties 20+.
P ☕ ♿ *shop*

CHILHAM CASTLE GARDENS
Near Canterbury, Kent

A Jacobean house and a mediaeval Castle Keep **(not open)** set in terraced gardens with many fine trees overlooking a lake.

Enjoy a day out in the gardens, seeing the birds of prey and walking round the lake. Special events through the season.

Tea Room and Gift Shop.
See Gazetteer for details.

Deal Castle — DEAL

Map 05 TR35
Victoria Rd
☎ (0304) 372762
Deal Castle was one of many forts built by Henry VIII in case of invasion by Catholic Europe. It is shaped like a many-leafed clover, with every wall rounded to deflect shot. At the centre is a massive keep. Iron Age weapons and relics of Deal's history are displayed.
Open all year, Apr-Sep, daily 10-6; Oct-Mar, Tue-Sun 10-4. (Closed 24-26 Dec & 1 Jan).
£1.80 (ch 90p, pen, students & UB40 £1.40).
♿ *shop*
(EH)

The Time-Ball Tower — DEAL

Map 05 TR35
Victoria Pde
☎ (0304) 360897
The tower is a unique four-storey museum of time and maritime communication, built in 1821, with a working time-ball which drops daily on the hour every hour.
Open 28 May-mid Sep, Tue-Sun & BH's 10-5.
£1 (ch & pen 60p).
shop ✠

Walmer Castle — DEAL

Map 05 TR35
Walmer, Kingsdown Rd (1m S on coast)
☎ (0304) 364288
Like Deal Castle, Walmer was built by Henry VIII and has a similar design. It is the official residence of the Lord Warden of the Cinque Ports, a post once held by the Duke of Wellington. His sparsely furnished bedroom can be seen, and there is a delightful garden.
Open all year, Apr-Sep, daily 10-6; Oct-Mar, Tue-Sun 10-4. (Closed 24-26 Dec & 1 Jan).
£2.50 (ch £1.30, pen, students & UB40 £1.90).
P ♿
(EH)

✲ An asterisk indicates that up-to-date information was not available at the time of our research – 1991 information has been published as an indication of what you may expect.

Crabble Corn Mill — DOVER

Map 05 TR34
Lower Rd (off A2)
☎ (0304) 823292
Visit this beautifully restored working Kentish water mill, enter the Victorian era and discover when traditional country life changed forever and today's technological world was born. Stoneground wholemeal flour always for sale.
Open all year, Etr-Oct Mon, Wed-Sat 10-5 (& Tue 10-5 in Aug) & Sun noon-5. Nov-Etr, Sat 10-5 & Sun noon-5.
£2.50 (ch 16 £1.25, students & pen £1.75)
P ☕ ♿ *shop* ✠

Dover Castle and Hellfire Corner — DOVER

Map 05 TR34
☎ (0304) 201628
The Norman castle has a massive keep built by Henry II in the 1180s, with chapels, a 242ft-deep well, and massive walls and towers. The castle was strengthened and adapted in later centuries. It stands on cliffs which have been fortified since Iron Age times, but the oldest building there now is the Roman lighthouse, the Pharos. The Saxon church of St Mary de Castros is also near the castle. It has been restored but still shows Saxon and Normanwork. Secret tunnels underneath the castle were built in Napoleonic times and were more recently used during the Second World War to plan the evacuation of Dunkirk. A new exhibition is based here called Hellfire Corner.
Open all year, Apr-Sep, daily 10-6; Oct-Mar, daily 10-4. (Closed 24-26 Dec & 1 Jan).
£4.50 (ch £2.30, students, pen & UB40 £3.40).
P ☕ ♿ *shop* ✠
(EH)

Old Town Gaol — DOVER

Map 05 TR34
Dover Town Hall, Biggin St
☎ (0304) 201066
High-tech animation, audio-visual techniques and 'talking heads' take visitors back to Victorian England to experience the horrors of life behind bars, listening, as they walk through the reconstructed courtroom, exercise yard, washroom and cells, to the stories of the felons and their jailers. You can even, if you so wish, try the prisoners' beds or find out what it is like to be locked in a 6ft x 4ft cell!
Open May-Oct, Mon-Sat 10-5. (Closed Mon & Tue in winter ex Public Hols). Telephone (0304) 242766 for recorded information.
✲ *£2.50 (ch & pen £1.25).*
P *(charged)* ♿ *shop* ✠

Roman Painted House — DOVER

Map 05 TR34
New St
☎ (0304) 203279
Visit five rooms of a Roman hotel built 1,800 years ago, now famous for its unique, well-preserved Bacchic frescos. The Roman underfloor heating system and part of a late-Roman defensive wall are also on view. There are extensive displays on Roman Dover with video and commentary. Foreign language commentaries available in French, German, Dutch and Italian. Parties are welcome; tours by arrangement. Special events are held throughout the year.
Open Apr-Oct, Tue-Sun 10-6 (5pm in Apr, Sep & Oct), also BH Mon & Mon Jul & Aug. Last admission half hour before closing.
✲ *£1 (ch & pen 50p)*
P ♿ *(touch table) shop* ✠

The White Cliffs Experience — DOVER

Map 05 TR34
Market Sq
☎ Deal (0304) 214566
The White Cliffs Experience tells the story of Britain's frontline town from the Roman Invasion to the Second World War. Comprising a Historium, Museum and Archaeological Gardens, and using the latest technology, history is brought to life in an informative way. Visitors can witness the Roman Invasion, talk to the Romans and even take a turn rowing in a Roman Galley.

Time and Tide is a living cartoon where Corporal Crabbe and Her Cliffness tell the story of Dover from Norman to Victorian Times. Finally, it's Dover 1944 and visitors can experience the blitzed streets complete with air-raid warning sirens.
Open all year, 24 Feb-1 Nov, daily 10-7; 4 Nov-23 Feb, Wed-Sun 10-5. Please telephone to confirm opening times.
£4 (ch £2.50, under 5 free, pen £3.50).
💺 ♿ *(Lifts, parking arranged) toilets for disabled shop* ✖

Dungeness Information Centre & Power Stations — DUNGENESS

Map 04 TR01
☎ Lydd (0679) 21815
The 'A' and 'B' power stations at Dungeness make an extraordinary sight in a landscape of shingle, fishing boats and owner-built houses. There is a high-tech information centre, with hands-on interactive videos and many other displays and models. This coupled with

a tour of either 'A' or 'B' power station, can make up a visit of more than two hours.
Open: Information centre daily Etr-Oct; Sun-Fri Oct-Etr. (Closed 2 wks Xmas). Tours of A & B power stations by appointment. No children under 5.
Free.
🅿 ♿ *(by arrangement)* ✖

Martello Tower — DYMCHURCH

Map 04 TR12
The tower is one of the series of circular towers built to defend the coast against the expected invasion by Napoleon in the early 19th century. It has a rooftop

mounting for a heavy gun.
Open Apr-Sep, daily 10-6.
Free.
(EH)

EDENBRIDGE
See Hever

✳ An asterisk indicates that up-to-date information was not available at the time of our research – 1991 information has been published as an indication of what you may expect.

Eynsford Castle — EYNSFORD

Map 04 TQ56
☎ (0322) 862536
The walls of this castle, still 30ft high, come as a surprise in the pretty little village. The castle was begun in the 11th century by William de Eynsford, who later retired to become a monk. Also to be seen are the remains of the castle hall

and ditch.
Open all year, Apr-Sep, daily 10-6; Oct-Mar, Tue-Sun 10-4. (Closed 24-26 Dec & 1 Jan).
Free.
🅿 ♿
(EH)

Lullingstone Castle — EYNSFORD

Map 04 TQ56
(1m SW of A225)
☎ Farningham (0322) 862114
The house was altered extensively in Queen Anne's time, and has fine state rooms and beautiful grounds. The 15th-century gate tower was one of the first gatehouses in England to be made entirely of bricks, and there is a church with family monuments. The National

Gardens Scheme will be held here on June 14th, and there will be an outdoor theatre production of 'Royal Hunt of the Sun' on June 26 and 28, and July 3rd and 4th.
Open, House Apr-Oct, Sat, Sun & BH 2-6; Wed, Thu & Fri by arrangement. House & Gardens £3 (ch £1 & pen £2.50).
🅿 💺 ♿ *shop* ✖

Lullingstone Roman Villa — EYNSFORD

Map 04 TQ56
(1.5m W off A225)
☎ (0322) 863467
The villa dates from the first and second centuries, and its rooms included an extensive bath complex. The mosaic floors are exceptionally well preserved, and fragments of painted wall plaster can also be seen. The site is roofed for

protection, with additional exhibits in a lighted gallery.
Open all year, Apr-Sep, daily 10-6; Oct-Mar, Tue-Sun 10-4. (Closed 24-26 Dec & 1 Jan).
£1.50 (ch 75p, students, pen & UB40 £1.10).
🅿 ♿ ✖
(EH)

Fleur de Lis Heritage Centre — FAVERSHAM

Map 04 TR06
13 Preston St
☎ (0795) 534542
A thousand years of history and architecture in Faversham are shown in award-winning displays, an audio-visual programme, and a working vintage telephone exchange, in this 16th-century

building (a former coaching inn). Tourist information centre.
Open all year, Etr-Sep, Mon-Wed, Fri & Sat 9.30-4.30; Oct-Etr 9.30-1 & 2-4. (Closed BH & 27 Dec-1 Jan).
£1 (ch, students & pen 50p). Party 10+ shop

Eurotunnel Exhibition Centre — FOLKESTONE

Map 04 TR23
St Martin's Plain, Cheriton High St (junc 12 off M20)
☎ (0303) 270111
Models, videos and displays explain the design and engineering of the huge project, which has been talked about for 200 years. Today's scheme is for three tunnels, one running each way with a

service tunnel in between, shuttling vehicles, passengers and freight between Britain and France.
Open all year, Tue-Sun 10-6 (5pm winter). Closed Mon & BH Mon.
£3 (ch & pen £1.80). Party 10+.
🅿 💺 ♿ *(ex observation tower) toilets for disabled shop* ✖

Museum & Art Gallery — FOLKESTONE

Map 04 TR23
Grace Hill
☎ (0303) 850123
In the 18th century Folkestone was noted for its fishing fleet; today it is best known as a Channel port. The museum has displays on its history up to World War II and also has fossils, natural

history and archaeology exhibits. There are new cases on weights and measures, ceramics and glass. Temporary art exhibitions are held.
Open all year Mon, Tue, Thu & Fri 9-5.30, Wed 9-1 & Sat 9-5. (Closed BH).
Free.
shop ✖

Old Town Hall FORDWICH

Map 04 TR15
The Square
☎ Canterbury (0227) 710610
The timber-framed Tudor town hall and courtroom is thought to be the oldest and smallest in England. It overlooks the River Stour, peaceful now but hectic in the Middle Ages, because Fordwich was the port for Canterbury. The old town jail can also be visited.
Open Etr, Jun-Sep, Mon-Fri 1-4 (Aug 11-4), Sat & Sun 2-4.
40p (ch 25p)
P ✗

Royal Engineers Museum GILLINGHAM

Map 04 TQ76
Prince Arthur Rd, Brompton
☎ Medway (0634) 406397
The work of the soldier-engineers from 1066 to 1945 is shown in a fascinating display, which includes memorabilia of General Gordon of Khartoum. Some displays are enlivened by sound effects.
Open all year, Tue-Fri & Spring/summer BH Mons 10-5, Sun 11.30-5.
£1 (ch, pen, students & UB40s 50p). Party 10+.
P & toilets for disabled shop ✗

Finchcocks GOUDHURST

Map 04 TQ73
(off A262)
☎ (0580) 211702
This fine early Georgian house stands in a spacious park with a beautiful garden, and contains an outstanding collection of keyboard instruments from the 17th century onwards. They have been restored to playing condition, and there are musical tours on all open days and private visits. Visually handicapped visitors may touch the instruments as well as hear them. Events for 1992 include a Spring Garden Fair (24/25 May), a series of chamber concerts on period instruments in September, and a craft fair on October 9-11th.
Open Etr-Sep, Sun & BH Mon 2-6; Aug, Wed-Sun 2-6. Private groups on other days by appointment Apr-Oct.
£4.50 (ch £2.50). Party. Private visits £4.50 (evening £5-£6).
P ♿ ✗ licensed & shop ✗

Kent Battle of Britain Museum HAWKINGE

Map 04 TR23
Aerodrome Rd (on A260)
☎ (030389) 3140
Once a Battle of Britain Station, today it houses the largest collection of authentic relics and related memorabilia of British and German aircraft involved in the fighting. Also shown are British and German uniforms and equipment, and full-size replicas of the Hurricane, Spitfire and Me 109 used in Battle of Britain films.
Open Etr-Sep, daily 11-5; Oct, daily 11-4.
P & shop ✗
Details not confirmed for 1992

"Brambles" Wildlife Park HERNE COMMON

Map 04 TR16
Wealdon Forest Pk
☎ Canterbury (0227) 712379
The 20-acre park has a nature trail leading through woodland where fallow and sika deer, mara, guanaco, wallaby, owls, Scottish wildcats and red foxes may be seen. Small rare breed farm animals, ponies and a miniature donkey may be fed with the food sold at the gate. There is also a walk-in rabbit enclosure and an indoor garden, an adventure playground and under-fives' playground.
Open Etr-Oct, daily 10-5.
£2 (ch £1.20, pen £1.50).
P ♿ & shop ✗

Every effort is made to provide accurate information, but details might change during the currency of this guide.

Hever Castle & Gardens HEVER

Map 04 TQ44
☎ Edenbridge (0732) 865224

This enchanting, double-moated, 13th-century castle was the childhood home of Anne Boleyn. In 1903 it was bought and restored by the American millionaire William Waldorf Astor, and now shows superb Edwardian craftsmanship and an exhibition on scenes from the life and times of Anne Boleyn. Astor also transformed the grounds, creating a Tudor village (available for conferences and corporate hospitality), a lake, a spectacular Italian garden filled with antique sculptures; maze and a fine topiary. Special events planned for 1992 include jousting tournaments throughout the summer and a traditional day of dance on 6th June. There are ramps in the gardens and purpose-built toilets for wheelchair users; some wheelchairs are available on request.
Open 17 Mar-8 Nov, daily. Castle 12-6, Gardens 11-6. Last admission 5pm. Private guided tours for pre-booked groups available all year.
Castle & Gardens £4.80 (ch 5-16 £2.40, pen £4.30). Family ticket £12. Gardens only £3.40 (ch 5-16 £2, pen £2.90). Family ticket £8.80. Party 15+.
P ✗ licensed & (Wheelchairs available) toilets for disabled shop garden centre

HYTHE

See map 04 TR13
Romney Hythe & Dymchurch Railway- For details see gazeteer entry under **New Romney.**

Ightham Mote IGHTHAM

Map 04 TQ55
(2.5m S off A227)
☎ Plaxtol (0732) 810378
This medieval manor house, complete with moat and attractive garden, was given to the National Trust in 1985. It has been extensively remodelled through the centuries but is still a splendid example of medieval architecture: particularly Great Hall, Old Chapel and crypt c.1340. The house also features many important additions from great periods and notable features include the drawing room with its Jacobean fireplace and frieze, its Palladian window and the hand-painted Chinese wallpaper. Large-scale repairs are in progress, with an excellent opportunity to see conservation in action with a major new exhibition in the Billiards Room. Five extra rooms will be open to the public in 1992.
Open Apr-Oct, daily ex Tue & Sat, 12-5.30 weekdays, 11-5.30 Sun. Pre-booked parties weekday am only. Open Good Fri & BH Mon.
Sun & BH's £3.70 (ch £1.90). Wkdays £3.20 (ch £1.60). Party.
P & toilets for disabled shop ✗ (NT)

OWL HOUSE GARDENS
Lamberhurst, Kent

Thirteen acres of romantic gardens surround this former wool smugglers' cottage, with spring flowers, roses, rare flowering shrubs, ornamental fruit trees. Expansive lawns lead to leafy woodland walks graced by English and Turkish oaks, elm, birch and beech trees. Rhododendrons, azaleas, camellias encircle peaceful informal sunken water gardens.
Gardens open daily, 11 to 6pm all year, including Bank Holiday weekends. Dogs on lead. Free car park. Coach parties welcome.

Admission: Adults £2.00. Children £1.00
(All proceeds towards Lady Dufferin's Charity, Maureen's Oast House for Arthritics)

Bayham Abbey   LAMBERHURST

Map 04 TQ63
(2m W in East Sussex)
☎ (0892) 890381
Set in the wooded Teise valley, these ruins date back to the 13th century and include parts of the old church, cloisters and gatehouse. Excavation and

preservation work is still in progress. *Open Apr-Sep, daily 10-6. £1.50 (ch 75p, pen, students & UB40 £1.10).*
🅿 & ✠
(EH)

Owl House Gardens   LAMBERHURST

Map 04 TQ63
(1m NE off A21)
☎ Tunbridge Wells (0892) 890230
The Owl House is a small, timber-framed 16th-century house, a former haunt of wool smugglers. Surrounding it are 13 acres of gardens offering the visitor romantic walks with spring flowers, azaleas, rhododendrons, roses,

shrubs and ornamental fruit trees. The sweeping lawns lead to lovely woodlands of oak and birch, and informal sunken water gardens.
Open all year, daily 11-6. (Closed 25-26 Dec & 1 Jan).
✱ *£2 (ch £1).*
🅿 &

Scotney Castle Garden   LAMBERHURST

Map 04 TQ63
(1m SE)
☎ (0892) 890651
The beautiful gardens at Scotney were carefully planned in the 19th century around the remains of the old, moated Scotney Castle. There is something to see at every time of year, with spring flowers followed by gorgeous

rhododendrons, azaleas and a mass of roses, and then superb autumn colours. *Open Apr-8 Nov, Wed-Fri 11-6, Sat, Sun & BH Mon 2-6. (Closed Good Fri). Old Castle open May-mid Aug same time. Wed-Sat: £2.40 (ch £1.20); Sun & BH Mon: £3 (ch £1.50).*
🅿 & *shop* ✠
(NT)

LEEDS

See Map 05 TQ85
For **Leeds Castle** see Maidstone

Lympne Castle   LYMPNE

Map 04 TR13
☎ Hythe (0303) 267571
Although this fortified manor house (originally built in the 12th century) was largely remodelled and restored in 1905, it retains much of its former character. The view from the castle includes the military canal, dug as part of the coastal

defences during the Napoleonic Wars, Romney Marsh and, in fine weather, across the Channel to the French Coast. *Open Etr-Sep & all BH's, daily 10.30-6. Other times by arrangement. (Closed occasional Sat).*
✱ *£1.50 (ch 50p).*
🅿

Port Lympne Zoo Park, Mansion & Gardens   LYMPNE

Map 04 TR13
☎ Hythe (0303) 264646
The only pair of Sumatran rhinos in the western world have their home in John Aspinall's 300-acre zoo park along with hundreds of other rare animals: Indian elephants, wolves, bison, black and snow leopards, Siberian and Indian tigers, monkeys and chimpanzees. The newly opened gorilla pavilion is now the home to Djoum and his family from Howletts. The mansion designed by Sir Herbert Baker is surrounded by 15-acres of spectacular gardens. Inside, the most notable features include the recently

restored Rex Whistler Tent Room, Moroccan Patio and hexagonal library where the Treaty of Paris was signed after the First World War. The recently completed Spencer Roberts mural room has illustrations of over 300 animals and birds from South East Asia adorning its walls. Safari trailers journey through some of the animal paddocks during peak times; please telephone to check availability.
Open all year, daily 10-5, 4pm in winter (Closed 25 Dec).
✱ *£6 (ch 4-14 & pen £4)*
🅿 ✕ *licensed & toilets for disabled shop* ✠

Leeds Castle   MAIDSTONE

Map 04 TQ75
(4m E on B2163 off M20/A20)
☎ (0622) 765400

Named after Led, Chief Minister of Ethelbert IV, King of Kent in AD 857, this castle was described by Lord Conway as 'the loveliest castle in the world'. Visitors may well agree with the sentiment. Built on two islands in the middle of a lake and set in 500 acres of landscaped parkland, it was converted into a royal palace by Henry VIII, and remained a royal residence for over three centuries. Today it has been beautifully restored and furnished; it has some beautiful pictures and other treasures, and, more unusual, a museum of medieval dog collars. Outside there are

the Culpeper Flower Garden, the greenhouses, aviaries and vineyard, the 14th-century barbican and mill, the maze and grotto, and water and woodland gardens. The Fairfax Hall, a 17th-century tithe barn, is the venue for 'Kentish Evenings' each Saturday night (except during Aug) and is a fully licenced self-service restaurant during normal opening hours. There are also many special events run throughout the year, including an Open Air Classical Concert, an International Balloon Fiesta, and a Festival of English Wines.
Open 16 Mar-Oct daily 11-5; Nov-Mar Sat & Sun 11-4. (Closed 27 Jun, 4 Jul & 7 Nov prior to special events). Open by special appointment at other times. Also daily in Xmas wk (26 Dec-1 Jan). Castle & park £6.20 (ch £4.20, students & pen £5.20); Park & gardens £4.70 (ch £2.70, students & pen £3.70). Family ticket £17.00, Park & gardens only £12.50. Party 20+.
🅿 ✕ *licensed & (Braille information, induction loops & wheelchair lift) toilets for disabled shop garden centre* ✠

See advertisement on page 107.

Maidstone Museum & Art Gallery   MAIDSTONE

Map 04 TQ75
Saint Faith's St
☎ (0622) 54497
Set in an Elizabethan manor house which has been much extended over the years, this museum houses a surprising and outstanding collection of fine and applied arts, including oil paintings and watercolours, furniture, ceramics, costume and a collection of Japanese art

and artefacts. Natural history collections and displays relating to local industry are also featured, together with the museum of the Queen's Own Royal West Kent Regiment.
*Open all year, Mon-Sat 10-5.30 & BH Mon 11-5.
Free.
shop* ✠

Museum of Kent Life   MAIDSTONE

Map 04 TQ75
Lock Ln, Sandling
☎ (0622) 763936
The story of the Kent countryside unfolds on this 27-acre site close to the River Medway. Exhibitions relating to farming history include displays of agricultural tools and machinery in farm buildings and livestock important to the county, and there are also displays of ancient local crafts. Events for 1992

include an Easter chicken hunt, an international folk weekend, a beer festival and hop picking weekend, and a plough day.
Open 28 Mar-Oct; daily 11-6; Nov-Mar, Sun 11-5. Open to booked parties throughout the year.
✱ *£1.20 (ch, pen & disabled 60p). Events £2.40 (£1.20)*
🅿 ♨ ✕ *licensed & toilets for disabled shop*

Tyrwhitt Drake Museum of Carriages   MAIDSTONE

Map 04 TQ75
The Archbishop's Stables, Mill St
☎ (0622) 54497
A wide array of horse-drawn carriages and vehicles is displayed in these late-medieval stables, which are interesting in themselves. The exhibits include state,

official and private carriages, and some are on loan from royal collections.
*Open all year, wkdays 10-1 & 2-5; Apr-Sep. BHs 11-5.
Free.*
& ✠

"The loveliest Castle in the whole world."

LEEDS CASTLE, KENT

Open every day from mid- March to October;
at weekends in winter; plus "Christmas Week"

Telephone: Maidstone (0622) 765400 Fax: (0622) 735616

Tudor House & Museum   MARGATE

Map 05 TR37
King St
☎ Thanet (0843) 225511
The main appeal of this small museum lies not in its exhibits (although these do illustrate much of the local history) but in its setting in the oldest domestic building in Margate. Dating from the early 16th century, the house is very well preserved, and has rich plaster ceilings and heavily moulded beams.
Open mid May-mid Sep, Tue-Sat 10-1 & 2-4.
    💪 *shop* ✈
Details not confirmed for 1992

This is just one of many guidebooks published by the AA.
The full range is available at any AA shop or good bookshop.

Badsell Park Farm   MATFIELD

Map 04 TQ64
Crittenden Rd
☎ Paddock Wood (0892) 832549 & 833436
A pleasant day in the country for all the family is offered at this attractive 180-acre fruit and arable farm. Children are able to handle young farm animals and pets in the Animal Park and Pet Area. There are nature trails to follow in beautiful countryside, a butterfly house with live tropical species, and picnic facilities. An Information Room gives details of farming and wildlife, including live insect displays. Strawberries, apples and other fruit and vegetables can be picked in season. Children's birthday parties are a speciality and pony and tractor rides are available by arrangement.
Open 25 Mar-15 Nov daily 10-5.30.
£2.50 (ch & pen £2)
🅿 🚽 💪 *shop* ✈ *(ex on nature trail)*

Places to visit in this guide are pinpointed on the atlas
at the back of the book.

Minster Abbey   MINSTER-IN-THANET

Map 05 TR36
☎ Ramsgate (0843) 821254
One of the first nunneries in England was built on this site in the 7th century. The house has been rebuilt in later centuries, but is still a religious community, and is run by Benedictine nuns. The ruins of the old abbey and the cloisters are open to the public and much of the Early English and Norman architecture can still be seen, and there is one wing dating back to 1027.
Open all year, May-Sep, Mon-Fri 11-12 & 2-4.30, Sat 11-12; Oct-Apr, Mon-Sat 11-12.
Donations
🅿 💪 *shop*

Romney Hythe & Dymchurch Railway   NEW ROMNEY

Map 04 TR02
☎ (0679) 62353 & 63256
The world's smallest public railway has its headquarters here. The concept of two enthusiasts coincided with Southern Railway's plans for expansion, and so the thirteen-and-a-half mile stretch of 15in. gauge railway came into being, running from Hythe through New Romney and Dymchurch to Dungeness Lighthouse.
Open daily Etr-Sep, also wknds in Mar & Oct. For times apply to: The Manager, RH & DR., New Romney, Kent.
Charged according to journey.
🅿 *(charged)* 🚽 💪 *shop*

Penshurst Place   PENSHURST

Map 04 TQ54
(on B2176)
☎ (0892) 870307

The original manor house was built by Sir John de Pulteney between 1340 and 1345 and is perfectly preserved. Successive owners enlarged it during the 15th, 16th and 17th centuries, and the great variety of architectural styles creates an elaborate and dramatic backdrop for the extensive collections of English, French and Italian furniture, tapestries and paintings. The world-famous, chestnut-beamed great hall is the oldest and finest in the country, and the collection in the Toy Museum is much loved by children. The house is surrounded by magnificent formal gardens laid out in authentic Tudor style. The leisure area includes an adventure playground, a countryside exhibition and nature trail. The Kent Craft and Hobby fair is held here on May 2-4 and September 18-20. There are also special activities and events on all Bank Holidays; telephone for details.
Open: House & gardens Apr-4 Oct, daily 12.30-5.30; Grounds & venture playground only open weekends from 7 Mar, 12.30-5, then until 1 Nov.
House & Grounds £4 (ch £2.25, pen & students £3.50). Grounds, Toy Museum & Venture playground £3 (ch £2, pen £2.50). Party 20+.
🅿 🚽 ✗ *licensed* 💪 *shop* ✈

See advertisement on page 108.

Old Soar Manor   PLAXTOL

Map 04 TQ65
Built by the famous Kentish family, the Culpeppers, in 1290, and amazingly intact, the solar, chapel, lavatorium and barrel-vaulted undercroft of Old Soar is joined to a lovely Georgian red-brick farmhouse. An ancient oak door displays 'graffiti' through the ages.
Open Apr-Sep, daily 10-6.
Free.
(EH & NT)

PENSHURST PLACE
Penshurst Tonbridge Kent

Penshurst Place welcomes you to a unique day out at one of England's finest stately homes.

Enjoy the delights of our lavishly furnished rooms, stroll amongst our landscaped gardens and enjoy the extensive Home Park.

There is plenty of fun for the children, including an exciting toy museum, thrilling venture playground, signposted nature trail and farm trail.

Watch the local press for our special events, Craft Fairs (2-4 May and 11-13 September) and many new activities.

NEW FOR '92
- LONGER OPENING TIMES
- FAMILY RESTAURANT
- NATURE TRAIL & FARM TRAIL
- MEMORIAL ARBORETUM

We have extended our opening arrangements and will be fully open **7 days a week** from 1st April until 4th October - 11.00 to 6.00pm (House 1.00 to 5.30pm)

The gardens, Home Park and Venture Playground will also be open at weekends from 7th March and will remain open after the season, at weekends, until 1st November.

Private guided tours available by special arrangement outside normal opening times.
The mediæval Baron's Hall and Sunderland Room can be booked for banqueting.
Enquiries welcome for corporate hospitality and country pursuit days.

Tel: **0892 870307**   Fax: **0892 870866**

Maritime Museum   RAMSGATE

Map 05 TR36
Pier Yard, Royal Harbour
☎ Thanet (0843) 587765
The museum is housed in four galleries in the restored Clock House, including the original Smeatons Dry Dock, and a collection of historic ships with the steam tug Cervia, and the Dunkirk little ship Sundowner. The museum complex outlines the study of the maritime heritage of the East Kent coast. Special events for 1992 include: 1 Jun-30 Sept, Summer Exhibition Fishing; 1 Sep-30 Sept, Columbus Exhibition, commemorating the 500th anniversary of the discovery of America.
Open all year, Apr-Sep Mon-Fri 9.30-4, Sat 2-5, Sun 1-6; Oct-Mar Mon-Fri 9.30-4.
* *Museum 75p (ch & pen 30p); Steam tug Cervia 40p (ch & pen 20p)*
shop ✶

Ramsgate Museum   RAMSGATE

Map 05 TR36
Ramsgate Library, Guildford Lawn
☎ Thanet (0843) 593532
This museum houses displays of objects, pictures and documents, which trace the history and development of Ramsgate. The town became an important port after Sandwich silted up. It gained popularity as a resort after George IV spent a season there in 1827.
Open all year, Mon-Wed 9.30-6, Thu & Sat 9.30-5, Fri 9.30-8. (Closed BH).
Free.
ᵬ *shop* ✶

---

* An asterisk indicates that up-to-date information was not available at the time of our research – 1991 information has been published as an indication of what you may expect.

Reculver Towers & Roman Fort   RECULVER

Map 05 TR26
☎ (02273) 66444
The Roman Regulbium was one of the forts built during the 3rd century to defend the Saxon Shore. The fort was in good condition until the 18th century, when erosion of the cliffs on which it stands caused part of the walls to collapse into the sea below.
During the 7th century an Anglo-Saxon church was built on the site, and its floor plan can still be traced. The church was extended and, during the 12th century, the Normans built on a west front and two huge towers. These are still almost intact, providing a mariners' landmark.
Open any reasonable time.
Free.
ᵬ ✶
(EH)

Richborough Castle   RICHBOROUGH

Map 05 TR36
☎ (0304) 612013
Close to Sandwich, these are the ruins of a Roman castle built to defend the Roman base of *Rutupiae*, the key fort in the defence of the Saxon Shore. The fort covered an area of about six acres and was mostly rebuilt in the 3rd century. Much remains of the Roman walls, parts of which were 12ft thick and up to 24ft high. Excavation has revealed the system of defensive ditches, and the remains of several buildings. There is a museum on the site.
Open all year, Apr-Sep, daily 10-6; Oct-Mar, Tue-Sun 10-4. (Closed 24-26 Dec & 1 Jan).
£1.40 (ch 70p, students, pen & UB40 £1).
P ᵬ ✶
(EH)

Charles Dickens Centre   ROCHESTER

Map 04 TQ76
Eastgate House, High St
☎ Medway (0634) 844176
Eastgate House is a fine late Tudor building, now showing local history exhibits and a waxwork display of Victorian life. The house itself appeared as Westgate House, in *Pickwick Papers*, and Nun's House in *Edwin Drood*. Also here is the chalet from Dickens' garden at Gad's Hill Place where he wrote *Edwin Drood*.
Open all year, daily 10-5.30. (Closed Xmas & 1 Jan).
ᵬ *shop* ✶
Details not confirmed for 1992

Guildhall Museum   ROCHESTER

Map 04 TQ76
High St
☎ Medway (0634) 848717
Built in 1687, the Guildhall has magnificent decorated plaster ceilings. Exhibits include local history and archaeology, arms and armour, dolls, toys and Victoriana, together with models of local boats, Short's flying boats, and some Napoleonic prisoner-of-war work. The city's civic plate, regalia and archives are housed here.
Open all year, daily 10-5.30. (Closed Good Fri, Xmas & 1 Jan).
ᵬ *shop* ✶
Details not confirmed for 1992

Rochester Castle   ROCHESTER

Map 04 TQ76
☎ Medway (0634) 402276
The castle was started in 1087, soon after the Norman Conquest, and the remarkable storeyed keep dates from 1126-39. On the way up are the site of a banqueting hall, a Norman chapel and mural galleries. Parts of the castle walls are still intact.
Open all year, Apr-Sep, daily 10-6; Oct-Mar, Tue-Sun 10-4. (Closed 24-26 Dec & 1 Jan).
£1.50 (ch 75p, pen, students & UB40 £1.10).
shop
(EH)

WITH 2,000 YEARS TO DISCOVER IT'S MUCH MORE THAN A DAY OUT!

A fascinating history has produced a City to delight the visitor of today.

If you are looking for true heritage and the perfect day out (or longer!) then why not visit the dramatic Norman Castle? Where King John used the fat of 40 pigs to save his bacon! Or Rochester Cathedral, the second oldest in the Country. Then there is the superbly restored Victorian High Street which is home to the 17th century Guildhall Museum and award winning Charles Dickens Centre where you can enter the grim reality

and curious world of the great Victorian novelist whose links with the City can be found everywhere.

Take a boat trip along the River Medway by paddlesteamer or river bus to the Historic Dockyard at Chatham where Britain's 'Hearts of Oak' were built. Or to the Country's finest Napoleonic Fortress, Fort Amherst, with its

2,000 yards of tunnels and military re-enactments.

Along with the colourful and lively festivals, superb tea rooms and shops, 2,000 years of history is just waiting to be discovered. All this and much more is only 30 miles from London and in a world of its own.

For further information contact the Rochester Tourist Information Centre at the address below, code 2000.

City of Rochester Upon Medway

Rochester Tourist Information, Eastgate Cottage, High Street, Rochester, Kent ME1 1EW. Tel: (0634) 843666

C M Booth Collection of Historic Vehicles   ROLVENDEN

Map 04 TQ83
Falstaff Antiques, 63 High St
☎ Cranbrook (0580) 241234
The collection is made up of historic vehicles and other items of interest connected with transport. The main feature is the unique collection of three-wheel Morgan cars, dating from 1913. Also here is the only known Humber

tri-car of 1904; and items include a 1929 Morris van, a 1936 Bampton caravan, motorcycles and bicycles. There is also a toy and model car display.
Open all year, Mon, Tue, Thu-Sat 10-6 & some Wed pm. Also some Sun & BHs. (Closed 25 Dec).
£1 (ch 50p)
shop

✘ The 'No Dogs' symbol does not normally apply to guide dogs – these are permitted in most establishments.

Knole   SEVENOAKS

Map 04 TQ55
☎ (0732) 450608
Thomas Bourchier, Archbishop of Canterbury, bought Knole in 1456 and set about transforming it from a simple medieval manor house into his palace; a century later the house was given to Henry VIII who extended it to even grander proportions. In the middle of the 16th century Knole was given to Thomas Sackville by Queen Elizabeth I; the Sackvilles kept the house for ten generations. Thomas lavished a fortune on the refurbishment and decoration of the house. Today, thanks to him, it is one of the largest houses in England. He employed an army of builders, plasterers, upholsterers and glaziers including 300 especially imported Italians; where most Elizabethan houses

had one Long Gallery, Knole has three. The State rooms are rich in architectural detail from the 17th and 18th centuries with fine portraits and outstanding furniture adding to their beauty. Outside, 26 acres of gardens contain formal walks among flower beds and fruit trees while beyond the encircling walls are further acres of undulating pasture and parkland.
Open Apr-Oct, Wed-Sat & BH Mon 11-5, Sun 2-5; Extra rooms shown Fri (ex Good Fri). Last admission 1hr before closing. Garden 1st Wed in month May-Sep. £3.50 (ch £1.80). Fri (ex Good Fri) £4 (ch £2). Garden 50p. Deer Park free to pedestrians.
🅿 *(charged)* ♨ ♿ *shop* ✘ *(ex in grounds)*
(NT)

Every effort is made to provide accurate information, but details might change during the currency of this guide.

Sissinghurst Garden   SISSINGHURST

Map 04 TQ73
(1.5m NE of town)
☎ Cranbrook (0580) 712850

The Tudor mansion of Sissinghurst Castle was bought in a neglected state in 1930 by Sir Harold Nicholson and his wife, the writer Vita Sackville-West. They set about restoring house and gardens and the gardens now rank among the most attractive and popular in England. Basing the design around the

existing high Tudor walls and two stretches of water, axial walks, usually ending with a statue or archway, have been combined with small geometrical gardens.
Each area is planted with a theme: either seasonal, such as the spring or summer garden; or colour, such as the White Garden or the Cottage Garden, planted mainly in orange or yellow. There is a rose garden with many old-fashioned varieties, a nuttery, a herb garden, a moat walk with a small lawn of thyme, an orchard and the beautiful Tower Lawn bordered with magnolias.
Open: Gardens Apr-15 Oct, Tue-Fri 1-6.30; Sat, Sun & Good Fri 10-6.30 (last admission 6pm).
Tue-Sat £4.50 (ch £2.30); Sun £5 (ch £2.50).
🅿 ✗ ♿ *shop* ✘
(NT)

For an explanation of the symbols and abbreviations, see page 2.

Smallhythe Place   SMALLHYTHE

Map 04 TQ82
☎ Tenterden (05806) 2334
Once a Tudor harbour master's house, this half-timbered, 16th-century building became Dame Ellen Terry's last home. It is now a museum of Ellen Terry

memorabilia and the barn has been made into a theatre.
Open Apr-Oct, Sat-Wed 2-6.
£2 (ch £1).
✘
(NT)

The Butterfly Centre   SWINGFIELD MINNIS

Map 04 TR24
McFarlanes Garden Centre
☎ (0303) 83244
A tropical greenhouse garden with scores of colourful free-flying butterflies from all over the world among exotic plants such as bougainvillea, oleander and

banana. The temperate section houses British butterflies, with many favourite species and some rarer varieties.
Open 28 Mar-11 Oct, daily 10-5.
£1.95 (ch £1.20 & pen £1.30). Family ticket £5.35-£5.85
🅿 ✗ ♿ *shop garden centre* ✘

Tenterden & District Museum — TENTERDEN

Map 04 TQ83
Station Rd
☎ (05806) 4310 (2-5pm) & 3350
The buildings and history of Tenterden, the Cinque Ports, and the Weald of Kent are featured at this local history museum. There are corporation records and insignia as well as exhibits on local trades, agriculture and hop growing, and also on display are the Tenterden Tapestry and Colonel Stephens light railway collection.
Open Apr-Oct daily 2-5 (10-5 Aug, ex Sun 2-5). Mar, Sat & Sun only 2-4.
Admission fee payable.
P *(charged)* ♿ *shop* 🐕

Tunbridge Wells Museum & Art Gallery — TUNBRIDGE WELLS

Map 04 TQ53
Civic Centre, Mount Pleasant
☎ Royal Tunbridge Wells (0892) 526121 ext 3171
The museum has exhibitions of local and natural history and archeology. There is also a fine display of Tunbridge ware. Toys, dolls, domestic and agricultural bygones. Regulary changing Art Gallery exhibitions include showings of the Ashton Bequest of Victorian oil paintings.
Open all year, daily 9.30-5. (Closed Sun, BH's).
Free.
♿ *shop* 🐕

Upnor Castle — UPNOR

Map 04 TQ77
☎ (0634) 718742
Built during Queen Elizabeth I's reign as a River Medway fort, Upnor Castle only saw real action in 1667 when its defences failed to deter the Dutch fleet sailing up the Medway. It is an attractive castle in ragstone brick, with turrets, a square gatehouse, mullioned windows and timber palisades around a neat lawn.
Open Apr-Sep, daily 10-6.
£1.50 (ch 75p, pen, students & UB40 £1.10).
♿
(EH)

Places to visit in this guide are pinpointed on the atlas at the back of the book.

Quebec House — WESTERHAM

Map 04 TQ45
(off A25)
☎ (0959) 62206
Westerham was the birthplace of General Wolfe who spent his childhood in the multi-gabled, square brick house now renamed Quebec House. The house probably dates from the 16th century but was extended and altered in the 17th century. It contains a Wolfe museum and an exhibition on Wolfe and the Quebec campaign.
Open Apr-Oct, daily (ex Thu & Sat) 2-6 (last admission 5.30pm).
£2 (ch £1).
🐕
(NT)

Squerryes Court — WESTERHAM

Map 04 TQ45
☎ (0959) 562345 & 563118
Owned and occupied by the Wardes for 260 years, this fine manor house was built about 1681. It overlooks a lake and attractive grounds with splendid azaleas and a formal garden. The house contains an excellent collection of pictures, china, tapestries and furniture. General Wolfe received his first commission here, at 14.
Open Apr-Sep, Wed, Sat & Sun, also BH Mon 2-6. Mar, Sun only. Last entry to house 5.30pm.
House & grounds £2.80 (ch 14 £1.40). Grounds £1.40 (ch 14 80p). Party 20+.
P ☕ ♿ *toilets for disabled shop* 🐕 *(ex in grounds)*

St Leonard's Tower — WEST MALLING

Map 04 TQ65
The fine early Norman tower is all that remains of a castle or fortified manor house built in about 1080 by Gundulf, Bishop of Rochester.
Open any reasonable time.
Free.
♿
(EH)

LANCASHIRE

Lewis Museum of Textile Machinery — BLACKBURN

Map 07 SD62
Exchange St
☎ (0254) 667130
A series of period rooms shows the development of the textile industry from the 18th century onwards. The gallery on the first floor has changing exhibitions. Building work may be in progress, please telephone ahead to check the museum is open.
Open all year, Tue-Sat 10-5. (Closed Good Fri, Xmas, 1 Jan & some BHs).
Free.
shop 🐕

Museum & Art Gallery — BLACKBURN

Map 07 SD62
Museum St
☎ (0254) 667130
Watercolours, oil paintings, Japanese prints and icons are among the works of art on display. The museum has fine books and manuscripts, militaria, coins and ceramics. There is also an Asian Centre, a 'time tunnel' and children's corner.
Open all year, Tue-Sat 10-5. (Closed Good Fri, Xmas, 1 Jan & some BHs).
Free.
♿ *toilets for disabled shop* 🐕

Grundy Art Gallery — BLACKPOOL

Map 07 SD33
Queen St
☎ (0253) 751701
Established in 1911, the gallery has a permanent collection of work by 19th- and 20th-century artists. There are also touring exhibitions.
Open Mon-Sat 10-5 (Closed BH).
♿ 🐕
Details not confirmed for 1992

Zoological Gardens — BLACKPOOL

Map 07 SD33
East Park Dr
☎ (0253) 65027
There are over four hundred of large and small animals kept in the 32 acres of landscaped gardens. There is a miniature railway and a children's play area, and also a mother and baby room..
Open all year daily, summer 10-6; winter 10-5 or dusk. (Closed 25 Dec).
* *£2.95 (ch & pen £1.50).*
P ☕ ✕ *licensed* ♿ *toilets for disabled shop* 🐕

Towneley Hall Art Gallery & Museums — BURNLEY

Map 07 SD83
☎ (0282) 24213
This 14th-century house contains the museum, which has oil paintings, English watercolours, furniture, ivories, 18th-century glassware and natural history exhibits. The Museum of Local Crafts and Industries includes displays on Burnley's recent social and industrial history. Special events are held throughout the year; telephone for details. There are nature trails and a Natural History Centre in the grounds which contains a new aquarium.
Open all year. Hall: Mon-Fri 10-5, Sun 12-5. Natural History Centre: Mon-Sat 10-5, Sun 12-5. (Closed Xmas & New Year).
P ☕ ✕ *licensed* ♿ *toilets for disabled shop* 🐕
Details not confirmed for 1992

Camelot Adventure Theme Park — CHARNOCK RICHARD

Map 07 SD51
☎ Eccleston (0257) 453044
This 130-acre theme park brings the legend and pageantry of the medieval world of Camelot to life every day with jousting tournaments, falconry displays, Merlin's Magic Show and Puppet Show. There are over 100 rides and attractions here, including The Tower of Terror and The Beast. There is also three-star hotel and conference centre in the grounds with 147 rooms in total, where family weekends and parties are a speciality.
Open Apr-Oct. Telephone for further details.
* *£7.45 (ch under 4 free).*
P ☕ ✕ ♿ *toilets for disabled shop* 🐕

Astley Hall — CHORLEY

Map 07 SD51
☎ (02572) 62166
A timber-framed 16th-century house with rich plasterwork, the hall stands in some 99 acres of park and woodland. It contains fine furnishings, pottery and pictures, and there are special exhibitions. Royal Lancashire Show held here.
Open daily Apr-Sep, 12-6; Oct-Mar, Mon-Fri 12-4, Sat 10-4 & Sun 11-4 (Last admission 30 mins before closing).
* *£1.55 (ch, pen & UB40's 75p). Family ticket £3.55.*
P ☕ ♿ *toilets for disabled shop* 🐕

Clitheroe Castle Museum — CLITHEROE

Map 07 SD74
☎ (0200) 24635
The museum in Castle House has a good collection of carboniferous fossils, and items of local interest. It is close to Clitheroe Castle, which ranks among Lancashire's oldest buildings and has one of the smallest Norman keeps in England. Displays include local history and the industrial archaeology of the Ribble Valley, while special features include the restored Hacking ferry boat, Victorian kitchen with taped commentary, printer's and clogger's shops. The grounds command magnificent views of the Ribble Valley.
Open Etr-May & Oct 12-4; Jun-Sep & BH wknds 11-4.30.
P ♿ *shop* 🐕
Details not confirmed for 1992

For an explanation of the symbols and abbreviations, see page 2.

City Museum (also 15 Castle Hill) — LANCASTER

Map 07 SD46
Market Sq
☎ (0524) 64637
The fine Georgian proportions of the old town hall are the setting for the museum of the King's Own Royal Lancaster Regiment, and a display of local social history and archaeological artefacts. Changing exhibitions occupy the ground floor. The Cottage Museum is furnished in the style of an artisan's house of around 1820.
Open all year, Mon-Sat 10-5, (Closed Xmas-New Year). 15 Castle Hill, Etr-Oct, daily 2-5.
City Museum free. 15 Castle Hill 40p (ch 20p).
♿ *shop* 🐕

Maritime Museum — LANCASTER

Map 07 SD46
St George's Quay
☎ (0524) 64637
Graceful Ionic columns adorn the front of the Old Customs House, built in 1764. Inside, the histories of the maritime trade of Lancaster, the Lancaster Canal and the fishing industry of Morecambe Bay are well illustrated. Special events for 1992 are the Easter Festival: 4 days of shanties, talks, walks and events, and the Georgian Festival in July when actors in residence relive events of a year in Georgian Lancaster.
Open all year, daily, Etr-Oct 11-5; Nov-Etr 2-5.
Apr-Oct £1 (ch & pen 50p). Rest of the year free.
P ☕ ♿ *toilets for disabled shop* 🐕

Shire Hall · LANCASTER

Map 07 SD46
Castle Pde
☎ (0524) 64998

The first fortifications were built on Castle Hill in the 11th century. The Norman keep was built in about 1170 and King John added a curtain wall and Hadrian's Tower, restored in the 18th and 19th centuries. A turret named after John of Gaunt was used as a beacon to warn of the approach of the Armada. The Shire Hall, chiefly noted for its Gothic revival design, was built within the castle boundaries and contains a splendid display of heraldry, with the coats of arms of all the sovereigns from Richard I. The Crown Court (still sited here) was notorious as having handed out the greatest number of death sentences of any court in the land, while another exhibition displays the grim relics of early prison life.
Open Etr-Sep, daily 10.30 (1st tour)-4 (last tour). Court requirements always take priority – it is advisable to telephone before visiting except in August.
£1 (ch 50p). Part tour when Court in session 80p (ch 40p, ch 5 free).
⅋ *shop* ✗

Leighton Hall · LEIGHTON HALL

Map 07 SD47
☎ Carnforth (0524) 734474

Early Gillow furniture is displayed among other treasures in the fine interior of this neo-Gothic mansion, which has a gallery with resident artist. Outside a large collection of birds of prey can be seen, and flying displays are given at 3.30pm each afternoon (weather permitting). Special events for 1992: 12-13 Sep, Rainbow Craft Fair; 18 Oct, Doll Fair.
Open May-Sep, Sun, Tue-Fri & BH Mon from 2pm. (Last admission 4.30). School parties pre-booked from 10am. Other times by arrangement.
£2.80 (ch £1.80, pen £2.30). Party 25 +.
🅿 ⅋ *toilets for disabled shop* ✗ *(ex in park)*

British Commercial Vehicle Museum · LEYLAND

Map 07 SD52
King St
☎ (0772) 451011

The largest commercial vehicle museum in Europe is located in a town long associated with the British motor industry. Over forty restored British vehicles are on display from horse drawn examples to modern. Special events for 1992: 19 Apr, Wreckers Day; 10 May, Spring Rally; 5 Jul, North West Vintage Motorcycle Rally; 27 Sep, Annual Autumn Rally; 15 Nov, Transport Fayre and Model Bus Show.
Open Apr-Sep, Tue-Sun 10-5; Oct & Nov, wknds 10-5; also BH.
£2 (ch & pen £1).
🅿 ⅋ *toilets for disabled shop* ✗

This is just one of many guidebooks published by the AA.
The full range is available at any AA shop or good bookshop.

Wildfowl & Wetlands Trust · MARTIN MERE

Map 07 SD41
☎ Burscough (0704) 895181

The Wildfowl Trust acquired 360 acres of the most primitive part of this old marsh and have re-created some of the open water habitats, many of which were lost when the land was drained for agriculture in the 17th century. The vast lake and variety of small ponds are now visited by thousands of wild geese, swans, ducks and waders; there are also three flocks of flamingoes among a permanent collection of birds numbering around 1600. In winter the refuge attracts Whooper swans from Iceland and more exciting still, Bewick's swans which have travelled well over 2000 miles from Siberia. The lake is overlooked by comfortable hides and the attractive visitor centre (built from Norwegian logs) contains an exhibition gallery, educational centre and a welcome coffee shop. Facilities for the disabled include wheelchair loan, purpose-built toilets for wheelchair users, braille notices around the grounds and tarmac paths. The Trust is signposted from the A565 at Mere Brow.
Open all year, daily 9.30-5.30 earlier in winter (ex 24-25 Dec).
🅿 ⅋ *toilets for disabled shop* ✗
Details not confirmed for 1992

Frontierland – Western Theme Park · MORECAMBE

Map 07 SD46
The Promenade
☎ (0524) 410024

Themed on the American Wild West, there are over 30 rides and attractions for all the family with wood and steel roller coasters, dark rides, American carousel, and an all-weather fun house with live country and western and magic shows in the main season. The Sky Ride offers great views across Morecambe Bay. Special events for 1992 include: 15-17 May, Country and Western Festival; 9 May and 12 Sept, Cub and Brownie Days; 4 Jul, Independence Day.
Open 12-26 Apr & 24 May-27 Sep, daily; 21 Mar-11 Apr & May Day-23 May, wknds only; Also school hol wk in Oct. Admission fee payable.
🅿 *(charged)* ⅋ *toilets for disabled shop*

Gawthorpe Hall · PADIHAM

Map 07 SD73
(0.75m E off A671)
☎ (0282) 78511

An early 17th-century manor house, Gawthorpe Hall was built around Britains most southerly Pele Tower, restored in 1850. The house contains fine panelling and moulded ceilings, a minstrel gallery and Jacobean long gallery. A collection of portraits from the National Portrait Gallery and the Kay-Shuttleworth Collections of costume, embroidery and lace are on show in the expanded exhibition areas. The coach house is home to a craft gallery.
Open all year, Garden: daily 10-6. Hall: Apr-1 Nov, Tue-Thu, Sat & Sun 1-5. Also open BH Mon. (Last admission 4.15). House: £2.30 (ch £1). Garden free. Party 15 +.
🅿 ⅋ *toilets for disabled shop* ✗ *(NT)*

Harris Museum & Art Gallery · PRESTON

Map 07 SD52
Market Square
☎ (0772) 58248

The Harris Museum and Art Gallery is an impressive Greek Revival building containing extensive collections of fine and decorative art. A Watercolour, Drawing and Prints gallery and gallery of Clothes and Fashion opened in 1989. The Story of Preston gallery covers the town's history and the lively exhibition programmes of contemporary art and social history are accompanied by events and activities throughout the year. Special events for 1992 include: 11 Jul-22 Aug, A Passion for Lancashire: Lowry's Landscapes.
Open all year, Mon-Sat 10-5. (Closed Sun & PHs).
Free.
⅋ *(Audio and tactile assistance. Wheelchair available) toilets for disabled shop* ✗

Museum of Childhood · RIBCHESTER

Map 07 SD63
Church St
☎ (0254) 878520

Twice winners of the Best of England's North-West Tourist Attractions Award, this nostalgic collection of toys, games, models, dolls, dolls' houses, miniatures and curios is housed in an atmospheric museum. There are over 250,000 objects on display and over fifty dolls houses. There is a working model fairground and special exhibitions including the Warneken Collection of embroidered dolls, the General Tom Thumb cabinet, the Titanic Bear and the famous Professor Tomlin's Flea Circus. There are normally at least four special events planned each year – details on application. From April there will be a special exhibition to commemorate the 80th anniversary of the liner Titanic.
Open all year, Tue-Sun, also BH Mon, 10.30-5. Last admission 4.30.
✱ *£1.95 (ch £1.25, pen £1.75). Faimly ticket £6.40.*
🅿 *shop*

Rufford Old Hall · RUFFORD

Map 07 SD41
(off A59)
☎ (0704) 821254

The hall was built by the Hesketh family in the 15th century, and added to later. The great hall has an intricate hammer-beam roof and movable wooden screen. The Carolean wing, altered in 1821, contains fine collections of 17th-century oak furniture, 16th-century arms, armour and tapestries.
Open Apr-1 Nov, Sat-Thu, Hall 1-5 (Last admission 4.30); Garden & shop 12-5.30, Sun 1-5.30.
£2.60 (ch £1.30). Garden only £1.30.
⅋ *shop* ✗ *(ex in grounds) (NT)*

Samlesbury Hall — SAMLESBURY

Map 07 SD53
Preston New Rd
☎ Mellor (0254) 812010 & 812229
A feature of this well restored half-timbered manor house, built during the 15th and 16th centuries, are the windows from nearby Whalley Abbey. Sales of antiques and collector's items, craft shows and temporary exhibitions are frequently held here.
Open 14 Jan-16 Mar 11.30-4; 17 Mar-19 Oct 11.30-5; 20 Oct-13 Dec 11.30-4.
£2 (ch 4-16 80p).
🅿 & *toilets for disabled shop* ✖

Turton Tower — TURTON BOTTOMS

Map 07 SD71
(1.5m N off B6391)
☎ Turton (0204) 852203
This historic house incorporates a 15th-century pele tower and Elizabethan half-timbered buildings. Restored in the 19th century, the house displays a major collection of carved wood furniture, mostly English, and period rooms depicting the Tudor, Stuart and Victorian eras. A product of the Renaissance, the house became associated with the Gothic revival and later typified the idealism of the Arts and Crafts movement. The gardens are being restored to show the wild formality that became popular in late Victorian times. Special events for 1992 will include, amongst others, a Summer Fair on 1 August.
Open May-Sep, Mon-Fri 10-12 & 1-5. Wknds 1-5; Mar, Apr & Oct Sat-Wed, 2-5; Nov & Feb, Sun 2-5. Other times by prior arrangement.
90p (ch 40p). Family ticket £2.30. Guided tour £1.50.
🅿 ☕ & *shop* ✖ *(ex in grounds)*

Places to visit in this guide are pinpointed on the atlas at the back of the book.

Saddleworth Museum & Art Gallery — UPPERMILL

Map 07 SD90
High St
☎ Saddleworth (0457) 874093 & 870336
This is the museum of a unique Pennine community and is based in an old mill next to the Huddersfield Narrow Canal. The exhibitions include Man and the Landscape, the Textile Industry – from cottage to mill, Victorian Life, Transport and Vintage Vehicles. There is also an Art Gallery. Temporary exhibitions, working days, craft demonstrations and special events are planned through the year. For 1992 these include a vintage vehicle gala on 14 Jun and lacemaking exhibition and demonstrations in August.
Open all year, Nov-Feb, daily 1-4; Mar-Oct, Mon-Sat 10-5, Sun 12-5.
70p (ch & pen 30p).
🅿 & *toilets for disabled shop* ✖

Whalley Abbey — WHALLEY

Map 07 SD73
☎ (0254) 822268
These ruins of a 13th-century Cistercian abbey are set in the delightful gardens of the Blackburn Diocesan Retreat and Conference House, a 16th-century manor house with gardens reaching down to the River Calder. The remains include two gateways, one of which had a chapel on the upper floor, a chapter house and the abbot's lodgings and kitchen.
Open all year Grounds; Apr-onwards. Craft centre, shop & visitor exhibition area, daily 11-5.
£1 (ch & pen 50p). Party 12 +.
🅿 ☕ & *(chair lift) shop*

LEICESTERSHIRE

Ashby-de-la-Zouch Castle — ASHBY-DE-LA-ZOUCH

Map 08 SK31
☎ (0530) 413343
The impressive ruins of a 14th century castle include a splendid 15th-century extension, the Warwick Tower. Mary Queen of Scots was imprisoned here; later, in the Civil War, the castle was held for over a year by royalists before being demolished. The remains include the tower, walls, solar and large kitchen.
Open all year, Apr-Sep, daily 10-6; Oct-Mar, Tue-Sun 10-4. (Closed 24-26 Dec & 1 Jan).
£1.10 (ch 55p, pen, students & UB40 85p).
🅿 & ✖
(EH)

Belvoir Castle — BELVOIR

Map 08 SK83
(between A52 & A607)
☎ Grantham (0476) 870262

Although Belvoir Castle has been the home of the Dukes of Rutland for many centuries, the turrets, battlements, towers and pinnacles of the house are a 19th-century fantasy. Amongst the many treasures to be seen inside are paintings by Van Dyck, Murillo, Holbein and other famous artists. Also here is the museum of the 17th/21st Lancers, the 'death or glory boys'. The castle's lovely terraced gardens are adorned with sculptures. Jousting tournaments will be held on 24-25 May, 28 Jun, 26 Jul, 30-31 Aug, 13 Sep.
Open Apr-Sep, Tue-Thu, Sat-Sun & BH Mon 11-5. Also Oct, Sun only.
£3.20 (ch & pen £2.20). Party 20 +.
Jousting days 50p extra per person.
🅿 ☕ *licensed* & *toilets for disabled shop garden centre* ✖

Rutland Railway Museum — COTTESMORE

Map 04 SK91
Cottesmore Iron Ore Mines, Sidings, Ashwell Rd (off B668)
☎ Stamford (0780) 62384 & 63092
The museum has an extensive collection of industrial locomotives and rolling stock, many of which were used in local ironstone quarries. A number are demonstrated in use over three quarters of a mile of the mineral branch built for the quarries. This line is also used to give passenger rides.
Open wknds for viewing, with free diesel-hauled rides on request, site conditions permitting. Steam operating days: 30 Mar-1 Apr, 5, 6 & 25-27 May, 7 Jul, 4 & 24-26 Aug & 29 Sep, 11-5.
🅿 ☕ & *shop*
Details not confirmed for 1992

Donington le Heath Manor House — DONINGTON-LE-HEATH

Map 04 SK41
(near Coalville)
☎ Coalville (0530) 31259
This is a rare example of a medieval manor house which has survived with very few alterations. The house was built in around 1280.
Open 30 Mar-2 Oct, Wed-Sun, also BH Mon & Tue 2-6.
🅿 ☕ & *shop* ✖
Details not confirmed for 1992

Kirby Muxloe Castle — KIRBY MUXLOE

Map 04 SK50
(off B5380)
☎ (0533) 386886
When Lord Hastings drew up designs for his castle in the late 15th century, he first had to obtain 'licence to crenellate'. The moated, fortified, brick-built manor house was never completed: Hastings was executed a few years later and building work ceased. Kirby Muxloe Castle now stands as a ruin in his memory.
Open all year, Apr-Sep, daily 10-6; Oct-Mar, Tue-Sun 10-4. (Closed 24-26 Dec & 1 Jan).
£1.10 (ch 55p, pen, students & UB40 85p)
🅿 &
(EH)

For an explanation of the symbols and abbreviations, see page 2.

Belgrave Hall — LEICESTER

Map 04 SK50
Church Rd, off Thurcaston Rd
☎ (0533) 666590
The early 18th-century house is finely furnished with period pieces, and coaches and implements are displayed in the stables and outbuildings. There are also gardens.
Open all year, Mon-Sat 10-5.30, Sun 2-5.30. (Closed Xmas & Good Fri).
& *shop* ✖
Details not confirmed for 1992

Jewry Wall Museum & Site — LEICESTER

Map 04 SK50
St Nicholas Circle
☎ (0533) 544766
Behind the massive fragment of Roman wall, a courtyard has been excavated revealing porticos leading into shops. Nearby are tessellated pavements with intricate and colourful designs, while coins, pottery and other finds are housed in the museum. The site offers a captivating insight into Roman Leicester (then known as *Ratae*).
Open all year, Mon-Sat 10-5.30, Sun 2-5.30. (Closed Good Fri, 25 & 26 Dec).
& *shop* ✖
Details not confirmed for 1992

Leicestershire Museum & Art Gallery — LEICESTER

Map 04 SK50
New Walk
☎ (0533) 554100
The unique collection of German expressionist art makes Leicester's town museum special. Otherwise there are attractive displays of 18th- to 20th-century English works of art, ceramics, silver, geology and natural history. It also boasts a very active educational programme.
Open all year, Mon-Sat 10-5.30, Sun 2-5.30. (Closed Good Fri, 25 & 26 Dec).
& *toilets for disabled shop* ✖
Details not confirmed for 1992

Leicestershire Museum of Technology — LEICESTER

Map 04 SK50
Abbey Pumping Station, Corporation Rd
☎ (0533) 661330
A knitting gallery, power gallery, transport gallery with original beam engines dating from the late 19th century, and a number of other displays all illustrate Leicester's past and present as an important industrial centre.
Open all year, Mon-Sat 10-5.30, Sun 2-5.30. (Closed Good Fri, 25 & 26 Dec).
🅿 & *shop* ✖
Details not confirmed for 1992

Leicestershire Record Office — LEICESTER

Map 04 SK50
57 New Walk
☎ (0533) 544566
The record office houses the county's rural and urban archives, both official and private.
Open all year, Mon-Thu 9.15-5, Fri 9.15-4.45, Sat 9.15-12.15. (Closed Sun & BH wknds Sat-Tue).
🅿 & *shop* ✖ 🖭
Details not confirmed for 1992

Museum of Royal Leicestershire Regiment — LEICESTER

Map 04 SK50
Oxford St
☎ (0533) 555889
Mementoes, battle trophies and relics of the Leicestershire Regiment are displayed in this museum in the Magazine Gateway.
Open all year, Mon-Sat 10-5.30, Sun 2-5.30. (Closed Good Fri, 25 & 26 Dec).
shop ✖
Details not confirmed for 1992

Newarke Houses   LEICESTER

Map 04 SK50
The Newarke
☎ (0533) 554100
A 19th-century street scene, 17th-century period furnished room and a collection of domestic memorabilia tell the story of the people of Leicester from

1500 to the present day. There is also a collection of clocks and musical instruments.
Open all year, Mon-Sat 10-5.30, Sun 2-5.30. (Closed Good Fri, 25 & 26 Dec).
& *shop* ✖
Details not confirmed for 1992

University of Leicester Botanic Gardens   LEICESTER

Map 04 SK50
Beaumont Hall, Stoughton Dr South, Oadby (3m SE A6)
☎ (0533) 717725
The grounds of four houses, now used as student residences and not open to the public, make up this 16-acre garden. A great variety of plants in different

settings provide a delightful place to walk, including rose, rock, water and sunken gardens, trees, borders, heathers and glasshouses.
Open all year, Mon-Thu 10-4.30, Fri 10-3.30. (Closed BHs).
Free.
& ✖

Wygston's House Museum of Costume   LEICESTER

Map 04 SK50
Applegate
☎ (0533) 554100
Reconstructions of 1920s draper's, milliner's and shoe shops are displayed, with English costume ranging from the

mid 17th-century to the present day.
Open all year, Mon-Sat 10-5.30, Sun 2-5.30. (Closed Good Fri & Xmas).
& *shop* ✖
Details not confirmed for 1992

Bell Foundry Museum   LOUGHBOROUGH

Map 08 SK51
Freehold St
☎ (0509) 233414
Located in the former fettling shop of the John Taylor Bell Foundry, the museum is part of the largest working bell foundry in the world. Exhibits follow the evolution of the bell founder's craft, showing techniques of

moulding, casting, turning and fitting, including modern craft practices.
Open all year, Tue-Sat 9.30-12.30 & 1.30-4.30. Evening tours by prior arrangement.
✱ *Museum only 75p (ch under 16 50p). Party 15 +.*
🅿 & *toilets for disabled shop* ✖

Great Central Railway   LOUGHBOROUGH

Map 08 SK51
Great Central Rd
☎ (0509) 230726

This private steam railway runs over seven miles from Loughborough Central

to Leicester, with all trains calling at Quorn and Woodhouse. The locomotive depot is at Loughborough Central, together with a museum. A buffet car is run on most trains. Special events for 1992 include three steam galas, two Thomas Tank Engine weekends, bonfire night fireworks display and Santa specials in December.
Open Sat, Sun & BH Mon & midweek May-Sep.
£5 (ch & pen £2.50). Family ticket £12.50.
🅿 ⬤ ✕ *licensed* & *(Disabled coach added to train by prior request) shop*

✖ The 'No Dogs' symbol does not normally apply to guide dogs – these are permitted in most establishments.

Bede House   LYDDINGTON

Map 04 SP89
☎ (0572) 822438
The vast diocese of the bishops of Lincoln, which stretched from the Humber to the Thames, necessitated an episcopal residence in Lyddington. Bede House was built for the purpose in the late 15th century and it remains a good example of the period. It passed out of

religious hands at the time of Henry VIII, and was later converted into an almshouse by the Earl of Exeter.
Open Apr-Sep, daily 10-6.
£1.10 (ch 55p, students, pen & UB40 85p).
& ✖
(EH)

The Battlefield Steam Railway Line   MARKET BOSWORTH

Map 04 SK40
(5m NW on unclass rd at Shackerstone station)
☎ Tamworth (0827) 880754 & (0827) 715790 (wknd)
Together with a regular railway service (mainly steam) from Shackerstone to Shenton, there is an extensive railway museum featuring a collection of rolling stock and a multitude of other relics from the age of steam rail travel. With the opening of the extension in April 1992 of the line to Shenton (site of the Battle of Bosworth Field), the return

passenger trip is 9 miles. Special events throughout the year include Friends of Thomas the Tank Engine days, a Teddy Bears' Picnic, Halloween Special, Bonfire Special and Santa Specials on December weekends.
Open all year, Station & Museum, Sat & Sun, 11.30-5.30. Passenger steam train service operates Apr-Oct, Sun & BH Mon only.
Shackerstone station: 50p (ch 5-15 free). Return train fare £4 (ch £2). Family ticket £11.
🅿 ⬤ & *shop*

Bosworth Battlefield
LEICESTERSHIRE
Visit the historic site of the Battle of Bosworth Field 1485
where King Richard III lost his crown, and his life, to the future Henry VII.

● **Award winning Battlefield Visitor Centre** with exciting exhibitions and models giving an insight into the Battle and mediaeval life; film theatre, book and gift shops, cafeteria.

● **Centre open every afternoon** Easter to end of October:
  Adults £1.50, Children/OAPs £1.00, Cars 30p.
  (Special Event Days excepted).

● **Illustrated Battle Trails** through picturesque countryside (open all year).

● **Series of Mediaeval Attractions** July - September.

● **Follow road signs** off A447, A444, A5 and B585 in vicinity of Market Bosworth, Leicestershire.

Project Manager Director of Property
Rural Practice Division
Leicestershire County Council

An enterprise of Leicestershire County Council England

Enquiries: Market Bosworth (0455) 290429
Bosworth Battlefield Visitor Centre & Country Park,
Sutton Cheney, Market Bosworth, Leicestershire.

Bosworth Battlefield Visitor Centre & Country Park   MARKET BOSWORTH

Map 04 SK40
Sutton Cheney (2.5m S)
☎ (0455) 290429
The Battle of Bosworth Field was fought in 1485 between the armies of Richard III and the future Henry VII. The visitor centre gives the viewer a comprehensive interpretation of the battle by means of exhibitions, models and a film theatre. There are also illustrated trails around the battlefield, and special medieval attractions are held in the summer months. Full details of

admission fees for special events and free leaflets are available on application.
Open all year – Country Park & Battle trails all year during daylight hours. Visitor Centre Apr-Oct, Mon-Sat 1-5.30, Sun & BH Mon 1-6. Parties all year by arrangement.
✱ *Visitor Centre £1.50 (ch & pen £1). Party 20 +. Special charges apply on event days.*
🅿 *(charged)* ⬤ & *(parts of footpath network not suitable) toilets for disabled shop* ✖ *(ex country park)*

Harborough Museum   MARKET HARBOROUGH

Map 04 SP78
Council Offices, Adam & Eve St
☎ (0858) 32468
Market Harborough has a long and varied history: it was a market town and social centre, a hunting centre and a medieval planned town. All these aspects

of its past are well illustrated in the local museum housed in the town's council offices.
Open all year. Mon-Sat 10-4.30, Sun 2-5. (Closed Good Fri & Xmas).
& *(ex Sat, Sun & BH) shop* ✖
Details not confirmed for 1992

Every effort is made to provide accurate information, but details might change during the currency of this guide.

Melton Carnegie Museum   MELTON MOWBRAY

Map 08 SK71
Thorpe End
☎ (0664) 69946
This historic town, the home of pork pies, Stilton cheeses and the Quorn Hunt, attracted 'quality' from all over the world for the hunting season in its 19th-century heyday. The Melton Carnegie Museum illustrates the

glamorous past, and the present life of the area.
Open all year, Etr-Sep, Mon-Sat 10-5, Sun 2-5; Oct-Etr, Mon-Fri 10-4.30, Sat 10.30-4 (Closed Sun, Good Fri, 25 & 26 Dec, 1 Jan).
shop ✖
Details not confirmed for 1992

Farmworld OADBY

Map 04 SK60
Stoughton Farm Park, Gartree Rd (off
A6 & A47)
☎ Leicester (0533) 710355
Winner of the 1989 Best of Tourism
Award for The Shires of Middle
England, Farmworld is a working farm
that offers a feast of fun and surprises for
all the family. Children will enjoy the
Children's Farmyard and the
playground, while their parents might
appreciate the Edwardian Ale-house and
the craft workshops and demonstrations.
There are also Shire horses and cart
rides, lakeside and woodland walks,
nature trails and ancient and modern
machinery displays.
*Open all year, daily 10-5.30 (5 in winter).
(Closed 25-26 Dec & 1 Jan).
£3.50 (ch 2-4 £1.25, ch 5-16 £1.75, pen
£2.50). Party.*
P ✉ ♿ *(specifically designed viewing
gallery) toilets for disabled shop* ✖

✖ The 'No Dogs' symbol does not normally apply
to guide dogs – these are permitted in
most establishments.

Oakham Castle OAKHAM

Map 04 SK80
off Market Place
☎ (0572) 723654
This splendid Norman hall houses a
unique collection of presentation
horseshoes.
Open all year. Grounds daily 10-5.30
*(4pm Nov-Mar). Great Hall Sun & BH
Mon 2-5.30, also Tue-Sat 10-1 & 2-5.30.
(Closed Good Fri & Xmas). Magistrates in
session on Mon.*
♿ *shop* ✖
Details not confirmed for 1992

Rutland County Museum OAKHAM

Map 04 SK80
Catmos St
☎ (0572) 723654
Local archaeological finds, especially
Roman and Anglo-Saxon pieces, are on
display here along with craft tools and
local history. A courtyard contains
agricultural implements and farm
wagons.
*Open all year, Apr-Oct Tue-Sat & BH
Mon 10-1 & 2-5, Sun 2-5; Nov-Mar,
Tue-Sat 10-1 & 2-5. (Closed Good Fri &
Xmas)*
♿ *toilets for disabled shop* ✖
Details not confirmed for 1992

Every effort is made to provide accurate information,
but details might change during the currency
of this guide.

Stanford Hall SWINFORD

Map 04 SP57
(1m E)
☎ Rugby (0788) 860250
This William and Mary house on the
River Avon, was built in the 1690s by
Sir Roger Cave. The Ballroom is notable
for its decoration and the chimney-piece
and the house contains antique furniture,
paintings and family costumes. There is
a replica of Percy Pilcher's flying
machine of 1898. In the grounds are a
walled rose garden, an old forge, and a
motor cycle museum. A craft centre
based in the old stables can be seen on
most Sundays. Outdoor pursuits include
fishing and a nature trail and the large
number of events arranged for 1992
include car and motorcycle owners club
rallies, National Hovercraft Racing
Championships on 23-25 May and
29-31 Aug, The 10th Rugby Raft Races
on 28 Jun and a craft fair on 3-4 Oct.
*Open Etr-Sep, Sat, Sun, BH Mon & Tue
following 2.30-6; noon on BH & Event
Days (House 2.30).
House & Grounds £2.80 (ch £1.30);
Grounds only £1.50 (ch 70p); Motorcycle
Museum 90p (ch 20p). Party 20+.*
P ✉ ♿ *(museum also accessible) toilets for
disabled shop* ✖ *(ex park)*

Twycross Zoo Park TWYCROSS

Map 04 SK30
(1.5m NW off A444)
☎ Tamworth (0827) 880250
Set up during the 1960s, Twycross Zoo
Park specialises in primates, and also
includes gibbons, gorillas, orang-utangs
and chimpanzees. There is a huge range
of monkeys from the tiny tamarins and
spider monkeys to the large howler
monkeys.
There are also various other animals
such as lions, tigers, elephants and
giraffes, and a pet's corner for younger
children. Other attractions include a
Sealion Pool with spectacular waterfall,
Penguin Pool with underwater viewing
and a Children's Adventure Playground.
*Open all year, daily 10-6 (4 in winter).
(Closed 25 Dec).
£3.80 (ch £2, pen £2.60). Party.*
P ✉ ♿ *toilets for disabled shop* ✖

LINCOLNSHIRE

Alford Manor House Folk Museum ALFORD

Map 08 TF47
West St
☎ (0507) 462143 & 466488
This thatched 17th-century manor house
is now a folk museum with local history
displays: a chemist's shop, shoemaker's
shop, veterinary display and a nursery
and maid's bedroom. There are also
displays of agricultural and craft tools,
sweet making equipment, a kitchen and
even a police cell.
*Open 4 May-2 Oct, Mon-Sat 10.30-4.30,
Sun 1-4.30.
50p (ch 25p).*
P ♿ ✖

GAINSBOROUGH OLD HALL
A MAGNIFICENT MEDIEVAL MANOR HOUSE
in the Centre of Gainsborough

Large unspoilt manor with original **medieval kitchens**, **great hall**, **tower** and **wings**.
Free Soundalive Tour. Shop. Tea Shop open daily.

1992 Events include:
MAY FAIR Mon May 4th
GRAND CRAFT FAIR Sat July 25th
17th century LIVING 26th &
HISTORY WEEKEND 27th Sept
CHRISTMAS CRAFT FAIR Sat Nov 28th

Lincolnshire County Council

Open all year: Mon-Sat 10.00-5.00
Summer Sundays: 2.00-5.30
Evening visits and meals by arrangement.
Admission: Adults £1.50. Under 16 & over 60 75p

TEL: 0427 612669 FOR MORE DETAILS

English Heritage

Belton House Park & Gardens BELTON

Map 08 SK93
(3m NE Grantham on A607)
☎ Grantham (0476) 66116

For many people Belton is the perfect
country house, a handsome but not
overwhelming grand mansion. It was the
home of the Brownlow family for nearly
three centuries before being given to the
National Trust, and the family still has a
flat in the house. The ground floor has a
succession of state rooms, with the
Marble Hall as its centrepiece. The
name comes from the black and white
marble floor, which is original. The
walls are decorated with intricate wood
carvings of birds, fruit, flowers and
foliage, which have been attributed to
Grinling Gibbons but are probably by
Edmund Carpenter. There are more
remarkable carvings in the formal
saloon, which also has ornate
plasterwork on the ceiling. Splendid
furnishings and decorations throughout
the house include tapestries and
hangings, both old and modern, lovely
garden scenes by Melchior
d'Hondecoeter, family portraits,
porcelain and fine furniture. Not to be
forgotten are the rolling grounds and
gardens, including an orangery and
formal Italian garden, laid out in the
19th century. There are some attractive
sculptures, and an adventure playground
for children. An open-air concert is
planned for 27 June.
*Open Apr-Oct, Wed-Sun & BH Mon
(Closed Good Fri). House open 1-5.30 (last
admission 5pm). Grounds open 11-5.30.
£3.80 (ch £1.90).*
P ✗ *licensed* ♿ *toilets for disabled shop* ✖
*(ex in grounds)
(NT)*

Battle of Britain Memorial Flight Visitor Centre CONINGSBY

Map 08 TF25
(on A153)
☎ (0526) 44041

View the aircraft of the Battle of Britain
Memorial Flight, comprising the only
flying Lancaster in Europe, five Spitfires,
two Hurricanes, DH Devon and a
Chipmunk. Because of operational
commitments, specific aircraft may not
be available. Ring the telephone number
given for information before planning a
visit.
*Open all year, Mon-Fri, conducted tours
10-3.30. (Closed BH's & 2 wks Xmas).
£2.50 (ch & pen £1.25).*
P ♿ *toilets for disabled shop* ✖

✳ An asterisk indicates that up-to-date information was
not available at the time of our research – 1991
information has been published as an
indication of what you may expect.

Old Hall GAINSBOROUGH

Map 08 SK88
Parnell St
☎ (0427) 612669
A complete medieval manor house
dating back to 1460-80 and containing a
remarkable Great Hall and original
kitchen with room settings. Richard III,
Henry VIII, the Mayflower Pilgrims and
John Wesley all in their day visited the
Old Hall. Special events for 1992
include: 4 May, May Fair; 25 Jul,
Grand Craft Fair; 26-27 Sep, 17th-
century living history weekend; 28 Nov,
Christmas Craft Fair.
*Open all year, Mon-Sat 10-5; Etr-Oct, Sun
2-5.30.
£1.50 (ch 75p).*
✉ ♿ *shop* ✖

GRANTHAM

See Map 08
See Belvoir

Grimsthorpe Castle
(A151 Bourne to Colsterworth Road. Off the A1)
LINCOLNSHIRE

Grimsthorpe Castle has been the home of the Barons Willoughby de Eresby since 1516. It has fine examples of Medieval, Tudor, Baroque and Neo-Gothic Architecture. The North Front being the work of Sir John Vanbrugh. There are 8 State Rooms, and 2 Picture Galleries open to the public, also Gardens, and park with picnic area.

Opening Times
Park & Gardens Easter Weekend. Sunday 19th and Monday 20th April. 12 noon to 6 pm (no entry after 5 pm).
From Saturday 2nd May to Sunday 13th September every Saturday, Sunday and Bank Holiday. 12 noon to 6 pm (No entry after 5 pm).
Castle Sunday 31st May to Sunday 13th September open Sundays and Bank Holidays 2 pm to 6 pm (last admission 5 pm).

Admission Prices
Park & Gardens Adults £1, OAPs and under 16 yrs 50p.
Castle In addition to the above charge, Adults £2, OAPs & under 16 yrs £1, under 5 yrs free.
The Coach House Cafeteria serves home made teas.

Grimsthorpe Castle   GRIMSTHORPE

Map 08 TF02
(8m E of A1 at Colsterworth on A151)
☎ Edenham (077832) 205
A stately home in the occupation of the Baron Willoughby de Eresby since 1516. The architecture comprises a medieval tower, Tudor quadrangular house with a Baroque north front by Vanbrugh. There are eight state rooms and two picture galleries with an important collection of furniture, pictures and tapestries. Formal gardens, parkland and lake. Grimsthorpe Country Fair is to be held on 7 June.
Open: Gardens & Park, 19-20 Apr & 2 May-13 Sep wknds & BH's. Castle open 30 May-13 Sep, Sun & BHs 2-6.
Gardens £1 (ch & pen 50p). Castle £2 (ch & pen £1).
P ☛ ₺ *toilets for disabled*

For an explanation of the symbols and abbreviations, see page 2.

The Pearoom   HECKINGTON

Map 08 TF14
Station Yard
☎ Sleaford (0529) 60765
The Pearoom has a craft shop, galleries and workshops for ten resident craft workers. Their products include pottery, wood-carving, jewellery, leather work, toys, and stained glass; and also there is a musical instrument restorer, a weaver-feltmaker, and a textile designer-printer.
An active programme of craft exhibitions runs throughout the year accompanied by a programme of weekend course activities. (For details tel. Exhibition Officer).
Open all year, Mon-Sat & BHs 10-5, Sun 12-5.
Free.
P ☛ ₺ *toilets for disabled shop* ✸

City & County Museum   LINCOLN

Map 08 SK97
Broadgate
☎ (0522) 530401
The county's main archaeology museum, housed in a magnificent medieval building, forms part of Greyfriars. Exhibitions in 1992 include a pre-history of Lincolnshire exhibition at the end of February; 4 Mar-27 May, Peru; 3 Jun- 26 Aug, Medieval Tiles; 9 Sep-Jan '93, Civil War.
Open all year, Mon-Sat 10-5.30, Sun 2.30-5.30 (Oct-Mar last entry 5). (Closed Good Fri & Xmas).
50p (ch 25p).
₺ *shop* ✸

Lincoln Castle   LINCOLN

Map 08 SK97
Castle Hill
☎ (0522) 511068

Situated in the centre of Lincoln, the Castle, built in 1068 by William the Conqueror, dominates the Bailgate area alongside the great Cathedral. In addition to its many medieval features, Lincoln Castle has strong 19th-century connections and the unique Victorian prison chapel is perhaps the most awe-inspiring. The beautiful surroundings are ideal for historical adventures, picnics and special events which take place throughout the year. Among these is a Folk Festival in May and a Vintage Vehicle Rally in September.
Open all year, British Summer Time Mon-Sat 9.30-5.30. Winter time Mon-Sat 9.30- 4, Sun 11-4. Last admission 30 mins before closing. (Closed 25-26 Dec & 1 Jan).
✳ *80p (ch, pen & students 50p). Party 20+.*
₺ *(video theatre also accessible) shop* ✸

Museum of Lincolnshire Life   LINCOLN

Map 08 SK97
Burton Rd
☎ (0522) 528448
The past two centuries of Lincolnshire life are illustrated by displays of domestic implements, industrial machinery, agricultural tools and a collection of horse-drawn vehicles. The Royal Lincolnshire Regiment museum is also housed here. From 4 April to 4 August 'How we used to live – the Victorians' will be exhibited.
Open all year, May-Sep, daily 10-5.30; Oct-Apr, Mon-Sat 10-5.30, Sun 2-5.30.
80p (ch 40p).
P ☛ ₺ *toilets for disabled shop* ✸

National Cycle Museum   LINCOLN

Map 08 SK97
Brayford Wharf North, Brayford Pool
☎ (0522) 545091
The National Cycle Museum houses the premier collection of cycles and cycling artefacts in the country, with over 140 cycles on display and related artefacts, including photographs, medals, trophies and more. Special events for 1992 include some temporary exhibitions: Dec 91-Mar 92, The Cycle in the Wars; Apr-Jul, a photographic exhibition The Life of a Cycling Club; Aug-Nov, Cycle Safety.
Open all year, daily 10-5 (Closed Xmas wk).
✳ *60p (ch 5-16 30p). Prices under review.*
₺ *shop* ✸

Usher Gallery   LINCOLN

Map 08 SK97
Lindum Rd
☎ (0522) 27980
Built as the result of a bequest by Lincoln jeweller, James Ward Usher, the Gallery houses his magnificent collection of watches, porcelain and miniatures, as well as topographical works, watercolours by Peter de Wint, Tennyson memorabilia and coins and medals. As the country's main visual arts venue, the Gallery also has an active exhibitions and outreach programme. There will be a Tennyson centenary exhibition from 4 July – 14 September.
Open all year, Mon-Sat 10-5.30, Sun 2.30-5. (Closed Good Fri & Xmas).
50p (ch 25p).
₺ *toilets for disabled shop* ✸

LONG SUTTON

See Map 08 TF42
see Spalding

Church Farm Museum   SKEGNESS

Map 08 TF56
Church Rd South
☎ (0754) 66658
A farmhouse and outbuildings that have been restored to show the way of life of a Lincolnshire farmer at the end of the 19th century, with farm implements and machinery plus household equipment on display. A timber-framed cottage and a barn have been re-erected. In the barn there is a temporary exhibition and, at weekends during the summer, craftsmen give demonstrations. Special exhibitions for 1992: April-July, Sporting Links; August-October, Off the Rails.
Open Apr-Oct, daily 10.30-5.30 70p (ch 30p).
P ☛ ₺ *toilets for disabled shop* ✸

Skegness Natureland Marine Zoo & Seal Sanctuary   SKEGNESS

Map 08 TF56
North Pde
☎ (0754) 764345
The Zoo houses a specialised collection of animals including seals, penguins, tropical birds, aquarium, reptiles, Pets' Corner etc. Also free-flight tropical butterflies (May-Oct). Natureland is well known for its rescue of abandoned seal pups, and has successfully reared and returned to the wild a large number of these beautiful creatures. The new Seal Hospital Unit incorporates a public viewing area. Additional attractions include the Seal Life exhibition, floral displays and an Animal Brass Rubbing House.
Open all year, Apr-Jun & Sep 10-5; Jul & Aug 10-6.30; Oct-Mar 10-4.30. (Closed 25-26 Dec & 1 Jan).
£2.50 (ch £1.50, pen £2). Party.
☛ ₺ *shop*

Butterfly & Falconry Park   SPALDING

Map 08 TF22
Long Sutton
☎ Holbeach (0406) 363833
The Park contains one of Britain's largest walk-through tropical houses, in which hundreds of butterflies from all over the world fly freely. Outside are 15 acres of butterfly and bee gardens, wildflower meadows, wildfowl and conservation ponds, nature trail, farm animals and a pets corner. At the new Falconry Centre, falcons, hawks and owls can be seen, the falcons give two displays every day.
Open 28 Mar-Sep, daily 10-6, Oct 10-5.
£2.80 (ch £1.80, pen £2.50). Party.
P ☛ ₺ *(wheelchairs available) toilets for disabled shop garden centre* ✸

Springfields Gardens   SPALDING

Map 08 TF22
Camelgate (on A151, signposted)
☎ (0775) 724843
The 25-acre gardens provide an amazing spectacle in the spring when more than a million bulbs are blooming among the lawns and lakes. There are also glasshouses and a magnificent bedding display with over 200,000 plants during the summer season. Flower parade early May; other events throughout the year will be held in the new Exhibition Centre which opens in April.
Open 27 Mar-4 Oct, daily 10-6.
£2.50 (accompanied ch free, pen £2.30). Special Events £3.
P ☛ ✕ *licensed* ₺ *(Free wheelchair hire) toilets for disabled shop garden centre* ✸

Burghley House   STAMFORD

Map 04 TF00
(1m SE off A1)
☎ (0780) 52451
This great Elizabethan palace was built by William Cecil, Queen Elizabeth I's first minister, and has all the hallmarks of that ostentatiously wealthy period. The vast house is three storeys high and on the roof is a riot of pinnacles, cupolas and paired chimneys in classic Tudor style.
However, inside there is very little of the Tudor period in evidence, as (apart from the kitchen) the house was restyled between 1680 and 1700. The state rooms are now Baroque, with silver fireplaces, elaborate plasterwork and painted ceilings. These were painted by Antonio Verrio, whose finest achievement here is the Heaven Room. The walls of the rooms are hung with superb tapestries and with pictures from the largest private collection of Italian Old Masters.
The grounds were landscaped during the 18th century by Capability Brown and each year, in September,
continued . . .

international horse trials are held.
Special events for 1992 include, amongst others; 23-25 May, Rainbow Craft Fair; 7 Jun, XK Jaguar Owners Club Rally; 10-13 Sep, Horse Trials.
Open 17 Apr-4 Oct, daily 11-5.

(Closed 12 Sep).
£4.10 (ch £2.50, pen £3.80). Family ticket £11. Party 20 +.
P ■ ✕ *licensed* ᵬ *(chairlift access to restaurant) toilets for disabled shop* ✻

Stamford Museum — STAMFORD

Map 04 TF00
Broad St
☎ (0780) 66317
The museum illustrates the history and archaeology of Stamford. Perhaps the most unusual exhibits are the clothes of Daniel Lambert (1770-1809), one of only three men in Britain recorded as weighing over 50 stone (317kg). These

are displayed with clothes of American midget, General Tom Thumb, who was 3ft 4in (102cm) when he died.
Open all year, Apr-Sep, Mon-Sat 10-5, Sun 2-5; Oct-Mar Mon-Sat 10-12.30 & 1.30-5.
25p (ch 10p).
ᵬ *shop*

Stamford Steam Brewery Museum — STAMFORD

Map 04 TF00
All Saints St
☎ (0780) 52186
An authentic steam brewery, with mash tuns, coppers, fermenting vessels and a steam engine. With the aid of an automatic sound system and illustrations

of Victorian working life, visitors are given an insight into the activities of a 19th-century brewery employee.
Open Apr-Sep, Wed-Sun 10-4. Also BH Apr-Sep. (Closed Wed during BH weeks).
ᵬ *shop*
Details not confirmed for 1992

Tattershall Castle — TATTERSHALL

Map 08 TF25
☎ Coningsby (0526) 42543
This large fortified house was built in 1440 by Ralph Cromwell, Treasurer of England, and has a keep 100ft high. On each of the four storeys is a fine heraldic chimneypiece: these were sold at one

point, but were retrieved in 1911. There is also a museum in the guardhouse.
Open all year, Apr-Oct, daily 10.30-6; Nov-Mar 12-4.30.
£1.90 (ch 90p).
P ᵬ *toilets for disabled shop* ✻
(NT)

Woolsthorpe Manor — WOOLSTHORPE

Map 08 SK92
☎ Grantham (0476) 860338
A fine stone-built, 17th-century farmhouse which was the birthplace of the scientist and philosopher Sir Isaac Newton, in 1642. He also lived at the house from 1665-66 during the Plague, after his time as an undergraduate at

Cambridge. An early edition of his *Principia Mathematica* (1687) is in the house.
Open Apr-Oct, Sat-Wed & BH Mon 1-5.30.
£2.30 (ch £1.10).
P ✻
(NT)

MERSEYSIDE

Birkenhead Priory — BIRKENHEAD

Map 07 SJ38
Priory St
☎ 051-666 1249
Founded in 1150, the Priory provided accommodation for the Prior and 16 Benedictine monks. Most of the buildings were neglected after the Dissolution, but not all are ruined. An interpretive centre traces the history and development of the site. St Mary's, the first parish church of Birkenhead, was opened in 1821 adjacent to the Priory:

only the tower now stands. However, the original clock mechanism and one bell have been re-installed with new displays. The tower offers superb views of the River Mersey, Cammel Laird's and the surrounding area.
Open all year, Tue-Sat 10.30-1.30 & 2-5, Sun 2-5 (Closed Xmas, New Year & some BH's).
Free.
P ᵬ *toilets for disabled* ✻

Williamson Art Gallery & Museum — BIRKENHEAD

Map 07 SJ38
Slatey Rd
☎ 051-652 4177
English watercolours and works by the Liverpool school are an outstanding feature of the gallery, which was specially built for the purpose. There is a large collection of pictures by P. Wilson Steer, and also on view are sculpture, ceramics (English, Continental and Oriental), glass, silver and furniture. Exhibitions are held throughout the year.
The museum is linked to the gallery,

and has displays on the history of the town and its port. Birkenhead was a hamlet before the 19th century, but grew large and rich through ship-building and the docks, so model ships are an important feature of this collection. Also on view are the Baxter Motor Collection, cars and motorbikes in a period garage setting. There is a full exhibition programme at the Gallery.
Open all year, Mon-Sat 10-5. Thu 10-9 & Sun 2-5. (Closed Xmas & Good Fri).
Free.
P ᵬ *shop* ✻

Animation World — LIVERPOOL

Map 07 SJ39
Britannia Pavilion, Albert Dock
☎ 051-707 1828
A permanent exhibition of cartoon and animation, including hands-on displays, workshops and model studios and fantasy sets. Also original sets, models

and drawings from children's favourite TV characters such as Count Duckula, Danger Mouse and Wind in the Willows.
Open all year, daily 10-6.
✱ *£3 (ch £2.50, pen & UB40 £2.70)*
P ᵬ *toilets for disabled shop* ✻

The Beatles Story — LIVERPOOL

Map 07 SJ39
Britannia Pavilion, Albert Dock
☎ 051-709 1963
Winner of the English Tourist Board's 'Come to Britain' award 1991, the sights and sounds of the sixties can be relived at The Beatles Story. You can take a trip to Hamburg, 'feel' the cavern beat, 'tune

in' to flower power, board the yellow submarine and battle with a Beatle brain computer.
Open all year, daily 10-6 (last admission 1 hr before closing). (Closed 25 & 26 Dec).
✱ *£3 (ch, pen & students £2, ch under 5 free). Family ticket £7.50*
P ■ ᵬ *toilets for disabled shop* ✻

Croxteth Hall & Country Park — LIVERPOOL

Map 07 SJ39
(5m NE of city centre)
☎ 051-228 5311
Visitors can step back in time and join an Edwardian house party when they visit the displays in Croxteth Hall: the Edwardian rooms are furnished with period pieces and character figures. The grounds of this former home of the Earls of Sefton contain a Victorian walled garden, a unique collection of rare breed animals, a miniature railway and an

adventure playground. Croxteth Hall is a popular venue for special events; it also boasts an award-winning educational service.
Open, all facilities daily 10.30-5 in season (phone for details); Some facilities remain open through winter, hours on request.
✱ *Hall 90p; Farm 90p; Walled Garden 50p. Inclusive ticket £2 (ch & pen £1).*
P ■ ᵬ *toilets for disabled shop* ✻ *(ex in park & grounds)*
See advertisement on page 117.

Liverpool Football Club Visitors Centre Museum — LIVERPOOL

Map 07 SJ39
Anfield Rd
☎ 051-263 2361
Come to Anfield and enjoy the magnificent display of trophies and memementos representing the achievement of one of soccers most successful clubs.

Experience and share some of the great moments in the club's history, captured on video.
Open all year, Mon-Fri. Tours starting at 2 & 3pm. (Closed Xmas wk).
✱ *£1.50 (ch & pen £1). Party 20 +.*
P ᵬ *shop* ✻

Liverpool Libraries & Arts — LIVERPOOL

Map 07 SJ39
William Brown Steeet
☎ 051-225 5429
The Picton, Hornby and Brown buildings house Liverpool's collection of over two million books, forming one of Britain's largest and oldest public libraries. First editions, prints and fine bindings are permanently displayed at

Hornby while the reference, international, scientific and technical collections are housed in the Picton and Brown buildings. Regular temporary exhibitions.
Open all year, Mon-Thu 9am-9pm (Fri & Sat 9-5). Closed PHs.
Free.
ᵬ *(lift) toilets for disabled* ✻

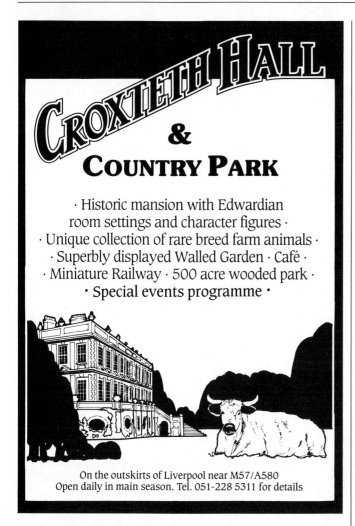

CROXTETH HALL & COUNTRY PARK

· Historic mansion with Edwardian room settings and character figures ·
· Unique collection of rare breed farm animals ·
· Superbly displayed Walled Garden · Café ·
· Miniature Railway · 500 acre wooded park ·
· Special events programme ·

On the outskirts of Liverpool near M57/A580
Open daily in main season. Tel. 051-228 5311 for details

Merseyside Maritime Museum
LIVERPOOL

Map 07 SJ39
Albert Dock
☎ 051-207 0001

A large award-winning museum in restored 19th-century docklands, which includes a Boat Hall, Cooperage, and the Albert Dock Warehouse, containing varied displays about the Port of Liverpool. There are floating craft, outdoor exhibits of maritime crafts and demonstrations. Permanent displays include Emigrants to a New World, Art and the Sea and World of Models Galleries. From 12 May-25 October the Tall Ships exhibition will be open – a major photographic display of the work of David E Smith showing ships and crew at work.
Open all year, daily 10.30-5.30 (last admission 4.30pm). (Closed Good Fri, 24-26 Dec & 1 Jan).
£1.50 (ch, pen, students & UB40's 75p). Family ticket £4.
🅿 *(charged)* ☕ ✗ *licensed* ♿ *(Lifts & free wheelchair) toilets for disabled shop* ✖

Museum of Labour History
LIVERPOOL

Map 07 SJ39
Islington
☎ 051-207 0001 Ext 279
Housed in the former County Sessions House built in 1884, the museum tells the story of working class Merseyside from 1840 to the present day. The Employment gallery illustrates different types of work from cargo-handling in the docks to mining in St Helens. The domestic scene is explored in the Housing gallery and there are also sections on Education, Building the Union and Leisure.
Open all year, Mon-Sat 10-5, Sun 2-5. (Closed Good Fri, 24-26 Dec & 1 Jan).
♿ *toilets for disabled shop* ✖
Details not confirmed for 1992

Tate Gallery
LIVERPOOL

Map 07 SJ39
Albert Dock
☎ 051-709 0507 & 051-709 3223
Housed in a converted warehouse in the Albert Dock complex, this is the National Collection of Modern Art in the North. Works on show include German sculptures, exhibits by Epstein and Moore, 'Out in the Wood' exhibition of wood sculpture and 20th-century German paintings. Special events for 1992 include: 5 Feb-22 Mar, Lucian Freud Exhibition; 7 Apr-21 Jun, Buddhism in Contemporary Korean Art; 6 Jul-4 Oct, Roy Lichtenstein Exhibition.
Open Wed-Sun 10-6, Tue 11-6. (Closed Mon ex BH Mon).
Free, a charge may be made for special exhibitions.
☕ ♿ *toilets for disabled* ✖

Walker Art Gallery
LIVERPOOL

Map 07 SJ39
William Brown St
☎ 051-207 0001
An outstanding collection of European paintings, and sculpture. Especially notable are the Italian, Netherlands, and Pre-Raphaelite and Victorian paintings. There is a new award-winning sculpture gallery and temporary exhibitions are held throughout the year.
Open all year, Mon-Sat 10-5, Sun 2-5. (Closed Good Fri, 24-26 Dec & 1 Jan).
☕ ♿ *(prior notice appreciated, wheelchair on request) shop* ✖
Details not confirmed for 1992

Port Sunlight Heritage Centre
PORT SUNLIGHT

Map 07 SJ38
95 Greendale Rd (junc 4 of M53 on B5137)
☎ 051-644 6466
The picturesque garden village was built by William Hesketh Lever for the workers in his soap factory, the first sod for the development being cut by Mrs Lever in 1888. The Heritage Centre tells the story of the village, the factory and its workers and a village trail incorporates the varied architecture, beautiful open spaces and the Lady Lever Art Gallery with its world-famous collection of pre-Raphaelite paintings and Wedgwood.
Open all year 12-4. Etr-Oct, daily. Nov-Etr, Mon-Fri.
✱ *20p (ch free).*
♿ *shop* ✖

Knowsley Safari Park
PRESCOT

Map 07 SJ49
☎ 051-430 9009
A five-mile drive through the reserves enables visitors to see lions, tigers, elephants, rhinos, monkeys and many other animals. Extra attractions include a children's amusement park and pets' corner plus sealion shows and a miniature railway.
Open, Game reserves Mar-Oct. Other attractions Etr-Sep. Daily 10-4.
✱ *£8 per car (incl all occupants). No soft-topped cars (safari bus available). Coach passengers £2.30 (ch 2-15 & pen £1.30).*
🅿 ☕ ♿ *toilets for disabled shop* ✖ *(kennels provided)*

Prescot Museum of Clock & Watch Making
PRESCOT

Map 07 SJ49
34 Church St
☎ 051-430 7787
An attractive 18th-century town house contains exhibits pertaining to the clock, watch and tool-making industries of the area. The display includes a reconstruction of part of a traditional watch-maker's workshop and examples of hand tools and machinery used to make the intricate parts of clock and watch movements.
Open all year, Tue-Sat & BH Mon 10-5, Sun 2-5 (Closed 24-26 Dec, 1 Jan & Good Fri).
Free.
♿ *shop* ✖

Pilkington Glass Museum
ST HELENS

Map 07 SJ59
Prescot Rd (on A58, 1m from town centre)
☎ (0744) 692499 & 692014
Since the 18th century, St Helens has gained a world-wide reputation for fine glass production. The glass museum traces the history of glassmaking from the Egyptians to the present day, with some of the finest examples of glass in the world. Other attractions are the hands-on interactive exhibits such as the working periscope, and the night vision display. A full programme of temporary exhibitions and a variety of craft demonstrations are planned for 1992.
Open all year, Mon-Fri 10-5; Sat, Sun & BH 2-4.30 (closed Xmas-New Year). Also evenings for groups by appointment.
Free.
🅿 ♿ *(by arrangement) toilets for disabled shop* ✖

Atkinson Art Gallery
SOUTHPORT

Map 07 SD31
Lord St
☎ (0704) 533133 ext 2111
The gallery specialises in 19th- and 20th-century oil paintings, watercolours, drawings and prints, as well as 20th-century sculpture. There is also a programme of visiting exhibitions including The Growth of Southport 1792-1992 and a children's art competition relating to the exhibition.
Open all year, Mon, Tue, Wed & Fri 10-5, Thu & Sat 10-1. (Closed 25-26 Dec & 1 Jan).
Free.
♿ *shop* ✖

Botanic Gardens Museum — SOUTHPORT

Map 07 SD31
Churchtown (2m N)
☎ (0704) 27547
The varied collections include items of local history including a lifeboat display. There is also a display on the nearby Ainsdale National Nature Reserve; and

also shown are a Victorian parlour and the Cecily Bate doll collection.
Open all year, Tue-Fri 11-3, Sat & Sun 2-5, BH's 12-4. (Closed 25, 26 Dec & 1 Jan also Fri following BH Mon).
Free.
🅿 ⅄ *toilets for disabled shop* ✶

Southport Railway Centre — SOUTHPORT

Map 07 SD31
Derby Rd
☎ (0704) 530693
A thousand feet of standard gauge rail connects the museum to the British Rail system. Within the museum, are ex-British Rail locomotives as well as several industrial locomotives, and also on display are local buses, tramcars, traction engines and a variety of other vehicles, making up what is possibly the largest preservation centre of its type in

north-west England. Special events are held from February to December (Santa Specials).
Open all year, Oct-May, Sat & Sun 1-5; Jun-Sep, Sat & Sun 11-5; Jun & first wk Sep wkdays 1-4.30; Jul & Aug wkdays 10.30-4.30. Also BH periods 11-5. Non Steam Days £1.50 (ch 80p, pen £1.20). Steam Days £1.80 (ch £1, pen £1.40).
🅿 🍴 ⅄ *toilets for disabled shop*

Southport Zoo — SOUTHPORT

Map 07 SD31
Princes Park
☎ (0704) 538102
Within its five acres, the zoo has large and small mammals, duck and flamingo pools, and an assortment of aviaries. An aquarium and a reptile house with an alligator beach are unusual attractions. There is also a mandrill house, a Pets' Corner, Penguin Pool and a variety of

monkeys. The new extension to the Zoo includes a giant tortoise house and enclosure, baby chimp house, and children's play area.
Open all year (ex 25 Dec) 10-6 in summer, 10-4 in winter,
✶ *£2.20 (ch £1.30, pen £1.70). Party 25 +*
🍴 ⅄ *toilets for disabled shop*

Speke Hall — SPEKE

Map 07 SJ48
The Walk
☎ 051-427 7231
This remarkable manor house was built around a square courtyard and originally had a moat. It is mainly Elizabethan, but was started in 1490, and is one of the most richly timbered houses in England. There is a vast Tudor great hall that contrasts with the later Victorian, small panelled rooms. The kitchen and the servant's hall are open and there is some elaborate 16th-and 17th-century

plasterwork to be seen in the great parlour. Additional delights are the priest's hole, examples of William Morris wallpaper, and the Mortlake tapestries.
House open; Apr-1 Nov, daily (ex Mon but open BH Mon) 1-5.30, 2 Nov-15 Dec, Sat & Sun 1-4.30. Garden open daily (ex Mon & Closed 24-26 Dec, 31 Dec & 1 Jan). £2.40 (ch £1.20). Family ticket £7.50. Party.
🅿 🍴 ⅄ *toilets for disabled shop* ✶
(NT)

NORFOLK

Baconsthorpe Castle — BACONSTHORPE

Map 09 TG13
The castle was really a moated and semi-fortified house, built by the Heydon family in the 15th century. It is now a ruin, but the gatehouses, curtain walls

and towers can still be seen.
Open any reasonable time.
Free.
🅿
(EH)

For an explanation of the symbols and abbreviations, see page 2.

Banham Zoo & Appleyard Craft Court — BANHAM

Map 04 TM08
The Grove (on B1113)
☎ Quidenham (095387) 771
Situated in over 20 acres of parkland and garden, this zoo specialises in rare and endangered species of animals and birds. Especially featured are the collection of monkeys and apes. There are also snow leopards, zebras, otters, seals, maned wolves, camels, macaws and flamingoes. Other facilities include an ice cream parlour, an indoor activity centre featuring a themed story room and new

children's outdoor play area, plus a putting green and appleyard craft courtyard, adjoining the zoo complex. Special events are planned throughout the year including an Owl Week in February and a Conservation Week in October.
Open all year, daily 10-6.30 (or dusk if earlier). (Closed 25-26 Dec).
✶ *£5 (ch 5-15 & pen £3). Disabled & party rates available.*
🅿 🍴 ⅄ *(wheelchair available) toilets for disabled shop* ✶

The Mill — BIRCHAM, GREAT

Map 09 TF73
(0.5m W off unclassified Snettisham rd).
☎ Syderstone (048523) 393
This windmill is one of the last remaining in Norfolk. Sails turn on windy days, and the adjacent tea room serves home-made cakes, light lunches

and cream teas. The working coal-fired oven in the bakehouse bakes bread which visitors can buy.
Open Sun, Wed & BH Mon from Etr-20 May; 20 May-Sep daily, 10-6 (Closed Sat). £2 (ch £1, pen £1.50)
🅿 🍴 *shop*

Blickling Hall — BLICKLING

Map 09 TG12
(on B1354)
☎ Aylsham (0263) 733084

Flanked by dark yew hedges and topped by pinnacles, the warm red brick front of Blickling makes a memorable sight. The house was built in the early 17th century, but the hedges may be earlier. They stand some 17ft tall and 10ft wide. The centrepiece of the house is the carved oak staircase which winds up in double flights from the hall. It was moved from another part of the house and adapted to fit a new 18th-century scheme. (There is also a lift.) On the first floor is Blickling's most celebrated room,

the Long Gallery, where the 125ft-long ceiling is covered in ornate Jacobean plasterwork. The work was done by Edward Stanyan, who charged £50.80 for the 'freat seeling'. Stanyard also provided the intricate decorations for the south drawing room, another of the original state rooms, at 'fyve shillings and six pence a yard square'. An equally remarkable room is the Chinese bedroom, which still has hand-painted Chinese wallpaper from the 18th-century. Amongst the house's fine furnishing tapestries is a set of eight 17th-century Mortlake works, and the many pictures include a Canaletto. The grounds include woodland and a lake, a formal parterre, and a moat filled with roses, camellias and other plants.
Open 28 Mar-1 Nov, Tue, Wed, Fri-Sun & BH Mon 1-5 (daily in Jul & Aug). Gardens open from noon. £4.90 (ch £2.40). Gardens only £2.30. Party 15 +
🅿 ✕ *licensed* ⅄ *toilets for disabled shop garden centre* ✶
(NT)

Bressingham Steam Museum & Gardens — BRESSINGHAM

Map 04 TM08
(on A1066)
☎ (037988) 386 & 382
Alan Bloom is an internationally recognised nurseryman and also a steam enthusiast, and has combined his interests to great effect at Bressingham. There are four steam-hauled trains: a 9.5in gauge, a 15in gauge running through five miles of the wooded Waveney Valley, a 2ft gauge running through two miles of Europe's largest hardy plant nursery and a standard gauge engine giving footplate rides alongside the driver. There are six acres of informal gardens, with 5000 species

of perennials and alpines, grouped in island beds; and there is a collection of 50 road and rail engines, mostly restored to working order. A steam roundabout is another attraction, and Norfolk fire museum is housed here. Various events are held here during the year including the 6th Annual Fire Rally on 2-6 August.
Open Apr-Oct, daily, 10-5.30. Also 29 Nov-20 Dec. Steam Days on Sun, Thu, BHs & Wed (Jul & Aug).
✶ *£3.50 (ch £2.50) Party 20+*
🅿 ✕ *licensed* ⅄ *toilets for disabled shop garden centre* ✶

Berney Arms Windmill — BURGH CASTLE

Map 05 TG40
☎ (0493) 700605
Access is by boat from Great Yarmouth or by rail to Berney Arms station: the road to the mill is unsuitable for cars. This lonely, seven-storey landmark dates back to the 19th century, and helped to drain the marshes. In earlier years it was also used to grind clinker for cement. The machinery for both functions can be seen.
Open Apr-Sep, daily 10-6.
75p (ch 40p, pen, students & UB40 55p)
&. ✗
(EH)

The Castle — BURGH CASTLE

Map 05 TG40
(off A143)
Burgh Castle was built in the third century AD by the Romans, as one of a chain of forts along the Saxon Shore – the coast where Saxon invaders landed. Sections of the massive walls still stand, (some parts faced with flint), and are protected by bastions where 'ballistae' or giant catapults may have been mounted.
Open any reasonable time.
Free.
(EH)

Caister Castle, Motor Museum, Tower & Grounds — CAISTER-ON-SEA

Map 05 TG51
Caister Castle
☎ Wymondham (057284) 251
The collection consists of vehicles from 1893 to the present day. In the same grounds is the moated castle built by Sir John Falstaff (the original of Shakespeare's Falstaff) when he returned from Agincourt. The walls surround a 98ft tower, and also here is the 1951 Festival of Britain Tree Walk, removed from Battersea Park.
Grounds open mid May-Sep daily ex Sat 10.30-5.
P ♿ &. *toilets for disabled shop*

Roman Town — CAISTER-ON-SEA

Map 05 TG51
The name Caister has Roman origins, and this was in fact a Roman naval base. The remains include the south gateway, a town wall built of flint with brick bonding courses, and part of what may have been a seamen's hostel.
Open any reasonable time.
Free.
(EH)

For an explanation of the symbols and abbreviations, see page 2.

Castle Acre Priory — CASTLE ACRE

Map 09 TF81
☎ Swaffham (0760) 755394
The priory was built for the Cluniac order by Earl Warren, son-in-law of William the Conqueror. Twenty-five monks once lived here in great state, but the priory fell into ruin after the Dissolution in 1536. Rising above the extensive remains is the glorious, arcaded west front of the priory church, a reminder of past splendour. The chapel can also be seen, and there is a 15th-century gatehouse.
Earl Warren also built a great castle, which was developed during the Middle Ages. Edward I was entertained there in 1297, at a time when the walls were 7ft thick. Today there are only ruins and earthworks, but even these are on an impressive scale.
Open all year, Apr-Sep, daily 10-6; Oct-Mar, Tue-Sun 10-4. (Closed 24-26 Dec & 1 Jan).
£1.80 (ch 90p, pen, students & UB40 £1.40).
P &. *shop*
(EH)

Castle Rising Castle — CASTLE RISING

Map 09 TF62
(off A149)
☎ (0553) 631330
The fine Norman keep was probably built by the Earl of Arundel. It stands in massive earthworks and the remains of a bridge and gatehouse can also be seen.
Open all year, Apr-Sep, daily 10-6; Oct-Mar, Tue-Sun 10-4. (Closed 24-26 Dec & 1 Jan).
£1.10 (ch 55p, pen, students & UB40 85p).
P &. *(exterior only) toilets for disabled shop*
✗
(EH)

Iceni Village & Museums — COCKLEY CLEY

Map 04 TF70
(off A1065)
☎ Swaffham (0760) 721339 & 24588
A village of the Iceni tribe has been reconstructed here, as it was 2,000 years ago, on the site where it was believed there was an Iceni encampment. There is also a museum, in a 15th-century cottage forge, with models and exhibits of local life from prehistoric times to the present day; and there is a museum of agricultural equipment, vintage engines and carriages. The nearby flint church dates back to around 630. There is also a nature trail and picnic area.
Open Apr-Oct, daily 12-5.30 (Jul-Sep 11-5.30).
£2.50 (ch 5-16 £1, pen & students £1.50). Party 10+.
P &. *toilets for disabled shop*

Cromer Museum — CROMER

Map 09 TG24
East Cottages, Tucker St
☎ (0263) 513543
The museum is housed in five 19th-century fishermen's cottages, one of which has period furnishings. There are pictures and exhibits from Victorian Cromer, with collections illustrating local natural history, archaeology, social history and geology.
Open all year, Mon-Sat 10-5, Sun 2-5. Closed Mon 1-2. (Closed Good Fri, Xmas & 1 Jan).
60p (ch 20p, pen, students & UB40s 30p).
shop ✗

Lifeboat Museum — CROMER

Map 09 TG24
☎ (0263) 512503
The museum in No 2 boat house at the bottom of The Gangway covers local lifeboat history and the RNLI in general. Also of interest is the Lifeboat Station on the pier, where a lifeboat has been stationed since 1804. The history of Cromer from 1804 to the present day is shown together with models of lifeboats. The museum will be housing the recently acquired lifeboat 'The H F Bailer' which served on the station from 1935 to 1945 and which saved 518 lives. The Blogg medals will be displayed in 1992.
Open May-Oct, daily 10-5.
Free.
&. *shop*

FAKENHAM
See Thursford Green

Felbrigg Hall — FELBRIGG

Map 09 TG23
(off B1436)
☎ West Runton (026375) 444
The name comes from the de Felbriggs, whose memorials can be seen in the isolated parish church at Felbrigg, but the house was built by the Windham family and was their home for 300 years. It is a splendid house of 1620 with a wing added in 1680, and has not changed on the outside since the 17th century; inside there are handsome rooms with paintings and furniture which have been in the house since the 18th century. Felbrigg Hall stands in a large park with fine old trees, and there is also a colourfully-restored walled garden overlooked by a dovecote built for 2000 birds.
Open: House 28 Mar-1 Nov, Mon, Wed, Thu, Sat, Sun & BH 1.30-5.30 (Closed Good Fri); House & Garden open 1.30-5.30. Woodland & Lakeside walks daily dawn-dusk. (Closed 25 Dec). House & garden £4.30 (ch £2.15). Garden £1.60 (ch 80p). Party 15 +
P ♿ ✗ *licensed* &. *toilets for disabled shop* ✗
(NT)

Thrigby Hall Wildlife Gardens — FILBY

Map 05 TG41
(on unclass road off A1064)
☎ Great Yarmouth (0493) 369477
The 250-year-old park of Thrigby Hall is now the home of animals and birds from Asia, and the lake has ornamental wildfowl. There are tropical and bird houses, a unique blue willow pattern garden and tree walk and a summer house as old as the park. An enormous jungled swamp hall is now open, with special features such as underwater viewing of large crocodiles.
Open all year, daily 10-5.
£3.30 (ch £2, pen £2.80).
P ♿ &. *(wheelchairs available) toilets for disabled shop* ✗

Shell Museum — GLANDFORD

Map 09 TG04
1.5m off B1156)
☎ Cley (0263) 740081
The appealing little museum with its Dutch gables was built in 1915 to house sea shells and curios collected from all over the world by Sir Alfred Jodrell of nearby Bayfield Hall. Glandford itself is an estate village of the hall, and its 1906 church is also worth seeing for its decorative carvings.
Open Feb-Nov, Mon-Thu 10-12.30 & 2-4.30, Fri & Sat 2-4.30pm. (Closed pm, Nov-Feb). Other times by prior arrangement.
40p (ch 16 20p)
P &. ✗

Gressenhall Norfolk Rural Life Museum & Union Farm — GRESSENHALL

Map 09 TF91
Beech House (2.5m NW on unclass rd at Gressenhall).
☎ Dereham (0362) 860563
This museum portrays the history of Norfolk over the past 200 years. Housed in what used to be a workhouse, it has displays on all aspects of rural life, with special emphasis on agriculture, rural crafts and village life, with working reconstructions. Union Farm is a typical small mixed farm of the 1920s with heavy horses and rare breeds of sheep, cattle, pigs and poultry. There is a nature trail around the farm.
Open 12 Apr-1 Nov, Tue-Sat 10-5, Sun 2-5.30. Also BH Mons 10-5.
✳ *£2 (ch 60p, concessions £1).*
P ♿ &. *toilets for disabled shop* ✗

Grimes Graves   GRIMES GRAVES

Map 04 TL88
☎ Thetford (0842) 810656
Grimes Graves is a network of hundreds of pits, dug by Neolithic people who were mining for flint between about 300BC and 1900BC. This is the largest known group of flint mines in Britain, and consisted of vertical shafts leading to galleries through the flint seams. Visitors today can go down a shaft to crouch in the gloom and imagine themselves prising out the flints with antler picks and wooden levers. Each shaft must have

provided about eight tons of flint, which went in rough form to other parts of the country to be turned into tools such as axes and knives.
Open all year, Apr-Sep, daily 10-6; Oct-Mar, Tue-Sun 10-4. (Closed 24-26 Dec & 1 Jan).
£1.10 (ch 55p, pen, students & UB40's 85p). A torch is useful.
🅿 ♿ *(exhibition area, grounds only; access track rough)* ✗
(EH)

Norfolk Lavender   HEACHAM

Map 09 TF63
Caley Mill (on A149 at junc with B1454)
☎ (0485) 70384
This is the largest lavender-growing and distilling operation in Britain. Different coloured lavenders are grown in strips and harvested in July and August. There are also rose and herb

gardens. Mini bus trips go to a large lavender field on Mondays, Wednesdays and Fridays from mid June until the end of November.
Open all year, daily 10-5. (Closed for 2 wks Xmas).
❋ *£1 for information tours.*
🅿 ♨ ♿ *(wheelchairs for loan) toilets for disabled shop*

Holkham Hall   HOLKHAM

Map 09 TF84
(off A149)
☎ Fakenham (0328) 710227

The Palladian mansion was built in 1734 and was later inherited by Thomas Coke, or 'Coke of Norfolk'. He became famous for pioneering work in the 'Agricultural Revolution' – and he also

started a fashion revolution by wearing country clothes at court.
The house has a splendid marble hall and other sumptuous state rooms, with paintings by Rubens, Van Dyck, Clande Poussin, Gainsborough and others. The park is equally fine, with deer, geese on the lake, and an impressive collection of trees, especially ilexes. Also of interest are the Holkham Pottery and the Holkham collection of agricultural and rural craft tools. Garden centre.
Open 26 May-Sep, Sun-Thu, 1.30-5. Etr, May, Spring & Summer BHs Sun & Mon 11.30-5.
🅿 *(charged)* ♨ ♿ *toilets for disabled shop garden centre* ✗ *(ex in park & gardens)*
Details not confirmed for 1992

Drainage Windmill   HORSEY

Map 09 TG42
The mill was built 200 years ago to drain the area, and then rebuilt in 1912 by Dan England, a noted Norfolk millwright. It has been restored since being struck by lightning in 1943, and overlooks Horsey Mere and marshes,

noted for their wild birds and insects.
Open 28 Mar-30 Aug, 11-5 (Jul & Aug till 6pm). Closed Good Fri.
£1.20 (£1 car park).
🅿 *(charged)*
(NT)

City of Norwich Aviation Museum   HORSHAM ST FAITH

Map 09 TG21
Old Norwich Rd
☎ Norwich (0603) 625309
Run entirely by enthusiastic volunteers, this museum offers displays relating to the aeronautical history of the local area, supported by a fine collection of aircraft, engines and equipment featuring the Vulcan bomber. Some of the aircraft

cockpits are open to visitors. The location of the museum also offers a good vantage point for viewing aircraft using the airport.
Open all year, Apr-Oct Sun 10-5 (also Tue & Thu eves 7.30pm-dusk May, Jun, Jul & Aug only); Nov-Mar Sun 10-3.30
75p (ch 25p & pen 50p)
🅿 ♿ *shop* ✗

Houghton Hall   HOUGHTON

Map 09 TF72
(1.25m off A148)
☎ East Rudham (048522) 569
This splendid Palladian house in beautiful parkland was built for Sir Robert Walpole. The staterooms have decorations and furniture by William Kent, and the harness room, coach house

and stables may be seen (complete with heavy horses and Shetland ponies). There is a model soldier collection.
Open Etr Sun-last Sun Sep, Thu, Sun & BH's 12.30-5.30.
🅿 ♨ ♿ *toilets for disabled shop*
Details not confirmed for 1992

Lynn Museum   KING'S LYNN

Map 09 TF62
Market St
☎ (0553) 775001
Once it was a walled city of considerable importance; its two great churches, two marketplaces and two Guildhalls testify to its size. King's Lynn was also a noted port and a stop on the Pilgrim's Way to Walsingham. The geology, archaeology and natural history of the area are the main collections in the local museum. Specimens include an icthyosaur and a golden eagle. Objects in the archaeology

gallery include Bronze Age weapons and the skeleton of a Saxon warrior. Relics from the medieval town of Lynn include an important collection of pilgrim badges. Farm tools, ship models and exhibits from a local fairground machinery firm are also on show.
Open all year, Mon-Sat, 10-5 (Closed BH, Xmas & New Year)
❋ *60p (ch 5-16 30p, pen, student & UB40 50p)*
♿ *shop* ✗

St George's Guildhall   KING'S LYNN

Map 09 TF62
Kings St
☎ (0553) 774725
Although it has been used for many purposes, the theatrical associations of this 15th-century Guildhall are strongest: Shakespeare himself is said to have performed here. Its present use as the town's theatre was brought about in the

1950s after an 18th-century theatre, incorporated into the hall, was restored and enlarged.
When not in use as a theatre or cinema open Mon-Fri 10-5, Sat 10-12.30. (Closed Good Fri, 25-26 Dec & 1 Jan).
Free.
✗ *licensed*
(NT)

Shirehall Museum   LITTLE WALSINGHAM

Map 09 TF93
Common Place
☎ Walsingham (0328) 820510
The museum is in an almost perfect Georgian courtroom with its original fittings, including a prisoner's lock-up. The displays show Walsingham's

history, with a special exhibition on the history of pilgrimage. There is also a tourist information centre.
Open Maundy Thu-Sep, daily; Oct wknds only.
60p (ch 20p, pen, students & UB40s 30p).
🅿 *shop* ✗

Walsingham Abbey Grounds   LITTLE WALSINGHAM

Map 09 TF93
☎ Walsingham (0328) 820259
In the grounds of the new abbey are the ruins of the original Augustinian priory built in the 1100s. The priory was built over the shrine of Our Lady of Walsingham which had been established in 1061. The remains include the east

wall of the church, the south wall of the refectory and one room, still intact.
Open Wed in Apr, then May-Jul Wed, Sat & Sun; Aug Mon, Wed, Fri, Sat & Sun; Sep Wed, Sat & Sun. Also BHs Etr-Sep.
♿ *shop*
Details not confirmed for 1992

Creake Abbey   NORTH CREAKE

Map 09 TF83
(1m N off B1355)
Church ruin with crossing and eastern arm belonging to a house of Augustinian

canons founded in 1206.
Open any reasonable time.
Free.
(EH)

Bridewell Museum   NORWICH

Map 04 TG20
Bridewell Alley
☎ (0603) 667228
Built in the late 14th century, this flint-faced merchant's house was used as a prison from 1583 to 1828. It now houses displays illustrating the trades and industries of Norwich during the past

200 years, including a large collection of locally made boots and shoes.
Open all year, Mon-Sat, 10-5. (Closed Good Fri, Xmas & New Year)
❋ *60p (ch 20p, pen, students & UB40 40p).*
shop ✗

The Guildhall   NORWICH

Map 04 TG20
Guildhall Hill
☎ (0603) 666071
Visitors may visit the Council Chamber and view civic plate and insignia dating

from 1549. The civic regalia is on view.
Open all year, Mon-Fri 10-5 (Jun-Aug, Sat by arrangement).
Free.
♿ *toilets for disabled* ✗

Norwich Castle Museum   NORWICH

Map 04 TG20
Castle Meadow
☎ (0603) 611277 & 223624
Norman Castle Keep built in the 12th century, and museum housing displays of art, archaeology, natural history, Lowestoft porcelain, Norwich silver, a large collection of paintings (with special emphasis on the Norwich School of Painters) and British ceramic teapots. There are also guided tours of the

dungeons and battlements. A major temporary exhibition – Norfolk Portraits – will be on display from 5 Sep-29 Nov.
Open all year, Mon-Sat 10-5, Sun 2-5. (Closed Good Fri, Xmas & New Year).
£1.30 (ch 50p, pen, students & UB40 £1). Party.
♨ ♿ *(lift to first floor, special parking by prior arrangement) shop* ✗

Royal Norfolk Regimental Museum   NORWICH

Map 04 TG20
Shirehall
☎ (0603) 223649
Museum displays deal with the social as well as military history of the county regiment from 1685, including the daily life of a soldier. It is housed in an old courtroom of the historic Shirehall. It is linked to the Castle Museum by a tunnel through which prisoners were

taken to court. This is followed by a reconstruction of a First World War communication trench. Audio-visual displays and graphics complement the collection. A programme of temporary exhibitions is planned for 1992.
Open all year, Mon-Sat 10-5, Sun 2-5.
❋ *60p (ch 5-16 30p, pen, students & UB40's 40p).*
♿ *shop* ✗

Sainsbury Centre for Visual Arts   NORWICH

Map 04 TG20
University of East Anglia
☎ (0603) 56060 & 592467
The collection of Sir Robert and Lady Sainsbury was given to the University in 1973. European art of the 19th and 20th centuries is on display together with ethnographical art. You can see African tribal sculpture and Oceanic

works along with North American and Pre-Colombian art. Egyptian, Asian and European antiquities are on show. Various other exhibitions are held during the year.
Open Tue-Sun 12-5. (Closed BH & University closure at Xmas).
🅿 ♨ ✗ ♿ *toilets for disabled shop* ✗
Details not confirmed for 1992

St Peter Hungate Church Museum — NORWICH

Map 04 TG20
Princes St (near Elm Hill)
☎ (0603) 667231
Built in 1460, this fine church has a hammer-beam roof and good examples of Norwich painted glass. It is now a museum of church art and a brass rubbing centre with a wide selection of brasses to rub from; charge includes materials and instructions.
Open all year, Mon-Sat 10-5. (Closed Good Fri, Xmas & New Year)
✱ *Free. Brass rubbing materials 50p-£5.*
✍ *shop* ✕

Strangers' Hall — NORWICH

Map 04 TG20
Charing Cross
☎ (0603) 667229
Strangers' Hall, once a medieval merchant's house, contains a series of rooms furnished in period styles from early Tudor to late Victorian. In addition there are displays of toys and changing exhibitions of costume and textiles including a children's book exhibition from 30 Mar-26 Apr.
Open all year, Mon-Sat, 10-5 (Closed Good Fri, Xmas & New Year)
60p (ch 30p, pen, students & UB40's 40p).
shop ✕

Oxburgh Hall — OXBOROUGH

Map 04 TF70
☎ Gooderstone (036621) 258
The outstanding feature of this 15th-century moated building is the 80ft high gatehouse which, unlike the rest of the hall, was spared from the alterations made in Victorian times. Two wings are built around a courtyard.
Henry VII lodged in the King's Room in 1487 and it is now furnished with a 17th-century bed, and wall hangings worked by Mary, Queen of Scots and Elizabeth Countess of Shrewsbury. A spiral staircase links the chambers to the room from which there are fine views across the countryside. A parterre garden of French design stands outside the moat, and there are woodland walks.
Open Gatehouse, principal rooms and garden 28 Mar-1 Nov, Sat-Wed 1.30-5.30. BH Mons 11-5.30. (Closed Good Fri).
£3.30 (ch £1.65). Party 15 +.
🅿 ✍ ✕ *licensed* ✍ *toilets for disabled shop* ✕
(NT)

Pettitts Feathercraft & Animal Adventure Park — REEDHAM

Map 05 TG40
(on B1140)
☎ Great Yarmouth (0493) 700094
Pettitts have aviaries where peacocks, ornamental pheasants, birds of prey and parrots are displayed. There are also waterfowl on show in their gardens, which are surrounded by a picnic area. The arts of feather craft and dip-and-carve American-style candles are demonstrated, and the products are on sale. Other attractions include a miniature horse stud, deer petting park, crazy golf, a large adventure playground with amusement rides, live entertainment and children's shows; and a half mile miniature railway. A gnome village and an American-style locomotive ride around the grounds are newly opened for 1992, also a 6-acre car park. Easy access makes Pettitts suitable for the elderly and disabled, there are purpose-built toilets for wheelchair-users and wheelchairs can be taken on a specially adapted truck on the train. Special events are planned throughout the season.
Open Etr Sun-Oct, daily 10-5.30. (Closed Sat).
£3.50 (ch & pen £2.50). Disabled & helpers £2.50. Party.
🅿 ✍ ✕ ✍ *toilets for disabled shop*

St Olaves Priory — ST OLAVES

Map 05 TM49
The fine brick undercroft seen in the cloister is one of the most notable features of the ruin of this small Augustinian priory: built in about 1216 it is an exceptionally early use of this material.
Open any reasonable time.
Free.
(EH)

Sandringham House, Grounds, Museum & Country Park — SANDRINGHAM

Map 09 TF62
(off A149)
☎ Kings Lynn (0553) 772675
Best known as the traditional Christmas home of the Royal Family, the 19th-century Sandringham House was bought by Queen Victoria for the Prince of Wales in 1862. Displayed in the public parts of the house are many paintings of the British and European royal families, furniture, china, sculpture and ornaments. The extensive grounds contain the parish church of St Mary Magdalene which attracts thousands of visits not only for its association with the royal family but also for its rich treasures: the solid silver altar and reredos for example, presented to Queen Alexandra in 1911. Both George V and George VI died at Sandringham and set into the chancel floor is a brass cross above which royal coffins have rested before their journey to Windsor. The Sandringham flower show will be held on 29 July.
Open Etr wknd & 19 Apr-1 Oct, Sun-Thu (House closed 20 Jul-8 Aug; Grounds closed 24 Jul-5 Aug). House 11-4.45 (noon Sun). Grounds 10.30-5 (11.30 Sun).
House, Museum & Grounds: £2.50 (ch £1.50, pen £2). Grounds & Museum £2 (ch £1, pen £1.50).
🅿 ✍ ✕ ✍ *toilets for disabled shop* ✕

Wolferton Station — SANDRINGHAM

Map 09 TF62
☎ Dersingham (0485) 540674
Used as retiring rooms for the Royal family and their guests en route to Sandringham, this small station building, dating from 1898, features many of the original fittings. The displays include period railway posters; Royal train furniture including Queen Victoria's travelling bed; letters and photographs. There is also an exhibition of Edwardian and Victorian fashion.
Open Apr-Sep & BHs, Mon-Fri 11-1 & 2-5.30, Sun 2-5.30.
🅿 ✍ *garden centre*
Details not confirmed for 1992

Mannington Gardens & Countryside — SAXTHORPE

Map 09 TG13
(2.25m NE)
☎ (026387) 4175
The moated manor house, built in 1460 and still a family home forms a centre-piece for the pretty gardens which surround it. Visitors can enjoy the roses – the chief feature of the gardens – and also lovely countryside walks. Special events take place throughout the season, including Nature Discovery Days for children. Special events for 1992 include: 24 May, Countryside Activities Day; 27-28 Jun, Rose Festival; 6 Sep, Charities Fair.
Open: Gardens May-Aug, Wed-Fri 11-5; also Sun noon-5 Etr-Oct. Walks open every day from 9am. Hall open by prior appointment only.
Garden £2 (accompanied ch 16 free, students & pen £1.50). Walks free (car park for walkers 50p).
🅿 *(charged)* ✍ ✍ *toilets for disabled shop garden centre* ✕

North Norfolk Railway — SHERINGHAM

Map 09 TG14
Sheringham Station
☎ (0263) 822045

A steam railway with trains operating on certain days from Easter to October, with extra days as the season progresses and a daily service in August. On Sundays, lunch is served on the train. At the station is a collection of steam locomotives and rolling stock, some of which are undergoing or awaiting restoration. These include several industrial tank engines and ex-Great Eastern mainline engines. The rolling stock includes suburban coaches, the Brighton Belle, Pullmans and directors' private saloons and a vintage buffet saloon. There is also a museum of railway memorabilia and a souvenir and book shop.
Open Etr-Oct; Aug (daily); Dec (Santa special). Telephone (0263) 825449 for timetable.
✱ *Return £4.50 (ch £2.30, pen £3.60). Family ticket £12.50. Party 20 +.*
✍ ✍ *shop*

Park Farm — SNETTISHAM

Map 09 TF63
☎ Dersingham (0485) 542425
You can see farming in action here with lambing in the spring, sheep shearing in May and deer and calving in June and July. Sheep, goats, lambs, rabbits, turkeys, ducks, chickens, ponies, piglets etc can be seen in the paddocks, there is a Sheep Centre and you can take a safari ride around the estate to see the magnificent herd of red deer. There is a large adventure playground, an indoor adventure area, mini golf and pedal buggies for the children and an indoor picnic area. Special events for 1992 include: 16-17 May, Craft Fayre; 23-25 May, Sheep Shearing with world champion shearer.
Open 29 Mar-1 Nov, daily 10.30-5.
✱ *£3 (ch £2, pen £2.50). Party 10 +.*
🅿 ✍ ✍ *toilets for disabled shop* ✕ *(ex on farm trails)*

The Fairhaven Garden Trust — SOUTH WALSHAM

Map 05 TG31
2 The Woodlands, Wymers Ln (on B1140)
☎ (060549) 449 & 683
These delightful water gardens lie beside South Walsham Broad. The Beech walk is a mass of flowers in spring; and rhododendrons and many rare plants line the waterways, which are spanned by small bridges. The tree known as the King Oak is said to be 900 years old. A bird sanctuary may also be visited by special arrangement with the warden.
Open 12 Apr-3 May, Sun & BH's 11-6; 6 May-13 Sep, Wed-Sun 11-6, Sat & BH's 2-6; 20 & 27 Sep, Sun 11-6. Primrose wknd 17-20 Apr & Candelabra Primula wknd 23-25 May 11-6, Sat 2-6. Walks with Warden at 2.30pm Sun in Jul. Autumn colours 1 Nov, 10-dusk. £1.80 (ch 80p, pen £1.30). Season tickets £6.
🅿 ✍ ✍

SWAFFHAM
See Cockley Cley

Places to visit in this guide are pinpointed on the atlas at the back of the book.

Ancient House Museum — THETFORD

Map 04 TL88
White Hart St
☎ (0842) 752599
An early Tudor timber-framed house with beautifully carved beam ceilings, it now houses an exhibition on Thetford and Breckland life. This has been traced back to very early times, and there are examples from local Neolithic settlements. Brass rubbing facilities are available and there is a small period garden recreated in the rear courtyard. Exhibitions for 1992 include: 5 May-5 Jun, Classic Plastics; 20 Jun-31 Jul, artwork from the Norfolk museum service collections selected by schools.
Open all year, Mon-Sat, 10-5 (closed 1-2); Jun-Sep also Sun 2-5. (Closed Good Fri, Xmas & New Year).
60p (ch 30p, concessions 40p) in Aug. Rest of year free.
shop ✕

Thetford Priory — THETFORD

Map 04 TL88
The Cluniac monastery was founded in 1103, and its remains are extensive. The 14th-century gatehouse of the priory stands to its full height, and the complete ground plan of the cloisters can be seen.
Open Apr-Sep, daily 10-6.
Free.
🅿 ✍ ✕
(EH)

Warren Lodge   THETFORD

Map 04 TL88
(2m NW, on B1107)
The remains of a two-storey hunting
lodge, built in 15th-century of flint with

stone dressings.
Open any reasonable time.
Free.
(EH)

Thursford Collection   THURSFORD GREEN

Map 09 TF93
(1m off A148)
☎ Fakenham (0328) 878477
This exciting collection specialises in
organs, with a Wurlitzer cinema organ,
fairground organs, barrel organs and
street organs among its treasures. There
are live musical shows every day;
featuring all the material organs and the
Wurtlizer show, extra Wurlitzer
concerts are given by the leading
organists on Tuesdays at 8pm

throughout the summer. The collection
also includes showmen's engines,
ploughing engines and a 2ft gauge steam
railway, as well as farm machinery.
There is a children's play area and a
breathtaking 'Venetian gondola'
switchback ride.
Open Apr-Oct, daily 1-5. (Jun-Aug 11-5).
✻ *£4 (ch 4-14 £1.80, pen £3.60, ch under*
4 free). Party 15 +.
🅿 ☕ ⅃ *toilets for disabled shop* ✕

🐕 The 'No Dogs' symbol does not normally apply
to guide dogs – these are permitted in
most establishments.

Weeting Castle   WEETING

Map 04 TL78
This ruined 11th-century fortified manor
house is situated in a rectangular moated
enclosure. It is interesting also for its
slight remains of a three-storeyed

cross-wing.
Open any reasonable time.
Free.
🅿
(EH)

Wells & Walsingham Light Railway   WELLS-NEXT-THE-SEA

Map 09 TF94
(A149 Cromer rd)
(Wells Station Sheringham Rd (A149).
Walsingham Station, Egmere Rd). The
railway covers the four miles between
Wells and Walsingham. It is unusual in
that it uses ten and a quarter inch gauge
track and is the longest track of this
width in Britain. The line passes through

some very attractive countryside,
particularly noted for its wild flowers
and butterflies. This is the home of the
unique Garratt Steam Locomotive
specially built for this line.
Open Good Fri-Sep, daily.
£3.50 (ch £2.20). Return.
🅿 ☕ ⅃ *shop*

Wildfowl & Wetlands Trust   WELNEY

Map 04 TL59
Pintail House, Hundred Foot Bank
(off A1101, N of Ely)
☎ Ely (0353) 860711

Probably the best time to visit this
refuge on the Ouse Washes is during the
winter, when the 920-acre site is home

to some 5000 migratory swans and vast
numbers of wild ducks and geese.
Bewick and whooper swans as well as
wigeon and pintail ducks can be seen.
  In the spring, the whole refuge is alive
with nesting birds including redshank,
snipe, ruff and blacktailed godwit, and in
the summer there is a trail to view the
resident wildfowl. There are numerous
hides and also a spacious observatory .
On winter evenings the lagoon is floodlit
to show hundreds of wild Bewick's
swans.
Open all year, daily 10-5. (Closed 24-25
Dec).
🅿 ☕ ⅃ *toilets for disabled shop* ✕
Details not confirmed for 1992

Norfolk Shire Horse Centre   WEST RUNTON

Map 09 TG14
West Runton Stables (on A149)
☎ (026375) 339
The Shire Horse Centre has a collection
of draught horses and nine breeds of
mountain and moorland ponies. There
are also exhibits of horse-drawn
machinery, waggons and carts, and
harnessing and working demonstrations
are given twice every day. Other
attractions include a photographic
display of draught horses past and

present, talks and a video show. There is
a riding school on the premises as well.
There are many events planned for 1992
from a programme of working
demonstrations, mornings and
afternoons, to day events such as sheep
dog days or timberloding days.
Open Good Fri-Oct, Sun-Fri, 10-5. Shire
Horse demonstrations 11.15 & 3. School
parties by appointment.
✻ *£3 (ch £1.50, pen £2). Party 10 +.*
🅿 ☕ ✕ ⅃ *toilets for disabled shop*

Norfolk Wildlife Park   WITCHINGHAM, GREAT

Map 09 TG12
(on A1067)
☎ Norwich (0603) 872274
This wildlife park offers a large
collection of British and European
wildlife. The animals can be viewed in
semi-natural surroundings set in 40 acres
of beautiful parkland. Britain's only
team of trained reindeer pull their

wheeled sledge round the park, and
there are tame animals to fascinate both
young and old. There are also exciting
Commando play areas, an electonic
Theme Hall, a narrow gauge Steam
Railway and a trout pool.
Open all year, daily 10.30-6 or dusk.
🅿 ☕ ⅃ *shop* ✕
Details not confirmed for 1992

Beeston Hall   WROXHAM

Map 09 TG31
Beeston St Lawrence (2.25m NE off
A1151).
☎ Horning (0692) 630771
A Georgian mansion built in Gothic
style with flint facing and a neo-classical
interior which has been lived in by
descendants of the Preston family since
1640. Under the house are interesting
wine cellars. There are attractive
woodland walks in the land around. For

those on a boating holiday, Beeston Hall
can be reached on foot from Barton
Broad disembarking at Neatishead
(twenty minutes walk). There is a
permanent exhibition of model toys
from home and abroad.
Open 16 Apr-13 Sep, Fri, Sun & BH
Mons. Also Wed in Aug. 2-5.30.
£2 (ch £1). Grounds only 50p (ch free).
🅿 ☕ ⅃ *shop* ✕

✻ An asterisk indicates that up-to-date information was
not available at the time of our research – 1991
information has been published as an
indication of what you may expect.

Elizabethan House Museum   YARMOUTH, GREAT

Map 05 TG50
4 South Quay
☎ Great Yarmouth (0493) 855746
A wealthy merchant built this house in
1596. Although it has a late Georgian
front, it contains 16th-century panelled
rooms, one with a magnificent plaster
ceiling. Other rooms have features from
later periods, some containing their
contemporary furniture and exhibits

illustrating domestic life in the 19th-
century. Children's toys, Lowestoft
porcelain and a collection of 18th- and
19th-century drinking glasses.
Open all year, Jun-Sep, daily (ex Sat) 10-1
& 2-5.30; Oct-May, Mon-Fri 10-1 &
2-5.30. (Closed Good Fri, Xmas & New
Year).
shop ✕
Details not confirmed for 1992

Maritime Museum For East Anglia   YARMOUTH, GREAT

Map 05 TG50
Marine Pde
☎ Great Yarmouth (0493) 842267
The sea and the fishing industry have
played an enormous part in East Anglia's
history and this Maritime Museum has
exhibits on each aspect. There are special
displays on the herring fishery, the
wherry, life-saving and the most recent

industry – oil and gas in the North Sea.
Open all year, Jun-Sep daily (ex Sat)
10-5.30; Oct, Mon-Fri 10-1 & 2-5.30,
Sun 1-5.30; Nov-May, Mon-Fri 10-1 &
2-5.30. 1 Jan 1-5.30. (Closed Good Fri &
Xmas).
shop
Details not confirmed for 1992

Merrivale Model Village   YARMOUTH, GREAT

Map 05 TG50
Wellington Pier Gardens, Marine Pde
☎ Great Yarmouth (0493) 842097
Set in attractive landscaped gardens, this
comprehensive miniature village is built
on a scale of 1:12. The layout includes a
two and a half inch gauge model
railway, radio-controlled boats, and over
200 models set in an acre of landscaped

gardens. There are additional
amusements, children's rides and remote-
controlled cars. During the summer,
from June to October, the gardens are
illuminated after dusk.
Open Etr 9.30-6, Jun-Sep 9.30-10
✻ *£2 (ch 3-14 £1)*
☕ ⅃ *shop*

Museum Exhibition Galleries   YARMOUTH, GREAT

Map 05 TG50
Central Library, Tolhouse St
☎ Great Yarmouth (0493) 858900
A regularly-changing series of travelling
exhibitions are displayed in the library.
Also exhibitions of local art, crafts and

other activities.
Open all year, Mon-Sat 9.30-5.30. (Closed
Sat 1-2, Etr, late May & Aug BH wknds,
Xmas & New Year).
⅃ ✕
Details not confirmed for 1992

This is just one of many guidebooks published by the AA.
The full range is available at any AA shop or good bookshop.

Old Merchant's House   YARMOUTH, GREAT

Map 05 TG50
Row 117
The 300-year-old house is behind the
grand buildings of the waterfront,
among narrow parallel lanes, or Rows,
of small dwellings. The Rows were so
narrow that a specially-built cart had to

be used. The restored house shows
examples of 17th- and 19th-century local
building craft.
Open Apr-Sep, daily 10-6.
Free.
✕
(EH)

Tolhouse Museum   YARMOUTH, GREAT

Map 05 TG50
Tolhouse St
☎ Great Yarmouth (0493) 858900
This late 13th-century building was once
the town's court house and gaol and has
dungeons which can be visited. The
rooms above contain exhibits on local
history. The museum has become a brass
rubbing centre and has a wide range of

replica brasses from which rubbings can
be made. Prices start at 50p and include
materials and instructions.
Open all year, Mon-Fri 10-1 & 2-5.30,
also Sun Jun-Sep only . (Closed Good Fri,
Xmas & New Year).
⅃ *(lift to ground & 2nd floor) shop* ✕
Details not confirmed for 1992

NORTH YORKSHIRE

Roman Town — ALDBOROUGH

Map 08 SE46
☎ Harrogate (0423) 322768
The pretty present-day village occupies the site of the northernmost civilian Roman town in Britain, with houses, courts, a forum and a temple, surrounded by a 9ft thick, 20ft high wall. All that can be seen today are two pavements, the position of the wall and excavated objects in the small museum.
Open all year, Apr-Sep, daily 10-6; Oct-Mar, grounds only. (Closed 24-26 Dec & 1 Jan).
£1.10 (ch 55p, pen, students & UB40 85p)
🚫🐕
(EH)

National Park Centre — AYSGARTH

Map 07 SE08
☎ Wensleydale (0969) 663424
A visitor centre for the Yorkshire Dales National Park, with maps, guides, walks and local information. Displays explain history and natural history of the area.
Open Apr-Oct, daily mid mornings to late afternoons. Nov-Mar limited Sun.
Free.
🅿 *(charged)* ☕ ♿ *toilets for disabled shop*
🚫🐕

Yorkshire Carriage Museum — AYSGARTH

Map 07 SE08
(G W Shaw Carriage Collection), Yore Mill (1.75m E on unclass rd N of A684)
☎ Richmond (0748) 823275
An old stone mill at Aysgarth Falls now houses over 60 horse-drawn vehicles, including some splendid coaches and carriages.
Open Etr-Oct, daily 11-5. (7pm wknds & BHs).
🚫🐕
Details not confirmed for 1992

Bedale Hall — BEDALE

Map 07 SE28
(On A684, 1.5m W of A1 at Leeming Bar)
☎ (0677) 424604
Housed in a building of 17th-century origin, with Palladian and Georgian extensions, the centre of this fascinating little museum is the Bedale fire engine dated 1742. Old documents, photographs, clothing, toys, craft tools and household utensils give an absorbing picture of the life of ordinary people.
Open Etr-Oct, Mon-Sat 10-4. Nov-Etr, Tue only 10-4. Other times by prior arrangement.
Donations.
🅿 ♿ *toilets for disabled shop* 🚫🐕

Beningbrough Hall — BENINGBROUGH

Map 08 SE55
(off A19. Entrance at Newton Lodge)
☎ (0904) 470666
Beningbrough was built around 1716, and its structure has hardly been altered since then. It houses 100 pictures from the National Portrait Gallery in London. Perhaps the finest feature of the house is the Great Staircase, built of oak with wide parquetried treads and delicate balusters carved to imitate wrought iron. Ornately carved wood panelling is a feature of several of the rooms, notably the drawing room. The other side of country house life can be seen in the restored Victorian laundry, which has its original stoves, drying racks and other equipment. The gardens include formal areas, a conservatory and a wilderness play area. Events for 1992 include: 4 Apr-4 May, exhibition of etchings by Janet Evans; 28 Jun, Edwardian picnic with music – in costume – 1-5pm; 16 Aug, Family fun day – 1pm.
Open 4 Apr-Jun & Sep-Oct, Tue-Thu, wknds, Good Fri & BH Mon; Jul-Aug, daily (ex Mon) 11-5. Last admission 4.30. Grounds, shop & restaurant 11-5.30. House, garden & exhibition: £4 (ch £2) Family ticket £10. Garden & exhibitions: £2.50 (ch £1.20) Family £6.20. Party.
🅿 ✕ *licensed* ♿ *toilets for disabled shop* 🚫🐕
(NT)

Brimham Rocks — BRIMHAM

Map 07 SE26
Brimham House, Summerbridge (off B6265)
☎ Harrogate (0423) 780688
A Victorian guidebook describes the rocks as 'a place wrecked with grim and hideous forms defying all description and definition'. The rocks have remained a great attraction, and stand on National Trust open moorland at a height of 950ft. An old shooting lodge in the area is now an information point and shop.
Open Information Centre, 21-24 Apr & 23 May-1 Nov daily. Also 4 Apr-May wknds & BH Mon, 11-5.
Cars £1.20. Minibuses £2. Coaches £5.
🅿 ♿ *(specially adapted path) toilets for disabled shop*
(NT)

Carlton Towers — CARLTON

Map 08 SE62
☎ Goole (0405) 861662
The Yorkshire home of the Dukes of Norfolk, Carlton Towers was first built in 1614, on land owned by the family since the Norman Conquest. It was altered in the 18th and 19th centuries, and its present appearance is a product of the 1870s, when it was remodelled in an ornate, High Victorian manner. The elaborate state rooms with their sumptuous decorations were designed by John Francis Bentley, the architect of Westminster Cathedral. A priest's hiding place can be seen, and there are collections of interesting paintings, furniture, silver and heraldry. Various events are held including: 23-26 May, a Spring Bank Holiday flower festival; 26 Jul, Annual Vintage Car Rally; 29-31 Aug, Festival of Fashion and Craft.
Open May-Sep, Sun & BHs. Parties any day by arrangement, plus Thu evening when a guided tour will be given, approx one and a half hours.
£2.50 (ch £1.50, under 5 free, pen £2). Guided tours 20+.
🅿 ☕ ♿ *toilets for disabled shop* 🚫🐕

CARLTON TOWERS
(Yorkshire Home of the Duke of Norfolk)

The most complete Victorian Gothic House, still a family home.
OPEN: 1.00-5.00pm (last admission 4.30pm)
ON: **Bank Holidays** –
Easter Saturday to Tuesday inclusive;
Early May Bank Holiday Sunday & Monday;
Spring Bank Holiday Saturday to Tuesday inclusive;
August Bank Holiday Saturday to Monday inclusive.
ALL SUNDAYS (May to end of September).
PARTY BOOKINGS ON ANY DAY, plus **THURSDAY EVENINGS,** by appointment (min. 20 in party), when guided tour will be given.
Situated 6 miles south of Selby and 1 mile north of Snaith (A1041), 6 miles from M62, Exit 34 (Whitley Bridge) and 36 (Goole); 30 mins from HUMBER BRIDGE.
Tel: Goole (0405) 861662
Parkland (FREE); Souvenir Shop; Rose Garden (FREE) with access to Stables, Tea Room.

Bolton Castle — CASTLE BOLTON

Map 07 SE09
(off A684)
☎ Wensleydale (0969) 23981 & 23981
The castle is set in the pretty surroundings of Wensleydale, and dates from 1379-97. It was a stronghold of the Scropes family. Mary Queen of Scots was imprisoned here in 1568-9; and the castle was besieged and taken in 1645 by Parliamentary forces. Tapestries, arms and armour, and other artefacts can be seen.
Open Mar-Nov 10-5, weekends in winter.
🅿 ☕ *shop*
Details not confirmed for 1992

CASTLE HOWARD
See Malton

Yorkshire Dales National Park Centre — CLAPHAM

Map 07 SD76
☎ (05242) 51419
A visitor centre with a display on 'The Limestone Dales'. There is an audio-visual theatre, and maps, walks, guides and local information are available.
Open Apr-Oct, daily mid morning-late afternoon.
Free.
🅿 *(charged) shop* 🚫🐕

Byland Abbey — COXWOLD

Map 08 SE57
☎ (03476) 614
The abbey was built for the Cistercians and is now a ruin, but enough still stands to show how beautiful it must have been. The ruins date back to the 12th and 13th centuries, and include well-preserved glazed floor tiles. Carved stones and other finds are displayed.
Open all year, Apr-Sep, daily 10-6; Oct-Mar, Tue-Sun 10-4. (Closed 24-26 Dec & 1 Jan).
£1.10 (ch 55p, students, pen & UB40 85p).
🅿 ♿ 🚫🐕
(EH)

The Moors Centre — DANBY

Map 08 NZ70
Lodge Ln
☎ Guisborough (0287) 660654
The former shooting lodge provides information on the North York Moors National Park, with an exhibition, video and bookshop information desk. There are riverside and woodland grounds, with terraced gardens, a children's play area and a brass-rubbing centre. Special events are held in summer.
Open all year, Apr-Oct, daily 10-5; Nov-Mar, Sun 11-4; (Guided walks Jul-Aug, Sun only).
Free.
🅿 ☕ ♿ *(woodland & garden trails) toilets for disabled shop* 🚫🐕

Easby Abbey   EASBY

Map 11 NZ10
Set beside the River Swale, the
Premonstratensian Abbey was founded
in 1155 and dedicated to St Agatha.
Extensive remains of the monks'
domestic buildings can be seen.

Open all year, Apr-Sep, daily 10-6; Oct-Mar, Tue-Sun 10-4. (Closed 24-26 Dec &
1 Jan).
Honesty box.
✗
(EH)

Yorkshire Air Museum & Allied Air Forces Memorial   ELVINGTON

Map 08 SE74
☎ (090485) 595
The aim of this museum is to preserve
part of a typical wartime airfield as a
memorial to the allied air and ground
crews who served in World War II – in
particular, the many thousands who
served in the Yorkshire and Humberside
area. Visitors can see many of the fine
aircraft including the last Lightning, and
enter the original Flying Control Tower.

Displays include engines, models and
photographs and there is even a friendly
NAAFI offering modern home cooking.
The whole museum recreates the sights,
sounds (and even the smells!) of an
authentic wartime base.
Open 29 Mar-10 Nov, Tue-Thu 11-4, Sat
& Sun noon-5, BH's 11-5.
🅿 ⬤ ✗ *licensed* ♿ *shop*
Details not confirmed for 1992

Places to visit in this guide are pinpointed on the atlas
at the back of the book.

Fairburn Ings Nature Reserve   FAIRBURN

Map 08 SE42
Newton Ln
☎ Sandy (0767) 680551
One-third of the 618-acre RSPB reserve
is open water, and over 200 species of
birds have been recorded. A visitor
centre provides information, and there is
an elevated boardwalk, suitable for

disabled visitors.
Access to the reserve from the village at all
times. Visitor Centre only open Sat, Sun &
BHs 10-5.
🅿 ♿ *(raised boardwalk for wheelchair)*
toilets for disabled shop
Details not confirmed for 1992

Gilling Castle   GILLING EAST

Map 08 SE67
☎ Ampleforth (04393) 238
The 14th- to 18th-century house is now
the preparatory school of Ampleforth
College, but the Elizabethan great
chamber can be visited on weekdays in
school term and is worth seeing for its

panelling, painted glass and ceiling.
There are also fine gardens.
Open Great Chamber and hall, weekdays
(during school term) 10-noon & 2-4;
garden only Jul-Sep, Mon-Fri.
✳ *Gardens 70p. House free.*
🅿 ✗

National Park Centre   GRASSINGTON

Map 07 SE06
Colvend, Hebden Rd
☎ (0756) 752774
The centre is a useful introduction to
the Yorkshire Dales National Park. It
has a video and a display on 'Wharfedale
– Gateway to the Park', and maps,
guides and local information are

available. There is also a 24-hr public
access information service through
computer screens.
Open Apr-Oct daily from mid morning to
late afternoon. Also limited wknds
Nov-Mar.
Free.
🅿 *(charged)* ♿ *toilets for disabled shop* ✗

Harlow Carr Botanical Gardens   HARROGATE

Map 07 SE35
Crag Lane, Otley Rd (off B6162)
☎ (0423) 565418
The gardens were begun in 1948 on a
rough site of pasture and woodland.
Today there are 68 impressive acres of
ornamental and woodland gardens,
including the northern trial grounds.
Various displays and exhibitions are held
including a 'Heritage Week: European

Plants' exhibition from 25 April to 4
May.
Open all year, Mar-Oct, daily 9-7.30 or
dusk. Nov-Feb, daily 9-5 or dusk.
✳ *£3 (accompanied ch free, pen £2.40).*
Party 20+.
🅿 ✗ *licensed* ♿ *(wheelchairs available, tape*
recorded tours) toilets for disabled shop
garden centre ✗

The Royal Pump Room Museum   HARROGATE

Map 07 SE35
Royal Pde
☎ (0423) 503340
The octagonal Pump Room building
contains displays of fine china and
jewellery of the 19th century. This part
of the building still houses the original
sulphur wells, now below modern street
level. The wells are enclosed by glass to

contain their pungent smell, but the
water can be tasted, by those brave
enough, at the original spa counter, now
the ticket counter.
Open all year, Tue-Sat 10-5, Sun 2-5.
(Closed 25-26 Dec & 1 Jan).
Admission fee payable.
♿ *toilets for disabled shop* ✗

Dales Countryside Museum & National Park Centre   HAWES

Map 07 SD89
Station Yard
☎ Wensleydale (0969) 667450
The Dales Countryside Museum
contains displays and an extensive
collection of bygones and farming
implements which explain the changing
landscapes and communities of the area.

There is a full national park and tourist
information service including 24-hr
public information terminals, maps,
guides, publications and souvenirs.
Open Apr-Oct, daily mid mornings-late
afternoon. Limited winter opening.
✳ *£1 (ch & pen 50p).*
🅿 *(charged)* ♿ *(restricted) shop* ✗

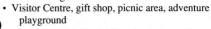
Duncombe Park   HELMSLEY

Map 08 SE68
(1m from town centre, off A170)
☎ (0439) 70213 & 71115
Duncombe Park stands at the heart of a
spectacular 30-acre early 18th-century
landscape garden which is set in 300
acres of dramatic parkland around the
River Rye. The house, originally built in
1713, was gutted by fire in 1879 and
rebuilt in 1895. Its principal rooms are a
fine example of the type of grand
interior popular at the turn of the
century. Home of the Duncombes for
300 years, for much of this century the
house was a girls school. In 1985 the
present Lord and Lady Feversham

decided to make it a family home again
and after major restoration, opened the
house to the public in 1990. It is a
British Tourist Authority 'Come to
Britain' award winner and special events
are planned from Easter to September.
This year these include an 'English Civil
War Spectacular' on 25-26 July.
Open 2 May-25 Oct, Sun-Thu, 11-6. Also
Sun in Apr & 17-21 Apr.
House & grounds £3.75 (ch 5-15 £2, pen
& students £3.25). Family ticket £9.50.
Grounds only £2.50 (ch £1.50). Party
15+.
🅿 ⬤ ♿ *toilets for disabled shop* ✗

Helmsley Castle   HELMSLEY

Map 08 SE68
☎ (0439) 70442
The ruined castle dates from the 12th
century and later, and stands within
enormous earthworks. It was besieged
for three months in the Civil War, and
destroyed in 1644.

Open all year, Apr-Sep, daily 10-6; Oct-Mar, Tue-Sun 10-4. (Closed 24-26 Dec &
1 Jan).
£1.50 (ch 75p, pen, students & UB40
£1.10).
(EH)

✳ An asterisk indicates that up-to-date information was
not available at the time of our research – 1991
information has been published as an
indication of what you may expect.

Flamingo Land Zoo & Family Funpark   KIRBY MISPERTON

Map 08 SE77
The Rectory (off the A169)
☎ (065386) 287
With an 18th-century house as a
backdrop, this vast 'adventure
playground' has appeal for all the family.
Fun-fair rides, exhibitions, a large lake

and over 1,000 animals are just some of
the many attractions.
Open Apr-Sep, daily 10-5 or 6 according to
season. Also school hol & wknds in Oct
10-5.
✳ *£6 (ch 4 free). Party 20+.*
🅿 ⬤ ♿ *(parking) toilets for disabled shop*

Kirkham Priory   KIRKHAM

Map 08 SE76
☎ Whitwell-on-the-Hill (065381) 768
Set on an entrancing site on the banks of
the River Derwent are the ruins of this
former house of Augustinian canons.
The remains of the finely sculptured
13th-century gatehouse and lavatorium,
where the monks washed in leaded

troughs, are memorable.
Open all year, Apr-Sep, daily 10-6; Oct-Mar, Tue-Sun 10-4. (Closed 24-26 Dec &
1 Jan).
£1.10 (ch 55p, pen, students & UB40 85p)
🅿 ♿ ✗
(EH)

Knaresborough Castle   KNARESBOROUGH

Map 08 SE35
☎ Harrogate (0423) 503340
High above the town of Knaresborough,
the ruins of this 14th-century Norman
castle look down over the gorge of the
river Nidd. This imposing fortress was
once the hiding place of Thomas
Becket's murderers and it also served as
a prison for Richard II, but all that
remains today is the keep (housing a
museum), the gatehouse and some of the

curtain wall. Nearby is the Old Court of
Knaresborough, part of which also dates
from the 14th century. It now houses a
local history museum, and entrance is
part of the combined ticket price.
Open Etr, 4 May-Sep, daily 10-5. Guided
tours on request.
Combined ticket 70p (ch 35p). Disabled and
local residents free.
🅿 ♿ *toilets for disabled shop* ✗ *(ex*
grounds)

Yorkshire Dales National Park Centre   MALHAM

Map 07 SD96
☎ Airton (0729) 830363
The national park centre has maps, guides and local information together with dispays on the remarkable natural history of the area, local community and work of conservation bodies. Audio-visuals are provided for groups. The centre underwent extensive refurbishment in 1991, and now benefits from new educational displays.
Open Apr-Oct, daily mid morning-late afternoon. Limited winter opening. Free.
🅿 *(charged)* ♿ *toilets for disabled shop* ✺

Castle Howard   MALTON

Map 08 SE77
☎ Coneysthorpe (065384) 333

In its dramatic setting of lakes, fountains and extensive gardens, this 18th-century palace was designed by Sir John Vanbrugh. Principal location for the TV series 'Brideshead Revisited', this was the first major achievement of the architect who later created the lavish Blenheim Palace near Oxford. Castle Howard was begun in 1699 for the 3rd Earl of Carlisle, Charles Howard, whose descendants still call the place 'home'. The striking façade is topped by an 80ft painted and gilded dome. The interior has a 192ft Long Gallery, as well as a Chapel with magnificent stained glass windows by the 19th-century artist, Edward Burne-Jones. Besides the collections of antique furniture, porcelain and sculpture, the Castle contains a number of important paintings, including a portrait of Henry VIII by Holbein and works by Rubens, Reynolds and Gainsborough. The grounds include the domed Temple of the Four Winds by Vanbrugh, and the richly designed family Mausoleum by Hawksmoor. The Rose Garden contains both old-fashioned and modern varieties of roses.
Ray Wood is a 30-acre area with unique collections of rare trees, shrubs, rhododendrons and azaleas, while Stable Court houses the internationally famous Costume Galleries which contain the largest private collection of period costume in Britain. Displays are changed annually and include a replica collection of Crown Jewels.
Open 1-24 Mar Grounds only. 25 Mar-1 Nov, Grounds & Plant Centre 10, House & Costume Galleries 11. Last admissions 4.30pm.
£5.50 (ch £2.50, pen £4.50). Party 12 + .
🅿 🍽 ✕ *licensed* ♿ *(chairlift, free adapted transport to house) toilets for disabled shop garden centre* ✺

Eden Camp Modern History Theme Museum   MALTON

Map 08 SE77
(junc of A64 & A169)
☎ (0653) 697777
The story of the peoples' war – the drama, the hardships, the humour – unfolds in this museum devoted to civilian life in World War II. The displays, covering the blackout, rationing, the Blitz, the Homeguard and others, are housed in a former prisoner-of-war camp built in 1942 for German and Italian soldiers. Large toilet cubicles with handles for wheelchair visitors; tapes and braille cards for the blind. On 30-31 May, a 50th anniversary display will include 50 years as a POW camp and 5 years as a museum.
Open 14 Feb-23 Dec, daily 10-5. Last admission 4pm.
£3 (ch & pen £2). Party 10 + .
🅿 🍽 ♿ *(taped tours, Braille guides) toilets for disabled shop*

Malton Museum   MALTON

Map 08 SE77
Old Town Hall, Market Place
☎ (0653) 695136
The extensive Roman settlements in the area are represented and illustrated in this museum, including collections from the Roman fort of Derventio. There are also displays of local prehistoric and medieval finds plus changing exhibitions of local interest. Exhibitions in 1992 will include phonographs, badgers and embroidery.
Open Apr-Oct, Mon-Sat 10-4, Sun 2-4; Nov-Dec, Sat 1-3. Parties by arrangement.
80p (ch, pen & students 50p). Family ticket £2.
♿ *shop* ✺

Theakston Brewery Visitor Centre   MASHAM

Map 08 SE28
The Brewery (on A6108)
☎ Ripon (0765) 689057
At the Visitor Centre adjacent to the Brewery visitors can discover how Theakston Traditional ales are brewed and see the ancient skills of the cooper, together with an exculsive video, a museum and a gift shop.
Open Good Fri-Oct, Wed-Sun, 10.30-4; Nov-Dec, Wed, Sat & Sun 10.30-1 & 2-4.
✱ *Visitor centre & Brewery tour £2.50 (ch 10-18 £2). Visitor centre only £1 (ch 10-18 50p).*
♿ *(ex brewery tours) toilets for disabled shop* ✺

Middleham Castle   MIDDLEHAM

Map 07 SE18
☎ Wensleydale (0969) 23899
The town of Middleham (much of which is a conservation area) is dominated by the 12th-century keep which saw its great days during the Wars of the Roses. The seat of the Neville family, the Earls of Warwick, it was the home for a time of the young King Richard III, then Duke of Gloucester, who married the Earl's daughter Anne Neville.
Open all year, Apr-Sep, daily 10-6; Oct-Mar, Tue-Sun 10-4. (Closed 24-26 Dec & 1 Jan).
£1.10 (ch 55p, pen, students & UB40 85p).
shop
(EH)

Newby Hall & Gardens   NEWBY HALL & GARDENS

Map 08 SE36
(4m SE off B6265)
☎ Boroughbridge (0423) 322583
This late 17th-century house had its interior and additions designed by Robert Adam, and contains an important collection of classical sculpture and Gobelins tapestries. In addition to the formal Gardens' 25 acres are a miniature railway, an adventure garden for children, and a woodland discovery walk. Special events take place throughout the year, including on 16-17 May, Carriage Driving; 14 June, Country Fair; 20-21 June and 19-20 Sep, Craft Fairs; 19 Jul, Historic Vehicle Rally..
Open 28 Mar-29 Sep, Tue-Sun & BH's; Gardens 11-5.30; House 12-5. Last admission 5pm.
House & Garden £4.80, (ch & disabled £2.70, pen £3.80). Gardens only £2.70 (ch & disabled £2, pen £2.30). Party.
🅿 🍽 ✕ *licensed* ♿ *(wheelchairs available, maps of wheelchair routes) toilets for disabled shop garden centre* ✺

See advertisement on page 127

Lightwater Valley Theme Park   NORTH STAINLEY

Map 07 SE27
(on the A6108)
☎ Ripon (0765) 635368 & 635321
Set in 125-acres of country park and lakeland, Lightwater Valley offers a selection of rides and attractions suitable for all the family. Enjoy the white-knuckle thrills of the world's biggest roller coaster, Soopa Loopa, the Rat and the Wave or, for the less adventurous, there is the steam train, boating lake or country sports. There is also live family entertainment and shopping malls.
Open 11-26 Apr; 2-4, 9-10, 16-17 & 23-31 May; Jun Wed-Sun; Jul-Aug daily; 1-6 Sep & wknds; Oct Sun only.
✱ *Telephone for details.*
🅿 🍽 ✕ *licensed* ♿ *toilets for disabled shop* ✺

See advertisement on page 126.

Nunnington Hall   NUNNINGTON

Map 08 SE67
(1.5m N of B1257)
☎ (04395) 283
This large 16th- to 17th-century house has panelled rooms and a magnificent staircase. The Carlisle collection of miniature rooms is on display. Special events for 1992 include: 29 Feb, Words and Music for Springtime, 7.30pm; 11 Apr, Halifax Gilbert and Sullivan Society, 7.30pm:
Open 4 Apr-1 Nov: 18-23 Apr & wknds, 2-6. May, Jun, Sep & Oct, Tue-Thu & wknds, 2-6. Jul-Aug, Tue-Thu, 2-6, wknds noon-6. BH Mon noon-6. Last admission 5pm.
House & garden £3 (ch £1.50); Gardens only £1.50 (ch 70p). Party.
🅿 🍽 ♿ *toilets for disabled shop* ✺
(NT)

Mount Grace Priory   OSMOTHERLEY

Map 08 SE49
(1m NW).
☎ Northallerton (0609) 83494
A ruined 14th-century Carthusian priory, next to a 17th-century house. One of the monks' cells has been fully restored to show where the monk lived and worked in solitude, and what life was like in this monastery.
Open all year, Apr-Sep, daily 10-6. Oct-Mar, Tue-Sun 10-4. (Closed 24-26 Dec & 1 Jan).
£1.80 (ch 90p, students, pen & UB40 £1.40).
🅿 ♿ *shop*
(EH & NT)

Every effort is made to provide accurate information, but details might change during the currency of this guide.

Parcevall Hall Gardens   PARCEVALL HALL GARDENS

Map 07 SEO6
☎ Burnsall (0756) 720311 (Admin) 720269 (Gardener)
Enjoying a hillside setting east of the main Wharfedale Valley, these beautiful gardens belong to an Elizabethan house.
Open Etr-Oct, daily 10-6. Winter visits by appointment.
£1.50 (ch 5-12 50p). Party.
🅿 🍽 *garden centre*

North Yorkshire Moors Railway   PICKERING

Map 08 SE78
Pickering Station
☎ (0751) 73535

Operating through the heart of the

North York Moors National Park between Pickering and Grosmont, steam trains cover a distance of 18 miles. Beautiful Newtondale Halt gives walkers easy access to forest and moorland. The locomotive sheds at Pickering are open to the public. 1992 marks the Railway's 25th anniversary.
Open Etr-Oct, daily. Dec, Santa Specials. Further information available from Pickering Station, North Yorkshire.
✱ *Return fr £4.80. Special rates for pen (ex Jun-Aug). Family ticket.*
🅿 *(charged)* 🍽 ✕ *licensed* ♿ *(ramp for trains) toilets for disabled shop*

Pickering Castle   PICKERING

Map 08 SE78
☎ (0751) 74989
Standing upon its mound high above the town, the 12th-century keep and baileys are all that is left of this favourite royal hunting lodge.
Open all year, Apr-Sep, daily 10-6; Oct-Mar, Tue-Sun 10-4. (Closed 24-26 Dec & 1 Jan).
£1.50 (ch 75p, students, pen & UB40 £1.10).
🅿 ♿ ✺
(EH)

Georgian Theatre Royal — RICHMOND

Map 11 NZ10
Victoria Rd
☎ (0748) 823710
Built in 1788, this is the oldest theatre in the United Kingdom still in its original form and still being used for live theatre. Having closed in 1848, it was restored and re-opened in 1962. The audience now watch the actors from the original gallery, boxes and pit. The museum contains old playbills and photographs, and the oldest complete set of painted scenery in the country.
Open Etr Sat-Oct, Mon-Sat 11-4.45, Sun 2.30-4.45. Parties by arrangement. £1 (ch & pen 70p). Party. shop ✻

Green Howards Museum — RICHMOND

Map 11 NZ10
Trinity Church Square, Market Place
☎ (0748) 2133
This award-winning museum traces the military history of the Green Howards from the late 17th century onwards. The exhibits include uniforms, weapons, medals and a special Victoria Cross exhibition. Regimental and civic plate is also displayed.
Open Feb, Mon-Fri 10-4.30; Mar, Mon-Sat 10-4.30; Apr-Oct, Mon-Sat 9.30-4.30 & Sun 2-4.30; Nov, Mon-Sat 10-4.30. ✳ £1 (ch 16 50p, pen 75p). ♿ shop ✻

Richmond Castle — RICHMOND

Map 11 NZ10
☎ (0748) 822493
Built high upon sheer rocks overlooking the River Swale, the castle was begun by Alan Rufus in 1071. It is ruined, but has a splendid 100ft high keep. Two of the towers are left on the massive curtain walls, and also well preserved is Scollard's Hall, which was built in 1080 and may be the oldest domestic building in Britain.
Open all year, Apr-Sep, daily 10-6; Oct-Mar, Tue-Sun 10-4. (Closed 24-26 Dec & 1 Jan). £1.50 (ch 75p, students, pen & UB40 £1.10). ♿ shop ✻ (EH)

Rievaulx Abbey — RIEVAULX

Map 08 SE58
☎ (04396) 228
The site for this magnificent abbey was given to a band of 12 Cistercian monks in 1131. Building began in about 1132 and most was completed by the end of the 12th century. The abbey was extremely prosperous, and under its third abbot, Aelred (1147-67), there were 140 monks and over 500 lay brothers. During the 15th century parts of the abbey were taken down as numbers fell, and by the time of the Dissolution there were only 22 monks left. Surrounded by wooded hills, this site in the Rye Valley is one of the most beautiful in England. The remains of the
continued . . .

high church and monastic buildings are extensive, and the choir is a notable example of a 13th-century work. The nave, which dates back to 1135, is the earliest large Cistercian nave in Britain. *Open all year, Apr-Sep, daily 10-6; Oct-*

Mar, Tue-Sun 10-4. (Closed 24-26 Dec & 1 Jan).
£1.80 (ch 90p, pen, students & UB40 £1.40).
P & shop ⚲
(EH)

Rievaulx Terrace & Temples   RIEVAULX

Map 08 SE58
(on B1257)
☎ Bilsdale (04396) 340
This curved terrace, half a mile long, overlooks the abbey, with views of Ryedale and the Hambleton Hills. It has two mock-Greek temples, one built for hunting parties, the other for quiet

contemplation. There are also remarkable frescoes by Borgnis, and an exhibition on English landscape design. *Open 1 Apr-1 Nov, daily 10.30-6 or dusk if earlier. Last admission 5.30pm. £1.80 (ch 90p). Party.*
P & *(runaround vehicle available) shop*
(NT)

Ripley Castle   RIPLEY

Map 07 SE26
(off A61)
☎ Harrogate (0423) 770152
This beautiful castle has been the home of the Ingilby family since 1320. The present castle dates mainly from the 16th century but has older and newer areas. The castle has Cromwellian connections and both James I and Cromwell stayed here. It is said that Cromwell was watched throughout the night by Trooper Jane Ingilby, who was armed with a pair of pistols. The castle has, among other things, a priest's hole which was discovered in 1964, and a collection of Royalist armour housed in the 1555 tower. The surrounding

gardens and grounds are very fine, and various events are held throughout the year. The gardens now house the national hyacinth collection and the Ripley tropical plant collection. A steam fair, country fair and craft fairs are planned for 1992.
Open Apr-May & Oct, Sat & Sun 11.30-4.30; Jun-Sep, Tue-Thu, Sat & Sun 11.30-4.30; Etr & BHs 11-4.30. Gardens, daily Etr-Oct, 11-5. Parties any day (ex 25 Dec & 1 Jan) by arrangement. Castle & Gardens £3.50 (ch £1.75, pen £3). Gardens only £2 (ch £1, pen £1.50). Party 25 +.
P 🍴 & *shop* ✖

Fountains Abbey & Studley Royal   RIPON

Map 07 SE37
(2m SW off B6265)
☎ Sawley (0765) 620333
Founded by Cistercian monks in 1132, Fountains Abbey is the largest monastic ruin in Britain. It was acquired by William Aislabie in 1768, and became the focal point of his landscaped gardens at Studley. These include formal water gardens, ornamental temples, follies and magnificent views. They are bordered by a lake and 400 acres of deer park. Other interesting features include Fountains Hall, built between 1598 and 1611 using the stone from the abbey ruins. Special events for 1992 include: 20 Jun, Music in the Water Garden – City of

London Sinfonia plus fireworks, 8pm; 26 Dec, Boxing Day Pilgrimage – Walk from Ripon Cathedral to Fountains Abbey (4 miles) and return.
Open all year. Abbey & garden: Jan-Mar, Nov & Dec, daily (ex 24 & 25 Dec, & Fri Nov-Jan), 10-5 or dusk if earlier; Apr-Jun & Sep 10-7; Jul & Aug 10-8; Oct 10-6 or dusk if earlier. Fountains Hall: Apr-Oct 11-6; Nov-Mar 11-4. St Mary's Church: 29 Mar-Sep, 1-5. Jan-Mar: £2.70 (ch £1.30). Family ticket £6.70. Apr-Oct: £3.50 (ch £1.60). Family ticket £8.60. Nov-Mar 1993: £3 (ch £1.50). Family ticket £7.50. Party 15 +.
P 🍴 & *toilets for disabled shop*
(NT)

Norton Conyers   RIPON

Map 07 SE37
(3.5m NW)
☎ Melmerby (0765) 640333
This late medieval house with Stuart and Georgian additions has belonged to the Grahams since 1624. The pictures and furniture reflect over 360 years of occupation by the same family. It was visited by James I, Charles I and James II. Another visitor was Charlotte Brontë: the house is one of the originals of 'Thornfield Hall' in Jane Eyre. There are displays of family costumes and

wedding dresses and relics of Charlotte Brontë. Please note that photography is by permission of the owner only, and that visitors are requested not to wear high-heeled shoes.
Open all year, Garden: Mon-Fri 9-5; 28 Mar-3 Oct, Sat & Sun 2-5.30. House: BH Sun & Mon, 17 May-13 Sep, Sun; 27 Jul-1 Aug, daily 2-5.30. Parties by appointment.
£2 (ch 4-14 £1, pen £1.50). Party 20 +.
P & *toilets for disabled shop garden centre*
✖ *(ex grounds)*

Ripon Prison & Police Museum   RIPON

Map 07 SE37
St Marygate
☎ (0765) 690799
This museum uses a variety of displays and exhibits to illustrate the history and development of Ripon's prison and

police force together with the history of the buildings (1686-1955).
Open Apr-Oct, Mon-Sun 1-5; Jul & Aug, Mon-Sat 11-5, Sun 1-5. Admission fee payable.
& *shop* ✖

Scarborough Castle   SCARBOROUGH

Map 08 TA08
☎ (0723) 372451
The ruins of Scarborough Castle stand on a narrow headland which was once the site of British and Roman encampments. The curtain wall was probably built several decades before the square keep, which dates from about 1155. The shell of the keep, the 13th-century Barbican and remains of

medieval chapels and a house is all that remains of this fine fortress.
Open all year, Apr-Sep, daily 10-6; Oct-Mar, Tue-Sun 10-4. (Closed 24-26 Dec & 1 Jan).
£1.50 (ch 75p, pen, students & UB40 £1.10).
& *(ex in keep)* ✖
(EH)

Craven Museum   SKIPTON

Map 07 SD95
Town Hall, High St
☎ (0756) 794079
The museum contains a collection dealing especially with the Craven district. There are important exhibits of folk life, lead mining and prehistoric and

Roman remains.
Open all year, Apr-Sep, Mon, Wed-Fri 11-5, Sat 10-noon & 1-5, Sun 2-5; Oct-Mar, Mon, Wed-Fri 2-5, Sat 10-noon & 1.30-4.30. Some BH's & PH's phone to check.
Free.

Skipton Castle   SKIPTON

Map 07 SD95
☎ (0756) 792442
Skipton is one of the most complete and well-preserved medieval castles in England. Some of the castle dates from the 1650s when it was rebuilt after being partially damaged following the Civil War. However, the original castle was erected in Norman times, and the gateway with its Norman Arch still exists. The castle became the home of the Clifford family in 1310 and was their home until 1676.

Entrance to the castle is through a massive round-towered gateway with the family motto 'Desormais' carved above it. The main buildings inside the walls are surrounded by well-kept lawns and cobblestones. Conduit Court is especially attractive with its ancient yew tree.
Open all year, daily from 10am (Sun 2pm). Last admission 6pm (4pm Oct-Feb) (Closed 25 Dec).
£2.40 (inc illustrated tour sh... £1.20, under 5 free)...
shop

✱ An asterisk indicates ...
not available ...
in... ...
in...

Sutton Park

Map 08 SE56
(on B1363)
☎ Easingwold (0347) 8102...
An early Georgian house (bu... Sutton Park contains some fine furniture by Chippendale and S... paintings and a good collection o... porcelain. The grounds have supe... terraced gardens, a lily pond and a Georgian ice house. There are also

Whitby Abbey

WHITBY

Map 08 NZ81
☎ (0947) 603568
Dominating the skyline above the fishing port of Whitby are the ruins of the 13th-century Benedictine abbey. The stone abbey was erected on the site of the wooden abbey of St Hilda, which was built in 657. It was badly damaged by shellfire during World War I.
Open all year, Apr-Sep, daily 10-6; Oct-Mar, Tue-Sun 10-4. (Closed 24-26 Dec & 1 Jan).
£1.10 (ch 55p, pen, students & UB40 85p).
🐕
(EH)

Whitby Museum

WHITBY

Map 08 NZ81
Pannett Park
☎ (0947) 602908
This museum and art gallery has a wide range of exhibits, many of which relate to Captain Cook: his ship Endeavour was built at Whitby. Other exhibits relate to the ship-building, whaling and jet industries, which have all been important to the town.
Open all year, weekdays 9.30-5.30, Sun 2-5; Oct-Apr, Mon & Tue 10.30-1, Wed-Sat 10.30-4, Sun 2-4.
✱ *£1 (ch 16 50p).*
&. *(by appointment) shop* 🐕

The ARC

YORK

Map 08 SE65
St Saviourgate
☎ (0904) 654324
The ARC is a 'hands-on' experience of archaeology, enjoyed by visitors of all ages. It is housed in the beautifully restored medieval church of St Saviour. Be an archaeologist yourself! Sift through the remains of centuries – bones, shell, pottery and much more. Piece together the lives of our ancestors. Solve the puzzle of how to open a Viking padlock, decipher Viking-age writing or learn to make a Roman shoe. Real archaeologists are on hand to assist you with your discoveries. Special events include children's activity mornings in school holidays, and for the Jorvik Viking Festival in 1992, there are events starting 14 February until 26 February.
Open Apr-Oct, Mon-Fri 10-5, Sat & Sun 1-5; Nov & Feb-Mar, Mon-Fri 10-5.
£2.75 (ch, pen, student & UB40's £1.75, ch under 5 free).
&. *(induction loop) toilets for disabled shop*
🐕

The Bar Convent

YORK

Map 08 SE65
17 Blossom St
☎ (0904) 643238
This elegant Georgian building is still in use as a practising convent but it is also much more. A museum outlines the early history of Christianity in the North of England and tells the story of Mary Ward foundress of the Institute of the Blessed Virgin and pioneer of women's education and of apostolic religious orders for women. A lively programme of exhibitions of religious and cultural heritage take place in the well-appointed exhibition gallery. Leisure Learning Centres are also offered to people of all ages.
Open Feb-Dec, Tue-Sat 10-5.
Museum & Gallery £1.75 (ch 16 £1, pen £1.50). Gallery only £1.
♨ &. *toilets for disabled shop* 🐕

Borthwick Institute of Historical Research

YORK

Map 08 SE65
St Anthony's Hall, Peasholme Green
☎ (0904) 642315
Originally built in the second half of the 15th century for the Guild of St Anthony, the hall, with its fine timber roof, was later used as an arsenal, a workhouse, a prison and the Bluecoat School from 1705 to 1946. Now part of York University, it houses ecclesiastical archives and exhibitions of documents.
Open all year, Mon-Fri 9.30-1 & 2-5. (Closed Etr & Xmas).
Free.
🐕 🚌

City Art Gallery

YORK

Map 08 SE65
Exhibition Square
☎ (0904) 623839
This gallery houses a treasure-house of European and British paintings spanning seven centuries and including the world-famous Lycett Green collection of Old Masters as well as works by the remarkable York-born painter of the nude, William Etty. You can also see the unrivalled Milner-White collection [of] stoneware pottery. In addition, there is a programme of temporary exhibitions, lectures and events including, amongst others: 29 Feb- 5 Apr, Shared Earth – contemporary landscapes from Britain and the Soviet Union; 13 Jun-25 Jul, A Taste of Pop.
Open all year, Mon-Sat 10-5, Sun 2.30-5, last admission 4.30 (Closed Good Fri, 25-26 Dec & 1 Jan).
Free.
&. *(chairlift) toilets for disabled shop* 🐕

[Cliffor]d's Tower

YORK

[Map 08 SE]65
☎ [... ...]040
[Cliffor]d's Tower, after Roger [... w]as hung from the [... Yor]k Castle was built in [... Conqu]eror as part [... th]e Saxons. [... t]opped with a [...s] of the River [... ...] down [...] during [... ...]King [... ...] was [... C]astle cracked from top to bottom in 1360, as a result of part of the mound subsiding into the moat. From the end of the 15th century the tower was largely unused. Since 1825 Clifford's Tower has been part of the prison and is now looked after by English Heritage. The wall walk provides one of the best views of York.
Open all year, Apr-Sep, daily 10-6; Oct-Mar, daily 10-4. (Closed 24-26 Dec & 1 Jan).
£1.10 (ch 55p, students, pen & UB40 85p).
🐕 🚌
(EH)

Fairfax House

YORK

Map 08 SE65
Castlegate
☎ (0904) 655543

An outstanding mid-18th-century house with a richly decorated interior, Fairfax House was acquired by the York Civic Trust in 1983 and restored. Prior to this it had been used as a cinema and a dance hall. The house contains fine examples of Georgian furniture, porcelain, paintings and clocks which form the Terry Collection. This collection was donated by Mr Noel Terry who was the great grandson of Joseph Terry the founder of the York-based confectionery business. There is a special display of a recreated meal dating from 1763 in the dining room and there are frequent other exhibitions including, in November and December, Images of Childhood – children in 18th-century portraiture.
Open 20 Feb-5 Jan, Mon-Sat 11-5, (Closed Fri). Sun 1.30-5. Last admission 4.30.
£2.50 (ch £1.25, pen £2).
&. *(with assistance. Phone before visit) shop*
🐕

Friargate Museum

YORK

Map 08 SE65
Lower Friargate
☎ (0904) 658775
This award-winning museum is celebrated for its role in bringing history to life. Over 60 lifesize waxwork figures are exhibited in carefully reconstructed, realistic sets, showing scenes like Drake and the Armada, the Dukes of York, and the Crown Jewels. There is even a lifelike Yeti or 'Abominable Snowman' for the very brave – sound effects as well! Among the figures on display are members of the royal family, Winston Churchill, Adolf Hitler, Mahatma Ghandi, Ronald Reagan and Mrs Thatcher.
The 'Chuckles' exhibition of unusual laughter machines forms an additional attraction. Special for 1992: 'Discovery' (Colombus and the New World).
Open Mar-Oct, daily 10-5; Nov-Feb, 10-dusk. (Closed Jan & 25 Dec).
£2.50 (ch £1.25, pen £1.75). Party 25 +.
&. *(touch tours for the blind) shop*

This is just one of many guidebooks published by the AA. The full range is available at any AA shop or good bookshop.

Guildhall

YORK

Map 08 SE65
Off Coney St
☎ (0904) 613161
The present Hall dates from 1446 but in 1942 an air raid virtually destroyed the building. The present Guildhall was carefully restored as an exact replica and was re-opened in 1960. There is an interesting arch-braced roof decorated with colourful bosses and supported by 12 solid oak pillars.
Although many of the windows in the Guildhall were unglazed until the 18th century, the west window contains stained-glass from 1682, by a York craftsman, and there is also a superb, modern stained glass window by Henry Harvey. This depicts the story of York through the ages. The Inner Chamber adjoining the Hall has two secret doors and a passageway beneath the Guildhall to the river.
Open all year, May-Oct, Mon-Thu 9-5, Fri 9-4.30, Sat 10-5, Sun 2.30-4.30; Nov-Apr, Mon-Thu 9-5, Fri 9-4.30. (Closed Good Fri, Spring BH, 25-26 Dec & 1 Jan).
&. *(electric chair lift) toilets for disabled* 🐕 🚌
Details not confirmed for 1992

Jorvik Viking Centre

YORK

Map 08 SE65
Coppergate
☎ (0904) 643211
Jorvik was the Viking name for York. Between 1976 and 1981 archaeologists made some remarkable discoveries about Jorvik, during a dig in an area known as Coppergate. In 1984 the Viking Centre was opened over the site of the original excavations. The dig shed a totally new light on the Viking way of life and has revealed many details of tools, clothing, crafts and trade. The Centre displays the archaeological remains – leather, textiles, metal objects and even timber buildings – in a detailed and vivid reconstruction. First there is an audio-visual display to explain exactly who the Vikings were. Then, 'time-cars' carry visitors through a 'time tunnel' from World War II back to Norman times and then to a full-scale reconstruction of 10th-century Coppergate. The busy street scene includes a crowded market, a river wharf with a fully-rigged sailing ship and a family at home. This is all made more authentic by voices speaking in Old Norse and even smells such as cooking, fish, pigsties and rubbish! Finally the tour passes through a reconstruction of Coppergate during the dig of the 1970s. The visit ends in the Skipper Gallery which has a display of some of the 15,000 small objects found during the dig. The Jorvik Viking Festival, 14-29 February celebrates Viking 'Jobalot'. Telephone the Viking Centre for the full programme.
Open all year, Apr-Oct daily 9-7; Nov-Mar daily 9-5.30. (Closed 25 Dec).
✱ *£3.50 (ch £1.75). (pen £2.60 Nov-Mar only).*
&. *(time car designed to take a wheelchair) toilets for disabled shop* 🐕

Merchant Adventurers' Hall

YORK

Map 08 SE65
Fossgate
☎ (0904) 654818
The Hall of the powerful Merchant Adventurers' Company was built in the 1350's and it is one of the finest in Europe. The building has an undercroft, chapel and a great hall, the largest timber-framed building in York.
Open all year, End Mar-early Nov, daily 8.30-5; Early Nov-late Mar, Mon-Sat 8.30-3.30. (Closed Xmas 2 wks).
£1.50 (ch 50p, pen £1.20).
&. *toilets for disabled shop*

Museum of Automata — YORK

Map 08 SE65
Tower St
☎ (0904) 655550
The Museum of Automata appeals to adults and children alike, with a unique collection of ingenious machines spanning 2000 years from simple articulated figurines from ancient civilisations to modern day robots. The French Gallery contains a throng of musicians, clowns, artists and eccentrics from Parisian cafe society, brought to life by video, sound and lighting. Visitors can crank exhibits into action in the Contemporary Gallery, and there's a reconstruction of a saucy 1950s seaside pier.
Open all year, daily 9.30-5.30. (Closed 25 Dec)
✱ *£2.85 (ch £1.50, pen & students £2.20)*
& *toilets for disabled shop* ✖

National Railway Museum — YORK

Map 08 SE65
Leeman Rd
☎ (0904) 621261

Wednesday 15 April 1992 will be the first time visitors will see the greatly expanded National Railway Museum with its new displays and exhibitions telling the story of British railways up to the present day. The opening of the Great Hall will enable the Museum to double its display space and focus on the technical aspects of railway development. Visitors will see famous locomotives explaining the evolution of motive power with displays highlighting design and safety on railways as well as the Channel Tunnel. The exhibition 'The Great Railway Show' will continue to highlight the social history connected with travelling by train, including the story of Royal travel.
Open all year, Mon-Sat 10-6, Sun 11-6. (Closed 24-26 Dec & 1 Jan).
✱ *£3 (ch £1.50 under 5 free, pen £2). Party 15+.*
🅿 *(charged)* ✕ *licensed* & *("Please Touch" evenings) toilets for disabled shop* ✖

Rail Riders World — YORK

Map 08 SE65
York BR Station, Tearoom Square
☎ (0904) 630169
One of the biggest and best model railway museums in Britain, Rail Riders World has two very intricate railway layouts. The larger one is set in town and country landscapes. It comprises hundreds of buildings, about 5,500 tiny trees, over 2,000 lights and around 2,500 people and animals. As many as 20 trains can run in this model at the same time, including the Royal Train, the Orient Express, Inter City 125 and the latest freight and passenger trains.
The second model is a much smaller layout and shows a typical German town at night, brightly lit by numerous tiny lights. There are push buttons for children, amid these detailed and accurate scale models.
Open daily 10-6 (Last admission 5.30). (Closed 24-26 Dec, 15 Jan-9 Feb & 19 Feb-1 Mar).
& *shop* ✖
Details not confirmed for 1992

Treasurer's House — YORK

Map 08 SE65
Chapter House St
☎ (0904) 624247
There has been a house on this site since Roman times and in the basement of this elegant 17th-century building is an exhibition of its history. The house was improved during the 18th century with the addition of a fine staircase. Restored between 1897 and 1930, it was left, with its fine furniture, to the National Trust. Exhibitions and events are planned from April to November including 25-26 Apr, Festival of Spring Flowers and 19-20 Sep, Festival of Autumn Flowers.
Open Apr-1 Nov, daily 10.30-5. Last admission 4.30.
£2.60 (ch £1.30). Party.
✕ *licensed shop* ✖
(NT)

York Castle Museum — YORK

Map 08 SE65
The Eye of York
☎ (0904) 653611
Four centuries of everyday life are exhibited in the Castle Museum, imaginatively displayed through reconstructions of period rooms and two indoor streets, complete with cobbles, a Hansom cab and a park. The museum is housed in the city's prison and is based on an extensive collection of 'bygones' acquired at the beginning of the century. It was one of the first folk museums to display a huge range of everyday objects in an authentic scene. The Victorian street includes a pawnbroker, a tallow candle factory and a haberdasher's. There is even a reconstruction of the original sweet shop of the York chocolate manufacturer, Joseph Terry. An extensive collection of many other items from musical instruments to costumes, and a gallery of domestic gadgets from Victorian times to the 1960s entitled 'Every home should have one' are further attractions to this remarkable museum. The museum also has one of Britain's finest collections of Militaria; this includes a superb example of an Anglo-Saxon helmet – one of only three known.
Open all year, Apr-Oct Mon-Sat 9.30-5.30, Sun 10-5.30; Nov-Mar, Mon-Sat 9.30-4, Sun 10-4. (Closed 25-26 Dec & 1 Jan).
£3.35 (ch, pen, students & UB40 £2.35). Family ticket £9.40. Party 20+.
🖢 & *toilets for disabled shop* ✖

The York Dungeon — YORK

Map 08 SE65
12 Clifford St
☎ (0904) 632599
The blood and thunder of Britain's past comes to life in the York Dungeon, where life-size tableaux depict superstition, pain, torture and death in spine-chilling detail. From the moment you enter, eerie sound effects and dramatic lighting create a fascinating atmosphere. The cold chill of horror is based on the realities of our ancestors' lives, through carefully researched historical facts.
Open all year, daily from 10am
✱ *£2.75 (ch & pen £1.75, under 5's free)*
& *shop*

The York Story — YORK

Map 08 SE65
The Heritage Centre, Castlegate
☎ (0904) 628632
The exhibition traces the history of York over the last 1000 years, helped by a large three-dimensional model of York. A model of part of the building of a medieval church, showing the scaffolding and other building techniques, is an unusual feature. There is a comprehensive audio-visual guide to the display of many notable pieces by modern artists and craftsmen and the treasures of the city.

The Heritage Centre is in the predominantly 15th-century church of St Mary which has the tallest spire in York, at 152ft.
Open all year, Mon-Sat 10-5, Sun 1-5. (Closed 25-26 Dec & 1 Jan).
✱ *£1.30 (ch, pen, students & UB40's 65p). Joint ticket with Castle Museum £4. Family ticket £9.40.*
& shop ✖

Yorkshire Museum & Gardens — YORK

Map 08 SE65
Museum Gardens
☎ (0904) 629745
The European award-winning Yorkshire Museum, set in 10 acres of botanical gardens in the heart of the historic city of York, displays some of the finest Roman, Anglo-Saxon, Viking and Medieval treasures ever discovered in Britain. The Middleham jewel, a fine example of English Gothic jewellery, is on display in the Medieval Gallery and, in the Roman Gallery, visitors can see a fine marble head of Constantine the Great and household utensils exhibited in a recreated kitchen, as well as many other artefacts. The Anglo-Saxon Gallery houses the magnificent, delicate silver-gilt Ormside bowl and the skilfully wrought Gilling sword. The Museum also has a fine collection of Rockingham porcelain.

Part of York's Roman city walls run through the Museum Gardens where, amongst a variety of flora and fauna, you can visit a working Observatory, the ruins of the Medieval St Mary's Abbey and its 14th-century guesthouse – the oldest timber-framed structure in Yorkshire. From March to 31 October there will be a major Natural History exhibition 'Dinosaurs from China'.
Open all year, Mar-Oct, daily 10-5; Nov-Mar, Mon-Sat 10-5, Sun 1-5. Last admission 4.30.
£2.50 (ch, pen, students & UB40's £1.25). Family ticket £6. Season ticket £4 (concessions £2.50). Family season ticket £10. Party 10+.
& *(lift) toilets for disabled shop* ✖

NORTHAMPTONSHIRE

Althorp Hall — ALTHORP

Map 04 SP66
☎ Northampton (0604) 770042
Althorp Hall has been the home of the Spencer family since 1508. The house was built in the 16th century, but has been changed since, most notably by Henry Holland in 1790. Restored in 1983, it contains magnificent pictures, furniture and china. Special party visits may be arranged for any day at extra cost, and include afternoon teas in the Sunderland Room of Althorp House.

The house is not suitable for small children, the frail or the disabled. Both house and grounds may be closed without notice for security reasons. Coaches will not be informed.
Open all year, daily 1-5; Jul-Aug & BH's 11-6.
✱ *£2.95 (ch £1.95). Wed Connoisseurs Day £3.95 (ch £2.25 no children under 8). Grounds & Lake only 50p (ch 25p). Party 8+.*
🅿 ⬤ & *shop* ✖

Canons Ashby House — CANONS ASHBY

Map 04 SP55
(on B4525)
☎ Blakesley (0327) 860044
Home of the Dryden family since the 16th century, this is an exceptional small manor house, with Elizabethan wall paintings and Jacobean plasterwork. It has restored gardens, a small park and a church – part of the original 13th-century Augustinian priory. On 25 July there will be 'Jazz in the Park' with the Temperance Seven.
Open Apr-Oct, Wed-Sun & BH Mon 1-5.30. Last admission 5pm.
£2.80 (ch £1.40).
🅿 ⬤ & *toilets for disabled shop (NT)*

For an explanation of the symbols and abbreviations, see page 2.

Deene Park — DEENE

Map 04 SP99
(off A43)
☎ Bulwick (078085) 223 & 278
Mainly 16th-century house of great architectural importance and historical interest. Home of the Brudenell family since 1514, including the 7th Earl of Cardigan who led the Charge of the Light Brigade. Large lake and park. Extensive gardens with old-fashioned roses, rare trees and shrubs.
Open BH's (Sun & Mon) Etr, May, Spring & Aug; Jun-Aug, Sun 2-5.
✱ *Admission fee payable.*
🅿 ⬤ & *toilets for disabled shop* ✖

Kirby Hall — DEENE

Map 04 SP99
(1.5m W)
☎ Corby (0536) 203230
The hall is a splendid Elizabethan mansion with some later alterations, perhaps by Inigo Jones. The gardens were famous in the 17th century, and have been restored to the original plan with roses and yews. There are also lawns, borders, shrubs and trees.
Open all year, Apr-Sep, daily 10-6; Oct-Mar, Tue-Sun 10-4. (Closed 24-26 Dec & 1 Jan).
£1.10 (ch 55p, pen, students & UB40 85p).
🅿 &
(EH)

Holdenby House Gardens — HOLDENBY

Map 04 SP66
(off A50 or A428)
☎ Northampton (0604) 770074
The gardens have been restored in the style of Elizabethan times (when this was the largest house in England), and have fragrant and silver borders. Also here are a museum, rare breeds of farm animals and a falconry centre. There is a children's farm and craft shop. Special events are planned for May; on Easter Sunday and Monday there will be an Easter Egg Hunt, and in September a Falconry Fair will be held.
Open Etr-Sep, BH & Sun 2-6; Jul & Aug, Thu 2-6. Parties 20+ by appointment Mon-Fri. Falconry Centre open Mon-Sat noon-5.
Gardens £2.50 (ch £1.20, pen £1.70). House & Gardens £3.50 (ch £1.20).
🅿 ⬤ & *(gravel paths) toilets for disabled shop garden centre* ✖

This is just one of many guidebooks published by the AA. The full range is available at any AA shop or good bookshop.

Alfred East Gallery — KETTERING

Map 04 SP87
Sheep St
☎ (0536) 410333
National, regional and local art, craft and photography are all displayed in around 20 exhibitions held each year at this well-run gallery. A collection of paintings by Sir Alfred East RA and Thomas Cooper Gotch on view by appointment, when not on display.
Open all year, Mon-Sat 9.30-5. (Closed BHs).
Free.
& ✖

Every effort is made to provide accurate information, but details might change during the currency of this guide.

Lyveden New Bield — LYVEDEN NEW BIELD

Map 04 SP98
☎ Benefield (08325) 358
The 'New Bield', or 'new building', is an unfinished shell of around 1600. It was designed by Sir Thomas Thresham to symbolise the Passion. The shape is a Greek cross, on which a frieze shows the cross, crown of thorns and other 'emblems of the Passion'. Even the building's dimensions are symbolic.
Open daily. Party by arrangement with the custodian.
£1 (ch 50p).
🚳
(NT)

Rockingham Castle — ROCKINGHAM

Map 04 SP89
(on A6003)
☎ (0536) 770240
Set on a hill overlooking three counties, Rockingham Castle was built on the instructions of William the Conqueror. The site of the original keep is now a rose garden, but the moat remains as do the foundations of the Norman Hall, and the twin towers of the gatehouse. The castle was a royal residence for 500 years. Then, in the late 16th century Henry VIII granted it to Edward Watson, and the Watson family have lived in it ever since.

The current building is basically Elizabethan, but every century since the 11th has had an influence somewhere, whether in architecture, furniture or works of art. James I was entertained here in 1603 and Charles Dickens, also a visitor, dedicated *David Copperfield* to the owners.
Open Etr Sun-Sep, Thu, Sun, BH Mon & following Tue (also Tue in Aug) 1.30-5.30.
£3.30 (ch £2 & pen £2.70). Gardens only £2.
Ⓟ ⬤ ⚇ *shop*

Triangular Lodge — RUSHTON

Map 04 SP88
☎ (0536) 710761
The curious construction of this lodge, built by Sir Thomas Tresham between 1593 and 1596, represents the Holy Trinity and the Mass. There are three walls, with three windows, and three

gables to each, on three storeys, topped by a three sided chimney.
Open Apr-Sep, daily 10-6.
£1.10 (ch 55p, students, pen & UB40 85p).
⚇ ✹
(EH)

Canal Museum — STOKE BRUERNE

Map 04 SP74
(4m S junc 15 M1)
☎ Northampton (0604) 862229
The three storeys of a former corn mill have been converted to hold a marvellous collection of bygones from over two centuries of the canals. The museum is near a flight of locks on the Grand Union Canal. Among the hundreds of exhibits is the reconstructed interior of a traditional narrow boat, complete with furniture, crockery,

brasssware and traditional art. There are genuine working narrowboats on show and the opportunity for a boat trip through the mile-long Blisworth Tunnel nearby. On 27-28 June there will be a national exhibition by waterways artists in a marquee by the canal, 11am-9pm, admission free.
Open Nov-Etr, Tue-Sun 10-4; Etr-Oct daily 10-6. (Closed Xmas).
£1.90 (ch & pen £1.20). Family ticket £5.
Ⓟ ⚇ *toilets for disabled shop* ✹

Sulgrave Manor — SULGRAVE

Map 04 SP54
Manor Rd
☎ (029576) 205
Sulgrave Manor was bought in 1539 by Lawrence Washington, wool merchant and twice Mayor of Northampton. It was here that George Washington's ancestors lived until 1656 when his great grandfather, John, emigrated to Virginia. The house that exists today is somewhat different from the one Lawrence Washington bought. His was larger, and much of the present house is a 20th-century restoration. Original parts include the porch, a screens passage, the great hall and the great Chamber. Over

the porch is carved the original of the American flag, with three stars and two stripes plus Elizabeth I's arms. Inside there are many relics of George Washington, such as his velvet coat, a lock of hair, documents and portraits. Special events take place throughout the year.
Open all year (ex Jan), daily (ex Wed) 10.30-1 & 2-5.30 (4pm Oct-Mar). Also open Feb for pre-booked parties only. (Closed 21 Jul).
£2.50 (ch £1.25). Party 12 +. Special event days £3.50 (ch £1.75).
Ⓟ ⬤ ⚇ *shop garden centre* ✹ *(ex in gardens)*

Old Dairy Farm Craft Centre — WEEDON BEC

Map 04 SP65
Upper Stowe (2m S of Weedon off A5)
☎ Weedon (0327) 40525
There are sheep, pigs, peacocks, ducks and donkeys. Features include a British wool collection, live sheep exhibits, craft workshop, gifts, Liberty materials,

antiques and farm shop. The Barn Restaurant serves homemade food.
Open all year, daily 10-5.30. (Closed 25 & 26 Dec).
Ⓟ ⬤ ✕ ⚇ *toilets for disabled shop* ✹
Details not confirmed for 1992

NORTHUMBERLAND

Alnwick Castle — ALNWICK

Map 11 NU11
☎ (0665) 510777

The old border town of Alnwick is dominated by this grey fortress, which is sometimes called the 'Windsor of the North'. It dates back to the 11th

century, became the property of the Percy family in 1309, and is still in Percy hands. It overlooks the River Aln, and has stone soldiers perched on the battlements to frighten enemies. The castle was restored by Salvin in the 19th century and decorated in classical style. The keep, armoury, museums and main apartments can be visited. and there are numerous treasures to be seen including paintings by Titian, Van Dyck and Canaletto. The castle also has a famous collection of Meissen china.
Opening dates, please telephone for details.
✱ *£2.50 (ch 16 £1 & pen £2). Party.*
Ⓟ *shop* ✹

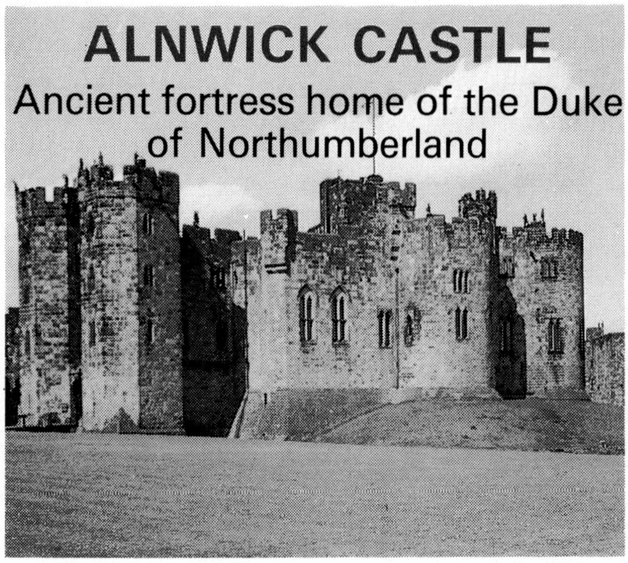

Bamburgh Castle — BAMBURGH

Map 11 NU13
☎ (06684) 208 & 515
Rising up dramatically on a rocky outcrop, Bamburgh Castle is a huge, square Norman castle. It was restored in the 19th century by Lord Armstrong, and has an impressive hall, an armoury with a large collection of armour from

HM Tower of London. Guide services are available.
Open daily, Apr-last Sun Oct; Jul & Aug from noon; Apr-Jun & Sep-Oct from 1pm.
✻ *£2.20 (ch £1, pen £1.80). Party.*
P *(charged)* ✆ ✿ *shop* ✖

See advertisement on page 131.

Grace Darling Museum — BAMBURGH

Map 11 NU13
Radcliffe Rd
☎ Seahouses (0665) 720037
Pictures, documents and other reminders of the heroine are on display, including the boat in which Grace Darling and her father, keeper of Longstone Lighthouse,

Farne Islands, rescued nine survivors from the wrecked 'SS Forfarshire' in 1838.
Open Etr-Sep, daily 11-6.
Free. Donations to R.N.L.I.
✿ *shop* ✖

Vindolanda (Chesterholm) — BARDON MILL

Map 11 NY76
Vindolanda Trust
☎ (0434) 344277
Vindolanda was a Roman fort and frontier town, with remains dating back to the 3rd and 4th centuries. It was started well before Hadrian's Wall, and became a base for 500 soldiers. The headquarters building is well preserved, and a special feature is a full-scale reconstruction of Hadrian's turf and stone wall, complete with turret and gate tower. The civilian settlement lay just west of the fort, and has been

excavated. A vivid idea of life for both civilians and soldiers can be gained at the excellent museum in the country house of Chesterholm nearby. It has displays and reconstructions, and its exhibits include homely finds such as sandals, shoes and a soldier's sewing kit. There are also formal gardens. Excavation will be in progress during the summer months.
Open daily from 10 am. (Closed Jan & Dec).
£2 (ch £1, student & pen £1.50).
P ✆ ✿ *toilets for disabled shop* ✖

Belsay Hall, Castle and Gardens — BELSAY

Map 11 NZ07
(on A696)
☎ (0661) 881636
Belsay Castle, with its splendid turrets and battlements, dates from 1370 and was home for generations of the Middleton family, until they built the Jacobean manor house beside it, and then the magnificent Grecian-style Hall.

Aside from the facinating buildings, Belsay has wonderful gardens and an excellent site exhibition.
Open all year, daily Apr-Sep 10-6; Oct-Mar 10-4. (Closed 24-26 Dec & 1 Jan).
P ✿ *toilets for disabled shop*
(EH)
Details not confirmed for 1992

Berwick Barracks — BERWICK-UPON-TWEED

Map 11 NT95
☎ (0289) 304493
These are Britain's oldest purpose-built barracks, constructed in the early 1700s because people objected to soldiers being billeted in public houses. The design has been attributed to Vanbrugh. The barracks now house the Museum of the King's Own Scottish Borderers, and the

Museum and Art Gallery.
Open all year, Apr-Sep, daily 10-6; Oct-Mar, Tue-Sun 10-4. (Closed 24-26 Dec & 1 Jan).
£1.80 (ch 90p, pen, students & UB40 £1.40).
P *shop* ✖
(EH)

Museum & Art Gallery — BERWICK-UPON-TWEED

Map 11 NT95
Berwick Barracks, Ravensdowne
☎ (0289) 330933
The museum is housed in the handsome barracks and has displays of local history, archaeology, fine art and decorative art, including an important collection donated by Sir William Burrell. Temporary exhibitions are held.
Open all year. Winter, Tue-Sat 10-12.30

✿ *1.30-4, Sun 10-1 & 2-4 (Closed Mon). Summer, Mon-Sat 10-12.30 & 1.30-6, Sun 10-1 & 2-6.*
✻ *£1.60 (ch 80p, pen & students £1.05). Party 11+. Admission includes entry to Museum of the King's Own Scottish Borderers & English Heritage exhibition 'By Beat of Drum'.*
✿ *toilets for disabled shop* ✖

Museum of The King's Own Scottish Borderers — BERWICK-UPON-TWEED

Map 11 NT95
The Barracks
☎ (0289) 307426
Designed by Vanbrugh in 1717, these are said to be the oldest barracks in Britain.

Open all year, Mon-Fri 9-4.30, Sat 9-noon. (Closed BH's).
£1.60 (ch & pen 80p). Includes admission to Town Museum and Heritage exhibition. shop ✖

Wallington House Garden & Grounds — CAMBO

Map 11 NZ08
(1m S on B6342)
☎ Scots Gap (067074) 283
Dating from the 17th and 18th centuries, the house is set in a great moorland estate of over 12,000 acres. It is famed for its delicate plasterwork, including fine porcelain work and rare British pieces. There are also displays of

dolls' houses and model soldiers, and the kitchen is filled with Victorian equipment. In the 19th century Ruskin and other writers and artists came here as guests of Sir William and Lady Trevelyan, who were renowned for their eccentricity and charm. One of the artists, William Bell Scott, painted the
continued ...

---

dramatic murals in the Central Hall. The gardens were partly laid out by 'Capability' Brown, and include formal and woodland areas, and a conservatory with magnificent fuchsias. A special event for 1992 is 'Shakespeare on the west lawn' between 23-27 June.
Open: House Apr-Oct, daily (ex Tue)

1-5.30; Last admission 5pm. Walled garden Apr-Sep, daily 10.30-7; Oct-Mar, daily 10.30-4.30. Grounds open all year. House, walled garden & grounds £3.80. Walled gardens & grounds only £1.80. Party.
P ✖ ✿ *toilets for disabled shop* ✖
(NT)

Roman Wall (Mithraic Temple) — CARRAWBROUGH

Map 11 NY87
(on B6318)
A farmer found the Mithraic Temple in 1949. It was excavated to reveal three altars to Mithras which date from the third century AD. They are now in the Museum of Antiquities in Newcastle,

but there are copies on the site. The temple is on the line of the Roman wall near the fort of Brocolitia.
Open any reasonable time.
Free.
P
(EH)

Chillingham Castle — CHILLINGHAM

Map 11 NU02
☎ Chatton (06685) 359 & 390
After a period of neglect, the castle has been brought back to life by a new owner. It dates back to the 12th century, and has a great hall and state rooms where antique furniture, tapestries, arms and armour are

displayed. There are formal gardens, woodland walks and a lake. A BASC country fair will take place on 10 May.
Open Etr wknd & May-Sep, daily (ex Tue) 1.30-5. (Last admission 4.30).
£2.50 (ch £1.80, ch under 5 Free, pen £2). Party 20+.
P ✆ *shop* ✖

Chillingham Wild Cattle Park — CHILLINGHAM

Map 11 NU02
(off B6348)
☎ Chatton (06685) 250
The park at Chillingham boasts an extraordinary survival: a herd of wild white cattle descended from animals trapped in the park when the wall was built in the 13th century; they are the sole surviving pure-bred examples of

their breed in the world. Binoculars are recommended for a close view. As the cattle are aggressive and should not be approached, visits are made with a warden.
Open Apr-Oct, daily 10-12 & 2-5, Sun 2-5. Closed Tue.
P
Details not confirmed for 1992

Corbridge Roman Site — CORBRIDGE

Map 11 NY96
☎ (0434) 632349
The remains of a Roman 'Corstopitum', built around AD210, include granaries, portico columns and the probable site of legionary headquarters. Finds from excavations of the site are displayed in a museum on the site.

Open all year, Apr-Sep, daily 10-6; Oct-Mar, Tue-Sun 10-4. (Closed 24-26 Dec & 1 Jan).
£1.80 (ch 90p, pen, students & UB40 £1.40).
P ✿ ✖
(EH)

Dunstanburgh Castle — EMBLETON

Map 11 NU22
(1.5m E)
☎ (0665) 576231
The skeletal ruins of the huge castle stand on cliffs 100ft above the North Sea. It was partly built by John of Gaunt, but was in ruins by Tudor times.

Its setting has made it a favourite with artists, and Turner painted it three times.
Open all year, Apr-Sep, daily 10-6; Oct-Mar, Tue-Sun 10-4. (Closed 24-26 Dec & 1 Jan).
£1.10 (ch 55p, students, pen & UB40 85p).
(EH)

Heatherslaw Corn Mill — FORD

Map 11 NT93
(signposted from A697)
☎ Crookham (089082) 338
This is a splendid example of a 19th-century water-driven double corn mill which is in daily use (water level permitting). Exhibitions and demonstrations are held; all processes are

visible to the visitor, from the huge water wheel to the finished flour.
Open Etr-Oct, daily 10-6. Winter by arrangement.
£1.50 (ch & pen 75p). Family ticket £4.
P ✿ *(Braille guide) toilets for disabled shop* ✖

Lady Waterford Hall — FORD

Map 11 NT93
(signposted from A697, N of Wooler)
☎ Crookham (089082) 224
The hall was built as the village school in 1862 by Louisa, Marchioness of Waterford. Its great attraction is the series of murals that she painted here, using local children and their parents as

models for Biblical scenes. She was a friend of John Ruskin who was not impressed by the work; today's visitors usually disagree with him however.
Open Etr-Oct, daily 10.30-12.30 & 1.30-5.30. Open by appointment in winter.
£1 (ch & pen 50p).
P ✿ *shop*

Birdoswald Roman Fort — GILSLAND

Map 11 NY66
(.25m S in Cumbria)
☎ (06977) 47602
This unique section of Hadrian's Wall enjoys a most picturesque setting overlooking the Irthing Gorge. There is no other point along the Wall where all the components of the Roman frontier system can be found together. But Birdoswald isn't just about the Romans,

it's also about border raids in the Middle Ages, about the Victorians, and about recent archaeological discoveries. A new Visitor Centre brings its fascinating history to life.
Open Apr-1 Nov, daily 10-5.30. Winter opening by prior arrangement only.
£1.50 (ch 75p, concessions £1).
P ✿ *toilets for disabled shop*

Lindisfarne Castle   HOLY ISLAND (LINDISFARNE)

Map 11 NU14
☎ Berwick (0289) 89244
The 16th-century castle was restored by Sir Edwin Lutyens in 1903 for the owner of *Country Life* magazine. The austere outside walls belie the Edwardian comfort within, and there is a little garden designed by Gertrude Jekyll. *Open Apr-Sep, daily*

(closed Fri ex Good Fri) 1-5.30; Oct Wed, Sat & Sun only 1-5.30. Last admission 5pm. Island not accessible two hours before & four hours after high tide. Other times by arrangement with Administrator.
£3.
✄
(NT)

Lindisfarne Priory   HOLY ISLAND (LINDISFARNE)

Map 11 NU14
☎ Berwick (0289) 89200
St Aidan and monks from Iona founded a monastery here in the 7th century and from it spread Christianity to much of Northern England. They also produced the beautifully illuminated Lindisfarne Gospels (now in the British Museum), but abandoned the monastery because of Viking raids in the 9th century. The beautiful priory ruins on Lindisfarne today date from the 11th century, and the history of life at the Priory is told in

the adjacent visitor centre. The island is reached by a causeway at low tide: tide tables are posted at each end of the causeway, or telephone the custodian on the above number.
Open all year, Apr-Sep, daily 10-6; Oct-Mar, Tue-Sun 10-4. Subject to tides. (Closed 24-26 Dec & 1 Jan).
£1.80 (ch 90p, students, pen & UB40 £1.40)
🅿 *shop* ✄
(EH)

Roman Wall (Housesteads Fort & Museum)   HOUSESTEADS

Map 11 NY76
Nr Bardon Mills
☎ Bardon Mill (0434) 344363

Vercovicium It has a spectacular site on Hadrian's Wall, and is also one of the best preserved Roman forts. It covers five acres, including the only known Roman hospital in Britain, and a 24-seater latrine with a flushing tank. There is also a museum.
Open all year, Good Fri-Sep, daily 10-6; Oct-Maundy Thu, daily 10-4. (Closed 24-26 Dec & 1 Jan).
✳ *£1.60 (ch 16 80p, students, pen & UB40s £1.20). Party reductions in winter.*
shop ✄
(EH & NT)

Housesteads was the Roman fort of

Brinkburn Priory   LONGFRAMLINGTON

Map 11 NU10
(off B6344)
☎ (0665) 570628
The priory was founded in 1135 for the canons of the Augustinian order, and stands on a bend of the river Coquet. After the Dissolution of Monasteries it fell into disrepair, but was restored in

1858; remaining medieval fittings include the font, double piscina and some grave slabs.
Open Apr-Sep, daily 10-6.
£1.10 (ch 55p, students, pen & UB40 85p)
🅿 ✄
(EH)

Castle   NORHAM

Map 11 NT94
☎ (0289) 382329
One of the strongest border fortresses, this castle has one of the finest Norman keeps in the country and overlooks the River Tweed.
Open all year, Apr-Sep, daily 10-6; Oct-

Mar, Tue-Sun 10-4. (Closed 24-26 Dec & 1 Jan).
£1.10 (ch 55p, students, pen & UB40 85p).
🅿 ✅ ✄
(EH)

Prudhoe Castle   PRUDHOE

Map 11 NZ06
☎ (0661) 33459
Standing on the River Tyne, this 12th- to 14th-century castle was the stronghold of the d'Umfravelles and Percys. The keep stands in the inner bailey and a notable gatehouse guards the outer bailey. Access is to the Pele

Yard only.
Open all year, Apr-Sep, daily 10-6; Oct-Mar, Tue-Sun 10-4. (Closed 24-26 Dec & 1 Jan).
£1.50 (ch 75p, pen, students & UB40 £1.10).
🅿 *shop* ✄
(EH)

Cragside House, Country Park & Garden   ROTHBURY

Map 11 NU00
(Entrance for cars 2m N on B6341)
☎ (0669) 20333

This splendid Victorian masterpiece was built for Sir William (later the first Lord) Armstrong in stages, between 1864 and

1895. It was designed for him by the architect Richard Norman Shaw and the interior of the house reflects the taste and style of both its architect and its owner. The drawing room is huge, with a curved glass roof and 10-ton marble-lined inglenook designed to soak up the heat of the peat fires. This was the first house in the world to be lit by electricity generated by water-power. The grounds, now 900 acres of country park, were transformed by Lord Armstrong. He planted seven million trees, diverted streams and created lakes, a waterfall, terraces, winding paths, gardens and orchards. Open in 1992:
continued . . .

formal garden including greenhouses, Italian terraces and rose loggia.
Open all year, Country Park & garden: daily, 10.30-7; Nov & Dec, Tue & wknds 10.30-4. House: Apr-Oct, daily (ex Mon, Open BH Mon's) 1-5.30. Last admission 5pm. Armstrong Energy Centre open Apr-Oct daily, 10.30-5.30; Nov & Dec, Tues

& wknds, 10.30-4;
House, Country Park, Garden & Energy Centre £5.20. Country Park, Garden & Energy Centre only £3.20. Party.
🅿 ▾ ✗ *licensed* ✅ *toilets for disabled shop*
✄
(NT)

Chesters Roman Fort & Museum   WALWICK

Map 11 NY97
(.5m E)
☎ Humshaugh (0434) 681379
One of the Roman forts on Hadrian's Wall is now in the park of Chesters, an 18th-century mansion. The fort named *Cilurnum* housed 500 soldiers and covered nearly 6 acres. The excavations were started in the 19th century by the owner of Chesters, and have revealed a great deal about life in a Roman fort. A large wall and six gatehouses were built to defend the fort, but evidence revealed that it was destroyed and rebuilt three times. The standard of living

appears to have been high: water was brought in by aqueduct, the commandant had underfloor heating in his house, and the soldiers' bath house had hot, cold, dry or steam baths, and latrines. The remains of the bath house are very substantial. There is a museum exhibiting artefacts from the site.
Open all year, Apr-Sep, daily 10-6; Oct-Mar, daily 10-4. (Closed 24-26 Dec & 1 Jan).
£1.80 (ch 90p, pen, students & UB40 £1.40).
🅿 ✅ *shop* ✄
(EH)

For an explanation of the symbols and abbreviations, see page 2.

Warkworth Castle   WARKWORTH

Map 11 NU20
☎ (0665) 711423
The castle is situated on a steep bank of the River Coquet, and dominates the town of Warkworth. It is a splendid ruin with its restored 15th-century keep and early 13th-century curtain wall. Near the castle is the 14th-century bridge over the river, with a rare bridge

tower. This can now only be used by pedestrians.
Open all year, Apr-Sep, daily 10-6; Oct-Mar, Tue-Sun 10-4. (Closed 24-26 Dec & 1 Jan).
£1.10 (ch 55p, pen, students & UB40 85p).
🅿 ✅ ✄
(EH)

Warkworth Hermitage   WARKWORTH

Map 11 NU20
Upstream from Warkworth Castle is the Hermitage, a refuge dug into the steep rockface of the riverbank by a 14th-century hermit. It consists of a chapel and two chambers to live in. The hermitage was occupied until the 16th

century. Nearby is Coquet island, which was also the home of hermit monks.
Open Apr-Sep, wknds only 10-6.
Free.
🅿 ✅ ✄
(EH)

NOTTINGHAMSHIRE

The D H Lawrence Birthplace Museum   EASTWOOD

Map 08 SK44
8A Victoria St
☎ Langley Mill (0773) 763312
D H Lawrence was born here on 11 September 1885, and the town and its surroundings influenced his writing throughout his life. The carefully restored house offers an insight into the author's early childhood and is also a

good example of a Victorian working class home. Audio-visual presentations are held.
Open all year, Apr-Oct, daily 10-5; Nov-Mar, daily 10-4. (Closed 24 Dec-1 Jan). Evenings by arrangement only.
shop ✄
Details not confirmed for 1992

White Post Modern Farm Centre — FARNSFIELD

Map 08 SK65
(1m W)
☎ Mansfield (0623) 882977 & 882026
This working farm gives an introduction to a variety of modern farming methods. It explains how farms work, with exhibits such as llamas, deer, pigs, cows, snails, quails, snakes and fish, through to 20 arable crop plots. A kennel is provided for dogs. There is also lots to see indoors including the owl houses, incubator room, mousetown and a

reptile house. Barn dances and wildlife and craft weekends will take place during the year (tel. for details).
Open all year, Mon-Fri 10-5. Wknds & BH's 10-6.
£1.95 (ch 4-16 £1.20, under 4 free, pen & people with special needs £1.50). Party 10+.
🅿 ☕ & *toilets for disabled shop* ✘ *(kennels available)*

See advertisement on page 133.

Museum & Art Gallery — MANSFIELD

Map 08 SK55
Leeming St
☎ (0623) 663088
'Images of Mansfield, past and present' uses objects and photographs to illustrate the history of the town. The museum has an important display of William Billingsley porcelain and the attractive

Buxton watercolours show the town at the turn of the century. The museum also presents a wide range of temporary exhibitions.
Open all year, Mon-Sat 10-5. (Closed Sun). Free.
& *shop* ✘

✱ An asterisk indicates that up-to-date information was not available at the time of our research – 1991 information has been published as an indication of what you may expect.

Millgate Museum of Social & Folk Life — NEWARK-ON-TRENT

Map 08 SK75
48 Millgate
☎ Newark (0636) 79403
By reconstructions of shop fronts and street areas from Victorian times to the 1950s, this enterprising museum illustrates the working and home life of local people through the years. A variety

of art and craft exhibitions is planned throughout the year.
Open all year, Mon-Fri 10-5, also Etr-Xmas, Sat & Sun 1-5. BH's 1-5. Last admission 4.30pm.
Free.
& *shop* ✘

Newark Air Museum — NEWARK-ON-TRENT

Map 08 SK75
The Airfield, Winthorpe
☎ Newark (0636) 707170
A diverse collection of transport, training and reconnaisance aircraft, jet fighters, bombers and helicopters, now numbering more than forty. A new Undercover Aircraft Display Hall (fifteen exhibits) and an Engine Display are now

open, making the museum an all-weather attraction.
Open all year, Apr-Oct, Mon-Fri 10-5, Sat & Sun 10-6; Nov-Mar, Mon-Fri 10-4.30, Sat & Sun 10-dusk. Closed 24, 25 & 26 Dec. Other times by appointment.
£2.50 (ch & pen £1.50). Party 10+.
🅿 & *toilets for disabled shop*

Newark Museum — NEWARK-ON-TRENT

Map 08 SK75
Appletongate
☎ Newark (0636) 702358
The museum displays the archaelogy and local history of the area. There is some natural history too. Visitors can see an exhibition of 17th-century Civil War items (to coincide with the 350th

anniversary of the Civil War) and a collection of militaria of the Sherwood Foresters.
Open all year Mon-Wed & Fri 10-1 & 2-5, Sat 10-1 & 2-5; Apr-Sep also Sun 2-5. BH's 2-5.
Free.
& *shop* ✘

Vina Cooke Museum of Dolls & Bygone Childhood — NEWARK-ON-TRENT

Map 08 SK75
The Old Rectory, Cromwell (5m N of Newark off A1)
☎ (0636) 821364
All kinds of childhood memorabilia are displayed in this 17th-century house: prams, toys, dolls' houses, costumes and a large collection of Victorian and Edwardian dolls including Vina Cooke

hand-made character dolls. There will be an Easter Monday extravaganza from 11am to dusk including Morris dancing, puppet shows etc.
Open all year, daily 10-noon & 2-5, appointment advisable. Also open evenings for booked parties.
£1 (ch 50p).
🅿 ☕ & *shop* ✘

Newstead Abbey — NEWSTEAD

Map 08 SK55
☎ Mansfield (0623) 793557
This beautiful historic house, set in extensive parklands, is best known as the home of the poet, Lord Byron, who made the house and its ghostly legends famous. Visitors can see Byron's own rooms, mementoes of the poet and other splendidly decorated rooms which date from medieval to Victorian times. The grounds of over 300 acres include waterfalls, ponds, water gardens and

Japanese gardens. Outdoor entertainment – jazz, classical, opera and popular music – is planned for the second and third weeks of July.
Open: Grounds all year, daily (ex last Fri in Nov); House Apr-Sep, daily 12-6. Last admission 5pm
✱ *House & Grounds £3 (concessions £1.40). Grounds only £1.35 (concessions 65p).*
🅿 ✗ *licensed* & *toilets for disabled shop*

Brewhouse Yard Museum — NOTTINGHAM

Map 08 SK53
Castle Boulevard
☎ (0602) 483504 ext 3602 or 3600
Housed in 17th-century buildings on a two acre site with unusual local plants, the museum depicts everyday life in Nottingham in post-medieval times. Rock-cut cellars show their past uses and

there are thematic displays. Many items may be operated by the public, and temporary exhibitions are changed regularly.
Open all year 10-5. Last admission 4.45pm. (Closed Xmas).
& *toilets for disabled* ✘
Details not confirmed for 1992

Canal Museum — NOTTINGHAM

Map 08 SK53
Canal St
☎ (0602) 598835
The history of the River Trent from the Ice Age to the present day is told in the ground and first floors and wharf of this 19th-century warehouse. Life size dioramas, models and an audio-visual presentation add impact to the displays

which include local canal and river navigation, boats, bridges and archaeology.
Open all year, Apr-Sep, Wed-Sat 10-12 & 1-5.45, Sun 1-5.45; Oct-Mar, Wed, Thu & Sat 10-12 & 1-5, Sun 1-5.
Free.
& *(wheelchairs available) toilets for disabled shop* ✘

Castle Museum — NOTTINGHAM

Map 08 SK53
☎ (0602) 483504
This 17th-century building has a much restored 13th-century gateway. Now a museum and art gallery, its visitors are taken on conducted tours through underground passages. Various special events are held throughout the year, with major temporary exhibitions, both historical and contemporary. There is an

automated car in the grounds for the disabled. Between 2 Aug-20 Sep two civil war exhibitions are planned.
Open all year, Summer 10-5.45; Winter 10-4.45. Grounds Mon-Fri 8-dusk, Sat, Sun, BH Mon 9-dusk. (Closed 25 Dec).
✱ *40p (ch 20p) Sun & BH. Otherwise free.*
☕ & *(chair lift) toilets for disabled shop* ✘

✘ The 'No Dogs' symbol does not normally apply to guide dogs – these are permitted in most establishments.

Green's Mill & Science Centre — NOTTINGHAM

Map 08 SK53
Windmill Ln, Sneinton
☎ (0602) 503635
Restored to working order, this tower mill can be seen in use when conditions allow. The adjacent Science Centre tells the story of George Green, one-time

miller here and distinguished mathematician. Flour is on sale.
Open all year Wed-Sun, 10-5, also BH's. (Closed 25 Dec).
Free.
🅿 & *toilets for disabled shop* ✘

The Lace Hall — NOTTINGHAM

Map 08 SK53
High Pavement
☎ (0602) 484221

The invention and development of the world-famous Nottingham lace is explained at Lace Hall. Working machines, bobbin lace demonstrations, period settings and talking figures create a lively and educational entertainment, and there are coffee and exhibition shops.
Open all year, daily. Summer 10-5.30, Winter 10-5. Last admission 4.30. (Closed 25-26 Dec).
£1.95 (ch, pen & students £1).
☕ ✗ *licensed* & *toilets for disabled shop* ✘

Every effort is made to provide accurate information, but details might change during the currency of this guide.

Museum of Costume & Textiles — NOTTINGHAM

Map 08 SK53
43-51 Castle Gate
☎ (0602) 483504
Costume from 1730 to 1960 is displayed in appropriate room settings. Other rooms contain 17th-century costume and embroidery, dress accessories, the Lord Middleton

collection and map tapestries. Knitted, woven and printed textiles are also on show, together with embroidery from Europe and Asia.
Open all year, daily 10-5. (Closed 25 Dec).
& *shop* ✘
Details not confirmed for 1992

Natural History Museum — NOTTINGHAM

Map 08 SK53
Wollaton Hall, Wollaton
☎ (0602) 281333 & 281130
Standing in a large deer park, this imposing Elizabethan mansion by Robert Smythson dates back to 1580. A wide variety of displays include birds, mammals, fossils and minerals.

Open all year, Apr-Sep, Mon-Sat 10-7, Sun 2-5; Oct, Mon-Sat 10-5.30, Sun 1.30-4.30; Nov-Mar, Mon-Sat 10-4.30, Sun 1.30-4.30.
✱ *Free, Mon-Sat 50p (ch 20p) Sun & BH. Ticket includes Industrial Museum.*
🅿 & *toilets for disabled shop* ✘

Nottingham Industrial Museum

NOTTINGHAM

Map 08 SK53
Courtyard Buildings, Wollaton Park
(3m W off A609 Ilkeston Rd)
☎ (0602) 284602
Housed in the 18th-century stable block,
displays illustrate Nottingham's
industrial history, in particular those of
lace and hosiery. Exhibits on the
pharmaceutical industry, engineering,
printing and the tobacco industry are
also here. A beam (pumping) engine and
heavy agricultural machinery are housed
in a new extension. Victorian street
furniture is displayed in a yard outside,
along with a horse gin from a local
coalmine.
*Open all year, Apr-Sep, Mon-Sat 10-6,
Sun 2-6; Oct-Mar, Thu & Sat 10-4.30,
Sun 1.30-4.30. 19th-century beam pump
engine in steam last Sun in each month &
BH.*
✻ *Free, Mon-Sat 50p (ch 20p) Sun &
BH. Ticket includes Natural History
Museum Wollaton Hall.*
🅿 ৬ *(hand & powered wheelchairs
available) toilets for disabled shop* ✕

The Tales of Robin Hood

NOTTINGHAM

Map 08 SK53
Maid Marian Way
☎ (0602) 483284
A marvel of special effects transporting
the visitor to medieval Nottingham and
the magical glades of the greenwood in
search of Robin Hood. Travelling in the
unique adventure cars the experience
happens below, around and above you
as the commentary is piped into each car
by portable compact disc players.
*Open all year, daily 10-5.
£3.95 (ch £2.50). Family ticket £9.95.*
🍴 ৬ *(chairlift) toilets for disabled shop* ✕

Sundown Kiddies Adventureland

RAMPTON

Map 08 SK77
(Sundown Pets Garden), Treswell Rd
(3m off A57 at Dunham crossroads)
☎ (077784) 274 due to change to 8274
Created specially with young children in
mind, the attractions include animated
nursery rhymes. Noah's Ark play area,
Westown Street with 'Crazy Critters'
Show. Large forts with climbing frames
etc., Smugglers' Cove, a Fantasy Castle
guarded by a watchful dragon, a Tudor
Street with secret passages and a
miniature farm with live animals are just
some of the goodies to delight
youngsters, including the recently
opened indoor play jungle.
*Open all year, daily 10-6, earlier in winter.
(Closed 25-26 Dec).
£2.75 (ch under 2 free).*
🅿 🍴 ৬ *toilets for disabled shop* ✕

Wetlands Waterfowl Reserve & Exotic Bird Park

SUTTON-CUM-LOUND

Map 08 SK68
Off Loundlow Rd
☎ Retford (0777) 818099
The collection of waterfowl includes
ducks, geese, swans, and flamingos on
two lagoons covering some 32 acres, and
many wild birds live here. There are also
parrots, a variety of trees and plants, and
a children's farm.
*Open all year, daily 10-6 (or dusk
whichever is earlier). (Closed 25 Dec).
Guided tours available on weekdays,
bookings only.*
🅿 🍴 ৬ *(wheelchair available) shop* ✕
Details not confirmed for 1992

OXFORDSHIRE

Banbury Museum

BANBURY

Map 04 SP44
8 Horsefair
☎ (0295) 259855
This small museum displays
photography and other items connected
with local history and archaeology.
There is a changing programme of
temporary exhibitions, including one of
the Civil War and local artists' work.
Also on the site is a tourism information
centre.
*Open all year, Oct-Mar, Tue-Sat 10-4.30;
Apr-Sep, Mon-Sat 10-5.
Free.*
🍴 ৬ *toilets for disabled shop* ✕

This is just one of many guidebooks published by the AA.
The full range is available at any AA shop or good bookshop.

Broughton Castle

BROUGHTON

Map 04 SP43
(2m W on B4035)
☎ Banbury (0295) 262624 & 812027
Originally owned by William of
Wykeham, and later by the first Lord
Saye and Sele, the castle is an early
14th- and mid-16th-century house with
a moat and gatehouse. Period furniture,
paintings and Civil War relics are
displayed.
*Open Etr & 18 May-14 Sep, Wed & Sun
(also Thu in Jul & Aug) & BH Sun &
Mon 2-5.
£2.80 (ch £1.40, pen & students £2.10).
Party 20+.*
🅿 🍴 ৬ *shop*

Cotswold Wildlife Park

BURFORD

Map 04 SP21
(2m S off A40 & A361)
☎ (0993) 823006
The 180-acre landscaped zoological
park, surrounding a Gothic-style manor
house, has a varied collection of animals
from all over the world, with tropical
birds, a large reptile collection, aquarium
and insect house. Other attractions
include an adventure playground, animal
brass-rubbing centre in the manor house
and train rides during the summer
months. Also during the summer there
are Snake Days, car rallies, Morris
dancers and falconry displays – dates on
application.
*Open all year, daily (ex Xmas Day) 10-6
or dusk if earlier.
£3.80 (ch 4 & pen £2.20). Party 20+*
🅿 🍴 ✕ *licensed* ৬ *toilets for disabled shop*

Buscot Park

BUSCOT

Map 04 SU29
(off A417)
☎ (0367) 240786
Much of the character of this 18th-
century house is due to two relatively
recent owners, the 1st Lord Faringdon,
who bought the house in 1889, and his
son. They amassed most of the
furniture, porcelain and other contents,
as well as the many pictures forming the
Faringdon Collection. It includes work
by Reynolds, Gainsborough,
Rembrandt, Murillo, several of the Pre-
Raphaelites, and some 20th-century
artists. Most memorable is the 'Legend
of the Briar Rose', a deeply romantic
series by Burne-Jones which fills the
walls of the saloon.
The charming formal water gardens
were laid out by Harold Peto in the
early 20th century. There is also an
attractively planted kitchen garden, with
unusual concentric walls.
*Open Apr-Sep, Wed, Thu & Fri 2-6. Also
every 2nd & 4th Sat & immediately
following Sun in each month 2-6 (last
admission on to house 5.30pm). (Closed BH
Mon).
£3.50. Grounds only £2.50*
🅿 🍴 ✕
(NT)

Great Coxwell Barn

COXWELL, GREAT

Map 04 SU29
William Morris said that the barn was
'as noble as a cathedral'. It is a 13th-
century stone-built tithe barn, 152ft long
and 44ft wide, with a beautifully crafted
framework of timbers supporting the
lofty stone roof. The barn was built for
the Cistercians.
*Open all reasonable times.
50p
(NT)*

Deddington Castle

DEDDINGTON

Map 04 SP43
The large earthworks of the outer and
inner baileys can be seen; the remains of
12th-century castle buildings have been
excavated, but they are not now visible.
*Open any reasonable time.
Free.
(EH)*

Didcot Railway Centre

DIDCOT

Map 04 SU58
(on A4130 at Didcot Parkway Station)
☎ (0235) 817200
The biggest collection anywhere of
Great Western Railway stock is housed
in the GWR engine shed, including 20
steam locomotives, a diesel railcar, and a
large amount of passenger and freight
rolling stock. A typical GWR station has
been re-created and original track has
been relaid. Events for 1992 include
'steamings' during Easter (17-20 Apr),
Spring Holidays (23-25 May) and
Christmas (29 Nov-20 Dec), Steamdays
for Midsummer (20 Jun), and for the
continued . . .

disabled (5 Jul), a Teddy Bears' Picnic (12 Jul), an Autumn Gala (26-7 Sep), and a Photographers' Evening (31 Oct). *Open all year, 4 Apr-27 Sep, daily 11-5 dusk in winter. Steam days first & last Sun of each month from Mar, BH's, all Sun's*

Jun-Aug & Wed in Aug. £2.70-£4.50 depending on event (ch £1.90-£4.50, over 60's £2.20-£3.60) ♥ & *(advance notice recommended) toilets for disabled shop*

Greys Court
HENLEY-ON-THAMES

Map 04 SU78
Rotherfield Greys (3m W)
☎ Rotherfield Greys (04917) 29
This appealing house has evolved over hundreds of years. The present gabled building has a pre-medieval kitchen, but dates mainly from the 16th century. It stands in the courtyard of its medieval predecessor, facing the mid-14th-century Great Tower. Additions were made in the 18th century and there are some fine 18th-century decorations and furniture. The complex of gardens includes a white garden and a rose garden planted with

old-fashioned varieties, which leads into the walled area with ancient wisterias. Beyond this is the kitchen garden, and from here a bridge leads to a symbolic brick maze laid out in 1980. Also of great interest is the wheelhouse with its huge wheel, once turned by a donkey to bring water up from the well.
Open: House Apr-Sep, Mon, Wed & Fri 2-6. Garden Mon-Wed & Fri-Sat 2-6. Last admission 5.30. (Closed Good Fri) Garden £2.50. House & Garden £3.50.
🅿 ♥ &
(NT)

Wellplace Bird Farm
IPSDEN

Map 04 SU68
☎ Checkendon (0491) 680473
Tropical birds, lambs, goats, monkeys, donkeys, otters, ponies and llamas are just some of the hundred varieties of animals and birds who make their homes at Wellplace Bird Farm; a delightful

place for adults and children.
Open all year, Apr-Sep, daily 10-5, Sun 10-6; Oct-Apr, wknds weather permitting.
✳ *£2 (ch 50p)*
🅿 ♥ & *toilets for disabled shop garden centre* ✕

Pendon Museum of Miniature Landscape & Transport
LONG WITTENHAM

Map 04 SU59
☎ Clifton Hampden (086730) 7365
This charming exhibition shows a highly detailed model railway and miniature village scenes transporting the visitor back into a 1930s country landscape.

Skilled modellers can often be seen at work on the exhibits
Open Sat & Sun 2-5, each day of summer BH wknds 11-5 (Closed 14 Dec-9 Jan). £1.50 (ch 16 & pen £1, ch 6 free).
🅿 ♥ *shop* ✕

For an explanation of the symbols and abbreviations, see page 2.

Mapledurham House
MAPLEDURHAM

Map 04 SU67
☎ Kidmore End (0734) 723350
The small community at Mapledurham includes the house, a water mill and a church, and is reached by travelling down a 'no through road', or by boat from the Caversham Promenade at Reading. The boat runs only when the house is open to the public but can be chartered by groups. The fine Elizabethan mansion, surrounded by quiet parkland which runs down to the River Thames, was built by the Blount family in the 16th century. Inside are paintings and family portraits collected

over three centuries, great oak staircases and moulded Elizabethan ceilings. Outside, a public footpath leads through beautiful beech woods where many woodland birds can be seen. Craft fairs will be held here over the 3-day Easter weekend and on 12-13 September
Open Etr-Sep, Sat, Sun & BH's 2.30-5. Picnic area 12.30-7. Last admission 5. Group visits midweek by arrangement.
✳ *Picnic area, grounds, house & watermill: £4 (ch £2). Picnic area, grounds & house: £3 (ch £1.50). Picnic area, grounds & watermill £2.50 (ch £1.30).*
🅿 ♥ & *shop* ✕ *(ex country park area)*

Mapledurham Watermill
MAPLEDURHAM

Map 04 SU67
☎ Kidmore End (0734) 723350
The last mill on the Thames to use wooden machinery stands close to Mapledurham House (above). It has been restored to full working order and grinds local grain: flour can be purchased. The mill can also be reached by river launch from Caversham Promenade at 1.45pm each day the house is open (details from the estate office). Craft fairs will be held here over

the 3-day Easter weekend and on 12-13 September.
Open Etr-Sep, Sat, Sun & BHs 1-5 (Sun in winter 2-4). Picnic area 12.30-7. Last admission 5. Groups midweek by arrangement.
✳ *Picnic area, grounds, house & watermill: £4 (ch £2). Picnic area, grounds & house: £3 (ch £1.50). Picnic area, grounds & watermill: £2.50 (ch £1.30).*
🅿 ♥ & *shop* ✕ *(ex in country park)*

Milton Manor
MILTON

Map 04 SU49
(off A34, signposted)
☎ Abingdon (0235) 831287 or 831871
This elegant 17th-century manor house, traditionally thought to have been designed by Inigo Jones, was bought in 1752 by Bevant Barrett, a Roman Catholic. It was he who added the splendid Strawberry Hill Gothic library, the wings, the chapel (where mass is still celebrated), the stables, ornamental lakes and the very pretty walled garden. The house is still a home to his direct

descendents, who have added their own collections of teapots, fine china and *objets d'art*. Events for 1992 include an Authors' Book Fair in June, an MG car rally in July, the Milton Manor Show in August, and a Medieval craft fair in September.
Open Etr Sat-Sep, wknds & BH's 2-5.30. House & gardens £2.50 (ch14 £1.25). Gardens £1.20
🅿 ♥ & *shop garden centre* ✕ *(ex in garden)*

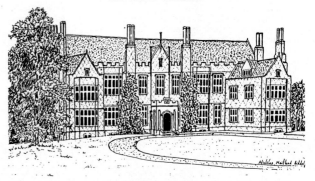
Minster Lovell Hall & Dovecot
MINSTER LOVELL

Map 04 SP31
☎ Witney (0993) 775315
Home of the ill-fated Lovell family, the ruins of the 15th-century house are steeped in history and legend. One of the main features of the estate is the medieval dovecote which has survived intact through the centuries. The village

of Minster Lovell is one of the prettiest in this outstanding area.
Open all year, Apr-Sep, daily 10-6; Oct-Mar, Tue-Sun 10-4. (Closed 24-26 Dec & 1 Jan). 95p (ch 50p, student, pen & UB40 70p). & *(ex Dovecot)* ✕
(EH)

North Leigh Roman Villa
NORTH LEIGH

Map 04 SP31
Excavations have found this villa to have been occupied between the second and fourth centuries and reconstructed later in the period. A tessellated pavement and a 2-3 feet high wall span, are on

show.
Open Apr-Sep, daily 10-6. Free.
✕
(EH)

OXFORD

Map 04 SP50
This ancient and picturesque University city dating back to the 8th century sits comfortably on the rivers Cherwell and Thames. The University, the oldest in Britain, probably dates from the 12th century and consists of a large number of colleges built over a period of several centuries, many of which are among the finest buildings of their age. Access to some colleges is restricted to certain times and details may be obtained from the Oxford Information Centre, St Aldgate's.

Ashmolean Museum of Art & Archaeology
OXFORD

Map 04 SP50
Beaumont St
☎ (0865) 278000

First opened in 1683 and the oldest museum in the country, the Ashmolean Museum was re-housed in C R Cockerell's building of 1845. Archaeological exhibits from Britain, Europe, the Mediterranean, Egypt and the Near East are on show and the Herbeden Coin Room contains coins and medals from all countries and periods. Italian, Dutch, Flemish, French and English oil paintings adorn the walls along with Old Masters and modern drawings, watercolours, prints and
continued . . .

miniatures. Chinese and Japanese porcelain, paintings and laquer-work are gathered here as well as European ceramics, Tibetan art, Indian sculpture and paintings, metalwork, and pottery from Islam and Chinese bronzes. Temporary exhibitions are held throughout the year, including The Art of Laughter (Feb-May), the Maxwell Webb Collection (May-Aug), and Indian Paintings from the Howard Hodgkin Collection (Oct-Dec).
Open all year, Tue-Sat 10-4, Sun 2-4. (Closed Etr & during St.Giles Fair in early Sep, Xmas & 1 Jan).
* *Free. Guided tours by arrangement.*
♿ *shop*

Carfax Tower — OXFORD

Map 04 SP50
☎ (0865) 792653
Excellent views of the city are to be seen from the top of this 14th-century west tower which is all that remains of St. Martin's Church. There is an historic display area on the first floor and an extensive souvenir stall on the ground floor. Bellringings are organised by the Oxford Bell Ringers Society, to celebrate special events.
Open end Mar-Oct, Mon-Sat 10-6, Sunday 2-6 (last entry 5.30)
80p (ch & pen 40p)
shop

Museum of Oxford — OXFORD

Map 04 SP50
St Aldate's
☎ (0865) 815559
Permanent displays depict the archaeology and history of the city from earliest times to the present day. There are temporary exhibitions and facilities for school parties and groups.
Open all year, Tue-Sat 10-5. (Closed 25-26 Dec & Good Fri).
Free.
shop

The Oxford Story — OXFORD

Map 04 SP50
6 Broad St
☎ (0865) 728822
The 800-year history of Oxford University is brought to life at this innovative exhibition. Sights, sounds . . . and smells from the past are described by Sir Alec Guinness or Timmy Mallett as visitors take a seat and ride through the exhibition. Foreign language commentaries are available.
Open all year, Apr-Jun & Sep-Oct daily 9.30-5, Jul-Aug 9.30-7 & Nov-Mar daily 10-4. (Closed 25 Dec)
£3.75 (ch under 16 £2.50, pen & students £3.25). Family ticket £11
♿ *toilets for disabled shop*

Every effort is made to provide accurate information, but details might change during the currency of this guide.

St Edmund Hall — OXFORD

Map 04 SP50
College of Oxford University
☎ (0865) 279000
This is the only surviving medieval academic hall and has a Norman crypt, 17th-century dining hall, chapel and quadrangle. Other buildings are of the 18th and 20th centuries.
Open all year. (Closed 21 Dec-1 Jan, 7-16 Apr & 25-28 Aug).
♿ *toilets for disabled shop*

University Arboretum — OXFORD

Map 04 SP50
Nuneham Courtenay (5m SE on A423 just S of the village).
☎ (0865) 276920
The gardens consist of 55 acres of mixed woodland, meadow, pond, rhododendron walks and fine specimen trees.
Open May-Oct, Mon-Sat 8.30-5, Sun 2-6.
Free.
P ♿

University of Oxford Botanic Garden — OXFORD

Map 04 SP50
High St (by Magdalen Bridge)
☎ (0865) 276920

Founded in 1621, these gardens are the oldest in the country and are of great botanical interest. There is a collection of over 8000 species of plants from all over the world.
Open all year, daily 9-5 (9-4.30 Oct-Mar), Greenhouses, daily 2-4. (Closed Good Fri & 25 Dec).
Jul-Aug £1, otherwise free
⅃ *Entry at wknds using Radar key.* ✈

For an explanation of the symbols and abbreviations, see page 2.

Rousham House — ROUSHAM

Map 04 SP42
(1m E of A4260.0.50m S of B4030)
☎ Steeple Aston (0869) 47110
This attractive mansion was built by Sir Robert Dormer in 1635. During the Civil War it was a Royalist garrison, and had shooting holes cut into its doors. Sir Robert's successors, Masters of Ceremonies at Court during eight reigns, embellished Rousham by employing Court artists and architects. Rooms were also decorated by William Kent and Roberts of Oxford, during the 18th century. The house contains over 150 portraits and other pictures, and also much fine contemporary furniture. The gardens are a masterpiece by William Kent, and are his only work to survive unspoiled. Extending to over 30 acres, with the River Cherwell flowing through, they include classical buildings, cascades, statues and views over the river.
Open all year, garden only, daily 10-4.30. House, Apr-Sep, Wed, Sun & BH 2-4.30. House £2; Garden £2. Party by arrangement. No children under 15.
🅿 ✈
See advertisement on page 137.

Rycote Chapel — RYCOTE

Map 04 SP60
(off B4013)
This small 15th-century private chapel was founded in 1449 by Richard Quatremayne. It has its original font, and a particularly fine 17th-century interior. The chapel was visited by both Elizabeth I and Charles I.
Open all year, Apr-Sep, daily 10-6; Oct-Mar, Tue-Sun 10-4. (Closed 24-26 Dec & 1 Jan).
Free.
🅿 ✈
(EH)

Stonor House & Park — STONOR

Map 04 SU78
(on B480).
☎ Turville Heath (049163) 587
Home of Lord and Lady Camoys and occupied by the Stonor family for 800 years, the house dates back to 1180 but features a Tudor façade. It has a medieval Catholic chapel which is still in use today, and shows some of the earliest domestic architecture in Oxfordshire. Its treasures include rare furniture, paintings, sculptures and tapestries from Britain, Europe and America. The house is set in beautiful gardens with commanding views of the surrounding deer park. The Chiltern craft show will be held here on 28-31 August.
Open Apr-Sep, Sun 2-5.30; May-Sep, Wed 2-5.30; Jul-Aug, Thu 2-5.30; Aug, Sat 2-5.30; BH Mon 12.30-5.30. Parties by appointment Tue, Wed & Thu. £3.25 (ch 14-18 & pen £2.65). Party 12+.
🅿 ⬛ ⅃ *shop* ✈ *(ex in grounds)*

✱ An asterisk indicates that up-to-date information was not available at the time of our research – 1991 information has been published as an indication of what you may expect.

Castle & White Horse   UFFINGTON

Map 04 SU38
The 'castle' is an Iron Age fort on the ancient Ridgeway Path over the Berkshire Downs. It covers about eight acres and has only one gateway. On the hill below the fort is the White Horse, a 375ft prehistoric figure carved in the chalky hillside. It was once thought to have been carved in 871 to celebrate

King Alfred's victory over the Danes, but is now thought to be at least 2000 years old. It is best seen from the B4508.
Open – both accessible any reasonable time.
Free.
P
(EH)

Vale & Downland Museum Centre   WANTAGE

Map 04 SU48
The Old Surgery, Church St
☎ (02357) 66838
The lively museum centre has displays on the geology, archaeology and local history of the Vale of the White Horse and the town of Wantage, birthplace of

King Alfred. There are frequent temporary exhibitions and occasional craft demonstrations.
Open all year, Tue-Sat 10.30-4.30 & Sun 2.30-5. (BH Mon enquire for times).
Free.
☛ ✗ ⅁ *toilets for disabled shop*

Waterperry Gardens   WATERPERRY

Map 04 SP60
☎ Ickford (0844) 339226 & 339254
The manor of Waterperry is mentioned in the Domesday Book, and the little church next to the current house incorporates Saxon work, although it dates from early Norman times. It has some very old stained glass, brasses, and woodwork showing the crests of the FitzEly and Curson families who owned Waterperry from about 1250 to 1830. The present house (not open) was rebuilt by Sir John Curson in 1713 and its elegant proportions reflect the classical tastes of the 18th century. The peaceful gardens and nurseries which surround the house were the home of a celebrated horticultural school between 1932 and

1971, and have fine herbaceous borders, a rock garden, riverside walk, shrub borders, lawns and trees. The horticultural centre now based at Waterperry maintains the earlier traditions with its extensive alpine, fruit, shrub and herbaceous nurseries, and the productive greenhouses. A limited number of wheelchairs are available for disabled visitors and there are ramps to the tea shop.
Open all year, Gardens (ex Xmas & New Year & during "Art in Action" 17-21 Jul). Apr-Sep 10-5.30, wknds 10-6; Oct-Mar 10-4.30 daily.
P ☛ ⅁ *garden centre*
Details not confirmed for 1992

For an explanation of the symbols and abbreviations, see page 2.

Cogges Farm Museum   WITNEY

Map 04 SP31
Church Ln, Cogges (0.5m SE off A4022)
☎ (0993) 772602
Farmhouse kitchens, a dairy, walled gardens and local breeds of animals form the central features of this Edwardian Oxfordshire farm. There is an historic

trail, and daily agricultural and craft demonstrations.
Open Apr-Nov, Tue-Fri & BH Mon 10.30-5.30, Sat & Sun noon-5.30. Mon, booked parties only.
✱ *Admission under review*
P ☛ ⅁ *toilets for disabled shop*

Blenheim Palace   WOODSTOCK

Map 04 SP41
☎ (0993) 811325

Once a Royal Manor, Woodstock was given to the Duke of Marlborough by Queen Anne as a reward for his brilliant military achievements in defeating the French. The Palace, begun in 1705, was designed by Sir John Vanbrugh. It was built on a very grand scale, covering three acres of ground, and was completed in 1722. The Palace has splendid State Rooms, a Long Library, magnificent tapestries and paintings as well as period furniture. Of particular

interest are the door frames carved by Grinling Gibbons and the Hall ceiling painted to depict the Battle of Blenheim by Sir James Thornhill.
The Palace is set in a 2000-acre park landscaped by Capability Brown who created a lake spanned by a 390-ft bridge. There are also formal Italian gardens and terraced water gardens. Sir Winston Churchill was born in the Palace in 1874 and he is buried nearby, at Bladon.
There is a garden centre, an adventure playground and nature trail through the parkland. Other attractions include a Motor launch, train and Butterfly House. Various events are held in the park throughout the year.
Open: Palace & Gardens mid Mar-Oct, daily 10.30-5.30 (last admission 4.45). Park all year 9-5.
£6 (ch 5-15 £3, ch under 5 free, pen £4.50)
P ☛ ✗ *licensed* ⅁ *toilets for disabled shop garden centre* ✖ *(ex in park)*
See advertisement on page 138.

The Oxfordshire County Museum   WOODSTOCK

Map 04 SP41
Fletcher's House
☎ (0993) 811456
Permanently displayed in Fletcher's House is an exhibition of the story of Oxfordshire and its people, from early times to the present day. The house, which is an elegant townhouse with

pleasant gardens, also has temporary exhibitions.
Open all year, Jan-Apr & Oct-Dec, Tue-Fri 10-4, Sat 10-5, Sun 2-5; May-Sep 10-5, Sat 10-6, Sun 2-6. (Closed Good Fri & 25-26 Dec)
Free.
☛ ⅁ *shop* ✖

SHROPSHIRE

Acton Burnell Castle   ACTON BURNELL

Map 07 SJ50
Now ruined, this fortified manor house was built in the late 13th century by Robert Burnell, the Chancellor of the time. It consisted of a central block with towers at the corners and a great hall and chapel on the upper floor. By 1420

the house was no longer being used, and part of it was converted into a barn in the 18th century.
Open at all reasonable times.
Free.
⅁
(EH)

Acton Scott Historic Working Farm   ACTON SCOTT

Map 07 SO48
Wenlock Lodge (off A49)
☎ Marshbrook (06946) 306 & 307

Expertly laid out in an old estate farm, the working museum gives a vivid introduction to traditional rural life. The animals are rare breeds, and the crops are types grown around 1900. They are cultivated on the old crop rotation

system, and all the work is done by hand or horse power, or with old machines such as steam-threshers. Butter-making takes place throughout the season, with daily craft demonstrations, and old machinery and equipment are displayed. Visitors may take part in some of the work, by becoming resident volunteers. Purpose-built toilets and picnic bench for wheelchair users; three wheelchairs for use on site; guide books in braille. Throughout the season there will be a variety of craft displays, weekend demonstrations of spinning, pottery and more, and seasonal festivals.
Open Apr-Nov, Tues-Sat 10-5; Sun & BH Mon 10-6.
£2.50 (ch & pen £1)
P ☛ ⅁ *(Braille guide) toilets for disabled shop* ✖

Attingham Park   ATCHAM

Map 07 SJ50
(on A5)
☎ Upton Magna (074377) 203

An imposing entrance front with massive portico, colonnades and pavilions greets the visitor to Attingham. The house was constructed around an earlier building, but most of what one sees today dates from the 18th and early 19th centuries. This even applies to the garden, where the planting remains very much as advised by Humphry Repton in 1797-8. The house was designed by George Steuart with the more 'masculine' rooms on the left of the entrance hall and the more 'feminine' rooms on the right. The entrance hall itself is elaborately

decorated to imitate marble. Other notable decorations can be seen in the boudoir, which has intricate and delicate designs, the Italian-style drawing room, the oriental Sultana room and the red dining room. The picture gallery was designed by Nash, who made early use of curved cast iron and glass for the ceiling. The River Tern flows through the park, which has a herd of fallow deer. The estate of the house is on the site of the Roman town of Viroconium, and is also crossed by two Roman roads. It is also notable for two fine bridges carrying the A5 over the Tern and Severn rivers.
House open 18 Apr-6 Sep, Sat-Wed 1.30-5, BH Mon 11-5. Pre-booked parties allowed daily ex Thu & Fri. Last admission 4.30. Grounds open all year, daily (ex 25 Dec), sunrise-sunset.
£3 (ch £1.50) Family ticket £7.50. Park & Grounds £1 (ch 50p).
P ☛ ⅁ *(electric scooter available for grounds) toilets for disabled shop* ✖ *(in Deer park)*
(NT)

Places to visit in this guide are pinpointed on the atlas at the back of the book.

Benthall Hall   BENTHALL

Map 07 SJ60
(on B4375)
☎ Telford (0952) 882159
The exact date of the house is not known, but it seems to have been started in the 1530s and then altered in the 1580s. It is an attractive sandstone building with mullioned windows, fine

oak panelling and a splendid carved staircase.
Open Apr-Sep, Wed, Sun & BH Mon 1.30-5.30. Last admission 5pm. Other days by appointment only.
House £2.20 (ch £1). Garden only £1.
P ⅁ ✖
(NT)

Boscobel House and The Royal Oak   BOSCOBEL

Map 07 SJ80
(off A5)
☎ Brewood (0902) 850244
The house was built around 1600 by John Giffard, a Catholic, and the structure includes a number of hiding places. One of them was used by King Charles II after his defeat at the Battle of Worcester in 1651. A descendant of the

oak tree where he also hid can be seen in the grounds.
Open all year, Apr-Sep, daily 10-6; Oct-Mar, Tue-Sun 10-4. (Closed 24-26 Dec & Jan).
£2.80 (ch £1.40, pen, students & UB40 £2.10).
P ☛ ⅁ *shop* ✖
(EH)

Whiteladies Priory (St Leonards Priory)   BOSCOBEL

Map 07 SJ80
Only the ruins are left of this Augustinian nunnery, which dates from 1158 and was destroyed in the Civil War. After the Battle of Worcester Charles II hid here and in the nearby

woods before going on to Boscobel House.
Open any reasonable time.
Free.
(EH)

Midland Motor Museum   BRIDGNORTH

Map 07 SO79
Stanmore Hall, Stourbridge Rd (2m on A458 Stourbridge Rd)
☎ (0746) 761761
A notable collection of over 100 well-restored sports and sports racing cars, and racing motor cycles dating from 1920 to 1980 (also a steam traction engine and a collection of toy model cars) are housed in the converted stables

of Stanmore Hall and surrounded by beautiful grounds with a nature trail and camping park. There are gatherings of various motor clubs at weekends from April to September.
Open all year, daily 10-5. (Closed 25 Dec). Evenings by appointment.
£3.50 (ch £1.75, pen £2.80). Family ticket £9.95.
P ☕ & *toilets for disabled shop* ✖

Severn Valley Railway   BRIDGNORTH

Map 07 SO79
☎ Bewdley (0299) 403816 & (0746) 764361
The leading standard gauge steam railway, with one of the largest collections of locomotives and rolling stock in the country. Services operate from Kidderminster and Bewdley to Bridgnorth through 16 miles of picturesque scenery along the River Severn. Special steam Galas take place in Apr, Jun and Sep and there is a Vintage Vehicle Weekend on 11 Oct. Saturday

evening 'Wine and Dine' and 'Sunday Luncheon' trains are a speciality. Steam, diesel and vehicle galas are arranged for 1992
Open wknds early Mar-Oct & daily mid May-early Oct. Also 21-28 Oct. Santa Steam & Mince Pie Specials wknds, end Nov-22 Dec, daily 16-20 Dec & 23-24 Dec.
✻ *Admission fee payable. Refundable in full if train tickets subsequently purchased.*
P ☕ ✗ *licensed* & *toilets for disabled shop*

Buildwas Abbey   BUILDWAS

Map 07 SJ60
☎ (095243) 3274
The beautiful, ruined, Cistercian abbey was founded in 1135, and stands in a picturesque setting. The church with its stout round pillars is roofless but otherwise almost complete.

Open all year, Apr-Sep, daily 10-6; Oct-Mar, Tue-Sun 10-4. (Closed 24-26 Dec & 1 Jan).
£1.10 (ch 55p, pen, students & UB40 85p).
& ✖
(EH)

Burford House Gardens   BURFORD

Map 07 SO56
(off A456)
☎ Tenbury Wells (0584) 810777
Surrounding the Georgian House (1723), the artistically designed gardens contain many rare and unusual plants including shrubs and herbaceous plants, species roses, and clematis in particular. The garden was started by John Treasure in 1954, and next to it is the

notable plant centre, Treasures of Tenbury, which holds the national clematis collection.
Open Mar-Oct, Mon-Sat 10-5, Sun 1-5. Winter Mon-Fri by appointment only. Plant Centre open all year.
✻ *Admission fee payable.*
P ☕ & *toilets for disabled garden centre*
✖ *(ex in Plant Centre)*

Aerospace Museum   COSFORD

Map 07 SJ70
(off A41)
☎ Albrighton (0902) 374872 & 374112
This is one of the largest aviation collections in the UK. Exhibits include the Victor and Vulcan bombers, the Hastings, York and British Airways airliners, the Belfast freighter and the last airworthy Britannia. The research and development collection include the notable TSR2, Fairey Delta 2, Bristol

188 and many more important aircraft. There is a British Airways exhibition hall, and a comprehensive missile display. 21 June is Royal Air Force Cosford open day.
Open all year daily, 10-4 (last admission). (Closed 24-26 Dec & 1 Jan).
£3.50 (ch, & pen £1.75). Family ticket £9. Party 20+.
P ☕ & *toilets for disabled shop* ✖

Haughmond Abbey   HAUGHMOND ABBEY

Map 07 SJ51
(off B5062)
☎ Upton Magna (074377) 661
The ruined abbey was founded for Augustinian canons in around 1135, and partly converted into a house during the Dissolution. The chapter house has a fine Norman doorway, and the abbot's lodging and the kitchens are well

preserved.
Open all year, Apr-Sep, daily 10-6; Oct-Mar, Tue-Sun 10-4. (Closed 24-26 Dec & 1 Jan).
£1.10 (ch 55p, students, pen & UB40 85p).
P & ✖
(EH)

Hodnet Hall Gardens   HODNET

Map 07 SJ62
☎ (063084) 202
Sixty acres of landscaped gardens offer tranquillity among pools, lush plants and trees. Big game trophies adorn the 17th-century tearooms, and plants are usually for sale in the kitchen gardens. The

house, rebuilt in Victorian-Elizabethan style, is not open.
Open daily Apr-Sep, Mon-Sat 2-5, Sun & BH 12.30-5.30.
£2.25 (ch £1, pen £2). Party.
P ☕ & *toilets for disabled shop*

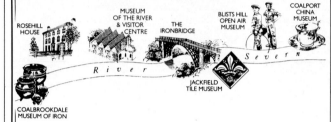

Ironbridge Gorge Museum   IRONBRIDGE

Map 07 SJ60
☎ (0952) 433522 & 432751 (wknds)
Ironbridge became famous when the world's first iron bridge was cast and built here in 1779, to span a narrow gorge over the River Severn. Now it is the site of a remarkable series of museums covering some six square miles. Perhaps the most appealing is the Blists Hill Open Air Museum. Set in 42 acres of woodland, the recreated Victorian town offers the visitor a chance to step into the past and see how people lived and worked in the 1890s. The Coalbrookdale Furnace Site uses a light and sound display to show the technique of smelting iron ore, perfected here by Abraham Darby. Associated with the furnace is the Museum of Iron. Another of the museums is housed in

the original buildings of the Coalport China Company, based in the area until the mid-1920s. It features workshop and social history displays. There is also the Jackfield Tile Museum. An introduction to the Ironbridge Gorge is given at the visitor centre in the Museum of the River, brought to life by a sound and light display.
Open all year, Jun-Aug 10-6, Sep-May 10-5.
✻ *£7.10 (ch £4.60, pen £6.10, family £20.50). Passport to all sites. A passport will admit visitors to all sites, in any order until all have been visited. It is therefore possible to return to Ironbridge on different days to ensure the whole atmosphere of this unique museum may be captured.*
P ☕ ✗ *licensed* & *toilets for disabled shop*
✖ *(ex at Blists Hill)*

Lilleshall Abbey   LILLESHALL

Map 07 SJ71
(1.5m SW off A518 on unclass road)
Some of the most impressive ruins in Shropshire stand in the beautiful grounds of Lilleshall Hall. Lilleshall Abbey was founded shortly before the middle of the 12th century and from the

high west front visitors can look down the entire 228ft length of the abbey church.
Open any reasonable time.
Free.
P ✖
(EH)

Ludlow Castle   LUDLOW

Map 07 SO57
☎ (0584) 873947

Ludlow Castle dates from about 1086 and was gradually greatly extended as ownership passed through the de Lacy and Mortimer families to the Crown. In 1473, Edward IV sent the Prince of Wales and his brother, later to become the Princes in the Tower, to live in Ludlow. Ludlow Castle then became a seat of government when the Council for Wales and the Marches was established there. Another royal resident was Prince Arthur, son of Henry Tudor
continued ...

and elder brother of Henry VIII. John Milton's *Comus* was first performed at Ludlow Castle in 1634; now contemporary performances of Shakespeare's plays are put on during the Ludlow Festival. In 1689 the Royal Welch Fusiliers were formed at Ludlow by Lord Herbert of Chirbury, into whose family, the Earls of Powis, ownership later passed. The Castle includes buildings ranging from the circular nave of the Norman chapel to an unusually complete range of medieval buildings and the Judges' Lodgings, built in the 16th century.
Open May-Sep daily 10.30-5; Oct-Nov & Feb-Apr 10.30-4. (Closed Dec & Jan). £2 (ch £1, pen £1.50). Family ticket £6. & *shop*

Ludlow Museum   LUDLOW

Map 07 SO57
Butter Cross
☎ (0584) 873857
Ludlow's importance dates from the founding of the Castle in about 1090. It was as a planned Norman town and subsequent capital of the Marches of Wales that it reached the height of prosperity with an important wool and cloth industry. Later it became a popular Georgian residential centre with glove making a major trade during the Napoleonic Wars, and after, a successful Victorian market town. The museum and its displays tell the story including an explanation of the geological significance of the Ludlow area; there is also a small section on the Whitcliffe Nature Trail.
Open 25 Mar-28 Sep, Mon-Sat 10.30-1 & 2-5. Also Sun 10.30-1 & 2-5 Jun-Aug only.
shop 💥
Details not confirmed for 1992

Walcot Hall   LYDBURY NORTH

Map 07 SO38
☎ (05888) 232
Built by Sir William Chambers for Lord Clive of India. The Georgian House possesses a free-standing and recently restored ballroom, stableyard with matching clock towers and extensive walled garden, in addition to its ice house, meat safe and dovecote. There is an arboretum, noted for its rhododendrons and azaleas, specimen trees, pools and a lake.
Open May-Sep, Thu 2.30-5.30. Also Sun in Jul-Aug & Sun & BH Mons 2.30-5.30. (Closed Xmas & New Year). £2.50 (ch under 15, free)

This is just one of many guidebooks published by the AA. The full range is available at any AA shop or good bookshop.

Castle   MORETON CORBET

Map 07 SJ52
A small 13th-century keep and the ruins of an impressive Elizabethan house are all that remain: the house was destroyed when the Parliamentary forces captured it in 1644.
Open all reasonable times.
Free.
🅿 &
(EH)

Much Wenlock Museum   MUCH WENLOCK

Map 07 SO69
High St
☎ (0952) 727773
Much Wenlock has kept its medieval flavour despite encroaching changes from the 20th century. Its museum, in the Old Market Hall, has an admirable collection illustrating the history of the town and its famous priory, together with displays on local trades.
Open Apr-Sep, Mon-Sat 10.30-1 & 2-5, also Sun Jun-Aug 10.30-1 & 2-5.
50p (ch, pen & UB40 free).
& *shop* 💥

Much Wenlock Priory   MUCH WENLOCK

Map 07 SO69
☎ (0952) 727466
The original priory was founded here as a convent in the 7th century. It was destroyed by the Danes but was rebuilt and grew over the years. The not inconsiderable remains of the 11th-century priory and subsequent additions are what the visitor will see today.
Open all year, Apr-Sep, daily 10-6; Oct-Mar, Tue-Sun 10-4. (Closed 24-26 Dec & 1 Jan).
£1.50 (ch 75p, pen, students & UB40 £1.10).
🅿 💥
(EH)

Cambrian Railway Museum & Oswestry Cycle Museum   OSWESTRY

Map 07 SJ22
Oswald Rd
☎ (0691) 661648
This Museum portrays bicycle history and the development of the bicycle through the ages. Displays include bicycle parts, signs and period costume. There is also a display of Dunlop's development of the pneumatic tyre. Over 60 bicycles can be seen and special events are held throughout the year. There is also a large display of steam engines and railway memorabilia at a joint museum with the Cambrian Railways.
Open all year, daily 9.30-4.
£1 (ch 50p)
🅿 & *shop*

Old Oswestry   OSWESTRY

Map 07 SJ22
(0.5m N)
This Iron Age hill-fort covers 68 acres, has five ramparts and an elaborate western portal. It is abutted by part of the prehistoric Wat's Dyke.
Open any reasonable time.
Free.
(EH)

Dudmaston   QUATT

Map 07 SO78
(4m SE of Bridgnorth on A442)
☎ Dudmaston (0746) 780866
The 17th-century flower paintings which belonged to Francis Darby of Coalbrookdale are exhibited in this house of the same period, with modern works, botanical art and fine furniture. The house stands in an extensive parkland garden. Dingle and lakeside walks.
Open Apr-Sep, Wed & Sun 2.30-6. (Last admission 5.30pm). Pre-booked parties Thu 2.30-6.
House & Garden £2.80 (ch £1.40). Family ticket £7. Garden only £1.80 (ch free).
🅿 ♨ & *(Braille guides, taped tours) toilets for disabled shop* 💥 *(ex in garden) (NT)*

Clive House Museum   SHREWSBURY

Map 07 SJ41
College Hill
☎ (0743) 354811
Town house with a long history, including a brief association in the 1760s with Robert, Lord Clive (Clive of India). There are outstanding displays of Coalport and Caughley porcelain, and paintings, in contemporary period room settings. Also domestic bygones, a children's room, and local social history 1750-1900.
Open all year, Mon 2-5, Tue-Sat 10-1 & 2-5.
80p (ch & pen 40p)
& *shop* 💥

Rowley's House Museum — SHREWSBURY

Map 07 SJ41
Barker St
☎ (0743) 361196
Impressive timber framed building and attached 17th-century brick mansion. Major displays of the archaeology, geology, prehistory, natural and local history of the region, including much of the material excavated from Roman Wroxeter. There is also a costume gallery, an innovative Medieval Shrewsbury gallery and a varied programme of temporary and touring exhibitions, including the 'Enamellers' Guild' on 21 Mar-20 Apr.
Open all year, Mon-Sat 10-5; Also Suns from Etr Sun-mid Sep 12-5.
£1 (ch & pen 50p)
& shop 🐾

The Shropshire Regimental Museum — SHREWSBURY

Map 07 SJ41
The Castle, Castle St
☎ (0743) 358516
The museum of The King's Shropshire Light Infantry, The Shropshire Yeomanry Cavalry and The Shropshire Royal Horse Artillery is housed within Shrewsbury's Norman castle. The museum contains weapons, silver, Colours, medals and uniforms of the three Regiments, as well as an American Colour taken when the White House was captured and burned, a lock of Napoleon's hair and the baton of Grand Admiral Donitz.
Open all year, Mon-Sat 10-5; Etr-Oct, Sun 10-5, (last admission 4pm).
80p (ch & pen 40p). Free admission to members of the regimental associations & their families.
& *(ground & 1st floor only) shop* 🐾

Stokesay Castle — STOKESAY

Map 07 SO48
☎ Craven Arms (0588) 672544
Well-preserved and little altered, this 13th-century manor house has a romantic setting. Special features are the fine gatehouse, the great hall and, reached by an outside staircase, a solar with 17th-century panelling.
Open 6 Mar-Oct, daily (ex Tue) 10-6, (10-5 Mar & Oct). Also Nov wknds only 10-dusk. Last admission half hour before closing.
🅿 *(charged)* & *shop* 🐾
Details not confirmed for 1992

🐾 The 'No Dogs' symbol does not normally apply to guide dogs – these are permitted in most establishments.

Tyn-y-Rhos Hall Museum & Chapel — WESTON RHYN

Map 07 SJ23
(2m W near Bron-y-Garth on unclass rd)
☎ Chirk (0691) 777898
This small manor house has been fully furnished in the style of the late 19th century. There are many interesting items of Victoriana on display and also a few from earlier periods such as the portrait of Charles I. The house has a family chapel which is still in use and services are held each Sunday.
Open all year, Sun tours at 11am, 2.30 & 5pm (except on Pilgrimage Days). Retreat Days Spring-Sep, Wed (with light meals). No charge but a small donation would be expected.
🅿 🍴 & 🐾
Details not confirmed for 1992

Roman Town — WROXETER

Map 07 SJ50
☎ (0743) 761330
These excavated remains of the Roman town of Virconium probably date from 140 – 150AD. There is a colonnade and a municipal bath. The museum has finds from both the Roman town and an earlier legionary fortress on the same site. It also offers educational facilities.
Open all year, Apr-Sep, daily 10-6; Oct-Mar, Tue-Sun 10-4. (Closed 24-26 Dec & 1 Jan).
£1.50 (ch 75p, students, pen & UB40 £1.10).
🅿 & *shop* 🐾
(EH)

SOMERSET

King John's Hunting Lodge — AXBRIDGE

Map 03 ST45
The Square
☎ (0934) 732012
Nothing to do with King John or with hunting, this jettied and timber-framed house was built around 1500. It gives a good indication of the wealth of the merchants of that time and is now a museum of local history, with old photographs, paintings and items such as the town stocks and constables' staves.
Open Etr-Sep, daily 2-5. Write for details of tours.
✱ *Admission fee payable.*
(NT)

Barrington Court Gardens — BARRINGTON

Map 03 ST31
(off A303)
☎ South Petherton (0460) 40601
The house dates from the 17th century, but the gardens were created in the 1920s, with the help (through the post) of Gertrude Jekyll. They are laid out in sections, and include a white garden, an iris garden, a lily garden and a spacious walled kitchen garden.
Open: Garden Apr-1 Nov, Sun-Thu 12-5.30. Last admission 5pm. House Apr-1 Nov, Wed only 1.30-5, Guided tours only.
£3 (ch £1.50). Guided tours 50p. Party.
🅿 ✗ *licensed* & 🐾 *(ex on farm trail)*
(NT)

Brympton House & Gardens — BRYMPTON

Map 03 ST51
Brympton d'Evercy (off A30 or A3088)
☎ Yeovil (0935) 862528

This Tudor and Stuart house has a wonderful setting within grounds which won the Christie's/Historic Houses Association Garden of the Year Award. Visitors can see the State rooms, the I Zingari Cricket Club Collection and a country life museum which includes the Brympton distillery (Brympton Apple Brandy is on sale). As well as the gardens, there is a vineyard, and art and photography exhibitions are held during the season.
Open Etr wknd, then May-Sep, daily (ex Thu & Fri) 2-6.
£3.90 (ch £1.50, NT members & pen £3.40).
🅿 🍴 & *toilets for disabled shop & plant sales* 🐾

Places to visit in this guide are pinpointed on the atlas at the back of the book.

Hadspen Garden & Nursery — CASTLE CARY

Map 03 ST63
Hadspen House (2m SE off A371)
☎ (0963) 50939
This is a sheltered, south-sloping garden of eight acres. It has a unique 17th-century curved-walled garden, with a modern planting scheme of rare species. The woodland area has unusual specimen trees, and there is a wild flower meadow. Adjoining plant nursery specializing in good garden plants as seen growing in the garden.
Open Mar-1 Oct, Thu-Sun & BHs 9-6.
£2 (ch 50p). Free admission for wheelchair users.
🅿 🍴 & *toilets for disabled garden centre* 🐾

Forde Abbey — CHARD

Map 03 ST30
☎ South Chard (0460) 20231
This 12th-century monastery was converted into a house by Cromwell's Attorney General. There are tapestries and a fine gatehouse, and 20-acres of some of the finest gardens in Dorset. A grand fête in aid of the Marie Curie Cancer Fund is to be held on 30 July.
Gardens, open all year, daily 10-4.30. Abbey & gardens Apr-Oct Sun, Wed & BH 1-4.30 (last admission).
✱ *Gardens £2.50 (pen £2.20). House & Gardens £3.80 (pen £3.30, ch free). Party*
🅿 🍴 & *toilets for disabled shop garden centre* 🐾 *(ex in grounds)*

Cheddar Showcaves — CHEDDAR

Map 03 ST45
Cheddar Gorge
☎ (0934) 742343
Britain's two most beautiful caves, Gough's Cave with its cathedral-like caverns and Cox's Cave with its delicate stalagmites and stalactites, are beneath the limestone cliffs of Cheddar Gorge. Climb Jacob's Ladder for spectacular views of this conservation area. There is an exhibition of 'Cheddar Man' Britain's oldest complete skelton, and his world 9,000 years ago. 'The Crystal Quest' is new. It is a fantasy adventure underground, while for the more daring, there is an exciting Adventure Caving Expedition (minimum age 12).
Open all year, Etr-Sep 10-5.30; rest of year 10.30-4.30. (Closed 24 & 25 Dec).
Combined ticket for all attractions £4.50 (ch 5-15 & pen £2.80, ch under 5 free).
Adventure Caving Expeditions (min 12yrs) £5.50. Inclusive ticket incl all attractions plus Adventure Caving & Orienteering £9 (ch 12-15 £7). Reductions for disabled on application.
🅿 🍴 ✗ *licensed* & *toilets for disabled shop*

✱ An asterisk indicates that up-to-date information was not available at the time of our research – 1991 information has been published as an indication of what you may expect.

East Somerset Railway — CRANMORE

Map 03 ST64
Cranmore Railway Station (on A361)
☎ (074988) 417
Nine steam locomotives and rolling stock can be seen at Cranmore station, which has an engine shed and workshops. The new art gallery displays David Shepherd's work. Steam train services (see timetable for Steam Days) include Santa Specials in December, and also here are a museum, wildlife information centre and play area.
Open daily May-Aug, 10-5.30. Apr, Sep & Oct 10-4. (wknds Nov, Dec & Mar 10-4). (Closed 2 Jan-Feb).
£3.30 (ch 4-16 & pen £1.70). Non-steam days £1.30 (ch 70p).
🅿 ✗ & *toilets for disabled shop*

Clapton Court Gardens — CREWKERNE

Map 03 ST40
Clapton (3m S on B3165)
☎ (0460) 73220 & 72200
The beautiful 10-acre gardens have formal and woodland settings with rare and unusual plants, brilliant spring bulbs and autumn colours. The plant centre sells choice and rare perennials, shrubs and trees, with fuchsias and pelargoniums a speciality. You can also see the oldest (500 years) and largest ash tree in Great Britain. On 25 April, from 11am-5pm there will be an annual rare plant sale.
Open Mar-Oct, Mon-Fri 10.30-5, Sun 2-5. Nov & Feb Mon-Fri 10.30-5.
£3 (ch 4-14 £1 & students £1.50). Party 20+.
🅿 ✗ *licensed* & *(special parking area) garden centre* 🐾

Wild Life Park — CRICKET ST THOMAS

Map 03 ST30
(on A30)
☎ Winsham (0460) 30755

The old and beautiful park of Cricket House has become a home for a wide variety of animals and birds, including elephants, camels, llamas, parrots and other exotic creatures. The wildlife enclosures have been designed to blend in with the surroundings as far as possible, and there have been successes with breeding, most notably of black swans. Shire horses can be seen at the National Heavy Horse Centre, and there is a woodland railway. The house became well known as 'Grantleigh Manor' in the BBC television series *To The Manor Born*. To celebrate 25 years of being open to the public, 25 charitable events are to be held in 1992, in addition to various other events such as the Wessex Custom and American Car Show on 10 May.
Open all year Apr-Oct, daily 10-6; Nov-Mar 10-5 or dusk (whichever is earlier). £5.50 (ch 3-14 £3 & pen £4.50). Wheelchair users free. Party 20+.
P ☕ ✕ *licensed & toilets for disabled shop garden centre*

Dunster Castle — DUNSTER

Map 03 SS94
(on A396)
☎ (0643) 821314
The setting of Dunster Castle is dramatic: it lies between Exmoor and the sea. Sub-tropical plants flourish in the 28-acre park and the terraced gardens are noted for exotica such as a giant lemon tree, yuccas, mimosa and palms. The castle's picturesque appearance is largely due to attractive 19th-century work, but handsome older features include intricately decorated ceilings, the superb 17th-century oak staircase and the gallery with its brightly painted wall-hangings. The castle was the home of the Luttrell family for 600 years, and there is a dramatic 16th-century portrait of Sir John Luttrell. Other notable features include the elaborate 'thrown chair' and the leather-look wallpaper of the comfortable 19th-century library.
Open: Garden & grounds Feb-Mar & Oct-Dec 11-4, Apr-Sep 11-5. Castle Apr-4 Oct, Sat-Wed 11-5; 5 Oct-1 Nov, Sat-Wed 11-4.
✱ *Castle & Garden £4.30 (ch 16 £2.10). Garden & Grounds only £2.20 (ch 16 £1.10). Party 15+.*
P & *(Braille guide, Batricar for grounds) toilets for disabled shop*
(NT)

Old Dovecote — DUNSTER

Map 03 SS94
☎ (0643) 821263
The 12th-century dovecote was built as part of a priory; it is especially unusual because it still has its 'potence' – the revolving ladder which was used for reaching the nesting boxes.
Open Etr-mid Oct, daily 10-dusk.
✱ *Charge for leaflet.*
✈

Every effort is made to provide accurate information, but details might change during the currency of this guide.

New Road Farm — EAST HUNTSPILL

Map 03 ST34
New Rd (Signposted from A38)
☎ Burnham-on-Sea (0278) 783250
One of the oldest farms in the area, this family run farm demonstrates both modern and traditional methods of farming. There are over 60 different breeds of animals and visitors are free to explore and make contact with the animals – or even try hand milking the cows. Somerset County Council's Levels Visitor Centre is also here, offering unusual audio-visual effects and 'hands-on' experiences for all ages. There is an 'I Spy' farm trail, an observation badger sett and a barn owl release scheme. Special events for 1992 include, amongst others, a sheepshearing demonstration at Whitsun, and a demonstration of bee keeping, horse shoeing and craft spinning in August.
Open Feb-Etr, wknds 10-5. Etr-Oct daily 10-6.
£3 (ch £2, pen £2.50). Party.
P ☕ ✕ & *toilets for disabled shop garden centre*

East Lambrook Manor Garden — EAST LAMBROOK

Map 03 ST41
(off A303)
☎ South Petherton (0460) 40328
Walter and Margery Fish created the cottage-style garden after buying the 15th-century manor in 1937. Margery Fish's book *We Made a Garden* described the work, and aroused so much interest that she started a nursery to sell the types of plants she used. Plants are still sold. The garden is now Grade I listed and has been fully restored.
Open Mon-Sat 10-5, also 25 May for National Gardens Scheme. (Closed Nov-28 Feb).
£1.90 (ch 50p). Party ✈
P *shop garden centre* ✈

Farleigh Hungerford Castle — FARLEIGH HUNGERFORD

Map 03 ST85
☎ (0225) 754026
The ruined 14th-century castle has a chapel with monuments to the Hungerfords, a powerful family who owned land from here to Salisbury. Family and castle are linked with various grim tales of hanging and murder.
Open all year, Apr-Sep, daily 10-6; Oct-Mar, Tue-Sun 10-4. (Closed 24-26 Dec & 1 Jan).
£1.10 (ch 55p, students, pen & UB40 85p).
P & ✈
(EH)

𝕲lastonbury 𝕬bbey

Enquiries: The Abbey Gatehouse, Glastonbury BA6 9EL. Telephone: 0458 832267

Extensive Ruins in 36 acres of ground.
First Christian Sanctuary in the British Isles.
Founded, according to legend, by Joseph of Arimathea in the First Century. Glastonbury Thorn flowers twice yearly. May and December.
Legendary burial place of King Arthur.
Mediaeval Gatehouse Museum contains fragments of the Wattle and Daub Church, some early Roman remains and a model of the Abbey.

Open:	All year except 25th December 0930 - dusk (approx) or 1800
Admission:	£1.50, Children £1.00 – under 5 free.

Glastonbury Abbey — GLASTONBURY

Map 03 ST43
☎ (0458) 832267
Few places in Britain are as rich in myth and legend as Glastonbury and an old tradition maintains that the impressive, medieval abbey ruins stand at the birth place of Christianity in Britain. This is where Joseph of Arimathea is said to have brought the Holy Grail (the chalice used by Christ at the Last Supper) and to have founded a chapel in AD61, on the site marked by a flowering thorn tree. Later, it is said, King Arthur and Guinevere were buried at Glastonbury; and the abbey was a place of pilgrimage in the Middle Ages. The present abbey ruins date from after a fire in 1184, and are mostly of the 12th and 13th centuries.
The abbey fell into decay after the Dissolution, during which the last abbot refused to submit to Henry VIII, and was dragged to the top of Glastonbury Tor to be hanged, drawn and quartered. The well preserved ruins are notable for the abbot's kitchen, and there is a model in the medieval gatehouse of the abbey as it was in 1539. Special event for 1992 is the West of England Pilgrimage on 27 June.
Open all year, daily, Jun-Aug 9-6; Sep-May 9.30-dusk or 6 whichever earlier (Closed 25 Dec).
£1.50 (ch 5-16 £1, pen £1.20).
& *toilets for disabled shop*

Glastonbury Tribunal — GLASTONBURY

Map 03 ST43
☎ (0458) 832949
The 15th-century Tribunal was the court house of the abbey officials. It now houses finds from the prehistoric Lake Village, a settlement of the times when Glastonbury was surrounded by water and marshes. The wooden artefacts have been preserved by the acid peat soil of the area.
Open all year, Apr-Sep, daily 10-6; Oct-Mar, Tue-Sun 10-4. (Closed 24-26 Dec & 1 Jan).
£1.10 (ch 55p, pen, students & UB40 85p).
& ✈
(EH)

For an explanation of the symbols and abbreviations, see page 2.

Somerset Rural Life Museum — GLASTONBURY

Map 03 ST43
Chilkwell St
☎ (0458) 831197
The museum is housed in the 14th-century abbey barn and farmhouse. The museum shows traditional skills of the region, including cider making, peat cutting and preparing willows for baskets. It also illustrates the life of a 19th-century Somerset labourer, and a typical farmhouse kitchen is shown.
Open all year, Mon-Fri 10-5, Sat & Sun 2-6 (Nov-Etr, Sat 11-4). (Closed Good Fri & 25 Dec).
✱ *£1.30 (ch 30p, pen 80p).*
P ☕ & *shop* ✈

Lytes Cary Manor   KINGSDON

Map 03 ST52
(off A303)
This charming manor, tucked away in the Somerset countryside, takes its name from the family who lived here for 500 years, the Lytes. Much of the present house was built by John Lyte in the 16th century although the oldest part, the chapel, dates from 1343. The Great Hall was a 15th-century addition and still boasts stained glass installed by John Lyte. His son, Henry, was a noted

horticulturalist and he transformed the gardens at the manor; unfortunately these have not survived, but the present formal gardens are being restocked with plants that were commonly grown in his day.
Open Apr-Oct, Mon, Wed & Sat 2-6 or dusk if earlier. Last admission 5.30.
£3 (ch £1.50)
🅿 ♿ ✖
(NT)

Combe Sydenham Country Park   MONKSILVER

Map 03 ST03
☎ Stogumber (0984) 56284
The 16th-century house was the home of Sir Francis Drake's second wife, Elizabeth, and is currently being restored. The Elizabethan-style garden has woodland walks, a corn mill and a children's play area. There is also fly fishing for the beginner, plus day tickets

for the more experienced fisherman, and a trout farm for the unsuccessful.
Open 9 Apr-2 Nov. Country Park: Sun-Fri. Court Room & Gardens: Mon-Fri. 10-5 (Last admission to Court Room & Garden 4pm).
🅿 ✖ *shop garden centre* ✖ *(ex in park)*
Details not confirmed for 1992

✖ **The 'No Dogs' symbol does not normally apply to guide dogs – these are permitted in most establishments.**

Montacute House   MONTACUTE

Map 03 ST41
(off A3088)
☎ Martock (0935) 823289

Set amidst formal gardens, Montacute House was built in honey-brown Ham stone by Sir Edward Phelips. He was a successful lawyer, and became Speaker of the House of Commons in 1604. The glittering expanse of windows and Flemish-style rounded gables date from his time, but the heraldic beasts and fluted columns were added in the 18th

century. Inside there are decorated ceilings, ornate fireplaces, heraldic glass and fine wood panelling. A collection of tapestries, paintings, furniture and ceramics bequeathed by Sir Malcolm Stewart has enabled the house to be furnished in fitting style. Better still, the Long Gallery displays a permanent collection of Tudor and Jacobean portraits from the National Portrait Gallery in London.
Open all year: Garden & Park daily (ex Tue) 11.30-5.30 or dusk if earlier. House: Apr-1 Nov, daily (ex Tue) 12-5.30. Last admission 5pm. (Closed Good Fri). Parties by appointment with the administrator.
✱ *House, Garden & Park £4.30 (ch £2.20); Garden & Park only £2.20. Party 15+.*
🅿 ✖ *licensed* ♿ *(Braille guide) toilets for disabled shop garden centre* ✖ *(ex park)*
(NT)

Muchelney Abbey   MUCHELNEY

Map 03 ST42
Encircled by marshes, Muchelney seemed a suitably remote spot to found a Benedictine Abbey in the 8th century. All that is left are the 15th and 16th century ruins; the southern range of cloister buildings, containing the Abbot's lodging, is fairly well preserved. Nearby

is a 14th-century priest's house, a rare example of domestic architecture from this period.
Open Apr-Sep, daily 10-6.
Free.
🅿 ♿ ✖
(EH)

Places to visit in this guide are pinpointed on the atlas at the back of the book.

Coleridge Cottage   NETHER STOWEY

Map 03 ST13
(off A39)
☎ (0278) 732662
It was in this small cottage that Coleridge was most inspired as a poet and here that he wrote *The Ancient Mariner*. The Coleridge family moved to Nether Stowey in 1796 and became friendly with the Wordsworths who lived nearby, but the group were

regarded with suspicion by the local population. The house was smaller and thatched, not tiled, in those days but otherwise little has changed.
Open Apr-4 Oct, Tue-Thu & Sun 2-5 (Parlour & Reading room only).
£1.40. (ch 70p). Parties by arrangement with caretaker.
🅿 ✖
(NT)

Nunney Castle   NUNNEY

Map 03 ST74
Built by Sir John de la Mere in 1373, and supposedly modelled on France's Bastille, this crenellated manor house has one of the deepest moats in England. It was ruined by the Parliamentarian forces

during the Civil War.
Open any reasonable time.
Free.
♿
(EH)

Tropical Bird Gardens   RODE

Map 03 ST85
☎ Frome (0373) 830326
The Tropical Bird Gardens consist of 17 acres of grounds, planted with trees and shrubs, in a pretty and little-visited village. An ornamental lake and a number of ponds surround the aviaries, where more than 200 species are kept. There is also a Pets Corner, a children's play area and an information centre. Plants are for sale; children must be accompanied by an adult. A Woodland

steam railway operates daily (Etr-mid Sep), weather permitting. Events for 1992 include a Steam Weekend (25-26 Apr), a Parrot Weekend (30-31 May), and a Clematis Weekend (11-12 Jul).
Open all year daily (ex 25 Dec); Summer 10-6.30pm (last admission 5.30pm); Winter 10-dusk (last admission 1hr before closing time).
£3.50 (ch 15 £1.75, pen £3).
🅿 ▣ ♿ *toilets for disabled shop* ✖

Haynes Sparkford Motor Museum   SPARKFORD

Map 03 ST62
(off Castle Cary/Fronfe Rd).
☎ North Cadbury (0963) 40804
This 47,000 sq ft museum is dedicated to the restoration and preservation of motorcars and motorcycles. The exhibits have all been restored to full working order, and, where possible, original parts

are used and the vehicles returned to mint condition.
Open all year, daily 9.30-5.30. Evenings by appointment. (Closed 25,26 Dec & 1 Jan).
🅿 ✖ ♿ *toilets for disabled shop* ✖
Details not confirmed for 1992

Willow & Wetlands Visitor Centre   STOKE ST GREGORY

Map 03 ST32
Meare Green Court
☎ North Curry (0823) 490249
The levels and moors of Somerset are the most important areas of 'wetland' left in England. This centre shows how today's landscape has been created from marsh and swamp. The wetland wild flowers, insects and bird are all illustrated. There are sections on

traditional industries based on locally found plants like withies and teasels. Models drawings and photographs are used to give a fascinating insight into this unique area.
Open all year, Mon-Fri 9-5 (guided tours 10-4), Sat (no tours) 10-5. Closed Sun.
£1.75 (ch £1, pen £1.25). Party.
🅿 *shop*

Stoke sub Hamdon Priory   STOKE-SUB-HAMDON

Map 03 ST41
This 15th-century house is built of Ham Hill stone and was once the home of the priests of the chantry belonging to the now vanished Beauchamp manor. The 14th- and 15th-century farm buildings and the screens passage of the chantry

remain, with part of the hall.
Open all year, daily 10-6. Hall only open to visitors.
Free.
🅿
(NT)

♿ **This symbol indicates that much or all of the attraction is accessible to wheelchairs. However, there may be some restrictions, so it would be wise to check in advance.**

The Shoe Museum   STREET

Map 03 ST43
C & J Clark Ltd, High St
☎ (0458) 43131
The museum is in the oldest part of the shoe factory set up by Cyrus and James Clark in 1825. It contains shoes from Roman times to the present, buckles, engravings, fashion plates, machinery,

hand tools and advertising material. One section illustrates the early history of the shoe firm and its role in the town.
Open Etr Mon-Oct, Mon-Fri 10-4.45, Sat 10-4.30. Winter months by appointment only.
♿ *toilets for disabled shop* ✖
Details not confirmed for 1992

Hestercombe Gardens   TAUNTON

Map 03 ST22
Fire Brigade Headquarters, Hestercombe House, Cheddon Fitzpaine (3m N, off A361 near Cheddon).
☎ (0823) 337222 ext 316
The late 19th-century house is now the headquarters of the Somerset Fire Brigade. The multi-level gardens and

orangery were originally planned in 1905 by Sir Edwin Lutyens and Gertrude Jekyll, with raised walks, sunken lawns and a water garden.
Open all year, May-Sep, Mon-Fri 9-5, wknds 2-5; Oct-Apr wkdays only 9-5, wknds groups by appointment only.
£1.50.
🅿 ♿

Sheppy's Cider   TAUNTON

Map 03 ST22
Three Bridges, Bradford-on-Tone (3.5m SW, A38)
☎ Bradford-on-Tone (0823) 461233
Sheppy's is a traditional cider farm which has been producing cider commercially since 1925. Today the farm has 20 acres of standard and 22 acres of bush orchards. Visitors are encouraged to walk round the orchards, press room and excellent farm/cider

museum, and see the video show of the cidermaking year. Various ciders may be sampled before purchase in the farm shop. The craft and cider country fayre is held her on 25-26 July.
Open all year, Mon-Sat, May-Sep 8.30-7; Oct-Apr 8.30-6. Sun (Etr-Xmas only) noon-2.
£1.50 (ch 14 £1, pen £1.25). Party 20+.
🅿 ♿ *toilets for disabled shop* ✖ *(ex orchard)*

Somerset County Museum — TAUNTON

Map 03 ST22
Taunton Castle, Castle Green
☎ (0823) 255504
The part of Taunton Castle that makes up the county museum dates from the 13th century, and has exhibits of local archaeology and history, glass, ceramics, costumes and dolls. The Military Museum has relics of the Somerset Light Infantry from 1685 to 1959. The castle's great hall witnessed part of Judge Jeffrey's 'Bloody Assize' after the Monmouth Rebellion of 1685.
Open all year, Mon-Sat 10-5. (Closed Good Fri, 25-26 Dec & 1 Jan).
✱ *£1.20 (ch 30p, pen 80p).*
🅿 ♿ *shop* ✖

Tintinhull House Garden — TINTINHULL

Map 03 ST51
(.5m S off A303)
An attractive, mainly 17th-century farmhouse with a Queen Anne façade, it stands in four acres of beautiful formal gardens and orchard. The gardens were largely created by Mrs Reiss, who gave the property to the National Trust in 1953.
Open Apr-Sep, Wed, Thu, Sat & BH Mons 2-6 (last admission 5.30pm).
£2.80.
🅿 ✖
(NT)

Cleeve Abbey — WASHFORD

Map 03 ST04
☎ (0984) 40377
The Cistercian abbey was founded at the end of the 12th century and is now a ruin. There is little left of the church, but the gatehouse, dormitory and refectory are in good condition, with traceried windows, a fine timbered roof and wall paintings to be seen.
Open all year, Apr-Sep, daily 10-6; Oct-Mar, Tue-Sun 10-4. (Closed 24-26 Dec & 1 Jan).
£1.50 (ch 75p, students, pen & UB40 £1.10).
🅿 ♿
(EH)

Tropiquaria — WASHFORD

Map 03 ST04
(on A39)
☎ (0984) 40688
Housed in a 1930s BBC transmitting station, the main hall has been converted into an indoor jungle with a 15-foot waterfall, tropical plants and free-flying birds. (Snakes, lizards, iguanas, spiders, toads and terrapins are caged!) Downstairs is the submarine crypt with local and tropical marine life. Other features include landscaped gardens, outdoor aviaries, a children's playground and the Shadowstring Puppet Theatre.
Open all year, Mar-Oct daily 10-6; Nov, Jan-Feb wknds & school hols 10-4; 27-31 Dec, 10-4. Closed 1-26 Dec.
£2.90 (ch £1.50, student & pen £2.40).
🅿 ♿ *shop* ✖

Bishop's Palace — WELLS

Map 03 ST54
☎ (0749) 678691
Close to the cathedral is the moated bishop's palace. The early part of the palace, the bishop's chapel and the ruins of the banqueting hall date from the 13th century. The undercroft remains virtually unchanged from this time. There are several state rooms and a long gallery which houses portraits of former Bishops. The palace is ringed with fortifications as well as the moat and access can only be gained through the 14th-century gatehouse. The name of the city is taken from the wells in the palace grounds. Exhibitions include 'Alive in God's World', held in the Cathedral and the Palace (1-12 Jul), Somerset Guild of Craftsmen Exhibition (21 Jul-9 Aug), and the Guild of Glass Engravers Exhibition (17-31 Aug).
Open Etr-30 Oct, Thu & Sun; daily in Aug & BHs 2-6. Last admission 5.30.
✱ *£1.50 (ch 16 50p, pen £1.50 & UB40's £1 (2 ch free). Party 10+.*
🍴 ♿ *shop* ✖ *(ex in grounds)*

Wookey Hole Caves & Papermill — WOOKEY HOLE

Map 03 ST54
☎ Wells (0749) 672243

The Caves are the main feature of Wookey Hole. Visitors enjoy a half mile tour through the Chambers, accompanied by a knowledgeable guide who points out the amazing stalagmites and stalactites, including the famous Witch of Wookey. The guides use remote controlled lighting to highlight geological features and illustrate the history and myths associated with the caves.
Visitors also take in the Traditional Papermill, at one time amongst the largest handmade paper mills in Europe, which sold exquisite paper all over the world. Also in the Mill are the Fairground Memories, historically important late 19th century and early 20th century fairground rides. The latest attraction is the Magical Mirror Maze, an enclosed passage of multiple image mirrors creating an illusion of endless reflections. After the fun of the maze, visitors move on to a typical Old Penny Arcade where they can purchase old pennies to operate the original machines.
Open all year, Mar-Oct 9.30-5.30; Nov-Feb 10.30-4.30. (Closed 17-25 Dec).
✱ *£4.60 (ch £3, pen £4). Party 10+. Disabled £3 (ch in wheelchairs & helpers free).*
🅿 ✖ *licensed* ♿ *(ex Papermill) toilets for disabled shop* ✖ *(ex in grounds)*

✖ The 'No Dogs' symbol does not normally apply to guide dogs – these are permitted in most establishments.

Fleet Air Arm Museum — YEOVILTON

Map 03 ST52
Royal Naval Air Station (on B3151)
☎ Ilchester (0935) 840565

Based at the Royal Naval Air Station, the museum portrays the history and achievements of the Royal Naval Air Service, with examples from the early days of kites and airships to the present day. A collection of more than 50 historical aircraft, plus ship and aircraft models, paintings and photographs tell the story of aviation at sea from 1908. There are many special exhibitions including World War's I and II, the Falklands War, the Wrens, War in the Pacific and the Swordfish story. Most recent exhibitions include The Harrier Jump-Jet Story and the Underwater Experience. Of particular interest is the prototype of Concorde 002 and the exhibition of the development of supersonic flight. There are airfield viewing galleries where the aircraft from the Naval base may be observed, a flight simulator and a children's adventure playground.
Open all year, daily (ex 24-26 Dec) 10-5.30 (4.30pm Nov-Feb).
£4.50 (ch, students & UB40's £2.50, pen £3.50). Disabled £2. Family ticket £12.50.
🅿 🍴 ✖ *licensed* ♿ *toilets for disabled shop* ✖

SOUTH YORKSHIRE

Monk Bretton Priory   BARNSLEY

Map 08 SE30
(1.5m E)
☎ (0226) 204089
The priory was an important Cluniac house, founded in 1135. The considerable remains of the gatehouse, church and other buildings can be seen, and include some well-preserved drains.
Open all year, Apr-Sep, daily 10-6; Oct-Mar, Tue-Sun 10-4. (Closed 24-26 Dec & 1 Jan).
75p (ch 40p, pen, students & UB40 55p).
P & ✻
(EH)

Conisbrough Castle   CONISBROUGH

Map 08 SK59
☎ Rotherham (0709) 863329
The splendid 12th-century keep soars up beside the River Don, and has good views of the surrounding industrial landscape. It is circular with six buttresses – a unique design – and is surrounded by a curtain wall with solid round towers. The castle features in Sir Walter Scott's *Ivanhoe*.
Open all year, Apr-Sep, daily 10-6; Oct-Mar, Tue-Sun 10-4. (Closed 24-26 Dec & 1 Jan).
£1.50 (ch 75p, pen & UB40 £1.10).
P & ✻
(EH)

Cusworth Hall Museum   CUSWORTH

Map 08 SE50
☎ Doncaster (0302) 782342
The 18th-century house is the home of this museum of South Yorkshire life. There are sections of special interest to children, and the extensive grounds have fishing (in ponds), cricket and football pitches. A children's study base and research facilities are provided and a programme of special exhibitions and events is planned for 1992.
Open all year, Mon-Fri 10-5, Sat 11-5 & Sun 1-5. (4pm Dec & Jan) (Closed Good Fri, Xmas & 1 Jan).
Free.
P & *(wheelchair available) shop* ✻ *(ex park)*

Doncaster Museum & Art Gallery   DONCASTER

Map 08 SE50
Chequer Rd
☎ (0302) 734293
The wide-ranging collections include British and European paintings and sculpture. There are also ceramics, glass, silver, and displays on history, archaeology and natural history. The historical collection of the Kings Own Yorkshire Infantry is housed here, and temporary exhibitions are held.
Open all year, Mon-Sat 10-5, Sun 2-5. (Closed Good Fri, 25-26 Dec & 1 Jan).
Free.
& *(lift) toilets for disabled shop* ✻

Roche Abbey   MALTBY

Map 08 SK59
(1.5m SE)
☎ (0709) 812739
The walls of the south and north transepts still stand to their full height in this 12th-century Cistercian abbey, providing a dramatic sight for the visitor. There is also a fine gatehouse to the north-west.
Open all year, Apr-Sep, daily 10-6; Oct-Mar, wknds only 10-4. (Closed 24-26 Dec & 1 Jan).
£1.10 (ch 55p, students, pen & UB40 85p).
P &
(EH)

Art Gallery   ROTHERHAM

Map 08 SK49
Walker Place
☎ (0709) 382121 ext 3628/3635
The gallery hosts a continuous programme of temporary exhibitions, including, at times, the work of 19th- and 20th-century painters from the museum collections.
Open all year, Tue-Fri 10-6, Sat 10-5. (Closed Sun, Mon & BH).
Free.
♿ & *shop* ✻

Museum   ROTHERHAM

Map 08 SK49
Clifton Park, Clifton Ln
☎ (0709) 382121 ext 3628/3635
Housed in a mansion designed by John Carr, the museum is noted for its collection of Roman relics from the site of a fort at Templeborough, and also for its Rockingham china. Other attractions include the 18th-century rooms, family portraits, the period kitchen, Victoriana, Natural History displays, local church silver and glassware.
Open all year, Mon-Thu & Sat 10-5, Sun 2.30-5 (4.30pm Oct-Mar).
Free.
P & *shop* ✻

Abbeydale Industrial Hamlet   SHEFFIELD

Map 08 SK38
Abbeydale Rd South (4m SW of Sheffield off A621)
☎ (0742) 367731
One of the first places to be preserved, and made accessible to the public, as an example of industrial archaeology, built around a late 18th-century and early 19th-century water-powered scythe and steelworks. The works, with their machinery, show production from raw material stage to the finished product. Some of the worker's houses and the manager's house have been restored and furnished in period style. There are special Abbeydale Working Days, when visitors can see craftsmen at their forges.
Open all year, Wed-Sat 10-5 & Sun 11-5. Also open BH Mon. (Closed Xmas & New Year).
£1.80 (ch & pen 90p). Family ticket £3.60. On working days £2.10 (ch & pen £1.05). Family ticket £4.20.
P ♿ & *shop* ✻

Bishops' House   SHEFFIELD

Map 08 SK38
Meersbrook Park, Norton Lees Ln
☎ (0742) 557701
This 15th- and 16th-century yeoman's house has been restored and opened as a museum of local and social history. Several rooms that have been furnished and there are displays of life in Tudor and Stuart times as well as a range of temporary exhibitions. Special educational facilities can be arranged for schools and colleges. Special exhibitions for 1992 will include 'A nice cup of tea' (a display of teapots and other accessories).
Open all year, Wed-Sat 10-4.30, Sun 11-4.30; also BH Mon 10-4.30. (Closed 24-26 Dec).
✻ *60p (ch & pen 30p, UB40's free). Family ticket £1.20.*
& *shop* ✻

City Museum   SHEFFIELD

Map 08 SK38
Weston Park (on A57)
☎ (0742) 768588
The museum houses exhibits on regional geology, natural history and archaeology. There is a particularly splendid display of cutlery and Sheffield plate, for which the city is famous, among exhibits on other local industries such as ceramics, clocks, watches and sundials. Educational facilities are available for schools and colleges.
Open all year, Tue-Sat 10-5, Sun 11-5 also BH Mons. (Closed 24-26 Dec & 1 Jan). Please telephone to check opening times.
Free.
& *(Inductive loop. Handling sessions for pre-booked groups) toilets for disabled shop* ✻

Sheffield Industrial Museum   SHEFFIELD

Map 08 SK38
Kelham Island, Alma St
☎ (0742) 722106
Housed in a former generating station, this lively museum tells the story of Sheffield's industrial development over the last 400 years. There are displays of working machinery and traditional cutlery craftsmen can be seen at work, using the time-honoured skills of the industry. These are complemented by exhibitions of a wide variety of goods made in Sheffield, both past and present, and film and slide shows.
Open all year, Wed-Sat & BH Mon, 10-5; Sun 11-5. (Closed Xmas)
P ♿ & *toilets for disabled shop* ✻
Details not confirmed for 1992

Sheffield Manor Ruins   SHEFFIELD

Map 08 SK38
Manor Ln
☎ (0742) 768588
The ruins of a manor house, which began as a medieval hunting lodge, and are currently undergoing restoration and excavation. The principal seat of the Earls of Shrewsbury between 1406 and 1616, the house was enlarged in the 16th century. It fell into disrepair in the 17th century and in the early 1900s the site was cleared of all except the surviving 16th-century structures.
Open Jul-Oct. Please telephone for details of opening times.
✻ *Small charge payable.*
P & *shop* ✻

Shepherd Wheel   SHEFFIELD

Map 08 SK38
Whiteley Woods, off Hangingwater Rd
☎ (0742) 367731
An early, water-powered, cutlery grinding works that was established in 1584. The works here employed 10 people and used less sophisticated methods than those exhibited in other local industrial museums. The water wheel is operated daily, water levels permitting.
Open all year, Wed-Sat 10-12.30 & 1.30-5, Sun 11-12.30 & 1.30-5 (4pm Nov-Feb).
Free.

STAFFORDSHIRE

Alton Towers   ALTON

Map 07 SK04
☎ Oakamoor (0538) 702200

This is the most famous and longest-established of Britain's theme parks, voted 'Britain's most outstanding tourist attraction' by the British Tourist Authority.

There are more than 125 attractions, grouped into five theme areas, centred on the ruined mansion which was formerly the home of the Earl of Shrewsbury. For those who don't enjoy the prospect of the rides, the lovely and extensive terraced gardens are a delight. For most people, however, Alton Towers means white-knuckle and white-water rides. Most famous of all is the Corkscrew Rollercoaster, but rivalling it for sheer terror is the Black Hole, introduced for the Alton Towers 1988 Silver Jubilee Year. White-water rides include the Grand Canyon Rapids and Log Flume, and on both of these you are liable to get quite wet – something to remember if the weather is cold. There are lots of gentler amusements too – from the Swanboat to the Scenic Skyride that takes you all around the park. For those who only want the illusion of adventure, there is a fantastic 3-D cinema with an enormous screen, and Kiddies Kingdom provides for the younger visitor.
Open mid Mar-early Nov 9am until 1 hr after attractions close. Attractions 10-5, 6 or 7 as shown daily at main entrance gate. Grounds & gardens daily mid Nov-mid Mar at reduced rates.
P ♿ ✗ *licensed & toilets for disabled shop. Details not confirmed for 1992*

Cheddleton Flint Mill

The Industrial Museum specialising in the history and preparation of the raw materials used in **the Pottery Industry.** This unique Watermill complements Gladstone Pottery, Museum & Stoke-on-Trent City Museum in Hanley. Cheddleton Flint Mill is a Charity.

Open almost every day.

Admission free, but donations very welcome

Biddulph Grange Garden · BIDDULPH

Map 08 SJ85
☎ (0782) 517999
This exciting and rare survival of a high Victorian garden has undergone extensive restoration which will continue for a number of years. Conceived by James Bateman, the fifteen acres are divided into a number of smaller gardens which were designed to house specimens from his extensive and wide-ranging plant collection. An Egyptian Court,

Chinese Pagoda, Willow Pattern Bridge and Pinetum together with many other settings all combine to make the Garden a miniature tour of the world.
Open Apr-Oct, Wed-Fri 12-6, Sat-Sun & BH Mon 11-6 (last admission 5.30 or dusk if earlier); Nov-20 Dec, Sat-Sun 12-4.
✱ *£3.50 (ch £1.75). Family ticket £8.75*
🅿 ☂ *shop* ✘
(NT)

For an explanation of the symbols and abbreviations, see page 2.

Bass Museum, Visitor Centre & Shire Horse Stables · BURTON-UPON-TRENT

Map 07 SK22
Horninglow St (on A50)
☎ Burton Upon Trent (0283) 42031
The museum is housed in the Engineers' Department and Company's Joiner's Shop, built in 1866. Three floors of entertaining and interesting exhibits trace the history of the brewing industry from its earliest times to the present day. Outside there are larger exhibits, such as a 1917 steam lorry and a Daimler van in the shape of a bottle of IPA. Other attractions are a model of Burton as it was in 1921, stables with Shire horses,

and a steam locomotive. There is a fine collection of drinking glasses, and there is also the beer. Special events take place on most weekends throughout the summer and there are brass band concerts every fourth Sunday lunchtime.
Open all year, Mon-Fri 10-5, Sat & Sun 11-5. Last admission 4pm. (Closed 25-26 Dec & 1 Jan).
✱ *£2.95 (ch £1.50, pen £1.95). Family ticket £7.75. Party. Brewery tours by arrangement only, at extra charge.*
🅿 ✘ *licensed & toilets for disabled shop* ✘

Heritage Brewery Museum · BURTON-UPON-TRENT

Map 07 SK22
Anglesey Rd
☎ Burton-on-Trent (0283) 69226
Heritage Brewery Museum as typical of the hundreds of Victorian Breweries built during the expansion of brewing in the last half of the century. Most are now mere memories but this one has been saved, together with its cottages,

stables and wagon sheds to become England's first independent working brewery museum.
Open Etr-Sep, Mon-Sat 10-4; Oct-Etr, Tue-Sat 10-2.
£2.50 (ch £1, concessions £2). Family ticket £5.50. Party 20+.
🅿 & *toilets for disabled shop* ✘

Flint Mill · CHEDDLETON

Map 07 SJ95
beside Caldon Canal, Leek Rd
☎ Barlaston (078139) 2561
Two water mills complete with wheels are preserved here, and both are in working order. The 17th-century south mill was used to grind corn, but the 18th-century north mill was built to grind flint for the pottery industry. The restored buildings have displays on aspects of the pottery industry. Exhibits

include examples of motive power, such as a Robey steam engine, and of transport, such as the restored 70ft horse-drawn narrow boat 'Vienna', which is moored on the Caldon Canal. There is also a haystack boiler of around 1770.
Open all year, Sat & Sun 2-5; Apr-Oct, Mon-Fri 10-5.
Donations.
🅿 &

Drayton Manor Park & Zoo · DRAYTON MANOR PARK & ZOO

Map 07 SK10
(on A4091)
☎ Tamworth (0827) 287979
A family leisure park with 160 acres of parkland, lakes, open-plan zoo and amusements. There are over 40 rides, including the Pirate Adventure, the looping roller coaster, log flume, Paratower, cable cars, Dinosaurland, Jungle Cruise, Flying Dutchman, Jungle Palladium Theatre, and the Pirate

Ship. Wristbands for unlimited rides are available or discount tickets for multiple or single rides.
Park & Zoo open Etr-Sep, daily 10.30-6 (Also Oct wknds & school holiday). Park (rides) 10.30-5, 6 or 7 (depending on season).
Free.
🅿 *(charged)* ☂ ✗ *licensed & toilets for disabled shop garden centre* ✘ *(ex in park)*
See advertisement on page 148.

✱ An asterisk indicates that up-to-date information was not available at the time of our research – 1991 information has been published as an indication of what you may expect.

Himley Hall · HIMLEY

Map 07 SO89
Himley Rd (off A449)
☎ Dudley (0384) 456000 ext 5514
The extensive parkland offers a range of attractions, from a model village to a nine-hole golf course and coarse fishing.

The hall is *not* open to the public.
Open all year, daily 8-8pm or half hour before dusk.
🅿 *(charged)* ☂ &
Details not confirmed for 1992

Hanch Hall · LICHFIELD

Map 07 SK10
(4m NW on B5014)
☎ Armitage (0543) 490308
A rare Regency four-poster bed, used by the poet Shelley; collections of needlework; antique dolls; early parchments; costumes and a postal display are all exhibited in this small country mansion, which has a fine

Jacobean staircase and an observation tower.
Open 31 Mar-29 Sep, Sun & BH Mon & following Tue 2-6; also Thu from 6 Jun & Sats in Jul & Aug 2-6. Parties by arrangement only.
🅿 ☂ & *shop* ✘
Details not confirmed for 1992

Lichfield Heritage Exhibition & Treasury · LICHFIELD

Map 07 SK10
St Mary's Centre Market Square
☎ (0543) 256611
Fine silver in the Treasury and lively presentations on the Civil War and the seige of Lichfield Cathedral, including a video entitled 'Lichfield – A Walk Through History', are featured here. The displays, housed in the ancient Guild Church of St Mary's, tell the

centuries-old story of the city.
Open all year, daily 10-5 (Closed Xmas, New Year & Spring BH Mon).
✱ *85p (ch, students & pen 40p). Family ticket £1.70. (Joint ticket with Samuel Johnson Birthplace Museum £1.20, concessions 60p). School parties by arrangement.*
✗ & *(lift) toilets for disabled shop* ✘

Samuel Johnson Birthplace Museum · LICHFIELD

Map 07 SK10
Breadmarket St
☎ (0543) 264972
A statue of Dr Johnson sits at one end of Market Square facing his birthplace on the corner of Breadmarket Street. The house, where Samuel's father has a bookshop, is now a museum containing many of Johnson's personal relics. His

favourite armchair and walking stick are among the collection.
Open daily 10-5. (Closed, Xmas & New Year).
90p (ch & pen 50p). Joint ticket with Lichfield Heritage Centre £1.50 (ch & pen 80p). Family ticket £2.30. Party.
shop ✘

Moseley Old Hall · MOSELEY

Map 07 SJ90
☎ Wolverhampton (0902) 782808
Charles II sheltered in Moseley Old Hall after the Battle of Worcester in 1651. He slept in the four-poster bed in the King's Room, and hid in a concealed space below a cupboard in the room. There are numerous pictures and other reminders of the king, and much of the furniture in the panelled room dates from around his time. The house itself is

an Elizabethan timber-framed building, which was encased in brick in the 19th century.
Open Apr-Oct, Wed, Sat, & Sun; Tue, Jul-Aug, 2-5.30. Also BH Mon 11-5. Pre-booked parties at other times.
£2.80 (ch £1.40). Family ticket £7. Party 15+.
🅿 ☂ ✗ *licensed & toilets for disabled shop* ✘
(NT)

Discover the dark secrets of the Caribbean Pirates on the amazing Pirate Adventure, it's the only ride like it anywhere in the U.K. It's big, it's exciting, it's at Drayton Manor Park.

160 ACRES OF PARKLAND AND LAKES

Over 50 rides and attractions from Roller Coasters and Sky Flyers to children's rides. Also Zoo, Museums and Zoo Farm, Jungle Cruise, Boating Lake, Woodland Walks, Restaurants, take-aways, Garden Centre, Shops, Green Grass Parking. There's never been so much for all ages.

Open Every Day 10.30 am – 5/6 pm Easter until end of October.

ONLY AT DRAYTON MANOR THE AMAZING **Pirate Adventure**

THE ONLY ONE IN THE U.K.

Drayton Manor Park and Zoo

Admission to Park, Zoo, Museums and Zoo Farm. Adult £2, Child £1 – Car 50p.

Wristband to ride all day including The Pirate Adventure £5.50 or discount tickets available.

ATTRACTIVE GROUP DISCOUNTS

Drayton Manor Park

Just off M42 (J9) on A 4091, Signposted. Nr. Tamworth, Staffordshire B78 3TW. Telephone: (0827) 287979.

Wolseley Garden Park   RUGELEY

Map 07 SK01
Wolseley Bridge (at junc of A51 & A513)
☎ (0889) 574766 & 574888
These beautiful ornamental gardens are the creation of Sir Charles and Lady Wolseley on land that has been in the Wolseley family for over a thousand years. Presently the gardens occupy forty-five acres and comprise excitingly different and beautiful theme gardens. There is the Spring Garden, the Rose Garden and the Scented Garden, whose fragrant herbs and shrubs offer particular enjoyment to the visually handicapped. Other areas of interest are the Water and Bog Garden, the Cathedral Garden and the Lakeside Walks. there is also a Museum and Garden Centre.
Open all year, daily 10-5.30 (or dusk if earlier). Open wknds only in severe winter weather. (Closed 25 Dec).
🅿 ⚫ ✗ *licensed* ♿ *(scented garden for the blind & audio guides) toilets for disabled shop garden centre* 🐕
Details not confirmed for 1992

🐕 The 'No Dogs' symbol does not normally apply to guide dogs – these are permitted in most establishments.

Shugborough Hall & Staffordshire County Museum   SHUGBOROUGH

Map 07 SJ92
(6m E of Stafford off A513)
☎ Little Haywood (0889) 881388
Shugborough Hall is the stately home of the Earls of Lichfield. It was begun in 1693 but was enlarged in the 18th and 19th centuries, largely by the architect Samuel Wyatt. There are magnificent state rooms with notable plasterwork, elegant Louis XV and XVI furniture, fine 18th- and 19-century silver and glassware and a collection of paintings. Among the offices, the kitchens, butler's pantry, laundry and brewhouse have been restored as museums but are fully operational.

The landscaped grounds are unusual in that they have seven large monuments scattered through them. These include a Chinese House, probably influenced by Admiral Anson's stay in China in the early 1700s, and also four monuments designed by James 'Athenian' Stuart in the Greek Revival style. There is also a working rare breeds farm, an agricultural museum and a restored corn mill in the park. Many special events, exhibitions and concerts take place throughout the year, including a classic car show (3-4 May), a goose fair (19 Jul), and The Great Bread Race (20 Sep).
Open 28 Mar-Oct, daily 11-5. Site open all year to pre-booked parties from 10.30am on weekdays.
✱ *Entry to Estate £1 per car. Mansion £3 (ch, pen & UB40's £2); Museum £3 (ch, pen & UB40's £2); Farm £3 (ch, pen & UB40's £2). Combined ticket £7.50 (ch, pen & UB40's £5). Family ticket £15.*
🅿 *(charged)* ⚫ ✗ ♿ *(wheelchairs provided) toilets for disabled shop garden centre* 🐕 *(ex in parkland)*
(NT)

Stafford Art Gallery   STAFFORD

Map 07 SJ92
Lichfield Rd
☎ (0785) 57303
The art gallery specialises in temporary exhibitions of contemporary art, craft and photography. There is also a craft shop selling a wide range of fine products from British craft workers, selected for quality by the Crafts Council. There will be a Brendan Neiland one-man exhibition from May to June.
Open all year, Tue-Fri 10-5, Sat 10-4. Free.
shop 🐕

Chatterley Whitfield Mining Museum   STOKE-ON-TRENT

Map 07 SJ84
Chatterley Whitfield Colliery, Tunstall (on A527)
☎ (0782) 813337
Chatterley Whitfield opened in 1979 as Britain's first underground mining museum on the site of the former million ton per annum Whitfield Colliery Complex. Established to preserve and present the story of coal mining in North Staffordshire, Chatterley Whitfield's purpose has broadened during the site's 11 year
continued . . .

history as a working museum of the mining industry. With British Coal's decision in 1989 to relocate their national collection of mining artefacts to Whitfield, the museum is now emerging as a major national archive for students of mining history.

The museum can offer visitors tours led by retired miner guides which include pit cage and manrider locomotive rides, together with retired pit ponies in their underground stalls. On the surface visitors can enjoy the sight of restored winding and compressor engines or marvel at the Museum's working steam railway. Visiting school and leisure groups can participate in Whitfield's Sandford award-winning Heritage Education Services. All visitors can take refreshments in the site's 1930s pit canteen. Events for 1992 include a rock and mineral fair on 2 May, and a bus rally on 7 June.
Open all year, daily 10-5, last tour 4pm (Closed 25-26 Dec).
✳ *£3.95 (ch 5-16 £2.95, pen, students & UB40 £2.95). Family ticket £11.95. Party.*
🅿 ⬤ ⬤ (surface only) toilets for disabled shop

City Museum & Art Gallery   STOKE-ON-TRENT

Map 07 SJ84
Bethesda St, Hanley
☎ (0782) 202173

A full picture of the Potteries is given here, with displays on social and natural history, archaeology and fine art as well as an exceptionally large and fine collection of ceramics. There is a particular emphasis on Staffordshire pottery and porcelain. Temporary exhibitions are held regularly.
Open all year, Mon-Sat 10-5, Sun 2-5. (Closed Good Fri & Xmas).
Free.
⬤ ⬤ (lift, induction loop in theatre) toilets for disabled shop ✈

For an explanation of the symbols and abbreviations, see page 2.

Ford Green Hall   STOKE-ON-TRENT

Map 07 SJ84
Ford Green Rd, Smallthorne (on the B5051)
☎ (0782) 534771
This timber-framed farmhouse was built in 1624 for the Ford family, and extended in the early 1700s. It is furnished with items and utensils used by a farming family from the 16th to the 19th century.
Open all year, Mon-Sun 1-5. (Closed Xmas & New Year). Tours available at 1.15, 2.15, 3.15 & 4.15.
Free.
🅿 ⬤ ⬤ toilets for disabled shop ✈

Gladstone Pottery Museum   STOKE-ON-TRENT

Map 07 SJ84
Uttoxeter Rd, Longton
☎ (0782) 319232
The museum has been created in a restored 'potbank', where day-to-day household chinaware was once produced. This small Victorian pottery is still complete with old warehouses, workshops and four huge bottle ovens. There are daily demonstrations by skilled craftsmen on the making and decorating of pottery. Also to be seen are galleries where colourful examples of tableware, tiles and sanitary ware are exhibited, and there is a history section. Pottery is sold in the shop.
Open all year, Mon-Sat 10-5, Sun 2-5. (Closed Mon & Sun, Nov-Feb). Limited opening Xmas & New Year.
£2.75 (ch £1.50, students & pen £2).
🅿 ⬤ ⬤ toilets for disabled shop

Minton Museum   STOKE-ON-TRENT

Map 07 SJ84
London Rd
☎ (0782) 744766
The Minton Museum shows fine examples of the factory's production from 1800 to the present day. The display includes many large exhibits such as the 5ft tall Minton majolica-glazed peacock, fawn, stork and heron. Minton china can be purchased.
Open all year, Mon-Fri 9-1 & 1.45-4.30 (Closed factory holidays). Shop Mon-Sat 9-5.30.
Free.
🅿 shop ✈

Sir Henry Doulton Gallery   STOKE-ON-TRENT

Map 07 SJ84
Nile St, Burslem
☎ (0782) 575454 ext 320
A tribute to Sir Henry Doulton, the gallery contains pottery treasures and artistry covering 150 years. There are nearly 300 figures on display, some very early pieces and some very rare. There are also displays showing the great variety of the Royal Doulton tradition, accompanied by archive material, sketches, pattern books and medals. There are additional displays of ceramic painting by outstanding artists as well as experimental ceramic work. Tours of the factory are also available.
Open all year, Mon-Fri 9.30-4.30. Factory tours by appointment. (Closed factory holidays). Shop Mon-Sat 9-5.30. Museum Free. Factory tours £2 (students & pen £1.75). Party 30+.
🅿 shop ✈

For an explanation of the symbols and abbreviations, see page 2.

Spode   STOKE-ON-TRENT

Map 07 SJ84
Church St
☎ (0782) 744011
This is the oldest manufacturing ceramic factory on its original site (established in 1770) where Josiah Spode first perfected the formula of bone china. Tours commence from the museum and visitors are shown production methods, under-glaze printing and processing to produce the finest tableware. Standard tours are one hour and connoisseur tours are two hours. Prior booking is essential.
Open Tours Mon-Thu 10 & 2, Fri 10 only (Closed during factory holidays). (ch under 12 precluded from factory tour). Shop Mon-Thu 9-5, Fri 9-4, Sat 9-1. (Closed BH's).
✳ *Standard tours £1.75; Connoisseur tour £5. By appointment only.*
🅿 ⬤ ⬤ shop ✈

Wedgwood Visitor Centre   STOKE-ON-TRENT

Map 07 SJ84
Barlaston (5m S)
☎ (0782) 204141 & 204218
The complex includes an art gallery with works by Reynolds, Stubbs and Romney, and a reconstruction of Wedgwood's original 18th-century Etruria workshops. There are demonstrations of the traditional skills in the production of Wedgwood ware, and a museum containing a comprehensive collection of the works of Josiah Wedgwood from 1750. A video gives the history of Wedgwood wares and demonstrates the craft of Wedgwood production; and there is a shop where products may be bought.
Open all year, Mon-Fri 9-5, Sat 10-4; Also Sun (Etr-Oct) 10-4. (Closed Xmas & 1 Jan).
£2.50 (ch, students & pen £1.25). Family ticket £6.50. Reductions Nov-Feb.
🅿 ⬤ ⬤ toilets for disabled shop ✈

The Childrens Farm

at ASH END HOUSE FARM, Middleton,
Nr. Tamworth, Staffs. *(signposted off A4091)*

OPEN ALL YEAR. Friendly farm animals, rare breeds, shire horses, play area, farm shop and tea room, picnic barns. Guided tours for schools, playgroups, playschemes, cubs, brownies, etc., and also **BIRTHDAY PARTIES ON THE FARM** (3 prices) — all by arrangement.
Open every day to the public (except Xmas and Boxing Day) 10.00am – 6.00pm (or dusk in winter).

Admission: £2.20 per child — includes: Bucket of animal food, Badge, Pony Ride, Fresh egg from nest boxes (when available).

ADULTS HALF PRICE £1.10!!

Toilet for the Disabled   Sorry, no dogs

Tamworth Castle — TAMWORTH

Map 07 SK20
The Holloway
☎ (0827) 63563
The castle is a mixture of Norman Gothic, Tudor, Jacobean and early 19th-century architecture, showing the tastes of its inhabitants over 700 years. It started as a Norman motte-and-bailey castle, with the walls of its keep 10ft thick at the base, and outer walls and a gatehouse were added in the 13th-century. The Tudor period brought additions of a more domestic sort, with a splendid, timber-roofed great hall and a warden's lodge.
The Jacobean state apartments have fine woodwork, furniture and heraldic friezes, including 55 oak panels painted with the arms of the lords of the castle up to 1787. There is a Norman exhibition with 'speaking' knight, a haunted bedroom, The Chapel, Annie Cook's bedroom and a Victorian nursery.
Outside are floral terraces and pleasure grounds with swimming pool and adventure playground.
Open all year, Mon-Sat 10-5.30; Sun 2-5.30. Last admission 4.30.(Closed 25 Dec).
ᵴ *shop* ✝
Details not confirmed for 1992

Wall Roman Site — WALL

Map 07 SK10
Watling St
☎ Shenstone (0543) 480768
Wall was originally the Roman fort of Letocetum. It was situated at the crossroads of Watling Street and Rykneild Street, and was an important military base from about AD50. Excavations started in the 19th century revealed the most complete bath house ever found in Britain. There are three baths: cold, tepid and hot as well as a furnace room and an exercise hall. A small museum at the site exhibits finds from this and other nearby Roman sites.
Open all year, Apr-Sep, daily 10-6; Oct-Mar, Tue-Sun 10-4. (Closed 24-26 Dec & 1 Jan).
£1.10 (ch 55p, pen, students & UB40 85p). (EH & NT)

Weston Park — WESTON PARK

Map 07 SJ81
(7m W of junc 12 of M6;3m N of junc 3 on M54)
☎ Weston-under-Lizard (095276) 207
Built in 1671, this fine mansion stands in elegant gardens and a vast park designed by 'Capability' Brown. Three lakes, a miniature railway, and a woodland adventure playground are to be found in the grounds, and in the house itself there is a notable collection of pictures, furniture and tapestries. Additional attractions are special events, including point-to-points, festivals of transport, craft fairs, dog shows, and others.
Open 17 Apr-21 Apr; 25 Apr-14 Jun wknds & BH (ex 4 May & Spring BH wk); 15 Jun-Jul daily (ex Mon & Fri); Aug daily; 1-20 Sep wknds only. Park 11-7 (last admission 5pm); House 1pm (last admission 5pm).
Park £3 (ch & pen £2). House £1 (ch & pen 75p).
P ⬛ ᵴ *(disabled route) toilets for disabled shop*

STAFFORDSHIRE

This Norman shell keep, in beautiful riverside grounds yet adjacent to the historic town centre, offers something for everyone. Amongst its features are the magnificent period rooms (3 new for 1992) depicting scenes from the lives of the Castle's former occupants, spanning nearly 800 years, plus firm favourites like the 'speaking' Norman Knight, Dungeon & Haunted Bedroom.
Open all year: 1000-1730 (1400-1730 Sun)   Last Admissions: 1630.
Easy access from M6 & M42 via A5.   **Tel: Tamworth (0827) 63563**

Staffordshire Regiment Museum, Whittington Barracks — WHITTINGTON

Map 07 SK10
☎ 021-311 3240/3229
Situated adjacent to the barracks, the museum displays a collection of regimental militaria. The exhibits include the regiment's battle honours, captured trophies, a variety of weapons of different ages, medals and uniforms past and present.
Open all year, Mon-Fri 9-4 (Closed BH & Xmas-New Year). Parties at other times by arrangement.
Free.
P ᵴ *shop*

The Dorothy Clive Garden — WILLOUGHBRIDGE

Map 07 SJ74
(on A51 between Nantwich & Stone)
☎ Pipegate (063081) 237
In the small village of Willoughbridge is a 200-year-old gravel quarry converted into a delightful woodland garden. The quarry is at the top of a small hill and the garden, which covers over 7 acres, has fine views of the countryside and adjoining counties. Among the tall oak trees are daffodils, rhododendrons and azaleas in profusion. There is also a variety of rare trees and shrubs, and water and rock gardens have been created among the steep banks. The garden provides colour and interest throughout the seasons from spring to glowing autumn tints.
Open Apr-Oct, daily 10-5.30.
£2 (ch 50p). Party 20+.
P ⬛ ᵴ *(wheelchairs for use) toilets for disabled*

SUFFOLK

Moot Hall Museum — ALDEBURGH

Map 05 TM45
☎ (0728) 452730
Standing close to the sea, the Moot Hall is a brick and timber-framed building of the 16th century. An outside staircase leads to the first-floor Council Chamber, where there are old maps and prints and objects of local historical interest with emphasis on maritime history and coastal erosion. Other exhibits include displays on archaeology, geology and natural history.
Open Etr-Jun & Sep, Sat & Sun 2.30-6; Jul-Sep daily 10.30-12.30 & 2.30-5. 35p (accompanied ch free)
shop ✝

The Otter Trust — BUNGAY

Map 05 TM38
Earsham (off A143)
☎ (0986) 893470
Otters are a rare sight in the wild nowadays, but at the Otter Trust it is possible to see these beautiful creatures at close quarters. While they are entertaining to watch, one of the Trust's main aims is to breed this endangered species in captivity in sufficient numbers so that it can re-introduce young otters into the wild every year wherever suitable habitat remains to reinforce the vanishing wild population. This re-introduction programme has been running very successfully since 1983 and is carried out in conjunction with English Nature. The Trust has now introduced captive-bred otters into the wild in Norfolk, Suffolk, Dorset, Hampshire and Hertfordshire and subsequent scientific monitoring has shown that nearly all these animals are breeding successfully. This has resulted in the wild otter population of Norfolk increasing to almost what it was twenty years ago. The Otter Trust covers 23 acres on the banks of the river Waveney. As well as the otter pens there are three lakes with a large collection of European waterfowl, lovely riverside walks and picnic areas.
Open Apr (or Good Fri if earlier)-Oct, daily 10.30-6.
✱ *£3 (ch £1.50, pen £2.50). Disabled person & pusher free.*
P ⬛ ᵴ *toilets for disabled shop* ✝

The Clock Museum — BURY ST EDMUNDS

Map 04 TL86
Angel Corner, 8 Angel Hill
☎ (0284) 757072 (Mon-Fri) & 757076 (wknds)
Angel Corner is a Queen Anne house owned by the National Trust, and is home to the wonderful Gershom-Parkington collection of clocks, watches and other timepieces. Important collections of fine art are also housed here.
Open all year Mon-Sat 10-5, Sun 2-5. (Closed Good Fri, 25 & 26 Dec).
Free.
ᵴ *shop* ✝
(NT)

Moyse's Hall Museum — BURY ST EDMUNDS

Map 04 TL86
Cornhill
☎ (0284) 757072 & 757488
This rare 12th-century house of flint and stone is now a museum of Suffolk history, archaeology and natural history. The clock tower is open by appointment. Temporary exhibitions are held throughout the year.
Open all year Mon-Sat 10-5, Sun 2-5. (Closed 25-26 Dec & Good Fri).
✱ *Donations welcome*
ᵴ *shop* ✝

Cavendish Manor Vineyards & Nether Hall — CAVENDISH

Map 04 TL84
☎ Glemsford (0787) 280221
The 15th-century manor house stands surrounded by its vineyards in the pretty Stour Valley village. Paintings and rural bygones are shown in the house and museum next to it. Tours of the vineyards and wine tasting are offered.
Open all year, daily 11-4.
£2 (pen £1.50, ch 16 free)
P ᵴ *shop* ✝

THE SUE RYDER FOUNDATION MUSEUM CAVENDISH SUFFOLK

This museum depicts the remarkable story of how the Foundation was established, its work today and its hopes for the future.

Open daily: 10am-5.30pm
Admission: Adults 80p,
Children 12 & under & OAPs 40p
Refreshments Rooms and delightful gardens adjoin the Museum. Lunches and light meals available. Lunch and Supper parties by arrangement. Menu on request. Gift Shop.

Advance bookings: Please write to:
The Sue Ryder Foundation, Cavendish, Suffolk CO10 8AY

Sue Ryder Foundation Museum   CAVENDISH

Map 04 TL84
Sue Ryder Home & Headquarters (on A1092)
☎ Glemsford (0787) 280252
The museum shows the work and history of the small but effective international foundation which cares for the sick and disabled. The home's garden and chapel are also open.
Open all year, daily 10-5.30. (Closed 25 Dec).
80p (ch 12 & pen 40p). Parties by appointment.
P ✗ & *toilets for disabled shop* ✗

This is just one of many guidebooks published by the AA. The full range is available at any AA shop or good bookshop.

Easton Farm Park   EASTON

Map 05 TM25
☎ Wickham Market (0728) 746475
Visitors can watch cows being milked at a modern dairy operation, alongside a Victorian dairy established by the Duke of Hamilton in 1870. Victorian dairy equipment is also on display, and the farm park has a collection of farming implements and vehicles. There is also a new exhibition on food and farming: Foodchains. There are Suffolk Punch horses and rare breeds of farm animals and other attractions include a picnic area, and adventure playground. There are also nature trails to follow through damp woodland and pasture alongside the River Deben. Interesting woodland and wetland plants and animals may be seen. There will be a country fair on 21 June.
Open 22 Mar-27 Sep, daily 10.30-6 Last admission 4.30.
£3.50 (ch3-16 £2, pen £2.75). Party 20+.
P ✠ & *toilets for disabled shop*

Places to visit in this guide are pinpointed on the atlas at the back of the book.

Euston Hall   EUSTON

Map 04 TL87
(on A1088)
☎ Thetford (0842) 766366
The 18th-century house is notable for its fine collection of pictures, by Stubbs, Lely, Van Dyck and other masters. The grounds were laid out by John Evelyn, William Kent and 'Capability' Brown, and include a 17th-century church in the style of Wren.
Open 4 Jun-24 Sep, Thu only & Suns 28 Jun & 6 Sep 2.30-5.
£2.25 (ch 50p, pen £1.50). Party 12+.
Wheelchairs free.
P ✠ & *shop* ✗

Norfolk & Suffolk Aviation Museum   FLIXTON

Map 05 TM38
(off A143, take B1062)
☎ Thurton (0508) 480778
This collection of aircraft and related items spans the history of aviation from the Wright Brothers onwards. There are 16 aircraft on display outside. Aircraft are displayed inside the museum's Blister Hanger. Special event for 1992 will be a display in a nissen hut called '2nd Air Division, 8th Air Force, USAAF'..'
Open Apr-Oct Sun & BH 10-5; Jun-Aug Wed & Thu 7pm-9pm also Jul & Aug Thu 11-5. Parties at other times by arrangement.
Free.
P & *shop* ✗

Framlingham Castle   FRAMLINGHAM

Map 05 TM26
☎ (0728) 723330
Built by Roger Bigod between 1177 and 1215, the castle has fine curtain walls, 13 towers and an array of Tudor chimneys. Queen Mary was told here that she was Queen of England. In the 17th century the castle was bequeathed to Pembroke College, which built almshouses inside the walls.
Open all year, Apr-Sep, daily 10-6; Oct-Mar, Tue-Sun 10-4. (Closed 24-26 Dec & 1 Jan)
£1.50 (ch 75p, pen, students & UB40 £1.10).
P & *shop*
(EH)

Ickworth   HORRINGER

Map 04 TL86
(2.5m S of Bury St Edmunds).
☎ (028488) 270
Ickworth was designed to show off works of art: it is a 100ft-high oval rotunda with two curved corridors, which were meant to be painting and sculpture galleries. The building was commissioned in 1796 by Frederick Hervey (pronounced Harvey), who collected many items for Ickworth, most of which were confiscated by Napoleon. The house is filled with treasures amassed by the family, however. It has fine furniture and porcelain, one of England's most splendid silver collections, sculptures, and paintings by Velasquez, Lawrence, Kauffmann, Gainsborough and others. The formal gardens are noted for fine trees and there are extensive park walks, a deer enclosure and a children's play area.
Open: House & Garden 28 Mar, Apr & Oct wknds only; Mar-Sep Tue, Wed, Fri, Sat, Sun & BH Mons 1.30-5.30. Park open daily 7-7pm.
House, Garden & Park £4.10 (ch £2); Garden & park £1.50. Party 15+
P ✗ *licensed* & *toilets for disabled shop* ✗
(NT)

Christchurch Mansion   IPSWICH

Map 04 TM14
Soane St (South side of Christchurch Park)
☎ (0473) 253246 & 213761

The original house, built in 1548 on the site of an Augustinian priory, was damaged by fire and largely rebuilt in the 17th century. At the end of the 19th century the house and parkland were saved by the Cobbold family from redevelopment; today Christchurch Mansion, set in a beautiful park, shows off its period furnished rooms. There is also an art gallery with a lively temporary exhibition programme; a Suffolk artists' gallery and a good collection of Constables and Gainsboroughs.
Open all year, Tue-Sat 10-5 (dusk in winter), Sun 2.30-4.30 (dusk in winter). (Closed Good Fri & 24-26 Dec).
Free.
& *(tape guide for partially sighted) shop* ✗

Ipswich Museum   IPSWICH

Map 04 TM14
High St
☎ (0473) 213761
The museum has sections on local geology and archaeology from prehistoric to medieval times, and there is also a 'Roman Suffolk' gallery. Another section explores the story of mankind all over the world and a temporary exhibition programme is held. There is a new 'Victorian' natural history gallery.
Open all year, Tue-Sat 10-5. (Closed Sun, BH's & 24-26 Dec).
Free.
& *shop* ✗

Lavenham Guildhall   LAVENHAM

Map 04 TL94
Market Place
☎ (0787) 247646
Although it has been much restored, there are still many of the original Tudor features left in this picturesque timber-framed building. The hall and its small museum are a testament to the time when East Anglia had a flourishing woollen industry.
Open 28 Mar-1 Nov, daily 11-5. (Closed Good Fri).
£2 (ch 60p)
✠ *shop* ✗
(NT)

The Priory   LAVENHAM

Map 04 TL94
Water St
☎ (0787) 247417
This fine medieval timber-framed building was built for Benedictine monks. It has been well restored, and photographs illustrating the restoration work are on display inside, together with drawings, paintings and stained glass by Erwin Bossanyi. Outside is a uniquely designed herb garden.
Open Apr-Oct daily, 10.30-5.30. Guided tours for groups by appointment.
£2 (ch £1).
✠ ✗ *shop* ✗

Leiston Abbey — LEISTON

Map 05 TM46
For hundreds of years this 14th-century abbey was used as a farm and its church became a barn. A Georgian house was built into its fabric and this is now used as a retreat house for the local diocese. The rest of the abbey is in ruins, but

remains of the choir and transepts of the church, and the ranges of cloisters still stand.
Open any reasonable time.
Free.
P &
(EH)

Long Shop Museum — LEISTON

Map 05 TM46
Main St
☎ (0728) 832189
The Long Shop Museum, winner of no fewer than seven national awards, features 200 years of Richard Garrett engineering, the town of Leiston and its surroundings. Exhibits include steam

engines, steam rollers, traction engines, and a large display of USAAF memorabilia from the World War II air base. Special events for 1992 include Steam Days and educational features.
Open Apr-Oct, Mon-Sat 10-5, Sun 11-5.
£1.20 (ch & pen 60p)
P & *toilets for disabled shop* ✱

St James's Chapel — LINDSEY

Map 04 TL94
Rose Green
Built mainly in the 13th century, this small thatched, flint-and-stone chapel incorporates some earlier work.

Open all year.
Free.
&
(EH)

Kentwell Hall — LONG MELFORD

Map 04 TL84
(off A134)
☎ Sudbury (0787) 310207
The major appeal of this Tudor manor house is its lived-in feeling: it is indeed a much-loved family home and great efforts have been made to retain its unique atmosphere. The mellow, red-brick, E-shaped building is surrounded by a broad moat and externally little has been altered. Appropriately enough, the

house displays an exhibition of Tudor style costume, while outside a brick-pave mosaic maze and rare breeds of farm animals are the chief attractions.
Open: House, Moat House, Gardens & Farm; 2-5 Apr, 28 May-2 Jun, 17 Jul-29 Sep, daily 12-5. Also 7 Apr-19 May, 9-16 Jun & 6-27 Oct, Sun only 12-5.
P & & *shop* ✱
Details not confirmed for 1992

Melford Hall — LONG MELFORD

Map 04 TL84
☎ Sudbury (0787) 880286
Queen Elizabeth I was a guest at this turreted, brick-built Tudor house in 1578, and it does not look very different on the outside today. It has its original panelled banquetting hall, and later features include an 18th-century drawing room, a Regency library and a Victorian bedroom. The house was owned for many years by the Parker family, which produced a number of admirals – hence the nautical flavour of the pictures.

There is also a large collection of Chinese porcelain, and a display on Beatrix Potter, who was related to the Parkers and often stayed here. The garden has a Tudor pavilion, which may have been built as a guardhouse.
Open 28 Mar-Apr, Sat, Sun & BH Mon 2-5.30; May-Sep, Wed, Thu, Sat, Sun & BH Mon 2-5.30; Oct, Sat & Sun 2-5.30. (Closed Good Fri).
£2.50 (ch £1.25). Party 15 +
P & *(stairlift) toilets for disabled* ✱
(NT)

East Anglia Transport Museum — LOWESTOFT

Map 05 TM59
Chapel Rd, Carlton Colville (3m SW, on B1384)
☎ (0502) 518459
A particular attraction of this museum is the reconstructed 1930s street scene which is used as a setting for working vehicles: visitors can ride by tram, trolley-bus and narrow gauge railway. Other motor, steam and electrical vehicles are exhibited on the three-acre woodland site. On 4-5 July the London

Event will be staged to commemorate the last day of tram operation in London in 1952. There will be London Transport vehicles to see, model displays and sales stands.
Open Etr Sun & Mon then all BH's & Sun's from May-Sep from 11; Jun-Sep Sat ;weekends during last week in Jul-Aug, from 2pm
£2.50 (ch & pen £1.20). Party
P & & *shop*

Maritime Museum — LOWESTOFT

Map 05 TM59
Sparrow Nest Gardens, Whapload Rd (on A12)
☎ (0502) 561963
Models of ancient and modern fishing and commercial boats are exhibited, together with fishing gear and

shipwrights' tools. There is an art gallery and a lifeboat display as well as a facsimile of a Drifter's Cabin complete with model fishermen – Bob and Frank!
Open May-Sep, daily 10-5
& *shop*
Details not confirmed for 1992

Pleasurewood Hills American Theme Park — LOWESTOFT

Map 05 TM59
Corton Rd (on A12)
☎ (0502) 513626
After the initial admission fee there is nothing more to pay at this exciting theme park. Apart from the breathtaking rides like the Waveswinger, Star Ride Enterprise and the Tempest visitors can slow down the pace at the Land that Time Forgot of Woody's Fairytale

Fantasy. Other attractions include the Sealion and Parrot shows, a Fun Factory and Cine 180. Train rides and chairlift make it easier to get around the park.
Open 29 Mar-7 Apr, 4 May-22 Sep & 21-27 Oct, daily. 13-14, 20-21, 27-28 Apr & 28-29 Sep, wknds. 6, 13 & 20 Oct, Sun. 10-6 (4 or 5 according to season).
P & & *toilets for disabled shop* ✱
Details not confirmed for 1992

National Horseracing Museum — NEWMARKET

Map 04 TL66
99 High St
☎ (0638) 667333

Newmarket has been the centre of the 'sport of kings' since 1605, and is still the headquarters of British racing. The

great story of the development of horseracing is told in the museum's five permanent galleries. There is a collection of videos of classic races and displays are changed each year. Equine tours give an opportunity to see horses at work on the historic gallops, at home in the yards, on the racecourse and at the National Stud, where some of the world's finest stallions are kept.
Open 24 Mar-6 Dec, Tue-Sat (also BH Mons & Mon in Jul & Aug) 10-5. Sun 2-5 (Jul & Aug 12-5).
✱ *£2.50 (ch 75p, pen £1.50). Party 20 +. Equine tour charges on request.*
P & ✗ *licensed* & *toilets for disabled shop* ✱

Orford Castle — ORFORD

Map 05 TM45
(on B1084)
☎ (0394) 450472
Built by Henry II circa 1165, this castle has three towers and incorporates an 18-sided keep.
Open all year, Apr-Sep, daily 10-6; Oct-

Mar, Tue-Sun 10-4. (Closed 24-26 Dec & 1 Jan).
£1.50 (ch 75p, students, pen & UB40 £1.10).
P
(EH)

For an explanation of the symbols and abbreviations, see page 2.

Bruisyard Winery, Vineyard & Herb Centre — SAXMUNDHAM

Map 05 TM36
Church Rd, Bruisyard (between Framlingham & Peasenhall)
☎ Badingham (072875) 281
This picturesque, 10-acre winery produces the award-winning Bruisyard St Peter English wine. There is also a herb garden, water gardens, a wooded

picnic area, and a children's play area. English wine, herbs, crafts and souvenirs are for sale.
Open Etr-Nov, daily 10.30-5.
✱ *£2.90 (ch £1.50 pen £2.65)*
P ✗ *licensed* & *shop garden centre* ✱ *(ex in vineyard)*

Saxtead Green Post Mill — SAXTEAD GREEN

Map 04 TM26
(on A1120)
☎ (0728) 685789
One of the finest examples of a traditional Suffolk post-mill can be seen at Saxtead Green. There has been a mill on the site at least since 1796 but the mill has been altered or rebuilt several times. The present structure dates from 1854; for those who climb the steep

staircase into the body of the mill there is the reward of finding the now redundant millstones and other machinery in perfect order.
Open Apr-Sep, Mon-Sat 10-6.
£1.10 (ch 55p, students, pen & UB40 85p)
& *(exterior only)* ✱
(EH)

Southwold Museum — SOUTHWOLD

Map 05 TM57
Bartholomew Green (A1095 E of A12 nr Blythburgh)
☎ (0502) 722375
Housed in a 17th-century Dutch gabled cottage, the museum contains relics of local and natural history and of the

Southwold light railway. There is also a display of pictures of the Battle of Sole Bay 1672, fought against the Dutch.
Open Etr, 5 & 6 May & 26 May-Sep Free.
& ✱

Museum of East Anglian Life — STOWMARKET

Map 04 TM05
☎ (0449) 612229
The extensive, 70-acre, all-weather museum is set in an attractive river-valley site. There are reconstructed buildings, including a water mill, a smithy and also a wind pump, and the Boby Building houses craft workshops, with a resident wood turner. There are videos of a cooper and basket maker at work, as well as a historic film show in a Bioscope cinema. Also here are displays

on Victorian domestic life, gypsies, farming and industry. These include working steam traction engines, the only surviving pair of Burrell ploughing engines of 1879, and a working Suffolk Punch horse.
Open 22 Mar-1 Nov, daily 10-5.
£3.25 (ch 3-16 £1.60, students & pen £2). Party.
P & & *(wheelchairs available, special parking facilities) toilets for disabled shop*

Gainsborough's House — SUDBURY

Map 04 TL84
46 Gainsborough St
☎ (0787) 72958
Birthplace in 1727 of Thomas Gainsborough, the portrait and landscape painter, the house contains 18th-century furniture and china together with paintings by Gainsborough and his contemporaries. A print workshop has been set up in the coach house. A series of temporary historic

and contemporary art and craft exhibitions are arranged throughout the year.
Open all year – House Tue-Sat 10-5, Sun & BH Mons 2-5; (4pm Nov-Maundy Thu). (Closed Good Fri & Xmas-New Year).
£2 (ch, students & disabled 75p pen £1.50). Party.
& *toilets for disabled shop* ✱

SURREY

RAMC Historical Museum · ASH VALE

Map 04 SU85
Keogh Barracks
☎ Aldershot (0252) 24431 ext Keogh 5212
Some 2,500 items related to the work of the Royal Army Medical Corps are displayed, including a horsedrawn ambulance, a 1942 Austin K2 ambulance, Falklands War items, and a mock-up of a patient on an operating table.
Open all year, Mon-Fri 8.30-4. (Closed Xmas, New Year & BH). Wknds & BH by appointment only.
🅿 ♿ *toilets for disabled shop* ✖
Details not confirmed for 1992

Polesden Lacey · BOOKHAM, GREAT

Map 04 TQ15
(2m S off A246)
☎ Great Bookham (0372) 458203
In Edwardian times, this attractive Regency house was owned by a celebrated society hostess, Mrs Ronnie Greville. King George VI and Queen Elizabeth (the Queen Mother) spent part of their honeymoon here, and photographs of other notable guests can be seen. The house is handsomely furnished with the Greville collection of tapestries, porcelain, Old Master paintings and other works of art. With its mixed Edwardian and Regency flavour, the house is full of charm, and it is set in spacious grounds. The gardens include a walled rose garden and there are good views and wide lawns. There is also an open-air theatre, where plays are performed in summer, this will run from 24 Jun-12 Jul.
Open all year. Grounds: daily 11-6. House: Mar & Nov, Sat & Sun, 1.30-4.30; Apr-Oct, Wed-Sun (inc Good Fri) 1.30-5.30. Also BH Mon & preceeding Sun 11-5.30.
✱ *Garden only: Apr-Oct £2; Nov-Mar £1.50. House: Sun & BH Mon £3.20; other open days £2.50.*
🅿 ♿ ✖ *licensed* ♿ *toilets for disabled shop* ✖
(NT)

Surrey Heath Museum · CAMBERLEY

Map 04 SU86
Surrey Heath House, Knoll Rd
☎ (0276) 686252
Museum of local history including geology, archaeology, natural history, and heathland crafts. A lively programme of temporary exhibitions of local and regional interest.
Open all year, Tue-Sat 11-5.
Free.
🅿 ♿ ♿ *(handling sessions & guided tours by appointment) toilets for disabled shop* ✖

Suffolk Wildlife & Rare Breeds Park · SUFFOLK WILDLIFE & RARE BREEDS PARK

Map 05 TM58
Kessingland (on A12)
☎ Lowestoft (0502) 740291
Set in an area of outstanding natural beauty this wildlife park has a wide selection of animals and birds, some of which are very rare. There are plenty of good sites for picnics, a children's play area, and also a 'Meet the Animals' show daily.
Open Etr-Oct, daily 10-6 (5pm Sep-Oct).
✱ *£3.50 (ch £2)*
🅿 ♿ ♿ *toilets for disabled shop* ✖

✱ An asterisk indicates that up-to-date information was not available at the time of our research – 1991 information has been published as an indication of what you may expect.

West Stow Anglo Saxon Village · WEST STOW

Map 04 TL87
West Stow Country Park (On A1101)
☎ Culford (0284) 728718
The village is a reconstruction of a pagan Anglo-Saxon settlement dated 420-650 AD. Six buildings have been reconstructed on the site of the excavated settlement, using the same techniques, tools and building materials as were used in the original farming village (free audio guides available). The village is situated in the 125-acre West Stow Country Park. There is a special Open Day each year and a new Visitors' Centre and children's play area. Facilities for the disabled include purpose-built toilets for wheelchair users and a braille guide to the park. Special event for 1992 will be a Saxon market held on 19 April.
Open all year, daily 10-5.
£2 (ch, pen & students £1.20).
🅿 ♿ *toilets for disabled shop* ✖

Woodbridge Tide Mill · WOODBRIDGE

Map 05 TM24
Tide Mill Way
☎ Ipswich (0473) 626618
The machinery of this 18th-century mill has been completely restored. There are photographs and working drawings on display. Situated in a busy quayside, this unique building looks over towards the romantic site of the Sutton Hoo Ship Burial. Every effort is made to run the machinery for a short time whenever the mill is open; details obtainable from tourist information offices or outside mill.
Open Etr, then daily May-Sep. Oct wknds only. 11-5
✱ *80p (ch 40p).*
♿ *shop*

Gatwick Zoo & Aviaries — CHARLWOOD

Map 04 TQ24
Russ Hill
☎ Crawley (0293) 862312
The zoo covers almost 10 acres and has hundreds of birds and mammals. The monkey island has spider and squirrel monkeys, and other animals and birds can be seen in large, naturalistic settings. Nearly all species breed each year. A play area for children up to 12 years old has been added.

Open all year, Mar-Oct, daily 10.30-6 (earlier by appointment for schools). Nov-Mar, wknds & school hols 10.30-4 or dusk if earlier. (Closed 25-26 Dec). No butterflies during winter.
£3.50 (ch 3-14 £2.50, pen £3 ex Sun & BH). Admission price includes Butterfly House.
🅿 ⊒ ♿ *toilets for disabled shop* ✖

See advertisement on page 153.

Chertsey Museum — CHERTSEY

Map 04 TQ06
The Cedars, 33 Windsor St
☎ (0932) 565764
The museum is housed in The Cedars, a late Georgian building. It contains the Matthews collection of costumes and accessories, local history displays including archaeology and silver, glass

and dolls. There is also a collection of Meissen porcelain figures, and various exhibitions are held during the year.
Open all year, Tue & Thu 2-5, Wed, Fri & Sat 10-1 & 2-5. (Closed Xmas).
Free.
♿ ✖

Thorpe Park — CHERTSEY

Map 04 TQ06
Staines Rd (on A320, off jct 11 or 13 of M25)
☎ (0932) 562633 & 569393
The park offers 500 acres of family fun; over 70 attractions are included in the admission price. The attractions include Loggers Leap, the highest log theme ride in the UK, Thunder River, Tea Cup ride, Thorpe Farm, Canada Creek

Railway, Carousel Kingdom, Magic Mills, lots of shows, and much more. There is free transport round the park by land train or water bus. The park is located one and three-quarter miles north of Chertsey on the A320.
Open 23 Mar-27 Oct, daily 10-6 (5 early & late season).
🅿 ⊒ ✖ ♿ *toilets for disabled shop* ✖
Details not confirmed for 1992

Watts Picture Gallery — COMPTON

Map 04 SU94
Down Ln
☎ Guildford (0483) 810235
This is a memorial gallery to the Victorian painter and sculptor George Frederick Watts, and is filled with his work. He is buried in the nearby Watts

Mortuary Chapel, a strange symbolic building erected by his widow.
Open all year, Chapel daily. Gallery: Apr-Sep, Fri-Wed 2-6 (Oct-Mar 2-4); also Wed & Sat 11-1.
🅿 ♿ *shop* ✖
Details not confirmed for 1992

CRAWLEY
See Charlwood

Hatchlands — EAST CLANDON

Map 04 TQ05
(E off A246)
☎ Guildford (0483) 222787
Robert Adam's first commission was to decorate the interior of this 18th-century house, and his work can be admired in the drawing room, library and other rooms. The attractive red brick house itself was probably designed by its first owner Admiral Boscawen, and is on seven different floor levels. It is given a regular appearance from the

outside by the use of false windows. In 1988 the Cobbe Collection of keyboard instruments, paintings and furniture was installed here and some of the instruments may be played on application to the administrator.
Open Apr-18 Oct, Tue-Thu, Sun & BH Mon 2-5.30. Last admission 5. (Closed Good Fri). Also open Sat in Aug.
✳ *£3.20 (ch £1.60).*
🅿 ✖ *licensed* ♿ *shop* ✖
(NT)

Birdworld & Underwaterworld — FARNHAM

Map 04 SU84
Holt Pound (3m S on A325)
☎ Bentley (0420) 22140
Eighteen acres of garden and parkland are home to a wide variety of birds, from the tiny tanager to the great ostrich and many rare and unusual species. There are waterfowl as well as land birds; a Sea Shore Walk and Tropical Walk; and an aquarium with tropical, freshwater and marine fish. The Owls Nest bookshop sells books on wildlife. Plant lovers will enjoy the extensive gardens. There are purpose-built toilets

for wheelchair users, wheelchairs are available on loan and there are good, solid paths around the grounds. Special events for 1992 will include: 14 Jun, Garden Day; 19 Jul, Teddy Bears Picnic, and at the end of August a Mad Hatter's party.
Open all year, daily from 9.30. (Closed 25 Dec).
Birdworld £3.40 (ch £1.80, pen £2.60); Underwater World 95p (ch 50p).
🅿 ⊒ ♿ *(wheelchairs available) toilets for disabled shop* ✖

Farnham Castle Keep — FARNHAM

Map 04 SU84
☎ (0252) 713393
The castle was started in the 11th century by Henry of Blois, Bishop of Winchester, at a convenient point on the way to London; his tower stood on the mound of the keep, which was later encased in high walls. Around the keep

are a ditch and bank topped by a wall.
Open Apr-Sep, daily 10-6.
£1.40 (ch 70p, pen, students & UB40 £1). Admission price includes a free Personal Stereo Guided Tour.
🅿 ✖
(EH)

Farnham Museum — FARNHAM

Map 04 SU84
38 West St
☎ (0252) 715094
Geology, archaeology, local history and art are displayed in Willmer House, which is worth seeing in itself for its handsome Georgian brickwork. William

Cobbett memorabilia are also shown, and there is a walled garden. Temporary exhibitions, on subjects of local interest, change at two-monthly intervals.
Open all year, Tue-Sat 10-5.
Free.
♿ *toilets for disabled shop* ✖

♿ **This symbol indicates that much or all of the attraction is accessible to wheelchairs. However, there may be some restrictions, so it would be wise to check in advance.**

Godalming Museum — GODALMING

Map 04 SU94
109A High St
☎ Guildford (0483) 426510
Displays on local history and temporary exhibitions are shown, and there is a

Jekyll-style garden.
Open all year, Tue-Sat 10-5. (Closed 25-26 Dec).
Free.
shop

Gallery 90 — GUILDFORD

Map 04 SU94
Ward St
☎ (0483) 444740
Gallery 90 is housed in a converted 19th-century Unitarian Church. There are changing exhibitions of painting, sculpture and craftwork. Special events for 1992 include an exhibition of Afghan artefacts on 7-28 March, and the

Guildford Festival exhibition – 'A taste of Europe' on 4-25 July.
Open Mon-Fri 10-4.30, Sat 10-12.30 & 1.30-4.30 (Closed a few days prior to each exhibition). For details of exhibitions please apply for leaflet.
Free.
shop ✖

Guildford Castle — GUILDFORD

Map 04 SU94
☎ (0483) 444701
The three-storey castle keep dates from the 12th century and gives fine views; and the castle ditch has been transformed into a colourful garden which is attractive throughout the

summer. Open-air theatre is also a feature of the summer months, and there is a brass-rubbing display.
Open: Grounds daily 8-dusk (Closed 25 Dec); Keep Apr-Sep 10.30-6.
65p (ch 35p).
♿

Guildford Museum — GUILDFORD

Map 04 SU94
Castle Arch
☎ (0483) 444750
A local museum with history, archaeology and needlework displays. Various events are planned for 1992

including a Mad Hatter's Tea Party on 5 July.
Open all year, Mon-Sat 11-5. (Closed 24-26 Dec & Good Fri).
Free.
♿ *toilets for disabled shop* ✖

Loseley House — GUILDFORD

Map 04 SU94
(2.5m SW)
☎ (0483) 304440
Familiar to many from yoghurt pots, the Elizabethan house has notable panelling, decorated ceilings, a carved chalk chimney piece and tapestries. It is also home of the Loseley dairy products, and

there are farm tours.
Open House: 29 May-28 Sep, Wed-Sat 2-5. Also BH Mon (27 May & 26 Aug).
Farm Tours: also May-Oct, Mon-Sat.
🅿 ✖ *licensed* ♿ *(wheelchair available, parking outside house) toilets for disabled shop* ✖
Details not confirmed for 1992

Winkworth Arboretum   HASCOMBE

Map 04 SU94
(1m NW on B2130)
☎ (048632) 477
This lovely woodland covers a hillside of
nearly 100 acres, with fine views over
the North Downs. The best times to
visit are May, for the azaleas, bluebells

and other flowers, and October for the
autumn colours.
Open all year, daily during daylight hours.
✳ £2.
🅿 ⬤ *shop (Apr-15 Nov, Tue-Sun 2-6)*
(NT)

Haxted Watermill & Museum   HAXTED

Map 04 TQ44
☎ Edenbridge (0732) 865720
The weatherboarded, late 16th-century
mill stands on 14th-century foundations,
next to the mill house on Eden Water.
Mill machinery including two working

water wheels can be seen, and there is a
picture gallery.
Open Apr-Sep, Wed, Sat-Sun & BH's 1-5.
Parties at other times by arrangement.
£2.50 (ch £1.75, pen £1.50).
🅿 ✕ *licensed shop* ✖

The Old Mill   OUTWOOD

Map 04 TQ34
Outwood Common (on A25)
☎ Smallfield (0342) 843458
This award-winning example of a post-
mill dates from 1665 and is the oldest
working windmill in England and one of
the best preserved in existence. Standing
400ft above sea level, it is surrounded by
common land and National Trust
property. Ducks, goats and horses
wander freely in the grounds, and there

is a small museum and a collection of
old coaches. Various events are planned
for 1992, including Morris dancing and
a horticultural show.
Open Etr Sun-last Sun in Oct, Sun & BH
Mons only 2-6. Other days & evening tours
by arrangement. School parties for
educational visits.
£1.25 (ch 75p, pen £1). Party.
⬥ *toilets for disabled shop*

Painshill Park   PAINSHILL PARK

Map 04 TQ06
(on A245)
☎ Cobham (0932) 868113
Painshill Park is an 18th-century
landscape garden created by the Hon.
Charles Hamilton. Well maintained for
almost 200 years, it fell into dereliction
following the Second World War. It
was not until 1981 when the Painshill
Park Trust, a charity, was formed that
the ambitious task of restoring the
gardens to their former splendour began.
Already Hamilton's masterpiece is
emerging from the wilderness and
visitors can follow the historic route,
taking in the lake, the Gothic temple,
Chinese bridge, grotto and water wheel,
together with numerous other follies
dotted around the landscape. As well as

a talented designer, Hamilton was a
knowledgeable plantsman and some of
the unusual trees and shrubs he planted
are still to be found in the Park, while
those that did not survive are being
carefully replanted.
Open Public open days Sun only, 12
Apr-18 Oct 11-6. Free optional guided
tours from 2pm. (Tours last one and a half
to two hours). Pre-booked parties (10+)
may be booked on any other day, all year,
ring (0932) 864674 for information.
£3 (ch 14 accompanied free, pen, students &
UB40's £2). Party 10+. Special
arrangements for school parties, contact
Education Trust (0932) 866743.
🅿 ⬤ ⬥ *(wheelchairs available) toilets for*
disabled shop ✖

✖ **The 'No Dogs' symbol does not normally apply
to guide dogs – these are permitted in
most establishments.**

Priory Museum   REIGATE

Map 04 TQ24
Bell St (off A217)
☎ (0737) 245065
Originally founded before 1200, this
house was later converted to a Tudor
mansion of which the hall fireplace is a
notable feature. Stucco painting of the
18th century changed the face of the

building, now used as a school. The
small museum has changing exhibitions.
There are 'hands on' facilities for the
disabled.
Open in term time only, Wed 2-4.30 &
first Sat in month 11-4.
Free.
🅿 ⬥ *("Hands On" facilities) shop* ✖

Old Windmill & Church   REIGATE HEATH

Map 04 TQ25
☎ Reigate (0737) 242610 & 221100
This 220-year-old windmill stands on
the Heath, just outside the town itself.
Converted into a church in 1882, it was
given a new set of sails and restored to
its original appearance in 1964, but is

not in working order. Services are held
at 3pm on the 3rd Sunday of each
month from May to October.
Open all year, dawn-dusk.
Free, donations.
🅿 ⬥ ✖

Rural Life Centre   TILFORD

Map 04 SU84
Reeds Rd (on A287)
☎ Frensham (025125) 2300 & 5571
The Old Kiln houses a collection of
farm implements and machinery, and
examples of the craft and trades allied to
farming may be seen. The larger exhibits
are displayed in the pleasant garden and
woodland surroundings which cover
some ten acres. In the old farm buildings

are a smithy and a wheelwright's shop,
hand tools and other artefacts. There is
also an arboretum and woodland walk.
On 26 July there will be a 'Rustic
Sunday' with craft demonstrations and
side shows.
Open Apr-Sep, Wed-Sun & BH 11-6.
£2 (ch £1, pen £1.50).
🅿 ⬤ ⬥ *toilets for disabled shop*

Clandon Park   WEST CLANDON

Map 04 TQ05
(on A247)
☎ Guildford (0483) 222482
An 18th-century house, built by Leoni
for the 2nd Lord Onslow, with fine
plasterwork and a fine collection of
furniture and pictures. Queens Royal
Surrey regimental museum. Concerts are

held in the Marble Hall.
Open Apr-Oct, incl Good Fri, Sat-Wed
1.30-5.30, also BH Mon & preceeding
Sun 11-5.30. Last admission 5pm.
✳ *£3.30.*
🅿 ✕ *licensed ⬥ toilets for disabled shop* ✖
(NT)

Wisley Garden   WISLEY

Map 04 TQ05
☎ Guildford (0483) 224234

These experimental gardens of the Royal
Horticultural Society were established in
1904 in Wisley village. The property
now covers over 300 acres, of which
half is devoted to garden, some to

vegetables and the rest to farm and
woodland. The gardens have a wide
variety of trees, shrubs and plants, many
of which are unusual in Britain, and
planted in their correct setting. There are
also greenhouses and specialist gardens.
The Royal Horticultural Society offer an
advisory service at Wisley. Purpose-built
toilets and wheelchairs are available for
disabled visitors
Open all year, Mon-Sat 10-7 or dusk
(4.30pm Jan, Nov & Dec). Sun members
only. (Closed 25 Dec). Glasshouses close at
4.15 or sunset Mon-Fri & 4.45 wknds &
BH.
£3.95 (ch 6-14 £1.25).
🅿 ⬤ ✕ *licensed ⬥ (free wheelchairs) toilets*
for disabled shop garden centre ✖

TYNE & WEAR

St Paul's Church & Monastery,   JARROW
Bede Monastery Museum

Map 08 NZ36
Jarrow Hall, Church Bank
☎ 091-489 2106

The 37 books, many of several volumes,
which the Venerable Bede wrote for his
students represented the collected
knowledge of his time in science,
literature, philosophy and the arts. His
most famous book is the Ecclesiastical
History of the English People, and he
also made the first translation of St
John's Gospel into English. St Paul's
Church was part of the monastery where
this impressive man lived from the age
of about thirteen until his death in 735;
with St Peter's, Monkwearmouth, the
other half of the monastery, it is now
regarded as the 'cradle of English

learning' and an important Christian
shrine. The chancel incorporates one of
the churches where Bede worshipped
and features some Saxon stained glass.
Very little remains of the original
monastery but archaeological finds from
excavations of the site are housed in the
Bede Monastery Museum, where the
story of this important monastery, and
its revered inhabitant, is told. The
Museum, which dates to about 1800,
also has an exhibition on its own
occupants; an audio-visual programme,
temporary exhibitions, tea room, craft
shop, herb garden and TIC. Special
events including concerts, day courses,
workshops and Anglo-Saxon feasts take
place throughout the year. Special events
arranged for 1992 include an exhibition
of silverwork from 18 Mar-26 Apr.
Open all year, Apr-Oct, Tue-Sat & BH
Mons 10-5.30, Sun 2.30-5.30; Nov-Mar,
Tue-Sat 11-4.30, Sun 2.30-5.30. Church
open Apr-Oct 10-4.30; Nov-Mar 11-4.30
Mon-Sat & Sun 2.30-4.30.
✳ *60p (ch, pen & UB40s 30p, students*
40p). UB40 family ticket 75p. Party.
🅿 ⬤ ⬥ *(Braille guide & taped tours)*
toilets for disabled shop ✖

Hancock Museum   NEWCASTLE UPON TYNE

Map 08 NZ26
The University
☎ 091-222 7418
One of the finest museums of natural
history in the country, the Hancock
Museum houses geological exhibits and
John Hancock's magnificent collection
of birds. One gallery is devoted to
Ethnographical and Egyptian collections,
with two spectacular mummies. The
Thomas Bewick Room demonstrates the

natural history woodcuts of the famous
Newcastle engraver, and Abel's Ark is
popular with children. The main
attraction in 1992 is 'Monsters of the
Deep' an eye-catching exhibition about
life in the sea, featuring whales, a sunken
wreck and live sharks. It will be open
from January to June.
Open all year, Mon-Sat, 10-5, Sun 2-5.
✳ *£1.50 (ch & concession's 75p). Party.*
🅿 ⬥ *shop* ✖

John George Joicey Museum   NEWCASTLE UPON TYNE

Map 08 NZ26
City Rd
☎ 091-232 4562
Built as an almshouse in 1681, this
Dutch-style building, formerly the Holy
Jesus Hospital, now illustrates aspects of
Newcastle's history. An audio-visual
presentation takes you through the
Great Fire of 1854 and the Tyne Flood
of 1771. There are also period rooms,
regimental collections of 15th/19th

King's Royal Hussars and displays of
regional significance about sporting guns
and the German swordmakers of
Shotley Bridge. Children's activities
include brass rubbing and colouring-in
sheets.
Open all year, Tue-Fri & BH 10-5.30, Sat
10-4.30.
🅿 ⬥ *shop* ✖
Details not confirmed for 1992

Laing Art Gallery   NEWCASTLE UPON TYNE

Map 08 NZ26
Higham Pl
☎ 091-232 7734 & 091-232 6989
British paintings and watercolours from
the 18th-century to the present day are
on display here, with works by Burne-
Jones, Reynolds, Turner and others,
including the Northumberland artist
John Martin. A pioneering interactive

display called Art on Tyneside shows
paintings, costume, silver etc in period
settings. There is also a programme of
temporary exhibitions.
*Open all year, Tue-Fri 10-5.30, Sat
10-4.30, Sun 2.30-5.30.
Free. Admission charged for special
exhibitions.*
🅿 ♿ *toilets for disabled shop* ✖

Museum of Antiquities   NEWCASTLE UPON TYNE

Map 08 NZ26
The University
☎ 091-222 7844
Artefacts from north east England from
prehistoric times to AD 1600 are on
display here. The principal museum for
Hadrian's Wall, this collection includes
models of the wall, life-size Roman

soldiers and a recently refurbished
reconstruction of the Temple of
Mithras. There is also a museum book
shop.
*Open all year, daily (ex Sun), 10-5 (Closed
Good Fri, 24-26 Dec & 1 Jan).
Free.*
♿ *shop* ✖

Museum of Science & Engineering   NEWCASTLE UPON TYNE

Map 08 NZ26
Blandford House, Blandford Sq (off
A6115/A6125)
☎ 091-232 6789
This museum houses a wealth of
artefacts and images from the industrial
heritage of the North East. Beautiful
ship models, powerful steam turbines,
guns, engines and even the humble light
bulb are displayed to tell the fascinating
story on one of Britain's greatest
industrial centres. Visitors can also

discover that science is fun in the
popular Science Factory Interactive
Science Centre – the only one in the
North East. In spring there will be the
North East Craft Roadshow and in
summer 1992, the Time Tunnel display
will open.
*Open all year, Tue-Fri 10-5.30, Sat
10-4.30, BH Mons 10-5.30. (Closed
25-26 Dec & 1 Jan).
Free.*
🅿 ♿ ♿ *toilets for disabled shop* ✖

Gibside Chapel & Grounds   ROWLANDS GILL

Map 08 NZ15
☎ (0207) 542255
Designed by James Paine as a
mausoleum, the classical chapel is part of
the remains of an 18th-century landscape
design. It has fine detail and a rare,
three-tier pulpit. The chapel is
approached along a terrace with an

avenue of oak trees. Walks are now
open in the grounds and a flower festival
is arranged for July.
*Open Apr-Oct, daily (ex Mon, Open BH
Mon's) 11-5. Last admission 4.30.
£2.*
🅿 ♿ *(Stairclimber at chapel) shop* ✖
(NT)

Arbeia Roman Fort & Museum   SOUTH SHIELDS

Map 08 NZ36
Baring St
☎ 091-456 1369
In South Shields town are the extensive
remains of Arbeia, a 2nd-century Roman
fort. It was the supply base for the
Roman army's campaign against
Scotland and was occupied for most of
300 years. The remains include fort
defences, stone granaries, gateways,
headquarter buildings, tile kilns and
latrines. On the site of the west gate is a

full-scale simulation of a Roman gateway
with interior scenes of life at the fort.
The museum exhibits site finds and gives
background information. Archaeological
excavations are in progress throughout
the year.
*Open all year, Tue-Fri 10-5.30, Sat
10-4.30. Sun (Etr-Sep only 2-5), also BH
Mon.
Free.*
🅿 ♿ *shop*

South Shields Museum & Art Gallery   SOUTH SHIELDS

Map 08 NZ36
Ocean Rd
☎ 091-456 8740
The museum shows the archaeology,
history and natural history of South
Shields. A maritime display includes a
section on the evolution of the lifeboat
and on local shipbuilding; and the
Catherine Cookson Gallery reflects the

life and environment of the hugely
popular, local-born author. There is a
programme of temporary exhibitions
one of which will be 'A Day at the
Seaside'.
*Open all year, Tue-Fri 10-5.30, Sat
10-4.30, Sun 2-5 & BH Mon.
Free.*
♿ *toilets for disabled shop* ✖

Grindon Museum   SUNDERLAND

Map 08 NZ35
Grindon Ln
☎ 091-514 1235
The museum specialises in Edwardian
period interiors. There are several
rooms, a chemist's shop and a dentist's
surgery.

*Open all year, Mon-Wed & Fri
9.30-12.30 & 1.30-5, Sat 9.30-12.15 &
1.15-4; Jun-Sep also Sun 2-5. (Closed Thu,
BH & Sat prior to BH).
Free.*
🅿 ✖

Monkwearmouth Station Museum   SUNDERLAND

Map 08 NZ35
North Bridge St
☎ 091-567 7075
The transport museum is housed in a
former station – one of the handsomest
anywhere. It was built in 1848 when the
railway baron George Hudson was the
local MP. The booking office, platforms
and footbridge have all been restored

and there is an outdoor display of rolling
stock. Inside, there are displays on
transport in north-east England and the
evolution of British steam locomotives.
*Open all year, Tue-Fri 10-5.30, Sat
10-4.30, Sun 2-5. (Closed Mon ex BHs).
Free.*
🅿 ♿ *toilets for disabled shop* ✖

Museum & Art Gallery   SUNDERLAND

Map 08 NZ35
Borough Rd
☎ 091-514 1235
The museum has a wide range of objects
on display, ranging from the wildlife and
geology of the north-east to silver and
paintings, set in period rooms. There is a
special section on Sunderland and its

industries, particularly glass, pottery and
shipbuilding. There is also a wide range
of temporary exhibitions.
*Open all year, Tue-Fri 10-5.30, Sat 10-4,
Sun 2-5. (Closed Mon ex BHs).
Free.*
♿ ♿ *toilets for disabled shop* ✖

Tynemouth Castle & Priory   TYNEMOUTH

Map 08 NZ36
☎ 091-257 1090
The Benedictine priory was built on the
site of a Saxon monastery in 1090. The
substantial ruins of the priory are
enclosed within the castle walls, built
during the 11th and 14th centuries.
Entrance is through the gatehouse, and
there are parts of the curtain wall, the

church nave and the chancel to be seen.
*Open all year, Apr-Sep, daily 10-6; Oct-
Mar, Tue-Sun 10-4. (Closed 24-26 Dec &
1 Jan).
£1.10 (ch 55p, pen, students & UB40
85p).*
♿ *shop* ✖
(EH)

For an explanation of the symbols and abbreviations, see page 2.

Washington Old Hall   WASHINGTON

Map 08 NZ35
☎ 091-416 6879
The home of George Washington's
ancestors from 1183 to 1613, the Old
Hall was originally an early medieval
manor, but was rebuilt in the 17th
century. The house has been restored
and filled with period furniture. The
property was given to the National

Trust in 1956. There will be
celebrations to mark American
Independence Day on 4 July.
*Open Apr-Oct, daily (closed Fri ex Good
Fri) 11-5. Last admission 4.30pm.
£1.80. Party.*
🅿 *shop* ✖
(NT)

The Wildfowl & Wetlands Trust   WASHINGTON

Map 08 NZ35
☎ 091-416 5454
Set in a busy industrial area, this
Wildfowl Trust park is a welcome
refuge on the north bank of the River
Wear. The 100-acre park has over 100
species of wildfowl, which form one of
the largest collections in the world. The
attractive landscaped park includes 70
acres for wild birds, which can be
viewed from several public hides. The

Visitor Centre, housed in an attractive
log cabin, also has a viewing gallery and
large picture windows giving excellent
views over the main collection area. The
centre provides information on the birds,
talks and guided walks as well as a
souvenir shop and bookshop.
*Open all year, daily 9.30-5 or dusk if
earlier. (Closed 24-25 Dec).*
🅿 ♿ ♿ *toilets for disabled shop* ✖
Details not confirmed for 1992

Souter Lighthouse   WHITBURN

Map 08 NZ46
☎ 091-529 3161
This 150ft-high lighthouse was built by
Trinity House in 1871 and contains a
bi-optic light, still in its original
condition, which was the first reliable
electrically powered lighthouse light.
The Engine and Battery Rooms are all
in working order and are included in the

guided tour, and also the light tower,
museum cottage and video. Open in
1992: an education room and restaurant.
*Open Apr-Oct, Tue-Sun 11-5. Last
admission 4.30. (Closed Mon ex BH's).
£2. Timed ticket at busy times. Party.*
🅿 *shop* ✖
(NT)

WARWICKSHIRE

Ragley Hall   ALCESTER

Map 03 SP05
(1.5m SW, on A435)
☎ (0789) 762090
Ragley Hall is set in four hundred acres
of parkland and gardens. The Great Hall
contains some of England's finest
Baroque plasterwork designed by James
Gibbs. Graham Rust's mural *The
Temptation* can be seen on the south
staircase. Ample picnic areas beside the
lake, as well as an Adventure
Playground, maze and woodland walks.

Events planned for 1992 include horse
trials in May and a craft fair in June.
*Open Etr-Sep, Tue-Thu, Sat, Sun & BH
Mon; Jul-Aug park & garden open
everyday. House 12-5, park & gardens
10-6.
Garden & Park £3.50 (ch & pen £2.50).
House (including garden & park) £4.50 (ch
& pen £3.50).*
🅿 ♿ ♿ *toilets for disabled shop* ✖ *(ex in
park & gardens)*

Baddesley Clinton House   BADDESLEY CLINTON

Map 04 SP27
(0.75m W off A4141)
☎ Lapworth (0564) 783294
This romantic moated manor house has
hardly changed since the 17th century.
It dates back to 1300, and has family
portraits and priest holes inside. There is
also a chapel, and a garden with ponds
and a lake walk.
Open 4 Mar-Sep, Wed-Sun & BH Mon

2-6, Grounds from 12.30; Oct Wed-Sun
12.30-4.30 (Closed Good Fri). Last
admissions to house 30 mins before closing.
✱ £3.50. Grounds only £2. Family ticket
£9.60. Parties by written appointment
only. Entry to house by timed numbered
ticket.
🅿 ♿ ♿ *toilets for disabled shop* ✖
(NT)

Charlecote Park

CHARLECOTE

Map 04 SP25
(on B4086)
☎ Stratford-upon-Avon (0789) 470277
The house is best known for its connections with Shakespeare: he is said to have been brought before the owner, Sir Thomas Lucy, for poaching deer in the 250-acre deer park. The park still has a herd of red and fallow deer, and also has Jacob sheep, introduced in 1756. The house was built in the 1550s, on a site where the Lucy family had lived since 1247, and was visited by Elizabeth I. The Great Hall (scene of the Shakespeare incident) can be seen, as can

the Victorian kitchen and rooms decorated in 1830s Elizabethan-revival style. There are carriages and a video display, and the picturesque gatehouse has a museum.
Open Apr-Oct, daily (ex Mon & Thu) Closed Good Fri but open BH Mon 11-1 & 2-5.30. Last admission to house 5. Evening guided tours for pre-booked parties Tue May-Sep 7.30-9.30.
£3.40 Family ticket £9.40.
🅿 🍴 ᣍ *(Braille guides available) toilets for disabled shop* ✖
(NT)

Coughton Court

COUGHTON

Map 03 SP06
(2m N,on E side of A435)
☎ Alcester (0789) 762435
The most imposing feature of Coughton Court is its immense, early 16th-century gatehouse, which leads into a courtyard flanked by Elizabethan wings with a number of hiding places for priests. This formerly moated, mainly Elizabethan house was attacked by both the Royalists and the Parliamentary forces during the Civil War, and suffered damage again during the reign of James II. Contents of the house include some

notable furniture, porcelain portraits and relics of the Throckmorton family who have lived here since 1409. There are also a lake, two churches, new formal gardens, and a riverside walk.
Open Apr wknds 1.30-5.30; Etr Sat-Thu, daily 1.30-5.30 Etr Mon 12.30-5.30; May-Sep, Tue-Thu & BH Mon 1.30-5.30; Oct wknds & 27-29 Oct 1.30-5. Last admission 30 mins before closing.
£3. Family ticket £8. Grounds £1
🅿 🍴 ᣍ *shop* ✖
(NT)

Farnborough Hall

FARNBOROUGH

Map 04 SP44
(off A423)
William Holbech began rebuilding the house around 1745, after his Grand Tour. He made it a Palladian villa with wonderful rococo decorations, and filled it with sculptures and pictures. He also built the garden terrace, with its temples and fine views. The entrance hall, staircase and two principal rooms are on

show.
House grounds & terrace walk open Apr-Sep, Wed & Sat &, May 2-6pm. Terrace walk Thu & Fri only, 2-6. Last admission 5.30.
£2.50 Garden & Terrace walk £1.50. Terrace walk only (Thu & Fri) £1.
🅿 ᣍ ✖
(NT)

Kenilworth Castle

KENILWORTH

Map 07 SP27
☎ (0926) 52078
The castle began life as a 12th-century wooden fortress but rapidly gained importance as first Norman, then Plantagenet and finally Tudor monarchs played a part in its development. John of Gaunt transformed it into a grand castle and in the 16th century it became the property of the newly created Earl of Leicester, John Dudley. Dudley made many further additions including the long barn and gatehouse; it was after his death that the castle went into decline,

until finally Cromwell ordered Kenilworth to be demolished. Today it stands as a noble ruin, although the 12th-century keep is still impressive and the outline of John of Gaunt's great hall is recognisable.
Open all year, Apr-Sep, daily 10-6; Oct-Mar, Tue-Sun 10-4. (Closed 24-26 Dec & 1 Jan).
£1.50 (ch 75p, pen, students & UB40 £1.10).
🅿
(EH)

Warwick District Council Art Gallery & Museum

LEAMINGTON SPA

Map 04 SP36
Av Rd
☎ Royal Leamington Spa (0926) 426559
Ceramics including Delft, Wedgwood, Whieldon, Worcester and Derby can be seen, with 18th-century glass. The art gallery specialises in British, Dutch and Flemish paintings of the 16th to 20th centuries. A new local history gallery

opens Mar 1992. There is also a regularly changing programme of temporary exhibitions throughout the year.
Open all year, Mon-Sat 10-1 & 2-5. Also Thu evenings 6-8. (Closed Sun, Good Fri, 25-26 Dec & 1 Jan).
Free.
ᣍ *shop* ✖

Ash End House Farm

MIDDLETON

Map 07 SP19
Middleton Ln, Middleton (signposted from A4091)
☎ 021-329 3240
Ash End House is a children's farm, specifically set up with children in mind. They love to learn and experience new things, and what better way than when having fun. Children's guided tours give them a unique opportunity to get close to friendly farm animals. A host of animals from the gigantic shire horse, through to hatching tiny chicks and fluffy ducklings can be seen daily. There are also rare breeds such as Bagot goats,

Saddleback pigs and Soay sheep. To celebrate the farm's 10th anniversary, from spring 1992, there will be a display of British wild animals in a natural scene in the old stables. Birthday party bookings are accepted and tours can also be arranged for Beavers, Brownies, Cubs etc.
Open daily 10-6 or dusk in winter. (Closed 25 & 26 Dec).
£1.10(ch £2.20 includes animal feed, badge, pony ride & fresh egg when available).
🅿 🍴 ᣍ *(shop not accessible) toilets for disabled shop* ✖

Middleton Hall

MIDDLETON

Map 07 SP19
(on A4091)
☎ (0564) 774350
Once the home of two great 17th-century naturalists, Francis Willoughby and John Ray, the Hall shows several architectural styles, from c1300 to an 11-bay Georgian west wing. The grounds include a nature reserve, lake, meadow, orchard and woodland – all Sites of Special Scientific Interest – plus two walled gardens. This is also the

home of the Middleton Hall Craft Centre, with craft studios and workshops in the former stable block. Events take place throughout the year, including an Easter craft fair (Apr 19 & 20) and a vintage car event (Jul 12); a programme is available on application to the Hon. Secretary.
Open Apr-Oct, Sun & BH's 2-5.30.
✳ *50p (ch 14 25p). Prices under review*
🅿 🍴 ᣍ *toilets for disabled shop* ♿

Packwood House

PACKWOOD HOUSE

Map 07 SP17
(on unclass road off A34)
☎ Lapworth (0564) 782024
Built as a modest 16th-century farmhouse, Packwood House was extended during the following century and outbuildings were added to make the carefully restored building we see today. Tapestry, needlework and furniture are displayed and Jacobean panelling may be seen. The most notable

feature of the gardens is the layout of 17th-century yews clipped to represent Christ's Sermon on the Mount.
Open Apr-Sep, Wed-Sun & BH Mon 2-6; Oct Wed-Sun 12.30-4.30 (Closed Good Fri). Last admission 30 mins before closing.
£2.80. Garden only £1.90. Family ticket £7.70.
🅿 ᣍ *(wheelchairs available) toilets for disabled shop* ✖
(NT)

The James Gilbert Rugby Football Museum

RUGBY

Map 07 SP57
Saint Matthew's St
☎ (0788) 536500
An intriguing collection of Rugby football memorabilia is housed in the shop in which Gilbert's have made their

world famous Rugby balls since 1842. Situated near to Rugby School and its famous playing field.
Open Mon-Fri 10-5, Sat 10-1 & 2-5. Free.
ᣍ *shop* ✖

Ryton Gardens

RYTON-ON-DUNSMORE

Map 04 SP37
National Centre for Organic, Gardening (on B4029)
☎ Coventry (0203) 303517
The gardens are the home of the Henry Doubleday Research Association, which researches organic farming and gardening. The whole site is landscaped with thousands of young trees, and every plant is grown organically. Visitors can stroll around the herb garden, the bee garden, fruit beds, vegetable gardens, shrub borders and many other

attractions, all showing how the organic gardener can use plants and planting schemes effectively. There is a garden centre selling organically grown products, seeds, equipment and other items for the organic gardener.
Open all year, Apr-Sep, 10-6; Oct-Mar, 10-4. (Closed Xmas).
✳ *£3 (ch 18, students, pen, disabled & UB40 £2). Family ticket £4.50. Party 10+*
🅿 🍴 ᣍ *toilets for disabled shop garden centre* ✖

For an explanation of the symbols and abbreviations, see page 2.

Anne Hathaway's Cottage

SHOTTERY

Map 04 SP15
☎ Stratford-upon-Avon (0789) 292100
Before her marriage to William Shakespeare, Anne Hathaway lived in this substantial 12-roomed thatched Tudor farmhouse with her prosperous yeoman family. The house now shows many aspects of domestic life in 16th-century England, and has a lovely garden and Shakespeare tree garden.

Open all year, Mar-Oct Mon-Sat 9-5.30, Sun 10-5.30; Nov-Feb Mon-Sat 9.30-4, Sun 10.30-4. (Closed Good Fri am, 24-26 Dec & 1 Jan am).
✳ *£2 (ch 90p). Inclusive ticket to all 5 Shakesperian properties £6 (ch £3). School and student party rates for groups visiting all five properties.*
🅿 *(charged)* 🍴 *shop* ✖

Hall's Croft

STRATFORD-UPON-AVON

Map 04 SP15
Old Town
☎ (0789) 292107
This lovely gabled Tudor house with a picturesque walled garden was the home of Dr John Hall, who married Shakespeare's daughter Susanna. There is an exhibition, on Dr John Hall and the medicine of his time; and a display of Elizabethan and Jacobean furniture.
Open all year, Mar-Oct Mon-Sat 9.30-5,

Sun 10.30-5; Nov-Feb Mon-Sat 10-4, Sun 1.30-4. (Closed Good Fri am, 24-26 Dec & 1 Jan am).
£1.60 (ch 70p). Town Heritage Walking tour (inc 3 town properties) £4.50 (ch £2). Inlcusive ticket to all 5 Shakesperian properties: £6.50 (ch £3). School & student party rates for groups visiting all 5 properties.
✖ ᣍ *toilets for disabled shop* ✖

The National Teddy Bear Museum

STRATFORD-UPON-AVON

Map 04 SP15
19 Greenhill St
☎ (0789) 293160
Ten settings are devoted to bears of all shapes and sizes. Many of the old bears are displayed and there are also mechanical and musical bears. Some of the bears belonged to famous people or are famous in their own right, such as

'Aloysius' from the television adaptation of *Brideshead Revisited*. This bear is actually named 'Delicatessen' and belonged to the actor Peter Bull. A bear festival will be held in the Civic Hall on 1 Feb.
Open all year, daily 9.30-6
✳ *£1.90 (ch 95p) Party 20+*
shop ✖

New Place / Nash's House
STRATFORD-UPON-AVON

Map 04 SP15
Chapel St
☎ (0789) 292325
Only the foundations remain of the house where Shakespeare spent the last five years of his life and died in 1616. The house was destroyed in 1759, but the picturesque garden has been planted as an Elizabethan knot garden. There is a small museum of furniture and local history in the adjacent Nash's House.

Open all year, Mar-Oct Mon-Sat 9.30-5, Sun 10.30-5; Nov-Feb Mon-Sat 10-4, Sun 1.30-4. (Closed Good Fri am, 24-26 Dec & 1 Jan am).
£1.60 (ch 70p) Town Heritage Walking Tour (inc 3 town properties) £4.50 (ch £2). Inclusive tickets for all 5 Shakesperian properties £6.50 (ch £3). School & student party rates for groups visiting all 5 properties.
& toilets for disabled shop ✻

Royal Shakespeare Company Collection
STRATFORD-UPON-AVON

Map 04 SP15
Royal Shakespeare Theatre, Waterside
☎ (0789) 296655
The permanent exhibition in the RSC Collection, Stages and Staging, contains over 1,000 items including costumes, props, pictures, photographs and sound recordings. They are used to illustrate the changes in staging from medieval times to the present use of a thrust stage in the Swan Theatre, and comparisons

of past RSC productions with the current season's plays. Temporary exhibitions include the work of the current artist(s) in residence.
Open all year, Mon-Sat 9.15-8, Sun 12-5 (Nov-Mar Sun 11-4).(Closed 25 Dec). Exhibition £1.50 (ch, pen & students £1). Theatre Tours £3.50 (ch, pen & students £2.50).
P (charged) ✿ ✗ licensed & toilets for disabled shop ✻

Shakespeare's Birthplace
STRATFORD-UPON-AVON

Map 04 SP15
Henley St
☎ (0789) 204016
Shakespeare was born in the timber-framed house in 1564. It contains numerous exhibits of the Elizabethan period and Shakespeare memorabilia, and a BBC Television Costume Exhibition is included in the admission price. The annual Shakespeare Birthday Celebrations will be held in April 1992.

Open all year, Mar-Oct Mon-Sat 9-5.30, Sun 10-5.30; Nov-Feb Mon-Sat 9.30-4, Sun 10.30-4. (Closed Good Fri am, 24-26 Dec & 1 Jan am).
£2.40 (ch £1). Town Heritage Walking Tour (inc 3 town properties) £4.50 (ch £2). Inclusive tickets to all 5 Shakesperian properties £6.50 (ch £3). School & student party rates for groups visiting all 5 properties.
& toilets for disabled shop ✻

World of Shakespeare
STRATFORD-UPON-AVON

Map 04 SP15
13 Waterside
☎ (0789) 269190
The atmosphere of Elizabethan England is recreated here with 25 life-size tableaux. Each one is brought to life by a combination of dramatic lighting,

sound techniques, original music and an audio-visual presentation.
Open all year, daily 9.05-5.30. Shows every hour & half hour. (Closed 25 Dec). £3 (ch, students & pen £2). Family ticket £7. Party 10+ .Children under 5 free.
& toilets for disabled shop ✻

Places to visit in this guide are pinpointed on the atlas at the back of the book.

Upton House
UPTON HOUSE

Map 04 SP34
(on A422)
☎ Edge Hill (029587) 266
A late 17th-century house built of a mellow local stone, with a modern interior adapted as a museum; it houses one of the finest collections of pictures and objets d'art in the country, assembled by the 2nd Lord Bearsted. Among these are Brussels tapestries, Sèvres porcelain, Chelsea figures, 18th-century furniture, and nearly 200 pictures from almost

every European school of art, including Flemish and Spanish. The terraced gardens contain fine herbaceous borders, lakes and woodland walks.
Open Apr & Oct, wknds & BHs (ex Good Fri) 2-6; May-Sep, Sat-Wed & BH Mon 2-6. (Last admission to house 5.30).
✻ £3.50. Family ticket £9.60. Garden only £2. Party.
P ✿ & (motorized buggy & driver available) toilets for disabled shop ✻ (NT)

Lord Leycester Hospital
WARWICK

Map 04 SP26
High St
☎ (0926) 492797
This lovely half-timbered building was built in 1383, and adapted into almshouses by the Earl of Leycester in 1571. It is still a home of rest for ex-servicemen and their wives. Originally it was built as a Guildhouse and the old

Guildhall, Great Hall, Chapel and courtyard remain. The building also houses the Regimental Museum of the Queen's Own Hussars.
Open all year, Mon-Sat 10-5.30 (4pm in winter). (Closed Good Fri & 25 Dec). Last admission half hour before closing.
£2 (ch 14 50p, pen £1). Party 20+.
P ✗ & shop

St John's House
WARWICK

Map 04 SP26
St John's (junct of A429 & A445 E of town).
☎ (0926) 410410 ext 2021
This fine 17th-century house was rebuilt by the Stoughton family on the site of an old hospital. It is now a branch of the county museum and has exhibits of costume and reconstructions of a

Victorian parlour, kitchen and schoolroom. On the first floor is the museum of the Royal Warwickshire Regiment.
Open all year, Tue-Sat & BH 10-12.30 & 1.30-5.30, Sun (May-Sep only) 2.30-5. Free.
P & shop ✻

Warwick Castle
WARWICK

Map 04 SP26
Off Castle Hill
☎ (0926) 495421

The first fortifications at Warwick were built by Ethelfleda, daughter of Alfred the Great, but the great castle that now stands over the River Avon was not begun until the end of the 11th century by William the Conqueror. The land was given then to Henry de Burgh, later the 1st Earl of Warwick; in the 16th century the castle was given to the Dudley family. None of the present buildings date from before the 13th century, when extensive work began on the castle. The outstanding buildings are

Caesar's Tower, built in 1356 (128ft high), and Guy's Tower (1394), which are on either side of the Gatehouse, or Clock Tower. The south range, overlooking the State Rooms, Private Apartments and Great Hall. In the Private Apartments there is an award-winning display by Madame Tussaud's entitled 'A Royal Weekend Party – 1898'.
There are also dungeons with a torture display and an armoury display. There is a rampart walk from Guy's Tower, and outside are magnificent grounds laid out by Capability Brown in the 18th century. The gardens are noted for their peacocks. Medieval banquets are held every Friday and Saturday night in the 14th-century Undercroft. Special events are planned for the summer – telephone for details.
Open daily 10-5.30 (4.30 Nov-Feb). (Closed 25 Dec).
✻ £5.75 (ch 4-16 £3.50 & pen £4). Family ticket £16-£18. Party 20+
P ✿ ✗ licensed & toilets for disabled shop ✻

Warwick Doll Museum
WARWICK

Map 04 SP26
Oken's House, Castle St
☎ (0926) 495546
The doll museum is based on a comprehensive collection of antique and period dolls and toys by Joy Robinson. The collection is exhibited in the half-timbered Elizabethan house which was

the birthplace of Thomas Oken, a benefactor of the town. The house has been carefully restored.
Open Etr-Sep, Mon-Sat 10-5 & Sun 2-5. Also school holidays throughout the year. Other times by arrangement.
85p (ch, students & pen 60p).
& shop ✻

Warwickshire Museum
WARWICK

Map 04 SP26
Market Place
☎ (0926) 412500 & 412501 (evenings)
The 17th-century market hall is now a museum displaying the geology, history and natural history of Warwickshire. The museum is notable for its giant fossil plesiosaur, habitat displays and the

Sheldon tapestry map of the county. It arranges children's activities during the summer and winter holidays.
Open all year, Mon-Sat 10-5.30, Sun (May-Sep only) 2.30-5.
Free.
shop

Warwickshire Yeomanry Museum
WARWICK

Map 04 SP26
The Court House Vaults, Jury St
☎ (0926) 492212
After a great fire in 1694, the court house was rebuilt between 1725 and 1728 in a style that befitted the wealthy merchants of the town. In the vaults there is now a museum displaying

militaria from the county Yeomanry, dating from 1794 to 1945. It includes regimental silver and some very fine paintings.
Open Good Fri-end Sep, Fri, Sat & Sun & BHs 10-1 & 2-4.
Free.
shop ✻ ▱

The Shakespeare Countryside Museum at Mary Arden's House
WILMCOTE

Map 03 SP15
(3m NW off A34)
☎ Stratford-upon-Avon (0789) 293455
Mary Arden was William Shakespeare's mother, and this picturesque, half-timbered Tudor house was her childhood home. The house is now a museum and the barns are given over to memorabilia of the countryside. There is a wide range of farm implements, other tools and bygones and there are displays of falconry daily throughout the year,

weather permitting.
Open all year, Mar-Oct Mon-Sat 9.30-5, Sun 10.30-5; Nov-Feb Mon-Sat 10-4, Sun 1.30-4. (Closed Good Fri am, 24-26 Dec & 1 Jan am).
£2.75 (ch £1.10). Family ticket £6.50. Inclusive ticket to all 5 Shakesperian properties £6.50 (ch £3). School & student party rates for groups visiting all 5 properties.
P ✿ & toilets for disabled shop ✻

WEST MIDLANDS

Aston Hall
BIRMINGHAM

Map 07 SP08
Trinity Rd, Aston
☎ 021-327 0062
Built by Sir Thomas Holt, Aston Hall is a fine Jacobean mansion complete with a panelled long gallery, balustraded staircase and magnificent plaster friezes and ceilings. It is also said to have the

ghost of Sir Thomas's daughter, who by tradition was locked up in a tiny room, went mad and died.
Open 23 Mar-3 Nov, daily 2-5. Guided tours available at other times if pre-booked.
P shop ✻
Details not confirmed for 1992

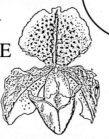

Blakesley Hall — BIRMINGHAM

Map 07 SP08
Blakesley Rd, Yardley
☎ 021-783 2193
Built around 1575, the Hall is a timber-framed yeoman's house, which has been furnished according to an inventory of 1684. There are displays on timber building, pottery and rural crafts, and on the parish of Yardley, as well as the history of the house.
Open 23 Mar-3 Nov, daily 2-5.
shop ✗
Details not confirmed for 1992

City Museum & Art Gallery — BIRMINGHAM

Map 07 SP08
Chamberlain Sq
☎ 021-235 2834
One of the world's best collections of Pre-Raphaelite paintings can be seen here, including important works by Burne-Jones, a native of Birmingham. Older schools of art are represented by French, Dutch, Italian and other works from the 14th century to the present day, and also on display are costumes and fine silver, ceramics and textiles. The wide-ranging archaeology section has prehistoric, Greek and Roman antiquities, and also objects from the Near East, Mexico and Peru. This section includes the Pinto Collection of wooden artefacts. Another popular display is the excellent collection of coins. There is a natural history section in the museum, and objects related to local history are also shown.
Open all year Mon-Sat 9.30-5, Sun 2-5. (Closed Xmas & 1 Jan). Guided tours Wed & Sat 2.30pm by prior arrangement.
☞ *shop* ✗
Details not confirmed for 1992

Museum of Science & Industry — BIRMINGHAM

Map 07 SP08
Newhall St (close to Post Office Tower)
☎ 021-236 1022
The displays range from the Industrial Revolution to the present day, with an emphasis on Birmingham's contribution to science and engineering. The Engineering Hall is a former Victorian plating works, and contains machine tools, electrical equipment, and working steam, gas and hot air engines. The Locomotive Hall was built to house the Stanier Pacific loco 'City of Birmingham; and the aircraft section has a World War II Spitfire and a Hurricane, as well as aircraft engines. The James Watt building houses the earliest still-functioning steam engine in the world, dated 1799. Other sections cover science, transport and arms. There are steam weekends in March and October, and an engine rally in May. Engines are steamed on the first and third Wednesday of each month.
Open all year, Mon-Sat 9.30-5, Sun 2-5 (Closed Xmas & 1 Jan).
& *toilets for disabled shop* ✗
Details not confirmed for 1992

Birmingham Botanical Gardens & Glasshouses — BIRMINGHAM

Map 07 SP08
Westbourne Rd, Edgbaston
☎ 021-454 1860
The gardens are a 15-acre 'oasis of delight' just 2 miles from the centre of Birmingham. Originally opened in 1832 they continue to be run by an independent educational charity. The Tropical House has a 24ft-wide lily pool and its lush tropical vegetation includes bromeliads, bananas, cocoa and other economic plants. Palm trees, ferns, orchids and insectiverous plants are displayed in the Palm House. The Orangery features a wide variety of citrus fruits and the Cactus House gives a desert scene with its giant agaves and opuntias. Outside there is colourful bedding on the Terrace and a tour of the gardens includes rhododendrons and azalea borders, Rose Garden, Rock Garden and a collection of over 200 trees. There are Domestic Theme Gardens, Herb and Cottage Gardens, a Children's Adventure Playground and Aviaries. Plant centre, gift shop, gallery and refreshment pavilion. Bands play every Sunday afternoon throughout the summer.
Open all year, wkdays 9-8 or dusk, Sun 10-8 or dusk whichever is earlier. (Closed 25 Dec).
£2.70 (£3 summer Sun, concessions £1.40). Party.
🅿 ☞ ✗ *licensed* & *(3 wheelchairs available free) toilets for disabled shop garden centre* ✗

For an explanation of the symbols and abbreviations, see page 2.

Birmingham Nature Centre — BIRMINGHAM

Map 07 SP08
Pershore Rd, Edgbaston (off A441, in Cannon Hill Pk)
☎ 021-472 7775
Animals of the British Isles and Europe can be seen in indoor and outdoor enclosures which are designed to resemble natural habitats. The grounds also have various ponds and a stream, to attract wild birds, butterflies and other creatures.
Open 23 Mar-3 Nov, daily 10-5. (Winter Sat & Sun 10-dusk).
🅿 ☞ & *toilets for disabled shop* ✗
Details not confirmed for 1992

Birmingham Railway Museum — BIRMINGHAM

Map 07 SP08
670 Warwick Rd, Tyseley
☎ 021-707 4696
This is a working railway museum with a fully equipped workshop. There are 12 steam locomotives and 36 historic carriages, wagons and other vehicles. Steam-hauled train rides can be taken.
Open daily 10-5. (Closed 25 & 26 Dec & 1 Jan). Steam Days every Sun & BH Etr-Oct & Dec.
🅿 ☞ ✗ & *shop*
Details not confirmed for 1992

The Patrick Collection — BIRMINGHAM

Map 07 SP08
180 Lifford Ln, Kings Norton
☎ 021-459 9111
Three halls are devoted to motoring from the beginning of the century to the present day, with cars ranging from a 1904 Wolseley to a 1991 Alfa Romeo SZ. There are also terraced gardens, a children's play area, children's electric go-karts and a new jetty for feeding the lakeside wildlife and fish. In spring 1992 a nature trail (accessible to disabled

visitors) will be opening. The Engine House, newly refurbished, will be exhibiting cut away engines and gear boxes from Jaguar, Scania, Rover etc.
Open 17 Apr-Oct, Wed, Sat & Sun 10.30-5.30. Also school holidays & BH's; Nov-Etr, Sun 10.30-5.30.
£3.50 (ch 14 £2.10, under 5 free, pen students & disabled £2.50). Family ticket £9. Party 10+.
🅿 ☕ ✗ *licensed* ♿ *(lift) toilets for disabled shop* ✖

Sarehole Mill — BIRMINGHAM

Map 07 SP08
Cole Bank Rd, Hall Green
☎ 021-777 6612
An 18th-century water mill, restored to working order and containing displays illustrating various aspects of milling, blade-grinding and English rural pursuits.

The writer J.R.R. Tolkein lived nearby and found inspiration for his book 'The Hobbit' here.
Open 23 Mar-3 Nov, daily 2-5.
shop ✖
Details not confirmed for 1992

Selly Manor Museum — BIRMINGHAM

Map 07 SP08
Maple Rd, Bournville (off A38)
☎ 021-472 0199
These two timber-framed manor houses date from the 13th and early 14th centuries, and have been re-erected in the 'garden suburb' of Bournville. There

is a herb garden and exhibitions are held, with an annual craft fair on the first Saturday in November.
Open mid Jan-mid Dec, Tue-Fri 10-5 (inc BH).
£1 (ch 50p).
♿ *toilets for disabled shop* ✖

Weoley Castle Ruins — BIRMINGHAM

Map 07 SP08
Alwold Rd
☎ 021-427 4270
Only some impressive remains can now be seen of the 13th-century fortified house, but there is a small site museum. It shows objects revealed during

excavations, such as coins, keys, a 13th-century shoe, and evidence of a 600-year-old chess game.
Open 26 Mar-1 Nov, Tue-Fri 2-5.
✖
Details not confirmed for 1992

Cadbury World — BOURNVILLE

Map 07 SP08
Linden Rd
☎ 021-433 4334
Not just a chocolate factory tour by any means. Visitors to Cadbury World are first of all transported to a tropical rainforest to see the Aztecs of the 16th century growing and trading cocoa beans, and may even sample Emperor Montezuma's favourite drink – a mixture of cocoa, honey and chilli peppers! The introduction of chocolate to Europe follows, with a reconstruction of a cobbled square in Georgian England complete with the notorious White's Chocolate House. Here the story of the

Cadbury family and their chocolate enterprise, including the creation of the Bournville factory and village, is related. There are further displays on packaging and marketing, early machinery, health and safety etc. Although there are no tours of the modern factory, the hand-processing unit shows all stages in the production of hand-made chocolates.
Open all year, Mon-Sat 10-5.30, Sun 12-6 (Closed 25 Dec).
£4 (ch 5-15 £3, pen £3.60). Family ticket £12.85.
🅿 ☕ ✗ *licensed* ♿ *(ex packaging plant) toilets for disabled shop* ✖

✱ An asterisk indicates that up-to-date information was not available at the time of our research – 1991 information has been published as an indication of what you may expect.

Coventry Cathedral & Visitor Centre — COVENTRY

Map 07 SP37
7 Priory Row
☎ (0203) 227597
Coventry's old cathedral was bombed during an air raid of November 1940 which devastated the city. The remains have been carefully preserved. The new cathedral was designed by Sir Basil Spence and consecrated in May 1962. It contains outstanding modern works of art, including a huge tapestry designed by Graham Sutherland, the west screen (a wall of glass engraved by John Hutton

with saints and angels), bronzes by Epstein, and windows by John Piper and others. There is also an opportunity to enjoy the art of modern technology in the visitors' centre.
Open all year, daily, Etr-Sep 9.30-7; Oct-Etr 9.30-5.30.
✱ *Visitor centre £1.25 (ch 6 free, ch 6-16, students & pen 75p). Party 10+. Cathedral £2 donation. Camera charge £1.*
✗ *licensed* ♿ *(lift) toilets for disabled shop* ✖

Coventry Toy Museum — COVENTRY

Map 07 SP37
Much Park St
☎ (0203) 227560
A collection of toys dating from 1740 to 1980, including trains, dolls, dolls'

houses and games, housed in a 14th-century monastery gatehouse.
Open all year, daily 2-6.
✱ *£1 (ch & pen 50p).*
shop ✖

Herbert Art Gallery & Museum — COVENTRY

Map 07 SP37
Jordan Well
☎ (0203) 832381
The collections cover social history, archaeology, folk life, industry, natural history and the visual arts. A special feature is the collection of Graham Sutherland's studies for the 'Christ in Glory' tapestry in Coventry Cathedral. Also here is the Frederick Poke

collection of fine 18th-century English furniture and silver, and the Allen collection of Chinese art. The natural history section includes a live animals display.
Open all year, Mon-Sat 10-5.30, Sun 2-5. (Closed Good Fri & part Xmas).
Free.
♿ *toilets for disabled shop* ✖

Lunt Roman Fort — COVENTRY

Map 07 SP37
Coventry Rd, Baginton (S side of city, off Stonebridge highway, A45)
☎ (0203) 832381
The fort which stood on this site around the end of the 1st century has been reconstructed, with an interpretation centre in the rebuilt granary. Other

features include a gateway gyrus and ramparts.
Open end May-Sep, daily ex Mon & Thu, 12-6.
£1 (ch, pen & UB40 50p). Guided tour by advanced booking.
🅿 ♿ *toilets for disabled shop* ✖

Museum of British Road Transport — COVENTRY

Map 07 SP37
St Agnes Ln, Hales St
☎ (0203) 832425
The museum illustrates the role of Coventry and the West Midlands in the development of transport throughout the world. There are over 400 exhibits, in displays of motor cars, commercial

vehicles, motor cycles and associated items. New for 1992 – a display of die-cast models.
Open all year, daily 10-5.
£2.50 (ch & pen £1.50). Family ticket £6.50.
♿ *toilets for disabled shop* ✖

St Mary's Guildhall — COVENTRY

Map 07 SP37
between Bayley Ln & Earl St
☎ (0203) 832373
The medieval guildhall of the city has a minstrel's gallery and a restored hall with portraits, Flemish tapestries and

'Caesar's watchtower'.
Open Etr-Oct, Mon-Sat 10-1 & 2-5.30, Sun 12-5.
Free.
shop ✖ 🚌

Black Country Museum — DUDLEY

Map 07 SO99
Tipton Rd (opposite Dudley Guest Hospital)
☎ 021-557 9643 & 021-520 8054

The museum is really a reconstruction of a Victorian Black Country village, complete with cottages, a chapel, chemist, baker and a pub serving real ale. One of the buildings is a chainmaker's house with a brewhouse, and demonstrations of chainmaking and glass cutting are given in traditional workshops. There is also a canal boat dock with a range of narrowboats, and boats set off daily for canal trips into the Dudley Tunnel, an eerie underground ride. Transport around the village is provided by an electric tramway. You can go underground in an 1850s mine, and see a replica of the world's first steam engine venture into a pit-pulled cottage (affected by subsidence due to mining). There will be a Working Boat gathering 26-27 Sep.
Open al year, Mar-Oct daily 10-5; Nov-Feb, Wed-Sun 10-4. (Closed 25 Dec).
£4.75 (ch 5 free, ch 18 £3.25, pen £4.25). Party 20+
🅿 ☕ ♿ *toilets for disabled shop* 🐕

Dudley Zoo & Castle — DUDLEY

Map 07 SO99
2 The Broadway
☎ (0384) 252401
The wooded grounds of Dudley Castle make a wonderful setting for the long-established, traditional zoo, which has animals from every continent. The castle ruins are impressive, and a chairlift and land train take you to the top of Castle Hill. An audio visual show of the castle's history is shown free of charge.
Open all year, Etr-mid Sep, daily 10-4.30; mid Sep-Etr, daily 10-3.30. (Closed 25 Dec).
* *£4 (ch & pen £2). Family ticket £11.50. Party 15+.*
🅿 *(charged)* ☕ ✕ *licensed* ♿ *(land train from gates to castle) toilets for disabled shop* 🐕

* An asterisk indicates that up-to-date information was not available at the time of our research – 1991 information has been published as an indication of what you may expect.

Museum & Art Gallery — DUDLEY

Map 07 SO99
St James's Rd
☎ (0384) 456000 ext 5570
The museum houses the Brooke Robinson collection of 17th-, 18th- and 19th-century European painting, furniture, ceramics and enamels, also Japanese netsuke and inro, and Greek, Roman and Oriental ceramics. A fine geological gallery has spectacular displays of fossils from the local 'Wenlock' limestone and coal measures, and a wide variety of temporary exhibitions throughout the year. Special events for 1992 include: 27 Jun-5 Sep, From Moon to Mars and Beyond; 28-29 Nov, Dudley Rock 'N' Fossil Fair.
Open all year, Mon-Sat 10-5. (Closed BHs).
Free.
♿ *shop* 🐕

Broadfield House Glass Museum — KINGSWINFORD

Map 07 SO88
Barnett Ln
☎ (0384) 273011
This magnificent collection of 19th- and 20th-century glass focuses on the cut, etched, engraved and coloured glass made in nearby Stourbridge during the last century. Highlights include cameo glass by Alphonse Lechevrel and George Woodall, and rock crystal engraving by William Fritsche. Also on display are the Michael Parkington collection of 18th-, 19th- and 20th-century British glass, the Hulbert of Dudley collection, and the Notley/Lerpiniere collection of Carnival Glass.
Open all year, Tue-Fri & Sun 2-5, Sat 10-1 & 2-5. BH's 2-5.
Free.
🅿 ♿ *shop* 🐕

Places to visit in this guide are pinpointed on the atlas at the back of the book.

National Motorcycle Museum — SOLIHULL

Map 07 SP17
Coventry Rd, Bickenhill (nr junc 6, of M42, off A45 nr NEC)
☎ 021-704 2784
Five exhibition halls showing British motorcycles built during the Golden Age of motorcycling. Spanning 90 years, the immaculately restored machines are the products of around 150 different factories.
Open all year, daily 10-6. (Closed 25 Dec).
£3.75 (ch 14 & pen £2). Party 20+.
🅿 ☕ ♿ *toilets for disabled shop* 🐕

Jerome K Jerome Birthplace Museum — WALSALL

Map 07 SP09
Belsize House, Bradford St
☎ (0922) 653135
Perhaps the most famous inhabitant of Walsall is Jerome K Jerome, author of *Three Men in a Boat*, published in 1899. Jerome was born in Walsall in 1859 and his home is now restored as a museum, housing documents and memorabilia of the author. One room has been reconstructed as an 1850s parlour.
Open all year wkdays. Please telephone for further details.
Free.
shop 🚌

Walsall Leather Centre Museum — WALSALL

Map 07 SP09
56-57 Wisemore
☎ (0922) 721153
Winner of the 'Museum of the Year' award (Social and Industrial History) this museum is housed in a former leather goods factory dating from 1891. In the atmospheric workshops, rich with the aroma of leather, visitors can see how traditional leather goods have been made, and (on most days of the week) talk to leatherworkers about their craft. Historical displays show beautiful products from the past, but this museum is not just about the past. Walsall firms of today supply such prestigious customers as Harrods. With 120 leather companies in the town there is still a wealth of experience here, reflected by the goods on sale in the museum shop. Regular exhibitions, events and activities are planned throughout the year for all ages. A special events leaflet will be available from April 1992.
Open all year, Tue-Sat 10-5 (Nov-Mar 4), Sun noon-5. Open BH Mon. Museum also available to parties in the evening by prior booking.
Free.
☕ ♿ *toilets for disabled shop* 🐕

This is just one of many guidebooks published by the AA. The full range is available at any AA shop or good bookshop.

Wightwick Manor — WOLVERHAMPTON

Map 07 SO99
☎ (0902) 761108

This house is unusual in that, although barely 100 years old, it is a gem of design and architectural interest. It was begun in 1887 and in its style of decoration it is one of the finest examples of the achievements of the late-19th century. The house was designed by Edward Ould, a follower of William Morris. All aspects of William Morris' talents are shown in this house – wallpapers, textiles, carpets, tiles, embroidery and even books. There are also paintings and drawings by Burne-Jones, D G Rosetti, Holman Hunt and others, glass by Kempe and tiles by de Morgan.
The garden was laid out by Alfred Parsons and Thomas Manson, and reflects late Victorian and Edwardian design.
Open Mar-Dec, Thu, Sat & BH Sun & Mon 2.30-5.30. (Closed 25-26 Dec, 1-2 Jan & Feb).
🅿 ♿
(NT)
Details not confirmed for 1992

WEST SUSSEX

Amberley Chalk Pits Museum — AMBERLEY

Map 04 TQ01
Houghton Bridge (off B2139)
☎ Bury (0798) 831370
A former chalk quarry and limeworks is the setting for this eye-opening display of industries in south-east England. A working blacksmith, potter and printer are based here, and there is a cobbler's

shop. Narrow-gauge railway; various events all year.
Open 20 Mar-27 Oct, Wed-Sun & BH Mon 10-6. Also Mon & Tue in school summer holidays. Last admission 5pm.
P ✖ ♿ *toilets for disabled shop*
Details not confirmed for 1992

Legh Manor — ANSTY

Map 04 TQ22
☎ Haywards Heath (0444) 413428
Three rooms and the hall can be visited in the interesting old house, and there is a garden laid out by Gertrude Jekyll.

Open May-Sep, 2nd and 3rd Wed and 2nd Sat in each month 2.30-5.30.
P ✖
Details not confirmed for 1992

Wakehurst Place Garden — ARDINGLY

Map 04 TQ32
(1.5m NW, on B2028)
☎ (0444) 892701
Woodland and lakes linked by a pretty watercourse make this large garden a beautiful place to walk, and it also has an amazing variety of interesting trees and shrubs. It is administered and maintained by the Royal Botanic

Gardens at Kew.
Open all year, Nov-Jan 10-4; Feb & Oct 10-5; Mar 10-6; Apr-Sep 10-7. (Closed 25 Dec & 1 Jan). Last admission 30 mins before closing.
✳ £3
P ✖ ♿ *toilets for disabled shop* ✖
(NT)

Arundel Castle — ARUNDEL

Map 04 TQ00
☎ (0903) 883136
This great Castle, home of the Dukes of Norfolk, dates from the Norman Conquest. Containing a very fine collection of furniture and paintings, it is still a family home reflecting the changes

of nearly a thousand years.
Open Apr-last Fri in Oct, Sun-Fri 12-5. Last admission 4pm (Closed Sat).
£3.60 (ch 5-15 £2.60, pen £3.10). Party 20+
P *(charged)* ✖ ✖ *licensed shop* ✖

This great castle, home of the Dukes of Norfolk, dates from the Norman Conquest. Containing a very fine collection of furniture and paintings Arundel Castle is still a family home, reflecting the changes of nearly a thousand years.

It is open from 1st April until 30th October Sundays to Fridays from 12.00 to 5.00pm. Last admission on any day is 4.00pm.

The castle is not open on Saturdays.

The restaurant serves homemade food for lunch or afternoon tea.

Pre-booked parties are welcome. Menus are available on request.

The shop sells many items chosen by the Countess of Arundel and is always open at the same time as the Castle.

Arundel Castle

For further information apply to:
The Comptroller, Arundel Castle, West Sussex, BN18 9AB.
Telephone (0903) 883136/882173

Arundel Toy & Military Museum — ARUNDEL

Map 04 TQ00
23 High St
☎ (0903) 883101 & 882908
A Georgian cottage in the heart of town displays a vast private collection of interesting old toys, games, dolls, teddy bears and toy soldiers. There are also royal commemoratives, boats, 'Goss' models, puppets, pocillovy (egg-cups), small militaria and curiosities collected

from all over the world. During the Arundel festival in August, the museum will hold a 'Design a Garden' competition – details on application.
Open every weekend 12-5, school & BH; Jun-Aug daily 10.30-5. Most days in Spring & Sep-Oct.
£1.25 (ch 15, students & pen £1). Party.
♿ *shop*

Wildfowl & Wetlands Trust — ARUNDEL

Map 04 TQ00
Mill Rd
☎ (0903) 883355
More than a thousand ducks, geese and swans from all over the world live here in 55 acres of well-landscaped pens, lakes and paddocks, and the site is also a sanctuary for many wild birds. Wild diving duck are attracted by the clear, spring-fed pools, while waders come to feed in the damp meadows and 'wader scrape'. Rarities include the shy water rail, which makes its nest among the reed beds. Its grunting, squealing call may be heard. There are hides

overlooking the different habitats, and the site also has a large viewing gallery and education complex. Facilities for the disabled include purpose-built toilet for wheelchair users, free wheelchair loan, access throughout the centre (including hides), and waitress service at the restaurant.
Open all year, daily. Summer 9.30-6.30; Winter 9.30-5.30. Last admission Summer 5.30; Winter 4pm. (Closed 25 Dec).
P ✖ *licensed* ♿ *toilets for disabled shop* ✖
Details not confirmed for 1992

Holly Gate Cactus Garden — ASHINGTON

Map 04 TQ11
Billingshurst Ln (B2133)
☎ Worthing (0903) 892930
A mecca for the cactus enthusiast, with more than 30,000 succulent and cactus plants, including many rare types. They come from both arid and tropical parts

of the world, and are housed in over 10,000 sq ft of greenhouses.
Open all year daily, 9-5. (Closed 25-26 Dec).
£1 (ch & pen 75p). Party 20+.
P ♿ *shop garden centre*

For an explanation of the symbols and abbreviations, see page 2.

Bignor Roman Villa & Museum — BIGNOR

Map 04 SU91
(between A29 & A285)
☎ Sutton (07987) 259
Rediscovered in 1811, this Roman house was built on a grand scale. It is one of the largest known, and has spectacular mosaics. The heating system can also be seen, and various finds from excavations are on show. The longest mosaic in Britain (82ft) is on display

here in its original position. A major archaeological dig is planned for Jun/Jul 1992. Visitors will have the opportunity to view and to talk to the archaeologists.
Open Mar-May & Oct 10-5 (Closed Mon ex BHs). Jun-Sep daily 10-6.
£2.10 (ch 16 £1.10, pen £1.45). Party 10+. Guided tours by arrangement
P ✖ ♿ *shop* ✖

Bramber Castle — BRAMBER

Map 04 TQ11
A former home of the Dukes of Norfolk, this ruined Norman stronghold lies on a ridge of the South Downs and

gives wonderful views.
Open all year, daily.
Free.
(NT)

Chichester District Museum — CHICHESTER

Map 04 SU80
29 Little London
☎ (0243) 784683
Housed in an 18th-century corn store, the museum has displays on local history, archaeology and geology.

Temporary exhibitions are held.
Open all year, Tue-Sat 10-5.30. (Closed BH & PH).
Free.
♿ *(staff will assist & accompany by arrangement) shop* ✖

Guildhall Museum — CHICHESTER

Map 04 SU80
Priory Park, Priory Rd
☎ (0243) 784683
The medieval Greyfriars church was later used as the city guildhall and now houses a branch of the District Museum. It displays local archaeological finds. The

mound of a Norman castle can be seen in the small public park.
Open Jun-Sep, Tue-Sat 1-5. Other times by arrangement.
Free.
♿ *(parking, 'phone for arrangements').*
shop ✖

Mechanical Music & Doll Collection — CHICHESTER

Map 04 SU80
Church Rd, Portfield (1m E off A27)
☎ (0243) 785421
Here is a unique opportunity to see and hear barrel, fair and Dutch street organs, musical boxes, polyphons etc – all fully restored and playing for your pleasure. The Doll Collection contains over one hundred fine examples of French and

German bisque-headed dolls. Also phonographs, stereoscopic viewers, veteran cycles and natural history exhibits.
Open all year, Etr-Sep, daily 10-5; Oct-Etr wknds only 10-5; Evening bookings by arrangement.
Admission fee payable.
P ♿ *shop* ✖

Pallant House

CHICHESTER

Map 04 SU80
9 North Pallant
☎ (0243) 774557
The gallery is housed in a restored Queen Anne town house. The rooms contain fine furniture, and there is an Edwardian kitchen. Permanent collections on display include the Modern British Art of the Hussey and Kearley bequests; the Geoffrey Freeman

collection of Bow porcelain and 18th-century English drinking glasses and enamels. There is a programme of temporary exhibitions, and the small garden is planted in 18th-century style.
Open all year, Tue-Sat 10-5.30. (Closed Sun, Mon & BHs). (Last admission 4.45pm).
£2.50 (ch £1, students & pen £1.70).
✻ *shop* ✻

Standen

EAST GRINSTEAD

Map 04 TQ33
(2m S, signposted from B2110)
☎ (0342) 323029
Standen is a showpiece of the 19th-century Arts and Crafts movement. It was designed by Philip Webb for the Beale family, and was meant from the start to be decorated with William Morris wallpapers and fabrics. The interior has been carefully preserved, and the Morris designs to be seen here include Sunflower, Peacock, Trellis, and Larkspur, among others. The furniture is also in keeping, and includes contemporary brass beds from Heal's,

furniture from the Morris firm, and ceramics by William de Morgan. Webb also designed some of the furniture and details such as the fire grates, finger plates for the doors, and the electric light fittings. There is a beautiful hillside garden.
Open Apr-Oct, Wed-Sun (inc Good Fri) House: 1.30-5.30, Garden: 12.30-5.30. Open BH Mon. Last admission 5pm.
✻ *House £3.50 (£4 wknds, Good Fri & BH Mons) ch half price. Garden only £2 (ch £1).*
🅿 ☕ ⚐ *shop* ✻
(NT)

Roman Palace

FISHBOURNE

Map 04 SU80
Salthill Rd
☎ Chichester (0243) 785859

This is the largest known Roman residence in Britain, but the reason for building such a magnificent house here is not known. It was occupied from the 1st to the 3rd centuries AD, when its hundred or so rooms must have been a

wonderful sight with their mosaic floors and painted walls; 25 of these mosaic floors can still be seen in varying states of completeness, including others rescued from elsewhere in the area. The museum gives an account of the history of the palace, and there is also an audio-visual theatre. There is a full-size reconstruction of a Roman dining room. The garden has been re-planted to its original first-century plan. There is a new mosaic making area for children.
Open all year, daily, Mar-Apr & Oct 10-5; May-Sep 10-6; Nov 10-4; Dec-Feb, Sun only 10-4.
£3 (ch £1.20, pen & students £2.30). Family ticket £7.50.
🅿 ☕ ⚐ *(self guiding tapes & tactile objects for the blind) toilets for disabled shop* ✻

Denmans Garden

FONTWELL

Map 04 SU90
(5m E of Chichester on A27)
☎ Eastergate (0243) 542808
This garden has been created from land which was part of an estate owned by Lord Denham in the 19th century. The present three-and-a-half-acre garden was begun in 1946 and has gradually developed over the last 40 years. There is a Walled Garden, bursting with

masses of perennials, herbs and old-fashioned roses, and a Gravel Stream with grasses, bamboo and a pond. The South Garden has fine maples and cherry trees. A school of Garden Design is housed in the Clock House.
Open 4 Mar-15 Dec, daily 9-5.
✻ *£1.95 (ch £1, ch under 5 free, pen £1.70). Party 12 +.*
🅿 ☕ ⚐ *shop garden centre* ✻

Goodwood House

GOODWOOD

Map 04 SU80
☎ Chichester (0243) 774107
The home of the Dukes of Richmond was acquired by the 1st Duke in 1697 so that he could ride with the local hunt. Horses and hunting remained a high priority, and the stable block added during 18th-century alterations outshines the house. The work was started by William Chambers, and taken over after his death by James Wyatt, who also designed an impressive classical building for the hounds. The 'Glorious Goodwood' horse races began in the 19th century. The glories of the house

itself, however, are its beautiful downland setting and its collection of paintings, including numerous Old Masters. There is also some fine furniture, porcelain, tapestries and mementoes of the family. Events planned for 1992 include antiques fairs (Feb, Jun, Nov), a craft fair (5-6 Dec), and a photographic exhibition (31 May).
Open 4 May-28 Sep, Sun & Mon 2-5. Also Etr Sun & Mon & Tue-Thu in Aug. (Closed 14 Jun & event days).
£3.20 (ch £1.50). Party 15 +.
🅿 ☕ ⚐ *toilets for disabled shop* ✻

Nymans Garden

HANDCROSS

Map 04 TQ22
(on B2114)
☎ (0444) 400321 & 400002
Set in the Sussex Weald, Nymans has flowering shrubs and roses, a flower garden in the old walled orchard, and a secret sunken garden. There are some fine and rare trees, although many were

lost in the storm of October 1987. Please telephone or send SAE for details.
Open Apr-Oct, daily (ex Mon & Fri) BH Mon & Good Fri 11-7 or sunset if earlier. Last admission 1 hour before closing.
✻ *£3 (ch £1.50)*
🅿 ☕ ⚐ *toilets for disabled shop* ✻
(NT)

Borde Hill Garden

HAYWARDS HEATH

Map 04 TQ32
(1.5m N)
☎ (0444) 450326
The 40-acre gardens have a huge collection of rhododendrons, and the azaleas, camellias and magnolias are also noteworthy. Close to the house are interesting herbaceous beds, and further

out there are woodland walks. Recent additions include a lake.
Open 28 Mar-25 Oct, daily 10-6.
✻ *Garden £2 (ch 75p & pen £1.25). Party 20+. Lake, picnic area & playground £1 per car.*
🅿 ☕ ✗ *licensed* ⚐ *(wheelchairs available) toilets for disabled shop*

Woods Mill Countryside Centre

HENFIELD

Map 04 TQ21
Shoreham Rd (1.5m S Henfield on A2037)
☎ (0273) 492630
The centre consists of a wildlife and countryside exhibition in an 18th-century watermill, and a trail through varied habitats. Nets are provided for a pond where children can identify

specimens. Special events are held throughout the season, including Focus on Amphibians (25-26 Apr), Focus on Bats (16-17 May), and Victorian Haymaking Day (19 Jul).
Open 17 Apr-27 Sep, Tue, Wed, Thu & Sat 2-6; Sun & BH's 11-6.
£1.80 (ch 90p, pen £1.40). Family £5.
🅿 ☕ ⚐ *shop* ✻

Highdown

HIGHDOWN

Map 04 TQ00
(N off A259 between Worthing & Littlehampton)
☎ Worthing (0903) 501054
These gardens were laid out in a chalk pit on Highdown Hill. There are rock

plants, flowering shrubs and daffodils, as well as excellent views.
Open all year, Mon-Fri 10-4.30; Apr-Sep, wknds & BH's 10-8.
Free.
🅿 ☕ ⚐ *toilets for disabled* ✻

Horsham Museum

HORSHAM

Map 04 TQ13
9 The Causeway
☎ (0403) 54959
The museum is in a timber framed Tudor house with diverse collections. On show in the recently opened Prehistory room are locally found dinosaur bones, in the new Transport gallery a fascinating collection of early bicycles. The Georgian room has an interesting ceramic collection. There is a display on shops and shopping, a

wheelwright's shop, a blacksmith's forge, and a gaol setting. The museum's walled garden has many unusual plants. Throughout the year there will be 5 temporary exhibitions drawing on the museum's superb collections. In July and August there will be a major exhibition centred round the poet, Shelley.
Open all year, Tue-Sat 10-5.
Free.
⚐ *toilets for disabled shop* ✻

Littlehampton Museum

LITTLEHAMPTON

Map 04 TQ00
Manor House, Church St
☎ (0903) 715149
The museum is situated in the manor house, built in the 1830s to serve the manor farm. Ship paintings, early photos of the town and its river, historic maps

and local archaeological finds are displayed along with some temporary exhibitions.
Open all year Tue-Sat (incl Summer BH); 10.30-4.30.
Free.
🅿 *(charged)* ⚐ *shop* ✻

Leonardslee Gardens

LOWER BEEDING

Map 04 TQ22
(3m SW from Handcross)
☎ Horsham (0403) 891212
Set on the edge of the ancient St Leonard's Forest, this wonderful landscaped garden was created by Sir Edmund Loder at the end of the 19th century. Listed Grade I in importance, there are over 200 acres open to the public. It is best seen in the spring when azaleas and rhododendrons clothe the banks of a series of six ancient hammer ponds. The autumn tints are impressive,

too and there are wallaby and deer parks. There is also a delightful Rock Garden and a Temperate Greenhouse. In 1991 a Japanese garden and Bonsai exhibition opened, and in 1992 a new Alpine house is due to open.
Open 17 Apr-Jun, daily 10-6; Jul-Oct, Mon-Fri 2-6, Sat & Sun 10-6.
May £3.50, May Sun & BH Mon £4 (ch £2); Apr, Jun & Oct £3; Jul-Sep £2.50 (ch £1).
🅿 ☕ ✗ *licensed shop garden centre* ✻
See advertisement on page 164.

Leonardslee Gardens
Lower Beeding, Nr Horsham, Sussex

Petworth House   PETWORTH

Map 04 SU92
☎ (0798) 42207
A 13-mile wall surrounds Petworth's acres. Rebuilt by the Duke of Somerset in the 17th century, all that remains of the 13th-century building is the chapel. The imposing 320ft west front faces the lake and great park, and was re-designed by Anthony Salvin between 1869 and 1872. The state rooms and galleries contain one of the finest art collections in England, including works by Gainsborough, Rembrandt and Van Dyck. Turner was a frequent visitor to Petworth, and a notable collection of his works is kept here. The carved room is said to be the most impressive in the house, with its lovely decoration by Grinling Gibbons. On 26-27 July open air concerts will be held, (telephone 0798 43748 for information).
Open Apr-Oct, daily (ex Mon & Fri; Open Good Fri & BH Mons, closed Tue following) 1-5.30. Gardens daily. Park 8-sunset.
✳ *£3.80.*
🅿 ♿ ⚹ *toilets for disabled shop* ✻ *(ex in park)*
(NT)

Parham House & Gardens   PULBOROUGH

Map 04 TQ01
Parham Park (3m SE off A283)
☎ Storrington (0903) 742021
Surrounded by a deer park, fine gardens and pleasure grounds in a beautiful downland setting, this Elizabethan family home contains a good collection of paintings, furniture, carpets and rare needlework. A brick and turf maze has been created in the grounds – designed with children in mind, it is called 'Veronica's Maze'. The garden at Parham has won the prestigious Christie's 1990 Garden of the Year Award. Plans for the garden in 1992 include a vegetable garden, with vegetable sales from the new garden shop. There is also a rose garden. Special events in the park include a steam rally in June, the Sussex Down RAFA Fete and a craft show. Details available from the Estate Office, 0903 742866.
Open Etr Sun-1st Sun in Oct, Wed, Thu, Sun & BH. Gardens 1-6; House 2-6 (last entry 5.30pm). Guided tours on Wed & Thu mornings by special arrangement.
✳ *House & Gardens £3.20 (ch 5-15 £1.50 & pen £2.50). Gardens £1.60 (ch 75p). Party 20+.*
🅿 ♿ ⚹ *(by arrangement) shop garden centre* ✻ *(ex in grounds)*

Marlipins Museum   SHOREHAM-BY-SEA

Map 04 TQ20
High St
☎ Brighton (0273) 462994
The Marlipins museum has a wide range of exhibits relating to local history and archaeology. There is also a maritime gallery, displaying a fine collection of ship portraits, ship models, and other items of local maritime interest. The building in which the museum is housed may have been built as a customs house. It dates from Norman times and has a superb knopped flint and stone
continued . . .

---

chequerwork façade. A topographical gallery displays drawings, watercolours, oil paintings and maps of the Shoreham area. The museum has been totally refurbished and reorganised, with many new exhibits, over the last three years.
Open May-Sep, Tue-Sat 10-1 & 2-4.50, Sun 2-4.30.
Donations.
shop ✻

Weald & Downland Open Air Museum   SINGLETON

Map 04 SU81
(6m N of Chichester on A286)
☎ (024363) 348

Situated in a beautiful Downland setting, this museum is of rescued historic buildings from south-east England. The buildings, ranging from early medieval houses to a 19th-century schoolhouse, have been re-erected to form a village and outlying farms and agricultural buildings. Among the exhibits there is a medieval farmstead working watermill, where corn is ground and flour is sold, a Tudor market hall, a blacksmith's forge, tollhouse and timber-framed building. There are displays of rural industries, including a charcoal burner's camp, and traditional crafts. Special events for 1992 include: 19-20 Apr, Traditional Food Fair; 25 May, Sheep Dog Trials; 7 Jun, Heavy Horses; 26 July, Show for Rare and Traditional Breeds; 24-25 Oct, Steam Threshing and Ploughing.
Open all year, Mar-Oct, daily 11-6; Nov-Feb, Wed & Sun 11-5. Also open BH's. Last admission 1hr before closing.
✳ *£3.50 (ch £1.75, pen £2.75). Family ticket £8.50. Party.*
🅿 ♿ ⚹ *toilets for disabled shop*

Uppark   SOUTH HARTING

Map 04 SU71
(1.5m S on B2146)
☎ (0730) 825317
On 30th August 1989 this late 17th-century house was partially destroyed by fire. The attic and the first floor were completely gutted, but the structure of the state rooms and basements survives largely intact. Many of the 18th-century contents were saved and are now in safe storage around the country. The garden, landscaped by Repton, and the magnificent views, can still be enjoyed.
Open: Grounds only, 5 Apr-Sep, Sun only 1.30-5.30. Last admission 5pm.
✳ *75p (ch free).*
🅿 ✻
(NT)

Tangmere Military Aviation Museum Trust   TANGMERE

Map 04 SU90
Tangmere Airfield (off A27)
☎ Chichester (0243) 775223
Based at an airfield which played an important role during the World Wars, this museum has a wide-ranging collection of relics relating to Tangmere and air war in the south-east of England.
There are photographs, documents, models, uniforms, aircraft and aircraft parts on display. There is an annual Aeromart in September.
Open Feb-Nov 10-5.30.
✳ *£2 (ch 75p).*
🅿 ⚹ *(wheelchairs available) shop*

West Dean Gardens   WEST DEAN

Map 04 SU81
(on A286 between Chichester & Midhurst)
☎ Singleton (024363) 303
The 35-acre garden is set in a scenic valley with magnificent specimen trees as well as a 300ft pergola, a gazebo, several summer houses and a wild garden. A Circuit Walk leads through the park and a 35-acre arboretum.
Open Mar-Oct, daily 11-6. Last ticket 5pm.
£2.25 (ch £1, pen £2). Party 20+.
🅿 ⚹ *toilets for disabled* ✻

Priest House   WEST HOATHLY

Map 04 TQ33
(off B2028)
☎ Sharpthorne (0342) 810479
The 15th-century house has been converted into a small folk museum with a variety of interesting exhibits including samplers, needlework and silver band instruments.
Open 25 Mar-Oct, Mon, Wed-Sat 11-5.30, Sun 2-5.30.
£1.50 (ch 5-16 50p). Party.
shop ✻

Worthing Museum & Art Gallery — WORTHING

Map 04 TQ10
Chapel Rd (on A24)
☎ (0903) 239999 ext 2528
A particularly rich collection of archaeological finds are displayed in this museum. There are artefacts from prehistoric, Roman, Romano-British and Anglo-Saxon times. There is a downland display, toys, pottery,

pictures and a large costume collection from the 18th to 20th centuries. A wheelchair is available for disabled visitors and there are entrance ramps and a lift.
Open all year, Mon-Sat 10-6 (summer), 10-5 (winter).
Free.
⟨ *(wheelchair available) shop* ✦

WEST YORKSHIRE

Bagshaw Museum — BATLEY

Map 07 SE22
Wilton Park (Best approached from Upper Batley Lane).
☎ (0924) 472514
The museum is housed in a 19th-century building, with displays of local history, Oriental arts, natural history, and a new gallery of Egyptology. There

is a full programme of exhibitions and events throughout the year – contact the curator for details.
Open all year, daily, telephone for opening times. (Closed Xmas).
Free.
P ⟨ *shop* ✦

Batley Art Gallery — BATLEY

Map 07 SE22
Market Place
☎ (0924) 473141
The permanent collection includes British oil paintings, watercolours, drawings and sculpture from the mid-19th century onwards. There are

also temporary loan exhibitions and special exhibitions throughout the year.
Open all year, Mon-Fri 10-6, Sat 10-4. (Closed Sun & BHs).
Free.
P ✦

Bolling Hall — BRADFORD

Map 07 SE13
Bowling Hall Rd
☎ (0274) 723057
A classic West Yorkshire manor house, complete with galleried 'housebody' (hall), Bolling Hall dates mainly from the 17th century but has medieval and 18th-century sections. It has panelled

rooms, plasterwork in original colours, heraldic glass and a rare Chippendale bed. There is also a 'ghost room'.
Open all year, Apr-Sep, Tue-Sun & BH Mon 10-6; Oct-Mar, Tue-Sun 10-5. (Closed Mon ex BH, Good Fri, 25 & 26 Dec).
P ⟨ *shop* ✦
Details not confirmed for 1992

Cartwright Hall Art Gallery — BRADFORD

Map 07 SE13
Lister Park
☎ (0274) 493313
Built in dramatic Baroque style in 1904, this art gallery has permanent collections of 19th- and 20th-century British art, contemporary prints, and older works by British and European masters, including

the 'Brown Boy' by Reynolds. There is an imaginative exhibition programme.
Open all year Apr-Sep, Tue-Sun & BH Mon 10-6; Oct-Mar, Tue-Sun 10-5 (Closed Mon ex BH, Good Fri, 25 & 26 Dec).
⟨ *toilets for disabled shop* ✦
Details not confirmed for 1992

Colour Museum — BRADFORD

Map 07 SE13
82 Grattan Rd
☎ (0274) 390955
A unique museum, run by the society of Dyers and Colourists, comprising two galleries packed with visitor-operated exhibits demonstrating the effects of light and colour, including optical

illusions, and the story of dyeing and textile printing. It even offers the chance to take charge of a modern dye-making factory. Declared Best Industrial Museum in 1988 by National Heritage. January 1992 will see the introduction of new interactive displays, and two
continued . . .

special exhibitions are planned for the year: Pigments (Jan) and Leather Colouration (Jul Aug).
Open all year, Tue-Fri 2-5, Sat 10-4.

Booked parties Tue & Fri mornings. (Closed Sun, Mon & BH's).
✳ *Admission fee payable.*
⟨ *(lift from street level) shop* ✦

Industrial Museum — BRADFORD

Map 07 SE13
Moorside Rd, Eccleshill
☎ (0274) 631756
The museum illustrates the growth of the woollen and worsted textile industry, and is housed in a former spinning mill. Motive power and transport are covered as well. The mill owner's house is also open and gives an idea of domestic life around 1900. The Victorian street is complete with a tramway and back-to-

back workers' cottages, and there are also working Victorian stables with three Shire horses. Visitors can ride on a horse-drawn tram, and there are also waggon rides. Temporary exhibitions are held monthly at weekends.
Open all year, Tue-Sun & BH Mon 10-5. (Closed Mon ex BH)
Free. Charges made for rides.
P ✿ ⟨ *(induction loop in lecture theatre) toilets for disabled shop* ✦

National Museum of Photography, Film & Television — BRADFORD

Map 07 SE13
Prince's View
☎ (0274) 727488
The National Museum of Photography, Film and Television portrays the past, present and future of the media using interactive displays and dramatic reconstructions – ride on a magic carpet, become a newsreader for the day or try your hand at vision mixing. Action Replay, the Museum's own theatre company, regularly performs highlights from the galleries. At the heart of the Museum is IMAX, UK's largest cinema

screen, which is over five storeys high. Vast brilliant images sweep you into another world, exploring the realms of space to the depths of the ocean or indeed any subject big enough to be turned into this extraordinary experience. Special event for 1992 is the opening of the new cinema development in April.
Open all year, Tue-Sun & BH's 11-6. (Closed Mon).
✳ *Museum free, IMAX Cinema £3.30 (ch 16 £1.75, concessions £2.25).*
✿ ⟨ *toilets for disabled shop* ✦

Treadwell's Art Mill — BRADFORD

Map 07 SE13
Upper Park Gate, Little Germany
☎ (0274) 306065
The largest collection of "Superhumanist" art in one building is housed in this four storey mill. Painting and sculpture by local, national and international artists is on display. Special events for 1992 include: Mar, Kevin

Harrison Exhibition; Mar, Hotchpotch – a playwriting competition with performances of winning entries; Jun, Bradford Festival.
Open all year, daily 10-6. (Closed 24-26 Dec).
✳ *£2.20 (ch 5-16, pen, students & UB40's £1.60). Party 12 +*
✿ ⟨ *toilets for disabled shop* ✦

Bramham Park — BRAMHAM

Map 08 SE44
(on A1 4m S of Wetherby)
☎ Boston Spa (0937) 844265
This fine Queen Anne house was built by Robert Benson and is the home of his descendants. The garden has ornamental ponds, cascades, temples and avenues. International horse trials are held here June 4-7.
Gardens open Etr, May Day & Spring BH wknds 1.15-5.30: House & gardens 14 Jun-Aug Sun, Tue, Wed & Thu including Aug BH Mon-1 Sep 1.15-5.30. (Last admission 5pm).
* *£3 (ch 5 £1, pen £1.50). Grounds only £2 (ch 5 50p, pen £1). Party 20+.*
P ♿ *toilets for disabled* 🚫 *(ex in grounds)*

Smith Art Gallery — BRIGHOUSE

Map 07 SE12
Halifax Rd
☎ (0484) 719222
The gallery shows temporary exhibitions of local artists' work and modern works throughout the year; in 1992, these will include Landscapes (Jan 25-Feb 23), Self Image (Jun 28-Aug 9), and Representative to Abstract (Nov 7-Dec 6).
Open all year, Mon-Sat (ex Wed) 10-5; also Apr-Sep, Sun 2-5. (Closed Xmas & 1 Jan).
Free.
P ♿ *toilets for disabled* 🚫

* An asterisk indicates that up-to-date information was not available at the time of our research – 1991 information has been published as an indication of what you may expect.

Bankfield Museum — HALIFAX

Map 07 SE02
Boothtown Rd, Akroyd Park
☎ (0422) 354823
Built by Edward Akroyd in the 1860s, this Renaissance-style building is set in parkland on a hill overlooking the town. It has an outstanding collection of costumes and textiles from many periods and parts of the world. There is also a section on toys, and the museum of the Duke of Wellington's Regiment is housed here. Temporary exhibitions are held, including 28 Mar-26 Apr, 'Hats Off'; 15 Aug-13 Sep, Halifax Art Society; 18 Sep-14 Nov, 'The People's Art', and textile workshops.
Open all year, Tue-Sat 10-5, Sun 2-5. (Closed Xmas & 1 Jan).
Free.
P ♿ *shop* 🚫

Calderdale Industrial Museum — HALIFAX

Map 07 SE02
Square Rd
☎ (0422) 358087
Over 100 machines represent local industries, from textiles to wrapping toffees. Other attractions include 1850s street scenes, and reconstructions of shops, a pub and a basement dwelling – all with authentic smells and sounds.
Open all year, Tue-Sat 10-5, Sun 2-5 (Closed Mon ex BH's, 25-26 Dec & 1 Jan).
£1 (ch, pen & UB40 50p).
♿ *(lift) toilets for disabled shop* 🚫

Piece Hall — HALIFAX

Map 07 SE02
☎ (0422) 358087
The merchants of Halifax built the elegant and unique hall in 1775, as a trading place for pieces of cloth. It has over 300 merchant's rooms around a courtyard, and now houses an industrial museum, art galleries and shops selling antiques, books and other specialities. There is an open market on Friday and Saturday, and a flea market on Thursday. Free entertainment most weekends. A tourist information point, art gallery and award winning Industrial museum are also available. Special events and exhibitions are planned throughout the year.
Open all year daily 10-5 (Closed 25-26 Dec). Industrial Museum Tue-Sat 10-5, Sun 2-5. Art Gallery Tue-Sun 10-5.
Free (ex small admission charge for the Industrial Museum & when special events are held).
☕ ✕ *licensed* ♿ *(lift to all floors) shop*

Shibden Hall & Folk Museum — HALIFAX

Map 07 SE02
Godley Ln
☎ (0422) 352246
The house dates back to the early 15th century, and its rooms have been laid out to illustrate life in different periods of its history. The vast 17th-century barn has a fine collection of horse-drawn vehicles. A special event will be 'Shibden by Candlelight' on 13 March, 7pm-9pm.
Open Mar-Nov, Mon-Sat 10-5, Sun 12-5; Feb, Sun 2-5. (Closed Dec-Jan).
£1.50 (concessions 75p).
P ☕ ♿ *shop* 🚫

Harewood House & Bird Garden — HAREWOOD

Map 07 SE34
(junc A61/A659 Leeds/Harrogate Rd)
☎ (0532) 886225

The 18th-century home of the Earl and Countess of Harewood contains fine furniture, porcelain and paintings, and its Capability Brown grounds offer lakeside and woodland walks. The Bird Garden has aviaries for over 150 species, and a tropical house. Adventure playground. Special events take place throughout the year.
Open Etr-Oct, daily Bird Garden from 10am, House from 11am.
P ☕ ✕ *licensed* ♿ *toilets for disabled shop garden centre* 🚫 *(in House or bird garden)*
Details not confirmed for 1992

Keighley & Worth Valley Railway & Museum — HAWORTH

Map 07 SE03
Keighley, Haworth, Oxenhope & Ingrow West
☎ Keighley (0535) 645214
The line was built mainly to serve the valley's mills, and goes through the heart of Brontë country. It begins at Keighley (also a BR station), and then climbs up to Haworth, the railway headquarters. The terminus is at Oxenhope, which has a museum and restoration building. There are 36 steam engines and eight diesels. Special events are planned throughout 1992, the 125th anniversary of the branch, including an enthusiasts weekend, two weeks before Easter.
All year wknd service, but daily all BH wks & Jul-1st wk Sep.
* *Full line ticket £3.50 reduced fares for ch & pen. Family ticket £9. Other fares on request.*
P *(charged)* ☕ ♿ *(wheelchairs can be accommodated in brake car). toilets for disabled shop*

Automobilia Transport Museum — HEBDEN BRIDGE

Map 07 SD92
Billy Ln, Old Town, Wadsworth
(Take A6033)
☎ (0422) 844775
The restored three-storey textile warehouse contains a collection of Austin and Morris cars, motorcycles and bicycles, together with other items of motoring nostalgia. There will be a Vintage weekend 1-2 August.
Open all year, Apr-Sep, Tue-Fri 10-5, wknds 12-5; Oct-Mar wkdays by prior arrangement, wknds 12-5. (Sun only Dec-Feb). (Closed 25-26 Dec).
* *£2.20 (ch 5-15 & pen £1.10, students & UB40's £1.65).*
P ♿ *shop* 🚫

Holmfirth Postcard Museum — HOLMFIRTH

Map 08 SE10
47 Huddersfield Rd
☎ (0484) 682231
Britain's first postcard museum, exhibiting a selection of Bamforth & Co sentimental and comic postcards and lantern slides. There are also video presentations of Bamforth's pioneering silent films and the dramatic story of the Holmfirth flood of 1852.
Open all year, Mon-Sat 10-5, Sun 1-5 (Closed 25-26 Dec & 1 Jan).
♿ *toilets for disabled shop* 🚫
Details not confirmed for 1992

Art Gallery — HUDDERSFIELD

Map 07 SE11
Princess Alexandra Walk
☎ (0484) 513808 ext 216
The permanent collections include British oil paintings, watercolours, drawings and sculpture from the mid-19th century onwards. Temporary loan exhibitions are also held throughout the year.
Open all year, Mon-Fri 10-6, Sat 10-4. (Closed Sun & BH).
Free.
♿ *toilets for disabled shop* 🚫

Tolson Memorial Museum | HUDDERSFIELD

Map 07 SE11
Ravensknowle Park (on A629)
☎ (0484) 530591
Displays on the development of the cloth industry and a collection of horse-drawn vehicles are shown, together with natural history, archaeology, toys and folk exhibits. There will be new galleries in 1992 and there is a full programme of temporary exhibitions and events planned..
Open all year, daily, telephone for further details.
Free.
🅿 ♿ *toilets for disabled shop* ✸

Manor House Gallery & Museum | ILKLEY

Map 07 SE14
Castle Yard, Church St
☎ (0943) 600066
The Elizabethan manor house is one of Ilkley's few buildings to pre-date the 19th century. The house was built on the site of a Roman fort and part of the Roman wall can be seen, together with Roman relics and displays on archaeology. Inside there is also a collection of 17th- and 18th-century farmhouse parlour and kitchen furniture, while the art gallery exhibits works by contemporary artists and craftsmen.
Open all year, Apr-Sep, Tue-Sun 10-6; Oct-Mar, Tue-Sun 10-5. Also open BH Mon. (Closed Good Fri, 25 & 26 Dec).
♿ *shop* ✸
Details not confirmed for 1992

Cliffe Castle Museum & Gallery | KEIGHLEY

Map 07 SE04
Spring Gardens Ln (NW of town on A629)
☎ Bradford (0274) 758230
French furniture from the Victoria and Albert Museum is displayed, together with collections of local and natural history, ceramics, dolls, geological items and minerals. The grounds of this 19th-century mansion contain a play area and an aviary.
Open all year, Apr-Sep Tue-Sun 10-6; Oct-Mar Tue-Sun 10-5. Also open BH Mon. (Closed Good Fri, 25 & 26 Dec).
🅿 🚻 ♿ *toilets for disabled shop* ✸
Details not confirmed for 1992

East Riddlesden Hall | KEIGHLEY

Map 07 SE04
Bradford Rd (1m NE of town)
☎ (0535) 607075
This charming 17th-century Yorkshire manor house is typical of its kind, although the plasterwork and oak panelling are contemporary. A small secluded garden is found in the grounds, which also feature one of the largest medieval tithe barns in the north of England. There is a programme of special events planned for 1992, from a Mothering Sunday Special on 29 March through to a Needlecraft Weekend on 19-20 September.
Open Apr, wknds & 17-22; May-1 Nov, Sat-Wed 12-5.30. Last admission 5pm. £2.50 (ch £1.30). Party.
🅿 🚻 ♿ *shop* ✸
(NT)

✳ An asterisk indicates that up-to-date information was not available at the time of our research – 1991 information has been published as an indication of what you may expect.

Armley Mills Museum | LEEDS

Map 07 SE33
Canal Rd, Armley (2m W of city centre)
☎ (0532) 637861
Once the world's largest woollen mill, when the shuttles fly and the bobbins spin Armley Mills evokes memories of the 18th-century woollen industry showing the progress of wool from the sheep to knitted clothing. The museum also illustrates the history of cinema projection, including the first moving pictures taken in Leeds, as well as 1920s silent movies. There are demonstrations of static engines and steam locomotives, and a unique exhibition of underground haulage.
Open all year, summer – Tue-Sat 10-6, Sun 2-6; winter – Tue-Sat 10-5, Sun 2-5. Last entry 1 hr before closing. (Closed Mon, 25-26 Dec & 1 Jan)
✳ *£1 (concessions 45p)*
🅿 ♿ *toilets for disabled shop* ✸

Kirkstall Abbey & Abbey House Museum | LEEDS

Map 07 SE33
Abbey Rd, Kirkstall (off A65, W of city centre)
☎ (0532) 755821
The most complete 12th-century Cistercian Abbey in the country stands on the banks of the River Aire. The abbey is also the venue for a major folk museum with full-size Victorian shops, workshops and cottages shown in minute detail. Exhibitions are planned throughout the year.
Open all year, Apr-Sep, Mon-Sat 10-6, Sun 2-6; Oct-Mar, Mon-Sat 10-5, Sun 2-5. Abbey site open dawn-dusk.
✳ *£1 (ch under 5 free; ch 16, pen, UB40s & single-parent families 45p). Abbey free.*
🅿 ♿ *shop* ✸

Middleton Colliery Railway | LEEDS

Map 07 SE33
Moor Rd, Hunslet
☎ (0532) 710320 (ansaphone)
This was the first railway authorised by an Act of Parliament (in 1758) and the first to succeed with steam locomotives (in 1812). Steam trains run each weekend in season from Tunstall Road roundabout to Middleton Park. Facilities include a picnic area, nature trail, playgrounds and fishing. Extensive programme of special events.
Open 6 Apr-29 Sep, Sat 1.30-4.30 & Sun 1-4.30 & Wed (Aug only), 1.30-4.30. Train trips every 45 minutes Sat & Wed (diesel-hauled), 30 minutes Sun. BH wknds from 11am.
🅿 ♿ *shop*
Details not confirmed for 1992

Temple Newsam House & Park — LEEDS

Map 07 SE33
(off A63)
☎ (0532) 647321 (House) & 645535 (Park)
This Tudor and Jacobean mansion boasts extensive collections of decorative arts in their original room settings, including the incomparable Chippendale collection. An extensive programme of renovation is restoring each room to its former glory, using original wall coverings and furniture.
Set in 1,200 acres of parkland (landscaped by Capability Brown), the Rare Breed Centre in the Home Farm delights visitors. The gardens have a magnificent display of rhododendrons, whilst a riot of roses bloom amid vibrant borders in the old walled garden. Events for 1992 include a steam spectacular (23-25 May), and Threshing Day (13 Sep). A programme of chamber music is planned for the 2nd Tuesday every month from Sep to May. Telephone for details.
Open all year – House, daily 10.30-6.15 or dusk, Wed, May-Sep until 8.30. (Closed Mon ex BH Mons). Phone for details of Xmas opening. Home Farm – summer Tue-Sun 10-5, winter Tue-Sun 10-4, last entry 30 mins before closing. Estate – daily dawn-dusk.
✳ *£1 (ch if accompanied & pen 45p). Estate & Home Farm, free.*
🅿 🍴 ♿ *toilets for disabled shop* ✕

Thwaite Mills — LEEDS

Map 07 SE33
Stourton (2m S of city centre)
☎ (0532) 496453
This water-powered mill sits marooned between the River Aire which drives the wheels, and the Aire and Calder Navigation. Two great swishing wheels continually drive a mass of coggs and grinding wheels which crushed stone for putty and paint throughout the 19th century. This was the hub of a tiny island community, and the Georgian mill-owner's house has been restored, and houses displays exploring the mill's history. Special events for 1992 include: 20 Apr, Easter Monday Funday; Aug, Craft Fair; 13 Dec, Christmas Fair.
Open all year, Tue-Sun 10-5 & BH Mon. (Closed 25-26 Dec & 1 Jan)
✳ *£1 (concessions 45p)*
🅿 ♿ *toilets for disabled shop*

Lotherton Hall — LOTHERTON HALL

Map 08 SE43
(10m E of Leeds, off B1217, near Aberford).
☎ Leeds (0532) 813259
Built in Edwardian times, the former home of the Gascoigne family is now a country house museum. It contains furniture, pictures, silver and ceramics from the Gascoigne collection, and works of art on loan from Leeds galleries. Other attractions include a gallery of Oriental art, a display of British fashion, contemporary crafts and frequent special exhibitions. Outside, the Edwardian garden, bird garden and deer park are
continued . . .

delightful places in which to stroll.
Open all year, Tue-Sun 10.30-6.15 or dusk; plus Thu (May-Sep) until 8.30.

The Yorkshire Mining Museum — MIDDLESTOWN

Map 07 SE21
Caphouse Colliery, New Rd (on A642 between Wakefield & Huddersfield)
☎ Wakefield (0924) 848806
A unique opportunity to go 450ft underground down one of Britain's oldest working mine shafts, where models and machinery depict methods and conditions of mining from the early 1800s to the present day. Visitors are strongly advised to wear sensible footwear and warm clothing. Surface displays (both indoor and outdoor), pit ponies, 'paddy' train rides, steam winder, nature trail and adventure playground. Many events are planned for 1992 including a Yorkshire Day on 1 August.
Open all year, daily 10-5. (Closed 25-26 Dec & 1 Jan).
✳ *£4.45 (ch £3.65, concessions £3.80). Party.*
🅿 🍴 ♿ *(induction loop, arrange in advance for underground tour) toilets for disabled shop*

Nostell Priory — NOSTELL PRIORY

Map 08 SE41
(6m SE of Wakefield, off A638)
☎ Wakefield (0924) 863892
Built by Paine in the middle of the 18th century, the priory has an additional wing built by Adam in 1766. It contains a notable saloon and tapestry room and displays pictures and Chippendale furniture. There is a lake in the grounds.
Open Apr-Jun & Sep-Oct, Sat noon-5, Sun 11-5; Jul-Aug daily ex Fri noon-5, Sun 11-5; BH's (Mon 11-5, Tue noon-5). House & Grounds £3.30 (ch £1.70). Grounds only £2 (ch £1). Party.
🅿 🍴 ♿ *(lift) toilets for disabled shop* ✕ *(NT)*

Oakwell Hall — OAKWELL HALL

Map 07 SE22
Nutter Lane, Birstall, Batley (6m SE of Bradford)
☎ Batley (0924) 474926
A moated Elizabethan manor house, furnished as it might have looked in the 1690s. Extensive Country Park with countryside centre. There are period gardens, an equestrian arena and an adventure playground. A full events programme is planned for 1992 including historical re-enactments, a country fair, craft days and summer holiday events.
Open all year, daily, telephone for opening times. (Closed Xmas).
✳ *Admission fee payable Mar-Oct. Otherwise Free ex major event days.*
🅿 🍴 ♿ *(herb garden for the blind) toilets for disabled shop (ex in gardens)*

Also open BH Mon. (Closed Xmas).
🅿 🍴 ✕ *licensed ♿ shop* ✕ *(ex in park)*
Details not confirmed for 1992

Pontefract Museum — PONTEFRACT

Map 08 SE42
Salter Row
☎ (0977) 797289
Displays on the history of Pontefract from prehistoric times to the present day, plus a wide range of temporary exhibitions.
Open all year, Mon-Sat 10.30-5, Sun 2.30-5 & all BH during summer & spring.
Free.
& ✗

✗ The 'No Dogs' symbol does not normally apply to guide dogs – these are permitted in most establishments.

Commonwealth Institute Northern Regional Centre — SHIPLEY

Map 08 SE13
Salts Mill, Victoria Rd, Saltaire
☎ (0274) 530251
The Commonwealth Institute Northern Regional Centre is attractively situated in Salts Mill in the heart of historic Saltaire. A programme of visual arts and crafts exhibitions, educational workshops and cultural events are organised to promote the 50 countries of the Commonwealth. Special events for 1992 include: a series of programmes, including touring exhibitions, visual, verbal and performing arts, conferences and workshops explore the encounter of Columbus with the Americas and their inhabitants.
Open all year, Mon-Fri 10-5. (Closed Good Fri, May Day, 24-26 Dec & 1 Jan).
Free.
& toilets for disabled ✗

Reed Organ & Harmonium Museum — SHIPLEY

Map 08 SE13
Victoria Hall, Victoria Rd, Saltaire
☎ Bradford (0274) 585601 after 6pm
Europe's only reed organ museum contains a collection of 50 models. The smallest is no bigger than a family bible and the largest, which belonged to Dr Marmaduke P Conway when he was organist at Ely Cathedral, has three manuals and pedals. If you are a player, you may have the chance to try some of the instruments. There are also harmoniums on display, which have featured on television and radio.
Open Sun-Thu, 11-4. (Closed 2 wks Xmas).
£1 (ch 65p, pen 75p). Family £2.75. Party 10+.
✗

Sooty's World — SHIPLEY

Map 08 SE13
Windhill Manor, Leeds Rd
☎ (0274) 531122
Sooty's World is now Sooty's official home, and fans can follow his rise to super-stardom through the sets, props, scripts, photos and films which chart the puppet's 40 year history. This permanent exhibition displays the many tiny special effects which have been used in Sooty shows over the years, including a miniature saxophone which cost more than a full-size instrument. Special events for 1992: for Sooty's 40th anniversary on television in 1992, many special events will be organised. Ring Bradford (0274) 531122 for details.
Open all year, Sat & Sun 10-5, Mon-Thu 10.30-4.30, Fri (school hols) 10.30-4.30. (Closed 25-26 Dec & 1 Jan).
✱ £1.75 (ch, pen & disabled £1.25)
✉ & shop ✗

Every effort is made to provide accurate information, but details might change during the currency of this guide.

Wakefield Art Gallery — WAKEFIELD

Map 08 SE32
Wentworth Ter
☎ (0924) 375402
Wakefield was home to two of Britain's greatest modern sculptors – Barbara Hepworth and Henry Moore. The art gallery, which has an important collection of 20th-century paintings and scultures, has special rooms devoted to these two local artists. There are frequent temporary exhibitions of both modern and earlier works.
Open all year, Mon-Sat 10.30-5, Sun 2.30-5. Also BH during spring & summer.
Free.
& shop ✗

Wakefield Museum — WAKEFIELD

Map 08 SE32
Wood St
☎ (0924) 295351
In addition to the exhibits of local archaeology and the history of Wakefield from prehistoric times to the recent past, the museum has the Waterton Collection – a substantial display of uniquely preserved animals and exotic birds. There are also temporary exhibitions.
Open all year, Mon-Sat 10.30-5, Sun 2.30-5. Also BH in spring & summer.
Free.
& ✗

Yorkshire Sculpture Park — WEST BRETTON

Map 07 SE21
Bretton Hall
☎ Wakefield (0924) 830302
The beautiful parkland of Bretton Hall provides a varied setting for exhibitions, permanently sited sculptures and works on loan. It is now recognised as one of the country's major art resources, with education and community programmes, workshops and residences offering the visitor unique opportunities to learn about and enjoy sculpture.
Open all year 10-6 (summer) 10-4 (winter). (Closed 25-26 Dec & 1 Jan)
🅿 ✉ & (scooters available for disabled) toilets for disabled shop
Details not confirmed for 1992

WIGHT, ISLE OF

The Needles Old Battery — ISLE OF WIGHT ALUM BAY

Map 04 SZ38
West High Down (.75m SW)
☎ Isle of Wight (0983) 754772
This former Palmerston fort, built in 1862, has recently been restored. It sits 77m above sea level. A 60m tunnel leads to a look-out position with spectacular views of the Needles chalk stacks and lighthouse, and across the bay to Dorset. In the fort are two of the original 12-ton gun barrels: they were hauled up from the sea and now lie in the parade ground. The powder house has an exhibition of the history of the Needles headland, from the establishment of the battery to the present day.
Open 29 Mar-1 Nov, Sun-Thu, open daily from 17-30 Apr & 25 May-1 Oct 10.30-5 (last admission 4.30).
£2 (ch £1).
✉ shop
(NT)

Haseley Manor — ISLE OF WIGHT ARRETON

Map 04 SZ58
☎ Isle of Wight (0983) 865420
This is the oldest and largest manor open to the public on the island. Parts of the south wing have some of the original building, c1350, but the rest of the house is a mixture of styles including Georgian and Victorian. The manor fell into disuse and was derelict by the 1970s but has since been carefully restored and now 20 rooms can be viewed, furnished in period style. Tableaux of figures in costume appear in many of the rooms.
Outside, there is a re-constructed 18th-century farm complete with animals, and a well-stocked herb garden. There is also a children's play area with a tree house, a small lake with an island castle and a floating Noah's Ark. Visitors can also see pottery and sweet-making demonstrations.
Open daily 10-5.30 Etr-Oct; Mon-Fri 10-5.30 Nov-Etr.
✱ £3 (ch £2.50, pen £2.60). Party.
🅿 ✉ ✗ & toilets for disabled shop

Robin Hill Adventure Park — ISLE OF WIGHT ARRETON

Map 04 SZ58
Robin Hill
☎ Isle of Wight (0983) 527352 & 528029
The 88 acres of magnificent downs and woodland incorporate a fascinating range of wildlife and activities. There is an exhilarating toboggan ride, a giant hillbilly slide, a Commando assault course, a maze, a boating lake, archery, BMX bikes, in fact everything for the adventurous! A 10-acre walk-through enclosure is home to fallow deer, sheep, llamas, wallabies, peacocks, geese, and ducks; snake handling demonstrations are held in a large tropical jungle house; there's a parrot playschool, and a nature trail through woodland. Events for 1992 include various 'fun days', a steam traction rally (3 May), and a clown convention (11 Jul).
Open Mar-Oct, daily from 10am.
£3.90 (ch 4-14 & pen £2.90). Party 15+
🅿 ✉ & toilets for disabled shop

Bembridge Windmill — ISLE OF WIGHT BEMBRIDGE

Map 04 SZ68
(off B3395)
☎ Isle of Wight (0983) 873945
The only windmill on the island to survive, Bembridge mill was built about 1700 and was in use until 1913. The stone-built tower with its wooden cap and machinery have been restored since it was given to the National Trust in 1961.
Open Apr-Oct, daily (ex Sat) & Etr Sat & Jul-Aug, daily 10-5. Last admission 4.45.
£1 (ch 50p)
🅿 shop ✗
(NT)

Isle of Wight Shipwreck Centre & Maritime Museum — ISLE OF WIGHT BEMBRIDGE

Map 04 SZ68
Providence House, Sherborne St
☎ Isle of Wight (0983) 872223 & 873125
Situated at the centre of Bembridge village, this fine museum brings alive the maritime history of the Isle of Wight. There are six galleries displaying a unique collection of salvage and shipwreck items, early diving equipment, ship models, HMS Swordfish, and a model of the harbour.
Open Mar-Oct, daily 10-5. (Other times by appointment)
£1.85 (ch £1 & pen £1.40).
🅿 ✉ ✗ licensed & shop ✗

Blackgang Chine Fantasy Park — ISLE OF WIGHT BLACKGANG

Map 04 SZ47
(on A3055)
☎ Isle of Wight (0983) 730330
Opened as scenic gardens in 1843 covering some 30 acres, the park is now divided into different theme areas. Set on the steep wooded slopes of the chine are Jungleland, Smugglerland (complete with pirate ship), Nurseryland, Dinosaurland and Frontierland. There is also Fantasy Land, Water Gardens and a maze. And the park incorporates two hertage exhibitions – Timberworld and St Catherine's Quay – set in the 1890s. Winner of the Isle of Wight Best Attraction Award.
Open 6 Apr-Oct daily, 10-5, late May-late Sep, daily 10-10 (floodlit).
Combined ticket to chine, sawmill & quay, £3.99 (ch 3-13 £2.99).
🅿 (charged) ✉ ✗ licensed & toilets for disabled shop ✗

Blackgang Sawmill & St Catherines Quay
ISLE OF WIGHT
BLACKGANG

Map 04 SZ47
☎ Isle of Wight (0983) 730330
St Catherine's Quay has a maritime exhibition showing the history of local and maritime affairs, including engines in steam. It is in an attractive park that has been 'themed' into different areas, with a complete replica of a Victorian water-
powered saw mill and a display of woodland skills and traditional crafts.
Open 6 Apr-late Oct, daily 10-5; late May-Sep daily 10-9.
Combined ticket with Chine & Quay £3.99 (ch 3-13 £2.99).
🅿 *(charged)* 🍴 ⅄ *shop* ✈

Animal World of Natural History
ISLE OF WIGHT
BRADING

Map 04 SZ68
High St (on A3055)
☎ (0983) 407286
Animal World is a Natural History Museum with a difference, with a collection of animals, birds and reptiles from all over the world. The exhibits are displayed in large, colourful scenes
depicting their natural surroundings.
Open all year, May-Sep 10-10pm; Oct-Apr 10-5.
✳ *£2.05 (ch 14 £1.55, under 3 free).*
Party 20+. Combined ticket with Isle of Wight Wax Museum available £3.70 (ch £2.65).
🅿 ⅄ ✈

Isle of Wight Wax Museum
ISLE OF WIGHT
BRADING

Map 04 SZ68
High St (on A3055)
☎ Isle of Wight (0983) 407286
Full of mystery and intrigue, this world-famous wax museum is set in the Ancient Rectory Mansion, part-dating from 1066. See the Chamber of Horrors in the Castle Dungeons. The picturesque
courtyards are floodlit at night.
Open all year, May-Sep 10-10pm; Oct-Apr 10-5.
✳ *£3.30 (ch 14 £2.35, under 3 free).*
Party 20+. Combined ticket with Animal World of Natural History available £3.70 (ch £2.65).
🅿 ⅄

✳ An asterisk indicates that up-to-date information was not available at the time of our research – 1991 information has been published as an indication of what you may expect.

Lilliput Doll & Toy Museum
ISLE OF WIGHT
BRADING

Map 04 SZ68
High St
☎ Isle of Wight (0983) 407231
This private museum contains one of the finest collections of dolls (and some toys) in Britain. There are over 2,000 exhibits, ranging in age from 200 BC to
1945 with examples of almost every seriously collectable doll.
Open daily (ex 15 Jan-15 Mar), 10-5 (winter), 9.30-9.30pm (summer).
£1.25 (ch & pen 85p, ch under 5 free).
Party.
⅄ *shop*

Morton Manor
ISLE OF WIGHT
BRADING

Map 04 SZ68
(off A3055 in Brading)
☎ Isle of Wight (0983) 406168
The manor dates back to 1249, but was rebuilt in 1680 with further changes during the Georgian period. The house contains furniture of both the 18th and 19th centuries, but its main attraction lies in the beautiful gardens and the vineyard. The garden is landscaped into terraces, with ornamental ponds, a sunken garden and a traditional
Elizabethan turf maze.
In recent years vine-growing for wine has become popular on the island, and Morton Manor is one of the places to have an established vineyard and winery. A museum of winemaking relics has been set up, and has some unusual exhibits.
Open Apr-Oct, daily 10-5.30 (Closed Sat).
£2.40 (ch £1.10 & pen £1.90). Party 15+.
🅿 ✕ *licensed* ⅄ *shop garden centre*

Nunwell House & Gardens
ISLE OF WIGHT
BRADING

Map 04 SZ68
(Off Ryde-Sandown Rd, A3055)
☎ (0983) 407240
Set in beautiful gardens, Nunwell is an impressive, lived-in and much loved house where King Charles I spent his last night of freedom. It has fine furniture, interesting collections of family militaria and a Home Guard
museum. In summer, concerts are occasionally held in the music room. Phone for details.
Open, House & Gardens, 5 Jul-24 Sep, Sun-Thu 10-5. Groups welcome when house open & at other times by appointment. Closed Fri & Sat.
£2.30 (ch 16 60p, pen £1.80).
🅿 ✕ *shop* ✈

Calbourne Watermill & Rural Museum
ISLE OF WIGHT
CALBOURNE

Map 04 SZ48
(On B3401)
☎ (098378) 227
There has been a mill here since at least 1299, and the present 17th-century machinery still works when turned by
the 20ft water wheel. The millpond and stream have been converted into an attractive water garden.
Open Etr-Oct, daily 10-6.
✳ *£1.50 (ch 70p & pen £1.20).*
🅿 🍴 *shop*

Carisbrooke Castle
ISLE OF WIGHT
CARISBROOKE

Map 04 SZ48
(on B3401)
☎ (0983) 522107

A Norman castle adapted from a Saxon fort, Carisbrooke is the only medieval castle on the island. It is set on a hill 150ft high, and the 12th-century keep is built on an artificial mound of about 60ft. The keep overlooks the later Elizabethan and Jacobean additions and
the strong castle walls.
There are two medieval wells in the castle. The keep has a 160ft-deep well, reached by climbing 71 steps, and the other is housed in a 16th-century wellhouse in the courtyard. The winding gear was traditionally driven by a donkey, and a team of donkeys now gives displays of the machinery working. Charles I was a prisoner in the castle from 1647-48, and the castle was the home of the Governor of the island. His lodge is now the Isle of Wight Museum.
Open all year, Apr-Sep, daily 10-6; Oct-Mar, daily 10-4. (Closed 24-26 Dec & 1 Jan).
£3 (ch £1.50, pen, students & UB40 £2.30).
🅿 🍴 ⅄
(EH)

Cowes Maritime Museum
ISLE OF WIGHT
COWES

Map 04 SZ49
Beckford Rd
☎ (0983) 293341
The exhibition is on permanent display in the public library, and includes ship models, photographs, paintings, books and other objects showing the island's
maritime past. A summer exhibition of Isle of Wight steamboats is planned for Aug-Oct 1992.
Open all year, Mon-Wed & Fri 9.30-5.30, Sat 9.30-4.30. (Closed BH's).
Free.
⅄ ✈

Barton Manor Vineyard & Gardens
ISLE OF WIGHT
EAST COWES

Map 04 SZ49
(on A3021)
☎ Isle of Wight (0983) 292835
Situated next to Osborne House, Barton Manor is one of England's finest vineyards. It covers about 10 acres next to some fine gardens, originally laid out by Queen Victoria and Prince Albert and later extended by Edward VII.
There is a winery and also a wine bar. BTA 'Come to Britain' Trophy Award Winner 1990.
Open May-11 Oct, daily (also Etr & wknds in Apr) 10.30-5.30.
✳ *£3.50 (ch 15 1 per adult free) Prices include guide leaflet, souvenir tasting glass & two tastings.*
🅿 🍴 ⅄ *toilets for disabled shop* ✈

Old Smithy Tourist Centre
ISLE OF WIGHT
GODSHILL

Map 04 SZ58
☎ Isle of Wight (0983) 840242 & 840364
The former blacksmith's forge has a garden shaped like the island, aviaries of exotic birds, and a herb garden. There
are shops with gifts, clothes, herbs and crafts on sale.
Open Etr-Nov, daily including evenings in mid summer.
70p (ch 40p).
🅿 🍴 ⅄ *shop*

⅄ This symbol indicates that much or all of the attraction is accessible to wheelchairs. However, there may be some restrictions, so it would be wise to check in advance.

Isle of Wight Steam Railway
ISLE OF WIGHT
HAVENSTREET

Map 04 SZ58
The Railway Station
☎ Isle of Wight (0983) 882204

When the Newport to Ryde railway was closed, Haven Street Station was taken over by a private company, the Isle of Wight Steam Railway. A number of volunteers restored the station, locomotives and rolling stock, and steam trains now run the five miles from Wootton, via Haven Street to Smallbrook Junction where there is a
direct interchange with the BR Ryde-Shanklin line. Locomotives in operation include former LSWR tank engine *Calbourne*, built in 1891, and LSBCR/Freshwater, Yarmouth & Newport Railway locomotive *Freshwater*, built in 1875. The rolling stock includes 60 70-year-old LBSCR/SECR carriages, plus vintage goods wagons.
At Haven Street, the old gas works houses a display of Island railway memorabilia.
Open 26 Mar-30 Apr, Thu, Sun & BH's; also 21 & 22 Apr; May, Wed, Thu & Sun also BH Mon & Tue, 5 & 26 May; 2 Jun-16 Jul, Tue-Thu & Sun; 19 Jul-4 Sep, daily (ex Sat); 6-30 Sep, Wed, Thu & Sun; Oct, Thu & Sun.
Return Fares £4 (ch 5-15 £3). Family ticket £14. Unlimited travel on day of issue.
🅿 🍴 ⅄ *(with assistance) toilets for disabled shop*

Roman Villa
ISLE OF WIGHT
NEWPORT

Map 04 SZ48
Cypress Rd
☎ (0983) 529720
Archaeologists have uncovered this 3rd-century Roman villa where visitors can now see the well-preserved baths and re-constructed rooms in which the family once lived. The site museum houses some of the finds from the excavation. Extensive refurbishment is planned for

1992, providing new displays in reconstructed rooms, a new audio-visual presentation on Roman Wight, a renewed artefact gallery, and a Roman garden.
Open Etr-Sep, Sun-Fri 10-4.30. Other times by appointment.
✽ £1 (ch & pen 50p)
& shop ✗

Old Town Hall
ISLE OF WIGHT
NEWTOWN

Map 04 SZ49
The town hall is unusual in that it stands alone, surrounded by grass and a few houses, not in a crowded high street. Although Newtown was once the island's capital, it was badly burned in 1377 and never fully recovered. In 1699 the town hall was rebuilt and has been

further restored recently.
Open Apr-Sep, Mon, Wed & Sun 2-5 (also open Etr & Jul-Aug, Tue & Thu). Last admission 4.45.
£1 (ch 50p)
✗
(NT)

✽ An asterisk indicates that up-to-date information was not available at the time of our research – 1991 information has been published as an indication of what you may expect.

Osborne House
ISLE OF WIGHT
OSBORNE HOUSE

Map 04 SZ59
(1m SE of East Cowes)
☎ Isle of Wight (0983) 200022

Designed by Prince Albert and Thomas Cubitt and built between 1845 and 1848, Osborne was the Royal Family's private residence and Queen Victoria's favourite home. She lived at Osborne most of the time and died there in 1901. The house was designed to resemble an

Italian villa, with terraced gardens overlooking Osborne Bay. The state and private apartments, which have been largely untouched since Victoria's death, are open to the public. The private apartments upstairs are cosy and comfortable and filled with all the paraphernalia of daily life. The large grounds are filled with every kind of English tree, a miniature fort and a Swiss cottage, where the Royal children learnt cooking and gardening. A horse-drawn carriage takes visitors to the Swiss cottage gardens and museum.
Open Apr-Sep, daily 10-5 (last admission 4.30), Grounds daily 10-6; Oct, House & Grounds daily 10-5 (last admission 4).
£5 (ch £2.50, students, pen & UB40 £3.80).
🅿 ➤ & shop ✗
(EH)

Tropical Bird Park
ISLE OF WIGHT
ST LAWRENCE

Map 04 SZ57
Old Park
☎ Isle of Wight (0983) 852583 & 853752
A bird park situated in the heart of the almost sub-tropical undercliff, in the grounds of Old Park. Enclosed by high stone walls are over 400 birds such as toucans, macaws and cockatoos. Woodland Trail is the home of eagles,

storks, vultures and owls. On an ornamental lake are spoonbills, flamingoes and ducks. An extra attraction is a showroom where Isle of Wight glass is blown and displayed.
Open Etr-Oct, 10-5; Oct-Etr, 10-4. (Closed 25 Dec).
✽ £2.20 (ch 7-15 £1.50, pen £1.75).
🅿 (charged) ➤ & shop ✗

Museum of Isle of Wight Geology
ISLE OF WIGHT
SANDOWN

Map 04 SZ58
Sandown Library, High St
☎ Isle of Wight (0983) 404344
The museum houses extensive collections of fossils and rocks. A special feature has been made of recently excavated dinosaur fossils. Modern

displays interpret millions of years of pre-history on the Isle of Wight.
Open all year, Mon-Fri 9.30-5.30, Sat 9.30-4.30. (Closed Sun).
Free.
shop ✗

Shanklin Chine
ISLE OF WIGHT
SHANKLIN

Map 04 SZ58
☎ Isle of Wight (0983) 866432
Shanklin Chine is a natural gorge of great scenic beauty and with a spectacular 45ft waterfall. A path winds down through the boulders, overhanging trees, ferns and other flora that cover its steep sides. The Heritage Centre features

details of nature trails, rare flora and life in Victorian Shanklin.
Open 16 Apr-23 May 10-5; 24 May-27 Sep 10am-10pm (illuminated at night); 28 Sep-18 Oct 10-4.
£1 (ch 40p, pen & students 75p)
➤ shop

Yafford Water Mill Farm Park
ISLE OF WIGHT
SHORWELL

Map 04 SZ48
☎ Isle of Wight (0983) 62117
The mill is situated in attractive surroundings with a large mill pond. The great overshot wheel still turns and all the milling machinery is in working order. An unusual attraction is the millpond, which is home to a pair of seals and their pup. The millstream has pools and falls with flowers and trees along its banks. There is a nature trail

along the stream and among the pools – home to ducks, coots and moorhen. Old farm wagons and machinery are displayed and there are some rare breeds of sheep and cattle and a trout farm. Across the lane there is a picnic area and an adventure playground.
Open Etr-Oct, daily 10-6. (Last admission 5pm).
£1.85 (ch & pen £1.25). Party 12+.
🅿 ➤ & shop ✗

Museum of the History of Smuggling
ISLE OF WIGHT
VENTNOR

Map 04 SZ57
Botanic Gardens
☎ Isle of Wight (0983) 853677
Situated underground in extensive vaults, this unusual museum shows methods of smuggling used over a 700-year period right up to the present day. Each year there is an 'Isle of Wight

Smuggling Pageant' in the middle of June. An adventure playground is near the entrance by the Botanic Gardens.
Open Etr-Sep, daily 10-5.30.
✽ £1.40 (ch & pen 70p). Parties by arrangement.
🅿 (charged) ✗ licensed shop

Appuldurcombe House
ISLE OF WIGHT
WROXALL

Map 04 SZ57
☎ Isle of Wight (0983) 852484
The manor house at Wroxall began as a priory in 1100. It later came into the hands of the Worsley family, who pulled down the original building and built Appuldurcombe in the Palladian style. Appuldurcombe has been a ruin since World War II, but the grounds,

landscaped by 'Capability' Brown, are still beautiful.
Open all year, Apr-Sep, daily 10-6; Oct-Mar, Tue-Sun 10-4. (Closed 24-26 Dec & 1 Jan).
£1.10 (ch 55p, pen, students & UB40 85p).
🅿 & ✗
(EH)

Fort Victoria Country Park
ISLE OF WIGHT
YARMOUTH

Map 04 SZ38
Sconce Point (1m W, off A3054)
☎ Isle of Wight (0983) 760860
Based around the remains of a fort built in 1852-3 to protect the western approach to Portsmouth, the wide grassy areas, coastal slopes, beach and sea wall have been made into a country park. Affording superb views of the Solent,

there are picnic and barbeque facilities, also guided walks, exhibitions and a Marine Aquarium.
Open park daily. Aquarium open end Mar-Nov 10-6.
✽ Park free. Aquarium £1.10 (ch 60p, pen 60p). Museum 80p (ch 40p, pen 50p).
🅿 ➤ & toilets for disabled shop

Yarmouth Castle
ISLE OF WIGHT
YARMOUTH

Map 04 SZ38
Quay St
☎ (0983) 760678
Now tucked away among newer buildings, this rather homely castle is in excellent repair. Visitors can see the Master Gunner's parlour and kitchen, plus an unusually small great hall. Built during the reign of Henry VIII as a

coastal defence, the open gun platform provides an excellent view of the harbour.
Open Apr-Sep, daily 10-6.
£1.50 (ch 75p, students, pen & UB40 £1.10).
& ✗
(EH)

WILTSHIRE

Avebury Manor
AVEBURY

Map 03 SU06
☎ (06723) 388
Avebury Manor has a monastic origin, and has been much altered since then. The present buildings date from the early 16th century, with notable Queen Anne alterations and Edwardian renovation. The flower gardens contain medieval walls, and there are examples

of topiary.
Open Garden – Apr-1 Nov, Tue-Wed & Fri-Sun 11-5.30 (last admission 5pm). House – due to restoration work, telephone for opening details.
House & garden £3 (ch £2.30); garden only £2 (ch £1.30).
✗
(NT)

Avebury Museum
AVEBURY

Map 03 SU06
(Alexander Keiller Museum)
☎ (06723) 250
This is one of the most important prehistoric sites in Europe, and was built before Stonehenge. In the midst of it is the pretty village of Avebury, which is surrounded by circles of massive sarsen stones and an impressive circular

embankment and ditch. An avenue of great stones leads to the site, which must have been a place of great religious significance. The small museum has recently been refurbished and contains many new exhibits. It is named after Alexander Keiller, the first archaeologist to analyse the site in a modern way. It
continued ...

shows finds from Avebury and from Windmill Hill, a Neolithic causewayed enclosure about 1.5 miles away, which is also part of the National Trust property. Educational facilities are provided.
Open all year, Apr-Sep, daily 10-6; Oct-

Mar, daily 10-4. (Closed 24-26 Dec & 1 Jan).
£1.20 (ch 60p, students, pen & UB40 90p).
🅿 ♿ ✠
(EH & NT)

Great Barn Museum of Wiltshire Life   AVEBURY

Map 03 SU06
☎ (06723) 555
Close to the prehistoric stones, the museum is housed in a fine 17th-century thatched barn with a splendid roof structure. There are displays on cheesemaking, thatching, saddlery, sheep and shepherds, and the work of blacksmiths, wheelwrights and other rural craftsmen. Regular craft sessions take place on Sundays between April

and September, and there is a rare breeds weekend on the early May Bank Holiday, followed by a craft fair at the end of the month. The Wiltshire Country Food Fair takes place on August Bank Holiday.
Open all year, mid Mar-Oct, daily 10-6. Nov-mid Mar, Sat 11-5, Sun 11-5.
95p (ch & pen 50p). Family ticket £2.30.
✗ *licensed* ♿ *shop*

Bedwyn Stone Museum   BEDWYN, GREAT

Map 04 SU26
☎ Marlborough (0672) 870043
This small but special open air museum explains the ancient secrets of the stonemason, showing how carvings have a language of their own. A fine sequence

of carvings can be seen in the nearby church.
Open all year.
Free.
♿ *toilets for disabled*

Crofton Beam Engines   BEDWYN, GREAT

Map 04 SU26
(6m SE of Marlborough, signposted from A338)
☎ Devizes (0380) 721279
The oldest working steam engine in the world, the Boulton and Watt 1812, is to be found in this rural spot. Its companion is a Harvey's of Hayle of 1845. Both are coal-fired, and pump water into the Kennet and Avon Canal with a lift of 40ft. During steam weekends telephone Marlborough

(0672) 870300 for information. The surroundings are pleasant, and walks can be taken on the canal towpath nearby. Trips can also be taken on the boat *Jubilee:* telephone 081-290 0031 to book places.
Open 17-20 Apr; 23-25 May; 25-28 Jun; 29-31 Aug; 25-27 Sep; 24-25 Oct.
✱ £2.50 (ch £1, pen £1.50). Family ticket £5.
🅿 ♨ ♿ *shop* ✠ *(ex in grounds)*

✱ **An asterisk indicates that up-to-date information was not available at the time of our research – 1991 information has been published as an indication of what you may expect.**

The Crocker Collection   BRADFORD-ON-AVON

Map 03 ST86
The Tithe Barn, Pound Ln
☎ Bradford on Avon (02216) 4783
This collection of farm machinery is housed in a medieval tithe barn. The oldest exhibit is a breast plough dating from around 1700, and there are larger

items such as carts and wagons. The reconstructed scenes of past days include a farm worker's kitchen and a dairy.
Open Apr-Oct, daily 10-6.
🅿 ♿ *shop*
Details not confirmed for 1992

Great Chalfield Manor   BRADFORD-ON-AVON

Map 03 ST86
(3m SW of Melksham)
Built during the Wars of the Roses, the manor is a beautiful, mellow, moated house which still has its great hall. It was restored in the 1920s. There is a small 13th-century church next to the house.

Open Apr-29 Oct, Tue-Thu. Tours starting at 12.15, 2.15, 3, 3.45, 4.30. (Closed on PH).
🅿 ✠
(NT)
Details not confirmed for 1992

Tithe Barn   BRADFORD-ON-AVON

Map 03 ST86
Over 160ft long by 30ft wide, the barn stands on Barton Farm, which belonged to Shaftesbury Abbey. It was probably used to store general farm produce as well as tithes of hay and corn. The roof is of stone slates, supported outside by

buttresses and inside by an impressive network of great beams and rafters.
Open any reasonable time.
Free.
♿
(EH)

Woodland Heritage Museum & Woodland Park   BROKERSWOOD

Map 03 ST85
☎ Westbury (0373) 822238 & 823880
Woodland Heritage Museum and Woodland Park nature walks lead through 80 acres of woodlands, with a lake and wildfowl. Facilities include a woodland visitor centre (covering wildlife and forestry), a children's adventure playground and guided walks and the Smokey Oak railway, over a

third of a mile long. (Special catering facilities for parties of 10 or more.) Barbeque sites and fishing permits available.
Open all year; Park open daily 10-sunset. Museum open Mon-Fri 9-4; Sat 2-6, Sun 10-6 (summer); Sun 2-4.30 (winter).
£2 (unaccompanied ch £1.25, accompanied ch free, pen £1.75).
🅿 ♨ ♿ *shop*

Bowood House & Gardens   CALNE

Map 03 ST96
(off A4 in Derry Hill village)
☎ (0249) 812102

Originally built in 1624, the house was unfinished when it was bought by the first Earl of Shelburne in 1754. He employed celebrated architects, notably Robert Adam, to complete the work, and what the visitor sees now is a handsome Georgian house. Adam's library is particularly admired, and also in the house is the laboratory where Dr Joseph Priestley discovered oxygen in

1774. There are fine paintings, sculpture, costume and other displays. The chief glory of Bowood, however, is its 2,000-acre expanse. 100 acres of which are pleasure gardens. They were laid out by Capability Brown in the 1760s and are carpeted with daffodils, narcissi and bluebells in spring. The centrepiece is a lake, while terraces, roses, clipped yews and sculpture are a perfect complement to the house. There is also a hermit's cave, a temple and cascade; and for children there is a huge adventure playground.
Open Apr-Nov, daily 11-6, including BH. Rhododendron Gardens (separate entrance off A342) open 6 weeks during May & Jun 11-6.
✱ *House & Grounds £4 (ch £1.90 pen £3.30). Party.*
🅿 ♨ ✗ *licensed* ♿ *(parking by arrangement) toilets for disabled shop garden centre* ✠

Places to visit in this guide are pinpointed on the atlas at the back of the book.

Sheldon Manor   CHIPPENHAM

Map 03 ST97
☎ (0249) 653120
The Plantagenet manor house has a 13th-century porch and a 15th-century chapel. There are beautiful informal terraced gardens, with a water garden, ancient yews and a connoisseur collection of old-fashioned roses.

Open 19 & 20 Apr, then every Sun, Thu & BH until 4 Oct, 12.30-6. House opens 2pm.
✱ *House & gardens £3 (pen £2.75). Garden only £1.75 (pen £1.50).*
🅿 ♨ ✗ *licensed* ♿ *(wheelchair available) shop*

Corsham Court   CORSHAM

Map 03 ST86
(4m W of Chippenham off the A4)
☎ (0249) 712214
The Elizabethan manor was built in 1582, and then bought by the Methuen family in the 18th century to house their collections of paintings and statues. Capability Brown made additions to the house and laid out the park, and later John Nash made further changes. There is furniture by Chippendale, Adam, Cobb and Johnson inside, as well as the Methuen collection of Old Master

paintings. The garden has flowering shrubs, herbaceous borders, a Georgian bath house, peacocks and a 15th-century gazebo.
Open Jan-Nov; Tue-Thu, Sat & Sun 2-4.30. (6pm Good Fri-Sep & also open Fri & bank hols) other times by appointment. Last admission half hour before closure.
£3 (ch £1.50). Gardens only £1.50 (ch £1). Party 20+
🅿 ♿ *shop* ✠

Devizes Museum   DEVIZES

Map 03 SU06
41 Long St
☎ (0380) 727369
Wiltshire archaeology, geology and history are explored in the museum, which also has a gallery on recent history and a new Bronze Age gallery

and art gallery with a John Piper window.
Open all year, Mon-Sat 10-5. (Closed PH's).
♿ *shop* ✠
Details not confirmed for 1992

The Courts   HOLT

Map 03 ST86
(3m N of Trowbridge, on B3107)
☎ Trowbridge (0225) 782340
Weavers came to The Courts to have their disputes settled until the end of the 18th century. The house is not open, but it makes an attractive backdrop to

the gardens – a network of stone paths, yew hedges, pools and borders with a strange, almost magical atmosphere.
Open Apr-1 Nov, daily (ex Sat) 2-5.
£2 (ch £1)
♿ ✠
(NT)

Lackham Gardens, Museum and Woodland   LACOCK

Map 03 ST96
(3m S of Chippenham, on A350)
☎ Chippenham (0249) 443111
Various visitor attractions are situated within the 210-hectare estate of the Lackam College of Agriculture. Thatched and refurbished farm buildings accommodate the farm museum and the grounds feature a walled garden, glasshouses, rhododendron glades, riverside and woodland walks, a children's adventure playground and two hectares of grassland devoted to rare breeds. There is a major collection of historical roses in the Italian Garden.

Also grown in this garden was the largest citron (large lemon) which earned a place in the Guinness Book of Records. The gardens are open in aid of the National Gardens Scheme on 3 May, 12 July and 4 October and on 17 May there is an open day with displays, tractor rides and more.
Open 21 Mar-1 Nov, 11-5 (last admission 4pm).
£3 (ch £1, concessions £2). Family ticket £8.
🅿 ♨ ✗ ♿ *(wheelchair available) toilets for disabled shop garden centre* ✠

Lacock Abbey — LACOCK

Map 03 ST96
(3m S of Chippenham, E of A350)
☎ (024973) 227
Lacock Abbey is not only historic and beautiful, it was also the venue for a series of innovative photographic experiments by William Henry Fox Talbot, which led to the world's first photographic negative being made here in 1835. The abbey, set in a carefully preserved village of 14th- to 18th-century houses, was founded by Ela, Countess of Salisbury in the 13th century. At the Dissolution it was sold to William Sherrington, who destroyed the church and turned the nuns' quarters into a grand home. The cloisters from the original convent remain and other ancient features include an octagonal Tudor tower and half-timbered gables in the courtyard. In 1754 Sanderson Miller was commissioned to design a new entrance hall; this stands today as a superb example of the Gothic Revival style. A museum devoted to Fox Talbot (one of Sherrington's descendants) is housed in an old barn.
Open Apr-1 Nov; House Wed-Mon 1-5.30; grounds & cloisters daily 12-5.30. Last admission 5pm. (Closed Good Fri). £3.80 (ch £1.90). Grounds & cloisters £1.60. Parties. No pushchairs in Abbey.
🅿 ♿ *(taped guides) toilets for disabled shop* 🚫
(NT)

Longleat House — LONGLEAT HOUSE

Map 03 ST84
(Entrance on Warminster-Frome Rd A362).
☎ Warminster (0985) 844551

The present Marquess of Bath was the first peer to open his house to the public on a regular basis, a trend which many would follow. The Longleat estate has now grown to offer the visitor a safari park (home to hundreds of wild animals, including Britain's only white tiger); an exciting Adventure Castle; a maze; pleasure boat; narrow-gauge railway and a multitude of exhibitions and other attractions. The centrepiece of all this tourist activity is the majestic Elizabethan house, built by Sir John Thynne in 1580 and decorated in the Italian Renaissance style in the late-19th century. It contains a mixture of furnishings and artefacts reflecting the tastes and interests of the Thynne family through the centuries, and the fully restored Victorian kitchens offer an interesting glimpse of life 'below stairs'. The magnificent grounds, laid out by Capability Brown, offer many lovely walks. Heaven's Gate is particularly spectacular when the rhododendrons are flowering. Rallies and other special events are planned throughout 1992 include the Radio Society of Great Britain Amateur Radio Rally on 28 June.
Open all year. House daily Etr-Oct 10-6, Nov-Etr 10-4. Safari park, mid Mar- end Oct 10-6, last car admitted 5.30 or sunset if earlier. All other attractions Etr-Oct 11-6 (some close or accept last visitor at 5.30). House: £3.50 (ch £1.50, pen £3). Safari Park: £5 (ch £3.50, pen £4). Discount tickets for all attractions: £10 (ch & pen £8). All attractions can be paid for separately.
🅿 ☕ ✕ *licensed* ♿ *toilets for disabled shop*

Ludgershall Castle — LUDGERSHALL

Map 04 SU25
(7m NW of Andover on A342)
Although a ruin since the 16th century, this was once a royal castle and hunting palace. The visitor can see large earthworks of the Norman motte-and-bailey castle and the flint walling of the later hunting palace. The medieval cross stands in the main street of the village.
Open all reasonable times.
🅿 ♿
(EH)

Lydiard House & Park — LYDIARD PARK

Map 03 SU18
Lydiard Tregoze
☎ Swindon (0793) 770401
Set in beautiful country park land, this fine Georgian house belonged to the St John family for 500 years up until 1943 when the house and parkland were purchased by the Swindon Corporation. Since then the sadly delapidated house has been gradually restored and refurbished with period furniture (in many cases original to the house) and a large St John family portrait collection (also original to the house). Exceptional plasterwork, early wallpaper and rare painted glass windows can also be seen. Adjacent, the church of St Marys has many fine and unusual memorials to the St John family. The Park, now operating as a Country Park, offers a variety of pleasant woodland walks, spacious lawns, lakes and children's adventure playground.
Open all year, Mon-Sat 10-1 & 2-5.30, Sun 2-5.30. (Closed Good Fri & Xmas). Winter closing 4pm. Free.
🅿 ☕ ♿ *shop* 🚫

For an explanation of the symbols and abbreviations, see page 2.

Heale Gardens & Plant Centre — MIDDLE WOODFORD

Map 03 SU13
(4m from Salisbury, between A360 & A345)
☎ (072273) 504
Heale House and its eight acres of beautiful garden, lie beside the River Avon at Middle Woodford. Much of the house is unchanged since King Charles II sheltered here after the Battle of Worcester in 1651. The garden provides a wonderfully varied collection of plants, shrubs, and musk and other roses, growing in the formal setting of clipped hedges and mellow stonework, which are at their best in June and July. Particularly lovely in spring and autumn is the water garden, planted with magnificent magnolia and acers, surrounding the authentic Japenese Tea House and Nikko Bridge which makes an exciting focus in this part of the garden.
Open all year, daily 10-5. £2 (ch under 14 accompanied, free). Party 20+.
🅿 ♿ *shop garden centre*

Mompesson House — SALISBURY

Map 03 SU12
Cathedral Close
☎ (0722) 335659
With its high wrought-iron railings and perfect proportions this Queen Anne house makes an impressive addition to the elegant Cathedral Close in Salisbury. Inside there are no disappointments: the stucco ceilings, carved oak staircase and period furniture are more than matched by the important collection of 18th-century glasses, china and some outstanding paintings.
Open Apr-1 Nov, daily (ex Thu & Fri) noon-5.30. Last admission 5pm. £2.60 (ch £1.30). Party.
☕ ♿ 🚫
(NT)

Museum of the Duke of Edinburgh's Royal Regiment — SALISBURY

Map 03 SU12
The Wardrobe, 58 The Close
☎ (0722) 414536
Yet another interesting and historic building in Cathedral Close displays the mementoes, relics, uniforms and weapons of this proud regiment.
Open May-Oct, daily; Apr & Nov, Sun-Fri 10-4.30; Feb & Mar, Mon-Fri 10-4.30. Dec & Jan closed. £1.50 (ch 50p, students & pen £1).
🅿 ♿ *shop* 🚫

Old Sarum — SALISBURY

Map 03 SU12
(2m N on A345)
☎ (0722) 335398
The story of Old Sarum began in pre-history: it was once the location for an Iron Age camp. What the visitor sees today, however, are the remains of a thriving community that grew up around a Norman cathedral and castle. When a new cathedral was built in nearby New Sarum, or Salisbury, the community was gradually abandoned, although until the Reform Bill of 1832 ten voters remained to return two members to parliament; at one time Pitt the Elder represented Old Sarum.
Open all year, Apr-Sep, daily 10-6; Oct-Mar, Tue-Sun 10-4. (Closed 24-26 Dec & 1 Jan). £1.20 (ch 60p, students, pen & UB40 90p).
🅿 *(charged)* ♿
(EH)

Salisbury & South Wiltshire Museum — SALISBURY

Map 03 SU12
The King's House, 65 The Close
☎ (0722) 332151
One of the most outstanding of the many beautiful buildings in Cathedral Close also houses the local museum. Covering an area that is so steeped in history – Stonehenge is not far away – there are many fascinating displays. Galleries include Stonehenge, Early Man, History of Salisbury, the Pitt-Rivers collection, ceramics and pictures and the Wedgwood room, and there is a reconstruction of a pre-NHS surgery. A costume, lace and embroidery gallery has recently been added to the museum.
Open all year Mon-Sat 10-5; also Suns Jul & Aug and Salisbury Festival, 2-5. (Closed Xmas). £2.25 (ch 50p, pen, students & UB40s £1.50). Party. Tickets give unlimited visits throughout year.
☕ ♿ *(parking by prior arrangement) toilets for disabled shop* 🚫

Stonehenge — STONEHENGE

Map 03 SU14
(off A344)
☎ (0980) 623108

Stonehenge is one of the most famous prehistoric monuments in Europe and has been the source of endless speculation by archaeologists and others. The henge was started about 5,000 years ago, but was redesigned several times during the following 1,500 years. The earliest parts are an encircling ditch and bank which were made about 2,800BC. About 700 years later, huge Blue Stones, 80 in all and each weighing 2 tons, were brought from south-west Wales. However, before the work on these was finished, enormous sarsen stones weighing over 50 tons each were dragged from the Marlborough Downs and the whole thing was reorganised into the design we see today. This is made up of an outer ring with mortis-and-tenon-fitted lintels and an inner horseshoe of five pairs of uprights with lintels. Later on, the Blue Stones were re-erected. The axis of the horseshoe points towards the midsummer sunrise. The whole area was obviously a centre of great ceremonial activity and there are a number of monuments, massive earthworks, and over 300 burial mounds within a relatively small area. Little is known about the Bronze Age society that organised such a vast undertaking, but there was no connection with the Druids.
Open all year, Apr-Sep, daily 10-6; Oct-Mar, daily 10-4. (Closed 24-26 Dec & 1 Jan). £2.50 (ch £1.30, students, pen & UB40 £1.90).
🅿 ☕ ♿ *shop* 🚫
(EH)

Stourhead House & Garden — STOURHEAD

Map 03 ST73
(Off B3092)
☎ Bourton (Dorset) (0747) 840348

The Palladian house was built in 1720 by Henry Hoare, a banker. It is not particularly outstanding, although it does contain some fine furniture. However, what makes Stourhead especially memorable are the superb gardens laid out by Henry Hoare II in 1741. He returned from his Grand Tour inspired by the gardens and landscapes he had seen in Italy, and was determined to create something similar in England. The result is one of the finest 18th-century landscape gardens in Europe. He built a

continued . . .

grotto and a temple to Flora around two springs and then dammed the River Stour to create a large triangular lake. He also erected a Pantheon in 1754 and over the next few years built other temples. Much of the comprehensive tree-planting was done by his grandson who, in 1791, began a planting programme around the lake. There are many varieties of oak, elm, willow and exotic trees, and the rhododendrons, which, with the azaleas, make spring so spectacular at Stourhead. These were first planted in 1791. Conifers were introduced in the 19th century, with further planting in the early 20th. The

Stourhead Fête Champêtre in the gardens will be held on the evenings of 22-25 July.
Open – House Apr-1 Nov, Sat-Wed 12-5.30 or dusk if earlier. Last admission 5pm. Garden daily all year 8-7 or dusk if earlier (ex 22-25 Jul when garden closes at 5pm).
House £4 (ch £2). Garden £3.60 (ch £1.80), Nov-Feb £2.60 (ch 1.30). Paries 15 + (ex Nov-Feb). No pushchairs or bulky bags in house.
P ✉ ✗ *licensed* ᵴ *toilets for disabled shop* ✗ *(ex in gardens Nov-Feb only)*
(NT)

Stourton House Garden — STOURTON

Map 03 ST73
(3m NW of Mere, on A303)
☎ Bourton (Dorset) (0747) 840417
Set in the attractive village of Stourton, the house has more than four acres of beautifully maintained gardens. Many grass paths lead through varied and colourful shrubs, trees and plants; and

Stourton House also specialises in unusual plants, many of which are for sale.
Open Apr-28 Nov, Wed, Thu, Sun & BH Mon 11-6 (or dusk if earlier). ✗
P ✉ ᵴ *shop plants for sale* ✗
Details not confirmed for 1992

Great Western Railway Museum — SWINDON

Map 03 SU18
Faringdon Rd
☎ (0793) 493189
The museum is in the Great Western Railway Village in Swindon, once one of the busiest railway towns in Britain, and now has a fascinating collection of locomotives and other exhibits relating to the GWR. Among the locomotives are the historic *Dean Goods* and *Lode Star* and a replica of the broad gauge locomotive *North Star*. There is a comprehensive display of nameplates, models, posters and tickets and other

railway paraphernalia, and a new exhibition 'Return to Swindon' celebrates Swindon's Railway Works and Village, complete with recreated Railway Workshop displays. There will be a Thomas the Tank Engine Christmas party in December.
Open all year, wkdays 10-5, Sun 2-5. (Closed Good Fri, 25 & 26 Dec). £1.80 (ch & pen 90p). Party. (Charge includes admission to the Railway Village museum.)
ᵴ *shop* ✗

Museum & Art Gallery — SWINDON

Map 03 SU18
Bath Rd
☎ (0793) 526161 ext 3188
The museum contains a small collection of items of local interest, and the art gallery has pictures by important British

20th-century artists, including Moore, Sutherland, Wadsworth etc.
Open all year, Mon-Sat 10-5.30, Sun 2-5.30 (Closed Good Fri, 25 & 26 Dec). Free.
shop ✗

Railway Village House — SWINDON

Map 03 SU18
34 Faringdon Rd (adjacent to GWR Museum)
☎ (0793) 526161 ext 4527
This restored foreman's house is furnished as a typical working-class home at the turn of the century. It was originally part of the model village built

in Bath stone by the GWR for its workers.
Open all year, Mon-Fri 10-1 & 2-5, Sun 2-5. (Closed Good Fri & Xmas). 75p (ch & pen 50p). Free to those paying for GWR Museum.
ᵴ *shop* ✗

Places to visit in this guide are pinpointed on the atlas at the back of the book.

Farmer Giles Farmstead — TEFFONT MAGNA

Map 03 ST93
☎ (0722) 716338
Working dairy farm with 20,000sq ft under cover without steps. The 150 cows are milked from 2.30 to 5pm, and there are calves, highland cattle, shire horses, donkeys, Shetland ponies, pigs, sheep, goats, rabbits and poultry in the paddocks. Children may bottle feed the lambs. Features include 'Dairying

Through the Ages', exhibitions and displays in the undercover area, and an adventure playground with tractor and beech belt nature walk. Special events including craft displays and a steam rally are held throughout the year.
Open 28 Mar-2 Nov, daily 10.30-6, wknds until Xmas. Party bookings all year. £2.50 (ch £1.50, pen £2)
P ✗ ᵴ *toilets for disabled shop*

Old Wardour Castle — TISBURY

Map 03 ST92
(2m SW)
☎ (0747) 870487
The old castle was a hexagonal building, and there are substantial remains. The walls still stand to their original 60ft and it is possible to climb nearly to the top. It was built in 1392 by John Lord Lovel with later additions after 1570. It was

twice besieged and badly damaged during the Civil War.
Open all year, Apr-Sep, daily 10-6; Oct-Mar, wknds only 10-4. (Closed 24-26 Dec & 1 Jan). £1.20 (ch 60p, pen, students & UB40 90p).
P ᵴ
(EH)

Westwood Manor — WESTWOOD

Map 03 ST85
(1.50m SW of Bradford on Avon, off B3109)
☎ Bradford on Avon (02216) 3374
The property of the National Trust, this late-15th-century stone manor house has some particularly fine Jacobean plasterwork. The house, which is

situated by the parish church, was altered in 1610 but still retains its late Gothic and Jacobean windows. Outside there is a superb modern topiary garden.
Open Apr-Sep, Sun, Tues & Wed 2-5 £2.80
P ✗
(NT)

Wilton House — WILTON (near Salisbury)

Map 03 SU03
(2.5m W of Salisbury, on the A30)
☎ Salisbury (0722) 743115
Built on the site of an abbey founded by King Alfred, the present Wilton House is the home of the Earl of Pembroke. The Pembroke family have lived at Wilton since the mid 1500s, when the abbey grounds were given to the 1st Earl by Henry VIII. The original house was probably designed by Hans Holbein, but a fire in 1647 destroyed most of it and little remains apart from a porch. After the fire, the house was redesigned by Inigo Jones and John Webb. Their contribution still remains in the seven state rooms, of which the unusual double and single cube rooms are the most magnificent. The single cube is exactly 30ft in height, length and width.

In 1800 James Wyatt made further extensive improvements, particularly to the north and west fronts. Inside the house there is a world-famous collection of paintings by Rubens, Van Dyck and Tinteretto among others, and some fine furniture and sculptures. There is also a display of 7,000 model soldiers and a dolls' palace.
The grounds are laid mainly to lawn, with superb old cedar trees and a Palladian bridge over the river as dramatic features. Documentary drama film presentations are planned for 1992.
Open 7 Apr-18 Oct, Mon-Sat 11-6, Sun 12-6. Last admission 4.30pm.
✱ *£4.50 (ch 5-16 £3.20, under 5 free, students & pen £4.20).*
P ✗ *licensed* ᵴ *toilets for disabled shop garden centre* ✗

Woodhenge — WOODHENGE

Map 03 SU14
(1m N of Amesbury)
Consisted formerly of six concentric rings of timber posts within a ditch. Positions of the posts are marked by concrete pillars. Discovered accidentally

by aerial reconnaissance in 1925.
Open all reasonable times. Free.
P ᵴ
(EH)

CHANNEL ISLANDS

Le Friquet Butterfly Centre — GUERNSEY CÂTEL (CASTEL)

Map 15
☎ Guernsey (0481) 54378
European and tropical butterflies fly freely in the lush setting of the Butterfly Farm greenhouse, and may be seen

hatching from their chrysalids. Other attractions include putting and croquet.
Open Etr-Oct, daily 10-5. £1.75 (ch & pen £1.25).
P ✉ ✗ *licensed* ᵴ *shop*

German Occupation Museum — GUERNSEY FOREST

Map 15
☎ Guernsey (0481) 38205
The museum has the Channel Islands' largest collection of authentic Occupation items, with tableaux of a kitchen, bunker rooms and a street during the Occupation. Tours of the

underground fortifications are arranged, and Liberation Day is commemorated on 9th May.
Open all year, Apr-Oct 10-5; Nov-Mar, Sun & Thu 2-4.30. (Closed Jan). £2 (ch £1, ch under 5 free).
P ✉ ᵴ ✗

Fort Grey — GUERNSEY ROQUAINE BAY

Map 15
☎ Guernsey (0481) 726518
The fort is a Martello tower, built as part of the Channel Islands' extensive defences against Napoleon. It is nicknamed the 'cup and saucer' because of its appearance, and houses a museum

devoted to wrecks on the treacherous Hanois reefs nearby.
Open mid Apr-mid Oct, 10.30-12.30 & 1.30-5.30. £1.50 (ch 50p, pen 75p). Family ticket £3.25. Party. Schools free.
P *shop* ✗

German Military Underground Hospital & Ammunition Store — GUERNSEY ST ANDREW

Map 15
La Vassalerie
☎ Guernsey (0481) 39100
This is the largest structure created during the German Occupation of the Channel Islands, a concrete maze of about 75,000sq ft, which took slave workers three-and-a-half years to complete, at the cost of many lives. The hospital was only used for about six weeks, to care for wounded German soldiers brought over from France after D-Day. The ammunition store, however,

which was larger than the hospital, was packed with thousands of tons of ammunition during its nine months of use. Most of the equipment has been removed, but the central heating plant, hospital beds and cooking facilities can still be seen.
Open Jul-Aug, daily 10-noon & 2-5; May-Jun & Sep, daily 10-noon & 2-4; Apr & Oct, daily 2-4; Mar & Nov, Sun & Thu 2-3.
✱ *£1.80 (ch 60p).*
P ᵴ *shop*

Sausmarez Manor
GUERNSEY ST MARTIN

Map 15
Sausmarez Rd
☎ Guernsey (0481) 35571
The Manor has been owned by the same family for many centuries, a family which has included artists, generals, admirals, privateers, judges, sportsmen, inventors, cartographers, explorers, adventurers and politicians – most of whom have left some mark on the house or its contents. Each room is a happy contrast in style to its neighbour, with collections of Oriental, French and English furniture and an eclectic variety of paintings. The Formal Garden has herbaceous borders in the style of Gertrude Jekyll, while the Woodland Garden, set around two small lakes and a stream, is inter-planted with colourful shrubs, bulbs and wild flowers, many designed to encourage butterflies, birds and other animal life. In a section of the wood, a 7.25 gauge ride-on railway runs for over a quarter of a mile over

embankments and through cuttings, while in the 16th-century Tudor Barn there is a 310sq ft model railway layout, with up to eight trains running continuously through meticulously scaled countryside, towns and villages. Another special layout is the Robus Playmobile Train Set is available for visitors to operate. New for 1992 is the Old Guernsey Working Museum with daily live demonstrations of a variety of old Guernsey crafts and activities, plus, in the Little Barn, a collection of dolls' houses dating from 1820 to the present day. There are a number of special events planned for 1992 ranging from fashion to bonsai to craft.
Open last BH in May-last Thu in Sep, Tue-Thu & BH Mons.
✱ *House £2 (ch 70p). Old Guernsey Museum £1.50. Dolls House £1. Railways £1.*
🅿 ⬤ ✗ ♿ *shop*

Castle Cornet
GUERNSEY ST PETER PORT

Map 15
☎ Guernsey (0481) 721657

Castle Cornet has been used in warfare from the 13th to 20th centuries, and has an impressive array of defences. During the Civil War it was garrisoned by the Royalist governor of the island, and although most islanders sympathised with Cromwell, it was not until 1651

that this last Royalist stronghold surrendered. In 1940 the castle was taken over by German troops and adapted for modern warfare. Today it houses the new Maritime Museum (opened in 1991), the Spenser collection of uniforms and badges, the Museum of Guernsey's Own 201 Squadron Royal Air Force, the Royal Guernsey Militia Museum, Art Gallery and Armoury. A gun is fired daily at noon on the order of a man who studies the town church clock through a telescope. There will be an open day on 13 June to mark the Queen's birthday.
Open Apr-Oct, daily 10.30-5.30.
£4 (ch £1.50, pen £2). Family ticket £9. Party. Schools free.
🅿 ⬤ *shop* ✖

Guernsey Museum & Art Gallery
GUERNSEY ST PETER PORT

Map 15
Candie Gardens
☎ Guernsey (0481) 726518
The island's first purpose-built museum tells the story of Guernsey and its people. The museum has an audio-visual theatre and an art gallery, and there are

special exhibitions throughout the year. It is surrounded by beautiful gardens.
Open all year, daily 10.30-5.30 (winter 4.30).
£2 (ch 75p, pen £1). Family tickets £4.50. Party. Schools free.
🅿 ⬤ ♿ *toilets for disabled shop* ✖

Hauteville House
GUERNSEY ST PETER PORT

Map 15
Maison de Victor Hugo, 38 Hauteville
☎ Guernsey (0481) 21911
Built around 1800, the house was bought by Victor Hugo, the great French writer, in 1856. He decorated it in a unique way, sometimes carving up

and recombining several different pieces of furniture or tapestry. There are fine collections of china, paintings and tapestries.
Open Apr-Sep, Mon-Sat, 10-11.30 & 2-4.30. (Closed Sun & BH)
♿ *shop* ✖
Details not confirmed for 1992

For an explanation of the symbols and abbreviations, see page 2.

Mont Orgueil Castle
JERSEY GOREY

Map 15
☎ Jersey (0534) 53292

The castle stands on a rocky headland, on a site which has been fortified since the Iron Age. It is one of the best-preserved examples in Europe of a medieval concentric castle, and dates from the 12th and 13th centuries. A series of tableaux with a commentary tells the history of the building.
Open Apr-Oct, daily 9.30-5.30.
£1.20 (ch 10 free, pen 60p).
⬤ ✖

La Hougue Bie
JERSEY GROUVILLE

Map 15
☎ Jersey (0534) 53823
This Neolithic burial mound stands 40ft high, and covers a stone-built passage grave which is still intact and may be entered. The passage is 50ft long, and is built of huge stones dragged from quarries; the mound is made from earth, rubble and limpet shells. On top of the mound are two medieval chapels, one of which has a replica of the Holy Sepulchre in Jerusalem below. Also on the site is an underground bunker built by the Germans as a communications

centre. It is now an Occupation museum. There are also archaeology and geology displays, an agricultural museum, and a railway exhibition in a former guard's van of the Jersey Eastern Railway. Excavations will be taking place during July, August and September.
Open all year, Mar-Oct, daily 10-5; Winter, Mon-Fri 10-3.
£1.50 (ch 10-16 & pen 75p). Passport for all 4 Jersey Museums Service sites £5 (student & pen £2.50).
🅿 ♿ *shop* ✖

Samarès Manor
JERSEY ST CLEMENT

Map 15
☎ Jersey (0534) 70551
There are guided tours of the manor, which stands in 14 acres of beautiful gardens. The Japanese Garden occupies an artificial hill, and has a series of waterfalls cascading over Cumberland

limestone. One of Britain's largest and most comprehensive herb gardens is here, with a herb and specialist hardy perennial nursery.
Open 6 Apr-17 Oct.
✱ *£2 (ch 80p, pen £1.50).*
🅿 ⬤ ✗ *licensed* ♿ *shop garden centre*

Elizabeth Castle
JERSEY ST HELIER

Map 15
(access by causeway or amphibious vehicle)
☎ Jersey (0534) 23971
The original Elizabethan fortress was extended in the 17th and 18th centuries, and then refortified by the Germans during the Occupation. There are many

buildings and defences to explore, a museum of the Jersey militia, a Granite and Gunpowder exhibition of cannon and fortifications in war and peace, and an exhibition of life in the castle.
Open Apr-Oct, daily 9.30-6.
✱ *£1.20 (ch 10 free, pen 60p).*
✗ *licensed* ♿ *shop* ✖

Jersey Museum
JERSEY ST HELIER

Map 15
Pier Rd
☎ Jersey (0534) 75940
The new Jersey Museum opens in March 1992. This designed, purpose-built building, houses 'The Story of Jersey', Jersey's Art Gallery, Temporary Exhibition Gallery, Lecture Room, AV

Theatre, café and giftshop. The Museum has full disabled facilities.
Open all year, Mon-Sat 10-5. (Closed Good Fri & 25 Dec).
✱ *£1.20 (ch 10 free, pen 60p). Passport ticket for all 4 Jersey Museums Service sites £3 (students & pen £1.50).*
shop ✖

German Underground Hospital
JERSEY ST LAWRENCE

Map 15
☎ Jersey (0534) 63442
The hospital was tunnelled out of solid rock by forced labour and slaves and civilians during the German Occupation, 1940-5. It was only ever half completed, but in a period of two-and-a-half years, 43,900 tons of rock were removed and 6,020 cubic metres of concrete were used to line the wards and corridors. Lighting and special effects re-create working conditions, and short video films tell the story of Jersey during the invasion, Occupation and liberation.

Photographs of war personalities, events, newspaper articles and German leaflets are displayed. There is also a collection of German firearms, and an escapee's boat. Special exhibition open all 1992: 'A Child's Occupation': images of childhood during the occupation of Jersey 1940-1945.
Open 2 Feb-5 Mar, Thu 12-5, Sun 2-5; 8 Mar-Oct, daily 9.30-5.30. Last admission 4.15pm.
£3.50 (ch £1.50).
🅿 ⬤ ♿ *toilets for disabled shop* ✖

Jersey Shire Horse Farm Museum
JERSEY ST OUEN

Map 15
Champ Donne, Rue de Trodez
☎ Jersey (0534) 82372
There are Shire horses and their foals to meet, and carriage rides can be taken along country lanes. There are also displays of harness, farming implements

and a museum.
Open Mar-Oct, daily (ex Sat) 10-5.30. Also all BH's.
£2.50 (ch £1.50, ch under 3 free, pen £2). Wheelchair users and the blind free.
🅿 ⬤ *shop* ✖

Kempt Tower Interpretation Centre
JERSEY ST OUEN

Map 15
Five Mile Rd
☎ Jersey (0534) 483651
The centre has displays on the past, and the wildlife, of St Ouen's Bay, including Les Mielles, which is Jersey's miniature national park. Nature walks are held every Thursday (May to September),

with bird walks most Sunday afternoons. Check local press for details.
Open 2 Apr & 27 Sep-29 Oct, Thu & Sun only 2-5; May-27 Sep, daily (ex Mon) 2-5.
Free.
🅿 *shop* ✖

Jersey Motor Museum
JERSEY
ST PETER

Map 15
St Peter's Village (jct off A12 & B41 at St Peters village)
☎ Jersey (0534) 82966 due to change to 482966
The museum has a fine collection of motor vehicles from the early 1900s. There are also Allied and German military vehicles of World War II, a Jersey Steam Railway section, aero-engines and other items. A pre-war Jersey AA box is shown, with a collection of AA badges of all periods.
Open mid Mar-Oct, daily 10-5. (Last admission 4.40pm).
✱ *£1.30 (ch 70p). Wheelchair users free.*
P ♿ *shop* 🚫

Le Moulin de Quetivel
JERSEY
ST PETER

Map 15
St Peters Valley (on B58 off A11)
☎ Jersey (0534) 83193
There has been a water mill on this site since 1309. The present granite-built mill was worked until the end of the 19th century, when it fell into disrepair; during the German Occupation it was reactivated for grinding locally grown corn, but after 1945 a fire destroyed the remaining machinery, roof and internal woodwork. In 1971 the National Trust for Jersey began restoration, and the mill is now producing stoneground flour again.
Open mid May-mid Oct, Tue-Thu 10-4. Dates to be confirmed.
P ♿ *shop* 🚫
(NT)
Details not confirmed for 1992

♿ This symbol indicates that much or all of the attraction is accessible to wheelchairs. However, there may be some restrictions, so it would be wise to check in advance.

St Peter's Bunker Museum
JERSEY
ST PETER

Map 15
St Peters Village (at junc of A12 & B41)
☎ Jersey (0534) 81048
German uniforms, motorcycles, weapons, documents, photographs and other items from the 1940-45 Occupation are displayed in a real wartime bunker. It accommodated 36 men and could be sealed in case of attack. One room has been refitted with authentic bunk beds and figures of soldiers.
Open mid Mar-early Nov, daily 10-5.
✱ *£1.30 (ch 60p).*
P *shop* 🚫

Jersey Zoological Park
JERSEY
TRINITY

Map 15
Les Augres Manor
☎ Jersey (0534) 64666 due to change to 864666
Les Augres Manor is the home of Gerald Durrell, and the Jersey Wildlife Preservation Trust, which has established here a unique sanctuary and breeding centre for endangered animals. Among the many exciting and attractive exhibits are Jambo, the world-famous Lowland gorilla and his large family, the Spectacled bears and their cubs, Snow leopards, marmosets and tamarins. The award-winning new enclosure for the Celebes macaques and the woodland home for the lemurs provide a memorable experience for visitors and a natural existence for the animals. The most important and prestigious new building is The Princess Royal Pavilion, where the fascinating story of the work of the Trust in every corner of the world is unfolded in a superb audio-visual presentation.
Open all year, daily 10-6 (dusk in winter). (Closed 25 Dec).
✱ *£4 (ch & pen £2).*
P ☕ ♿ *(trail for the blind, auditory loop in pavilion) toilets for disabled shop* 🚫

ISLE OF MAN

Curraghs Wild Life Park
ISLE OF MAN
BALLAUGH

Map 06 SC39
☎ Sulby (062489) 7323
Developed adjacent to the reserve area of the Ballaugh Curraghs is the wildlife park, which exhibits a variety of animals and birds in natural settings.
Open Etr-Sep, daily 10-6. Last admission 5.15pm.
£2 (ch £1). Party 25+.
P ☕ ♿ *toilets for disabled shop* 🚫

For an explanation of the symbols and abbreviations, see page 2.

Castle Rushen
ISLE OF MAN
CASTLETOWN

Map 06 SC26
☎ Douglas (0624) 675522
On view to the visitor are the state apartments of this 14th-century stronghold. There is also a Norman keep, flanked by towers from its later rebuilding, with a clock given by Elizabeth I in 1597. The castle is available for private hire.
Open Etr-Sep, daily 10-5.
✱ *£2.50 (ch & pen £1.25).*
☕ ♿ *shop* 🚫

Nautical Museum
ISLE OF MAN
CASTLETOWN

Map 06 SC26
☎ Douglas (0624) 675522
The island's colourful relationship with the sea is illustrated here. There is an 18th-century Manx yacht and interesting Cabin Room and Quayle Room. Other areas comprise displays of net-making equipment and sailing ships.
Open Etr-late Sep, daily 10-5.
✱ *£1.50 (ch & pen 75p).*
♿ *shop* 🚫

🚫 The 'No Dogs' symbol does not normally apply to guide dogs – these are permitted in most establishments.

Cregneash Village Folk Museum
ISLE OF MAN
CREGNEISH

Map 06 SC16
(2m from Port Erin/Port St Mary)
☎ Douglas (0624) 675522
A group of traditional Manx cottages with their gardens and walled enclosures. Inside the cottages furniture and the everyday equipment used by typical Manx crofting communities are displayed. A crofter-fisherman's home, a farmstead, a turner's shed, smithy and a weaver's shed are all represented in realistic settings. Spinning demonstrations are given on certain days and sometimes a blacksmith can be seen at work. In the field adjoining the turner's shed, Manx Loghtan sheep can often be viewed; this ancient breed survives in very small numbers. The rams have a tendency to produce four, or even six, horns.
Open Etr-Sep, daily 10-5.
✱ *£1.50 (ch & pen 75p).*
P ☕ ✕ ♿ *shop* 🚫 *(ex in grounds)*

Manx Museum
ISLE OF MAN
DOUGLAS

Map 06 SC37
☎ (0624) 675522
The 'Story of Man' begins at Manx Museum, where a specially produced film portrayal of Manx history compliments the award-winning gallery displays. This showcase of Manx heritage provides the ideal starting-point to a journey of rich discovery embracing the length and breadth of the island.
Open all year, Mon-Sat 10-5. (Closed Sun, Xmas, New Year, Good Fri & am of Tynwald Day 5 Jul).
Free.
P ☕ ♿ *toilets for disabled shop* 🚫

Laxey Wheel
ISLE OF MAN
LAXEY

Map 07 SC48
☎ Douglas (0624) 675522
Constructed to keep the lead mines free from water, this big wheel, known as the 'Lady Isabella', is an impressive sight at 72.5ft in diameter. It is the largest working wheel in the world.
Open Etr-Sep, daily 10-5.
✱ *£1.50 (ch & pen 75p).*
P ♿ *shop* 🚫

Every effort is made to provide accurate information, but details might change during the currency of this guide.

Peel Castle
ISLE OF MAN
PEEL

Map 06 SC28
(on Patricks Isle, facing Peel Bay)
☎ Douglas (0624) 675522
The castle was built to protect the cathedral of St German's, perhaps founded by St Patrick. A phantom black dog, the Moddey Dhoo, is said to have haunted the castle. Sir Walter Scott used the story in *Peveril of the Peak*.
Open Etr-Sep, daily 10-5.
✱ *£1.50 (ch & pen 75p).*
P *shop* 🚫

'The Grove' Rural Life Museum
ISLE OF MAN
RAMSEY

Map 07 SC49
(on W side of Andreas Road)
☎ Douglas (0624) 675522
For an intimate glimpse into the everyday life of a previous era this Victorian villa is well worth a visit. Inside there are many of the original furnishings and personal belongings of the former owners, the Gibb family, displayed among the minutiae of Victorian life, both upstairs and downstairs. Outbuildings house a collection of early agricultural equipment including a horse-driven threshing mill; one of the few to survive in working order. There is also an exhibition on bees and bee-keeping.
Open Etr-Sep, daily 10-5.
✱ *£1.50 (ch & pen 75p).*
P ☕ ♿ *shop* 🚫

Murray's Museum
ISLE OF MAN
SNAEFELL MOUNTAIN

Map 06 SC38
Bungalow Corner (Junction A14 & A18)
☎ Laxey (0624) 861719
The TT races are perhaps the best-known feature of the Isle of Man, and not surprisingly the island has a motorcycle museum. Situated at the Bungalow corner on the TT course, this is an historic collection of 150 motorcycles and cycles, plus motoring and motorcycling memorabilia and equipment.
Open 25 May-25 Sep daily 10.30-5.
P ☕ ♿ *shop*
Details not confirmed for 1992

SCOTLAND

BORDERS

Broughton Place · BROUGHTON

Map 11 NT13
☎ (08994) 234
The house was designed by Sir Basil Spence in 1938, in the style of a 17th-century Scottish tower house. The drawing room and main hall are open to the public, and have paintings and crafts by living British artists for sale. The

gardens are open for part of the summer, and give fine views of the Tweeddale hills.
Open – Gallery 29 Mar-22 Oct & 22 Nov-20 Dec, daily (ex Wed) 10.30-6. Gallery free; Garden donations.
🅿 ᵺ shop ✈

The Hirsel · COLDSTREAM

Map 11 NT84
(0.5m W on A697)
☎ (0890) 2834
The Hirsel is the seat of the Home family, and its grounds are open all year. The focal point is the Homestead Museum, craft centre and workshops. From there, nature trails lead around the

lake, along the Leet Valley and into a wood which is noted for its rhododendrons and azaleas. May Fair 2-4 May, Crafts for Christmas Weekend in Nov.
Open all year, daylight hours.
£1 (ch free, pen concessions). Party.
🅿 ♨ ᵺ toilets for disabled shop

Dryburgh Abbey · DRYBURGH

Map 11 NT53
(5m SE of Melrose on B6404)
☎ 031-244 3101
The abbey was one of the Border monasteries founded by David I, and stands in a lovely setting on the River Tweed. The ruins are equally beautiful, and the church has the graves of Sir

Walter Scott and Earl Haig.
Open all year, Apr-Sep, weekdays 9.30-6, Sun 2-6; Oct-Mar weekdays 9.30-4, Sun 2-4. (Closed 25-26 Dec & 1-2 Jan).
£1.70 (concessions 90p). Family ticket £4.50.
🅿 shop ✈
(AM)

Jim Clark Room · DUNS

Map 11 NT75
44 Newtown St
☎ (0361) 82600 ext 36
Motor racing trophies won by Jim Clark are on display, including two world championship trophies of 1963 and 1965, and other Grand Prix awards. Clark was the first Honorary Burgess of Duns. He was killed in Germany in

1968, and his parents gave the trophies to the town. There is also a growing collection of photographs and other memorabilia.
Open Etr-Oct, Mon-Sat 10-1 & 2-5, Sun 2-5.
50p (ch 16 25p, under 5 free, pen 25p).
🅿 ᵺ ✈

Manderston · DUNS

Map 11 NT75
(1.25m E off A6105)
☎ (0361) 83450
This grandest of grand houses gives a fascinating picture of Edwardian life both above and below stairs. It was built for the millionaire racehorse owner Sir James Miller. The architect was told to spare no expense, and so the house boasts features such as the world's only silver staircase, a ballroom painted in Sir James's racing colours, and painted

ceilings. The state rooms are magnificent, and the domestic quarters are also quite lavish. Outside buildings include the handsome stable block and marble dairy, and there are fine formal gardens, with a woodland garden and lakeside walks.
Open 9 May-29 Sep, Thu & Sun 2-5.30 (also May & Aug BH Mon).
✱ *House & grounds £3.75. Grounds only £2.*
🅿 ♨ ᵺ shop

Coldstream Museum

Market Square Coldstream
Tel: (0890) 2630

A local history museum which uses many items loaned and donated by local people. The first floor of the museum is devoted to a fascinating display of items which belong to the Regiment of the Coldstream Guards.

OPEN EASTER TO LATE OCTOBER
Monday to Saturday 10-1, 2-5
Sunday 2-5

Small admission charge with reductions. Disabled access to ground floor and good parking.

MANDERSTON
DUNS BERWICKSHIRE

THE SWAN SONG OF THE GREAT CLASSICAL HOUSE
A house in which no expense has been spared. Superb, sumptuous staterooms decorated in the Adam manner and the only silver staircase in the world. "Below Stairs" gives an intriguing insight into life in a large house in the nineteen hundreds. A Biscuit Tin Museum was opened in 1984. Cream Teas and Gift Shop.
OPEN 2-5.30pm. Thursday and Sunday afternoons. May 14 to September 27, plus the Bank Holiday Mondays of May 25 and August 31
Parties at any time by appointment. **Telephone: Duns (0361) 83450**

Eyemouth Museum · EYEMOUTH

Map 11 NT96
Auld Kirk, Market Place
☎ (08907) 50678
The museum was opened in 1981 as a memorial to the 129 local fishermen lost in the Great Fishing Disaster of 1881. Its main feature is the 15ft Eyemouth tapestry, which was made for the

centenary. There are also displays on local history, and exhibitions are held.
Open Apr-Jun & Oct, Mon-Sat 10-4.30; Jul-Aug, Mon-Sat 9.30-5.30; Sep, Mon-Sat 10-5, Sun 2-3.30.
£1 (ch & pen 50p, ch 5 free). Party.
ᵺ shop

Every effort is made to provide accurate information, but details might change during the currency of this guide.

Nether Mill (Peter Anderson Ltd) · GALASHIELS

Map 11 NT43
Huddersfield St
☎ (0896) 2091
Opened in 1983, the museum brings the town's past to life with photographs and captions. The focal point is a display on the town's important woollen industry, and there are everyday items of the past

on show. Guided tours of the mill take about 40 minutes.
Open all year, Mon-Sat 9-5, Sun 12-5. Mill tours Mon-Fri at 10.30, 11.30, 1.30 & 2.30.
✱ *Museum free. Mill tour £1 (ch free).*
🅿 ᵺ toilets for disabled shop

Mellerstain House · GORDON

Map 11 NT64
(3m S on unclass road)
☎ (057381) 225
One of Scotland's finest Georgian houses, Mellerstain was begun by William Adam and completed by his son Robert in the 1770s. It has beautiful plasterwork, period furniture and

pictures; terraced gardens and a lake. Vintage Car Rally 7th June; Craft Festival 25th-27th July; RNLI fête 14 June.
Open Etr, then May-Sep, Mon-Fri & Sun 12.30-5 (Last admission 4.30pm).
£3 (ch £1.50, pen £2.50). Party 20+.
🅿 ♨ ᵺ shop ✈

Hawick Museum & Scott Art Gallery · HAWICK

Map 11 NT51
Wilton Lodge Park
☎ (0450) 73457
Wilton Lodge Park forms a beautiful setting for this museum on the history, trades and wildlife of the Borders. There is an interesting range of exhibitions, including new wildlife displays. The art gallery has exhibitions throughout the

year, and the park has riverside walks and gardens.
Open all year, Apr-Sep, Mon-Sat 10-noon & 1-5, Sun 2-5; Oct-Mar, Mon-Fri 1-4, Sun 2-4.
70p (ch, pen, students & UB40's 35p). Party 20+.
🅿 ᵺ shop ✈

Hermitage Castle · HERMITAGE

Map 11 NY59
(5.5m NE of Newcastleton off A7)
☎ 031-244 3101
An old Douglas stronghold, mainly 14th-century, and well restored.
Open all year, Apr-Sep weekdays 9.30-6,

Sun 2-6; Oct-Mar wknds only 2-4. (Closed 25-26 Dec & 1-2 Jan).
£1 (concessions 50p).
🅿 ᵺ shop ✈
(AM)

Robert Smail's Printing Works · INNERLEITHEN

Map 11 NT33
7/9 High St
☎ (0896) 830206
These buildings contain a Victorian office, a paper store with reconstructed waterwheel, a composing room and a press room. The printing works is in full

working order and visitors may view the printer at work.
Open Apr-Oct Mon-Sat 10-1 & 2-5, Sun 2-5. (Last admission 1hr before closing).
£1.50 (ch & pen 80p). Party
shop ✈
(NTS)

TRAQUAIR HOUSE

Scotland's oldest inhabited and most romantic house. Over 1000 years old, Traquair has seen over 27 Scottish monarchs pass through its doors including strong associations with Mary Queen of Scots and Bonnie Prince Charlie.
18th century working brewery, maze, craft workshops, 1745 Cottage available for light lunches and teas.
Opening times 1992: April 18th-26th incl., Sundays and Mondays in May. May 30th-September 30th daily; 1.30pm-5.30pm. July and August 10.30am-5.30pm.

Traquair House, Innerleithen, Peeblesshire EH44 6PW. Tel (0896) 830323.

See also gazetteer entry under Traquair.

Castle Jail & Museum — JEDBURGH

Map 11 NT62
Castlegate
☎ (0835) 63254
The social history of 19th-century Jedburgh, a town with a colourful past, is revealed in a museum at the Castle Jail. The jail itself is interesting as possibly the last surviving example of its kind. Built in the 1820s on the site of a medieval castle, it served as a county prison, and the three blocks were used to incarcerate different types of offenders.
Open Etr-Sep, Mon-Sat 10-5, Sun 1-5. 70p (ch, pen, students & UB40's 35p). Party 20+.
& ✸

Jedburgh Abbey — JEDBURGH

Map 11 NT62
4-5 Abbey Bridgend
☎ 031-244 3101

Standing as the most entire of the Border monasteries, although it has been sacked and rebuilt many times, Jedburgh Abbey has been described as 'the most perfect and beautiful example of the Saxon and early Gothic in Scotland'. It was founded as a priory in the 12th century by David I and remains of some of the domestic buildings have been uncovered during excavations.
Open all year, Apr-Sep, weekdays 9.30-6, Sun 2-6; Oct-Mar, weekdays 9.30-4, Sun 2-4. (Closed 25-26 Dec & 1-2 Jan). £1.70 (concessions 90p). Family ticket £4.50.
P & (limited access) toilets for disabled shop ✸
(AM)

Mary Queen of Scots House — JEDBURGH

Map 11 NT62
Queen St
☎ (0835) 63331
Mary Queen of Scots visited Jedburgh in 1566, and had to prolong her stay because of ill-health. Her home here is now a museum devoted to her memory and tragic history. An unusual feature of this 16th-century fortified dwelling ('bastle house') is the left-handed spiral staircase: the owners of the house, the Ker clan, were left-handed and the special staircase allowed the men to use their sword hands. The museum presents a thought-provoking interpretation of her tragic life, and as 1992 is the 450th anniversary of the birth of Mary Queen of Scots, special events will be held, including medieval fayres, music and dancing in the house and grounds, and children's competitions.
Open Etr-mid Nov, daily 10-5. £1.10 (ch, pen, students & UB40's 55p). Party 20+.
& shop ✸

For an explanation of the symbols and abbreviations, see page 2.

Floors Castle — KELSO

Map 11 NT73
☎ (0573) 23333

Sir Walter Scott described this fairy-tale castle as 'altogether a kingdom for Oberon and Titania to dwell in'. Today it is the home of the 10th Duke of Roxburghe and its lived-in atmosphere enhances the superb collection of tapestries and paintings contained inside. The house was designed by William Adam in 1721 and extended by W H Playfair over a century later; it boasts a window for each day of the year and looks out over the graceful River Tweed. A holly tree in the grounds is said to mark the spot where James II was killed; and a magnificent walled garden, garden centre and play area are among the attractions outside. Pipe bands play on 3 and 24 May, 7 Jun, 12 Jul, and 30 Aug.
Open Etr & Apr-Jun & Sep (Sun-Thu), Jul-Aug (daily) 10.30-5.30; Oct, Sun & Wed, 10.30-4. Walled Garden & Garden Centre open daily. £3 (ch £1.50, pen £2.40). Family ticket £8. Party.
P ✦ ✗ licensed & (lift) toilets for disabled shop garden centre ✸ (ex in grounds)

Kelso Abbey — KELSO

Map 11 NT73
☎ 031-244 3101
Founded by David I in 1128 and probably the greatest of the four famous Border abbeys, Kelso became extremely wealthy and acquired extensive lands. In 1545 it served as a fortress when the town was attacked by the Earl of Hertford, but now only fragments of the once-imposing abbey church give any clue to its long history.
Open at any reasonable time. Free.
&
(AM)

Kelso Museum — KELSO

Map 11 NT73
Turret House, Abbey Court (off A698)
☎ (0573) 25470
The history of Kelso Abbey is explained more fully in Kelso's museum, located in one of the town's oldest and most attractive buildings. Together with a tourist information centre, the museum shows the visitor a reconstructed skinner's workshop and a 19th-century market place, reflecting Kelso's own Flemish-style, cobbled market square.
Open Etr-Oct, Mon-Sat 10-12 & 1-5, Sun 2-5. Free.
& shop ✸
(NTS)

Thirlestane Castle — LAUDER

Map 11 NT54
(off A68)
☎ (05782) 430
This fairy-tale castle has been the home of the Maitland family, the Earls of Lauderdale, since the 12th century, and part of the family still live in one of the wings. Some of the most splendid plasterwork ceilings in Britain may be seen in the 17th-century state rooms. The former family nurseries now house a sizeable collection of antique toys and dolls, while in the basement there are several interesting displays illustrating Border country life. The informal grounds, with their riverside setting and views of nearby grouse moors, include a woodland walk.
Open 17-20 Apr, May-Jun & Sep, Wed-Thu & Sun; Jul-Aug, daily (ex Sat) 2-5 (last admission 4.30). Grounds open on dates listed above noon-6. £3. Family ticket £8. Grounds only £1. Party.
P ✦ & toilets for disabled shop ✸ (ex in grounds)

✸ The 'No Dogs' symbol does not normally apply to guide dogs – these are permitted in most establishments.

Abbotsford House — MELROSE

Map 11 NT53
(2m W off A6091)
☎ Galashiels (0896) 2043
Set on the River Tweed, Sir Walter Scott's romantic mansion remains much the same as it was in his day. Inside there are many mementoes and relics of his remarkable life and also his historical collections, armouries and library, with some 9000 volumes. The mansion was built between 1817 and 1822, and Sir Walter Scott lived here until his death ten years after its completion.
Open 19 Mar-Oct, Mon-Sat 10-5, Sun 2-5. £2.20 (ch £1.10). Party.
P ✦ & toilets for disabled shop ✸

Melrose Abbey & Abbey Museum — MELROSE

Map 11 NT53
☎ 031-244 3101
The ruin of this Cistercian abbey is probably one of Scotland's finest, and has been given added glamour by its connection with Sir Walter Scott. The abbey was repeatedly wrecked during the Scottish wars of independence, but parts of the nave and choir survive from the 14th century, and include some of the best and most elaborate traceried stonework in Scotland. Most of the ruins belong to a 15th-century reconstruction. The abbey has many interesting features: the heart of Robert the Bruce is buried somewhere within the church; note too the figure of a pig playing the bagpipes, set on the roof. The museum, sited at the entrance to the ruins and housed in the 16th-century Commendator's House, is an interesting addition to this historic ruin.
Open all year, Apr-Sep weekdays 9.30-6, Sun 2-6; Oct-Mar, weekdays 9.30-4, Sun 2-4. £1.70 (concessions 90p). Family ticket £4.50.
P & shop ✸
(AM)

Melrose Motor Museum — MELROSE

Map 11 NT53
Annay Rd
☎ St Boswells (089682) 2624
A short walk from the abbey ruins, this is a fascinating collection of cars, cycles, motorcycles and accessories.
Open Etr-Whitsun, please telephone for opening times. Whitsun-Oct, daily 10-5.30. Last admission 4.45. £1.80 (ch 50p, pen £1.30). Party 10+ by arrangement.
P & shop ✸

Priorwood Garden — MELROSE

Map 11 NT53
(off A6091)
☎ (089682) 2965
This small garden specialises in flowers which are suitable for drying. It is formally designed with herbaceous and everlasting annual borders, and the attractive orchard has a display of 'apples through the ages' including ancient varieties.
Open Apr & Nov-24 Dec, Mon-Sat 10-5.30; May-Oct, Mon-Sat 10-5.30, Sun 2-5.30. Free.
& shop
(NTS)

Kailzie   PEEBLES

Map 11 NT23
(2.5m SE on B7062)
☎ (0721) 20007
These extensive grounds with their fine old trees provide a burnside walk flanked by bulbs, rhododendrons and azaleas. A walled garden contains herbaceous, shrub rose borders, greenhouses and a small formal rose garden, and there is a waterfowl pond and an art gallery. Various art exhibitions are held throughout the year.
Open 27 Mar-25 Oct, daily 11-5.30. Grounds close 6pm.
✱ *May-Sep £1.80 (ch 50p, pen £1.50). Rest of year £1.50 (ch 50p, pen £1).*
🅿 ☕ ✕ *licensed & toilets for disabled shop garden centre*

Neidpath Castle   PEEBLES

Map 11 NT23
(1m W on A72)
☎ (0721) 20333
Successively owned by the families of Fraser, Hay (Earl of Tweeddale), Douglas (Earl of March) and Wemyss (Earl of Wemyss & March), Neidpath Castle occupies a spectacular position on the Tweed. The 14th-century stronghold has been interestingly adapted to 17th-century living; it contains a rock hewn well, pit prisons, a small museum, and a tartan display, and has picturesque views.
Open 16 Apr-Sep, Mon-Sat 11-5, Sun 1-5. £1.50 (ch 50p, pen £1). Party 20+.
🅿 *shop*

Bowhill House & Country Park   SELKIRK

Map 11 NT42
(3m W of Selkirk off A708)
☎ (0750) 20732
An outstanding collection of pictures, including works by Van Dyck, Canaletto, Reynolds, Gainsborough and Claude Lorraine, are displayed in this, the Border home of the Duke of Buccleuch and Queensberry KT. In addition to these there is an equally stunning collection of porcelain and furniture, much of it made in the Paris workshop of André Boulle. Memorabilia and relics of people such as Queen Victoria and Sir Walter Scott, and a restored Victorian kitchen add further interest inside the house. Outside, the wooded grounds are perfect for walking, cycling and riding (there is bicycle hire and a riding centre). Children will enjoy the adventure playground and, no doubt, the gift shop. There is also a theatre and an audio-visual display. Art courses are held here.
Open, Grounds: May-Aug 12-5 (ex Fri), Riding centre all year. House & grounds: Jul, daily 1-4.30. House & grounds £3 (ch 5 free, pen £2). Grounds only £1. Party 20+.
🅿 ☕ ✕ *licensed & (guided tours for the blind) toilets for disabled shop (Jul) ✖ (ex in grounds)*

Halliwells House Museum   SELKIRK

Map 11 NT42
Halliwells Close, Market Place
☎ (0750) 20096
The former role of Selkirk's oldest surviving dwelling has been recreated in this enterprising museum. The home and ironmonger's shop, lovingly restored, can be seen together with the story of the town's development and frequent temporary exhibitions.
*Open Apr-Oct, Mon-Sat 10-12.30 & 1.30-5 (Jul & Aug until 6), Sun 2-4; Nov-Dec, daily 2-4.
Free.*
🅿 & *toilets for disabled shop ✖*

Smailholm Tower   SMAILHOLM

Map 11 NT63
(1.5m SW on B6937)
☎ 031-244 3101
An outstanding example of a classic Border tower-house, probably erected in the 15th century. It is 57ft high and well preserved. The tower houses an exhibition of dolls and a display based on Sir Walter Scott's book 'Minstrels of the Border'. It consists of tapestries and costume figures.
*Open Apr-Sep, weekdays 9.30-6, Sun 2-6. (Closed in winter).
£1 (concessions 50p)*
🅿 *shop ✖*
(AM)

Dawyck Botanic Garden   STOBO

Map 11 NT13
(8m SW of Peebles on B712)
☎ (07216) 254
Dawyck is a specialist garden of the Royal Botanic Garden, Edinburgh. The garden is particularly noted for its arboretum, especially the 'Dawyck beeches' and a larch believed to have been planted by the Swedish botanist Linnaeus in 1725.
Open 15 Mar-22 Oct, daily 10-6. £1 (ch & concessions 50p).
🅿 & *toilets for disabled ✖*

Traquair House   TRAQUAIR

Map 11 NT33
(1m S of Innerleithen on B709).
☎ Innerleithen (0896) 830323 & 830785

This is said to be Scotland's oldest inhabited, and most romantic, house. It dates back to the 10th century and 27 English and Scottish kings have stayed here. William the Lion Heart held court at Traquair, and the house has rich associations with Mary Queen of Scots and the Jacobite risings. The large Bear Gates were closed in 1745, not to be reopened until the Stuarts should once again ascend the throne.
The house contains a fine collection of historical treasures and a unique 18th-century brewhouse which is licensed to make and sell its own beer. Outside there is a maze, croquet, and the opportunity for woodland walks by the River Tweed. There are also craft workshops and an art gallery. Events for 1992 include Traquair Fair (1-2 Aug) and a sheep and wool day (26 Jul).
*Open Etr wk & 18-26 Apr, Sun & Mons in May, then daily from 30 May-Sep, 1.30-5.30 (ex Jul & Aug 10.30-5.30). Last admission 5pm. Grounds open Apr-Sep, 10.30-5.30.
£3 (ch £1.50). Party.*
🅿 ☕ ✕ *licensed & shop*

CENTRAL

Bannockburn Heritage Centre   BANNOCKBURN

Map 11 NS89
Glasgow Rd (2m S off M80/M9 junc 9)
☎ (0786) 812664
The Heritage Centre stands close to the Borestone site, which by tradition was King Robert the Bruce's command post before the Battle of Bannockburn, June 1314, at which the Scots trounced the English. It was a turning-point in Scottish history, and Bruce is commemorated by a bronze equestrian statue, unveiled in 1964. The site is enclosed by the Rotunda. The centre has an exhibition, 'The Kingdom of the Scots', and an audio-visual display on the battle. Wheelchairs are available on loan.
*Open – Rotunda & site always open. Visitor Centre etc Apr-Oct daily 10-6. (Last audio-visual showing 5.30).
£1.30 (ch & pen 70p). Party.*
🅿 & *(Induction loop for the hard of hearing) toilets for disabled shop ✖ (ex site only)*
(NTS)

The Birkhill Clay Mine   BIRKHILL

Map 11 NS97
☎ Bo'ness (0506) 825855
No simulations here, this is a real clay mine deep in the steep wooded Avon Gorge. Experience life underground, and visit the original mill, clay handling buildings and haulage gear. Work is in progress on a car park, picnic area, underground walks and a nature trail.
Open Etr-Sep, Sat & Sun 12-4; daily, mid Jul-Aug 12-4.
🅿 *shop*
Details not confirmed for 1992

Blair Drummond Safari & Leisure Park   BLAIR DRUMMOND

Map 11 NS79
(Exit 10 off M9, A84 between Doune/Stirling)
☎ Doune (0786) 841456
Wild animals can be seen roaming in natural surroundings. There is a lion and a tiger reserve with an aerial walkway above the lions. Other attractions include a pets' farm, boat safari around Chimp Island, sealion shows, Splash Cats and pedal boats, Astra Glide, and flying fox cable slide across the lake. Amusement area and Adventure Playground.
*Open late Apr-5 Oct, daily 10-5.30. Last admission 4.30.
£5 (ch 3-14 & pen £3).*
🅿 ☕ & *toilets for disabled ✖*

Bo'ness & Kinneil Railway   BO'NESS

Map 11 NS98
Bo'ness Station, Union St
☎ (0506) 822298
The Scottish Railway Preservation Society has reclaimed land on the foreshore at Bo'ness and used it to re-create the days of steam, with many relocated historic railway buildings and Scotland's largest collection of locomotives and rolling stock. There is a seven-mile round trip by steam train through woodland and countryside for a visit underground to Birkhill Fireclay Mine. Work is in progress to extend the line to Manuel Junction (5.5 miles). Santa Specials are held at weekends in December, and other special events take place throughout the year, including a Victorian Day (24 May), a vintage vehicle rally (21 Jun), and a diesel enthusiasts' weekend.
Open wknds 11 Apr-18 Oct; Mon 20 Apr, 4 & 25 May; daily 18 Jul-Aug; School weeks Mon-Fri 25-29 May & 1-5 Jun. Return fare £3 (ch 5-15 £1.50, pen £2). Family ticket £7.50. Event days £4 (ch 3-15 & pen £2). Family ticket £10.
🅿 ☕ & *shop*

Kinneil House   BO'NESS

Map 11 NS98
☎ 031-244 3101
Standing in a public park, Kinneil House has a 16th-century tower which became part of the 17th-century home of the Dukes of Hamilton. There are decorated ceilings and 16th- to 17th-century wall paintings inside. James Watt developed the steam engine in an outhouse in the grounds.
*Open at all reasonable times.
Free.*
(AM)

Kinneil Museum & Roman Fortlet BO'NESS

Map 11 NS98
Duchess Anne Cottages, Kinneil Estate
☎ (0506) 824318
The musuem is in a converted stable block of Kinneil House. The ground floor has displays on the industrial history of Bo'ness, while the upper floor looks at the history and environment of the Kinneil estate. The remains of the

Roman fortlet can be seen nearby. An audio visual theatre shows 2000 years of history, and there are guided tours by costumed interpreter during the summer (Weds and Sat).
Open all year, Apr-Sep, Mon-Fri 10-12.30 & 1.30-5, Sat 10-5 & May-Aug, Sun 10-5; Oct-Mar, Sat 10-5.
Free.
🅿 ♿ *shop* ✈

Kilmahog Woollen Mill CALLANDER

Map 11 NN60
(1m W on A84)
☎ (0877) 30268
An old water-wheel has been preserved in working order at the former woollen mill, famous for handwoven blankets and tweeds. A showroom is open for the

sale of woollens, tweeds, tartans and Scottish gifts.
Open all year, Summer, Mon-Sat 9-5.30, Sun 10-5.30; Winter, Mon-Sat 10-4, Sun 12-4.
Free.
🅿 ✗ ♿ *shop* ✈

Rob Roy and Trossachs Visitor Centre CALLANDER

Map 11 NN60
Ancaster Square (on A84)
☎ (0877) 30342
The fascinating story of Scotland's most famous outlaw, Rob Roy MacGregor is vividly portrayed through an exciting multi-media theatre and explained in the carefully researched 'Life and Times' exhibition. Also full tourist information centre covering the beautiful Trossachs

area, Scottish bookshops and specially themed souvenirs. Evening entertainment, including slide presentations and pipe band displays, is arranged from Jun-Oct; telephone for details.
Open Mar-May & Oct-Nov 10-5; Jun & Sep 10-7; Jul-Aug 9-10, Dec 10-5.
£1.75 (ch & pen £1.35).
🅿 ♿ *toilets for disabled shop* ✈

✈ The 'No Dogs' symbol does not normally apply to guide dogs – these are permitted in most establishments.

Wallace Monument CAUSEWAYHEAD

Map 11 NS89
☎ Stirling (0786) 72140
The 220ft tower was built in 1869, and Sir William Wallace's two-handed sword is preserved inside. Seven battlefields and a fine view towards the Highlands can be seen. Displays include a Hall of

Heroes, an audio-visual show on the life of Wallace, the Forth Panorama, and a sound-and-light show on famous Scots.
Open Feb, Mar & Oct 10-5; Apr & Sep 10-6; May-Aug 10-7.
✱ £1.20 (ch 60p). Party 15 +.
🅿 ☕ *shop* ✈

Castle Campbell & Dollar Glen DOLLAR

Map 11 NS99
(10m W of Stirling on A91)
☎ 031-244 3101
The 15th- to 17th-century tower stands in the picturesque Ochil Hills and gives wonderful views. It can be reached by a walk through the magnificent Dollar Glen. Care must be taken in or after rain when the path may be dangerous.

Open Glen at reasonable times. Castle open Apr-Sep, Mon-Sat 9.30-6, Sun 2-6; Oct-Mar, Mon-Sat 9.30-4, Sun 2-4. (Closed Thu pm & Fri in winter, 25-26 Dec & 1-2 Jan).
Castle £1.50 (concessions 80p).
🅿 *shop* ✈
(AM & NTS)

Doune Castle DOUNE

Map 11 NN70
(8m S of Callander on A84)
☎ 031-244 3101
The 14th-century stronghold with its two fine towers has been restored. It stands on the banks of the River Teith, and is associated with Bonnie Prince Charlie and Sir Walter Scott.

Open all year, Apr-Sep, weekdays 9.30-6, Sun 2-6; Oct-Mar 9.30-4, Sun 2-4. (Closed Thu pm & Fri in winter; 25-26 Dec & 1-2 Jan).
£1.50 (concessions 80p).
🅿 *shop* ✈
(AM)

This is just one of many guidebooks published by the AA. The full range is available at any AA shop or good bookshop.

Doune Motor Museum DOUNE

Map 11 NN70
(8m NW of Stirling on A84)
☎ (0786) 841203
Around 50 cars are displayed, and motoring events are held throughout the

season.
Open Etr-Oct, daily 10-5.
✱ £1.60 (ch 80p, pen £1).
🅿 ☕ ♿ *toilets for disabled shop* ✈

Falkirk Museum FALKIRK

Map 11 NS88
15 Orchard St
☎ (0324) 24911 ext 2472
Displays trace the development of the district from earliest times to the present

day. A variety of exhibitions is held.
Open all year, Mon-Fri 10-12.30 & 1.30-5, Sat 10-5.
Free.
♿ *shop* ✈

Rough Castle FALKIRK

Map 11 NS88
(1m E of Bonnybridge)
☎ 031-244 3101
The impressive earthworks of a large Roman fort on the Antonine Wall can be seen here. The buildings have disappeared, but the mounds and terraces are the sites of barracks, granary

and bath buildings. Running between them is the military road which once linked all the forts on the wall and is still well defined.
Open any reasonable time.
Free.
🅿 ✈
(AM)

Inchmahome Priory PORT OF MENTEITH

Map 11 NN50
☎ 031-244 3101
Walter Comyn founded this Augustinian house in 1238, and it became famous as the retreat of the infant Mary Queen of Scots in 1543. The ruins of the church and cloisters are situated on an island in the Lake of Monteith.

Open Apr-Sep, weekdays 9.30-6, Sun 2-6. (Closed in winter). Ferry subject to cancellation in adverse weather conditions, advisable to phone.
£1.70 (concessions 90p). Family ticket £4.50. Includes ferry.
shop ✈
(AM)

Mar's Wark STIRLING

Map 11 NS79
Broad St
☎ 031-244 3101
Now partly ruined, this Renaissance-style mansion was built in 1570 by the 1st Earl of Mar, Regent of Scotland. With its gatehouse enriched with sculptures, it is one of several fine

buildings on the road to Stirling Castle. The Earls of Mar lived there until the 6th Earl fled the country after leading the 1715 Jacobite Rebellion.
Open at all times.
Free.
(AM)

Museum of Argyll & Sutherland Highlanders STIRLING

Map 11 NS79
☎ (0786) 75165
Situated in King James V's Palace in Stirling Castle, the museum tells the history of the Regiment from 1794 to the present day. Displays include uniforms, silver, paintings, colours, pipe banners, and commentaries. There is a

fine medal collection covering the period from the Battle of Waterloo to the present day.
Open Etr-Sep, Mon-Sat 10-5.30, Sun 11-5; Oct, Mon-Fri 10-4.
✱ *Entry to museum free but entry fee to castle.*
☕ *shop* ✈

Smith Art Gallery & Museum STIRLING

Map 11 NS79
Dumbarton Rd
☎ (0786) 71917
This lively, award-winning museum and gallery presents a variety of exhibitions drawing on its own rich collections and works from elsewhere. A range of programmes and events offers the opportunity to see, find out about and

join in art, history, craft and design. There is a small shop.
Open all year, Apr-Oct, Tue-Sat 10.30-5, Sun 2-5; Nov-Mar Tue-Fri 12-5, Sat 10.30-5 & Sun 2-5.
☕ ♿ *(wheelchair lift) toilets for disabled shop* ✈
Details not confirmed for 1992

Places to visit in this guide are pinpointed on the atlas at the back of the book.

Stirling Castle STIRLING

Map 11 NS79
Upper Castle Hill
☎ 031-244 3101

Sitting on top of a 250ft rock, Stirling Castle has a strategic position on the Firth of Forth. As a result it has been the scene of many events in Scotland's history. Much of the castle that remains today is from the 15th and 16th

centuries, when it became a favourite royal residence. James II was born at the castle in 1430. Mary Queen of Scots spent some years there, and it was James IV's childhood home. The old towers were built by James IV, as was the fine great hall. Among its finest features are the splendid Renaissance palace built by James V, and the Chapel Royal, rebuilt by James VI.
Open all year, Oct-Dec & 4 Jan-Mar, Mon-Sat 9.30-4.20 (last ticket sold), Sun 12.30-3.35 (last ticket sold). Apr-Sep, Mon-Sat 9.30-5.15, (last ticket sold). Sun 10.30-4.45 (last ticket sold). (Closed 24-26 Dec & 31 Dec-3 Jan).
£2.30 (concessions £1.20). Family ticket £6.
🅿 ☕ *shop* ✈
(AM)

Stirling Castle Visitor Centre STIRLING

Map 11 NS79
Upper Castle Hill, Castle Esplanade
☎ (0786) 62517
The centre has an exhibition with an audio-visual display on the history of Stirling Castle. It is situated in a restored old building overlooking the River Forth. There is also a shop.
Open Visitor Centre all year (ex Jan); Oct-

Mar, Mon-Sat 9.30-5.05, Sun 12.30-4.20; Apr-Sep, Mon-Sat 9.30-6 & Sun 10.30-5.30. (Last entry 45 minutes before closing).
Charge for audio visual, 60p (ch & pen 30p).
🅿 ☕ ♿ *(Induction loop for the hard of hearing) shop* ✈
(NTS)

DUMFRIES & GALLOWAY

Ardwell House Gardens   ARDWELL

Map 10 NX14
(10m from Stranraer, on A716)
Country house gardens and grounds
with flowering shrubs and woodland
walks. Plants for sale. House not open
to the public.
Open Mar-Oct, 10-6.
✻ *£1 (ch & pen 50p).*
🅿

Caerlaverock Castle   CAERLAVEROCK

Map 11 NY06
Glencaple (8m SE of Dumfries on
B725)
☎ 031-244 3101
This ancient seat of the Maxwell family
is a splendid medieval stronghold dating
back to the 13th century. It has high
walls and round towers, with
machicolations added in the 15th
century.
*Open all year, Apr-Sep, weekdays 9.30-7,
Sun 2-7; Oct-Mar 9.30-4, Sun 2-4.
(Closed 25-26 Dec & 1-2 Jan).
£1.20 (concessions 60p).*
🅿 & *shop* ✖
(AM)

Wildfowl & Wetlands Trust   CAERLAVEROCK

Map 11 NY06
Eastpark Farm
☎ Glencaple (038777) 200
This is an exciting wildlife refuge of over
100 acres on the north Solway shore.
There are outstanding hide facilities,
observation towers and an observatory
giving impressive views of the huge
numbers of wildfowl that spend most of
the winter here. The barnacle geese are
the most impressive sight. Thousands of
them fly in from their Spitsbergen
breeding grounds to rest and feed in the
waters and marshes. Pink-footed and
greylag geese can also be seen, as can
waders, whooper swans and ducks such
as pintails and wigeons. These in turn
may attract interesting predators such as
peregrines and merlins. The 'merse', or
salt marsh, is also a home of the rare
natterjack toad.
*Open mid Sep-Apr, 9.30-5 (Closed 24-25
Dec).*
🅿 & ✖
Details not confirmed for 1992

✻ An asterisk indicates that up-to-date information was
not available at the time of our research – 1991
information has been published as an
indication of what you may expect.

Cardoness Castle   CARDONESS CASTLE

Map 11 NX55
(1m SW of Gatehouse of Fleet off A75)
☎ 031-244 3101
A 15th-century stronghold overlooking
the Water of Fleet. It was once the
home of the McCullochs of Galloway.
*Open all year, Apr-Sep, weekdays 9.30-6,
Sun 2-6; Oct-Mar, wknds only. (Closed
25-26 Dec & 1-2 Jan).
£1 (concessions 50p).*
🅿
(AM)

Threave Castle   CASTLE DOUGLAS

Map 11 NX76
(3m W on A75)
☎ 031-244 3101
Archibald the Grim built this lonely
castle in the late 14th century. It stands
on an islet in the River Dee, and is four
storeys high with round towers guarding
the outer wall. Access to the island is by
rowing boat.
*Open Apr-Sep, Mon-Sat 9.30-6, Sun 2-6.
Ferry charge £1 (concessions 50p).*
🅿 *shop* ✖
(AM)

Threave Garden   CASTLE DOUGLAS

Map 11 NX76
(1m W of Castle Douglas off A75)
☎ (0556) 2575

The best time to visit is in spring when
there is a dazzling display of some 200
varieties of daffodil. The garden has
something to see all year round,
however, and includes a walled garden
and glasshouses. The house is the
National Trust for Scotland's School of
Horticulture.
*Open all year. Garden, daily 9-sunset.
Visitor centre, Shop & Exhibition Apr-Oct
daily 9-5.30. (Last entry 30 minutes before
closing).
£2.80 (ch & pen £1.40). Party.*
🅿 ✖ *licensed* & *(wheelchairs available)
toilets for disabled shop garden centre* ✖
(NTS)

Comlongon Castle   CLARENCEFIELD

Map 11 NY06
☎ (038787) 283
An exceptionally well-preserved 15th-
century Border castle currently being
restored. It contains many original
features including dungeons, kitchen,
great hall, Heraldic devices, and bed
chambers with 'privies'. It's set in
gardens and woodland with secluded
walks, and is haunted by a 16th-century
suicide. Special events for 1992 include:
Guided walks by candlelight, followed
by candle-lit dinners.
*Open Mar-Oct
£1.10 (ch & pen 75p)*
🅿 & ✖

Creetown Gem Rock Museum   CREETOWN

Map 11 NX45
Chain Rd (follow signs from A75)
☎ (067182) 357 & 554
The museum displays gemstones and
minerals collected by the owners from
around the world. The beautiful
collection also includes gemstone *objets
d'art*. There are three large exhibition
halls and a gemstone workshop. The
Crystal Cave is a major new display,
built to commemorate the museum's
tenth anniversary. There is also a new
display of replicas of the world's largest
diamonds, all 'facet cut'.
*Open Etr-Oct, daily 9.30-6; Nov-24 Dec &
Mar-Etr, wknds 10-4. (Closed Xmas &
New Year). By appointment only Jan-Feb.*
✻ *£1.50 (ch 5-15 75p, students & pen
£1).*
🅿 ☕ & *shop*

Places to visit in this guide are pinpointed on the atlas
at the back of the book.

Drumcoltran Tower   DRUMCOLTRAN TOWER

Map 11 NX86
(7m NE of Dalbeattie)
☎ 031-244 3101
The 16th-century tower house stands
three storeys high and has a simple,
functional design.
*Open at any reasonable time.
Free.*
✖
(AM)

Burns House   DUMFRIES

Map 11 NX97
Burns St
☎ (0387) 55297
Robert Burns lived in the house for
three years before his death in 1796, and
his wife, Jean Armour, lived here until
she died in 1834. Various relics of the
poet are displayed.
*Open all year, Mon-Sat 10-1 & 2-5, Sun
2-5. (Closed Sun & Mon, Oct-Mar).*
✻ *70p (ch, pen, students & UB40's 35p).*

Burns Mausoleum   DUMFRIES

Map 11 NX97
St Michael's Churchyard
☎ (0387) 55297
The mausoleum is in the form of a
Greek temple, and contains the tombs of
Robert Burns, his wife Jean Armour,
and their five sons. A sculptured group
shows the Muse of Poetry flinging her
cloak over Burns at the plough.
*Viewed at any time, for access contact
attendant at Burns House.
Free.*

Dumfries Museum & Camera Obscura   DUMFRIES

Map 11 NX97
The Observatory, Church St
☎ (0387) 53374
The museum has large collections on the
Solway area, and is also worth visiting
for its camera obscura. A branch
museum is the Old Bridge House (on
the Old Bridge) with period rooms
showing local life in the past.
*Open all year, Mon-Sat 10-1 & 2-5, Sun
2-5. (Closed Sun & Mon, Oct-Mar;
Camera Obscura closed Oct-Mar).
Free except Camera Obscura 75p
(concessions 35p).*
& *toilets for disabled shop*

Robert Burns Centre   DUMFRIES

Map 11 NX97
Mill Rd
☎ (0387) 64808
The centre has an exhibition and an
audio-visual display on the poet.
*Open all year, Apr-Sep, Mon-Sat 10-8,
Sun 2-5; Oct-Mar, Tue-Sat 10-1 & 2-5.
Free except audio-visual theatre 75p
(concessions 35p).*
🅿 ☕ ✖ *licensed* & *(Induction loop
hearing system in auditorium) toilets for
disabled shop*

Dundrennan Abbey   DUNDRENNAN

Map 11 NX74
(6.5m SE of Kirkcudbright)
☎ 031-244 3101
The ruined abbey was founded for the
Cistercians. Mary Queen of Scots is
thought to have spent her last night in
Scotland here on 15 May 1568, before
seeking shelter in England, where she
was imprisoned and eventually executed.
*Open all year, Apr-Sep, weekdays 9.30-6,
Sun 2-6; Oct-Mar, weekdays 9.30-4, Sun
2-4. (Closed 25-26 Dec & 1-2 Jan). Key
with keeper in winter.
£1 (concessions 50p).*
🅿 ✖
(AM)

Ellisland Farm   ELLISLAND FARM

Map 11 NX98
☎ Dumfries (0387) 74426
Robert Burns lived at this farm on the
west bank of the Nith from 1788 to
1791. He tried to introduce new
farming methods, but eventually had to
give up and became an exciseman. While
here, he composed *Tam o'Shanter*,
Auld Lang Syne and other poems and
songs. Material associated with the poet
is displayed.
*Open all year, daily 10-5. Groups are
advised to telephone in advance.*
🅿 & *shop*
Details not confirmed for 1992

Glenluce Abbey   GLENLUCE

Map 10 NX15
(2m N of village)
☎ 031-244 3101
The abbey was founded for the
Cistercians in 1192 by Roland, Earl of
Galloway. The ruins include a vaulted
chapter house, and stand in a beautiful
setting.
*Open all year, Apr-Sep, weekdays 9.30-6,
Sun 2-6; Oct-Mar, wknds only 2-4. (Closed
25-26 Dec & 1-2 Jan).
£1 (concessions 50p).*
🅿 ☕ ✖
(AM)

Arbigland Gardens   KIRKBEAN

Map 11 NX95
(1m SE, adjacent to Paul Jones cottage).
☎ (038788) 283
Extensive woodland, formal and water gardens are set around a delightful sandy bay which is ideal for children. John Paul Jones, the US Admiral, worked in the gardens as a young boy (his father

was the gardener here in the 1740s). His birthplace can be seen nearby; it will be opened officially as a museum mid-July.
Open Gardens May-Sep, Wed-Sun 2-6. House 21-31 May. Also open BH Mon. £2 (ch 50p).
🅿 🚻 ♿ *toilets for disabled shop*

MacLellan's Castle   KIRKCUDBRIGHT

Map 11 NX65
☎ 031-244 3101
This handsome structure has been a ruin since the mid-18th-century: it was once an imposing castellated mansion, elaborately planned with fine architectural detail. Something of its

16th-century grandeur still remains.
Open all year, Apr-Sep, weekdays 9.30-6, Sun 2-6; Oct-Mar, Sat 9.30-4, Sun 2-4. (Closed 25-26 Dec & 1-2 Jan). £1 (concessions 50p).
♿ *shop* ✗
(AM)

Stewartry Museum   KIRKCUDBRIGHT

Map 11 NX65
Saint Mary St
☎ (0557) 31643
A large and varied collection of archaeological, social history and natural history exhibits relating to the

Stewartry district.
Open Etr-Oct, Mon-Sat 11-4 (Jul-Aug 7.30pm & Sun 2-5); Nov-Etr, Sat only 11-4.
£1 (ch free, pen & concessions 50p).
♿ *shop* ✗

For an explanation of the symbols and abbreviations, see page 2.

Craigcleuch Collection   LANGHOLM

Map 11 NY38
(2m NW Langholm on B709)
☎ (03873) 80137
Baronial stone mansion house with collection of ancient artefacts in wood, jade, ivory and coral, and hundreds of rare tribal sculptures and Prehistoric stone pipes, carved as animals and birds.

Also Oriental paintings and panoramic views overlooking the 'Gates of Eden' woodland walks.
Open Etr wknd, BH & May-15 Sep, Mon-Sat 10-5.30. Other times by appointment.
🅿 ♿ *shop*
Details not confirmed for 1992

New Abbey Corn Mill   NEW ABBEY

Map 11 NX96
(8m S of Dumfries on A710)
☎ 031-244 3101
Built in the late 18th century, this water-driven corn mill is still in working order.
Open all year, Apr-Sep, weekdays 9.30-7,

Sun 2-7; Oct-Mar, weekdays 9.30-4, Sun 2-4. (Closed Thu pm & Fri in winter; 25-26 Dec & 1-2 Jan).
£1.20 (concessions 60p).
shop ✗
(AM)

Shambellie House Museum of Costume   NEW ABBEY

Map 11 NX96
(0.25m N on A710)
☎ (038785) 375 & 031-225 7534
Displayed in this small mid-Victorian house is a collection of fashionable European dress, dating from the late 1700s to the early part of this century.

Each year there is a new exhibition of material from Charles Stewart's admirable collection.
Open May-Sep, Thu-Mon 10-5.30, Sun noon-5.30.
Free.
🅿 *shop* ✗

Sweetheart Abbey   NEW ABBEY

Map 11 NX96
☎ 031-244 3101
Lady Devorgilla of Galloway founded Balliol College in Oxford in memory of her husband John Balliol; she also founded an abbey in his memory in 1273. When she died in 1289 she was buried in front of the high altar with the heart of her husband resting on her bosom; hence the name 'Sweetheart Abbey'. This monument, inspired by

love and loyalty, now stands as one of Scotland's most beautiful ruins. It features an unusual precinct wall of enormous boulders.
Open all year, Apr-Sep weekdays 9.30-6, Sun 2-6; Oct-Mar, wkdys 9.30-4, Sun 2-4. (Closed 25-26 Dec & 1-2 Jan). £1 (ch 50p).
🅿 ♿ *(with assistance) shop* ✗
(AM)

Orchardton Tower   PALNACKIE

Map 11 NX85
(6m SE of Castle Douglas)
☎ 031-244 3101
John Cairns built this rare example of a circular tower in the late 15th century.

Open all reasonable times, on application to key keeper. (Closed 25-26 Dec & 1-2 Jan).
Free.
🅿 ✗
(AM)

Logan Botanic Garden   PORT LOGAN

Map 10 NX04
☎ Stranraer (0776) 86231
This specialist section of the Royal Botanic Garden of Edinburgh contains a wide range of plants from the warm, temperate regions of the southern

hemisphere, protected in a walled garden.
Open 15 Mar-Oct, daily 10-6.
£1.50 (ch & concessions £1).
🅿 🚻 ♿ *toilets for disabled shop* ✗

SAVINGS BANK MUSEUM
Situated at Ruthwell on the Solway Coast Heritage Trail. The exhibition highlights the life of the Founder and the international spread of the Banking movement. No admission charge. Large parties by appointment.
Telephone: Clarencefield 640
Open: Daily all year 10am-1pm and 2pm-5pm, except Sundays and Mondays from October to March

Ruthwell Cross   RUTHWELL

Map 11 NY16
(off B724)
☎ 031-244 3101
Now in a specially built apse in the parish church, the carved cross dates from the 7th or 8th centuries. Two faces show scenes from the Life of Christ; the others show scroll work, and parts of an ancient poem in Runic characters. It was

broken up in the 18th century, but pieced together by a 19th-century minister.
Open all reasonable times. Key from Key Keeper, Kirkyett Cottage, Ruthwell.
Free.
🅿 ✗
(AM)

Savings Banks Museum   RUTHWELL

Map 11 NY16
(6m W of Annan)
☎ Clarencefield (038787) 640
Housed in the building where Savings Banks first began, the museum traces their growth and development from 1810 up to the present day. Exhibits include original letters, books and

papers.
The museum also traces the life of Dr Henry Duncan, father of savings banks, and restorer of the Ruthwell Cross.
Open all year, daily (ex Sun & Mon Oct-Mar), 10-1 & 2-5.
Free.
🅿 ♿ *(touch facilities for blind)* ✗

Castle Kennedy Gardens   STRANRAER

Map 10 NX06
Stair Estates (3m E on A75)
☎ (0776) 2024
Situated on a peninsula between two lochs, the gardens around the Old Castle were first laid out in the early 18th century and, after years of neglect, were restored and developed in the 19th. They are noted for their flowering shrubs (at their best in May and early

June) and walled kitchen garden with fine herbaceous borders (best in August and September). The gardens contain many avenues and walks amid some beautiful scenery.
Open Apr-Sep, daily 10-5.
✱ *£1.80 (ch 15 50p, pen £1). Party 30+.*
🅿 🚻 ♿ *toilets for disabled shop garden centre*

Places to visit in this guide are pinpointed on the atlas at the back of the book.

Drumlanrig Castle   THORNHILL

Map 11 NX89
(4m NW off A76 on west bank of River Nith).
☎ (0848) 31682 & 30248

This unusual, pink sandstone castle was built in the late 17th century in Renaissance style. Ringed by rugged hills, the castle was erected on the site of

earlier Douglas strongholds. It contains a celebrated collection of paintings by Rembrandt, Da Vinci, Holbein, Murillo and many others. There is also French furniture, mainly Louis XIV, as well as silver and relics of Bonnie Prince Charlie. The old stable block has a craft centre with resident craft workers, a gift shop, tearoom and a visitor's centre. The grounds offer an extensive garden, and adventure woodland play area and woodland walks.
Open – Castle May-Aug, wkdays 11-5, Sun 1-5 (Closed Sat). Last admission 4pm. Grounds May-Sep, daily.
✱ *House & Grounds £3 (ch 5-16 £1, pen & student £2). Grounds only £1. Party.*
🅿 🚻 ♿ *(lift) toilets for disabled shop* ✗ *(ex in park)*

Tongland Tour   TONGLAND

Map 11 NX65
☎ Kirkcudbright (0557) 30114
This tour of part of the Scottish Power Galloway hydro-electricity scheme includes a video presentation and a visit to the dam and the power station. There is a fish ladder at the dam which

provides the chance to see salmon returning to their spawning grounds.
Open 22 May-5 Sep, Mon-Sat 10 & 11.30, 2 & 3.30, by telephone appointment.
Admission fee payable.
🅿 *shop* 🚌

CASTLE KENNEDY GARDENS

STRANRAER : WIGTOWNSHIRE

The Gardens are situated on a peninsula between two lochs and are nationally famous for their rhododendrons, azaleas, magnolias and embothriums. They are set in extensive grounds and offer a range of interesting and varied walks.

OPEN DAILY EASTER TO END SEPTEMBER 10 a.m. to 5 p.m.

Situated 3 miles East of Stranraer on the A75 Stranraer-Dumfries Road.

PLANT CENTRE.
Light refreshments available.

Admission:
Adults £1.80, OAPs £1.00, Children 50p.
Discount for groups over 30 people.

For further information contact:
Stair Estates, Estates Office, Rephad, Stranraer.
Phone 0776-2024

Museum of Lead Mining — WANLOCKHEAD

Map 11 NS81
(on B797 at N end of Mennock Pass).
☎ Leadhills (0659) 74387
The museum conserves, displays and interprets the physical and written evidence of lead mining in Scotland. There is also an interesting collection of local gold, silver and other minerals on display. A one-and-a-half-mile walkway takes the visitor to an 18th-century lead mine, smelt mill and miners' cottages furnished in the styles of 1740 and 1890. An unusual feature is a Miners'

Reading Society library, which was founded in 1756. In 1992 the museum will display a new collection of rare minerals, all found locally. There will also be a new exhibition on gold to celebrate Wanlockhead's hosting of the 1992 world gold panning championships.
Open 17 Apr-mid Oct, daily 11-4.30 (last mine tour 4pm).
£2.50 (ch 5-16 £1, concessions £1.80).
🅿 ♿ *toilets for disabled shop*

✳ An asterisk indicates that up-to-date information was not available at the time of our research – 1991 information has been published as an indication of what you may expect.

Whithorn Dig — WHITHORN

Map 11 NX44
45-47 George St
☎ (09885) 508
Archaeologists are carefully uncovering 1,500 years of history of Scotland's first-recorded Christian settlement. There are site tours and viewing platforms. Admission also includes the new visitor

centre, picture show, exhibitions, Whithorn Priory (see below), museum and crypts, herb garden, gift shop, craft demonstrations and children's play area.
Open Etr-Oct.
✳ *£2.50 (ch, pen & UB40's £1.25).*
Family ticket £7. Season ticket. Party.
♿ *toilets for disabled shop*

Whithorn Priory — WHITHORN

Map 11 NX44
☎ 031-244 3101
The first Christian church in Scotland was founded here by St Ninian in 397, but the present ruins date from the 12th century. The ruins are scanty but there is a notable Norman door, the Latinus stone of the 5th century and other early

Christian monuments.
Open all year, Apr-Sep weekdays 9.30-6, Sun 2-6; Oct-Mar, wkdys 9.30-4, Sun 2-4. (Closed Mon-Fri in winter, 25-26 Dec & 1-2 Jan).
£1 (concessions 50p).
♿ ✖
(AM)

FIFE

Aberdour Castle — ABERDOUR

Map 11 NT18
☎ 031-244 3101
The earliest surviving part of the castle is the 14th-century keep. There are also later buildings, and the remains of a terraced garden, a bowling green and a fine 16th-century doocot (dovecote).

Open all year, Apr-Sep, Mon-Sat 9.30-6, Sun 2-6; Oct-Mar, Mon-Sat 9.30-4, Sun 2-4. (Closed Thu pm, Fri in winter, 25-26 Dec & 1-2 Jan).
£1.20 (concessions 60p).
🅿 ♿ *shop* ✖
(AM)

Scottish Fisheries Museum — ANSTRUTHER

Map 11 NO50
St Ayles, Harbour Head
☎ (0333) 310628
A cobbled courtyard at the harbour is the setting for the displays on Scotland's fishing history. Chief attractions are the boats (real and model), the marine aquarium, and the fishermans cottage. The museum is housed in a range of

16th-19th century buildings. A special exhibition, 'The Viking legacy', will be held between Mar and Apr.
Open all year, Apr-Oct, Mon-Sat 10-5.30, Sun 11-5; Nov-Mar, Mon-Sat 10-5, Sun 2-5. (Closed 25 Dec & 1 Jan).
✳ *£1.60 (ch & pen 90p). Party 12+.*
🎫 ♿ *toilets for disabled shop* ✖

Burntisland Edwardian Fair Museum — BURNTISLAND

Map 11 NT28
102 High St
☎ Kirkcaldy (0592) 260732
All the fun of the fair at this Scottish Museum of the Year award winner. Burntisland Museum has recreated a walk through the sights and sounds of the town's fair in 1910, based on a

painting of the scene by local artist Andrew Young. See rides, stalls and side shows of the time and view the local history gallery.
Open all year, Mon-Sat 10-1 & 2-5. (Closed Sun & BH Mon's).
Free.
🅿 ✖

This is just one of many guidebooks published by the AA. The full range is available at any AA shop or good bookshop.

Fife Folk Museum — CERES

Map 11 NO41
The Weigh House, High St (on B939)
☎ (033482) 380 (curator's home)
This comprehensive regional collection is displayed in a 17th-century weigh house and other buildings. Local crafts, farming and trades are illustrated with tools and

other items of a social and domestic nature in an attractive and informative way.
Open Apr-Oct, Mon & Wed-Sun 2.15-5.
✳ *£1.30 (ch 50p, pen £1).*
♿ *shop* ✖

Culross Abbey — CULROSS

Map 11 NS98
☎ 031-244 3101
The Cistercian monastery was founded by Malcolm, Earl of Fife, in 1217. The choir is still used as the parish church, and parts of the old nave remain. The

fine central tower still stands complete.
Open at all reasonable times. (Closed 25-26 Dec & 1-2 Jan).
Free.
✖
(AM)

Culross Palace — CULROSS

Map 11 NS98
☎ (0383) 880608
Dated 1597 and 1611, and noted for the painted rooms and terraced gardens. The palace is closed for restoration for up to two years, but visitors are welcome to

view the building externally.
Open all year. Under repair, interior not accessible, can be viewed from outside. Admssion fee payable.
✖
(NTS)

Town House & The Study — CULROSS

Map 11 NS98
(off A985)
☎ New Mills (0383) 880359
Culross is unique – a Royal Burgh that has remained virtually unchanged for 200 years. It dates mostly from the 16th and 17th centuries, when it prospered by the coal and salt trades developed by Sir George Bruce. When business declined in the 1700s, Culross stayed as it was, unable to afford improvements like wider streets. Its present appearance is due to the National Trust for Scotland, which has been gradually restoring the burgh since the 1930s. The aim has been to provide modern living standards without destroying the burgh's character, and the small houses with their red-pantiled roofs are still lived in by local people.

The Trust has a visitor centre and exhibition in the Town House (1626). The house called The Study (1610) is also open for visitors to view the Norwegian painted ceiling in the drawing room. The first building bought by the Trust in Culross was The Palace, home of Sir George Bruce. It has terraced gardens and painted rooms (closed during '92 for restoration). Many other buildings can be seen from the outside.
Open – House 17-20 Apr & May-Sep, daily 11-1 and 2-5. Study 4 Apr-Oct, Sat & Sun 2-4 also by appointment. House 90p (ch & pen 50p). Study 60p (ch & pen 30p).
⛬ ✠
(NTS)

Hill of Tarvit Mansion House & Garden — CUPAR

Map 11 NO31
(2.5m S off A916)
☎ (0334) 53127
Sir Robert Lorimer virtually rebuilt this Edwardian house. It has a notable collection of furniture, tapestries and paintings, regular exhibitions of local artists' work, a walled garden, nursery,

video and adventure playground.
Open 4-30 Apr, Sat & Sun; 17-20 Apr & May-Oct, daily 2-6. (Last admission 5.30). Garden & grounds all year, daily 10-sunset.
✱ *House & Garden £2.80 (ch & pen £1.40). Garden only £1 (ch 50p). Party.*
🅿 ☕ ⛬ shop ✠
(NTS)

The Scottish Deer Centre — CUPAR

Map 11 NO31
Bow-of-Fife (3m W on A91)
☎ Letham (033781) 391
Guided tours take about 30 minutes and allow visitors to meet and stroke deer. Children can help with bottle-feeding young fawns, and facilities include farm, nature and heritage trails. A film presentation and exhibition are provided. Aerial walkways and observation platforms are a special feature, allowing

better views of several species of deer and the landscape. There is a large Adventureland and indoor playroom for children.
Open daily, Apr-Oct 10-5 (summer 6pm). Nov-Dec & Mar Sat-Sun only 10-5 (or dusk). (Closed Jan-Feb).
✱ *£3.05 (ch £1.95, concessions £2.50). Family ticket £8.25. Party 10+.*
🅿 ✗ *licensed* ⛬ *(special parking bay, loan of wheelchairs) toilets for disabled shop* ✠

Places to visit in this guide are pinpointed on the atlas at the back of the book.

Andrew Carnegie Birthplace Museum — DUNFERMLINE

Map 11 NT08
Moodie St
☎ (0383) 724302
The museum tells the story of the humble handloom weaver's son who was born here in 1835, created the biggest steel works in the USA, and then became a philanthropist on a huge scale. The present-day work of the philanthropic Carnegie Trust is also

explained. Weaving days will be held on the first Friday of every month (May-Oct); on these days, the restored jacquard handloom will be worked by a member of the Angus Handloom Weavers.
Open all year, Apr-Oct, Mon-Sat 11-5, Sun 2-5; Nov-Mar 2-4.
✱ *Free. Donations.*
🅿 ☕ ⛬ *toilets for disabled shop* ✠

Dunfermline Abbey — DUNFERMLINE

Map 11 NT08
Pittencrieff Park
☎ 031-244 3101

The monastery was a powerful Benedictine house, founded by Queen Margaret in the 11th century. The foundations of her church still lie

beneath the nave of a later, more elaborate Norman nave. The site of the choir is occupied by a modern parish church, at the east end of which are the remains of the 13th-century St Margaret's shrine. The grave of King Robert the Bruce is marked by a modern brass in the choir. The monastery guest house became a royal palace, and was the birthplace of Charles 1. The ruins of other monastic buildings can be seen.
Open all year, Apr-Sep, weekdays 9.30-7, Sun 2-7; Oct-Mar, weekdays 9.30-4, Sun 2-4. (Closed Thu pm & Fri in winter; 25-26 Dec & 1-2 Jan).
£1.20 (concessions 60p).
🅿 ⛬ *(Nave and perimeter only) shop* ✠
(AM)

Dunfermline District Museum — DUNFERMLINE

Map 11 NT08
Viewfield Ter
☎ (0383) 721814
Interesting and varied displays on local history are shown, including domestic articles and damask linen – an important local product. The Small Gallery has

changing art and craft exhibitions every month, and special exhibitions are a regular feature.
Open all year, Mon-Sat 11-5. (Closed Sun & PHs).
Free.
shop ✠

Pittencrieff House Museum — DUNFERMLINE

Map 11 NT08
Pittencrieff Park
☎ (0383) 722935
The fine 17th-century mansion house stands in a park in the rugged glen, with lawns, hothouses and gardens, and the 11th-century tower of Malcolm Canmore. In the house itself there are

galleries with displays of costume and local history. Temporary art exhibitions are shown in the top gallery.
Open 1st wknd May-last wknd-Oct, Wed-Mon 11-5.
Free.
⛬ *shop* ✠

Falkland Palace & Garden — FALKLAND

Map 11 NO20
(off A912)
☎ (0337) 57397

The hunting palace of the Stuart Kings and Queens, situated below the Lomond Hills. The French Renaissance style of

the south range is admired as the best of its kind in Britain. The palace is also noted for the beautiful interiors of the Chapel Royal and the King's Bedchamber, and for the royal tennis court of 1539, the oldest in Britain. There is a visitor centre, and in the town hall, a display of the history of the palace and the royal burgh.
Open Apr-Sep, Mon-Sat 10-6, Sun 2-6. Oct, Mon-Sat 10-5, Sun 2-5. (Last admission 1hr before closing). Palace & Garden £3 (ch & pen £1.50). Garden only £2 (ch & pen £1).
🅿 ⛬ *shop* ✠
(NTS)

Kellie Castle & Gardens — KELLIE CASTLE & GARDENS

Map 11 NO50
(3m NW of Pittenweem on B9171)
☎ Arncroach (03338) 271
The oldest part of this castle dates from about 1360, but it is as a fine example of 16th- and 17th-century domestic architecture that Kellie is renowned. Inside the most notable features are the plasterwork and the panelling, which is painted with romantic landscapes, and furniture designed by Sir Robert Lorimer. The castle has a Victorian nursery, an old kitchen, and four acres

of gardens. There are also audio-visual shows.
Open – Castle 4-30 Apr, Sat-Sun 2-6; 17-20 Apr & May-Oct, daily 2-6 (last admission 5.30). Gardens & grounds open all year 10-sunset. Castle & gardens £2.80 (ch & pen £1.40); Gardens only £1 (ch accompanied by adult & pen 50p). Party 20+.
🅿 ☕ ⛬ *(Induction loop for the hard of hearing) shop* ✠
(NTS)

Museum & Art Gallery — KIRKCALDY

Map 11 NT29
War Memorial Gardens (next to Station)
☎ (0592) 260732
A unique collection of Scottish paintings, arts, crafts and historical displays with unusual 'please touch' sections, make a visit to this inspiring

museum well worthwhile. 1992 sees the introduction of a major exhibition on the history of linoleum.
Open all year, Mon-Sat 11-5, Sun 2-5. (Closed Local Hols).
Free.
🅿 ☕ ⛬ *toilets for disabled shop* ✠

Ravenscraig Castle — KIRKCALDY

Map 11 NT29
☎ 031-244 3101
Although it is now little more than an impressive ruin, the 15th-century edifice of Ravenscraig Castle is noted for its symmetrical design; it was perhaps the first British castle to be built with defence by firearms in mind.

Open all year, Apr-Sep, weekdays 9.30-6, Sun 2-6; Oct-Mar, wkdys 9.30-4, Sun 2-4. (Closed Thu pm & Fri in winter; 25-26 Dec & 1-2 Jan). 80p (concessions 40p).
🅿 ⛬
(AM)

Earlshall Castle — LEUCHARS

Map 11 NO42
☎ (0334) 839205
Built with 5ft-thick walls, battlements and gun loops, Earlshall Castle is a fine example of a 16th-century Scottish stronghold. A renowned feature of its interior is the painted ceiling in the Long Gallery depicting mythological beasts and the arms of the principal families of Scotland. There is also a wealth of old timber panelling, Jacobite relics, arms

and armour, antique furniture, porcelain and paintings exhibited throughout the castle. The gardens contain a notable feature too, in the form of topiary yew chessmen, and the wooded parkland has a nature trail and picnic facilities. There is a Craft Festival 13 Jul-3 August.
Open Etr Fri-Mon, Sun in Apr then daily May-Sep, 2-6. (Last admission 5.15). £2.80 (ch £1, pen £2.20). Party.
🅿 ☕ *shop* ✠

British Golf Museum — ST ANDREWS

Map 11 NO51
Bruce Embankment
☎ (0334) 78880
Tells the history of golf with highly visual displays, complemented by the use of visitor-activated touch screens throughout the galleries. Exhibits take the visitor from the misty origins of the game, through to the present day. You'll see amazing images, fascinating

collections of clubs, balls, fashion and memorabilia, two period workshops and historic documents. An audio-visual theatre shows historic golfing moments.
Open all year, May-Oct daily 10-5.30; Mar-Apr Thu-Tue 10-5; Nov Thu-Tue 11-3; Jan-Feb & Dec Thu-Mon 11-3. £3 (ch £1, pen & students £2). Family ticket £7.50
🅿 *(charged)* ⛬ *toilets for disabled shop* ✠

Castle — ST ANDREWS

Map 11 NO51
☎ 031-244 3101
This 13th-century stronghold castle was the setting for the murder of Cardinal Beaton in 1546. Only its ruins now remain.

Open all year, Apr-Sep, weekdays 9.30-6, Sun 2-6; Oct-Mar, weekdays 9.30-4, Sun 2-4. (Closed 25-26 Dec & 1-2 Jan).
£1 (ch & pen 50p).
&. shop ✖
(AM)

✖ The 'No Dogs' symbol does not normally apply to guide dogs – these are permitted in most establishments.

Cathedral (& Museum) — ST ANDREWS

Map 11 NO51
☎ 031-244 3101
The cathedral was the largest in Scotland, and is now an extensive ruin. The remains date mainly from the 12th and 13th centuries, and large parts of the precinct walls have survived intact. Close by is St Rule's church, which the cathedral was built to replace. St Rule's probably dates from before the Norman Conquest, and is considered the most interesting Romanesque church in Scotland.

The museum is housed in a 14th-century building and contains an important collection of Celtic and medieval sculpture and artefacts. There is also a fascinating array of later gravestones on display.
Open all year, Apr-Sep, weekdays 9.30-7, Sun 2-7; Oct-Mar, weekdays 9.30-4, Sun 2-4. (Closed 25-26 Dec & 1-2 Jan).
£1.20 (ch & pen 60p).
&. shop ✖
(AM)

GRAMPIAN

Aberdeen Art Gallery — ABERDEEN

Map 13 NJ90
Schoolhill
☎ (0224) 646333
The gallery's 16th- to 20th-century Scottish art includes an outstanding collection of modern paintings. Also here are watercolours, sculpture and decorative arts, and a print room and art

library. Special exhibitions and events all year.
Open all year, Mon-Sat 10-5 (8pm Thu) Sun 2-5. (Closed 25 & 26 Dec, 1 & 2 Jan).
🍴 &. toilets for disabled shop ✖
Details not confirmed for 1992

Aberdeen Maritime Museum — ABERDEEN

Map 13 NJ90
Provost Ross's House, Shiprow
☎ (0224) 585788
The museum is in Provost Ross's House, Aberdeen's third oldest building (1593). It highlights the city's maritime history, and its oil industry, in dramatic fashion. National Trust for Scotland

visitor centre and shop is open part of the year; at other times the area is used for special maritime exhibitions.
Open all year, Mon-Sat 10-5 (Closed 25-26 Dec & 1,2 Jan).
&. toilets for disabled shop ✖
Details not confirmed for 1992

Cruickshank Botanic Garden — ABERDEEN

Map 13 NJ90
University of Aberdeen, St Machar Drive,
☎ (0224) 272704
Developed at the end of the 19th century, the 11 acres include rock and water gardens, a heather garden, herbaceous plants and a patio garden.

There are collections of spring bulbs, gentians and alpine plants, and a fine array of trees and shrubs.
Open all year, Mon-Fri 9-4.30; also Sat & Sun, May-Sep 2-5.
Free.
&. ✖ 🚌

Every effort is made to provide accurate information, but details might change during the currency of this guide.

James Dun's House — ABERDEEN

Map 13 NJ90
61 Schoolhill
☎ (0224) 646333
This 18th-century house is used as a museum and puts on temporary exhibitions with special appeal for

families.
Open all year, Mon-Sat, 10-5. (Closed 25-26 Dec,1 & 2 Jan)
✖
Details not confirmed for 1992

Provost Skene's House — ABERDEEN

Map 13 NJ90
Guestrow
☎ (0224) 641086
The handsome old town mansion has notable decorated ceilings and panelling, and is now a museum of local history and social life, with rooms furnished in

period style. There is also an audio-visual display on the history of the house.
Open all year, Mon-Sat 10-5. (Closed 25 & 26 Dec, 1 & 2 Jan)
🍴 &. shop ✖
Details not confirmed for 1992

Satrosphere ("Hands-On" Science & Technology Centre) — ABERDEEN

Map 13 NJ90
19 Justice Mill Ln
☎ (0224) 213232
Satrosphere, the Discovery Place, is different from many museums or exhibition centres. It is a Science and Technology Exhibition Centre where everything is 'hands-on'. Displays aren't locked in glass cases and there are certainly no *Do Not Touch* signs. The emphasis is on doing and finding out, not just looking and standing back. There is a shop with exciting and unusual presents. Special events include

visits by 'Starlab' (an inflatable planetarium), Captain Cook, Sir Isaac Newton and many others. Theme events run for approximately one month and include such topics as Colour, Communication (Jan), Electricity (Feb), Festival of Toys, Health (Mar), and The Ground Beneath Your Feet (Apr).
Open all year, Mon-Sat 10-4, Sun 1.30-5. (Closed Tue, 25-26 & 31 Dec & 1 Jan).
✳ £2.75 (ch £1.25, concessions £1.25). Family ticket £4.25-£7.50.
🅿 (charged) 🍴 &. toilets for disabled shop ✖

Alford Valley Railway — ALFORD

Map 13 NJ51
☎ (09755) 62326
Narrow-gauge passenger railway in two sections: Alford-Haughton Park and Haughton Park-Murray Park approx one mile each. Steam on peak weekends.

Diesel traction. Exhibitions.
Open Apr, May & Sep wknds from 1-5, Jun-Aug daily from 11 (30 min service). Party bookings also available at other times. £1.30 (ch 70p) return fare.
🅿 &. shop

Grampian Transport Museum — ALFORD

Map 13 NJ51
☎ (09755) 62292
There is a strong local theme to this road and rail museum. Its large collection of vintage vehicles includes cycles and motorcycles, horse-drawn and steam vehicles, cars and lorries. 1992 events include Alford Cavalcade vintage

vehicle rally (26 July), Grampian Motorcycle Convention (16 September), Alford Auction and Autojumble (27 September).
Open 29 Mar-Oct, daily 10.30-5.
✳ £2 (ch 80p, pen £1.50).
🅿 &. toilets for disabled shop

The Glenlivet Distillery — BALLINDALLOCH

Map 13 NJ13
(Off B9008 10m N of Tomintoul).
☎ Glenlivet (08073) 427 & 471
(05422) 7471(winter)
The first licensed distillery in the Highlands. Produces the famous The Glenlivet 12-year-old single malt whisky. Visitors are shown round in parties of

not more than ten, and are offered a free sample. Exhibition area, audio visual display.
Open Etr-Oct, Mon-Sat 10-4. (Jul-Aug 10-7).
Free.
🅿 🍴 &. toilets for disabled shop ✖

Balmoral Castle Grounds & Exhibition — BALMORAL

Map 13 NO29
(on A93)
☎ Crathie (03397) 42334 & 42335

Balmoral is the focal point of what is now known as Royal Deeside, a landscape of woodlands and plantations sweeping up to grouse moors and distant

mountains. Queen Victoria and Prince Albert first rented Balmoral Castle in 1848, and Prince Albert bought the property four years later. He commissioned William Smith to build a new castle, which was completed by 1855 and is still the Royal Family's Highland residence. The wooded grounds and gardens can be visited from May to July when the Royal Family is not in residence. Country walks and pony trekking can be enjoyed, and an exhibition of paintings and other works of art can be seen in the castle ballroom.
Open May-Jul, Mon-Sat 10-5.
£1.75 (ch free, pen £1.25).
🍴 &. (wheelchairs available) toilets for disabled shop ✖ (ex in grounds)

BANCHORY
See map 13
See Crathes

Banff Museum   BANFF

Map 13 NJ66
High St
☎ Peterhead (0779) 77778
The museum has an exhibition of British birds, set out as an aviary. The bird display won the Glenfiddich Living

Scotland Award in 1989. Armour and items of local history are also on display.
Open Jun-Sep, Fri-Wed 2-5.20.
Free.
& shop ✝

Duff House   BANFF

Map 13 NJ66
(0.5m S, access south of town).
☎ (0261) 22872
The house was designed by William Adam for William Duff, later Earl of Fife. The main block was roofed in 1739, but the planned wings were never built. Although it is incomplete, the

house is still considered one of Britain's finest Georgian baroque buildings. There is an exhibition on its history.
Under repair, interior not accessible, can be viewed from outside.
Admission fee payable.
P ✝
(AM)

Braemar Castle   BRAEMAR

Map 13 NO19
(0.5m N on A93)
☎ (03397) 41219 & 41224 (out of season)
A picturesque castle beside the River Dee, Braemar was built in 1628 by the Earl of Mar, but burned in 1689 by The Black Colonel, and was largely rebuilt as

a garrison post after the 1745 rising. It is now a fully furnished residence of great charm, with many items of historic interest to be seen.
Open Etr-mid Oct, daily 10-6.
£1.45 (ch 13 75p). Special rate for pen & parties.
P & shop ✝ *(ex in grounds)*

This is just one of many guidebooks published by the AA.
The full range is available at any AA shop or good bookshop.

Brodie Castle   BRODIE CASTLE

Map 13 NH95
(4.5m W of Forres, off A96)
☎ Brodie (03094) 371
The Brodie family were granted land in this area in 1160, and lived in the castle for hundreds of years. It was passed to the National Trust for Scotland by the 25th Chief of the family in 1980. It is a handsome, gabled Scottish castle, and contains numerous treasures acquired over the centuries: fine furniture, porcelain, and an impressive collection of paintings including 17th-century Dutch works, 19th-century English watercolours and French Impressionists. The extensive grounds have woodland

walks, daffodils and a wildlife hide. There is also an adventure playground. Facilities for the disabled include wheelchair loan, purpose-built toilets for wheelchair users, audio tape and information in braille.
Open Apr-27 Sep, Mon-Sat 11-6, Sun 2-6; 3-18 Oct, Sat 11-6, Sun 2-6 (last admission 5.15). Other times by prior appointment. Grounds open all year, 9.30-sunset.
£3 (ch & pen £1.50). Party.
P ▼ & *(audio tape & information sheet in Braille)* ✝
(NTS)

Buckie Museum & Peter Anson Gallery   BUCKIE

Map 13 NJ46
☎ Forres (0309) 73701
This maritime museum illustrates the fishing industry with exhibits on coopering, navigation, lifeboats and fishing methods. Selections from the

Peter Anson watercolour collection of fishing scenes are on display.
Open all year, Mon-Fri 10-8, Sat 10-noon. (Closed PHs).
Free.
P & shop ✝

Corgarff Castle   CORGARFF

Map 13 NJ20
(8m W of Strathdon village)
☎ 031-244 3101
The 16th-century tower was beseiged in 1571 and is associated with the Jacobite risings of 1715 and 1745. It later

became a military barracks.
Open Apr-Sep, Mon-Sat 9.30-6, Sun 2-6.
£1.50 (ch & pen 80p).
P ✝
(AM)

Crathes Castle & Garden   CRATHES

Map 13 NO79
(3m E of Banchory on A93)
☎ (033044) 525

This impressive 16th-century castle with magnificent interiors and painted ceilings has royal associations dating from 1323. There is a walled garden of over 3 acres and a notable collection of unusual plants. Yew hedges date from 1702, and

seasonal herbaceous borders are a special feature. Wild gardens, extensive grounds and five nature trails, including one for the disabled, are among the attractions, plus a wayfaring course and children's adventure playground. There is entertainment within the grounds on most Sundays.
Open Castle & Visitor Centre 17 Apr-Oct, daily 11-6. (Last admission 5.15). Other times by appointment only. Garden & grounds open all year, daily 9.30-sunset. Castle, Garden & Grounds £3.50 (ch & pen £1.80). Grounds £1.30 (ch & pen 70p). Party.
P ✕ *licensed* & *toilets for disabled shop* ✝ *(ex in grounds)*
(NTS)

See advertisement on page 185.

Balvenie Castle   DUFFTOWN

Map 13 NJ33
☎ 031-244 3101
The ruined castle was the ancient stronghold of the Comyns, and became a stylish house in the 16th century.

Open Apr-Sep, Mon-Sat 9.30-6, Sun 2-6.
£1 (ch & pen 50p).
P & ✝
(AM)

Dufftown Museum   DUFFTOWN

Map 13 NJ33
The Tower, The Square
☎ Forres (0309) 73701
This small museum has displays on the local area, including the ancient religious site of Mortlach with a history from the 6th-century to the present day. Other

displays show aspects of social history.
Open 20 Mar-1 Apr, Mon-Sat 10-5.30; 8-31 May & 1-14 Oct, Mon-Sat 10-5.30; Jun & Sep, Mon-Sat 10-6, Sun 2-5.30; Jul-Aug, Mon-Sat 9.30-6.30, Sun 2-6.
Free.
& shop ✝

Glenfiddich Distillery   DUFFTOWN

Map 13 NJ33
(N of town, off A941)
☎ (0340) 20373
Set close to Balvenie Castle, the distillery was founded in 1887 by Major William Grant and has stayed in the hands of the family ever since. Visitors can see the whisky-making process in its various stages, and then sample the finished

product. A theatre provides an audio-visual show (in six languages) on the history and manufacture of whisky, and there is a Scotch whisky museum.
Open all year Mon-Fri 9.30-4.30, also Etr-mid Oct Sat 9.30-4.30, Sun 12-4.30. (Closed Xmas & New Year).
P & *toilets for disabled shop* ✝
Details not confirmed for 1992

Duffus Castle   DUFFUS

Map 13 NJ16
(off B9012)
☎ 031-244 3101
The remains of the mighty motte-and-bailey castle are surrounded by a moat. Within the eight-acre bailey is a 15th-

century hall, and the motte is crowned by a 14th-century tower.
Open at all reasonable times.
Free.
P ✝
(AM)

Elgin Cathedral   ELGIN

Map 13 NJ26
North College St
☎ 031-244 3101
Founded in 1224, the cathedral was known as the Lantern of the North and the Glory of the Kingdom because of its beauty. In 1390 it was burnt, with most of the town, by the Wolf of Badenoch – Alexander Stewart, Earl of Buchan – who had been excommunicated by the bishop. Although it was rebuilt, it fell into ruin after the Reformation. The

ruins are quite substantial, however, and there is still a good deal to admire, including the fine west towers and the octagonal chapter house.
Open all year, Apr-Sep, weekdays 9.30-6, Sun 2-6; Oct-Mar, weekdays 9.30-4, Sun 2-4. (Closed Thu pm & Tue in winter; 25-26 Dec & 1-2 Jan).
£1 (ch & pen 50p).
shop
(AM)

Elgin Museum   ELGIN

Map 13 NJ26
1 High St
☎ (0343) 543675
The most notable feature of the museum is its world-famous fossil collection, including fossil fish and reptiles. Other items relating to the history and natural history of Elgin and Moray from

prehistoric to modern times are also shown.
Open Apr-Sep, Tue-Fri 10-5, Sat 11-4.
£1 (ch, pen & student 50p). Family ticket £2.50.
& *(handrails inside & out. All case displays at sitting level) toilets for disabled* ✝

Pluscarden Abbey   ELGIN

Map 13 NJ26
(6m SW on unclass road)
☎ Dallas (034389) 257 & 388 (Information)
The original monastery was founded by Alexander II in 1230 and then burnt, probably by the Wolf of Badenoch who also destroyed Elgin Cathedral. It was restored in the 14th and 19th centuries, and then reoccupied in 1948 by Benedictines from Prinknash. It is now once more a religious community. Special events for West Wing

restoration appeal. New Exhibition Centre with models, plans, etc. Guides on duty at weekends and busy periods. Natural beeswax polish and natural apiary remedies now available. Engrave-a-slate provided for visitors. New women's retreat-hostel opened 1990. There is a variety of concerts planned for 1992.
Open all year, daily 5am-8.30pm.
Free.
P & *shop*

Fasque   FETTERCAIRN

Map 13 NO67
(0.5m N on B974)
☎ (033045) 227
Fasque has been the home of the Gladstone family since 1829, and W E Gladstone, four times Prime Minister, lived here from 1830 to 1851. There are impressive state rooms and a handsome, sweeping staircase, but more interesting in many ways are the extensive servants'

quarters. The life and work of the large household staff is illustrated, and there are also collections of farming machinery and other local items. The spacious park has red deer and Soay sheep.
Open May-Sep, Sat-Thu 1.30-5.30. (Last admission 5pm).
✱ *£2 (ch 90p). Party 25 +.*
P & *shop* ✝

Baxters Visitor Centre — FOCHABERS

Map 13 NJ35
(on A96)
☎ (0343) 820393
The Baxters food firm started here over 120 years ago and now sells its products in over 60 countries. Visitors can see the Victorian kitchen and the shop where the story began, take a guided tour of the factory, and watch an audio-visual display.
Open 6 Jan-24 Dec, Mon-Fri 9.30-4.30, also 2 May-27 Sep, wknds 11-4.30. No guided tours on factory holidays.
Free.
🅿 ✗ *licensed* ♿ *(parking facilities) toilets for disabled shop* ✠

Fochabers Folk Museum — FOCHABERS

Map 13 NJ35
High St
☎ (0343) 820362
This converted church exhibits the largest collection of horse drawn vehicles in the North of Scotland. There are also displays of the many aspects of village life through the ages, including model engines, clocks, costumes, a village shop and Victorian parlour.
Open all year, daily 9.30-1 & 2-6. Winter closing 5pm.
60p (ch & pen 40p). Family ticket £1.50.
🅿 ♿ *shop* ✠

Dallas Dhu Distillery — FORRES

Map 13 NJ05
(1m S of Forres)
☎ 031-244 3101
A perfectly preserved time capsule of the distiller's art. It was built in 1898 to supply malt whisky for Wright and Greig's 'Roderick Dhu' blend. Visitors are welcome to wander at will through this fine old Victorian distillery, or to take a guided tour, dram included.
Open Apr-Sep, Mon-Sat 9.30-6, Sun 2-6.
£1.50 (ch & pen 80p).
🅿 ♿ *toilets for disabled shop* ✠
(AM)

Falconer Museum — FORRES

Map 13 NJ05
Tolbooth St
☎ (0309) 73701
This museum was founded by bequests made by two brothers, Alexander and Hugh Falconer. Hugh was a distinguished scientist, a friend of Darwin, recipient of many honours and Vice-President of the Royal Society. On display are fossil mammals collected by him, and items relating to his involvement in the antiquity of mankind. Other displays are on local wildlife, geology, archaeology and history. Regular temporary exhibitions.
Open all year. May, Jun, Sep & Oct, Mon-Sat 10-12.30 & 1.30-5.30; Jul & Aug, Mon-Sat, 9.30-12.30 & 1.30-6.30, Sun 2-5; Nov-Apr, Mon-Fri 10-12.30 & 1.30-4.30.
Free.
♿ *shop* ✠

Suenos' Stone — FORRES

Map 13 NJ05
☎ 031-244 3101
The 20ft-high stone was elaborately carved in the 9th or 10th century, with a sculptured cross on one side and groups of warriors on the other. Why it stands here no one knows, but it may commemorate a victory in battle.
Open & accessible at all times.
Free.
🅿 ✠
(AM)

Huntly Castle — HUNTLY

Map 13 NJ53
☎ 031-244 3101
The original medieval castle was rebuilt a number of times and destroyed, once by Mary Queen of Scots. It was rebuilt for the last time in 1602, in palatial style, and is now an impressive ruin, noted for its ornate heraldic decorations. It stands in wooded parkland.
Open all year, Apr-Sep, weekdays 9.30-6, Sun 2-6; Oct-Mar 9.30-4, Sun 2-4. (Closed Thu pm & Fri in winter; 25-26 Dec & 1-2 Jan).
£1.50 (ch & pen 80p).
🅿 *shop* ✠
(AM)

Huntly Museum — HUNTLY

Map 13 NJ53
The Square
☎ Peterhead (0779) 77778
The museum has local history displays, and also holds changing special exhibitions every year.
Open all year, Tue-Sat 10-noon & 2-4.
Free.
shop ✠

Inverurie Museum — INVERURIE

Map 13 NJ72
Town House, The Square
☎ Peterhead (0779) 77778
This busy shopping and business centre is ringed by many prehistoric sites; and in more recent times the canal to Aberdeen was started from one of its suburbs. Together with enterprising thematic exhibitions (changed about three times a year) Inverurie's fine museum displays canal relics and items on local history and archeology.
Open all year, Mon-Tue & Thu-Fri 2-5, Sat 10-noon & 2-5.
Free.
shop ✠

Castle Fraser — KEMNAY

Map 13 NJ71
(3m S, off B993).
☎ Sauchen (03303) 463
The massive Z-plan castle was begun about 1575 and completed in 1636. Its architectural embellishments were mainly carried out by two notable families of master masons, Bell and Leiper, and their work helped to make it one of the grandest of the Castles of Mar. An earlier fortified tower house is incorporated in the design.
Open Castle May-Jun & Sep, daily 2-6; Jul-Aug, daily 11-6; Oct, Sat & Sun 2-5. (Last tour 45 mins before closing). Garden & grounds open all year, daily 9.30-sunset. Castle £3 (ch & pen £1.50). Garden & grounds by donation. Party.
🅿 ♨ ♿ *garden centre* ✠ *(ex restricted areas/grounds)*
(NTS)

The KILDRUMMY CASTLE GARDENS

in their unique setting were planted about 1904; within the curtain of silver firs and the drapery of larch and tsuga.
Water Garden. The Alpine Garden in the ancient quarry faces south, quietly enjoying the entrapped sun.
Old mill stones, quern stones and stack-stones have been arranged on the ancient quarry waste tip, among the Specie Rhododendrons. There is a small Museum, a Video Room, a Children's play Area, Wheelchair Facilities. A few plants and shrubs are for sale. Walks
Admission: £1.50, Children 20p, 8yr-16yr 50p
CAR PARK inside hotel entrance (free), Coach Park 2nd Entrance
OPEN DAILY 10 a.m. – 5 p.m. APRIL – OCTOBER
ALFORD STRATHDON ROAD, ABERDEENSHIRE (A97 off A944)
Coaches – write or Telephone: 09755 71264 & 71277

Kildrummy Castle — KILDRUMMY

Map 13 NJ41
(10m W of Alford)
☎ 031-244 3101
An important part of Scottish history, at least until it was dismantled in 1717, this fortress was the seat of the Earls of Mar. Now it is a ruined, but splendid example of a 13th-century castle, with four round towers, hall and chapel all discernible. Some parts of the building, including the Great Gatehouse, are from the 15th and 16th centuries.
Open all year, Apr-Sep, weekdays 9.30-6, Sun 2-6; Oct-Mar, Sat 9.30-4, Sun 2-4. (Closed 25-26 Dec & 1-2 Jan).
£1 (ch & pen 50p).
🅿 ♿ *toilets for disabled shop* ✠
(AM)

Kildrummy Castle Garden Trust — KILDRUMMY

Map 13 NJ41
(on A97)
☎ (09755) 71264 & 71277
With the picturesque ruin as a backdrop, these gardens are not only beautiful but also noted for their botanic interest. An alpine garden in an ancient quarry and a water garden are just two of its features, while the surrounding woods give interesting short walks. There is also a small museum, a video room showing a 15-minute film of the changes in the garden through the seasons, a children's play area and a sales area selling unusual plants.
Open Apr-Oct, daily 10-5.
£1.50 (ch 3-9 20p, 10-16 50p).
🅿 ♿ *toilets for disabled shop*

Tamdhu Distillery — KNOCKANDO

Map 13 NJ14
☎ Carron (03406) 221 & 320
A guided tour and viewing gallery offer visitors the chance to see the whole process of whisky distilling in action. There is also a large graphic display for further explanation.
Open Etr-May, Mon-Fri 10-4; Jun-Sep, Mon-Sat 10-4.
Free.
🅿 ♿ *shop* ✠

Storybook Glen — MARYCULTER

Map 13 NO89
(5m W of Aberdeen on B9077)
☎ Aberdeen (0224) 732941
This is a children's fantasy land, where favourite nursery rhyme and fairytale characters are brought to life. Grown-ups can enjoy the nostalgia and also the 20 acres of Deeside country, full of flowers, plants, trees and waterfalls.
Open Mar-Oct, daily 10-6; Nov-Feb, Sat & Sun only 11-4.
£2.10 (ch £1.05).
🅿 ♨ ✗ *licensed* ♿ *toilets for disabled shop* ✠

Glenfarclas Distillery — MARYPARK

Map 13 NJ13
(On A95 between Grantown-on-Spey & Aberlour)
☎ Ballindalloch (08072) 245
Home of one of the finest Highland malt whiskies, this distillery provides an interesting exhibition illustrating the whisky's history and production. There is also a craft shop and visitor centre. A recent addition is a cask-filling store where visitors may watch new whisky being poured into oak casks.
Open all year, Mar-Oct, Mon-Fri 9-4.30 (Jun-Sep also Sat 10-4); Nov-Feb, Mon-Fri 10-4. (Closed 25 Dec & 1-3 Jan). Other times by appointment.
Free.
🅿 ♿ *toilets for disabled shop* ✠

Haddo House — METHLICK

Map 13 NJ83
(4m N of Pitmedden off B999)
☎ Tarves (06515) 440
Haddo House is renowned for its Choral Society and is the venue for international concerts which attract top performers from around the world. It is a splendid Palladian-style mansion built in the 1730s to designs by William Adam. Home to the Earls of Aberdeen, the house was refurbished in the 1880s in the 'Adam Revival' style and still retains much of its original flavour. The adjoining country park, run by Grampian Regional Council, offers a network of enchanting woodland paths and attracts all kinds of wildlife. Hundreds of birds can be seen roosting on the loch and there is an observation hide for visitors. James Giles exhibition.
Open – House 17 Apr-May & Sep, daily 2-6; Jun-Aug, daily 11-6; Oct, Sat-Sun 2-5 (last admission 30 mins before closing). Garden & country park open all year, daily 9.30-sunset.
£3 (ch & pen £1.50). Garden by donation. Party.
🅿 ♨ ✗ *licensed* ♿ *(lift & wheelchair) toilets for disabled shop* ✠ *(ex in grounds)*
(NTS)

Aden Country Park — MINTLAW

Map 13 NJ04
(1m W Mintlaw off A950)
☎ (0771) 22857
The grounds of a former estate provide over 200 acres of beautiful woodland and open farmland for the visitor to explore. A network of footpaths winds through a specially developed nature trail, and gives a chance of seeing many varieties of plants and animals. A countryside ranger service is available by appointment. New wildlife centre is open weekends only.
Open all year. Farm Heritage centre May-Sep, daily 11-5; Apr & Oct wknds only 12-5. Last admission 30 mins before closing.
✱ *Park free. Admsiion charge to Farm Heritage Centre.*
🅿 🍴 ♿ *(access via Radar key. Garden for blind) toilets for disabled shop ✈ (ex in park)*

NE Scotland Agricultural Heritage Centre — MINTLAW

Map 13 NJ04
Aden Country Park (1m W on A950)
☎ (0771) 22857 & Banff (0261) 812521
The award-winning heritage centre is housed in 19th-century farm buildings, once part of the estate which now makes up the Aden Country Park (above). Two centuries of farming history and innovation are illustrated in an exciting exhibition, a pleasant way to take a break from enjoying the surrounding countryside. The story of the Aden estate is also interestingly illustrated. The newly reconstructed farm of Hareshowe shows how a family in the north-east might have farmed during the 1950s – access by guided tour only.
Open May-Sep, daily 11-5; Apr & Oct, wknds only noon-5. Park open all year. Last admission 30 mins before closing.
✱ *£1 (ch 16 free).*
🅿 🍴 ♿ *(garden for blind) toilets for disabled shop ✈*

Deer Abbey — OLD DEER

Map 13 NJ94
(10m W of Peterhead)
☎ 031-244 3101
The remains of the Cistercian Abbey, founded in 1218, include the infirmary, Abbot's House and the southern claustral range. The University Library at Cambridge now houses the famous Book of Deer.
Open at all reasonable times.
Free.
🅿 ✈
(AM)

Drum Castle — PETERCULTER

Map 13 NJ80
(3m W of Peterculter off A93)
☎ Drumoak (03308) 204
The great Square Tower was built in the late-13th century and is one of the three oldest tower houses in Scotland. It has associations with King Robert the Bruce. The handsome mansion was added in 1619. There is a collection of family memorabilia in the Irvine Room, and the grounds contain the 100-acre Wood of Drum.
Open May-Sep, daily 2-6, Oct Sat & Sun 2-5. (Last admission 45 mins before closing). Grounds open all year, 9.30-sunset. Walled garden May-Oct.
£3 (ch & pen £1.50). Grounds only £1.20 (ch & pen 60p). Party.
🅿 🍴 ♿ *shop ✈ (ex in grounds)*
(NTS)

Arbuthnot Museum & Art Gallery — PETERHEAD

Map 13 NK14
St Peter St
☎ (0779) 77778
Specialising in local exhibts, particularly those relating to the fishing industry, this museum also displays Arctic and whaling specimens and a British coin collection.
Open all year, Mon-Sat 10-noon & 2-5. (Closed PH).
Free.
shop ✈

Pitmedden Garden — PITMEDDEN

Map 13 NJ82
(1m W on A920)
☎ Udny (06513) 2352
The fine late 17th-century garden has been recreated here, and sundials, pavilions and fountains are dotted among the elaborate floral designs. The Museum of Farming Life and visitor centre are also open and there are less formal walks to be taken from the garden.
Open – Garden, Museum of Farming Life & Visitor Centre open May-Sep, daily 10-6 (last admission 5.15). Grounds open all year, daily 9.30-sunset.
Garden, Museum of Farming Life & Visitor Centre £2.40 (ch & pen £1.20). Party.
🅿 🍴 ♿ *(wheelchairs available) toilets for disabled shop ✈*
(NTS)

Tolquhon Castle — PITMEDDEN

Map 13 NJ82
(2m NE off B999)
☎ 031-244 3101
Now roofless, a late 16th-century quadrangular mansion encloses an early 15th-century tower. There is a fine gatehouse and courtyard.
Open all year, Apr-Sep, weekdays 9.30-6, Sun 2-6; Oct-Mar wknds only 2-4. (Closed 25-26 Dec & 1-2 Jan).
£1 (ch & pen 50p).
🅿 ♿ *toilets for disabled shop ✈*
(AM)

Leith Hall & Garden — RHYNIE

Map 13 NJ42
(3.5m NE on B9002)
☎ Kennethmont (04643) 216
Home of the Leith family for over 300 years, the house dates back to 1650, and has a number of Jacobite relics and a major exhibition: 'For Crown and Country: the military Lairds of Leith Hall'. It is surrounded by charming gardens and extensive grounds.
Open – House May-Sep, daily 2-6; Oct, wknds 2-5. (Last admission 45 mins before closing). Grounds open all year 9.30-sunset.
£3 (ch & pen £1.50). Party.
🅿 🍴 ♿ *(scented garden for the blind) toilets for disabled shop ✈ (ex in grounds)*
(NTS)

Glen Grant Distillery — ROTHES

Map 13 NJ24
(On A941, in Rothes)
☎ (03403) 413 (Apr-Sep) & (05422) 7471
Established in 1840, the whisky produced in this distillery is used in many first-class blends as well as being sold as the single Glen Grant malt in the bottle. Traditional malt whisky methods of distillation are used, together with the most up-to-date equipment. There is a shop on the premises, and a free whisky is provided.
Open Apr-Sep, Mon-Fri 10-4.
Free.
🅿 ♿ *(reception centre & still house) toilets for disabled shop ✈*

Tugnet Ice House — SPEY BAY

Map 13 NJ36
☎ Forres (0309) 73701
The largest ice house in Scotland, built in 1830, now contains exhibitions on the history and techniques of commerical salmon fishing on the River Spey, with an audio-visual programme. There are sections on the geography, wildlife and industries of the Lower Spey area, such as ship-building at nearby Kingston.
Open Jun-Sep 10-4 & any reasonable time.
Free.
🅿 ♿ *toilets for disabled shop ✈*

Dunnottar Castle — STONEHAVEN

Map 13 NO88
(1.5m S off A92)
☎ (0569) 62173
Set on a truly spectacular clifftop site are the partly-restored ruins of Dunnottar Castle. The ruins date from the late-12th to the 18th centuries. The Scottish crown jewels were kept here during the 17th century, but they were smuggled out during a seige by Cromwell's troops, to be hidden in Kinneff church.
Open all year, Apr-Oct, Mon-Sat 9-6, Sun 2-5. Nov-Mar, Mon-Fri 9-dusk. Last admission 30 mins before closing. (Closed Xmas & New Year).
shop
Details not confirmed for 1992

Stonehaven Tolbooth — STONEHAVEN

Map 13 NO88
Old Pier
☎ Peterhead (0779) 77778
This was once a 16th-century storehouse of the Earls of Marischal. It was later used as a prison but is now a fishing and local history museum.
Open Jun-Sep, Mon & Thu-Sat 10-noon & 2-5; Wed & Sun 2-5.
Free.
♿ *shop ✈*

Every effort is made to provide accurate information, but details might change during the currency of this guide.

Tomintoul Museum — TOMINTOUL

Map 13 NJ11
The Square
☎ Forres (0309) 73701
The museum has displays on the local landscape, geology, climate and wildlife, as well as local history and folklife, with a reconstructed farm kitchen and blacksmith's shop.
Open Apr, May & Oct, Mon-Sat 9.30-1 & 2-5.30, Sun 2-5.30; Jun & Sep, Mon-Fri 9.30-6, Sat 9.30-1 & 2-6, Sun 2-6; Jul & Aug, Mon-Fri 9-6.30, Sat 9-1 & 2-6.30, Sun 11-1 & 2-6.30.
Free.
🅿 ♿ *(handling display for visually impaired) shop ✈*

Fyvie Castle — TURRIFF

Map 13 NJ75
Fyvie (8m SE of Turriff on A947)
☎ (0651) 891266
This superb castle dating from the 13th century has five towers, each built in a different century by one of the families who lived here. It is now one of the grandest examples of Scottish baronial architecture. The castle contains the finest wheel stair in Scotland, and a 17th-century morning room which, along with other rooms, has been decorated and furnished in lavish Edwardian grandeur. There is an exceptional collection of portraits, with works by Batoni, Raeburn, Romney, Gainsborough, Opie and Hoppner: and arms, armour and 16th-century tapestries can also be seen.
Open 17 Apr-May & Sep, daily 2-6; Jun-Aug, daily 11-6; Oct Sat & Sun 2-5 (last admission 45 mins before closing). Grounds open all year, daily 9.30-sunset.
£3 (ch & pen £1.50). Party.
🅿 🍴 ♿ *toilets for disabled shop ✈ (ex in grounds)*
(NTS)

HIGHLAND

Dalmore Farm Centre — ALNESS

Map 13 NH66
☎ (0349) 883978
An old-fashioned Highland welcome awaits visitors to this family-run working farm. Attractions include a restaurant serving home cooking and baking, a farm shop, garden centre, farm museum, children's play area and pets' corner. Visitors will see the animals in their natural surroundings and are welcome to watch farm activities, such as sheep clipping and sheep dipping.
Open all year, Mon-Sat 10-5, Sun 1-5. Farm open Etr-Oct.
Free.
🅿 🍴 ✕ ♿ *toilets for disabled shop garden centre*

Strathspey Steam Railway — AVIEMORE

Map 13 NH81
Aviemore Speyside Station, Dalfaber Rd
☎ (0479) 810725
This steam railway covers the five miles from Boat of Garten to Aviemore, where trains can also be boarded. The journey takes about 20 minutes, but allow around an hour for the round trip. Timetables are available from the station

and the tourist information centre. Special events for 1992 include a Boat of Garten beer festival, a crafts fair and a Thomas the Tank Engine weekend – please telephone for details.
Open 23 May-4 Sep daily; 28 Mar-28 Oct selected days. Also 19-20, 26-27 & 31 Dec. £3.60 Basic return; £9 Family return.
🅿 ☕ ✕ ♿ shop

Balmacara (Lochalsh House & Garden) — BALMACARA

Map 12 NG82
☎ (059986) 207
Balmacara is a huge estate surrounding the Kyle of Lochalsh. It offers magnificent West Highland scenery, including the Five Sisters of Kintail and Beinn Fhada. The landscape is dotted with small lochs ('lochans'), and there are wonderful views of the coast. The delightful woodland garden of Lochalsh House offers pleasant walks, and there is a natural history display in the coach

house. Independent or guided walks can be taken from Balmacara on the Kyle to Plockton Peninsula. Haunt of artists and holidaymakers. A Ranger Naturalist Service is available.
Open all year. Woodland & Garden, daily 9.30-sunset. Coach house & Information Kiosk 2 May-27 Sep, Mon-Sat 10-1 & 2-6, Sun 2-6.
£1 (ch & pen 50p).
🅿
(NTS)

Strathnaver Museum — BETTYHILL

Map 13 NC76
☎ (06412) 421
The village is named after Elizabeth, Countess of Sutherland, who built it for families evicted in the Highland Clearances. (The 'clearing' of the Sutherland estates was notorious.) The museum has displays on the clearances, with a fine collection of homemade furnishings, domestic and farm implements, and Gaelic books. There is also a Clan Mackay room. The

museum's setting is a former church, a handsome stone building with a magnificent canopied pulpit dated 1174. The churchyard contains a carved stone known as the Farr Stone, which dates back to the 10th century and is a fine example of Celtic art. A Neil Gunn exhibition is planned for March 1992.
Open Apr-Oct, Mon-Sat 10-1 & 2-5; Nov-Mar by appointment only.
£1 (ch 30p).
♿ ✖

Landmark Visitor Centre — CARRBRIDGE

Map 13 NH92
(off A9)
☎ (047984) 614
The innovative centre has an exhibition on the history of the Highlands and a multi-screen, sound-and-vision presentation, 'The Highlander', which tells of the break-up of Europe's last tribal society. The Forestry Heritage Park has a 65ft forest viewing tower, a working steam-powered sawmill and

various exhibitions and buildings. Attractions include trails, a maze, an adventure play area, a craft and book shop, restaurant, and snack bar with picnic area.
Open all year, daily, Apr-Jun & Sep-Oct 9.30-6; Jul-Aug 9.30-8 & Nov-Mar 9.30-5.
Apr-Jun £3.85 (ch £2.40); Jul-Sep £3.95 (£2.60).
🅿 ✕ licensed ♿ toilets for disabled shop

Cawdor Castle — CAWDOR

Map 13 NH85
(on B9090 off A96)
☎ (06677) 615

Home of the Thanes of Cawdor since the 14th century, the castle has a drawbridge, an ancient tower built round a tree, and a freshwater well inside the house. There are nature trails, pitch-and-putt and a putting green.
Open May-4 Oct, daily 10-5.30. (Last admission 5pm).
£3.50 (ch 5-15 £1.90, pen £2.80). Family ticket £10. Party 20+. Gardens, grounds & nature trails only £1.80.
🅿 ☕ ♿ toilets for disabled shop ✖

Clava Cairns — CLAVA CAIRNS

Map 13 NH74
(6m E of Inverness)
☎ 031-244 3101
On the south bank of the River Nairn, this group of circular burial cairns is surrounded by three concentric rings of great stones. It dates from around

1,600BC, and ranks among Scotland's finest prehistoric monuments.
Open all times.
Free.
🅿 ✖
(AM)

Hugh Miller's Cottage — CROMARTY

Map 13 NH76
☎ (03817) 245
Hugh Miller, a stonemason who became an eminent geologist and writer, was born in the cottage in 1802. It was built by his great-grandfather in the early 18th century, and now has an exhibition and

video on Miller and his work. The cottage garden was redeveloped in 1988.
Open Apr-27 Sep, Mon-Sat 10-12 & 1-5, Sun 2-5.
£1.20 (ch & pen 60p)
✖
(NTS)

Culloden Battlefield — CULLODEN MOOR

Map 13 NH74
(5m E of Inverness)
☎ (0463) 790607

A cairn built in 1881 recalls the last battle fought on mainland Britain, on 16 April 1746, when 'Bonnie' Prince Charles Edward Stuart's army was bloodily routed by the Duke of Cumberland's forces. The battle was fought around Old Leanach Cottage, which has been furnished in the style of

the period, complete with a figure of a mother and baby. The Graves of the Clans and the Well of the Dead can also be seen. There is a visitor centre with a display, audio-visual show, (also in Gaelic, German, French, Italian and Japanese), bookshop and restaurant.
Open – site always. Visitor Centre open Feb-Mar & Nov-30 Dec, daily 10-4. (Closed 25 & 26 Dec); Apr-22 May & 14 Sep-Oct, daily 9.30-5.30; 23 May-13 Sep, daily 9-6.30. Audio visual show & restaurant closed 30 mins before Visitor Centre.
Admission to visitor centre & museum (includes audio-visual programme & Old Leanach Cottage) £1.50 (ch & pen 80p). Party 20+.
🅿 ✕ ♿ (induction loop for hard of hearing) toilets for disabled shop ✖ (ex in grounds)
(NTS)

Eilean Donan Castle — DORNIE

Map 12 NG82
☎ (059985) 202
The castle is in a beautiful mountain setting at the meeting point of Lochs Duich, Alsh and Long, and is connected to the mainland by a causeway. It was

first built in 1220 and then destroyed in 1719 after being held by Jacobite troops. It was restored in 1912.
Open Etr-Sep, daily 10-5.45.
🅿 shop ✖
Details not confirmed for 1992

Official Loch Ness Monster Exhibition — DRUMNADROCHIT

Map 12 NH52
Loch Ness Centre
☎ (04562) 573 & 218
A fascinating computer-controlled, multi-media presentation lasting 40 minutes. Ten themed areas cover the story from the pre-history of Scotland, through the cultural roots of the legend of the monster in Highland folklore, and into the fifty year controversy which

surrounds it. The exhibition was totally renewed in July 1989 and the centre encompasses the Nessie Giftshop, Iceberg Glassblowers and a kilt-maker.
Open all year, peak season 9am-9.30pm, otherwise times on application.
✱ £3.50 (ch reduced rate, students £2.50).
🅿 ☕ ✕ licensed ♿ toilets for disabled shop ✖ (ex in grounds)

Urquhart Castle — DRUMNADROCHIT

Map 12 NH52
☎ 031-244 3101
The castle was once Scotland's biggest and overlooks Loch Ness. It dates mainly from the 14th century, when it was built on the site of an earlier fort, and was destroyed before the 1715

Jacobite rebellion.
Open all year, Apr-Sep, weekdays 9.30-6, Sun 2-6; Oct-Mar, weekdays 9.30-4, Sun 2-4. (Closed 25-26 Dec & 1-2 Jan).
£1.50 (ch & pen 80p). Family ticket £4.
🅿 shop ✖
(AM)

Places to visit in this guide are pinpointed on the atlas at the back of the book.

Laidhay Croft Museum — DUNBEATH

Map 13 ND12
(1m N on A9)
☎ (05933) 244
The museum gives visitors a glimpse of a long-vanished way of life. The main building is a thatched Caithness longhouse, with the dwelling quarters, byre and stable all under one roof. It dates back some 200 years, and is

furnished as it might have been 100 years ago. A collection of early farm tools and machinery is also shown. Near the house is a thatched winnowing barn with its roof supported on three 'Highland couples', or crucks.
Open Etr-mid Oct, daily 10-6.
✱ 50p (ch 20p).
🅿 ☕ ♿

Fort George — FORT GEORGE

Map 13 NH75
(11m NE of Inverness)
☎ 031-244 3101
The fort was begun in 1748, as one of a chain of three designed to keep peace in the Highlands. It was visited by Dr Johnson and Boswell in 1773 and is admired today as one of Europe's finest

18th-century artillery fortifications.
Open all year, Apr-Sep, weekdays 9.30-6, Sun 2-6; Oct-Mar, weekdays 9.30-4, Sun 2-4. (Closed 25-26 Dec & 1-2 Jan).
£2 (ch & pen £1). Family ticket £5.
🅿 ♿ shop ✖
(AM)

Queen's Own Highlanders Regimental Museum — FORT GEORGE

Map 13 NH75
☎ Inverness (0463) 224380
Fort George (above) has been a military barracks since it was built in 1748-69, and was the Depot of the Seaforth Highlanders until 1961. The museum of the Queen's Own Highlanders (Seaforth and Camerons) is sited in the former Lieutenant Governor's house, where

uniforms, medals and pictures are displayed.
Open Apr-Sep, Mon-Fri 10-6, Sun 2-6; Oct-Mar, Mon-Fri 10-4. (Closed Good Fri-Etr Mon, Xmas, New Year & BH).
Free. Admission charged for entry to Fort George.
🅿 ♿ toilets for disabled shop ✖

Inverlochy Castle — FORT WILLIAM

Map 12 NN17
(2m NE)
☎ 031-244 3101
The castle was began in the 13th century and added to later. It is noted in Scottish history for the battle fought nearby in 1645, when Montrose

defeated the Campbells.
Open Apr-Sep. Key available from keykeeper.
Free.
✴
(AM)

West Highland Museum — FORT WILLIAM

Map 12 NN17
Cameron Square
☎ (0397) 702169
The displays illustrate traditional Highland life and history, with numerous Jacobite relics. One of them is the 'secret portrait' of Bonnie Prince

Charlie, which looks like meaningless daubs of paint but reveals a portrait when reflected in a metal cylinder.
Open all year, Mon-Sat, Jul-Aug 9.30-7; Sep-Jun 10-5.
70p (ch 20p, pen 40p).
shop ✴

Gairloch Heritage Museum — GAIRLOCH

Map 12 NG87
Achtercairn
☎ Badachro (044583) 243
A converted farmstead now houses the award-winning museum, which shows ways of life in this typical West Highland parish from early times to the 20th century. There are reconstructions

of a croft house room, a school room, a shop, and the inside of a local lighthouse. Restored fishing boats are also shown.
Open Etr-Sep, Mon-Sat 10-5.
£1 (ch 20p).
P ⬤ ✕ *licensed* ♿ *shop* ✴

Glencoe & North Lorn Folk Museum — GLENCOE

Map 12 NN15
Two heather-thatched cottages in the main street of Glencoe now house items connected with the Macdonalds and the Jacobite risings. A variety of local domestic and farming exhibits, dairying

and slate-working equipment, costumes and embroidery is also shown.
Open mid May-Sep, Mon-Sat 10-5.30.
✴ *60p (ch 30p).*
P ♿ *shop*

Glencoe Visitor Centre — GLENCOE

Map 12 NN15
(on A82)
☎ Ballachulish (08552) 307
Glencoe has stunning scenery and some of the best climbing (not for the unskilled) and walking country in the Highlands. Its wildlife includes red deer and wildcats, golden eagles and ptarmigan. The A82 Glasgow to Fort William road runs through the glen, so it is also more accessible than some. It is best known, however, as the scene of the massacre of February 1692, when a party of troops billeted here tried to

murder all their Macdonald hosts – men, women and children. The Visitor Centre is at the north end of the glen, close to the scene of the massacre. It has a display on the history of mountaineering in the glen, and provides information on walks. Ranger service.
Open Visitor Centre 1 Apr-22 May & 7 Sep-18 Oct, daily 10-5.30; 23 May-6 Sep, daily 9.30-6.30.
30p (ch & pen 15p). Includes parking.
P ⬤ ♿ *toilets for disabled shop* ✴
(NTS)

Jacobite Monument — GLENFINNAN

Map 12 NM88
☎ Kinlocheil (039783) 250
The monument commemorates Highlanders who fought and died for Bonnie Prince Charlie in 1745. It was built in 1815, and has an awe-inspiring setting at the head of Loch Shiel. There is a visitor centre with information

(commentary in four languages) on the Prince's campaign.
Open – Visitor Centre, Apr-22 May & 7 Sep-18 Oct, daily 10-1 & 2-5.30; 23 May-6 Sep, daily 9.30-6.30.
£1 (ch & pen 50p). Includes parking.
P ⬤ ♿ *(information centre only) shop*
(NTS)

Dunrobin Castle — GOLSPIE

Map 13 NH89
(1m NE on A9)
☎ (0408) 633177 & 633268
The ancient seat of the Earls and Dukes of Sutherland takes its name from Earl Robin, who built the original square keep in the 13th century. The castle is now a splendid, gleaming, turreted structure, thanks largely to 19th-century rebuilding, and has a beautiful setting overlooking the sea. Paintings (including Canalettos), furniture and family heirlooms are on display inside, and the

gardens are on a grand scale to match the house (they were modelled on those at Versailles). A summer house in the grounds is now a museum with a variety of exhibits.
Open May, Mon-Thu 10.30-12.30; Jun-Sep, Mon-Sat 10.30-5.30 & Sun 1-5.30. (Last admission 5pm).
£3 (ch £1.50, pen £2). Family ticket £7.50. Party.
P ⬤ ♿ *(access by arrangement only) shop*
✴

Castle Stuart — INVERNESS

Map 13 NH64
Petty Parish (5m E of Inverness, off A96)
☎ (0463) 790745
Ancient home of the Earl of Moray and the Stuart family, constructed in 1621 when the Royal House of Stuart had ruled the United Kingdoms of England and Wales, Scotland and Ireland for some twenty years. It is located within

the sound of the cannon's roar from High Culloden Moor, where the last attempt to restore the Stuart monarchy ended in defeat. The interior has been restored to its former glory with Jacobean furnishings, armour and historic relics.
Open daily May-Sep 10.30-5.
P *shop* ✴
Details not confirmed for 1992

Highland Wildlife Park — KINCRAIG

Map 13 NH80
(on B9152)
☎ (05404) 270 due to change to (0540) 651270
In a magnificent natural setting, native animals from Scotland's past and present can be viewed: wolves, bears, reindeer, wildcats and European bison are some of the many animals who have their home

and breed here. Eagles and capercaillie are kept in the aviaries. For children, a pets' corner provides amusement, and grown-ups will find the 'Man and Fauna' exhibition fascinating.
Open Apr-Oct, daily 10-6.
✴ *£8 per car.*
P ♿ *toilets for disabled shop* ✴

Highland Folk Museum — KINGUSSIE

Map 13 NH70
Duke St
☎ (0540) 661307
The Highland way of life is illustrated with an interesting display of crafts and furnishings, a farming museum, a reconstructed Hebridean mill and a primitive 'black house'. Demonstrations

of crafts are held every day throughout Jul and Aug, including weaving, spinning and baking.
Open all year, Apr-Oct, Mon-Sat 10-6, Sun 2-6; Nov-Mar, Mon-Fri 10-3. (Closed Xmas-New Year).
£1.70 (ch & pen 85p). Subject to review.
P ♿ *toilets for disabled shop*

Ruthven Barracks — KINGUSSIE

Map 13 NH70
(0.5m SE of Kingussie)
☎ 031-244 3101
Despite being blown up by Bonnie Prince Charlie's Highlanders, these infantry barracks are still the best preserved of the four that were built after the Jacobite uprising. The

considerable ruins are the remains of a building completed in 1716 on the site of a fortress of the 'Wolf of Badenoch'.
Open at any reasonable time.
Free.
P ✴
(AM)

Moniack Castle (Highland Winery) — KIRKHILL

Map 12 NH54
(7m from Inverness on A862)
☎ Drumchardine (046383) 283
A unique Scottish enterprise is undertaken in the former fortress of the Loval chiefs: commercial wine-making is not a usual Scottish industry, but nevertheless a wide range of 'country'-

style wines is produced, including elderflower and silver birch; and also mead and sloe gin. A wine bar and bistro are added temptations.
Open all year, Mon-Sat 10-5.
Free.
P ⬤ ✕ *licensed shop* ✴

Clan Macpherson House & Museum — NEWTONMORE

Map 13 NN79
Main St
☎ (05403) 332
Containing relics and memorials of the clan chiefs and other Macpherson families as well as those of Prince Edward Stuart, this museum also displays the Prince's letters to the Clan Chief of 1745 and one to the Prince from his father the Old Pretender, along with royal warrants and the green

banner of the clan. Other interesting historic exhibits include James Macpherson's fiddle, swords, pictures, decorations and medals. Highland games take place on the first Saturday in August, and the Clan Macpherson Rally in the same day.
Open May-Sep, Mon-Sat 10-5.30, Sun 2.30-5.30. Other times by appointment.
Free. Donations.
P ♿ *shop* ✴

Inverewe Garden — POOLEWE

Map 12 NG88
(6m NE of Gairloch, on A832)
☎ (044586) 200
The presence of the Atlantic Drift enables this remarkable garden to grow rare and sub-tropical plants. At its best in early June, but full of beauty from March to October, Inverewe has a backdrop of magnificent mountains and

stands to the north of Loch Maree.
Open – Garden all year, daily 9.30-sunset. Visitor Centre Apr-22 May & 7 Sep-18 Oct, Mon-Sat 10-5, Sun 2-5; 23 May-6 Sep, Mon-Sat 9.30-6, Sun 12-6.
£2.80 (ch £1.40). Party.
P ✕ *licensed* ♿ *toilets for disabled shop* ✴
(NTS)

AEA Technology Dounreay

REAY

Map 13 NC96
(2m NE off A836)
☎ (0847) 802701 & 802235
Situated on the spectacular north coast of Scotland, the Centre has two floors of information, models and hands-on exhibits to interest all ages. Dounreay is the home of Britain's first fast reactor, the development of which is explained in easy-to-follow terms, as are Dounreay's other diverse activites such as nuclear

fuel processing and research into renewable energy resources. Everyone over 12 can also tour the PFR (Prototype Fast Reactor) Reactor Hall and stand on top of the fast reactor.
Open mid Apr-Sep, Tue-Sun 9-4.30. Reactor tours 11.45-2.15pm. Tours last approximately 1 hour.
Free. Donations.
P ☂ & *shop*

Strathpeffer Station Visitor Centre

STRATHPEFFER

Map 12 NH45
☎ Kessock (046373) 505
The centre is in a renovated Victorian railway station of 1885. Attractions include an exhibition of photographs, a museum of childhood, and various craft

shops. In mid-June Victorian days are held. Strathpeffer also has Highland Games in early August.
Open Etr-Oct, daily.
Donations.
P & *shop*

Countryside Centre

TORRIDON

Map 12 NG85
(N of A896).
☎ (044587) 221
Set amid some of Scotland's finest mountain scenery, the centre offers audio-visual presentations on the local wildlife. At the Mains nearby there are live deer to be seen, and there is also a static display on the life of the red deer.

Open – Visitor Centre 2 May-27 Sep, Mon-Sat 10-6, Sun 2-6.
Ranger/naturalist service. Deer Museum un-manned, all year.
Deer Museum 80p (ch & pen 40p). Audio-visual display by donation.
P
(NTS)

This is just one of many guidebooks published by the AA.
The full range is available at any AA shop or good bookshop.

Caithness Glass Factory & Visitor Centre

WICK

Map 13 ND34
Airport Industrial Estate
☎ (0955) 2286
All aspects of glassmaking are on view, from the initial processing of the raw materials to the finished article. There is a shop, which also sells factory seconds,

and a restaurant.
Open all year, Factory shop & restaurant Mon-Sat 9-5 (Sun, Etr-Sep 11-5). Glassmaking Mon-Fri 9-4.30.
Free.
P ✕ *licensed* & *toilets for disabled shop* ✖
(ex in shop)

Castle of Old Wick

WICK

Map 13 ND34
(1m S)
☎ 031-244 3101
A ruined four-storey, square tower that is probably of the 12th century. It is also known as Castle Oliphant.

Open except when adjoining rifle range is in use.
Free.
✖
(AM)

Wick Heritage Centre

WICK

Map 13 ND34
20 Bank Row
☎ (0955) 5393
The heritage centre is near the harbour in a complex of eight houses, yards and outbuildings. The centre illustrates local history from Neolithic times and there is a prize-winning exhibition on the herring

fishing industry. In addition, there is a complete working 19th-century lighthouse, and the famous Johnston collection of photographs.
Open Jun-Sep, daily 10-5. (Closed Sun).
£1 (ch 50p).
P & *toilets for disabled*

LOTHIAN

Myreton Motor Museum

ABERLADY

Map 11 NT47
☎ (08757) 288
This is a charming and wide-ranging collection, with cars and motorcycles from 1896, cycles from 1863 and commercial vehicles, historic British

military vehicles, advertising signs and automobilia.
Open all year, daily 10-6 (summer); 10-5 (winter). (Closed 25 Dec & 1 Jan).
❋ *£1.80 (ch 16 50p).*
P & ✖

Malleny Garden

BALERNO

Map 11 NT16
(off Bavelaw Rd)
☎ 031-449 2283
The delightful gardens are set around a 17th-century house (not open). There is a good selection of shrub roses, a woodland garden, and a group of four clipped yews, the survivors of a group of

12 which were planted in 1603. The National Bonsai Collection for Scotland is also at Malleny.
Open daily 10-sunset.
£1 (ch & pen 50p). Charge Box.
P & ✖
(NTS)

Cairnpapple Hill Sanctuary & Burial Cairn

BATHGATE

Map 11 NS96
(3m N)
☎ 031-244 3101
Cairnpapple is one of the most important prehistoric sites in Scotland. It is a sanctuary and burial place which was used for around 3,000 years, from Neolithic times to the first century BC, but mainly in the second millenium BC. Bodies were cremated before being put inside the chamber. Finds such as flint arrowheads, a cup-and-ring-marked stone

and Beaker Folk pottery have all been found in the area and have helped to date the site. Today Cairnpapple is protected by a modern dome. It is set on a high point of the Bathgate Hills, and on clear days gives wide views right across Scotland, from the Isle of May to Arran.
Open Apr-Sep, Mon-Sat 9.30-6, Sun 2-6.
£1 (ch & pen 50p).
P ✖
(AM)

Crichton Castle

CRICHTON

Map 11 NT36
(2.5m SW Pathhead)
☎ 031-244 3101
The castle dates back to the 14th century, but most of what remains today was built over the following 300 years. A notable feature is the 16th-century wing built by the Earl of Bothwell in

Italian style, with an arcade below.
Open all year, Apr-Sep weekdays 9.30-6, Sun 2-6; Oct-Mar, wknds only. (Closed 25-26 Dec & 1-2 Jan).
£1 (ch & pen 50p).
P ✖
(AM)

Dalkeith Park

DALKEITH

Map 11 NT36
Buccleuch Estate
☎ 031-663 5684 & 031-665 3277
The extensive grounds of Dalkeith House offer pleasant woodland and riverside walks, and nature trails. A beautiful Adam bridge and an orangery

can be seen, and there is a fine woodland adventure playground and a farm park. Ranger-led walks are available, as are hay rides.
Open end Mar-Oct, daily 10-6.
£1.50. Family ticket £4. Party 20+.
P & *toilets for disabled*

Edinburgh Butterfly & Insect World

DALKEITH

Map 11 NT36
(At Dobbie's Melville Gdn World 1m N on A7)
☎ 031-663 4932
Richly coloured butterflies from all over the world can be seen flying among exotic plants, trees and flowers. The tropical pools are filled with giant waterlilies and colourful fish, and

surrounded by lush vegetation. Also displayed are scorpions, tarantulas and other dangerous creatures, and there is a unique honeybee display.
Open 12 Mar-Oct, daily 10-5.30.
£2.85 (ch 5 free, ch £1.60, pen & students £2.20). Family ticket £8.20. Party 10+.
P ☂ & *toilets for disabled shop garden centre* ✖

Dirleton Castle

DIRLETON

Map 11 NT58
☎ 031-244 3101
The oldest part of this romantic castle dates from the 13th century. It was besieged by Edward I in 1298, rebuilt and expanded, and then destroyed in 1650. Now the sandstone ruins have a beautiful mellow quality. Within the castle grounds is a garden established in

the 16th century, with ancient yews and hedges around a bowling green.
Open all year, Apr-Sep weekdays 9.30-6, Sun 2-6; Oct-Mar, weekdays 9.30-4, Sun 2-4. (Closed 25-26 Dec & 1-2 Jan).
£1.50 (ch & pen 80p).
P & ✖
(AM)

Every effort is made to provide accurate information, but details might change during the currency of this guide.

Museum of Flight

EAST FORTUNE

Map 11 NT57
East Fortune Airfield (Signposted from A1 near Haddington)
☎ (0620) 88308 or 031-225 7534

Aircraft on display include a Supermarine Spitfire MK 16, De Haviland Sea Venom, Hawker Sea Hawk and Comet (4). The museum is set out in a former airship base, and also has a section on Airship R34 which flew from here to New York and back in 1919. There is also an extensive display of rockets and aero-engines.
Open Etr-Sep, daily 10.30-4.30.
Free.
P ☂ & *toilets for disabled shop* ✖

Hailes Castle

EAST LINTON

Map 11 NT57
(1m SW on unclass rd).
☎ 031-244 3101
The castle was a fortified manor house of the Gourlays and Hepburns. Bothwell brought Mary Queen of Scots here when they were fleeing from Borthwick Castle. The substantial ruins include a

16th-century chapel.
Open all year, Apr-Sep, weekdays 9.30-6, Sun 2-6; Oct-Mar, weekdays 9.30-4, Sun 2-4. (Closed Wed pm & Thu in winter, 25-26 Dec & 1-2 Jan). Key with Keeper.
Free.
✖
(AM)

Preston Mill
EAST LINTON

Map 11 NT57
☎ (0620) 860426
This is the oldest working water-driven meal mill to survive in Scotland, and was last used commercially in 1957. It has a conical roof and red pantiles. A short walk leads to Phantassie Doocot

(dovecote), built for 500 birds.
Open 17 Apr-Sep, Mon-Sat 11-1 & 2-5, Sun 2-5; Oct, Sat 11-1 & 2-4, Sun 2-4. Last entry 30 mins before closing.
£1.20 (ch & pen 60p). Party.
P & shop ✈
(NTS)

EDINBURGH

Map 11 NT27
Edinburgh has a glorious setting, with unexpected views of the sea and hills wherever you happen to be, and a skyline dominated by the great crag, on which the castle stands. From here the medieval Old Town runs down to the Palace of Holyrood House, and through the heart of the Old Town runs the Royal Mile, lined with historic buildings like the Outlook Tower with its camera obscura, the tall tenement of Gladstone's Land, Lady Stair's house and a number of museums, all full of interest. It is also well worth spending time exploring the many 'wynds' and alleys that run down steeply from either side of the Royal Mile. Edinburgh's second main area is the New Town, a place of elegant squares and terraces built for the city's merchants and aristocrats in the late-18th century, seen at its grandest in Charlotte Square. There is a third town as well – the districts of grand Victorian houses – and Edinburgh is also a city of villages, each with their own character. Always fascinating to visit, Edinburgh becomes a riot of theatre and music both on and off the streets during the International Festival and Fringe Festival in August. An especially popular event is the military searchlight tattoo held in front of the castle.

Camera Obscura
EDINBURGH

Map 11 NT27
Outlook Tower Visitor Centre, Castle Hill, Royal Mile
☎ 031-226 3709
Step inside this magical 1850s 'cinema' for a unique experience of Edinburgh. As the lights go down a brilliant moving image of the surrounding city appears. The scene changes as a guide operates the camera's system of revolving lenses and mirrors. As the panorama unfolds

the guide tells the story of the city's historic past. Also of interest is the Rooftop Terrace, and exhibitions on Holography, Pinhole Photography and Victorian Edinburgh.
Open all year, daily, Apr-Sep 9.30-6; Oct-Mar 10-5. (Closed 25-26 Dec & 1 Jan).
£2.75 (ch £1.40, pen & students £2).
Family ticket £7.15.
& shop ✈

Craigmillar Castle
EDINBURGH

Map 11 NT27
(2.5m SE)
☎ 031-244 3101
Mary Queen of Scots retreated to this 14th-century stronghold after the murder of Rizzio, and the plot to murder Darnley, her second husband, was also hatched here. There are 16th-

and 17th-century apartments.
Open all year, Apr-Sep, weekdays 9.30-6, Sun 2-6. Oct-Mar, weekdays 9.30-4, Sun 2-4. (Closed Thu & Fri in winter, 25-26 Dec & 1-2 Jan).
£1.20 (ch & pen 60p).
P & ✈
(AM)

Edinburgh Castle
EDINBURGH

Map 11 NT27
☎ 031-244 3101

This historic stronghold stands on the precipitous crag of Castle Rock. One of the oldest parts is the 11th-century chapel of the saintly Queen Margaret, but most of the present castle evolved later, during its stormy history of sieges and wars, and was altered again in Victorian times. The apartments of Mary Queen of Scots can be seen, including the bedroom where James I of England and VI of Scotland was born. Also on the rock is James IV's 16th-

century great hall. The vaults underneath have graffiti by 19th-century French prisoners of war. The Scottish crown and other royal regalia are displayed in the Crown Room, and the spectacular Military Tattoo is held on the Esplanade, built in 1753 – shortly after the castle's last seige in 1745. Also notable is the Scottish National War Memorial, opened in 1927 on the site of the castle's church. There is still a military presence in the castle, and some areas cannot be visited.
Open all year, 4 Jan-Mar & Oct-Dec, Mon-Sat 9.30-4.20 (last ticket sold), Sun 12.30-3.35 (last ticket sold). Apr-Sep, Mon-Sat 9.30-5.05 (last ticket sold), Sun 10.30-4.45 (last ticket sold). Castle closes 45 mins after above times.
£3.40 (ch & pen £1.70). Family ticket £5.50. War Memorial Free.
P *(charged)* & *(with limitations) toilets for disabled shop* ✈
(AM)

Edinburgh Zoo
EDINBURGH

Map 11 NT27
The Scottish National, Zoological Park, Corstorphine Rd (2m W on A8)
☎ 031-334 9171
The zoo is set in 80 acres of grounds, and is notable for its colony of penguins, which perform the Penguin Parade daily at 2.30pm in summer. A visitor centre explains the role of zoos in conservation, research and education, and there are

panoramic views of Edinburgh and the countryside.
Open all year, Mon-Sat 9-6, Sun 9.30-6 in summer, but closes 5pm or dusk in winter.
✱ *£3.85 (ch, pen & UB40's £2). Party 10+.*
P *(charged)* ☕ ✗ *licensed* & *toilets for disabled shop garden centre* ✈

General Register House
EDINBURGH

Map 11 NT27
(East end of Princes St)
☎ 031-556 6585
The headquarters of the Scottish Record Office and repository for the national archives of Scotland, designed by Robert Adam and founded in 1774. The historical and legal search rooms are available to researchers, and changing

exhibitions are held, including Scotland and Europe (from Mar) and Robert Adam and Scotland: 1792-1992 (Jul 6-26 Sep).
Open Mon-Fri 9-4.45. Exhibitions 10-4. (Closed certain PHs & part of Nov).
Free.
& *toilets for disabled shop* ✈

Georgian House
EDINBURGH

Map 11 NT27
7 Charlotte Sq
☎ 031-225 2160
The house is part of Robert Adam's splendid north side of Charlotte Square, the epitome of New Town architecture. The lower floors of No 7 have been restored in the style of 1800, when the house was new. It gives a vivid

impression of Georgian life, in both the grand public rooms and the servants' areas.
Open Apr-Oct, Mon-Sat 10-5, Sun 2-5. Last admission 4.30pm.
£2.40 (ch & pen £1.20); (includes audiovisual show). Party.
(induction loop for hard of hearing) shop ✈
(NTS)

Gladstone's Land
EDINBURGH

Map 11 NT27
477b Lawnmarket
☎ 031-226 5856
Built in 1620, this six-storey tenement still has its arcaded front – a rare feature now. Visitors can also see unusual tempera paintings on the walls and ceilings. It is furnished as a typical home

of a 17th-century merchant, complete with ground-floor shop front and goods of the period.
Open Apr-Oct, Mon-Sat 10-5, Sun 2-5. Last admission 4.30pm.
£2.20 (ch & pen £1.10).
shop ✈
(NTS)

Huntly House
EDINBURGH

Map 11 NT27
142 Canongate
☎ 031-225 2424 ext 6689 & 031-225 1131 after 5pm & wknds.
This is one of the best-preserved 16th-century buildings in the Old Town. It was built in 1570 and later became the headquarters of the Incorporation of Hammermen. It is now the main

museum of local history, and has collections of silver, glassware, pottery and other items such as street signs.
Open all year, Mon-Sat, Jun-Sep 10-6, Oct-May 10-5. (During Festival period only Sun 2-5).
Free.
& *shop* ✈

& This symbol indicates that much or all of the attraction is accessible to wheelchairs. However, there may be some restrictions, so it would be wise to check in advance.

John Knox House
EDINBURGH

Map 11 NT27
The Netherbow, 43-45 High St
☎ 031-556 9579
John Knox is said to have died in the house, which was built by the goldsmith to Mary Queen of Scots. Renovation work has revealed the original floor in the Oak Room, and a magnificent painted ceiling. The house is traditionally associated with John Knox the Reformer and contains an exhibition

about his life and times. Events for 1992 include the Edinburgh Puppet Festival (13-25 Apr), Old Town Week (20-28 Jun), and the Scottish Storytelling Festival (17-31 Oct).
Open all year, Mon-Sat 10-5. (Closed Xmas & New Year). Last admission 30 mins before closure.
£1.20 (ch 50p, students & pen £1). Party 20+.
☕ & *toilets for disabled shop* ✈

Lady Stair's House
EDINBURGH

Map 11 NT27
off Lawnmarket
☎ 031-225 2424 ext 6593 & 031-225 1131 after 5pm & wknds.
Lady Stair lived in the 18th century and once owned this town house, but it dates back to 1622. It is now a museum housing various objects associated with

Robert Burns, Sir Walter Scott and Robert Louis Stevenson.
Open all year, Mon-Sat, Jun-Sep 10-6; Oct-May 10-5. (During Festival period only Sun 2-5).
Free.
shop ✈

Lauriston Castle
EDINBURGH

Map 11 NT27
Cramond Rd South, Davidson's Mains (NW outskirts of Edinburgh, 1m E of Cramond)
☎ 031-336 2060
The castle is a late 16th-century mansion, but is most notable as a classic example of the Edwardian age. It has a beautifully preserved Edwardian interior by one of Edinburgh's leading decorators, and still has the feel of an

Edwardian country house. There are spacious, pleasant grounds. Edwardian Extravaganza in late May and other special events throughout the year (tel 031-225 2424 Ext 6682).
Open all year, Apr-Oct, Sat-Thu 11-1 & 2-4; Nov-Mar wknds 2-4. (Last tour approx 3.20).
✱ *£2 (ch £1). Grounds only free.*
P & *shop* ✈

Museum of Childhood
EDINBURGH

Map 11 NT27
42 High St (Royal Mile)
☎ 031-225 2424 ext 6645
One of the first museums of its kind, it was reopened in 1986 after major expansion and reorganisation. It has a wonderful collection of toys, games and other belongings of children through the ages, to delight visitors both old and young.
Open all year, Mon-Sat, Jun-Sep 10-6; Oct-May 10-5. (During Festival period only Sun 2-5. (Closed Xmas).
Free.
&. *(3 floors only) toilets for disabled shop* ✠

National Gallery of Scotland
EDINBURGH

Map 11 NT27
The Mound
☎ 031-556 8921
Recognised as one of Europe's best smaller galleries, the National Gallery of Scotland occupies a handsome neo-classical building designed by William Playfair. It contains notable collections of works by Old Masters, Impressionists and Scottish artists. Among them are the *Bridgewater Madonna* by Raphael, Constable's *Dedham Vale*, and works by Titian, Velázquez, Van Gogh and Gauguin. Drawings, watercolours and original prints by Turner, Goya, Blake and others are shown on request, Monday to Friday 10-12.30 and 2-4.30. Special exhibitions for 1992 include Leonardo da Vinci: 'Madonna of the Yarnwinder' (15 May-12 Jul), and 'A Reflection of Taste: Dutch Art and Scotland' (13 Aug-18 Oct).
Open all year, Mon-Sat 10-5, Sun 2-5; (during Festival period Mon-Sat 10-6, Sun 11-6). Winter (Oct-Mar) some rooms may be closed. (Closed May Day, 25-26 Dec & 1-3 Jan).
Free. Admission charged to major exhibitions.
&. *shop* ✠

Nelson Monument
EDINBURGH

Map 11 NT27
Calton Hill
☎ 031-556 2716
Designed in 1807 and erected on Calton Hill, the monument dominates the east end of Princes Street. Visitors climbing to the top will enjoy superb views of the city. Every day except Sunday the time ball drops at 1pm as the gun at the castle goes off.
Open all year, Apr-Sep Mon 1-6 Tue-Sat 10-6; Oct-Mar Mon-Sat 10-3.
🅿 *shop* ✠
Details not confirmed for 1992

Places to visit in this guide are pinpointed on the atlas at the back of the book.

Palace of Holyroodhouse
EDINBURGH

Map 11 NT27
(at east end of Canongate)
☎ 031-556 7371 & 031-556 1096 (info)

The palace grew from the guesthouse of the Abbey of Holyrood, said to have been founded by David I after a miraculous apparition. Mary, Queen of Scots, had her court here from 1561 to 1567, and Bonnie Prince Charlie held levees at the palace during his occupation of Edinburgh. The castle is still used by the royal family, but can be visited when they are not in residence. Little remains of the original abbey except the ruined 13th-century nave of the church. The oldest part of the palace proper is James V's tower, with Mary's rooms on the second floor. A plaque marks the spot where Rizzio was murdered. The audience chamber where she debated with John Knox can also be seen. There are fine 17th-century state rooms, and the picture gallery is notable for its series of Scottish monarchs, starting in 330 BC with Fergus I. The work was done by Jacob de Wet in 1684-5, so many of the likenesses are based on imagination. The grounds are used for royal garden parties in summer. Special events for 1992 include: Until Mar, Exhibition of Watercolours of the Interior of Royal Residences commissioned by Queen Victoria and Prince Albert.
Open Winter, 6 Jan-28 Mar 9.30-3.45. (Closed Sun). Summer 29 Mar-Oct, wkdays 9.30-5.15, Sun 10.30-4.30. (Closed 11-26 May & 9 Jun-28 Jul). Subject to closure at short notice at other times telephone 031-556 1096.
£2.50 (ch £1.30, pen £2). Family ticket £6.50.
&. *shop* ✠

Parliament House
EDINBURGH

Map 11 NT27
Supreme Courts
☎ 031-225 2595
Scotland's independent parliament last sat in 1707, in this 17th-century building hidden behind an 1829 facade. It is now the seat of the Supreme Law Courts of Scotland and has been adapted to its changed use, but the Parliament Hall still has its fine old hammerbeam roof.
Open all year, Mon-Fri 10-4.
Free.
🍴 ✗ &. *toilets for disabled* ✠

The People's Story
EDINBURGH

Map 11 NT27
Canongate Tolbooth, 163 Canongate
☎ 031-225 2424 ext 6638/6687 or 031-225 1131 after 5 pm & wknds
The museum, housed in the 16th-century tolbooth, tells the story of the ordinary people of Edinburgh from the late 18th century to the present day. Reconstructions include a prison cell, 1930s pub and 1940s kitchen supported by photographs, displays, sounds, smells and a video.
Open Jun-Sep, Mon-Sat 10-6; Oct & May, Mon-Sat 10-5. Also, open Sun during Edinburgh Festival 2-5.
Free.
&. *(first floor accessible by lift) toilets for disabled shop* ✠

Royal Botanic Garden
EDINBURGH

Map 11 NT27
Inverleith Row
☎ 031-552 7171
The gardens offer 70 acres of peace and greenery close to the city centre. They were founded as a physick garden in 1670 at Holyrood, and came to Inverleith in 1823. The largest rhododendron collection in Britain can be seen here, and the different areas include an arboretum, a peat garden, a woodland garden, and rock and heath gardens. There is a splendid herbaceous border, and the plant houses have orchids, cacti and other specialities from a variety of climates. The gardens have colour all year round, even in winter when the plants with coloured bark come into their own. The exhibition hall has informative displays, and Inverleith House Gallery has art exhibitions. All major routes and areas of interest are accessible to wheelchairs, and there are purpose-built toilets for wheelchair users. Wheelchairs are available at the entrance.
Open all year Garden. (Closed 25 Dec & 1 Jan).
Free. Donations.
✗ *licensed* &. *(wheelchairs available at east/west gates) toilets for disabled shop* ✠

Royal Museum of Scotland (Chambers St)
EDINBURGH

Map 11 NT27
Chambers St
☎ 031-225 7534
This magnificent museum houses extensive international collections covering the Decorative Arts, Natural History, Science, Technology and Working Life, and Geology. A lively programme of special events including temporary exhibitions, films, lectures and concerts takes place throughout the year.
Open all year, Mon-Sat 10-5, Sun 2-5. (Closed 25-26 Dec & 1-2 Jan).
Free.
🍴 &. *toilets for disabled shop* ✠

Royal Museum of Scotland (Queen St)
EDINBURGH

Map 11 NT27
1 Queen St
☎ 031-225 7534
History and everyday life in Scotland, from the Stone Age to modern times are illustrated in this museum. There are artefacts from the Picts, Romans, Vikings and others. A new permanent gallery displays 'Dynasty: The Royal House of Stewart' – 300 years of Stewart rule in Scotland, illustrated by portraits and objects from the Scottish national collections.
Open all year, Mon-Sat 10-5, Sun 2-5. (Closed 25-26 Dec & 1-2 Jan).
Free.
🍴 &. *toilets for disabled shop* ✠

Royal Observatory Visitor Centre
EDINBURGH

Map 11 NT27
Blackford Hill
☎ 031-668 8405
The visitor centre explains the work of Scotland's national observatory both at home and overseas. There are displays on the latest discoveries about the universe, and a wide range of exhibits including two large telescopes and many antique examples. The Visitor Centre rooftop gives panoramic views over the city and the Braid Hills. A permanent exhibition includes the latest NASA photography, and there are also videos and computer games. Evening observing and winter breaks from October to March. Special events for 1992 include: Apr, The Universe Exhibition.
Open all year, Apr-Sep, Mon-Fri 10-4, wknds & PHs noon-5; Oct-Mar, daily 1-5. £1.50 (ch 75p). Season ticket £5. Family season ticket £10.
🅿 &. *(lift) toilets for disabled shop*

Scottish National Gallery of Modern Art
EDINBURGH

Map 11 NT27
Belford Rd
☎ 031-556 8921
This is the home of the national collection of 20th-century painting, sculpture and graphic art. Among the many modern artists represented are Derain, Picasso, Giacometti, Magritte, Henry Moore, Hepworth and Lichtenstein. There is also the national collection of modern Scottish art, with paintings and sculpture by Peploe, Fergusson, Cadell, Bellamy, Paolozzi and Conroy. Exhibitions for 1992 include Otto Dix: The Dresden Collection of Work on Paper (29 Feb-10 May), and James Pryde (14 Aug-11 Oct).The print room and library are open by appointment.
Open all year, Mon-Sat 10-5 & Sun 2-5. (During Festival Mon-Sat 10-6, Sun 11-6). (Closed May Day, 25-26 Dec & 1-3 Jan).
Free. Admission charged to major exhibitions.
🅿 🍴 &. *(lift) toilets for disabled shop* ✠

Scottish National Portrait Gallery
EDINBURGH

Map 11 NT27
Queen St
☎ 031-556 8921
The striking red Victorian building brings Scottish history to life with portraits of royals, rebels, soldiers, scientists, writers and many others, in all media including sculpture. The development of Highland dress is also illustrated, and there is an extensive reference section of engravings and the Scottish photography archive. A major exhibition is planned for 1 Aug-27 Sep 1992 – Allan Ramsay.
Open all year, daily, Mon-Sat 10-5, Sun 2-5. (During Festival, Mon-Sat 10-6, Sun 11-6). Winter lunchtime closure 12.30-1.30. (Closed May Day, 25-26 Dec & 1-3 Jan).
Free. Admission charged to major exhibitions.
🍴 &. *(lift) toilets for disabled shop* ✠

Scottish United Services Museum
EDINBURGH

Map 11 NT27
Edinburgh Castle
☎ 031-225 7534
The museum is in Edinburgh Castle. Exhibitions include 'The Story of the Scottish Soldier'.
Open all year, Apr-Sep, Mon-Sat 9.30-5.05, Sun 11-5.05; Oct-Mar, Mon-Sat 9.30-4.20, Sun 12.30-3.35.
✱ *Free admission after paying entrance fee to the Castle.*
&. *toilets for disabled shop* ✠

West Register House   EDINBURGH

Map 11 NT27
Charlotte Square
☎ 031-556 6585
The former church of St George (1811) was designed by Robert Reid in Greco-Roman style and is now the modern record branch of the Scottish Record

Office. It houses the exhibition '800 Years of Scottish History', and the Search Room is available to researchers. *Open Mon-Fri 9-4.45. Exhibitions 10-4. (Closed certain PHs & part of Nov).* *Free.*
& ✗ ▨

Suntrap Garden & Advice Centre   GOGAR

Map 11 NT17
43 Gogarbank (1m S off A8 Edinburgh to Glasgow road)
☎ 031-339 7283 & (0506) 854387
The three-acre garden comprises of many gardens within a single garden, including Italian, Rock, Rose, Peat and Woodland. Details from the Principal, Oatridge Agricultural College,

Ecclesmachan, Broxburn, West Lothian, EH52 6NH. Special events for 1992 include: 6 Jun, Open Day. *Open all year: Garden daily 9.30-dusk. Advice Centre Mon-Fri 9.30-4.30 (also open Sat & Sun, Apr-Sep 2.30-5). 50p (accompanied ch free).* 🅿 & *toilets for disabled*

Scottish Agricultural Museum   INGLISTON

Map 11 NT17
(National Museums of Scotland), Royal Highland Showground
☎ 031-225 7534 ext 313
Rural Scotland through the ages: the tools and equipment, the workers and their families, homes and lifestyles are all

illustrated by the models and exhibits devoted to Scottish agriculture. *Open mid Apr-Sep, Mon-Fri 10-4.30 & some Sun in summer Free.* 🅿 ⬛ & *toilets for disabled shop* ✗

Inveresk Lodge Garden   INVERESK

Map 11 NT37
☎ 031-336 2157
With a good deal of appeal, this charming garden specialises in plants, shrubs and roses suitable for growing on small plots. The 17th-century house makes an elegant backdrop and is open to the public for occasional exhibitions,

which are advertised locally. *Open all year, Mon-Fri 10-4.30, Sun 2-5. Last admission 30 mins before closing. Lodge open for temporary exhibitions only. 50p (ch accompanied by adult & pen 25p).* ✗ *(NTS)*

Blackness Castle   LINLITHGOW

Map 11 NS97
(4m N)
☎ 031-244 3101
Once this was one of the most important fortresses in Scotland. Used as a state prison during covenanting time and in the late-19th century as a powder magazine, it was one of four castles left fortified by the Articles of Union. Most

impressive are the massive 17th-century artillery emplacements. *Open all year, Apr-Sep weekdays 9.30-6, Sun 2-6. Oct-Mar, weekdays 9.30-4, Sun 2-4. (Closed Thu pm & Fri in winter; 25-26 Dec & 1-2 Jan). £1 (ch & pen 50p).* 🅿 *shop* ✗ *(AM)*

House of The Binns   LINLITHGOW

Map 11 NS97
(4m E off A904)
☎ Philipstoun (050683) 4255
An example of changing architectural tastes from 1612 onwards, the House of the Binns now stands as a Regency-style mansion. It was once a tall, grey, three-storeyed building with small windows and twin turrets; and after additions, reshaping and refacing it has evolved into a pretty U-shaped house, with crenellations and embellished windows. The most outstanding features are the beautiful early 17th-century moulded

plaster ceilings inside. This is the historic home of the Dalyell family – General Tam Dalyell raised the Royal Scots Greys here in 1681. Panoramic views from a site in the grounds. *Open Etr (18-20 Apr) Sat-Mon, daily 2-5, then 2 May-Sep, daily (ex Fri) 2-5. (Last admission 4.30pm). Parkland and panoramic viewpoint all year 10-7. £2.80 (ch & pen £1.40). Party. Members of the Royal Scots Dragoon Guards free when in uniform.* 🅿 & *(braille sheets)* ✗ *(NTS)*

Linlithgow Palace   LINLITHGOW

Map 11 NS97
☎ 031-244 3101
This 15th- to 17th-century royal palace was the birthplace of Mary Queen of Scots; a fire in 1746 left it a splendid ruin overlooking the south shore of the loch. A fine chapel, the great hall and a richly carved 16th-century fountain in

the quadrangle can still be seen. *Open all year, Apr-Sep, weekdays 9.30-6, Sun 2-6; Oct-Mar, weekdays 9.30-4, Sun 2-4. (Closed 25-26 Dec & 1-2 Jan). £1.50 (ch & pen 80p). Family ticket £4.* 🅿 & *shop* ✗ *(AM)*

Scottish Mining Museum   NEWTONGRANGE

Map 11 NT36
Lady Victoria Colliery (on A7)
☎ 031-663 7519
Newtongrange is the largest surviving coal company village in Scotland, and after a working life of almost 90 years, Lady Victoria Colliery is being restored and developed as a museum. An exhibition of talking tableaux in the

visitor centre portrays characters involved in the creation of the mine and its day-to-day organisation. The steam winding machine and pit-head can also be visited. Guided tours by a former miner are available. *Open Apr-Sep, daily 11-4. Last tour 3pm. £1.95 (ch & pen £1).* 🅿 ⬛ & *toilets for disabled shop* ✗

North Berwick Museum   NORTH BERWICK

Map 11 NT58
School Rd
☎ (0620) 3470
The former Burgh School contains a small museum with sections on natural history, local history, archaeology and domestic life. Exhibitions are held throughout the summer. Special events

for 1992 include: The Bass Rock, and Woodland Matters. *Open Etr-May & Oct, Fri & Sun 2-5, Sat & Mon 10-1 & 2-5; Jun-Sep, Mon-Sat 10-1 & 2-5, Sun 2-5. Free.* 🅿 *shop* ✗

Tantallon Castle   NORTH BERWICK

Map 11 NT58
(3m E on A198)
☎ 031-244 3101
A famous 14th-century stronghold of the Douglases facing towards the lonely Bass Rock from the rocky Firth of Forth shore. Nearby 16th- and 17th-century earthworks.

Open all year, Apr-Sep, weekdays 9.30-6, Sun 2-6; Oct-Mar, weekdays 9.30-4, Sun 2-4. (Closed Thu pm & Fri in winter; 25-26 Dec & 1-2 Jan). £1.50 (ch & pen 80p). Family ticket. 🅿 & *shop* ✗ *(AM)*

Edinburgh Crystal Visitor Centre   PENICUIK

Map 11 NT26
Eastfield Industrial Estate (on A701)
☎ (0968) 75128
A tour around the factory allows visitors to see the various stages in the art of glassmaking, including glass blowing, the 'lehr', cutting, polishing, engraving and sand etching. Audio-visual presentations

further explain the process. *Open all year. Factory tours Mon-Fri 9-3.30. (Closed Xmas, New Year & staff holidays). Visitor Centre Mon-Sat 9-5, Sun 11-5. Tours £1 (ch 50p). Party.* 🅿 ✗ *licensed* & *toilets for disabled shop* ✗

✱ An asterisk indicates that up-to-date information was not available at the time of our research – 1991 information has been published as an indication of what you may expect.

Scottish Mining Museum   PRESTONPANS

Map 11 NT37
Prestongrange (on B1348)
☎ 031-663 7519
The oldest documented coal mining site in Britain with 800 years of history, this museum shows a Cornish Beam Engine and on-site evidence of associated industries such as brickmaking and pottery, plus a 16th-century customs port. The 'Cutting the Coal' exhibition, in the David Spence Gallery, has an

underground gallery, a coalface, a reconstruction of a colliery workshop and a wonderful collection of coal-cutting machines and equipment. There is a guided tour of the site by a former miner. Special events for 1992 include: Apr-Sept, Steam Sundays on the first Sunday of each month. *Open Apr-Sep, daily 11-4. Last tour 3pm. £1 (ch & concessions 50p).* 🅿 ⬛ & *toilets for disabled shop* ✗

Dalmeny House   SOUTH QUEENSFERRY

Map 11 NT17
☎ 031-331 1888
This is the home of the Earl and the Countess of Rosebery, whose family have lived here for over 300 years. The house, however, only dates from 1815 when it was built in Tudor Gothic style. There are vaulted corridors and a splendid Gothic hammerbeamed hall, but the main rooms are in classical style. Dalmeny House has a magnificent situation on the Firth of Forth and there are delightful walks in the wooded

grounds and along the shore. Inside, it has fine French furniture, tapestries and porcelain from the Rothschild Mentmore collection. Early Scottish furniture is also shown, with 18th-century portraits, Rosebery racing momentoes and a display of pictures and items associated with Napoleon. *Open May-Sep, Sun-Thu 2-5.* ✱ *£3 (ch £1.50, students £2.50). Party 20+.* 🅿 ⬛ & *toilets for disabled* ✗ *(ex in grounds)*

Hopetoun House   SOUTH QUEENSFERRY

Map 11 NT17
(2m W on unclassified road)
☎ 031-331 2451

Scotland's greatest Adam mansion is the home of the 4th Marquess of Linlithgow. It was built in 1699 to a design by William Bruce, but between 1721 and 1754 it was enlarged by William and Robert Adam. The magnificent reception rooms have notable paintings by artists such as Canaletto, Gainsborough and Raeburn,

and there are also fine examples of furniture and a collection of china. A museum in the stables features an exhibition entitled 'Horse and Man' in Lowland Scotland.
The grounds are extensive, and include deer parks with red and fallow deer, and a herd of the rare St Kilda sheep. There are formal gardens as well, and it is possible to play croquet or petanque for a fee. Walks along the coast give views of the Forth bridges, which can also be seen from a special viewing platform. Facilities include a garden centre, a nature trail and a free Ranger Service. If prior notice is given special arrangements can be made for blind and disabled visitors. *Open 17 Apr-4 Oct, daily 10-5.30 (last admission 4.45). £3.30 (ch £1.60). Grounds £1.70 (ch 50p).* 🅿 ⬛ & *toilets for disabled shop garden centre*

Inchcolm Abbey — SOUTH QUEENSFERRY

Map 11 NT17
Inchcolm Island (1.5m S of Aberdour Access by ferry Apr-Sep)
☎ 031-244 3101
Situated on a green island on the Firth of Forth, the Augustinian abbey was founded in about 1123 by Alexander I. The well-preserved remains include a fine 13th-century octagonal chapter

house and a 13th-century wall painting.
Open all year, Apr-Sep, weekdays 9.30-6, Sun 2-6; Oct-Mar, weekdays 9.30-4, Sun 2-4. (Closed Thu pm & Fri in winter; 25-26 Dec & 1-2 Jan).
£1.50 (ch & pen 80p). Additional charge for ferry trip.
✠
(AM)

Torphichen Preceptory — TORPHICHEN

Map 11 NS97
☎ 031-244 3101
This was one of the principal seats of the Knights Hospitallers of St John. The central tower and the transepts of their church were rebuilt in the 18th century. There is also an exhibition on the

history of the knights in Scotland and overseas.
Open Apr-Sep, Mon-Sat 9.30-6, Sun 2-6.
£1 (ch & pen 50p).
🅿 ✠
(AM)

STRATHCLYDE

Burns' Cottage — ALLOWAY

Map 10 NS31
(2m S of Ayr)
☎ (0292) 41215
Thatched cottage built in 1757, now a museum, birthplace of Robert Burns in 1759.

Open all year, Jun-Aug 9-7 (Sun 10-7); Apr-May & Sep-Oct 10-5 (Sun 2-5); Nov-Mar 10-4 (Closed Sun).
✱ *£1.50 (ch & pen 75p) includes entry to Burns Monument & Gardens.*
🅿 ☕ ⓒ shop ✠ *(ex in grounds)*

Burns' Monument — ALLOWAY

Map 10 NS31
(2m S of Ayr)
☎ (0292) 41321
Robert Burns was born in the thatched cottage in 1759, two years after it was built. It is now a museum. The monument was built in 1823 to a fine design by Thomas Hamilton Junior,

with sculptures of characters in Burns' poems by a self-taught artist, James Thorn.
Open as for Burns' Cottage (ex closed Nov-Mar).
✱ *Admission included in entrance to Burns' Cottage*
🅿 ⓒ shop ✠ *(ex in grounds)*

Land O'Burns Centre — ALLOWAY

Map 10 NS31
Murdoch's Loan
☎ (0292) 43700
The centre gives a potted introduction to the life of Robert Burns, with an audio-visual, multi-screen presentation

and an exhibition area. There are also landscaped gardens.
Open daily, Oct-May 10-5; Jun & Sep 10-5.30; Jul-Aug 10-6.
✱ *Audio visual theatre 40p (ch 20p).*
🅿 ☕ ⓒ toilets for disabled shop ✠

Auchindrain – Old West Highland Township — AUCHINDRAIN

Map 10 NN00
(5.5m SW of Inverary)
☎ Furnace (04995) 235
Auchindrain is an original West Highland township, or village of great antiquity, and the only communal tenancy township to have survived on its centuries-old site. The township buildings, which have been restored and

preserved, are furnished and equipped in the style of various periods to give the visitor a taste of what life was really like for the Highlander in past ages.
Open Apr-May & Sep, Sun-Fri 10-5; Jun-Aug, daily 10-5.
£2.20 (ch £1.40, pen £1.70). Family ticket £6.80.
🅿 ☕ shop

Maclaurin Art Gallery & Rozelle House — AYR

Map 10 NS32
Rozelle Park, Monument Rd
☎ Alloway (0292) 45447
A modern art collection in the house and Henry Moore sculptures are permanent fixtures, with art, craft, photography and sculpture all featured in temporary shows. The park has a

nature trail and there is a small military museum. Social history exhibitions and park centre under development.
Open all year, Mon-Sat 10-5, Sun (Apr-Oct only) 2-5. (Closed Xmas & New Year).
Free.
🅿 ☕ ✕ ⓒ shop ✠

Balloch Castle Country Park — BALLOCH

Map 11 NS38
☎ Alexandria (0389) 58216
Set beside Loch Lomond, the country park spreads over a hillside with woodland trails, a walled garden, and lawns for picnics giving wonderful views. Overlooking the lawns is Balloch Castle, built in 1808. Its visitor centre gives an

introduction to local history and wildlife.
Open Visitor Centre, Apr-Sep daily 10-6. Country Park 8-dusk. Garden 10-6 (4.30 winter).
Free.
🅿 ⓒ toilets for disabled shop

Sea Life Centre — BARCALDINE

Map 10 NM94
Loch Creran (10m N of Oban on A828)
☎ Ledaig (0631) 72386
This ultra-modern centre has Britain's largest collection of native marine life. The unique layout is designed for greater understanding, and includes a tidepool touch tank and intertidal dump tank. Seals can be seen underwater, with a

twice-daily talk and feeding time. During the summer young seals can be viewed prior to their release back into the wild. A full talks programme is available throughout the day during the peak season.
Open mid Feb-late Nov, daily 9-6. (Jul-Aug 7pm).
Admission fee payable.
🅿 ✕ licensed ⓒ toilets for disabled shop ✠

Roman Bath-House — BEARSDEN

Map 11 NS57
Roman Rd
☎ 031-244 3101
Considered to be the best surviving visible Roman building in Scotland the bath-house was discovered in 1973 during excavations for a construction

site. It was originally built for use by the Roman garrison at Bearsden Fort, which is part of the Antonine Wall defences.
Open all reasonable times.
Free.
ⓒ ✠
(AM)

Younger Botanic Garden — BENMORE

Map 10 NS18
(7m N of Dunoon on A815)
☎ Sandbanks (036985) 261

This is a woodland garden on a grand scale, with many species of conifers, and

rhododendrons. It became a specialist garden of the Royal Botanic Garden in Edinburgh in the 1930s, but the garden's origins go back much further. The colours are especially good in late spring and early summer, and there are fine views. About half the garden is accessible to the disabled. Wheelchairs are available on loan and there are purpose-built toilets for wheelchair users. The garden is famous for its Redwood Avenue, and has some of the largest conifers in the British Isles.
Open 15 Mar-Oct, daily 10-6.
£1.50 (ch 50p, concessions £1).
🅿 ☕ ⓒ toilets for disabled shop

Gladstone Court Museum — BIGGAR

Map 11 NT03
(entrance by 113 High St)
☎ (0899) 21050
An old-fashioned village street is portrayed in this museum, which is set out in a century-old coach-house. On display are reconstructed shops, complete with old signs and adverts; a

bank, a telephone exchange, a photographer's booth and other interesting glimpses into the recent past.
Open Etr-Oct, daily 10-12.30 & 2-5, Sun 2-5.
✱ *£1 (ch 50p, pen 80p). Family ticket £2.50. Party.*
🅿 ⓒ shop ✠

Greenhill Covenanters House — BIGGAR

Map 11 NT03
Burn Braes
☎ (0899) 21050
This 17th-century farmhouse was brought, stone by stone, ten miles from Wiston and reconstructed at Biggar. It has relics of the turbulent 'Covenanting' period, when men and women defended

the right to worship in Presbyterian style. Rare breeds of sheep and poultry are also kept.
Open Etr-mid Oct, daily 2-5.
✱ *50p (ch 30p, pen 40p). Family ticket £1.20. Party.*
🅿 ⓒ ✠

Moat Park Heritage Centre — BIGGAR

Map 11 NT03
☎ (0899) 21050
The centre illustrates the history and geology of the Upper Clyde and Tweed valleys with interesting displays.
Open all year, Apr-Oct, daily 10-5, Sun

2-5; Nov-Feb, weekdays during office hours. Other times by prior arrangement.
✱ *£1.50 (ch 80p, pen £1.20). Family ticket £4. Party.*
🅿 ⓒ *(with assistance) toilets for disabled shop* ✠

THE DAVID LIVINGSTONE CENTRE BLANTYRE

BIRTHPLACE OF SCOTLAND'S GREATEST EXPLORER

Africa is now just off the M74 — turn off at junction 5 — and explore the David Livingstone Centre. Besides our prize winning Museum we have extensive parkland and grounds, a Tearoom and newly expanded free coach and car parking. Other attractions include Adventure Playground and Gift Shop.

Adults £1.70 · OAP £1 · Children 85p
(Discounts available for groups)

Telephone: Blantyre (0698) 823140

David Livingstone Centre — BLANTYRE

Map 11 NS65
☎ (0698) 823140
David Livingstone was born in a single-roomed house in Shuttle Row, Blantyre, and the whole row is now an unusual museum. It has displays on the town, and on Livingstone's life and his work in Africa. The story continues in the African Pavilion, which looks at the continent today. Special events for 1992 include: Opening of Exhibition from Zambia.
Open Apr-Oct, Mon-Sat 10-6, Sun 2-6. Last admission 5.15. Other times by appointment only.
✱ £1.50 (ch 75p, pen 75p).
🅿 ♿ toilets for disabled shop (ex in grounds)

Bothwell Castle — BOTHWELL

Map 11 NS75
(entrance at Uddington by traffic lights)
☎ 031-244 3101
Besieged, captured and 'knocked about' several times in the Scottish-English wars, the castle is a splendid ruin. Archibald the Grim built the curtain wall; later, in 1786, the Duke of Buccleuch carved graffiti — a coronet and initials — beside a basement well.
Open all year, Apr-Sep, weekdays 9.30-6, Sun 2-6; Oct-Mar, weekdays 9.30-4, Sun 2-4. (Closed Thu pm & Fri in winter; also 25-26 Dec & 1-2 Jan).
£1 (ch & pen 50p).
🅿
(AM)

Strone House — CAIRNDOW

Map 10 NN11
☎ (04996) 284
The pinetum was established in 1860, and the garden also has rhododendrons, azaleas, daffodils and various exotic plants. Also here is the tallest tree in Britain (205ft).
Open Apr-Oct, 9-dusk.
🅿♿
Details not confirmed for 1992

For an explanation of the symbols and abbreviations, see page 2.

Carnassarie Castle — CARNASSARIE CASTLE

Map 10 NM80
(2m N of Kilmartin off A816)
☎ 031-244 3101
Built in the 16th-century by John Carswell, first Protestant Bishop of the Isles, the castle was taken and partly destroyed in Argyll's rebellion of 1685.
It consists of a tower house with a courtyard built on to it.
Open at all reasonable times.
Free.
🅿
(AM)

Summerlee Heritage Trust — COATBRIDGE

Map 11 NS76
West Canal St
☎ (0236) 31261
Twenty-five acres of a former iron works are used here to illustrate the story of the Industrial Revolution and its effect on Scottish culture and society. Special events for 1992 include: May, Spring Fling; Jun, Historic Vehicle Festival and Autojumble; Sept, Model and Engineering Fair.
Open daily 10-5pm. (Closed 25-26 Dec & 1-2 Jan).
Free.
🅿 ♿ (wheelchair available & staff assistance) toilets for disabled shop

Culzean Castle — CULZEAN CASTLE

Map 10 NS21
(4m W of Maybole, off A77)
☎ Kirkoswald (06556) 274
This great 18th-century castle stands on a clifftop site in spacious grounds (see below) and was designed by Robert Adam for David, 10th Earl of Cassillis. It is noted for its oval staircase, circular drawing room and plasterwork. The Eisenhower Room explores the general's links with Culzean. There are numerous events taking place here throughout the year.
Open Castle, Visitor Centre, restaurant & shops Apr-25 Oct, daily 10.30-5.30 (last admission 5pm). Other times by appointment.
£3 (ch & pen £1.50). Party.
🅿 (charged) ♿ ✕ licensed ♿ (lift) toilets for disabled shop
(NTS)

Culzean Country Park — CULZEAN CASTLE

Map 10 NS21
(4m W of Maybole, off A77)
☎ Kirkoswald (06556) 269
The country park and castle together make one of the most popular days out in Scotland. Culzean was Scotland's first country park, and covers 563 acres with a wide range of attractions — shoreline, woodland walks, parkland, an adventure playground, and gardens, including a walled garden of 1783. The visitor centre has various facilities and information, and is also the base of the ranger naturalists who provide guided walks and other services. Various events are held each year.
Open all year.
Country Park £4.50 per car, £7 minibus/caravan, £1.10 motor cycles, free to members & pedestrians. Party.
🅿 (charged) ♿ ✕ licensed ♿ (wheelchairs available) toilets for disabled shop garden centre
(NTS)

Dumbarton Castle — DUMBARTON

Map 11 NS37
☎ 031-244 3101
The castle is set on the 240ft Dumbarton Rock above the River Clyde, and dominates the town (the capital of the Celtic kingdom of Strathclyde). Most of what can be seen today dates from the 18th and 19th centuries, but there are a few earlier remains, and the rock gives spectacular views.
Open all year, Apr-Sep, weekdays 9.30-6, Sun 2-6; Oct-Mar, weekdays 9.30-4, Sun 2-4. (Closed Thu & Fri pm in winter also 25-26 Dec & 1-2 Jan).
£1 (ch & pen 50p).
🅿 shop
(AM)

Achamore Gardens — GIGHA ISLAND

Map 10 NR64
☎ Gigha (05835) 267
The wonderful woodland gardens of rhododendrons and azaleas were created by Sir James Horlick Bt, who bought the little island of Gigha in 1944. Many of the plants were brought in laundry baskets from his former home in Berkshire, and others were added over the following 29 years. Sub-tropical plants flourish in the rich soil and virtually frost-free climate, and there is a walled garden for some of the finer specimens.
Open all year, daily.
£2 (ch & pen £1).
🅿♿

GLASGOW

Map 11 NS56
Glasgow was the second city of the British Empire, a 'dear, dirty city' which was a hub of the Industrial Revolution. Now it is clean, and has become a major attraction for visitors, who are discovering its artistic and architectural riches and its inimitable atmosphere. The biggest surprise for newcomers is the amount of open space in the city, which has over 70 richly varied public parks and several public golf courses. Glasgow Green has been open common land for centuries, but the heyday of the park was in the 19th century, when numerous stretches of land were bought and laid out for the public. In the heart of the city is the medieval cathedral, close to Provand's Lordship, Glasgow's oldest house, and to an array of splendid Victorian buildings. At the end of the Victorian era, Charles Rennie Mackintosh led the way in making Glasgow a centre for Art Nouveau; his style is epitomised by the Willow Tea Rooms, which are serving tea once more. Mackintosh's home has been reconstructed in the Hunterian Art Gallery, one of Glasgow's impressive galleries and museums. The most astonishing is the Burrell Collection, but there are many others in easy reach of the city centre.

Bellahouston Park — GLASGOW

Map 11 NS56
Ibrox
☎ 041-427 4224
The park was the site of the Empire Exhibition in 1938, and covers 171 acres only three miles from the city centre. There are sweeping lawns, a sunken garden and a walled garden, with a multi-purpose sports centre at the west end and an all-weather athletics track next to it. A Charles Rennie Mackintosh-designed house is under construction. The Glasgow Show and world pipe band championships are held in the park.
Open all year, 8am-dusk.
🅿 ♿ toilets for disabled (ex in park)
Details not confirmed for 1992

Botanic Gardens — GLASGOW

Map 11 NS56
Queen Margaret Dr, off Great Western Rd
☎ 041-334 2422
The gardens were established in 1817 from an older university physick garden, and moved to this site in 1842. There is an outstanding plant collection, but the most remarkable feature is the 23,000 sq ft Kibble Palace, a spectacular glasshouse with soaring tree ferns inside, set off by a number of Victorian sculptures. There are more conventional glasshouses too, showing orchids and other exotica. The grounds are laid out with lawns and beds, including a chronological border and a herb garden. At the northern edge the ground slopes down to the River Kibble, which is crossed by footbridges.
The Kibble Palace open 10-4.45 (4.15 in winter). The main glasshouse open Mon-Sat 1-4.45 (4.15 in winter), Sun 12-4.45 (4.15 in winter). Gardens open daily 7-dusk.
♿ toilets for disabled (ex in grounds)
Details not confirmed for 1992

Burrell Collection — GLASGOW

Map 11 NS56
Pollok Country Park
☎ 041-649 7151
John Julius Norwich has said that 'in all history, no municipality has ever received from one of its native sons a gift of such munificence'. The Burrell Collection was amassed over some 80 years by Sir William Burrell, who presented it to Glasgow in 1944. It is now beautifully housed in a specially designed gallery, opened by HM The Queen on 21 October 1983.
Among the 8,000 items in the collection are Ancient Egyptian alabaster; Chinese
continued . . .

ceramics, bronzes and jade; Japanese prints; Near Eastern rugs and carpets; Turkish pottery; and European medieval art, including metalwork, sculpture, illuminated manuscripts, ivories, and two of the world's best collections of stained glass and tapestries. There are also medieval doorways and windows, now set in the walls of mellow sandstone; British silver and needlework; and paintings and sculptures, ranging from the 15th to the early 20th centuries,

with work by Cranach, Bellini, Rembrandt, Millet, Degas, Manet, Cezanne and others. Wise visitors come back more than once, partly because there is too much to see at one go, and partly to revisit their favourite treasures.
Open all year, Mon-Sat 10-5, Sun noon-6. (Closed 25 Dec & 1 Jan).
Free.
🅿 (charged) ✕ licensed ᾅ (wheelchairs available, tape guides for blind) toilets for disabled shop ✘

Cathedral   GLASGOW

Map 11 NS56
Castle St
☎ 031-244 3101
This is the most complete medieval cathedral surviving on the Scottish mainland. It was founded in the 6th century by St Kentigern, better known as Mungo ('dear one'), Glasgow's patron saint, and dates from the 13th and 14th centuries. The Cathedral was threatened at the time of the Reformation, but the city's trade guilds formed an armed guard to ensure that no damage was done. The choir pews are named after

those guilds, and after more modern city organisations which helped with renovation work in the 1950s. The Cathedral is on two levels, and the lower church contains the tomb of St Kentigern, covered by an embroidered cloth. Nearby is the St Kentigern tapestry, presented in the 1970s.
Open all year, Apr-Sep, weekdays 9.30-6, Sun 2-6; Oct-Mar, weekdays 9.30-4, Sun 2-4. (Closed 25-26 Dec & 1-2 Jan).
Free.
✘
(AM)

Places to visit in this guide are pinpointed on the atlas at the back of the book.

Craigie Hall   GLASGOW

Map 11 NS56
6 Rowan Rd, off Dumbreck Rd
☎ 041-427 6884
Craigie Hall is one of Glasgow's finest Victorian residences where, in 1897, the famous music or organ room was fitted providing a rare example of a Mackintosh instrument. The house was

owned by the famous Green family – Glasgow's entertainment moguls – until the late 1970s, when it was bought and restored by its present owners.
Telephone for opening details
✱ £1.50 (ch 75p, pen & students £1)
🅿 shop ✘

Glasgow Art Gallery & Museum   GLASGOW

Map 11 NS56
Kelvingrove
☎ 041-357 3929

The gallery's extraordinary wealth of pictures includes works by Giorgione and Rembrandt, and is especially strong on the French Impressionists, Post-Impressionists, and Scottish artists from

the 17th century to the present day. The painting which has attracted the most attention, however, is Salvador Dali's *Christ of St John of the Cross*, which raised a storm when it was bought in the 1950s. Other areas show sculpture, porcelain, silver, and a magnificent display of arms and armour. One section is devoted to the 'Glasgow Style', with furniture by Charles Rennie Mackintosh and others. Archaeology, ethnography and natural history are also featured, and special attention is paid to Scottish wildlife.
Open all year, Mon-Sat 10-5, Sun noon-6. (Closed 25 Dec & 1 Jan).
Free.
🅿 ☛ ✕ ᾅ toilets for disabled shop ✘

For an explanation of the symbols and abbreviations, see page 2.

Greenbank Garden   GLASGOW

Map 11 NS56
Flenders Rd, Clarkston (off B726 on southern outskirts of the city)
☎ 041-639 3281
The spacious walled and woodland gardens are attractively laid out in the grounds of an elegant Georgian house (not open), and are best seen between April and October. The aim is to help local owners of small gardens, and a very wide range of flowers and shrubs is grown to show what is possible. There is

also a garden and greenhouse designed for disabled enthusiasts, with special gardening tools. A programme of the many walks and other events is available on request.
Garden open all year, daily 9.30-sunset. (Closed Xmas & New Year).
£1.50 (ch 16 & pen 80p). Party.
🅿 ☛ ᾅ (wheelchairs available) toilets for disabled shop (& plant sales) ✘
(NTS)

HMS Plymouth   GLASGOW

Map 11 NS56
Plantation Quay, Govan Rd
☎ 041-427 1407
Here is a chance to see Scotland's own Falklands frigate, bombed and battered

but home safely.
Open all year, daily 10-dusk.
✱ £2 (ch & pen £1).
🅿 ☛ ✕ shop ✘

Haggs Castle   GLASGOW

Map 11 NS56
100 St Andrews Dr
☎ 041-427 2725
Adults are welcome, but the museum is really meant for children. The house was built in the 1580s, taken over by the Army in World War II, converted into flats and finally transformed into a museum in the 1970s. Children are encouraged to find out its history through worksheets and quizzes, and can

explore the house, from the old-style kitchen up to the 17th-century bedroom and Victorian nursery. The hands-on approach to education extends to weekend and holiday activities, including learning traditional crafts. Regular temporary exhibitions are held.
Open all year, Mon-Sat 10-5, Sun noon-6. (Closed 25 Dec & 1 Jan).
Free.
ᾅ shop ✘

Hunterian Art Gallery   GLASGOW

Map 11 NS56
The University of Glasgow
☎ 041-330 5431
The core of the collection is a group of paintings bequeathed in the 18th century by Dr William Hunter, but it has grown a good deal since his time. There are important works by James McNeill Whistler, an ever-growing collection of 19th- and 20th-century Scottish paintings, contemporary British art and sculpture, and a remarkable re-creation of Charles Rennie Mackintosh's home, including the windows and front door. The print collection has some 15,000 items, from Old Masters to modern, and

there is a changing programme of print exhibitions. Special events for 1992 include: 15 Feb-16 Apr, A Century of Scottish Drawings and Watercolours; 2 May-27 Jun, Avant-Garde British Printmaking 1914-1960 from the British Museum; 11 Jul-10 Oct, Works on Paper by James McNeill Whistler.
Open all year. Main gallery Mon-Sat 9.30-5. Mackintosh House Mon-Sat 9.30-12.30 & 1.30-5. Telephone for PH closures.
Free.
ᾅ (lift, wheelchair available) toilets for disabled shop ✘

Hunterian Museum   GLASGOW

Map 11 NS56
The University of Glasgow (2m W of city centre)
☎ 041-330 4221
The museum is named after the 18th-century physician, Dr William Hunter, who bequeathed his large and important collections of coins, medals, fossils, geological specimens and archaeological and ethnographic items to the university. Since the museum opened in 1807 there have been many additions, and the

emphasis is now on Geology, Archaeology, Coins and Anthropology. The exhibits are shown in the main building of the university, and temporary exhibitions are held.
Open all year, Mon-Sat 9.30-5. (Closed certain PH's). Possible extension of summer hours.
Free.
☛ ᾅ (access by lift, prior arrangement) shop ✘

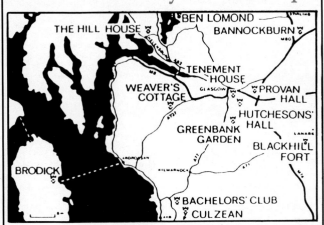
Hutchesons' Hall   GLASGOW

Map 11 NS56
158 Ingram St
☎ 041-552 8391
This handsome 19th-century building was designed by David Hamilton and is now the National Trust for Scotland's regional office. There is a visitor centre and a shop.

*Open – Visitor centre & Function Hall Mon-Fri 9-5, Sat 10-4. Shop Mon-Fri 9-5, Sat 10-4. (Closed PH's & 1-5 Jan). Hall on view subject to functions in progress.
Free.*
⌕ *toilets for disabled shop* ✖
(NTS)

Linn Park   GLASGOW

Map 11 NS56
Cathcart (southern outskirts of Glasgow).
☎ 041-637 1147
The park covers 200 acres of hillside by White Cart Water, with riverside and woodland walks, a nature trail, a children's zoo and a collection of British ponies and Highland cattle. The 18-hole golf course is another attraction, and

also in the park is a ruined 14th-century castle. Countryside ranger service; various events. Adventure playground for the disabled adjacent to park (Netherlee Road).
Open all year, daily 7am-dusk.
P ⌕ *(some parts of river walkway unsuitable)*
Details not confirmed for 1992

✶ An asterisk indicates that up-to-date information was not available at the time of our research – 1991 information has been published as an indication of what you may expect.

McLellan Galleries   GLASGOW

Map 11 NS56
270 Sauchiehall St
☎ 041-331 1854
The McLellan Galleries were officially re-opened on 2nd March 1990 by Her Majesty The Queen, on her visit to inaugurate Glasgow as European Cultural Capital 1990. With over 1,200 sq metres of top gallery space, the McLellan Galleries provide Glasgow Museums with the opportunity to bring

to Glasgow major exhibitions and establish Glasgow as Britain's second art city, with a popular and international exhibition programme.
*Open Mon-Sat 10-5, Sun noon-6 during exhibitions. 17 Jan-22 Mar "The Alan Davie Retrospective"; 14 May-28 Sep "The America Project". For details of other 1992 exhibitions please write or telephone.
Admission fee payable.*
⌕ *(lift) toilets for disabled shop* ✖

Museum of Transport   GLASGOW

Map 11 NS56
Kelvin Hall, 1 Bunhouse Rd
☎ 041-357 3929
The first Museum of Transport was an old tram depot, but in 1988 the collections were handsomely rehoused in Kelvin Hall. The new museum is a feast of nostalgia for older Glaswegians and a fascinating look at the past for younger visitors, with Glasgow buses, a reconstruction of a Glasgow side street in the year 1938, and Glasgow trams (last used in 1962, when they made their way around the city in a grand, final

procession). There are Scottish-made cars, fire engines, horse-drawn vehicles, cycles and motorcycles, and a walk-in car showroom with vehicles from the 1930s to the present day. Railways are represented by steam locomotives and a Glasgow subway station; and the already notable collection of ship models has been expanded.
*Open all year, Mon-Sat 10-5, Sun noon-6. (Closed 25 Dec & 1 Jan).
Free.*
P ⌕ ⌕ *(wheelchair available) toilets for disabled shop* ✖

People's Palace   GLASGOW

Map 11 NS56
Glasgow Green
☎ 041-554 0223

This museum looks at the work and leisure of the ordinary people of Glasgow, with exhibits ranging from a 2nd-century Roman bowl to mementoes of the Jacobite risings, football games

and boxing matches. Glasgow's trades and industries are illustrated with fine products of the city's potteries, textile mills and foundries; and there is an interesting section on Glasgow's tobacco trade and immensely rich 'Tobacco Lords'. There are also numerous banners, posters and other material from Glasgow's days of campaigning for wider voting rights, votes for women and recognition of trade unions.
Beyond the main museum building is the glass-and-iron expanse of the Winter Gardens, a huge conservatory with tropical plants.
*Open all year, Mon-Sat 10-5, Sun noon-6. (Closed 25 Dec-1 Jan).
Free.*
P ⌕ ⌕ *toilets for disabled shop* ✖

Pollok Country Park   GLASGOW

Map 11 NS56
2060 Pollokshaws Rd ˙
☎ 041-632 9299 & 041-649 0331
The leafy 361-acre park was presented to the city in 1966 by Mrs Anne Maxwell Macdonald, whose family owned the Pollok estates for nearly 700 years. It is home to two major museums, the Burrell Collection and Pollok House, and its many outdoor attractions range from a jogging track to a display rose garden and a demonstration garden. Amateurs are given advice here on a wide range of gardening matters. There are waterside

and woodland trails to follow. The Countryside Rangers' Centre gives information on these and on the park's history and wildlife (ranger service available). The park is also home to a championship herd of Highland cattle, which represents the City of Glasgow at agricultural shows around the country.
Open – Park always. Demonstrations & display garden open Mon-Thu 8-4, Fri 8-3, wknds 8-6.30 (winter wknds 8-4pm).
P ✖ ⌕ *toilets for disabled shop (at Ranger Centre)*
Details not confirmed for 1992

Pollok House   GLASGOW

Map 11 NS56
(3m S)
☎ 041-632 0274

Given to the city at the same time as the land for Pollok Country Park, the house contains the remarkable Stirling Maxwell collection of Spanish paintings, including works by El Greco, Murillo and Goya. Silver, ceramics and furniture collected by the family over the generations are also on display.
*Open all year, Mon-Sat 10-5, Sun noon-6. (Closed 25 Dec & 1 Jan).
Free.*
P ⌕ ⌕ *shop* ✖

Provan Hall   GLASGOW

Map 11 NS56
Auchinlea Rd
☎ 041-771 6372
This 15th-century mansion house has remained virtually unchanged since before the Reformation – a remarkable survivor in a built-up part of Glasgow. Once the country residence of the

Prebend of Provan (a canon of Glasgow Cathedral), it stands in Auchinlea Park, which has a formal and informal gardens, including a garden for the blind.
Telephone for opening hours.
🅿 ⅃ ✠ *(ex in grounds)* 🚐
Details not confirmed for 1992

Provand's Lordship   GLASGOW

Map 11 NS56
3 Castle St
☎ 041-552 8819
The Prebend of Provan (see Provan Hall) used this house as his city residence. It was built in 1471 as a manse for the Cathedral and St Nicholas Hospital, and is the city's oldest house. Mary Queen of Scots is reputed to have stayed here; in Victorian times it was used as an alehouse; in the early 1900s it was a sweet shop; and the city hangman used to live in a lean-to next door (now

demolished). The house has been carefully restored and displays furniture, pictures and stained-glass panels from various periods in the city's history. There is a fine collection of 17th-century Scottish furniture, and the machines which made the sweets in the house's sweetshop days can be seen.
Open all year, Mon-Sat 10-5, Sun noon-6. (Closed 25 Dec & 1 Jan).
Free.
shop ✠

Rouken Glen Park   GLASGOW

Map 11 NS56
Giffnock
☎ 041-638 1101
Fine walks can be taken along riverside pathways through the deep, wooded glen, and the waterfall at the head of the glen is a noted beauty spot. The park also offers the pleasures of a large walled

garden and spreading lawns, a picturesque loch for boating, a large enclosed children's play area (dog free) and an 18-hole pitch and putt course.
Open all year, daily, dawn-dusk.
Free.
🍽 ✗ *licensed* ⅃ *shop garden centre*

For an explanation of the symbols and abbreviations, see page 2.

Tenement House   GLASGOW

Map 11 NS56
145 Buccleuch St, Garnethill (N of Charing Cross)
☎ 041-333 0183
This National Trust for Scotland property shows an unsung but once-typical side of Glasgow life: it is a first-floor flat, built in 1892, with a parlour, bedroom, kitchen and bathroom, furnished with the original box beds, kitchen range, sink, and coal bunker, a rosewood piano and other articles. It was the home of Miss Agnes Toward from 1911 to 1965, and was bought by

an actress who carefully preserved its 'time capsule' quality until the Trust acquired and restored it. Today the contents of the flat are interesting for the vivid picture they give of one section of Glasgow society. Two flats on the ground floor provide reception, interpretative and educational facilities.
Open Apr-1 Nov, daily 2-5; 7 Nov-Mar, Sat-Sun 2-4.(Last admission 30 mins before closing).
£1.50 (ch 80p). Party (not exceeding 15).
✠
(NTS)

University of Glasgow Visitor Centre   GLASGOW

Map 11 NS56
University Av
☎ 041-330 5511
The University of Glasgow's Visitor Centre is a spacious, pleasant attraction with leaflets, publications and video displays explaining how the university works, what courses are available and which university events are open to the public. It forms the starting point for

guided tours of the university's historic attractions, including the Hunterian Museum, Memorial Chapel, Bute and Randolph Halls, Professors' Square, Lion and Unicorn Staircase, and Main Gates.
Open all year, Mon-Sat 9.30-5. Also May-Oct, Sun 2-5.
Free.
🍽 ⅃ *toilets for disabled shop* ✠

Victoria Park   GLASGOW

Map 11 NS56
Whiteinch
☎ 041-959 2128
Workmen who were digging a path in the park in 1887 came across stone-like tree stumps which turned out to be fossil remains, some 230 million years old. They are the best-known examples, and

can be seen in the Fossil Grove building. Elsewhere the park has tree-lined walks, an arboretum and formal beds.
Fossil Grove Building open Mon-Fri 8-4, wknds pm only. Park open daily 7-dusk.

Details not confirmed for 1992

✠ The 'No Dogs' symbol does not normally apply to guide dogs – these are permitted in most establishments.

Museum of the Cumbraes   GREAT CUMBRAE ISLAND MILLPORT

Map 10 NS15
Garrison House
☎ (0475) 530741 (Mon-Fri)
The Garrison House was built in 1745 by Captain Crawford as a barracks for his crew of 'The Royal George', a customs ship. It now houses a small museum which displays the history and

life of the Cumbraes. Along with artefacts from the collection, the museum displays a major exhibition each summer. There is also a fine collection of local photgraphs.
Open Jun-Sep, Tue-Sat 10-4.30.
Free.
⅃

Every effort is made to provide accurate information, but details might change during the currency of this guide.

McLean Museum & Art Gallery   GREENOCK

Map 10 NS27
15 Kelly St
☎ (0475) 23741
James Watt was born in Greenock, and various exhibits connected with him are shown. The museum also has an art collection, and there are displays on

shipping (including river paddle steamers and cargo vessels), natural history and ethnography.
Open all year, Mon-Sat 10-noon & 1-5. Closed local & national PH.
Free.
⅃ *shop* ✠

Chatelherault Country Park

Situated on the A72, 1½ miles south of Hamilton, Chatelherault Country Park is a unique addition to Scotland's range of tourist attractions. At its centre is Chatelherault Lodge, a carefully restored hunting lodge of the 1730's, designed by William Adam for the 5th Duke of Hamilton.

You can have a great day out at Chatelherault. The Information Centre tells you about life at Chatelherault in the early 18th C. There are woodland walks, picnic areas, a childrens' play area, the unique herd of wild white cattle, an Iron Age Fort, and the famous Cadzow Oaks – 500 years old and still thriving!

Whether you're interested in history, botany, archaeology, or whether you just want a day out in the Country Chatelherault's for you!

Opening hours:
Summer:
House – 11.00am to 4.30pm
V.Centre – 10.30am to 5.30pm
last admissions

Winter:
House – 11.00am to 4.00pm
V.Centre – 10.30am to 4.30pm
last admissions

Open all year round except for Christmas and New Year holidays

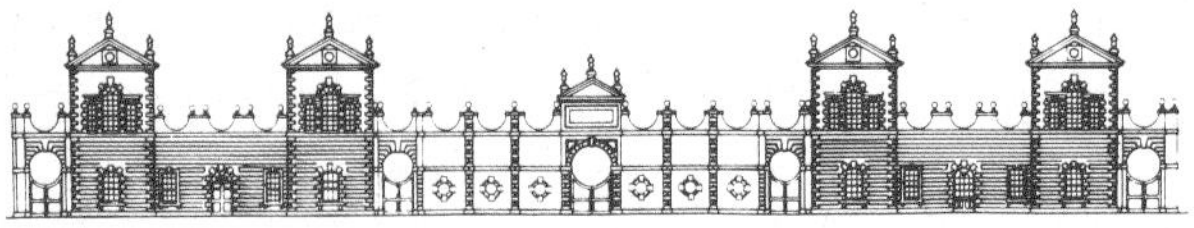

Chatelherault Country Park, Ferniegair nr. Hamilton
Telephone: Hamilton (0698) 426213

HAMILTON DISTRICT COUNCIL

Hamilton District Museum — HAMILTON

Map 11 NS75
129 Muir St
☎ (0698) 283981
This local history museum is housed in a 17th-century coaching inn complete with its old stables and an 18th-century assembly room. It has a reconstruction of a Victorian kitchen and a transport section; various items of local interest are also displayed. Special events for 1992 include: Exhibition Openings and Private Viewings, and Musical Concerts, to be arranged.
Open all year, Mon-Sat 10-5 (closed noon-1 on Wed & Sat).
Free.
P ♿ *shop* ✕

The Hill House — HELENSBURGH

Map 10 NS28
Upper Colquhoun St (off B832, between A82 & A814)
☎ (0436) 3900
The Hill House is a handsome example of Charles Rennie Mackintosh's work, modern but part-inspired by Scottish tower houses. It was commissioned by the publisher Walter Blackie. The gardens are being restored to Blackie's design, with features reflecting the work of Mackintosh. There is also a special display about Mackintosh.
Open Apr-23 & 28-29 Dec, daily 1-5. Last admission 4.30.
£2.40 (ch £1.20). Party.
✕
(NTS)

For an explanation of the symbols and abbreviations, see page 2.

Hunterston Power Station — HUNTERSTON

Map 10 NS15
☎ West Kilbride (0800) 838557
This is a nuclear power station of the advance gas-cooled reactor (AGR) type. Parties of about 32 are taken on guided tours and shown a video presentation on the generation of nuclear power.
Open May-Sep, Mon-Sat at 10, 11.30, 2 & 3.30; Sun 2 & 3.30.
P ✕
Details not confirmed for 1992

Bell Tower of All Saint's Church — INVERARAY

Map 10 NN00
The Avenue
☎ Inverary (0499) 2259
The tower was built in the 1920s and stands at 126ft. It has the world's third heaviest ring of ten bells, installed as a Campbell War Memorial in 1931. An exhibition on campanology is mounted inside and there are visiting bell ringers who give recitals, usually once a month. A splendid view rewards those who climb to the roof.
Open May-Sep, Mon-Sat 10-1 & 2-5, Sun 2-5.
* *70p (ch & pen 35p).*
♿ *shop*

Inveraray Castle — INVERARAY

Map 10 NN00
☎ (0499) 2203
The third Duke of Argyll (the chief of Clan Campbell) engaged Roger Morris to build the present castle in 1743; in the process the old Burgh of Inverary was demolished and a new town built nearby. The beautiful interior decoration was commissioned by the 5th Duke from Robert Mylne; the great armoury hall and staterooms are of particular note but the furniture, tapestries and paintings throughout are well worth viewing. The gardens are open by appointment.
Open Apr-Jun & Sep-Oct, Sat-Thu, 10-1 & 2-6, Sun 1-6; Jul-Aug, Mon-Sat 10-6, Sun 1-6. Last admissions 30 mins before closing.
£3 (ch 16 £1.50, pen £2). Family ticket £7.50.
P ☕ ♿ *shop* ✕

Inveraray Jail — INVERARAY

Map 10 NN00
Church Sq
☎ (0499) 2381
Enter Inveraray Jail and step back in time. See furnished cells and experience prison sounds and smells. Ask the 'prisoner' how to pick oakum, or help him make herring nets. Turn the heavy handle of an original crank machine, take 40 winks in a hammock or listen to Matron's tales of day-to-day prison life as she keeps one eye on the nursing mother, barefoot thieves and the lunatic in her care. Visit the magnificent 1820 courtroom, see trials in progress and imaginative exhibitions including 'Torture, Death and Damnation'.
Open all year, Nov-Mar, daily 10-5 (last admisssion 4); Apr-Oct, daily 9.30-6 (last admission 5pm). (Closed 25-26 Dec & 1 Jan). Extended hours in summer.
£3.25 (ch £1.60, pen £1.75). Family ticket £8.90. Party.
P ♿ *toilets for disabled shop*

Places to visit in this guide are pinpointed on the atlas at the back of the book.

Glasgow Vennel Museum & Burns Heckling Shop — IRVINE

Map 10 NS34
10 Glasgow Vennel
☎ (0294) 75059
The Glasgow Vennel Museum has a reputation for exciting and varied exhibitions, ranging from international artists to local school groups. Behind the museum is the Heckling Shop where Robert Burns, Scotland's most famous poet, spent part of his youth learning the trade of flax dressing. In addition to the audio-visual programme on Burns, there is also a reconstruction of his lodgings to be seen. For 1992, there will be exhibits of the work of artists from Germany and Russia, (Apr and May).
Open all year – Jun-Sep, Mon-Sat 10-5, Sun 2-5 (Closed Wed); Oct-May, Tue, Thu-Sat 10-5 (Closed Mon & Wed). Closed for lunch 1-2.
Free.
♿

HAMILTON DISTRICT MUSEUM

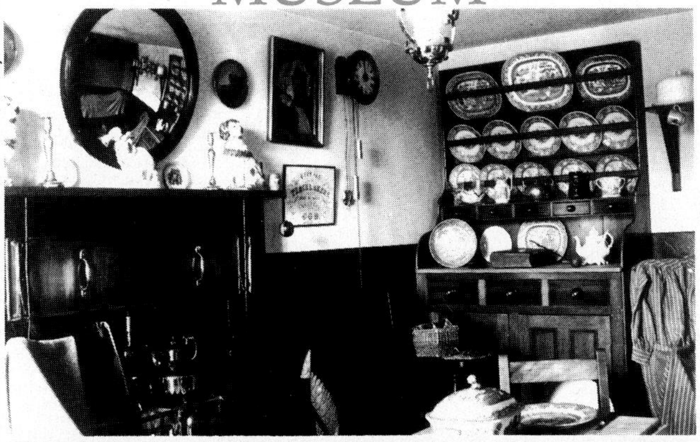

Step into the past at Hamilton District Museum, the oldest building in the town. It was originally the Hamilton Arms Inn, built in 1696, and London coaches stopped here daily. Re-live that era in our restored stable and fascinating transport gallery with four-in-hand coach and other early vehicles. Stroll through the elegant 18th century Assembly Room with its original plasterwork and musician's gallery, and then savour the atmosphere of our reconstructed Victorian kitchen. We also have a wide range of local history displays, including costume, archaeology, lacemaking, handloom weaving, coalmining and much more.

129 MUIR STREET, HAMILTON
Telephone 283981

Scottish Maritime Museum — IRVINE

Map 10 NS34
Harbour St
☎ (0294) 78283
The museum has displays which reflect all aspects of Scottish Maritime History. Vessels are displayed afloat in the harbour as in undercover displays. A 1910 tenement house shows a shipyard

worker's house. There will be a special exhibition 'Puffers' from April to October, and a Scottish Boat Jumble on May 3rd.
Open Apr-Oct, daily 10-5.
£1.50p (ch & pen 75p). Family ticket £3.
🅿 ♨ & shop ✗

Weaver's Cottage — KILBARCHAN

Map 11 NS46
Shuttle St, The Cross
☎ (05057) 5588
Together with a fascinating display of weaving equipment, occasional demonstrations of the craft are given in this characterful museum. Also displayed in the 18th-century weaver's cottage is a

collection of early domestic utensils.
Open 2 Apr-28 May & 1 Sep-1 Nov, Tue, Thu, Sat & Sun 2-5; 30 May-30 Aug, daily 2-5. Last admission 4.30.
£1.20 (ch 60p). Party.
♨ ✗
(NTS)

Dean Castle — KILMARNOCK

Map 11 NS43
Dean Rd
☎ (0563) 26401 ext 136 & 22702
This fine castle has a 14th-century fortified keep and 15th-century palace, and is the ancestral home of the Boyd family. The restoration work which has taken place shows the building in almost its original splendour, and inside there is an outstanding collection of medieval arms and armour, musical instruments, tapestries and a display of Burns'

manuscripts. The castle is set in a beautiful wooded country park with rivers, gardens, woodlands, adventure playground, children's corner and avaries. A jazz festival will be held on 1st and 2nd August.
Open all year, daily noon-5. (Closed 25-26 Dec & 1-2 Jan).
✳ £1 (ch free).
🅿 ♨ & (special disabled garden) toilets for disabled shop ✗ (ex in grounds)

Dick Institute — KILMARNOCK

Map 11 NS43
Elmbank Ave
☎ (0563) 26401
Museum exhibiting geology, natural history, engineering, archaeology and local history. Newly modernised art gallery with an important permanent collection of paintings and touring exhibitions of prints, photography and crafts. Works by contemporary artists

often for sale. A series of special exhibitions will be held in 1992 to mark the 400th anniversary of the Burgh of Kilmarnock.
Open all year, Gallery: Mon, Tue, Thu & Fri 10-8, Wed & Sat 10-5. Museum: May-Sep, Mon, Tue, Thu & Fri 10-8, Wed & Sat 10-5; Oct-Apr Mon-Sat 10-5.
Free.
🅿 & toilets for disabled shop ✗

Dunadd Fort — KILMARTIN

Map 10 NR89
(1m W of Kilmichael Glassary)
☎ 031-244 3101
Dunadd was one of the ancient capitals of Dalriada from which the Celtic kingdom of Scotland was formed. Near to this prehistoric hill fort (now little more than an isolated hillock) are

carvings of a boar and a footprint; these probably marked the spot where early kings were invested with their royal power.
Open & accessible at all reasonable times.
Free.
✗
(AM)

Kilmun Hill: Arboretum & Forest Walks — KILMUN

Map 10 NS18
(on A880 1m from junc with A815)
☎ (036984) 666
The Argyll Forest Park extends over a large area of hill ground and forest, noted for its rugged beauty. Numerous forest walks and picnic sites allow the

forest to be explored in detail. The Arboretum walks and the route from the Younger Botanic Gardens to Packs Glen are of special scenic quality.
Open all year.
Free.
🅿 🚲

Colzium House & Estate — KILSYTH

Map 11 NS77
Colzium-Lennox Estate (on A803)
☎ (0236) 823281
The old castle was associated with Montrose's victory over the Covenanters in 1645; the museum, courtyard, ice-house and walled garden make interesting viewing and the grounds

include a children's zoo and forest walks.
Open – House Etr wknd-Sep wknd, Mon-Fri, 9-5 & Sun, 10-6. (Closed when booked for private functions). Grounds open at all times. Museum open Wed 2-8.
Free.
🅿 ♨ &

Souter Johnnie's Cottage — KIRKOSWALD

Map 10 NS20
(on A77)
☎ (06556) 603 or 274
'Souter' means cobbler and the village cobbler who lived in this 18th-century cottage was the inspiration for Burns' character Souter Johnnie, in his ballad *Tam o'Shanter*. The cottage is now a Burns' museum and life-size stone figures

of the poet's characters can be seen in the restored ale-house in the cottage garden.
Open Apr-25 Oct, daily 12-5. Also by appointment.
£1.20 (ch accompanied & pen 60p). Party.
& ✗
(NTS)

Finlaystone Country Estate — LANGBANK

Map 10 NS37
(1m W on A8)
☎ (047554) 285 & 505
A charming exhibition of Victorian flower books and an international collection of dolls, are displayed in a homely family house with historical connections to John Knox and Robert Burns. The house, though, is only a foil to the considerable natural beauty; most visitors to Finlaystone are drawn by the formal gardens, walled gardens, woodland walks and adventure

playgrounds. Disabled visitors will enjoy the small scented garden, and there is purpose-built toilet for wheelchair users in the visitor centre; lift to second floor in the Mansion House.
Open all year. Woodland & Gardens daily. House with doll collections Apr-Aug, Suns only 2.30-4.30 or by appointment.
✳ Garden & Woods £1.20 (ch & pen 80p); House £1.20 (ch & pen 80p).
🅿 ♨ (lift to second floor) toilets for disabled

Kelburn Country Centre — LARGS

Map 10 NS25
(2m S off A78)
☎ Fairlie (0475) 568685
Eighteenth-century farm buildings have been neatly converted here to resemble a village square, with craft shops, workshops, display rooms, special exhibitions and a café. The setting is the historic estate of the Earls of Glasgow, which also provides the visitor with beautiful gardens and magnificent scenery. The most famous part of the estate is Kelburn Glen, areas of which are still in a wild state, with waterfalls and pools. There are also rare trees,

nature trails, a pets' corner, pony-trekking centre and adventure playgrounds. For those looking for some real action, there is a Marine Commando assault course and various special events during the year, including a wood and forestry fair (Apr 25/26), a Scottish teddy bears' picnic (May 10), and a Viking day (Aug 30).
Open all year, Etr-mid Oct, daily 10-6; Grounds only mid Oct-Etr, daily 11-5. Kelburn Castle 20 Apr-27 May.
£3 (ch & pen £1.50). Low season £1.50 (ch & pen £1).
🅿 ♨ ✗ licensed & shop

Cruachan Power Station — LOCHAWE

Map 10 NN12
(3m W off A85, near Pass of Brander)
☎ Taynuilt (08662) 673
A vast cavern inside Ben Cruachan contains a 400,000 kilowatt hydro-electric power station which is driven by water drawn from a high-level reservoir

up the mountain. A guided minibus tour starts from the visitor centre which also provides fascinating displays on the site. The picnic area gives spectacular views.
Open late Mar-late Oct, daily 9-4.30.
✳ £1.50 (ch 8-16 50p).
🅿 ♨ & toilets for disabled shop ✗

Lochwinnoch Community Museum — LOCHWINNOCH

Map 10 NS35
Main St
☎ (0505) 842615
Local agriculture, industry and village life are reflected in the series of changing exhibitions displayed in this enterprising

museum.
Open all year, Mon, Wed & Fri 10-1, 2-5 & 6-8; Tue & Sat 10-1 & 2-5.
Free.
🅿 & ✗
£

RSPB Nature Centre — LOCHWINNOCH

Map 10 NS35
Largs Rd (on A760)
☎ (0505) 842663
An attractive Norwegian timber building in the Lochwinnoch Nature Reserve, incorporating an observation tower offering fine views of the reserve and the surrounding countryside, an RSPB shop, and an exhibition and lecture room with a video system and displays. A nature trail leads from the centre, through deciduous woodland to two observation

hides. An attractive second trail, featuring a boardwalk across the marsh, leads from the centre to a third birdwatching hide; this one has been designed specifically for the convenience of disabled visitors.
Open all year, Sun-Wed & Fri-Sat 10-5. (Closed Thu & Xmas-New Year).
£1 (ch 50p).
🅿 & (wheelchairs available) toilets for disabled shop ✗

For an explanation of the symbols and abbreviations, see page 2.

Crossraguel Abbey — MAYBOLE

Map 10 NS20
(2m S)
☎ 031-244 3101
The extensive remains of this 13th-century Cluniac monastery are impressive and architecturally important. The monastery was founded by Duncan,

Earl of Carrick and the church, claustral buildings, abbot's house and an imposing castellated gatehouse can be seen.
Open Apr-Sep, Mon-Sat 9.30-6, Sun 2-6.
£1 (ch & pen 50p).
🅿 & ✗
(AM)

Crarae Gardens — MINARD

Map 10 NR99
☎ (0546) 86614 & 86607

Set in a Highland Glen beside Loch Fyne, these gardens are among Scotland's loveliest. They are noted for their rhododendrons, azaleas, conifers and ornamental shrubs, which include a number of rare species.
Open all year, daily, summer 9-6; winter during daylight hours. Visitor centre 10-5.
🅿 ♨ & toilets for disabled shop
Details not confirmed for 1992

Dunstaffnage Castle　　　　　　　　　OBAN

Map 10 NM83
(3m N on peninsula)
☎ 031-244 3101
Now ruined, this four-sided stronghold
has a gatehouse, two round towers and
walls 10ft thick. It was once the prison

of Flora MacDonald.
Open Apr-Sep, Mon-Sat 9.30-6, Sun 2-6.
£1.20 (ch & pen 60p).
P ✖
(AM)

Oban Glassworks　　　　　　　　　　OBAN

Map 10 NM83
Lochavullin Estate
☎ (0631) 63386
Visitors can watch the art of making
paperweights here, and can buy seconds
in the large shop.

Open all year, Factory Shop: Mon-Fri 9-5
(May-Sep, Sat 9-1). Glassmaking Mon-Fri
9-5.
Free.
P ঠ *shop* ✖

Bargany Gardens　　　　　　　　OLD DAILLY

Map 10 NX29
Girvan (4m NE on B734 from Girvan)
☎ (046587) 227 or 249
Woodland walks display snowdrops,
daffodils and blubells in spring, and a
fine show of azaleas and rhododendrons
is to be seen around the lilypond in May
and June. Ornamental trees give autumn

colour, and visitors can buy plants from
the gardens.
Open Gardens Mar-Oct, daily 7pm (or
dusk).
✱ *Contribution Box.*
P ঠ

See advertisement on page 195.

Coats Observatory　　　　　　　　　PAISLEY

Map 11 NS46
49 Oakshaw St West
☎ 041-889 2013
Astronomy, meteorology and space
flight, along with the history of the
building, are the subjects of displays on
show in this observatory built in 1883.
Recent renovations have installed
modern technology, and the observatory
has resumed an important role in

astronomy and meteorology.
Introductory astronomy lectures will
take place in Jan 1992.
Open all year, Mon, Tue & Thu 2-8,
Wed, Fri & Sat 10-5. Oct-Mar Thu 7-9
weather permitting. (Closed Xmas & New
Year).
Free.
shop ✖

Paisley Museum & Art Galleries　　　PAISLEY

Map 11 NS46
High St
☎ 041-889 3151
Pride of place here is given to a world-
famous collection of Paisley shawls.
Other collections illustrate local
industrial and natural history, while the
emphasis of the art gallery is on 19th-

century Scottish artists. There is also a
study centre for studio ceramics. Events
for 1992 include a children's art
exhibition (Jun), and an international
organ festival (Aug 1-9).
Open all year, Mon-Sat 10-5. (Closed PH).
Free.
ঠ *toilets for disabled shop* ✖

Newark Castle　　　　　　　PORT GLASGOW

Map 10 NS37
☎ 031-244 3101
The one-time house of the Maxwells,
dating from the 15th and 17th centuries.
The courtyard and hall are preserved.
Fine turrets and the remains of painted

ceilings can be seen, and the hall carries
an inscription of 1597.
Open Apr-Sep, Mon-Sat 9.30-6, Sun 2-6.
£1 (ch & pen 50p).
P ✖
(AM)

North Ayrshire Museum　　　　　SALTCOATS

Map 10 NS24
Manse St, Kirkgate
☎ (0294) 64174
This museum is housed in a prime
example of mid-18th-century Scottish
church architecture. On display is a rich
variety of artefacts from the North
Ayrshire area, including archaeological
and social history material. The museum
also houses a fine collection of Ayrshire

Whitework, a town hall clock and a
recreation of a turn-of-the-century
kitchen. There is a continuing
programme of temporary exhibitions.
Open all year, Jun-Sep, Mon-Sat (ex Wed)
10-1 & 2-5; Oct-May, Tue, Thu-Sat 10-1
& 2-5.
Free.
ঠ *toilets for disabled* ✖

Bonawe Iron Furnace　　　　　　TAYNUILT

Map 10 NN03
(0.75m NE off B845)
☎ 031-244 3101
The furnace is a restored charcoal blast-
furnace for iron-smelting and making
cast-iron. It was established in 1753 and
worked until 1876. The most complete

furnace and ancillary buildings in
Britain, the works exploited the Forest
of Lorne to provide charcoal for fuel.
Open Apr-Sep, Mon-Sat 9.30-6, Sun 2-6.
£1.50 (ch & pen 80p).
P ✖
(AM)

Glasgow Zoo　　　　　　　　UDDINGSTON

Map 11 NS66
Calderpark
☎ 041-771 1185
The developing, open-plan zoo has birds,
mammals and reptiles housed in spacious
new enclosures and buildings. There are
many rare animals and the zoo's

specialities are cats and reptiles. Other
attractions include ample picnic sites,
children's shows and free guided tours.
Open all year, daily 10-5 (or 6pm
depending on season).
P ✖ ঠ *shop* ✖
Details not confirmed for 1992

TAYSIDE

Arbroath Abbey　　　　　　　　ARBROATH

Map 11 NO64
☎ 031-244 3101
The Declaration of Arbroath – declaring
Robert the Bruce as king – was signed at
the 12th-century abbey on 6 April
1320. The abbot's house is well
preserved, and the church remains are

also interesting.
Open all year, Apr-Sep, Mon-Sat 9.30-6,
Sun 2-6; Oct-Mar, Mon-Sat 9.30-4, Sun
2-4. (Closed 25-26 Dec & 1-2 Jan)
£1 (ch & pen 50p).
P ঠ ✖
(AM)

Arbroath Museum　　　　　　　ARBROATH

Map 11 NO64
Signal Tower, Ladyloan
☎ (0241) 75598
Fishing, flax and engineering industries
including Shanks lawnmowers are all
shown in this museum of Arbroath's
history. It is housed in a signal tower
which was once the shore base for Bell

Rock lighthouse – also featured
prominently in the displays.
Open all year, Apr-Oct Mon-Sat 10.30-1
& 2-5, also Sun 2-5 Jul & Aug; Nov-
Mar, Mon-Fri 2-5, Sat 10.30-1 & 2-5.
P ঠ *shop* ✖
Details not confirmed for 1992

Atholl Country Collection　　　　BLAIR ATHOLL

Map 13 NN86
The Old School
☎ (079681) 232
Artefacts and photographs illustrate local
life and trades from 1850 onwards.
Displays include a crofter's kitchen, a
'smiddy' (smithy), dress,
communications, a byre (with stuffed

Highland cow) and a gamekeeper's
corner. There is a Kiddies' Kist, where
everything can be lifted up and
examined.
Open end May-mid Oct 1.30-5.30 also
from 9.30am Jul-Aug & Sep weekdays.
£1 (ch 50p).
P ঠ *toilets for disabled shop*

Blair Castle　　　　　　　　BLAIR ATHOLL

Map 13 NN86
(7m NW of Pitlochry, off A9)
☎ (079681) 207 due to change to
(0796) 481207

Home of the Duke of Atholl, chief of
the Murrays, and his unique private
army, the Atholl Highlanders. The castle
dates back to the 13th century but was
altered in the 18th century and later

given a castellated exterior. The oldest
part is Cumming's Tower, built in about
1270. There are 32 rooms open to the
public, with paintings, Jacobite relics,
lace, tapestries, china, arms and armour,
and Masonic regalia to be seen. The
extensive grounds include a deer park,
and visitors may follow nature trails or
go pony trekking. Numerous events are
held throughout the year, including
Highland games (May 24), a charity day
(Jul 2), and the Glenfiddich Fiddle
Championships Nov 1).
Open 28 Mar-25 Oct, daily 10-6 (Sun in
Apr, May & Oct 2-6). Last admission 5pm.
✱ *£4 (ch & pen £2.50). Family ticket*
£11.50. Party.
P ▪ ✕ *licensed* ঠ *(restaurant accessible to*
disabled) toilets for disabled shop ✖ *(ex in*
grounds)

Clan Donnachaidh (Robertson) Museum　　　BRUAR

Map 13 NN86
☎ Calvine (079683) 264 due to change
to (0796) 483264
Robes, uniforms, weapons, silver, glass,
books and pictures associated with the
clan are shown. The Battle of
Bannockburn and the Jacobite risings are

also featured.
Open Apr-Oct, Mon-Sat 10-1 & 2-5, Sun
2-5. Other times by arrangement. (Closed
on Tue).
Free.
P ঠ *shop* ✖

Scottish Tartans Museum　　　　　　COMRIE

Map 11 NN72
Drummond St (A85 town centre)
☎ (0764) 70779
Just about every aspect of tartan is
covered here. There are details of nearly
2,200 tartans, with over 450 tartans on
display, and the period costume room
shows costumes and artefacts from the
early 18th century to the present day.
At the rear is a reconstructed weaver's
cottage and a dye plant garden, which
grows the plants which were
traditionally used to dye the wool for
tartans. The Scottish Tartans Society can

also offer a research service into
surnames associated with clans or
tartans. Children's corner. There are also
spinning demonstrations every weekday
afternoon during the summer months.
Open Jan-Mar & Nov-Dec, Mon-Fri 10-5,
Sat 10-1 (Closed Sun); Apr-May & Sep-
Oct, Mon-Sat 10-6, Sun 11-5; Jun-Aug,
Mon-Sat 9.30-6.30, Sun 11-5. (Closed
25-26 Dec & 1-2 Jan).
£1.40 (ch & pen 95p, ch under 5 free).
Family ticket £3.50. Party.
ঠ *shop* ✖

Glenturret Distillery　　　　　　　CRIEFF

Map 11 NN82
The Hosh (1.5m NW off A85)
☎ (0764) 2424
The distillery dates from 1775 and is the
oldest in Scotland. It uses the pure water
of the Turret Burn to make award-
winning whiskies, sold at eight, twelve,

fifteen and twenty-one years of age.
Open Mar-Dec, Mon-Sat 9.30-5.30 (last
tour 4.30); Jan-Feb, Mon-Fri 11.30-2.30.
Guided tours and Audio visual exhibition
£2.20 (ch 12-17 £1.10 ch under 12 Free).
P ✕ *licensed* ঠ *shop* ✖

Innerpeffray Library CRIEFF

Map 11 NN82
(4.5m SE on B8062)
☎ (0764) 2819
This is Scotland's oldest free lending library. It was founded in 1691 and is still open every day except Thursdays. It is housed in a late-18th-century building which is interesting in itself, and contains a notable collection of bibles

and rare books. Adjacent is St Mary's Chapel, the original site for the library and the Drummond family burial place.
Open all year, Mon-Wed & Fri-Sat 10-12.45 & 2-4.45, Sun 2-4. (Closed Thu).
P ⛟ shop ✹
Details not confirmed for 1992

Barrack Street Natural History Museum DUNDEE

Map 11 NO43
Barrack St
☎ (0382) 23141
Displays on Scottish wildlife of the Lowlands and Highlands are shown, including the skeleton of the Great Tay whale. New displays are currently being

developed on the ground floor. A major gallery for changing exhibitions explores nature and environmental themes.
Open all year, Mon-Sat 10-5.
Free.
shop ✹

Broughty Castle Museum DUNDEE

Map 11 NO43
Broughty Ferry (4m E)
☎ (0382) 76121
The 15th-century castle was rebuilt to defend the estuary in the 19th century. It now houses displays on Dundee's maritime history, including harpoons and other exhibits from the long-gone days of whaling – a major industry for

Dundee, which built most of Britain's whaling ships. Other sections display arms and armour, local history and seashore life.
Open all year, Mon-Thu & Sat 10-1 & 2-5. (Sun 2-5 Jul-Sep only)
Free.
P *shop* ✹

Camperdown Country Park DUNDEE

Map 11 NO43
(off A923)
☎ (0382) 621993 & 23141 ext 4296
The 19th-century mansion of Camperdown House was built for the son of Admiral Lord Duncan, who defeated the Dutch at the Battle of Camperdown in 1797. The house is set in nearly 400 acres of fine parkland with

a wide variety of trees, some of them rare. Most notable is the Camperdown elm, a weeping form of wych-elm. The park also offers attractions such as a golf course, a wildlife centre with a big collection of native and domestic animals, and an award-winning adventure play area with the Battle of
continued . . .

Camperdown as its theme. There is an extensive network of footpaths and forest trails to follow, and the house itself has a restaurant and function area. The Templeton Ranger Centre has interpretive displays and offers guided

walks.
Open all year – park. Wildlife Centre – daily 10-4.
✱ *Park free. Wildlife Centre £1 (ch 20p). Party 12+.*
P ⛟ ✕ ♿ *toilets for disabled shop*

Claypotts Castle DUNDEE

Map 11 NO43
(junc of A92 & B978)
☎ 031-244 3101
Claypotts is an excellent example of the tower house type of fortified home. It was built in the late 16th century and later belonged to John Graham of

Claverhouse, the Bonnie Dundee of the 1688-9 uprising.
Open Apr-Sep, Mon-Sat 9.30-6, Sun 2-6. £1 (ch & pen 50p).
✹
(AM)

✱ An asterisk indicates that up-to-date information was not available at the time of our research – 1991 information has been published as an indication of what you may expect.

HM Frigate Unicorn DUNDEE

Map 11 NO43
Victoria Dock
☎ (0382) 200900
The *Unicorn* is the oldest British warship still afloat, and is Scotland's only example of a wooden warship. Today she makes an apt setting for a fascinating

museum of life in the Royal Navy during the days of sail, with guns, models and displays.
Open all year, daily 10-5.
✱ *£1.50 (concessions £1).*
P ♿ *shop* ✹

McManus Galleries Museum DUNDEE

Map 11 NO43
Albert Square
☎ (0382) 23141 ext 65136
A resplendent Victorian building in the city centre is the home of Dundee's main museum. It has collections of silver, ceramics, glass and furniture, and displays on local archaeology, civic and

social history, trades and industries. The major art gallery has an important collection of Scottish and Victorian works of art, and touring exhibitions are a regular feature.
Open all year, Mon-Sat 10-5.
Free.
♿ *toilets for disabled shop* ✹

Mills Observatory   DUNDEE

Map 11 NO43
Balgay Park, Glamis Rd
☎ (0382) 67138 & 23141
The observatory was built in 1935, and
has a Victorian 10in Cooke refracting
telescope among its instruments. The
gallery has displays on astronomy and

space exploration, and there is a small
planetarium. Regular slide shows.
*Open all year, Apr-Sep, Mon-Fri 10-5, Sat
2-5; Oct-Mar, Mon-Fri 3-10, Sat 2-5.
Free.*
P *shop* ✹

Royal Research Ship Discovery   DUNDEE

Map 11 NO43
Victoria Dock
☎ (0382) 201175
Built by the Dundee Shipbuilding
Company, the *Discovery* was the first
purpose-built research vessel to be
constructed in Britain. She was
commissioned for Captain Scott's
1901-4 Antarctic expedition, and came
to be seen as a symbol of shipbuilding
quality and of human endurance. The

Discovery is undergoing a five-year
restoration, but can be visited and is
already a focal point of the docks.
*Open 27 Mar-3 May & 2 Sep-13 Oct,
wkdays 1-5, wknds & PHs 11-5; Jun-1
Sep, daily 10-5.
£2.20 (concessions £1.70).*
P & *(induction loop, radio hearing link
with guides) toilets for disabled shop* ✹

See advertisement on page 203.

Little Houses   DUNKELD

Map 11 NO04
(off A9, 15m N of Perth)
☎ (03502) 460
The National Trust for Scotland owns
two rows of 20 houses in Dunkeld, and
has brought them up to modern
standards without destroying their
character. Most were built after the
Battle of Dunkeld in 1689. There is a

Trust display and audio-visual show in
the tourist information centre.
*Open Jun-Aug Mon-Sat 10-5, Sun 2-5;
Apr-May & Sep-23 Dec Mon-Sat 10-1 &
2-5. (Closed 28 Oct-4 Nov).
Free.
shop* ✹
(NTS)

& This symbol indicates that much or all of the
attraction is accessible to wheelchairs.
However, there may be some restrictions,
so it would be wise to check
in advance.

Edzell Castle   EDZELL

Map 13 NO56
☎ 031-244 3101
The 16th-century castle has a remarkable
walled garden built in 1604 by Sir David
Lindsay. Flower-filled recesses in the
walls are alternated with heraldic and
symbolic sculptures of a sort not seen
elsewhere in Scotland, with niches for
birds to nest in above. There is also a

garden house.
*Open all year, Apr-Sep, weekdays 9.30-6,
Sun 2-6; Oct-Mar, weekdays 9.30-4, Sun
2-4. (Closed Thu pm & Tue in winter;
25-26 Dec & 1-2 Jan).
£1.50 (ch & pen 80p).*
P & *toilets for disabled* ✹
(AM)

Angus Folk Museum   GLAMIS

Map 13 NO34
Kirkwynd Cottages (off A94 in Glamis)
☎ (030784) 288
A row of stone-roofed, early 19th-
century cottages now houses the
splendid Angus Folk Collection of
domestic equipment and cottage
furniture, and there is an agricultural

annexe with farm equipment. There is
also a bothy exhibition with audio-visual
display.
*Open 17-20 Apr & May-Sep, daily 11-5.
(Last admission 4.30pm).
£1.50 (ch & pen 80p).*
P & ✹
(NTS)

Glamis Castle   GLAMIS

Map 13 NO34
(5m W of Forfar on A94)
☎ (030784) 242
The splendid, turreted and battlemented
castle is the family home of the Earls of
Strathmore, and was the childhood
home of HM The Queen Mother. The
present castle dates from the 15th
century, but parts of the tower are much
older, and there is known to have been a
building here for many centuries. One of
the oldest parts is known as Duncan's
Hall, a reminder of the murder of King
Duncan in Shakespeare's *Macbeth* ('All
hail, Macbeth! hail to thee, Thane of
Glamis!'). Other noteworthy rooms are

the chapel with its painted panels, and
the drawing room. There are fine
collections of china, pictures, tapestries
and furniture, and the grounds can also
be explored. Various events during the
summer, including Strathmore Vehicle
Vintage Club Extravaganza, 12th July.
*Open 17 Apr-12 Oct noon-5.30, (11-5.30
Jul-Aug). Last tour 4.45. Other times by
prior appointment.
Castle & grounds £3.70 (ch £2, pen
£2.90). Grounds only £1.50 (ch & pen
70p).*
P ✕ *licensed* & *toilets for disabled shop* ✹
(ex in grounds)

Glengoulandie Deer Park   GLENGOULANDIE DEER PARK

Map 13 NN75
(8m NW of Aberfeldy on B846).
☎ Kenmore (08873) 509 & 261
Various native birds and animals are
kept in surroundings as similar to their
natural environment as possible, and

there are herds of red deer and Highland
cattle. Pets must not be allowed out of
cars.
*Open Apr-Oct, 9am-1hr before sunset.
* 75p. Cars £3.
P *shop* ✹

Killiecrankie Visitors Centre   KILLIECRANKIE

Map 13 NN96
(3m N of Pitlochry on A9)
☎ Pitlochry (0796) 3233
The visitors' centre at this historic spot
features an exhibition illustrating the
battle that took place near here in 1689;
there are also displays on the natural
history of the area and ranger services.
The battle site was where the Jacobite
army, led by 'Bonnie Dundee' (who was
mortally wounded in the attack) routed

King William's troops. The wooded
gorge is a notable beauty spot admired
by Queen Victoria, and there are some
splendid walks.
*Open Visitor Centre, Exhibition, shop &
snack bar Apr-May & Sep-Oct, daily 10-5;
(Jun-Aug, daily 9.30-6).
30p (ch free)*
P *(charged)* ▼ *shop*
(NTS)

Kinross House Gardens   KINROSS

Map 11 NO10
☎ (0577) 63467
Yew hedges, roses and herbaceous
borders are the elegant attractions of
these formal gardens. The 17th-century

house was built by Sir William Bruce,
but is not generally open to the public.
*Gardens only open May-Sep, daily 10-7.
* £2 (ch 50p).*
P & ✹

Loch Leven Castle   KINROSS

Map 11 NO10
Castle Island
☎ 031-244 3101
Mary Queen of Scots was imprisoned
here in this five-storey castle in 1567 –
she escaped 11 months later and gave
the 14th-century castle its special place

in history.
*Open Apr-Sep, Mon-Sat 9.30-6, Sun 2-6.
Ferry charge £1.50 (ch & pen 80p).
Family ticket £4.*
P ✹
(AM)

Barrie's Birthplace   KIRRIEMUIR

Map 13 NO35
9 Brechin Rd
☎ (0575) 72646
The creator of Peter Pan, Sir James
Barrie, was born in Kirriemuir in 1860.
The upper floors of No 9 Brechin Road
are furnished as they may have been
when Barrie lived there, and the adjacent

house, No 11, houses a new exhibition
about his literary and theatrical works.
*Open 17-20 Apr & May-Sep, Mon-Sat
11-5.30 & Sun 2-5.30. Last admission
5pm.
£1.20 (ch & pen 60p). Party.*
✹
(NTS)

Burleigh Castle   MILNATHORT

Map 11 NO10
☎ 031-244 3101
Dating from 1582 this tower house has
an enclosed courtyard and roofed angle
tower.

*Open all year, daily.
Free.*
✹
(AM)

House of Dun   MONTROSE

Map 13 NO75
(4m W, on A935)
☎ Bridge of Dun (067481) 264
A Palladian house, overlooking the
Montrose Basin, built in 1730 for David
Erskine, Lord Dun, to designs by
William Adam, and particularly noted
for its exuberant plasterwork. The house
was opened to the public in 1989 after
extensive restoration, along with the

courtyard buildings housing exhibitions,
a working loom and tearoom.
*Open 17-20 Apr & May-18 Oct, daily
11-5.30 (last admission 5pm). Garden &
Grounds open all year.
£3 (ch & pen £1.50). Party.*
P ▼ & *(braille sheets) toilets for disabled
shop* ✹ *(ex in grounds)*
(NTS)

✱ An asterisk indicates that up-to-date information was
not available at the time of our research – 1991
information has been published as an
indication of what you may expect.

Montrose Museum & Art Gallery   MONTROSE

Map 13 NO75
Panmure Place
☎ (0674) 73232
Pictish stones, whaling artefacts,
Napoleonic items (including a cast of his
death mask) and Montrose silver and
pottery are all displayed to illustrate the
history of this town and port from
prehistoric times up until the local

government reorganisation. There are
also paintings and local views by Angus
artists, and sculpture by W Lamb.
*Open all year, Apr-Oct, Mon-Sat 10.30-1
& 2-5, Sun (Jul & Aug only) 2-5;Nov-
Mar. Mon-Fri 2-5, Sat 10.30-1 & 2-5.*
& *shop* ✹
Details not confirmed for 1992

Drummond Castle Gardens   MUTHILL

Map 11 NN81
(1m N)
☎ (076481) 257
The gardens of Drummond Castle were
originally laid out in 1630 by John
Drummond, 2nd Earl of Perth. In 1830,
the parterre was changed to an Italian
style, and embellished with fine figures
and statues from Italy. Probably one of

the most interesting pieces of statuary is
the sundial, designed and built by John
Mylne, Master Mason to King Charles
I. There is a garden open day on 2 Aug
at 2pm.
*Open – Gardens May-Sep, daily 2-6 (Last
admission 5pm).
£2 (ch & pen £1).*
P &

Black Watch Regimental Museum — PERTH

Map 11 NO12
Balhousie Castle, Hay St
☎ (0738) 21281 ext 8530
The treasures of the 42nd/73rd
Highland Regiment from 1739 to the
present day are on show in this
museum, together with paintings, silver,
colours and uniforms.
*Open all year, Etr-Sep, Mon-Fri 10-4.30,
Sun & BH 2-4.30; Oct-Etr 10-3.30
(Closed 24 Dec-5 Jan). Other times &
Parties 16+ by appointment.
Donations.*
P shop ✖

Branklyn Garden — PERTH

Map 11 NO12
Dundee Rd (on Dundee Rd, A85)
☎ (0738) 25535
Described as the finest garden of its size
in Britain, Branklyn covers little more
than two acres and is noted for its
collection of rhododendrons, shrubs and
alpines.
*Open Mar-Oct, daily 9.30-sunset.
£1.50 (ch & pen 80p). Party.*
P & ✖
(NTS)

Caithness Glass Visitor Centre — PERTH

Map 11 NO12
Inveralmond Industrial Est
☎ (0738) 37373
All aspects of paperweight-making can
be seen from the viewing gallery at this
purpose-built visitors' centre. There is a
collectors' museum and a factory
seconds shop.
*Open all year, Factory shop Mon-Sat 9-5,
Sun 11-5 (Oct-Mar, Sun 1-5).
Glassmaking Mon-Fri 9-4.30.
Free.*
P ✖ *licensed* & *toilets for disabled shop*

Elcho Castle — PERTH

Map 11 NO12
(3m SE on S bank of River Tay).
☎ 031-244 3101
This well-preserved 16th-century
stronghold features wrought-iron
window grilles.
*Open Apr-Sep, Mon-Sat 9.30-6, Sun 2-6.
£1.20 (ch & pen 60p).*
P ✖
(AM)

Huntingtower Castle — PERTH

Map 11 NO12
(2m W)
☎ 031-244 3101
Formerly known as Ruthven Castle and
famous as the scene of the so-called
'Raid of Ruthven' in 1582, this structure
was built in the 15th and 16th centuries
and features a painted ceiling.
*Open all year, Apr-Sep, weekdays 9.30-6,
Sun 2-6; Oct-Mar, weekdays 9.30-4, Sun
2-4. (Closed Thu pm & Fri in winter;
25-26 Dec & 1-2 Jan).
£1 (ch & pen 50p).*
P ✖
(AM)

Perth Museum & Art Gallery — PERTH

Map 11 NO12
78 George St
☎ (0738) 32488
This purpose-built museum houses
collections of fine and applied art, social
and local history, natural history and
archaeology.
*Open all year, Mon-Sat 10-5.
Free.*
& *shop* ✖

✱ An asterisk indicates that up-to-date information was
not available at the time of our research – 1991
information has been published as an
indication of what you may expect.

Edradour Distillery — PITLOCHRY

Map 13 NN95
(2.5m E on the A924)
☎ (0796) 2095
It was in 1825 that a group of local
farmers founded Edradour, naming it
after the bubbling burn that runs
through it. It is Scotland's smallest
distillery and is virtually unchanged since
Victorian times. Visitors can see the
distillers' art practised here today as it
has been for over 160 years and then
retire to the Malt Barn for a 'wee dram'.
*Open 4 Mar-2 Nov, daily 9.30-5. Winter
months, Mon-Sat 10-4.*
P *(charged)* & *toilets for disabled shop* ✖
Details not confirmed for 1992

Faskally — PITLOCHRY

Map 13 NN95
Forestry Commission (1m N on the
B8019)
☎ Dunkeld (03502) 284
On the shores of man-made Loch
Faskally, the woodland incorporates
forest walks, a nature trail and picnic
facilities.
*Open Apr-Oct, dawn to dusk.
Free.*
P & *toilets for disabled* 🚐

Pitlochry Power Station, Dam & Fish Pass — PITLOCHRY

Map 13 NN95
☎ (0796) 3152
The hydro-electric visitor centre consists
of a souvenir shop; an exhibition
showing how electricity is brought from
the power station to the customer;
access to the turbine viewing gallery and
video shows. The salmon ladder viewing
chamber allows visitors to see the fish as
they travel upstream to their spawning
ground. There is also a walkway across
the top of the dam.
*Open Apr-25 Oct, daily 9.40-5.30.
£1.50 (ch 60p, student £1). Family ticket
£2.50.*
P & *toilets for disabled shop* ✖

Queen's View Visitor Centre — QUEEN'S VIEW

Map 13 NN85
(7m W of Pitlochry on B8019)
☎ Dunkeld (03502) 284
Queen Victoria admired the view on a
visit here in 1866, and there is a
splendid viewpoint which also has access
for the disabled. Forest walks take the
visitor to viewpoints, an excavated ring
fort and a reconstructed 18th- century
farm village. The Visitor Centre has an
exhibition describing the history of the
area and places to visit.
*Open 25 Mar-26 Oct, daily 10-5.30.
Free.*
P *(charged)* 🍴 & *toilets for disabled shop*

Scone Palace — SCONE

Map 11 NO12
☎ (0738) 52300
Scottish kings were crowned at Scone
until 1651; it was the seat of
government in Pictish times; and it was
the site of the famous coronation Stone
of Destiny, brought there in the 9th
century until it was seized by the English
in 1296. The castellated edifice of the
present palace dates from 1803 but
incorporates the 16th-century and earlier
buildings. The displays inside include a
magnificent collection of porcelain,
furniture, ivories, clocks and 16th-
century needlework; one of the bed
hangings was worked by Mary Queen of
Scots. The grounds include an
outstanding Pinetum, woodland garden
and brilliant displays of rhododendrons
and azaleas (at the right time of the
year). Although one of the most
historical houses in Scotland, its chief
attraction lies in its much-loved and
'lived-in' atmosphere – it still remains a
family home. Events for 1992 include
horse trials (May 2-3), a Coronation
pageant (Jun 28), and a Scottish game
fair (Jul 4-5).
*Open 17 Apr-12 Oct, Mon-Sat 9.30-5,
Sun 1.30-5 (Jul-Aug 10-5). Special parties
outside normal opening hours & during
winter by arrangement.
Palace & Grounds £3.70 (ch £2). Grounds
only £1.85 (ch £1). Family £11. Party
20+.*
P ✖ *licensed* & *toilets for disabled shop*
✖ *(ex in grounds)*

The Retreat — TARFSIDE

Map 13 NO47
(1m E)
☎ (03567) 254
This former shooting lodge is now a
museum of local country life and
handicrafts.
*Open Etr-May, Sat & Mon; Jun-Sep, daily
2-6, Sun 1-6.*
✱ *70p (ch 30p, ch under 5 free).*
P 🍴 & *shop* ✖

Castle Menzies — WEEM

Map 13 NN85
(1.5m from Aberfeldy on B846)
☎ Aberfeldy (0887) 20982
Seat of the Chiefs of Clan Menzies, the
castle is now being restored. It is a fine
example of a 16th-century Z-plan
fortified tower house, and currently
houses a small museum. There is a clan
gathering each year in August and music
recitals are held occasionally. There is a
Menzies Clan Gathering planned for
Aug 7-9.
*Open Apr-mid Oct, wkdays 10.30-5, Sun
2-5.
£2 (ch 50p, pen £1).*
P & *shop* ✖

SCOTTISH ISLANDS

Brodick Castle, Garden & Country Park — ISLE OF ARRAN BRODICK

Map 10 NS03
☎ (0770) 2202
The site of Brodick Castle has been
fortified since Viking times, but the
present castle dates from the 13th
century, with extensions added in 1652
and 1844. It was a stronghold of the
Dukes of Hamilton and more recently
became the home of the late Duchess of
Montrose. Splendid silver, fine porcelain
and paintings acquired by generations of
owners can be seen, including many
sporting pictures and trophies.
There is a formal garden, dating from
the 18th century and restored in
Victorian style, but the most impressive
part of the grounds is the woodland
garden. It was started by the Duchess in
1923, and is world-famous for its
continued . . .

rhododendrons and azaleas. A self-guided walk leads to its heart, and there are weekly guided walks in summer. The grounds also have an ice house and an adventure playground, ranger service and display centre.
Open all year, Country Park & Goatfell, daily 9.30-sunset. Castle open 1-17 Apr &

3-24 Oct, Mon, Wed, Sat 1-5; 18 Apr-Sep, daily 1-5. (Last admission 4.30). House & Gardens £3 (ch & pen £1.50). Garden only £2 (ch & pen 90p).
P ■ *(Braille sheets & wheelchairs available) shop* ✕ *(ex in park)* (NTS)

Isle of Arran Heritage Museum
ISLE OF ARRAN BRODICK

Map 10 NS03
Rosaburn
☎ (0770) 2636
The setting is an 18th-century croft farm, including a cottage restored to its pre-1920 state and a 'smiddy' where a blacksmith worked until the late 1960s. There are farming and shipping displays,

as well as a heritage project carried out in conjunction with a local high school. There are also occasional demonstrations of horseshoeing, sheepshearing and of the horse mill working.
Open Apr-Oct, Mon-Sat 10-5.
✱ *£1 (ch 50p, pen 75p).*
P ■ & *shop*

Ardencraig
ISLE OF BUTE ROTHESAY

Map 10 NS06
Lochgilphead (1m off A844, S of Rothesay)
☎ (0700) 504225
Particular attention has been paid to improving the layout of the garden and introducing rare plants. The greenhouse and walled garden produce plants for

floral displays throughout the district. A variety of interesting fish is kept in the ornamental ponds and the aviaries have some interesting birds.
Open all year.
Free.
P ■ & ✕ 🚌

Bute Museum
ISLE OF BUTE ROTHESAY

Map 10 NS06
Stuart St
☎ (0700) 502248
The contents are all from the Isle of Bute, and are divided into sections. The natural history room has birds, mammals and seashore items; and the history room has varied collections of recent bygones, such as models of Clyde steamers. There is a collection of early Christian crosses, and the prehistoric section has flints and pots from two

Neolithic burial cairns. A comprehensive geological survey of the island can be seen, and there is also a children's 'touch table'. Details of nature trails on the island are on sale. A special exhibition of local interest is held during Highland Week.
Open all year, Apr-Sep, Mon-Sat 10.30-4.30, Sun 2.30-4.30; Oct-Mar, Tue-Sat 2.30-4.30 (Closed Sun & Mon).
✱ *70p (ch 20p, pen 40p).*
P & *(touch table for blind) shop* ✕

Rothesay Castle
ISLE OF BUTE ROTHESAY

Map 10 NS06
☎ 031-244 3101
The focal point of Rothesay is this 13th-century castle. It has lofty curtain walls defended by drum towers and enclosing a circular courtyard.
Open all year, Apr-Sep, weekdays 9.30-6,

Sun 2-6; Oct-Mar, weekdays 9.30-4, Sun 2-4. (Closed Thu am & Fri in winter; also 25-26 Dec & 1-2 Jan).
£1 (ch 50p).
& ✕
(AM)

Black House Museum
ISLE OF LEWIS ARNOL

Map 12 NB34
☎ 031-244 3101
A traditional Hebridean dwelling is built without mortar and roofed with thatch on a timber framework. It has a central peat fire in the kitchen, no chimney and a byre under the same roof. The Black

House museum is an excellent example and it retains many of its original furnishings.
Open Apr-Sep, Mon-Sat 9.30-6.
£1 (ch & pen 50p).
P & ✕
(AM)

Callanish Standing Stones
ISLE OF LEWIS CALLANISH

Map 12 NB23
(12m W of Stornoway)
☎ 031-244 3101
An avenue of 19 monoliths leads north from a circle of 13 stones with rows of more stones fanning out to south, east and west. Probably constructed between

3000 and 1500BC, this is a unique cruciform of megaliths.
Open & accessible at all times.
Free.
P
(AM)

Dun Carloway Broch
ISLE OF LEWIS CARLOWAY

Map 12 NB24
(1.5m S of Carloway)
☎ 031-244 3101
Brochs are late-prehistoric circular stone towers, and their origins are mysterious. One of the best examples can be seen at

Dun Carloway, where the tower still stands about 30ft high.
Open at all reasonable times.
Free.
P
(AM)

Mull & West Highland Narrow Gauge Railway
ISLE OF MULL CRAIGNURE

Map 10 NM73
Craignure (old pier) Station
☎ (06802) 494 (in season) or Aros (0680) 300389
The first passenger railway on a Scottish island opened in 1983. Both steam and diesel trains operate on the ten-and-a-quarter inch gauge line, which runs from Craignure to Torosay Castle. The line is

1.25 miles long, and there are extensive and dramatic woodland and mountain views.
Open Etr-mid Oct.
Return £1.75 (ch £1.20); Single £1.20 (ch 90p). Family ticket return £4.70, single £3.30.
P & *(provision to carry person seated in wheelchair on trains) shop*

Torosay Castle & Gardens
ISLE OF MULL CRAIGNURE

Map 10 NM73
(1m S of Ferry Terminal at Craignure)
☎ (06802) 421
Much of this Victorian castle is open to the public together with its delightful Italian terraced gardens, designed by Lorimer. The Scottish baronial architecture is complemented by the magnificent setting and inside the house there are displays of portraits and wildlife pictures, family scrapbooks and a study of the Antarctic. The Edwardian library and archive rooms particularly

capture the flavour of their era. Allures of the garden include a statue walk and water garden, an avenue of Australian gum trees, a Japanese garden and many rare shrubs.
Open May-Oct, daily 10.30-5.30. Gardens all year.
✱ *Castle & garden £3.50. Garden only £1.50 (Reductions for ch, pen, students & groups).*
P ■ & *toilets for disabled shop* ✕ *(ex in gardens)*

The Brough of Birsay
ORKNEY DOUNBY

Map 13 HY22
(6m NW)
☎ 031-244 3101
This ruined Romanesque church stands next to the remains of a Norse village. The nave, chancel and semicircular apse

can be seen along with claustral buildings. Crossings must be made on foot at low-water – there is no boat.
Open at all reasonable times.
Free.
(AM)

Click Mill
ORKNEY DOUNBY

Map 13 HY22
(NE of village, off B9057)
☎ 031-244 3101
This is an example of the rare Orcadian horizontal watermill, and is in working

condition.
Open at all reasonable time.
Free.
(AM)

Skara Brae
ORKNEY DOUNBY

Map 13 HY22
(4m SW)
☎ 031-244 3101
Engulfed in drift sand, this remarkable group of well-preserved Stone-Age dwellings is the most outstanding survivor of its kind in Britain. Stone furniture and a fireplace can be seen.

Open all year, Apr-Sep, weekdays 9.30-6, Sun 2-6; Oct-Mar, weekdays 9.30-4, Sun 2-4. (Closed 25-26 Dec & 1-2 Jan).
£1.70 (ch & pen 90p). Family ticket £4.50.
✕
(AM)

Maes Howe Chambered Cairn
ORKNEY FINSTOWN

Map 13 HY31
(9m W of Kirkwall)
☎ 031-244 3101
The masonry of Britain's finest megalithic tomb is in a remarkable state of preservation. Dating from neolithic times it contains Viking carvings and

runes.
Open all year, Apr-Sep, weekdays 9.30-6, Sun 2-6; Oct-Mar, weekdays 9.30-4, Sun 2-4. (Closed 25-26 Dec & 1-2 Jan).
£1.50 (ch & pen 80p). Family ticket £4.
P ✕
(AM)

Stenness Standing Stones
ORKNEY FINSTOWN

Map 13 HY31
(3m SW off A965)
☎ 031-244 3101
Dating back to the second millenium BC, the remains of this stone circle are near the Ring of Brogar – a splendid

circle of upright stones surrounded by a ditch.
Open at any reasonable time.
Free.
P
(AM)

Orkney Farm & Folk Museum
ORKNEY HARRAY

Map 13 HY31
☎ (0856) 77411 & 77268
The museum consists of two Orkney farmhouses with outbuildings. Kirbuster (Birsay) has the last surviving example of a 'Firehoose' with its central hearth; Corrigall represents an improved farmhouse and steading of the late

1800s. Both display period furnishings, farm implements and native breeds of sheep among their exhibits.
Open Mar-Oct, Mon-Sat 10.30-1 & 2-5, Sun 2-7.
£1 (ch, students, pen & UB40 free).
P & *shop* ✕

Bishop's Palace
ORKNEY
KIRKWALL

Map 13 HY41
☎ 031-244 3101
This ruined palace dates from the 12th century. The round tower was built by Bishop Reid and other additions were made in the 1600s by Patrick Stewart,

Earl of Orkney.
Open Apr-Sep, Mon-Sat 9.30-6, Sun 2-6. £1 (ch & pen 50p).
🅿 ✖
(AM)

Earl Patrick's Palace
ORKNEY
KIRKWALL

Map 13 HY41
☎ 031-244 3101
Although roofless, much still remains of this palace. Considered one of the finest Renaissance buildings in Scotland, its

oriel windows are of particular interest.
Open Apr-Sep, Mon-Sat 9.30-6, Sun 2-6. £1 (ch 50p).
🅿 ✖
(AM)

Tankerness House Museum
ORKNEY
KIRKWALL

Map 13 HY41
Broad St
☎ (0856) 3191
One of the finest vernacular town houses in Scotland, this 16th-century building now contains a museum of

Orkney history, including the islands' fascinating archaeology.
Open all year, Mon-Sat 10.30-12.30 & 1.30-5 (May-Sep Sun 2-5).
£1 (ch, students, pen & UB40's free).
& *shop* ✖

✖ The 'No Dogs' symbol does not normally apply to guide dogs – these are permitted in most establishments.

Orkneys Natural & Maritime History Museum
ORKNEY
STROMNESS

Map 13 HY20
52 Alfred St
☎ (0856) 850025
Founded by the Orkney Natural History Society in 1837, this museum includes exhibits on birds, shells, butterflies, whaling and fishing. There are items

relating to Hudson Bay and the German Fleet in Scapa Flow.
Open Mon-Sat 10.30-12.30 & 1.30-5 (May-Sep 10.30-5). (Closed Sun, Xmas, New Year & 3 wks Feb-Mar).
✱ *40p (ch 10p).*
& *shop* ✖

Pier Arts Centre
ORKNEY
STROMNESS

Map 13 HY20
☎ (0856) 850209
The collection is housed in a warehouse standing on its own stone pier. There are galleries for children's work and visiting exhibitions, and an arts library

and reading room.
Open all year, Tue-Sat 10.30-12.30 & 1.30-5 & Sun 2-5 (Jun-Aug only) shop.
& *shop* ✖
Details not confirmed for 1992

Noltland Castle
ORKNEY
WESTRAY

Map 13 HY44
☎ 031-244 3101
Started in the 16th century, this ruined castle was never completed. It has a fine hall, vaulted kitchen and a notable winding staircase.

Open all reasonable times. Application to key keeper.
Free.
✖
(AM)

Every effort is made to provide accurate information, but details might change during the currency of this guide.

Clickhimin
SHETLAND
LERWICK

Map 13 HU44
(0.5m S)
☎ 031-244 3101
The remains of a prehistoric settlement that was fortified at the beginning of the Iron Age with a stone-built fort. The site was occupied for over 1,000 years. The

remains include a partially demolished broch (round tower) which still stands to a height of 17ft.
Open at all reasonable time.
Free.
(AM)

Fort Charlotte
SHETLAND
LERWICK

Map 13 HU44
(overlooking harbour)
☎ 031-244 3101
An artillery fort, begun in 1665 to protect the Sound of Bressay during the Anglo-Dutch War. The fort was burned by the Dutch in 1673, together with the town of Lerwick. It was repaired in

1781 during the American War of Independence. The fort is pentagonal with high walls and seaward-facing gunports.
Open at all reasonable time.
Free.
(AM)

Shetland Museum
SHETLAND
LERWICK

Map 13 HU44
Lower Hillhead
☎ (0595) 5057
The massive brass propeller blade outside the building is from the 17,000-ton liner *Oceanic*, wrecked off Foula in 1914. The museum itself has a fascinating range of items recovered from shipwrecks, and houses a permanent collection of artefacts, models, displays and specimens which illustrate the

history of Shetland from pre-historic times to the present day. Exhibits include replicas of the St Ninian's Isle Treasure. Regular exhibitions of photographs and paintings are held in the Back Gallery.
Open all year Mon, Wed, Fri 10-7, Tue, Thu, Sat 10-5.
Free.
🅿 & *(lift, wheelchair available) toilets for disabled shop* ✖

Mousa Broch
SHETLAND
MOUSA ISLAND

Map 13 HU42
(Accessible by boat from Sandwick)
☎ 031-244 3101
This broch is the best-preserved example of an Iron Age drystone tower in Scotland. The tower is nearly complete

and rises to a height of 40ft. The outer and inner walls both contain staircases that may be climbed to the parapet.
Open at all reasonable time.
Free.
(AM)

Scalloway Castle
SHETLAND
SCALLOWAY

Map 16 HU33
☎ 031-244 3101
The ruins of a castle designed on the medieval two-step plan. The castle was actually built in 1600 by Patrick Stewart, Earl of Orkney. When the Earl, who was renowned for his cruelty, was

executed in 1615, the castle fell into disuse.
Open at all reasonable time.
Free.
🅿
(AM)

Jarlshof Prehistoric Site
SHETLAND
SUMBURGH

Map 13 HU30
(At Sumburgh Head, approx 22m S of Lerwick)
☎ 031-244 3101
One of the most remarkable archeological sites in Europe. There are remains of Bronze Age, Iron Age and Viking settlements as well as a medieval farm. There is also a 16th-century Laird's House, once the home of the

Earls Robert and Patrick Stewart, and the basis of 'Jarlshof' in Sir Walter Scott's novel *The Pirate*.
Open all year, Apr-Sep, weekdays 9.30-6, Sun 2-6; Weekends only in winter. (Closed 25-26 Dec & 1-2 Jan).
£1.50 (ch & pen 80p).
🅿 ✖
(AM)

& This symbol indicates that much or all of the attraction is accessible to wheelchairs. However, there may be some restrictions, so it would be wise to check in advance.

Clan Donald Centre
ISLE OF SKYE
ARMADALE

Map 12 NG60
(0.5m from Armadale Pier A851)
☎ Ardvasar (04714) 305 & 227
Skye's award-winning Visitor Centre is situated at the south end of the island. Armadale Castle and Gardens were built in 1815 as the home of Lord Macdonald. The sculptured ruins of the castle now house the Museum of the Isles, with an exhibition and slide-show. A library and study centre offer genealogical research and access to historical records. Surrounding the castle are 40 acres of beautiful woodland gardens and nature trails. The

Countryside Ranger Service provides a full summer programme of walks, talks and children's afternoons. The stables serve as a gift shop and licensed restaurant during the day, and in the evenings as a theatre for plays and music. Events for 1992 include classical pipes and harp competitions, and sheep dog trials. Telephone for details.
Open Mar-Oct, daily 9.30-5.30. Limited winter opening.
£2 (concessions £2). Family ticket £8. Party.
🅿 ⬤ ✗ *licensed & (wheelchairs available) toilets for disabled shop*

Dunvegan Castle
ISLE OF SKYE
DUNVEGAN

Map 12 NG24
☎ (047022) 206
This fortress stronghold set on the sea loch of Dunvegan has been the home of the Chief of Macleod for 790 years. On view are books, pictures, arms and treasured relics of the clan. There is a display that traces the history of the family and the clan from their days as Norsemen until the present day. There are boat trips from the jetty to a nearby

seal colony, and musical events in July and August. There are also shops and a restaurant.
Open 23 Mar-Oct, Mon-Sat 10-5.30, Sun, castle 1-5.30, gardens 10-5.30. Last admission 5pm. Nov-Mar by appointment only.
✱ *£3.30 (ch £1.70, pen £2.80). Gardens £1.70 (ch 90p). Seal boats £2.80 (ch £1.70)*
🅿 ⬤ ✗ *licensed shop* ✖ *(ex in grounds)*

WALES

CLWYD

Bodelwyddan Castle — BODELWYDDAN

Map 07 SJ07
(adjacent to A55)
☎ St Asaph (0745) 584060
The castle has been authentically restored as a Victorian mansion and it houses a major collection of 19th-century portraits and photography from the National Portrait Gallery. These are complemented with a remarkable collection of furniture from the Victoria and Albert Museum and the Royal Academy of Arts. The extensive walled gardens have been restored to their former glory and provide a magnificent display of flowering plants, water features, aviary and woodland walks. For children, there is an adventure woodland and play areas. Temporary exhibitions and events throughout the year.
Special events for 1992 include: 11 Apr-1 Sep, Discovery Dome, hands on science exhibition; 30-31 May, North Wales Antiques Fair; 24-25 October, Conservation and Countryside Fair.
*Open all year, Etr-Jun & Sep-1 Nov, daily (ex Fri) Jul-Aug daily 10-5. Last admission one hour before closing. Please phone for details of winter opening.
£3.50 (ch 4-16, pen, student & UB40 £2). Family ticket £9. Grounds only £2 (ch 4-16, pen, student & UB40 £1). Family ticket £5. Party.*
🅿 ⬤ ✕ *licensed* ⬤ *(lift to first floor) toilets for disabled shop garden centre* ✖

Llyn Brenig Information Centre — CERRIGYDRUDION

Map 07 SH94
(on B4051)
☎ (049082) 463
The 1,800-acre estate has a unique archaeological trail and round-the-lake walks of 10 miles (completion certificate available). There is also a nature trail and a nature reserve with a number of rare plants and birds. A hide is available: best viewing is November to March. Disabled anglers are catered for with a specially adapted boat and an annual open day. The centre has a bi-lingual exhibition on geology, archaeology, history and natural history.
Open all year, mid Mar-3 Oct daily 8-6; 1 Nov-mid Mar, Mon-Fri 8-4. (Access in winter may be limited by snow; cross-country skiing is then available).
❄ *Free. (ex water sports & fishing).*
🅿 *(charged)* ⬤ ⬤ *(boats for disabled & fishing open days) toilets for disabled shop* ✖

You can see the National Portrait Gallery in London. Or in a stunning Victorian mansion in North Wales.

Not only is Bodelwyddan Castle a painstakingly restored, authentic Victorian mansion, but also home of an extensive 19th Century collection from the National Portrait Gallery.

Add to this our remarkable collection of furniture from the V & A and sculptures from the Royal Academy and it is clear why we became Museum of the Year — and one of the most popular attractions in the North West.

For opening times see editorial entry
Tel: (0745) 584060

BODELWYDDAN CASTLE
Off the A55 near St. Asaph

Chirk Castle — CHIRK

Map 07 SJ23
(off A5, 0.5m W Chirk village, 1.5m driveway)
☎ (0691) 777701

Chirk is one of a chain of late-13th-century Marcher castles. Its high walls and drum towers have hardly changed, but the inside shows the varied tastes of 700 years of occupation. One of the least-altered parts is Adam's Tower. Elsewhere, many of the medieval-looking decorations were by Pugin in the 19th century. The elegant stone staircase and delicate plasterwork of the staterooms date from the 18th century when Chirk was transformed in neo-classical style. There is a 17th-century Long Gallery, and the servants' hall has its old list of rules. The equally varied furnishings include fine tapestries. Outside is a formal garden with clipped yew hedges, and a landscaped park with splendid wrought-iron gates by the Davies brothers.
*Open 1 Apr-27 Sep daily (ex Mon & Sat) (open BH Mon) 12-5. 3 Oct-1 Nov Sat & Sun only 12-5. Grounds open 12-6. Last admission 4.30pm.
£3.40 (ch £1.70) Family ticket £8.50. Party.*
🅿 ⬤ ⬤ *shop* ✖
(NT)

✖ The 'No Dogs' symbol does not normally apply to guide dogs – these are permitted in most establishments.

Welsh Mountain Zoo & Flagstaff Gardens — COLWYN BAY

Map 07 SH87
Old Highway (off bypass, A55)
☎ (0492) 532938

The zoo and gardens are set in a 37-acre estate overlooking Colwyn Bay, with magnificent panoramic views. The animals are housed in natural settings, interspersed with gardens and woodland. The traditional range of zoo animals can be seen, from lions and elephants to penguins and parrots, and the zoo also attracts a variety of local wildlife. There are falconry displays during the summer months, and Californian sealions can be seen performing tricks at feeding time. A new attraction is the Chimpanzee World complex, featuring the unique Chimp Encounter. There is also a Jungle Adventureland and Tarzan Trail activity area, and a Children's Farm. Special events for 1992 include: Easter, 4th Annual Safari; 10 Oct, Cub Scouts' Fun Day.
Open all year, 9.30-last admission 5pm. (4pm Nov-Feb).
❄ *£4 (pen & ch £2). Party*
🅿 ⬤ ✕ *licensed* ⬤ *(free admission for the blind & wheelchair visitors) toilets for disabled shop* ✖

Denbigh Castle — DENBIGH

Map 07 SJ06
(via A525, A543 & B5382)
☎ (074571) 3979
The castle was begun by Henry de Lacy in 1282 and has an inspiring and impressive castle gatehouse, with a trio of towers and a superb archway, which is surmounted by a figure believed to be that of Edward I.
Open all year, 27 Oct-24 Mar wkdays 9.30-4, Sun 2-4; 25 Mar-26 Oct, daily 9.30-6.30. (Closed 1 Jan & 24-26 Dec).
🅿 ✖
(AM Cadw)
Details not confirmed for 1992

Town Walls & Leicester's Church — DENBIGH

Map 07 SJ06
Noted for their almost complete circuit, the town walls were started in 1282 at the same time as the castle. The remains include one of the gateways and the unfinished Leicester's Church, built by the Earl of Leicester, favourite of Elizabeth I, who meant it to become the cathedral of the diocese.
Open all year, 27 Oct-24 Mar wkdays 9.30-4, Sun 2-4; 25 Mar-26 Oct daily 9.30-6.30. (Closed 24-26 Dec & 1 Jan)
(AM Cadw)
Details not confirmed for 1992

Ewloe Castle — EWLOE

Map 07 SJ26
(NW of village on B5125)
The remains of Ewloe Castle stand in Ewloe Woods. It was a native Welsh castle, and Henry II was defeated nearby in 1157. Part of the Welsh Tower in the upper ward still stands to its original height, and there is a well in the lower ward. Remnants of walls and another tower can also be seen.
Open at all times.
(AM Cadw)
Details not confirmed for 1992

Flint Castle — FLINT

Map 07 SJ27
☎ (03526) 3222
The castle was started by Edward I in 1277 and overlooks the River Dee. It is exceptional for its great tower, or Donjon, which is separated by a moat. It may have been the castle's chief residence. Other buildings would have stood in the inner bailey, of which parts of the walls and corner towers remain.
Open all year, 27 Oct-24 Mar, wkdays 9.30-4, Sun 2-4; 25 Mar-26 Oct, daily 9.30-6.30. (Closed 24-26 Dec & 1 Jan).
🅿 ✖
(AM Cadw)
Details not confirmed for 1992

Chwarel Wynne Mine & Museum — GLYN CEIRIOG

Map 07 SJ23
Wynne Quarry (on B4500)
☎ (069172) 343
This is a mine, museum and education centre, where visitors can watch a video on the history of the slate industry, and take a half-hour conducted tour of the underground workings. The mine has a beautiful setting in a 12-acre site, and there is a nature trail.
Open Etr-Oct, daily 10-5. Parties welcome at other times by prior appointment.
✻ *£2 (ch & students £1, pen £1.50) Party & family tickets available.*
🅿 ☕ ♿ *shop garden centre*

Horse Drawn Boats and Canal Exhibition Centre — LLANGOLLEN

Map 07 SJ24
The Wharf, Wharf Hill
☎ (0978) 860702 & 823548(eve)
Visitors can enjoy horsedrawn boat trips along the beautiful Vale of Llangollen, as well as a fascinating museum illustrating the heyday of canals in Britain. The imaginative displays include working and static models, photographs, murals and slides.
Open wknd afternoons Apr-Oct (pm daily Jul-Aug). Trips also run during May, Jun & Sep at various times, phone for details
✻ *Museum 70p (ch 45p).*
☕ ♿ *shop*

Every effort is made to provide accurate information, but details might change during the currency of this guide.

Llangollen Station — LLANGOLLEN

Map 07 SJ24
☎ (0978) 860951 & 860979
The restored Great Western Railway Station is situated in the town centre and beside the River Dee. Locomotives and rolling stock are displayed, and passenger trains run on a seven-mile round trip between Llangollen and Deeside Halt. A special coach for the disabled is sometimes available. Events for 1992 will include Thomas the Tank Engine weekends, Santa Specials, and special 'Wine and Dine' trains on Saturday evenings (summer only) and Sunday lunchtimes.
Open – Station wkds, Steam hauled trains Mar-Oct Sun & daily in Jul & Aug, diesel trains May-Oct Sat, daily during Jun. Santa specials during Dec.
✻ *Station Free; Return Fares 1st class £3.70 (ch £1.85) 2nd class £3.20 (ch £1.60). Single Fare 1st class £2.50 (ch £1.40) 2nd class £2.20 (ch £1.20)*
☕ ♿ *(special coach for disabled parties) toilets for disabled shop (at stations)*

Plas Newydd — LLANGOLLEN

Map 07 SJ24
Butler Hill
☎ Wrexham (0978) 861514

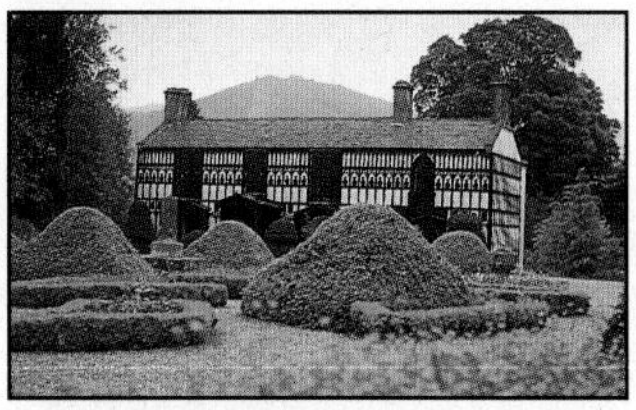

The 'Ladies of Llangollen', Lady Eleanor Butler and Sarah Ponsonby lived here from 1780 to 1831. The original stained glass windows, carved panels, leather wall coverings and domestic miscellany of two lives are exhibited along with prints, pictures and letters.
Open Apr10-5; May-Sep Mon-Sat 10-7, Sun 10-5; Oct daily 10-5 Sun 10-4; rest of year, by arrangement.
✻ *£1.10 (ch 60p)*
🅿 ⊘ *(ex in grounds)*

✻ An asterisk indicates that up-to-date information was not available at the time of our research – 1991 information has been published as an indication of what you may expect.

Valle Crucis Abbey — LLANGOLLEN

Map 07 SJ24
(on B5103, off A5 W of Llangollen)
☎ (0978) 860326
Set in a deep, narrow valley, the abbey was founded for the Cistercians in 1201 by Madog ap Grufydd. Substantial remains of the church can be seen, and some beautifully carved grave slabs have been found. There is a small exhibition on the Cistercian monks and the abbey.
Open all year, 27 Oct-24 Mar wkdays 9.30-4, Sun 2-4; 25 Mar-26 Oct, daily 9.30-6.30. (Closed 24-26 Dec & 1 Jan)
🅿 ♿ *shop* ⊘
(AM Cadw)
Details not confirmed for 1992

The Bersham Industrial Heritage Centre — WREXHAM

Map 07 SJ35
Bersham (2m SW)
☎ (0978) 261529
Bersham was a centre of the ironworking industry and the Industrial Heritage Centre is part of an industrial history trail which covers eight miles. The centre is housed in a Victorian schoolhouse and has an exhibition on the history of ironworking in the Bersham area plus workshops and demonstrations of smithing. There are free guided tours of the Bersham and Clywedog Trail throughout the summer and also lectures and temporary exhibitions, including a display of black and white photographs entitled 'Miners of North Wales' (Oct 24-Dec 14), 'Kites of the Far East' (Dec 19-Jan 18), and 'Forging Links', an exhibition of iron and steel (Feb 27-Mar28).
Open Etr-Oct, Tue-Sat & BH 10-12.30 & 1.30-4, Sun 2-4; Nov-Etr, Tue-Sat 10-12.30 & 1.30-4.
Free.
🅿 ♿ *shop* ⊘

Erddig — WREXHAM

Map 07 SJ35
(off the A525, 2m S of Wrexham)
☎ (0978) 355314

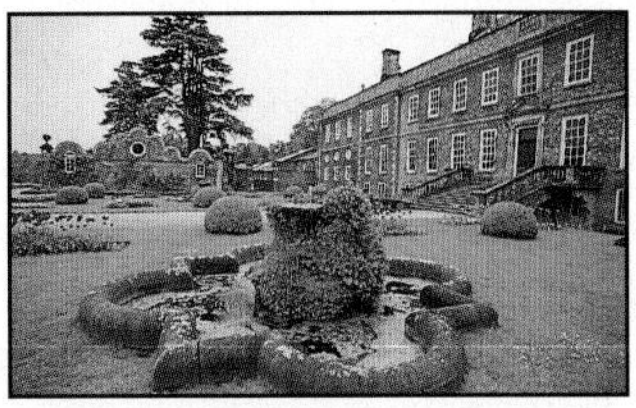

Owned by the National Trust, Erddig is a treasure house of furnishings, utensils and tools of a country house since the 1700s. Built in 1680, the house was enlarged and improved during the next half century by a wealthy London lawyer with a passion for gilt and silver furniture. The house still has its original furnishings including a magnificent state bed in Chinese silk.
The house is especially notable for the view it gives of both 'upstairs' and 'downstairs' life. There is a range of restored outbuildings which show the workings of the laundry, the bakehouse – where bread is still baked – and the estate smithy and sawmill.
The gardens are unusual in that they have been very little changed since the 18th century.
Open Apr-Sep, daily (ex Thu & Fri, open Good Fri); 11-6 (house 12-5); last entry 4pm. Family rooms close in Oct, 3 Oct-1 Nov belowstairs servants quarters only. Family rooms (inc below stairs, outbuildings & gardens) £4.50 (ch £2.25). Below stairs (inc gardens & outbuildings) £2.80 (ch £1.40). Party.
🅿 ✕ *licensed* ♿ *toilets for disabled shop* ⊘
(NT)

DYFED

Carmarthen Museum — ABERGWILI

Map 03 SN42
(2m E of Carmarthen, on A40)
☎ Carmarthen (0267) 231691
Housed in the old palace of the Bishop of St David's and set in seven acres of grounds, the museum offers a wide range of local subjects to explore, from geology and prehistory to butter making and pottery and Welsh furniture and folk art. There are Roman and medieval displays, and temporary exhibitions are held.
Open all year, Mon-Sat 10-4.30. (Closed Xmas-New Year).
✻ *50p (ch free, pen, students & unemployed 25p). Party 10+.*
🅿 ♿ *toilets for disabled shop* ⊘

National Library of Wales — ABERYSTWYTH

Map 07 SN58
Penglais Hill
☎ (0970) 623816
The huge library is one of Britain's six copyright libraries, and specialises in Welsh and Celtic literature. It has music, prints and drawings, as well as books in all languages, and picture exhibitions are held here.
Open all year, Library & reading rooms Mon-Fri 9.30-6, Sat until 5. (Closed BH's & first wk Oct). Exhibition Gallery only, open Whit & Aug BH
🅿 ☕ ♿ *toilets for disabled* ⊘
Details not confirmed for 1992

Colby Woodland Garden — AMROTH

Map 03 SN10
☎ (0834) 811885
The tranquillity and seclusion of this sheltered valley combined with the splendour of the woodland garden makes Colby one of the most beautiful National Trust properties in Pembrokeshire. There are many pleasant meadow and woodland walks. From early spring to the end of June the garden is a blaze of colour, from the masses of daffodils to the rich hues of rhododendrons, azaleas and bluebells.
Open 30 Mar-Oct, daily 10-5.
✻ *£2 (ch 70p).*
🅿 ☕ *shop* ⊘
(NT)

Rheidol Power Station & Information Centre — CAPEL BANGOR

Map 07 SN68
Cwm Rheidol (Off A44 at Capel Bangor)
☎ (097084) 667
A guided tour of the power station can be taken. It lies in a secluded valley, and other facilities include a fish farm, forest walks and a lakeside picnic area. There is an information centre.
Open Etr-Sep, daily 11-4.30 & Oct noon-4pm for tours of the Power Station & information centre.
£1.50 (ch 16 50p, pen & students £1). Family ticket £3.50.
🅿 ♿ *shop*

Cardigan Wildlife Park — CARDIGAN

Map 03 SN14
Cilgerran (entrance near village off A478)
☎ (0239) 614449
This is an unusual park and sanctuary, with a wide range of animals, birds and plants. It also has disused slate quarries and there are nature walks and fishing on the River Teifi. The ancient art of coracle fishing is demonstrated regularly during the season, and various events are held through the year.
Open from Etr, daily 10-sunset (last admission 5.30pm).
🅿 ☕ ♿ *shop* ⊘
Details not confirmed for 1992

Carew Castle & Tidal Mill — CAREW

Map 02 SN00
(on A4075, 5m E of Pembroke)
☎ (0646) 651657 & 651782
This magnificent Norman castle – later an Elizabethan residence – has royal links with Henry Tudor and was the setting for the Great Tournament of 1507. Special events for the year include theatre interpretation, a schools programme, holiday activities and concerts – details available spring 1992.
continued . . .

Nearby is the Carew Cross (Cadw), an impressive 13ft Celtic cross dating from the 11th century. Carew Mill is one of only three restored tidal mills in Britain, with records dating back to 1558. The fine four-storey building houses a theatre showing an introductory film, and there are talking points explaining the milling process.
Open Etr-Oct, daily 10-5.
✻ *£1.75 (ch & pen 90p). Single ticket (castle or mill) £1.15 (ch 60p).*
🅿 ⅃ *shop*

Carreg Cennen Castle — CARREG CENNEN CASTLE

Map 03 SN61
☎ Llandeilo (0558) 822291

A steep path leads up to the castle, which is spectacularly sited on a limestone crag. It was first built as a stronghold of the native Welsh and then rebuilt in the late 13th century. Most remarkable among the impressive remains is a mysterious passage, cut into the side of the cliff and lit by loopholes. The farm at the site operates a rare breeds centre and a tea room.
Open all year, 27 Oct-24 Mar wkdays 9.30-4, Sun 2-4; 25 Mar-26 Oct daily 9.30-6.30. (Closed 24-26 Dec & 1 Jan).
🅿 ⅃ *shop* 🍴
(AM Cadw)
Details not confirmed for 1992

Cilgerran Castle — CILGERRAN

Map 03 SN14
(off A484 & A478)
☎ Cardigan (0239) 615136
Set picturesquely above a gorge of the River Teifi – famed for its coracle fishermen – Cilgerran Castle dates from the 11th to 13th centuries. It decayed gradually after the Civil War, but its great round towers and high walls give a vivid impression of its former strength.
Open all year, 27 Oct-24 Mar wkdays 9.30-4, Sun 2-4; 25 Mar-26 Oct wkdays 9.30-6.30, Sun 2-6.30. (Closed 24-26 Dec & 1 Jan).
⅃ *toilets for disabled shop* 🍴
(AM Cadw)
Details not confirmed for 1992

Castell Henllys Fort — CRYMYCH

Map 03 SN13
Pant-Glas, Meline (Off A487)
☎ Crosswell (023979) 319
This Iron Age hill fort is set in the beautiful Pembrokeshire Coast National Park. Excavations began in 1981 and three roundhouses have been reconstructed. A forge, smithy, and primitive looms can be seen, with other attractions such as adventure trails and a herb garden.
Open Etr-Oct, daily 10-6 (closes 5pm from mid-Sep).
✻ *£2 (ch & pen £1).*
🅿 *shop*

For an explanation of the symbols and abbreviations, see page 2.

Museum of the Welsh Woollen Industry — DRE-FACH FELINDRE

Map 03 SN33
☎ Velindre (0559) 370929
Housed in part of the Cambrian Mills, which are still working, the museum is a branch of the National Museum of Wales. Its collection of textile machinery and tools dates back to the 18th century, and there are displays tracing the history of the industry from the Middle Ages to the present. A factory trail can be followed.
Open all year, Apr-Sep, Mon-Sat 10-5; Oct-Mar, Mon-Fri 10-5. (Closed Good Fri, 24-26 Dec & 1 Jan). Evening visits by prior arrangement.
£1 (ch 50p, pen 75p). Family ticket £2.50. Party.
🅿 ⅃ *toilets for disabled shop* 🍴

Dryslwyn Castle — DRYSLWYN

Map 03 SN52
The ruined 13th-century castle was a stronghold of the native Welsh. It stands on a lofty mound, and was important in the struggles between English and Welsh.
Open – entrance by arrangement with Dryslwyn Farm.
🅿
(AM Cadw)
Details not confirmed for 1992

Haverfordwest Castle, Museum, Art Gallery & Record Office — HAVERFORDWEST

Map 02 SM91
☎ (0437) 763708
The ruined 12th-century castle was used as a jail and a police headquarters before it became a museum. Exhibits include items linked with the Pembroke Yeomanry, and there is an art gallery.
Open all year. Museum Mon-Sat 10-4.30. (Closed Good Fri, 25 Dec-2 Jan). Record Office Mon-Thu 9-4.45, Fri 9-4.15. Parties book in advance. Castle ruins daily during daylight, at visitors' own risk.
✻ *50p (ch free, pen & unemployed 25p).*
🅿 ⅃ *shop* 🍴 *(ex in grounds)*

Kidwelly Castle — KIDWELLY

Map 03 SN40
(via A484)
☎ (0554) 890104
This is an outstanding example of late-13th-century castle design, with its 'walls within walls' defensive system. There were later additions made to the building, the chapel dating from about 1400. Of particular interest are two vast circular ovens.
Open all year, 27 Oct-24 Mar wkdays 9.30-4, Sun 2-4; 25 Mar-26 Oct, daily 9.30-6.30. (Closed 25-26 Dec & 1-2 Jan).
🅿 ⅃
(AM Cadw)
Details not confirmed for 1992

Kidwelly Industrial Museum — KIDWELLY

Map 03 SN40
☎ (0554) 891078

Two of the great industries of Wales are represented in this museum: tinplate and coal mining. The original buildings and machinery of the Kidwelly tinplate works, where tinplate was hand made, are now on display to the public. There is also an exhibition of coal mining with pit-head gear and a winding engine, while the more general history of the area is shown in a separate exhibition.
Open Etr-Sep, Mon-Fri 10-5 (6pm Jul-Aug), Sat-Sun 2-5 (6pm Jul-Aug). Last admission 4pm (5pm Jul-Aug). Other times by arrangement for parties only.
✻ *£1 (ch, pen, students & UB40s 50p). Family ticket £2.50. Party.*
🅿 ⅃ *toilets for disabled shop* 🍴 *(ex in grounds)*

Places to visit in this guide are pinpointed on the atlas at the back of the book.

Lamphey Palace — LAMPHEY

Map 02 SN00
☎ Pembroke (0646) 672224
This ruined 13th-century palace once belonged to the Bishops of St Davids.
Open all year, 27 Oct-24 Mar, wkdays 9.30-4, Sun 2-4; 25 Mar-26 Oct wkdays 9.30-6.30, Sun 2-6.30. (Closed 1 Jan & 24-26 Dec).
🅿 ⅃ *toilets for disabled shop* 🍴
(AM Cadw)
Details not confirmed for 1992

Dylan Thomas' Boat House — LAUGHARNE

Map 03 SN31
Dylans Walk (14m W of Carmarthen)
☎ (0994) 427420
Under Milk Wood was written here by Wales's most prolific 20th- century poet and writer. The waterside house, set on the 'heron priested' shore of the Taf estuary, contains much original furniture, family photographs, an art gallery and displays on the life and works of Dylan Thomas. There is an audio-visual presentation available. Nearby is the writing shed where Dylan Thomas actually wrote so many of his well-known poems and short stories.
Open all year, Etr-Oct, daily 10-6 (last admission 5.15); Nov-Etr, Sun-Fri 11-4 (last admission 3.15).
✻ *£1.35 (ch & pen 85p). Party 10+.*
⅃ *shop* 🍴

Parc Howard Art Gallery & Museum — LLANELLI

Map 03 SN50
☎ (0554) 773538
Llanelli pottery, local museum exhibits and a permanent collection of paintings are housed in this gallery, which is set in a pleasant park.
Open all year, daily. Apr-Sep 11-1 & 2-6; Oct-Mar 11-1 & 2-4.
Free.
⅃ 🍴

Llansteffan Castle — LLANSTEFFAN

Map 03 SN31
The ruins of this 11th- to 13th-century stronghold stand majestically on the west side of the Towy estuary.
Open – access throughout the year.
(AM Cadw)
Details not confirmed for 1992

Penrhos Cottage — LLANYCEFN

Map 02 SN02
☎ Clarbeston (0437) 731328
Local tradition has it that cottages built overnight on common land could be claimed by the builders, together with the ground a stone's throw away from the door. This cottage is an example, built with help from friends and family; and it remained in the same family from the time it was built until the late 1960s, when the county council bought it. Its character has been maintained, and it gives the visitor an insight into traditional Welsh country life. Various outbuildings complete the picture.
Open Etr & mid May-Sep, Tue-Sat 10-1 & 2-5 & Sun afternoons.
✻ *20p (ch free, pen & UB40 10p).*
⅃ *shop* 🍴 *(ex in grounds)*

Llawhaden Castle — LLAWHADEN

Map 02 SN01
☎ (09914) 201
The castle was first built in the 12th century to protect the possessions of the bishops of St David's. The 13th- and 14th-century remains of the bishops' hall, kitchen, bakehouse and other buildings can be seen, all surrounded by a deep moat.
Open all year, 27 Oct-24 Mar wkdays 9.30-4, Sun 2-4; 25 Mar-26 Oct, wkdays 9.30-6.30, Sun 2-6.30. (Closed 24-26 Dec & 1 Jan). Key keeper arrangement.
🍴
(AM Cadw)
Details not confirmed for 1992

Oakwood Adventure & Leisure Park — NARBERTH

Map 03 SN11
Canaston Bridge (signposted off the A40)
☎ Martletwy (0834) 891376
The activities offered here are numerous and include rollercoaster, waterfall and bobsleigh rides, miniature trains, go-karts and assault courses. There is a huge undercover playland as well as an outdoor children's play area. A 400- seat theatre has recently opened.
Open 11 Apr-Sep, daily from 10am. Restricted in Oct.
Admission fee payable.
🅿 ✕ *licensed* ⅃ *toilets for disabled shop* 🍴

Felin Geri Mill · NEWCASTLE EMLYN

Map 03 SN34
Cwmcou (2m N on unclass rd off
B4333 at Cwmcou)
☎ (0239) 710810
Felin Geri Mill is one of the last
watermills in the UK to use the original
methods of production to grind corn on
a regular, commercial basis. Visitors are
shown all the stages of production of
stoneground wholemeal flour. There is
also a water-powered sawmill and a mill
museum. Children can have fun in the
large adventure playground and there are
walks to enjoy. With trout ponds, a
woodland interpretation centre and craft
workshops there is plenty to see and do.
Open Etr-Oct, daily 10-6.
P ✕ *licensed* &. *shop*
Details not confirmed for 1992

Pentre Ifan Burial Chamber · NEWPORT

Map 02 SN03
(3m SE from B4329 or A487)
Found to be part of a vanished long
barrow when excavated in 1936-37, the
remains of this chamber include the
capstone, three uprights and a circular
forecourt.
Open – access throughout the year.
(AM Cadw)
Details not confirmed for 1992

*Every effort is made to provide accurate information,
but details might change during the currency
of this guide.*

Castle Hill Museum (The Museum of the Home) · PEMBROKE

Map 02 SM90
7 Westgate Hill
☎ (0646) 681200
A pleasant domestic setting provides an
opportunity to view some of the objects
that have been part of everyday life over
the past three hundred years.
*Open Etr-Oct, Sun-Wed & Fri
10.30-5.30.*
£1 (ch & pen 70p). Party.
✕ 🏷

Pembroke Castle · PEMBROKE

Map 02 SM90
☎ (0646) 681510
This 12th- to 13th-century fortress has
an impressive 80ft high round keep.
There is also a new Interpretative
Centre.
*Open all year, daily, Apr-Sep 9.30-6; Mar
& Oct 10-5; Nov-Feb, Mon-Sat 10-4.
(Closed 24-26 Dec & 1 Jan).
£2 (ch 16 & pen £1.20, ch 5 &
wheelchairs free). Family ticket £5. Party.*
🍴 &. *toilets for disabled shop*

Graham Sutherland Gallery · PICTON CASTLE

Map 02 SN01
(5m E of Haverfordwest, S of A40)
☎ (0437) 751296
Graham Sutherland was enchanted with
Wales, and this unique gallery reflects
the artist's fascination. A large collection
of Sutherland paintings hangs here, and
visitors can discover for themselves the
lanes and estuaries that inspired one of
Britain's greatest artists. Videos on
Sutherland can be seen in the lecture
theatre. Special events for 1992 include:
7 Apr-21 Jun, The Language of Flowers
– ceramics and paintings from the
collection of the National Museum of
Wales; 3 Jul-9 Aug, The Valleys Project
– photographs by William Tsui; 15
Aug-Sep, South Bank Centre Touring
Exhibition.
*Open 29 Mar-4 Oct, Tue-Sun
10.30-12.30 & 1.30-5. Also open BH
Mons.*
✳ *£1 (ch 5-15 50p, pen, UB40 & disabled
75p). Family ticket £2.50*
P &. *toilets for disabled shop* ✕

Bwlch Nant-Yr-Arian Forest Visitor Centre · PONTERWYD

Map 07 SN78
(3m W)
☎ Crossword (09743) 404
Operated by the Forestry Commission,
the centre interprets all the aspects of the
forest. There are forest walks in the
vicinity.
*Open Etr-Sep, daily 10-5 (6pm in
Jul-Aug).
Free.*
P &. *toilets for disabled shop* ✕ *(ex in
grounds)*

Llywernog Silver-Lead Mine · PONTERWYD

Map 07 SN78
(11m E of Aberystwyth on A44)
☎ (097085) 620
The Llywernog Silver-Lead Mine is an
internationally known mining heritage
centre. The mountains of Mid Wales
form a backdrop to the museum
displays, Miner's Trail, underground
tunnel, working water-wheels, tea rooms
and picnic site. Displays and
demonstrations of silver panning take
place regularly in season. A special event
for 1992 is Miners' Gala Day on 4 July.
*Open Etr-Oct, daily 10-6 (Oct 5pm). Last
admission 1 hour before closing time.
Winter by appointment.
£2.75 (ch 5-15 £1.50, students & pen
£2.25). Family ticket £7.50.*
P 🍴 &. *shop*

*This is just one of many guidebooks published by the AA.
The full range is available at any AA shop or good bookshop.*

Dolaucothi Gold Mines · PUMSAINT

Map 03 SN64
☎ (05585) 359

Here is an opportunity to spend a day
exploring the gold mines and to wear a
miner's helmet and lamp while touring
the underground workings. The
information centre and a walk along the
Miners' Way disclose the secrets of
2,000 years of gold mining. A unique
blend of history and beauty, this is the
only place in Britain where the Romans
mined gold.
*Open 30 Mar-Oct, daily (incl BH's) 10-6.
Underground tours May-Sep, daily every
half hour. (Last admission 5pm).*
✳ *£2-£4 (ch £1.20-£2).*
P 🍴 *shop* ✕
(NT)

St Davids Bishop's Palace · ST DAVID'S

Map 02 SM72
(on A487)
☎ (0437) 720517
These extensive and impressive ruins are
all that remain of the principle residence
of the Bishops of St Davids. The palace
shares a quiet valley with the cathedral,
which was almost certainly built on the
site of a monastery founded in the 6th
century by St David. The Bishop's
Palace houses an exhibition: 'Life in the
Palace of a Prince of the Church'.
*Open all year, 27 Oct-24 Mar wkdays
9.30-4, Sun 2-4; 25 Mar-26 Oct, daily
9.30-6.30. (Closed 24-26 Dec & 1-2 Jan).*
&. *toilets for disabled shop* ✕
(AM Cadw)
Details not confirmed for 1992

Manor House Wildlife & Leisure Park · ST FLORENCE

Map 02 SN00
Ivy Tower (on B4318)
☎ Carew (0646) 651201
The park is set in 12 acres of delightful
wooded grounds and award-winning
gardens. The wildlife includes exotic
birds, reptiles and fish. Also here are a
pets' corner, a children's playground,
amusements and radio-controlled
models. Other attractions include a giant
astraglide slide, a go-kart track and
model railway exhibition. There are
falconry displays twice a day (except
Sat).
Open Etr-Sep, daily 10-6.
✳ *£2 (ch & pen £1). Party 20+.*
P 🍴 &. *toilets for disabled shop garden
centre* ✕

Scolton Manor Museum & Country Park · SCOLTON

Map 02 SM92
(5m N of Haverfordwest, on B4329)
☎ Clarbeston (0437) 731328 (Mus) &
731457 (Park)
The early Victorian mansion, stables and
a large exhibition hall are given over to
illustrating the history and natural
history of Pembrokeshire. The 60 acres
of grounds are rich in fine trees and
ornamental shrubs while a 'tree and
nature trail' provide interesting
diversions.
*Open all year, Country Park. Museum:
May-Sep, Tue-Sun & BH's 10-4.30.*
✳ *50p (ch free, pen & UB40 25p). Party
10+.*
P 🍴 &. *shop* ✕ *(ex in grounds)*

Solva Nectarium   SOLVA

Map 02 SM82
☎ St Davids (0437) 721323
At the Nectarium, live butterflies from all around the world can be seen at close quarters. There are specimens from places as far apart as the rain forests of India, Malaysia and the Amazon, as well as many from more temperate climates. In an insect gallery, butterflies can be

seen emerging from their pupae. There are several shops in the complex selling perfumery, designer clothing and furnishings for the home.
Open Etr-Sep, Mon-Sat 10-6, Sun 2-6. (Last admission 5).
✱ *£2 (ch 5-14 £1, under 5 free, pen £1.50).*
🐦 *shop*

Strata Florida Abbey   STRATA FLORIDA ABBEY

Map 03 SN76
☎ Pontrhydfendigaid (09745) 261
Little remains of the Cistercian abbey founded in 1164, except the ruined church and cloister. Strata Florida was an important centre of learning in the Middle Ages, and it is believed that the 14th-century poet Dafyd ap Gwilym

was buried here.
Open all year, 27 Oct-24 Mar wkdays 9.30-4, Sun 2-4; 25 Mar-26 Oct, wkdays 9.30-6.30, Sun 2-6.30. (Closed 24-26 Dec & 1 Jan).
🅿 ✖
(AM Cadw)
Details not confirmed for 1992

✱ An asterisk indicates that up-to-date information was
not available at the time of our research – 1991
information has been published as an
indication of what you may expect.

Talley Abbey   TALLEY

Map 03 SN63
☎ (05583) 444
Only beautiful ruins now remain of this once magnificent abbey, including two pointed archways, set in the remains of the north and east walls of the church's central tower. The abbey was founded in 1197 by Rhys app Gruffud, and was virtually destroyed in the uprising led

by Owain Glyndwr.
Open all year, 27 Oct-24 Mar wkdays 9.30-4, Sun 2-4; 25 Mar-26 Oct, wkdays 9.30-6.30, Sun 2-6.30. (Closed 24-26 Dec & 1 Jan). Key keeper arrangement.
🅿 ✖
(AM Cadw)
Details not confirmed for 1992

Tenby Museum   TENBY

Map 03 SN10
Castle Hill
☎ (0834) 2809
The town museum is situated on Castle Hill and covers local history, with particular reference to the town's development as a 19th-century seaside resort. There are maritime and picture

galleries, as well as exhibits on local geology, archaeology and natural history.
Open all year, Etr-Oct, daily 10-6; Nov-Etr, Mon-Fri 10-12 & 2-4.
✱ *60p (ch 30p, pen 50p).*
♿ *shop* ✖

Tudor Merchant's House   TENBY

Map 03 SN10
Quay Hill
☎ (0834) 2279
Recalling Tenby's history as a thriving and prosperous port, the Tudor Merchant's house is a fine example of gabled 15th-century architecture. There is a good Flemish chimney and on three

walls the remains of frescoes can be seen. The ground floor is now a National Trust information centre.
Open 30 Mar-Oct, Mon-Fri 11-6, Sun 2-6. (Closed Sat).
✱ *£1.50 (ch 70p).*
shop ✖
(NT)

GWENT

Abergavenny Castle & District Museum   ABERGAVENNY

Map 03 SO21
☎ (0873) 854282
Craft tools, a Welsh kitchen, a saddler's shop, carriage room and local exhibits are displayed at the museum, and the remains of the castle's walls, towers and gateway can be seen.

Open all year. Museum open Mar-Oct, Mon-Sat 11-1 & 2-5; Sun 2-5. Nov-Feb, Mon-Sat 11-1 & 2-4. Castle open daily 8-dusk.
✱ *70p (ch, pen & students 35p)*
🅿 ♿ *shop* ✖

Big Pit Mining Museum   BLAENAVON

Map 03 SO20
☎ (0495) 790311
The 'Big Pit' closed as a working mine in 1980, but today visitors can don safety helmets and cap lamps, and descend the 300ft shaft to find out what life was like for generations of miners in South Wales. There is an exhibition in the old pithead baths and changing rooms, and a reconstructed miner's cottage can also be seen. Stout shoes and

warm clothes are recommended for tours of the mine.
Open Mar-Oct, daily 9.30-5. (Last tour 3.30). Nov-Feb telephone for opening details.
Underground & surface £4.50 (ch £3.25 & pen & students £4.25) surface only £1.50 (ch 75p, pen & students £1.25). Family ticket £14.
🅿 🐦 ♿ *(underground tours by prior arrangement) toilets for disabled shop*

Caerleon Fortress Baths, Amphitheatre & Barracks   CAERLEON

Map 03 ST39
(on B4236)
☎ Newport (0663) 422518

Caerleon was an important Roman military base, with accommodation for

thousands of men. The foundations of barrack lines and parts of the ramparts can be seen, with remains of the cookhouse, latrines and baths. The amphitheatre nearby is one of the best examples in Britain. The Fortress Baths were excavated in the 1970s and represent the most complete example of a Roman legionary bath building in Britain.
Open all year, 27 Oct-24 Mar wkdays 9.30-4, Sun 2-4; 25 Mar-26 Oct daily 9.30-6.30. (Closed 1 Jan & 24-26 Dec).
🅿 ♿ *N shop* ✖
(AM Cadw)
Details not confirmed for 1992

Roman Legionary Museum   CAERLEON

Map 03 ST39
High St
☎ (0633) 423134
The museum illustrates the history of Roman Caerleon and the daily life of its garrison. On display are arms, armour and equipment, with a collection of engraved gemstones, a labyrinth mosaic and Roman finds from the legionary

base at Usk.
Open all year, 15 Mar-15 Oct, daily 9.30-6.30; 16 Oct-14 Mar, wkdays 9.30-4, Sun 2-4pm. (Closed 24-26 Dec, 1 Jan, Good Fri & May Day).
£1.25. Reductions for ch & pen. Also joint ticket available with Roman Baths & Amphitheatre.
♿ *toilets for disabled shop* ✖

Caerwent Roman Town   CAERWENT

Map 03 ST49
(beside A48)
A complete circuit of the town wall of 'Venta Siluarum', together with excavated areas of houses, shops and a

temple.
Open – access throughout the year.
(AM Cadw)
Details not confirmed for 1992

Caldicot Castle, Museum & Countryside Park   CALDICOT

Map 03 ST48
(on B4245)
☎ (0291) 420241
The restored Norman border castle has a sandstone keep which was probably built by Humphrey de Bohun in the 13th century. It houses a museum and exhibitions, and overlooks a country park where herons and other water-

loving birds may be seen. There is also an adventure playground. Around the castle are tranquil gardens, the scene of fashionable parties in the 19th century.
Open Mar-Oct, Mon-Fri 11-12.30 & 1.30-5, Sat & BH 10-1 & 1.30-5, Sun 1.30-5.
🅿 ♿ *toilets for disabled shop*
Details not confirmed for 1992

Chepstow Castle   CHEPSTOW

Map 03 ST59
☎ (02912) 4065
Built by William FitzOsbern soon after the Norman Conquest, Chepstow is the first recorded Norman stone castle. It was used as a base for advances into Wales, and stands in a strategic spot above the Wye. Not only could it easily be defended, but it also overlooked a harbour. The castle was strengthened in the following centuries, but was not besieged (as far as is known) until the Civil War, when it was twice lost to the Parliamentarians. The remains of the domestic rooms are evidence of past splendour, and the massive gatehouse

with its portcullis grooves and ancient gates is still impressive, as are the walls and towers with their variety of slots for arrows and guns. An extension of the castle was the Port Wall, which ran round the town. An exhibition, 'Chepstow – A Castle at War', provides visitors with an insight into the building of the medieval castle and its role in the civil war.
Open all year, 27 Oct-24 Mar wkdays 9.30-4, Sun 2-4; 25 Mar-26 Oct daily 9.30-6.30. (Closed 24-26 Dec & 1 Jan).
🅿 *shop* ✖
(AM Cadw)
Details not confirmed for 1992

✖ The 'No Dogs' symbol does not normally apply
to guide dogs – these are permitted in
most establishments.

Chepstow Museum   CHEPSTOW

Map 03 ST59
Gwy House, Bridge St
☎ (0291) 625981
Now set out in a fine 18th-century house, the museum has exhibitions of the history of Chepstow, the lower Wye

Valley and the surrounding area. Exhibition themes change monthly.
Open Mar-Oct, Mon-Sat 11-1 & 2-5, Sun 2-5.
♿ *toilets for disabled shop* ✖
Details not confirmed for 1992

Cwmcarn Forest Drive   CWMCARN

Map 03 ST29
(9m N of Newport on A467)
☎ Newport (0663) 400205
A seven-mile scenic drive with spectacular views over the Bristol Channel and surrounding countryside. Facilities include barbecues, picnic and

play areas, and forest and mountain walks. The area is run by the Forestry Commission.
Open Etr-Oct, daily 11-7pm.
✱ *Cars & Motorcycles £2, Minibus fr £6, Coaches £20.*
🅿 ♿ *shop*

Garden Festival Wales — EBBW VALE

Map 03 SO10
Victoria (2m S)
☎ (0495) 305545
Garden Festival Wales will be a five-month long celebration of new life, growth and fun with one and a half million trees, shrubs and plants bringing the 142-acre valley setting alive with colour and excitement. Events will include street theatre, opera and sporting events, with spectacular horticultural

shows. Special events include: 2-10 May, The Celtic Connection; 13-22 Jun, Kiss a Frog Week; 19-25 Sept, The Orient Expressed.
Open Jun-Aug, daily 10-8; May, Sep-Oct 10-7.
£8.50 (ch 5-16, pen, students, UB40 & disabled £5.50). Family ticket £26
P ■ ✕ *licensed* & *toilets for disabled shop garden centre* ✕

Grosmont Castle — GROSMONT

Map 03 SO42
(on B4347)
Grosmont is one of the 'trilateral' castles of Hubert de Burgh (see also Skenfrith and White Castle). It stands on a mound with a dry moat, and the considerable remains of its 13th-century great hall can

be seen. Three towers once guarded the curtain wall, and the western one is well preserved.
Open – access throughout the year.
(AM Cadw)
Details not confirmed for 1992

Llanthony Priory — LLANTHONY

Map 03 SO22
In the early 12th century William de Lacey discovered the remains of a hermitage dedicated to St David, built six centuries earlier; by 1108 a church had been consecrated on the site and just over a decade later the priory was complete. Forty years after an uprising in 1135, when the priory was brought to a state of seige, Hugh de Lacey provided the funds for a new church, and it is this that makes the picturesque

ruin seen today. Its architectural styles range from Norman to Early English, and the visitor can still make out the west towers, north nave arcade and south transept. The former priest's house is part of a hotel. The priory is reached by narrow roads through lovely scenery.
Open – access throughout the year.
P
(AM Cadw)
Details not confirmed for 1992

Hen Gwrt — LLANTILIO CROSSENNY

Map 03 SO31
(off B4233)
The rectangular enclosure of the former medieval house, still surrounded by a moat.

Open – access throughout the year.
✕ ⛳
(AM Cadw)
Details not confirmed for 1992

The Nelson Museum & Local History Centre — MONMOUTH

Map 03 SO51
New Market Hall, Priory St
☎ (0600) 3519
The bulk of the Nelson Museum collection was formed by Lady Llangattock who lived near Monmouth. On show are commemorative glass, china, silver, medals, books, prints and the prize exhibit: Admiral Nelson's fighting sword. The local history displays deal with Monmouth's past as a

fortress market town in the Wye Valley, and include a section on the co-founder of the Rolls Royce company, Charles Stewart Rolls, who was also a pioneer balloonist, aviator and, of course, motorist.
Open all year, Mon-Sat 10-1 & 2-5; Sun 2-5 (Closed Xmas & New Year).
£1 (ch & pen 50p). Party 10+.
& *shop* ✕

Museum & Art Gallery — NEWPORT

Map 03 ST38
John Frost Sq
☎ (0633) 840064
The archaeology and history of Gwent, including Roman finds, are on display in the museum. There are sections on the Chartist movement of 1838-40, a weather centre, natural history and geology as well as watercolours, oil

paintings, contemporary art, and the John Wait teapot collection on show in the art gallery.
Open all year, Mon-Thu 9.30-5, Fri 9.30-4.30, Sat 9.30-4. (Closed BH & PH).
Free.
& *(lift) shop* ✕

Tredegar House & Park — NEWPORT

Map 03 ST38
Coedkernew
☎ (0633) 815880
Tredegar was home to one of the greatest of Welsh families, the Morgans, later Lords Tredegar, for over five centuries, but for years their house has remained relatively unknown. Today it stands out as one of the most magnificent 17th-century houses in Britain. A tour of the interior vividly illustrates what life was like for the Morgans and their servants, giving visitors a fascinating insight into life 'above' and 'below' stairs.
The gardens are currently being restored but their past history – and that of the Orangery and Stables – and of the

famous Cefn Mill Mabli shovelboard, is magically brought to life. The house and gardens are set within a 90-acre landscape park. Carriage rides, self-guided trails, craft workshops, boating, and an exciting adventure playfarm provide a wide variety of things to do and see. Special events for 1992 include: 15-17 May, Folk Festival; 20-21 Jun, Antiques Fayre; 28-30 Aug, Newport Show.
Open Good Fri-end Sep, Wed-Sun & BHs 11.30-4.(Tue during school holidays. Wknds only in Oct. Special Xmas opening).
✳ *House £3.20 (ch & pen £2.20) Family ticket £8. Garden only £1.*
P *(charged)* ■ ✕ *licensed* & *(wheelchairs for loan) toilets for disabled shop*

Penhow Castle — PENHOW

Map 03 ST49
☎ (0633) 400800
This, the oldest inhabited castle in Wales, was originally a small border fortress and was the first British home of the famous Seymour family. The building presents a fascinating picture of life from the 12th to 19th centuries. The ramparts, with views of three counties, are 12th century, while the great hall, its reconstructed screen and minstrels' gallery are of the 15th century. The

kitchen represents life in the 17th century, and there is a housekeeper's room of the Victorian era. Walkman tours, pioneered here, are included in the admission price.
Open Etr-Oct, Wed-Sun & BH 10-5.15; "Candlelit Tours" by arrangement; Aug open daily; Winter Wed only 10-5.
£2.75 (ch £1.50. Family ticket £7. Party 20+
P & *shop* ✕

The Valley Inheritance — PONTYPOOL

Map 03 SO20
Park Buildings (off A4042)
☎ (0495) 752036
Housed in the Georgian stable block of Pontypool Park House, exhibitions and films tell the story of a South Wales valley. Temporary exhibitions are also held. Special events for 1992 include:

15-21 June, Welsh Week (aimed at English speakers) with choirs, music, drama, poetry and lectures.
Open Feb-Dec, Mon-Sat 10-5 & Sun 2-5 (Closed 25 Dec).
£1.20 (ch 60p).Family ticket £2.40. Party.
🅿 ▄ ⟁ *toilets for disabled shop* ✖

Raglan Castle — RAGLAN

Map 03 SO40
☎ (0291) 690228
This magnificent 15th-century castle is noted for its 'Yellow Tower of Gwent'. It was built by Sir William Thomas and slighted during the Civil War, after a long siege. The ruins are still impressive, however, and the castle's history is illustrated in an exhibition situated in the

closet tower and two rooms of the gate passage.
Open all year, 27 Oct-24 Mar wkdays 9.30-4, Sun 2-4; 25 Mar-26 Oct, daily 9.30-6.30. (Closed 24-26 Dec & 1 Jan).
🅿 ✖
(AM Cadw)
Details not confirmed for 1992

Skenfrith Castle — SKENFRITH

Map 03 SO42
This 13th-century castle has a round keep set within an imposing towered curtain wall. It was built by Hubert de Burgh as one of three 'trilateral' castles

to defend the Welsh Marches.
Open – access throughout the year. Key keeper arrangement.
(AM Cadw & NT)
Details not confirmed for 1992

Tintern Abbey — TINTERN

Map 03 SO50
(via A466)
☎ (0291) 689251

Standing serenely beside the banks of the River Wye, the ruins of the Cistercian monastery church are still surprisingly intact. The monastery was established in 1131 and it continued to thrive and become increasingly wealthy well into

the 15th century. During the Dissolution, the monastery was closed and most of the buildings, other than the church, were completely destroyed. During the 18th century the ruins of Tintern were considered to be one of the essential sites to visit. Many poets and artists came to see the majestic arches, fine doorways and elegant windows, and recorded their experiences in poetry and paintings. An exhibition, situated near the new shop, illustrates the lifestyles of the monks.
Open all year, 27 Oct-24 Mar wkdays 9.30-4, Sun 2-4; 25 Mar-26 Oct, daily 9.30-6.30. (Closed 24-26 Dec & 1 Jan).
🅿 ⟁ *toilets for disabled shop* ✖
(AM Cadw)
Details not confirmed for 1992

Gwent Rural Life Museum — USK

Map 03 SO30
Malt Barn, New Market St
☎ (02913) 3777
An award-winning collection of farm tools, machinery, wagons and domestic items.

Open Etr-Oct, daily 10-5 (ex Sat & Sun am). Winter hours contact the Museum.
£1.50 (ch 75p,pen £1). Party.
🅿 ⟁ *(special tape recording of tour for deaf) shop*

White Castle — WHITE CASTLE

Map 03 SO31
(7m NE of Abergavenny, unclass rd N of B4233)
The impressive 12th- to 13th-century moated stronghold was built by Hubert de Burgh to defend the Welsh Marches. Substantial remains of walls, towers and a gatehouse can be seen. This is the finest of a trio of castles, the others

being at Skenfrith and Grosmont.
Open all year, 27 Oct-24 Mar wkdays 9.30-4, Sun 2-4; 25 Mar-26 Oct, wkdays 9.30-6.30, Sun 2-6.30. (Closed 24-26 Dec & 1 Jan).
🅿 ⟁ ✖
(AM Cadw)
Details not confirmed for 1992

GWYNEDD

Penrhyn Castle — BANGOR

Map 07 SH57
(3m E at Landegai on A5122)
☎ (0248) 353084

The splendid castle with its towers and battlements was commissioned in 1827 as a sumptuous family home. The architect was Thomas Hopper, who was also responsible for the panelling, plasterwork and furniture, still mostly in the 'Norman' style of the mid-19th century. Notable rooms include the great hall, heated by the Roman method of hot air under the floor, the library with its heavily decorated ceiling and great arches, and the dining room, which is covered with neo-Norman decoration.
continued . . .

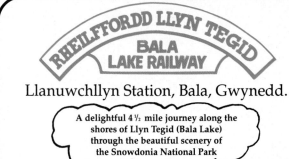

Among the furniture is a slate bed weighing over a ton, and a decorated brass bed made specially for Edward VII at the then huge cost of £600.

A natural history collection in the house shows species native to Snowdonia and there are two museums. Lady Penrhyn's bedroom suite is a doll museum and has dolls from all parts of the world, with an annexe showing Victorian nursery toys. The Penrhyn Castle Industrial Railway Museum occupies the stableyard.

The 40-acre grounds include a walled garden, wild garden and attractive woodland. There are wonderful views over Anglesey, Puffin Island, the North Wales coast and Snowdonia.
Open Apr-1 Nov, daily (ex Tue) 12-5 (Jul-Aug 11-5). Last admission 4.30pm. Last audio tour 4pm. Grounds open 11-6.
£3.80 (ch £1.90). Family ticket £9.50. Party. Garden only £2 (ch £1).
🅿 ▄ ⟁ *toilets for disabled shop* ✖
(NT)

Beaumaris Castle — BEAUMARIS

Map 07 SH67
☎ (0248) 810361

Beaumaris was the last of the great castles built by Edward I around the coast of North Wales, and there is an exhibition on his castles in the Chapel Tower. The building took from 1295 to 1312 to complete and involved a huge workforce: a record for 1296 mentions 400 masons and 2,000 labourers, besides 100 carts and wagons and 30 boats carrying stone and seacoal. In the early

1400s it was captured by Owain Glyndwr and then retaken, and in later centuries it was plundered for its lead, timber and stone. Despite this it remains one of the most impressive and complete castles built by Edward I. It has a perfectly symmetrical, concentric plan, with a square inner bailey and curtain walls, round corner towers and D-shaped towers in between. There are also two great gatehouses, but these were never finished. Around it is an outer curtain wall with small towers, and a moat which has been restored. The original defended dock for shipping has also survived.
Open all year, 27 Oct-24 Mar wkdays 9.30-4, Sun 2-4; 25 Mar-26 Oct daily 9.30-6.30. (Closed 24-26 Dec & 1 Jan).
🅿 ⟁ ✖
(AM Cadw)
Details not confirmed for 1992

Beaumaris Gaol & Courthouse — BEAUMARIS

Map 07 SH67
☎ (0248) 750262 ext 269
With its treadmill and grim cells, the gaol is a vivid reminder of the tough penalties exacted by 19th-century law. One particularly gruesome feature is the route that condemned prisoners took to the scaffold. Also here is the George Scott exhibition of police memorabilia. The courthouse, built in 1614 and

renovated early in the 19th-century, is a unique survival of a Victorian court room.
Open Etr, end May-Sep, daily 11-6. Court 11.30-5.30 (ex when in session). Other times by arrangement only.
Gaol £2.20 (ch & pen £1.50). Courthouse £1.30 (ch & pen £1). Combined ticket £2.70 (ch & pen £2). Family ticket £6.50.
⟁ *(audio tape tour available) shop* ✖

Museum of Childhood — BEAUMARIS

Map 07 SH67
1 Castle St (on B4375)
☎ Bangor (0248) 712498
Many rare and valuable exhibits are shown in the nine rooms of the museum, which illustrates the life and interests of children and families over 150 years. They include money boxes, dolls, educational toys and games, early clockwork trains, cars and aeroplanes, push toys and cycles. Also shown are things that were used rather than played with by children, such as pottery and glassware, and pieces of furniture. A

gallery shows paintings and prints of children, with early samplers and needlework pictures worked by children. Winner of the BTA and National Heritage Museum of the Year Awards. In 1990, the museum was voted 'Star Choice' out of 35 top museums by the Sunday Express Magazine travel writers.
Open daily 10-6, Sun 12-5. (Closed 25 Dec & 2nd wk Jan-2nd wk Mar).
✱ *£2.50 (ch £1.25, pen £1.50). Family ticket £6. Free entry for wheelchairs.*
🅿 ⟁ *shop* ✖

Sygun Copper Mine — BEDDGELERT

Map 07 SH54
☎ *(076686) 595*
With the help of an expert guide, visitors can explore the workings of this 19th-century copper mine set deep within the Gwynant Valley. The less energetic can enjoy a continuous audio-visual presentation and a display of artefacts found during excavations.
Open all year, daily 10-6. (Last tour 5.15pm).
* *£3.60 (ch £2.25, pen £3).*
P ♿ *toilets for disabled shop* 🐕

Conwy Valley Railway Museum — BETWS-Y-COED

Map 07 SH75
Old Goods Yard
☎ (0690) 710568
The two large museum buildings have displays on both the narrow- and standard-gauge railways of North Wales, including railway stock and other memorabilia. There are working model railway layouts and a steam-hauled miniature railway in the grounds, which cover over four acres. The latest addition is a 15in gauge tramway to the woods.
Open Etr-Oct, daily 10-5.30.
£1 (ch & pen 50p). Family ticket £2.50. Steam train/Tram ride 75p.
P ☕ ♿ *toilets for disabled shop*

Ffestiniog Pumped Storage Power Station — BLAENAU FFESTINIOG

Map 07 SH64
Ffestiniog Information Centre, Tan-Y-Grisiau (off A496)
☎ (0766) 830310
The scheme was the first hydro-electric pumped storage scheme, and was opened by Her Majesty the Queen in 1963. Water is released from an upper dam, through turbines, to generate electricity when needed, and then pumped back up when demand is low. Guided tours are available, and the information centre includes a souvenir shop and café.
Open Etr-Oct 10-4.30. Other times by prior arrangement.
P ☕ *shop* 🐕 *(ex in grounds)*
Details not confirmed for 1992

Gloddfa Ganol Slate Mine — BLAENAU FFESTINIOG

Map 07 SH64
(1m N on A470)
☎ (0766) 830664
Visitors can put on safety helmets and go into the extensive underground workings of this slate mine, which is the world's largest. There are special conducted tours by Land Rover for the more adventurous, which explore some of the miles of chambers and tunnels hundreds of feet up in the mountain. The massive machinery used in slate mining is displayed in the mill, and the art of slate splitting is demonstrated. Gloddfa Ganol is an active mine. Today's open cast blasting operations can be seen from the safety of the Mining Museum, and with the help of video films, exhibitions and

continued . . .

demonstrations visitors achieve a valuable insight into the complex nature of the slate industry.
Open Etr-Oct, Mon-Fri, also Sun 19 Jul-1 Sep 10-5.30.
£3 (ch £1.75).
P ☕ ✕ *licensed* ♿ *shop*

Llechwedd Slate Caverns — BLAENAU FFESTINIOG

Map 07 SH64
☎ (0766) 830306
The miners' underground tramway carries visitors into areas where early conditions have been recreated, while the Deep Mine is reached by an incline railway and has an unusual audio-visual presentation. Free surface attractions include several exhibitions and museums, slate mill and the Victorian village which has Victorian shops, money-house, Miners Arms pub, lock-up and working smithy.
Open all year, daily from 10am. Last tour 5.15 (Oct-Feb 4.15). (Closed 25-26 Dec & 1 Jan).
Single Tour £4.25 (ch £3, pen £3.75). Combined Tour £6.50 (ch £4.50, pen £5.25).
P ☕ ✕ *licensed* ♿ *toilets for disabled shop* 🐕 *(ex on surface)*

Hen Blas Country Park — BODORGAN

Map 07 SH36
☎ (0407) 840152
The focal point is the manor house, which dates back to the 15th century, and is one of Anglesey's oldest properties. There are 230 acres of parkland, with an 18th-century barn, shire horses, and a nature reserve and trail. There is also a large undercover play area.
Open all year, daily 10-5.30. (Restricted facilities at other times).
P ☕ ✕ ♿ *shop*
Details not confirmed for 1992

Bryn Celli Ddu Burial Chamber — BRYN-CELLI-DDU

Map 07 SH57
(3m W of Menai Bridge off A4080)
Excavated in 1865, and then again in 1925-9, this is a prehistoric circular cairn covering a passage grave with a polygonal chamber.
Open at all times.
P
(AM Cadw)
Details not confirmed for 1992

Anglesey Sea Zoo — BRYNSIENCYN

Map 07 SH46
The Oyster Hatchery
☎ (0248) 430411
The sea zoo is a unique collection of marine life found around Anglesey and the North Wales coast. The sea creatures are housed in glass-sided and open-topped tanks of all shapes and sizes, which are intended to provide as natural and unrestricted an environment as possible. Another important

continued . . .

consideration has been providing cover for visitors. There are also shoaling tanks, a wave tank, tide tank, wreck room and touch pools. A new attraction is an exhibit called 'The Big Fish Forest'. This is a huge kelp forest enclosed by the largest unsupported acrylic panel in Britain.
Open 7 Jan-Dec, from 10am. Last admission 5pm (Nov-Feb 3pm).
£3.80 (ch £2.60, pen £3.30). Family ticket £10.50. Party 12+.
P **✕** *licensed* **&** *(wheelchair available) toilets for disabled shop*

Caernarfon Castle   CAERNARFON

Map 07 SH46
☎ (0286) 77617

Edward I began building the castle and extensive town walls in 1283 after defeating Llywelyn the Last (last of the native Welsh princes). Completed in 1328, it has unusual polygonal towers, notably the 10-sided Eagle Tower, and the walls have bands of colour. There is a theory that these features were copied from the walls of Constantinople, to reflect a tradition that Constantine the Great was born nearby, at the Roman fort of Segontium. Caernarfon was the largest of Edward I's castles in Wales, and the Chamberlain Tower has an exhibition on the castles of Edward I. His son and heir was born and presented to the Welsh people here, setting a precedent that was followed in 1969, when Prince Charles was invested as Prince of Wales – there is a 'Prince of Wales' exhibition in the North-East Tower and a display of investiture robes. A wall walkway links the Eagle Tower to the Queen's Tower, which houses the museum of the Royal Welsh Fusiliers. The regiment dates back to 1689 and eight Victoria Crosses are on display. There is also a 'Prospect of Caernarfon' exhibition on the ground floor of the Eagle Tower.
Open all year, 27 Oct-24 Mar wkdays 9.30-4, Sun 2-4; 25 Mar-26 Oct daily 9.30-6.30. (Closed 24-26 Dec & 1 Jan)
P *shop* **✕**
(AM Cadw)
Details not confirmed for 1992

✕ The 'No Dogs' symbol does not normally apply to guide dogs – these are permitted in most establishments.

Segontium Roman Fort & Museum   CAERNARFON

Map 07 SH46
☎ (0286) 5625
The Roman fort dates from AD78 and was an important base for 300 years. It was rebuilt a number of times, and remains from the various phases can be seen, including four gateways and an underground storeroom. Sir Mortimer Wheeler directed excavations in the 1920s, and the museum shows finds from the site.
Open all year, Nov-Feb, Mon-Fri 9.30-4, Sun 2-4; Mar-Apr & Oct, closes 5.30; May-Sep, closes 6pm. (Closed 24-26 Dec, 1 Jan, Good Fri & May Day).
✱ *50p (ch & pen 25p).*
P **&** *shop* **✕**
(AM Cadw)

Coed-y-Brenin Forest Park & Visitor Centre   COED-Y-BRENIN

Map 07 SH72
☎ Dolgellau (0341) 422289
Located in the heart of Coed-y-Brenin the visitor centre provides an excellent introduction to the area with its range of displays and audio-visual programmes. Coed-y-Brenin means King's Forest, and it was named to commemorate the Silver Jubilee of King George V in 1935. There are over 50 miles of waymarked walks, delightful picnic spots and a wildlife conservation hide. Guide leaflets on the surrounding trails are provided by the centre, where visitors can also see a fascinating display on the gold mines which were once worked in this area.
Open Etr-Oct 10-5. Other dates by prior bookings.
P *(charged)* **♨** **&** *toilets for disabled shop*
Details not confirmed for 1992

Aberconwy House   CONWY

Map 07 SH77
☎ (0492) 592246
This house dates from the 14th century; it is the only medieval merchant's house in Conwy to have survived the turbulence, the fire and pillage of this frontier town for nearly six centuries. Furnished rooms and an audio-visual presentation show daily life in the house at different periods in its history.
Open Apr-1 Nov, daily (ex Tue) 11-5.30. Last admission 5pm.
£1.40 (ch 70p). Family ticket £3.50. Party.
shop **✕**
(NT)

Conwy Castle   CONWY

Map 07 SH77
(by A55 or B5106)
☎ (0492) 592358
The castle is a magnificent fortress, built from 1283-9 by Edward I. There is an exhibition on Edward I and his castles in Wales within the shop area. The castle forms part of the same defensive system as the extensive town walls, 1,400yds long and some 30ft high, which are among the most complete in Europe. They have 21 (originally 22) towers, and sweep up and down hills as they encircle the town. The best view of the castle and walls is from the other side of the river, which is spanned by three bridges designed to complement the scene. The graceful suspension bridge was built by Telford in 1826, the tubular bridge by Stephenson in 1848, and the road bridge was completed in 1958.
Open all year, 27 Oct-24 Mar, wkdays 9.30-4, Sun 2-4; 25 Mar-26 Oct daily 9.30-6.30. (Closed 24-26 Dec & 1 Jan)
P *shop* **✕**
(AM Cadw)
Details not confirmed for 1992

Plas Mawr   CONWY

Map 07 SH77
High St
☎ Aberconwy (0492) 593413
Plas Mawr is an excellent example of an Elizabethan town mansion, and is practically the same as when it was built between 1570 and 1580. Temporary exhibitions are held here.
Open Feb-Mar & Nov Wed-Sun 10-4; Apr-Sep daily 10-6; Oct daily 10-4. Art exhibitions Mar-Nov.
£1 (ch 25p, ch under 5 free, pen & students 50p). Party.
shop

Smallest House   CONWY

Map 07 SH77
The Quay
☎ (0492) 593484
The 'Guinness Book of Records' lists this as the smallest house in Britain. Just 6ft wide by 10ft high, it is furnished in the style of a mid-Victorian Welsh cottage. A series of events is planned for 1992, from March onwards, entitled 'Conway Celebrates'.
Open Apr-mid Oct daily 10-6 (10-9.30/10pm in Jul & Aug). In winter by arrangement.
50p (ch 5 free).
& *shop*

Railway Museum   CORRIS

Map 07 SH70
The museum is housed in a century-old railway building, and has photographs of Corris narrow-guage railway from 1890 to 1948. Items connected with the railway are constantly being added, and old wagons are on show. Half a mile of track has been reinstated, but passengers are not carried. Children's playground nearby.
Open 30 Mar-1 Apr, 25-27 May, 22 Jul-Aug, Mon-Fri & BH wknds 10.30-5; 2-5 Apr, 28 May-19 Jul, 2-27 Sep, Mon-Fri.
P **&** *shop*
Details not confirmed for 1992

Criccieth Castle   CRICCIETH

Map 07 SH43
☎ (0766) 522227
The castle dates from the 13th century and was taken and destroyed by Owain Glyndwr in 1404. Evidence of a fierce fire can still be seen. The gatehouse leading to the inner ward remains impressive, and parts of the walls are well preserved. There are two exhibitions – one on the castles of native Welsh Princes and another on Gerald of Wales and the Welsh Princes. Perched on its rocky peninsula, the castle commands superb views over the resort and Tremadog Bay.
Open all year, 27 Oct-24 Mar wkdays 9.30-4, Sun 2-4; 25 Mar-26 Oct, daily 9.30-6.30. (Closed 24-26 Dec & 1Jan)
P *shop* **✕**
(AM Cadw)
Details not confirmed for 1992

Cymer Abbey   CYMER ABBEY

Map 07 SH71
(2m NW of Dolgellau on A494)
☎ Dolgellau (0341) 422854
The abbey was built for the Cistercians in the 13th century. It was never very large, and does not seem to have been finished. The church is the best-preserved building, with ranges of windows and arcades still to be seen. The other buildings have been plundered for stone, but low outlines remain.
P **&** **✕**
(AM Cadw)
Details not confirmed for 1992

Meirion Mill   DINAS MAWDDWY

Map 07 SH81
☎ (06504) 311
This working woollen mill stands in the grounds of the old Mawddwy railway station in a pretty village at the southern end of Snowdonia National Park. Facilities include a visitor centre, shop, children's adventure playground, and dog exercise area. There is a packhorse bridge which is an ancient monument.
Open Etr-Oct, daily incl BH. Limited during winter.
Free.
P **♨** **✕** *licensed* **&** *shop*

Dolwyddelan Castle   DOLWYDDELAN

Map 07 SH75
☎ (06906) 366
The castle is reputed to be the birthplace of Llywelyn the Great. It was captured in 1283 by Edward I, who immediately began strengthening it for his own purposes. A restored keep of around 1200, and a 13th-century curtain wall can be seen. An exhibition on the castles of the Welsh Princes is located in the keep.
Open all year, 27 Oct-24 Mar, wkdays 9.30-4 & Sun 2-4; 25 Mar-26 Oct daily 9.30-6.30. (Closed 24-26 Dec & 1 Jan).
P **✕**
(AM Cadw)
Details not confirmed for 1992

Fairbourne Railway   FAIRBOURNE

Map 07 SH61
Beach Rd
☎ (0341) 250362

One of the most unusual of Wales's 'little trains' – it was built in 1890 as a horse-drawn railway to carry building materials for the seaside resort of Fairbourne. It was later converted to steam, and now runs one-and-a-half miles from Fairbourne to the end of the peninsula and the ferry for Barmouth. Its route passes one of the loveliest beaches in Wales, with views of the beautiful Mawddach Estuary. An enjoyable round trip can be made from Barmouth in summer, crossing the Mawddach by ferry, catching the miniature train to Fairbourne and then taking the British Rail train – or walking – across the Mawddach Viaduct. At
continued . . .

Gorsaf Newydd terminus visitors can see locomotive sheds and engineering works.
Open Etr-Sep, times vary according to season and events.
P ✕ *licensed* & *shop*
Details not confirmed for 1992

Felin Isaf Watermill
GLAN CONWY

Map 07 SH87
(on A470, 1m S from junc A55 & A470).
☎ Aberconwy (0492) 580646
This award-winning 17th-century mill has recently been restored, and stands in its own secluded gardens. There is a mini golf course, fishing and craft shops.

A working water wheel will be ready for 1992. School groups are a speciality. Children can take part in a Discovery Project.
Open Etr-Nov, daily 10-dusk.
£1.50 (ch & disabled £1).
P & *shop* ✖

Harlech Castle
HARLECH

Map 07 SH53
(from A496)
☎ (0766) 780552
Harlech Castle was built in 1283-80 by Edward I, with a sheer drop to the sea on one side. Owain Glyndwyr starved the castle into submission in 1404 and made it his court and campaigning base. Later, the defence of the castle in the Wars of the Roses inspired the song *Men of Harlech*.
Today the sea has slipped away, and the

castle's great walls and round towers stand above the dunes. The gatehouse is especially impressive, and there are magnificent views of Snowdonia and across Tremadoc Bay.
Open all year, 27 Oct-24 Mar wkdays 9.30-4, Sun 2-4; 25 Mar-26 Oct, daily 9.30-6.30. (Closed 24-26 Dec & 1 Jan)
P *shop* ✖
(AM Cadw)
Details not confirmed for 1992

Din Llugwy Ancient Village
LLANALLGO

Map 07 SH58
(1m NW off A5205)
The remains of a 4th-century village can be seen here. There are two circular and seven rectangular buildings, still standing up to head height and encircled by a

pentagonal stone wall some 4 to 5ft thick.
Open at all times.
(AM Cadw)
Details not confirmed for 1992

Maes Artro Village
LLANBEDR

Map 07 SH52
☎ (034123) 467
An old wartime RAF camp has been imaginatively converted to display a varied range of exhibitions and activities. An original air raid shelter has been restored with light and sound effects; the history of RAF Llanbedr is illustrated; and a Spitfire, used in the TV series *A Piece of Cake*, is on show. Old farm

implements, a 'Village of Yesteryear', a log fort playground and nature trails are all set among the lovely wooded grounds. Most recent attraction is the Marine Life Aquarium. Musicians play live in the village most days.
Open Etr-Sep, daily 10-5.30
✱ *£2.30 (ch & pen £1.70)*
P ✖ ✕ *licensed* & *toilets for disabled shop garden centre*

Dolbadarn Castle
LLANBERIS

Map 07 SH56
Built by Llywelyn the Great in the early 13th century, this Welsh castle overlooks Llyn Padarn in the Llanberis pass.
Open all year, 27 Oct-24 Mar, wkdays

9.30-4, Sun 2-4; 25 Mar-26 Oct, daily 9.30-6.30. (Closed 24-26 Dec & 1 Jan).
P ✖
(AM Cadw)
Details not confirmed for 1992

Llanberis Lake Railway
LLANBERIS

Map 07 SH56
Padarn Country Park (off A4086)
☎ (0286) 870549
Steam locomotives dating from 1889 to 1948 carry passengers on a four-mile return journey to Gilfach Ddu, adjacent to the Welsh Slate Museum and the

centre of the Padarn Country Park. The railway was formerly used to carry slate.
Open Etr-late Oct. Trains run frequently every day (ex Sat), 11-4.30 in peak season.
£3.40 (ch £2). Family ticket.
P ✿ & *toilets for disabled shop* ✖ *(train & shop)*

Museum of the North/Power of Wales
LLANBERIS

Map 07 SH56
☎ Caernarfon (0286) 870636
The rich natural environment of Snowdonia has given rise to this purpose-built centre, which aims to explain and illustrate the relationship between man and these unique

surroundings. A variety of exhibitions is held throughout the year.
Open all year, Nov-Mar, Mon-Fri (Parties by arrangement); Mar-Oct, daily 9.30-6pm. (Closed Good Fri & 24-26 Dec).
✱ *£3.50 (ch £1.75, pen £2.60).*
P & *toilets for disabled shop* ✖

Snowdon Mountain Railway
LLANBERIS

Map 07 SH56
(on A4086)
☎ (0286) 870223
On the route of an old pony track, Britain's only rack-and-pinion railway is operated by 7 vintage steam and 3 modern diesel locomotives. The journey of just over four-and-a-half miles takes passengers more than 3000ft up to the summit of Snowdon; breathtaking views include, on a clear day, the Isle of Man

and the Wicklow Mountains in Ireland. The railway was opened in 1896.
Open 15 Mar-1 Nov, daily from 9am (weather permitting).
✱ *Return £12 (ch £8.50). Single (Llanberis-summit) £8.50 (ch £6). Party 15+ by prior arrangement (out of season only).*
P *(charged)* ✿ & *(2 carraiges suitable for disabled) toilets for disabled shop* ✖

Welsh Slate Museum
LLANBERIS

Map 07 SH56
Gilfach Ddu (.25m off A4086)
☎ (0286) 870630
Until its closure in 1969 the Dinorwic Quarry was one of the largest in Britain, employing over three thousand men in its heyday. The workshops, most of the machinery and plant have been preserved, including the foundry and the Dinorwic water wheel. The museum which was subsequently founded on the site includes displays and audio-visual

presentations depicting the life here, and much of the original atmosphere still prevails. Nearby is a group of craft workshops and a woodcraft centre where visitors can watch craftsmen at work.
Open daily, Etr Sat-Apr 9.30-5.30; May-Sep 9.30-6.30. (Closed May Day).
✱ *£1 (ch 50p, pen 75p).*
P & *shop*
(AM Cadw)

Childhood Revisited
LLANDUDNO

Map 07 SH78
5 Bodhyfryd Rd
☎ (0492) 870424
The Llandudno Doll Museum and the Llandudno Motorcycle Museum form part of this "collection of collections". Exhibits range from 16th-century dolls and those made from wood, wax, china, bisque and terracotta to present day dolls, and there are various playthings

and accessories of childhod. The centrepiece of the display is a model working railway, combined with hundreds of old toys, models, games and books.
Open Mar-1 Nov, daily 10-6 (last admission 5).
£2.50 (ch 3-15 £1.50 & pen £2)
✿ & *shop*

St Cybi's Well
LLANGYBI

Map 07 SH44
Cybi was a sixth-century Cornish saint, known as a healer of the sick; and St Cybi's Well (or Fynnon Gybi) has been famous for its curative properties through the centuries. The corbelled

beehive vaulting inside the roofless stone structure is Irish in style and unique in Wales.
Open at all times.
(AM Cadw)
Details not confirmed for 1992

Bryn Bras Castle & Grounds
LLANRUG

Map 07 SH56
(.5m SE of A4086)
☎ Llanberis (0286) 870210
Against a backdrop of high mountains, this extravagant neo-Norman style mansion, thought to be the work of Thomas Hopper, was built in 1830. The charm of the interior lies in its 'lived-in' atmosphere, and the richly carved furniture, stained glass, interesting ceilings and galleried staircase are special features. The grounds are splendid with

herbaceous borders, rhododendrons, roses and hydrangeas, waterfalls, pools and streams. Perhaps the chief attraction is the walled knot garden, but the woodland and mountain walks with their panoramic views are strong contenders.
Open Spring BH-Sep, Mon-Fri & Sun 1-5; mid Jul-Aug 10.30-5.
✱ *£2.50 (ch £1.25).*
P ✿ & *shop* ✖

Every effort is made to provide accurate information, but details might change during the currency of this guide.

Gwydyr Uchaf Chapel
LLANRWST

Map 07 SH86
(.5m SW off B5106)
☎ (0492) 640578
Built in the 17th century by Sir John Wynn of Gwydir Castle, the chapel is noted for its painted ceiling and

wonderfully varied woodwork.
Open all year, wkdays 8.30-4.
✖
(AM Cadw)
Details not confirmed for 1992

Bala Lake Railway
LLANUWCHLLYN

Map 07 SH83
The Station (off A494)
☎ (06784) 666
Steam locomotives which once worked in the slate quarries of North Wales now haul passenger coaches for four-and-a-half miles from Llanwchllyn Station along the lake to Bala. The railway has one of the four remaining GWR signal boxes, installed in 1896. Some of the coaches are open and some closed, so passengers can enjoy the beautiful views of the lake and

mountains in all weathers; the latest corridor coach has facilities for the disabled. Special events for 1992 include: 20-21 Jun, Grand Summer Gala; 5-6 Sep, Model Engineers' Weekend.
Open 23 Mar-7 Apr, 25 May-2 Jun & 29 Jul-8 Sep,daily; 9 Apr-23 May, 4-27 Jun & 18-29 Sep, daily (ex Mon & Fri).
£4 return (ch £2). Family ticket £9.10. (single fares also available).
P ✿ & *shop*
See advertisement on page 214.

Lloyd George Memorial Museum & Highgate Victorian Cottage
LLANYSTUMDWY

Map 07 SH43
(on A497)
☎ (0766) 522071
David Lloyd George, the Liberal Prime Minster, spent his childhood in the village and eventually came back to live and die at the house of Ty Newydd in 1945. The museum has various memorabilia and gives an interesting

picture of his life and times.
Open Etr-Sep, daily 10-5. Other times by appointment, telephone (0286) 679098 for details.
✱ *£1.80 (ch & pen £1.20). Family ticket £5. Party.*
P & *(limited access to Highgate) toilets for disabled shop* ✖
See advertisement on page 218.

THE NEW LLOYD GEORGE MUSEUM AND HIGHGATE HIS CHILDHOOD HOME LLANYSTUMDWY, CRICCIETH

Explore the life & times of David Lloyd George in the newly extended museum with its improved exhibitions, audio visual theatre, Victorian schoolroom and 'talking head'. Highgate Cottage and his Uncle Lloyd's shoemaking workshop are recreated as they were when he lived there as a boy until 1880.

SEE GAZETTEER FOR DETAILS

Penarth Fawr   PENARTH FAWR

Map 07 SH43
(3.5m NE of Pwllheli off A497)
The hall, buttery and screen are preserved in this house which was probably built in the 15th century.
Open at all times.
(AM Cadw)
Details not confirmed for 1992

Penmachno Woollen Mill   PENMACHNO

Map 07 SH75
(2m N on A5)
☎ Betwys-y-Coed (0690) 710545
The 17th-century quarrymen and farmers wore flannel shirts made from cloth woven by local cottage weavers. The cloth was washed and finished in the Pandy (fulling mill). Power looms introduced in the 19th century now weave lightweight tweed and rug cloth. The Story of Wool exhibition explains the process and its history, and there is a mill shop and café. Mill is worked by hydro-electric turbine, powered by the River Machno.
Open Etr-2 Nov, daily.
Free.
🅿 ⚓ *shop* ✸

Plas Newydd   PLAS NEWYDD

Map 07 SH56
☎ Llanfairpwll (0248) 714795
Built by James Wyatt in the 18th century, this house stands on the Menai Strait in unspoilt surroundings, and enjoys uninterrupted views of the Snowdonia mountain range. Beautiful lawns and parkland surround the house and there is a fine spring garden. An exhibition of Rex Whistler's work is on show with his largest wall painting. Relics of the first Marquess of Anglesey and the Battle of Waterloo are kept here, along with the Ryan collection of military uniforms and headdresses. Plas Newydd is to be found one mile SW of Llanfairpwll on the A4080 to Brysiencyn. Turn off the A5 at Llanfairpwll on the western end of Brittania Bridge.
Open Apr-27 Sep, daily (ex Sat) noon-5 (garden 11-5 Jul-Aug); 2 Oct-1 Nov, Fri & Sun noon-5. Last admission 4.30.
£3.30 (ch £1.65). Family ticket £8.25. Party.
🅿 ⚓ 🔆 *toilets for disabled shop* ✸
(NT)

Plas yn Rhiw   PLAS-YN-RHIW

Map 06 SH22
(on unclass road 4.5m NE of Aberdaron)
☎ Rhiw (075888) 219
House with gardens and woodlands down to the sea on west shore of Porth Neigwl (Hell's Mouth Bay). This is a small manor house, part medieval, with Tudor and Georgian additions and ornamental gardens with flowering trees and shrubs including sub-tropical specimens, divided by box hedges and grass paths. There is a stream and waterfall, rising behind the snowdrop wood.
Open Apr-27 Sep, daily (ex Sat) noon-5; 4 Oct-1 Nov, Sun only. (Last admission 30 mins prior to closing).
£2 (ch £1). Family ticket £5. Party 20+.
🅿 🔆 *toilets for disabled* ✸ 🚻
(NT)

Ffestiniog Railway   PORTHMADOG

Map 07 SH53
Harbour Station
☎ (0766) 512340 & 831654
Opened in 1836 to serve the slate mines at Blaenau Festiniog, the line carried slate to the sea at Porthmadog on trucks which ran from the production point by gravity. The railway carried its first passengers on steam trains in 1865 and was closed in 1946. The narrow-gauge railway was re-opened by enthusiasts and operates steam locomotives including a unique Fairlie-type articulated locomotive. Most trains carry licensed buffet cars.
Open late Mar-early Nov, daily service and also 26 Dec-1 Jan & wnds Mar. Also limited service on certain days in Nov & Feb.
✱ *Charges vary according to distance travelled. First & third class available.*
🅿 ⚓ 🔆 *shop*

Ffestiniog Railway Museum   PORTHMADOG

Map 07 SH53
Harbour Station
☎ (0766) 512340
The harbour station is home to exhibits including an old four-wheeled hearse converted from a quarryman's coach, one of the original steam locos from 1863, a slate wagon and model steam engine. Maps and diagrams illustrate the history of the famous narrow-gauge railway.
Open Mar-Nov when train services operating (see Ffestiniog Railway).
Donations.
🅿 ⚓ 🔆 *shop*

Porthmadog Pottery   PORTHMADOG

Map 07 SH53
Snowdon Mill, Snowdon St
☎ (0766) 512137
Housed in the engine rooms of an old flour mill dating from 1862, the history of pottery is displayed here. The town's past is featured in a 1,300sq ft mural showing the building of the Cob walls to reclaim land from the sea, and the loading of locally built slate-carrying ketches. Visitors can watch pottery being made, and even make a piece themselves. Activities for the disabled include 'Throw a Pot', 'Paint a Plate' and 'Colour a Pot'.
Open Etr-Sep, Mon-Fri 9-5.30.
25p (ch free). Activity (Potters Wheel, Paint A Plate or Colour A Pot) £2.25.
🅿 ⚓ 🔆 *shop*

Portmeirion   PORTMEIRION

Map 07 SH53
☎ Porthmadog (0766) 770457

Welsh architect Sir Clough Williams Ellis built his fairy-tale, Italianate village on a rocky, tree-clad peninsula on the shores of Cardigan Bay. The nucleus of the estate is a sumptuous waterfront hotel, rebuilt from the original house and containing a fine 18th-century fireplace and a library moved here from the Great Exhibition of 1851. A bell-tower, castle and lighthouse mingle with a watch-tower, grottoes and cobbled squares among pastel-shaded picturesque cottages let as holiday accommodation. A number of shops sell a variety of goods and the whole village is set in 175 acres of sub-tropical coastal cliff and wooded gardens.
One of the finest wild gardens in Wales is here – the 60-acre Gwyllt Gardens. They include miles of dense woodland paths and are famous for their fine displays of rhododendrons, azaleas, hydrangea and sub-tropical flora. There is a mile of sandy beach and a playground for children. Toll-paying visitors can see the place where Noel Coward wrote 'Blithe Spirit', and the location for the cult TV series 'The Prisoner'.
Open all year, daily 9.30-5.30.
£2.70 (ch £1.20, pen £2.20). Party 20+.
🅿 ⚓ ✕ *licensed* 🔆 *toilets for disabled shop*
✸

This is just one of many guidebooks published by the AA. The full range is available at any AA shop or good bookshop.

Museum of Old Welsh Country Life   TAI'N LON

Map 07 SH45
Felin Faesog
☎ Clynnogfawr (028686) 311
Set in a 17th-century watermill in the hills by the River Desach, the museum has a wide range of exhibits from Wales of the past, including displays on the old farming year, the women's week, children's work and play, a miller's room, and clog making.
Open Good Fri-Sep, daily (ex Sat) 10-5.
✱ *80p (ch 16 40p). Party 15+.*
🅿 ⚓ 🔆 *shop* ✸ *(ex in grounds)*

Bodnant Garden   TAL-Y-CAFN

Map 07 SH77
(8m S of Llandudno & Colwyn Bay on A470)
☎ Tyngroes (0492) 650460
Situated above the River Conwy with beautiful views over Snowdonia, these gardens are a delight. They were first laid out in 1875 but in 1900 the 2nd Lord Aberconway started to improve them dramatically. Five terraces in the Italian style were constructed below the house, and between two large, existing cedars he placed a lily pool. On the lowest terrace is a canal pool with an open-air stage at one end and a reconstructed Pin Mill at the other. Part of the grounds have been made into a beautiful woodland garden in a sheltered valley. This is notable for its rhododendrons and other delicate shrubs. There are also many azaleas, a rock garden, and a laburnum walk.
Open 14 Mar-Oct, daily 10-5 (last admission 4.30pm).
£3 (ch £1.50). Party 20+.
🅿 ⚓ ✕ 🔆 *shop garden centre* ✸
(NT)

Trefriw Woollen Mill   TREFRIW

Map 07 SH76
Trefriw Woollen Mills Ltd (on B5106)
☎ Llanrwst (0492) 640462
Established in 1859, the mill is situated beside the fast-flowing Afon Crafnant, which is used to drive two hydro-electric turbines to power the looms. All the machinery of woollen manufacture can be seen here: blending, carding, spinning, dyeing, warping and weaving. The mill produces tapestries and tweeds, and there is a large shop selling its products. In the Weaver's Garden, there are plants traditionally used in the textile industry, mainly for dyeing.
Mill open Etr-Oct, Mon-Fri 9-5.30. (Closed BHs & 3rd Mon Oct). Weaving demonstrations & turbine house: open all year, Mon-Fri 9-5.30 (5 in winter). Also Spring BH-Aug, Sat & BH's 10-5, Sun 2-5.
Free (ex school parties which must be pre-booked).
⚓ 🔆 *shop* ✸

Narrow-Gauge Railway Museum   TYWYN

Map 07 SH50
Wharf Station
☎ (0654) 710472
An interesting small museum displaying a number of locomotives, wagons and signalling equipment used on the non-standard narrow-gauge railways. There are also displays of other relics, from tools to signs.
Open 6 Apr-Oct, daily 10-5. Winter by arrangement.
50p (ch 10p).
🅿 *(charged)* ⚓ 🔆 *toilets for disabled shop*
✸

TALYLLYN RAILWAY
Tywyn, on the Mid Wales Coast

Historic narrow gauge steam trains through Welsh hill scenery. Train services Easter to October inclusive and during Christmas/New Year Holiday. Forest walks, waterfalls, Narrow Gauge Railway Museum, shops and refreshments.
See Gazetteer for further details or contact Wharf Station, Tywyn, Gwynedd LL36 9EY. Tel. Tywyn (0654) 710472.

Talyllyn Railway — TYWYN

Map 07 SH50
Wharf Station
☎ (0654) 710472
This is the oldest 27in gauge railway in the world. It was built in 1865 to run from Tywyn on Cardigan Bay to Abergynolwyn slate mine some seven miles inland. The railway was also the first to be saved by a voluntary preservation society, after the slate quarry closed in 1947. The railway climbs the steep sides of the Fathew valley and on the way there are stops to admire the Dolgoch falls or to allow passengers to visit the Nant Gwernol

forest. The train takes 2 hours and 30 minutes to cover the round trip. Each year in August there is a 'Race the Train' charity competition. This will be held on 15 August in 1992. Nearly 1,000 runners follow the track and usually as many as 100 will beat the train.
Open 6 Apr-Oct, daily. Santa special 19 Dec, Xmas holiday serice 26 Dec-3 Jan. Timetable available.
✱ £5.50 return ticket. Family ticket £12.50-£14.50.
P (charged) ♿ (by prior arrangement on trains) toilets for disabled shop

MID GLAMORGAN

Newcastle — BRIDGEND

Map 03 SS97
☎ (0656) 2964
The small castle dates back to the 12th century. It is ruined, but a rectangular tower, a richly carved Norman gateway and massive curtain walls enclosing a

polygonal courtyard can still be seen.
Open – accessible throughout the year. Key keeper arrangement.
P
(AM Cadw)
Details not confirmed for 1992

Caerphilly Castle — CAERPHILLY

Map 03 ST18
(on A469)
☎ (0222) 883143
The concentrically planned castle was begun in 1268 by Gilbert de Clare and completed in 1326. It is the largest in Wales, and has extensive land and water defences. A unique feature is the ruined

tower – the victim of subsidence – which manages to out-lean even Pisa!
Open all year, 27 Oct-24 Mar wkdays 9.30-4, Sun 2-4; 25 Mar-26 Oct, daily 9.30-6.30. (Closed 24-26 Dec & 1 Jan).
P ♿ toilets for disabled shop
(AM Cadw)
Details not confirmed for 1992

Coity Castle — COITY

Map 03 SS98
☎ Bridgend (0656) 652021
A 12th- to 16th-century stronghold, with a hall, chapel and the remains of a square keep.
Open all year, 27 Oct-24 Mar wkdays

9.30-4, Sun 2-4; 25 Mar-26 Oct, wkdays 9.30-6.30, Sun 2-6.30. (Closed 24-26 Dec & 1 Jan). Key keeper arrangement.
P
(AM Cadw)
Details not confirmed for 1992

Brecon Mountain Railway — MERTHYR TYDFIL

Map 03 SO00
Pant Station Dowlais (2.5m NE to the N of A465)
☎ (0685) 4854 due to change to 384854

After eight years of planning and construction, this narrow-gauge railway was opened in 1980. It follows part of an old British Rail route which was closed in 1964 when the iron industry in South Wales fell into decline. The present route starts at Pant Station, three miles north of Merthyr Tydfil, and continues through the beautiful scenery of the Brecon Beacons National Park, as far as the two-and-a-half-mile long Taf Fechan reservoir. The train is pulled by a vintage steam locomotive, a delight in itself, and for lovers of vintage locomotives the workshops at Pant
continued ...

Station are well worth a visit. The display includes engines built in Germany and the USA as well as Great Britain, and some have spent their days on railways in far-flung corners of the earth.
Opening times on application to The Brecon

Mountain Railway, Pant Station, Merthyr Tydfil, Mid Glamorgan. Return fares £3.60 (ch 16 £1.80, free when travelling with adult paying full return fare). Party.
P ♥ ✗ licensed ♿ toilets for disabled shop

Cyfarthfa Castle Museum & Art Gallery — MERTHYR TYDFIL

Map 03 SO00
Cyfarthfa Park
☎ (0685) 723112
The home of the Crawshay family, who took over the Cyfarthfa Ironworks which employed 1,500 men by the turn of the century, is an imposing Gothic mansion. It was built in 1825 and the magnificent gardens, designed at around the same time, still survive today. The state rooms are given over to a museum which not only covers the social and industrial life of the area, but also houses

collections of fine and decorative art, natural history items, archaeology and Egyptology. Temporary exhibitions are held; in June there is a Vintage Car Rally and in July a Heritage Day..
Open all year, Apr-Oct, Mon-Sat 10-6, Sun 2-5. Oct-Mar, Mon-Sat, 10-1 & 2-5, Sun 2-5. (Last admission 30 mins before closing). Closes one hour earlier every Fri.
✱ 50p (ch, pen & UB40's 30p).
P ♿ (stair lift & wheelchair available) shop ♈

🐕 The 'No Dogs' symbol does not normally apply to guide dogs – these are permitted in most establishments.

Garwnant Forest Centre — MERTHYR TYDFIL

Map 03 SO00
Cwm Taf (5m N, off A470).
☎ (0685) 723060
Old farm buildings on the southern edge of the Brecon Beacons National Park have been converted into this visitor centre for the surrounding forest area. It offers a wealth of information about the facilities and forest trails, and has displays of models and photographs to illustrate the main features of the area: farming, forestry and water. The

verandah looks out over the LLwyn-On reservoir, and the character of the old buildings has been carefully preserved. It is a pleasant spot to start a walk in the surrounding forest, the Coed Taf Fawr. There is also a children's adventure play area.
Open Etr-Sep wkdys 10.30-4.45. Apr, May & Sep, wknds 2-5 (inc BH). Jun-Aug, wknds 2-6 (inc BH).
P ♥ ♿ shop
Details not confirmed for 1992

Joseph Parry's Cottage   MERTHYR TYDFIL

Map 03 SO00
4 Chapel Row (off A470)
☎ (0685) 83704 & 73117
The cottage was the birthplace of the musician and composer, Joseph Parry, and contains an exhibition devoted to his life and works. Also shown here are displays of the industrial and social history of 19th-century Merthyr Tydfil during its heyday as an industrial centre. The ground floor of the cottage has been restored and furnished in the style of the 1840s. An excavated section of the Glamorganshire Canal provides an open-air exhibition. Heritage Day is to be held on 12 July. A bus service will link all heritage sites and events in Merthyr Tydfil.
Open Etr-Oct, Mon-Fri 2-5, Sat, Sun & BH 2-5. Other times by appointment.
25p (ch 6-16 10p).
🅿 & *shop* ✖

Ynysfach Engine House   MERTHYR TYDFIL

Map 03 SO00
Ynysfach Rd (off A470)
☎ (0685) 721858 & 83704
Opened in July 1989 by HRH The Duchess of York, this heritage centre once housed the beam-blowing engine of the Ynysfach Iron Works. Exhibitions in the superbly restored building introduce the history of Merthyr Tydfil's once-famed iron industry with an 18-minute audio-visual programme narrated by actor Philip Madoc, full-size models, maps and photographs. Winner of the Prince of Wales Award in 1989 and two others in 1990. Heritage Day will be held on 12 July. There will be a bus service linking all heritage sites and events in Merthyr Tydfil.
Open Mar-Oct, Mon-Fri 11-5, wknds & BH 2-5. Nov-Feb, Mon-Fri 10-4, wknds 1-4. (Closed Xmas.)
90p (ch 6-16, students, pen & UB40's 50p). Party.
🅿 ☕ *shop* ✖

Ogmore Castle   OGMORE

Map 03 SS87
Standing on the river Ogmore, the west wall of this castle is 40ft high. A hooded fireplace is preserved in the 12th-century, three-storey keep and a dry moat surrounds the inner ward.
Open – access throughout the year. Key keeper arrangement.
(AM Cadw)
Details not confirmed for 1992

Rhondda Heritage Park   TREHAFOD

Map 03 ST09
Coed Cae Rd (off A470)
☎ Porth (0443) 682036
Lewis Merthyr colliery buildings are now huge industrial theatres that house the multi-million pound 'Black Gold' exhibition. Audio-visual presentations and special effects help bring alive the 'story of coal'. Ex-miners will guide you around and give their own accounts of life underground.
Open all year, daily 10-6. Last admission 4.30pm. Closed 25 & 26 Dec.
✳ *£2.75 (ch, student, pen, disabled & UB40 £1.75p).*
🅿 ☕ & *toilets for disabled shop* ✖

See advertisement on page 219.

POWYS

Dan-Yr-Ogof Showcaves   ABERCRAF

Map 03 SN81
(3m N on A4067)
☎ (0639) 730284

Winner of eleven major tourism awards,

Dan-Yr-Ogof Showcave is the longest in Britain. Cathedral Showcave is the largest single chamber in any British showcave and Bone Cave was home to man 3,000 years ago. There is also a Dinosaur Park, a museum and audio-visual theatre, and a craft shop with information centre. Instruction is also given on the artificial ski slope (opening times on request). Special event for 1992 is 'Music in the Mountains' on 30-31 August.
Open Apr-Oct, daily from 10am.
£4.50 (ch £4).
🅿 ☕ & *toilets for disabled shop*

Brecknock Museum   BRECON

Map 03 SO02
Captain's Walk
☎ (0874) 624121
A wealth of local history is explored at the museum, which has archaeological and historical exhibits, with sections on folk life, decorative arts and natural history.
Open all year, Mon-Sat 10-1 & 2-5 (also Sun Apr-Sep) . Closed Good Fri & Xmas-New Year.
Free.
🅿 & *(parking available, must be accompanied by able-bodied) shop* ✖

The South Wales Borderers (24th Regiment) Museum   BRECON

Map 03 SO02
The Barracks, The Watton
☎ (0874) 623111 ext 2310
This is the museum of the South Wales Borderers and Monmouthshire Regiment, which was raised in 1689 and has been awarded 23 Victoria Crosses. Amongst the collections is the Zulu War Room, devoted to the war and in particular to the events at Rorke's Drift, 1879, when 121 men fought 4,500 Zulus.
Open all year, Apr-Sep Mon-Sat; Oct-Mar, Mon-Fri 9-1 & 2-5. (Closed Xmas & New Year).
✳ *50p*
🅿 & *shop* ✖

Llandrindod Wells Museum   LLANDRINDOD WELLS

Map 03 SO06
Temple St
☎ (0597) 824513
An appealing town museum with displays including the Paterson doll collection, a Victoria spa gallery with costumes and 19th-century chemist's equipment, and archaeological finds from the area. A number of temporary exhibitions are held throughout the year.
Open all year, Mon-Sun 10-12.30 & 2-5. (Closed Sat pm & Sun Oct-Apr).
& *shop* ✖
Details not confirmed for 1992

Welshpool & Llanfair Light (Steam) Railway   LLANFAIR CAEREINION

Map 07 SJ10
(on A458)
☎ (0938) 810441
Austrian and Colonial locomotives are among those operated on the eight miles of track between Welshpool and Llanfair Caereinion.
Open Etr-4 Oct, wknds; Etr, May Day BH, Spring BH wk; 16 Jun-16 Jul, Tue-Thu; 18 Jul-6 Sep, daily. 8-17 Sep, Tue-Thu. Trains from Llanfair at 10.45, 1.30 & 4.15pm; from Welshpool 12, 2.45 & 5.15. Extra trains at BHs.
£5.80 return (ch 5-15 £2.90). Family ticket £14.
🅿 ☕ & *(one coach adapted for wheelchairs) toilets for disabled shop (at Llanfair station)*

Old Market Hall   LLANIDLOES

Map 07 SN98
☎ Llandrindod Wells (0597) 824513
A small local history museum is housed on the upper floor of this delightful half-timbered building, which stands on open arches.
Open Etr, then Spring BH-Sep daily 11-1 & 2-5
✖
Details not confirmed for 1992

Centre for Alternative Technology   MACHYNLLETH

Map 07 SH70
Llwyngwern Quarry (2.5m N on A487)
☎ (0654) 702400
An old slate quarry, overlooking Snowdonia National Park, provides the site for this intriguing centre which demonstrates technologies designed to improve the environment. The latest feature is a water-powered cliff railway. Research, low-energy studies, monitoring of equipment, and horticulture are all carried out here, along with demonstrations of windpower, solar energy and organic gardening. Residential courses are available.
Open all year, daily 10-7 or dusk, last admission 5pm. (Closed Xmas). Admission fee payable.
🅿 ☕ ✖ *licensed* & *shop garden centre* ✖

Tretower Court & Castle   TRETOWER

Map 03 SO12
☎ Brecon (0874) 730279
The castle is a substantial ruin of an 11th-century motte and bailey, with a three-storey tower and 9ft-thick walls. Nearby is the Court, a 14th-century fortified manor house which has been altered and extended over the years. The two buildings show the shift from medieval castle to more domestic accommodation over the centuries, and an audio-cassette tour is available.
Open all year, 27 Oct-24 Mar wkdays 9.30-4, Sun 2-4; 25 Mar-26 Oct, wkdays 9.30-6.30, Sun 2-6.30. (Closed 24-26 Dec & 1 Jan).
P ⓖ *toilets for disabled* ✖
(AM Cadw)
Details not confirmed for 1992

✳ An asterisk indicates that up-to-date information was not available at the time of our research – 1991 information has been published as an indication of what you may expect.

Powis Castle   WELSHPOOL

Map 07 SJ20
☎ (0938) 554336

This medieval castle was built in about 1200 for a Welsh prince and has been continuously inhabited ever since. Later improvements to the castle have added 16th-century plasterwork and panelling and a fine 17th-century staircase. There are also murals by Lanscroon. Over the centuries many articles and treasures have been collected by both the Herbert family and the Clive family, who lived here and formed one of the finest country-house collections in Wales, including paintings, tapestries and early Georgian furniture. The most celebrated of the Clive family was Clive of India, and there are relics of his life and career in the house. The gardens at Powis, with their magnificent early 18th-century terraces, are of great horticultural and historical importance.
Open Apr-Jun & Sep-1 Nov, Wed-Sun; Jul-Aug, Tue-Sun & BH Mon. Castle: noon-5; Museum & garden: 11-6. Last admission 30 mins prior to closing. Gardens & Museum Sun 2-4 in winter. Castle, Museum & Gardens £5.40 (ch 2.70). Museum & Gardens only £3.20 (ch £1.60) Family ticket £8. Party.
P ⓦ ⓖ *toilets for disabled shop* ✖
(NT)

SOUTH GLAMORGAN

Welsh Hawking Centre   BARRY

Map 03 ST16
Weycock Rd (on A4226)
☎ (0446) 734687
There are over 200 birds of prey here, including eagles, owls and buzzards as well as hawks and falcons. They can be seen and photographed in the mews and some of the breeding aviaries, and there are flying demonstrations at regular intervals during the day. A variety of tame, friendly animals, such as donkeys, goats, pigs, lambs, cows and rabbits will delight younger visitors.
Open all year, daily 10.30-5, 1hr before dusk in winter. (Closed 25 Dec). £2.75 (ch & pen £1.75).
P ⓦ ⓖ *shop*

Cardiff Castle   CARDIFF

Map 03 ST17
Castle St
☎ (0222) 822083

The Norman castle was built on the site of a Roman fort, and Roman walls some 10ft thick can still be seen. There is also a Norman keep and a 13th-century tower. Apartments were started in the 15th century, but the present-day character of the castle comes from its transformation in the 19th century, when the immensely rich 3rd Marquess of Bute employed William Burges to restore and rebuild it. Together they created a romantic fantasy of a medieval castle, decorated with wall paintings, tapestries and colourful carvings of birds, animals, knights and ladies. Also here are the military museums of the Royal Regiment of Wales and Queen's Dragoon Guards. Special events for 1992 include: 27 Jun, Beating Retreat Ceremony; 17-19 Jul, Hot Air Balloon Festival; 30-31 Jul, Marching Massed Bands Display.
Open all year, daily (ex Xmas & New Year BH's). Conducted tours Mar, Apr & Oct, daily 10-12.30 & 2-4 (Castle closes 5). May-Sep, daily 10-12.40 & 2-5 (Castle closes 6); Nov-Feb daily 10.30-3.15 (Castle closes 4.30). Only short tours when functions in progess. Conducted tours all year.
Conducted tour, military museums, green, Roman Wall & Norman Keep £3 (ch & pen £1.50). Short tour, military museum, green, Roman Wall & Norman Keep £2.50 (ch & pen £1.25) Green, Roman Wall, Norman Keep, & military museums £2 (ch & pen £1).
ⓦ ⓖ *shop* ✖ *(ex in grounds)*

✖ The 'No Dogs' symbol does not normally apply to guide dogs – these are permitted in most establishments.

Dyffryn Gardens   CARDIFF

Map 03 ST17
St Nicholas (6m W of city centre off A48)
☎ (0222) 593328
The 50 acres of gardens have rare trees and shrubs, and seasonal bedding displays. There are also plant houses, a temperate house, a succulent house and many small themed gardens. Various events are held throughout the year.
Open all year, daily.
✳ *£1.50 (ch & pen £1). Party 20+.*
P ⓦ ✗ *licensed* ⓖ *(parking available) toilets for disabled shop*

National Museum Of Wales (Main Building)   CARDIFF

Map 03 ST17
Cathays Park
☎ (0222) 397951
Treasurehouse of the principality, the National Museum of Wales' main building at the heart of Cardiff's elegant Civic Centre boasts excellent collections including paintings, silver and ceramics, coins and medals, fossils, minerals, shells, archaeological artefacts and even dinosaur skeletons. The recent refurbishment of the East Wing has provided a splendid new setting for the museum's impressive art collections and, for the first time, shows them in their European context. New galleries, planned for 1993, will enable the museum to focus more attention on contemporary art, and among the highlights will be a new setting for the renowned Davies collection of French Impressionists. In addition to the permanent gallery displays, the museum regularly mounts special exhibitions.
Open all year, Tue-Sat 10-5, Sun 2.30-5. (Closed Mon (ex BHs), Good Fri, 24-26 Dec & 1 Jan). £2 (ch £1, pen £1.50).
ⓦ ⓖ *toilets for disabled shop* ✖

This is just one of many guidebooks published by the AA. The full range is available at any AA shop or good bookshop.

Techniquest   CARDIFF

Map 03 ST17
72 Bute St, Pier Head
☎ (0222) 460211
Science and technology made accessible – and fun – at Britain's largest hands-on science centre, where visitors of all ages can participate in the activities and experiment with the exhibits. See yourself as others see you, instead of the mirror-image you are used to. Understand how aircraft fly . . . Techniquest makes it easy. Special events take place throughout the year.
Open all year, Tue-Fri 9.30-4.30; Sat-Sun & BH's 10.30-5. Also Mon during scool hols.
P ⓦ ⓖ *toilets for disabled shop* ✖
Details not confirmed for 1992

HISTORY COMES TO LIFE

AT THE WELSH FOLK MUSEUM, ST. FAGANS, CARDIFF.

BTA 'Come to Britain' Special Award Winner

Walk into the Welsh Folk Museum and experience
a glimpse of the past.
Turn the corner and discover the Castle, a farmhouse or maybe
the quarry worker's humble cottage. There's more, including a
valley store, a saddler and a pottery.
Everything is authentic, from the craftsmen's skills to the
farmyard animals.

Why not visit our special events as we bring history to life
through the seasons.

We're only four miles from Cardiff City Centre.
For further information on **The Welsh Folk Museum**, and all
other **National Museum of Wales** branches, please contact....

Marketing Department.
Welsh Folk Museum, St. Fagans,
Cardiff CF5 6XB. Tel (0222) 555105

AMGUEDDFA GENEDLAETHOL CYMRU

NATIONAL MUSEUM OF WALES

Welsh Industrial & Maritime Museum — CARDIFF

Map 03 ST17
Bute St
☎ (0222) 481919
In Cardiff's dockland, among the world's
most famous maritime districts, the
museum stands at the heart of the
Cardiff Bay Development Area and tells
visitors the story of industrial and
maritime Wales. Within a Hall of
Power, working exhibits show the
evolution of methods of driving
machinery, with waterwheel, steam
engine, gas engine, steam turbine and
Rolls Royce jet engine all on show. A
transport gallery includes a replica of
Trevithick's Locomotive and the
Railway and Shipping galleries complete
the picture of how Wales communicated
with the world.
Newly opened is '126 Bute Street –
Coal out of Cardiff' which is housed in
the former Cardiff Ship Stores. The
displays tell the tale of Cardiff's growth
from small town quay to coal port, with
photographic displays, a mock street
scene and the replica wheelhouse of a
typical Cardiff tramp steamer where a
West Walian sea captain regales visitors
with stories of his voyages. Cargoes and
the port's history all combine to paint a
picture of the economic rise and fall of
Cardiff's docklands.
'Q Shed' was once the warehouse and
booking office for the much-loved P and
A Campbell pleasure steamers. Today a
wide range of frequently changing,
exciting and dynamic events are held
here. These appeal to all ages but
especially younger visitors.
Open all year, Tue-Fri 10-5, Sun 2.30-5.
(Closed Mon (ex BHs), 24-26 Dec, 1 Jan,
Good Fri).
£1 (ch 50p, pen 75p).
ఉ *(wheelchair available) toilets for disabled*
shop ✖

Cosmeston Medieval Village — PENARTH

Map 03 ST17
Cosmeston Lakes Country Park,
Lavernock Rd
☎ Cardiff (0222) 708686
Deserted during the plagues and famines
of the 14th century, the original village
was rediscovered through archaeological
excavations. Now the buildings have
been faithfully reconstructed on the
excavated remains, within the
Cosmeston Lakes Country Park, creating
a living museum of medieval village life.
Special events throughout the year.
Open all year, Mon-Fri 8.30-4.30 & Sat-
Sun 9-5. (Closed Sat, Nov-Mar, 24-26
Dec, 31 Dec & 1 Jan).
ఐ ఉ *toilets for disabled shop*
Details not confirmed for 1992

Turner House — PENARTH

Map 03 ST17
Plymouth Rd
☎ Cardiff (0222) 708870
This small gallery holds temporary
exhibitions of pictures and *objets d'art*
from the National Museum of Wales
and other sources.
Open all year, Tue-Sat 11-12.45 & 2-5,
Sun 2-5. (Closed Good Fri, May Day &
Xmas).
Free.
shop ✖

Welsh Folk Museum — ST FAGANS

Map 03 ST17
(junc 33 of M4)
☎ Cardiff (0222) 569441

Once the home of the Earls of
Plymouth, St Fagans is a 16th-century
house built within the curtain walls of
the original 13th-century castle. Donated
to the National Museum in 1947, it is
now the home of the extensive Welsh
Folk Museum.

The museum is designed to represent
the life and culture of Wales, and there
is a huge amount to see. Old
farmhouses, cottages, a tannery, a school
and a chapel have been reconstructed,
and are just a part of the range of the
building styles and living conditions to
be seen. Numerous skills are also
demonstated throughout the year, and
traditional Welsh cooking is part of the
facilities. Events for 1992 include the
Old May Day Fair (1-4 May), a
Midsummer Folk Festival (20 Jun), and
a Harvest Festival (26-27 Sep).
Open all year, Apr-Oct, daily 10-5; Nov-
Mar, Mon-Sat 10-5. (Closed Good Fri,
24-26 Dec & 1 Jan).
£3.50 (ch £1.75, pen £2.60).
ఐ ఐ ✖ *licensed* ఉ *(wheelchairs available)*
toilets for disabled shop ✖ *(ex in grounds)*

Old Beaupre Castle — ST HILARY

Map 03 ST07
(1m SW)
This ruined manor house was rebuilt
during the 16th century. Its most
notable features include an Italianate
gatehouse and porch. The porch is an
unusual three-storeyed structure and
displays the Basset arms.
Open – access throughout the year. (Closed
Sun). Key keeper arrangement.
(AM Cadw)
Details not confirmed for 1992

ఉ This symbol indicates that much or all of the
attraction is accessible to wheelchairs.
However, there may be some restrictions,
so it would be wise to check
in advance.

Castell Coch — TONGWYNLAIS

Map 03 ST18
☎ (0222) 810101
Castell Coch is Welsh for red castle, a
good name for this fairy-tale building
with its red sandstone walls and conical
towers rising out of the wooded hillside.
The castle was originally built in the
13th century but fell into ruins, and the
present castle is the late-19th-century
creation of William Burges and the 3rd
Marquis of Bute, who commissioned
him to restore it. An exhibition provides
an illustrated history of Bute, of Burges
and of the building they created. It has
three round towers with conical roofs, a
drawbridge and portcullis. Inside, the
castle is decorated in fantasy style with
many murals, giltwork, statues and
carvings. The most spectacular room is
probably Lady Bute's bedroom, which
has a domed ceiling painted on the
theme of the Sleeping Beauty.
Open all year, 27 Oct-24 Mar wkdays
9.30-4, Sun 2-4; 25 Mar-26 Oct, daily
9.30-6.30. (Closed 24-26 Dec & 1 Jan).
ఐ *shop* ✖
(AM Cadw)
Details not confirmed for 1992

WEST GLAMORGAN

Aberdulais Falls — ABERDULAIS

Map 03 SS79
☎ Neath (0639) 636674

A short walk through the wooded gorge
reveals one of the most famous
waterfalls in the Vale of Neath, whose
waters have been harnessed since the
16th century for a range of industries,
from copper-smelting to tinplate. A
beautiful and historic site. A unique
hydro-electric scheme is currently
underway to harness this great natural
resource; due to ongoing development
work, it may be necessary to close the
property or restrict access at short
notice. Visitors are advised to check
before embarking on a visit.
Open Apr-Oct, Mon-Fri 10-5, Sat-Sun &
PH 11-6; Nov-24 Dec, daily 11-4. Due to
development work, site may have to close.
Telephone for details.
✱ *£2 (ch 70p).*
ఉ *shop*
(NT)

Penscynor Wildlife Park — CILFREW

Map 03 SN70
☎ Neath (0639) 642189
Tropical birds, penguins, sea lions and
parrots are seen here in an attractive
setting among trees, streams and ponds,
where visitors can also feed rainbow
trout or see their tropical relatives. A
chair lift goes to the cliff top for
bobsleigh rides, and there is a children's
playground.
Open all year, daily 10-6, dusk in winter.
(Closed 25 Dec).
✱ *£3 (ch 3 free, ch & pen £2). Party*
20+.
ఐ *(charged)* ఐ ఉ *toilets for disabled shop*
✖

Down County Museum & St Patrick Heritage Centre — DOWNPATRICK

Map 14 E5
The Mall
☎ (0396) 615218 & 615022
The museum occupies the old county gaol built between 1789 and 1796. The Saint Patrick Heritage Centre in the former gatehouse, tells the story of Ireland's patron saint. In the recently restored governor's residence are galleries relating to the human and natural history of County Down. The story of man's settlement from 7,000 BC to recent times, is told with texts and artefacts ranging from flint arrowheads

to Dinky toys. In Spring 1991, the renovation work on the three-storey cell block was completed and some of the 18th-century cells on the ground floor are now open, together with additional exhibition areas. Special events for 1992 include: 6 Jun, 1st Northern Ireland Stationery Engine Club Rally.
Open all year, Jul-mid Sep, Mon-Fri 11-5, wknds 2-5; rest of year, Tue-Fri 11-5 & Sat 2-5.
Free.
P ✉ ᕕ toilets for disabled shop ✈

Inch Abbey — DOWNPATRICK

Map 14 E5
(on River Quoile)
☎ (0232) 235000
Beautiful riverside ruins of a Cistercian abbey founded by John de Courcy around 1180. Of particular note is the

tall, pointed triple east window.
Open Apr-Sep 10-7. Oct-Mar free access.
✳ Apr-Sep 50p (ch 25p)
P ᕕ
(AM)

Loughinisland Churches — DOWNPATRICK

Map 14 E5
(4m W)
The ruins of these three ancient churches stand on an island in the lough, accessible by causeway.

Open all times
Free.
P ᕕ ♿
(AM)

Mound of Down — DOWNPATRICK

Map 14 E5
(on the Quoile Marshes, from Mount Crescent)
Hill fort from the Early Christian period, conquered by Anglo-Norman troops in 1177, who then built an earthwork castle on top. This mound in

the marshes, beside the River Quoile, was the first town before the present Downpatrick.
Open all times
Free.
P
(AM)

Struell Wells — DOWNPATRICK

Map 14 E5
Pilgrims come to collect the healing waters from these holy drinking and eye wells which are fed by a swift underground stream. Nearby are the ruins of an 18th-century church, and, even more interesting, single-sex bath-

houses. The men's bath-house is roofed, has an anteroom and a sunken bath, while the ladies' is smaller and roofless.
Open all times
Free.
P ♿
(AM)

Legananny Dolmen — DROMARA

Map 14 E6
(5m S)
Theatrically situated on the slopes of Slieve Croob, this tripod dolmen with its three tall uprights and huge capstone is the most graceful of Northern Ireland's

Stone-Age monuments. There are views to the Mourne mountains.
Open at all times
Free.
ᕕ ♿
(AM)

Hillsborough Fort — HILLSBOROUGH

Map 14 E6
☎ (0846) 683285
On a site that dates back to early Christian times, the existing fort was built in 1650 by Colonel Arthur Hill to command a view of the road from Dublin to Carrickfergus. The building was ornamented in the 18th century. It

is set in a forest park with a lake and pleasant walks.
Open all year; Tue-Sat 10-7, Sun 2-7 summer, Tue-Sat 10-4, Sun 2-4 winter.
Free.
P ᕕ
(AM)

Ulster Folk and Transport Museum — HOLYWOOD

Map 14 E6
153 Bangor Rd (on A2)
☎ Belfast (0232) 428428
Opened in 1964, in the grounds of Cultra Manor, this museum is in two parts. The Folk Museum, which covers a 136-acre site, has a wonderful collection of rural and urban buildings that have been taken from original settings all over Northern Ireland, dismantled stone by stone and re-erected here. There is a terraced row of Ulster Street houses, simple one-roomed labourers' houses, cottages, a substantial rectory, a school, a church, mill and much more besides – all re-erected in

the most fitting setting and authentically furnished. There are also displays of traditional farming methods throughout the year. The Transport Museum is principally concerned with Northern Ireland's shipbuilding and aircraft industries, as well as the history of transport in general. One of the main attractions is the three-masted schooner Result built at Carrickfergus.
Open all year May-Sep, Mon-Sat 11-6, Sun 2-6; Oct-Apr, Mon-Sat 11-5, Sun 2-5.
P ✉ ᕕ toilets for disabled shop
Details not confirmed for 1992

Greencastle — KILKEEL

Map 14 E5
(5m SW)
Looking very much like an English Norman castle with its massive keep, gatehouse and curtain wall, this 13th-century royal fortress stands on the shores of Carlingford Lough, with fine views of the Mourne Mountains. One of

the main English strongholds from the late-15th century, it was destroyed by Cromwellian troops in 1652.
Open Apr-Sep, Tue-Sat 10-7, Sun 2-7.
✳ 50p (ch 25p).
P ᕕ
(AM)

Sketrick Castle — KILLINCHY

Map 14 E6
(3m E on W tip of Sketrick Islands)
Badly ruined tall tower house, probably 15th century. Ground floor rooms include boat bay and prison. Underground passage leads from NE

corner of bawn to freshwater spring.
Open at all times.
Free.
P
(AM)

Duneight Motte and Bailey — LISBURN

Map 14 E6
(2m S beside Ravernet River)
☎ Belfast (0232) 230560
Impressive Anglo-Norman earthwork castle with high mound-embanked

enclosure, making use of defences of earlier pre-Norman fort.
Open at any reasonable time.
Free.
(AM)

✳ An asterisk indicates that up-to-date information was not available at the time of our research – 1991 information has been published as an indication of what you may expect.

Dundrum Castle — NEWCASTLE

Map 14 E5
(4m N)
☎ Belfast (0232) 230560
This medieval castle, one of the finest in Ireland, was built in 1777 by John De Courcy in a strategic position overlooking Dundrum Bay, a position which offers visitors fine views over the sea and to the Mourne Mountains. The castle was captured by King John in 1210 and was badly damaged by

Cromwellian troops in 1652. Still an impressive ruin, it shows a massive round keep with walls 16m high and 2m thick, surrounded by a curtain wall, and a gatehouse which dates from the 13th century.
Open all year, Apr-Sep, Tue-Sat 10-7, Sun 2-7. Oct-Mar, Tue-Sat 10-4, Sun 2-4.
✳ 50p (ch & pen 25p).
P ᕕ toilets for disabled
(AM)

Maghera Church — NEWCASTLE

Map 14 E5
(3m N)
☎ Belfast (0232) 235000
The stump of a round tower, blown down in a storm in the early 18th century, survives from the early

monastery, with a ruined 13th-century church near by.
Open at any reasonable time.
Free.
P ᕕ
(AM)

Mount Stewart House, Garden & Temple of the Winds — NEWTOWNARDS

Map 14 E6
Greyabbey (5m SE)
☎ Greyabbey (024774) 387

On the east shore of Strangford Lough, this 18th-century house was the home of the Stewart family (who later became Marquesses of Londonderry) and the place where Lord Castlereagh, Foreign Secretary from 1812 to 1823, grew up. The house is the work of three architects – James Wyatt in the 1780s and George Dance and probably Vitruvius

Morrison in the early 19th century. Much of the house's contents have associations with Castlereagh, and there are interesting paintings, including one by Stubbs, as well as silver and porcelain. Outside, in the lovely, inspired gardens (among the very best of the National Trust's), many rare and subtropical trees thrive, while by the shore of Strangford Lough is the Temple of the Winds, built by James Stewart in 1782 for the first Marquess.
Open House Apr wknds (17-26 daily); May-Aug, Wed-Mon 1-6; Sep-Oct wknds only 1-6. Temple of The Winds open dates as house 2-5. Garden Apr-Aug, daily; Sep & Oct, wknds 12-6.
✳ House Garden & Temple £3.30 (ch £1.65); Garden & Temple £2.70 (ch £1.35). Party.
P ✉ ᕕ (wheelchair available) toilets for disabled shop
(NT)

Scrabo Tower — NEWTOWNARDS

Map 14 E6
Scrabo Country Park, 203A Scrabo Rd (1m W)
☎ (0247) 811491
Built in memory of the third Marquis of Londonderry in 1857, this 135ft tower stands on Scrabo Hill and offers superb

views over Strangford Lough and the north Down landscape.
Open Etr, May-Sep, Tue-Sun 11.30-7. Country park open all year, daily.
Free.
P shop ✈
(AM)

Northern Ireland Aquarium   PORTAFERRY

Map 14 E6
The Ropewalk, Castle St
☎ (02477) 28062
Interpretative centre for Strangford
Lough, including Ireland's only public
Aquarium Hall. Dry displays explain
why the marine life of Strangford Lough
is unique: and 23 aquaria, with a total
volume of 90 tonnes of sea water,
exhibit a wide range of the marine
animals found in the lough. Also on the

site are tea rooms, wildfowl pond, tennis
courts, bowls, putting, touring caravan
site, children's play area, picnic areas and
woodland walks.
*Open all year, Apr-Aug, Mon-Sat 10-6,
Sun 1-6; Sep-Mar, Tue-Sat 10.30-5, Sun
1-5.*
✱ *£1.38 (ch, pen, UB40 & disabled 77p).
Family ticket £3.58.*
🅿 ▣ ⅄ *toilets for disabled shop* ✖

Rowallane Garden   SAINTFIELD

Map 14 E6
(1m S on A7)
☎ (0238) 510131
Beautiful, exotic, 50-acre gardens started
by the Rev John Moore in 1860 and
continued by his nephew Hugh
Armytage. The gardens contain exquisite
plants from all over the world.
Particularly noted for its rhododendrons
and azaleas and for the wonderful floral
displays in spring and summer. Events

for 1992 include an evening 'Garden in
Spring' walk (6 May), a horse drive (21
Jun), and a Yuletide market (12-13 Dec).
*Open Apr-Oct, Mon-Fri 10.30-6, Sat &
Sun 2-6; Nov-28 Mar, Mon-Fri 9-5.
Etr-Nov £2.30 (ch £1.15); Nov-Mar
£1.20 (ch 60p). Party.*
🅿 *(charged)* ▣ ⅄ *(parking facilities) toilets
for disabled shop*
(NT)

Audley's Castle   STRANGFORD

Map 14 E6
(1.5m W by shore of Strangford Lough)
☎ Belfast (0232) 230560
Fifteenth-century tower house on
Strangford Lough which offers lovely
views from its top floor. The internal

fittings are complete.
*Open Apr-Sep, daily 10-7.
Free.*
🅿 ✖
(AM)

✱ An asterisk indicates that up-to-date information was
not available at the time of our research – 1991
information has been published as an
indication of what you may expect.

Castle Ward   STRANGFORD

Map 14 E6
(0.5m W on A25)
☎ (039686) 204
The curious diversity of styles in this
house is due to the fact that its owner,
Bernard Ward, later First Viscount
Bangor, and his wife could never agree;
so the classical style preferred by the
Viscount and the more elaborate Gothic
look favoured by his wife were both
incorporated in the house. Not
altogether surprisingly, the couple
separated shortly after the house was
completed! The servants' living quarters
are separate from the house and are
reached by an underground passage.

Fully equipped laundry in the courtyard.
Small theatre in part of the large barn.
Castle Ward is beautifully placed
overlooking Strangford Lough. The
gardens, complete with a small lake,
home to a collection of waterfowl, and a
classical summerhouse, are richly planted
and especially beautiful in spring.
*House open Etr, daily; Apr & Sep-Oct,
wknds; May-Aug, daily (ex Thu) 1-6.
Estate grounds all year, daily dawn-dusk.
✱ House £2.30 (ch £1.15). Estate £3 per
car (Nov-Mar £1.50). Party.*
🅿 *(charged)* ▣ ✖ ⅄ *(wheelchair available)
toilets for disabled shop*

Strangford Castle   STRANGFORD

Map 14 E6
A three-storey tower house built in the
16th century, overlooking the small
double harbour of Strangford.

*Key available from house opposite.
Free.*
✖
(AM)

Narrow Water Castle   WARRENPOINT

Map 14 E5
(1m NW)
☎ Belfast (0232) 235000
Both picturesque and complete in detail,
this 16th-century battlemented tower
house is surrounded by a wall and juts

out into the river estuary which it was
originally built to defend.
*Open Apr-Sep, Tue-Sat 10-7.
✱ 50p (accompanied ch 25p).*
🅿
(AM)

CO FERMANAGH

Belleek Pottery   BELLEEK

Map 14 C6
☎ (036565) 501
Known worldwide for its fine Parian
china, this pottery was started in 1857
by the Caldwell family. Although the
Caldwells originally used felspar from
the Castle Caldwell estate, today it is

imported, mainly from Norway. Visitors
can watch craftsmen at work, admire the
showpieces on display and visit the shop.
*Open all year, Mar-Sep, Mon-Fri 9-6, Sat
10-6, Sun 2-6; Oct-Feb, Mon-Fri 9-5.30.*
🅿 ✖ ⅄ *shop* ✖
Details not confirmed for 1992

White Island Church   CASTLE ARCHDALE BAY

Map 14 C6
(in Castle Archdale Bay; ferry from
marina)
☎ Belfast (0232) 235000
Lined up on the far wall of a small,
roofless 12th-century church are eight
uncanny carved-stone figures. Part
Christian and part pagan in appearance,

their significance has been the subject of
great debate. The church ruins sit on an
early monastic site.
Open Jul-Aug, Tue-Sat 10-7, Sun 2-7.
✱ *£1.50 (ch 75p).*
🅿 ✖ ▣
(AM)

Tully Castle   DERRYGONNELLY

Map 14 C6
(3m N, on W shore of Lower Lough
Erne)
☎ Belfast (0232) 235000
Extensive ruins of a Scottish-style
stronghouse with enclosing bawn
overlooking Lough Erne. Built by Sir
John Hume in the early 1600s, the
castle was destroyed, and most of the

occupants slaughtered, by the Maguires
in the 1641 Rising. There is a replica of
a 17th-century garden in the bawn.
*Open all year, daily, Apr-Sep 10-7; Oct-
Mar 10-4.*
✱ *50p (ch 25p).*
🅿 ⅄ ✖
(AM)

✖ The 'No Dogs' symbol does not normally apply
to guide dogs – these are permitted in
most establishments.

Castle Coole   ENNISKILLEN

Map 14 C5
(1.5m SE on A4)
☎ (0365) 322690
One of the finest classical mansions in
Northern Ireland, if not in the British
Isles. No expense was spared in the
building of this mansion for the First
Earl of Belmore between 1789 and
1795. James Wyatt was the architect,
the lovely plasterwork ceilings were by
Joseph Rose, and the chimney pieces the
work of Richard Westmacott. Vast
amounts of Portland stone were specially
imported, together with an Italian expert

in stonework, and joiners from England
were brought in to make the shutters
and doors. The house is filled with
beautiful Regency furniture. Don't miss
the sumptuous state bed in scarlet silk.
Outside the lawns slope gently towards
Lough Coole which is home to a flock
of greylag geese.
*Open 17-21 Apr, daily; Apr-May & Sep,
wknds & BH's; Jun-Aug, daily (ex Thu)
2-6.*
£2.20 (ch £1.10). Party.
🅿 ⅄ *toilets for disabled*

Devenish Island   ENNISKILLEN

Map 14 C5
(2m N)
☎ Belfast (0232) 235000
Two miles downstream from the city
centre, this island (once the site of a
monastery founded in the 6th century
by St Molaise – regarded as one of the
12 apostles of Ireland) has a considerable
number of interesting ecclesiastical
remains. The ruins of Teampull Mor,
with its fine south window, date back to
the 13th century, while St Molaise's
house – the remains of a tiny but sturdy
church (roofless now) – to the 12th

century. Facing this little church is a
perfect 80ft-tall round tower. Also
dating back to the 12th century, this
tower is built on five floors accessible by
ladders. The ruins of the Augustinian
priory of St Mary's has an elaborately
carved north chancel door and a pretty
15th-century cross in the graveyard.
Open Apr-Sep, Tue-Sat 10-7, Sun 2-7.
✱ *£1.50 (incl ferry access to museum &
tower); 50p (tower & museum only)
shop* ✖
(AM)

This is just one of many guidebooks published by the AA.
The full range is available at any AA shop or good bookshop.

Enniskillen Castle   ENNISKILLEN

Map 14 C5
☎ (0365) 325000
Overlooking Lough Erne this castle – a
three-storey keep, surrounded by
massive stone-built barracks and with a
turreted fairytale 17th-century water
gate – now houses two museums. In the
castle keep is a small museum displaying
Royal Enniskillen Fusiliers regimental
exhibits, while the other rooms contain

the Fermanagh County Museum's
collection of local antiquities. 1992 will
see the opening of a new heritage centre
inside the castle.
*Open all year, Mon-Fri 10-1 & 2-5, also
BH's.*
Free.
🅿 ⅄ *shop* ✖
(AM)

Florence Court   ENNISKILLEN

Map 14 C5
(8m SW)
☎ (036582) 249
Named after the wife of the first owner,
John Coles, and later the seat of the
Earls of Enniskillen, this 18th-century
mansion overlooks wild and beautiful
scenery towards the mountain of
Cuilcagh. The interior of the house,
particularly noted for its flambuoyant
rococo plasterwork, was gutted by fire in
1955, but has been miraculously
restored. The mansion is situated in

beautiful parkland full of fine old trees,
including the Florence Court Yew –
mother of all Irish yews. There are
lovely views and fine walks to be
enjoyed within the grounds and in the
larger surrounding forest park.
*Open Etr, daily 1-6; Apr, May & Sep
wknds & BH's 1-6; Jun-Aug, daily (ex
Tue) 1-6.*
£2.20 (ch £1.10). Party.
🅿 ▣ ⅄ *(wheelchair available) toilets for
disabled shop*
(NT)

Marble Arch Caves — ENNISKILLEN

Map 14 C5
Marlbank Scenic Loop (off A4
Enniskillen-Sligo road)
☎ (0365) 8855

Magical cave system – one of Europe's
finest – under the Mountains of
Cuilcagh. Here visitors are given a tour
round a wonderland of stalagmites,
stalactites, underground rivers and lakes,
which starts with a boat trip on the
lower lake. The streams which flow
down and then disappear into the
mountain, feed the caves and then
emerge at 'Marble Arch', a huge 30ft
detached limestone bridge.
*Open Apr-Oct, daily (weather permitting).
Tours Mon-Sat 11-4.30, Sun 11-6.*
P ▭ *shop* ✈
Details not confirmed for 1992

Monea Castle — ENNISKILLEN

Map 14 C5
(6m NW)
☎ Belfast (0232) 235000
A fine example of a plantation castle still
with much of its enclosing bawn wall
intact, built around 1618. Of particular
interest is the castle's stone corbelling –

the Scottish method of giving additional
support to turrets.
*Open at any reasonable time.
Free.*
P &
(AM)

Castle Balfour — LISNASKEA

Map 14 D5
☎ Belfast (0232) 235000
Dating from 1618 and refortified in
1652, this is a T-plan house with vaulted
rooms. Badly burnt in the early 1800s,

this house has remained in ruins.
*Open at all times.
Free.*
&
(AM)

CO LONDONDERRY

Hezlett House — COLERAINE

Map 14 D7
(4m W on Coleraine/Downhill coast rd)
☎ Castlerock (0265) 848567
A low, thatched cottage built around
1690 with an interesting Cruck Truss
roof, constructed by using pairs of
curved timbers to form arches and
infilling around this frame with clay,

rubble and other locally available
materials.
*Open Etr, daily; Apr-Jun & Sep wknds &
BH's; Jul-Aug, daily (ex Tue) 1-5.
£1.20 (ch 60p). Party.*
P ✈
(NT)

Mount Sandel — COLERAINE

Map 14 D7
☎ Belfast (0232) 230560
This 200ft oval mound overlooking the
River Bann is believed to have been
fortified in the Iron Age. Nearby is the
earliest known inhabited place in
Ireland, where post holes and hearths of
wooden dwellings, and flint implements

dating back to 6,650BC have been
found. The fort was a stronghold of de
Courcy in the late 12th century and was
refortified for artillery in the 17th
century.
*Open at all times.
Free.*
(AM)

For an explanation of the symbols and abbreviations, see page 2.

Springhill — COOKSTOWN

Map 14 D6
(5m NE on B18)
☎ Moneymore (0648) 748210
Dating back to the 17th century, this
attractive, pleasingly symmetrical manor
house was originally the home of the
Scottish Conyngham family. Today
much of the family furniture, books and
bric-a-brac has been retained. Outside,
the laundry, stables, brewhouse, and old
dovecote make interesting viewing, as do
the old Irish cottage kitchen and the

excellent costume museum. Events for
1992 include 'Music in May' – an
evening of 18th-century music with a
Georgian supper (May 22), Summer
Sleuthing – family fact-finding fun (Jul
25-26), and a Victorian archery shoot
(Sep 13).
*Open Etr, daily 2-6; Apr-Jun & Sep,
wknds & BH's 2-6; Jul-Aug, daily (ex
Thu) 2-6.
£1.80 (ch 90p). Party.*
P ▭ & *toilets for disabled shop*

Tullaghoge Fort — COOKSTOWN

Map 14 D6
(2m S)
☎ Belfast (0232) 230560
This large hilltop earthwork, planted
with trees, was once the headquarters of
the O'Hagans, Chief Justices of the old
kingdom of Tyrone. Between the 12th
and 16th centuries the O'Neill Chiefs of
Ulster were also crowned here – the
King Elect was seated on a stone

inauguration chair, new sandals were
placed on his feet and he was then
anointed and crowned. The last such
ceremony was held here in the 1590s; in
1600 the stone throne was destroyed by
order of Lord Mountjoy.
*Open at all times.
Free.*
P
(AM)

Wellbrook Beetling Mill — COOKSTOWN

Map 14 D6
Corkhill (4m W)
☎ Tulnacross (06487) 51735

This 18th-century water-powered linen

mill was used for bleaching and, until
1961, for finishing Irish linen. Beetling
was the name given to the final process
in linen making, when the material was
beaten by 30 or so hammers (beetles) to
achieve a smooth and slightly shiny
finish. The National Trust acquired the
mill and restored it to working order.
*Open 17-21 Apr, daily; 8 Apr-Jun & Sep,
wknds & BH's; Jul-Aug, daily (ex Tue)
2-6.
£1.20 (ch 60p). Party.*
P & *shop*
(NT)

Mussenden Temple Bishop's Gate and Black Glen — DOWNHILL

Map 14 D7
Mussenden Rd (1m W of Castle Rock)
Spectacularly placed on a cliff edge
overlooking the Atlantic, this perfect
18th-century rotunda was modelled on
the Temple of Vesta at Tivoli. Frederick
Hervey, Bishop of Derry and 4th Earl of
Bristol, had the temple built as a
summer library for his cousin, but sadly
she died before its completion, so he
studied there himself. The temple, with
its magnificent views of the Antrim and

Donegal coasts, is only a part of the Earl
Bishop's Downhill demesne; visitors
entering by the Bishop's Gate can enjoy
a beautiful glen walk up to the headland
where the temple stands.
*Open 1-12 Apr, booked parties only;
Temple: Etr (29 Mar-7 Apr), daily,
noon-6; Apr-Jun & Sep, weekends & BH's
noon-6; Jul-Aug, daily noon-6.
Free.*
P &
(NT)

Every effort is made to provide accurate information,
but details might change during the currency
of this guide.

Banagher Church — DUNGIVEN

Map 14 D6
(2m SW)
☎ Belfast (0232) 235000
This church was founded by St
Muiredach O'Heney in 1100 and
altered in later centuries. Today
impressive ruins remain. The nave is the
oldest part and the square-headed
lintelled west door is particularly
impressive. Just outside, the perfect
miniature stone house, complete with
pitched roof and the sculpted figures of a

saint at the doorway, is believed to be
the tomb of St Muiredach. The saint
was said to have endowed his large
family with the power of bringing good
luck. All they had to do was to sprinkle
whoever or whatever needed luck with
sand taken from the base of the saint's
tomb.
*Open at all times.
Free.*
P
(AM)

Dungiven Priory — DUNGIVEN

Map 14 D6
(SE of town overlooking River Roe)
☎ Belfast (0232) 235000
Up until the 17th century Dungiven was
the stronghold of the O'Cahan chiefs,
and the Augustinian priory, of which
extensive ruins remain, was founded by
the O'Cahans around 1150. The church,
which was altered many times in later
centuries, contains one of Northern
Ireland's finest medieval tombs. It is the

tomb of Cooey na Gall O'Cahan who
died in 1385. His sculpted effigy,
dressed in Irish armour, lies under a
stonework canopy. Below are six kilted
warriors.
*Open – Church at all times, chancel only
when caretaker available. Check at house at
end of lane.
Free.*
✈ ▭
(AM)

Rough Fort — LIMAVADY

Map 14 D7
(1m W)
Early Christian rath.
Open at all times.

Free.
▭
(NT)

City Walls — LONDONDERRY

Map 14 D6
☎ Belfast (0232) 235000
Finest and most complete city walls to
be found in Ireland. The walls – 20-
25ft high – are mounted with ancient
cannon, and date back to the 17th
century. The walled city is a

conservation area with many fine
buildings. Visitors can walk round the
city ramparts – a circuit of one mile.
*Open all times.
Admission free from various points.*
P *(charged)* &
(AM)

Maghera Church — MAGHERA

Map 14 D6
(E approach to the town)
☎ Belfast (0232) 235000
Important 6th-century monastery
founded by St Lurach, later a bishop's
see and finally a parish church. This
much-altered church has a magnificently
decorated 12th-century west door. A

cross-carved stone to the west of the
church is supposed to be the grave of the
founder.
*Key from Leisure Centre.
Free.*
P &
(AM)

CO TYRONE

Ardboe Cross   ARDBOE

Map 14 D6
(off B73)
☎ Belfast (0232) 230560
Situated at Ardboe Point, on the western shore of Lough Neagh, is the best example of a high cross to be found in Northern Ireland. Marking the site of an ancient monastery, the cross has 22 sculpted panels, many recognisably biblical, including Adam and Eve and the Last Judgment. It stands over 18ft high and dates back to the 10th century. It is still the rallying place of the annual

Lammas, but praying at the cross and washing in the lake has been replaced by traditional music-making, singing and selling of local produce. The tradition of 'cross reading' or interpreting the pictures on the cross, is an honour passed from generation to generation among the men of the village.
Open at all times.
Free.
🅿 ♿
(AM)

U S Grant Ancestral Homestead & Visitor Centre   BALLYGAWLEY

Map 14 D6
Dergenagh, Ballygawley Rd (off A4, 3m on Dergenagh road)
☎ Aughnacloy (066252) 7133
Ancestral homestead of Ulysses S Grant, 18th President of the United States of America. The homestead and farmyard have been restored to the style and appearance of a mid-19th-century Irish smallholding. The small thatched cottage consists of two rooms, furnished with replica period pieces, and the farmyard contains examples of agricultural

implements used by the 19th-century farmer. The Visitor Centre houses a shop and a display area with exhibitions on the Ulster Scots Plantation and the U S Grant story. There is also a small audio-visual theatre, and a small cafeteria in which each the five tables represents a different period in local history.
Open Etr-Sep, Tue-Sat 10-6, Sun 2-6. Other times by arrangement. (Closed 25-26 Dec & 1 Jan).
60p (ch & pen 30p).
🅿 ♨ ♿ *shop*

Beaghmore Stone Circles and Alignments   BEAGHMORE

Map 14 D6
☎ Belfast (0232) 235000
Discovered in the 1930s, these impressive, ritualistic stones have been dated back to the early Bronze, and maybe even Neolithic Ages. There are three pairs of stone circles, one single circle, stone rows or alignments and

cairns, which range in height from one to four feet. This is an area littered with historic monuments, many discovered by people cutting turf.
Open at all times.
Free.
🅿 ♿
(AM)

Benburb Castle   BENBURB

Map 14 D6
☎ Belfast (0232) 235000
The castle ruins – three towers and massive walls – are dramatically placed on a cliff-edge 120ft above the River Blackwater. The northwest tower is newly restored and has dizzy cliff-edge views. The castle, built by Sir Richard

Wingfield around 1615, is actually situated in the grounds of the Servite Priory. There are attractive walks down to the river.
Open at all times.
Free.
🅿 ♿ ♨
(AM)

Castlecaulfield   CASTLECAULFIELD

Map 14 D6
☎ Belfast (0232) 235000
Sir Toby Caulfield, an Oxfordshire knight and ancestor of the Earls of Charlemont, built this manor house in 1619 on the site of an ancient fort. It was badly burnt in 1641, repaired and lived in by the Caulfield/Charlemont family until 1670. It boasts the rare

distinction of having had Saint Oliver Plunkett and John Wesley preach in its grounds. Some fragments of the castle are re-used in the fine, large 17th-century parish church.
Open at all times.
Free.
♿
(AM)

Donaghmore Cross   DUNGANNON

Map 14 D6
(2m NW, at W end of Main Street)
☎ Belfast (0232) 235000
This 15ft-tall cross, situated at the top of the main street, dates back to the 9th or 10th century. It is carved with biblical scenes: Old Testament one side, New Testament the other. As the patterns of

the top and bottom parts don't match, the probability is that what we now see is a combination of two crosses.
Open at all times.
Free.
♿
(AM)

Mountjoy Castle   MOUNTJOY

Map 14 D6
(on western shores of Lough Neagh)
☎ Belfast (0232) 235000
Ruins of an early 17th-century brick and stone fort, with four rectangular towers, overlooking Lough Neagh. The fort was built for Lord Deputy Mountjoy during his campaign against Hugh O'Neill, Earl

of Tyrone. It was captured and re-captured by the Irish and English during the 17th century and was also used by the armies of James II and William III.
Open at all times.
Free.
🅿
(AM)

Harry Avery's Castle   NEWTOWNSTEWART

Map 14 D6
☎ Belfast (0232) 235000
The hilltop ruins of a Gaelic stone castle, built around the 14th century by one of the O'Neill chiefs, are the remains of the oldest surviving Irish-built

castle in the north. Only the great twin towers of the gatehouse are left.
Open at all times.
Free.
♨ 🚐
(AM)

For an explanation of the symbols and abbreviations, see page 2.

Omagh Mellon House and Ulster American Folk Park   OMAGH

Map 14 D6
(5m NW Omagh)
☎ (0662) 243292 & 243293
An outdoor museum, established in 1976, that traces the history of Ulster's links with America and the emigration of Ulster residents to North America during the 18th and 19th centuries. The 15-acre site is divided into two parts – Old World and New World. The Old World is centred around the restored farmhouse of Thomas Mellon, who emigrated to Pennsylvania in 1818, and later founded the Mellon Bank of Pittsburgh. In the New World are log houses and outbuildings – all are suitably furnished. A recent addition is the cottage of John Joseph Hughes, who

emigrated from Augher in 1817, became first Catholic Archbishop of New York and initiated the building of St Patrick's Cathedral there in 1858. There are also demonstrations of Old and New World crafts, such as horseshoeing and thatching. A modern visitor centre, with exhibitions and audio-visual presentations, provides further information. There is also a new gallery area, complete with dockside buildings and immigrant ship.
Open Etr-early Sep, daily 11-6.30, Sun & BH 11.30-7; Sep-Etr Mon-Fri 10.30-5. Last admission 1hr 30mins before closing.
🅿 ♨ ♿ *toilets for disabled shop* ♨
Details not confirmed for 1992

Gray's Printing Press   STRABANE

Map 14 D6
49 Main St
☎ (0504) 884094
Strabane was once an important printing and book-publishing centre, the only relic of which is a small shop in Main Street – Gray's Printing Shop. The shop now houses a Printing Museum containing three 19th-century presses, while upstairs the development of printing techniques over sixty years is illustrated. Two young men who served their apprenticeships in Strabane during the 18th century went on to great

things: John Dunlap emigrated to Philadelphia, where he founded 'The Pennsylvania Packet' – America's first 'daily'; James Wilson who also emigrated to Philadelphia becoming a printer, newspaper editor and judge whose grandson was President Woodrow Wilson.
Open Apr-Sep, daily (ex Thu, Sun & BH's) 2-5.30. Other times by prior arrangement.
£1.20 (ch 60p). Party.
shop ♨
(NT)

REPUBLIC OF IRELAND

CO CLARE

Bunratty Castle & Folk Park BUNRATTY

Map 14 B3
☎ Limerick (061) 361511
Rebuilt in 1353 and still in use, this is Ireland's most complete medieval castle. It houses the Lord Gort collection of furniture, objects of art, and paintings and tapestries dating from before 1650. One-day tours operate in season from Limerick and include a medieval banquet at the castle. Irish village life at the turn of the century is tellingly recreated in the folk park in the grounds, with its typical 19th-century rural and urban dwellings. There are eight farmhouses, a watermill, a blacksmith's forge, and a village street complete with shops and pub.
Open all year, daily 9.30-5 (last admission 4.15). Also Folk Park remains open Jun-Aug until 7 (last admission 6).
IR£3.60 (ch IR£1.80 & pen IR£2.35). Family ticket IR£9
🅿 ⬛ ✕ *licensed* ♿ *(castle not accessible) toilets for disabled shop*

O'Brien's Tower & Cliffs of Moher LISCANNOR

Map 14 B3
(4m N)
☎ Ennis (065) 81171
Just north of Liscannor on the coast of West Clare, are the famous Cliffs of Moher, defiantly standing as giant natural ramparts against the aggressive might of the Atlantic Ocean. They rise in places to 700ft, and stretch for almost 5 miles. O'Brien's Tower was built in the early 19th century as a viewing point for Victorian tourists on the highest point. From here you can view the Clare coastline, the Aran Islands and mountains as far apart as Kerry and Connemara. There is a visitor centre with tourist information.
Open – Cliffs of Moher accessible all year. O'Briens Tower May-Sep, daily 10-5.30. IR65p (ch IR40p)
🅿 ⬛ ♿ *toilets for disabled shop*

For an explanation of the symbols and abbreviations, see page 2.

Craggaunowen Bronze Age Project QUIN

Map 14 B3
☎ Limerick (061) 367178
Contains a full-scale reconstruction of a crannog, a Bronze Age lake dwelling. The project includes a reconstructed ring fort and replicas of furniture, tools and utensils. Also on display is the *Brendan*, a replica of the leather boat used by St Brendan the Navigator in the 6th century. The boat was sailed across the Atlantic Ocean in 1976 and 1977.
Open all year, daily 9.30-6 (last admission 5).
IR£2.70 (ch, pen & students IR£1.60). Family ticket IR£7.40
🅿 ⬛ ♿ *shop*

CO CORK

Bantry House BANTRY

Map 14 B2
☎ (027) 50047
A Georgian mansion surrounded by gardens.
Open all year. (Closed 25 Dec)
IR£2.50 (ch free if accompanied, pen & students IR£1.50)
🅿 ⬛ ✕ *licensed* ♿ *shop* ✖ *(ex in grounds)*

Blarney Castle & Rock Close BLARNEY

Map 14 B2
☎ (021) 385252 & 385669
The site of the famous Blarney Stone, known the world over for the eloquence it is said to impart to those who kiss it. The stone is in the upper tower of the castle, and the visitor, held by his feet, must lean backward down a shaft in order to receive the gift of the gab.
Open – Blarney Castle & Rock Close, Jun-Jul Mon-Sat 9-8.30; Aug Mon-Sat 9-7.30; May Mon-Sat 9-7; Sep Mon-Sat 9-6.30; Apr & Oct Mon-Sat 9-sunset; summer Sun 9.30-5.30; winter Sun 9.30-sunset. Blarney Castle House & Gardens Jun-mid Sep Mon-Sat noon-5. Blarney Castle & Rock Close IR£3 (ch IR£1, pen & students IR£1.50). Blarney Castle House & Gardens IR£2.50 (ch IR£1, pen & students IR£1.50)
🅿 ♿ *shop* ✖

Cork Public Museum CORK

Map 14 C2
Fitzgerald Park, Mardyke (N of University College)
☎ (021) 270679
Displays illustrating the history of the city are housed in this museum. The collections cover the economic, social and municipal history from the Mesolithic period, with emphasis on civic regalia, and the trades and crafts of the 19th and 20th centuries. There are fine collections of Cork Silver and Glass and Youghal Needlepoint Lace.
Open all year, Jun-Aug Mon-Fri 11-1 & 2.15-6, Sun 3-5; Sep-May Mon-Fri 11-1 & 2.15-5, Sun 3-5. (Closed Sat, BH wknds & PH)
Mon-Fri free; Sun IR20p (ch IR10p) shop ✖

CO DUBLIN

Newbridge House and Traditional Farm DONABATE

Map 14 E4
☎ Dublin (01) 436534 & 452655
Newbridge House was designed by George Semple and built in 1737 for Charles Cobbe, Archbishop of Dublin. The Cobbe family continued to live there until 1985 when the house, estate and much of its contents was bought by Dublin County Council. It offers many interesting features, including the Inner Hallway and Museum of Curiosities, and an outstanding example of an early 18th-century kitchen containing many original fittings.
Open all year, Apr-Oct Tue-Fri 10-1 & 2-5, Sat 11-6, Sun & PH 2-6; Nov-Mar Sat-Sun & PH 2-5. Parties at other times by arrangement.
IR£2.20 (ch IR£1.20, pen & students IR£1.80). Family ticket IR£6.50.
🅿 ⬛ ♿ *shop* ✖ 🚐

DUBLIN

Map 14 E4
Dublin is a delightful city with many outstanding examples of 18th-century architecture. Birthplace and inspiration of many great authors, its contrasts are apparent everywhere: sweeping avenues and intimate sidestreets, chic shops and smokey pubs, stately museums and colleges, and terraces with faded exteriors emanating character. A good place to begin a tour of this compact city is O'Connell Bridge, leading to the city's main shopping area, O'Connell Street, where the best buys are local products, such as linen and lace, homespun tweeds and knitwear. City attractions include Parnell Square, one of Dublin's earliest and most attractive squares of handsome brick-faced Georgian houses; Charlemont House, containing the Hugh Lane Municipal Gallery of Modern Art; Nassau Street, with its bookstores; the National Gallery, housing more than 2000 works of art; the National Museum's fascinating collection of Irish treasures; the Civic Museum, and Trinity College Library. Dublin Castle's state apartments have guided tours every half-hour, and the Guinness brewery offers visitors a 30-minute film show, followed by a tasting.

Dublin's Writers Museum DUBLIN

Map 14 E4
18/19 Parnell Square North
☎ (01) 722077
The Dublin Writers Museum and Living Writers Centre is housed in two restored 18th-century buildings which retain many of their Georgian characteristics, and a modern annexe with lecture rooms and exhibition spaces. Dublin's rich literary heritage can be followed through fascinating displays tracing the written tradition in Ireland from the Book of Kells in the 8th century to the present day. Paintings, letters, photographs and artefacts are also on show.
Open all year, Mon-Sat 10-5, Sun & BH 2-6.
IR£2 (ch IR50p, pen & students IR£1). Family ticket IR£5
⬛ ✕ *licensed shop* ✖

Guinness Hop Store DUBLIN

Map 14 E4
Crane St
☎ (01) 536700
Established in 1876, the Hop Store remained crammed with hopsacks until 1957, when a new hop store came into use. It has now been converted to 'The World of Guinness' which shows the history of the famous brewery through museum exhibits and audio-visual presentations. In 'The Cooperage', there is a comprehensive collection of cooper's tools and oak casks displayed in an authentic brewery setting. There is also a Transport Gallery and a Sample Bar, where you can taste the famous drink.
Open all year, Mon-Fri 10-4 (last complete tour 3.30). (Closed Sat-Sun & PH/BH)
IR£2 (ch & pen IR50p). Party 20+
🅿 ♿ *toilets for disabled shop* ✖

See advertisement on page 232.

Howth Castle Rhododendron Gardens DUBLIN

Map 14 E4
Howth (9m NE)
☎ (01) 322624 & 322256
On the northern boundary of Dublin Bay, the castle is justly famous for its attractive gardens and it is especially lauded for its rhododendron walk. The walk is open all year, but is at its floral best in May and June. There are views north to the Mourne Mountains and West of Dublin Bay.
Open all year, daily 8am-dusk. (Closed 25 Dec).
Free.
🅿 ✕ *licensed*

Hugh Lane Municipal Gallery of Modern Art DUBLIN

Map 14 E4
Charlemont House, Parnell Square
☎ (01) 741903
The gallery occupies Charlemont House, a lovely Georgian mansion. Included here are collections of Irish works and art from the modern French and British schools.
Open all year, Tue-Fri 9.30-6, Sat 9.30-5, Sun 11-5. (Closed Mon).
Free.
✕ *licensed* ♿ *toilets for disabled shop* ✖

National Botanic Gardens DUBLIN

Map 14 E4
Glasnevin
☎ (01) 374388 & 377596
The gardens encompass 50 acres of grounds planted with common and uncommon varities of flowers, shrubs and trees. Especially noteworthy are the collections of orchids and palms. The gardens were founded by direction of the Irish Parliament in 1795, and have been modified and improved over the years.
Open all year, summer Mon-Sat 9-6, Sun 11-6; winter Mon-Sat 10-4.30, Sun 11-4.30. (Closed 25 Dec).
Free.
♿ *toilets for disabled* ✖

THE HOME OF GUINNESS

Visit the World of Guinness Exhibition at the Guinness Hop Store, Crane Street, Dublin 8 — including interesting audio-visual presentation, brewing equipment and machinery, coopers' tools, transport used in the industry, advertising. Sample some of the famous 'brew' and browse through the Guinness Souvenir Shop.

For further information phone Dublin 536700, Extension 5155

**Open Monday to Friday —
10 a.m. to 4.30 p.m.**

THE GUINNESS HOP STORE

Royal Zoological Society of Ireland — DUBLIN

Map 14 E4
Phoenix Park
☎ (01) 771425
The gardens were founded in 1830 and today exhibit many species of birds and animals, notably lions and other large cats. Inhabitants occupy spacious buildings and outdoor enclosures in beautifully landscaped grounds. Two

large lakes are the home of pelicans and flamingoes, and the largest collection of waterfowl in Ireland.
Open all year, Mon-Sat 9.30-6, Sun 11-6. Gardens close sunset in winter. (Closed 25 & 26 Dec)
✻ *IR£4.20 (ch & pen IR£1.80). Family ticket IR£12. Party 20 +*
🍴 ✕ *licensed & toilets for disabled shop* 🐕

James Joyce Tower — DUN LAOGHAIRE

Map 14 E4
Sandycove
☎ (01) 2809265 & 2808571
Built by the British as a defence against a possible invasion by Napoleon, the tower has walls approximately 18ft thick and an entrance door 13ft above the ground. Once reached by a rope ladder, the door is now accessible via a wrought-iron stairway. The tower was once the temporary home of James

Joyce, who depicted this setting in the opening scene of *Ulysses*. The structure is now a museum devoted to the author. Special events for 1992 include: 16 Jun, Bloomsday.
Open May-Sep Mon-Sat 10-1 & 2-5, Sun & PHs 2-6.
IR£1.60 (ch IR90p, pen & students IR£1.30)
& *shop* 🐕

🐕 The 'No Dogs' symbol does not normally apply to guide dogs – these are permitted in most establishments.

Fry Model Railway — MALAHIDE

Map 14 E4
Malahide Castle
☎ Dublin (01) 452758 & 452655
The Fry Model Railway is a rare collection of "0" Gauge Trains and Trams, depicting the history of Irish rail transport from the first train that ran in 1834. Cyril Fry began to build his model collection in the late 1920s, in the attic of his home. All the models are built to scale, and they are now housed

in a purpose-built setting adjacent to Malahide Castle.
Open all year Apr-Oct Mon-Thu 10-1 & 2-5, Sat 11-1 & 2-6, Sun & PH 2-6 (also Jul-Aug Fri 10-1 & 2-5); Nov-Mar Sat-Sun & PH 2-5. Parties at other times by arrangement.
IR£2 (ch IR£1.15, pen & students IR£1.45). Family ticket IR£6.
🅿 & *shop* 🐕

Malahide Castle — MALAHIDE

Map 14 E4
☎ Dublin (01) 452655 & 452371
One of Ireland's oldest castles, with a late medieval core as the nucleus to the romantic and beautiful structure. Tours offer views of Irish period furniture and historical Irish portrait collections. Additional paintings from the National Gallery depict Irish life from the last

few centuries.
Open all year, Apr-Oct Mon-Fri 10-12.45 & 2-5, Sat 11-6, Sun & PH 2-6; Nov-Mar Mon-Fri 10-12.45 & 2-5, Sat-Sun & PH 2-5.
IR£2.45 (ch IR£1.25, pen & students IR£1.85). Family ticket IR£7
🅿 🍴 ✕ *licensed & shop* 🐕

CO GALWAY

Clonfert Cathedral — CLONFERT

Map 14 C4
☎ (0509) 51269
Founded in the 6th century by St Brendan, "The Navigator". In addition to the ruins and rebuilt edifices here, an

Irish Romanesque doorway survives intact.
Open all year, daily.
Free. Donations accepted.
🅿 & 🐕

Spanish Arch Civic Museum — GALWAY

Map 14 B4
City Hall, College Rd
☎ (091) 68151
In the south-west quarter, the arch dates from the days when Spain and Ireland had trading ties. Galway City Museum

at the arch is devoted to the city's history.
Open Whitsun-mid Oct, daily 10-5.
✻ *IR50p*
🐕

Thoor Ballylee — GORT

Map 14 B4
☎ (091) 63081
This tower house is the former home of the poet William Butler Yeats and where he completed most of his literary works. The tower has been restored to appear exactly as it was when he lived

there, and houses an Interpretative Centre with audio-visual presentations and displays of his work.
Open daily 10-6.
IR£2.50 (ch IR75p). Family ticket IR£5
🅿 🍴 & *toilets for disabled shop* 🐕

Dunguaire Castle — KINVARRA

Map 14 B4
☎ (091) 37108
Dunguaire Castle has stood for hundreds of years on the site of the 7th-century stronghold of Guaire, the King of Connaught. The castle bridges 13 centuries of Irish history from the skirmishes, battles and sieges that characterise its colourful past to the

literary revival of the early 20th century. Today the restored castle gives an insight into the lifestyle of the people who lived there from 1520 to modern times.
Open mid Apr-Sep, daily 9.30-5.30 (last admission 4.30).
IR£1.80 (ch IR£1)
🅿 *shop*

CO KILDARE

Castletown House — CELBRIDGE

Map 14 D4
☎ Dublin (01) 6288252
Considered by many to be Ireland's finest Georgian country house. Built for William Connolly, speaker of the Irish House of Commons in 1715-19, the restored house contains excellent plasterwork, Irish furniture and paintings of the period, the Pompeian Long Gallery with its Venetian chandeliers, and an 18th-century print room. A mile-long avenue of lime trees leads to the house. Special events for 1992 include:

Mid-Jun, Opening and final nights of GPA Music in Great Irish Houses Festival; Aug, Castletown Horse Trials. Information on other concerts and events, ring 01-628 8252.
Open all year, Apr-Sep Mon-Fri 10-6, Sat 11-6, Sun & BH 2-6; Oct Mon-Fri 10-5, Sun & BH 2-5; Nov-Mar Sun & BH 2-5.
IR£2.50 (ch IR£1, pen & students IR£2). Family ticket IR£6.
🅿 🍴 *shop* 🐕

CO LIMERICK

Lough Gur Stone Age Centre — HOLYCROSS

Map 14 C3
Bruff Rd
☎ (061) 85186
Lough Gur introduces visitors to the habitat of Neolithic Man on one of Ireland's most important archaeological sites. Near the lake is an interpretative centre which tells the story of 5,000 years of man's presence at Lough Gur. The centre features an audio-visual

presentation, models of stone circles, burial chambers and facsimiles of weapons, tools and pottery found in the area. Walking tours covering the archaeological features of the area are conducted at regular intervals.
Open mid May-Sep, daily 10-6 (last admission 5.30)
IR£1.70 (ch IR90p)
🅿 *shop*

Hunt Museum — LIMERICK

Map 14 B3
University of Limerick
☎ (061) 333644
The Hunt Museum at the University of Limerick holds Ireland's finest collection of Celtic to Medieval treasures outside Dublin's National Museum. On display is a treasury of antiquities and art objects from Europe and Ireland, including some excellent examples of ancient Irish metal work, with European objects crafted in medieval bronzes, ivories and Limoges enamels.
Open May-Sep, daily 9.30-5.30 (last admission 5).
IR£1.60 (ch IR90p)
🅿 ⚊ ♿ *toilets for disabled shop* ✖

King John's Castle — LIMERICK

Map 14 B3
Castle St, King's Island
☎ (061) 411201
A national monument marked by an imposing twin-towered gatehouse and battle-scarred walls. The 13th-century King John's Castle is an impressive Anglo-Norman fortress where imaginative models and three-dimensional displays demonstrate 800 years of Limerick's and Ireland's history. An audio-visual show depicts the wars, sieges and treaties of its past, and in the courtyard there are copies of ancient war machines.
Open all year, May-Oct daily 9.30-5.30 (last admission 4.30); Nov-Apr, daily (subject to demand). The Castle may also be open evenings in summer.
IR£3 (ch IR£1.50 & pen IR£2.50).
Family ticket IR£7
♿ *toilets for disabled shop* ✖

CO WEXFORD

The Irish Agricultural Museum — WEXFORD

Map 14 D2
Johnstown Castle Old Farmyard
☎ (053) 42888
Open all year, Jun-Aug Mon-Fri 9-5 & Sat-Sun 2-5; Apr-May & Sep-11 Nov Mon-Fri 9-12.30 & 1.30-5, Sat-Sun 2-5; 12 Nov-Mar Mon-Fri 9-12.30 & 1.30-5. *(Closed 25 Dec-2 Jan).*
IR£1.50 (ch & students IR75p). Parking charge May-Sep.
🅿 ⚊ ♿ *toilets for disabled shop*

See Johnstown Castle Gardens for description.

Johnstown Castle Gardens — WEXFORD

Map 14 D2
(4m SW)
☎ (053) 42888
A 19th-century mansion incoprorating the remains of a 15th-century castle. It now houses a research centre of the Agriculture Institute and is closed to visitors. The Irish Agricultural Museum may be visited, and it houses extensive displays on rural transport, farming, and the activities of the farmyard and the farmhouse. Also the grounds, which contain 200 different types of trees and shrubs, three ornamental lakes with wildfowl, and walled gardens and hothouses.
Open all year, daily 9-5. (Closed 25 Dec).
✳ *Car (plus passengers) IR£2. Pedestrians IR£1 (ch & students IR50p)*
🅿 ⚊ ♿ *shop*

✖ The 'No Dogs' symbol does not normally apply to guide dogs – these are permitted in most establishments.

CO WICKLOW

Powerscourt Gardens — ENNISKERRY

Map 14 E4
Powerscourt Estate
☎ Dublin (01) 2867676
Includes a large deer park, beautiful Italian and Japanese gardens and walled gardens, herbacious borders and a famous collection of trees. It is one of the last formal gardens to have been created in Europe. The waterfall is the highest in Ireland (400ft) and is very spectacular. Special events for 1992 include: Aug, Vintage and Veteran Car Rally; Jun, Launch of Wicklow Gardens Festival; Apr, World Cup Motocross Championships at Waterfall.
Open – Gardens Mar-Oct daily 9.30-5.30; Waterfall Mar-Oct daily 9.30-7; winter daily 10.30-dusk.
Gardens: IR£2.50 (ch IR£1.50 & students IR£2). Waterfall: IR£1.50 (ch IR80p & students IR£1). Under 5's free. Party 20 +
🅿 ⚊ ♿ *toilets for disabled shop garden centre*

About Britain Quiz

Competition Winners 1991

1	Mr Smith of Rotherham, Yorkshire
2	Mrs Meacham of Chepstow, Gwent
3	Mr Gordon of Brentford, Middlesex
4	Mrs Dauler of Tewkesbury, Gloucestershire
5	Mr Evans of Twickenham, Middlesex
6	Mr Baker of Stowmarket, Suffolk

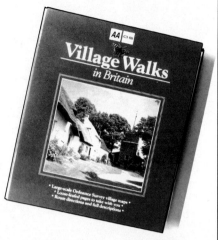

KEY TO ATLAS

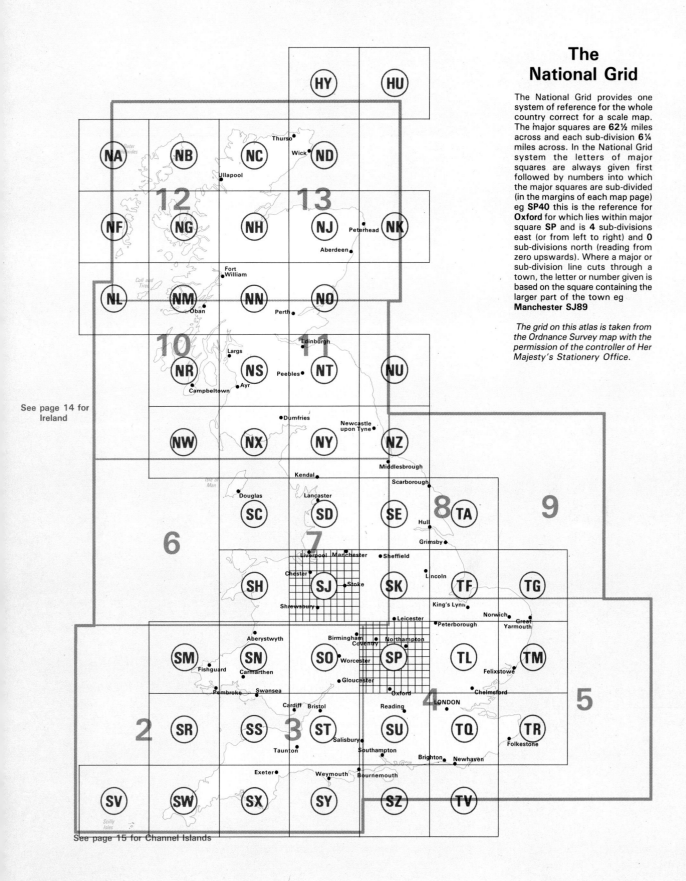

The National Grid

The National Grid provides one system of reference for the whole country correct for a scale map. The major squares are **62½ miles** across and each sub-division **6¼** miles across. In the National Grid system the letters of major squares are always given first followed by numbers into which the major squares are sub-divided (in the margins of each map page) eg **SP40** this is the reference for **Oxford** for which lies within major square **SP** and is **4** sub-divisions east (or from left to right) and **0** sub-divisions north (reading from zero upwards). Where a major or sub-division line cuts through a town, the letter or number given is based on the square containing the larger part of the town eg **Manchester SJ89**

The grid on this atlas is taken from the Ordnance Survey map with the permission of the controller of Her Majesty's Stationery Office.

See page 14 for Ireland

See page 15 for Channel Islands

Maps produced by

Information Services Division, AA Commercial Services Ltd., Fanum House, Basingstoke, Hants. RG21 2EA
©The Automobile Association 1992.

Scale 16 miles to 1 inch

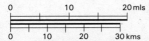

0   10   20 mls

0   10   20   30 kms

The atlas is for location purposes only:

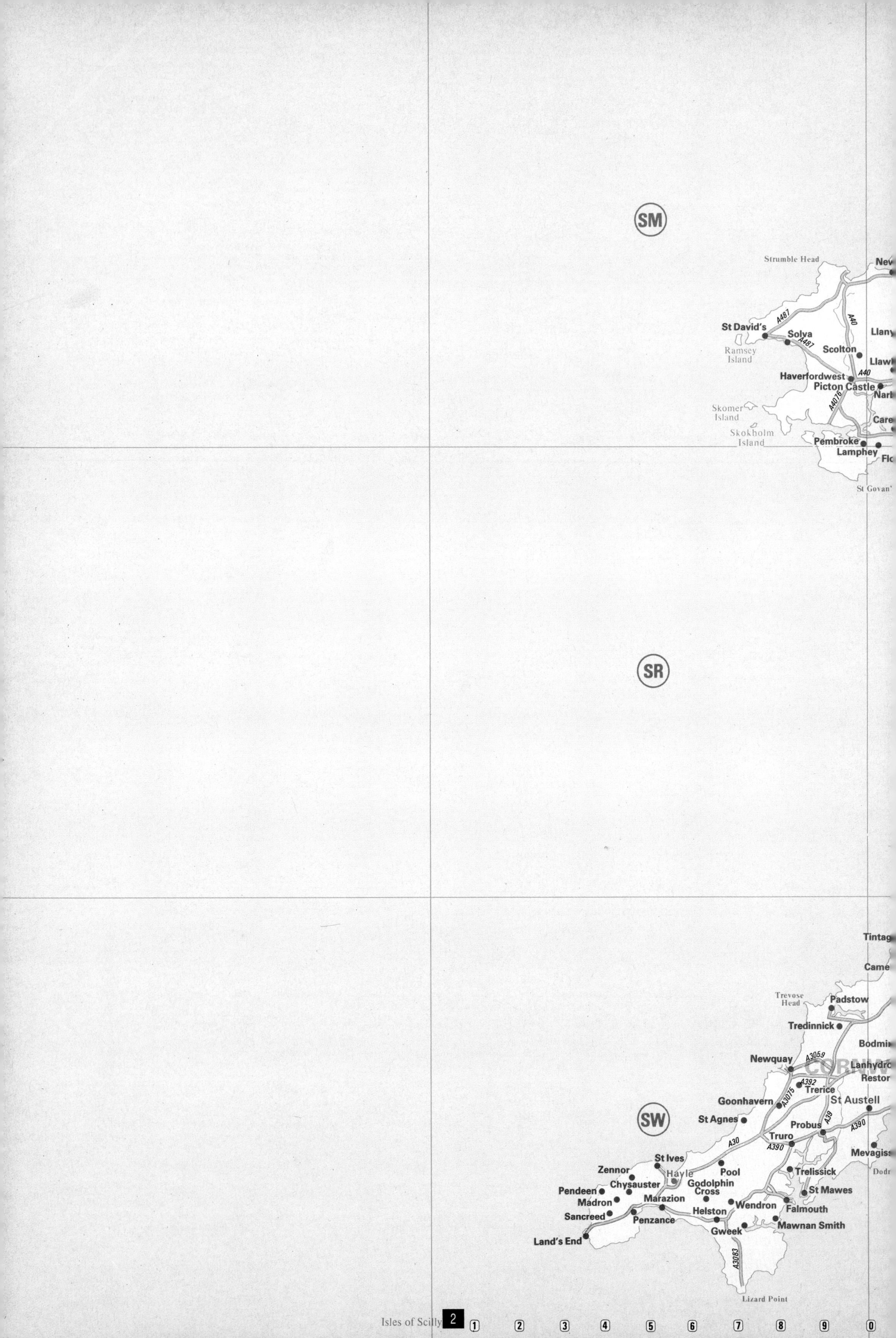

SM

Strumble Head

Nev

St David's

Solva

A487

A487

A40

Llany

Scolton

Llawh

Ramsey
Island

Haverfordwest

A40

Picton Castle

Narl

A4076

Skomer
Island

Care

Skokholm
Island

Pembroke

Lamphey

Flo

St Govan'

SR

Tintag

Camé

Trevose
Head

Padstow

Tredinnick

Bodmi

A305.9

Newquay

Lanhydro

A392

Restor

Trerice

A3075

Goonhavern

St Austell

A39

SW

St Agnes

Probus

A390

Truro

Mevagiss

A30

A390

St Ives

Trelissick

Dodr

Zennor

Hayle

Pool

Chysauster

Godolphin
Cross

St Mawes

Pendeen

Madron

Marazion

Wendron

Falmouth

Sancreed

Helston

Penzance

Mawnan Smith

Gweek

Land's End

A3083

Lizard Point

Isles of Scilly 2 ① ② ③ ④ ⑤ ⑥ ⑦ ⑧ ⑨ ⓪

Horsey

xham

TG

Filby
Caister-on-Sea
th
sham
Great Yarmouth

Burgh Castle

Reedham
St Olaves
A143
A12

Lowestoft
A146

Bungay
Suffolk Wild Life Park
A144
A145
ixton

Southwold
A12

mlingham
Saxmundham
iston
Leiston
A10.94
Aldeburgh

Orford
TM
oodbridge
Orford Ness

vich

Naze

Margate
ulver
North Foreland
A253
Broadstairs
Ramsgate
Minster-in-Thanet
Richborough

Deal
TR
A258

tone

④   ⑤   ⑥

E L

ISLE
OF
MAN

10

Ballaug

Peel

A4

A3

A31

Craigneish

Castletow

Dre

Carmel Head

Holy Island

Bord

Plas-
yn-Rhiw

A4

Bardsey
Island

C a r d i

B a

SM

2

Strumble Head

Cardigan

Newport

Newc
Em

Cilgerran

Dr
Fe

Crymych

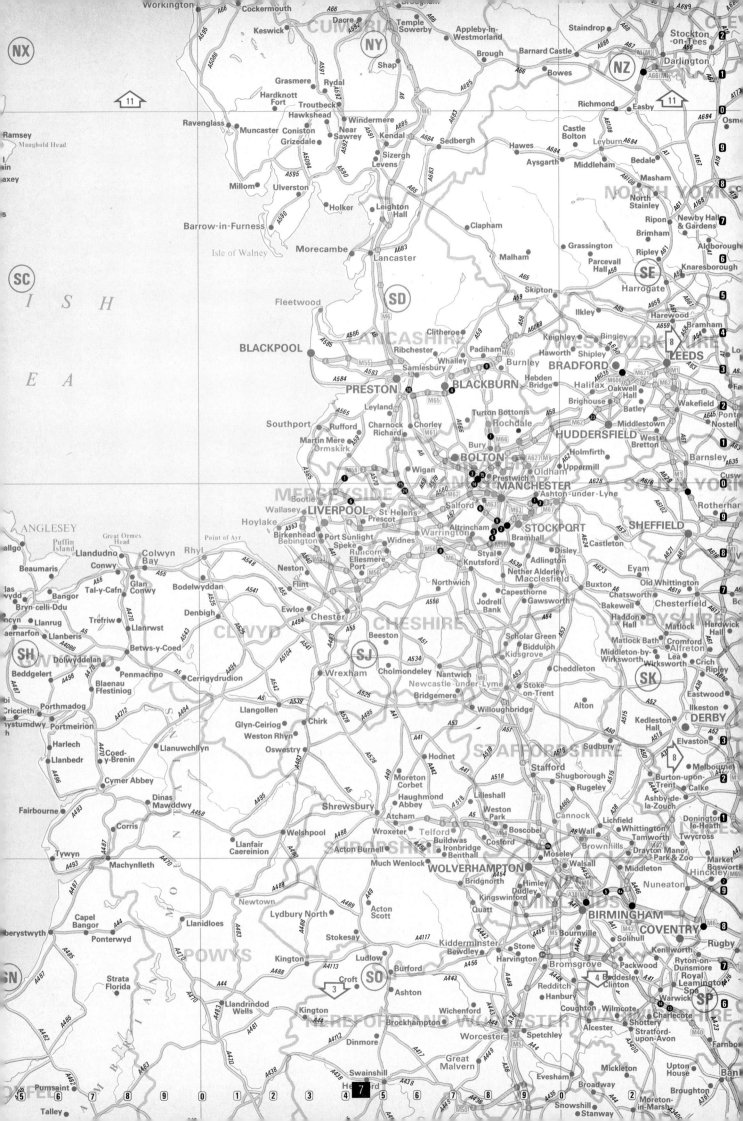

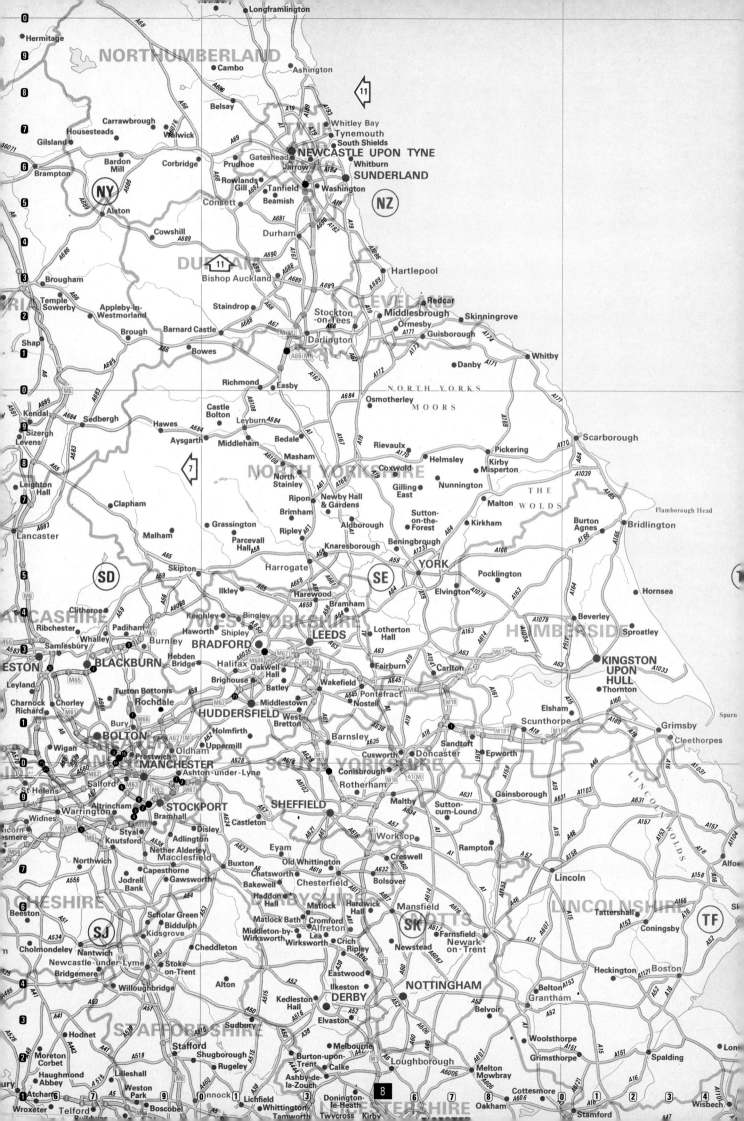

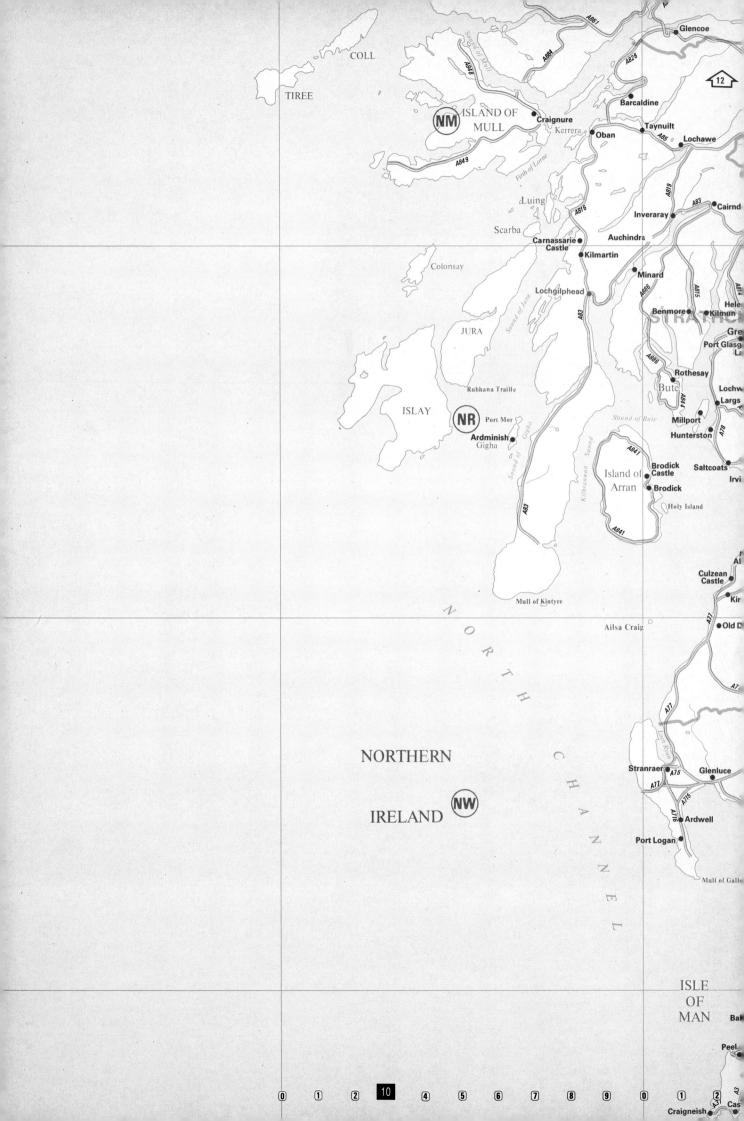

TIREE

COLL

Sound of Mull

A884

A848

A861

Glencoe

A828

Barcaldine

ISLAND OF
MULL

NM

Craignure

Kerrera

Taynuilt

A85

Oban

Lochawe

Firth of Lorne

A819

A816

Luing

Inveraray

A83

Cairnd

Scarba

Auchindra

Carnassarie
Castle

Kilmartin

Colonsay

Minard

A886

A815

A814

Lochgilphead

A83

Benmore

A815

Hele

Kilmun

STRATHC

Gre

Port Glasg

A886

La

JURA

Rothesay

Sound of Jura

Bute

Lochw

Rubhana Traille

A844

Largs

ISLAY

NR

Port Mor

Sound of Bute

Millport

A78

Ardminish

Gigha

Hunterston

Sound of Gigha

A841

Island of
Arran

Brodick
Castle

Saltcoats

Brodick

Irvi

Kilbrannan Sound

Holy Island

A83

Culzean
Castle

Al

A841

Mull of Kintyre

Kir

A77

N
O
R
T
H

Ailsa Craig

Old D

A7

A77

NORTHERN

Loch Ryan

C
H
A
N
N
E
L

Stranraer

A75

Glenluce

A77

A715

IRELAND

NW

A716

Ardwell

Port Logan

Mull of Galle

ISLE
OF
MAN

Bal

Peel

A3

A31

Cas

Craigneish

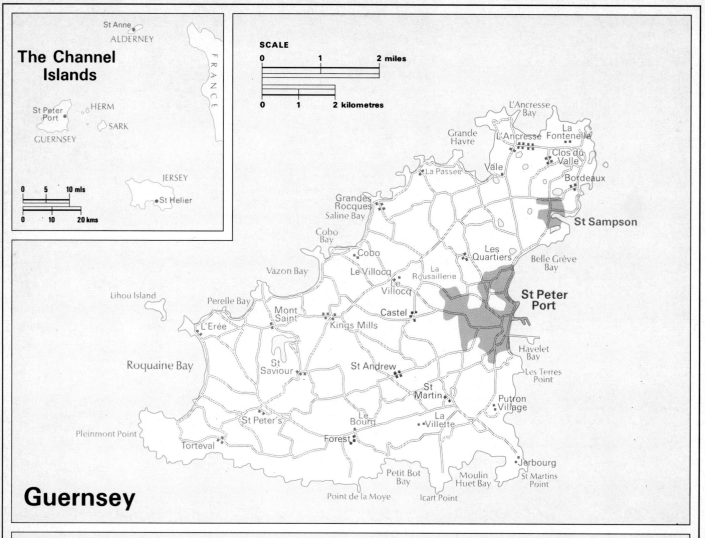

The Channel Islands

ALDERNEY
St Anne

FRANCE

St Peter Port
HERM
SARK
GUERNSEY

JERSEY
St Helier

SCALE
0   1   2 miles
0   1   2 kilometres

0   5   10 mls
0   10   20 kms

L'Ancresse Bay
La Fontenelle
L'Ancresse
Grande Havre
Clos du Valle
Vale
Bordeaux
La Passee
St Sampson
Grandes Rocques
Saline Bay
Les Quartiers
Belle Grève Bay
Cobo Bay
Cobo
La Rousaillerie
St Peter Port
Le Villocq
Vazon Bay
Le Villocq
Castel
Lihou Island
Perelle Bay
Mont Saint
Kings Mills
Havelet Bay
L'Erée
St Saviour
St Andrew
Les Terres Point
Roquaine Bay
St Martin
Putron Village
Le Bourg
La Villette
St Peter's
Pleinmont Point
Torteval
Forest
Jerbourg
Petit Bot Bay
Moulin Huet Bay
St Martins Point
Point de la Moye
Icart Point

Guernsey

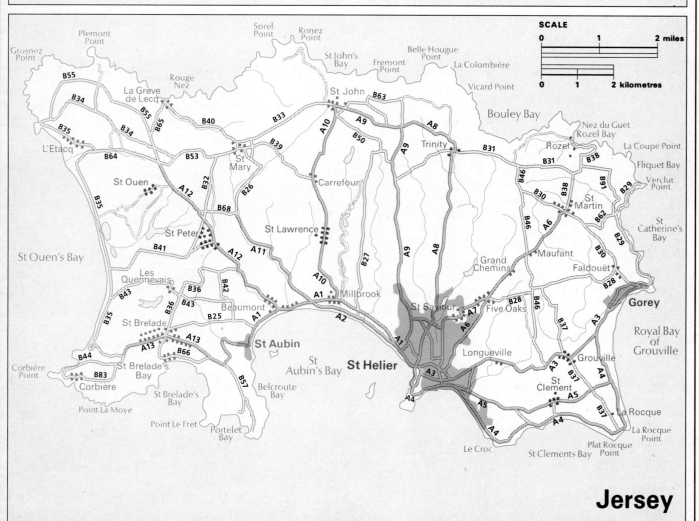

SCALE
0   1   2 miles
0   1   2 kilometres

Plemont Point
Sorel Point
Ronez Point
Grosnez Point
St John's Bay
Belle Hougue Point
Fremont Point
La Colombière
Vicard Point
Rouge Nez
La Grève de Lecq
St John
B63
Bouley Bay
B55
B34
B55
B65
B40
B33
A10
A9
A8
Nez du Guet
Rozel Bay
B35
B34
B39
B50
Trinity
B31
Rozel
La Coupe Point
L'Etacq
B64
B53
St Mary
Fliquet Bay
B31
B38
St Ouen
A12
B32
B26
Carrefour
A9
B49
B38
B91
B29
Verclut Point
B68
B30
St Martin
B62
St Peter
St Lawrence
B46
A6
St Catherine's Bay
B41
A12
A11
B27
A9
A8
B29
St Ouen's Bay
A10
Grand Chemins
Maufant
B30
Les Quennevais
B36
B42
A1
Millbrook
Grand Chemins
Faldouet
B43
B36
Beaumont
A1
St Saviour
A7
Five Oaks
B28
B46
B28
Gorey
B35
B25
A7
A2
A6
Longueville
B37
A3
Royal Bay of Grouville
St Brelade
A13
A13
St Aubin
St Aubin's Bay
St Helier
A3
Grouville
A4
B44
B66
A4
St Clement
A5
Corbière Point
B83
St Brelade's Bay
Belcroute Bay
A3
B37
B37
la Rocque
Corbière
St Brelade's Bay
A5
La Rocque Point
Point La Moye
B57
A4
Point Le Fret
Portelet Bay
A4
Le Croc
St Clements Bay
Plat Rocque Point

Jersey

INDEX